HISTORY OF DOGMA

HISTORY OF DOGMA

BY

Dr. ADOLPH HARNACK

ORDINARY PROF. OF CHURCH HISTORY IN THE UNIVERSITY, AND FELLOW OF
THE ROYAL ACADEMY OF SCIENCE, BERLIN

*TRANSLATED FROM THE THIRD GERMAN
EDITION*

BY

NEIL BUCHANAN

VOLUME IV
and
VOLUME V

DOVER PUBLICATIONS, INC.

NEW YORK

Published in the United Kingdom by Constable
and Company Limited, 10 Orange Street, London
W. C. 2.

This new Dover edition, first published in 1961,
is an unabridged republication of the English translation of the third German edition that appeared
circa 1900. This Dover edition is an unaltered republication except that minor typographical errors
in Volume VII have been corrected.

The original English edition appeared as seven
separate volumes, whereas this Dover edition is
published complete in four separate volumes.

Library of Congress Catalog Card Number: 61-4455

Manufactured in the United States of America

Dover Publications, Inc.
180 Varick Street
New York 14, N.Y.

HISTORY OF DOGMA

BY

Dr. ADOLPH HARNACK

Volume IV

EDITORIAL NOTE.

THE volume now issued finishes Volume II. of the original, of which a portion appears in Volume III. of the English Translation. The first chapter of this volume corresponds to Chapter VII. of Volume II. of the original, which treats of the Divinity of Christ. The remaining third volume of the German Edition will occupy three volumes in the English Translation, making seven volumes in all.

A. B. BRUCE.

CONTENTS.

CHAPTER I.[1]

THE DOCTRINE OF THE HOMOUSIA OF THE SON OF GOD WITH GOD HIMSELF.[2]

Is the Divine which appeared on the earth and has made its presence actively felt, identical with the supremely Divine that rules heaven and earth? Did the Divine which appeared on the earth enter into a close and permanent union with human nature, so that it has actually transfigured it and raised

[1] *Vide* Preface.

[2] See the Opp. Athanas., and in addition the works of the other Church Fathers of the fourth century, above all, those of Hilary, the Cappadocians and Jerome; the Church Histories of Sulpicius, Rufinus, Socrates, Sozomen, Theodoret, Gelasius, the Vita Constantini of Eusebius, the Panarion of Epiphanius, and the Codex Theodosianus ed. Hænel; on the other side, the fragments of the Church History of Philostorgius; of the secular historians, Ammian in particular. For the proceedings of the Councils see Mansi Collect. Conc. v. II. and III.; Hefele, Conciliengesch. 2nd ed. v. I. and II.; Walch, Historie der Ketzereien v. II. and III.; Münscher, Ueber den Sinn der nicän. Glaubensformel, in Henke's Neues Magazin, VI., p. 334 f.; Caspari, Quellen zur Gesch. des Taufsymbols, 4 vols., 1866 ff.; Hahn, Bibliothek der Symbole, 2nd ed. 1877; Hort, On the Constantinop. Creed and other Eastern Creeds of the fourth century, 1876; Swainson, The Nicene and Apostles' Creeds, 1875; Bright, Notes on the Canons of the first four General Councils, 1882; my art. "Konstantinop. Symbol" in Herzog's R.-Encykl., 2nd ed. Besides the historical works of Baronius, Tillemont, Basnage, Gibbon, Schröckh, de Broglie, Wietersheim, Richter, Kaufmann, Hertzberg, Chastel, Schiller, Victor Schultze, and Boissier, above all, Ranke, (also Löning, Gesch. d. deutschen Kirchenrechts, vol. I.) and others, the references in Fabricius-Harless, the careful biographies of the Fathers of the fourth century by Böhringer, and the Histories of Dogma by Petavius, Schwane, Baur, Dorner (Entw. Gesch. d. L. v, d. Person Christi), Newman (Arians of the fourth century), Nitzsch, Schultz, and Thomasius may be consulted. On Lucian: see my article in Herzog's R.-Encyklop. v. VIII. 2, and in my Altchristl. Lit. Gesch. vol. I. On Arius: Maimbourg, Hist. de l'Arianisme, 1673, Travasa, Storia della vita di Ario, 1746; Hassenkamp, Hist. Arianæ controversiæ, 1845; Revillout, De l'Arianisme des peuples germaniques, 1850; Stark, Versuch einer

it to the plane of the eternal? These two questions necessarily arose out of the combination of the incarnation of the Logos and the deification of the human nature (See Vol. III., p. 289 ff.) Along with the questions, however, the answers too were given. But it was only after severe conflicts that these answers were able to establish themselves in the Church as dogmas. The reasons of the delay in their acceptance have been partly already indicated in Vol. III., pp. 167 ff. and will further appear in what follows. In the fourth century the first question was the dominant one in the Church, and in the succeeding centuries the second. We have to do with the first to begin with. It was finally answered at the so-called Second Œcumenical Council, 381, more properly in the year 383. The Council of Nicæa (325) and the death of Constantine (361) mark off the main stages in the controversy.

I. FROM THE BEGINNING OF THE CONTROVERSY TO THE COUNCIL OF NICÆA.

At the great Oriental Council which met at Antioch about the year 268, the Logos doctrine was definitely accepted,

Gesch. des Arianism, 2 vols., 1783 f.; Kölling, Gesch. der arianischen Häresie, 2 vols., 1874, 1883; Gwatkin, Studies of Arianism, 1882. On Athanasius: Möhler, Athan. d. Gr., 1827; Voigt, Die Lehre d. Athan., 1861; Cureton, The Festal Letters of Athan., 1848; Larsow, Die Festbriefe des hl. Athan., 1852; Sievers, Ztschr. f. d. hist. Theol., 1868, I.; Fialon, St. Athanase, 1877; Atzberger, Die Logoslehre d. hl. Athan., 1880 (on this ThLZ., 1880, No. 8) Eichhorn, Athan. de vita ascetica, 1886. On Marcellus: Zahn, M. von Ancyra, 1867; Klose, Gesch. d. L. des Marcel and Photin, 1837. Reinkens, Hilarius, 1864; Krüger, Lucifer, 1886, and in the Ztschr. f. wiss. Theol., 1888, p. 434 ff.; Klose, Gesch. und Lehre des Eunomius, 1833; Rode, Gesch. der Reaction des Kaiser Julian, 1877 (also the works of Naville, Rendall and Mücke); Ullmann, Gregor v. Naz., 2nd ed. 1867; Dräseke, Quæst. Nazianz. Specimen, 1876; Rupp, Gregor v. Nyssa, 1834; Klose, Basilius, 1835; Fialon, St. Basile, 2nd edit. 1869; Rade, Damasus, 1882; Förster, Ambrosius, 1884; Zöckler, Hieronymus, 1875; Güldenpenning and Ifland, Theodosius d. Gr., 1878; Langen, Gesch. d. röm. Kirche, I. 1881. In addition the articles on the subject in Herzog's R.-Encykl. (particularly those by Möller) and in the Dict. of Christ. Biography, and very specially the article Eusebius by Lightfoot. The most thorough recent investigation of the subject is that by Gwatkin above mentioned. The accounts of the doctrines of Arius and Athanasius in Böhringer are thoroughly good and well-nigh exhaustive. The literary and critical studies of the Benedictines, in their editions, and those of Tillemont form the basis of the more recent works also, and so far they have not been surpassed.

while the "Homoousios" on the other hand was rejected. [1]
The most learned man whom the East at that time possessed,
Lucian (of Samosata?) took up the work of the excommunicated
metropolitan, Paul of Samosata. First educated at the school
of Edessa, where since the days of Bardesanes a free and
original spirit had prevailed, then a follower of Paul, he got
from the latter his dislike to the theology of "the ancient
teachers", and with this he united the critical study of the
Bible, a subject in which he became a master. He founded
in Antioch an exegetical-theological school which, during the
time of the three episcopates of Domnus, Timäus and Cyril,
was not in communion with the Church there, but which afterwards, shortly before the martyrdom of Lucian, made its peace
with the Church.

This school is the nursery of the Arian doctrine, and Lucian,
its head, is the Arius before Arius. Lucian started from the
Christology of Paul, but, following the tendency of the time,
and perhaps also because he was convinced on exegetical
grounds, he united it with the Logos Christology, and so
created a fixed form of doctrine. [2] It is probable that it was
only gradually he allowed the Logos doctrine to have stronger
influence on the Adoptian form. This explains why it was not
till towards the end of his life that he was able to bridge over
his differences with the Church. He was revered by his pupils
both as the teacher *par excellence,* and in his character as
ascetic; his martyrdom, which occurred in the year 311 or 312,
increased his reputation. The remembrance of having sat at
the feet of Lucian was a firm bond of union amongst his
pupils. After the time of persecution they received influential
ecclesiastical posts. [3] There was no longer anything to recall

---

[1] See Vol. iii., pp. 40, 45.

[2] It is extremely probable that Lucian's study of Origen too had convinced him
of the correctness of the Logos doctrine. We have to regard his doctrine as a
combination of the doctrines of Paul and Origen. Lucian and Origen are classed
together by Epiph., H. 76, 3, as teachers of the Arians.

[3] Amongst Lucian's pupils were Arius, Eusebius of Nicomedia, Menophantus of
Ephesus, Theognis of Nicæa, Maris of Chalcedon, Athanasius of Anazarbus (?),
the sophist Asterius, and Leontius, afterwards bishop of Antioch, and others. In Syria
the pupils of Dorotheus—namely, Eusebius of Cæsarea and Paulinus of Tyre were

the fact that their master had formerly been outside of the
Church. These pupils as a body afterwards came into conflict
more or less strongly with the Alexandrian theology. So far
as we know, no single one of them was distinguished as a
religious character; but they knew what they wanted; they
were absolutely convinced of the truth of their school-doctrine,
which had reason and Scripture on its side. This is what
characterises the school. At a time when the Church doctrine
was in the direst confusion, and was threatening to disappear,
and when the union of tradition, Scripture, and philosophical
speculation in the form of dogma had been already called for,
but had not yet been accomplished, this school was conscious
of possessing an established system of doctrine which at the
same time permitted freedom. This was its strength. [1]

The accounts of Lucian's Christology which have been handed
down are meagre enough, still they give us a sufficiently clear
picture of his views. God is One; there is nothing equal to
Him; for everything besides Him is created. He has created

supporters of Arius, as were also many of Origen's admirers. As regards the other
partisans of Arius who are known to us by name, we do not know whether they
were pupils of Lucian or not. Egypt and Libya are represented by Theonas of
Marmarica, Secundus of Ptolemais and the presbyter Georgius of Alexandria, and
further, according to Philostorgius, by Daches of Berenice, Secundus of Tauchira,
Sentianus of Boräum, Zopyrus of Barka and Meletius of Lykopolis. In other provinces
we have Petrophilus of Scythopolis, Narcissus of Neronias, Theodotus of Laodicea,
Gregorius of Berytus and Aëtius of Lydda. Philostorgius further mentions others,
but he also reckons as belonging to his party those old bishops who did not live
to see the outbreak of the controversy and who accordingly have been claimed by
the orthodox side as well; see Gwatkin l. c., p. 31. For other names of presbyters
and deacons at Alexandria who held Arian views, see the letters of Alexander in
Theodoret, I. 4, and Socrates, I. 6.

[1] These pupils of Lucian must have displayed all the self-consciousness, the
assurance, and the arrogance of a youthful exclusive school (ἐκ τῆς αὐτῆς δηλητηρίου φρατρίας, says Epiphanius in one place, H. 69, 5), haughtily setting themselves
far above the "ancients" and pitying their want of intelligence. Highly characteristic
in this respect is the account of Alexander, their opponent, after making all
allowance for the malevolent element in it; see very specially the following
passage, Theodoret, H. E. I. 4): οἵ οὐδὲ τῶν ἀρχαίων τινὰς συγκρίνειν ἑαυτοῖς ἀξιοῦσιν,
οὐδὲ οἷς ἡμεῖς ἐκ παίδων ὡμιλήσαμεν διδασκάλοις ἐξισοῦσθαι ἀνέχονται· ἀλλ᾽ οὐδὲ
τῶν νῦν πανταχοῦ συλλειτουργῶν τινὰ εἰς μέτρον σοφίας ἡγοῦνται· μόνοι σοφοὶ καὶ
ἀκτήμονες καὶ δογμάτων εὑρεταὶ λέγοντες εἶναι, καὶ αὐτοῖς ἀποκεκαλύφθαι μόνοις,
ἅπερ οὐδενὶ τῶν ὑπὸ τὸν ἥλιον ἑτέρῳ πέφυκεν ἐλθεῖν εἰς ἔννοιαν. One may further
compare the introduction to the Thalia.

the Logos or Wisdom—who is to be distinguished from the *inner* divine Logos—out of the things that are not (ἐξ οὐκ ὄντων), and sent him into the world.[1] This Logos has taken a human body though not a human soul, and accordingly all the feelings and spiritual struggles of Christ are to be attributed to the Logos. Christ has made known the Father to us, and by being man and by his death has given us an example of patience. This exhausts his work, by means of which—for so we may complete the thought—he, constantly progressing, has entered into perfect glory. It is the doctrine of Paul of Samosata, but instead of man it is a created heavenly being who here becomes "Lord". Lucian must have put all the emphasis on the "out of the things that are not" (ἐξ οὐκ ὄντων) and on the "progress" (προκοπή). The creaturehood of the Son, the denial of his co-eternity with the Father, and the unchange-ableness of the Son achieved by constant progress and constancy, constitute the main articles in the doctrine of Lucian and his school. Just because of this he refuses to recognise in the Son the perfectly equal image of the *ousia* or substance of the Father (Philost. II. 15).[2] There can be no doubt as to the

[1] He is thus a created "God."

[2] For the proofs of what is here said regarding Lucian see my article "Lucian" in Herzog's R.-Encykl., 2nd ed. Vol. VIII. Here I give merely the following. For the close connection between Arius and Lucian we possess a series of witnesses. Alexander of Alex. says expressly in his letter to Alexander (Theodoret H. E. I. 4) that Arius started from Lucian. Arius himself in his letter to Eusebius of Nicomedia describes himself and his friend as Συλλουκιανιστής; Philostorgius enumerates the pupils of Lucian, whom he regards as the friends of Arius (II. 14), and lets us see (II. 3, 13—15 and III. 15) that at the beginning of the fifth century Lucian was still regarded as the patriarch and teacher of the Arians. Epiphanius (Hær. 43. 1) and Philostorgius (l. c.) inform us that Lucian was revered by the Arians as a martyr. Epiphanius and Marius Victorinus call the Arians "Lucianists" (see also Epiph. H. 76. 3). Sozomen relates that the Fathers of Arian or semi-Arian views asscmbled in Antioch in the year 341 accepted a confession of faith of Lucian's (III. 5). This confession is, it is true, given by Athanasius (de synodis 23), Socrates (II. 10) and Hilary (de synod. 29) without any statement as to its having originated with Lucian; but Sozomen informs us that a semi-Arian synod which met in Caria in 367 also recognised it as Lucianist (VI. 12). According to the author of the seven dialogues on the Trinity, who was probably Maximus Confessor, the Macedonians did the same (Dial. III. in Theodoreti Opp. V. 2, p. 991 sq., ed. Schultze and Nöss). The semi-Arians also at the synod of Seleucia in 359 seem to have ascribed the Confession to Lucian (see Caspari, Alte und neue Quellen zur

philosophy to which Lucian adhered. He worked with the means supplied by the critical and dialectic philosophy of Aristotle, although indeed his conception of God was Platonic, and though his Logos doctrine had nothing in common with the teaching of Aristotle. His opponents have expressly informed us that his pupils turned to account the Aristotelian philosophy. [1] If one recollects that in the third century the Theodotian-Adoptian Christology was founded by the help of what was supplied by Aristotelianism, and that the Theodotians were also given to the critical study of the Bible, [2] the connection between Arianism and Adoptianism thus becomes clear. It is incorrect to trace the entire opposition between the Orthodox and the Arians to the opposition between Platonism and Aristotelianism, incorrect if for no other reason because a strong Platonic element is contained in what they possess in common—namely, the doctrine of God and of the Logos; but it is correct to say that the opposition cannot be understood if regard is not had to the different philosophical methods employed. [3] *In Lucian's teaching Adoptianism is combined* [4] *with the doctrine of the Logos as a creature (κτίσμα), and this form of doctrine is developed by the aid of the Aristotelian philosophy and based on the*

Gesch. d. Taufsymbols, p. 42 f., n. 18). Since Sozomen himself, however, questions the correctness of the view which attributes it to Lucian, and since, moreover, other reasons may be alleged against it, we ought with Caspari to regard the creed as a redaction of a confession of Lucian's. This fact too shews what a high reputation the martyr had in those circles. That Lucian's school was pre-eminently an exegetical one is evident amongst other things from Lucian's well-known activity in textual criticism, as well as from Philostorg. (III. 15).

[1] See on Arius, *e.g.*, Epiphan. H. 69 c. 69, on Aëtius, who was indirectly a pupil of Lucian (Philostorg. III. 15), the numerous passages in the Cappadocians and Epiphanius H. 76 T. III., p. 251, ed. Oehler. Besides, in almost every sentence of what is left us of the writings of Aëtius we see the Aristotelian. Philostorgius testifies to the fact that he specially occupied himself with Logic and Grammar; see above all, the little work of Aëtius in 74 theses, which Epiphanius (H. 76) has preserved for us. In his application of Aristotelianism Aëtius, however, went further than Arius, as is peculiarly evident from the thesis of the knowableness of God.

[2] See Vol. III., p. 24.

[3] Correctly given in Baur, L. v. d. Dreieinigkeit I., p. 387 ff.—not at all clear in Dorner *op. cit.* I., p. 859.

[4] It is self-evident that this combination deprived Paul's system of doctrine of all the merit which it contained.

critical exegesis of the Bible. Aristotelian Rationalism dominated
the school. The thought of an actual redemption was put in
the background. The Christian interest in monotheism is
exhausted by the statement that the predicate "underived"
attaches to one single being only. This interest in the "unbegotten begetter", and also, what is closely connected with
it, the ranging of all theological thoughts under the antithesis
of first cause or God, and creation, are also Aristotelian.
Theology here became a "Technology", that is, a doctrine of
the unbegotten and the begotten [1] which was worked out in
syllogisms and based on the sacred codex.

A pupil of Lucian named Arius, perhaps a Lybian by birth,
became when already well up in years, first deacon in Alexandria, and afterwards presbyter· in the church of Baukalis. The
presbyters there at that period still possessed a more independent position than anywhere else. [2] Owing, however, to the
influence of the martyr bishop Peter (+ 311) a tendency
had gained ascendency in the episcopate in Alexandria, which
led to Christian doctrine being sharply marked off from the
teachings of Greek philosophy (μαθήματα τῆς Ἑλληνικῆς
φιλοσοφίας) the presence of which had been observed in
Origen, and in general shewed itself in a distrust of

---

[1] According to Theodoret (Hær. fab. IV. 3) it was Aëtius himself who called
theology "technology." Perhaps the most characteristic example of how this technology
treated purely religious language is to be found in the benediction with which
Aëtius concluded one of his works (Epiphan. H, 76. T. III., p. 222, ed. Oehler).
Ἐρρωμένους καὶ ἐρρωμένας ὑμᾶς ὁ ὤν αὐτογέννητος Θεός, ὁ καὶ μόνος ἀληθινὸς Θεὸς
προσαγορευθεὶς ὑπὸ τοῦ ἀποσταλέντος Ἰησοῦ Χριστοῦ, ὑποστάντος τε ἀληθῶς πρὸ
αἰώνων καὶ ὄντος ἀληθῶς γεννητῆς ὑποστάσεως, διατηρήσει ἀπὸ τῆς ἀσεβείας, ἐν
Χριστῷ Ἰησοῦ τῷ κυρίῳ ἡμῶν, δι᾽ οὗ πᾶσα δόξα τῷ πατρὶ καὶ νῦν καὶ ἀεὶ καὶ
εἰς τοὺς αἰῶνας τῶν αἰώνων. Ἀμήν. This reminds us *mutatis mutandis* of the
benediction of the modern rationalistic preacher, "The grace of our Lord Jesus
Christ, the great teacher and friend of men, be with you all." I am glad further
to see that Rupp too (Gregor von Nyssa, p. 137) has connected the conception of
ἀγεννησία, as being a central one in Eunomius, with the πρῶτον κινοῦν ἀκίνητον
of Aristotle.

[2] Spite, however, of what we know of the Meletian schism in Alexandria and
of the temporary connection of Arius with it, (cf. also the schism of Colluthus) it
is not very clear if the outbreak of the Arian controversy· is connected with the
opposition between episcopate and presbyterate (against Böhringer). The Alexandrian
Presbyters were at that time actual Parochi. There are some obscure references in
the letter of Alexander (Theodoret I. 4), see Gwatkin, p. 29.

"scientific" theology, while at the same time the thought
of the distinction between the Logos and the Father was
given a secondary place. [1] Arius nevertheless fearlessly advanced
the views he had learned from Lucian. The description we
get of him is that of a man of grave appearance and a strict
ascetic, but at the same time affable and of a prepossessing
character, though vain. He was highly respected in the city;
the ascetics and the virgins were specially attached to him.
His activity had been recognised also by the new bishop
Alexander who began his episcopate in 313. The outbreak of
the controversy is wrapped in obscurity, owing to the fact
that the accounts are mutually contradictory. According to the
oldest testimony it was an opinion expressed by Arius when
questioned by the bishop on a certain passage of Scripture, and
to which he obstinately adhered, which really began the controversy, [2] possibly in the year 318. Since the persecution had
ceased, the Christological question was the dominant one in the
Alexandrian Church. Arius was not the first to raise it. On
the contrary he was able later on to remind the bishop how
the latter had often both in the Church and in the Council of
Presbyters (ἐν μέσῃ τῇ ἐκκλησίᾳ καὶ συνεδρίῳ πλειστάκις) refuted
the Valentinian Christology, according to which the Son is an
emanation,—the Manichæan, according to which the Son is a
consubstantial part of the Father (μέρος ὁμοούσιον τοῦ πατρός),
—the Sabellian, according to which the Godhead involves the
identity of the Son and Father (υἱοπάτωρ),—that of Hieracas,
according to which the Son is a torch lighted at the torch of
the Father, that Son and Father are a bipartite light and so
on,—and how he, Arius, had agreed with him. [3] It was only
after considerable hesitation and perhaps vacillation too, that

----

[1] See Vol. III., p. 99 ff.

[2] See Constantine's letter in Euseb., Vita Constant. II. 69; the notices in the
Church historians and in Epiphanius (H. 69. 4) can hardly be reconciled with it.
Along with Constantine's statements the account of Socrates is specially worthy of
consideration (I. 5).

[3] Ep. Arii ad Alex. in Athanas. de synod. 16 and Epiphan. H. 69. 7. According
to Philostorg. I. 3, the exertions of Arius had very specially contributed to bring
about the election of Alexander as bishop, although he could then have become
bishop himself.

Alexander resolved on the excommunication of Arius. It took place at a Synod held in 321 or 320 in presence of about one hundred Egyptian and Lybian bishops. Along with Arius some presbyters and deacons of Alexandria, as well as the Lybian bishops Theonas and Secundus, were deposed. This did not quieten Arius. He sought and forthwith found support amongst his old friends, and above all, got the help of Eusebius of Nicomedia. This student-friend had an old cause of quarrel with Alexander, [1] and, contrary to ecclesiastical law, had been transferred to Nicomedia by Berytus, the most influential bishop [2] at the court of the Empress, a sister of Constantine. Arius, driven out of Alexandria "as an atheist", had written to him from Palestine. [3] He was able to appeal to a number of eastern bishops, and above all, to Eusebius of Cæsarea; in fact he asserted that *all* the eastern bishops agreed with him and had on this account been put under the ban by Alexander (?). Eusebius of Nicomedia espoused the cause of Arius in the most energetic fashion in a large number of letters. [4] Alexander on his part also looked about for allies. He wrote numerous letters to the bishops, two of which have been preserved—namely, the Encyclica, *i.e.*, the official report of what had occurred, [5] and the epistle to Alexander, Bishop of Constantinople. (?) [6] In the

---

[1] Ep. Alexandri in Socr. I. 6 on Eusebius. Τὴν πάλαι γὰρ αὐτοῦ κακόνοιαν τὴν χρόνῳ σιωπηθεῖσαν νῦν διὰ τούτων (by letters) ἀνανεῶσαι βουλόμενος, σχηματίζεται μὲν ὡς ὑπὲρ τούτων γράφων· ἔργῳ δὲ δείκνυσιν, ὡσ ὅτι ὑπὲρ ἑαυτοῦ σπουδάζων τοῦτο ποιεῖ. His lust of power is characterised by Alexander in the words (l. c.) νομίσας ἐπ᾽ αὐτῷ κεῖσθαι τὰ τῆς ἐκκλησίας.

[2] He is supposed to have been related to the Emperor. According to a letter of Constantine's of a later date (in Theodoret. H. E. I. 19) he remained faithful to Licinius and had before the catastrophe worked against Constantine.

[3] Theodoret H. E. I. 5, Epiph. H. 69 6.

[4] See the letter to Paulinus of Tyre—which is put later by some—in Theodoret, H. E. I. 6. In this letter Eusebius praises the zeal of the Church historian Eusebius in the matter and blames Paulinus for his silence. He too ought to come to the help of Arius by giving a written opinion based on the theology of the Bible. There is a fragment of a letter of Eusebius to Arius in Athanasius, de synod. 17, where there are also other letters of the friends of Arius.

[5] See Socrat. H. E. I. 6 and Athanas., Opp. I., p. 313 sq. (ed. Paris, 1689, p. 397 sq.).

[6] Theodoret, H. E. I. 4. The address is probably incorrect; the letter is written to several persons.

latter letter, which is written in a very hostile tone, Alexander
sought to check the powerful propaganda of Arianism. He
appealed to the bishops of the whole of Egypt and the Thebaid
and further to the Lybian, Pentapolitan, Syrian, Lycio-Pam-
phylian, Asiatic, Cappadocian, and other bishops. Arius betook
himself to Nicomedia and from there addressed a conciliatory
epistle to the Alexandrian bishop which we still possess. [1] He
also composed at that time his " Thalia," of whose contents which
were partly in prose and partly in verse, we cannot form any
very correct idea from the few fragments handed down to us
by Athanasius. His supporters thought a great deal of this
work while his opponents condemned it as profane, feeble, and
affected. [2] A Bithynian Synod under the leadership of Eusebius
decided for Arius, [3] and Eusebius of Cæsarea entered into
communication with Alexander of Alexandria in the character
of mediator, in order to induce him to take a more favourable
view of the doctrine of the excommunicated presbyter. [4] It
may have been, more than anything else, the political state of
things which allowed Arius to find his way back once more
to Alexandria. Under the patronage of some distinguished
bishops with whom he had entered into correspondence, but
who were not able to bring about any amicable arrangement
with Alexander, Arius resumed his work in the city. [5] In the
autumn of 323 Constantine, after his victory over Licinius, became sole ruler in the Roman Empire. The controversy had
already begun to rage in all the coast-provinces of the East.
Not only did the bishops contend with each other, but the
common people too began to take sides, and the dispute was
carried on in such a base manner that the Jews scoffed at the

---

[1] See note 3, p. 8.

[2] On the Thalia see Athan., Orat. c. Arian I. 2—10; de synod. 15. Philostorgius II. 2 tells us that Arius put his doctrine also into songs for sailors, millers,
and travellers etc., in order thus to bring it to the notice of the lower classes.
Athanasius also mentions songs. We can see from this that Arius made no distinction between faith and philosophical theology. He followed the tendency of the
time. His opponents are for him "heretics."

[3] Sozom. I. 15.

[4] The letter is in the Acts of the Second Nicene Council, Mansi XIII., p. 315.

[5] Sozom. I. 15.

thing in the theatres, and turned the most sacred parts of the doctrine of the Church into ridicule. [1] Constantine forthwith interfered. The very full letter which he sent to Alexander and Arius, [2] in 323—24, is one of the most important monuments of his religious policy. The controversy is described as an idle wrangle over incomprehensible things, since the opponents are, he says, at one as regards the main point. [3] But the letter had no effect, nor was the court-bishop, Hosius of Cordova, who brought it, and who as an Occidental appeared to be committed to neither side, able to effect a reconciliation between the parties. In all probability, however, Hosius had already come to an understanding [4] in Alexandria with Alexander, and the latter shortly

---

[1] Euseb., Vita Const. II. 61 ; Socrates I. 7 ; Theodoret I. 6 ; the discord extended even into families.

[2] Vita Const. II. 64—70.

[3] Constantine wrote the letter not as a theologian, but as Emperor, which ought in fairness to be reckoned to his credit. The introduction is very skilfully worded : the Emperor trusted that he would be able with the help of the Eastern bishops to compose the Donatist schism, and now he sees the East torn by a far more destructive schism. He offers his services as mediator and accordingly takes up an absolutely impartial position. " Alexander should not have asked the questions and Arius should not have answered them; for such questions lie outside the " Law " ; and above all, care ought to have been taken not to bring them to the notice of the people. The opponents, who at bottom presumably had the same convictions, ought to come to an agreement and compose their differences; this is what is done in the schools of philosophy ; those who attend them dispute, but they afterwards formulate terms of agreement upon a common basis. It is only the common people and ignorant boys who quarrel about trifles." The close of the letter expresses the very great anxiety felt by the Emperor lest the grand work of restoring peace and unity entrusted to him by Providence should be hindered. He accordingly most earnestly urges peace, even if they cannot actually agree. *In necessariis unitas, in dubiis libertas* and—reserve, is thus the watchword of the Emperor; in faith in Providence and in the conception of the Supreme Being they are certainly one : for the upholder of all has given to all a common light; differences of opinion on separate points are unavoidable and are perfectly legitimate when there is radical unity in dogma. "Restore to me my peaceful days and my undisturbed nights and do not allow me to spend what remains of my life in joylessness." The close is once more very effective: he had already started, he says, for Alexandria, but had turned back when he heard of the split; the combatants may make it possible for him to come by becoming reconciled. This letter can hardly have been written under the influence of Eusebius of Nicomedia; still Nicomedia had already before this been the starting-point of a movement for bringing about union, as the conciliatory epistle of Arius and the pacific letter of his friends prove.

[4] If according to Socrat. III. 7, he at this time agitated in Alexandria the

after took a journey to Nicomedia, thoroughly completed the
understanding, talked over some other bishops there, and so
prepared the way for the decision of the Council of Nicæa. [1]
The Emperor was won over by Hosius after he perceived the
fruitlessness of his union-policy. [2] He now summoned a General
Council to meet at Nicæa, apparently on the advice of Hosius, [3]
and the latter had the main share also in determining the
choice of the formula proposed. [4]

But before we take up the Council of Nicæa, we must get
some idea of the doctrines of the contending parties.

We still know what were the Christological formulæ of Bishop
Alexander which were attacked by Arius. [5] They were the
words: 'Αεὶ θέος, ἀεὶ υἰός, ἅμα πατήρ, ἅμα υἰός, συνυπάρχει ὁ
υἰὸς ἀγεννήτως [6] τῷ θεῷ, ἀειγενής, ἀγενητογενής, οὔτ' ἐπινοίᾳ, οὔτ'

question about οὐσία and ὑπόστασις, it must have been in the western-orthodox
sense. On the other hand, it is said (l. c.) that Hosius when in Alexandria
endeavoured to refute the doctrine of Sabellius. He might thus, as a matter of
fact, regard himself as a mediator, namely, between the Arian and Sabellian
doctrinal propositions; see on this below. It is probable that a Synod was held
in Alexandria during his stay there.

[1] This, it is true, is the account only of Philostorgius (I. 7), but there is no
reason for mistrusting him.

[2] In Egypt the tumults were so serious that even the image of the Emperor
was attacked (Vita Const. III. 4).

[3] This is the account given by Sulpicius Severus, Chron. II. 40 ; " Nicæna synodus
auctore Hosio confecta habebatur."

[4] Athan. hist. Arian. 42; οὗτος ἐν |Νικαίᾳ πίστιν ἐξέθετο. On Hosius see the
lengthy article in the Dict. of Christ. Biogr. The life of this important and influential
bishop covers the century between the death of Origen and the birth of Augustine.

[5] From the letter of Arius to Eusebius of Nicomedia.

[6] Lightfoot (S. Ignatius Vol. II., p. 90 ff.) has published a learned discussion
on ἀγένητος (underived) and ἀγέννητος (unbegotten) in the Fathers up till Athanasius. Ignatius (Eph. 7) called the Son as to His Godhead " ἀγέννητος." In the
first decades of the Arian controversy no distinction was made between the words,
i.e., the difference in the writing of them was not taken account of, and this
produced frightful confusion. Still Athanasius saw clearly from the first that though
the conception of generation might hold good of the Son, that of becoming or
derivation did not; s. de synod 3: τὸν πατέρα μόνον ἄναρχον ὄντα καὶ ἀγέννητον
γεγεννηκέναι ἀνεφίκτως καὶ πᾶσιν ἀκαταλήπτως οἴδαμεν· τὸν δὲ υἰὸν γεγεννῆσθαι
πρὸ αἰώνων καὶ μηκέτι ὁμοίως τῷ πατρὶ ἀγέννητον εἶναι καὶ αὐτὸν, ἀλλ' ἀρχὴν
ἔχειν τὸν γεννήσαντα πατέρα. Spite of this he could say (l. c. c. 46) : τοῦτο τὸ
ὄνομα—scil. ἀγέννητος, as if it were identical in form with ἀγένητος—διάφορα ἔχει
τὰ σημαινόμενα. καὶ οἱ μέν, τὸ ὂν μὲν μήτε δὲ γεννηθέν, μήτε ὅλως ἔχον τὸν αἴτιον,

ἀτόμῳ τινὶ προάγει ὁ θεὸς τοῦ υἱοῦ, ἀεὶ θεός, ἀεὶ υἱός, ἐξ αὐτοῦ τοῦ
θεοῦ ὁ υἱός; always God, always Son, at the same time Father,
at the same time Son, the Son exists unbegotten with the
Father, everlasting, uncreated, neither in conception nor in any
smallest point does God excel the Son, always God, always
Son, from God Himself the Son.

λέγουσιν ἀγέννητον, οἱ δὲ τὸ ἄκτιστον; see also the tiresome distinctions in the
work "de decret. synod. Nic." 28 sq. The distinction in fact between γεννᾶν, γίγ-
νεσθαι, κτίζειν was not yet itself a definite one. At a later period there was no
hesitation in asserting that the Son both as God and as Man is γεννητός; s. Joh.
Damasc. I. 8: χρὴ γὰρ εἰδέναι, ὅτι τὸ ἀγένητον, διὰ τοῦ ἑνὸς ν γραφόμενον, τὸ
ἄκτιστον ἤ τὸ μὴ γενόμενον σημαίνει, τὸ δὲ ἀγέννητον, διὰ τῶν δύο ν γραφόμενον,
δηλοῖ τὸ μὴ γεννηθέν. From this he infers that the Father only is ἀγέννητος, while
the Son as God is γεννητός and indeed μόνος γεννητός. One can see from the
wonderful word of Alexander's, ἀγεννητογενής, what difficulties were created at first for
the orthodox by the ἀγέν[ν]ητος. Athanasius would have preferred to banish entirely
the fatal word and not to have used it even for the Father. That it, as is the case
with ὁμοούσιος also, was first used by the Gnostics and in fact by the Valentinians
is evident from the striking passage in the letter of Ptolemäus to Flora c. 5, which
has hitherto escaped the notice of those who have investigated the subject. Ptolemäus is there dealing with the only good primal God, the primal ground of all
Being and all things, with the true demiurge and Satan. He writes amongst other
things: καὶ ἔσται (ὁ δημιουργὸς) μὲν καταδεέστερος τοῦ τελείου Θεοῦ, ἅτε δὴ καὶ
γεννητὸς ὢν καὶ οὐκ ἀγέννητος—εἷς γὰρ ἐστιν ἀγέννητος ὁ πατήρ, ἐξ οὗ τὰ πάντα ...
μείζων δὲ καὶ κυριώτερος τοῦ ἀντικειμένου γενήσεται καὶ ἑτέρας οὐσίας τε καὶ
φύσεως πεφυκὼς παρὰ τὴν ἑκατέρων τούτων οὐσίαν ... τοῦ δὲ πατρὸς τῶν ὅλων τοῦ
ἀγεννήτου—that is thus the characteristic!—ἡ οὐσία ἐστὶν ἀφθαρσία τε καὶ φῶς
αὐτοόν, ἁπλοῦν τε καὶ μονοειδές, ἡ δὲ τούτου (scil. τοῦ δημιουργοῦ) οὐσία διττὴν μέν
τινα δύναμιν προήγαγεν, αὐτὸς δὲ τοῦ κρείττονός ἐστιν εἰκών. μηδέ σε τὰ νῦν τοῦτο
θορυβείτω, θέλουσαν μαθεῖν, πῶς ἀπὸ μιᾶς ἀρχῆς τῶν ὅλων οὔσης τε καὶ ὁμολογου-
μένης ἡμῖν καὶ πεπιστευμένης, τῆς ἀγεννήτου καὶ ἀφθάρτου καὶ ἀγαθῆς, συνέστησαν
καὶ αὗται αἱ φύσεις, ἥ τε τῆς φθορᾶς καὶ ἡ τῆς μεσότητος, ἀνομοούσιοι αὗται καθεσ-
τῶσαι, τοῦ ἀγαθοῦ φύσιν ἔχοντος τὰ ὅμοια ἑαυτῷ καὶ ὁμοούσια γεννᾶν τε γαὶ προ-
φέρειν· μαθήσῃ γὰρ ἑξῆς καὶ τὴν τούτου ἀρχήν τε καὶ γέννησιν. This is how Ptolemäus
wrote c. 160. His words already contain the ecclesiastical terminology of the future!
We also already meet with the term "σοφία ἀνυπόστατος" in a passage of his
l. c. c. 1. Many passages prove, moreover, that not only the words employed later
on, but also the ideas from which sprang the Church doctrine of the immanent
Trinity in its subsequent form, were present in the writings of the Valentinians,
as, e.g., the following from Hipp. Philos. VI. 29 (Heracleon): ἥν ὅλως γεννητὸν
οὐδέν, πατήρ δὲ ἥν μόνος ἀγέννητος ... ἐπεὶ δὲ ἥν γόνιμος, ἔδοξεν αὐτῷ ποτὲ τὸ
κάλλιστον καὶ τελεώτατον, ὃ εἶχεν ἐν αὐτῷ, γεννῆσαι καὶ προαγαγεῖν· φιλέρημος
γὰρ οὐκ ἥν· Ἀγάπη γάρ, φησίν, ἥν ὅλος, ἡ δὲ ἀγάπη οὐκ ἔστιν ἀγάπη, ἐὰν μὴ ᾖ τὸ
ἀγαπώμενον ... τελειότερος δὲ ὁ πατήρ, ὅτι ἀγέννητος ὢν μόνος. In what follows
the whole discussion is conditioned by the problem that the begotten Æons are
in their nature indeed ὁμοούσιοι with the Father, but that they are imperfect as
γεννητοί and are inferior to the μόνος ἀγέννητος. Here therefore the field for the

Alexander thus maintains the beginningless, eternal co-existence of Father and Son: the Father is never to be thought of
without the Son who springs from the Father. It is not improbable that Alexander was led thus to give prominence to
the one side of the Logos doctrine of Origen, owing to the
influence of the theology of Irenæus or Melito. [1] The doctrine
which Arius opposed to this is above all dominated by the
thought that God, the Only One, is alone eternal, and that
besides Him there exists only what is created, and that this
originates in His will, that accordingly the Son also is not
eternal, but a creation of God out of the non-existent. [2] From
this thesis there necessarily follows the rejection of the predicate ὁμοούσιος for the Son. Arius and his friends already before
the Council of Nicæa give expression to it, incidentally indeed,
but without ambiguity. [3]

The doctrine of Arius is as follows: [4]

Arian-Athanasian controversy is already marked out. But it is to be noticed further
that the three terms, μονογενής, πρωτότοκος, and εἰκών contain and define the entire
Valentinian Christology, which is of an extremely complicated character. (See Heinrici,
die Valentin. Gnosis. p. 120). In the fourth century, however, they became the
catchwords of the different Christologies.

[1] It is impossible to come to any certain decision on this point, so long as it
is not proved that the pieces which are ascribed to Alexander are really his, and
at the same time so long as it is uncertain if the sentences from them which also
bear the names of Irenæus and Melito really belong to these writers and have
been made use of by Alexander. See on this question Cotterill, Modern Criticism and
Clement's Epp. to the Virgins, 1884, on this ThLZ., 1884, p. 267 f; Pitra, Analecta Sacra T. IV. pp. 196 sq., 430 sq. On this Loofs, ThLZ. 1884, Col. 572 f.,
and very specially Krüger, Ztschr. f. wiss. Theol. 1888, p. 434 ff.; Melito of Sardes
and Alex. of Alexandria. Socrates asserts (I. 5) that Arius believed that Alexander
wished to introduce the doctrinal system of Sabellius. But the Christology of Irenæus has also been understood in a "Sabellian" sense. The important address
of Alexander on soul and body, in which he also treats of the Incarnation, is
to be found in Migne T. 18.

[2] This was the original point of dispute. Διωκόμεθα, writes Arius to Eusebius,
ὅτι εἴπομεν, Ἀρχὴν ἔχει ὁ υἱός, ὁ δὲ Θεὸς ἄναρχός ἐστι. Διὰ τοῦτο διωκόμεθα, καὶ
ὅτι εἴπομεν, Ἐξ οὐκ ὄντων ἐστίν.

[3] See the fragment from the Thalia in Athan. de synod. 15, the letter of
Eusebius of Nicomedia to Paulinus, also that of Arius to Alexander.

[4] The fragments of the Thalia and the two letters of Arius which have been
preserved are amongst the most important sources: cf. also the confession of faith
of Arius in Socr. I. 26 (Sozom. II. 27). Then we have the statements of his earliest
opponents, very specially the two letters of Alexander and the verbal quotations

(a) God, the Only One, besides whom there is no other, is alone unbegotten, without beginning and eternal; He is inexpressible, incomprehensible, and has absolutely no equal. These are the notes which express His peculiar nature. He has *created* all things out of His free will, and there exists nothing beside Him which He has not created. The expression "to beget" is simply a synonym for "to create". If it were not, the pure simplicity and spirituality of God's nature would be destroyed. God can put forth nothing out of His own essence; nor can He communicate His essence to what is created, for this essence is essentially uncreated. He has accordingly not been Father always; for otherwise what is created would not be created, but eternal. [1]

of the propositions of Arius in Athanasius; see especially ep. ad episc. Ægypt 12 and de sentent. Dionys. 23, also the Orat. c. Arian. In the third place, we can adduce the propositions laid down by the earliest Arians, or by the patrons of Arius. Opponents made little difference between them and Arius himself, and the actual facts shew that they were justified in so doing; see the letter of Eusebius of Nicomedia to Paulinus and the fragments of Arian letters in Athanas. de synod. 17, also the fragments from Asterius. Finally, we have to consider what the Church historians and Epiphanius have to tell us regarding the doctrinal propositions of Arius. There was no "evolution" of Arianism, we can only distinguish different varieties of it. Even Eunomius and Aëtius did not "develop" the doctrinal system, but only gave it a logically perfect form. Lucian had already completed the entire system, as is specially evident from the letter of Eusebius of Nicomedia to Paulinus; see also the introduction to the Thalia in Athan., Orat. c. Arian. I. 5, which, moreover, presents the character of Arius in an unfavourable light: κατὰ πίστιν ἐκλεκτῶν Θεοῦ, συνετῶν Θεοῦ, παίδων ἁγίων, ὀρθοτόμων, ἅγιον Θεοῦ πνεῦμα λαβόντων, τάδε ἔμαθον ἔγωγε ὑπὸ τῶν σοφίης μετεχόντων, ἀστείων, θεοδιδάκτων, κατὰ πάντα σοφῶν τε· τούτων κατ' ἴχνος ἦλθον ἐγὼ βαίνων ὁμοδόξως ὁ περικλυτός, ὁ πολλὰ παθὼν διὰ τὴν Θεοῦ δόξαν, ὑπό τε Θεοῦ μαθὼν σοφίαν καὶ γνῶσιν ἐγὼ ἔγνων.

[1] In the doctrine of God as held by Arius and his friends two main ideas appear all through as those upon which everything depends: (1) that God alone is ἀγέννητος; (2) that all else has been created out of nothing by God's free will. In accordance with this they get rid of everything designated as προβολὴ ἀγέννητος, ἐρυγή, γέννημα, μέρος ὁμοούσιον, ἐξ ἀπορροίας τῆς οὐσίας, μονὰς πλατυνθεῖσα, ἕν εἰς δύο διῃρημένον, etc.; even the old pictorial expressions "Light of Light", "Torch of Torch" are rejected, and they will have nothing to do with the transformation of an originally impersonal eternal essence or substance in God into a personally subsisting essentiality; see the epp. Arii ad Euseb. et Alexand. Εἰ τό; Ἐκ γαστρός, καὶ τό· Ἐκ πατρὸς ἐξῆλθον καὶ ἥκω, ὡς μέρος τοῦ ὁμοουσίου καὶ ὡς προβολὴ ὑπό τινων νοεῖται, σύνθετος ἔσται ὁ πατὴρ καὶ διαιρετὸς καὶ τρεπτὸς καὶ σῶμα... καὶ τὰ ἀκόλουθα σώματι πάσχων ὁ ἀσώματος Θεός; It was Eusebius Nic. specially in his letter to Paulinus, who developed the thought that "to beget" is equal to "to create" and he, for the rest, allows that if

(b) Wisdom and Logos dwell within this God as the powers (not persons) which are coincident with His substance, and are by their very nature inseparable from it; there are besides many *created* powers. [1]

(c) Before the world existed, God of His free will created an independent substance or hypostasis (οὐσία, ὑπόστασις) as the instrument by means of which all other creatures were to be created, since without it the creatures would not have been able to endure the contact of the Godhead. This Being is termed in Scripture Wisdom, also Son, Image, Word; this Wisdom, which, compared with the inner divine Wisdom, is called Wisdom only in a loose sense, has like all creatures been created out of nothing. It originates in God only in so far as it has been created by God; it is in no sense of the substance or essence of God. It has had a beginning; it accordingly did not always exist, there was a time in which it was not. That the Scriptures use the word "begotten" of this Substance does not imply that this is peculiar to it any more than is the predicate "Son"; for the other creatures are likewise described here and there as "begotten," and men are called "sons of God". [2]

the Son were begotten out of the substance of the Father the predicate ἀγέννητος would attach to Him, and He would possess the ταυτότης τῆς φύσεως with the Father. In laying down their doctrine of God, Arius and his friends express themselves with a certain amount of fervour. One can see that they have a genuine concern to defend monotheism. At the same time they are as much interested in the negative predicates of the Godhead as the most convinced Neo-platonists. On πατήρ see the Thalia in Athan., Orat. I. c. Arian c. 5 : οὐκ ἀεὶ ὁ Θεὸς πατὴρ ἦν, ἀλλ᾿ ἦν ὅτε ὁ Θεὸς μόνος ἦν καὶ οὔπω πατὴρ ἦν, ὕστερον δὲ ἐπιγέγονε πατήρ.

[1] Thalia l. c.: δύο σοφίας εἶναι. μίαν μὲν τὴν ἰδίαν καὶ συνυπάρχουσαν τῷ Θεῷ, τὸν δὲ υἱὸν ἐν ταύτῃ τῇ σοφίᾳ γεγενῆσθαι καὶ ταύτης μετέχοντα ὠνομάσθαι μόνον σοφίαν καὶ λόγον· ἡ σοφία γὰρ τῇ σοφίᾳ ὑπῆρξε σοφοῦ Θεοῦ βελήσει. Οὕτω καὶ λόγον ἕτερον εἶναι λέγει παρὰ τὸν υἱὸν ἐν τῷ Θεῷ καὶ τούτον μετέχοντα τὸν υἱὸν ὠνομάσθαι πάλιν κατὰ χάριν λόγον καὶ υἱόν... Πολλαὶ δυνάμεις εἰσί, καὶ ἡ μὲν μία τοῦ Θεοῦ ἐστιν ἰδία φύσει καὶ αἴδιος, ὁ δὲ Χριστὸς πάλιν οὐκ ἔστιν ἀληθινὴ δύναμις τοῦ Θεοῦ, ἀλλὰ μία τῶν λεγομένων δυνάμεων ἐστι καὶ αὐτός, ὧν μία καὶ ἡ ἀκρὶς καὶ ἡ κάμπη κ.τ.λ.

[2] See the foregoing note and Thalia l. c.: οὐκ ἀεὶ ἦν ὁ υίός, πάντων γὰρ γενο-μένων ἐξ οὐκ ὄντων καὶ πάντων ὄντων κτισμάτων καὶ ποιημάτων γενομένων, καὶ αὐτὸς ὁ τοῦ Θεοῦ λόγος ἐξ οὐκ ὄντων γέγονε, καὶ ἦν ποτε ὅτε οὐκ ἦν, καὶ οὐκ ἦν πρὶν γένηται, ἀλλ᾿ ἀρχὴν τοῦ κτίζεσθαι ἔσχε καὶ αὐτός... Ἦν μόνος ὁ Θεὸς καὶ οὔπω ἦν ὁ λόγος καὶ ἡ σοφία, εἶτα βέλησις ἡμᾶς δημιουργῆσαι, τότε δὴ πεποίηκεν

(*d*) As regards his Substance, the "Son" is consequently an unrelated and independent being totally separated from, and different from, the substance or nature of the Father. He has neither one and the same substance together with the Father, nor a nature and constitution similar to that of the Father. If he had, then there would be two Gods. On the contrary, like all rational creatures he has a free will and is capable of change. He might consequently have been good or bad; but he made up his mind to follow the good, and continued in the good without vacillation. Thus he has by means of his own will come to be unchangeable. [1]

ἕνα τινὰ καὶ ὠνόμασεν αὐτὸν λόγον καὶ σοφίαν καὶ υἱόν, ἵνα ἡμᾶς δι' αὐτοῦ δημιουργήσῃ. Ep. Arii ad Euseb.: Πρὶν γεννηθῇ ἤτοι κτισθῇ ἤτοι ὁρισθῇ ἢ θεμελιωθῇ, οὐκ ἦν, ἀγένητος γὰρ οὐκ ἦν. Since the Son is neither a part of the Father nor ἐξ ὑποκειμένου τινός, he must be ἐξ οὐκ ὄντων; θελήματι καὶ βουλῇ ὑπέστη πρὸ χρόνων καὶ πρὸ αἰώνων ὁ υἱός. Ep. Arii ad Alex: ... γεννήσαντα υἱὸν μονογενῆ πρὸ χρόνων αἰωνίων, δι' οὗ καὶ τοὺς αἰῶνας καὶ τὰ ὅλα πεποίηκε ... κτίσμα τοῦ Θεοῦ τέλειον ... θελήματι τοῦ Θεοῦ πρὸ χρόνων καὶ πρὸ αἰώνων κτισθέντα, καὶ τὸ ζῆν καὶ τὸ εἶναι παρὰ τοῦ πατρὸς εἰληφότα καὶ τὰς δόξας συνυποστήσαντος αὐτῷ τοῦ πατρός. Οὐ γὰρ ὁ πατὴρ δοὺς αὐτῷ πάντων τὴν κληρονομίαν ἐστέρησεν ἑαυτὸν ὧν ἀγεννήτως ἔχει ἐν ἑαυτῷ. πηγὴ γὰρ ἐστι πάντων, ὥστε τρεῖς εἰσιν ὑποστάσεις ... Ὁ υἱὸς ἀχρόνως γεννηθεὶς οὐκ ἦν πρὸ τοῦ γεννηθῆναι οὐδὲ γάρ ἐστιν ἀΐδιος ἢ συναΐδιος ἢ συναγένητος τῷ πατρὶ οὐδὲ ἅμα τῷ πατρὶ τὸ εἶναι ἔχει ... Ἀρχὴ αὐτοῦ ἐστιν ὁ Θεός, ἀρχεῖ γὰρ αὐτοῦ ὡς Θεὸς αὐτοῦ καὶ πρὸ αὐτοῦ ὤν. Ep. Euseb. ad Paulin.: κτιστὸν εἶναι καὶ θεμελιωτὸν καὶ γενητὸν τῇ οὐσίᾳ, according to Proverbs 8: ... Οὐδέν ἐστιν ἐκ τῆς οὐσίας τοῦ Θεοῦ, πάντα δὲ βουλήματι αὐτοῦ γενόμενα. Ep. Euseb. Nic. ad Arium.: τὸ πεποιημένον οὐκ ἦν πρὶν γενέσθαι, τὸ γενόμενον δὲ ἀρχὴν ἔχει τοῦ εἶναι. Athan. Nazarb., ep. ad. Alex.: "Why do you blame the Arians because they say that the Son κτίσμα πεποίηται ἐξ οὐκ ὄντων καὶ ἕν τῶν πάντων ἐστίν? We are to understand by the hundred sheep of the parable all created beings, and thus the Son too is included." Georg. Laod. ep. ad. Aiex.: "Don't blame the Arians because they say ἦν ποτε ὅτε οὐκ ἦν ὁ υἱὸς τοῦ Θεοῦ, Isaiah too came later than his father." Georg. Laod. ep. ad. Arianos. "Don't be afraid to allow that the Son is *from* the Father; for the Apostle says that all things are *from* God, although it is certain that all things are ἐξ οὐκ ὄντων." Thalia (de synod. 15): ἡ μόνας ἦν, ἡ δυὰς δὲ οὐκ ἦν πρὶν ὑπάρξει. Arius for the rest seems to have considered the creation of this "Son" as simply a necessity, because God *could* not create directly, but *required* an intermediate power.

[1] Ep. Euseb. ad Paulin.: "Εν τὸ ἀγένητον, ἓν δὲ τὸ ὑπ' αὐτοῦ ἀληθῶς καὶ οὐκ ἐκ τῆς οὐσίας αὐτοῦ γεγονός, καθόλου τῆς φύσεως τῆς ἀγενήτου μὴ μετέχον, ἀλλὰ γεγονὸς ὁλοχερῶς ἕτερον τῇ φύσει κ. τῇ δυνάμει. The ταυτότης τῆς φύσεως is rejected. Ep. Arii ad Alex.: υἱὸν ὑποστήσαντα ἰδίῳ θελήματι ἄτρεπτον καὶ ἀναλλοίωτον. Who says, therefore, that the Son is in everything like the Father introduces two "ἀγέννητοι." Thalia: τῇ μὲν φύσει ὥσπερ πάντες οὕτω δὲ αὐτὸς ὁ λόγος ἐστὶ τρεπτός, τῷ δὲ ἰδίῳ αὐτεξουσίῳ, ἕως βούλεται, μένει καλός· ὅτε μέν τοι θέλει

(*e*) Since the Son is, as regards his substance, unrelated to the Godhead, [1] he is not truly God, and accordingly has not by nature the divine attributes; he is only the so-called Logos and Wisdom. As he is not eternal, neither is his knowledge in any sense perfect; he has no absolute knowledge of God, but only a relative knowledge, in fact he does not even know his own substance perfectly, accordingly he cannot claim equal honour with the Father. [2]

(*f*) Still the Son is not a creature and a product like other creatures; he is the perfect creature, κτίσμα τέλειον; by him everything has been created; he stands in a special relation to God, but this is solely conditioned by grace and adoption; the bestowal of grace on the other hand, is based on the steadfast inclination of this free being to the good which was fore-

δύναται τρέπεσθαι καὶ αὐτὸς ὥσπερ καὶ ἡμεῖς, τρεπτῆς ὤν φύσεως... As all things so far as their substance is concerned are unrelated to God and unlike Him, so too is the Logos ἀλλότριος καὶ ἀνόμοιος κατὰ πάντα τῆς τοῦ πατρὸς οὐσίας καὶ ἰδιότητος. Μεμερισμέναι τῇ φύσει καὶ ἀπεξενωμέναι καὶ ἀπεσχοινισμέναι καὶ ἀλλότριοι καὶ ἀμέτοχοί εἰσιν ἀλλήλων αἱ οὐσίαι τοῦ πατρὸς καὶ τοῦ υἱοῦ καὶ τοῦ ἁγίου πνεύματος; they are even ἀνόμοιοι πάμπαν ἀλλήλων ταῖς τε οὐσίαις καὶ δόξαις ἐπ' ἄπειρον. τὸν γοῦν λόγον φησὶν εἰς ὁμοιότητα δόξης καὶ οὐσίας ἀλλότριον εἶναι πολυτελῶς ἑκατέρων τοῦ τε πατρὸς καὶ τοῦ ἁγίου πνεύματος. ὁ υἱὸς διῃρημένος ἐστὶν καθ' ἑαυτὸν καὶ ἀμέτοχος κατὰ πάντα τοῦ πατρός. Thalia (de Synod. 15): Ἄρρητος Θεὸς Ἴσον οὐδὲ ὅμοιον οὐχ ὁμόδοξον ἔχει. ὁ υἱὸς ἴδιον οὐδεν ἔχει τοῦ Θεοῦ καθ' ὑπόστασιν ἰδιότητος οὐδὲ γὰρ ἐστιν Ἴσος ἀλλ' οὐδὲ ὁμοούσιος αὐτῷ. The Triad is not of ὁμοίαις δόξαις: ἀνεπίμικτα ἑαυταῖς εἰσιν αἱ ὑποστάσεις αὐτῶν, μία τῆς μιᾶς ἐνδοξότερα δόξαις ἐπ' ἄπειρον. Ξένος τοῦ υἱοῦ κατ' οὐσίαν ὁ πατήρ, ὅτι ἄναρχος ὑπάρχει. According to the letter of Eusebius to Paulinus it looks as if Eusebius held the unchangeableness of the Son to belong to his substance; he probably, however, only means that it had come to be his substance. At a later date many Arians must have attributed to the Son an original unchangeableness as a *gift* of the Father, for Philostorgius mentions as a peculiarity of the Arian bishop Theodosius that he taught (VIII. 3): ὁ Χριστὸς τρεπτὸς μὲν τῇ γε φύσει τῇ οἰκείᾳ.

[1] Because of this sundering of the Father and the Son the Arians at a later date are also called " Diatomites " (Joh. Damasc. in Cotellier, Eccl. Gr. monum. I., p. 298).

[2] Thalia (Orat. c. Arian I. 6): οὐδὲ Θεὸς ἀληθινός ἐστιν ὁ λόγος. He is only called God, but he is not truly God, καὶ τῷ υἱῷ ὁ πατὴρ ἀόρατος ὑπάρχει καὶ οὔτε ὁρᾶν οὔτε γιγνώσκειν τελείως καὶ ἀκριβῶς δύναται ὁ λόγος τὸν ἑαυτοῦ πατέρα, ἀλλὰ καὶ ὃ γιγνώσκει καὶ ὃ βλέπει ἀναλόγως τοῖς ἰδίοις μέτροις οἶδε καὶ βλέπει, ὥσπερ καὶ ἡμεῖς γιγνώσκομεν κατὰ τὴν ἰδίαν δύναμιν. Ὁ υἱὸς τὴν ἑαυτοῦ οὐσίαν οὐκ οἶδε. Euseb. Cæs. ep. ad Euphrat.: Χριστὸς οὐκ ἔστιν ἀληθινὸς Θεός. The conviction that the Son is not truly God, and that all lofty predicates attach to him only in a nuncupative sense, that he does not know the Father, is very strongly expressed in the fragment of the Thalia de synod. 15.

seen by God. Through God's bestowal of grace and by his own steady progress he has become God, so that we may now call him "only-begotten God", "strong God" and so on. [1]

(*g*) All that Scripture and tradition assert in reference to the incarnation and the humanity of this being holds good; he truly took a human body (σῶμα ἄψυχον); the feelings shewn by the historical Christ teach us that the Logos to whom they attach—for Christ had not a human soul—is a being capable of suffering, not an absolutely perfect being, but one who attains by effort absolute perfection. [2]

(*h*) Amongst the number of created powers (δυνάμεις) the Holy Ghost is to be placed beside the Son as a second, independent Substance or Hypostasis, (οὐσία, ὑπόστασις); for the Christian believes in three separate and different substances or persons, (οὐσίαι, ὑποστάσεις); Father, Son and Spirit. Arius apparently, like his followers, considered the Spirit as a being created by the Son and subordinate to him. [3]

---

[1] Arii Ep. ad Euseb.: πλήρης Θεὸς μονογενής, ἀναλλοίωτος (in virtue of his will). Arii ep. ad Alex.: υἱὸν μονογενῆ... κτίσμα τοῦ Θεοῦ τέλειον, ἀλλ᾽ οὐχ ὡς ἕν τῶν κτισμάτων, γέννημα, ἀλλ᾽ οὐχ ὡς ἓν τῶν γεννημάτων... Πατὴρ δοὺς αὐτῷ πάντων τὴν κληρονομίαν... Ὁ υἱὸς μόνος ὑπὸ μόνου τοῦ πατρὸς ὑπέστη. Thalia: τὸν υἱὸν ἐν ταύτῃ τῇ σοφίᾳ γεγενῆσθαι καὶ ταύτης μετέχοντα ὠνομάσθαι μόνον σοφίαν καὶ λόγον... Διὰ τοῦτο καὶ προγιγνώσκων ὁ Θεὸς ἔσεσθαι καλὸν αὐτόν, προλαβὼν αὐτῷ ταύτην τὴν δόξαν δέδωκεν, ἣν ἄνθρωπος καὶ ἐκ τῆς ἀρετῆς ἔσχε μετὰ ταῦτα· ὥστε ἐξ ἔργων αὐτοῦ, ὧν προέγνω ὁ Θεός, τοιοῦτον αὐτὸν νῦν γεγονέναι πεποίηκε... Μετοχῇ χάριτος ὥσπερ καὶ οἱ ἄλλοι πάντες οὕτω καὶ αὐτὸς λέγεται ὀνόματι μόνον Θεός... Θεὸς ἔνεγκεν εἰς υἱὸν ἑαυτῷ τόνδε τεκνοποιήσας· ἴδιον οὐδὲν ἔχει τοῦ Θεοῦ καθ᾽ ὑπόστασιν ἰδιότητος... The Son is Wisdom, Image, Reflection, Word; God cannot produce a greater than He; Θεοῦ θελήσει ὁ υἱὸς ἡλίκος καὶ ὅσος ἐστίν, ἐξ ὅτε καὶ ἀφ᾽ οὗ καὶ ἀπὸ τότε ἐκ τοῦ Θεοῦ ὑπέστη, ἰσχυρός Θεὸς ὤν, but he extols the greater Father. Arius ap. Athan. Orat. I. c. Arian. 9: μετοχῇ καὶ αὐτὸς εθεοποιήθη. It is evident from Alexander's letter to Alexander that Arius strongly emphasised the προκοπή, the moral progress of the Son.

[2] Owing to the general uncertainty regarding the extent of the "humanity" which prevailed at the beginning of the controversy, the latter assertion of the Arians was not so energetically combatted as the rest. That the limitation of the humanity of Christ to a body originated with Lucian, is asserted by Epiph. Ancorat. 33.

[3] In the writings of Arius οὐσία and ὑπόστασις are used as synonymous terms. The impersonal Spirit (Logos, Wisdom) indwelling in God the Father as *Power*, was naturally considered by the Arians to be higher than the Son. On this point they appeal like the old Roman Adoptianists to Matt. XII. 31 (see Vol. III., p. 20 ff.). It is indeed not even certain whether Arius and the older Arians when they speak of a Trinity, always included the Holy Spirit. According to Athanasius de synod.

Alexander expressly notes that the Arians appeal to Scripture in support of their doctrine, and Athanasius says that the Thalia contained passages of Scripture.[1] The passages so frequently cited later on by the Arians; Deut. VI. 4, XXXII. 39; Prov. VIII. 22; Ps. XLV. 8; Mt. XII. 28; Mk. XIII. 32; Mt. XXVI. 41, XXVIII. 18; Lk. II. 52, XVIII. 19; John XI. 34, XIV. 28, XVII. 3; Acts II. 36; 1 Cor. I. 24, XV. 28; Col. I. 15; Philipp. II. 6 f.; Hebr. I. 4, III. 2; John XII. 27, XIII. 21; Mt. XXVI, 39, XXVII. 46, etc., will thus already have been used by Arius himself. Arius was not a systematiser, nor were his friends systematisers either. In this respect their literary activity was limited to letters in which they stirred each other up, and which were soon put together in a collected form. The only one amongst them before Eunomius and Aëtius who undertook to give a systematic defence of the doctrinal system, was the Sophist Asterius, called by Athanasius the advocate (συνήγορος) of the sects. He was a clever, clear-headed man, but he was quite unable to wipe out what was in everybody's eyes the blot on his character, his denial of the Faith during the time of persecution.[2] There were various shades of

---

15, we may conclude that their Trinity consisted of the following hypostases: (1) God as primordial without the Son; (2) God as Father; (3) the Son. Still this is not certain.

1 Orat. I. c. Arian. 8.

2 On Asterius see Athan., Orat. c. Arian. I. 30—33; II. 37; III. 2, 60; de decret. syn. Nic. 8, 28—31; de synod. 18, 19, 47. Epiphan. H. 76, 3; Socrat. I. 36; Philostorg. II. 14, 15; Hieron. de vir. inl. 94. Marcellus of Ancyra wrote against the principal work of Asterius, see Zahn, p. 41 ff. Athanasius attacked a συνταγμάτιον of his. One of the main theses of this book was that there are two ἀγένητα. Asterius also discussed 1 Cor. I. 24, and indeed he took the correct view. His explanation too of the passage John XIV. 10, is worthy of note: εὔδηλον ὅτι διὰ τοῦτο εἴρηκεν ἑαυτὸν μὲν ἐν τῷ πατρὶ, ἐν ἑαυτῷ δὲ πάλιν τὸν πατέρα, ἐπεὶ μήτε τὸν λόγον, ὅν διεξήρχετο, ἑαυτοῦ φησιν εἶναι, ἀλλὰ τοῦ πατρὸς δεδωκότος τὴν δύναμιν. Upon this passage Athanasius remarks (Orat. III. 2) that only a child could be pardoned such an explanation. It is a point of great importance that Asterius, like Paul of Samosata, reckoned the will as the highest thing. Accordingly, to create of His free will is more worthy of God too than to beget (l. c. III. 60). Athanasius says that Arius himself made use of the work of Asterius, and in this connection he gives us the important statement of Asterius (de decret. 8) that created things are not able τῆς ἀκράτου χειρὸς τοῦ ἀγεννήτου ἐργασίαν βαστάξαι, and that on account of this the creation of the Son as an intermediary was necessary. (See Orat. c. Arian II. 24.)

opinion amongst the followers and supporters of Arius. In Arianism in its more rigid form the tradition of Paul of Samosata and Lucian predominated, in its milder form the subordination doctrine of Origen. Both types were indeed at one as regards the form of doctrine, and the elements traceable to Origen won over all enlightened "Conservatives". We may count Asterius too amongst, the latter, at all events the unbending Philostorgius was not at all pleased with him, and Asterius subsequently approached near to the Semiarians.

Previous to the Council of Nicæa, the letters of the bishop Alexander are, for us at all events, the sole literary manifestos of the opposite party. The Encyklica already shews that the writer is fully conscious he has got to do with a heresy of the very worst type. The earlier heresies all pale before it; no other heretic has approached so near to being Antichrist. Arius and his friends are the enemies of God, murderers of the divinity of Christ, people like Judas. Alexander did not enter into theoretical and theological explanations. After giving a brief but complete and excellent account of the Logos doctrine of Arius, he sets in contrast with the statements contained in it, numerous passages from the Gospel of John and other quotations from Scripture. [1] The sole remarks of a positive kind he makes are that it belongs to the substance or essence of the Logos, that he perfectly knows the Father, and that the supposition of a time in which the Logos was not, makes the Father ἄλογος καὶ ἄσοφος. The latter remark, which for that matter of it does not touch Arius, shews that Alexander included the Logos or Son *in the substance of the Father as a necessary element*. The second epistle goes much more into details, [2] but it shews at the same time how little Alexander, in solving the

---

[1] John I. 1, 13, 18, X. 15, 30, XIV. 9, 10; Hebr. I. 3, II. 10, XIII. 8; Ps. XLV. 2; CX. 3; Mal. III. 6. The passages continued to be regarded by the orthodox as the most important.

[2] Theodoret I. 4. Exaggerations and calumnies of the worst kind are not wanting in this writing. The reproach, too, that the Arians acted like the Jews is already found here. Of more importance, however, is the assertion that the Arian christology gave countenance to the heathen ideas of Christ and that the Arians had also in view the approval of the heathen. Ebion, Artemas (see Athanas., de synod. 20) and Paul are designated their Fathers.

problem, was able definitely to oppose fixed and finished formulæ to those of the Arians. The main positions of Arius are
once more pertinently characterised and refuted.

Alexander is conscious that he is contending for nothing less
than the divinity of Christ, the universal Faith of the Church,
when he refutes the statements that the Son is not eternal, that
He was created out of the non-existent, that He is not by
nature (φύσει) God, that He is capable of change, that He went
through a moral development (προκοπή), that He is only Son
by adoption, like the sons of God in general, and so on. [1] He
not only adduces proofs from the Bible in large numbers, [2] he
has unmistakably in his mind what is for him a central, religious
thought. Christ must *belong to God and not to the world*, because all other creatures require such a being in order to attain
to God and become the adopted sons of God. In order to make
clear the possibility of such a being, Alexander uses by preference
for the Son the expression which had been already preferred
by Origen—"the perfect image," "the perfect reflection." But
even this expression does not suffice him; it gains deeper meaning
by the thought that the Son as the image of the Father at the
same time first clearly expresses the peculiar character of the
Father. In the Wisdom, the Logos, the Power, the "Son is made
known and the Father is characterised. To say that the reflection
of the divine glory does not exist is to do away also with the
archetypal light of which it is the reflection; if there exists no
impress or pattern of the substance of God, then he too is done
away with who is wholly characterised by this pattern or express
image:"—γνωρίζεται ὁ υἱὸς καὶ ὁ πατὴρ χαρακτηρίζεται. Τὸ γὰρ
ἀπαύγασμα τῆς δόξης μὴ εἶναι λέγειν συναναιρεῖ καὶ τὸ πρωτότυπον
φῶς, οὗ ἐστιν ἀπαύγασμα... τῷ μὴ εἶναι τὸν τῆς ὑποστάσεως τοῦ

---

[1] The two last theses are rejected in a specially emphatic manner. Alexander
repeatedly complains in this connection of the procedure of Arius in taking from
the Holy Scriptures only such passages as have reference to the humiliation of the
Logos for our sakes, and then referring them to the substance of the Logos. "They
omit the passages which treat of the divinity of the Son. Thus they arrive at the
impious supposition that Paul and Peter would have been like Christ if they had
always persisted in the good."

[2] John I. 1—3, I. 18, X. 30, XIV. 8, 9, 28; Matt. III. 17, XI. 27; 1 John V. 1 ;
Coloss. I. 15, 16; Rom. VIII. 32; Heb. I. 2 f.; Prov. VIII. 30 ; Ps. II. 7, CX. 3
XXXV. 10; Is. LIII. 8.

Θεοῦ χαρακτῆρα συναναιρεῖται κἀκεῖνος, ὁ πάντως παρ᾽ αὐτοῦ χαρακτηριζόμενος. While in laying down this thesis and others of a similar kind, *e.g.*, that the Son is the inner reason and power of the Father Himself, he approaches "Sabellianism," the latter doctrine is repudiated in the most decided and emphatic way. But on the other hand again, not only is the supposition of two unbegottens (αγεν[ν]ητα) rejected as a calumny, but he repeatedly emphasises in a striking fashion the fact that the begetting of the Son is not excluded by the application to Him of the predicate always (ἀεί), that the Father alone is unbegotten, *and that He is greater than the Son.* [1] Alexander thus asserts both things—namely, the inseparable unity of the substance of the Son with that of the Father [2] and their difference, and yet the one is held to be unbegotten and the other to be not unbegotten. In order to be able to maintain these contradictory theses he takes up the standpoint of Irenæus, that the mystery of the existence and coming forth of the Son is an inexpressible one even for Evangelists and angels, and is no proper object of human reflection and human statement. Even John did not venture to make any pronouncement regarding the ἀνεκδιήγητος ὑπόστασις τοῦ μονογενοῦς Θεοῦ, [3]—the ineffable substance of the only begotten God. "How could anyone waste his labour on the substance of the Logos of God, unless indeed he were afflicted with melancholy?" Πῶς ἄν περιεργάσαιτό τις τὴν τοῦ Θεοῦ λόγου ὑπόστασιν, ἐκτὸς εἰ μὴ μελαγχολικῇ διαθέσει ληφθεὶς τυγχάνοι. [4]

---

[1] From this it is plainly evident that the real point in dispute was not as to subordination and coördination, but as to unity of substance and difference of substance. That the archetype is greater than the type is for Alexander a truth that is beyond doubt. He goes still farther and says: οὐκοῦν τῷ ἀγεννήτῳ πατρὶ οἰκεῖον ἀξίωμα φυλακτέον, μηδένα τοῦ εἶναι αὐτῷ τὸν αἴτιον λέγοντας, τῷ δὲ υἱῷ τὴν ἁρμόζουσαν τιμὴν ἀπονεμητέον, τὴν ἄναρχον αὐτῷ παρὰ τοῦ πατρὸς γέννησιν ἀνατιθέντας.

[2] The expression "ὁμοούσιος" does not occur in Alexander.

[3] On this expression, which was used by Arius, see Hort, Two Dissertations, 1876.

[4] The respective passages in the letter have so many points of contact with expressions of Irenæus (see Vol. II., pp. 230 f., 276 f.) as to make the supposition, which also commends itself for other reasons, very probable (see above, p. 14, note 1), that Alexander had read Irenæus and had been strongly influenced by him. That Irenæus was known in Alexandria, at least at the beginning of the third century, follows from Euseb., H. E. VI. 14. (Strange to say it has undoubtedly not been proved that Athanasius ever quotes from Irenæus.) Alexander shews that he is not throughout dependent on Origen.

Alexander's actual standpoint is undoubtedly plainly expressed here. He does not wish to speculate; for the complete divinity of Christ is for him not a speculation at all, but a judgment of faith, and the distinction between Father and Son is for him something beyond doubt. But he sees that he is under the necessity of opposing certain formulæ to the doctrine of Arius. These are partly vague and partly contradictory : [1] "The Son is the inner reason and power of God," "Father and Son are two inseparable things" (δύο ἀχώριστα πράγματα), "Between Father and Son there is not the slightest difference" (διάστημα), "not even in any thought" (οὐδ᾽ ἄχρι τινὸς ἐννοίας), "There is only one unbegotten," "The Son has come into being in consequence of a γένεσις καὶ ποίησις" (an act of generation and production), "The Son has, compared with the world, an ineffable substance peculiarly his own" (ἰδιότροπος ἀνεκδιήγητος ὑπόστασις), "He is μονογενὴς Θεὸς" (only begotten God), "His Sonship is by its nature in possession of the deity of the Father" (κατὰ φύσιν τυγχάνουσα τῆς πατρικῆς θεότητος), [2] "Father and Son are two natures in the hypostasis" (τῃ ὑποστάσει δύο φύσεις [3]), between the Underived and he who has come into being out of the non-existent there is a μεσιτεύουσα φύσις μονογενής (the Son) δι᾽ ἧς τὰ ὅλα ἐξ οὐκ ὄντων ἐποίησεν ὁ πατὴρ τοῦ Θεοῦ λόγου, ἢ ἐξ αὐτοῦ τοῦ ὄντος πατρὸς γεγέννηται," (a mediating only begotten nature by which the Father of the God-Logos has made all things out of the non-existent, and which has been begotten out of the existent Father), "The Son has not proceeded out of the Father κατὰ τὰς τῶν σωμάτων ὁμοιότητας, ταῖς τομαῖς ἢ ταῖς ἐκδιαιρέσεων ἀπορροίαις (in the manner in which bodies are formed, by separation or by the emanation of parts divided off) ; "

---

[1] Alexander made no distinction between οὐσία, ὑπόστασις, φύσις.

[2] Ὃν τρόπον γὰρ ἡ ἄρρητος αὐτοῦ ὑπόστασις ἀσυγκρίτῳ ὑπεροχῇ ἐδείχθη ὑπερκειμένη πάντων οἷς αὐτὸς τὸ εἶναι ἐχαρίσατο, οὕτως καὶ ἡ υἱότης αὐτοῦ κατὰ φύσιν τυγχάνουσα τῆς πατρικῆς θεότητος ἀλέκτῳ ὑπεροχῇ διαφέρει τῶν δι᾽ αὐτοῦ θέσει υἱοτεθέντων.

[3] On John X. 30: ὅπερ φησὶν ὁ κύριος οὐ πατέρα ἑαυτὸν ἀναγορεύων οὐδὲ τὰς τῃ ὑποστάσει δύο φύσεις μίαν εἶναι σαφηνίζων, ἀλλ᾽ ὅτι τὴν πατρικὴν ἐμφέρειαν ἀκριβῶς πέφυκεν σώζειν ὁ υἱὸς τοῦ πατρός, τὴν κατὰ πάντα ὁμοιότητα αὐτοῦ ἐκ φύσεως ἀπομαξάμενος καὶ ἀπαράλλακτος εἰκὼν τοῦ πατρὸς τυγχάνων καὶ τοῦ πρωτοτύπου ἔκτυπος χαρακτήρ.

still we may speak of a fatherly generation! (πατρικὴ θεογονία) which certainly is beyond the power of human reason to grasp." "The expressions ἦν, ἀεὶ, etc., (was, always), used of the Son, are undoubtedly too weak, but on the other hand, they are not to be conceived so as to suggest that the Son is unbegotten (ἀγέννητος); the unbeginning genesis from the Father (ἄναρχος γέννησις παρὰ τοῦ πατρὸς) is his,—"the Father is greater than the Son, to Him honour in the strict sense (οἰκεῖον ἀξίωμα) is due, to the Son the dignity that is fitting (τιμὴ ἁρμόζουσα)." [1]

These confused thoughts and formulæ contrast unfavourably with the clear and definitely expressed statements of Arius. Alexander's opponents had a better right to complain of the chameleon-like form of this teaching than he had of that of theirs. When they maintained that it offered no security against dualism (two unbegotten, [ἀγένητα]), [2] or against Gnostic emanationism (προβολή, ἀπόρροια), or against Sabellianism (υἱοπάτωρ), or against the idea of the corporeality of God, and that it contained flagrant contradictions, [3] they were not far wrong. But they cannot have been in the dark as to what their opponents meant to assert, which was nothing else than the inseparable, essential unity of Father and Son, the complete divinity of Christ who has redeemed us and whom every creature must necessarily have as redeemer. Along with this they taught a real distinction between Father and Son, though they could assert this distinction only as a mystery, and when they were driven to describe it, had recourse to formulæ which were easily refuted.

---

[1] In the Confession of Faith which Alexander had put at the close of his letter, the Spirit, the Church, and so on, are mentioned. According to Alexander, too, the Logos got only a body from Mary, who, for the rest, is called θεοτόκος (see Athan. Orat. III. 29, 33). Möhler and Newman (Hist. Treatises, p. 297) consider Athanasius as the real author of Alexander's encyclical epistle. Their arguments, however, are not convincing.

[2] Hence the reproach so frequently brought against this doctrine, that according to it Father and Son are "brothers"; see, e.g., Orat. c. Arian I. 14. Paul of Samosata had already brought this reproach against all the adherents of the Logos doctrine. The Arians sought to make a reductio ad absurdum of the doctrine that the Son is the perfect image of the Father, by pointing out that in this case the Son too must beget as well as the Father (Or. c. Arian. I. 21).

[3] See some of those adduced by them in Orat. c. Arian. I. 22: they are said to have pointed them out to children and women.

We may at this point give an account of the doctrine of Athanasius; for although it was not till after the Nicene Council that he took part in the controversy as an author, [1] still his point of view coincides essentially with that of Bishop Alexander. It underwent no development, and considered from the standpoint of technical theology it partly labours under the same difficulties as that of Alexander. Its significance does not lie in the nature of his scientific defence of the faith, but solely in the triumphant tenacity of the faith itself. His character and his life are accordingly the main thing. The works he composed, like all the theological formulæ he uses, were wrung out of him. The entire Faith, everything in defence of which Athanasius staked his life, is described in the one sentence: *God Himself has entered into humanity.* [2]

The theology and christology of Athanasius are rooted in the thought of Redemption, and his views were not influenced by any subordinate considerations. [3] Neither heathenism nor Judaism has brought men into fellowship with God, the point on which everything turns. It is through Christ that we are transported into this fellowship; He has come in order to make

---

[1] That he took an active interest in the Nicene Council is undoubted; see Theodoret I. 26, Sozom, I. 17 fin., but, above all, Apol. Athan. c. Arian. 6 and the work "de decretis." The Arians drew special attention to the influence exercised by Athanasius, when deacon, on his bishop Alexander, and Athanasius did not contradict their statements; see also Gregor Naz. Orat. 21, 14.

[2] His chief works against the Arians are the four Orationes c. Arian—his most comprehensive work, containing mainly his refutation of the Arian Bible exegesis; the fourth Oration is, however, either merely a sketch, or else it is not in its proper place along with the others; further, the treatises de decret. Nic. synodi, de sentent. Dionys. Alex., historia Arian. ad monachos, apologia c. Arian., apologia ad imp. Constantium, de synodis Arimini et Seleuciæ habitis, the Tomus ad Antioch., and in addition the festival-orations and some lengthy letters, *e.g.*, that ad Afros episcopos.

[3] To prove this it would be necessary to quote hundreds of passages. In none of his larger works has Athanasius omitted to base his anti-Arian christology on the thought of redemption, and wherever he gives this as the basis one feels that he is adducing what is his most telling argument. The manner too in which he was able, starting from this as the central point of his whole view of the subject, to justify what were purely derivative formulæ by referring them back to it, is well worthy of notice; cf. the Orat. c. Arian., espec. II. 67—70. The fact that his knowledge of scientific theology was slender is hinted at by Gregor Naz., Orat. 21. 6.

us divine, *i e.*, to make us by adoption the sons of God and gods. But Christ would not have been able to bring us this blessing if He Himself had possessed it merely as a gift *secundum participationem*, for in this case He only had just as much as He needed Himself and so could not proceed to give away what was not His own. [1] Therefore Christ must be of the substance of the Godhead and be one with it. Whoever denies that is not a Christian, but is either a heathen or a Jew. [2] This is the fundamental thought which Athanasius constantly repeats. Everything else is secondary, is of the nature of necessary controversy. In the Son we have the Father; whoever knows the Son knows the Father. [3] This confession is at bottom the entire Christian confession. The adoration of Christ, which according to tradition, has been practised from the first, and which has not been objected to by their opponents, already, he says, decides the whole question. God alone is to be adored; it is heathenish to worship creatures. [4] Christ therefore shares in the divine

---

[1] Specially striking is what he says de synod. 51 : Christ could not make others gods if He himself had, to begin with, been made God ; if He possessed His godhead merely as something bestowed upon Him, He could not bestow it, for it would not be in His own power, and He would not have more than He needed Himself. Similarly Orat. I. 39, I. 30 : Οὐκ ἄρα καταβὰς ἐβελτιώθη ἀλλὰ μᾶλλον ἐβελτίωσεν αὐτὸς τὰ δεόμενα βελτιώσεως· καὶ εἰ τοῦ βελτιῶσαι χάριν καταβέβηκεν, οὐκ ἄρα μισθὸν ἔσχε τὸ λέγεσθαι, υἱὸς καὶ Θεός, ἀλλὰ μᾶλλον αὐτὸς υἱοποίησεν ἡμᾶς τῷ πατρὶ καὶ ἐθεοποίησε τοὺς ἀνθρώπους γενόμενος αὐτὸς ἄνθρωπος. Οὐκ ἄρα ἄνθρωπος ὢν ὕστερον γέγονε Θεός, ἀλλὰ Θεὸς ὢν ὕστερον γέγονεν ἄνθρωπος, ἵνα μᾶλλον ἡμᾶς θεοποιήσῃ. II. 69, I. 16 : αὐτοῦ τοῦ υἱοῦ μετέχοντες τοῦ Θεοῦ μετέχειν λεγόμεθα, καὶ τοῦτό ἐστιν ὃ ἔλεγεν ὁ Πέτρος ἵνα γένησθε θείας κοινωνοὶ φύσεως.

[2] The frequent designation of the Arians as Jews and heathen, and together with this the designation " Ariomanites," were employed by Athanasius in a really serious sense; see de decret. 1—4, 27 ; Encycl. ad. ep. Ægypt. et Lib. 13, 14 ; Orat. I. 38, II. 16, 17, III, 16, 27 sq. " Abomination of the impious " XI. Festbrief, p. 122 (Larsow).

[3] Orat. I. 12 : To the demand of Philip, "Shew us the Father," Christ did not reply : βλέπε τὴν κτίσιν, but " He who sees me, sees the Father." Orat. I. 16 : τοῦ υἱοῦ μετέχοντες τοῦ Θεοῦ μετέχειν λεγόμεθα... ἡ τοῦ υἱοῦ ἔννοια καὶ κατάληψις γνῶσίς ἐστι περὶ τοῦ πατρός, διὰ τὸ ἐκ τῆς οὐσίας αὐτοῦ ἴδιον εἶναι γέννημα. I. 21.

[4] This is a point which is very frequently emphasised; see Orat. I. 10, II. 20, 24, but chiefly III. 16 : Διατί οὖν οἱ Ἀρειανοὶ τοιαῦτα λογιζόμενοι καὶ νοοῦντες οὐ συναριθμοῦσιν ἑαυτοὺς μετὰ τῶν Ἑλλήνων; καὶ γὰρ κἀκεῖνοι, ὥσπερ καὶ οὗτοι, τῇ κτίσει λατρεύουσι παρὰ τὸν κτίσαντα τὰ πάντα Θεόν· ἀλλὰ τὸ μὲν ὄνομα τὸ Ἑλληνικὸν φεύγουσι, διὰ τὴν τῶν ἀνοήτων ἀπάτην, τὴν δὲ ὁμοίαν ἐκείνοις διάνοιαν ὑποκρίνονται. καὶ γὰρ καὶ τὸ σοφὸν αὐτῶν, ὅπερ εἰώθασιν λέγειν, οὐ λέγομεν δύο ἀγέννητα,

substance. Athanasius did not draft any system of theology or christology. The real point at issue appeared to him to be quite simple and certain. We have to put together his doctrinal system for ourselves, and the attempts to construct such a system for him is not something to be entered upon lightly. A body of theoretical propositions resulted solely from the polemic in which he was engaged and also from his defence of the "'Ομοούσιος." Throughout, however, his thought in the final resort centres not in the Logos as such, [1] but in the Divine, which had appeared in Jesus Christ. He has no longer any independent Logos doctrine, on the contrary he is a Christologist. We accordingly give merely some of the main lines of his teaching.

1. To acknowledge that the substantial or essential element in Christ is "God," is to assert that there is nothing of the creature in this, that it does not therefore belong in any sense to what has been created. Athanasius insisted as confidently as Arius on the gulf which exists between created and uncreated. This constitutes the advance made by both in clearness. [2] Arius, however, drew the dividing line in such a way that with him

φαίνονται πρὸς ἀπάτην τῶν ἀκεραίων λέγοντες· φάσκοντες γάρ· " οὐ λέγομεν δύο ἀγέννητα," λέγουσι δύο Θεοὺς καὶ τούτους διαφόρους ἔχοντας τὰς φύσεις, τὸ μὲν γενητήν, τὸ δὲ ἀγένητοι. Εἰ δὲ οἱ μὲν Ἕλληνες ἑνὶ ἀγενήτῳ καὶ πολλοῖς γενητοῖς λατρεύουσιν, οὗτοι δὲ ἑνὶ ἀγενήτῳ καὶ ἑνὶ γενητῷ, οὐδ᾽ οὕτω διαφέρουσιν Ἑλλήνων. This was the view of it which was still held at a later period also. The expression in the Vita Euthymii (Cotel. Monum. II., p. 201) c. 2, is full of meaning: Τοῦ Ἑλληνισμοῦ λήξαντος ὁ τοῦ Ἀρειανισμοῦ πόλεμος ἰσχυρῶς ἐκράτει.

[1] It is very characteristic of Athanasius' way of looking at things that with him the Logos in general retires into the background, and further that he expressly declines to recognise or to define the divine in Christ from the point of view of his relation to the world or in terms of the predicate of the eternal. Image, Reflection and Son are the designations which he regards as most appropriate. See, e.g.. Orat. III. 28: οὐ τοσοῦτον ἐκ τοῦ ἀϊδίου γνωρίζεται κύριος, ὅσον ὅτι υἱός ἐστι τοῦ Θεοῦ· υἱὸς γὰρ ὢν ἀχώριστός ἐστι τοῦ πατρός., . καὶ εἰκὼν καὶ ἀπαύγασμα ὢν τοῦ πατρὸς ἔχει καὶ τὴν ἀϊδιότητα τοῦ πατρός.

[2] Beyond Origen and the Origenists, who, though they too certainly make a sharp distinction between the Godhead and the creation, attribute with Philo an intermediate position to the Logos. The Eusebians held fast to this, and that is why Athanasius always treats them as Arians; for in connection with this main point the maxim in his opinion held good "Whosover is not with us is against us." See Orat. IV. 6, 7; Encycl. ad ep. Ægypt, et Lib. 20; de decret. 6, 19, 20; ad Afros 5, 6, and the parallel section in the work "de synodis."

the Son belongs to the world side, while with Athanasius He, as belonging to God, stands over against the world.

2. Since the Divine, which has appeared in Christ, is not anything created, and since there can be no "middle" substance,[1] it follows, according to the reasoning of Athanasius, that this Divine cannot in any sense be postulated as resulting from the idea of the creation of the world. God did not require any agent for the creation of the world; He creates direct. If He had required any such intervening agent in order to effect a connection with the creature that was to come into existence, this Divine could not have supplied Him with it, for it itself really belongs to His substance. *In this way the idea of the Divine, which in Christ redeemed men, is severed from the world idea;*[2] *the old Logos doctrine is discarded; Nature and Revelation no longer continue to be regarded as identical.* The Logos-Son-Christ is at bottom no longer a world principle, but, on the contrary, a salvation principle.[3]

[1] Orat. I. 15 : If the Son is Son then that wherein He shares is not outside of the substance of the Father : τοῦτο δὲ πάλιν ἐὰν ἕτερον ᾖ παρὰ τὴν οὐσίαν τοῦ υἱοῦ τὸ ἴσον ἄτοπον ἀπαντήσει, μέσου πάλιν εὑρισκομένου τούτου ἐκ τοῦ πατρὸς καὶ τῆς οὐσίας τοῦ υἱοῦ, ἥτις ποτέ ἐστι. In putting it thus Athanasius corrected not only an incautious expression of Bishop Alexander (see above p. 24 f.), but very specially the thesis of the Origenists of "The image and reflection which sprang from and was created out of the will" (see *e.g.*, Euseb. Demonstr. IV. 3). But Arius himself, spite of all his efforts to avoid it, also arrived at the idea of a "middle substance" between the Godhead and the creature, because according to him God had necessarily to make use of such a being in order to be able to create at all.

[2] In contrast to this it holds good of the Arians that τὸν δημιουργὸν τῶν ὅλων τοῖς ποιήμασι συναριθμήσωσι (Orat. I. c. Arian. T. I., p. 342).

[3] It is this which constitutes the most significant advance made by Athanasius, the real fruit of his speculation which took its start from the thought of redemption. *The Logos of the philosophers was no longer the Logos whom he knew and adored.* The existence of the Logos who appeared in Christ is independent of the idea of the world. The creation of the world—abstractly speaking—might even have taken place without the Logos. This is the point in which he is most strongly opposed to the Apologists and Origen. No traces of this advance are to be found as yet in the works "c. Gent" and "de incarnat." See, on the other hand, Orat. II. 24, 25: οὐ κάμνει ὁ Θεὸς προστάττων, οὐδὲ ἀσθενεῖ πρὸς τὴν τῶν πάντων ἐργασίαν, ἵνα τὸν μὲν υἱὸν μόνος μόνον κτίσῃ, εἰς δὲ τὴν τῶν ἄλλων δημιουργίαν ὑπουργοῦ καὶ βοηθοῦ χρείαν ἔχῃ τοῦ υἱοῦ. οὐδὲ γὰρ οὐδὲ ὑπέρθεσιν ἔχει, ὅπερ ἂν ἐθελήσῃ γενέσθαι, ἀλλὰ μόνον ἠθέλησε καὶ ὑπέστη τὰ πάντα, καὶ τῷ βουλήματι αὐτοῦ οὐδεὶς ἀνθέστηκε. Τίνος οὖν ἕνεκα οὐ γέγονε τὰ πάντα παρὰ μόνου τοῦ Θεοῦ τῷ προστάγματι, ᾧ γέγονε καὶ ὁ υἱός... ἀλογία μέν οὖν πᾶσα παρ' αὐτοῖς· φασὶ δὲ ὅμως περὶ τούτου, ὡς ἄρα

3. Scripture and tradition know of only *one* Godhead; they, however, at the same time pronounce Christ to be God: they call the Divine which has appeared in Christ, Logos, Wisdom and Son; they thus distinguish it from God, the Father. Faith has to hold fast to this. But in accordance with this we get the following propositions:

(a) The Godhead is a unity (μονάς). Therefore the Divine which appeared in Christ, must form part of this unity. There is only one underived or unbegotten principle; this is the Father. [1]

(b) The very name Father implies, moreover, that a second exists in the Godhead. God has always been Father, and who-

θέλων ὁ Θεὸς τὴν γενητὴν κτίσαι φύσιν, ἐπειδὴ ἑώρα μὴ δυναμένην αὐτὴν μετασχεῖν τῆς τοῦ πατρὸς ἀκράτου χειρὸς καὶ τῆς παρ' αὐτοῦ δημιουργίας, ποῖει καὶ κτίζει πρώτως μόνον ἕνα καὶ καλεῖ τοῦτον υἱὸν καὶ λόγον, ἵνα τούτου μέσου γενομένου οὕτως λοιπὸν καὶ τὰ πάντα δι' αὐτοῦ γενέσθαι δυνηθῇ· ταῦτα οὐ μόνον εἰρήκασιν, ἀλλὰ καὶ γράψαι τετολμήκασιν Εὐσέβιός τε καὶ Ἀρεῖος καὶ ὁ θύσας Ἀστέριος. As against this view Athanasius shews that God is neither so powerless as not to be able to create the creatures nor so proud as not to be willing to create them (εἰ δὲ ὡς ἀπαξιῶν ὁ Θεὸς τὰ ἄλλα ἐργάσασθαι, τὸν μὲν υἱὸν μόνον εἰργάσατο, τὰ δὲ ἄλλα τῷ υἱῷ ἀνεχείρισεν ὡς βοηθῷ· καὶ τοῦτο μὲν ἀνάξιον Θεοῦ· οὐκ ἔστι γὰρ ἐν θεῷ τύφος); he shews further from Matt. X. 29, VI. 25 f. that God cares for all things in the most direct way, and therefore has also brought them into existence. The same proof is given in de decret. 8. Athanasius thus did away with the latent dualism between the godhead and the creature which had existed in Christian theology since the time of Philo. *God is creator in the directest way.* This, however, implies that the Logos is discarded. If spite of this Athanasius not only retained the name, but also recognised the function of a mediator of creation and type of all rational beings, the reason was that he understood Scripture as implying this, and because he was not able wholly to free himself from the influence of tradition. But the Divine in Christ is no longer for him the world-reason, on the contrary it is the substance of the Father which—accidentally, as it were—has also the attributes of creative power and of the reason that embraces and holds ideas together. For Athanasius, in fact, the Son is the substance of the Father *as the principle of redemption and sanctification.* The most pregnant of his formulæ is in Orat. III. 6. in support of which he appeals to 2 Cor. V. 19: τὸ ἴδιον τῆς τοῦ πατρὸς οὐσίας ἐστὶν ὁ υἱός, ἐν ᾧ ἡ κτίσις πρὸς τὸν Θεὸν κατηλλάσσετο.

[1] That the Godhead is a unity, is a thought which Athanasius emphasised in the strongest way over and over again (μονὰς τῆς θεότητος), (2) also that there are not two underived or unbegotten principles (ἀρχαί), and finally (3) that the Father is the ἀρχή, which because of this may be identified with the μονάς also. He retorts the charge of Polytheism brought against him by the Arians; they, he says, adore two gods (see above, note 4, p. 27). The best summary of his view is in Orat. IV. 1: μονάδα τῆς θεότητος ἀδιαίρετον καὶ ἄσχιστον· λεχθείη μία ἀρχὴ θεότητος καὶ οὐ δύο ἀρχαί ὅθεν κυρίως καὶ μοναρχία ἐστιν.

ever calls Him Father posits at the same time the Son ; for the Father is the Father of the Son, and only in a loose sense the Father of the world and of men ; for these are created, but the divine Trinity is uncreated, for otherwise it might either decrease again, or further increase in the future. [1]

(c) This Son, the offspring of the Father (γέννημα τοῦ πατρός), [2] was not, however, begotten in a human fashion as if God were corporeal. On the contrary, He has been begotten as the sun begets light and the spring the brook; He is called Son, because He is the eternal, perfect reflection of the Father, the image [3] proceeding from the substance of the Father ;

[1] Orat. III. 6: πατέρα οὐκ ἄν τις εἴποι, μὴ ὑπάρχοντος υἱοῦ· ὁ μὲν τοι ποιητὴν λέγων τὸν Θεὸν οὐ πάντως καὶ τὰ γενόμενα δηλοῖ· ἔστι γὰρ καὶ πρὸ τῶν ποιημάτων ποιητής· ὁ δὲ πατέρα λέγων εὐθὺς μετὰ τοῦ πατρὸς σημαίνει καὶ τὴν τοῦ υἱοῦ ὕπαρξιν. διὰ τοῦτο καὶ ὁ πιστεύων εἰς τὸν υἱὸν εἰς τὸν πατέρα πιστεύει· εἰς γὰρ τὸ ἴδιον τῆς τοῦ πατρὸς οὐσίας πιστεύει, καὶ οὕτως μία ἐστιν ἡ πίστις εἰς ἕνα Θεόν. II. 41. De decret. 30 fin.: λέγοντες μὲν γὰρ ἐκεῖνοι τὸν Θεὸν ἀγένητον ἐκ τῶν γενομένων αὐτὸν ποιητὴν μόνον λέγουσιν, ἵνα καὶ τὸν λόγον ποίημα σημάνωσι κατὰ τὴν ἰδίαν ἡδονήν· ὁ δὲ τὸν Θεὸν πατέρα λέγων εὐθὺς ἐν αὐτῷ καὶ τὸν υἱὸν σημαίνει. The Son is a second in the Godhead, see Orat. III. 4: δύο μὲν εἰσιν, ὅτι ὁ πατὴρ πατήρ ἐστι καὶ οὐχ ὁ αὐτὸς υἱός ἐστι· καὶ ὁ υἱὸς υἱός ἐστι καὶ οὐχ ὁ αὐτὸς πατήρ ἐστι· μία δὲ ἡ φύσις. IV. 1: ὥστε δύο μὲν εἶναι πατέρα καὶ υἱόν, μονάδα δὲ θεότητος ἀδιαίρετον. The idea that the Triad must be from all eternity and be independent of the world, if it is not to be increased or diminished, is developed in Orat. I. 17. There is a strong polemic against the Sabellians in Orat. IV.

[2] In the theoretical expositions of his teaching Athanasius uses the expression γέννημα in preference to υἱός, in order to exclude the idea of human generation.

[3] "Reflection", "Image", "God of God", are the expressions which always appeared to Athanasius to be the most appropriate. He preferred the first of these in order to exclude the thought that the Son proceeded from the will of the Creator. The light cannot do otherwise than l ghten, and it always shines or lightens, otherwise it would not be light. The archetype projects its type necessarily. Following Origen he puts the whole emphasis on the eternal (Orat. I. 14: ἀίδιός ἐστιν ὁ υἱὸς καὶ συνυπάρχει τῷ πατρί) and necessary. If the Son were begotten by the will of the Father, He would be something contingent, a creation, and would have a beginning: though certainly He was not, on the other hand, begotten contrary to this will, as the Arians charge their opponents with believing (Orat. III. 62, 66), nor from some necessity superior to God, nor does the blessed Godhead undergo any kind of suffering (Orat. I. 16), on the contrary He proceeded from the substance of God οὐ παρὰ γνώμην. Only the expression ἐκ τῆς οὐσίας suffices, as Athanasius over and over again makes plain; any intervention of the will here degrades the Son; for "the substance is higher than the will." See the characteristic passage Orat. III. 62: ὥσπερ ἀντίκειται τῇ βουλήσει τὸ παρὰ γνώμην, οὕτως ὑπέρκειται καὶ προηγεῖται τοῦ βουλεύεσθαι τὸ κατὰ φύσιν. οἰκίαν μὲν οὖν τις βουλευόμενος κατασκευάζει,

He is called Wisdom and Logos not as if the Father were imperfect without Him, [1] but as the creative power of the Father. [2] "To be begotten" simply means completely to share by nature in the entire nature of the Father, implying at the same time that the Father does not therefore suffer or undergo anything. [3]

(d) Consequently the assertions of the Arians that the Son is God, Logos, and Wisdom in a nominal sense only, that there was a time in which the Son was not, that He has sprung from the will of the Father, that He was created out of the non-existent or out of some other substance, that He is subject to change, are false. [4] On the contrary He is (1) co-eternal with the

υἱὸν δὲ γεννᾷ κατὰ φύσιν. καὶ τὸ μὲν βουλήσει κατασκευαζόμενον ἤρξατο γίνεσθαι καὶ ἔξωθέν ἐστι τοῦ ποιοῦντος· ὁ δὲ υἱὸς ἴδιόν ἐστι τῆς οὐσίας τοῦ πατρὸς γέννημα καὶ οὐκ ἔστιν ἔξωθεν αὐτοῦ· διὸ οὐδὲ βουλεύεται περὶ αὐτοῦ, ἵνα μὴ καὶ περὶ ἑαυτοῦ δοκῇ βουλεύεσθαι· ὅσῳ οὖν τοῦ κτίσματος ὁ υἱὸς ὑπέρκειται, τοσούτῳ καὶ τῆς βουλήσεως τὸ τὸ κατὰ φύσιν. The Father wills the Son in so far as He loves Him and wills and loves Himself (Orat. III. 66), but in so far as "willing" involves τὴν ἐπ' ἄμφω ῥοπήν, *i.e.*, includes the ability not to will, the Son is not from the will of the Father.

[1] Athanasius rarely repeats the unguarded utterances of Bishop Alexander and others belonging to the orthodox party. The Father is for him, on the contrary, in and for Himself—if one may so put it—personal; He is νοῦς and He is τῆς ἰδίας ὑποστάσεως θελητής. In one passage in his later writings (de decret. 15) he has, however, curiously enough, argued that the Father would be ἄλογος and ἄσοφος, if the Logos were not from all eternity.

[2] In order to give meaning to the expressions "Logos", "Wisdom", Athanasius could not avoid describing the divine in Christ as the wisdom, prudence, strength, might, creative power in God, see Orat. I. 17, III. 65. Still he rarely has recourse to these terms.

[3] After the beginning of the Arian controversy, though not before it (see c. Gent. 2), Athanasius made a thorough distinction between "to beget" and "to create." "Begetting" held good of the Father only in reference to the Son. It means the production of a perfect image of Himself which, while originating in His substance, has by nature a share in the *entire* substance. That the Son shares in the *entire* substance of the Father is a thought which was constantly repeated by Athanasius, Orat. I. 16: τὸ ὅλως μετέχεσθαι τὸν Θεὸν ἴσόν ἐστι λέγειν ὅτι καὶ γεννᾷ. The begotten is thus ἴδιον τῆς οὐσίας τοῦ Θεοῦ γέννημα (Orat. II. 24), which φύσει ἔχει τὴν πατρικὴν οὐσίαν and in fact τελείαν. That God does not in consequence of this suffer or undergo anything, and that there is here no question of an emanation, are points which he urges as against the Valentinians.

[4] The refutation of these propositions given by Athanasius takes a great number of forms; we may distinguish the religious-dogmatic, the dialectic-philosophic, the patristic and the biblical refutations (see Böhringer, Athanasius, pp. 210—240).

Father and (2) He is of the substance of the Father, [1] for otherwise He would not be God at all, (3) He is by His own nature
in all points similarly [2] constituted as the Father, and finally He is
all this, because He has *one and the same substance in common
with the Father* and together with Him constitutes a unity, [3]

For Athanasius himself the religious and biblical argument is the chief thing. Besides numerous passages from the Gospel of John, Athanasius quotes specially
1 John V. 20; Rev. I. 4; Matt. III. 17, XVII. 5; Rom. I. 20, VIII. 32, IX. 5;
Hebr. I. 3, XIII. 8; Ps. II. 7; XLV. 2, CII. 28, CXLV. 13; Is. XL. 28. Matt.
XXVIII. 19 had for him supreme importance. Amongst the theses laid down by
the Arians he had a special objection to that of the προκοπή of the Logos.
Hence the strong emphasis he lays on the ἄτρεπτος.

[1] "From the Father," as Athanasius says in several passages, would be sufficient
if it were not possible to say, using the words in an improper sense, that everything is from God because it has been created by God. It is because the Eusebians
make capital out of this that we must avow: ἐκ τῆς οὐσίας τοῦ πατρός; see de
decret. 19; de synod. 33 sq.: ad Afros 5. He entirely rejects the idea of a mere
unity of feeling or doctrine between the Father and the Son (*e.g.*, Orat. III. 11)
for this would mean the disappearance of the Godhead of the Son.

[2] The word "ὅμοιος" means something more than our word "resembling" and
something less than our word "similar"; our "similarly constituted" comes nearest
it. The "ὅμοιος" alone did not satisfy Athanasius, because it implicitly involves a
difference and, above all, a *distinction*, and he says, moreover, that even dog and
wolf, tin and silver are ὅμοια. He, however, certainly applied the word in connection with substance (φύσις οὐσία) or with "κατὰ πάντα" (*e.g.*, de decret. 20) to
the relation between Father and Son (ὁμοίωσις τοῦ υἱοῦ πρὸς τὸν πατέρα κατὰ τὴν
οὐσίαν καὶ κατὰ τὴν φύσιν, de synod. 45). But still he found it necessary as a
rule, at least at a later date, expressly to emphasise the ἑνότης—where he expresses
himself in a less strict way we also find ὁμοιότης alone—and in opposition to the
Homoiousians was driven to add "ἐκ τῆς οὐσίας" to "ὁμοιούσιος" in order to
banish any idea of separateness. (de synod. 41). Yet he recognised at the same time
(l. c. c. 53 sq.) that ὅμοιος is really an unsuitable word; for it cannot be used of
substances, but only of σχήματα καὶ ποιότητες. In connection with substances we
say ταυτότης. Men resemble each other in general outline and character, but in
substance they are ὁμοφυεῖς; vice versa, man and dog are not unlike, but yet they
are ἑτεροφυεῖς. Thus ὁμοφυές and ὁμοούσιον match each other, and in the same
way ἑτεροφυές and ἑτεροούσιον. The phrase ὅμοιος κατ᾽ οὐσίαν always suggests a
μετουσία; το γὰρ ὅμοιον ποιότης ἐστίν, ἥτις τῇ οὐσίᾳ προσγένοιτ᾽ ἄν. Thus it is
correct to say of created spiritual beings that they resemble God, not however in
substance, but only in virtue of sonship. Ὁμοιούσιος is in fact nothing, and
when used of the real Son is consequently either nonsense or false.

[3] This is the key to the whole mode of conception: Son and Father are not a duality,
but a *duality in unity, i.e.*, the Son possesses entirely the substance which the Father
is; He is a unity with the unity which the Father is. Athanasius did not defend the
idea of the co-ordination of the two as opposed to a subordination view, but the unity
and inseparability as opposed to the theory of difference and separateness. He, however,

but "substance" in reference to God means nothing else than "Being." [1] It is not the case that the Father is one substance expresses this as follows: in substance Father and Son are one; or, the Son has one and the same substance with the Father. Thus the expression "μία φύσις" is often used for both; and so we have: οὐσία ἕν ἐστιν αὐτὸς γεννήσας αὐτὸν πατήρ (de synod. 48). The Son has the ἑνότης πρὸς τὸν πατέρα (de decret. 23); He constitutes with Him a ἀδιαίρετος ἑνότης; there subsists between both ἑνότης ὁμοιώσεως κατὰ τὴν οὐσίαν καὶ κατὰ τὴν φύσιν. He expresses his meaning most plainly in those passages in which he attaches the ταυτότης to Father and Son without prejudice to the fact that the Father is the Father and not the Son. Identity of substance, as Athanasius (de synod. 53) explains, is ταυτότης. Thus he says (Orat. I. 22): ὁ υἱὸς ἔχει ἐκ τοῦ πατρὸς τὴν ταυτότητα. In a passage of earlier date he had already said (c. Gent. 2): δοὺς τῷ υἱῷ καὶ τῆς ἰδίας ἀϊδιότητος ἔννοιαν καὶ γνῶσιν, ἵνα τὴν ταυτότητα σώζων κ.τ.λ. Later on, (de decret. 23): ἀνάγκη καὶ ἐν τούτῳ τὴν ταυτότητα πρὸς τὸν ἑαυτοῦ πατέρα σώζειν, 20: μὴ μόνον ὅμοιον τὸν υἱὸν ἀλλὰ ταὐτὸν τῇ ὁμοιώσει ἐκ τοῦ πατρὸς εἶναι ... οὐ μόνον ὅμοιος ἀλλὰ καὶ ἀδιαίρετος ἐστι τῆς τοῦ πατρὸς οὐσίας, καὶ ἕν μέν εἰσιν αὐτὸς καὶ ὁ πατήρ. 24: ἑνότης καὶ φυσικὴ ἰδιότης ... τὴν ἑνότητα τῆς φύσεως καὶ τὴν ταυτότητα τοῦ φωτὸς μὴ διαιρῶμεν. Orat. IV. 5 (and elsewhere): πατὴρ ἐν τῷ υἱῷ, υἱὸς ἐν τῷ πατρί ... ἡ τοῦ υἱοῦ θεότης τοῦ πατρός ἐστι ... ἡ θεότης καὶ ἡ ἰδιότης τοῦ πατρὸς τὸ εἶναι τοῦ υἱοῦ ἐστί. Thus ὅμοιος is unsatisfactory not only because it does not express complete likeness, but, above all, because it does not express the unity upon which everything depends. The Son cannot, like human sons, go away from the Father, (de decret. 20) for He is in a more intimate relation to Him that a human son is to his father; He is connected with the Father not as an accident of which we might make abstraction (l. c. 12), but as τὸ ἴδιον τῆς πατρικῆς ὑποστάσεως (Orat. III. 65) or as τὸ ἴδιον τῆς οὐσίας τοῦ πατρός (frequently in de decret. Orat. I. 22), or as ἴδιον τῆς οὐσίας τοῦ Θεοῦ γέννημα. Athanasius uses the words "ἴδιος", "γνήσιος" frequently; they give the conception of Son a more extended meaning than it naturally has, so that the Son may not appear as ἔξωθεν ἀπλῶς ὅμοιος and consequently as ἑτεροούσιος (de decret. 23). *The substantial unity of Father and Son is the fundamental thought of Athanasius.* Atzberger therefore correctly says (op. cit. p. 117) "There can be no doubt but that Athanasius conceived of the unity of the Father and the Son as a numerical unity of substance." In Orat. III. 3 ff. where he puts himself to great trouble to state the problem that two are equal to one, he says: Εἰ καὶ ἕτερόν ἐστιν ὡς γέννημα ὁ υἱός, ἀλλὰ ταὐτόν ἐστιν ὡς Θεός· καὶ ἕν εἰσιν αὐτὸς καὶ ὁ πατὴρ τῇ ἰδιότητι καὶ οἰκειότητι τῆς φύσεως καὶ τῇ ταυτότητι τῆς μιᾶς θεότητος. We cannot therefore help being astonished (with Zahn p. 20) to find that Athanasius declines to use the word μονοούσιος of the Son (see Expos. fidei 2: οὔτε υἱοπάτορα φρονοῦμεν ὡς οἱ Σαβέλλιοι, λέγοντες μονοούσιον καὶ οὐχ ὁμοούσιον καὶ ἐν τούτῳ ἀναιροῦντες τό εἶναι υἱὸν); still he always says: μίαν οἴδαμεν καὶ μόνην θεότητα τοῦ πατρός. If the question is raised as to whether Athanasius thought of the Godhead as a numerical unity or as a numerical duality, the answer is: *as a numericat unity.* The duality is only a relative one—if we may write such an absurdity—the duality of archetype and type. That the Arians called the Catholics "Sabellians" is expressly stated by Julian of Eclan. (August., op. imperf. V. 25).

[1] Θεότης, οὐσία, ὑπόστασις, ἰδιότης τῆς οὐσίας, οἰκειότης τῆς οὐσίας (ὑποστάσεως) are all used by Athanasius in reference to the Godhead as perfectly synonymous.

by itself and the Son another substance by itself and that these
two are similarly constituted. This would do away with the
unity of the Godhead. On the contrary, the Father is the
Godhead ; this Godhead, however, contains in it a mystery which
can only be approximately conceived of by men. It conceals
within itself in the form of an independent and self-acting
product something which issues from it and which also possesses
this Godhead and possesses it from all eternity in virtue, not of any
communication, but of nature and origin,—the true and real Son,
the image which proceeds from the substance. There are not two
divine ousias, not two divine hypostases or the like, but *one* ousia
and hypostasis, which the Father and the Son possess. Thus the
Son is true God, inseparable from the Father and reposing in the
unity of the Godhead, not a second alongside of God, but simply
reflection, express image, Son within the *one* Godhead which cannot

He had no word by which to describe Father and Son as different subjects, and
indeed he never felt it necessary to seek for any such word. We cannot call
ἰδιότης τῆς οὐσίας anything special; for Athanasius by the very use of the word
ἰδιότης asserted the unity of the Father and Son. Ὑπόστασις and οὐσία are
repeatedly described by him as identical; see de decret. 27; de synod. 41; ad
Afros 4; ἡ δὲ ὑπόστασις οὐσία ἐστί, καὶ οὐδὲν ἄλλο σημαινόμενον ἔχει ἢ αὐτὸ τὸ
ὄν, ὅπερ Ἱερεμίας ὕπαρξιν ὀνομάζει λέγων... ἡ γὰρ ὑπόστασις καὶ ἡ οὐσία ὕπαρξίς
ἐστιν (so still in the year 370). Tom. ad Antioch. 6: ὑπόστασιν μὲν λέγομεν
ἡγούμενοι ταὐτὸν εἶναι εἰπεῖν ὑπόστασιν καὶ οὐσίαν. The divine substance is, however, nothing other than τὸ ὄν (pure Being); see ad Afr. l. c. and the decret. 22;
Godhead is the οὐσία ἀκατάληπτος... τὸ· Θεός, οὐδὲν ἕτερον ἢ τὴν οὐσίαν αὐτοῦ
τοῦ ὄντος σημαίνει. As opposed to this φύσις is the nature which attaches to the
substance as the complex of its attributes; Athanasius distinguishes it from οὐσία;
hence the formula often used : κατὰ τὴν οὐσίαν καὶ κατὰ τὴν φύσιν (*e.g.*, de synod.
45) see also Tom. ad Antioch 6, where Athanasius after the words above quoted,
continues: μίαν δὲ φρονοῦμεν διὰ τὸ ἐκ τῆς οὐσίας τοῦ πατρὸς εἶναι τὸν υἱὸν καὶ
διὰ τὴν ταυτότητα τῆς φύσεως· μίαν γὰρ θεότητα καὶ μίαν εἶναι τὴν ταύτης φύσιν
πιστεύομεν. Orat. I. 39: The Son is φύσει κατ' οὐσίαν ταῦτα. When, however,
Athanasius asserts the numerical unity of the Ousia of Father, Son, (and Spirit)
he is thinking of it both as being that which we call " substance " and also as
what we call "subject", so that here again, too, what is obscure is not the unity,
but the duality (triad) as in Irenæus. In de synod. 51 the conception of the Ousia
as involving three substances, *i.e.*, a common genus and two co-ordinate "brothers"
ranged under it, is expressly rejected as Ἑλλήνων ἑρμηνεῖαι. It is only the one
passage: Expos. fid. 2, (see above) where Athanasius rejects μονοούσιος, that betrays
any uncertainty on his part. It stands quite by itself. Otherwise by οὐσία he
understands the individual or single substance which, however, as applied to God,
is the fulness of all Being, a view which allows him to think of this substance
as existing in wonderful conditions and taking on wonderful shapes.

and ought not to be thought of apart from reflection, express
image, and Son. He has everything that the Father has, for
He actually possesses the ousia of the Father; He is ὁμοούσιος, [1]
of the same substance. Only He is not actually the Father, for
the latter is also His source and root, the Almighty Father,
the only unbegotten principle. [2]

[1] The meaning of this word will be clear from what was said in the preceding
discussion. It signified oneness of substance, not likeness of substance, "unius
substantiæ." Father and Son possess in common one and the same substance,
substance in the sense of the totality of all that which they are. This is how
Athanasius always understood the word, as Zahn (op. cit., pp. 10—32) was the
first to point out in opposition to the long current erroneous interpretations of it.
It is in fact equal to ταυτούσιος, the meaning which the Semiarians also attached
to it (Ephiph. H. 73. 11). Athanasius neither discovered the word, nor had he any
special preference for it; but he always recognised in it the most fitting expression
wherewith to repel Arians and Eusebians; see on the adoption of the word into
the Nicene Creed and the history of its interpretation, the discussions which follow.

[2] This is an important point in the Athanasian doctrine and balances in some
degree the thoughts comprised in the word "ὁμοούσιος." From some passages it
certainly appears as if the statement that the Son has everything in common with
the Father (according to Holy Scripture) except the name of Father (see Orat. III. 4
fin; III. 6; de synod. 48, 49; frequently as in Orat. I. 61, the language is paradoxical to the verge of absurdity) expressed a merely nominal distinction between
Father and Son. According to this, He is either identical with the Father, or a
part of the Father's substance, or an attribute of God, or a kind of pendicle
which has emanated from the Father; but all these modes of conception were
considered at the time to be "Sabellian": they were condemned already. In order
to escape them or rather because he himself considered them to be false, Athanasius in the proper place strongly emphasised the idea that the Father is the entire
monad, that He is the ἀρχή for the Son too, that it is in fact the ousia of the
Father which the Son has received, that thus the conception of the Father as the
sole Θεὸς παντοκράτωρ maintains the unity of the Godhead. The Father is the
μία ἀρχή (Orat. IV. 1); there are not two or three Fathers (III. 15); there is ἕν
εἶδος θεότητος, which is the Father, but τὸ εἶδος τοῦτό ἐστι καὶ ἐν τῷ υἱῷ (l. c.);
the Father is ὁ Θεός. He alone is αὐτὸς ὁ Θεός, He alone is the unbegotten God
(Expos. fid. I); the Son is a γέννημα, even though He has not come into being.
Accordingly the Father is sufficient for Himself (Orat. II. 41), and ἡ οὐσία τοῦ
πατρός ἐστιν ἀρχὴ καί ῥίζα καὶ πηγὴ τοῦ υἱοῦ. The "ὁμοούσιος" does not thus
include any absolute co-ordination. According to Athanasius all men are ὁμοούσιοι
relatively to each other, because they are ὁμογενεῖς and ὁμοφυεῖς (de synod. 52 sq,)
and yet spite of this we find amongst them superiority and subordination. The
same is the case here. Athanasius maintains the inseparable unity of substance of
Father and Son, the unity of the Godhead; but this idea is for him applicable
only in virtue of another, according to which the Father has everything of Himself while the Son has everything from the Father. *Father and Son, according to
Athanasius, are not co-ordinate equal substances, but rather one single substance,*

(4) The language used of Christ in Scripture to express what is human and belonging to the creature, has, always and only, reference to the human nature which He took upon Him in order to redeem men. Since He who is by nature God took upon Him a body in order to unite with Himself what is by nature man in order that the salvation and deification of man might be surely accomplished, He also along with the body took to Himself human feelings. So complete, however, is the identity of the humanity of Christ with the nature of humanity as a whole that we may, according to Athanasius, refer the statements of Scripture as to a special endowment and exaltation of Christ, to the whole humanity. [1] Complete too, however, was the union of the Son of God with humanity, which Athanasius, like Arius up to the time of the Apollinarian controversy, usually thought of as " Flesh," "vesture of the Flesh." [2] Because the body of the Logos was really His own body—although we must discard the thought of variation, of change [3]—and because this union had become already perfect in Mary's body, [4] everything that holds good of the flesh holds

---

which involves the distinction of ἀρχή *and* γέννημα, *and thus of principle and what is deduced, and in this sense involves a subordination,* which, however, is not analogous to the subordination in which the creature stands to God.

[1] See Orat. I. 41: Τῆς ἀνθρωπότητός ἐστιν ἡ ὕψωσις, *i.e.*, not of the humanity of Christ, but of humanity as a whole: c. 42: When Scripture uses the word "ἐχαρίσατο" in reference to what God does to Christ, this is not said of the Logos, but on our account: δι' ἡμᾶς καὶ ὑπὲρ ἡμῶν τοῦτο πάλιν περὶ αὐτοῦ γέγραπται. ὥσπερ γὰρ ὡς ἄνθρωπος ὁ Χριστὸς ἀπέθανε καὶ ὑψώθη, οὕτως ὡς ἄνθρωπος λέγεται λαμβάνειν ὅπερ εἶχεν ἀεὶ ὡς Θεός, ἵνα εἰς ἡμᾶς φθάσῃ καὶ ἡ τοιαύτη δοθεῖσα χάρις. The human race is thereby enriched. c. 43: By our kinship with the body of Christ we too have become a temple of God and are henceforth made sons of God, so that already in us the Lord is adored. "Therefore hath God also exalted Him"—this signifies our exaltation.

[2] So correctly Baur. I have not found Dorner's statement that the presupposition of a human soul occupies the background of the whole view of Athanasius "of the incarnation and redemption as affecting the totality of man" (op. cit. I. p. 957) to be supported by evidence. From what is alleged by Dorner it merely follows that Athanasius did not reflect on the subject. Baur, however, meanwhile goes too far when he expresses the opinion that Athanasius *designedly* left the human soul of Christ out of account; on the contrary, by the term "Flesh" he understood the whole substance of man, (see Orat. III. 30) and did not feel there was any necessity for studying the question as to the position occupied by the soul.

[3] Orat. IV. 31.

[4] Orat. IV. 32—34.

good of the Logos also, and this is true of all sufferings even,—
although He was not affected by them so far as His Godhead
is concerned, [1]—and Mary is the mother of God. Athanasius
also refers to the incarnate Logos the *locus classicus* of the
Arians, Prov. VIII. 22, 23, [2] with which Eustathius of Antioch
likewise occupied himself. [3] Finally, Athanasius spoke also of a
προκοπή or progress in reference to the incarnate Logos, of an
increase in the manifestation of God in the body of Christ, by
which he means that the flesh was more and more completely
irradiated by the Godhead: τὸ ἀνθρώπινον ἐν τῇ σοφίᾳ προέκοπτεν,[4]
(the human advanced in wisdom).

How are the two mutually opposed doctrines to be judged
from the standpoint of history, of reason, and of the Gospel?
Each party charged the other with holding doctrines which
involved contradictions, and, what is of more consequence,
they mutually accused each other of apostasy from Christianity,
although the Arians never advanced this charge with such
energy as the opposite party. We have first of all to ascertain
definitely how much they had in common. *Religion and doctrine are with both thoroughly fused together,* [5] and, indeed,
formally considered, the doctrine is the same in both cases,
i.e., the fundamental conceptions are the same. The doctrine
of the pre-existent Christ, who as the pre-existent Son of God
is Logos, Wisdom, and world-creating Power of God, seems
to constitute the common basis. Together with this both have
a common interest in maintaining the *unity* of God and in

---

[1] Orat. I. 45, III. 30—33.

[2] Almost the whole second oration against the Arians is devoted to the task
of refuting the use made by them of this passage.

[3] Theodoret, H. E. I. 8.

[4] Orat. III. 53: Αὐξάνοντος ἐν ἡλικίᾳ τοῦ σώματος, συνεπεδίδοτο ἐν αὐτῷ καὶ ἡ
τῆς θεότητος φανέρωσις... τὸ ἄνθρώπινον προέκοπτεν, ὑπεραναβαῖνον κατ᾽ ὀλίγον τὴν
ἀνθρωπίνην φύσιν καὶ θεοποιούμενον καὶ ὄργανον τῆς σοφίας πρὸς τὴν ἐνέργειαν τῆς
θεότητος καὶ τὴν ἔκλαμψιν αὐτῆς γενόμενον,

[5] Both thus occupy the stage of development which was described in Vol. III.,
pp. 113—118. We may say meanwhile, and what follows will prove it, that the fusion
of a theoretical doctrine with religion was more thorough in the case of Arianism
than with Athanasius.

making a sharp distinction between Creator and creature. Finally, both endeavour to base their doctrines on Scripture and at the same time claim to have tradition on their side, as is evident in the case of Arius from the introduction to the Thalia. Both are, however, convinced that the final word lies with Scripture and not with tradition.

I. We cannot understand Arianism unless we consider that it consists of two entirely disparate parts. It has, first of all, a Christ who gradually becomes God, who therefore develops more and more in moral unity of feeling with God, progresses and attains his perfection by the divine grace. This Christ is the Saviour, in so far as he has conveyed to us the divine doctrine and has given us an example of goodness perfectly realised in the exercise of freedom. When Arius calls this Christ Logos it appears as if he did this by way of accommodation. The conception of Arius here is purely Adoptian. But, secondly, with this is united a metaphysic which has its basis solely in a cosmology and has absolutely no connection with soteriology. This metaphysic is dominated by the thought of the antithesis of the one, inexpressible God, a God remote from the world, and the creature. The working-out of this thought accordingly perfectly corresponds with the philosophical ideas of the time and with the one half of the line of thought pursued by Origen. In order that a creation may become possible at all, a spiritual being must first be created which can be the means whereby a spiritual-material world can be created. This cannot be the divine reason itself, but only the most complete image of the divine reason stamped on a created, freely acting, independent being. With this we have arrived at the Neo-platonic origination. Whether in order to find a means of transition to the world we are to speak of "God, the essential νοῦς of God, the created Logos," or "God, the created Logos, the world-spirit," or are to arrange the terms in some other way, is pretty much a matter of indifference, and to all appearance Arius laid little stress on this. It is the philosophical triad, or duad, such as we meet with in Philo, Numenius, Plotinus etc. These created beings which mediate between God and the creature are, however, according to Arius, to be adored, *i.e., it is only as a cosmologist that he is a strict monotheist, while as a theologian he is a polytheist.* This again perfectly corresponds to the dominant Hellenic view. Arius in fact occupies a place, so to speak, on the extreme left, for the energetic way in which he emphasises the thought that the second ousia has been created out of the free will of God, that it is foreign to the substance of God, that as a creaturely substance it is capable of change and definable, and, above all, the express assertion that this "Logos" and "Son" is "Logos" and "Son" merely nominally, that in no sense whatever is an emanation or anything of that kind to be thought of here, but simply a *creation*, is surprising even in the sphere of Hellenic philosophy. That this created Logos which made possible the further creation has appeared in Jesus Christ and has in human vesture developed into God and has therefore not been lowered, but on the contrary has been exalted by His being man, is accordingly what constitutes the uniting thought between the two parts of the system.

In the other case, as here, the expressions "pre-existent Son of God," "Logos," "Wisdom" are plainly only an accommodation. They are unavoidable, but not necessary, in fact they create difficulties. It clearly follows from this, however, that the doctrine of Origen does not constitute the basis of the system—in so far as its Christology is concerned—and that what it has in common with the orthodox system is not what is really characteristic of it, but is on the contrary what is secondary. The Arian doctrine has its root in Adoptianism, in the doctrine of Lucian of Samosata, [1] as is proved, above all, by the strong emphasis laid on the creaturehood of the Redeemer and by the elimination of a human soul. We know what signification this had for Origen. Where it is wanting we can no longer speak of Origenism in the full meaning of the word. But it is correct that the cosmological-causal point of view of Origen, this one side of his complicated system, was appropriated

---

[1] See above p. 3, and in addition Athan. Orat. III. 51 : The view of Lucian of Samosata is the idea of the pure creaturehood and humanity of the Redeemer ὅ τῇ μὲν δυνάμει καὶ ὑμεῖς φρονεῖτε, τῷ δὲ ὀνόματι μόνον ἀρνεῖσθε διὰ τοὺς ἀνθρώπους. This is no mere trick of logic, although the alleged motive of the correction of the Adoptianist doctrine is assuredly incorrectly described.

by Arius, that is by Lucian. Meanwhile it has to be added that it was not peculiar to Origen. He made an effort to get beyond it; he balanced the causal-cosmological point of view, according to which the Logos is a heavenly κτίσμα, by the soteriological, according to which He is the essential and recognisable image of the Father, which constitutes an essential unity with the Father. Of this there is nothing in Arius.[1]

Arianism is a *new doctrine* in the Church; it labours under quite as many difficulties as any other earlier Christological doctrine; it is, finally, in one important respect, really Hellenism which is simply tempered by the constant use of Holy Scripture. It is a new doctrine; for not only is the frank assertion of the creaturehood and changeableness of the Logos in this sharply defined form, new, spite of Origen, Dionysius Alex., Pierius and so on, but, above all, the emphatic rejection of any essential connection of the Logos with the Father. The images of the source and the brook, the sun and the light, the archetype and the type, which are almost of as old standing in the Church as the Logos-doctrine itself, are here discarded. This, however, simply means that the Christian Logos- and Son-of-God-doctrine has itself been discarded. Only the old names remain. But new too, further, is the combination of Adoptianism with the Logos-cosmology, and if the idea of two distinct Logoi and two Wisdoms is not exactly new, it is a distinction which had never before this been permitted.

Athanasius exposed the inner difficulties and contradictions, and in almost every case we may allow that he has right on his side. A son who is no son, a Logos who is no Logos, a monotheism which nevertheless does not exclude polytheism, two or three ousias which are to be revered, while yet only *one* of them is really distinct from the creatures, an indefinable being who first becomes God by becoming man and who is yet neither God nor man, and so on. In every single point we have apparent clearness while all is hollow and formal, a boyish enthusiasm for playing with husks and shells, and a

---

[1] We do not know whether or not Arius appealed to Origen. The later Arians undoubtedly quoted him in support of their views; they seem, however, to have appealed most readily to Dionysius of Alex. See Athan. de sentent. Dionysii.

childish self-satisfaction in the working out of empty syllogisms. [1]
This had not been learned from Origen, who always had facts
and definite ends in view when he speculated.

But all this might be put up with if only this doctrine were in
any way designed to shew how communion with God is arrived
at through Christ. This is what we must necessarily demand;
for what the ancient Church understood by "redemption" was
in part a physical redemption of a very questionable kind, and
it would not necessarily have been anything to be regretted if
anyone had emancipated himself from this "redemption." But
one has absolutely nowhere the impression that Arius and his
friends are in their theology concerned with communion with
God. Their *doctrina de Christo* has nothing whatever to do
with this question. The divine which appeared on earth is not
the Godhead, but one of its creations. God Himself remains
unknown. Whoever expresses adherence to the above propositions and does this with unmistakable satisfaction, stands up
for the unique nature of God, but does this, however, only that
he may not endanger the uniformity of the basis of the world,
and otherwise is prepared to worship besides this God other
"Gods" too, creatures that is; whoever allows religion to disappear in a cosmological doctrine and in veneration for a heroic
teacher, even though he may call him "perfect creature,"
κτίσμα τέλειον, and revere in him the being through whom this
world has come to be what it is, is, so far as his religious way
of thinking is concerned, a Hellenist, and has every claim to be
highly valued by Hellenists. [2]

The admission that the Arians succeeded in getting a grasp
of certain features in the historical Christ presented to us by
the New Testament, cannot in any way alter this judgment.
In this matter they were far superior to their opponents; but
they were absolutely unable to make any *religious* use of what
they perceived. They speak of Christ as Paul of Samosata
does, but by foisting in behind the Christ who was exalted to
be Lord, the half divine being, logos-creature, λόγος-κτίσμα,

[1] See the tractate of Aëtius preserved in Epiphanius; but the older Arians had
already acted in the same way.

[2] There are some good remarks on Arianism in Kaufmann, Deutsche Geschichte I.,
pp. 232, 234; also in Richter, Weström. Reich, p. 537.

they deprived the most valuable knowledge they had of all practical value. Paul could say in a general way: τὰ κρατού-μενα τῷ λόγῳ τῆς φύσεως οὐκ ἔχει ἔπαινον· τὰ δὲ σχέσει φιλίας κρατούμενα ὑπεραινεῖται (what was accomplished by the Logos of nature deserves no praise, but what was accomplished in the state of love is to be praised exceedingly). Such a statement was made impossible for the Arians by the introduction of cosmological speculation. What dominates Paul's whole view of the question—namely, the thought that the unity of love and feeling is the most abiding unity, scarcely ever finds an echo amongst the Arians, for it is swallowed up by that philosophy which measures worth by duration in time and thinks of a half-eternal being as being nearer God than a temporal being who is filled with the love of God. We cannot therefore finally rate very high the results of the rational exegesis of christological passages as given by the Arians; they do not use them to shew that Jesus was a man whom God chose for Himself or that God was in the man Jesus, but, on the contrary, in order to prove that this Jesus was no complete God. Nor can we put a high value on their defence of monotheism either, for they adored creatures. What is alone really valuable, is the energetic emphasis they lay on freedom, and which they adopted from Origen, but even it has no religious significance.

Had the Arian doctrine gained the victory in the Greek-speaking world, it would in all probability have completely ruined Christianity, that is, it would have made it disappear in cosmology and morality and would have annihilated religion in the religion. "The Arian Christology is inwardly the most unstable, and dogmatically the most worthless, of all the Christologies to be met with in the history of dogma."[1] Still it had its mission. The Arians made the transition from heathenism to Christianity easier for the large numbers of the cultured and half-cultured whom the policy of Constantine brought into the Church. They imparted to them a view of the Holy Scriptures and of Christianity which could present no difficulty to any one at that period. The Arian monotheism was the best transition from polytheism to monotheism. It asserted the truth that there is

[1] Schultz, Gottheit Christi, p. 65.

one supreme God with whom nothing can be compared, and thus rooted out the crude worship of many gods. It constructed a descending divine triad in which the cultured were able to recognise again the highest wisdom of their philosophers. It permitted men to worship a demiurge together with the primal substance, πρώτη οὐσία; it taught an incarnation of this demiurge and, on the other hand again, a *theopoiesis*, and was able skilfully to unite this with the worship of Christ in the Church. It afforded, in the numerous formulæ which it coined, interesting material for rhetorical and dialectic exercises. It quickened the feeling of freedom and responsibility and led to discipline, and even to asceticism. And finally, it handed on the picture of a divine hero who was obedient even to death and gained the victory by suffering and patience, and who has become a pattern for us. When transmitted along with the Holy Scriptures, it even produced a living piety [1] amongst Germanic Christians, if it also awakened in them the very idea to which it had originally been specially opposed, the idea of a theogony. What was shewn above—namely, that the doctrine was new, is to be taken *cum grano salis;* elements which were present in the teaching of the Church from the very beginning got here vigorous outward expression and became supreme. The approval the doctrine met with shews how deeply rooted they were in the Church. We cannot but be astonished at the first glance to find that those who sought to defend the whole system of Origen partly sided with Arius and partly gave him their patronage. But this fact ceases to be striking so soon as we consider that the controversy very quickly became so acute as to necessitate a decision for or against Arius. But the Origenists, moreover, had a very strong antipathy to everything that in any way suggested "Sabellianism"; for Sabellianism had no place for the pursuit of Hellenic cosmological speculation, *i.e.*, of scientific theology. Their position with regard to the doctrine of Athanasius was thereby determined. They would rather have kept to their rich supply of musty formulæ, but they were forced to decide for Arius.

[1] The figure of Ulfilas vouches for this; his confession of faith (Halm, § 126) is the only Arian one which is not polemical.

II. Nothing can more clearly illustrate the perverse state of the problem in the Arian-Athanasian controversy than the notorious fact that the man who saved the character of Christianity as a religion of living fellowship with God, was the man from whose Christology almost every trait which recalls the historical Jesus of Nazareth was erased. Athanasius undoubtedly retained the most important feature—namely, that Christ promised to bring men into fellowship with God. But while he subordinated everything to this thought and recognised in redemption a communication of the divine *nature*, he reduced the entire historical account given of Christ to the belief that the Redeemer shared in the nature and unity of the Godhead itself, and he explained everything in the Biblical documents in accordance with this idea.[1] That which Christ is and is for us, is the Godhead; in the Son we have the Father, and in what the Son has brought, the divine is communicated to us. This fundamental thought is not new, and it corresponds with a very old conception of the Gospel. It is not new, for it was never wanting in the Church before the time of Athanasius. The Fourth Gospel, Ignatius, Irenæus, Methodius, the so-called Modalism and even the Apologists and Origen—not to mention the Westerns—prove this; for the Apologists, and Origen too, in what they say of the Logos, emphasised not only His distinction from the Father, but also His unity with the Father. The Samosatene had also laid the whole emphasis on the unity, although indeed he was not understood.[2] But not since the days in which the Fourth Gospel was written do we meet with any-

---

[1] Anyone, on the other hand, who, like Arius, held to the idea of a developing and struggling Christ was not able to conceive of Him as Redeemer, but only as teacher and example. This was the situation: the Bible accounts of Christ did not favour and establish the sole idea which was held at the time regarding fellowship with God and redemption, but, on the contrary, they interfered with it.

[2] Athanasius always appealed to the collective testimony of the Church in support of the doctrine which he defended. In the work, de decret, 25 sq., he shews that the words ἐκ τῆς οὐσίας and ὁμοούσιος were not discovered by the Nicene Fathers, but, on the contrary, had been handed down to them. He appeals to Theognostus, to the two Dionysii and Origen, to the latter with the reservation that in his case it is necessary to distinguish between what he wrote γυμναστικῶς and what he wrote of a positive character. It is one of the few passages in which he has thought of Origen.

one with whom the conviction is so definite, thought out with such an assurance of victory, expressed so strongly and so simply, and of such an absolute kind, as it is with Athanasius. All the rest by introducing qualifying thoughts in some way or other, brought an element of uncertainty into their feeling of its truth, and impaired its strength. That in the age of Constantine during the greatest revolution which the Church has experienced and which was so fraught with consequences, the faith represented by Athanasius was confessed with such vigour, is what saved the Christian Church. Its faith would probably have got entirely into the hands of the philosophers, its confession would have become degraded or would have been turned into an imperial official decree enjoining the worship of the "clear-shining Godhead", if Athanasius had not been there and had not helped those who shared his views to make a stand and inspired them with courage.

But at the beginning of the Fourth Century the form of expression for the belief in the unity of the eternal Godhead and its appearance in Jesus Christ was already sketched out. It was as little allowable to think of a unity of living feeling, of will and aim alone, as of the perfect identification of the persons. The doctrines of the pre-existing Son of God, of the eternal Logos, but, above all, the view that everything valuable is accomplished in the *nature* only, of which feeling and will are an annex, were firmly established. Athanasius in making use of these presuppositions in order to express his faith in the Godhead of Christ, *i.e.*, in the essential unity of the Godhead in itself with the Godhead manifested in Christ, fell into an abyss of contradictions.

Unquestionably the old Logos doctrine too, and also Arianism, strike us to-day as being full of contradictions, but it was Athanasius who first arrived at the *contradictio in adjecto* in the full sense of the phrase. That the Godhead is a numerical unity, but that nevertheless Son and Father are to be distinguished within this unity as two—this is his view. He teaches that there is only one unbegotten principle, but that nevertheless the Son has not come into being. He maintains that the Divine in Christ is the eternal "Son", but that the Son

is as old as the Father. This Son is not to be thought of
either as created, or as an attribute of God, or as an emanation or a part of God, and is therefore something wholly indefinable. The thought of a theogony is rejected as emphatically as that of a creation, and yet the thought of an active
attribute is not in any sense to be entertained. The Father is
perfect for Himself and is sufficient for Himself; indeed, although
Father and Son have one substance, in the sense of a single
nature, in common, still the Father alone is "the God", and
is the principle and root of the Son also. *Quot verba, tot
scandala!*

Whatever involves a complete contradiction cannot be correct,
and everyone is justified in unsparingly describing the contradiction as such. This the Arians sufficiently did, and in so far
as they assumed that a contradiction cannot be seriously
accepted by anyone, and that therefore the view of Athanasius
must at bottom be Sabellian, they were right. Two generations
and more had to pass before the Church could accustom itself
to recognise in the complete contradiction the sacred privilege
of revelation. There was, in fact, no philosophy in existence
possessed of formulæ which could present in an intelligible
shape the propositions of Athanasius. What he called at one
time Ousia and at another Hypostasis, was not an individual
substance in the full sense of the word, but still less was it a
generic conception.

If anything is clear, it is the fact that the thought of Athanasius—namely, the unity of the Godhead which rested in and
appeared in Christ, could not be expressed under the traditional
presuppositions of the pre-existing Son of God and the personal
Logos existing from all eternity. We have here to do with the
most important point in the whole question. The very same series
of ideas which created the most serious difficulties for the
Arians and which have been shewn to occupy a secondary place
in their system, seriously hamper the doctrinal utterances of
Athanasius; namely, the Logos doctrine of Origen and the
cosmological-metaphysical conceptions which form the background of statements regarding an historical person. The
Arians required to have a created being, created before the

world, changeable, of the same nature as men, for their Christ,
and had to banish all other determinations from their conception, and so they could not make use of the Logos of Philo
and the Apologists; Athanasius required a being who was
absolutely nothing else than the Godhead, and so the Logos
referred to did not in any sense fit in with his doctrine. *In
both cases the combined Logos doctrine of Philo and Origen
was the disturbing element.* And at bottom,—though unfortunately not actually,[1]—they both discarded it; Arius when he
distinguishes between the Logos *nuncupativus* which Christ is,
and the actual Logos of God; Athanasius when he banishes
the world-idea from the content of the substance which he
adores in Christ. In the view of Arius, Christ belongs in every
sense to the world, *i.e.*, to the sphere of created things; in
that of Athanasius he belongs in every sense to God, whose
substance He shares.

Arius and Athanasius both indeed occupy the standpoint of
the theology of Origen which no one could now abandon; but
their religious and theological interests do not originate in it.
In the gnosis of Origen everything spiritual stands to God in
a two-fold relation; it is His created work and yet it is at the
same time His nature. This holds good in a pre-eminent sense
of the Logos, which comprises all that is spiritual in itself and
connects the graduated spheres of the spiritual substances,
which, like it, have an eternal duration, with the supreme Godhead. To this idea corresponds the thought that the creatures
are free and that they *must* return from their state of estrangement and their Fall to their original source. Of this we find
nothing either in Arius or in Athanasius. In the case of the
former, the sober Aristotelian philosophy on the one hand
reacts against this fundamental thought, and on the other, the
tradition of the Christ who is engaged in a conflict, who increases and progresses towards perfection. In the case of

---

[1] They were not able, and did not dare, to discard it actually, because of
John I. 1 f., on account of the Church tradition, and because of the scientific
views of the time. As regards Athanasius, we have to keep in mind his idea of
the Father as the $\rho i \zeta \alpha$ of the Son, and his other idea, according to which the
world was actually made by the Son.

Athanasius what reacts against it is the ancient belief of the Church in the Father, the Almighty Creator of all things, and in the Son in whom the Father reveals Himself and has stooped to hold fellowship with man.

It is thus not the case that the gnosis of Origen was simply halved between Arius and Athanasius; on the contrary, it underwent a fundamental correction in the teaching of both. But it was no longer possible to avoid the "*vis inertiæ*" of the gnosis of Origen, the contrary formulæ which were held together by the idea of the Logos-cosmology as the basis for Christology.[1] And now the question was which of the two was to be adopted, the Logos-κτίσμα or the Logos-ὁμοούσιος formula. The former freed from the latter was indeed deprived of all soteriological content, but was capable of intelligent and philosophical treatment—namely, rational-logical treatment; the latter taken exclusively, even supposing that the distinction between the Son and the Father and the superiority of the Father were maintained in connection with it, simply led to an absurdity.

Athanasius put up with this absurdity;[2] without knowing it he made a still greater sacrifice to his faith—the historical Christ. It was at such a price that he saved the religious conviction that Christianity is the religion of perfect fellowship with God, from being displaced by a doctrine which possessed many lofty qualities, but which had no understanding of the inner essence of religion, which sought in religion nothing but "instruction," and finally found satisfaction in an empty dialectic.

---

[1] Dionysius of Alexandria was a genuine pupil of Origen, for he was equally prepared to maintain the other side of the system of Origen, when his namesake pointed out to him that by his one-sided emphasising of the one side, he had lost himself in highly questionable statements. Eusebius of Cæsarea took up the same position.

[2] The Nicene Creed sanctioned it. One of its most serious consequences was that from this time onward Dogmatics were for ever separated from clear thinking and defensible conceptions, and got accustomed to what was anti-rational. The anti-rational—not indeed at once, but soon enough—came to be considered as the characteristic of the sacred. As there was everywhere a desire for mysteries, the doctrine seemed to be the true mystery just because it was the opposite of the clear in the sphere of the profane. Even clear-headed men like the later members of the school of Antioch were no longer able to escape from absurdity. The complete contradiction involved in the Ὁμοούσιος drew a whole host of contradictions after it, the further thought advanced.

It was intended that the General Church-Council which was summoned by the Emperor to meet at Nicæa should, besides settling some other important questions, compose the controversy which already threatened to produce division amongst the Eastern bishops.[1] It met in the year 325, in summer apparently. There were present about 300 (250, 270) bishops, hardly so many as 318 as asserted by Athanasius at a later time; the correctness of this latter number is open to suspicion. The West was very poorly represented;[2] the Roman bishop was not there, but he had sent two presbyters. The most important of the Eastern bishops were present. It is not clear how the business was arranged and conducted. We do not know who presided, whether Eustathius, Eusebius of Cæsarea, or Hosius. It is undoubted, however, that Hosius exercised a very important influence in the Council. The Emperor at first gave the Council a free hand,[3] though he at once put a stop to private wrangling, and he energetically interfered at the most decisive moment, and in the character of a theologian interpreted himself the formula to be adopted.[4] We may assume that at first he reckoned on the possibility that the Council would itself find some formula of agreement. He had, however, resolved, under the influence of Hosius, that in the case of this not being successfully carried out, he would enforce the formula which Hosius had agreed upon with Alexander. As

[1] For the sources and the literature referring to the Council of Nice see Herzog's R-Encykl., Vol. X. 2, p. 530 ff. The accounts are meagre and frequently self-contradictory. We do not yet possess an exhaustive study of the subject. In what follows the main points only can be dealt with. I must renounce the idea of giving here the detailed reasons in support of the views I hold. See Gwatkin, p. 36 ff.

[2] No one was present from Britain; though there were probably bishops from Illyria, Dacia, Italy, Gaul, Spain, Africa and also a Persian bishop. Eusebius (Vita III. 8) compares the meeting with that described in Acts II.

[3] Sozom. I. 18; we certainly cannot form any clear picture of what took place from the account given in this passage.

[4] This follows from the letter of Eusebius of Cæsarea to his Church (Theodoret, H. E. I. 11), which we may regard as trustworthy in connection with this matter. Eusebius there distinguishes quite plainly two parties; (1) the party to which he himself belongs and (2) the party which he introduces with "οἱ δὲ" (οἱ δὲ προφάσει τῆς τοῦ ὁμοουσίου προσθήκης τήνδε τὴν γραφὴν πεποιήκασιν, the Nicene Creed follows) and which he does not describe in more definite terms than by "αὐτοί" (καὶ δὴ ταύτης τῆς γραφῆς ὑπ᾽ αὐτῶν ὑπαγορευθείσης).

regards the composition of the Council, the view expressed by the Macedonian Sabinus of Heraclea (Socr. I. 8), that the majority of the bishops were uneducated, is confirmed by the astonishing results. The general acceptance of the resolution come to by the Council is intelligible only if we presuppose that the question in dispute was above most of the bishops.[1] Of the "cultured" we have to distinguish three parties—namely, Arius and the Lucianists, who had Eusebius of Nicomedia for their leader; the Origenists, the most important man amongst whom was Eusebius of Cæsarea, who was already highly celebrated;[2] and Alexander of Alexandria with his following, to which the few Westerns also belonged.[3] The Arians came to the Council confident of victory; as yet nothing was prejudged; the Bishop of Nicæa himself was on their side and they had relations with the Court.

All were apparently at one in thinking that the Council could not break up without establishing a standard of doctrine, ($\pi i \sigma \tau \iota \varsigma$, $\mu \acute{\alpha} \theta \eta \mu \alpha$.) Those in the East possessed neither a uniform nor a sufficiently authoritative symbol by which the controversy could be settled. The Lucianists accordingly—who may have been about twenty in number, not more at any rate—produced, after deliberation, a confession of faith which was communicated by Eusebius of Nicomedia and embodied their doctrine in unambiguous terms. They did this without having previously come to an understanding with the Origenists. This was a tactical blunder. The great majority of the bishops rejected this rule of faith which was decisively in favour of Arianism.[4] Even the "Conservatives" must have been unpleasantly affected by the naked statement of the Arian doctrinal system. The sup-

---

[1] With the exception of the bishops whom their contemporaries and our earliest informants have mentioned by name, there do not seem to have been any capable men at the Council.

[2] It is worthy of note that Eusebius in the letter just cited does not introduce the Arians as a special party, but merely hints at their existence. The middle party stood, in fact, very near to them.

[3] Athanasius (de decret. 19 sq. ad Afros 5, 6, de synod. 33—41) mixes up the two opposition-parties together.

[4] See Theodoret I. 6: fin.; he relies upon the account of Eustathius. In addition Athanas., Encycl. ad epp. Ægypt 13, de decret. 3.

porters of Arius were now in the greatest perplexity owing to the unforeseen turn which events had taken. In order to be able to keep their position at the Council at all, they, with the exception of two who remained firm, withdrew this sketch of their doctrine, and now made up their minds to follow the lead of the Origenists in order to secure at least something. Eusebius of Cæsarea now came to the front. No one was more learned than he; no one was more intimately acquainted with the teaching of the Fathers. He had good reason to hope that he would be able to speak the decisive word. If there was a general conviction that in everything it was necessary to abide by the ancient doctrine of the Church, then there seemed to be no one more fitted to define that ancient doctrine than the great scholar who was also, moreover, in the highest favour with the Emperor. His formulæ were, "the created image", "the reflection originating in the will", "the second God" etc.[1] He could, if needful, have accepted the Arian formulæ; those of Alexander he could not adopt, for he saw in them the dreaded Sabellianism which meant the death of theological science. Eusebius accordingly laid a creed before the Council.[2] He was convinced that all could and must unite on the basis supplied by it, and as a matter of fact no better conciliatory formula could be imagined.[3] Still Eusebius considered it neces-

---

[1] See the characteristic passage Demonstr. IV. 3 : ἡ μὴν αὐγὴ οὐ κατὰ προαίρεσιν τοῦ φωτὸς ἐκλάμπει. κατά τι δὲ τῆς οὐσίας συμβεβηκὸς ἀχώριστον. ὁ δὲ υἱὸς κατὰ γνώμην καὶ προαίρεσιν εἰκών ὑπέστη τοῦ πατρός. βουληθεὶς γὰρ ὁ Θεὸς γέγονεν υἱοῦ πατὴρ καὶ φῶς δεύτερον κατὰ πάντα ἑαυτῷ ἀφωμοιωμένον ὑπεστήσατο.

[2] According to Eustathius (in Theodoret I. 7) the creed of the strict Arians was composed by Eusebius of Nicomedia; at least I think that it must be the latter who is referred to in what is said in that passage : ὡς δὲ ἐζητεῖτο τῆς πίστεως ὁ τρόπος, ἐναργὴς μὲν ἔλεγχος τὸ γράμμα τῆς Εὐσεβίου προὐβάλλετο βλασφημίας. ἐπι πάντων δὲ ἀναγνωσθὲν αὐτίκα συμφορὰν μὲν ἀστάθμητον τῆς ἐκτροπῆς ἕνεκα τοῖς αὐτηκόοις προὐξένει, αἰσχύνην δ᾽ἀνήκεστον τῷ γράψαντι παρεῖχεν. It is impossible that it can be the creed of Eusebius of Cæsarea which is referred to here, for the latter (l. c. I. 11) expressly notes that his creed after having been communicated to the Council was substantially accepted. Whether we have a right to call the creed which he produced simply "Baptismal Creed of the Church of Cæsarea," is to me questionable, judging from the introduction to it given in the letter to his Church.

[3] The creed is contained in the letter of Eusebius to his Church. See Theodoret I. 1 : Πιστεύομεν εἰς ἕνα Θεὸν πατέρα παντοκράτορα, τὸν τῶν ἁπάντων ὁρατῶν τε καὶ

sary to tack on to it an anti-Sabellian addition.[1] According to Eusebius the Creed was unanimously pronounced orthodox,[2] still the imperial will already made its influence felt here. The Arians were doubtless well pleased to get off on these terms. But Alexander and his following demanded a perfectly plain rejection of Arianism. They went about it in an extremely adroit fashion inasmuch as they accepted the basis of the Creed of Cæsarea, but demanded that its terms should be made more precise. We know from Eusebius himself that the Emperor sided with them, and so far as he was concerned resolved to incorporate in the Creed the word "ὁμοούσιος", which was suggested to him by Hosius.[3] But the matter was not settled by the mere insertion of a word. It was pointed out that the Creed of Cæsarea contained formulæ which might favour the Arian view. Its supporters were already put in the position of defendants. Accordingly, the Alexandrian party presented a very carefully constructed doctrinal formula which was represented as being a revised form of the Creed of Cæsarea[4] and

ἀοράτων ποιητήν, καὶ εἰς ἕνα κύριον Ἰησοῦν Χριστόν, τὸν τοῦ Θεοῦ λόγον, Θεὸν ἐκ Θεοῦ, φῶς ἐκ φωτός, ζωὴν ἐκ ζωῆς, υἱὸν μονογενῆ, πρωτότοκον πάσης κτίσεως, πρὸ πάντων τῶν αἰώνων ἐκ τοῦ πατρὸς γεγεννημένον, δι᾽ οὗ καὶ ἐγένετο τὰ πάντα, τὸν διὰ τὴν ἡμετέραν σωτηρίαν σαρκωθέντα καὶ ἐν ἀνθρώποις πολιτευσάμενόν καὶ παθόντα καὶ ἀναστάντα τῇ τρίτῃ ἡμέρᾳ καὶ ἀνελθόντα πρὸς τὸν πατέρα καὶ ἥξοντα πάλιν ἐν δόξῃ κρῖναι ζῶντας καὶ νεκρούς, καὶ εἰς ἓν πνεῦμα ἅγιον.

[1] Τούτων ἕκαστον εἶναι καὶ ὑπάρχειν πιστεύοντες, πατέρα ἀληθινῶς πατέρα, καὶ υἱὸν ἀληθινῶς υἱόν, πνεῦμά τε ἅγιον ἀληθινῶς πνεῦμα ἅγιον, καθὰ καὶ ὁ κύριος ἡμῶν ἀποστέλλων εἰς τὸ κήρυγμα τοὺς ἑαυτοῦ μαθητὰς εἶπε· Matt. XXVIII. 19 follows.

[2] Ταύτης ὑφ᾽ ἡμῶν ἐκτεθείσης τῆς πίστεως οὐδεὶς παρῆν ἀντιλογίας τόπος, ἀλλ᾽ αὐτός τε πρῶτος ὁ θεοφιλέστατος ἡμῶν βασιλεὺς ὀρθότατα περιέχειν αὐτὴν ἐμαρτύρησεν. οὕτω τε καὶ ἑαυτὸν φρονεῖν συνωμολόγησε· καὶ ταύτῃ τοὺς πάντας συγκατατίθεσθαι, ὑπογράφειν τε τοῖς δόγμασι καὶ συμφωνεῖν τούτοις αὐτοῖς παρεκελεύετο (I. 11).

[3] According to Eusebius, however, the Emperor himself added an interpretation of the Ὁμοούσιος. We read in the letter of Eusebius, immediately after the words cited in the foregoing note: ἑνὸς μόνου προσεγγραφέντος ῥήματος τοῦ Ὁμοουσίου, ὃ καὶ αὐτὸς ἡρμήνευσε λέγων ὅτι μὴ κατὰ σωμάτων πάθε λέγοιτο Ὁμοούσιος, οὔτε κατὰ διαίρεσιν, οὔτε κατά τινα ἀποτομὴν ἐκ τοῦ πατρὸς ὑποστῆναι ... θείοις δὲ καὶ ἀπορρήτοις λόγοις προσήκει τὰ τοιαῦτα νοεῖν. The word is thus only intended to express the mystery!

[4] Eusebius in an ill-concealed tone of reproach says οἱ δὲ (i.e., the Alexandrians) προφάσει τῆς τοῦ Ὁμοουσίου προσθήκης τήνδε τὴν γραφὴν (i.e., the Nicene Creed) πεποιήκασι, that is, they have corrected my proposed creed not only here but in other passages also.

in which some think they can recognise, in addition to the
contributions of the Alexandrians, the hand of Eustathius of
Antioch and of Makarius of Jerusalem.¹ (1) In place of ἀπάντων
ὁρατῶν etc., ("of all seen things whatsoever"), there was put by
preference πάντων ὁρατῶν ("of all seen things"), in order to exclude the creation of the Son and Spirit;² (2) *in place of the
Logos at the beginning of the second article, the "Son" was
put, so that all that follows refers to the Son;*³ (3) the words
Θεὸν ἐκ Θεοῦ ("God of God") were extended to γεννηθέντα ἐκ
τοῦ πατρὸς μονογενῆ Θεὸν ἐκ Θεοῦ ("begotten of the Father only
begotten God of God"), but in the final discussion, however,
between μονογενῆ and Θεόν the words τοῦτ' ἐστὶν ἐκ τῆς οὐσίας
τοῦ πατρός ("that is of the substance of the Father") were
further inserted, because it was observed that otherwise the
opposition party might be able to put their doctrine into the
proposition;⁴ (4) the unsatisfactory descriptions ζωὴν ἐκ ζωῆς
("life of life"), πρωτότοκον πάσης κτίσεως ("the first-born of every
creature"), πρὸ πάντων αἰώνων ἐκ τοῦ πατρὸς γεγεννημένον ("begotten of the Father before all ages"), before δι' οὗ, etc., were
deleted, and in their place the following was put: Θεὸν ἀληθινὸν
ἐκ Θεοῦ ἀληθινοῦ, γεννηθέντα, οὐ ποιηθέντα, δι' οὗ τὰ πάντα ἐγένετο
("true God of true God, begotten, not made, by whom all
things were"). At this point, however, a further insertion was
made, and this once more in the course of the discussion itself, ⁵
at what too was not at all a suitable place—namely, after
"ποιηθέντα" ("made"), the words ὁμοούσιον τῷ πατρί ("of the
same substance with the Father"), because it was observed that
none of the other terms excluded the Arian evasions; (5) the
indefinite ἐν ἀνθρώποις πολιτευσάμενον (" having lived amongst
men ") was replaced by the definite ᾽ενανθρωπήσαντα ("having

---

¹ See Hort., l. c., p. 59 and my article in Herzog, R.-Encyklop., Vol. VIII., p. 214 ff.

² See Gwatkin, p. 41.

³ The "Logos" is wholly absent from the Nicene Creed; after what has been
adduced above this will cause as little astonishment as the fact that neither Atha-
nasians nor Arians took any offence at its exclusion.

⁴ See on this what is told us by Athanasius, l. c. The clumsy position of the
words which mutilate the conception μονογενῆ Θεὸν, further proves that they are
an insertion made at the very last.

⁵ See Athanasius, l. c.

become incarnate"); and (6) finally, in order to exclude all ambiguity, the condemnation of the Arian catchwords was added on to this.[1]

The opposition parties did not yield without debates, in which the Emperor himself took part.[2] We do not know the details of the discussions, but we gather from the accounts of Athanasius that the Eusebians made still further proposals of a conciliatory kind and attempted to produce new catchwords.[3] The nature of their objections to the Alexandrian outline of doctrine may be gathered from the irenic explanation which Eusebius gave to his Church in Cæsarea as well as from the objections which later on were brought against the Nicene Creed. They fought against ἐκ τῆς οὐσίας ("of the substance") and ὁμοούσιος because (1) they believed they saw in these words a materialising of the Godhead, which made it a composite substance comprising emanations or parts; because (2) they could not help seeing in the ὁμοούσιος a Sabellian definition too, and because (3) the words did not occur in Holy Scripture. This last reason was specially decisive. In many parts of the Church there was still a shrinking from the definite adoption of unbiblical terms for the expression of the Faith.[4] In addition to

---

[1] The doctrinal formula in accordance with this was worded as follows. (The differences above discussed between it and the Creed of Cæsarea are to be explained as the result of the influence exercised by the Jerusalem and Antiochian Creed). The textual proofs are enumerated in Walch, Bibl. symb., p. 75 sq., Hahn, § 73, 74, and Hort. l. c.;—slight variations occur—: Πιστεύομεν εἰς ἕνα Θεὸν πατέρα παντοκράτορα, πάντων ὁρατῶν τε καὶ ἀοράτων ποιητήν, καὶ εἰς ἕνα κύριον Ἰησοῦν Χριστόν, τὸν υἱὸν τοῦ Θεοῦ, γεννηθέντα ἐκ τοῦ πατρός μονογενή—τοῦτ᾽ ἐστὶν ἐκ τῆς οὐσίας τοῦ πατρός—Θεὸν ἐκ Θεοῦ, φῶς ἐκ φωτός, Θεὸν ἀληθινὸν ἐκ Θεοῦ ἀληθινοῦ, γεννηθέντα οὐ ποιηθέντα—ὁμοούσιον τῷ πατρί—δι᾽ οὗ τὰ πάντα ἐγένετο, τὰ δε ἐν τῷ οὐρανῷ καὶ τὰ ἐν τῇ γῇ, τὸν δι᾽ ἡμᾶς τοὺς ἀνθρώπους καὶ διὰ τὴν ἡμετέραν σωτηρίαν κατελθόντα καὶ σαρκωθέντα, ἐνανθρωπήσαντα, παθόντα, καὶ ἀναστάντα τῇ τρίτῃ ἡμέρᾳ, ἀνελθόντα εἰς [τοὺς] οὐρανούς, ἐρχόμενον κρῖναι ζῶντας καὶ νεκρούς, καὶ εἰς τὸ ἅγιον πνεῦμα.

Τοὺς δὲ λέγοντας· Ἦν ποτὲ ὅτε οὐκ ἦν καὶ πρὶν γεννηθῆναι οὐκ ἦν, καὶ ὅτι ἐξ οὐκ ὄντων ἐγένετο, ἢ ἐξ ἑτέρας ὑποστάσεως ἢ οὐσίας φάσκοντας εἶναι [ἢ κτιστὸν] ἢ τρεπτὸν ἢ ἀλλοιωτὸν τὸν υἱὸν τοῦ Θεοῦ [τούτους] ἀναθεματίζει ἡ καθολικὴ [καὶ ἀποστολικὴ] ἐκκλησία.

[2] Eusebius in Theoderet, H. E. I. 11: ἐρωτήσεις τοιγαροῦν καὶ ἀποκρίσεις ἐντεῦθεν ἀνεκινοῦντο, ἐβασανίζετο ὁ λόγος τῆς διανοίας τῶν εἰρημένων.

[3] See Athan. de decret. 19, 20; ad Afros 5, 6.

[4] Still Gwatkin, p. 43, goes too far when he asserts that "the use of ἄγραφα in

this there was the fact that the ὁμοούσιος had before this been
rejected at Antioch.¹ But the will of the Emperor decided the
matter. Respect for the Emperor, his express declaration that
there was a desire not to endanger the absolute spirituality of
the Godhead, the wish to conclude a grand work of peace—
a creed was a positive revolution in the Church." It is quite impossible to maintain this in view, for example, of the Creed of Gregorius Thaumaturgus.

¹ See on μοούσιος, which the Gnostics were the first to use, and on its meaning and
history Vol. III. 141 f., 221; above pp. 15 f., 32—35; I. 257; II. 259, 352, 354;
iii. 45. On the older ecclesiastical use of οὐσία, ὑπόστασις, ὑποκείμενον, above all in
Origen, see the scholarly discussions by Bigg (the Christian Platonists, p. 164 ff.).
"Ousia is properly Platonic, while hypostasis, a comparatively modern and rare
word, is properly Stoic"... Hypokeimenon already in Aristotle means the *substantia materialis*, ὕλη quæ determinatur per formam or οὐσία cui inhærent πάθη
συμβεβηκότα... the theological distinction between the terms οὐσία and ὑπόστασις
is purely arbitrary." On the conception of hypostasis see Stentrup, Innsbrucker
Zeitschr. f. Kath. Theologie. 1877, p. 59 ff. The question as to who brought forward the ὁμοούσιος again after it had been condemned at Antioch, is an important
one. It does not occur in the letters of Bishop Alexander. Athanasius had never
any special preference for the *word*. It is found only once in the Orat. c. Arian
(Orat. I. 9), and in the undoubtedly conciliatory work, de synod., 41, he admits
that importance does not attach so much to the word as to the thing. The conceptions "ἑνότης" and "ἐκ τῆς οὐσίας" would have served the purpose so far as he
himself was concerned. Such being the state of the case one may reasonably
assume that the word was not revived by any one belonging to the Eastern Church,
since its rejection at Antioch must have stood in the way of this, but rather that
some one in the West went back upon it, and Hosius is the only one we can
think of as the likely person. This hypothesis is strengthened by the following
considerations: (1) According to the testimony of Eusebius of Cæsarea there can be
no doubt that the Emperor himself energetically defended the word ὁμοούσιος, but
the Emperor was dependent on Hosius; (2) Athanasius (hist. Arian. 42) says of
Hosius: οὗτος ἐν Νικαίᾳ πίστιν ἐξέθετο; (3) the Western-Roman doctrine was the
substantial unity of Father and Son; the Alexandrian bishop was accused before
the Roman bishop Dionysius on the ground that he was unwilling to use "ὁμοούσιος'"
and in Rome the accused excuses himself for not using it, and it is the Roman
bishop who in his letter stated in energetic language the κήρυγμα τῆς μοναρχίας,
the ἡνῶσθαι τῷ Θεῷ τὸν λόγον, and the οὐ καταμερίζειν τὴν μονάδα. I therefore
conjecture that the word had been retained in Rome, *i.e.*, in the West, since the
time of the controversy of the Dionysii, that when the occasion offered it was once
more produced in the East, and that the Alexandrians then accepted the word
because they themselves had no better short catchword at their command. This
explains why Athanasius always treats the expression as one which was suitable
so far as the actual fact to be expressed was concerned, but which as regards its
form was for him a foreign term. He could not, it is true, go quite so far as
Luther (Opp. reform. V., p. 506): "Quod si odit anima mea vocem homousion et
nolim ea uti, non ero hæreticus. Quis enim me coget uti, modo rem teneam, quæ
in concilio per scripturas definita est? Etsi Ariani male senserunt in fide, hoc

this doctrinal declaration [1] of the entire Church was, moreover, something new and imposing—induced the Conservatives, *i.e.*, the Origenists and those who did not think for themselves, to fall in with what was proposed. They all subscribed with the exception of two, and at the same time salved their consciences in different ways by mental reservations.[2] The Lucianists

tamon optime, sive malo sive bono animo, exegerunt, ne vocem profanam et novam in regulis fidei statui liceret." Finally, the statement of Socrates (III. 7) which indeed has been rejected by most, is decisive. According to this Hosius during his stay in Alexandria—before the Nicene Council—had discussed οὐσία and ὑπόστασις. At the first glance that undoubtedly seems unworthy of belief, because it is a ὕστερον-πρότερον; but as soon as we remember the work of Tertullian, adv. Prax., which is the most important dogmatic treatise which the West produced previous to Augustine and which cannot have been unknown to Hosius, everything becomes clear. In this work in which Tertullian bears witness to the strong influence exercised upon him by Monarchianism spite of the fact that he is opposing it, no thought is so plainly expressed as this, that Father, Son, and Spirit are *unius substantiæ*, *i.e.*, ὁμοούσιοι (Vol. II., p. 259 ff.). Along with this, however, we have the idea clearly developed, that Father, Son, and Spirit are different " personæ " (see *e.g.*, c. 3: "proximæ *personæ*, consortes *substantiæ* patris", 15; "visibilem et invisibilem deum deprehendo sub manifesta et *personali distinctione* condicionis utriusque"; see also the conception of "personales substantiæ" in adv. Valent. 4). These personæ are also called by Tertullian "formæ cohærentes", "species indivisæ", "gradus" (c. 2, 8), and in fact even simply "nomina" (c. 30), and this gives his representation as much a Monarchian appearance as the appearance of an immanent Trinity (for a more detailed examination, see the appendix to this chapter). It is from this source, and also from Novatian who in his work, de trinitate, adopted the thoughts of Tertullian, that the theology of Hosius is derived. He may very probably, along with Tertullian, have already spoken of "personæ", side by side with the "unius substantiæ" which the entire West possessed belief in, in accordance with the baptismal formula, for this is what it was understood to be. (See Hilar., de trinit. II. 1. 3; Ambros. de myster. 5 fin). That his formula was: "unius substantiæ tres personæ" where persona is certainly to be conceived of rather as species or forma—not as "substance"—is very probable. The Western Hippolytus, moreover, (c. Noët. 14) also spoke of *one* God and several *prosopeia*, and so too did the Western Sabellius, and Tert. (l. c. c. 26) says bluntly: "ad singula nomina in personas singulas tinguimur." Only this point must remain undecided—namely, whether Hosius already actually translated "persona" by "ὑπόστασις." It is not probable, since in the so-called Creed of Sardica he used ὑπόστασις as = οὐσία (substantia). That his main catchword was μία οὐσία follows from what he says in his letter to Narcissus of Neronias (Euseb. c. Marcell., p. 25).

1 This is what the Nicene Creed was primarily intended to be, and not a baptismal creed, as the anathemas prove.

2 Theonas of Marmarika and Secundus of Ptolemais refused and were deposed and banished, and the same thing happened in the case of Arius and some presbyters. Arius was specially forbidden by the Council to enter Alexandria, Sozom I. 20.

who up till now had to all appearance been united together in an indissoluble friendship, were unprincipled enough to sacrifice their old comrade Arius.[1] He was condemned as the scapegoat, and the Emperor, anxious to protect with the strong hand the unity which had been won, gave orders that the books of Arius should be burned and that his adherents should henceforth be called "Porphyrians", *i.e.*, should be placed on a level with the worst enemies of Christ.[2] To the Alexandrian Church he wrote: ὅ τοῖς τριακοσίοις ἥρεσεν ἐπισκόποις οὐδὲν ἔστιν ἕτερον ἢ τοῦ Θεοῦ γνώμη, μάλιστά γε ὅπου τὸ ἅγιον πνεῦμα τοιούτων καὶ τηλικούτων ἀνδρῶν ταῖς διανοίαις ἐγκείμενον τὴν θείαν βούλησιν ἐξεφώτισεν[3] ("what satisfied the three hundred bishops is nothing else than the judgment of God, but most of all where the Holy Spirit being present in the thoughts of men such as

The evasions to which the Lucianists and Origenists had recourse in order to justify their conduct to themselves, can be studied in the letter of Eusebius to his Church. Eusebius interprets "ἐκ τῆς οὐσίας τοῦ πατρὸς" as equal to "He has His existence from the Father" (!), "γεννηθέντα οὐ ποιηθέντα" as equivalent to "the Son is not a creature like the rest of the creatures", ὁμοούσιος as ὁμοιούσιος, meaning μόνῳ τῷ πατρὶ τῷ γεγεννηκότι κατὰ πάντα τρόπον ὅμοιος and not out of a foreign substance. The worst shift of all is undoubtedly when Eusebius writes to his Church that he has (now) rejected the formula ἦν ποτὲ ὅτε οὐκ ἦν, because we ought not to use any unbiblical expressions whatsoever (but Ὁμοούσιος !) and because the Son did indeed exist already before His incarnation. But that was not the point at all! Πέπονθέ τι δεινόν, says Athanasius (de decret. 3), with justice, of this passage in the letter.

[1] They afterwards asserted no doubt that they had not subscribed the anathemas, but only the positive doctrine of the Nicene Creed (Socr. I. 14). However, Eusebius of Nicomedia and Theognis of Nicæa were, notwithstanding this, banished soon after; they were suspected by the Emperor of being Arians and intriguers; see the strongly hostile letter of Constantine in Theodoret I. 19.

[2] Socr. I. 9; those with Arian books in their possession were even to be punished with death.

[3] L. c. Other writings of Constantine in the same place. The synodal-epistle in Theodoret I. 9, Gwatkin, p. 50, has proved that in the respect shewn by Athanasius for the Nicene Council there is no trace "of the mechanical theory of conciliar infallibility." It is necessary to guard against exaggerated ideas of the extent to which the decree of the Nicene Council was accepted. It can be proved that in the East (see *e.g.*, Aphraates' Homilies) and still more in the West, there were numerous bishops who did not trouble themselves about the decree and for whom it had no existence. It was not till after the year 350 that men began to think over the Nicene Creed in the West, and to perceive that it contained more than a mere confirmation of the ancient Western belief in the doctrine of monarchy.

these and so ripe in years, made known the Divine will"). He persecuted the Arians, and the orthodox approved of what he did. They are thus responsible along with him for the persecution. The Arians at a later date only carried on what the orthodox had begun.

The correct faith had triumphed and—the Bishop of Alexandria.[1] The Council of Nicæa is the first step taken by the Bishop of Alexandria in aspiring to the primacy of the East.

2.   TO THE DEATH OF CONSTANTIUS.[2]

Never again in the history of the Church has there been a victory so complete and so quickly secured as that at Nicæa, and no other decision of the Church approaches it in importance. The victors had the feeling that they had set up for all ages[3] a "warning notice against all heresies" (στηλογραφία κατὰ πασῶν αἱρέσεων), and this estimate of the victory has continued to be the prevailing one in the Church.[4] The grand innovation, the elevation of two unbiblical expressions to the rank of catchwords of the Catholic Faith, insured the unique nature of this Faith. At bottom not only was Arianism rejected, but also Origenism; for the exclusive Ὁμοούσιος separated the Logos from all spiritual creatures and seemed thus to do away with scientific cosmology in every form.

But it was just because of this that the strife now began. The Nicene Creed effected in the East a hitherto unprecedented concord, but this was amongst its opponents, while its friends, on the other hand, felt no genuine enthusiasm for its subtle formulæ. The schismatic Meletians of Egypt made common cause with the Arians and Origenists; those of the bishops

---

[1] The victory of the Bishop of Alexandria may be studied above all in the Canons of Nicæa. They have not so far been treated of from this point of view.

[2] In what follows I give merely a sketch; the details belong to Church history.

[3] Athanas. ad Afros II. and elsewhere.

[4] Up to time of the Chalcedonian Creed the conceptions Homoousia and Orthodoxy were quite identical; the latter involved no more than the former. Thus the orthodoxy of Origen is for Socrates (VI. 13) undoubted, just because none of his four chief opponents (Methodius, Eustathius, Apollinaris, and Theophilus) charge him with heresy in reference to his doctrine of the Trinity.

who were indifferent or stupid were induced to oppose it by
the bugbear of Sabellianism and by the unbiblical shape in
which the new faith was formulated. Society was still for the
most part heathen, and this heathen society openly sided with
the anti-Nicenes; the Jews too, who were still influential, ranged
themselves on this side. The clever sophist Asterius was able,
as "travelling professor", to interest large numbers in "the
one Unbegotten". But, above all, the two Eusebiuses sought again
to be masters of the situation. The one necessarily strove in
the first instance to regain his seat, the other to make the
weight of his untouched personal authority once more felt in
theology also. What their mutual relationship was is not clear;
in any case they marched separately and struck unitedly.[1]
The Nicomedian always thought first of himself and then of
his cause; the Bishop of Cæsarea saw science and theology
disappear in the movement which received its impulse from
Alexandria. Both, however, had made up their minds not to
part company with the Emperor if they could not otherwise
succeed in managing him. The great mass of the bishops
always were, in accordance with this policy, purely "imperial".
With regard to the *strict* Arians, however, it must be admitted
to their credit that during the whole controversy they were as
little willing to accept as authoritative the decisions of the
Emperors in matters of faith as were Athanasius, Hilary, and
Lucifer.

When Constantine interfered in the great controversy, he had
only just come to the East. He was under the guidance of
Western bishops, and it was Western Christianity alone with
which he had hitherto been acquainted. And so after an abortive
attempt to compose the controversy, he had accomplished the
"work of peace" at Nicæa in accordance with Western views.
But already during the years which immediately followed he
must have learned that the basis upon which he had reared it
was too narrow, that, above all, it did not meet the requirements of

---

[1] The best investigation regarding Eusebius of Nicomedia is contained in the
article in the Dict. of Chr. Biogr. We know Eusebius, it is true, almost exclusively
from the picture which his opponents have drawn of him. But in his actions he
has portrayed himself as an imperious prince of the Church of a secular type, for
whom all means were justifiable.

the "common sense" of the East. As a politician he was prudent enough not to take any step backward, but, on the other hand, as a politician he knew that every law gets its meaning quite as much from the method in which it is carried out as from the letter of it. Feeling this—to which has to be added the presence of Arian influences at the Court—he had since about the year 328 resolved, under cover of the Nicene Creed, to reinstate the broader doctrinal system of older days whose power he had first got to know in Asia, in order to preserve the unity of the Church which was endangered.[1] But Constantine did not get the length of doing anything definite and conclusive. He merely favoured the anti-Nicene coalition to such an extent that he left to his sons a ruptured Church in place of a united one. The anti-Nicene coalition, however, had already become during the last years of Constantine's life an anti-Athanasian one. On the eighth of June, 328, Athanasius, not without opposition on the part of the Egyptian bishops,[2] had mounted the Episcopal throne in Alexandria. The tactics of the coalition were directed first of all towards the removal of the main defenders of the Nicene faith, and it was soon recognised that the youthful bishop of Alexandria was the most dangerous of these. Intrigues and slanders of the lowest kind now began to come into play, and the conflict was carried on sometimes by means of moral charges of the worst kind, and sometimes by means of political calumnies. The easily excited masses were made fanatical by the coarse abuse and execrations of the opponents, and the language of hate which hitherto had been bestowed on heathen, Jews, and heretics, filled the churches. The catchwords of the doctrinal formulæ, which were unintelligible to the laity and indeed even to most of the bishops themselves, were set up as standards, and the more successful they were in keeping up the agitation the more surely did the pious-minded turn away from them and sought satisfaction in asceticism and polytheism in a Christian garb. In every diocese, however, personal interests, struggles about

[1] If Eusebius is right the Emperor had already at Nice also advocated a broad application of the orthodox formula.

[2] The matter, so far as the particulars are concerned, is quite obscure.

sees and influence, were mixed up with the controversy, and this was the case in the West too, especially in Rome, as we may gather from the events of the year 366. Thus a series of bloody town-revolutions accompanied the movement.

In the midst of all this Athanasius alone in the East stood like a rock in the sea. If we measure him by the standard of his time we can discover nothing ignoble or mean about him. The favourite charge of hierarchical imperiousness has something naive about it. His stern procedure in reference to the Meletians was a necessity, and an energetic bishop who had to represent a great cause could not be anything else but imperious. It is certainly undeniable that for years he was formally in the wrong, inasmuch as he would not admit the validity of his deposition. He regarded it as the task committed to him, to rule Egypt, to regulate the Church of the East in accordance with the standard of the true faith, and to ward off any interference on the part of the State. He was a Pope, as great and as powerful a one as there ever has been.

When the sons of Constantine entered upon the inheritance of their father, the heads of the Nicene party in the East had been deposed or exiled; Arius, however, was dead.[1] The exiled

---

[1] The dates put shortly are as follows. Some three years after the Nicene Council, years which for us are absolutely dark (the letter of Constantine in Gelas., Hist. Conc. Nic. III. 1 is probably not genuine), Constantine begins to turn round. (Was this owing to the influence of Constantia and her court-clergyman?) The recall of Arius, Eusebius of Nicom. and Theognis (the latter's letter in Socrat. I. 14, is perhaps not genuine). Eusebius gains a decisive influence over the Emperor. At an Antioch synod 330. Eustathius of Antioch, one of the chief champions of the Nicene Creed is deposed (for adultery) at the instigation of the two Eusebiuses. Arius presents to the Emperor a diplomatically composed confession of faith which satisfies him, (Socr. I. 26) is completely rehabilitated, and demands of Athanasius that he be allowed to resume his position in Alexandria. Athanasius refuses, and succeeds in making good his refusal and in clearing himself from the personal charges brought against him on the part of the Eusebians. At the Synod of Tyre 335 (not 336) held under the presidency of the Church historian Eusebius, the coalition nevertheless succeeds in passing a resolution for the deposition of Athanasius on account of certain alleged gross excesses, and in persuading the Emperor to proceed against him as a disturber of the peace, and this spite of the fact that in the year 334 Athanasius, in opposition to the Synod of Cæsarea, had convinced the Emperor of his perfect innocence and of the base intrigues of the Meletian bishops. Athanasius notwithstanding this succeeded a second time in inducing the Emperor to give his case an impartial trial, by hastening to Constantinople and making a personal statement to the Emperor, who was taken by surprise. His

bishops in accordance with a resolution [1] come to in common by the Emperors, were free to return as a body. This was the case in the latter part of the autumn of 337. But as soon as Constantius became master in his own domain he continued the policy of his father. He wished to rule the Church as the latter had done; he perceived that this was possible in the East only if the Nicene innovation, or at least the exclusive application of it, were got rid of, and he did not feel himself bound to the Nicene Creed as his father had done. One cannot but admit that the youthful monarch shewed statesmanlike insight and acted with energy, and with all his devotion to the Church he never allowed churchmen to rule as his brother did. He had not, however, the patience and moderation of his father, and though he had indeed inherited from the latter the gift of ruling, he had not got from him the art of managing men by gentle force. The brutal trait which Constantine knew how to keep in check in himself, appeared in an undisguised fashion in his son, and the development of the Emperor into an Oriental despot advanced a stage further in Constantius. [2] First of

opponents, who had meanwhile been commanded to go from Tyre to Jerusalem, now expressly declared that the doctrinal explanations given by Arius and his friends were sufficient, and already made preparations for burying the Nicene Creed in their pretentious assembly, and also for bringing to trial Marcellus, the friend of Athanasius. They were, however, summoned by the Emperor to come to Constantinople and to carry on their deliberations. Only the worst of Athanasius' opponents complied with this demand, and they succeeded by bringing forward new accusations (at the beginning of the year 336), in inducing the Emperor to banish Athanasius (to Trier). Still it is at least doubtful if the Emperor did not wish him to escape for a while from his enemies. His chair in any case was *not* filled. Marcellus, who had also appealed to the Emperor, was deposed and condemned on account of erroneous doctrine. The solemn induction of Arius into his Church—against the wish of the bishop, Alexander of Constantinople—was immediately robbed of its significance by his sudden death. The Emperor sought to carry on his energetic peace-policy by the banishment of other "disturbers of the peace," such as the Meletian leading spirit, and Paulus, the newly elected bishop of Constantinople. He died, however, in May 337, in his own opinion in the undoubted Nicene faith. His son maintained that he had himself further resolved on the restitution of Athanasius. Sources: besides the Church historians and Epiphanius, chiefly Athan. Apolog. c. Arian.; in addition, the Festival letters, the Hist. Arian. ad monach. de morte Arii ad Serapionem, Ep. ad epp. Æg. 19, and Euseb , Vita Constant. IV.

[1] On this resolution see Schiller II., p. 277 f.

[2] The best characterisation is in Ranke IV., p. 35 ff.; see also Krüger, Lucifer, p. 4 ff., Gwatkin, p. 109 sq., Schiller II., p. 245 ff.

all, Paul of Constantinople was deposed for the second time; Eusebius of Nicomedia at last secured the seat he had so long striven after. Eusebius of Cæsarea died, and his place was taken by a man deserving of little respect, Acacius, a friend of the Arians. The tumults which took place in Egypt after the return of Athanasius made it easier for his enemies, who regarded him as deposed and once more pronounced the sentence of deposition at a Synod in Atioch, to move the Emperor to proceed against him. His energetic conduct in his diocese and the violence of his Egyptian friends (Apol. c. Arian. 3—19) aggravated the situation. Constantius listened to the Eusebians, but did not sanction the choice of Bishop Pistus whom they had set apart for Alexandria. He decreed the deposition of Athanasius, and sent as bishop to Alexandria, a certain Gregory, a Cappadocian who had nothing to commend him save the imperial favour. Athanasius anticipated a violent expulsion by leaving Alexandria—in the spring of 339. He betook himself to Rome, leaving his diocese behind him in a state of wild uproar.

The Eusebians were now masters of the situation, but just because of this they had a difficult task to perform. What had now to be done was to get the Nicene Creed actually out of the way, or to render it ineffective by means of a new formula. This could only be done in conjunction with the West, and it would have to be done in such a way that they should neither seem to be giving the lie to their own vote in Nicæa—and therefore they would have to make it appear that they were attacking only the form and not the contents of the confession— nor seem to the Church in the West to be proclaiming a new faith. It is in the light of these facts that we are to regard the symbols of Antioch and the negotiations with Julius of Rome. They found themselves shut up in a position from which they could not escape without a certain amount of evasion. The *faith* of Athanasius must not be attacked any more than that of the Westerns.[1] The condemnation of the great bishop

---

[1] This explains why the canons of the Synod of Antioch came to enjoy a high reputation and why Hilary (de synod. 32) designated the assembly a ' synodus sanctorum.' All the same such a description is not quite intelligible; we know too little both of the character and of the proceedings of the Synod.

had thus always throughout to be based on personal accusations. As regards the doctrinal question, the whole stress had
to be laid on getting the Homousios put quietly aside, on the
ground that it was unbiblical and gave an inlet to Sabellianism. In this respect the doctrine of Marcellus of Ancyra was
very welcome to the Eusebians, for they sought, not without
justice, to shew from it to what destructive results a theology
which based itself on the Homousios must lead.[1] But the

[1] Marcellus is an extremely interesting phenomenon in the history of theology;
he did not, however, succeed in effecting any change in the history of dogma or
in creating any noteworthy number of followers. At the Council of Nicæa he
belonged to the few who zealously championed the Homousios (Apol. c. Arian. 23, 32).
After the Council he was, besides Eustathius, at first the sole literary representative
of orthodoxy, since he wrote a comprehensive treatise περὶ ὑποταγῆς by way of
reply to the work of the Arian Asterius. This work, in which he defends the
unity of substance of the Logos, drew upon him from the dominant party the
accusation of Sabellianism and Samosatenism. His case was dealt with at the
Councils of Tyre, Jerusalem, and Constantinople, since he also personally defended
Athanasius and opposed the restoration of Arius. Spite of his appeal to the Emperor
he was at Constantinople deprived of his office as a teacher of erroneous doctrine,
another bishop was sent to Ancyra, and Eusebius of Cæsarea endeavoured in two
works (c. Marcell., de ecclesiast. theolog.) to refute him. These works are for us
the source for the teaching of Marcellus. Marcellus did not recognise the common
doctrinal basis of Arianism and orthodoxy; he went back behind the traditional
teaching of Origen, like Paul of Samosata, and consequently got rid of the element
which caused the trouble to Arianism and, in a higher degree, to orthodoxy. His
doctrinal system presents, on the one hand, certain points of agreement with that
of the old Apologists, though these are more apparent than real, and on the other
with that of Irenæus; still it cannot be proved that there is any literary dependence.
Marcellus was at one with Arius in holding that the conceptions "Son", "begotten"
etc., involve the subordination of the being thus designated. But just because of
this he rejected these conceptions as being inapplicable to the divine in Christ. He
clearly perceived that the prevalent theology was on a wrong track owing to its
implication with philosophy ; he wished to establish a purely biblical system of
doctrine and sought to shew that these conceptions are all used in the Scriptures
in reference to *the incarnate one*, the view of most in the older days, *e.g.*, Ignatius.
The Scripture supplies only *one* conception to express the eternal-divine in Christ,
that of the Logos (the Logos is image or type only in connection with man created
in his image): the Logos is the indwelling *power* in God, which has manifested
itself in the creation of the world as δύναμις δραστική, in order then for the first
time to become *personal* with the view of saving and perfecting the human race.
Thus the Logos is in and for itself, in its essential nature, the *unbegotten* reason
of God indwelling in God from all eternity and absolutely inseparable from him ;
it begins its actuality in the creation of the world, but it first becomes a personal
manifestation distinct from God in the incarnation, through which the Logos as the
image of the invisible God becomes visible. In Christ consequently the Logos has

Roman bishop was not to be corrupted, he did not even sacrifice Marcellus; and the creeds of Antioch which were not actually heterodox, but which were not sincere, did not at all meet with his approval. He did not concern himself with the attempt, justifiable from the point of view of the Orientals and

become a person and son of God—a person who is as surely ὁμοούσιος τῷ Θεῷ as he is the active working of God Himself. After the work has been completed, however, the Son subordinates Himself to the Father in such a way that God is again all in all, since the hypostatic form of the Logos now *ceases* (hence the title of M.'s work: περὶ ὑποταγῆς; the idea is an old one, see Vol. II.). M. confessed that he did not know what became of the humanity of Christ. The stumbling-blocks which this system presented to that age were (1) that M. called only the incarnate one Son of God, (2) that he taught no real pre-existence, (3) that he assumed the Kingdom of Christ would have an end, and (4) that he spoke of an extension of the indivisible monad. Marcellus having been recalled (337) and then expelled again from his diocese (338), like Athanasius, betook himself to Rome, and by means of a confession in which he disguised his doctrine, induced Bishop Julius to recognise his orthodoxy. (The confession is in the letter to Julius in Epiph. H. 72. 2: Zahn, Marcell. p. 70 f., vainly attempts to dispute the fact of a "disguising." In the letter he avows his belief in the Roman Creed also.) The Roman synod of the year 340 declared him to be sound in the faith. It scarcely fully understood the case; what is of much more importance is that Athanasius and consequently also the Council of Sardica did not abandon Marcellus, and the Council indeed remarked that the Eusebians had taken as a positve statement what he had uttered only *tentatively* (ζητῶν). That Athanasius spite of all remonstrances should have pronounced Marcellus orthodox, is a proof that his interest in the matter was confined to one point, and centred in the godhead of the historical Jesus Christ as resting upon the *unity of substance* with God. Where he saw that this was recognised, he allowed freedom of thought on other points. At a later period, it is true, when it became possible still more to discredit Marcellus through his pupil Photinus, there was a disagreement of a temporary kind between him and Athanasius. Athanasius is said to have refused to have intercourse with him and Marcellus is said to have dropped him. Athanasius also combatted the *theology* of M. (Orat. c. Arian. IV), though he afterwards again recognised the truth of his *faith*. Epiphanius informs us (72. 4) that he once put some questions to the aged Athanasius regarding M.: Ὁ δὲ οὔτε ὑπεραπελογήσατο, οὔτε πάλιν πρὸς αὐτὸν ἀπεχθῶς ἠνέχθη, μόνον δὲ διὰ τοῦ προσώπου μειδιάσας ὑπέφηνε, μοχθηρίας μὴ μακρὰν αὐτὸν εἶναι, καὶ ὡς ἀπολογησάμενον εἶχε. Marcellus' followers in Ancyra also possessed at a later date an epistle of Athanasius (Epiph. 72. 11) which was favourable to them. The East, however, stuck firmly to the condemnation of Marcellus, and so too did the Cappadocians at a later period—a proof this also of a radical difference between them and Athanasius The further history of this matter has no place here (see Zahn op. cit. and Möller, R.-Encykl., 2nd Ed., p. 281 f.). Marcellus died in the year 373, close on a hundred years old, after that his theology had repeatedly done good service to the opponents of orthodoxy, without, however, helping them to discredit Athanasius.

of Constantius, to create for the East a doctrinal form of expression which was more in accordance with the convictions of the majority. The most important result of the operations of the Eusebians at Antioch, and the one which was of the greatest consequence, was that they had to bring themselves to renounce Arianism in order to gain over the West. Arianism was now condemned on all sides in the Church; nevertheless the Eusebians did not attain their aim.[1]

---

[1] The negotiations between Bishop Julius and the Eusebians assembled at Antioch (Rom. Council, autumn 340; Council at Antioch, summer and autumn 341) are from the point of view of Church politics of great significance, and more particularly the letter of Bishop Julius to the Eusebians after the Roman Council (Apol. c. Arian. 21) is a masterpiece. But we cannot enter on this matter here. The four formulæ of Antioch (it is to them that the reproach brought by Athanasius against his opponents chiefly refers—namely, that they betrayed their uncertainty by the new forms of faith they were constantly publishing,—see de decret. 1: de synod. 22—23: Encycl. ad epp. Ægypt. 7 sq.: Ep. ad. Afros 23) are in Athan., de synod. 22 sq. (Hahn § 84, 115, 85, 86). There are some good remarks in Gwatkin, p. 114 sq. The zealous efforts made by the Eusebians to arrive at a harmonious agreement with the West were probably closely connected also with the general political situation. After the fall of Constantine II. (spring 340) Constans had promptly made himself master of the whole of his brother's domain Constantius, whose attention was claimed by severe and incessant wars on the eastern boundary, was unable to hinder this. From the year 340 Constans thus had the decisive preponderance in the Empire. The first Antiochian formula still supports Arius, though with the odd qualification that those who were in favour of him had not followed him (πῶς γὰρ ἐπίσκοποι ὄντες ἀκολουθήσαν πρεσβυτέρῳ), but had tested his teaching: it limits itself to describing the Son as μονογενῆ, πρὸ πάντων τῶν αἰώνων ὑπάρχοντα καὶ συνόντα τῷ γεγεννηκότι αὐτὸν πατρί, but it already contains the anti-Marcellian proposition descriptive of the Son: διαμένοντα βασιλέα καὶ Θεὸν εἰς τοὺς αἰῶνας. The second, so-called Lucian, formula already gathers together all designations for the Son which could possibly be used of His Godhead from an Origenistic standpoint (above all, μονογενῆ Θεὸν, Θεὸν ἐκ Θεοῦ, ἄτρεπτον τε καὶ ἀναλλοίωτον, τῆς θεότηρος οὐσίας τε καὶ βουλῆς καὶ δυνάμεως καὶ δόξης τοῦ πατρὸς ἀπαράλλακτον εἰκόνα, Θεὸν λόγον); it then adopts once more the addition which Eusebius had appended to the outline of his belief presented at Nicæa (see p. 52), and formulates the following proposition against Marcellus; τῶν ὀνομάτων οὐχ ἁπλῶς οὐδὲ ἀργῶς κειμένων σημαινόντων ἀκριβῶς τὴν οἰκείαν ἑκάστου τῶν ὀνομαζομένων ὑπόστασιν (N.B.═οὐσίαν) καὶ τάξιν καὶ δόξαν, ὡς εἶναι τῇ μὲν ὑποστάσει τρία, τῇ δὲ συμφωνίᾳ ἕν; but on the other hand, without mentioning Arius, it expressly rejects the Arian catchwords objected to at Nicæa. The third, submitted by the Bishop of Tyana, has a still stronger anti-Marcellan colouring (Ἰ. Χρ. ὄντα πρὸι τὸι Θεὸν ἐν ὑποστάσει ... μένοντα εἰς τοὺς αἰῶνας), repudiates Marcellus, Sabellius, and Paul of Samosata by name, but otherwise in place of all other possible designations it has the Nicene sounding: Θεὸν τέλειον ἐκ Θεοῦ τελείου. At length the fourth formula, drawn up some months later, became the

During the following years Constantius' hands were tied by
the Persian war, and he was forced to keep on good terms
with his brother so as to avoid having trouble on the western
boundary of his kingdom also. At the same time, just after the
death of Eusebius of Nicomedia, which took place in the autumn
of 342, the party amongst the conservatives of the East who,
partly no doubt for political reasons, were actually set on
coming to an agreement with the West, gained the lead.
A general Council which was summoned by Constans to meet
at Sardica in the summer of 343 and was approved of by
Constantius, was to restore the unity of the Church. But the
Western bishops, about a hundred in number, rejected the preliminary demand of the Eastern bishops for the deposition of
Athanasius and Marcellus, both of whom were present in Sardica; pronounced sentence of deposition upon the leaders of the
Orientals after the exodus of the latter; after an investigation
declared the bishops attacked to be innocent, that is to say,
orthodox; avowed their belief in the Nicene Creed, and under
the guidance of Hosius took up the most rigid attitude possible
on the doctrinal question.[1] In opposition to this the bishops,

final one. It is constructed as far as possible on the model of the Nicene Creed;
at the end too some Arian catchwords are expressly condemned. The most important propositions run thus: καὶ εἰς τὸν μονογενῆ αὐτοῦ υἱόν, τὸν κύριον ἡμῶν Ἰ.
Χρ., τὸν πρὸ πάντων τῶν αἰώνων ἐκ τοῦ πατρὸς γεννηθέντα, Θεὸν ἐκ Θεοῦ, φῶς ἐκ
φωτός … λόγον ὄντα καὶ σοφίαν καὶ δύναμιν καὶ ζωὴν καὶ φῶς ἀληθινόν, at the
close of this section (against Marcellus): οὗ βασιλεια ἀκατάλυτος οὖσα διαμενεῖ εἰς
τοὺς ἀπείρους αἰῶνας· ἔσται γὰρ καθεζόμενος ἐν δεξιᾷ τοῦ πατρὸς οὐ μόνον ἐν τῷ
αἰῶνι τούτῳ, ἀλλὰ καὶ ἐν τῷ μέλλοντι. All four formulæ have this in common,
that they are compatible with the theology of Origen; the three last, that Arianism
in the strict sense is repudiated. The fourth was communicated to the Emperor
Constans by a deputation in Gaul. For the rest it ought not to be forgotten that the
Eusebians formally adhered to the basis of the Nicene Creed; see Hefele I., p. 502 ff.

[1] Sardica was situated in the territory of Constans. The most influential of the
Eastern bishops were present. Hosius took the lead. (Histor. Arian 15.) The
formal restatement of the Nicene Creed desired by some of them was not proceeded
with. (Athan. Tom. ad Antioch. 5 against Socrates II., 20); but the description of
the Faith which will be found at the close of the encyclical letter, although it is
not to be regarded as an official declaration, is a document whose importance has
hitherto not been sufficiently recognised. It originated with Hosius and Protogenes
of Sardica, and *is the most unambiguous expression of the Western view in the
matter*, so unambiguous that for the moment it seemed even to the orthodox Orientals themselves to be questionable (the formula is in Theodoret II. 8, lat. trans-

who met together in the neighbouring Philippopolis, framed a circular letter, dated from Sardica, in which they set forth the illegality of the procedure of their opponents, and confessed the faith in terms essentially identical with those of the fourth formula of Antioch.[1]

The endeavours of Constantius to give efficacy [2] to the resolutions of his bishops fell through; in fact, the shameless attempt to set a trap for the two Western bishops sent as a deputation from Sardica to Constantius and provided with a letter of introduction from Constans, and who were to try and effect the recall of the banished bishops, turned out to their advantage.[3] Constantius, so at least it seems, had not for a while any real confidence in his own party; or was it that he was afraid to rouse his brother? In a long-winded formula drawn up at Antioch in the summer of 344 they once more sought to hint to the West their orthodoxy and to suggest the minimum of their demands.[4] The Church in the West, it is true, rejected at

lation discovered by Maffei). It is here first of all that the proposition is found: μίαν ὑπόστασιν, ἣν αὐτοὶ οἱ αἱρετικοὶ οὐσίαν προσαγορεύουσι (for ὑπόστασιν we have in the Latin "substantiam"), τοῦ πατρὸς καὶ τοῦ υἱοῦ καὶ τοῦ ἁγίου πνεύματος. Καὶ εἰ ζητοῖεν, τίς τοῦ υἱοῦ ἡ ὑπόστασίς ἐστιν, ὁμολογοῦμεν ὡς αὕτη ἦν ἡ μόνη τοῦ πατρὸς ὁμολογουμένη. In the second place the doctrine of the Son is put in such a way that one can very easily understand how the Westerns refused to condemn Marcellus; there are turns of expression which approach the doctrine of Marcellus. (A comparison with the Christology of Prudentius is instructive in this connection.) Ursacius and Valens amongst others were declared deposed. Their bishoprics were situated in the territory of Constans, but they were of an Arian way of thinking. Hefele, op. cit. p. 533 ff., treats in great detail the canons and acts of the Council.

[1] Above all, the Eusebians repeated their old statement that the decrees of deposition pronounced by Councils in reference to bishops are irrevocable. So too they held to the charges against Marcellus (of erroneous doctrine) and against Athanasius (of flagrant abuse of his power). There is a wish to introduce something entirely new, "ut orientales episcopi ab occidentalibus judicarentur"; but whoever holds by Marcellus and Athanasius let him be Anathema. The doctrinal formula (Hilarius Fragm. III. and de synod, 34) differs little from the fourth formula of Antioch and thus condemns Arianism. *Formally* the Easterns were in the right as regards Athanasius.

[2] Histor. Arian. 18, 19.

[3] Histor. Arian. 20; Theodoret II. 9, 10. Bishop Stephanus of Antioch, who had tried the trick, was deposed.

[4] Their motive in bringing forward the new formula was by almost completely meeting the demands of the Westerns in reference to the doctrinal question, to

both the Councils held at Milan in the years 345 and 347, the teaching of Photinus of Sirmium, who, in a surprising fashion, had developed an Adoptian doctrinal system out of the doctrine of Marcellus,[1] but otherwise remained firm; and the ship of the Eusebians already appeared to be in so great danger that its two chief pilots, Ursacius and Valens, preferred to go over to induce them to give way on the personal question. (Ekthesis macrostichos, see Athan., de synod. 26: Socrat II. 19). It begins with the fourth formula of Antioch, then follow detailed explanations of the faith as against the Arians, Sabellians, Marcellus, and Photinus who is mentioned here for the first time. Spite of the polemic against the proposition of Athanasius—who is, however, not mentioned by name—that the Son is begotten οὐ βουλήσει οὐδὲ θελήσει, this formula indicates the greatest approach conceivable on the part of the Eusebians towards meeting the views of their opponents. They emphasise in the strongest way the unity of the one Godhead (c. 4): οὔτε μήν, τρία ὁμολογοῦντες πράγματα καὶ τρία πρόσωπα (it has to be noticed that the bishops avoid the expression three "substances or hypostases" and use the Western πρόσωπον which had been brought into discredit by Sabellius) τοῦ πατρὸς καὶ τοῦ υἱοῦ καὶ τοῦ ἁ. πνεύματος κατὰ τὰς γραφάς, τρεῖς διὰ τοῦτο Θεοὺς ποιοῦμεν, and they expressed themselves in such a way in c. 9, that the words must pass for an unobjectionable paraphrase of the Homousios. They are practically the very same expressions as those used by Athanasius to describe the relation of Father and Son. "Homousios" is, however, wanting: but, on the other hand, we find here, so far as I know, for the first time: κατὰ πάντα ὅμοιον. Socrates, II. 20, has candidly remarked on the formula macrostichos: ταῦτα οἱ κατὰ τὰ ἑσπέρια μέρη ἐπίσκοποι διὰ τὸ ἀλλογλώσσους εἶναι καὶ διὰ τὸ μὴ συνιέναι οὐ προσεδέχοντο, ἀρκεῖν τὴν ἐν Νικαίᾳ πίστιν λέγοντες. On the Acts of a Synod at Köln, from which we gather that Bishop Euphrates of Köln who was sent to Antioch from Sardica, had afterwards fallen away to Arianism, see Rettberg (K.-G. Deutschlands, I., p. 123 ff.) and Hauck (K.-G. Deutschlands, I., p. 47 f.), who are opposed to their genuineness; Friedrich (K.-G. Deutschland, I., p. 277 f.) and Söder (Stud. u. Mitth. aus. d. Benedict. Orden, fourth year's issue, I., p. 295 f., II., p. 344 f., fifth year, I., p. 83 f.) who are in favour of it.

[1] Photinus of Sirmium, a fellow-countryman and pupil of Marcellus, developed the doctrinal system of the master in such a way as to represent even the ἐνέργεια δραστική of God as not assuming a concrete hypostatic form in Jesus Christ, (or if it did take a concrete form as a hypostasis, then this was a purely human one— the matter is not quite clear). He thus rigidly held fast the single personality of God, and accordingly, like Paul of Samosata, saw in Jesus a man miraculously born (Zahn, op. cit., p. 192 combats this; but neither is the evidence that Photinus denied the birth from the Virgin Mary certain enough, nor is it in itself credible that a catholic bishop in the fourth century should have departed so far from the tradition), predestined to his office by God, and who in virtue of his moral development has attained to divine honour. We thus have here the last inherently logical attempt to guard Christian monotheism, entirely to discard the philosophical Logos-doctrine, and to conceive of the Divine in Christ as a divine *effect*. But this attempt was no longer in harmony with the spirit of the age; Photinus was charged on all sides with teaching erroneous doctrine. His writings have dis-

the opposite party and to make their peace with Athanasius.[1] Constantius, very sorely pressed by the Persians, sought to have peace in the Church at any price and even granted the prayer of his brother's protégé, Athanasius, and allowed him to return to Alexandria (in October 346), where Gregory meanwhile had died (in June 345 [2]). The bishop got an enthusiastic welcome in his city. The protest of the Eastern Council at Sirmium—the first Council of Sirmium—had no effect. A large number of the Eastern bishops were themselves tired of the controversy, and it almost looked as if the refusal of the West to condemn Marcellus together with the word ὁμοούσιος, now virtually constituted the only stone of offence.[3]

appeared: compare the scattered statements regarding him in Athanasius, Hilary, the Church historians, Epiph. H. 72 and the anathemas of various Councils, see also Vigilius Taps. adv. Arian., Sabell. et Photin.). The two Milan Councils, the date of which is not quite certain, condemned him, so too did a Sirmian Council of Eusebians which was perhaps held as early as 347. Still he remained in office till 351, held in high respect by his congregation. That the macrostic Confession of the Orientals ought not all the same to be accepted as so orthodox as it from its wording appears to be, is evident from the fact that the Eastern bishops who were deputed to take it to the West declined at Milan to condemn Arianism too. (Hilarius, Fragm. V.)

[1] For the documents relating to their conversion, which was hypocritical and dictated entirely by policy, and to their complete recognition of Athanasius, see Athanas. Apol. c. Arian. 58, Hilar., Fragm. II.

[2] Schiller (op. cit. p. 282). "As a matter of fact Constans wished to establish a kind of supremacy in relation to his brother, which in spiritual matters was to be exercised through the Bishop of Rome. Trusting to his support, deposed bishops on their own authority returned to their dioceses, without having received the sanction of the Emperor. The restoration of Athanasius resolved on by the Council was a direct interference with the sovereignty of Constantius ... But Constans was able once more to make such a skilful use of the existing Persian difficulty that his brother yielded." The fact is that the recall of Athanasius was altogether forced upon Constantius; the relation of the great bishop to his Emperor at this time was not that of a subject, but that of a hostile power with which he had to treat. This is naturally glossed over in the papers issued by Constantius referring to the recall. It is specially characteristic that Athanasius did not personally present himself before Constantius till after repeated invitations; see, above all, Apol. c. Arian. 51—56, Hist. Arian. 21—23.

[3] A Council of Jerusalem held in 346 under Maximus actually recognised Athanasius as a member of the Church. (Apol. c. Arian. 57). Cyril's Catecheses shew the standpoint of the Oriental extreme Right; they are undoubtedly based on Orig. de princip.; but they faithfully express the Christological standpoint of the formula macrostichos; the ὁμοούσιος only is wanting; as regards the matter of the Faith, Cyril is orthodox. The polemic directed against Sabellius and Marcellus

But the death of Constans in 350 and the overthrow of the usurper Magnentius in 353 changed everything. If in these last years Constantius had been compelled by the necessities of the situation to submit to the bishops, his own subjects, who had ruled his deceased brother, now that he was sole sovereign he was more than ever resolved *to govern the Church* and to pay back the humiliations which he had undergone.[1] Already in the year 351 the Easterns had at Sirmium—the second Council—again agreed upon taking common action, and Ursacius and Valens promptly rejoined them.[2] The great thing now was to humiliate the stubborn West. Constantius set about the task with wisdom, but what he wanted done he carried out by the sheer force of terror. He demanded only the condemnation of Athanasius, his mortal enemy, as a rebel, and purposely put the doctrinal question in the background. He forced the Western bishops, at Arles in 353 and at Milan in 355, to agree to this, by terrorising the Councils. The moral overthrow of the Westerns was scarcely less complete than that of the Easterns at Nicæa. Though the great majority were unaware of the struggle and were not forced to adopt a new confessional

(Catech. 15, 27) is severe and very bitter; Arianism is also refuted, but without any mention of names. Jews, Samaritans, and Manicheans are the chief opponents referred to, and Cyril is at great pains everywhere to adduce the biblical grounds for the formulæ which he uses. The Catecheses of Cyril are a valuable document in illustration of the fact that amongst the Eastern opponents of the Nicene formula there were bishops who, while fully recognising that Arianism was in the wrong, could not bring themselves to use a doctrinal formula which seemed to them a source of ceaseless strife and to be unbiblical besides.

[1] Schiller (p. 283 f.) supposes that Constantius was apprehensive before this that Athanasius would declare for Magnentius. Hence his friendly letter to Athanasius after the death of Constans, Hist. Arian. 24.

[2] Photinus was deposed here. The Creed of this Council, the first formula of Sirmium (in Athanas., de synod. 27, Hilar. de synod. 38 and Socr. II., 30), is identical with the Fourth Formula of Antioch, but numerous anathemas are added to it in which formulæ such as "two gods", (2), "$\pi\lambda\alpha\tau\upsilon\sigma\mu\grave{o}\varsigma$ $\tau\tilde{\eta}\varsigma$ $o\upsilon\sigma\acute{\iota}\alpha\varsigma$ $\grave{\epsilon}\sigma\tau\grave{\iota}\nu$ $\acute{o}$ $\upsilon\acute{\iota}\acute{o}\varsigma$" (7), "$\lambda o\gamma o\varsigma$ $\grave{\epsilon}\nu\delta\iota\acute{\alpha}\theta\epsilon\tau o\varsigma$ $\mathring{\eta}$ $\pi\rho o\phi o\rho\iota\varkappa\acute{o}\varsigma$" (8) are condemned, and already several explanations of Bible passages are branded as heretical (11, 12, 14—18). The subordination of the Son is expressly (18) avowed in this Creed, which otherwise strongly resembles the Nicene Creed. The anathemas 20—23 have to do with the Holy Ghost. In No. 19 the formula $\acute{\epsilon}\nu$ $\pi\rho\acute{o}\sigma\omega\pi o\nu$ is rejected. Nos. 12, 13, deny that the divine element in Christ is capable of suffering. One can see that new questions have emerged.

formula, still the fact could not be concealed from those who better understood the state of things, that the projected condemnation of Athanasius meant something more than a personal question. The few bishops who refused were deposed and exiled.[1] The order for his deposition was communicated to Athanasius in February 356. Yielding only to force, he made his escape into the desert where the Emperor could not reach him. Egypt was in a state of rebellion, but the revolt was put down by the Emperor with blood.[2] The unity of the Church was restored; above all, it was once more brought under the imperial sway. And now, forsooth, the orthodox bishops who had formerly secured so much by the help of Constans began to recollect that the Emperor and the State ought not to meddle with religion. Constantius became "Antichrist" for those who would have lauded him as they had his father and his brother, if he had given them the help of his arm.[3]

But the political victory of the Eastern bishops directly led to their disunion; for it was only under the tyranny of the West and in the fight against Athanasius and the word

[1] Of the Western bishops—leaving out Pannonia—almost all were orthodox. The Councils—that of Arles was a provincial Council, that of Milan a General Council, but apparently badly attended—were also managed by the new Pope Liberius (since 352), but ended quite contrary to his will. The best description is in Krüger Lucifer, pp. 11—20. At Arles Paulinus of Trier was the only one who remained firm, and he was exiled to Phrygia; even the Papal legates yielded. At Milan Lucifer and Eusebius of Vercelli were exiled, and also Dionysius of Milan, although he had agreed to the condemnation of Athanasius. Soon after Hosius, Liberius, and Hilary had to follow them into exile. In Milan Constantius actually ruled the Church, but with a brutal terrorism. There are characteristic utterances of his in Lucifer's works and in Athanasius.

[2] Already in the years immediately preceding, an incessant agitation had again been kept up against Athanasius; see Socr. II., 26, Sozom. IV., 9, Athan. Apol. ad Const. 2 sq., 14 sq., 19 sq. He betook himself to the desert, but later on he seems to have remained in hiding in Alexandria. No one, it would appear, cared to secure the price set upon his head. We have several writings of his belonging to this period. His successor, George, was pretty much isolated in Alexandria.

[3] The watchword of the "independence" of the Church of the State was now issued by Athanasius, Hilary, and above all by the hot-blooded Lucifer. Hilary, who first emerges into notice in 355, speedily gained a high reputation. He was the first theologian of the West to penetrate into the secrets of the Nicene Creed, and with all his dependence on Athanasius was an original thinker, who, as a theologian, far surpassed the Alexandrian Bishop. On his theology see the monograph by Reinkens, also Möhler, op. cit. 449 ff., and Dorner.

"ὁμοούσιος" that they had become united. Above all, Arianism
in its rigid, aggressive form again made its appearance. Aëtius
and Eunomius, two theologians of spirit who had been trained
in the Aristotelian dialectic, and were opponents of Platonic
speculation, expressed its tenets in the plainest possible way,
would have nothing to do with any mediation, and had no
scruple in openly proclaiming the conversion of religion into
morality and syllogistic reasoning. The formulæ which they
and their followers, Aëtians, Eunomians, Exukontians, Heterou-
siasts, Anomœans, defended, ran thus: "ἑτερότης κατ᾽ οὐσίαν",
"ἀνόμοιος καὶ κατὰ πάντα καὶ κατ᾽ οὐσίαν" ("different in substance", "unlike in everything and also in substance"). If they
allowed that the Son perfectly knows the Father, this was not
in any way a concession, but an expression of the thought that
there is no kind of mystery about the Godhead, which on the
contrary can be perfectly known by every rightly instructed
man. And so too the statement that the Logos had his superior
dignity from the date of his creation, and did not first get it
by being tested, was not intended at all as a weakening of
the Arian dogma, but as an expression of the fact that God
the Creator has assigned its limit to every being.[1] The great
majority of the Eastern bishops, for whom the Origenistic formulæ in very varied combinations were authoritative, were
opposed to this party. The old watchword, however, "the
unchangeable image", which was capable of different interpretations, now received in opposition to Arianism, in its strict
form, and on the basis of the formulæ of Antioch, more and
more a precise signification as implying that the Son is of like
nature with the Father in respect of substance also, and not
only in respect of will (ὅμοιος κατὰ πάντα καὶ κατὰ τὴν οὐσίαν),
and that his begetting is not an act at all identical with creation.
The *likeness* of the qualities of Son and Father was more and
more recognised here; on the other hand, the substantial *unity*
was disallowed, so as to avoid getting on the track of Marcel-

---

[1] After the full account given of the theology of Arius there was no need
for any detailed description of the theology of Aëtius and Eunomius; for it is
nothing but logical Arianism; see on the Ἔκθεσις πίστεως and the Ἀπολογητικός
of Eunomius Fabricius-Harless T. IX. The rejection of all conciliatory formulæ is
characteristic.

lus; *i.e.*, these theologians did not, like Athanasius, advance from the unity to the mystery of the duality, but, on the contrary, still started from the duality and sought to reach the unity by making Father and Son perfectly co-ordinate. They therefore still had a Θεὸς δεύτερος, and in accordance with this excluded the idea of full *community* of substance. The leaders of these Homoiousians, also called semi-Arians, were George of Laodicea,[1] Eustathius of Sebaste, Eusebius of Emesa, Basilius of Ancyra, and others.

The point of supreme importance with the Emperor necessarily was to maintain intact the unity between those who up till now had been united, but this was all the more difficult as the Homoiousians more and more developed their doctrinal system in such a way that their ideas came to have weight even with those Westerns who lingered in exile in the East and whose theology was on Nicene lines.[2] Some bishops who were devoted to Constantius and who represented simply and solely the interests of the Emperor and of the Empire, now sought by means of a formula of the most indefinite possible character to unite Arians and semi-Arians. These were Ursacius, Valens, Acacius of Cæsarea, and Eudoxius of Antioch. If up till 356 the Nicene Creed had, strictly speaking, been merely evaded, now at last a Confession was to be openly brought forward in direct opposition to the Nicene Creed. Simple *likeness of nature* was to be the dogmatic catchword, all more definite characterisations being omitted, and in support of this, appeal was made to the insoluble mystery presented by the Holy Scriptures (ὅμοιος κατὰ τὰς γραφάς—like according to the Scriptures). This ingenious formula, along with which, it is true, was a statement expressly emphasising the subordination, left it free to every one to have what ideas he chose regarding the extent of the qualities of Father and Son, which were thus declared to be of like kind. The relative ὅμοιος did not neces

---

[1] Dräseke (Ges. patristische Unters., 1889, p. 1 ff.) wishes to credit him with the anonymous work against the Manicheans, which Lagarde discovered (1859) in a MS. of Titus of Bostra.

[2] With Hilary, for example, as his work "de synodis" proves. It is very characteristic that Lucifer, the strictest of the Nicenes, never came to have a clear idea of the meaning of the formulæ, ὁμοούσιος and ὁμοιούσιος; see Krüger, p. 37 f.

sarily exclude the relative ἀνόμοιος, but neither did it exclude the ὁμοιούσιος. Already at the third Council of Sirmium (357), after Constantius, on a visit to Rome, had overthrown his enemies, a formula was set forth by the Western bishops of as conciliatory a character so far as Arianism was concerned as could possibly be conceived. It was proclaimed in presence of the Emperor, who under the influence of his consort came more and more to have Arian sympathies. This is the second Sirmian formula.[1] But the bishops assembled at Ancyra did not acquiesce in the move towards the Left (358).[2] What a

[1] The Confession is in Hilary, de Synod. 11, Athan. de synod. 28, Socrat. II. 30. Valens, Ursacius and Germinius of Sirmium took the lead. The words ὁμοούσιος and ὁμοιούσιος were *forbidden* as being unbiblical and because no one could express the generation of the Son. It is settled that the Father is greater, that the Son is subordinate. Here too the Christological problem of the future is already touched upon. Hilary pronounces the formula blasphemous. It marks the turning-point in the long controversy to this extent that it is the first public attempt to controvert the Nicene Creed. Against it Phobadius wrote the tractate " de filii divinitate", which is severely Western-Nicene in tone, and in this respect is markedly different from the conciliatory work of Hilary "de synodis"; see on it Gwatkin, p. 159 sq. The Eastern bishops Acacius and Uranius of Tyre, who shared the sentiments of the court-bishops, accorded a vote of thanks to the latter at a Council at Antioch, held in 358. Hosius subscribed the second Sirmian formula (Socr. II. 31).

[2] Aëtius was in high favour with Eudoxius of Antioch, and his pupils occupied the Eastern bishoprics. The manifesto of Sirmium appeared like an edict of toleration for strict Arianism. At the instigation of George of Laodicea some Semi-Arians joined together to oppose it at the Council of Ancyra. The comprehensive synodal-letter of Ancyra (Epiph. p. 73, 2—11, see Hilar. de synod) indicates the transition on the part of the Semi-Arians to the point of view at which the Niceans were able to meet them. It was re-echoed in the writings of Hilary and Athanasius de synodis (358—359). The Semi-Arians at Ancyra took up a position based on the fourth Antiochian formula, which was also that of Philippopolis and of the First Sirmian Council, but they explained that the new Arianism made it necessary to have precise statements. The following are the most important explanations given; (1) the name Father by its very form points to the fact that God must be the author of a substance of like quality with Him (αἴτιος ὁμοίας αὐτοῦ οὐσίας): πᾶς πατὴρ ὁμοίας αὐτοῦ οὐσίας νοεῖται πατήρ—this does away with the relation of Logos-Son and world-idea—(2) the designation "Son" excludes everything of a created kind and involves the full ὁμοιότης, (3) "the Son" is consequently Son in the peculiar and unique sense, and the analogy with men as sons of God is thus done away with. The likeness in substance is further based on Bible statements, and in the 19 anathemas together with Sabellianism *all* formulæ are rejected which express less than likeness in substance. Finally, however, "ὁμοούσιος" too, together with the characteristic addition "ἢ ταυτοούσιος" has an anathema attached to it, *i.e.*, the substantial *unity* of essence is rejected as Sabellian.

change! Easterns now defended purity of doctrine against
Arianising Westerns! A deputation from this Council succeeded
in paralysing the influence of the Arians with Constantius, and
in asserting at the Fourth Council of Sirmium, in 358, their
fundamental principles to which the Emperor lent the weight
of his authority.[1] But the triumph of the Homoiousians led
by Basilius Ancyranus was of short duration. The Emperor
saw that the Church could not be delivered up either to
Nicæans, to semi-Arians, or to Arians. The alliance between
the two first mentioned, which was so zealously pushed on by
Hilary, was not yet perfect. A grand Council was to declare
the imperial will, and Homoiousians and Arians vied with each
other in their efforts to get influencing it. The Homœans alone,
however, both in their character as leaders and as led, concurred with the Emperor's views. They were represented by
Ursacius, Valens, Marcus of Arethusa, Auxentius of Milan, and
Germinius of Sirmium. The fourth Sirmian formula (359), an
imperial cabinet-edict and a political masterpiece, was intended
to embody what was to be laid before the Council.[2] The latter

The Conservatives of the East have undoubtedly here quite changed their ground.
A definitely defined doctrine has taken the place of prolix formulæ, at once
cosmological and soteriological in drift, and derived from Origen, Lucian, and
Eusebius.

[1] The victory of the Semi-Arians at the court is a turn of affairs which we
cannot clearly explain. The fact is incontestable. The third formula of Sirmium,
drawn up at the Fourth Council of Sirmium, is identical with the fourth Antiochian
formula. That Constantius should have fallen back on this is perhaps to be explained from the fact that the disturbances at Rome made it necessary for him to
send Liberius back there, though the most he could hope for was to get him to
subscribe that formula, but not the manifesto of the year 357. He actually got him
to do this, i.e., Liberius subscribed several older confessional formularies which
originated at a time when the Nicene Creed had been only indirectly attacked. It
was not only, however, that Liberius bought his freedom at that time, but it was
actually for the time being a question of a general victory of the Homoiousians,
which they used too entirely in their own interest, after all the bishops present at
Sirmium, including Ursacius and Valens, had had to make up their minds to subscribe the synodal decrees. Eudoxius of Antioch and Aëtius and in addition 70
Anomœans were banished at the instigation of Basil of Ancyra and there were
many instances of the violent use of power. One cannot be certain if these same
violent proceedings did not bring about once more a quick change of feeling on
the part of the Emperor.

[2] The Council was intended to bring about at last a general peace; at first the
Emperor evidently intended to summon it to meet at Nicæa (Soz. IV. 16), then

was summoned to meet at Rimini and Seleucia because the circumstances in the East and West respectively differed so very much. In May 359 more than four hundred Western bishops assembled at Rimini. They were instructed to treat only of matters relating to the Faith and not to leave the Council till the unity aimed at had been attained. But the Emperor's confidants failed to induce the great majority of the members to accept the Sirmian formula. The bishops, on the contrary, took their stand on the basis of the Nicene Creed which had been abandoned during these last years, rejected Arianism and declared its friends deposed. But when they sought by means of a Deputation to get the Emperor to give his sanction to their decisions, they did not get a hearing. The Deputation was not admitted to the Emperor's presence, was at first detained and then conducted to Nice in Thrace, where the members at last shewed themselves docile enough to sign a formula—the formula of Nice—which was undoubtedly essentially identical with the Confession which the Westerns had themselves drawn up two years earlier at Sirmium, at the third Synod in 357—("the Son is like the Father [κατὰ πάντα is omitted] according to the Scriptures"). Armed with this docu-

---

Nicomedia was next considered as a likely place, but it was destroyed by an earthquake. Then it was that Nicæa was again thought of; Basil of Ancyra had still a great influence at the time. Finally, the party opposed to this was victorious, and the plan of a division of the Councils was carried through. But it was just this opposition-party which now wished to unite all parties in a Homœan Confession and gained over the Emperor to assent to this. The actual result, however, was that Homœans and Anomœans on the one hand, Homoiousians and Homousians on the other, more and more drew together. Hilary, who was staying in the East, had indeed already explained to his Gallic compatriots that it was possible to attach an "unpious" meaning to ὁμοούσιος quite as readily as to ὁμοιούσιος. The bishops assembled in presence of the Emperor now composed in advance for the Council a Confession which, since Semi-Arians were also present, might serve as a means of reconciling Homœan and Homoiousian conceptions. It was already evident at the time of signing it that it was differently interpreted. The catchwords ran thus : ὅμοιον πατρὶ κατὰ τὰς γραφάς—ὅμοιον κατὰ πάντα ὡς οἱ ἅγιαι γραφαὶ λέγουσιν. Valens signed it and at the same time simply repeated the word ὅμοιον without the κατὰ πάντα; Basil in signing it expressly remarked that πάντα included being also. The formula is in Athan. de synod. 8, Socrat. II. 37; see Sozom. IV. 17. The dogmatic treatise of Basil in Epiph. H. 73, 12—22, has reference to this formula, which Athanasius (de synodis) had already scoffed at because of its being dated, i.e., because it bore the signs of its newness on its front.

ment Ursacius and Valens made their way to Rimini, taking the deputies with them, and by means of threats and persuasions finally induced the Assembly there to accept the formula into which one could indeed read the Homoiousia, but not the Homousia. In the autumn of 359 the Eastern Synod met at Seleucia. The Homoiousians, with whom some Niceans already made common cause, had the main say. Still the minority led by Acacius and Eudoxius, which defended the Sirmian formula and clung to the likeness while limiting it, however, to the will, was not an insignificant one. There was an open rupture in the Synod. The majority finally deposed the heads of the opposition-party.[1] But as regards the East as well, the decision lay with the court.[2] The Emperor, importuned on all sides, had resolved to abandon the strict Arians, and accordingly Aëtius was banished and his Homœan friends had to leave him, but he was also determined to dictate the formula of Nice to the Easterns too.[3] Their representatives finally condescended to recognise the formula, and this event was announced at the Council of Constantinople in 360, and the Homœan Confession was once more formulated.[4] Although the new Imperial Confession involved the exclusion of the extreme Left, this did not constitute its peculiar significance. Had it actually been what it appeared to be, a formula of union for all who rejected the

---

[1] Socr. II. 37 explains that Nice was chosen with the view of giving to the new formula a name which sounded the same as that of the Nicene Creed. The formula is in Athan. de synod. 30, and Theodoret II. 21: ὅμοιον κατὰ τὰς γραφάς, οὗ τὴν γέννησιν οὐδεὶς οἶδεν. In addition: τὸ δὲ ὄνομα τῆς οὐσίας ὅπερ ἁπλούστερον ἐνετέθη ὑπὸ τῶν πατέρων, ἀγνοούμενον δὲ τοῖς λαοῖς σκάνδαλον ἔφερε, διὰ τὸ ἐν ταῖς γραφαῖς τοῦτο μὴ ἐκφέρεσθαι, ἤρεσε περιαιρεθῆναι καὶ παντελῶς μηδεμίαν μνήμην οὐσίας τοῦ λοιποῦ γίνεσθαι ... μήτε μὴ δεῖν ἐπὶ προσώπου πατρὸς καὶ υἱοῦ καὶ ἁγίου πνεύματος μίαν ὑπόστασιν ὀνομάζεσθαι. One might be pleased with this rational explanation if polytheism did not in fact lurk behind it.

[2] Hilary was present in Seleucia and made common cause with the Homoiousians against the others. Acacius in face of the superior numbers of the Homoiousians sought to save his party by drawing up a creed in which he expressly repudiated the Anomœans and proclaimed the *likeness in will*, (see the creed in Athanas. de synod. 29, Epiph. H. 73, c. 25, Socr. II. 40). But this did not protect him and his party.

[3] It was on the night of the last day of the year 359 that the Emperor achieved the triumph of the ὅμοιος in his empire.

[4] The Confession is in Athanas. de synod. 30 and Socr. II. 41.

unlikeness, it would not have been something to be condemned, from the standpoint of the State at all events. But in the following year it was recklessly used as a weapon against the Homoiousians.[1] They had to vacate all positions of influence, and by way of making up for what had been done to the one Aëtius, who had been sacrificed, his numerous friends were installed as bishops.[2] Under cover of the "likeness in nature" a mild form of Arianism was actually established in the Church, modified chiefly only by the absence of principle. In Gaul alone did the orthodox bishops once more bestir themselves after Julian had in January 360 been proclaimed Augustus at Paris.[3] Constantius died in November 361, during the campaign against the rebels.

3. TO THE COUNCILS OF CONSTANTINOPLE 381. 383.

The three possible standpoints—the Athanasian, the Lucianist-Arian, and the Origenist, which in opposition to the Arian had gradually narrowed itself down to the Homoiousian—had been set aside by Constantius in the interest of the unity of the Church. But the Homœan formula, which had no firm theological conviction behind it, meant the domination of a party which gravitated towards Arianism, i.e., which resolved faith in Jesus Christ into a dialectical discussion about unbegotten and begotten and into the conviction of the *moral* unity of Father and Son. It was for twenty years, with the exception of a brief interval, the dominant creed in the East. This fact finds its explanation only in the change, or narrowing, which came over what was at an earlier date the middle party. The Arianising Homœans were now *conservative* and in their way even conciliatory. They disposed of the ancient tradition of the East as

---

[1] People like Eudoxius and Acacius were real victors; they got a perfectly free hand for themselves against the Homoiousians at the cost of the condemnation of Aëtius, and made common cause with Valens and Ursinus. The Creed of Nice was sent all over the Empire for signature under threat of penalty.

[2] Eunomius became bishop of Cyzikus; Eudoxius of Antioch received the chair of Constantinople.

[3] See the epistle of the Synod of Paris (360 or 361) in Hilar. Fragm. XI. It did not at that time require any courage to declare against Constantius.

the Eusebians had done before them; for their formula " of like nature according to Holy Scripture" contained that latitude which corresponded to the old traditional doctrine. With this we may compare the standpoint of Eusebius of Cæsarea. The old middle party had, however, in the ὁμοιούσιος made for themselves a *fixed* doctrinal formula. [1]　This was a change of the

---

[1] The dogmatic dissertation of the Homoiousians in Epiphan. 73, 12—22, is of the highest importance; for it shews in more than *one* respect a dogmatic advance: (1) the differentiation of the conceptions οὐσία, ὑπόστασις, πρόσωπον begins here. The first of these is used in order to express the idea of the essence or substance which imprints itself in the form of a definite quality; accordingly the action of the Fathers who in protesting against Paul of Samosata attributed a *special* οὐσία to the Son, is by an explanation excused. They did this in order to do away with the idea that the Logos is a mere ῥῆμα, a λεκτικὴ ἐνέργεια. The proper expression, however, is ὑπόστασις. It is because the Logos is an ὑπόστασις, *i.e.*, because he does not, like the other words of God, lack being, that the Fathers called τὴν ὑπόστασιν οὐσίαν (c. 12). The ἀκρίβεια τῆς τῶν προσώπων ἐπιγνώσεως must be strictly maintained as against Sabellius (c. 14); but no one is to be led astray by the word ὑποστάσεις (Pl.); it does not mean that there are two or three Gods: διὰ τοῦτο γὰρ ὑποστάσεις οἱ ἀνατολικοὶ λέγουσιν, ἵνα τὰς ἰδιότητας τῶν προσώπων ὑφεστώσας καὶ ὑπαρχούσας γνωρίσωσιν. The word "Hypostasis" is thus merely meant to give the word πρόσωπον a definite meaning, implying that it is to be taken as signifying independently existing manifestations (c. 16), while οὐσία is in the tractate interchangeable with φύσις or πνεῦμα, and is thus still used only in the singular; (2) quite as much attention is already given to the Holy Ghost as to the Son, and the τρόποι ὑπάρξεως are developed, *i.e.*, an actual doctrine of the Trinity independent of any ideas about the world, is constructed (c. 16): Εἰ γὰρ πνεῦμα ὁ πατήρ, πνεῦμα καὶ ὁ υἱός, πνεῦμα καὶ τὸ ἅγιον πνεῦμα, οὐ νοεῖται πατὴρ ὁ υἱός· ὑφέστηκε δὲ καὶ τὸ πνεῦμα, ὃ οὐ νοεῖται υἱός, ὃ καὶ οὐκ ἔστι... Τὰς ἰδιότητας προσώπων ὑφεστώτων ὑποστάσεις ὀνομάζουσιν οἱ ἀνατολικοί, οὐχὶ τὰς τρεῖς ὑποστάσεις τρεῖς ἀρχὰς ἢ τρεῖς θεοὺς λέγοντες... Ὁμολογοῦσι γὰρ μίαν εἶναι θεότητα... ὅμως τὰ πρόσωπα ἐν ταῖς ἰδιότησι τῶν ὑποστάσεων εὐσεβῶς γνωρίζουσι, τὸν πατέρα ἐν τῇ πατρικῇ αὐθεντίᾳ ὑφεστῶτα νοοῦντες, καὶ τὸν υἱὸν οὐ μέρος ὄντα τοῦ πατρός, ἀλλὰ καθαρῶς ἐκ πατρὸς τέλειον ἐκ τελείου γεγεννημένον καὶ ὑφεστῶτα ὁμολογοῦντες, καὶ τὸ πνεῦμα τὸ ἅγιον, ὃ ἡ θεία γραφὴ παράκλητον ὀνομάζει, ἐκ πατρὸς δι᾽ υἱοῦ ὑφεστῶτα γνωρίζοντες... Οὐκοῦν ἐν πνεύματι ἁγίῳ υἱὸν ἀξίως νοοῦμεν, ἐν υἱῷ δὲ μονογενεῖ πατέρα εὐσεβῶς καὶ ἀξίως δοξάζομεν, (3) the Christological problem based on Philipp. II. 6 and Rom. VIII. 3 (ὁμοίωμα) is already introduced for the elucidation of the Trinitarian: ἀπὸ τοῦ σωματικοῦ εὐσεβῶς καὶ τὴν περὶ τοῦ ὁμοίου ἔννοιαν ἡμᾶς καὶ ἐπὶ τοῦ ἀσωμάτου πατρός τε καὶ υἱοῦ διδαχθῆναι (c. 17, 18). As Christ's flesh is *identical* with human flesh, but is, on the other hand, on account of its wonderful origin only ὅμοιος, κατὰ τὸν ὅμοιον τρόπον καὶ ὁ υἱὸς πνεῦμα ὢν καὶ ἐκ τοῦ πατρὸς πνεῦμα γεννηθείς, κατὰ μὲν τὸ πνεῦμα ἐκ πνεύματος εἶναι τὸ αὐτό ἐστιν, κατὰ δὲ τὸ ἄνευ ἀπορροίας καὶ πάθους καὶ μερισμοῦ ἐκ τοῦ πατρὸς γεννηθῆναι ὅμοιός ἐστι τῷ πατρί. Accordingly we have now the decisive statement: Οὐκοῦν διὰ τῆς πρὸς Φιλιππησίους ἐπιστολῆς ἐδίδαξεν ἡμᾶς πῶς ἡ ὑπόστασις τοῦ υἱοῦ ὁμοία ἐστὶ

most decisive kind. We may still further say *it was not the "Homousios" which finally triumphed, but on the contrary the Homoiousian doctrine, which fixed on the terms of agreement with the "Homousios."* The doctrine which Hosius, Athanasius, Eustathius, and Marcellus had championed at Nicæa, was overthrown. The new Origenism which was based on the "Homousios" succeeded in establishing itself. A form of doctrine triumphed which did not exclude scientific theology, a subject in which Athanasius and the Westerns of the older days never shewed any interest. But Athanasius himself contributed to the revolution thus accomplished, [1] though it is very doubtful if he ever came to see the full extent of it.

τῇ ὑποστάσει τοῦ πατρός· πνεῦμα γὰρ ἐκ πατρός. Καὶ κατὰ μὲν τὴν τοῦ πνεύματος ἔννοιαν (and therefore thought of in essence as a generic conception) ταὐτόν, ὡς κατὰ τὴν τῆς σαρκὸς ἔννοιαν ταὐτόν. Οὐ ταὐτὸν δὲ ἀλλὰ ὅμοιον, διότι τὸ πνεῦμα, ὅ ἐστιν ὁ υἱός, οὐκ ἔστιν ὁ πατήρ, καὶ ἡ σάρξ, ἣν ὁ λόγος ἀνέβαλεν, οὐκ ἔστιν ἐκ σπέρματος καὶ ἡδονῆς, ἀλλ᾽ οὕτως ὡς τὸ εὐαγγέλιον ἡμᾶς ἐδίδαξεν ... ὁ πατὴρ πνεῦμα ὢν αὐθεντικῶς ποιεῖ, ὁ δὲ υἱὸς πνεῦμα ὢν οὐκ αὐθεντικῶς ποιεῖ ὡς ὁ πατὴρ ἀλλ᾽ ὁμοίως. Οὐκοῦν καθὰ μὲν σάρξ καὶ σάρξ ταὐτόν, ὥσπερ καθὸ πνεῦμα καὶ πνεῦμα ταὐτόν. καθὸ δὲ ἄνευ σπορᾶς οὐ ταὐτὸν ἀλλ᾽ ὅμοιον, ὥσπερ καθὸ ἄνευ ἀπορροίας καὶ πάθους ὁ υἱὸς οὐ ταὐτὸν ἀλλ᾽ ὅμοιον. Thus these Homoiousians already admit the ταὐτόν if they also reject the ταὐτοούσιος (= ὁμοούσιος), *i.e.*, Father and Son are ταὐτόν as regards substance, in so far as they are both πνεῦμα, but in so far as they are different Hypostases they are not identical, but of like nature. (4) These Homoiousians have expressly rejected the designations ἀγέννητος for God and γεννητός for the Son, and indeed not only because they are unbiblical, but because "Father" includes much more than "Unbegotten", and because "γεννητός" includes much less than "Son", and further because the conjunction "unbegotten—begotten" does not express *the relation of reciprocity* between Father and Son (the γεννησίως γεγεννημένῳ), which is emphasised as being the most important (c. 14, 19): διὸ κἂν πατέρα μόνον ὀνομάζωμεν, ἔχομεν τῷ ὀνόματι τοῦ πατρὸς συνυπακουομένην τὴν ἔννοιαν τοῦ υἱοῦ, πατὴρ γὰρ υἱοῦ πατὴρ λέγεται· κἂν υἱὸν μόνον ὀνομάσωμεν, ἔχομεν τὴν ἔννοιαν τοῦ πατρός, ὅτι υἱὸς πατρὸς λέγεται. Whoever names the one names the other at the same time, and yet does not posit him merely in accordance with his name, but with his name καὶ τῆς φύσεως οἰκειότητα; on the other hand, ἀγέννητον οὐ λέγεται γεννητοῦ ἀγέννητον, οὐδὲ γεννητὸν ἀγεννήτου γεννητόν. Athanasius could scarcely wish more than this, or rather: we have already here the main outlines of the theology of the three Cappadocians, and it is not accidental that Basil of Ancyra is himself a Cappadocian.

[1] The work of Athanasius, de synodis, written in the year 359, is of the highest importance for the history of the Arian controversy. It is distinguished as much by the firmness with which his position is maintained—for Athanasius did not yield in any point—as by its moderation and wisdom. The great bishop succeeded in combining these qualities in his book, because he was not concerned with the

Julian granted liberty to all the bishops to return, and in so doing did away with the artificial state of things created by Constantius. The Niceans were once more a power, and Athanasius who returned to Alexandria in February 362, at once re-assumed the leadership of the party. A Synod was held at Alexandria in summer, and this prepared the way for the triumph of orthodoxy in the year 381.[1] It was here resolved that the Nicene Creed was to be accepted *sans phrase, i.e.,* that those were to be recognised as Christian brethren who *now* acknowledge the ὁμοούσιος, and condemn the Arian heresy together with its chief supporters, irrespective of any former departure on their part from the faith. But still further, the question as to whether it was necessary to believe in *one* hypostasis or in *three* was left an open one. (At Alexandria the Holy Spirit had already been the subject of discussion as well as the Son.) Both statements were disapproved of since the ὁμοούσιος was considered to be sufficient, but it was explained that both might be understood in a pious sense.[2] These resolutions were not passed without strong opposition.[3] Not only did some bishops demand that

formula itself, but solely with the thought which in his view the formula attacked best expressed. We must, he said, speak like brethren to brethren to the Homoiousians who hold almost the same view as the Nicæans and are merely suspicious about a word. Whoever grants that the Son is in nature of like quality with the Father and springs from the substance of the Father is not far from the ὁμοούσιος; for this is a combination of ἐκ τῆς οὐσίας and ὁμοιούσιος (c. 41 ff.). While expressly making an apology to Basil of Ancyra, he endeavours to remove the stumbling-blocks presented by ὁμοούσιος, but seeks at the same time to shew that ὁμοιούσιος either involves an absurdity or is dogmatically incorrect (c. 53 f.).

[1] The most important source of information for the Synod of Alexandria is the Tomus of Athanas. ad Antioch., and in addition Rufin. X. 27—29, Socr. III. 7, Athan. ep. ad Rufinian. I need not here (after the work published by Revillout) enter upon any discussion of the σύνταγμα διδασκαλίας of the Synod, which is identical with Opp. Athanas. ed. Migne XXVIII., p. 836 sq.; cf. Eichhorn, Athan., de vita ascet. testim., 1886, p. 15 sq. On the Synod cf. also Gregor. Naz. Orat. 21, 35.

[2] Tom. ad Antioch. 5. 6. This was probably the largest concession which Athanasius ever made. When Socrates affirms that at the Synod the employment of "Ousia" and "Hypostasis" in reference to the Godhead was forbidden, his statement is not entirely incorrect; for it is evident from the Tomus that the Synod did actually disapprove of the use of the terms in this way.

[3] This is sufficiently shewn in the Tomus; the Lucifer schism has its root here; see Krüger, op. cit., pp. 43—54. Lucifer was, moreover, not a man of sufficient education to appreciate the real question at issue. He did not wish to have

those who had subscribed the Fourth Sirmian Formula should be denied the communion of the Church, but, what was of much greater importance, there was a party which insisted on the interpretation of the Nicene Creed which had been settled by some of the Western bishops at Sardica, and which as a matter of fact was the original one. [1] But they did not press their views, and they seem to have acquiesced in the decision of the Synod. This marked a complete change. [2] If up till now orthodox faith had meant the recognition of a mysterious plurality in the substantial unity of the Godhead, it was now made permissible to turn the unity into a mystery, *i.e.*, to reduce it to equality and to make the threefoldness the starting-point; but this simply means that that Homoiousianism was recognised which resolved to accept the word ὁμοούσιος. And to this theology, which changed the substantial *unity* of substance expressed in the ὁμοούσιος into a mere likeness or *equality* of substance, so that there was no longer a threefold unity, but a trinity, the future belonged, in the East, though not to the same extent in the West. The theologians who had studied Origen regarded it with favour. The Cappadocians started from the ὁμοούσιος, [3]

the *venia ex pœnitentia* accorded to the Semi-Arians who were passing over to orthodoxy. It was thus a Novatian-Donatist element which determined his position.

[1] See above, p. 68, and the Tom. c. 5. init. These bishops thus demanded the acknowledgment of the μία ὑπόστασις. The West never at bottom abandoned this demand, but in the Meletian-Antiochian schism it, however, finally got the worst of it and had to acquiesce in the Eastern doctrinal innovation. That at the Synod of Alexandria, however, the Homoiousians also attempted to get their catchword, or, their interpretation of the ὁμοούσιος, adopted, is evident from the letter of Apollinaris to Basil; see Dräseke Ztschr. f. K.G., VIII., p. 118 f.

[2] Just as it is to Zahn that, speaking generally, we primarily owe the understanding of the original meaning of Ὁμοούσιος, so it is he too who, so far as I know, first plainly noticed this complete change. (Marcell, p. 87 f., also Gwatkin, p. 242 sq.)

[3] This is specially evident from the letter of Basil to Apollinaris (in Dräseke, op. cit. 96 ff.) of the year 361. Basil communicates to the great teacher (of whom later) his doubts as to whether it is justifiable to use the word ὁμοούσιος. For biblical and philosophical dogmatic reasons he is inclined to prefer the formula ἀπαραλλάκτως ὅμοιος κατ' οὐσίαν. Apollinaris accordingly explains to him (p. 112 ff.) that the ὁμοούσιος is more correct, but his own explanation of the word is no longer identical with that of Athanasius. He finds both expressed in it, the ταυτότης as well as the ἑτερότης, and according to his idea the Son is related to the Father as men are to Adam. Just as it may be said of all men, they are Adam, they were in Adam, and just as there is only *one* Adam, so too is it with the Godhead. Basil

though this is certainly true of Gregory of Nyssa only indirectly. They ackowledged the ὁμοούσιος and accordingly set up a system of doctrine which neither disavowed the theology of Origen, that is, science in general, nor yet remained in the terminologically helpless condition of Athanasius. But they succeeded in attaining terminological clearness—they could not improve on the *matter* of the doctrine—only because they modified the original thought of Athanasius and developed the theology which Basil of Ancyra had first propounded in his tractate. Οὐσία now got a meaning which was half way between the abstract "substance" and the concrete "individual substance", still it inclined very strongly in the direction of the former.[1] Ὑπόστασις got a meaning half way between "Person" and "Attribute", (Accident, Modality), still the conception of Person entered more largely into it.[2] Πρόσωπον was avoided because it had a Sabellian sound, but it was not rejected. The unity of the Godhead, as the Cappadocians conceived of it, was not the same as the unity which Athanasius had in his mind. Basil the Great was never tired of emphasising the new distinction implied in οὐσία and ὑπόστασις. For the central doctrine of the incarnation of God they required a conception of God of boundless fulness. Μία οὐσία (μία θεότης) ἐν τρισὶν ὑποστάσεσιν, (*one*

at any rate started from Homoiousianism, and it is because this has not been taken into consideration that the letter in question has been pronounced not genuine. For the rest, the efforts of the Benedictines in the third volume of their edition of the Opp. Basil. (Præf.) to vindicate Basil's orthodoxy shew that, leaving this letter out of account, his perfect soundness in the faith is not—in all his utterances— beyond doubt. Later on Basil understood the ὁμοούσιος exactly in the sense given to it by him in the letter to Apollinaris and which at that time made him hesitate to use it; see Krüger, p. 42 f. See further the characteristic statements made at an earlier date in ep. 8. 9: ὁ κατ᾽ οὐσίαν Θεὸς τῷ κατ᾽ οὐσίαν Θεῷ ὁμοούσιος!

[1] Basil has frequently so expressed himself as to suggest that he regarded the idea of the generic unity of Father and Son as sufficient (see, *e.g.*, ep. 38, 2). Zahn (p. 87): "the οὐσία with Basil designates the κοινόν, the ὑπόστασις the ἴδιον (ep. 114, 4). He is never tired of holding forth on the difference between the two expressions, and goes so far as to assert that the Nicene Fathers were well aware of this difference, since they would surely not have put the two words side by side without some purpose (ep. 125)." It is interesting to note that already at the Council of Antioch in 363 it had been explained that οὐ κατά τινα χρῆσιν Ἑλληνικὴν λαμβάνεται τοῖς πατράσι τὸ ὄνομα τῆς οὐσίας. Assuredly not! It was a terminology which was expressly invented.

[2] And yet in Gregory of Nyssa the persons appear also as συμβεβηκότα (accidents).

divine substance (one divine nature) in three *subjects*,) was the formula. In order to give clear expression to the actual distinction of the Persons within the Godhead, Gregory of Nyssa attached to them τρόποι ὑπάρξεως, (modes of existence,) ἰδιότητες χαρακτηρίζουσαι, ἐξαίρετα ἰδιώματα, (characteristic peculiarities, special characters). To the Father he attributed ἀγεννησία, the quality of being unbegotten, and in consequence of this the word which had formerly been forbidden by the Niceans was once more restored to a place of honour, no longer, however, as referring to substance, but as expressing a mode of being (σχέσις) of God the Father. To the Son he attributed γεννησία, the quality of being begotten, and even the older Homoiousians shewed more reserve on this point than Gregory did. To the Spirit he attributed ἐκπόρευσις—procession.[1] But what is more,

---

[1] See the treatises of Gregor. Nyss. περὶ διαφορᾶς οὐσίας καὶ ὑποστάσεως—περὶ τοῦ οἴεσθαι λέγειν τρεῖς Θεούς—πρὸς "Ελληνας ἐκ τῶν κοινῶν ἐννοιῶν. "Prosopon" is no longer for Gregory a technical term in the strict sense of the word, but on the other hand he also avoids the expression "three ἄτομα". The word φύσις maintained itself alongside of οὐσία, and in the same way ἰδιότης was used along with ὑπόστασις. The God who was common to the Three was supposed to be a real substance, not, however, a fourth alongside of the Three, but on the contrary the unity itself! On the characteristics of the Hypostases, see Gregor. Naz. Orat. 25. 16: Κοινὸν τὸ μὴ γεγονέναι καὶ ἡ θεότης. "Ιδιον δὲ πατρὸς μὲν ἡ ἀγεννησία, υἱοῦ δὲ ἡ γέννησις, πνεύματος δὲ ἡ ἔκπεμψις. The two others expressed their views in almost similar terms in their works against Eunomius, unless that Gregory of Nyssa alone put the doctrine of the Holy Ghost in a logically developed form (see below), while as regards it, Basil (see de spir. s. ad Amphiloch.) advanced least of them all. The pronounced attitude taken up by them all, especially by Basil, against Marcellus, is characteristic. The theological orations of Gregory of Nazianzus (Orat. 27—31) may, more than anything else, have spread the doctrinal system far and wide. (It is important to note that in opposition to it Athanasius in his letter ad Afros. [c. 369] expressly said that ὑπόστασις and οὐσία were to be used as identical in meaning.) It follows from Orat. 31 (33) that Gregory did *not* wish to apply the *number* one to the Godhead; a unity was for him only the κίνησις and φύσις (μίαν φύσιν ἐν τρισὶν ἰδιότησι, νοεραῖς τελείαις, καθ᾽ ἑαυτὰς ὑφεστώσαις, ἀριθμῷ διαιρεταῖς καὶ οὐ διαιρεταῖς θεότητι). So too was he doubtful about the suitability of the old image, "source, stream", for the Trinity, not only because it represents the Godhead as something changeable, something flowing, *but also because it gave the appearance of a numerical unity to the Godhead.* He is equally unwilling, and in fact for the same reasons, to sanction the use of the old comparison of sun, beam, and brightness. He is always in a fighting attitude towards "Sabellianism". The doctrine of the *one* God is to him Jewish—that is the new discovery. "We do not acknowledge a Jewish, narrow, jealous, weak Godhead" (Orat. 25. 16). Gregory had, moreover, already begun those odd speculations about the

the entire Origenistic speculation regarding the Trinity, with which Athanasius would have nothing to do, that is, of which he knew nothing, was rehabilitated. The moment or element of finitude within the Trinitarian evolution was no doubt struck out, still the Absolute has nevertheless not only *modi* in itself, but also in some degree, stages. The (eternal) *generation* or begetting, in the sense of a Godhead extending itself to the limits of the creaturely, was again put in the foreground. In this way the subordination-conception, which was an irreducible remainder in Athanasius' whole way of looking at the question, again acquired a peculiar significance. The idea that the Father in Himself is to be identified with the entire Godhead again became one of the ground-principles of speculation. He is the starting-point of the Trinity, just as He is the Creator of the world. The idea that He is source, beginning, cause of the Godhead (πηγή, αρχή, αἰτία τῆς θεότητος), the cause (τὸ αἴτιον) and consequently God in the proper sense (κυρίως Θεός), while the other Hypostases again are effects (αἰτιατά),[1] meant something different to the Cappadocians from what it did to Athanasius. For the Logos-conception, which Athanasius had discarded as theistic-*cosmical*, again came to the front, and in their view Logos and Cosmos are more closely related than in that of Athanasius. The unity of the Godhead does not rest here on the Homousia, but in the last resort, as with Arius, on the "monarchy" of God the Father; and the Spiritual on earth is, in fine, not a mere creature of God, but—at any rate

immanent substance of God which, though they are mere bubble-blowing, are still highly thought of. The divine loftiness, according to him, shews itself in this, that in His immanent life also God is a *fruitful* principle; the life of the creature has its vital manifestation in the tension of dualities, but it is in this opposition that its imperfection also consists; the Trinity is the "sublation", or abrogation of the duality, living movement and at the same time rest, and not in any way a sublimation into multiplicity. The Orat. 23 in particular is full of thoughts of this sort, see c. 8: τριάδα τελείαν ἐκ τελειῶν τριῶν, μονάδος μὲν κινηθείσης διὰ τὸ πλούσιον, δυάδος δὲ ὑπερβαθείσης, ὑπὲρ γὰρ τὴν ὕλην καὶ τὸ εἶδος, ἐξ ὧν τὰ σώματα, τριάδος δὲ ὁρισθείσης διὰ τὸ τέλειον, πρώτη γὰρ ὑπερβαίνει δυάδος σύνθεσιν, ἵνα μήτε στενὴ μένῃ ἡ θεότης μήτε εἰς ἄπειρον χέηται· τὸ μὲν γὰρ ἀφιλότιμον, τὸ δὲ ἄτακτον, καὶ τὸ μὲν Ἰουδαϊκὸν παντελῶς, τὸ δὲ Ἑλληνικὸν καὶ πολύθεον.

[1] Gregor. Nyss., ἐκ τῶν κοινῶν ἐννοιῶν T. II. p. 85; ἕν καὶ τὸ αὐτὸ πρόσωπον τοῦ πατρός, ἐξ οὗ ὁ υἱὸς γεννᾶται καὶ τὸ πνεῦμα τὸ ἅγιον ἐκπορεύεται, διὸ καὶ κυρίως τὸν ἕνα αἴτιον ὄντα τῶν αὐτοῦ αἰτιατῶν ἕνα Θεόν φαμεν.

with Gregory of Nyssa—as in the view of Origen, is a being
with a nature akin to His.[1] "Science" concluded an alliance
with the Nicene Creed; that was a condition of the triumph
of orthodoxy. If at the beginning of the controversy the
scientific thinkers—including those amongst the heathen—had
sympathised with Arianism, men were now to be found as the
defenders of the Nicene Creed to whom even a Libanius yielded
the palm. These men took their stand on the general theory
of the universe which was accepted by the science of the time;
they were Platonists, and they once more naïvely appealed to
Plato in support even of their doctrine of the Trinity.[2] Those
who were on the side of Plato, Origen,[3] and Libanius—Basil
indeed had recommended the latter to his pupils as one who
could help them in advanced culture,—those who were on
a footing of equality with the scholars, the statesmen, and
highest officials, could not fail to get sympathy. The literary
triumphs of the Cappadocians who knew how to unite devotion
to the Faith and to the practical ideals of the Church with
their scientific interests, the victories over Eunomius and his
following were at the same time the triumphs of Neo-platonism
over an Aristotelianism which had become thoroughly arid and
formal.[4] Orthodoxy in alliance with science had a spring which
lasted from two to three decades, a short spring which was
not followed by any summer, but by destructive storms. Spite
of all the persecutions, the years between 370 and 394 were

---

[1] It is here that we have the root of the difference between Athanasius and
Gregory.

[2] From this time this once more became the fashion amongst the scientific
orthodox. The confession of Socrates (VII. 6) is very characteristic. He cannot
understand how the two Arian Presbyters, Timotheus and Georgius can remain
Arians and yet study Plato and Origen so industriously and esteem them so highly:
οὐδὲ γὰρ Πλάτων τὸ δεύτερον καὶ τὸ τρίτον αἴτιον, ὡς αὐτὸς ὀνομάζειν εἴωθεν, ἀρχὴν
ὑπάρξεως εἰληφέναι φησί, καὶ Ὠριγένης συναΐδιον πανταχοῦ ὁμολογεῖ τὸν υἱὸν τῷ
πατρί. It is instructive further to note how Philostorgius too (in Suidas) asserts
that in the matter of the vindication of the ὁμοούσιος Athanasius was deemed a
boy in comparison with the Cappadocians and Apollinaris.

[3] See the Philocalia.

[4] This is one of the strongest impressions we carry away from a reading of
the works against Eunomius.

very happy ones for the orthodox Church of the East. It was engaged on a great task, and this was to restore the true faith to the Churches of the East, and to introduce into them the asceticism which was closely allied with science.[1] It was in the midst of a struggle which was more honourable than the struggles of the last decades had been. Men dreamt the dream of an eternal league between Faith and Science. Athanasius did not share this dream, but neither did he disturb it. He did not go in for the new theology, and there is much to shew that it did not quite satisfy him.[2] But he saw the aim of his life, the recognition of the complete Godhead of Christ, brought nearer accomplishment, and he continued to be the patriarch and the recognised head of orthodoxy, as the letters of Basil in particular shew. When, however, orthodoxy had attained its victory, there arose after a few years within its own camp an opponent more dangerous to its scientific representatives than Eunomius and Valens—the traditionalism which condemned all science.

Nothing more than an outline can here be given of the development of events in particular instances. The Synod of Alexandria was not able by means of its resolution to unite the parties which had separated at Antioch: the party of the

---

[1] This aspect of the activity of the Cappadocians cannot be too highly valued. But in this respect too, though in quite a new fashion, they took up the work of Athanasius. The dominant party on the contrary were supported by an Emperor (Valens) who no doubt for good reasons persecuted monarchism. (See the law in the Cod. Theodos. XII. 1, 63 of the year 365.) The aversion of the Homœans to monasticism is evident from the App. Const. Basil's journey to Egypt was epoch-making. The relation in which he stood to Eustathius of Sebaste, the ascetic and Semi-Arian, is also of great importance.

[2] For the sake of peace and in order to secure the main thing, Athanasius at the Synod of Alexandria, which may be called a continuation of the Synod of Ancyra, himself concluded the alliance with the new Oriental orthodoxy and acknowledged Meletius. But his procedure later on in the Antiochian schism (see Basil., ep. 89, 2), the close relation in which he stood throughout to Rome as contrasted with the East, the signal reserve he exhibited towards Basil (Basil. ep. 66, 69), and finally the view he took of the Marcellian Controversy which was still going on—Basil saw in Marcellus a declared Sabellian heretic, while the judgment passed on him and his following by Athanasius was essentially different—prove that he never came to have a satisfying confidence in the neo-orthodox Niceans who were associated with Meletius; see on this Zahn, pp. 83 ff., 88 ff., Rade, Damasus, p. 81 ff.

orthodox who clung to the old faith and that of the Homoiousians who under the leadership of Meletius acknowledged the
Homousios. This Antiochian split remained an open wound,
and the history of the attempts to get it healed makes it
abundantly evident that different doctrines were really in
question, that Alexandria and the East had not lost their feeling of distrust of Meletius, and that the Cappadocians who
were at the head of the new orthodoxy in the East were not
able to suppress the suspicion of Sabellianism in the light of
the old orthodoxy.[1]

Jovian, who was inclined to orthodoxy, once more recalled
Athanasius who had been banished for the last time by Julian.[2]
Athanasius somewhat prematurely announced the triumph of
the true faith in the East.[3] Under the new ruler, Acacius, at
a Synod held in Antioch in 363, found himself obliged to
agree with Meletius and to join with him in declaring his
adherence to the ὁμοούσιος, explaining at the same time that it
expressed as much as the ἐκ τῆς οὐσίας (of the substance) and
the ὁμοιούσιος together [4] (see Athan., de Synod.) But the accession of Valens in the following year changed everything. An
attempt on the part of the semi-Arians at the Synod at Lamp-
sacus in 364 to get the upper hand, miscarried.[5] Eudoxius of
Constantinople and the adroit Acacius who again made a change
of front, became masters of the situation, and Valens resolved

---

[1] See the art. "Meletius" in Herzog's R.-Encykl. IX., p. 530 f. and the discussion by Rade, op. cit., p. 74 ff. The Westerns had the same kind of feeling in
reference to the opponent of Meletius in Antioch, Paulinus, as they formerly had
in reference to Athanasius; he alone was for them orthodox; but they did not
succeed in getting their view adopted. Hieron. ep. 15. 16 shews what scruples the
formula, τρεῖς ὑποστάσεις, gave rise to in the minds of the Westerns.

[2] Julian, spite of his aversion to all Christians, seems nevertheless to have been
somewhat more favourably disposed towards Arianism than towards orthodoxy, i.e.,
than to Athanasius, who, moreover, incurred his suspicions on political grounds.

[3] See his letter to Jovian in the Opp. and in Theodoret. IV. 3. Here the
matter is so represented as to suggest that there were now only a few Arian Churches
in the East. The attack on those who do indeed accept the ὁμοούσιος, but give it
a false interpretation, is worthy of note.

[4] See the Synodical-epistle in Socrat. III. 25, Mansi III., p. 369.

[5] Socrat. IV. 2 sq. 12, Sozom. VI, 7 sq. In the following decade the view of
Eudoxius of Constantinople was the authoritative one.

to adopt once more the policy of Constantius, to maintain the Arian Homœism in its old position, and to make all bishops who thought differently [1] suffer. Orthodox and Homoiousians had again to go into banishment. From this time onwards many Homoiousians turned to the West, having made up their minds to accept the ὁμοούσιος in order to get support. The West after the brief episode of the period of oppression (353 —360) was once more Nicene. There were but few Arians, although they were influential. After various Councils had met, the Homoiousians sent deputies from Pontus, Cappadocia, and Asia [2] to Liberius to get the doctrinal union brought about. Liberius, whose sentiments were the same as those of Hilary, did not refuse their request. The announcement of this happy event was made at Tyana in 367; [3] but at a Carian Council a Homoiousian minority persisted in rejecting the ὁμοούσιος. [4] From this time Basil, who became bishop in 370, [5] took an active part in affairs and he was soon after followed by the other Cappadocians, and they threw not only the weight of science, but also that of asceticism, into the scale in favour of orthodoxy. The new bishop of Rome, Damasus, took a decided stand against Arianism at the Roman Synods held in 369 (370) and 377, then against the Pneumatomachians (see below) and the Apollinarian heresy, while Marcellus and Photinus were also condemned. The rigid standpoint of the bishops Julius and Athanasius again became the dominant one in the West, and it was only after some hesitation that the Western bishops re-solved to offer the hand of friendship to the new-fashioned orthodoxy of the East. The representatives of the latter did not indeed settle the Antiochian schism at the well-attended Council at Antioch in September 379, but they subscribed the

[1] The Altercatio Heracliani et Germinii is instructive; see Caspari, Kirchenhist. Anecdota, 1883.

[2] Cappadocia was the native land of the new orthodoxy; see the Cappadocian self-consciousness of Gregor. Naz.; up till this time, however, it had been the prin-cipal seat of Arianism.

[3] Socrat. IV. 12.

[4] Sozom. VI. 12.

[5] He was at the same time the patriarch of the diocese of Pontus.

Roman pronouncements of the last years, and thus placed themselves at the standpoint of Damasus.[1]

But meanwhile very great changes had taken place in the
State. In November 375 Valentinian died. He had not taken
any part in Church politics, and had in fact protected the Arian

[1] It was Athanasius who roused Damasus to take up an attitude of energetic
opposition to the Arian Bishop Auxentius of Milan, and thus, speaking generally,
led him to follow in the track of Bishop Julius; see Athan. ep. ad Afros. It was
at the Roman Council of 369 that the Western episcopate first formally and solemnly
renounced the resolution of Rimini. On the text of the epistle of this Council, see
Rade, p. 52 ff. Auxentius of Milan was condemned; but this sentence was a futile
one since the Court protected him. No mention was yet made at this Council of
the difficulties of the East. The years from 371 to 380 are the epochs during
which the new-fashioned orthodoxy of the East, under the leadership of Basil and
Meletius, attempted to induce the West to bring its influence to bear on Valens and
the Homœan-Arian party, by means of an imposing manifesto, and thus to
strengthen orthodoxy in the East, but at the same time to pronounce in favour of
the Homoiousian-Homoousian doctrine and to put the orthodox Niceans in the
wrong. These attempts were not successful; for Damasus in close league, first with
Athanasius, then after his death (373), with his successor Peter, was extremely
reserved, and in the first instance either did not interfere at all or interfered in
favour of the old Niceans, of Paulinus that is, at Antioch. (This Peter, like Athanasius before him, had fled to Rome, and the alliance of Rome with Alexandria
was part of the traditional policy of the Roman bishop from the days of
Fabian to the middle of the fifth century.) The numerous letters and embassies
which came from the East of which Basil was throughout the soul, shew what
trouble was taken about the matter there. But the letters of Basil did not please
the "ἀκριβέστεροι" in Rome; at first, indeed, intercourse with the East was carried
on only through the medium of Alexandria, and on one occasion Basil had his
letter simply returned to him. He complained that at Rome they were friendly with
everybody who brought an orthodox confession and did not mind anything else.
He referred to the friendship shewn towards those who were inclined to the views
of Marcellus, further to the friendly intercourse of the Roman bishop with Paulinus,
who was always suspected of Sabellianism by Basil, and to the occasional recognition of an Apollinarian. In letter 214 Basil brought the charge of Sabellianism
against the entire Homoousian doctrine in its older form. It was in the year 376
that the West first promised help to the East. (The decretals of Damasus = 1
Fragment of the letter of Damasus designated by Coustant as ep. 4.) Basil now (ep.
263) pleads for active interference—where possible an imposing Council—against
the heretics who are heretics under cover of the Nicene Creed, and he designates
as such the Macedonian Eustathius of Sebaste, Apollinaris and *Paulinus*, i.e., the
man who taught pretty much the same doctrine as Athanasius; according to Basil,
however, he is a Marcellian. The accusations against Paulinus were naturally received
with anything but favour in the West. Peter of Alexandria who was still in Rome
at the time, called Meletius, Basil's honoured friend, simply an Arian. A Synod
was nevertheless held in Rome at which Apollinarianism was for the first time
rejected (377); to it we owe the pieces 2 and 3 in the ep. Damasi, 4 ed. Coustant.

bishops as he did the orthodox bishops, and had never had any difference with his brother regarding their religious policy. His successor, the youthful Gratian,[1] yielded himself wholly to the guidance of the masterful Ambrose. He firmly established the State Church as against the heterodox parties, by passing some severe laws, and in doing this he followed Ambrose "whom the Lord had taken from amongst the judges of the earth and placed in the Apostolic chair." (Basil ep. 197, 1.) In August 378 Valens fell at the battle of Adrianople, fighting with the Goths; and on the 19th of January, 379, the Western Theodosius was made Emperor of the East by Gratian. The death of Valens was quite as much a determining cause of the final triumph of orthodoxy as its alliance with science; for the inner force of a religious idea can never secure for it the dominion of the world. Theodosius was a convinced Western Christian who took up the policy of Gratian, but carried it out in a perfectly independent fashion.[2] He was determined to rule

Basil died in January 379. He did not attain the aim of all his work, which was to unite the orthodoxy of the East and the West on the basis of the Homoiousian interpretation of the Homoousios. But soon after his death, in September 379, Meletius held a synod in Antioch, and this synod subscribed all the manifestoes of the Romans, i.e., of the West, issued during the previous years 369, 376, 377, and thus simply submitted to the will of the West in dogmaticis, and despatched to Rome the Acts which contained the concessions. The triumph of the old-orthodox interpretation of the Nicene Creed thus seemed perfect. The West, under the guidance of Ambrose, from this time forth recognised the Meletians also as orthodox. It was from there (see the Synod of Aquileia 380, under Ambrosius) that the proposal emanated that if one of the two anti-bishops in Antioch should die, no successor should be chosen, and thus the schism would be healed. The fact that the Meletians thus came round to the orthodox standpoint is explicable only when we consider the complete changes which had taken place in the political situation since the death of Valens. On the involved state of things in the years from 369 to 378 see the letters of Basil, 70, 89—92, 129, 138, 214, 215, 239, 242, 243, 253—256, 263, 265, 266. It was the investigation of the matter by Rade, op. cit. pp. 70—121, which first threw light on this. On Damasus and Peter of Alex. see Socrat. IV. 37, Sozom. VI. 39, Theod. IV. 22. All were agreed in holding Athanasius in high respect. It was this that kept the combatants together. Gregory begins his panegyric (Orat. 21) with the words: Ἀθανάσιον ἐπαινῶν ἀρετὴν ἐπαινέσομαι, and in saying this he said what everybody thought.

[1] See on Gratian's religious policy my art. in Herzog's R.-Encykl. s. h. v.

[2] Valentinian was the last representative of the principle of freedom in religion, in the sense in which Constantine had sought to carry it out in the first and larger half of his reign, and also Julian.

the Church as Constantius had done, but to rule it in the spirit of rigid orthodoxy. He had himself been baptised [1] in the year 380, and immediately after appeared the famous edict which enjoined the orthodox faith on all nations. It is, however, in the highest degree characteristic of his whole policy that this faith is more definitely described as the Roman and Alexandrian faith, *i.e.*, the new doctrinal orthodoxy of Cappadocia and Asia is passed over in silence.[2] After his entry into Constantinople Theodosius took all their churches from the Arians and handed them over to the orthodox.[3] In the year 381 he issued a regulation in which he prohibited all heretics from holding divine service in the towns. In the same year, however, the Emperor summoned a large Eastern Council to meet at Constantinople, and its resolutions were afterwards regarded as ecumenical and strictly binding, though not till the middle of the fifth century, and in the West not till a still later date. This Council denotes a complete change in the policy of Theodosius. His stay in the East had taught him that it was necessary for him to recognise as orthodox all who acknowledged the Nicene Creed however they might interpret it, and at the same time to make an attempt to gain over the Macedonians. He had come to see that in the East he must rely upon the *Eastern* form of orthodoxy, the new orthodoxy, that he would have to suppress the aspirations of the Alexandrian bishops, and that he must do nothing which would have the appearance of anything like tutelage of the East by the West.

---

[1] During a severe illness, by the orthodox bishop of Thessalonica.

[2] Impp. Gratianus Valentinianus et Theodosius AAA. ad populum urbis Constantinop.: "Cunctos populos, quos clementiæ nostræ regit temperamentum in tali volumus religione versari, quam divinum Petrum apostolum tradidisse Romanis religio usque ad nunc ab ipso insinuata declarat quamque pontificem Damasum sequi claret et Petrum Alexandriæ episcopum virum apostolicæ sanctitatis, hoc est, ut secundum apostolicam disciplinam evangelicamque doctrinam patris et filii et spiritus sancti unam deitatem sub pari majestate et sub pia trinitate credamus (this is the Western-Alexandrian way of formulating the problem). Hanc legem sequentes Christianorum catholicorum nomen jubemus amplecti, reliquos vere dementes vesanosque judicantes hæretici dogmatis infamiam sustinere, divina primum vindicta, post etiam motus nostri, quem ex cælesti arbitrio sumpserimu s, ultione plectendos" (Cod. Theod. XVI. 1, 2; Cod. Justin I. 1.

[3] With the exception of Egypt most of the Churches in the East were at this time in the hands of the Arians.

This reversal of his policy is shewn most strikingly by the fact that Meletius of Antioch was called upon to preside at the Council, the very man who was specially suspected by the orthodox of the West.[1] He died shortly after the Council met, and first Gregory of Nazianzus,[2] and then Nectarius of Con-

[1] The relations which existed in the years 378—381 between the East and the West (Alexander was closely allied with the latter) are complicated and obscure. Their nature was still in all essential respects determined by the continuance of the schism in Antioch. The following is certain (1) Theodosius, as soon as he came to perceive the true state of things in the East, had ranged himself on the side of the orthodox there; he wished to suppress Arianism not by the aid of the West and of the Alexandrian bishop Peter who was closely allied with Rome and who had already acted as if he were the supreme Patriarch of the Greek Church, but by the orthodox powers of the East itself. The proof of this is (1) that he transferred in a body to Meletius the Arian Churches in Antioch,—Paulinus was shelved; (2) that in the Edict (Cod. Theodos. XVI. 1, 3) he does not mention Damasus, but on the contrary enumerates the orthodox of the East as authorities (July 30th, 381) and this Gwatkin, p. 262, rightly terms an "amended definition of orthodoxy"; (3) that he refused to accede to the repeated and urgent demands of the Westerns who wished him to settle impartially the dispute at Antioch with due respect to the superior claims of Paulinus, and also refused their request for the summoning of an Ecumenical Council at Alexandria; (4) that he summoned an Eastern Council to meet at Constantinople without troubling himself in the slightest about the West, Rome and Alexandria, made Meletius president of it, heaped honours upon him, and sanctioned the choice of a successor after his death, and this in spite of the advice of the Westerns that the whole Antiochian Church should now be handed over to Paulinus, an advice which had the support of Gregory of Nazianzus himself. Nor can there be any doubt in view of the manner in which the Council was summoned to meet, that its original intention was to draw up a formula of agreement with the Macedonians. It is certain (II.) that the orthodox Fathers who assembled at Constantinople gladly recognised and availed themselves of the opportunity thus presented of freeing themselves from the tutelage of Alexandria and the West, and of recalling by a distinct act the concessions which they had made under compulsion two years previously at Antioch. "It is in the East that the sun first rises, it was starting from the East that the God who came in the flesh flashed upon the world." By their united attitude, their choice of Flavian as the successor of Meletius, who had died during the Council, by passing the third Canon—on the importance of the chair of Constantinople—and by their rejection of Maximus who was proposed for the chair of Constantinople by Alexandria and patronised by Rome and the West, they inflicted the severest possible defeat on Alexandria and the West, and specially on the policy of Peter and Damasus. It is certain (III.) finally, that shortly before the Council of Constantinople, during the Council, and immediately after it rose, the relations between the Egyptians and Westerns and the East were of the most strained character, and that a breach was imminent. (See the letter in Mansi III., p. 631.)

[2] The choice of him as president (on this and on the general procedure of the Council see his Carmen de vita sua) was not any more than that of Meletius

stantinople presided over its deliberations. The opposition at
the Council between the old orthodox party, orthodox in the
Alexandrian and Western sense, who were few in numbers,
and the new orthodox party composed of Antiochians, Cappadocians and Asiatics, was of the most pronounced character,
though we are only partially acquainted with it.[1] The confusion
was so great that Gregory of Nazianzus resigned and left the
Council with the most bitter feelings.[2]   Still union was finally

approved of by Alexandria and Rome. His support of Paulinus may find its
explanation in the fact that he aimed at getting into the good graces of Rome
after he had himself attained the Patriarchate. Gregory had a Tasso-like nature.
Quite incapable of effecting anything in the sphere of Church government or politics, he did not really desire office ; but he wished to have the honour and distinction which are connected with office. So long as he did not have office he was
ambitious, when he had it he threw it away.

[1] The Egyptians even went the length of separating themselves from the majority
at the Council; they did not approve of the decisions come to by the neo-orthodox;
see Theodoret V. 8.

[2] The Egyptian bishops felt it ,to be intolerable that the Cappadocian and not
their man, Maximus, should get the position of Patriarch in Constantinople The
resignation of Gregory of Nazianzus was the price demanded by the Egyptians
for yielding; see Gregory's farewell address to the Council, Orat. 42. The Canons
1—4 of the Council—for these only are in all probability genuine, while those
which follow belong to the Council of 382—are strongly anti-Alexandrian and are
intended to bring down the claims of the Alexandrian which were already pitched
high. Canon 3 is directed not so much against Rome as against Alexandria (Τὸν
μέντοι Κωνσταντινουπόλεως ἐπίσκοπον ἔχειν τὰ πρεσβεῖα τῆς τιμῆς μετὰ τὸν τῆς
Ῥώμης ἐπίσκοπον, διὰ τὸ εἶναι αὐτὴν νέαν Ῥώμην). Canon 2 is intended to put a
stop to the attempt of the Bishop of Alexandria to rule other Eastern Churches.
But this very Canon plainly proves (cf. the sixth Canon of Nice) that as a matter
of fact the Bishop of Alexandria had a position in the East which was wholly
different from that of the other bishops. He only is mentioned in the singular
number—τὸν μὲν Ἀλεξανδρείας ἐπίσκοπον ... τοὺς δὲ τῆς Ἀνατολῆς ἐπισκόπους .. ;
φυλαττομένων τῶν πρεσβείων τῇ Ἀντιοχέων ἐκκλησίᾳ .. , τοὺς τῆς Ἀσιανῆς διοική-
σεως ἐπισκόπους ... τοὺς τῆς Ποντικῆς ... τοὺς τῆς Θρᾳκικῆς. The peculiar position
of the Alexandrian bishop which the latter wished to develop into a position of
primacy, was chiefly due to three causes. (It is quite clear that Athanasius and
Peter wished so to develop it, and perhaps even Dionysius the Great; the intention of the Alexandrian scheme to place Maximus on the episcopal seat of Constantinople, was to secure a preponderating influence upon the capital and the imperial
Church by the aid of this creature of Alexandria.) These three causes were as
follows; (1) Alexandria was the second city of the Empire and was recognised as
such *in the Church also* at least as early as the middle of the third century; see,
e.g., the conciliar epistle of the great Council of Antioch of the year 268, addressed
"to the bishops of Rome and *Alexandria* and to all Catholic churches." (Alexandria

secured, although the attempt to win over the Macedonians failed. The "150 bishops" unitedly avowed their adherence to the Nicene faith, and, as we are told, accepted in addition to this a special explanation of the doctrine of the Trinity in which the complete Homousia of the Spirit also was expressed. In the first canon containing the decisions, after the ratification of the Nicene Creed, Eunomians (Anomeans) Arians (Eudoxians) Semi-Arians (Pneumatomachians) Sabellians, Marcellians, Photinians and Apollinarians were expressly anathematised. The Nicene Creed thus gained an unqualified victory so far as its actual terms were concerned, but understood according to the interpretation of Meletius, the Cappadocians, and Cyril of Jerusalem. *The community of substance in the sense of equality or likeness of substance, not in that of unity of substance, was from this time the orthodox doctrine in the East.* But the Creed which since the middle of the fifth century in the East, and since about 530 in the West, has passed for the ecumenical-Constantinopolitan Creed, is neither ecumenical nor Constantinopolitan; for the Council was not an ecumenical one, but an Eastern one, and it did not in fact set up any new

ranks as the second, Antioch as the third city of the Empire in Josephus, de bello Jud. 4, 11, 5, cf. the chronograph of the year 354, Stryzygowski, Jahrb. d. k. deutschen archäol. Instituts. Supplementary vol., 1888, I., die Kalenderbilder des Chronographen v. j. 354, p. 24 f. The chronograph gives the series thus, Rome, Alexandria, Constantinople, Trèves. Lumbroso, L'Egitto dei Greci e dei Romani, 1882, p. 86, proves that all the authors of the first to the third centuries agree in giving the first place after Rome to Alexandria, see, *e.g.*, Dio Chrysostomus, Orat. 32, 1, p. 412: ἡ γὰρ πόλις ὑμῶν τῷ μεγέθει καὶ τῷ τόπῳ πλεῖστον ὅσον διαφέρει καὶ περιφανῶς ἀποδέδεικται δευτέρα τῶν ὑπὸ τὸν ἥλιον. In the "ordo urbium nobilium" of Ausonius we have for the first time the cities given in the following order: Rome, Constantinople, Carthage, Antioch, Alexandria, Trèves. So long as Alexandria was the second city in the Empire, it was the first city in the East. (2) Alexandria had this in common with Rome, that it had no cities in its diocese which were of importance in any way. The bishop of Alexandria was always the bishop of Egypt (Libya and Pentapolis), as the bishop of Rome was always the bishop of Italy. The case was quite otherwise with Antioch and Ephesus; they always had important episcopates alongside of them. (3) The lead in the great Arian controversy had fallen to the Bishop of Alexandria; he had shewn himself equal to this task and in this way had come to be the most powerful ecclesiastic in the East. The hints which I have given as to the policy of the Alexandrian Patriarch here and in Chap. III. 2, have been further developed in an instructive fashion by Rohrbach (die Patriarchen von Alexandrien) in the Preuss. Jahrb. Vol. 69, Parts 1 and 2.

Creed. This Creed, on the contrary, is the Baptismal Creed of
the Jerusalem Church which was issued in a revised form soon
after 362 and furnished with some Nicene formulæ and with
a *regula fidei* in reference to the Holy Spirit, and which was
perhaps brought forward at the Council of 381 and approved
of, but which cannot pass for its creed. How it subsequently
came to rank as a decision of the Council is a matter regarding which we are completely in the dark. This much, however, is clear, that if this Creed had any connection at all with
the Council of 381, the *neo-orthodox* character of the latter is
thereby brought out in a specially striking way; *for the so-called
Creed of Constantinople can in fact be taken simply as a formula of union between orthodox, Semi-Arians, and Pneumatomachians.* The most contested phrase of the Nicene Creed "ἐκ
τῆς οὐσίας τοῦ πατρός" is wanting in it, and it presents the
doctrine of the Holy Spirit in a form which could not have
appeared wholly unacceptable even to the Pneumatomachians.[1]

---

[1] On the Creed of Constantinople see my article in Herzog's R.-Encyklop. VIII.,
pp. 212—230, which summarises the works of Caspari and particularly of Hort, and
carries the argument further. The following facts are certain. (1) The Council of 381 did
not set up any new creed, but simply avowed anew its adherence to the Nicene
Creed (Socrat. V. 8, Sozom. VII. 7, 9, Theodoret V. 8, Greg. Naz. ep. 102 [Orat. 52]
the testimony of the Latin and Constantinople Councils of 382). (2) If we take the years
from 381 to 450, we do not find in any Synodal Act, Church Father, or heterodox
theologians during that period any certain trace whatsoever of the existence of the
Creed of Constantinople, much less any proof that it was used then as the Creed
of Constantinople or as the official Baptismal Creed; it is simultaneously with the
recognition of the Council of 381 as an ecumenical Council—about 451 in the East,
in the West fifty years later—that the Creed in question, which now emerges, is first
described as the Creed of Constantinople. (3) It did not, however, then first come into
existence, but is on the contrary much older; it is found already in the Ancoratus of
Epiphanius which belongs to the year 374, and there is no reason for holding that it is
an interpolation here; on the contrary (4) the internal evidence goes to shew that it is a
Nicene redaction of the Baptismal Creed of Jerusalem composed soon after 362.
The Creed is thus not any extension of the Nicene Creed, but rather belongs to
that great series of Creeds which sprang up after the Council of Alexandria (362)
in the second creed-making epoch of the Eastern Churches. At that time the
opponents of Arianism in the East, now grown stronger, resolved to give expression
to the Nicene doctrine in connection with the solemn rite of baptism. It was
possible to do this in three different ways, that is to say either by embodying the
Nicene catchwords in the old provincial church creeds, by enlarging the Nicene
Creed for the special purpose of using it as a baptismal Creed, or, finally, by
adopting it itself, without alteration, for church use as a baptismal Creed, in spite

For this very reason it is certainly out of the question to regard the Creed as the Creed of the Council of 381. It did indeed assert the complete Homousia of the divine Persons. But the legendary process in the Church which attached this Creed to that Council performed a remarkable act of justice;

of its incompleteness and its polemical character. These three plans were actually followed. In the first half of the fifth century the third was the one most widely adopted, but previously to this the two first were the favourites. To this series belong the revised Antiochian Confession, the later Nestorian Creed, the Philadelphian, the Creed in the pseudo-Athanasian ἑρμηνεία εἰς τὸ σύμβολον, the second, longer, Creed in the Ancoratus of Epiphanius, the Cappadocian-Armenian, the exposition of the Nicene Creed ascribed to Basil, a Creed which was read at Chalcedon and which is described as "Nicene." To this class our Creed also belongs. If it be compared with the Nicene Creed it will be easily seen that it cannot be based on the latter; if, on the other hand, it be compared with the old Creed of Jerusalem (in Cyril of Jerusalem) it becomes plain that it is nothing but a Nicene redaction of this Creed. But this is as much as to say that it was probably composed by Cyril of Jerusalem. Moreover, its general character also perfectly corresponds with what we know of Cyril's theology and of his gradual approximation to orthodoxy. (Socrat. V. 8, Sozom. VII. 7) "Cyril's personal history presents in various respects a parallel to the transition of the Jerusalem Creed into the form of the so-called Creed of Constantinople." That is to say, in the Creed which afterwards became ecumenical the words of the Nicene Creed "τοῦτ᾽ ἐστὶν ἐκ τῆς οὐσίας τοῦ πατρός" and the Nicene anathemas are omitted. The christological section accordingly runs thus : "καὶ εἰς ἕνα κύριον Ἰησοῦν Χριστόν, τὸν υἱὸν τοῦ Θεοῦ τὸν μονογενῆ, τὸν ἐκ τοῦ πατρὸς γεννηθέντα πρὸ πάντων τῶν αἰώνων, φῶς ἐκ φωτός, Θεὸν ἀληθινὸν ἐκ Θεοῦ ἀληθινοῦ, γεννηθέντα οὐ ποιηθέντα, ὁμοούσιον τῷ πατρί, δι᾽ οὗ τὰ πάντα ἐγένετο." From the writings of the Homoiousians and the Cappadocians we can accordingly easily gather that the "ἐκ τῆς οὐσίας τοῦ πατρός" presented a far greater difficulty to the half-friends of the Nicene Creed than the ὁμοούσιος; for ὁμοούσιος not without some show of fairness might be interpreted as ὅμοιος κατ᾽ οὐσίαν, while on the contrary the "ἐκ τῆς οὐσίας", both in what it said and in what it excluded—the will, namely—seemed to leave the door open to Sabellianism. It follows also from Athan. de Synodis that he considered the "ἐκ τῆς οὐσίας" as of supreme importance; for in a way that is very characteristic of him he observes that ὁμοούσιος is equal to ὁμοιούσιος ἐκ τῆς οὐσίας, that is, whoever intentionally avows his belief in the ὁμοούσιος without the "ἐκ τῆς οὐσίας" avows his belief in it as a Homoiousian. *The Christological formula in the Creed of Jerusalem, i.e., what was later on the Nicene-Constantinopolitan Creed, is thus almost homoiousian,* even although it retains the ὁμοούσιος. It corresponds exactly to the standpoint which Cyril must have taken up soon after 362. The same holds good of what the Creed says regarding the Holy Spirit. The words: "καὶ εἰς τὸ πνεῦμα τὸ ἅγιον, τὸ κύριον, τὸ ζωοποιόν, τὸ ἐκ τοῦ πατρὸς ἐκπορευόμενον, τὸ σὺν πατρὶ καὶ υἱῷ συνπροσκυνούμενον καὶ συνδοξαζόμενον, τὸ λαλῆσαν διὰ τῶν προφητῶν" are in entire harmony with the form which the doctrine of the Holy Spirit had in the sixties. A Pneumatomachian could have subscribed this formula at a pinch; and just because of this it is certain that the Council of 381 did not accept this Creed. We can only conjecture how it came for in tracing back to this Council "an enlarged Nicene Creed" without the "ἐκ τῆς οὐσίας τοῦ πατρός", "of the substance of the Father", without the Nicene anathemas, and without the avowal of the Homousia of the Spirit, and in attesting it as orthodox, it, without wishing to do so, preserved the recollection of the fact that the Eastern orthodoxy of 381 had really been a neo-orthodoxy, which in its use of the word Ὁμοούσιος did not represent the dogmatic conviction of Athanasius. In the *quid pro quo* involved in this substitution of one Creed for another, we have a judicial sentence which could not conceivably have been more discriminating; but it involves still more than that—namely, the most cruel satire. From the fact that in the Church the Creed of Constantinople gradually came to be accepted as a perfect expression of orthodoxy, and was spoken of as the Nicene Creed while the latter was forgotten, it follows that the great difference which existed between the old Faith and the Cappadocian neo-orthodoxy was no longer understood, and that under cover of the Ὁμοούσιος a sort of Homoiousianism had in general been reached, the view which has really been the orthodox one in all Churches until this day. The father of the official doctrine of the Trinity in the form in which the Churches have held to it, was not Athanasius, nor Basil of Cæsarea, but Basil of Ancyra.

All the same, the thought of the great Athanasius, though in

to be the Creed of Constantinople (see Hort., pp. 97—106 f. and my article pp. 225 f., 228 f.). It was probably entered in the Acts of the Council as the Confession by which Cyril had proved to the Council that his faith was orthodox and which the highly esteemed Epiphanius had also avowed as his. The Bishop of Constantinople took it from among the Acts shortly before the year 451 and put it into circulation. The desire to foist into the churches a *Constantinopolitan* Creed was stronger in his case than his perception of the defects of this very Creed. It was about 530 that the Creed of Constantinople first became a Baptismal Creed in the East and displaced the Nicene Creed. It was about the same time that it first came into notice in the West, but it, however, very quickly shoved the old Apostolic Baptismal Creeds into the background, being used in opposition to Germanic Arianism which was very widely spread there. On the "filioque" see below. We may merely mention the extreme and wholly unworkable hypothesis of the Catholic Vincenzi (De process. Spiritus S., Romæ, 1878) that the Creed of Constantinople is a Greek made-up composition belonging to the beginning of the seventh century, a fabrication the sole aim of which was to carry back the date of the rise of the heresy of the procession of the Holy Spirit *ex patre solo* into the Fourth Century

a considerably altered form, had triumphed. Science and the
revolution which took place in the political world had paved
the way for its victory; *suppressed*, it certainly never could
have been.

The Westerns were anything but pleased in the first instance
with the course things had taken in the East. At Councils held
at the same time in Rome and Milan, in the latter place under
the presidency of Ambrose, they had made representations to
Theodosius and had even threatened him with a withdrawal
of Church privileges.[1] But Theodosius answered them in a very
ungracious manner, whereupon they sought to justify their
attitude.[2] The Emperor was prudent enough not to fall in
with the proposal of the Westerns that an ecumenical Council
should be summoned to meet at Rome. He followed the policy
of Constantius also in keeping the Churches of the two halves
of the Empire separate, as his choice of Rimini and Seleucia
proves. And by his masterly conduct of affairs he actually
succeeded in introducing a *modus vivendi* in the year 382,
spite of the attempts made to thwart him by his colleague
Gratian who was led by Ambrose. Gratian summoned a General
Council to meet at Rome, to which the Eastern bishops were
also invited. But Theodosius had already got them together
in Constantinople. They accordingly replied in a letter in which
they declined the invitation, and its tone which was as praiseworthy as it was prudent, helped in all probability to lessen
the tension between the East and the West. They appealed,
besides, not only to the decisions of the Council of 381, but
also to their resolution of 378 in which they had made advances
to the West,[3] and they explained finally that they had adopted

---

[1] See the letter "Sanctum" in Mansi III., p. 631.

[2] See the letter "Fidei" in Mansi III., p. 630.

[3] The important letter is in Theodoret V. 9. It contains a description of the
persecutions which had been endured, of the struggles which still continued, thanks
that they ὡς οἰκεῖα μέλη should have received an invitation to the Council so that
they may rule along with the West and that it may not rule alone, regret that they
are prevented from appearing at it; then follows the exposition of the Faith, after
the despatch of the three envoys had been announced: "What we have suffered
we suffered for the Evangelical Faith which was settled at Nicæa, ταύτην τὴν
πίστιν καὶ ὑμῖν καὶ ἡμῖν καὶ πᾶσι τοῖς μὴ διαστρέφουσι τὸν λόγον τῆς ἀληθοῦς

a recent detailed dogmatic declaration of the Western bishops, of Damasus that is, and were ready to recognise the Paulinists in Antioch as orthodox, which meant that they no longer suspected them of Marcellianism. [1] The despatch of three envoys to Rome where, besides Jerome, the distinguished Epiphanius happened to be just at this time, could not but help towards

πίστεως συναρέσκειν δεῖ· ἣν μόλις ποτὲ [sic] πρεσβυτάτην τε οὖσαν καὶ ἀκόλουθον τῷ βαπτίσματι καὶ διδάσκουσαν ἡμᾶς πιστεύειν εἰς τὸ ὄνομα τοῦ πατρὸς καὶ τοῦ υἱοῦ καὶ τοῦ ἁγίου πνεύματος, δηλαδὴ θεότητός τε καὶ δυνάμεως καὶ οὐσίας μιᾶς τοῦ πατρός καὶ τοῦ υἱοῦ καὶ τοῦ ἁγίου πνεύματος πιστευομένης, ὁμοτίμου τε τῆς ἀξίας καὶ συναϊδίου τῆς βασιλείας, ἐν τρισὶ τελείαις ὑποστάσεσιν ἤγουν τρισὶ τελείοις προσώποις, ὡς μήτε τὴν Σαβελλίου νόσον χώραν λαβεῖν συγχεομένων τῶν ὑποστάσεων, εἴγουν τῶν ἰδιοτήτων ἀναιρουμένων, μή τε μὴν τὴν τῶν Εὐνομιανῶν καὶ Ἀρειανῶν καὶ Πνευματομάχων βλασφημίαν ἰσχύειν, τῆς οὐσίας ἢ τῆς φύσεως ἢ τῆς θεότητος τεμνομένης καὶ τῇ ἀκτίστῳ καὶ ὁμοουσίῳ καὶ συναϊδίῳ τριάδι μεταγενεστέρας τινὸς ἢ κτιστῆς ἢ ἑτεροουσίου φύσεως ἐπαγομένης. The Easterns did not yield anything here and yet they expressed their belief in as conciliatory a form as possible since they were silent about Marcellus, called Sabellianism a "disease", but Arianism a "blasphemy". Next follows the reference to the acts of the Councils of 379 and 381, then an explanation regarding the new appointment to the "as it were newly founded Church of Constantinople" and to the bishopric of Antioch where—this is directed against Rome and Alexandria—the name Christian first arose. So too the recognition of Cyril of Jerusalem, who had suffered so much for the Faith, is justified. Jerusalem is called in this connection "the mother of all Churches." The Easterns at the close beseech the Westerns to give their consent to all this, τῆς πνευματικῆς μεσιτευούσης ἀγάπης καὶ τοῦ κυριακοῦ φόβου, πᾶσαν μὲν καταστέλλοντος ἀνθρωπίνην προαπάθειαν, τὴν δὲ τῶν ἐκκλησιῶν οἰκοδομὴν προτιμοτέραν ποιοῦντος τῆς πρὸς τὸν καθ᾽ ἕνα συμπαθείας ἢ χάριτος. Then will we no longer say, what is condemned by the Apostles: "I am of Paul, and I of Apollos, and I of Cephas", but we shall all appear as belonging to Christ, who is not divided in us, and will with the help of God preserve the body of the Church from division.

[1] The so-called fifth Canon of the Council of 381 (see Rade, pp. 107, 116 f., 133) belongs to the Synod of 382, as also the sixth; the seventh is later. It runs: περὶ τοῦ τόμου τῶν Δυτικῶν καὶ τοὺς ἐν Ἀντιοχείᾳ ἀπεδεξάμεθα τοὺς μίαν ὁμολογοῦντας πατρὸς καὶ υἱοῦ καὶ ἁγίου πνεύματος θεότητα. It can only be the Paulinists in Antioch who are here referred to. But as regards the Western Tomos we must with Rade, op. cit., apparently take it to be the twenty-four Anathemas of Damasus (in Theodoret V. II.). This noteworthy document, which perhaps originated in the year 381, presents in a full and definite way the standpoint of the Westerns in regard to the different dogmatic questions. It is specially worthy of notice that the doctrine of Marcellus is condemned without any mention being made of its author. The ninth anathema is further of importance and also the eleventh: "If anyone does not confess that the Son is from the Father, i.e., is born of His Divine substance, let him be accursed." Compare with this the so-called Creed of Constantinople in which the ἐκ τῆς οὐσίας is wanting. The fulness with which the doctrines of the Incarnation and the Holy Spirit are already treated, is significant.

the conclusion of a treaty of peace. The opposition to Nectarius of Constantinople and Cyril of Jerusalem was now allowed
to drop in Rome; but the Western bishops could not yet bring
themselves to acknowledge Flavian in Antioch, and, moreover,
Paulinus, his opponent, was himself present at the Council in Rome.
There was once more a strong reaction against Apollinarianism.[1]

If Arianism, or Homœism, from the time when it ceased
to enjoy the imperial favour tended rapidly to disappear in
the Empire, if too it had no fanatic as Donatism had, it was
nevertheless still a power in the East in 383; large provinces
had still Arian tendencies, the common people[2] in them above
all; while in the West it had supporters[3] in the Empress Jus-

---

[1] To this period, according to Rade's pertinent conjecture, the work of Damasus
given in Theodoret V. 10 against Apollinarianism, also belongs. It probably came
from the pen of Jerome, soon after 382, and gives expression to the supreme self-
consciousness of the occupant of the chair of Peter. Jerome always flattered Damasus.

[2] The Church historians, Philostorgius in particular, give us some information
about this, but they do not enter much into particulars. Eunomius kept his ground
firmly and courageously and declined all compromises. He did not even so much
as recognise the baptism and ordination of the other Church parties (Philostorg. X. 4).
The Conciliar epistle of the Easterns of the year 382 (see above) further shews
what difficulties the attempt to carry through the Homoousios gave rise to.

[3] See the struggles of Ambrose against Arianism in Upper Italy, which went
on still the year 388. After the death of his mother, Valentinus II. declared for
orthodoxy; see Cod. Theodos. XVI. 5, 15. The knowledge that Maximus the usurper had
owed his large following to the fact of his being strictly orthodox helped to bring
about this decision. The assertion of Libanius that Maximus entered into an alliance
even with the unruly and rebellious Alexandrians is one which is calculated to
make us reflect. The fact that in the days of Theodosius Ambrose was at the
head of the Church in the West, probably contributed largely to bring about an
adjustment of the differences between the Western-Alexandrian and the Cappado-
cian-neo-orthodox doctrines of the Son. This bishop had learned from Philo, Origen,
and Basil, and he had friendly intercourse with the last mentioned; but he never
shewed any interest in or appreciation of the difference between the form of
doctrine in East and West, and he did not go into the speculations of the theologians of the East. It was thus merely in a superficial fashion that he accepted the
theological science of the East. But this very fact was of advantage to him so far
as his position was concerned; for it meant that he did not separate himself from
the common sense of the West, while, on the other hand, he had a great respect
for the Cappadocian theology and consequently was admirably suited for being a
peace-maker. *Ex professo* he did not handle the Trinitarian problem; his formulæ
bear what is essentially the Western stamp, without, however, being pointed against
the "Meletians", and in fact, he himself accepted the statement: "nulla est discre-
pantia divinitatis et operis; non igitur in utroque una persona, sed una substantia

tinia and her son. Theodosius was more concerned to win
over the Arians than to drive them out of the Church. In the
first years of his reign while shewing a firm determination to
establish orthodoxy, he had at the same time followed a sort
of *conciliatory* policy which, however, to the honour of the
Arians be it said, did not succeed. Just as in 381 he invited
the Macedonians to the Council, so in the year 383 he made
a further attempt to unite all the opposing parties at a Constantinopolitan Council and if possible to bring about concord.
The attempt was sincere—even Eunomius was present—but
it failed; but it is very memorable for two reasons: (1)
the orthodox bishop of Constantinople made common cause
on this occasion with the Novatian bishop, a proof of how
insecure the position of orthodoxy in the capital itself still was;[1]
(2) an attempt was made at the Council to transfer the whole
question in dispute between orthodox and Arians into the
region of tradition. The Holy Scriptures were to be dispensed
with, *and the proof of the truth of orthodoxy was to be furnished
solely by the testimony of the ante-Nicene Fathers to whose
authority the opposite party must as good Catholics bow.* This
undertaking was a prophecy of the ominous future which was
before the Church, and proved at the same time that the actual

est"; but on the other hand: "non duo domini, sed unus dominus, quia et pater
deus et filius deus, sed unus deus, quia pater in filio et filius in patre—nevertheless—unus deus, quia una deitas" (see Förster, Ambrosius, p. 130). Ambrose did not
engage in any independent speculations regarding the Trinity, as Hilary did (see Reinkens, op. cit., and Schwane, D G. d. patrist. Zeit., p. 150 ff.). The fact, however, that
in the fourth century the greatest theologian of the West—namely, Jerome, and the
most powerful ecclesiastical prince of the West, Ambrose, had learned their theology
from the Greeks, was the most important cause of the final union of East and
West in the matter of the doctrine of the Trinity. Hosius, Julius of Rome, Lucifer
and Damasus of Rome would not have been able to accomplish the dogmatic
unity of the two halves of the Empire. As a matter of fact the dogmatic unity did
not spring from the alliance of Athanasius, Julius, Peter, and Damasus, Alexandria
and Rome that is, but from the alliance of Athanasius, Hilary, Basil, Jerome, and
Ambrose.

[1] On the Novatians in the East in the Fourth Century and their relations to the
orthodox, particularly in the city of Constantinople, see my articles s. v. "Novatian", "Socrates", in Herzog's R.-Encykl. The Novatians, strange to say, always
had been and continued to be Nicene. The explanation of this may be found in
the fact that they originated in the West, or in the fact of their connection with
the West.

interest in the controversy in the East had already once more
taken a secondary place compared with the conservative interest.
Nothing grows faster than tradition, and nothing is more convenient when the truth of a proposition has to be defended
than to fall back on the contention *that it has always been so.*[1]

After this Council Theodosius discontinued his efforts in
favour of union and from this time sought to suppress Arianism. Ambrose seconded his plans in Upper Italy. The orthodox
State-Church, which was, however, on the other hand, a Church-
State, was established.   Severe laws were now passed against
all heretics with the exception of the Novatians.[2]   The State
had at last secured that unity of the Church which Constantine
had already striven after.   But it was a two-edged sword.   It
injured the State and dealt it a most dangerous wound. Amongst
the Greeks Arianism died out more quickly than Hellenism.
Violent schisms amongst the Arians themselves seem to have
accelerated its downfall,[3] but the different stages are unknown

---

[1] Socr. V. 10 (Sozom. VII. 12) has given us some information regarding the
proceedings at the Council of Constantinople in 383. Theodosius wished to have
an actual conference between the opposing parties. Sisinius, the reader to the
Novatian bishop Agelius, is then said to have advised that instead of having a
disputation the matter should be settled simply on the basis of passages from the
Fathers; the patristic proof alone was to be authoritative. Socrates tells us that
with the consent of the Emperor this was actually the course followed, and that
on the part of the orthodox only those Fathers were appealed to who had lived
before the Arian controversy. The raising of the question, however, as to whether
the various parties actually recognised these Fathers as authoritative, produced a
Babylonian confusion amongst them, and indeed even amongst the members of one
and the same party, so that the Emperor abandoned this plan of settling the
dispute. He next collected together Confessions composed by the different parties
(the bold one composed by Eunomius is still preserved, see Mansi III., p. 646 sq.),
but rejected them all with the exception of the orthodox one, and ungraciously sent
the parties home. The Arians, it is said, consoled themselves for the Emperor's
unkind treatment of them, with the saying that "many are called but few chosen".
This narrative, so far as the particulars are concerned, is too much a made-up
one to be implicitly trusted. But the attempt to decide the whole question on the
authority of tradition was certainly made. If we consider how at first both parties
proceeded almost exclusively on the basis of the Holy Scriptures we can perceive
in the attempt an extremely significant advance in the work of laying waste the
Eastern Churches.

[2] See Cod. Theodos. XVI. 1, 4 of the year 386 and the other laws of Theodosius and his sons. Things became particularly bad from about 410 onwards.

[3] See Sozom. in Books VII. and VIII., especially in VIII. 1.

to us. The history of its fortunes amongst the German peoples
until the seventh century does not fall within the scope of
this work. The educated laity, however, in the East regarded
the orthodox formula rather as a necessary evil and as an
unexplainable mystery than as an expression of their Faith.
The victory of the Nicene Creed was a victory of the priests
over the faith of the Christian people. The Logos-doctrine had
already become unintelligible to those who were not theologians. The setting up of the Nicene-Cappadocian formula as the
fundamental Confession of the Church made it perfectly impossible for the Catholic laity to get an inner comprehension
of the Christian Faith taking as their guide the form in which
it was presented in the doctrine of the Church. The thought
that Christianity is the revelation of something incomprehensible became more and more a familiar one to men's minds.
This thought has for its obverse side the adoration of the
mystery, [1] and for its reverse side indifference and subjection to
mystagogues.[2] The priests and theologians could certainly not
give the people more than they possessed themselves; but it is
alarming to note in the ecclesiastical literature of the Fourth
Century and the period following how little attention is given
to the Christian *people*. The theologians had always the clergy,
the officials, good society in their minds. The people must
simply believe the Faith; they accordingly did not live in this
Faith, but in that Christianity of the second rank which is

---

[1] Athanasius had already described the whole substance of the Christian religion
as a " doctrine of the mysteries "—see, *e.g.*, his Festival-letters, p. 68 (ed. Larsow).

[2] We have here, above all, to remember the attitude taken up by Socrates,
which is typical of that of the ecclesiastically pious laity of the East. His standpoint is—we ought silently to adore the mystery. Whatever the generation the last
but one before his own has fixed, is for him already holy; but he will have nothing to do with dogmatic disputes in his own time, and one may even find in
what he says traces of a vague feeling on his part that the laity as regards their Faith
had in fine been duped by the bishops and their controversies. His agreement with
what was said by Euagrius in reference to the Trinity (III. 7) is characteristic of
his position in the matter: πᾶσα πρότασις ἢ γένος ἔχει κατηγορούμενον ἢ εἶδος ἢ
διαφορὰν ἢ συμβεβηκὸς ἢ τὸ ἐκ τούτων συγκείμενον· οὐδὲν δὲ ἐπὶ τῆς ἁγίας τριάδος τῶν
εἰρημένων ἐστὶ λαβεῖν. σιωπῇ προσκυνείσθω τὸ ἄρρητον. He will have nothing to do
with οὐσία and ὑπόστασις. The case too of Procopius of Cæsarea illustrates the
attitude of reserve taken up by the laity in the sixth century to the whole dogmatic
system of the Church.

represented in the legends of the saints, in apocalypses, in image-worship, in the veneration of angels and martyrs, in crosses and amulets, in the Mass regarded as magical worship, and in sacramental observances of all sorts. Christ as the ὁμοούσιος became a dogmatic form of words; and in place of this the bones of the martyrs became living saints, and the shades of the old dethroned gods together with their worship, revived once more.

APPENDIX.

I. IN the baptismal formula, along with the confession of belief in the Father and Son, there had always been from early times a confession also of belief in the Holy Spirit. This belief expressed the thought that Christianity has within it the Spirit of the Father—the Spirit of Christ—the living, illuminating, divine principle. The Spirit is the *gift* of God. But after the Montanist controversies the combination of Spirit and Church, Spirit and individual Christians came to have a secondary place in regular theological thought. The World-Church and its theologians busied themselves instead with the Spirit in so far as it spoke through the prophets, in so far as it had before this brooded "over the waters", in so far as it descended on Christ at His baptism, etc.—though this soon became a minor point— or took part in His human origin. But there was quite an accumulation of difficulties here for rational theology. These difficulties lay (1) in the notion itself, in so far as $\pi\nu\varepsilon\tilde{\upsilon}\mu\alpha$ also described the substance of God and of the Logos; (2) in the impossibility of recognising any specific activity of the Spirit in the present; (3) in the desire to ascribe to the Logos rather than to the Spirit the active working in the universe and in the history of revelation. The form of the Spirit's existence, its rank and function were accordingly quite uncertain. By one the Holy Spirit was considered as a gift and as an impersonal— and therefore also an unbegotten—power which Christ had promised to send and which consequently became an actual fact only after Christ's Ascension; by another as a primitive power in the history of revelation; by a third as an active power in the world-process also. Others again attributed to it a personal existence misled by the expression "the Paraclete". Of these some regarded it as a created divine being, others as the highest spiritual creature made by God, the highest angel; others again as the second προβολή or " derivatio " of the Father, and thus as a permanently existing Being sharing in the Godhead itself; while once more others identified it with the eternal Son Himself. There were actually some too who were inclined to regard the Spirit, which is feminine in Hebrew, and which was identified with the " Wisdom " of God, as a female principle. [1] The views held regarding its rank and functions also were accordingly very different. All who regarded the Spirit as personal, subordinated it to the Father and probably also as a rule to the Son when they distinguished it from the latter, for the relation of Father and Son did not seem to permit of the existence of a third being of the same kind, and, besides, Christ had expressly said that he would send the Spirit, and therefore it looked as if the latter were His servant or messenger. The other idea that the Logos is the organ of the Spirit or Wisdom is very rarely met with. This or an idea similar to it was the one reached by those who distinguished between the impersonal Logos or Wisdom eternally inherent in God and the created Logos or Wisdom, and then identified the divine in Christ with the latter. As to its functions, we meet with no further speculations regarding their peculiar nature after the attempts of the Montanists to define them, until a very much later date when at last theologians had learned to commit a special department of the mysteries to the care of the Spirit. All that was meanwhile said regarding the activity of the Spirit in the world-process, in the history of revelation, in regeneration, including illumination and sanctification, was of a wholly vague kind, and was frequently either the expression of perplexity or of exegetical learning, but never gave evidence of any special theological interest in the question. We must not, however, overlook the fact that in Church theology in its oldest form as we see it in Irenæus

---

[1] The fact that in the original draft of the Apostolical Constitutions (II. 26) a parallel is drawn between the deaconess and the Holy Spirit is perhaps connected with this too.

and Tertullian, we find an attempt made to give to the Spirit,
which had necessarily to be ranked as a being of special dignity
within the Godhead, an immanent relation to the Father and
the· Son. The passages in Irenæus referring to the Spirit are
of special importance, though Tertullian was the first to call
Him "God". One can trace within theology a well-marked line
of development running from Justin through Tertullian to Origen.[1]
After Sabellius, starting from totally different premises, had by
his speculations drawn attention to the Holy Spirit, Origen
here too supplied a definite conception on the subject just as
he had in connection with the doctrine of the Logos. While
admitting the want of any certainty in what was given by tradition, he treated *the doctrine of the Holy Spirit entirely according
to the analogy of the doctrine of the Logos*, and even *demanded*
that it should be so treated. The Holy Spirit forms part of the
Godhead, it is a permanently existing divine Being, but it is at
the same time a creature, and a creature, in fact, which occupies
a stage lower than the Son, because it, like everything created,
has come into being by the Son or Logos. The sphere of its
activity is correspondingly smaller than that of the Son. Origen
declared that intensively it was more important, but he did not
give this its due value, since for him the categories of magnitude,
space, and causality were in the last resort the highest.[2] The
fact that the doctrine of the Holy Spirit was treated in Tertullian (adv. Prax.) and Origen in a way perfectly analogous to
that followed in the case of the doctrine of the Logos, is the
strongest possible proof that there was no specific theological
interest taken in this point of doctrine.[3] Nor was it different in

[1] But it is only in so far as Origen teaches the pre-temporal "processio" of
the Spirit that his doctrine betokens an advance on that of Tertullian, who still
essentially limits the action of the Spirit to the history of the world and of revelation. By the "unius substantiæ" which he regards as true of the Spirit also, Tertullian comes nearer the views which finally prevailed in the Fourth Century than
Origen. For the remarkable formula used by Hippolytus in connection with the
Spirit, see Vol. II., p. 261.

[2] On the doctrine of the Holy Spirit before Origen and in Origen see Vol. II.
passim, Kahnis, L. vom. h. Geist, 1847, Bigg, The Christian Platonists, 171 sq.,
Nitzsch, pp. 289—293.

[3] It is in Irenæus alone that we find indications of any specific speculation
regarding the Holy Spirit.

the period following. The Arian and the Arianising formulæ of the Fourth Century still at least embody the attempt to state in reference to the Spirit what, according to the old Church tradition, describes the character of its active working, little as that is; the pompous formula of orthodoxy, however, merely gives expression to the general thought that there is no foreign element in the Godhead, and shews, moreover, that the doctrine of the hypostasis of the Holy Spirit was already beginning to be an embarrassing one for the Church.

The doctrine of Origen that the Holy Spirit is an individual hypostasis and that it is a created being included within the sphere of the Godhead itself, found only very partial acceptance for more than a century. And even in the cases in which, under the influence of the baptismal formula, reference was made to a Trinity in the Godhead—which came to be more and more the practice,—the third Being was still left in the vague, and, as at an earlier period, we hear of the promised *gift* of the Holy Spirit. Nevertheless the philosophical theologians became more and more convinced that it was necessary to assume the presence not merely of a threefold economy in the Godhead, but of three divine beings or substances. In the first thirty years after the commencement of the Arian controversy, the Holy Spirit is scarcely ever mentioned,[1] although the Lucianists and consequently Arius too regarded it as indeed a divine hypostasis, but at the same time as the most perfect creature, which the Father had created through the Son and which therefore was inferior to the Son also in nature, dignity, and position.[2] In their Confessions they kept to the old simple tradition: πιστεύομεν καὶ εἰς τὸ πνεῦμα τὸ ἅγιον, τὸ εἰς παράκλησιν καὶ ἁγιασμὸν καὶ τελείωσιν τοῖς πιστεύουσι διδόμενον,[3] " and we believe

---

[1] See Basil., ep. 125: ὁ δὲ περὶ τοῦ πνεύματος λόγος ἐν παραδρομῇ κεῖται, οὐδεμιᾶς ἐξεργασίας ἀξιωθείς, διὰ τὸ μηδέπω τότε κεκινῆσθαι τὸ ζήτημα, *i.e.*, at the time of the Nicene Council.

[2] See above, p. 19. The view of Eunomius is representative of the whole group; see the documents which originated with him and Basil c. Eunom. III. 5. Epiphanius has pithily summarised the Arian doctrine (H. 69 c. 56): τὸ ἅγιον πνεῦμα κτίσμα πάλιν κτίσματός φασιν εἶναι διὰ τὸ διὰ τοῦ υἱοῦ τὰ πάντα γεγενῆσθαι (John I. 3).

[3] See the so-called Confession of Lucian, *i.e.*, the Second Creed of Antioch.; cf. besides the third and fourth formulæ of Antioch, the so-called formula of

in the Holy Spirit given to believers for consolation, and sanctification, and perfection." They recognised three graduated
hypostases in the Godhead. The fact that Athanasius did not
in the first instance think of the Spirit at all, regarding which
also nothing was fixed at Nicæa, is simply a proof of his intense
interest in his doctrine of the Son. The first trace of the
emergence of the question as to the Spirit is found, so far as I
know, in the Anathemas (20 ff.) of the very conservative Creed
of the Eusebian Council of Sirmium (351). Here the identification of the Holy Spirit with the unbegotten God and with the
Son, as also the designation of it as μέρος τοῦ πατρὸς ἢ τοῦ υἱοῦ,
(part of the Father and of the Son,) are forbidden.[1] It was
towards the end of the fifties that Athanasius directed his
attention to the doctrine of the Holy Spirit, and he at once
took up a firm position.[2] If the Holy Spirit belongs to the
Godhead it must be worshipped, if it is an independent being
then all that holds good of the Son holds good of it *also*, for
otherwise the Triad would be divided and blasphemed and the
rank of the Son too would again become doubtful—this is for
him a conclusive argument. There can be nothing foreign,
nothing created in the Triad which is just the one God (ὅλη
τριὰς εἷς Θεός ἐστιν). Athanasius was not only able to adduce
a number of passages from Scripture in support of this assertion,
but he also endeavoured to verify his view by a consideration
of the functions of the Holy Spirit. The principle of sanctification cannot be of the same nature as the beings which it sanctifies; the source of life for creatures cannot itself be a creature;

Sardica—a proof that the orthodox theologians of the West had not yet given
attention to the question; their statement: πιστεύομεν τὸν παράκλητον, τὸ ἅγιον
πνεῦμα, ὅπερ ἡμῖν αὐτὸς ὁ κύριος καὶ ἐπηγγείλατο καὶ ἔπεμψεν· καὶ τοῦτο πιστεύομεν πεμφθέν, καὶ τοῦτο οὐ πέπονθεν, ἀλλ᾽ ὁ ἄνθρωπος, if it has been correctly
handed down, shews, besides, a highly suspicious want of clearness; further the formula
macrostich., the formulæ of Philippopolis and the later Sirmian and Homœan
formulæ; in the formula of 357 we have "spiritus paracletus per filium est."

[1] The theology of Marcellus might certainly have drawn the attention of the
theologians to the doctrine of the Spirit; for Marcellus discussed this doctrine
although not with fulness; see Zahn, op. cit., p. 147 ff. According to Marcellus
the Spirit proceeds from the Father *and* from the Logos, and forms part of the
divine substance; its special work does not, however, begin till after that of the Son.

[2] See Athanas. ad Serap.

he who is the medium whereby we enter into fellowship with the Divine nature must himself possess this nature.[1] On the other hand, He who works as the Father and the Son work, or to put it more accurately, He who bestows one and the same grace—for there is only *one* grace, namely, that of the Father through the Son in the Holy Spirit—is part of the Godhead, and whoever rejects Him separates himself from the Faith generally. Thus everything is really already expressed in the baptismal formula; for without the Holy Spirit it would be destroyed, since it is the Spirit who throughout *completes* or perfects what is done. The personality of the Spirit is simply presupposed by Athanasius in the indefinite form in which he also presupposed the personality of the Son. The attempts to distinguish the peculiar nature of the activity of the Spirit from that of the Father and the Son did not indeed get beyond empty words such as perfection, connection, termination of activity, etc. The question as to why the Son could not do all this Himself, and why, if there was here a third, the existence of a Fourth was not also possible, was left unanswered. It is necessary to believe in the Trinity as handed down by tradition: "and it is manifest that the Spirit is not one being of the many nor an angel [one of many], but one unique being, or rather, He belongs to the Logos who is one, and to God who is one, and is also of the same substance" (καὶ οὐκ ἄδηλον, ὅτι οὐκ ἔστι τῶν πολλῶν τὸ πνεῦμα, ἀλλ᾽ οὐδὲ ἄγγελος, ἀλλ᾽ ἕν ὄν. μᾶλλον δὲ τοῦ λόγου ἑνὸς ὄντος ἴδιον καὶ τοῦ Θεοῦ ἑνὸς ὄντος ἴδιον καὶ ὁμοούσιόν ἐστιν).[2] The "Tropicists" as he calls those who teach erroneous doctrine in reference to the Holy Spirit, are in his view no better than the Arians.

---

[1] Passages op. cit., above all, I. 23, 24: εἰ κτίσμα δὲ ἦν τὸ πνεῦμα τὸ ἅγιον, οὐκ ἄν τις ἐν αὐτῷ μετουσία τοῦ Θεοῦ γένοιτο ἡμῖν· ἀλλ᾽ ἢ ἄρα κτίσματι μὲν συνηπτόμεθα, ἀλλότριοι δὲ τῆς θείας φύσεως ἐγινόμεθα, ὡς κατὰ μηδὲν αὐτῆς μετέχοντες ... εἰ δὲ τῇ τοῦ πνεύματος μετουσία γινόμεθα κοινωνοὶ θείας φύσεως, μαίνοιτ᾽ ἄν τις λέγων τὸ πνεῦμα τῆς κτιστῆς φύσεως, καὶ μὴ τῆς τοῦ Θεοῦ· διὰ τοῦτο γὰρ καὶ ἐν οἷς γίνεται οὗτοι θεοποιοῦνται· εἰ δὲ θεοποιεῖ, οὐκ ἀμφίβολον, ὅτι ἡ τούτου φύσις Θεοῦ ἐστι.

[2] Ad Serap. I. 27. Athanasius also appeals in support of this belief to the tradition of the Catholic Church (c. 28 sq.), though he is able to construe it ideally only and does not quote any authorities.

The letters of Athanasius to Serapion of Thmuis were called
forth by the complaints of this bishop about the intrigues of
those who taught false doctrine regarding the Holy Spirit. As
a matter of fact, amongst the Semi-Arians the doctrine of the
Holy Spirit was now purposely developed in opposition to the
Homousia. It was in particular the highly esteemed chief of
the Thracian Semi-Arians, Macedonius, at a later date the deposed
bishop of Constantinople, who defended the doctrine that the
Spirit is a creature similar to the angels, a being subordinate
to the Father and the Son and in their service.[1] It is worth
noting with regard to these Semi-Arians that the more their
common opposition to the Homœans and Anomœans drove
them to side with the Nicæans the more firmly they stuck to
their doctrine of the Spirit. It looked as if they wished to
preserve in their doctrine of the Holy Spirit the Conservativism
which they had had to abandon as regards the doctrine of the
Son. It was at the Synod of Alexandria (362) that the orthodox
first took up the definite position with regard to this question
that whoever regards the Holy Spirit as a creature and separates
it from the substance of Christ, in so doing divides up the
Holy Trinity, gives a hypocritical adherence to the Nicene
Faith, and has merely in appearance renounced Arianism.[2] But
what was thus firmly established by the Alexandrians by no
means at once became law for the orthodox in the East. The
statements regarding the Spirit[3] were indeed further amplified

---

[1] On Macedonius see the articles in the Diction. of Chr. Biogr. and in Herzog's
R.-Encykl, and in addition Gwatkin, pp. 160—181, 208. The doctrine is given
in Athan. ad Serap. I. 1 f. Socrat. II. 45, 38, Sozom. IV. 27, etc., Basil, ep. 251,
Theodoret. II. 6. The Macedonians laid stress on the difference between the particles ἐκ, διά, ἐν, as used of the hypostases, and emphasised the fact that the Holy
Scripture does not describe the Holy Spirit as an object of adoration, and pointed
out that the relation of Father and Son did not admit of a third. What the τρίτη
διαθήκη of the Macedonians was (see Gregor. Naz. Orat. 31. 7), I do not know.

[2] See Athan., Tom. ad Antioch. 3, see also 5: τὸ ἅγιον πνεῦμα οὐ κτίσμα οὐδὲ
ξένον ἀλλ᾽ ἴδιον καὶ ἀδιαίρετον τῆς οὐσίας τοῦ υἱοῦ καὶ τοῦ πατρός.

[3] The formula of the revised Creed of Jerusalem, i.e., the later Creed of Constantinople, is characteristic. It only demands the complete adoration and glorifying
of the Spirit along with the Father and Son, but otherwise confines itself to general
predicates: " τὸ κύριον, τὸ ζωοποιόν, τὸ ἐκ τοῦ πατρὸς ἐκπορευόμενον, τὸ λαλῆσαν
διὰ τῶν προφητῶν." These are undoubtedly of a very exalted kind and seem also

in subsequent years in connection with the remodelling of the
old Confessions, but amongst the Homoiousians who were becoming Homousians, the greatest uncertainty continued to prevail
up till 380. The thirty-first oration of Gregory of Nazianzus
which was composed at that time, proves this.[1] Meanwhile it
was just the Cappadocians who did most towards getting the
orthodox conception naturalised in the Church, namely, Basil
in his work against Eunomius (lib. III.) and in the tractate "de
spiritu sancto," Gregory of Nazianzus in several of his orations
(31, 37, 44), and Gregory of Nyssa in his amplifications of
Trinitarian doctrine. They had apparently learned something
from the letters of Athanasius ad Serap., for they repeat his
arguments and give them more formal development. But neither
in Basil nor in Gregory of Nazianzus is there the stringency
which marks the thought of Athanasius. The absence of any
tangible tradition exercised a strong influence [2] on them, and
at bottom they are already satisfied—Basil at any rate—with
the avowal that the Spirit is not in any sense a creature.[3]

to exclude the idea of the dependence of the Spirit on the Son, but nevertheless
they do not get the length of the complete Homousia.

[1] He writes, "Of the wise amongst us some consider the Holy Spirit to be an
energy, others a creature, others God, while others again cannot make up their
minds to adopt any definite view out of reverence for Scripture, as they put it,
because it does not make any very definite statement on the point. On this
account they neither accord to Him divine adoration nor do they refuse it to
Him, and thus take a middle road, but which is really a very bad path. Of those
again who hold Him to be God, some keep this pious belief to themselves, while
others state it openly. Others to a certain degree measure the Godhead since like
us they accept the Trinity, but they put a great distance between the three by
maintaining that the first is infinite in substance and power, the second in power,
but not in substance, while the third is infinite in neither of these two respects."
For the details see Ullmann, p. 264 f.; at pages 269—275 he has set forth
the doctrine of Gregory regarding the Holy Spirit, together with the Scriptural
proofs.

[2] Gregory of Nazianzus has consequently (Orat. 31.2) to begin by remarking
that he had been accused of introducing a Θεὸς ξένος καὶ ἄγραφος. He himself
practically admits the want of any explicit Scriptural proof, and has recourse to
the plea (c. 3) that "love of the letter is a cloak for impiety." Basil undoubtedly
appealed (de s. s. 29) to Irenæus, Clemens Alex., Origen, and Dionysius of Rome
in defence of his doctrine, but he felt all the same that there was little evidence
in support of it. Gregory made a similar admission.

[2] Cf. also the remarkable words of Gregory of Naz. Vol. III., p. 230. The striking
utterances of the Cappadocians regarding the letter of Holy Scripture, tradition

Gregory of Nyssa as an Origenist and speculative Trinitarian carried the doctrine further.[1] As the theologians were at a loss how to accord to the Spirit a peculiar mode of being in relation to the Father, they hit upon the plan of attributing to it, following some passages in St John, eternal sending

kerygma, and dogma all owe their origin to the troublesome situation created by the doctrine of the Holy Spirit. The Greeks of later days no longer found themselves in such a predicament of this kind, and consequently they did not require to repeat the bold statements regarding tradition.

[1] See also the work of Didymus, περὶ τριάδος, edid. Mingarelli, particularly the Second Book, c. 6 sq., written about 380, which contains the fullest Fourth Century proof of the complete Godhead of the Holy Spirit which we possess. Previous to this Didymus had already composed a tractate "de spiritu sancto". Of special interest further is the "οἰκονομία", that is, the pædagogic or politic reticence which the Cappadocians permitted themselves and others in connection with the doctrine of the Holy Spirit. According to Gregory of Naz. God Himself merely *indicated* the Godhead of the Holy Spirit in the N. T. and did not plainly reveal it till later on in order not to lay too great a burden on men (!)—a theory which overthrows the whole Catholic doctrine of tradition. It is thus also permitted to the faithful now to imitate this divine "economy" and *to bring forward the doctrine of the Spirit with caution and to introduce it gradually*. "Those who *regard* the Holy Spirit as God are godly men illuminated with knowledge, and those who *say that He is God, when this is done in presence of well-disposed hearers, have something heroic about them; but if it be done in presence of the vulgar-minded it shews that they do not possess the true teaching wisdom* (εἰ δὲ ταπεινοῖς, οὐκ οἰκονομικοι), because they are casting their pearls into the mud, or are giving strong meat instead of milk," and so on (Orat. 41.6). Gregory defends the conduct of Basil also, who, watched by the Arians in his lofty post in Cæsarea, guarded against openly calling the Holy Spirit "God" because the γυμνὴ φωνή that the Holy Spirit is God would have cost him his bishopric. (Orat. 43.68.) He acknowledged the Godhead of the Spirit "economically" only, *i.e.*, when the time was suitable for so doing. He was sharply blamed for this conduct by the rigidly orthodox clerics, as Gregory tells us (Ep. 26, al. 20). They complained that while Basil expressed himself admirably regarding the Father and the Son, he tore away the Spirit from the divine fellowship as rivers wash away the sand on their banks and hollow out the stones; he did not frankly confess the truth, but acted rather from policy than from truly pious feeling, and concealed the ambiguity of his teaching by the art of speech. Gregory who was regarded as a suspected person himself, stood up for his friend; a man, he said, occupying such an important post as Basil did, must surely proceed with some prudence and circumspection in proclaiming the truth (βέλτιον οἰκονομηθῆναι τὴν ἀλήθειαν) and make some concession to the haziness of the spirit of the time so as not to still further damage the good cause by any public pronouncement. The difference between Athanasius and the *religious*-orthodox on the one hand, and the *theological*-orthodox on the other, comes out here with special clearness. Athanasius would have indignantly rejected that "οἰκονομηθῆναι τὴν ἀλήθειαν", because he did not regard God Him-

forth (ἔκπεμψις) and procession (ἐκπόρευσις). Just as in the second century the begetting of Christ whereby he came to exist on this earth had been made into a super-terrestrial begetting then became an eternal begetting, while the "being begotten" next came to be regarded as the supreme characteristic of the second hypostasis, so in the fourth century an "eternal sending" of the Spirit was made out of the promised "sending" of the Holy Spirit and was regarded as descriptive of the essential characteristic of the third hypostasis within the Holy Trinity. Nowhere can the work of imaginative conception be more plainly recognised than here. Behind a history already in itself a wonderful one, and the scene of which is laid partly in the Godhead and partly within humanity, there was put by a process of abstraction and reduplication a second history the events of which are supposed to pass entirely within the Godhead itself. The former history is to get its stability through the latter which comprises "the entire mystery of our Faith."

The matter was much more quickly settled in the West. Hilary, it is true, was anything but clear as regards doctrine, but this was merely because he had eaten of the tree of Greek theology. The general unreasoned conviction in the West was that the Holy Spirit, belief in whom was avowed in the Apostles' Creed, is the one God likewise.

When the question as to the personality of the Spirit emerged, it was as quickly settled that it must be a *persona*, for the nature of God is not so poor that His Spirit cannot be a person.—(It has to be noted that *persona* and our "person" are not the same thing.) The views of Lactantius again on this point were different. Since the year 362 the orthodox at several Councils in the West and then in Asia had pronounced in favour of

self as a politician or a pedagogue, who acts κατ᾽ οἰκονομίαν, but as the Truth. If he had ever acted as the Cappadocians did, the Homœans would have been the victors. Still, on the other hand, we ought not to judge the Cappadocians too severely. As followers of Origen they regarded the loftiest utterances of the Faith as *Science*; but Science admits, in fact often demands a pedagogic and economic or accommodating method of procedure. Just as Basil made a distinction between κηρύγματα and δόγματα, so Gregory (Orat. 40) concluded his Decalogue of Faith with the words: ἔχεις τοῦ μυστηρίου τὰ ἔκφορα, καὶ ταῖς τῶν πολλῶν ἀκοαῖς οὐκ ἀπόρρητα· τὰ δὲ ἄλλα εἴσω μαθήσῃ, τῆς τριάδος χαριζομένης, ἃ καὶ κρύφεις παρὰ σεαυτῷ σφραγῖδι κρατούμενα.

the complete Godhead of the Spirit [1] in opposition to the Arians, as we see from the Confession of Eunomius, and also to the Pneumatomachians. [2] The big Eastern Council summoned to meet at Constantinople in 381 by Theodosius orginally included thirty-six Macedonians amongst its members. But they could not be got to assent to the new doctrine of the Holy Spirit, spite of all the imperial efforts made to win them over. They were accordingly compelled to leave the Council. [3] The latter reaffirmed the Nicene Creed, but gave to it a detailed dogmatic explanation which has not been preserved, in which the complete homousia of the Spirit was avowed, and in the same way the first canon of the Council passes condemnation on the Semi-Arians or "Pneumatomachians". [4] The pronouncements of the years following confirmed the final result; see the epistle of the Council of Constantinople of 382, [5] but above all, the anathemas of Damasus. [6] The doctrine of the homousia of the Spirit from this time onward was as much a part of orthodoxy as the doctrine of the homousia of the Son. But since according to

---

[1] Their leaders, in addition to Macedonius, were Eustathius of Sebaste, Eleusius of Cyzikus, and probably also Basil of Ancyra. In Marathonius of Nicomedia the party had a member who was held in high honour both because of his position and his ascetic life. The Macedonians in general made a deep impression on their contemporaries by their ascetic practices and by their determined struggle against the Homœans. In the countries on the Hellespont they were the most important party.

[2] The most important utterances are the Epistle of the Alexandrian Council of 363, the declarations of the Westerns under Damasus in the years 369, 376, 377, the resolution of an Illyrian Council, (given in Theodoret IV. 9), the Council at Antioch in 379, which is decisive as regards the East in so far as those present avowed their belief in the Western doctrine including the doctrine of the Spirit. Compare, besides, the Confession of Basil (Hahn, § 121): βαπτίζομεν εἰς τριάδα ὁμοούσιον, that of Epiphanius in the Ancorat. (374): πνεῦμα ἄκτιστον, and that produced by Charisius (Hahn, § 144): πνεῦμα ὁμοούσιον πατρὶ καὶ υἱῷ.

[3] See Socr. V. 8; Sozom. VII. 7, 9; Theodoret V. 8.

[4] It follows from a communication of the Council held at Constantinople in 382, that the Council issued a "tomus" on the doctrine of the Trinity. That the formula in reference to the Holy Spirit which is given in the so-called Creed of Constantinople, did not proceed from the Council of 381 and cannot have proceeded from it, since it is not sufficiently different from the view of the Macedonians, has been shewn above, p. 93.

[5] Theodoret V. 9.

[6] C. 16 f., see Theodoret V. 11.

the Greek way of conceiving of the matter, the Father continued to be regarded as the root of the Godhead, the perfect homousia of the Holy Spirit necessarily always seemed to the Greeks to be called in question whenever he was derived from the Son *also*. He consequently seemed to be inferior to the Son and thus to be a grandchild of the Father, or else to possess a double root. Then, besides, the dependence of the Spirit on the Son was obstinately maintained by the Arians and Semi-Arians on the ground that certain passages in the Bible supported this view, and in the interest of their conception of a descending Trinity in *three* stages. Thus the Greeks had constantly to watch and see that the procession of the Spirit from the Father *alone* was taught, and after the revised Creed of Jerusalem became an ecumenical Creed, they had a sacred text in support of their doctrine, which came to be as important as the doctrine itself.

II. The Cappadocians [1] and their great teacher, Apollinaris of Laodicea, [2] before them, reached *the* doctrine of the Trinity, which remained the dominant one in the Church, though it always continued to be capable of being differently restated by

---

[1] Athanasius prepared the way in his letters ad Serapionem.

[2] As is proved by his correspondence with Basil and as his own writings shew, Apollinaris was the first who completely *developed* the orthodox doctrine of the Trinity. He was, however, more strongly influenced by Aristotle than the Cappadocians were, and accordingly in his case the conception of the *one* divine substance was a shade nearer the idea of a mere generic conception than with them, although he too was in no way satisfied with the genuine conception (see above p. 84). Apollinaris further retained the old image of αὐγή, ἀκτίς, ἥλιος, not, however, as it would appear, in order by it to illustrate the unity, but rather the difference in the greatness of the persons (περὶ τριάδ. 12, 17). (The Logos had already a side turned in the direction of finitude.) His followers afterwards directly objected to the doctrine of the Cappadocians and vice versa. We are now better acquainted with Apollinaris's doctrine of the Trinity than formerly, since Dräseke (Ztschr. f. K.-Gesch. VI., p. 503 ff.) has shewn it to be very probable that the pseudo-Justinian Ἔκθεσις πίστεως ἤτοι περὶ τριάδος is by him, and that the detailed statements of Gregory of Nazianzus in the first letter to Kledonius refer to this work (op. cit., p. 515 ff.). From the work, κατὰ μέρος πίστις, which Caspari has rightly claimed for Apollinaris (Alte und neue Quellen, 1879, p. 65 f.), and which represents a dogmatic advance as compared with the tractate περὶ τριάδος, it likewise follows that Apollinaris is to be reckoned amongst the founders of the orthodox doctrine of the Trinity,—also because of his advanced doctrine of the Holy Spirit in which he teaches the homousia—and that in fact he ought to be called the very first of these.

theologians. We are to believe in *one* God, because we are to believe in *one* divine substance or essence (οὐσία, φύσις, essentia, substantia, natura) in three distinct subjects or persons (ὑπόστασις, persona [πρόσωπον]). The substance is to be thought of neither as a mere generic conception nor, on the other hand, as a fourth alongside of the three subjects, but as a reality, *i.e.*, the unity must coincide with the real substance. The subjects again are not to be represented as mere attributes nor, on the other hand, as separate persons, but as independent, though apart from their mutual relationship, unthinkable, partakers of the divine substance. Their likeness of nature which is involved in their community of substance finds expression in the identity of their attributes and activities, their difference in the characteristic note (τρόπος ὑπάρξεως, ἰδίωμα) of their *manner* of existence as signified by the ideas, unbegotten, begotten, proceeding from (ἀγεννησία, γεννησία, ἐκπόρευσις). The special characteristic attached to the Father implies that He is the source, the root, the first principle of the Godhead, while the two other persons—*within* the divine substance—are "caused". The Father is greater than the other two in so far as He is the first principle and the cause (κατὰ τὸν τῆς ἀρχῆς καὶ αἰτίας λόγον). The Godhead is consequently in itself and *apart from all relation to the world*, an inexhaustible living existence and no rigid and barren unity, "as the Jews teach." Yet neither is it a divided multiplicity "as the heathen think", but, on the contrary, unity in Trinity and Trinity in unity. Because the Godhead is what is common to the Three, there is only one God. At the same time the hypostatic difference is not to be regarded as a merely nominal one, but it has not reference to the substance, the will, the energy, the power, time, and consequently not to the rank of the persons. From the unity results the unity of activity. Every divine act is to be understood as a working of the Father through the Son in the Holy Spirit as is expressed in the terms, primal source, mediating power, and completion. See, above all, Gregor. Naz. Orat. 27—32.

This doctrinal system shews itself to be a radical modification of the system of *Origen* under the influence of the religious thought defended by Athanasius and the West, that the Godhead which appeared, Jesus Christ, and the Godhead which is still active in the Church, the Holy Spirit, are the Godhead themselves.[1] The Cappadocians were pupils both of Origen[2] and of Athanasius. This fact explains their doctrinal system.

Before them, however, there had been a theologian in the ancient Church who had come under influences wholly similar to those which had affected them, and who because of this, also anticipated in a striking way their formulæ when he saw that he must amplify the doctrine of God. *This was Tertullian.* Tertullian's theology was dependent on the one hand on Justin and the Apologists, and on the other on Irenæus, but besides this the modalistic Monarchianism which at that time held sway in the West and which he combatted, exercised a strong influence upon him. Consequently the conditions under which Tertullian composed his work " adv. Praxean "were, *mutatis mutandis,* the same as those by which the Cappadocians were surrounded, and they accordingly led to a similar result, so that we may say: *the orthodox doctrine of the Trinity already announced its presence even in its details, in Tertullian—and only in him and in his pupil Novatian.*[3] Did not Hosius carry it into the East? (See above p. 57.)

[1] Gregory designates as opponents of the correct doctrine of the Trinity (1) the Sabellians, (2) the Arians, (3)—this is extremely remarkable—the hyper-orthodox who teach the doctrine of three Gods equal in substance (οἱ ἄγαν παρ' ἡμῖν ὀρθό-δοξοι, Orat. 2, 37). The true orthodoxy is always represented as the *middle-path.* For details, see Ullmann, pp. 232—275.

[2] The theology of Origen was transplanted into the Pontus country by Gregorius Thaumaturgus. It is thus that Marcellus also probably became acquainted with it and combatted it.

[3] Owing to the importance of the matter it may be allowable here to go back again to Tertullian (see Vol. ii., p. 258 f.). The crude part of his doctrine and the points in which it diverges from Cappadocian orthodoxy are indeed sufficiently obvious. Son and Spirit proceed from the Father solely in view of the work of creation and revelation; the Father can send forth as many "officiales" as He chooses (adv. Prax. 4); Son and Spirit do not possess the entire substance of the Godhead, but on the contrary are " portiones " (9); they are subordinate to the Father (minores); they are in fact transitory manifestations: the Son at last gives everything back again to the Father; the Father alone is absolutely invisible, and though the Son is indeed invisible too, He can become visible and can do things which would be simply unworthy of the Father, and so on. All these utterances along with other things shew that Tertullian was a theologian who occupied a position between Justin and Origen. But the remarkable thing is that at the same time we have a view in a highly developed form which coincides with the Cappadocian view, and—this is genuinely Western—in some points in fact approaches nearer

The Christological dogma with its formula had already had a share in the establishment of the Trinitarian dogma. Tertullian had already made use of the same conceptions for giving a fixed form both to his doctrine of God and to his Christology (adv. Prax.). The form taken by the Trinitarian doctrine of the

Modalism and the teaching of Athanasius than that of Gregory and has a strong resemblance to the doctrine of an immanent Trinity, without actually being such: the Godhead in substantia, status, potestas, virtus, is one (2 ff.), there is only *one* divine substance and therefore there are not two or three Gods or Lords (13, 19). In this one substance there is no separatio, or divisio, or dispersio, or diversitas (3, 8, 9), though there is indeed a distributio, distinctio, dispositio, dispensatio (9, 13), an οἰκονομία in short, a differentia per distinctionem (14). Accordingly the unitas substantiæ is not in any way a singularitas numeri (22, 25)—God is not unicus et singularis (12)—but it comprises three nomina or species, formæ gradus, res, *personæ*, (Tertullian here, however, usually avoids the use of all substantives), see 2, 8 etc. No one of these is a mere attribute, on the contrary each is a substantiva res ex ipsius dei substantia (26); there are thus tres res et tres species unius et indivisæ substantiæ (19); these, however, are most intimately connected together (conjuncti 27); they are tres cohærentes (8, 25) without, however, being one (masc.) [rather are they one (neut. 22, 25)], because the second and the third spring ex unitate patris (19) and are accordingly God as He is, individui et inseparati a patre (18). In the divine substance there are in fact conserti et connexi gradus (8). These three gradus or persons are different from each other in proprietas and conditio, but not in substance (8, 11, 14, 15, 17, 18, 24, 25). The peculiar property of the Father is that He is a nullo prolatus et innatus (19) and also absolutely invisible. The Son is also invisible in virtue of the substance, but visible as to his conditio (14). In virtue of the substance there is in fact a perfect *societas nominum*; even the Son in accordance with this is "almighty" (17, 18). It is thus necessary to believe in the unitas ex semetipsa derivans trinitatem. This has already become an established truth as against Jews and heathen. What is most instructive of all, however, is to notice Tertullian's use of "persona" as distinguished from "substantia", because it is here that he has most plainly prepared the way for the later orthodox phraseology. The Latin Bible supplied Tertullian with the word "persona"; for (adv. Prax. 6) in Proverbs VIII. 30 it had "cottidie oblectabar in *persona* ejus" and in Lamentations IV. 20 (adv. Prax. 14) "spiritus personæ ejus Christus dominus." (The LXX. has πρόσωπον in both passages.) Both passages must have attracted special notice. But Tertullian was further a jurist, and as such the conceptions "persona" and "substantia" were quite familiar to him. I accordingly conjecture—and it is probably more than a conjecture—that Tertullian always continued to be influenced in his use of these words by the juristic usage, as is specially evident from his naive idea of a substantia impersonalis and from the sharp distinction he draws between persona and substantia. From the juristic point of view there is as little objection to the formula that several persons are possessors of one and the same substance or property, that they are in uno statu, as to the other formula that one person possesses several substances unmixed. (See Tertullian's Christology adv. Prax. 27; Vol. ii., p. 281.) The fact that Tertullian, so far as I know, never renders "substance" by "natura"—although he takes the latter to in-

Homoiousians, as represented by Basil of Ancyra and of Apollinaris, was likewise determined by their Christological speculations.
(It was Christological speculation which produced the " ὁμοίωμα "

clude substance—seems to me as conclusively in favour of my view as the other
fact that, in the introduction to his work (3), he attempted to elucidate the problem
by making use of an image drawn from the spheres of law and politics. "Monarchy does not always require to be administered by *one* despot ; on the contrary he
may name proximæ personæ officiales, and exercise authority through them and
along with them ; it does not cease to be *one* government, especially when the
Son is the co-administrator. Son and Father are, however, consortes substantiæ
patris." Tertullian's exposition of the doctrine in which he hit upon the spirit of
the West was, however, hardly understood in the East. In the East the question
was taken up in a philosophical way, and there the difficulties first made themselves felt, which in the juristic way of looking at the matter had been kept in
the background. In the latter "persona" is sometimes manifestation, sometimes
ideal subject, sometimes fictive subject, sometimes "individuum", and "substantia" is the property, the substance, the Real, the actual content of the subject
as distinguished from its form and manifestation (persona). It is significant that
Tertullian is also able to use nomen, species, forma, gradus, and in fact even res
for "persona", so elastic is the conception, while for "substantia" he has deitas,
virtus, potestas, status. On the other hand, when the question is viewed philosophically it is difficult, it is in fact actually impossible to distinguish between nature
and person. The following passages will illustrate Tertullian's use of words, (ad
v. persona): adv. Valent. 4: "personales substantiæ", sharply distinguished from
"sensus, affectus, motus"; adv. Prax. 7: "filius ex sua persona profitetur patrem";
ibid: " Non vis eum substantivum habere in re per substantiæ proprietatem, ut res
et persona quædam videri possit" (scil. Logos); ibid: "quæcumque ergo substantia
sermonis (τοῦ λόγου) fuit, illam dico personam"; 11: "filii personam ... sic et
cetera, quæ nunc ad patrem de filio vel ad filium, nunc ad filium de patre vel ad
patrem, nunc ad spiritum pronuntiantur, unamquamque personam in sua proprietate constituunt"; 12: "alium autem quomodo accipere debeas jam professus sum,
personæ, non substantiæ, nomine, ad distinctionem non ad divisionem"; 13: "si
una persona et dei et domini in scripturis inveniretur, etc."; 14: "si Christus personæ paternæ spiritus est, merito spiritus, cujus personæ erat, id est patris, eum
faciem suam ex unitate scilicet pronuntiavit"; 15: "manifesta et personalis distinctio conditionis (this too is a juristic conception) patris et filii"; 18: "pater prima
persona, quæ ante filii nomen erat proponenda.'; 21: " quo dicto (Matt. XVI. 17)
Christus utriusque personæ constituit distinctionem"; 23: (on John XII. 28) "quot
personæ tibi videntur, Praxea?" ..."Non propter me ista vox (John XII. 30)
venit, sed propter vos, ut credant et hi et patrem et filium in suis quemque nominibus et personis et locis"; 24: " duarum personarum conjunctio (in reference to
John XIV. 10 " apparet proprietas utriusque personæ ")"; 26: " nam nec semel sed
ter ad singula nomina in personas singulas tinguimur "; 27: " Father and Son
must not be distinguished in una persona "; c. 27: " videmus duplicem statum non
confusum sed conjunctum in una persona, deum et hominem Jesum "; 31: " sic
voluit deus renovare sacramentum, ut nove unus crederetur per filium et spiritum,
ut coram iam deus in suis propriis nominibus et personis cognosceretur."

[likeness] and which gave currency to the analogy of the conceptions. "Humanity" and "Adam" in relation to individual
men.)[1] But the Cappadocians learned from them. Quod erat
in causa, apparet in effectu! An Aristotelian and a Subordinationist element lurks in the orthodox doctrine of the Trinity
as well as this element of dependence upon Christological
dogma. The Christological controversies accordingly could not
but re-act on the form given to the dogma of the Trinity.
That their influence was not stronger than the historical evidence
shews it actually to have been, is to be explained solely by
the rigid form taken by the dogma so quickly rendered sacred
by tradition. Anything in the way of modification was unsuccessful, and accordingly the attempts in this direction belong
not to the history of dogma, but of theology. Some Monophysites who were influenced by the Aristotelian philosophy and
who were thus scholars of the same type as Apollinaris, but
who were also Chalcedonian theologians, attempted to give a
dialectic shape to the ambiguous conceptions of "Nature" and
"Person" in the Church. In doing this they naturally landed
either in Tritheism or in Unitarianism, which their opponents could
also represent as Quaternity whenever the three persons were
reckoned as belonging to the one real Substance as Reals and
not as attributes. The departure on the part of the Monophysites from orthodox dogma had not a philosophical cause only,
though the period was one in which there had been a revival
of Aristotelian study, but was also the result of their Christology. Since in their Christology they regarded φύσις (nature)
as equal to ὑπόστασις (hypostasis),[2] it naturally suggested itself
to them to carry out the same equation in reference to the

---

[1] Natural theology also exercised an influence here and did good service to the
Homousios. If it is certain that man has been created καθ' ὁμοίωσιν of God, and
if the view—a view which was indeed rejected—could even suggest itself, that
his spirit is a portio dei (substantia divina), then the Logos appeared to have no
advantage over man if the Homoousia were not attributed to Him.

[2] Οὐκ ἔστι φύσις ἀνυπόστατος—said both Monophysites and Nestorians in setting
forth their Christology. This was applied to the Trinity. But the orthodox too in
so far as they were Aristotelians, shunned the platonic—which was also the juristic—
fiction of a φύσις ἀνυπόστατος, and this was bound to create difficulties in connection
with their doctrine of the Trinity. The Theopaschian controversy is connected with
this; see Chap. III.

Trinity. But if οὐσία or φύσις be regarded as equivalent to ὑπόστασις then we have Unitarianism; while if on the other hand, in making this equation we start from the hypostasis, we have three gods. Both of these doctrines were taught amongst the Monophysites in the sixth century, or to put it more accurately, from about 530.[1] In opposition to the Tritheists Johannes Damascenus, although he was himself strongly influenced by Aristotle and based his theology on the work of the Cappadocians, gave a Modalistic turn to the theological exposition of the dogma of the Trinity, and in so doing sought to get rid of the last remains of Subordinationism. It is true that he also grants that the Father is greater than the Son (de fide orthodox. I. 8) because He is the Principle of the Son, a view which Athanasius too, founding on John XIV. 28, had always maintained, but he nevertheless conceives of the being unbegotten (ἀγεννησία) in a still higher fashion than the Cappadocians had done—namely, as a mode of being of the same kind as the being begotten (γεννησία) and procession (ἐκπόρευσις), and in order to put the unity of the Hypostases on a firm basis he not only emphasises much more strongly the "in one another" (ἐν ἀλλήλοις) which had already been maintained before this, rejecting the Apollinarian analogy of human-substance and man, and teaching that each person is not less dependent on others than on himself, but he also uses the questionable formula that the difference between them exists only for thought (ἐπινοία), and that there exists between them a pervasion (περιχώρησις) with-

---

[1] Of the Monophysite Tritheists the most important are Askusnages, Johannes Philoponus against whom Leontius of Byzantium wrote "de sectis", and Peter of Kallinico. On the works of John, see the article in the Dict. of Christ. Biogr.; an important fragment in Joh. Damasc., de hær. 83 from the "Diætetes" of John. Here it may be plainly seen that Christology determined the form of John's doctrine of the Trinity, but that he sought to give out as Church doctrine his Aristotelian conception of the Hypostasis, viz., Nature reaching manifestation in an "individuum", Nature itself existing only in the single substance, or in the Idea. From Leontius we gather that John spoke of τρεῖς μερικαὶ οὐσίαι and accepted the notion of an οὐσία κοινή which, however, exists only in conception. This doctrine caused divisions amongst the Monophysites, and these led the Coptic patriarch Damian to emphasise so strongly the reality of the one substance, that he could be represented as a Tetradite, although at the same time he probably took away from the independence of the persons. Cf. the Art. "Tritheistic' ɔr Streit" by Gass in the R.-Encykl.

out, however, any blending (συναλοιφή) and mixture (σύμφυρσις)
(I. 8). In his case too this way of putting the dogma was
determined by the Christological dogma.[1]

In the Eastern Church the further development of the dogma
of the Trinity beyond the limit reached by the Cappadocians
had no appreciable result.[2] It was too unimportant in itself,
and, above all, it left untouched the point in connection with
which the placing of the Father above the other Hypostases
came most plainly to the front. John also (I. 8) taught
that the Holy Spirit proceeds *from the Father*.[3] He further
simply repeated the old statements that the Spirit proceeds
through the Son, that He is the image of the Son as the latter
is of the Father, and that He is the mediation between Father
and Son, although in his day the doctrine of the Latins—the
filioque—was already known in the East.[4] The Easterns clung
to the statements in support of which they alleged countless
passages from the writings of the Fathers of the Fourth Century,
that the Spirit proceeds from the Father, or from the Father
through the Son. As against the Arians and Semi-Arians they
emphasised the Spirit's independence of the Son, in so far as

---

[1] See on this Bach, DG. des MA. I., pp. 53 ff., 67 ff. In the Tritheistic propositions and in the counter-movement we have the beginning of the mediæval
controversy regarding Realism and Nominalism.

[2] On the other hand the fact that the most distinguished teacher of the East
propounded a doctrine of the Trinity which seems to be akin to that of Augustine
was of importance for Western theology. We cannot assume that Augustine influenced John. Moreover, after this theologians were still to be found in the
East who, perhaps under the influence of Mohammedanism, worked out the doctrine
of the Trinity in a modalistic way. Thus in the eleventh century Elias of Nisibis
in his book "On the proof of the truth of the Faith", written against the Mohammedans, says (Horst, 1886, p. 1 f.); "Wisdom and Life are two *attributes* of God,
which no one except Him possesses. For this reason Christians also say that He
is three persons, *i.e.*, possesses three essential attributes—namely, Essence, Wisdom
which is His Word, and Life; He is, however, a single substance ... 'Three persons'
expresses the same as is expressed by the statement—the Almighty is God, wise,
and living. The Essence is the Father, the Wisdom is the Son, the Life is the
Holy Spirit." God is thus purely a single being. I am not able to say whether
Elias is alone amongst the Nestorians in teaching this heterodox doctrine.

[3] The addition " and rests in the Son" does not require to be taken account
of; see Langen, Joh. v. Damaskus, p. 283 ff.

[4] John expressly rejects the view (l. c.) that the Spirit is from the Son or that
it has its ὕπαρξις from the Son (Hom. de Sabb. s.).

dependence meant that the Spirit was a creation of the Son, and they always continued to stick to the "from the Father". If in the following centuries they seldom *purposely* emphasised it, still they always laid stress on it as being a self-evident expression of the thesis that the Father is the First Principle (ἀρχή) in the Trinity, and that accordingly the Spirit appears as depotentiated, or double caused, if it is regarded as proceeding from the Son also.[1] The doctrine of the procession of the Holy Spirit from the Father alone thus clearly shews that in the East the mutual indwelling of the Hypostases was not thought of as complete, and that the Father was regarded as greater than the Son. The spiritual representation of the Trinity was of a different kind in the East and in the West respectively, especially from the time of Augustine onwards. It is accordingly at this point that Photius (867) took up the subject, since he, in searching for a dogmatic disputed point, charged the West with introducing innovations into doctrine, and strengthened this charge by alleging the still graver accusation against the West, of having falsified the most holy Creed of Constantinople by the addition of the "filioque"—"worst of

---

[1] Παρὰ τοῦ υἱοῦ or διὰ τοῦ υἱοῦ was the expression used; *i.e.*, it was assumed from what was stated in Holy Scripture that there was a μεσιτεία on the part of the Son in connection with the ἐκπόρευσις of the Spirit; *e.g.*, Athan. ad Serap. I. 20, so that Athanasius himself could say, "what the Holy Spirit has, it has from (παρὰ) the Son" (Orat. IV. 24), but the Father alone is the *cause* of the Spirit; cf. Basil. ep. 38. 4, de sp. s. 6 f.; Gregor., Naz., Orat. 31. 7, 8, 29; Gregor., Nyss., Orat. cat. 3 and many passages in his work against Eunomius. This system of doctrine continued to be the dominant one, and it makes no difference to it that a passage has always been pointed to in Epiphanius and Cyril according to which the Spirit is ἐξ ἀμφοῖν. Marcellus had already expressed himself on this point in his own fashion when he wrote (Euseb., de eccl. theol. III. 4): Πῶς γάρ, εἰ μὴ ἡ μονὰς ἀδιαίρετος οὖσα εἰς τριάδα πλατύνοιτο, ἐγχωρεῖ, αὐτὸν περὶ τοῦ πνεύματος ποτὲ μὲν λέγειν, ὅτι ἐκ τοῦ πατρὸς ἐκπορεύεται, ποτὲ δὲ λέγειν, ἐκεῖνος ἐκ τοῦ ἐμοῦ λήψεται καὶ ἀναγγελεῖ ὑμῖν. In reference to this point the dominant theology found it possible only to distinguish between the immanent processio and the processio in the historical revelation, or to analyse the "παρά" into "ἐκ" (Father) and "διά". In the Nestorian controversy the use of the proposition that the Spirit proceeds from the Son was formally disallowed. Theodoret, it is true, maintained in opposition to Cyril the view that the Holy Spirit is ἴδιον υἱοῦ, but he declared it to be an impiety to teach that the Holy Spirit is ἐξ υἱοῦ or has δι' υἱοῦ τὴν ὕπαρξιν (Opp. V. p. 47 ed. Schultze). Maximus Confess. further repeated this in the ep. ad Marinum, and so too did Joh. Damasc. It is to be found also in the Confession of Theodore v. Mops. (Hahn, § 139, p. 230).

evils is the addition to the holy Creed" (κακῶν κάκιστον ἡ ἐν
τῷ ἁγίῳ συμβόλῳ προσθήκη). As a matter of fact "filioque", as
a word in the Creed and indeed in the doctrine itself too, was
an innovation, but in reality it was merely the correct expression for the original Western conception of the one God in
whom the Trinity coheres. This is not the place to describe
the endless controversy; for the countless and ever new arguments adduced on both sides, so far as they do not spring
from a different way of conceiving of the Trinity and from the
determination to hold by what had once been delivered to the
Church, are worthless. Nor have the attempts to reconcile the
opposing views any interest for the history of dogma, because,
as a rule, they were dictated by ecclesiastical policy. It is,
however, worthy of note that the Greeks gradually came to be
suspicious of the old "διὰ τοῦ υἱοῦ", "through the Son", too,
but that they otherwise continued to hold by the Cappadocian
doctrine of the Trinity. [1] This together with the dogma of the
Incarnation continued to be the Faith of the Church, the mystery
κατ᾽ ἐξοχήν. The whole of the material, however, which had

---

[1] Photius, Mystag. (ed. Hergenröther) p. 15: Εἰ δύο αἰτίαι ἐν τῇ θεαρχικῇ καὶ
ὑπερουσίῳ τριάδι καθορᾶται, ποῦ τὸ τῆς μοναρχίας πολυύμνητον καὶ θεοπρεπὲς κράτος;
The tracing back of the Holy Spirit to the Father and the Son is compared to
Manichean dualism. The controversial works are innumerable and those in the
Slav languages are also very numerous, dating chiefly from the ninth, eleventh,
thirteenth, (Council of Lyons) fifteenth (Synod of Florence) and seventeenth (Cyril-
lus Lucaris) centuries. In our own day, owing to the Old-Catholic movement and
its projects of Union, the question has again been revived. For the carrying out
of their plans of Union with Eastern Churches, which have already been in a large
measure successful, the Romans have always found it necessary to have controversialists of a conciliatory disposition, e.g., Leo Allatius; while for their condemnation
of the obstinate Greeks they have always required fanatical controversialists. The
Greeks in order to protect themselves against the threatening encroachment on the
part of the Romans, still continue to lay great stress on dogmatic controversy, as
is proved by the existence of numerous works and essays, and even by the Greek
newspapers which appear in Constantinople. Besides the large works on the
Schism by Pichler, and on Photius by Hergenröther, cf. Walch, Hist. controv. de
process. s. s. 1751; Theophanes, de process. s. s. 1772; Gass, Symbolik d. griech.
K. p. 130 ff.; Kattenbusch, op. cit. I., p. 318 ff.; Vincenzi, op. cit.; Langen, Die tri-
nitar. Lehrdifferenz, 1876; Swete, On the History of the Procession of the Holy
Spirit, 1876; Stanley, The Eastern Church, 1864; Kranich, Der h. Basil, i. s. Stellung z. filioque, 1882; Pawlow, Kritische Versuche zur Geschichte der ältesten
griechish-russischen Polemik gegen die Lateiner (Russian) 1878; Bach, Dogmengesch. des M.-A. II. p. 748 ff.

been taken over from Greek philosophy was turned to account in giving a definite form to this dogma, and was to a certain extent exhausted here. Accordingly in the Trinitarian theology we also meet with what the Church inherited from the downfall of the ancient world of thought, though certainly it presents itself in a very much abridged and stunted form. Owing to the way in which it was employed and owing to its being united with separate Biblical expressions which came to be taken as philosophical-theological conceptions—the τρόποι ὑπάρξεως, modes of existence for example—it doubtless underwent the most astonishing modification. Still the doctrine of the Trinity in the theological treatment given to it, became the vehicle by which the Platonic and Aristotelian philosophy was transmitted to the Slavic and Germanic peoples. It contains a most peculiar blend of the Christian thought of the revelation of God in Jesus and the legacy of ancient philosophy.

In the West, Augustine, following an ancient Western tendency, destroyed the last remains of subordinationism, though just because of this he advanced in the direction of Modalism. According to him in constructing the doctrine of God we should not start from the person of the Father. On the contrary the conception of the Godhead ought from the very first to be personal and Trinitarian, so that the Father is regarded as being conditioned in His existence by the Son in the same way as the Son is by the Father. Augustine wishes the unity of the three persons to be so conceived of that the three are equal to each one singly, and the triple personality is understood as existing within the absolute simplicity of God. The differences or characteristic notes of the three persons are still to hold good when the Godhead is so conceived of; but they appear merely as relations in the one Godhead, and their characteristics are done away when it is considered that in connection with the act of production or procession Son and Spirit are to be regarded as active agents. Augustine searched for analogies to the threefoldness which is found in the one divine essence, in creation, in the conceptions of basis and substance, form and idea, persistence, and in the human spirit in object, subjective picture of the object, intention of perception—mens ipsa, notitia

mentis, amor—memoria, intelligentia, voluntas. The doctrine in
its entirety is the effort of a man whose mind was as sceptical
as it was intellectually powerful, but who revelled in the incomprehensible, who had laid hold of a new thought, but who both
as sceptic and as theosophist felt himself bound to tradition,
and who for this reason was for his punishment driven about
between the poles of a *docta ignorantia* and a knowledge which
was replete with contradictions. This speculation, which attempts
to construe the most immanent of immanent Trinities and to
sublimate the Trinity into a unity, just because it does this,
discards everything in the way of a basis in historical religion
and loses itself in paradoxical distinctions and speculations, while
at the same time it is not able to give clear expression to its
new and valuable thought. The great work of Augustine, "De
Trinitate", can scarcely be said to have promoted piety anywhere or at any time.   It, however, became the high-school not
only for the technico-logical culture of the understanding, but also
for the metaphysics of the Middle-Ages. The realistic scholasticism
of the Middle-Ages is not conceivable apart from this work,
because it itself already contains Scholasticism. [1]

[1] The larger histories of dogma go very fully into Augustine's doctrine of the
Trinity. For the history of dogma, however, it is sufficient to get a knowledge
of the main outlines of this doctrine. The chief source is the great work " de trinitate", the letters Nos. 11 and 120 are specially instructive; the former because, written
immediately after Augustine's conversion, it nevertheless already contains his fundamental thought, although still in a simple form and accompanied by a confidence
in the power of sanctified reason to understand the mystery; letter 120, because in
a proportionately brief form it sets forth the doctrine in its matured shape. (The
Quaternity is rejected in c. 7, 13.) Besides this, attention should be given to lib. XI.
10 de civit. dei, amongst other passages; cf. the monographs by Bindemann and
Dorner jun., and also Gangauf, Augustin's specul. Lehre v. Gott., 1865. According
to Augustine it is not the divine substance or the Father that is the monarchical
principle, but, on the contrary, the Trinity itself is the one God (unus deus est ipse
trinitas, pater et filius et spiritus s. est unus deus; see de trin. V. 9, c. serm. Arian.
c. 4). Consequently the equality and unity are conceived of by him in a much
stricter fashion than by the Cappadocians. He is not afraid of the paradox that
two persons are equal to three, and again that one is equal to three (VII. 11,
VI. 10); for "singula sunt in singulis et omnia in singulis et singula in omnibus
et omnia in omnibus et unum omnia." Accordingly the Son too takes an active
part in His own sending (II. 9: "a patre et filio missus est idem filius, quia verbum
patris est ipse filius"); the immanent function of the persons as well as their
economic function are never to be thought of as separated, for "sunt semper uni-
cem, neuter solus" (VI. 7); it is therefore true that the Trinity—in the O. T.—

It was for Augustine a self-evident truth that the Holy Spirit proceeds also from the Son, and he expressly maintained has also been seen (II.), a fact which the Greeks denied, and that the unity is actually a numerical one. It is accordingly also self-evident that the equality is a perfect one; the Father in all His acts is no less dependent on the Son than the Son is on Him (c. serm. Arian. 3 : 1. c. 4 is therefore striking: "solus pater non legitur missus, quoniam solus non habet auctorem, a quo genitus sit vel a quo procedat"); the special qualities do not establish anything in the way of superiority or inferiority. Nor are the persons to be conceived of as independent substances or as accidents, but as *relations*, in which the inner life of the Godhead is present (V. 4, VII. 11, VI. 60, V. 5: " in deo nihil quidem secundum accidens dicitur, quia nihil in eo mutabile est; nec tamen omne quod dicitur, secundum substantiam dicitur. Dicitur enim ad aliquid, sicut pater ad filium et filius ad patrem, quod non est accidens, quia et ille semper pater et ille semper filius" etc. V. 6 : amplification of the " relative ", see also ep. 233). We can see that Augustine only gets beyond Modalism by the mere assertion that he does not wish to be a Modalist, and by the aid of ingenious distinctions between different ideas. His strength and the significance of his book consist in the attempts he makes to base the doctrine of the Trinity on analogies, together with these distinctions in thought. In connection with these Augustine has given us some extraordinarily acute and valuable discussions on psychology, the theory of knowledge, and metaphysics, which supplied the subsequent centuries with philosophical education. The Scholastics made use of these investigations not only in connection with the doctrine of the Trinity, in discussing which they do not get beyond Modalism—but also in connection with the conception of God in itself and theology generally. It is impossible, however, to understand the labyrinths of the work " de trinitate ", on which Augustine was occupied for fifteen years, if we do not keep the fact in view that the great thinker has attempted to express in his formula for the Trinity a thought which this formula not only does not contain, but, on the contrary, implicitly disowns—namely, that the Godhead is personal and is consequently one person, that θεότης and Θεός mean the same thing. Obliged to believe in " the three persons in the one essence " by tradition, but obliged also by his Christian experience to believe in the single personality of God (see the Confessions), spite of the value which he too puts upon the " Essence " this situation could only result in a contradiction. Had Augustine been able to make a fresh start in putting the Christian religion into a doctrinal system, he would have been the last to have thought of the Greek formula. One who could write (V. 9) " dictum est ' tres personæ ' non ut illud diceretur, sed ne taceretur," would not have discovered the three persons in the one substance ! But though thus involved in contradiction this great mind was nevertheless able to instruct posterity in a hundred ways, for Augustine employed the whole resources of his philosophy in the endeavour to overcome the contradiction which could not be overcome. It is moreover, of importance that his acquaintance with the Cappadocian theology was of such a very superficial kind. When (V. 9) he translates the formula, μίαν οὐσίαν τρεῖς ὑποστάσεις, by "una essentia tres substantiæ " it is evident that he had not entered into the spirit or grasped the point of view of that theology. The addition, however, "sed quia nostra loquendi consuetudo iam obtinuit, ut hoc intelligatur cum dicimus essentiam, quod intelligitur cum dicimus substantiam, non audemus dicere: unam essentiam tres substantias, sed unam essentiam vel substantiam, tres

this.[1] In doing this he merely gave expression to the view which
was implicitly contained in the ancient Western doctrine of the
autem personas, quemadmodum multi Latini ista tractantes et digni auctoritate
dixerunt, cum alium modum aptiorem non invenirent, quo enuntiarent verbis quod
sine verbis intellegebant," proves that spite of the agreement come to with the
East, the West was not yet conscious of possessing a common terminology. The
studies of Reuter (Ztschr. f. K. G. V., p. 375 ff., VI. p. 155 ff.) have thrown light
on Augustine's relation to the Trinitarian conclusions of the East. We may assent
to his thesis (p. 191) " In his discussion of the doctrine of the Trinity Augustine
seldom expressly falls back on the formulæ of the Nicene Creed. His doctrine is
not anti-Nicene, but neither is it for the most part Nicene in its wording. He
made very little use of the discussions of Greek or even of Latin authors." The
Nicene Creed is not once mentioned in the work " de trinitate ". We ought not in
fact to measure the acquaintance which the West had with the theological development in the East by the careful attention given to it by the Roman bishops.
Reuter is right in saying (p. 383 f.) that it is not so much the Nicene Creed or
indeed any formula whatever which Augustine takes for granted as expressing the
Church doctrine of the Trinity, but rather a fixed series of fundamental thoughts.
The West was never so deeply impressed by the Nicene Creed as the East had
been. In the writings of Tertullian, Novatian, Dionysius of Rome amongst others,
it possessed the " series of fundamental thoughts " which proved sufficient and in
which was still contained a trace of that ἕν πρόσωπον maintained by Calixt. (Philos.
IX. 12) and the presence of which is still manifested in the " non ut illud diceretur
[to wit, ' tres personæ ']" of Augustine. Just for this very reason the West did not
require the Nicene Creed, or required it only when it came to close quarters with
Arianism, as we may gather from what is said by Ambrose. We have finally to
refer to an important element in the position of Augustine in reference to the
doctrine of the Trinity. Augustine was positively and negatively influenced by Neo-
Platonism as represented by Plotinus and Porphyry. Negatively, in so far as he
was there confronted with a doctrine of the Trinity, but with one which was based
on a descending series of emanations; positively, in so far as he took over from
Plotinus the thought of the simplicity of God and attempted actually to make use
of it. To Augustine as a philosopher the construction of a doctrine of the Trinity
was already a matter of course. All the more was it necessary for him to strive
to construct a peculiarly *Christian* doctrine of the Trinity, and, because of the idea
of simplicity which could no longer be referred to the Father alone, to bring the
other two persons into unity with the Father. With the philosophical postulate of
the simplicity of God was blended the religious postulate of the personality of
God, a point regarding which indeed Augustine never got to have theoretically
clear views. Here accordingly the other two " persons" had to be fused, and in
this way originated the logical work of art represented by his doctrine of the
Trinity, which no one had taught him and which appeared even to himself to be
so difficult that he did not count on its being understood by outsiders (Reuter, p. 384).
Prudentius (see, *e.g.*, Cath. XI. 13 sq.) has a very ancient doctrine of the Trinity,
which partly recalls that of Tertullian and partly that of Marcellus.

  [1] The Father Himself is only relatively principium, the Son and the Holy
Spirit are also to be termed principium; but they form together one principium (V. 13). The statement accordingly holds good: " fatendum est, patrem

Trinity[1] inasmuch as the procession of the Spirit from Father and Son implied in it could never be regarded as the procession from *two* First Principles. The first mention of the doctrine after Augustine is in the Confession of Faith of a Synod of Toledo which probably met in 447, hardly in 400, "paracletus a patre filioque procedens" (Hahn, § 97) and in the words of Leo I. (ep. ad Turib. c. 1): "de utroque processit"; see further the so-called Athanasian Creed and the Confession of the Synod of Toledo in the year 589 (Reccared's Confession, Hahn, § 106). It was at this Synod that the "filioque" was first put into the text of the Creed of Constantinople, which had probably then or shortly before first reached Spain. We have no further information regarding the reception it met with;[2] it is likely that in opposition to the West Gothic Arianism there was a desire to give expression to the doctrine of the equality of Father and Son. From Spain the addition reached the Carlovingian Frankish Empire,[3] and already in the first decades of the ninth century it had been there embodied in the official form of the Creed—by the order of Charles the Great. In Rome the Augustinian doctrine of the Holy Spirit had indeed been long ago sanctioned, but as late as the beginning of the ninth century the Creed as accepted there was still without that addition, as the table constructed by Leo III. and his answer to the Frankish ambassadors in the year 809 prove. Soon after this, however,—when and under what circumstances it is impossible to say—it was adopted into the Creed in Rome too; see the ordo Romanus de div. off. (Max Bibl. Patr. XIII.,

et filium principium esse spiritus sancti, non duo principia." It is, however, worthy of note that Augustine in this very place (V. 14) rejects the view that the Son was born of the Holy Spirit also.

[1] It seems to have appeared again in the teaching of Priscillian as avowed Modalism; see the Anathemas of the Spanish Synod of 447 in Hefele, op. cit. II., p. 307 f., and Leo I., ep. ad Turibium.

[2] See the Acts of the Council in Mansi IX., pp. 977—1010, Gams, K. Gesch. Spaniens II. 2, p. 6 ff., Hefele III., p. 48 ff. Rösler (Prudentius, p. 362 ff.) regards the Confession in question as being that of the Council of 400.

[3] The first controversy, (with the Easterns,) arose at the Council of Gentilly in the year 767. Already in the libri Carolini the East is censured for not accepting the filioque.

p. 677*a*), which perhaps belongs to the second half of the ninth century, and the controversy with Photius. [1]

So far as popular Christian thought is concerned, the Cappadocian manner of formulating the doctrine exercised in the end a more decisive influence even in the West than the Augustinian view which dissolves the persons into conceptions and leaves little room for the play of ordinary or pictorial thought. But for the Church and for Science [2] Augustine's view came to be authoritative. What contributed most to this result was the fact that it was embodied as the doctrine of Athanasius in a formula which came to have the authority of a universal and binding Confession of Faith. It is extremely probable that the so-called Athanasian Creed, so far as the first half of it is concerned, is a Gallican Rule of Faith explanatory of the Creed of Nicæa. As such it was from the fifth century onwards, by means of the theology of Augustine and Vincentius of Lerinum, gradually made into a course of instruction for the clergy, *i.e.*, the monks, suitable for being committed to memory. As a *regula fidei* meant to explain the Nicene Creed it was called " fides catholica " or " fides Athanasii ", though it had other names also, and perhaps as early as 500 it began with the words " Quicunque vult salvus esse." It is probable that in the course of the sixth century it essentially received its present technical form in Southern Gaul where the West-Gothic Spanish Arianism still continued to provoke opposition. In the middle of the sixth century it, or at least a recension very similar to it, was already current as the authoritative course of instruction for the clergy in Southern Gaul, and was together with the Psalms learned by heart. It got into the decisions of single Councils from the Psalm-books and breviaries of the monks and clergy, in so far as the practice had here begun of appealing to single statements in this rule of faith. Starting from here it gradually came to be the Confession of the Frankish Church in the eighth and ninth centuries. It was perhaps then that the second Christological half was added, the origin of which is completely

[1] See Abelard, Sic et Non IV., p. 26 sq. ed. Cousin, and the works cited above; in addition Köllner, Symbolik I., p. 1 f., p. 28 ff.

[2] See Erigena's doctrine of the Trinity, which is entirely drawn from Augustine, de div. nat. I. 62, II. 32, 35, homil. in prolog. ev. sec. Joann.

wrapped in obscurity; it was of course put together before the ninth century. The Frankish Church by its relations with Rome was the means of communicating the Creed as the Confession of Athanasius to the entire Western Church during the period from the ninth to the eleventh centuries. As Rome and—through Rome—the West finally received the Gallico-Frankish form of the so-called Apostles' Creed and gave up the primitive Apostles' Creed, so too Rome adopted as a second Creed the Gallico-Frankish statement of the Augustinian doctrine of the Trinity. This, at any rate, is the relatively most probable view that can be taken of the obscure history of the origin and reception of the so-called Athanasian Creed.[1] The three

---

[1] For the older works on the Athanasian Creed which begin with the disquisition of Voss (1642), see Köllner, Symbolik I., p. 53 ff. In more recent times, besides Caspari, the English, who use the Creed at divine service and nevertheless have come to feel it to be inconvenient, have published valuable discussions on it; see Ffoulkes The Athan. Creed, 1871; Swainson, The Nicene and Apost. Creeds, etc., 1875; Ommaney, Early History of the Athan. Creed, 1875; two prize-essays by Peabody and Courtney Stanhope Kenny, 1876, which are known to me only from the Jena Lit. Ztg., 1877, No. 21. In addition the discussions on the Utrecht Psalter by Hardy (1874), Aratz (1874), and Springer (1880). It is since the non-Athanasian origin of the Creed has been established beyond doubt both on internal and external grounds, that positive work has begun to be done, and this has not yet been brought to a conclusion. The question as to how far its transmission in writing takes us back has already been the subject of important controversies. It is doubtful if the manuscript takes us back as far as the time of Charles the Great or Charles the Bald. But the question of origin cannot be decided by the settlement of this point. Swainson gives 850 as the date of its origin—amongst the Neustrian clergy—and sees in it a piece of intentional deception. Ffoulkes endeavours to prove that it originated at the end of the eighth century and is also inclined to believe there was deception in the matter; Caspari suggests the sixth century; others go as far back as the fifth, beyond the middle of which, at any rate, we cannot, for internal reasons, go. The question of origin is a complicated one since the Rule of Faith originated by stages and only gradually came to be authoritative. There is no reason for thinking of deception. What I have given in the text is based on independent studies, but to describe these at length would take us too far. The most certain traces seem to me to point to Southern Gaul, and North Africa may also have had something to do with it. The Athanasian Creed does not belong to the same category as the pseudo-Isidorian Decretals as Swainson holds; nor was it set up by Charles the Great as a sharp boundary line between East and West, which is the view of Ffoulkes; on the contrary, it was a syllabus of instruction based on the doctrine of Athanasius, which in uncritical times was turned into a creed of Athanasius. The necessity for a detailed creed of this kind was coincident with the desire to possess a compendium of the sacred paradoxes of Augustine and at the same time a sharp weapon against the Trinitarian, *i.e*, Arian, errors which had for so long haunted the West.

so-called ecumenical Creeds are consequently all "apocryphal." The Apostles' Creed did not originate with the Apostles, though so far as its basis is concerned, it belongs to the post-Apostolic age; the Nicene-Constantinopolitan Creed originated neither in Nicæa nor in Constantinople, but in Jerusalem or Cyprus, though it got its main contents from Nicæa; the Athanasian Creed is not the work of Athanasius. Nor are they ecumenical, on the contrary it is at most the Nicene-Constantinopolitan Creed which can be so termed [1] since the East knew nothing of the other two.

The doctrine of the Trinity in the Athanasian Creed is strictly Augustinian, and yet it has certain traits which are not to be traced either to Augustine or to Vincentius. No other Creed went so far in the development of the doctrine of the Trinity as an article of faith necessary to salvation, as this one. This can be explained only by the fact of its having originated in mediæval times. The Franks regarded the Faith handed down to them by the ancient Church simply as a legal statute, and accordingly only required faith in the Faith, obedience, that is, *fides implicita* therefore, since they did not yet possess what was required for a religious or philosophical appropriation of the system of belief. Under the form of *fides implicita*, however, *i.e.*, a faith of obedience, the most developed theology can be looked for from every one. *In the Athanasian Creed as a Creed we have the transformation of the doctrine of the Trinity as an article of Faith to be inwardly appropriated, into an ecclesiastical legal statute on the observance of which salvation depends.* [2]

---

[1] The Armenian Church possesses a Creed which is closely akin to the Creed of Constantinople, but not identical with it.

[2] The Creed is in Hahn, § 81. Careful attention has been bestowed on the separate statements by those who have investigated the subject, and their origin has been ascertained. The verses 9—12 are not to be directly traced to Augustine. Four times over in the Creed salvation is made dependent on carefully defined belief. This is not like Augustine; see ep. 169. 4. He did not intend his amplifications of Trinitarian doctrine to be taken as Church doctrine (de trin. I. 2). The most recent work on the Creed is in Lumby's History of the Creeds, third ed., 1887. Lumby comes to the conclusion based on a very careful examination of the MSS., and tradition, that the Creed in its present shape is not older than the time of Charles the Bald.

For Athanasius the fundamental religious thought was the "Ὁμοούσιος", and just because of this he could not treat it technically. For the Cappadocians the "Ὁμοούσιος" and the doctrine of the Trinity came to be the sum of theological knowledge. For the Westerns after Augustine these doctrines became a sacred legal statute, to which, above all, obedience must be rendered. This is the course of things which is constantly repeated in the history of religion. Men pass from the religious thought to the philosophical and theological doctrinal proposition, and from the doctrinal proposition which requires knowledge to the legal proposition which demands obedience, or to the sacred relic the common veneration for which constitutes a bond of union for the community, whether it be that of the nation, the state, or the Church. And thus the process of formulating comes to have an ever-increasing importance, and the Confession with the mouth becomes the foundation of the Church. But in reference to this the Valentinian Herakleon had as early as the second century correctly remarked:—

"There is an agreement in faith and life on the one hand and in word on the other; the agreement in word is also an agreement based on authorities which many hold to be the only agreement, though this is not a sound opinion; for hypocrites can subscribe to this kind of agreement." (Ὁμολογίαν εἶναι τὴν μὲν ἐν τῇ πίστει καὶ πολιτείᾳ, τὴν δὲ ἐν Φωνῇ· ἡ μὲν οὖν ἐν Φωνῇ ὁμολογία καὶ ἐπὶ τῶν ἐξουσιῶν γίνεται, ἣν μόνην ὁμολογίαν ἡγοῦνται εἶναι οἱ πολλοί, οὐχ ὑγιῶς· δύνανται δὲ ταύτην τὴν ὁμολογίαν καὶ οἱ ὑποκριταὶ ὁμολογεῖν.)

CHAPTER II.

THE DOCTRINE OF THE PERFECT LIKENESS OF THE NATURE OF THE INCARNATE SON OF GOD WITH THAT OF HUMANITY.

WHILE the question whether the Divine which had appeared on the earth was identical with the supreme Godhead, was still agitating men's minds, the second question arose as to the nature of the union of the Divine in Christ with humanity. In this question, comprising as it does two closely connected problems, the problem, namely, as to the character of the humanity of Christ, and the problem as to how the union of divinity and humanity is to be conceived of, that which constituted the supreme concern of Greek theology has its culmination. It accordingly had already necessarily emerged in the Arian controversy, for it was in reference to the thought of the union of Godhead and humanity that the whole controversy was carried on by Athanasius.[1]

The problem was not a new one; on the contrary, it had already engaged the attention of the old theologians who had carried on the struggle against Marcion and Valentin,[2] and since the time of Irenæus it had occupied a central place in men's thoughts. The doctrine that the flesh of Christ was actual human flesh had been for long an established one,[3]

---

[1] See Vol. III., Chap. VI.

[2] The Valentinians themselves had already handled it with supreme technical skill, though no unanimity was attained in their own schools. With them the whole stress was laid on complicated distinctions within the person of Christ. On the other hand, all the elements of the composite nature of Jesus Christ were by some of the leaders of the schools elevated to the heavenly sphere.

[3] See Tertull., de carne Christi.

although platonising theologians still continued to find it possible to combine with it dogmatic thoughts and a refined Valentianism;[1] in fact, no single outstanding Church teacher really accepted the humanity in a perfectly unqualified way. Further than that it was necessary to believe in an actual "incarnation of the Logos" (σάρκωσις τοῦ λόγου) all else was uncertain. What in the way of intensification or modification the conception of the σάρξ was susceptible of in order still to rank as human flesh, was a point which was as uncertain as the question as to the relation between σάρξ and ἄνθρωπος, and as the other question as to whether the σάρξ must maintain itself as such in union with the Divine and whether it could or could not do this. All the Christological problems which had before given rise to controversies with the Gnostics returned in a more subtle form, since it was still possible to posit a real σάρξ of Christ in the statement of the problem, and then actually to do away with it again in the course of speculation.

A Christological theory had undoubtedly been propounded by Origen, according to which the presence of a human *soul* also in Jesus is to be expressly admitted. Others before him had long ago demanded this, perhaps partly because they already felt that everything turned on the human personal life, and that a human body without a soul involves a merely seeming humanity, though they did not actually draw the logical conclusions.[2] But the theory of Origen was not determined by this thought alone. He was also influenced by a cosmological postulate. He required a middle term between the Logos and matter to bind them together, and this was to be found in the human soul of Christ, concerning which he taught that it had not shared in the general antemundane fall of the spirits.[3] Moreover, he was certainly acute enough to perceive that the free human will also must be located in the personality of Christ and that Holy Scripture affirms that it is. But his theory of the human

---

[1] So, above all, the Alexandrians.

[2] See I Clem. ad Cor. 49, 6: τὸ αἷμα αὐτοῦ ἔδωκεν ὑπὲρ ἡμῶν Ἰησοῦς Χριστὸς ... καὶ τὴν σάρκα ὑπὲρ τῆς σαρκὸς ἡμῶν καὶ τὴν ψυχὴν ὑπὲρ τῶν ψυχῶν ἡμῶν. Iren. V. I. I : τῷ ἰδίῳ αἵματι λυτρωσαμένου ἡμᾶς τοῦ κυρίου καὶ δόντος τὴν ψυχὴν ὑπὲρ τῶν ἡμετέρων ψυχῶν καὶ τὴν σάρκα τὴν ἑαυτοῦ ἀντὶ τῶν ἡμετέρων σαρκῶν.

[3] For details, see Vol. II., p. 369 ff.

soul and of the nature of the union of the divine and human in Christ scarcely passed beyond the circle of his own pupils.[1] It was too closely connected with the most peculiar and most questionable fundamental presuppositions of the great philosopher and was also too difficult to win approval. Even in Alexandria in the time of Alexander and Athanasius it would appear that attention was no longer given to Origen's way of putting the doctrine; in those cases in which his view was retained its effect at best was merely still further to increase the elasticity of all the conceptions attached to the person of Jesus.

The general stagnation which marked theology in the first half of the Fourth Century, shewed itself no less in the different views of the Incarnation than in the doctrine of the Godhead of Christ. Most theologians contented themselves with the idea of the ensarkosis, and in connection with this clung to the most naive doketic views as regard details.[2] If this already involved a reassertion of the opinions held in the oldest theological schools which Christianity possessed, namely, the Valentinian, others went still further in reasserting these opinions and directly

---

[1] Hilary (de trinit. X. 22) will not entertain the idea of a human soul. His view of the origin of souls is certainly, speaking generally, creationist. "He has taken the soul from Himself which, moreover, was never communicated by men as something emanating from those who beget.... The soul of the body (of Christ) must have been from God."

[2] The detailed discussions of Hilary amongst other things (de trinitate) shew the length to which these doketic views had gone and the extent to which they had spread. According to him the body of Christ was exalted above all πάθη and always took these upon itself voluntarily only. The normal condition of the body of Christ was always the condition of glorification, the appearance in ordinary material form with the ordinary needs was on every occasion a voluntary act (X. 23, 25: "in natura Christi corporis infirmitatem naturæ corporeæ non fuisse" etc.). Christ in Gethsemane did not tremble and pray for himself, but for his disciples (X. 37, 41) He did not feel pain; His sufferings affected Him as an arrow passes through fire and air (X. 23). His nature was absolutely incapable of suffering. Amongst the confused ideas of Hilary, that of a depotentiation of the Logos by an act of self-emptying, is also met with. But the passages to which the modern supporters of the kenotic theory appeal (de trin. IX. 14, XI. 48, XII. 6) are not in place; for when Hilary is dealing with the idea of self-humiliation he always takes back in the second statement what he has asserted in the first, so that the unchangeableness of God may not suffer. Hence the statement: "Christus in forma dei manens formam servi accepit." This statement must be taken along with the strongly kenotic statements of Hilary.

taught the doctrine of the heavenly σάρξ of Christ, [1] the Homousia of this σάρξ with the Godhead of the Logos, and so on. [2] Others adopted the theory of a transformation. According to them the σάρξ originated with the Logos Himself, who in view of its appearance or manifestation, by an act of transformation made for Himself a body capable of suffering and thus in part re-nounced His own nature. We can trace the influence here of the old monarchian theologoumena of the ὑιοπάτωρ who is incapable of suffering when He wills and capable of suffering when He wills. [3] Speculative Pantheistic views, such as afterwards plainly reappeared amongst the Monophysites and which had formerly been propounded by the Gnostics, may already have been in existence at this time, ideas such as those of the moment of finitude in the essence of God Himself, and of the Cosmos as the natural body of the Godhead. In opposition to these views some taught the doctrine of a perfect incarnation (ἐνανθρώ-πησις), feeling probably that a mere ensarkosis or appearing in the flesh was not sufficient. But they were perfectly in the dark in regard to the question as to whether the Godhead really became a man or adopted human nature. As no one had yet decided this question, so no one knew whether the incarnate Logos had two natures or one, though the great majority clung to the idea of one nature without knowing, however, how to conceive of it. No one knew whether the Logos was blended with humanity or merely joined with it, whether He had trans-formed Himself into it or whether He had put it on as a dress

---

[1] "Corpus cæleste" says Hilary himself, l. c. X. 18. The Pauline speculations regarding the second Adam and the heavenly man, had come to have very disastrous consequences for the theologians of the Fourth and Fifth Centuries as they had already had for the Gnostics before them. By the attention which was given to these speculations the problem, which was otherwise already a complicated one, got into the direst confusion. It was, however, doketism in particular, both in its coarse and in its refined forms, which turned them to account, and modern theo-logians have shown a fondness for fishing in these muddy waters in order to extract from them their very different fancies regarding Christ as the heavenly type of humanity and as the ideal-man.

[2] See Vol. III., p. 299 ff.

[3] That the Logos himself formed His own body (from Mary) seems to have been the almost universal opinion; see Hilary X. 18 (also 22) "Christ Himself is the source of His body."

and dwelt in it as in a temple, whether in becoming man
He had taken it up into the Godhead, or in deifying it had
left its peculiar nature intact; or had not deified it at all, but
had merely associated it with the Godhead. Further, no one
knew in what way the Gospel statements were to be employed
in connection with the complicated nature of the God-man. Was
the flesh, the man, born of the Virgin Mary, or was the Logos
born of her together with the flesh. Who suffers, who hungers,
who thirsts, who trembles and is afraid, who asks and is anxious,
who confesses his ignorance, who describes the Father as the
only Good, who dies, the man or the God-man? And again :
who does miracles, commands nature, forgives sins, in short,
who is the Redeemer, God or the God-Man? There was no
fixed, generally accepted answer. Further, no one was able to
make any definite statement regarding the permanence of the
humanity[1] of Christ and its nature after the Resurrection, and yet
the question as to the effect of the Incarnation turned entirely
on this point. Finally, the question as to whether the Logos did
or did not undergo a change owing to the Incarnation, was one
on which complete uncertainty prevailed. The questions regarding
exaltation, humiliation, depotentiation, assumption emerged and
affected the always half-concealed fundamental question, as to
the relation of the Divine and human generally. The theologians, however, groped uncertainly about, and however paradoxical many of the doctrines already were of a suffering without
suffering, of a humiliation without humiliation, still the most
paradoxical by no means passed yet for the most certain.[2] We
can easily see that we are here at the very central point of
the old Greek theology; at the time of the Nicene Creed this
was, however, no rock, but a slippery bit of country shelving
down on all sides. The religious thought : Θεὸς σαρκωθεὶς δι᾽

---

[1] See the peculiar doctrine of Marcellus in Zahn, Marcell., p. 177 f., given differently by Dorner and Baur.

[2] Examples of these disputed questions are supplied by all the writings of the
Fathers dealing with the subject, down to the middle of the Fourth Century. A
specially characteristic example is to be found in Philostorg., H. E., IX. 14. He tells
us that in Constantinople, in the time of Valens, Demophilus, e.g., preached τὸ σῶμα
τοῦ υἱοῦ ἀνακραθὲν τῇ θεότητι εἰς τὸ ἀδηλότατον κεχωρηκέναι, as a drop of milk
disappears when it trickles into the ocean.

ἡμᾶς,—God made flesh for us,—stood firm, but the theology which sought to grasp it slipped off it at every point. How could it possibly be put in intelligible conceptions so long as theologians concerned themselves with the "Natures"! A human nature made divine which nevertheless remains truly human, is a *contradictio in adjecto*. What those in after times succeeded in doing was accordingly not to give a clear explanation, but simply a paraphrase which as formulated was by no means perfectly suited to express the thought, and whose value consisted in this, that it surrounded the speculative theologians with a hedge and prevented them from falling into abysses.

The Christological problem, however, as it was treated in the ancient Church was not only connected in the closest way with the Trinitarian, and, further, had not only the element of contradiction in common with it, but it also in the last resort issued in the same formulæ. If in the case of the latter the singular of the substance or nature and the plurality of the persons were the accepted terms, it was the reverse way in the case of the other, where the accepted terms came finally to be the plurality of the substances and the unity of the persons. The distinction between "Nature" and "Person" was also the subject of discussion in both cases. That this distinction, with which the West had been long acquainted without, however, using it as a speculative starting-point, supplied the means of escape from the difficulties connected with both problems, theologians had begun to perceive as early as the middle of the Fourth Century, though undoubtedly in a slow and hesitating fashion. This was the anchor to which they fastened themselves, although it was not supplied by any philosophy; they had to provide it for themselves. While, however, so far as the Trinitarian problem was concerned, the distinction once introduced quickly established itself in the East, it was a century before it triumphed there as regards the Christological problem, and this triumph, far from uniting the parties, permanently separated them.

What is the explanation of this remarkable phenomenon? It may be said that neither in connection with the Trinitarian question did the perfect unity of the substance succeed in establishing itself (see pp. 120, 125); but it very nearly did so, and the controversy accordingly ceased. Why then did the formula of the unity of the person not in the same way prove satisfactory in connection with the Christological problem?

This question may already be raised here, though it cannot be settled till the next chapter. Attention must, however, be directed to one point. The antecedents of the "solution" of the Trinitarian and Christological problem which proved victorious in the Eastern Church and consequently in the Catholic Church generally, are to be found only partly in the East; it was naturalised in the West. The Tertullian who in the work "adv. Prax." created the formula of the "una substantia" and the "tres personæ", in the same work constructed the formulæ of the "utraque substantia (duplex status non confusus—this is the ἀσυγχύτως—sed conjunctus) in una persona" (the substance of two kinds in one person, the twofold state not confused but joined together in one person); "duæ substantiæ in Christo Jesu, divina et humana" (two substances in Christ Jesus, divine and human); "salva est utriusque proprietas substantiæ in Christo Jesu" (the property of each substance in Christ Jesus is not interfered with). [1] He thus laid the foundation for the formally similar treatment of both problems, and created the terminology which was accepted by the East after more than two hundred years. Had he the same interest in the Christological problem as the later Eastern theologians had? Was the deification of humanity a matter of importance to him? By no means. And what philosophy did he make use of? Well, no philosophy at all; on the contrary, *he used the method of legal fictions*. By the aid of the distinction current among jurists between "substance" and "person" he with great facility explained and securely established as against the Monarchians both the ancient ecclesiastical and, *par excellence*, Western formula, "Christus deus et homo", and also the formula, "pater, filius et spiritus sanctus—unus deus." Substance—for Tertullian never uses the word "nature"—is in the language of the jurists not anything personal, but rather corresponds to "property" in the sense of possession, or to the essence as distinguished from the manifestation or "status"; the person again is not in itself anything

---

[1] See Vol. II., p. 280 ff. and above, p. 121.

substantial, but the subject or individual as capable of entering into legal relations and possessing property, who can quite well possess different substances, just as on the other hand it is possible for one substance to be in the possession of several persons. Tertullian introduced these legal terms into theology. That this is what they were in his use of them, and not philosophical terms, is shewn by the words themselves, shewn too by the application made of them and by the utter disregard of the difficulty which their application must necessarily create for every philosophical thinker. And it was these legal fictions which the East had to accept as philosophy, *i.e.*, theology, or change into philosophy! This became the basis of the "philosophy of revelation."(!) This was more than the boldest Neo-Platonic philosophy in its strangest intellectual phantasies had ever asked. No wonder that difficulties were made about accepting it, especially when, besides, it did not cover what was still the preponderating interest of the Faith, the interest in the deification of humanity. People always shrank from positing an οὐσία ἀνυπόστατος, a substance without an hypostasis, because when used in reference to a living being it was simply absurd, and because the unity of the person of Christ, "salva utriusque substantiæ proprietate", gave no security for the unity of the Godhead and humanity. The jurist Tertullian, however, could manage quite well with "person" and substance", as if the distinction between them were self-evident, because he did not here develop the logical results of the doctrine of redemption, but gave expression [1] to a matter of fact which was ostensibly

---

[1] The Westerns did the same after him; amid all the odd ideas that some of them produced they always clung to the humana et divina substantia, to the filius dei et filius hominis, and this distinction which had been supplied by the Creed, together with the unity of the person, became for them the rudder when it came to be a question of sailing through the stormy waves which had arisen in the East. See already Novatian, then Hilary, Ambrose, Augustin, Leo I. and also the less important theologians. It is extremely characteristic that Vincentius (Comm. 17, 18) still uses not the designation two natures, but two substances, and as against Apollinaris he finds the thesis perfectly sufficient "that Christ had two substances, the one divine, the other human, the one from the Father, the other from His Mother." Hilary very frequently employs the expressions "utraque natura", "persona"; he also writes de trin. IX. 14: "utriusque naturæ persona." In the "Statuta ecclesiæ antiqua" (Mansi III., p. 950) we have: "qui episcopus ordinandus est, antea exami-

contained in the Creed, and because he did not, properly speaking, indulge in philosophical speculation, but applied the artificial language of the jurists. If we accordingly perceive that many centuries afterwards, the philosophical-realistic method of handling the main problem was in Western scholasticism completely displaced by a formal-logical or legal method of treatment, there is nothing surprising in this; for the foundation of such a method of handling the problem was in fact laid by Tertullian.

Irenæus had already clearly discerned and plainly expressed the thought of the most perfect union. The great Western theologians about the year 200 were further advanced in respect of Christology in consequence of the struggle with Gnosticism and Patripassianism, than the East was a hundred years later.[1] But what they had secured in the heat of battle did not possess even in the West itself any general validity; while in the East the greatest uncertainty reigned, having been brought in by the "scientific" Christology of Origen.[2] It delayed or threw back the development, which had certainly begun in a strictly scientific form. Thus at the beginning of the Fourth Century the East had once more to take up the question entirely anew. If we are to estimate correctly what was finally accomplished, it must not be measured by the Gospel, but by the dead state of things which had prevailed a hundred years before.

––––––––

The assertion of Arius and his pupils that the Logos took only a human body gave the impulse to renewed consideration of the problem. Like Paul of Samosata the Lucianists would have nothing to do with two natures, but they taught the doctrine of one half-divine nature which was characterised by

netur ... si incarnationem divinam non in patre neque in spiritu s. factam, sed in filio tantum credat, ut qui erat in divinitate dei patris filius, ipse fieret in homine hominis matris filius, deus verus ex patre, homo verus ex matre, carnem ex matris visceribus habens et animam humanam rationalem, simul in eo ambæ naturæ, i.e., deus et homo, una persona, unus filius, unus Christus." For details see below.

[1] See Vol. II., p. 275 ff.

[2] Nevertheless he strongly emphasised the thought of the deification of the human nature. On the other hand it is possible to attribute to him a doctrine of two natures.

human feelings, limited knowledge and suffering.[1] Like Paul of Samosata they also found fault with the orthodox on the ground that their Christology led to the assumption of two Sons of God or two natures; for these were still regarded as identical. The reply made by the orthodox at first to this charge lacked theological precision. Just because Athanasius was as much convinced of the necessity of the Incarnation (ἐναν-θρώπησις) as of the unity of the personality of Christ as Redeemer, he did not put the doctrine in fixed formulæ. On the one hand, as against Arius, he made a sharp distinction between what the God and what the man in Christ had done, in order to keep the Logos Omoousios free of everything human; on the other hand, however, he wished the divine and human to be thought of as a perfect unity; for it is to a strictly uniform being that we owe our salvation, the Word made flesh, the λόγος σαρκωθείς.[2]

[1] Most instructive in this connection is the otherwise interesting Creed of Eudoxius of Constantinople (Caspari, Quellen IV., p. 176 ff.): πιστεύομεν εἰς ἕνα, τὸν μόνον ἀληθινόν, Θεὸν καὶ πατέρα, τὴν μόνην φύσιν ἀγέννητον καὶ ἀπάτορα, ὅτι μηδένα σέβειν πέφυκεν ὡς ἐπαναβεβηκυῖα· καὶ εἰς ἕνα κύριον, τὸν υἱόν, εὐσεβῆ ἐκ τοῦ σέβειν τὸν πατέρα, καὶ μονογενῆ μέν, κρείττονα πάσης τῆς μετ᾽ αὐτὸν κτίσεως, πρωτότοκον δέ, ὅτι τὸ ἐξαίρετον καὶ πρώτιστόν ἐστι τῶν κτισμάτων, σαρκωθέντα, οὐκ ἐνανθρω-πήσαντα, οὔτε γὰρ ψυχὴν ἀνθρωπίνην ἀνείληφεν, ἀλλὰ σὰρξ γέγονεν, ἵνα διὰ σαρκὸς τοῖς ἀνθρώποις ὡς διὰ παραπετάσματος Θεὸς ἡμῖν χρηματίσῃ· οὐ δύο φύσεις, ἐπεὶ μὴ τέλειος ἦν ἄνθρωπος, ἀλλ᾽ ἀντὶ ψυχῆς Θεὸς ἐν σαρκί· μία τὸ ὅλον κατὰ σύνθεσιν φύσις· παθητὸς δι᾽ οἰκονομίαν· οὔτε γὰρ ψυχῆς ἢ σώματος παθόντος τὸν κόσμον σώζειν ἐδύνατο· Ἀποκρινέσθωσαν οὖν, πῶς ὁ παθητὸς καὶ θνητὸς τῷ κρείττονι τούτων Θεῷ, πάθους τε καὶ θανάτου ἐπέκεινα, δύναται εἶναι ὁμοούσιος. In the same way Eunomius, see Epiph. H. 69. 19, Ancor. 33.

[2] Curiously enough Athanasius throughout merely touched on the Christology of Arius. He afterwards stated his views in greater detail in opposition to Apollinaris, see Atzberger, Logoslehre d. h. Athan., p. 171 ff. In the "Orations against the Arians" the distinction between the divinity and humanity of Christ is brought prominently forward. The unity is next secured again by means of the deceptive formula that the flesh of the Logos was just his own flesh, his humanity (Orat. III. 32: "οθεν τῆς σαρκὸς πασχούσης οὐκ ἦν ἐκτὸς ταύτης ὁ λόγος· διὰ τοῦτο γὰρ αὐτοῦ λέγεται τὸ πάθος); see also the particularly characteristic word ἰδιοποίησις used for the assumption of the flesh. In the case of Athanasius it may already be very clearly seen that it was not religious feeling, but solely the biblical tradition regarding Christ (His weakness and His capacity for being affected in a human way,) which led him in the direction of the doctrine of the two natures. That tradition was a serious stumbling-block. But Athanasius used neither the formula "δύο φύσεις" nor the other "μία φύσις". (See also Reuter, Ztschr. f. K.-Gesch. VI., p. 184 f.) He speaks of divinity and humanity or of Θεὸς λόγος and σάρξ. So far as I know the formula μία φύσις was brought into use by Apollinaris, while, so far as I know,

The prolix amplifications of Hilary [1] were still more uncertain,
so much so that there was some justification for the charge
brought against orthodoxy by its opponents, that it led to
a division of the Son of God from the Son of Man. But
Athanasius had not reflected on this; in this connection too
he had stated the mystery simply and forcibly, frequently
in the words of Irenæus. The Logos not only had a man, did
not only dwell in a man, but was man. He united what was
ours with Himself in order to give us what was His. The
Logos is not, however, thereby lowered, but on the contrary, the
human is raised higher. [2] The question as to the extent of
what was comprised in the human nature was one which
Athanasius did not think out. He preferred to speak of a
natural union, an ἕνωσις φυσική, in Christ, but in this connection
he uniformly disregarded the human personality. The *free will*
was the category used, roughly speaking, at that period to
express what is called in modern times "human personality".
But Athanasius had not yet thought of this term in connection
with Christ, because he had not learned anything from Origen.
In all probability he found in fact no problem here, but, like
Irenæus, a comforting mystery which could not be other than

we first meet with the other, the δύο φύσεις, in Origen, and next in the mouths of
the Arians who reproached the orthodox with their use of it—with the exception
of a doubtful fragment of Melito, where, moreover, we have δύο οὐσίαι. The Cappadocians were the first to make use of the expression again in attacking Apollinaris,
inasmuch as they made a sharp distinction between "two natures" and "two
Sons". Owing to its use by the Cappadocians the formula of "two natures" had
almost already become orthodox and had been regularly introduced into ecclesiastical language, or, to put it otherwise, the tradition which had come down from
Origen and the presence of which is scarcely anywhere noticeable in Athanasius
himself, penetrated into the Church in connection with this matter also by means
of the Cappadocians. Cyril himself accordingly employed the expression. Thus the
problem raised by Reuter, op. cit. 185 f., as to how it comes about that Cyril
employs an Origenistic formula, which nevertheless is not to be found in Athanasius, is solved. We have to remember that there was a revival of Origenism in
consequence of the theological work of the Cappadocians. For the rest " δύο
φύσεις " as distinguished from " duo substantiæ " is to be regarded as a realistic
speculative formula.

[1]   See especially lib. X. de trinit., Dorner I., pp. 1037—1071.

[2]   See the collection of passages referring to the matter in Dorner I., pp. 948—
955. The Arian doctrine of the σῶμα ἄψυχον of Christ had already been combated
by Eustathius, see Dorner, op. cit. 966—969.

it was. He did not see that the mind must necessarily go astray on this matter either in the direction of the Gnostic doctrine of two natures or in that of the doctrine of unity, in the sense in which it was held by Valentinian, the doctrine of a heavenly humanity, or in the sense in which it was held by Arius. He believed that the doctrine of one composite being would serve his purpose which in any given case allowed of the distinction being made between what belonged to the divinity and what belonged to the humanity respectively. Neither did the great theologian who attached himself to Athanasius—namely, Marcellus—perceive yet the full difficulty of the problem. His energetic and practical theology could, however, only bring him nearer to the doctrine of a complete unity. The Logos is the Ego of the Personality of Christ; the nature which serves as an organ for the incarnate Logos and gives outward expression to his self-manifestation, is impersonal. The Logos is the ἐνέργεια δραστική, the divine energy; the body is the matter which is moved by it, which is transformed into a perfect instrument for the Logos. Marcellus was still further than Athanasius from assuming the existence of two separate, independent natures. He does indeed incidentally attack the Arian idea of the unity and he also employs the expression σύναφεια, connection, for the union of the Logos with humanity, but at bottom he sees at every point in the incarnate God-Logos a perfect unity.[1] He thus thought about the matter as the great Christologist did after him, who first felt the difficulty of the problem and created a formula which did not harm Greek religious feeling, but rather gave it a secure basis, and which in doing this nevertheless left unnoticed an element of tradition which was indeed concealed, but was not to be rooted out.

Apollinaris of Laodicea[2] whose divine teachers were Pythagoras, Plato, and Aristotle, who had learned from Athanasius,

---

[1] See Dorner I., p. 871 ff.; Zahn, Marcell., pp. 155—165.

[2] Dräseke, Zeitfolge d. dogmat. Schriften des A. v. Laod. (Jahrb. f. protest. Theol., 1887, Part 4). The same author, Apoll. v. Laodicea, nebst einem Anhange, Apollinarii Laod. quæ supersunt dogmatica (Texte u. Unters. z. Altchristl. Litt. Gesch. VII, 3, 4) in addition Jülicher in the Gött. Gel. Anz., 1893, No. 2.

whose theological method was the Aristotelian one, and who
because of this had been strongly influenced by the Arian
theology, the zealous and acute opponent of Origen and Porphyry, the sober-minded exegete who preserved the most brilliant traditions of the school of Antioch and had a reverence for
the letter of Scripture, made it the task of his life to combat
the Origenistic and Arian theologies,—their doctrine of the
Trinity and their Christology. Nemesius and Philostorgius have
termed him the most important theologian of his age,[1] and
that in fact he was. The most striking proof of his importance is supplied by the fact that many of his works create
the impression of having been written in later centuries, so
energetically has he thought out the Christological problem
and overtaken the coming generations. His syllogistic-dialectic
and his exegetic method is akin to that of the later Antiochians, and consequently the Fourth Century possessed in Marcellus, Eunomius, Apollinaris and the Antiochians a series of
theologians, who, although not unacquainted with Plotinus and
Origen, did not all the same adhere to the Origenistic, Neo-Platonic
speculative views, theologians who were united by their employment of the same philosophico-theological method, but who
nevertheless arrived at wholly different results.[2]

[1] According to Suidas, referring back to Philostorgius, Athanasius seemed a
child alongside of Apollinaris, Basil, and Gregory of Nazianzus.

[2] The fullest account of the Apollinarian Christology (after Walch) is that given
by Dorner I., p. 985 ff. (but cf. now Dräseke). Since that account was written,
however, thanks to the labours of Caspari (Alte und neue Quellen z. Gesch. des
Taufsymbols, 1879) and Dräseke, a new and rich supply of material has been
brought forward. These scholars have shewn that the Apollinarians have foisted
(from about 400) writings by their master on recognised authorities, such as Gregor.
Thaum., Athanasius, Felix of Rome, Julius of Rome, in order to accredit their
theology. We still possess the greater part of these writings; see Caspari, Quellen,
IV., p. 65 ff. (on the κατὰ μέρος πίστις); Dräseke in the Ztschr. f. K. Gesch. Vol.
VI., VII., VIII., IX.; Jahrb. f. protest. Theol., IX., X., XIII.; Ztschr f. wiss. Theol.,
XXVI., XXIX., XXX., collected together in the Monograph (Texte u. Unters. VII.
3, 4 by Loofs, Leontius von Byzanz, p. 92 ff.). The sources for Apollinaris
previously known, i.e., the places where fragments are found, are besides Epiph.,
H. 77, Socrat., Sozom., the works of Athanasius (the genuineness of the work adv.
Apoll. is disputed), of the Cappadocians, of Theodore and Theodoret.; see in
addition the resolutions of Councils from 362 onwards, Mai, Script. Vet. nova Coll.
T. VII. Spicil. X. 2 and catenas. Epiphanius treated Apollinaris in a friendly
fashion, Athanasius corresponded with him, the Cappadocians at first revered him

Apollinaris in combating Arius and his changeable Christ, Χριστὸς τρεπτός, started by allowing that the assumption that in Christ the God-Logos who was equal in substance with God united Himself with a physically perfect man, necessarily led to the idea of two Sons of God, one natural and one adopted.[1] A perfect God and a perfect man can never make a uniform being,[2] and in this he was in agreement with Paul of Samosata, Marcellus and the Arians. They constitute on the contrary a hybrid form, *i.e.*, a fabulous Minotaur, a cross breed, etc. But if there is no such thing as a union between a perfect God and a perfect man, then, if these premises are valid, the idea of the incarnation of God which is the whole point in question, disappears. And further the unchangeableness and sinlessness of Christ disappears also, for changeableness and sin belong to the nature of the perfect man. We are, therefore, not to see in the Redeemer a perfect man, we are on the contrary to assume and believe that the Logos assumed human nature, namely, the animated σάρξ, but that He Himself became the principle of self-consciousness and self-determination (πνεῦμα) in this σάρξ. Freedom too is an attribute of the perfect man, but—this as against Origen— Christ cannot possibly have possessed this freedom; for the Godhead in Him would have destroyed it. God, however, destroys nothing He has created.[3]

Apollinaris sought to prove his doctrine out of the central convictions of Greek piety, and at the same time to establish

and always held him in high respect, while the Arian theologians extolled him as their ablest opponent. Cf. on this Vincent., Common. 15—20.

[1] Gregor. Antir. 42. According to Apollinaris two knowing and willing beings could not possibly be united in *one* being. Here we can see the Antiochian tradition which had come from Paul of Samosata : δύο τέλεια ἓν γένεσθαι οὐ δύναται. (So Apollinaris according to what purports to be the work of Athanasius against him, I. 2 Migne, Vol. 26, p. 1096.)

[2] Εἰ ἀνθρώπῳ τελείῳ συνήφθη Θεὸς τέλειος, δύο ἂν ἦσαν, εἷς μὲν φύσει υἱὸς Θεοῦ, εἷς δὲ θετός (Dräseke, Texte u. Unters. VII. 3, 4, p. 388).

[3] There are three theses which Apollinaris everywhere attacks, and from these we can easily understand what his own theology is. He wishes to disown (1) the view that there are two Sons, (2) the idea that Christ was an ἄνθρωπος ἔνθεος, the view he attributed to Marcellus, since heathens and Jews could also believe in a Christ of this kind, (3) the view that Christ was a free and therefore a changeable being. He accordingly directs his attacks (1) against the Gnostic division of Christ and Jesus, (2) against Paul, Marcellus, and Photinus, (3) against Origen and Arius.

it by Biblical and speculative arguments. In a lying age he
stated it with the most refreshing candour. Everything that
Christ had done for us God must have done, otherwise it has
no saving power: "The death of a man does not abolish death"
—ἀνθρώπου θάνατος οὐ καταργεῖ τὸν θάνατον.[1] Everything that He
did must be perfect else it avails us nothing. There is here
thus absolutely no room for a human ego. This would do away
with the redemption. If it had been present in Him, then Paul
of Samosata would be right, and Christ would be merely an
inspired man, ἄνθρωπος ἔνθεος; but such a being cannot give us
any help; for if he had not essentially united humanity with
Himself how could we expect to be filled with the divine
nature? Further, if he had been a man he would have been
subject to weaknesses, but we require an unchangeable spirit
who raises us above weaknesses.[2] Therefore He must have
assumed our nature in such a way that He made it the perfect
organ of His Godhead and Himself became its νοῦς—the human
nature of Christ "is not moved separately"—οὐ κινεῖται ἰδιαζόν-
τως. But this is also the doctrine of Scripture. It says that the
Logos became flesh, and by this is denoted the animated body,
not the νοῦς. It does not say "He assumed a man", but that "He
was found as a man"—ὡς ἄνθρωπος. It teaches that He appeared
in the likeness of sinful flesh—ἐν ὁμοιώματι σαρκὸς ἁμαρτίας, and
was in the likeness or according to the likeness of men—ἐν
ὁμοιώματι ἀνθρώπων or καθ' ὁμοίωσιν. It shews finally that there
was in Him the most perfect unity of the human and the divine,
so that it says of the humanity what holds good of the divinity
and vice versa; God was born and died, and so on. At the same
time, however, the Godhead is not to be thought of as capable of
suffering. Owing to the intimate union with the σάρξ which was

---

[1] Antir. 51.

[2] Athan. adv. Apoll. I. 2: ὅπου τέλειος ἄνθρωπος, ἐκεῖ ἁμαρτία. It is just from
the νοῦς that sin springs. In addition Antir. 40, 51 : Ἡ σὰρξ ἐδεῖτο ἀτρέπτου νοῦ,
μὴ ὑποπίπτοντος αὐτῇ διὰ ἐπιστημοσύνης ἀσθένειαν, ἀλλὰ συναρμόζοντος αὐτὴν
ἀβιάστως ἑαυτῷ... Οὐ δύναται σώζειν τὸν κόσμον ὁ ἄνθρωπος μὲν ὢν καὶ τῇ κοινῇ
τῶν ἀνθρώπων φθορᾷ ὑποκείμενος. We must accordingly seriously accept the thought
that in Christ the Godhead was not a force, but τὸ ὑποκείμενον. Antir. 39: Οὐ
σώζεται τὸ ἀνθρώπινον γένος δι' ἀναλήψεως νοῦ καὶ ὅλου ἀνθρώπου, ἀλλὰ διὰ προσ-
λήψεως σαρκός. Apollinaris was conscious that he was the first to perceive what the
incarnation of God meant.

wholly and entirely *its* σάρξ, it shared in a complete fashion in the suffering, and the efficacy of redemption consists only in the fact that it did so share in it. And conversely the σάρξ is entirely taken up into the nature of the Logos. "The flesh therefore is divine, because it is united with God, and it indeed saves"—θεϊκὴ ἄρα σάρξ, ὅτι Θεῷ συνήφθη καὶ αὕτη μὲν σώζει.[1] Starting from this Apollinaris attempted to give his doctrine a speculative basis. This also rests on Scripture passages, but at the same time it refers back to a peculiar metaphysic. The attempt indeed to reach it was made long before his day, and it is uncertain how far he himself followed it out, since those who tell us about it had here an occasion for special pleading. Apollinaris starts from the Scriptural statement that Christ is the heavenly man, the second spiritual, heavenly Adam. (See also John III. 13.) Close upon this idea he, like Marcellus, puts in the more general idea of Aristotle that the divine is always related to the human as the moving to the moved.[2] As such

---

[1] Apollinaris assumes the existence in Christ of what is indeed a composite nature, but which is nevertheless a nature possessing oneness. The μία φύσις τοῦ λόγου σεσαρκωμένη is his formula (see the letter to the Emperor Jovian in Hahn, Symbole 2, § 120: ὁμολογοῦμεν . . . οὐ δύο φύσεις τὸν ἕνα υἱόν, μίαν προσκυνητὴν καὶ μίαν ἀπροσκύνητον, ἀλλὰ μίαν φύσιν τοῦ Θεοῦ λόγου σεσαρκωμένην καὶ προσ-κυνουμένην μετὰ τῆς σαρκὸς αὐτοῦ μιᾷ προσκυνήσει.) He, besides, expressly teaches that the σαρκωθεὶς οὔκ ἐστιν ἕτερος παρὰ τὸν ἀσώματον; he demands a perfect ἀντιμεθίστασις τῶν ὀνομάτων and he here reasons again mainly from the standpoint of Greek religious feeling: "Ἀλλης καὶ ἄλλης οὐσίας μίαν εἶναι καὶ τὴν αὐτὴν προσ-κύνησιν ἀθέμιτον, τουτέστιν ποιητοῦ καὶ ποιήματος, Θεοῦ καὶ ἀνθρώπου. Μία δὲ ἡ προσκύνησις τοῦ Χριστοῦ, καὶ κατὰ τοῦτο ἐν τῷ ἐνὶ ὀνόματι νοεῖται Θεὸς καὶ ἄνθρωπος. Οὐκ ἄρα ἄλλη καὶ ἄλλη οὐσία Θεὸς καὶ ἄνθρωπος· ἀλλὰ μία κατὰ σύνθεσιν Θεοῦ πρὸς σῶμα ἀνθρώπινον, or: ἀδύνατον τὸν αὐτὸν καὶ προσκυνητὸν ἑαυτὸν εἰδέναι καὶ μή. Ἀδύνατον ἄρα τὸν αὐτὸν εἶναι Θεόν τε καὶ ἄνθρωπον ἐξ ὁλοκλήρου, ἀλλ᾽ ἐν μονότητι συγκράτου φύσεως θεϊκῆς σεσαρκωμένης, see still other passages in Dorner I., p. 999 ff. The flesh must therefore be adored also; for it constitutes an inseparable part of the *one* substance: ἡ σάρξ τοῦ κυρίου προσκυνεῖται καθὸ ἕν ἐστι πρόσωπον καὶ ἕν ζῶον μετ᾽ αὐτοῦ.

[2] Mai VII., p. 70 (the letter of the Apollinarian Julian): Ἐκ κινητοῦ καὶ ἀκινήτου, ἐνεργητικοῦ τε καὶ παθητικοῦ, τὸν Χριστὸν εἶναι μίαν οὐσίαν καὶ φύσιν σύνθετον, ἑνί τε καὶ μόνῳ κινουμένην θελήματι· καὶ μιᾷ ἐνεργείᾳ τά τε θαύματα πεποιηκέναι καὶ τὰ πάθη, μόνος καὶ πρῶτος ὁ πατὴρ ἡμῶν Ἀπολλινάριος ἐφθέγξατο, τὸ κεκρυμμένον πᾶσι καταφωτίσας μυστήριον; see also l. c., p. 301, where Apollinaris himself has developed the thought of the one being (ἕν ζῶον) composed of the ruling moving principle of activity, and the σῶμα, the passive principle: σὰρξ, Θεοῦ σὰρξ γενομένη, ζῶόν ἐστι μετὰ ταῦτα συντεθεῖσα εἰς μίαν φύσιν. P. 73: Οὐδεμία διαίρεσις τοῦ λόγου καὶ τῆς σαρκὸς αὐτοῦ ἐν θείαις φέρεται γραφαῖς· ἀλλ᾽ ἔστι μία φύσις, μία ὑπόστασις, μία ἐνέργεια.

they stand opposed. This relation first reached perfect outward embodiment and manifestation in the word made flesh, the λόγος σαρκωθείς. But the Logos as "the mover" was from all eternity destined to become the λόγος σαρκωθείς. He has always been in mysterious fashion "mind incarnate"—νοῦς ἔνσαρκος, and "spirit made flesh"—πνεῦμα σαρκωθέν. Therefore He could be and had to be the λόγος σαρκωθείς, the Logos made flesh. He certainly did not bring His flesh with Him from heaven, but He is nevertheless the "heavenly man"; because it was intended that He should become flesh, His flesh is consubstantial with His Godhead; His Godhead comprised within it the future moment of the incarnation from all eternity, because only thus was it destined to be in the most perfect way the authoritative principle, the ἡγεμονικόν, of the creature. And just for this reason the historical incarnation which cannot be denied, is the direct opposite of anything like the accidental and arbitrary inspiration of a man. It is the realisation of an idea which always had its reality in the essence of the Logos, the heavenly man, the mediator (μεσότης) between God and humanity. After the incarnation too everything in this heavenly man is divine; for death could be overcome only if it was God who suffered and died. The human is purely the passive element only, the organ of the Godhead and the object of redemption.[1]

1 Apollinaris has not himself put in words those furthest reaches of his speculations in any of the numerous confessional formulæ of his which we possess. (See, e.g., the two Confessions in the κατὰ μέρος πίστις.) Much, too, of what is said by Gregory in his letters to Kledonius and by Gregory of Nyssa in the Antir. may be exaggerated, but as regards the main point Apollinaris's own words prove that he really went the length of attributing the moment of the σάρξ in some form or other to the Logos in the pre-temporal existence. He conceived of the nature of the Logos as that of the mediator; it was only by so conceiving of it that the μία φύσις could get justice done to it, and he accordingly does not hesitate to take something from the Godhead itself, without detriment to its homousia. The essential characteristic of the πνεῦμα which the Logos is, consists in this, that it includes the idea of the mediator, i.e., the type of humanity. In this sense he could say: ἡ θεία σάρκωσις οὐ τὴν ἀρχὴν ἀπὸ τῆς παρθένου ἔσχεν (Antir. 15), or (c. 13), προϋπάρχει ὁ ἄνθρωπος Χριστός, οὐχ ὡς ἑτέρου ὄντος παρ' αὐτὸν τοῦ πνεύματος, τοῦτ' ἔστι τοῦ Θεοῦ, ἀλλ' ὡς τοῦ κυρίου ἐν τῇ τοῦ θεανθρώπου φύσει θείου πνεύματος ὄντος. The Logos was already man before He appeared on earth, since the statement holds good: αὐτὴν τοῦ υἱοῦ θεότητα ἐξ ἀρχῆς ἄνθρωπον εἶναι. This conception, however, which was not meant to take from the historical fact of the incarnation, but was intended, on the contrary, to make its reality certain, now led him further to the

This doctrine, estimated by the presuppositions and aims of the Greek conception of Christianity as religion, is complete. Apollinaris set forth in a way that cannot be surpassed, energetically developed and in numerous works untiringly repeated, with the pathos of the most genuine conviction, what at heart all pious Greeks believed and acknowledged. Every correction made on his Christology calls in question the basis or at least the vitality of Greek piety. Only this perfect unity of the person guarantees the redemption of the human race and its acquiring of a divine life. "Oh new creation and wondrous mingling. God and flesh produced one nature!" (ὦ καινὴ κτίσις καὶ μίξις θεσπεσία, Θεὸς καὶ σάρξ μίαν ἀπετέλεσαν φύσιν!) All else in the Redeemer is non-existent for faith. The assumption of a human separate personality

idea that neither is the Godhead present in the Logos, in its totality : οὐδεμία μεσότης ἑκατέρας ἔχει τὰς ἀκρότητας ἐξ ὁλοκλήρου, ἀλλὰ μερικῶς ἐπιμεμιγμένας. As the middle colour between black and white has not merely the white in it in an imperfect way, but also the black, as spring is half winter and half summer, as the mule is neither wholly horse nor wholly ass, so the mixture of divinity and humanity in the Logos, at least in the Logos as appearing on the earth, is of such a kind that neither element is entirely perfect: οὔτε ἄνθρωπος ὅλος οὔτε Θεός. How far the doctrine of Apollinaris did actually lead to this conclusion—and we have here a clear example of the imperfect way in which the Homousia was understood amongst the neo-orthodox of the East; how far his opponents, including not only the Gregories, but also Theodoret, H. F. IV. 8, were justified in asserting that his Trinity was composed of a great, a greater, and a greatest; how far he made use of the old traditional image of the sun and the sunbeam in order to build up on the basis of the Homousia a graduated Trinity, are points which still require to be thoroughly investigated in the light of the new material we now possess. But if his Christ actually was the middle being his opponents represent it to have been, one can only be astonished to observe how in the case of Apollinaris speculation regarding Christ has returned to the point it started from. For this Christ is actually the Pauline Christ, the heavenly spiritual being (ἐν μορφῇ Θεοῦ), who assumed the body, *i.e.*, the flesh, neither ὁ Θεός nor man, but *as* God and *as* a man, who is nevertheless the mediator or reconciler between God and man because being without sin He has done away with sin and death in His body and consequently for humanity generally—the second Adam, the heavenly man. It cannot be doubted either but that Apollinaris formed his views chiefly on the New Testament; for he was above all an exegete—though unfortunately what is his in the numerous collections of passages, in those of Cramer pre-eminently, has up till now not been ascertained nor has any test been applied to find out what belongs to him—and he endeavoured to be true to the words of the Bible without applying the allegorical method of Origen, as his notable adherence to the primitive Christian eschatology, the reign of a thousand years, proves.

in Christ does away with His power as Redeemer. Thousands before Apollinaris felt this and had a vague idea of its truth. He alone understood and preached it. He did not juggle with what was a matter of indifference to Faith or dangerous to Faith, but did away with it.[1] But he perceived at the same time that that separate personality is present whenever a human νοῦς is attributed to Christ. This decided the matter so far as he was concerned. Christ possessed no human νοῦς. He was honest enough not to say anything more about the perfect humanity of Christ, but openly avowed that Christ was not a complete man.[2] The fact that Apollinaris, when called on to decide between the interests of the Faith and the claims of tradition, unhesitatingly decided in favour of the former, is fitted to call forth our admiration, and is a clear proof of the great bishop's piety and love of truth. But the very frankness of his language reminded the Church that the Gospel and partly tradition also demand a complete human nature for Christ. Even before the appearance of Apollinaris the conflict with Arius had, from about the year 351, taken a turn which made it as necessary to emphasise the complete human nature of the incarnate one as to reject the

---

[1] The confessional formulæ of Apollinaris and his pupils emphasised as a rule only the homousia of the Logos, the assumption of flesh from Mary and the perfect unity (ἐν πρόσωπον καὶ μίαν τὴν προσκύνησιν τοῦ λόγου καὶ τῆς σαρκός). The somewhat long creed in the κ. μ. πίστις is the most instructive, see Caspari IV., p. 18, there too, p. 20, will be found the shorter one, and at p. 24 that of the Apollinarian Jobius. In the latter we have: ὁμολογῶ τὸν κύριον Ἰησοῦν Χριστόν, ἐξ αἰῶνος μὲν ἄσαρκον Θεὸν λόγον, ἐπ᾽ ἐσχάτων δὲ αἰώνων σάρκα ἐξ ἁγίας παρθένου ἐνώσαντα ἑαυτῷ, εἶναι Θεὸν καὶ ἄνθρωπον, ἕνα καὶ τὸν αὐτόν, ὑπόστασιν μίαν σύνθετον καὶ πρόσωπον ἓν ἀδιαίρετον, μεσίτευον Θεῷ καὶ ἀνθρώποις καὶ συνάπτον τὰ διῃρημένα ποιήματα τῷ πεποιηκότι, ὁμοούσιον Θεῷ κατὰ τὴν ἐκ τῆς πατρικῆς οὐσίας ὑπάρχουσαν αὐτῷ θεότητα, καὶ ὁμοούσιον ἀνθρώποις κατὰ τὴν ἐκ τῆς ἀνθρωπίνης φύσεως ἡνωμένην αὐτῷ σάρκα, προσκυνούμενον δὲ καὶ δοξαζόμενον μετὰ τῆς ἰδίας σαρκός· ὅτι δι᾽ αὐτῆς ἡμῖν γέγονεν λύτρωσις ἐκ θανάτου καὶ κοινωνία πρὸς τὸν ἀθάνατον· ἄκρως γὰρ ἡνωμένη ἡ σάρξ τῷ λόγῳ καὶ μηδέποτε αὐτοῦ χωριζομένη, οὐκ ἔστιν ἀνθρώπου, οὐ δούλου, οὐ κτιστοῦ προσώπου, ἀλλ᾽ αὐτοῦ τοῦ Θεοῦ λόγου, τοῦ δημιουργοῦ, τοῦ ὁμοουσίου τῷ Θεῷ, τουτέστιν τῇ ἀσωμάτῳ οὐσίᾳ τοῦ ἀρρήτου πατρός. It is difficult to say whether the long Creed printed by Caspari, p. 163 f., and which in its formalism bears a resemblance to the Athanasian, is Apollinarian or Monophysite.

[2] Apollinaris did not deny the homousia of Christ with humanity, but he conceived of it as a likeness in nature = ὁμοίωμα. The later Apollinarians even emphasised the homousia, but they were thinking of a body and the ψυχὴ σαρκική.

thought of a transformation of the Logos into flesh or of a depotentiation. The Christological question became involved with the Trinitarian, and the latter was illustrated by the aid of the former. The full humanity was supposed to prove the full Godhead *ex analogia*; it had been reached in the struggle against Gnosis, and it was required in order to explain the Gospel accounts which otherwise cast a shadow on the Godhead of the Redeemer. Accordingly the complete humanity of Christ was first expressly asserted at the Council of Alexandria in 362 and, in fact, in opposition[1] to the views of Apollinaris.[2] The great literary activity of the bishop who was equally distinguished as exegete and apologist and as a systematic theologian, and who gathered around him a band of enthusiastic pupils, falls within the sixties.[3] With the beginning of the seventieth year of the century the Cappadocians came forward in opposition to their old master, shewed now their unconcealed

---

[1] See Dräseke, Texte und Unters. VIII. 3. 4., p. 28 f.

[2] Athan.. Tom. ad. Antioch. 7. He first establishes the truth that the Word of God did not come in Christ to a holy man as it came to the prophets, on the contrary : αὐτὸς ὁ λόγος σὰρξ ἐγένετο, καὶ ἐν μορφῇ Θεοῦ ὑπάρχων ἔλαβε δούλου μορφήν, ἔκ τε τῆς Μαρίας τὸ κατὰ σάρκα γεγένηται ἄνθρωπος δι' ἡμᾶς, καὶ οὕτω τελείως καὶ ὁλοκλήρως τὸ ἀνθρώπινον γένος ἐλευθερούμενον ἀπὸ τῆς ἁμαρτίας ἐν αὐτῷ καὶ ζωοποιούμενον ἐκ τῶν νεκρῶν εἰσάγεται εἰς τὴν βασιλείαν τῶν οὐρανῶν. Then it is further said: ὡμολόγουν γὰρ καὶ τοῦτο, ὅτι οὐ σῶμα ἄψυχον οὐδ' ἀναίσθητον οὐδ' ἀνόητον εἶχεν ὁ σωτήρ, οὐδὲ γὰρ οἷόν τε ἦν, τοῦ κυρίου δι' ἡμᾶς ἀνθρώπου γενομένου, ἀνόητον εἶναι τὸ σῶμα αὐτοῦ, οὐδὲ σώματος μόνου, ἀλλὰ καὶ ψυχῆς ἐν αὐτῷ τῷ λόγῳ σωτηρία γέγονεν. Finally, however, the identity of the Son of God and the Son of man is strongly emphasised. It was the same person who asked about Lazarus and who raised him from the dead. He asked ἀνθρωπίνως, He raised from the dead θεϊκῶς.

[3] In the way in which it kept firmly together, in its veneration for the master, in its activity and vivacity and finally in the efforts made by the members of it to carry their point in the Church, the school of Apollinaris reminds us of the school of Lucian. Like the latter it was chiefly an exegetical school, and at the same time like it it was a school for theologico-philosophical method after the manner of the Aristotelian dialectic. Such conditions always give rise to a peculiar arrogance and to a confident feeling of superiority to everybody else. "It was our father Apollinaris who first and who alone uttered and put in a clear light the mystery which had been hidden from all—namely, that Christ became one being out of the moving and the immovable": it is thus that one Apollinarian writes to another and in so doing shews that the real interest of the school was in the methodical and the formal. The fact that afterwards falsification was carried to such an extraordinary extent in the school is a sign that the Epigoni aspired to secure power at all costs.

indignation and sought to cast suspicion on his doctrine of the Trinity also. Apollinaris accordingly retorted by treating them as they treated him. How far Athanasius himself was mixed up with the controversy is a point which is still uncertain. Apollinaris separated from the Church about the year 375. Soon after he consecrated Vitalius bishop of Antioch.[1] It was the West led by Bishop Damasus which hastened to the assistance of the orthodoxy of the East held in fetters under Valens, and which at the Roman Council of 377 condemned Apollinarianism.[2] It could do this with a good conscience since it had always understood the "filius hominis" in the thesis in the full extent of the term and had had no difficulties about the unity. Basil had been the denouncer of the Apollinarian heresy (Ep. 263). The Council of Antioch of 379 sided with the Romans, and that held at Constantinople in 381 in its first canon expressly condemned the heresy of the Apollinarians. The anathemas of Damasus which belong perhaps to the year 381, condemn (No. 7) "those who say that the Word of God dwelt in human flesh in place of the rational and intellectual soul of man, since the Son Himself is the Word of God and was not in His body in place of a rational and intellectual soul, but assumed and saved our soul, i.e., a rational and intellectual soul without sin," ("eos, qui pro hominis anima rationabili et intelligibili dicunt dei verbum in humana carne versatum, quum ipse filius sit verbum dei et non pro anima rationabili et intelligibili in suo corpore fuerit, sed nostram id est rationabilem et intelligibilem sine peccato animam susceperit atque salvaverit."[3] Before this those are condemned on the other hand "who assert the existence of two sons, one before time and another after the assumption of flesh from the Virgin"—"qui duos filios asserunt, unum ante sæcula et alterum post assumptionem carnis ex virgine"—With all the zeal of a fanatic who had nevertheless not made the matter his own, Damasus, under the guidance of Jerome, soon

[1] Sozom. H. E. VI. 25; Epiph. H. 67. 21, 23—25; Gregor. Naz., ep. ad Cledon. II. 2; Basil, ep. 265, 2. On him see Dräseke, Ges. patrist. Abhandl. (1889), p. 78 ff.

[2] See the fragment "Illud sane miramur", Rade, p. 113 f., Mansi III., p. 461; see also the fragment "Ea gratia", Mansi III., p. 460.

[3] See Hahn, op. cit., p. 200.

after the year 382, once more took up the question and warned
the Church against the doctrine of Apollinaris and his pupil
Timothy: "Christ the Son of God by His passion brought the
most complete redemption to the human race in order to free
from all sin the whole man who lies in sin. If therefore anyone says something was wanting either in the humanity or
divinity of Christ, he is filled with the spirit of the devil and
proves himself to be a son of hell.[1] Why therefore do you
once more demand of me the condemnation of Timothy? He
has already been deposed here by the sentence of the Apostolic
chair, Bishop Peter of Alexandria being also present at the
time, together with his teacher Apollinaris, and must await on
the day of judgment the chastisement and punishment due to
his sin."[2] Apollinaris was condemned. One after another the
representatives of the non-Alexandrian theology, Paul, Marcellus,
Photinus, Apollinaris were cut off from the Church. The Antiochians will follow them, but the turn of Origen and his pupils is
also to come; the Cappadocians only will be saved "so as by fire."

The homousia or the identity in nature,—for both words were
used,—of the humanity of the Redeemer and humanity, was thus
acknowledged. And as a matter of fact many and important
arguments could be alleged in support of it. One has to make
use of the most desperate exegesis in order to banish it from
the Synoptics. And further Christ redeemed only what He
assumed; if He did not assume a human soul then the latter
has not been redeemed, and this appeared a very obvious
argument. Finally, it was only by the assumption of the completeness of the human nature in Christ that His divinity seemed to
be secured against sinking down into the region of human
feelings and suffering. But what signified these advantages if
the unity was insecure? And Apollinaris was perfectly right: it
was insecure. His opponents, the Cappadocians, might indeed
be able to refute him as regards separate points,[3] but they

---

[1] See the fragment "Illud sane miramur": "If an imperfect man was assumed
then the gift of God is imperfect, because the whole man has not been redeemed."

[2] Theodoret, H. E. V. 10.

[3] See several letters of Basil, the two letters of Gregory of Nazianzus to Kledonius
and his ep. ad. Nectar. sive Orat. 46, also the Antirrhet. of Gregory of Nyssa and

could not escape from the reproach he brought against them that they reduced the doctrine to the idea of an inspired man. In proportion, however, as they sought to escape it, their assertion of the completeness of the human nature in Christ became a mere assertion. Their long-winded, obscure, and hazy deductions made in truth a miserable appearance alongside of the unambiguous, coherent, and frank avowals of their opponent. There are two natures,[1] but yet there is only one; there are not two Sons, but the divinity effects one thing, the humanity another; Christ possessed human freedom, and nevertheless He acted within the limits of divine necessity. On the other hand, the whole position of the later Monophysites, thought out to all its conceivable conclusions, is already to be found in Apollinaris; but his opponents had not yet at their command a fixed terminology whereby to preserve the contradiction and to protect it against disintegration. At bottom their views were the same as those of Apollinaris, they did not think of two strictly separate natures; but they were unwilling to give up the perfect human nature, and they had learned too much from Origen to sacrifice the thought of freedom to the constitution of the God-man.[2]

his work ad Theophil. They enter upon an examination of the Scripture proofs of Apollinaris and also of his argument that the Logos could not have assumed a rational, free nature, since in this case he must necessarily have destroyed freedom, which is not, however, the Creator's way of doing: φθορὰ τοῦ αὐτεξουσίου ζώου τὸ μὴ εἶναι αὐτεξούσιον· οὐ φθείρεται δὲ ἡ φύσις ὑπὸ τοῦ ποιήσαντος αὐτὴν· οὐκ ἄρα ἑνοῦται ὁ ἄνθρωπος Θεῷ (Antirrh. 45). Gregory's remarks on this are extremely weak. The only striking thing is to be found in the detailed arguments in which it is shewn that the picture of the Christ of the Gospels includes a human soul; for it was neither the God-Logos nor the irrational flesh which was sad, which trembled, feared, etc., but the human spirit; see also Athan. c. Apoll. I., 16—18.

1 The definite formula "δύο φύσεις" without some qualifying clause is rarely met with in the East before the time of the great Antiochians, though it is otherwise in the West. But expressions such as that of Eusebius, H. E. I. 2, 1, are, however, frequent: Διττοῦ ὄντος τοῦ κατ' αὐτὸν τρόπου, καὶ τοῦ μὲν σώματος ἐοικότος κεφαλῇ ᾗ Θεὸς ἐπινοεῖται, τοῦ δὲ ποσὶ παραβαλλομένου, ᾗ τὸν ἐν ἡμῖν ἄνθρωπον ὁμοιοπαθῆ τῆς ἡμῶν αὐτῶν ἕνεκεν ὑπέδυ σωτηρίας, γένοιτ' ἂν ἡμῖν, etc. The Arian theologians always reproached the orthodox with teaching the doctrine of δύο φύσεις.

2 It is unnecessary to give any summary of the numerous different forms in which the Cappadocians set forth their view as against Apollinaris (see Ullmann, Gregor. v. Naz., p. 276 ff.; Dorner I., pp. 1035 f., 1075 f.; Schwane II., pp. 366—390), for what they wish and do not get at—the unity, namely—is obvious, while their terminology on the other hand is still uncertain. At this time expressions and

Probably an historical and biblical element had a share in turning them against Apollinaris, the thought of the man Jesus as he is presented in the Gospels, this, however, not as something which had a well-understood religious value, but as a part of the tradition of the schools and as a relic of antiquity. None of the religious thoughts current at that time led to the idea of a "perfect man" with a free will, *i.e.*, as an individual.

images of the most varied kind were in use (δύο φύσεις, δύο οὐσίαι, μία φύσις, σάρκωσις, ἐνανθρώπησις, θεάνθρωπος, ἕνωσις οὐσιώδης, ἕνωσις φυσική, ἕνωσις κατὰ μετουσίαν, σύγκρασις, μίξις, συνάφεια, μετουσία, ἐνοίκησις, the humanity of Christ was described as καταπέτασμα or παραπέτασμα, as ναός, as οἶκος, as ἱμάτιον, as ὄργανον. In the writings of the Cappadocians most of these terms are still found side by side; the only idea which is definitely rejected is that of the change into flesh whether by kenosis or by actual transmutation. The unchangeable, the divinity, remains unchangeable; it merely takes to itself what it did not possess. How the unlimited united with the limited is just the point which is left obscure. We might imagine we were listening to a teacher of the period before Irenæus when we hear Gregory of Nazianzus say that the unlimited dealt with us through the medium of the flesh as through a curtain, because we were not capable of enduring His pure Godhead (Orat. 39, 13, similarly Athanasius). He also teaches that Christ by assuming humanity did not become two out of one (masc.), but out of two became one (neut.). We can imagine it is Apollinaris who is speaking when he further declares that God is both, the one who assumes and what is assumed, and uses the word σύγκρασις in this connection (Orat. 37. 2, this word is frequently met in Methodius). This thought is expressed in an almost stronger form in Orat. 38. 13 (see Orat. 29. 19): "Christ is one out of the two opposite things, out of flesh and spirit, of which the one deifies while the other was deified, ὢ τῆς καινῆς μίξεως, ὢ τῆς παραδόξου κράσεως! The eternally existing comes into being, the uncreated is created, the unlimited limits itself, since—and now the thought takes an Origenistic turn—the rational soul is the means whereby a union is brought about between the Godhead and the gross flesh." As if it were possible to stop short at this function of the human soul, as if the human soul did not include the free will regarding which Gregory here maintains a prudent silence. On the other hand, however, Gregory maintains in opposition to Apollinaris that "there are undoubtedly two natures, God and man; soul and body are also in Him, but there are not two Sons or Gods, since there are not two men in one, because Paul speaks of an inner and an outer man"—this argument is specially weak since it is just the argument which Apollinaris could make use of. "To put it in a word: He is one and again He is another, in so far as He is Saviour, but He is not one person and again another person—God forbid. For both exist in the union which has been accomplished since God is made human and man is made divine, or however it may be expressed" (Ep. ad. Cledon. I.). Gregory as a pupil of Origen sees no difficulty in putting two different substances together into one. But neither does he follow the Chalcedonian Creed since with him it was not a question of a union of divinity and humanity in a third, but a question of fusion, and this spite of the δύο φύσεις. In their struggle with Apollinaris the Cappadocians nowhere intentionally arrived

The idea that the human νοῦς cannot have been saved if Christ did not assume it too, was one which they themselves could not honestly believe in, for they stripped His humanity of the principle of individuality and of more than that. In Apollinaris, on the contrary, it was really the sovereignty of faith which supplied him with his doctrine. He merely completed the work of Athanasius inasmuch as he added to it the Christology which was demanded by the Homousia of the Logos. They both made a supreme sacrifice to their faith in that they took from the complicated and contradictory tradition regarding Christ those elements only which were in harmony with the belief that He was the Redeemer from sin and death. They neglected everything else: λόγος ὁμοούσιος ἐν σαρκί, (μία φύσις σύνθετος)—the co-substantial Logos in the flesh, (one composite nature)—was the watchword of Apollinaris, in the sense of a perfectly uniform being. This Apollinarianism dressed in orthodox garb exercised the strongest possible influence upon Church doctrine in the Fifth Century. The Church, however, rejected this particular

at the line of thought followed by the school of Antioch at a later time, though, what is very rare, a formula here and there has an Antiochian appearance. They are at bottom Monophysites, although they were the first to make the ominous "two natures" of Origen fit for church use. It was only because they were compelled that they trouble themselves about the question of freedom in Christ, and the thought once occurred to Gregory of Nyssa (Antir. 48) that Christ would not have possessed any ἀρετή if He had been without αὐτεξούσιον. What most strongly impressed the Christian world in general was certainly the view that Christ had to give His body as a ransom for our body, His soul for our soul, His spirit for our spirit. There was undoubtedly some real justification for this thought since Apollinaris, or his pupils, seem to have carried their Paulinism so far (for so at least it would appear from some undoubtedly uncertain indications in the work of Athan. adv. Apollo, sec. I., 2 sq., II. 11) as to assert that Christ had only done away with the sin and death belonging to the flesh and thus renewed the flesh, but that the purification of the spirit was something which each individual had to carry out for himself by the imitation of Christ on the basis of that purification; in this sense redemption was not yet perfect. Σαρκὸς μὲν καινότητα Χριστὸς ἐπιδέδεικται καθ᾽ ὁμοίωσιν, τοῦ δὲ φρονοῦντος ἐν ἡμῖν τὴν καινότητα διὰ μιμήσεως καὶ ὁμοιώσεως καὶ ἀποχῆς τῆς ἁμαρτίας ἕκαστος ἐν ἑαυτῷ ἐπιδείκνυται (I. 2) or τῇ ὁμοιώσει καὶ τῇ μιμήσει σώζεσθαι τοὺς πιστεύοντας καὶ οὐ τῇ ἀνακαινίσει (II. 11). In opposition to this thesis, which probably really originated with Apollinaris since it is in harmony with the traditions of the school of Antioch, his opponents had certainly good reason for emphasising the full extent of the work of Christ if the whole structure of the faith of that time were not to be rendered insecure. Kenotic statements such as we meet with in Hilary are, so far as I know, not to be found in the writings of the Cappadocians.

form of unity and maintained the idea of "the perfect man ", "the perfect humanity" in the unity.   The Church knew what it wanted to do—to unite contradictions; there were not to be two sons, but two natures; not two natures, but one substance; though it certainly did not know how this was to be conceived of.   Nor did it know how the contradiction was to be expressed. But while it thus loaded its own faith with a heavy burden and thereby weakened its power, by preserving the thought of the perfect humanity of Christ, it did an inestimable service to later generations.   And there was further one good result which even those times got the benefit of.   The Gnostic specu- lations regarding the heavenly origin of the flesh of Christ, the transformation of God into a man, and such like, were now forbidden, or at least were rendered excessively difficult.

CHAPTER III.

THE DOCTRINE OF THE PERSONAL UNION OF THE DIVINE AND HUMAN NATURES IN THE INCARNATE SON OF GOD.

THE course of theological development in ecclesiastical antiquity may in some parts be compared to the windings of a descending spiral. Starting from any given point we seem to be always getting further away, and finally we come back to it again; only we are a stage lower down. The great Trinitarian controversy of the Fourth Century has its starting-point in the Christological doctrine of Paul of Samosata: Christ, the deified man inspired by the power of God and one with God in loving affection and in energy of will. Opposed to this doctrine was the belief that Christ is co-substantial with God, the Θεός ὁμοούσιος, who has become man. This article of faith established itself after Arianism and other middle doctrines had been rejected. But when in the course of the development both the perfect Godhead and the perfect humanity of Christ had been elevated to the rank of an article of faith, it looked as if the unity could be secured only by once more following the path taken by Paul of Samosata, by emphasising the spiritual and moral unity of God and man. This idea of the unity was indeed made more difficult now that the God in Christ had to be conceived of as a personal being, but any other unity no longer offered itself to thinking people who were unwilling to give up clear views on the subject. And it was still permissible to hold this view of the unity; for though the doctrine of Apollinaris had been repudiated, no fixed idea was thereby arrived at as to the nature of the union of the divine and the human. All the conceivable forms in which the conception of the union of the divine and the human might be put, were still at anyone's disposal, especially as no single term was yet in regular use.

As it was the Antiochian Apollinaris who worked out to its logical conclusion the doctrine of the Trinity as regards Christology, so it was his compatriots who worked out to its logical conclusion the formula "perfect God and perfect man." This conclusion was indeed the opposite of the doctrine of Apollinaris. He had shewn every clear thinker that it was impossible to carry out the idea of the incarnation without deducting something from the essence of humanity, and that the incarnate one could have only one nature (μία φύσις). But if the human nature in the incarnate one was nevertheless to be complete,— and the Church maintained that it was,— then the conception of the incarnation would have to get a new form. And if piety should suffer in the process, well, there was and there still is a stronger interest than that of piety—namely, that of truth.

§ 1. *The Nestorian Controversy.*

I. The most zealous opponents of Apollinaris were his compatriots and scientific friends, the Antiochian theologians, distinguished by methodical study of Scripture, sober thinking in imitation of Aristotle, and the strictest asceticism. They alone had during many decades worked out the Christological dogma in a scientific way in opposition to Arius and Apollinaris. Following the example of Diodorus of Tarsus, Theodorus of Mopsuestia treated it with the greatest fulness by making use of the philosophical theological fundamental conceptions which Paul of Samosata had already employed, and by turning to account the biblical results of the exegetical labours of the school of Antioch. The Antiochians based their position on the Ὁμοούσιος and did not wish either to interfere with the divine personality of the Logos. But at the same time they fully accepted the perfect humanity of Christ. The most important characteristic of perfect humanity is its freedom. The thought that Christ possessed a free will was the lode-star of their Christology. To this was added the other thought that the nature of the Godhead is absolutely unchangeable and incapable of suffering. Both of these thoughts have at least no concern with the belief in the real redemption of humanity from sin and death through the God-man. *The Christology of the Antiochians was therefore not soteriologically determined;* on the contrary, the realistic-soteriological elements were attached to it by way of supplement. [1]

In the view of the Antiochians it followed from the premises above mentioned, that Christ possessed, strictly speaking, two natures and that the supposition of a natural union (ἕνωσις φυσική, ἕνωσις καθ' ὑπόστασιν) was prejudicial both to the humanity and the divinity of Christ, as the doctrines of Arius and Apollinaris shewed. It was, on the contrary, necessary to maintain that the God-Logos assumed a perfect man of the race of David and united him with Himself. He dwelt (ἐνοίκησις) in the man Jesus from the time of the conception. This indwelling [2] is to be

---

[1] In respect of scientific method we may regard Paul of Samosata, Dorotheus, Lucian, the Lucianists such as Arius and Eusebius of Nicomedia, Eusebius of Emesa, Theodore of Heraklea, Eustathius, Marcellus, Cyril of Jerusalem, Apollinaris, Diodorus, Theodore, Polychronius, Chrysostom, Theodoret, etc., as forming a union of like-minded scholars as opposed to the school of Origen. Regarded in a theological aspect their differences are manifold. Diodorus of Tarsus (+ shortly before 394) and his school constitute a special group here. Diodorus "the ascetic who was punished in his body by the Olympian gods", was the recognised head. His numerous works, of which only fragments are preserved, are specified in the Diction. of Chr. Biogr. I., p. 836 sq. He was as prolific an apologist, controversialist, and dogmatist as he was an exegete. His most important pupils were Theodore of Mopsuestia (+ 428) and Chrysostom. The former is the typical representative of the whole tendency. Of the astounding mass of his works a good deal has been preserved. To what is printed in Migne, T. 66, we have to add, above all, the edition of his commentary on the Pauline letters by Swete, 2 vols., 1882; the fragments of the dogmatic works are given in the second volume, pp. 289—339. Sachau edited, in 1869, Syrian fragments with a Latin translation; in addition Bäthgen in the Ztschr. f. Atlich. Wissensch. V., p. 53 ff.; Möller, in Herzog's R.-Encykl. XV. 2, p. 395 ff.; Gurjew, Theodor von Mopsu., 1890 [Russian]. On the Antiochian School Münscher (1811), Kihn (1866), Hergenröther (1866). Specht, Theodor v. M. u. Theodoret, 1871; Kihn, Theodor v. Mops. 1880. Glubokowski has written a very comprehensive and thorough monograph on Theodoret in Russian (2 vols. 1890). Bertram, Thedoreti doctrina christologica. Hildesiæ, 1883. On Theodoret's brother, Polychronius, see Bardenhewer, 1879. Chrysostom did not take any part in the work of giving Christology a sharply outlined form. Theodoret taught the same doctrine as Theodore, but finally capitulated.

[2] Athanasius also used the word in a natural way, *e.g.*, de incarn. 9.

conceived of according to the analogy of the indwelling of God
in men generally. It is not a substantial indwelling, not κατ'
οὐσίαν, for this involves a transmutation or else limits the Godhead. Nor is it any mere indwelling of inspiration, but a gracious
indwelling, κατὰ χάριν (κατ' εὐδοκίαν), i.e., God out of grace and
in accordance with His own good pleasure has united Himself
with the man Jesus in the way in which He unites Himself
with every pious soul, only that in the case of Jesus the union
was besides a perfect one in virtue of the perfection of his
piety. It is to be thought of as a species of combination (συνάφεια), or we may express it thus: God dwells in the man as in
a temple.[1] The human nature, therefore, as nature remains purely
unchanged, for grace leaves the nature as it is. This nature,
then, like all human nature, was also a free self-developing
nature. As man Jesus Christ had to pass through all the stages
of moral growth as a free self-acting agent. Over him and in
him God did undoubtedly always hold sway as a supporting
power, but He did not interfere with the development of the
character belonging to his human nature, which by independent action confirmed itself in the good.

In accordance with this the union was only a relative one
(ἕνωσις σχετική) and was at the outset only relatively perfect, i.e.,
the God-Logos united Himself with the man Jesus as early as
the time of his conception, forseeing of what sort he would be
(κατὰ πρόγνωσιν ὁποῖός τις ἔσται), but this union merely began
then in order to become a more intimate union at every stage
of the human development.[2] It consisted in the common feeling
and energy of the two natures as well as in the common direction given to the will; it was therefore essentially a moral union.
By means of it, however, there appeared at the close of the
human development of Jesus and in virtue of the elevation
which was granted to him as the reward of his perseverance,

---

[1] Athanasius also employed this image, e.g., l. c. c. 20.

[2] It was always and from the first dependent on God's good pleasure in the virtue
of the man Jesus; for to Theodore the general proposition held good without any
exception that God bestows grace solely in proportion to the free exercise of virtue.
Grace is always reward; see the large fragment from the seventh book of the
work περὶ ἐνανθρωπήσεως in Swete II., p. 293 sq. Theodore paid special attention
to the baptism of Jesus also.

a subject or individual worthy of adoration, (I separate the natures, I unite the adoration: χωρίζω τὰς φύσεις, ἑνῶ τὴν προσκύνησιν). Still we must not speak of two sons or two lords, but, on the contrary, we have to adore one person, whose unity, however, is not a substantial one, but κατὰ χάριν. *The formula of the distinction of the natures and the unity of the person is to be found in Theodore.* But the unity of the person is the unity of names, of honour, of adoration.[1] Since, however, each nature in Christ is at the same time person, it was here that the peculiar difficulty of the Antiochian Christology made its appearance. The union does not at bottom result in any unity of the person; it is merely nominal. The Antiochians had two persons in Christ, a divine and a human (δύο ὑποστάσεις or πρόσωπα). When, spite of this, they spoke of one, this was really a third, or rather, to put it more correctly, it was only in the combination (συνάφεια), and indeed in the last resort it was only in the relation of believers to Jesus Christ that the latter appeared as a unity.

It was in accordance with this that the conception of the Incarnation took its shape. Two natures are two subjects; for a subjectless or impersonal spiritual nature does not exist Since accordingly one subject cannot become the other, for if it did it would either have to cease to exist itself or would have to transform itself, it is also impossible that the Logos can have become man. It is only in appearance that He became something through the incarnation, through "becoming man"; in reality He assumes something in addition to what He had. Since the sphere of the unity is solely the will, the attributes, experiences, and acts of the two natures are to be kept strictly apart. It was the man only who was born; it was he who suffered, trembled, was afraid, died. To maintain that this could be said of God is both absurd and blasphemous. So too accordingly Mary is not to be called the mother of God, not at least in the proper sense of the term.[2] But the Christian

---

[1] "Unam offer venerationem."

[2] The designation θεοτόκος was already quite current about 360. Instances of its use at an earlier period may be found in Pierius and Alexander of Alexandria, see accordingly Julian c. Christ., p. 276 E.

adores Jesus Christ as the one Lord, because God has also raised to divine dignity the man who in feeling was united with the Logos so as to form a unity.

In accordance with this conception, though certainly *invitis autoribus*, the humanity in the person of Christ came again to the front as a humanity which experienced merely the effects produced by the divine Logos who remained in the background. Since the distinction between person and nature was not fundamental, was not made in a realistic way, that is, and since the possibility of the substantial union of two persons was denied as we can see already from the case of Paul of Samosata, since further, in opposition to Paul, the Godhead in Christ was recognised as being a substantial Godhead, unity was *not* attained, as opponents at a later time justly observed. When again, as in the case of the Antiochians, an approach was made towards this unity, then the divine factor, contrary to the presupposition which was strictly clung to, threatened to become an inspiring and supporting power, and hence the reproach brought against them of Ebionitism, Samosatenism, Photinianism, or of Judaising. It would appear that the Antiochians rarely took the doctrine of redemption and perfection as the starting-point of their arguments, or when they did, they conceived of it in such a way that the question is not of a restitution, but of the still defective perfection of the human race, a question of the new second katastasis. The natural condition of humanity, of which liability to death forms a part, can be improved; humanity can be raised above itself by means of a complete emancipation from the sense life and by moral effort. This possibility, which lies open to everyone who summons up courage to raise himself by the exercise of free will above his inherited nature, has become a fact through Christ the second Adam. This fact has an immeasurable significance, for its effects now uphold everyone who honestly strives so to raise himself. The second Adam who has already appeared will once more appear from heaven ἐπὶ τῷ πάντας εἰς μίμησιν ἄγειν ἑαυτοῦ — in order to bring all to imitate him. He already points out to all "the path to the angelic life", and, judging from the way in which they sometimes work out the thought, it almost looks as if in the

view of the Antiochians the whole thing reduced itself to this
alone. The hints given here towards a spiritual conception of
the redemption through Christ have not, as one can see, resulted
from perceiving that everything depends on a transformation
of the feelings and will, and in the case of the Antiochians
themselves they have by no means entirely displaced the realistic
and mystical conception of redemption. In the indefinite form
which is peculiar to them, they were thoughts of reason and
results of exegesis, but not thoughts of faith. We hail them as
cheering proofs of the fact that the feeling of the spiritual
character of the Christian religion had not at that time wholly
died out amongst the Greeks; but there can be no doubt of this,
that these Antiochians were further away from the thought of
redemption as the forgiveness of sins and regeneration than
from the idea of a realistic redemption.   While in Christology
they illustrated in an admirable way the weak side and in fact
the impossibility of this idea, they did not understand how to
point these out in reference to soteriology itself. The latter was
with them always vague and tinged with a strongly moralistic
element. Its connection with the Christology was loose and
indefinite, while the development of the latter in the form of
positive doctrines was no less questionable, contradictory and
uncouth than the theses of their opponents; for the Antiochians
out of one being made two and thereby introduced an innovation into the Church of the East.   Only Gnostics had before
them taught the doctrine of two strictly different natures in
Christ.   The fact too that the redemption work of Christ was
essentially attributed to the man Jesus and not to God was a
further innovation. It was a flagrant contradiction that Theodore
would not entertain the idea of two Sons although he assumed
the presence of two natures and rejected the thought of an
impersonal nature. But though we might criticise the Christology
of the Antiochians still more severely, we must not forget that
*they held up before the Church the picture of the historical
Christ at a time when the Church in its doctrinal formulæ
was going further away from Him.* One has indeed to add that
they also directed attention to the incomprehensible essence
of the God-Logos which ostensibly remained behind this picture,

and did not on that account possess the power of presenting the historical Christ to the minds of men in a forcible way. But still that these theologians should have done what they did at that time was of immeasurable importance. It is to them the Church owes it that its Christology did not entirely become the development of an idea of Christ which swallowed up the historical Christ. And there is still something else for which these Antiochians are to be praised. Although they professed to preserve the traditional elements of dogma as a whole, they nevertheless essentially modified them by perceiving that every spiritual nature is a person and that what gives character and value to the person is feeling and will. This view, which was inherited from the Adoptionists and Paul, restores to the Christian religion its strictly spiritual character. But the Antiochians as Easterns were able to get possession of this knowledge only in a way which led from religion to moralism, because they based the spiritual on freedom, while again they understood freedom in the sense of independence even in relation to God. It was Augustine in his thought of liberty as "adhærere deo" and as "necessitas boni" who first united the most ardent piety with the recognition of Christianity as the spiritual-moral religion. It is, however, worth remembering that alone of all the Easterns the Antiochians and the theologians who sympathised with them took an interest in the Augustinian-Pelagian controversy— though they undoubtedly sided with Pelagius. For this interest proves that spite of the Eastern fog of mysteries, they were accessible to the freer air in which that controversy was fought out. Their opponents in the East wished to have mystery and spiritual freedom side by side; they, however, strove to lift the whole of religion up into the sphere of the latter—and they led it in the direction of moralism. [1] What confused the Antiochian

---

[1] Compare, above all, the full Confession of Theodore in Mansi IV., p. 1347 sq. (Hahn, § 139) which gives an admirable view of the Christology of Theodore and of its tendency. The word συνάπτεσθαι (συνάφεια) occurs more than a dozen times (so far as I know the word is first found within Christology in a fragment of Hippolytus [ed. Lagarde, p. 202]; ἵνα ὁ πρωτότοκος Θεοῦ πρωτοτόκῳ ἀνθρώπῳ συναπτόμενος δειχθῇ, Julius Afr. in his letter to Aristides [ed. Spitta, p. 121] uses συνάφεια in the sense of blood-relationship); λόγος ἄνθρωπον εἴληφε τέλειον ἐκ σπέρματος ὄντα 'Αβραὰμ καὶ Δαυΐδ is the principal thesis (also τέλειον τὴν φύσιν). The exaltation is strongly emphasised; then we have: δέχεται τὴν παρὰ πάσης τῆς

theology and involved it in contradictions was apparently the
load of tradition, *i.e.*, the adhesion to the belief that Jesus
Christ possessed a divine nature. This belief, however, constituted

κτίσεως προσκύνησιν, ὡς ἀχώριστον πρὸς τὴν θείαν φύσιν ἔχων τὴν συνάφειαν,
ἀναφορᾷ Θεοῦ καὶ ἐννοίᾳ πάσης αὐτῷ τῆς κτίσεως τὴν προσκύνησιν ἀπονεμούσης.
Καὶ οὔτε δύο φαμὲν υἰοὺς οὔτε δύο κυρίους... κύριος κατ' οὐσίαν ὁ Θεὸς λόγος, ᾧ
συνημμένος τε καὶ μετέχων θεότητος κοινωνεῖ τῆς υἱοῦ προσηγορίας τε καὶ τιμῆς· καὶ
διὰ τοῦτο οὔτε δύο φαμὲν υἰοὺς οὔτε δύο κυρίους. In what follows the doctrine of
the two sons is again disowned and this with a certain irritation, as is also the
idea that our Sonship can be compared with that of Christ, (μόνος ἐξαίρετον ἔχων
τοῦτο ἐν τῇ πρὸς τὸν Θεὸν λόγον συναφείᾳ τῆς τε υἱότητος καὶ κυριότητος μετέχων,
ἀναιρεῖ μὲν πᾶσαν ἔννοιαν δυάδος υἱῶν τε καὶ κυρίων). Theodore thus did not teach
the doctrine of two sons, one natural and one adopted, but that of one son
who communicated his name, his authority, and his glory to the man Jesus in
virtue of the συνάφεια. This was indeed the impossible shift of one in a dilemma. At
the end of the Creed the doctrine of the two Adams—a specially Antiochian doctrine
cf. Apoll.—and that of the two states are developed in detail. The commentaries of
Theodore ought to be studied in order that it may be seen how γνώμη and μίμησις—
as opposed to φύσις—were for him the main thing. Both in our case and in that of
Christ everything was to depend upon freedom, disposition, and the direction of the
will. In what follows I quote some passages from the dogmatic works of Theodore
by way of explaining and illustrating the account given in the text; Diodorus is in
complete agreement with Theodore so far as it is still possible for us to check
his statements. Theodore, de myster. I. 13 (Swete, p. 332): "Angelus diaboli est
Samosatenus Paulus, qui purum hominem dicere præsumpsit dominum J. Chr. et
negavit existentiam divinitatis unigeniti, quæ est ante sæcula"; cf. adv. Apollin. 3
(Swete, p. 318), where Theodore places Paul together with Theodotus and Artemon
and condemns him. Theodore, περὶ ἐνανθρωπήσεως l. 1 (Swete, p. 291): "præcipuum
Christo præter ceteros homines non aliquo puro honore ex deo pervenit, sicut in
ceteris hominibus, sed per unitatem ad deum verbum, per quam omnis honoris ei
particeps est post in cœlum ascensum"; l. 2 (p. 291): "homo Jesus similiter omnibus
hominibus, nihil differens connaturalibus hominibus, quam quia ipsi gratiam dedit;
gratia autem data naturam non immutat, sed post mortis destructionem donavit ei deus
nomen supra omne nomen... o gratia, quæ superavit omnem naturam!... sed mei
fratres dicunt mihi: "non separa hominem et deum, sed unum eundemque dic,
hominem dicens connaturalem mihi deum"; si dicam connaturalem deum, dic quomodo homo et deus unum est? numquid una natura hominis et dei, domini et servi,
factoris et facturæ? homo homini consubstantialis est, deus autem deo consubstantialis est. Quomodo igitur homo et deus unum per unitatem esse potest, qui salvificat
et qui salvificatur, qui ante sæcula est et qui ex Maria adparuit"? l. c. l. 2 (p. 292):
"quando naturas quisque discernit, alterum et alterum necessario invenit... hoc
interim item persona idem ipse invenitur, nequequam confusis naturis, sed propter
adunationem quæ facta est adsumpti et adsumentis... sic neque naturarum con-
fusio fiet neque personæ quædam prava divisio, maneat enim et naturarum ratio
inconfusa et indivisa cognoscatur esse persona; illud quidem proprietate naturæ...
illud autem adunatione personæ, in una adpellatione totius considerata sive adsumentis sive etiam adsumpti natura"; l. c. l. 7 (p. 294): οὐσίᾳ μὲν οὖν λέγειν ἐνοι-

the strong foundation of the theology of their opponents.   Their
Christology was built up on this thesis.   For the Antiochians

κεῖν τὸν Θεὸν τῶν ἀπρεπεστάτων ἐστίν ... οὔτε οὐσίᾳ λέγειν οὔτε μὴν ἐνεργείᾳ οἷόν
τε ποιεῖσθαι τὸν Θεὸν τὴν ἐνοίκησιν (both would draw him into the sphere of ἀνάγκη
and limit him). Δῆλον οὖν ὡς εὐδοκίᾳ λέγειν γίνεσθαι τὴν ἐνοίκησιν προσήκει, εὐδοκία
δὲ λέγεται ἡ ἀρίστη καὶ καλλίστη θέλησις τοῦ Θεοῦ ἣν ἂν ποιήσηται ἀρεσθεὶς τοῖς
ἀνακεῖσθαι αὐτῷ ἐσπουδακόσιν ἀπὸ τοῦ εὖ καὶ καλὰ δοκεῖν αὐτῷ περὶ αὐτῶν ...
ἄπειρος μὲν γὰρ ὢν ὁ Θεὸς καὶ ἀπερίγραφος τὴν φύσιν πάρεστιν τοῖς πᾶσιν· τῇ δὲ
εὐδοκίᾳ τῶν μὲν ἔστιν μακράν, τῶν δὲ ἐγγύς. This ἐνοίκησις, however, as is shewn
in what follows, has different τρόποι; in its unique and perfect form it is in the
"Son" only; l. c. (p. 297): Ἰησοῦς δὲ προέκοπτεν ... χάριτι παρὰ Θεῷ—χάριτι δὲ,
ἀκόλουθον τῇ συνέσει καὶ τῇ γνώσει τὴν ἀρετὴν μετιών, ἐξ ἧς ἡ παρὰ τῷ Θεῷ χάρις
αὐτῷ τὴν προσθήκην ἐλάμβανεν ... δῆλον δὲ ἄρα κἀκεῖνο, ὡς τὴν ἀρετὴν ἀκριβέστερόν
τε καὶ μετὰ πλείονος ἐπλήρου τῆς εὐχερείας ἢ τοῖς λοιποῖς ἀνθρώποις ἦν δυνατόν,
ὅσῳ καὶ κατὰ πρόγνωσιν τοῦ ὁποῖός τις ἔσται ἑνώσας αὐτὸν ὁ Θεὸς λόγος ἑαυτῷ ἐν αὐτῇ
διαπλάσεως ἀρχῇ, μείζονα παρεῖχεν τὴν παρ᾽ ἑαυτοῦ συνέργειαν πρὸς τὴν τῶν δεόντων
κατόρθωσιν ... ἥνωτο μὲν γὰρ ἐξ ἀρχῆς τῷ Θεῷ ὁ ληφθεὶς κατὰ πρόγνωσιν· ἐν αὐτῇ
τῇ διαπλάσει τῆς μήτρας τὴν καταρχὴν τῆς ἑνώσεως δεξάμενος; l. c. l. 8. (p. 299):
πρόδηλον δὲ ὡς τὸ τῆς ἑνώσεως ἐφαρμόζον· διὰ γὰρ ταύτης συναχθεῖσαι αἱ φύσεις ἓν
πρόσωπον κατὰ τὴν ἕνωσιν ἀπετέλεσαν (Matt. XIX. 6, is now brought in as an
analogy; we also no longer speak κατὰ τὸν τῆς ἑνώσεως λόγον of two persons,
but of one, δηλονότι τῶν φύσεων διακεκριμένων; ὅταν μὲν γὰρ τὰς φύσεις διακρί-
νωμεν, τελείαν τὴν φύσιν τοῦ Θεοῦ λόγου φαμέν, καὶ τέλειον τὸ πρόσωπον· οὐδὲ γὰρ
ἀπρόσωπον ἐστιν ὑπόστασιν εἰπεῖν· τελείαν δὲ καὶ τὴν τοῦ ἀνθρώπου φύσιν καὶ τὸ
πρόσωπον ὁμοίως· ὅταν μέντοι ἐπὶ τὴν συνάφειαν ἀπίδωμεν, ἓν πρόσωπον τότε φαμέν:
l. c. l. 9 (p. 300): Λόγος σὰρξ ἐγένετο—ἐνταῦθα τὸ "ἐγένετο" οὐδαμῶς ἑτέρως
λέγεσθαι δυνάμενον εὑρήκαμεν ἢ κατὰ τὸ δοκεῖν ... τὸ δοκεῖν οὐ κατὰ τὸ μὴ εἰληφέναι
σάρκα ἀληθῆ, ἀλλὰ κατὰ τὸ μὴ γεγενῆσθαι: ὅταν μὲν γὰρ "ἔλαβεν" λέγῃ, οὐ κατὰ
τὸ δοκεῖν ἀλλὰ κατὰ τὸ ἀληθὲς λέγει· ὅταν δὲ "ἐγένετο", τότε κατὰ τὸ δοκεῖν· οὐ
γὰρ μετεποιήθη εἰς σάρκα; l. c. l. 10 (p. 301): καταβέβηκεν ἐξ οὐρανοῦ μὲν τῇ εἰς
τὸν ἄνθρωπον ἐνοικήσει· ἔστιν δὲ ἐν οὐρανῷ τῷ ἀπεριγράφῳ τῆς φύσεως πᾶσιν παρών;
l. c. l. 12 (p. 303): ἀληθῆ υἱὸν λέγω τὸν τῇ φυσικῇ γεννήσει τὴν υἱότητα κεκτη-
μένον· ἑπομένως δὲ συνεπιδεχόμενον τῇ σημασίᾳ καὶ τὸν κατὰ ἀλήθειαν τῆς ἀξίας
μετέχοντα τῇ πρὸς αὐτὸν ἑνώσει. For the explanations given of Luke I. 31 f. ; 1
Tim. III. 16; Matt. III. 14, IV. 4, see p. 306 f., l. c. l. 12 (p. 308): ἑνώσας αὐτὸν
ἑαυτῷ τῇ σχέσει τῆς γνώμης, μείζονά τινα παρεῖχεν αὐτῷ τὴν χάριν, ὡς τῆς εἰς
αὐτὸν χάριτος εἰς πάντας τοὺς ἑξῆς διαδοθησομένης ἀνθρώπους· ὅθεν καὶ τὴν περὶ τὰ
καλὰ πρόθεσιν ἀκέραιον αὐτῷ διεφύλαττεν; see the sequel where the thought is
developed that the man Jesus voluntarily willed the good, his will being protected
by the God-Logos; l. c. l. 15 (p. 309): "utrumque iste filius vocatur, una existente
persona, quam adunatio naturarum effecit" l. c. c. 15 (p. 310): Mary may as well
be called θεοτόκος as ἀνθρωποτόκος, but the latter τῇ φύσει τοῦ πράγματος the
former τῇ ἀναφορᾷ. Adv. Apollin. l. c. (p. 313): the distinction between ναός (the
man Jesus) and ὁ ἐν ναῷ Θεὸς λόγος· next: ἔστιν μὲν γὰρ ἀνόητον τὸ τὸν Θεὸν ἐκ
τῆς παρθένου γεγεννῆσθαι λέγειν. In the eighth Sermon of the "Catechism" Theodore has employed the Aristotelian category "secundum aliquid" in order to shew,
that a thing may be a unity in one respect and a duality in another.

it was simply a fact to which they had to adapt themselves, although they had not themselves felt its truth in this form.

The view adopted by the Alexandrians, above all by Cyril, is undoubtedly the ancient view, that namely of Irenæus, Athanasius, and the Cappadocians, even when we make allowance for the falsification of tradition by the Apollinarians. The interest they had in seeing in Christ the most perfect unity of the divine and human, and therefore their interest in the reality of our redemption, determined the character of the development of the doctrines. Up till the year 431, and even beyond that time, this was wanting in formal thoroughness and scientific precision. This is as little an accident as the fact that Athanasius supplied no scientific doctrine of the Trinity. The belief in the real incarnation of God was only capable of the scientific treatment which Apollinaris had given it. If this were forbidden then theologians were debarred from all treatment of the subject with the exception of the merely analytic and descriptive or scholastic mode of treatment. This latter was not, however, yet in existence. But also apart from this, belief in the real incarnation simply demanded a forcible and definite statement of the secret, nothing more: σιωπῇ προσκυνείσθω τὸ ἄρρητον—let the secret be adored in silence. We must live in the feeling of this secret. This is why Cyril also stated his faith in what was essentially a polemical form only; he would not have taken long to have given a purely positive statement of it. Therefore it is that without knowing it he has recourse to Apollinarian works when he wishes to bring forward a plain and intelligible formula in opposition to the Antiochians and so to make the mystery clearer—and he is continually in danger of overstepping the limits of his own religious thought—and therefore it is finally, that his terminology has so little fixity about it.[1]

---

[1] In many respects his language is more certain than that of the Cappadocians and Athanasius: he no longer speaks, so far as I know, of mingling, fusion and so on, but in other respects his language is not behind theirs in uncertainty, and in denying "freedom" to Christ, he comes nearer to Apollinaris than they, for they in fact made use also of the conception of "two natures." The works of Cyril are in Aubert. Vol. VI. and VII., Migne Vols. 75—77. Most of what bears on the subject under discussion will be found also in Mansi T. IV., V. Specially notable are his letters to the Egyptian monks, to Nestorius (3) to John of Antioch,

Still he vindicated the religious thought of Greek piety: ("If the God-Logos did not suffer for us in a human way then He did not accomplish our salvation in a divine way, and if He was only man or a mere instrument then we are not truly redeemed." "Our Immanuel would not in any way have benefited us by His death if He had been a man; but we are redeemed because the God-Logos gave His own body to death.") Neither Cyril's personal character nor the way in which he devised and carried on the controversy ought to be allowed to lead us astray as regards this fact: for his Christianity did not succeed in making him just.

It was as easy for Cyril to formulate the thought of faith as it was for Athanasius and the Cappadocians. Faith does not in his case start from the historical Christ, but from the Θεὸς λόγος, and is occupied only with Him. By the Incarnation the God-Logos incorporated with Himself the whole human nature and still remained the same. He did not transform Himself, but He took up humanity into the unity of His substance, without losing any of it; on the contrary, He honoured it and raised it into His divine substance. He is the same with human nature as He was before the Incarnation, the one indivisible subject which merely added something to itself just in order to take up into its nature this something thus added. Everything which the human body and the human soul of the God-Logos endured, He Himself endured, for they are *His* body and *His* soul.[1] The characteristic *moments* in this

to Succensus (2) to the Constantinopolitan and Alexandrian Churches, the liber de recta in Jesum fide addressed to Theodosius, the book and the oration on the same subject addressed to the Empress, the explanation of the 12 anathemas and their vindication as against Theodoret, the five books against Nestorius, the dialogue on the Incarnation of the only-begotten, the other dialogue: "Οτι εἷς ὁ Χριστός and the tractate κατὰ τῶν μὴ βουλομένων ὁμολογεῖν θεοτόκον τὴν ἁγίαν παρθένον. On Cyril's theology see Dorner, Thomasius, (Christology) and H. Schultz. Koppalik, Cyril, Mainz 1881. That the work published by Mai (Script. Vet. Nova Coll. I., VIII.) περὶ τῆς τοῦ κυρίου ἐνανθρωπήσεως does not belong to Cyril has been shewn by Ehrhard (the work attributed to Cyril of Alex. περὶ τ. τ. κυρ· ἐνανθ., a work of Theodoret of Cyrus. Tübingen, 1888). In this treatise will be found a full and thorough account of the Christological formulæ of Cyril.

[1] I purposely cite no passages; they would not, taken separately, prove the doctrine here summarised, but would, on the contrary, point now in one direction and now in another. That the group of phrases given in the text embodies Cyril's

conception are "one and the same" (εῖς κἀι ὁ αὐτός) that
is, the God-Logos, "the making the flesh His own by way of
accommodation" (ἰδίαν ποιεῖν τὴν σάρκα οἰκονομικῶς), "He remembered who He was" (μεμένηκε ὅπερ ἦν), "out of two natures
one" (ἐκ δύο φύσεων εἷς), or "the joining of two natures in an
unbroken union without confusion and unchangeably" (συνέλευσις
δύο φύσεων καθ' ἕνωσιν ἀδιάσπαστον ἀσυγχύτως καὶ ἀτρέπτως), "the
Logos with His own flesh" (ὁ λόγος μετὰ τῆς ἰδίας σαρκός), hence
the "physical union" (ἕνωσις φυσική) or "hypostatic union" (καθ'
ὑπόστασιν), and finally, "one nature of the God-Logos made
flesh" (μία φύσις τοῦ Θεοῦ λόγου σεσαρκωμένη), [1] yet "not so that the
difference of the two natures is done away with by the union'
(οὐχ' ὡς τῆς τῶν φύσεων διαφορᾶς ἀνῃρημένης διὰ τὴν ἕνωσιν).
Cyril scarcely touched upon the distinction between φύσις
(οὐσία) and ὑπόστασις, which had nevertheless already come to
be current among the Antiochians so far as Christology was concerned; still he never says "of two hypostases" (ἐκ δύο ὑποστασεων)
or "a union in nature" (ἕνωσις κατὰ φῦσιν). [2] He was not able
to make that distinction, because in his view φύσις and ὑποστασις
meant the same thing as applied to the divine nature, but not
as applied to the human. *What rather is really characteristic
in Cyril's position is his express rejection of the view that an
individual man was present in Christ, although he attributes to
Christ all the elements of man's nature.* [3] For Cyril, however,
everything depends on the possibility and actuality of such a
human nature, on the fact, namely, that in Christ a hypostatic
union was reached and that this union forthwith purified and
view and in a measure embodies it completely, will be allowed by everyone
acquainted with the subject. Nor as regards Christology can I hope much from a
careful monograph on Cyril on the lines of a history of dogma, such as has
recently been asked for; for beyond what is adduced above Cyril had no theological interest; his way of formulating his views might, however, easily lead to his
having a very complicated "Christology" attributed to him.

[1] According to an expression taken from a work of Apollinaris which Cyril
considered as Athanasian, because the Apollinarians had fathered it on Athanasius.

[2] See Loofs, Leontius, p. 45.

[3] The Ep. ad Succens. supplies the most important proof-passages here. Cyril's
thought is that the substance (οὐσία) of the human nature in Christ does not sub-
sist on its own account, but that it is nevertheless not imperfect since it has its
subsisting element in the God-Logos. This either means nothing at all or it
is Apollinarianism.

transfigured human nature generally. Christ can be the second
Adam for men only if they belong to him in a material sense
as they did to the first Adam, and they do belong to Him
materially only if He was not an individual man like Peter and
Paul, but the real beginner of a new humanity. Cyril's view,
moreover, was determined as a whole by the realistic thought of
of redemption.[1] Still it is not a matter of accident that he so
frequently uses σάρξ for "human nature", although in opposition
to Apollinaris he acknowledged the human conscious soul in
Christ. It was only σάρξ that he could freely employ straight
off in this connection, not πνεῦμα and ψυχή. The proposition
that *before* the Incarnation there were two φύσεις, but *after*
it only one, is, however, of special importance for Cyril's conception of the Incarnation. This perverse formula, which Cyril
repeats and varies endlessly, regards the humanity of Christ as
having existed before the Incarnation, and therefore in accordance
with the Platonic metaphysic, but does not do away with the
humanity after the Incarnation, on the contrary, it merely transfers
it entirely to the substance of the God-Logos. Both natures are
now to be distinguished θεωρίᾳ μόνῃ—a phrase which he uses
very frequently, *i.e.*, it is in virtue of the physical or natural
unity that the Logos has actually become man. This physical
unity does not, however, mean that the Godhead thereby becomes capable of suffering: but the Logos suffers in His own
flesh and was born of Mary as regards His own humanity. He
is thus God crucified, (Θεὸς σταυρωθείς)—the Logos suffered without suffering, *i.e.*, in His flesh (ἔπαθεν ὁ λόγος ἀπαθῶς, *i..e*, ἐν
σαρκί)—and Mary is θεοτόκος, in so far as the σάρξ which she
bore constitutes an indissoluble unity with the Logos. (What
belonged to the Logos thus became the property of the humanity, and again what belonged to the humanity became the property
of the Logos—γέγονε τοίνυν ἴδια μὲν τοῦ λόγου τὰ τῆς ἀνθρωπότητος,
ἴδια δὲ πάλιν τῆς ἀνθρωπότητος τὰ αὐτοῦ λόγου). Therefore this

---

[1] Orat. ad imp. Theodos. 19, 20 (Mansi IV. 641): An apparent body would
have been sufficient if the God-Logos had merely required to show us the path to
the angelic life. But He became a perfect man, ἵνα τῆς μὲν ἐπεισάκτου φθορᾶς τὸ
γήϊνον ἡμῶν ἀπαλλάξῃ σῶμα, τῇ καθ᾽ ἕνωσιν οἰκονομίᾳ τὴν ἰδίαν αὐτῷ ζωὴν ἐνιείς,
ψυχὴν δὲ ἰδίαν ἀνθρωπίνην ποιούμενος ἁμαρτίας αὐτὴν ἀποφήνῃ κρείττονα, τῆς ἰδίας
φύσεως τὸ πεπηγός τε καί ἄτρεπτον, οἷάπερ ἐρίῳ βαφήν, ἐγκαταχρώσας αὐτῇ.

σάρξ of Christ can in the Lord's Supper be the means of producing
divine life, although it has not disappeared as human flesh.[1]

Is this conception Monophysitism? It is necessary to distinguish
here between the phraseology and what is actually stated. As
regards their actual substance all conceptions may be described
as Monophysite or Apollinarian which reject the idea that Christ
was an individual man; for between the doctrine of the hypostatic
union and the most logical Apthartodocetism there are only
grades of difference. No hard and fast line can be drawn here,
although very different forms of monophysitism were possible
according as the consequences of the Incarnation for the divinity
of Christ on the one hand, or for His humanity on the other
were conceived of in a concrete way and definitely stated. But
according to ecclesiastical phraseology only those parties are to be
described as monophysite who rejected the deliverance of the
Council of Chalcedon. But this deliverance presupposes the
existence of factors which did not yet lie within the mental
horizon of Cyril. In these circumstances we must content ourselves with saying that nowhere did Cyril intentionally deviate
to the right hand, or to the left, from the line of thought followed
by the Greek Church and its great Fathers in their doctrine
of redemption. He was a Monophysite in so far as he taught
that the Logos after the Incarnation continues to have as before
one nature only; but as the opponent of Apollinaris he did not
wish to mix the human nature with the divine in Christ.[2] The
assertion of a perfect humanity, unmingled natures, must be
allowed to stand, for it is really impossible to put in an intel-

---

[1] Cyril connected the Christological dogma in the form in which he put it, with
the Lord's Supper and also with baptism.

[2] Similarly also Loofs op. cit., p. 48 f. As Loofs rightly remarks, the distinction between the natures which Cyril wished to have made was nevertheless not
one solely in thought, but I cannot find any word which expresses what he wanted.
It is obvious that as regards the docetic and Apollinarian ideas (apparent-humanity,
κρᾶσις, σύγχυσις, τροπή), which were current and which were still widely spread
at the time, Cyril's influence was of a wholesome kind. It is wonderful how firm
he was here. Perhaps it is herein that his greatest significance lies. And yet the
best of what he had he had got from Apollinaris. Moreover, before Cyril, Didymus in Alexandria had already put together and used the words ἀτρέπτως,
ἀσυγχύτως in his formula for the Incarnation; see Vol. III., p. 299. They were
therefore not a monopoly of the Antiochians.

ligible form any part of these speculations which treat of substances as if they had no connection whatever with a living person. It is really not any more difficult to put up with the contradiction here than it is to tolerate the whole method of looking at the question. Both constitute the great mystery of the faith. Monophysitism, which limits itself to the statement that in Christ out of two perfect natures, divinity and humanity, one composite or incarnate divine nature has come into existence, and which will have nothing to do with the idea of a free will[1] in Christ, is dogmatically consistent. It has indeed no longer the logical satisfying clearness of the Apollinarian thesis; it involves an additional mystery, or a logical contradiction, still in return for this it definitely put into words the by no means unimportant element of "perfect humanity". But this Monophysitism, when distinctly formulated as ἕνωσις φυσική, certainly made it plain to the Greeks themselves that it was no longer possible to reconcile the Christ of faith with the picture of Christ given in the Gospels; for the idea of the physical unity of the two natures and of the interchange of properties, which Cyril had worked out in a strict fashion, swallowed up what of the human remained in Him. Arrived at this point three possible courses were open. It was necessary either to revise the doctrine of redemption and perfection which had the above-mentioned statement as its logical result—a thing which was not to be thought of,—or else theologians would have to make up their minds still further to adapt the picture of the historical Christ to the

---

[1] Like Apollinaris, Cyril also regarded with the deepest abhorrence the thought that Christ possessed a free will. Everything seemed to them to be made uncertain if Christ was not ἄτρεπτος. We can quite understand this feeling; for all belief in Christ as Redeemer is, to say the least of it, indifferent to the idea that Christ might have done other than He did. But that age was in the direst dilemma; for "freedom" was at that time the only formula for the "personality" of the creature, and yet it at the same time necessarily involved the capability of sin. In this dilemma the true believers resolved to deny freedom to Christ. With these accordingly the Apollinarians who had been excluded from the Church were able once more to unite. "All with the exception of a few," writes Theodoret H. E. V. 3, cf. V. 37, "came over to the Church and again took part in Church fellowship; they had not, however, all the same, got rid of their earlier disease, but still infected many with it who before had been sound. From this root there sprang up in the Church the doctrine of the μία τῆς σαρκὸς καὶ τῆς θεότητος φύσις, which attributes suffering to the Godhead too of the only begotten."

dogmatic idea, *i.e.*, to destroy it altogether, which was logical Monophysitism, or finally, it would be necessary to discover a word, or a formula, which would mark off the dogma of faith from Apollinarianism with still greater sharpness than had been done by the catchword "perfect humanity". It was therefore necessary to intensify the contradictions still further, so that it was no longer only the concrete union of the natures which appeared as the secret, but the conception of the union itself already involved a *contradictio in adjecto* and became a mystery. If it could be maintained that the natures had become united without being united, then on the outside everything seemed to be as it should be, and Apollinaris was as certainly beaten as Paul of Samosata—and this was maintained. But certainly no pupil of Athanasius or Cyril hit on a notion such as this, which paralysed the force of the thought: λόγος σαρκωθείς. A danger lurked here which had finally a momentous result. The expression of the faith which was constantly being burdened with fresh contradictions so that no legitimate element might be wanting to it, had to forfeit its strength.[1] Its place was finally taken by a complicated formula which it was no longer possible to make one's own through feeling, the mystery of conceptions put in the form of concrete ideas. If theologians might no longer teach as Apollinaris taught and in fact no longer quite in the way in which Cyril taught, they saw themselves under the necessity of using a complicated formula. But to begin with it seemed as if Cyril had carried his point.[2]

The controversy broke out in Constantinople and was throughout carried on with ambitious designs and for the purposes of ecclesiastical policy. In the person of Nestorius an ascetic Antiochian was again raised to the dignity of Bishop of Constantinople (428). The bishop of the capital just because he was

---

[1] Thomasius in his description of the Christology of Cyril sees only difficulties, but no contradictions. Nor has he fully understood the relation between Apollinaris and Cyril.

[2] Cyril never sought subsequently to tone down in appearance the paradox of the mystery of the Incarnation by means of logical distinctions. In this connection it is important to note that he allows that Nestorius wishes a ἕνωσις τῶν προσώπων (Ep. ad C P. Mansi IV., p. 1005), but that he himself rejects such a union because the important thing is the union of the natures.

the bishop was an object of jealousy to the Alexandrian Patriarch
and as an Antiochian he was doubly so. A conceited preacher and
one who plumed himself on being an enemy of heretics, but
not a man with any meanness about him, Nestorius, who was
supported by his presbyter Anastasius, gave offence in the capital
by using the catchwords of the Antiochian dogmatic and by
the contest he engaged in against the description of Mary as
θεοτόκος. With great frankness Nestorius described the statements
regarding the God who was wrapped in swaddling clothes and
fastened to the Cross, as heathen fables. His Christology[1] was
that of Theodore; it cannot be said that he developed it further;
on the contrary, one can see the influence of Chrysostom. Nestorius seems scarcely to have mentioned the human development
of Jesus, and he seems to have laid greater emphasis on the
idea of the union than Theodore ("one Christ"), if also only
in the form of the συνάφεια and προσκύνησις; but he was, above
all, concerned in getting rid of "the corruption of Arius and Apollinaris." Cyril took advantage of the excitement in the Capital,
which would perhaps have quieted down spite of some unruly
priests and monks, in order to stir up the Egyptian monks, the
Egyptian clergy in Constantinople, and the imperial ladies. The
result was an angry correspondence with Nestorius, who was,
moreover, protected by the Emperor. Cyril wrote in a more
dignified way than his rival, but the hierarchs since the days
of Cyprian had always known better how to take up an outwardly
dignified attitude than their opponents. The narrow-minded
patriarch of the capital was characterised by a simple pride.[2]
He expressed himself in an inconsiderate and imprudent way

[1] Some of his writings in Mansi IV., V., see also VI., VII., IX. On the beginning
of the controversy Socrat. H. E. VII. 29 sq. cf. the letters of Cœlestin and Vincent.
Common. 17 sq. The sermons of Nestorius, above all, deserve attention. The
history is in Hefele, op. cit. II. 2, pp. 141—288, who is indeed wholly biassed.
See Walch, Ketzergesch., Vol. V.; Largent, S. Cyrille et le concile d'Éphèse (Rev.
des quest. hist., 1872, July). Older accounts by Tillemont and Gibbon.

[2] Luther ("Von den Conc. u. K K.", Vol. 25, pp. 304 ff., 307), falling back
on Socrates, has rehabilitated Nestorius: "One can see from this that Nestorius,
though a proud and foolish bishop, is in earnest about Christ; but in his folly he
does not know what he is saying and how he is saying it, like one who was not
able to speak properly of such things and yet wished to speak as if he knew all
about it.

in his letters, and his conduct in his diocese was no less inconsiderate and imprudent, for there he went on with the work
of deposition and attacked "Apollinarianism" as if it had been
a red rag.

The formulæ employed by the two opponents were no longer
very different. Everything depended on how they were accentuated. Both spoke of two natures and one Christ, and the one
wished as little to be an Apollinarian as the other did to be a
"blasphemous"[1] Samosatene. Cyril did not deny that the Godhead was incapable of suffering, and Nestorius was prepared to
use even the formula θεοτόκος with a qualification.[2] But in reality
they were undoubtedly separated from each other by a deep gulf
represented in the former case by the ἕνωσις φυσική, (the physical
union,) and in the latter by the ἕνωσις κατὰ συνάφειαν, (the union
by combination,) and they can scarcely be blamed if they indulged
in specious arguments; for both views were intelligible only
when one went behind the formulæ, and in the case of many
if not actually in that of the leaders, ideas which went a great
deal further were as a matter of fact concealed behind the
formulæ.[3] Nestorius addressed himself to the Roman bishop
Cœlestin as a colleague of co-ordinate rank, Cyril did the same
soon after as an informant moved by a sense of duty, and
therewith the controversy came to have a universal importance.
But owing to the interference of the Roman bishop on behalf
of Cyril it also took a wholly unexpected turn; for there is not

---

[1] So Nestorius himself in the third letter to Cœlestin.

[2] This was the case from the first; see already the first letter to Cœlestin. In
the third letter he proposed to the Pope that the latter should see that neither
θεοτόκος nor ἀνθρωποτόκος was used, but χριστοτόκος; "This controversy about
words," he adds moreover, "will not in my opinion occasion any difficult enquiry
at the Council nor will it interfere with the doctrine of the divinity of Christ."

[3] In this contest Nestorius directs his attack against Photinianism, as representing
the idea that the Word had first originated with the Virgin, against Apollinarianism,
against the idea that the flesh of Christ was no longer flesh after the Resurrection,
and therefore against the "deificatio" of the flesh, and against the mingling of
the natures (first letter to Cœlestin). As a matter of fact nothing of all this applied
to Cyril. The latter fought against Nestorius as if it were a matter of combating
Paul of Samosata, and in this Cœlestin made common cause with him (see his
first letter to the Church of Constantinople c. 3). The real difference was: Did
God *become* man or did He not?

perhaps in the history of dogma a second fact of equal importance which so thoroughly deserves to be pronounced a scandal
nor one which at the same is so little to the credit of its author,
as the interference of the Pope on behalf of Cyril.

He had indeed sufficient reason for doing this. Since the
time of Athanasius and Julius, and in fact from the days even
of Demetrius and Fabian, it had always been the traditional
dogmatic policy of the Roman Chair to support the Alexandrian
Patriarch, as conversely the latter in his struggle against the
ambitious patriarch of New Rome necessarily looked for his
natural ally in old Rome.[1] Further Nestorius had shewn himself unwilling to excommunicate right off the Pelagians who
had been condemned by the Pope and who had fled to Constantinople. Finally, he had not in his writing generally given
token of the submission which the Apostolic Chair already
demanded. But what does that signify in face of the fact that
Cœlestin in interfering on behalf of Cyril disowned his western
view and in the most frivolous fashion condemned Nestorius
without having considered his teaching. That he did both things
may be easily shewn. In his letter to the Pope Nestorius laid
before the latter the formula "utraque natura quæ per conjunc-
tionem summam et inconfusam in una persona unigeniti adoratur"[2]
("the two natures which, perfectly joined together and without
confusion, are adored in the one person of the only-begotten").
*This was substantially the Western formula, and Cœlestin him-
self held no other view.*[3] He did not, however, trouble himself

---

[1] The solidarity between Rome and Alexandria is emphasised also in the letters
of Cœlestin to Cyril (I. 1), to John of Antioch (c. 2) and to Nestorius (c. 11).

[2] Ep. II. Nest. ad Cœlest. (Mansi IV., p. 1024.)

[3] It was substantially the Western formula: see on this above, p. 145, and
Reuter, Ztschr. für K.-G. VI., p. 156 ff. Augustine, Cœlestin's authority, had
taught the doctrine of una persona and two natures, or still more frequently the
"duæ substantiæ" which corresponds more closely with the Western conception;
he had further used "deus (ex patre) et homo (ex matre), or "verbum et homo"
or "deus-homo." He had rejected every view which taught the changeableness
of God, and explained that the "forma dei" remained together with the "forma
servi" after the "assumptio carnis". He had not himself questioned the relative
correctness of the idea of the indwelling of the Godhead in Christ after the
fashion of the indwelling of the Godhead in believers, *i.e.*, as in a temple, if he
also clung to the view that the Word *became* flesh. It is undoubted that accord-

about the formula, put his own Christology on one side and declared in favour of Cyril, while he made everything depend on the one point "θεοτόκος" in order at least to produce an appearance of difference, although this was just the very point regarding which Nestorius was prepared to make concessions.

ing to Augustine, "Christ is the collective person comprising a duality" in connection with which we have to distinguish between what relates to the forma dei and the forma servi. It is only with certain qualifications that the formula "God was crucified" is to be employed, the perfectly correct statement is only "Christus crucifixus est in forma servi." The passages in which Augustine speaks of "caro dei", "natus ex femina deus" etc., are extremely rare, and for him these formulæ have in my opinion no real importance; for the reconciling work of Christ belongs according to Augustine to his humanity; see above. Here he is therefore in agreement with the Antiochians. (The fact that in one passage Augustine, like Tertullian, speaks of "mingling", is of no importance). We meet with the same thing in Ambrose (de incarn. Sacram.) and again in Vincentius and Leo I. They all go back together to Tertullian (see above). Ambrose like Augustine speaks of two substances (natures) and he is "still more zealously intent than the latter in preserving the two in their integrity": "Servemus distinctionem divinitatis et carnis." Apollinaris has no more violent opponent than Ambrose. According to him the Johannine "becoming flesh" first gets its true meaning through "He dwelt among us." When we speak of the death and passion of Christ we ought to add "secundum carnem". And naturally in this connection emphasis is also laid on the "unus et idem", but the co-existence of the formæ dei et servi is maintained. And here, as in Augustine, we meet with the formula that the Logos assumed a man. In fact Ambrose, the keenest opponent of Apollinaris, turned against the ἀντιμετάστασις τῶν ὀνομάτων as against a dangerous, Apollinarian mode of speech, and went so far in regard to the distinction of the natures as even to hazard (c. 2, § 13) the bold statement: "Fieri non protest, ut, per quem sunt omnia, sit unus ex nobis." (More detailed information in Förster, Ambrosius, p. 128 f., 136 f.) The remaining evidence, moreover, which we possess in the shape of Papal letters etc., proves that the Westerns since the time of Tertullian and Novatian—in the latter also we find the "utraque substantia" (not "natura") and the "sociatus homo et deus"—possessed a christological formula on which they were all agreed, based on their creed, and to which they had strictly adhered, (see the admirable remarks of Reuter op. cit. p. 191 f.). *This form was closely akin to that of the Antiochians, although it rested on a different basis.* The Antiochians, without being influenced by the West, had reached quite independently the formula "two natures, one person." Not only the "mild" Antiochians (Loofs op. cit., p. 49 f.), but Theodore also (see above) and Nestorius had employed it. We must certainly admit that there is a radical difference, the Antiochian formula would strictly have run thus: The two natures, which are two hypostases, constitute together one prosopon or person who is to be adored, i.e., in the view of the Antiochians nature and hypostasis coincided and the undivided subject possessed its unity only in the union, the name, in the position of authority and in adoration. On the other hand we should have to paraphrase the Western form of the doctrine which was outlined by Tertullian, developed by Ambrose and handed on to the theologians

The Pope had determined to put down Nestorius. A Roman
Synod (430) demanded of him immediate recantation on pain
of excommunication. As if by way of insult Cyril was charged
by the Pope himself with the duty of carrying the sentence
out. Nestorius himself, whose Church was revolutionised, now

of subsequent times, thus: Jesus Christ as one and the same possesses two substances (properties) or two co-existent forms (status, forma). The difference is obvious at the first glance. The former formula is of a speculative kind and from
general conceptions constructs a personal being, the latter on the contrary assigns
"the state of life" to a person, it is, so to speak (see above), of a legal or political kind. The two formulæ are thus quite disparate (the Antiochian and Alexandrian are on the contrary formally similar) and therefore it is very possible that
the Western form in fine, considered from the *religious* point of view, contains a
side which is more akin to the Alexandrian than to the Antiochian form. But in
the formulæ Nestorius was in agreement with Cœlestin, and it cannot be proved
that the Pope was able to look behind the formulæ (see the "simplicior" in Mansi V.,
p. 702). In fact the opposite can be proved. In all his numerous letters he took
good care in connection with this affair not to state his own Christological view.
If anything escapes him it does not remind us at all of Cyril's views, see, *e.g.*,
the letter to the Church of Constantinople (Mansi IV., p. 1044): "Nestorius denies
that the Logos assumed a man for our sakes." He fastens solely on the θεοτόκος
to which objection had been taken by Nestorius and he adduces a sort of argument
in proof of its antiquity taken from a poem of Ambrose. Beyond this nothing
else occurs in his letters to shew what was really to blame in the Christology of
Nestorius. In place of this he from the very start loads him with abuse, with
threats from the Bible and with imprecations of a wholly general character, denounces
him to his Church as a heretic and writes him a letter (Mansi IV., p. 1026 sq.),
which in its unfairness and bare-faced audacity is one of the vilest compositions we
have of the fourth and fifth centuries. In his instructions to his legates too and in
his letter to the Council, he carefully guarded against using any Christological formula
at all, and he knew very well why. As Nestorius had expressed himself, particularly
towards the end, his Christology came so near to that of Augustine that Cœlestin at all
events was not able to distinguish the one from the other. Cœlestin's main concern,
however, was by no means with the Christology, but rather with the person of Nestorius
because the latter had not treated the Pelagians *ad nutum papæ*. He accordingly,
instructed his legates simply to take Cyril's side, and in his letter to the Council
contented himself with an exhortation to the members to preserve the old faith without
saying what the old faith was. There is, however, not the slightest ground for the assumption that Augustine's affair with the Gallican monk and presbyter Leporius (about
426, Mansi IV., pp. 518, 519 sq.) probably had an influence upon Cœlestin. This
controversy, which was quickly settled, undoubtedly shews that on the basis of the
formulæ of Tertullian and Novatian, discussions regarding the mystery of the person
of Christ had been started in the West too, which led to considerable division of
opinion, and that in opposition to this the Westerns held firmly to their "unus et
idem" which, however, was something different from the Antiochian ἓν πρόσωπον
(Leporius would have nothing to do with the idea of a deus natus et passus; Augustine
and Aurelius of Carthage forced him to recant: the Confession of Leporius is in

urged the Emperor to call a General Council, and in addition
to this collected a number of accusations against Cyril for the
way in which he had discharged the duties of his office. To the
twelve anathemas which an Alexandrian Council under the
presidency of Cyril had served on him, and which embodied
the teaching of Cyril in sharply cut phrases (θεοτόκος γεγέννηκε
σαρκικῶς σάρκα γεγονότα τὸν ἐκ Θεοῦ λόγον—ἕνωσις καθ᾽ ὑπόστασιν—
ἕνωσις φυσική—σὰρξ τοῦ κυρίου ζωοποιός,—the mother of God bore
flesh born after the manner of flesh, the Logos of God—hypostatic
union—natural union—the life-giving flesh of the Lord) he replied
by twelve counter-anathemas.[1] This sealed the breach. The
Emperor, displeased with Cyril, summoned a Council to meet
at Ephesus at Whitsuntide 431. Cyril who appeared with some
50 bishops, here shewed how an Emperor, such as Theodosius
was, ought to be treated. Without waiting for the arrival of
the Syrians under John of Antioch, the cautious friend (?) of
Nestorius,[2] the Egyptian party supported by the bishop of
Ephesus, Memnon, on its own authority and spite of the opposition of the Imperial commissioner, constituted itself the Council,
treated Nestorius who naturally did not appear at this meeting,
but waited in the city for the Syrians, as an accused person,
approved of all Cyril's declarations as being in harmony with

Hahn, Symbole 2, § 138). But in the affair with Nestorius Cœlestin nowhere referred
to the heresy of Leporius and to his recantation. The commonitorium of Vincentius best shews how little disposed those in the West were to have their own
Christological form of doctrine interfered with by the East or by the recognised
Council of Ephesus. In this book, written soon after 431, the Creed of Ephesus is
highly praised and Nestorius is abused, but at the same time the Christological
formula of Tertullian and no other is used, and what is said exhibits complete uncertainty regarding the teaching of Nestorius.

[1] Mansi IV., pp. 1081 sq., 1099 sq., Hahn, § 142, 143. In the third thesis of
Nestorius the permanence of the difference of the two natures also after the Incarnation is strongly emphasised. The fifth thesis runs thus: "Si quis post assumptionem hominis naturaliter dei filium unum esse audet dicere, anathema sit." It
is the most questionable one.

[2] John of Antioch was perhaps also one of the false friends of Nestorius. The
matter is still not quite clear—spite of the Coptic sources which are now at our
command. Probably John came so late intentionally, in order to be able to turn
the scale; from the first his attitude towards Nestorius had been an equivocal one.
We may indeed assume that he wished to get rid both of Nestorius and of Cyril
in order to secure for himself the supreme influence over the Church.

Holy Scripture and the Nicene Creed, pronounced the deposition
of Nestorius and declared him to have forfeited priestly fellowship. In opposition to this petty assembly, which did not set up any
new creed, but which on the contrary took up the position that
the sole question had reference to the Nicene Creed which was
in danger, Nestorius and his friends, as soon as the Syrians
arrived, held the legal Council under the presidency of the
Imperial Commissioner and pronounced sentence of deposition
on Cyril and Memnon. It was only now that the Papal legates
arrived in Ephesus and they at once took the side of Cyril.[1]
In accordance with their instructions they reopened the case
pro forma, in order to exalt the authority of the Apostolic
Chair. Cyril's party complied with this, and the Legates then
agreed to everything which had been done, after all the documents had been once more read over.[2] With the cry, "the whole
Council thanks the new Paul Cœlestin, the new Paul Cyril,
Cœlestin the guardian of the faith, Cœlestin who concurs with
the Council: One Cœlestin, one Cyril, one faith of the Council,
one faith of the whole world,"[3] this assembly closed, which sought
to maintain the ancient Nicene faith and did maintain it, at
which, however, there was no discussion, but at which unanimity was reached solely on the basis of a selection of authorities.[4]

[1] Otherwise the Westerns were not present at all.

[2] Besides Cœlestin's letter to the Council a similar one from the Carthaginian
Archbishop Capreolus who excused the absence of the Africans was read again.
This letter too is instructive because the bishop does not go beyond counselling
that no change should be made on the ancient faith. He expresses no opinion
on the question in dispute, (Mansi IV., p. 1207 sq.).

[3] Mansi l. c. p. 1287. At the close the Council did the Pope the further favour
of condemning the Pelagians. Thus both parties were quits. Cœlestin condemned
Nestorius without knowing what his teaching was and thereby disparaged his own
doctrine, and the followers of Cyril condemned the Pelagians without thoroughly
examining their theses and condemned themselves in condemning them. We may
put it thus and yet not mistake the peculiar solidarity which existed between the
Antiochians and the Pelagians; for the Ephesian judges knew nothing of this.
It was Cassian who first drew attention to it (libr. VII., de incarn. Chr.).

[4] See the Acts in Mansi; Vicentius too in the so-called Second Commonitorium
describes the procedure; they interrogated antiquity. "Peter of Alex., Athanasius,
Theophilus of Alex., the three Cappadocians, Felix and Julius of Rome were quoted
at Ephesus as teachers, councillors, witnesses and judges (what, however, was

The following will be found in the historical accounts. The
Emperor, instead of standing up for the right, allowed himself
to be overawed. At first it is true the resolutions of Cyril's
Council were annulled, but thereafter the controversy was to be
settled in true Byzantine fashion by the removal of the leaders.
The Emperor gave the force of law both to the deposition of
Cyril and Memnon and to that of Nestorius. The Alexandrians,
however, were united and followed one master, but this was not
the case with the opposite party. Nestorius who was violent but
not tenacious, resigned; soon, however, his isolation was to change
to imprisonment. In the eyes of the Emperor the doctrine which
he represented was by no means condemned; but Cyril succeeded
in getting permission to resume possession of his bishopric, and
by means of intrigue and bribery his party continued more and
more to gain ground at the Court and the capital. Still he could not
reckon on a victory as regards the dogmatic question; he had
to be content with knowing that a man who was acceptable to
him occupied the chair of Constantinople. The Emperor sought
to bring about a union, and the friends of Nestorius became
disunited. One section under the leadership of John of Antioch
was prepared to come to terms, and to this party Theodoret, [1]
the most distinguished Antiochian scholar, also belonged, though
undoubtedly with a certain reserve. Another section actively
resisted. Cyril's behaviour in the year 432—433 is little to his
credit. To him it was of more importance to get the condemnation of his mortal enemy, Nestorius, carried through in the
Church, than to preserve his dogmatic system pure. Thus he
subscribed the creed submitted by the moderate Antiochians,
without, however, retracting his earlier opinions, and in return
for this got some of the heads of the opposite party, above all,
John of Ephesus, to abandon Nestorius. Cyril could save his
consistency by interpreting this Antiochian creed in accordance
with his Christology; the friends of Nestorius were not able to

---

quoted from them originated with Apollinaris!), and also Cyprian and Augustine."
According to Vincentius these constituted "the hallowed decalogue". But in
addition to these the opinions of others were also adduced.

[1] He was now the spiritual leader of the Antiochians. He fought untiringly
for the view that God was incapable of suffering.

escape the disgrace which they had brought upon themselves by their treachery towards their ill-used friend. But in a question which was for him a matter of faith Cyril had agreed to a compromise, in proof of the fact that all hierarchs are open to conviction when they are in danger of losing power and influence.[1] He could, moreover, reckon on the victory of his opponents being a Pyrrhic victory. His own reputation and that of his dogmatic system went on increasing; thousands of monks were busy spreading it, and Cyril himself was constantly working at the Court and in Rome. The condemnation of Nestorius was followed by the most disgraceful treatment of the unfortunate bishop. In consequence of the confusion which arose because he was condemned while his teaching was tolerated by others, the whole party was weakened; the strict Nestorians separated from the others,[2] and since Cyril had not been under the necessity

---

[1] The Creed of Union is in Mansi V., pp. 781, 291, 303. (Hahn § 99). It was composed as early as the year 431, probably by Theodoret, and was sent from Ephesus to be submitted to the Emperor, Cyril subscribed it in the year 433. The Creed is a dogmatic work of art in which the Antiochians, however, could without much difficulty recognise their views, but not so Cyril. The second, and really important half runs thus: δύο γὰρ φύσεων ἕνωσις γέγονε· διὸ ἕνα Χριστόν, ἕνα υἱόν, ἕνα κύριον ὁμολογοῦμεν. Κατὰ ταύτην τὴν τῆς ἀσυγχύτου ἐνώσεως ἔννοιαν ὁμολογοῦμεν τὴν ἁγίαν παρθένον θεοτόκον, [Nestorius had already admitted this, and he might in fact have subscribed this creed without any scruples of conscience] διὰ τὸ τὸν Θεὸν λόγον σαρκωθῆναι καὶ ἐνανθρωπῆσαι, καὶ ἐξ αὐτῆς τῆς συλλήψεως ἑνῶσαι ἑαυτῷ τὸν ἐξ αὐτῆς ληφθέντα ναόν. Τὰς δὲ εὐαγγελικὰς καὶ ἀποστολικὰς περὶ τοῦ κυρίου φωνὰς ἴσμεν τοὺς θεολόγους ἄνδρας τὰς μὲν κοινοποιοῦντας, ὡς ἐφ᾽ ἑνὸς προσώπου, τὰς δὲ διαιροῦντας, ὡς ἐπὶ δύο φύσεων (Cyril admitted that!) καὶ τὰς μὲν θεοπρεπεῖς κατὰ τὴν θεότητα τοῦ Χριστοῦ, τὰς δὲ ταπεινὰς κατὰ τὴν ἀνθρωπότητα αὐτοῦ παραδιδόντας. This formula of union which reflects no discredit on the Antiochians, especially as they, like the Arians and Semi-Arians before them, had a theological rather than a religious interest in the problem, is markedly different from the later Chalcedonian formula. It does not abandon an intelligible position as that was understood by the Antiochians. Cyril had to content himself with the words ἕνωσις and θεοτόκος and had to put up with the absence of συνάφεια. He naturally clung firmly to the μία φύσις σεσαρκωμένη, declaring that the creed of union merely excluded the misinterpretations of the doctrine he had hitherto taught, misinterpretations which he had himself always disavowed; in fact he went so far as to assert that the Antiochians too understood the difference of the natures after the incarnation as being purely a distinction *in thought*.

[2] This was a slow process which began with the emigration to Edessa and was concluded only at the end of the fifth century with the formation of a strictly exclusive Nestorian Church. It maintained itself in the extreme East of Christendom, in East Syria and Persia, and soon took on a national colouring; on the

of retracting anything, he was able to direct his energies towards getting the decrees of his assembly accepted as orthodox, as ecumenical decrees, under cover of the union-creed. He did actually succeed in a few years in getting this done in the East; in the West they had ranked as such from the first. The situation continued to be perplexed and became more and more disingenuous.

§ 2. *The Eutychian Controversy.*

Cyril died in the year 444; there were in his own party some who so far as he was concerned had never forgiven him the union of 433 which had led Cyril to agree to the expression "δύο φύσεις".[1] His successor was Dioscurus who, according to the testimony of his own adherents, though not indeed the equal of his predecessor, was also not unlike him. The Alexandrian bishops from Athanasius to Dioscurus have something in common. They strove to make themselves the masters of Egypt and the leaders of the Church of the East.[2] Their resistance to the power of the State was not less strong than their hatred of the

strongly marked national consciousness of the Nestorians in Church matters, see Horst, Elias von Nisibis, p. 112 ff. The Emperor Zeno put an end to their existence in the Empire in 489. All the successors of Theodosius II. persecuted them. How the latter came to have such a ferocious hatred of Nestorius whom he had once protected has not, however, been yet explained. The Emperor gave orders that all the writings of Nestorius were to be burned and that his followers were to be called "Simonists". The result was that the writings of Diodorus and Theodore were all the more eagerly circulated in the East and translated into other languages. Edessa in particular did a great deal in the way of getting the Greek-Antiochian literature put into Syrian (Persian, Armenian). Much that is of a free and antique character has been preserved in the Nestorian-Persian or Chaldean Church; Assemani, Bibl. Orient. III., 2; Silbernagl, Kirchen des Orients p. 202 ff.; Kattenbusch, op. cit. I., p. 226 ff. For the history of dogma, in the strict sense of the word, the Nestorians are no longer of any importance.

[1] See Isidor Pelus. epp. I., Nos. 323, 334; Acacius of Melitene, ep. ad Cyril. in Mansi V., p. 860 (998 sq.). Cyril himself (ep. ad Eulog. Migne, Vol. 77, p. 225) says that people are now speaking reproachfully of him: διὰ τί δύο φύσεις ὀνομαζόντων αὐτῶν ἠνέσχετο ἢ καὶ ἐπῄνεσε ὁ τῆς ᾿Αλεξανδρείας. Fuller details in Ehrhard, op. cit., p. 42 f.

[2] See, above all, the Church History of Socrates, who thoroughly understood this aspiration of theirs.

parvenu, the bishop of New Rome, whose aspirations after power they wished to put a stop to. We can only compare them with the great Popes, and the comparison is so far a just one inasmuch as they aimed at making Egypt a sort of independent ecclesiastical State. Each bishop in the series from Athanasius to Dioscurus came nearer accomplishing this design.[1] In following out this policy they relied upon three powerful forces, on Greek piety and monasticism, on the masses of the lower classes, and on the Roman Bishop who had an equal interest in keeping down the bishop of Constantinople, and in making head against the State. In the respect first mentioned, Theophilus' change of front is specially characteristic. He abandoned science, *i.e.*, Origenism, as soon as he perceived that a stronger force was present in the Church,—namely, the orthodoxy of the monks and of the religious communities. From that time onwards the Alexandrian bishop stood at the head of ecclesiastical traditionalism; he decisively rejected Greek science. But in doing this he surrendered what was an important element in the influence he could exercise on the rest of the churches, and the loss of this was a momentous one. He became a national Coptic bishop. This brings us to the second point. Like all

---

[1] Of all the great bishops of the Empire the Roman and Alexandrian bishops alone possessed a traditional policy which was strictly adhered to, and acted in accordance with it. They accordingly really became forces in history. The Chair of Antioch never had a policy; in the conflicts with the Arians it became a mere puppet after the Church already sixty years before this had had to come to its assistance, and it possessed no fixed traditions. The position taken up in the Nestorian controversy by the feeble and unreliable John is typical of the bishops of Antioch (see his letter to Sixtus of Rome). It is customary to complain of the hierarchial imperiousness of Athanasius, of the violent actions of Theophilus, Cyril, and Dioscurus, and of the unfeeling policy of the Roman bishops, and to contrast them with the Bishops of Antioch. But people do not reflect that when forces manifest themselves they have to adapt themselves to the material upon which they are to work, and quite as little do they try to imagine what appearance the history of the Church would have presented without the " violences " of the Roman and Alexandrian bishops. Those who at the present day complain, together with their dogmatic system, would not at all events have been here at all if these tyrannical and unfeeling princes of the Church had not existed, and the tame dogmatic of the present time would never have made its appearance apart from the fanatical dogmatic of those despots. It may be incidentally remarked that we ought hardly to conclude from Mansi VI., p. 1008, that Dioscurus wished to restore Origen's reputation.

despots, the great Alexandrian bishops sought the support of
the masses. They were demagogues. They flattered the people
and sought to please them, while they hampered and crushed
the aristocracy composed of the bishops, the scholars and the
upper classes.

Athanasius had already begun this policy, in fact he was not
in all probability the first to follow it. Each of his successors
went a step further on these lines. But the Copts were not the
Romans; the master of the eternal city could always think of
ruling the world. A Coptic despot, however, who had rejected
all that belonged to the Greek world, could only dream of
world-empire.[1] Cyril had the Egyptian clergy and people completely under his power; but the less wise Dioscurus by his
unconcealed despotism created an aristocratic reaction in the
country. In him we see the downfall and overthrow of the
policy of the Alexandrian chair. Had he been a man like Leo I.,
Christianity might perhaps have got a second Rome in Alexandria.[2] But there was no room in the world for two such chairs.
The traditional policy of common action which had for so long
united Rome and Alexandria, was bound to reach a point at
which it turned into bitter enmity. The Byzantine patriarch
accordingly turned this enmity to account. It is indeed possible
to trace back the whole difference between the Roman and the
Alexandrian bishop to the brusque and imprudent conduct of
Dioscurus, or, with a still greater show of justice, to Leo's love
of power;[3] but this would be to take a narrow view of the

---

[1] Hellenism in the East received its death-blow owing to the downfall of the
Alexandrian bishop in the year 451; with Theophilus the process of estrangement
between the Church and Hellenism had undoubtedly already begun.

[2] The unique position of the Alexandrian Chair till 450 and its policy, have
up till now not had justice done them in our histories. The bishop of Alexandria
ranked as the second in Christendom (see above, at the Council of 381) and
corresponding to this position was a certain right which is indeed difficult to define—
of oversight, or better, the exercise of an oversight over the churches of the East
in the Fourth and Fifth centuries, which was being more and more widely
recognised. The Alexandrian bishops attempted to develop the position which
they thus occupied to a position of primacy.

[3] Sixtus III., Cœlestin's successor, as his letters prove, continued on the best of
terms with Cyril and silently repulsed the attempt made by two Nestorian bishops,
Eutherius and Helladius, to break up the union between Rome and Alexandria

matter. About the middle of the fifth century the Alexandrian bishop was on the point of becoming master of Egypt and at the same time master of the East. Rome would not have been Rome if she had looked calmly on at a result such as this, to which indeed she had herself contributed so long as she was concerned in defending herself against a more powerful enemy. It is here that we have the key to the proper understanding of the direction taken by Roman policy in the East, and it is owing to it that the history of dogma too has taken a wholly unexpected turn. For once that opposition had sprung up between Rome and Alexandria it could not be but that the profound dogmatic difference between the two which Cœlestin had disregarded in order to humble the Emperor and the Constantinopolitan bishop, should find expression. But if Rome came off victorious, then the dogmatic development of the East was bound to enter a new, and what was essentially, a foreign channel. Conversely again, the permanent victory of the Second Council of Ephesus (449) would, owing to the weakness of the State, have been equivalent to the victory of Egypt in the Church and probably also in the Empire; for Empire and Emperor had come to be entirely dependent on the Church which culminated in the Alexandrian chair and its monks. Pope and Emperor therefore made common cause; in the years 450—451 they had a common enemy and realised the solidarity of their interests. But the political victory of Rome did not correspond with the victory of Leo in the dogmatic question over the East under the leadership of Alexandria. The Emperor went about the matter in an extremely clever way. While making use of

(see the letter of the two amongst the letters of Sixtus). His epistle to John of Ephesus proves (ep. 6) that he had inherited his predecessor's hatred of Nestorius. On the other hand the sole letter of Leo I. to Dioscurus which we possess, and which was written soon after his enthronement (445), surprises us by its tone which recalls the letters of Victor and Stephanus, and by its demands. Dioscurus could not have forgotten a letter such as this. Still it is not till the time of the Council of Ephesus that we have plain evidence of the dissension between the two bishops (see Leo's ep. 43 sq.). The way in which Dioscurus treated Leo's epistle and the legates secured for him the bitter enmity of the Pope. The question now was : Rome or Alexandria? Previous to this Leo himself, like his predecessors, had in Christology used a form of statement which was Cyrillian, or Tertullian-Augustinian. He says Serm. 34. 4 : " dei filius naturæ carnis immixtus ", and 23. 1 : " naturæ alteri altera miscebatur."

the Roman bishop in so far as he found him necessary in order
to carry out his purpose, which was to deliver the Empire and
the Church from the despotism of Alexandria based as it was
on dogmatics, he at the same time deprived him of the power
of extending in any way his influence in the East by raising
his own court-patriarch to a position of equal rank and importance with the Pope. Simultaneously with the downfall of his
Alexandrian colleague Leo I. had to direct his attention once
more to his Constantinopolitan colleague, behind whom stood
no less a person than the Emperor himself—the Byzantine idea
of the state. He now promptly resumed the traditional policy of
his chair and sought to form a connection with Proterius, the
successor of Dioscurus. He, however, no longer found in Alexandria a powerful monarch, but only the shadow of such a ruler,
the Melchitian bishop of a small party who soon fell a victim
to the fanaticism of the Egyptians. But on the other hand the
Emperor had dearly bought his victory over the hankering
after independence on the part of the Church in the East, in
the form in which it had been fostered by the monkish church
of the Copts under the Alexandrian patriarchs. He plunged the
East into a state of frightful confusion, and his policy, which
was a clever one for the moment, resulted in being the direst
calamity for the Eastern Empire, since it set free the centrifugal
and national forces of the Eastern provinces. It was possible to
overthrow the Egyptian ecclesiastical State, but this done, it
was no longer possible permanently to retain Egypt. It was
possible to deliver the Empire and Constantinople from the
domination of a dogmatic which was hostile to the State, but
it was not possible to force a foreign dogmatic on the people
of the East. The Roman bishop, however, also soon saw that
he was further from the attainment of his aim than ever, and
the proud language employed by Leo's successors towards the
Emperor and the East and which reminds us of the mediæval
Popes, is not so much a token of actual power as a proof of the
breach and estrangement between East and West which had occurred, and so of the actual powerlessness of Rome. The Emperor
could no longer get at the Pope, but neither could the Pope
get at the Emperor and the East; he came to have no influence.

A section of the Easterns could come to terms with the dogmatic decree of Chalcedon—it is always possible to come to terms with dogmatic decrees—and while acknowledging its authority could nevertheless give expression to what was truly essential in the Faith of the East; but the twenty-eighth Canon of Chalcedon, which had reference to the Roman bishop, was no "noumenon" which could be got over by scholastic refinement. Rome had the satisfaction of having dictated its Christological formula to the Byzantine State-Church, just as it had previously taken the biggest share in the work of getting the Trinitarian formula accepted, but this very Church now took up a position of extreme isolation relatively to Rome and the West. The Byzantine Patriarch, although his power was always more and more restricted within the domain in the East over which he ruled, was an invincible opponent; for he was simply the exponent of all the peculiar powers still possessed at the time by the State of Constantine and Theodosius I. and by the Greek Church.

This is the general outline of the circumstances we have to take into account in studying the history of the "Eutychian Controversy." What happened here was, *mutatis mutandis,* repeated in the controversy about images in so far as the State in this struggle in the same way resisted the authority of the Church which sought to crush it. It was successful in both instances. The power which had opposed the State in Egyptian Monophysitism and set itself against it in the matter of the adoration of images, was one and the same. But the nature of the victory was different in the two cases. In the middle of the Fifth Century the State, unfortunately for itself, did not possess the power of putting up with the dogmatic teaching of its opponent while humiliating the opponent himself; or shall we say: it did not think of the power it had, and to its own loss lent an ear to the suggestions of a foreign power, namely, the Roman bishop. In the ninth century, however, it was able to let its opponent have its own way in the domain of dogma and worship—for the adoration of images was restored,—and yet to make it submit to its laws and attach it to its interests. A powerful ruler, who would have accepted the dogmatic decree

of the second Council of Ephesus but who would have been
at the same time able to break the political power of Dioscurus
and to compel the monks and Copts to submit—would perhaps—if it is permissible to make such a reflection—have been
able to maintain the unity of the Empire of Constantius and
to preserve for the Eastern provinces the Græco-Christian culture. Of what incalculable importance this would have been!
But it is useless to pursue a line of thought such as this.

It follows from these considerations that the history of dogma
has to be regarded almost exclusively in its connection with
politics, not merely after the Council of Chalcedon, but already
previous to this. The forces which from 444 onwards determined
the great decisions and actions were throughout political. It
was individuals only who really thought of the Faith when they
spoke of the Faith; they brought about crises, but they no
longer determined the course things were to take. Nor is it
the case that what was dogmatically "the right thing" gained
acceptance here as if by a wonderful arrangement of things;
for if, as is reasonable to suppose, "the right thing" here can
only be what is in harmony with Greek religious feeling, then
it did not gain entire acceptance. And in pronouncing an
opinion on this, whether we take our stand at a very much
earlier or at a very much later period, it may certainly be
maintained that the decision of Chalcedon was the happiest
amongst those that were at all possible at the time; but to see
this can in no way alter the opinion that the Council of Chalcedon, which to distinguish it from the Robber Council [1] we might
call the Robber and Traitor Council, betrayed the secret of
Greek Faith. It is only with the forces of history that the
historian is concerned; and so, from about 444 onwards, the
political historian almost entirely takes the place of the historian
of dogmas. If the latter is willing to keep strictly to his own
domain but a small extent of ground is left to him, which,
since what does not change awakens no interest, gets smaller
and smaller from century to century.

---

[1] Thomasius (Dogmengesch. I. 2, p. 367) also pronounces the Council of Chalcedon "hardly less stormy" than that of the year 449.

If it be asked, what is the saddest and most momentous event in the history of dogma since the condemnation of Paul of Samosata, we must point to the union of the year 433. The shadow of this occurrence rests on the whole subsequent history of dogma.[1] It bore two sorts of evil fruit. In the first place it permanently prohibited Greek piety from establishing the formula which was alone appropriate to it: μία φύσις θεοῦ λόγου σεσαρκωμένη—one incarnate nature of the divine Logos. (The relief which the Creed of Ephesus of 449 was supposed to bring, came too late.) In the second place it introduced such a stagnation into the dogmatic question that every one who attempted to state his Christological views ran the risk of being regarded as a heretic, while on the other hand people found it possible when they so desired, to give a favourable turn to every dogmatic utterance. It threw the East into

---

[1] The documentary material bearing on the Eutychian controversy has been for the most part printed in Mansi T. V. sq.; where also will be found the letters of Leo I. (cf. the edition of Ballerini) and those of Theodoret having reference to the subject. Historical accounts in Prosper, Liberatus, Facundus, in the hist. eccl. of Zacharias of Mytilene hitherto published only in Syrian, in the breviculus hist. Eutych. (Sirmond's App. ad Cod. Theodos.), in Euagrius, Theophanes, and many later Greek and particularly Oriental chroniclers. To these have been added in recent times, apart from Zacharias (see Krüger, Monophys. Streitigkeiten, 1884) first of all the hitherto unknown Appellations of Flavian and Eusebius of Doryläum to Leo I. (see Guerrino Amelini, S. Leone magno e l'Oriente. Roma 1882, Grisar i. d. Ztschr. f. Kath. Theol. VII., 1883, p. 191 f., Mommsen, Neues Archiv. XI. 2, 1886, p. 361 f.); second, the Acts of the Robber-Council according to a Syrian MS., in German by Hoffmann (Kiel 1873), in an English translation with rich additions from other Syrian MSS. by Perry, The Second Synod of Ephesus 1881, and previously published by the same writer, An Ancient Syriac Docum. etc., Oxford 1867; Martin, Actes du Brigand. d'Éphese, traduct. faite sur le texte Syriaque, 1875; by the same, Le Pseudo-Synode connu dans l'hist. sous le nom de Brigandage d'Éphese, étudié d'après ses actes retrouvés en Syriaque, 1875, thirdly the publication of Révillout, Récits de Dioscore, exilé à Gangres, sur le concile de Chalcédoine, translated into French from the Coptic, (Rev. Egyptol. 1880, p. 187 sq., 1882, p. 21 sq., 1883, p. 17 sq.); see Krüger op. cit. p. 12 f. Accounts in Baronius, Tillemont, Gibbon, Walch, Schröckh, Neander and Hefele; cf. the works on Leo I. by Quesnel, Arendt, Perthel. Spite of these works we do not yet possess a critical account of the history of the Church and of dogma for the all important years previous to the Council of Chalcedon. The most important preliminary work in this direction would be a monograph on Theodoret, the man who in my opinion was the most truth-loving and the least guided by consider-ations of policy of the Fathers of that period. This has been done by a Russian, Glubokowski (see above); but it is unfortunately not accessible to German science.

a state of confusion and made of Christology an armoury of poisoned weapons for the warfare of ecclesiastical politics. A middle party was formed from each of the two sides. To one of these Theodoret belonged, and to another Dioscurus (Cyril). But the representatives of these middle parties were no nearer each other than the two extremes. If they employed the same formulæ they nevertheless gave them a different meaning, and they were at the same time intent upon protecting their extreme associates so far as possible.

The Alexandrians had acquired the sovereignty of the East at the price of union. The "high-priest Emperor" and his eunuchs abandoned themselves more and more to their guidance. Under the feeble Theodosius the Empire was in danger of becoming an ecclesiastical state led by Alexandria. In addition to this, under cover of the formula of concord the doctrine of the one nature was propagated, and even the extravagances of earlier times again made their appearance. Cyril himself who was so cautious otherwise in his use of formulæ, had not been able to avoid the use of the questionable Apollinarian conception, according to which the nature or hypostasis of the incarnate Logos is a "certain middle something", [1] and accordingly it is not astonishing to find that his followers went still further. The brave and indefatigable Theodoret [2] did indeed keep a look-out against the ἕνωσις φυσική, "the suffering God", the κρᾶσις or mixture, in short, against the anathemas of Cyril, while at the same time he parried the attacks of Cyril on Theodore of Mopsuestia. But spite of the great prudence shewn by Theodoret in keeping to a middle path Dioscurus succeeded in calumniating him at the Court, after he had himself in his character as supreme bishop interfered in the affairs of Antioch. [3]   Theodoret was instructed to keep to his diocese.

[1] See, e.g., de recte fida ad Theodos. (Mansi IV., p. 673): 'Ι. Χρ. ἀνθρωπίνοις τε αὖ καὶ τοῖς ὑπὲρ ἄνθρωπον ἰδιώμασιν εἰς ἕν τι τὸ μεταξὺ συγκείμενος.

[2] See, above all, his " Eranistes ". The work of the Catholic Bertram, Theodoreti doctrina christologica, 1883, is painstaking but biassed; sec. Theol. Lit. Ztg., 1883, No. 24; Möller in Herzog's R.-Encyklop. sec ed. XV., p. 401 ff. The question of Theodoret's orthodoxy is certainly a very troublesome one for a Catholic.

[3] Dioscurus treated the metropolitan Irenæus of Tyre, and Theodoret in the year 448, in the style of one who was primate of the whole Greek Church and was recognised by the Emperor as such.

Still greater was the hatred of the Alexandrians against the bold and worldly-minded Bishop Ibas of Edessa, Theodore's enthusiastic supporter. Dioscurus had apparently made up his mind to bring the East under his authority and gradually to exterminate all who in a half way or who wholly accepted the Antiochian theology. The formula: two natures or hypostases, one Christ, was to disappear from the Church.

In the capital the old and respected Archimandrite Eutyches supported his views, taking his stand on the Christology of Cyril. Still it was no mere calumny when his opponents maintained that in the course of the violent attack on the Nestorians he had himself fallen into the error of making Apollinarian statements. Already in the year 448 Bishop Domnus of Antioch had denounced him on these grounds to the Emperor. But no action was taken until Bishop Eusebius of Doryläum brought a similar charge against him before Flavian who was bishop of Constantinople at the time. Eutyches afterwards asserted that he had done this from personal hatred, and one cannot get rid of the suspicion that he was right; for Eusebius himself had formerly been one of most bitter opponents of Nestorius. In any case a certain obscurity hangs over the outbreak of the controversy, and the energy too with which Flavian at once took the matter up is strange. He was on bad terms with the court and particularly with the all-powerful Chrysaphius with whom Eutyches stood in high favour. The bishop probably felt that he was hampered by the Archimandrite and wanted to get rid of him. It is useless to look for any religious motives in the case of Flavian, whose Christological statements bear a pretty close resemblance to those of Cyril, though they did actually fall short of them. [1] The Council of Constantinople

---

[1] Flavian takes his stand on the Union of 433 though he inclines to the Antiochian interpretation of it; see his confession in Mansi VI., p. 541: καὶ γὰρ ἐν δύο φύσεσιν ὁμολογοῦντες τὸν Χριστὸν μετὰ τὴν σάρκωσιν τὴν ἐκ τῆς ἁγίας παρθένου καὶ ἐνανθρώπησιν, ἐν μιᾷ ὑποστάσει καὶ ἐν ἑνὶ προσώπῳ (a distinction is thus drawn between φύσις and ὑπόστασις, while ὑπόστασις and πρόσωπον are regarded as parallel terms, and accordingly the way is paved for the Chalcedonian formula in the East also), ἕνα Χριστόν, ἕνα υἱόν, ἕνα κύριον ὁμολογοῦμεν, καὶ μίαν μὲν τοῦ Θεοῦ λόγου φύσιν σεσαρκωμένην μέντοι καὶ ἐνανθρωπήσασαν λέγειν οὐκ ἀρνούμεθα— the letter is addressed to Leo, and Flavian was apparently not yet aware what

(448) which followed on this and with whose procedure we are
well acquainted, shewed the frivolity of the attack on Eutyches,
though it shewed too how the influential archimandrite set his
bishop at defiance. In reference to the dogmatic question
Eutyches acted with great prudence, and, though indeed with
some hesitation, gave his assent to the formula of the Creed
of Union, "of two natures, one Christ" (one hypostasis, one
person). But one can plainly see that this formula, in so far
as it was taken as implying the continued existence of the two
natures after the union, was one which Eutyches would regard
as objectionable. "Two natures after the union" was rightly
felt to be Nestorian and above all to be an "innovation".
Eutyches, indeed, corrected the incautious statements he had made
at an earlier time, divergent from the middle path of the formula of
unity—my God is not of the same substance with us ;[1] He has no
"body of a man" (σῶμα ἀνθρώπου), but only a "human body"
(σῶμα ἀνθρώπινον). But this was of no avail. It was insisted that
he taught a "blending" (σύγκρασις) and "confusion" (σύγχυσις),
and after the most disgraceful proceedings the records of which
were besides falsified, he was deposed "amid tears" on account
of Valentinian and Apollinarian heresy. This was done by
people who themselves professed to acknowledge Cyril's second
letter to Nestorius and its approval by the Synod of Ephesus,

---

Leo's views were and whether perhaps he did not adhere entirely to the doctrine
of Cyril. The prudent patriarch accordingly "confesses" two natures after the
incarnation also and yet one!—διὰ τὸ ἐξ ἀμφοῖν ἕνα καὶ τὸν αὐτὸν εἶναι τὸν κύριον
ἡμῶν ᾽Ι. τὸν Χρ. Τοὺς δὲ δύο υἱοὺς ἢ δύο ὑποστάσεις etc.; a condemnation of Nestorius follows. Here at all events the way is paved for the Chalcedonian formula
but, characteristically enough, by a bishop who sought to take up a safe position
relatively to both sides.

[1] The statement when compared with Cyril's doctrine can scarcely be regarded
as open to suspicion. Eutyches recognised the existence of two natures previous
to the incarnation, i.e., allowed that the distinction in thought was an ideal moment,
but he could not admit the perfect homousia of the body of the Logos with
our body after the incarnation, since that body was to be thought of as having
been deified. Cyril had not indeed openly said that the actual body of the Logos
was not ὁμοούσιος with our body, but still he could scarcely avoid that conclusion.
Eutyches rejected as a calumny the charge brought against him of teaching that
Christ brought his flesh from heaven, on the contrary indeed he was the first to
declare in the course of the debate that the Holy Virgin is *homousios* with us and
that from her our God became flesh. He wished in this way to escape making any
direct admission.

as well as the epistle of Cyril to John of Antioch. Both parties laboured to secure the favour of the Court, the capital, and the Roman bishop, and the Court sided with Eutyches. People's views were still everywhere ruled by the condemnation of Nestorius and there was no inclination to change sides. Flavian, "the moderate Antiochian" played a dangerous game when he sought to increase the authority of his chair in face of the court and the ruling system of dogma. Leo I. who was applied to by Eutyches first, was for some weeks uncertain which course to take (Leon. epp. 20 sq.). He was disposed to regard the Constantinopolitan Patriarch as his born enemy; but he had soon to recognise the fact that his strongest enemy was to be looked for elsewhere. Dioscurus, who substantially agreed with Eutyches and who long ere this took an active part in different provincial Synods in the East as supreme bishop, had already annexed the question and moved the Emperor to summon a Council. The Pope's policy was now marked out for him. He must not strike either upon the Constantinopolitan Scylla or upon the Alexandrian Charybdis, but on the contrary, as his predecessor Julius had done, he must attempt to bring the true faith and with it himself to the East. Dioscurus was determined to use every means to exploit the Council in his own interests. It was to establish the authority of the Alexandrian Patriarch and of the Alexandrian Christology in the Church of the East. He was prudent enough all the same to employ no new formula while attempting this. The Nicene Creed was alone to be regarded as authoritative, of course according to the interpretation put upon it by the anathemas of Cyril. Whoever went a word beyond this was to be considered an innovator, a heretic. This was his standpoint and he found a pliant Emperor and a minister who were favourably disposed toward him and who were prepared to hand over the Church to him in order to humiliate the occupant of the episcopal chair of the capital for the time being whom they hated, a policy which was treachery to the State. [1] Dioscurus was equipped with full

---

[1] See the letter of the Empress Eudokia to Theod. II. (Leo. ep 57): ἐγράφη γὰρ ἐνταῦθα πᾶσαν φιλονεικείαν κεκινῆσθαι, ὥστε Φλαυιανὸν τὸν ἐπίσκοπον ἐκ τῶν ἀνθρωπίνων πραγμάτων ἐπαρθῆναι.

powers as master of the Synod. It was called together in
accordance with his ideas, even a representative of the monastic
order was present—a novelty at a Council—and Theodoret
was excluded.

Leo had meanwhile discovered that Eutyches was a heretic [1]
(ep. 27) and bethought himself of the Western Christological
form of doctrine which his predecessors, Cœlestin and Sixtus,
and he himself seem up to this time to have forgotten. The
summoning of a Council caused him grave anxiety; Flavian,
who had seriously displeased the Pope by his independent
attitude, nevertheless suddenly became his dear friend who had
been attacked, and along with the legates who attended the
Council Leo sent numerous letters to all in the East concerned
in the affair (epp. 28—38), to Flavian (28, 36, 38), to the Emperor
(29, 37), to Pulcheria (30, 31), to the Constantinopolitan archi-
mandrites (32), to the Council (33) and to Bishop Julian of Kos
(34, 35). He repeatedly observes that a synodal decision was
not at all necessary, and that the Council was superfluous. [2]
But what he was now above all concerned with was to furnish
Flavian with dogmatic instructions and to draw the attention of
the Council to the unique dignity of the Roman Chair which
had already decided the question. The latter of these two
things he did in Epistle 33, which contains a daring attempt to
misrepresent [3] the conditions under which the Council had come

---

[1] Leo's admission is amusing reading (ep. 34 1): "Diu apud nos uncertum fuit,
quid in ipso Eutyche catholicis displiceret." Now Eutyches is the child of the
devil who denies the reality of the body of Christ. Leo represents him in the
bluntest fashion as the out and out doketist.

[2] Ep. 36 ad Flav.: "Et quia clementissimus imperator pro ecclessiæ pace solli-
citus synodum voluit congregari, quamvis evidenter appareat, rem, de qua agitur,
nequaquam synodali indigere tractatu" etc.; ep. 37 ad Theod. II.: "præsertim cum tam
evidens fidei causa sit, ut rationabilius ab indicenda synodo fuisset abstinendum " etc.

[3] Leo writes here as if in this affair of Eutyches the Emperor had had recourse
to him first as the successor of Peter, and as if he had at once unfolded the true
doctrine of the Incarnation on the basis of the confession of Peter and thereby
refuted Eutyches ("religiosa clementissimi principis fides sciens ad suam gloriam
maxime pertinere, si intra ecclesiam catholicam nullius erroris germen exsurgeret,
hanc reverentiam divinis detulit institutis, ut ad sanctæ dispositionis effectum auctoritatem apostolicæ sedis adhiberet, tamquam ab ipso Petro cuperet declarari, quid
in eius confessione laudatum sit, quando dicente domino: quem me esse dicunt
homines filium hominis?" etc.). The Council is merely an opus superadditum,

together, while he accomplished the former by the dogmatic epistle he sent to Flavian. It contains a paraphrase of the Christological section of the work of Tertullian adv. Prax. (cf. Novatian de trinitate) in accordance with the views, and in part in the words, of Ambrose and Augustine, with special reference to Eutyches, and in combating the views of the latter it accordingly undeniably goes a step beyond what had hitherto been accepted in the West, though not any further than the situation for the moment demanded. This document, which was highly lauded in subsequent times and is to the present day, contains nothing new. What, however, is of importance in it is that the West, *i.e.*, the Pope, has here kept in view the peculiar character of its Church. It is consequently an evidence of power, and the Christology set forth in it may at the same time have actually corresponded with the inclinations of the Pope. But on the other hand it ought not to be forgotten that the situation, as represented by Nestorianism already condemned and Eutychianism about to be rejected, appeared directly to call for the old Western formula " duæ substantiæ (naturæ) in una persona ", and that the Pope expressed himself more fully regarding it than tradition justified.[1] The Pope

"ut pleniori iudicio omnis possit error aboleri." Thus the condemnation of Eutyches is already decided upon and the Council has merely to repeat it. The Pope enjoins this.

[1] The letter to which not till a later date, however, (see Mansi VI., p. 962 sq.) though by Leo himself, proofs were appended from Hilary, Augustine, Gregory of Nazianzus, Chrysostom and Cyril, begins with a reference to the Roman Creed which in the view of Leo decides the whole question in its opening words; for the three statements: " Credere in patrem omnipotentem, et in Christum Iesum filium eius unicum dominum nostrum, qui natus est de spiritu sancto et Maria virgine", demolish " the devices of almost all heretics." They involve the nativitas divina, and the nativitas temporalis which in no way injures the former. We should not have been able to overcome the author of sin and death if the deus ex deo had not assumed our nature. If Eutyches was unable to recognise that this was taught in the Creed, then certain passages (which the Pope now adduces) ought to have convinced him—as if Eutyches had ever denied the truth of this thought! The idea of a non-human body of Christ cannot be proved from the miraculous birth; for the Holy Spirit merely gave the impulse ; the reality of the body of Christ was got from the body of Maria semper virgo (c. 2). This is followed by the proposition in the style of Tertullian : " Salva igitur proprietate utriusque naturæ et substantiæ (both words should be noted) et in unam coeunte personam suscepta est a maiestate humilitas", attached to which we have a series of expressions

throughout puts the interests of our salvation in the foreground;
he wants exactly what Cyril and Eutyches also want, but he
goes on to give an explanation which Cyril at any rate would have
entirely repudiated, [Cyril said that the idea of redemption
demands the deification of the human nature, Leo went on to
shew that this same idea demands a true human nature which

which are supported by statements in Damasus, Ambrose, Augustine, and partly
also in Tertullian; thus, "natura inviolabilis unita est naturæ passibili", "mediator dei et hominum homo Iesus Christus", "mori potest ex uno, mori non potest
ex altero", "in integra veri hominis perfectaque natura verus natus est deus,
totus in suis, totus in nostris", "assumpsit formam servi sine sorde peccati,
humana augens, divina non minuens", "exinanitio inclinatio fuit miserationis, non
defectio potestatis", "tenet sine defectu proprietatem suam utraque natura, et sicut
formam servi dei forma non adimit, ita formam dei servi forma non minuit."
This was the way in which God met the cunning of the devil, in order that we
should not be lost contra dei propositum (c. 3). Next follow the old Western
paradoxes of the "invisibilis factus visibilis" etc. The fourth chapter contains the
detailed development of the doctrine. The human nature in Christ was not
absorbed by the divine; on the contrary "agit utraque forma cum alterius communione, quod proprium est verbo scilicet operante quod verbi est et carne exse-
quente quod carnis est." The flesh never loses the "natura nostri generis". In
accordance with this the evangelic history is apportioned between the human and
the divine nature of him "qui unus idemque est". "Quamvis enim in domino
J. Chr. dei et hominis (!) una persona sit, aliud tamen est, unde in utroque communis est contumelia, aliud unde communis est gloria". "Propter hanc unitatem
personæ", as it is put in c. 5, "in utraque natura intelligendam et filius hominis
legitur descendisse de cœlo" etc., that means as Leo now shews, that we can and
must interchange the *opera*. "That the Son of God was crucified and buried,
we all confess in the Creed." Christ established this article of faith in the 40
days after the Resurrection, after Peter had already before this ackowledged the
identity of the Son of God and the Son of Man. All ought accordingly to see
that the "proprietas divinæ humanæque naturæ" "individua permanet" in Him,
and consequently know that "Word" and "Flesh" are not the same, but that the
one Son of God is Word and Flesh. Eutyches, who has by the most barefaced
fictions emptied of its meaning the mystery to which alone we owe our redemption and separates the human nature from Jesus, incurs the sentence pronounced
in 1 John IV. 2, 3. He must also necessarily deny the reality of the passion and
death of Christ and thus subvert everything, the Spirit of sanctification, the water
and the blood.

In his concluding chapter Leo discusses the statement of Eutyches that before
the union there were two natures and one after it and expresses his astonishment
that "none of the judges censured such a foolish and perverse avowal and passed
over such an absurd and blasphemous utterance as if they had heard nothing to
which to take exception." The first half of the statement is as impious as the
second; this statement which had been passed over ought "si per inspirationem
misericordiæ dei ad satisfactionem causa perducitur," to be made a clean sweep of

remains absolutely unchanged], and which, so far, goes beyond
the use and wont doctrine of the West and actually approaches
Nestorianism, inasmuch as the Pope uses by preference "nature"
in place of substance and speaks of a peculiar mode of action
on the part of each nature, and thus really hypostatises each
nature. In Leo's view the "Person" is no longer entirely the

as a pestilential opinion. The Pope hopes that Eutyches will amend and in this
case the greatest mercy will be shewn him. The statements in this twenty-eighth
letter were further supplemented in letter 35 addressed to Julian. Here (c. 1)
Nestorius too is regarded as a heretic; as against Eutyches the view is made good
that it is not only a question of the Creator being known, but also of the creature
being redeemed. Here we meet with the statement "in susceptione hominis non
unius substantiæ, sed unius eiusdemque personæ", here the unity of the person is
made intelligible (see Cyril) by pointing to unity of body and soul in man, and
here finally the statement of Eutyches examined in the sixth chapter of letter 28
and which was not censured at Constantinople, is further dealt with. Leo understands it as meaning that the human nature of Christ had been already created
before the Incarnation and accordingly classes it along with the statement of
Origen regarding the pre-existence of the soul which had been already condemned.
See also letter 59.

A few remarks on the catchwords ἀσυγχύτως, ἀτρέπτως will perhaps not be out
of place here. (The words ἀδιαιρέτως and ἀχωρίστως do not require any special
genetic explanation.) They have sprung from two sources in the history of dogma.
The first of these is to be found in Tertullian's work adv. Prax. Tertullian c. 27
wrote in opposition to certain monarchian ideas, according to which the spiritus
(= deus = pater = Christus) was either changed into the caro (= homo = filius
= Jesus) or else was united and mingled with the caro so as to form a tertium
quid and therefore a new being, and thus disappeared in the new being. The
view thus developed became universally known through Novatian who adopted it
in part, but particularly by means of Leo's doctrinal letter. It runs: "Si enim
sermo ex transfiguratione et demutatione substantiæ caro factus est, una iam erit
substantia ex duabus, ex carne et spiritu, mixtura quædam, ut electrum ex auro et
argento et incipit nec aurum esse, id est spiritus, neque argentum, id est caro, dum
alterum altero mutatur et tertium quid efficitur." Thus Jesus would be no longer
either God or Man: ita ex utraque neutrum est; aliud longe tertium est quam
utrumque. But both the passages in the Psalms (LXXXVII. 5) and the Apostle
(Rom. I. 3) teach de utraque eius substantia. Videmus duplicem statum, non confusum sed coniunctum, in una persona, deum et hominem Iesum ... Et adeo salva
est utriusque proprietas substantiæ, ut et spiritus res suas egerit in illo, i.e., virtutes
et opera et signa, et caro passiones suas functa sit, esuriens sub diabolo, sitiens sub
Samaritide ... denique et mortua est. Quodsi tertium quid esset, ex utroque confusum, ut electrum, non tam distincta documenta parerent utriusque substantiæ.
Sed et spiritus carnalia et caro spiritalia egisset ex translatione aut neque carnalia
neque spiritalia, sed tertiæ alicuius formæ ex confusione ... Sed quia substantiæ
ambæ in statu suo quæque distincte agebant, ideo illis et operæ et exitus sui
occurrerunt." The second source is to be found in the Eastern and Western

one subject with two "properties", but the union of two
hypostatic natures. In a word, the unity is neither made intelligible by Leo nor did he consider what was the supreme
concern of the pious Greeks in this matter, namely, to see in
the humanity of Christ the real deification of human nature
generally. Nor is there any trace in the doctrinal letter of any-

authors who wrote against Apollinaris; these maintained the ἀσυγχύτως and
ἀτρέπτως, and this was quite the current view in the time of Cyril. Cyril,
in a great number of passages asserts that according to his doctrine the two
natures are joined together ἀσυγχύτως, ἀτρέπτως, ἀναλλοιώτως, ἀμεταβλήτως,
without there having been any kind of mingling (σύγχυσις, σύγκρασις, συνουσίωσις)
(see adv. Nest. l. 5, c. 4—ad Theodos. n. 6, 10—ep. 3 ad Nestor. Migne, Vol. 77,
p. 109—adv. neg. deip. n. 2—epil. ad. I—adv. Theodoret. ad. 4, 5, 8, 10—adv.
Orient. ad 1, 10, 11—ep. ad Maxim., Vol. 77, p. 152—ad Acac. Ber. 160—ad
Joan. 180—ad Acac. Mel. 192—ad Eulog. 225—ad Valerian. 257—1 ad Succ. 232,
36—2 ad Succ. 237, 40—ad Euseb. 288—Explan. Symb. 304—Quod un. Christ.
Vol. 75, p. 1361—Hom. XV., Vol. 77, p. 1092—in Luc., Vol. 72, p. 909—c. Julian.
I., 10, Vol. 76, p. 1012—Hom. ad Alex., Vol. 77, pp. 1112, 1113—in ep. ad Hebr.,
Vol. 74, p. 1004—Resp. ad Tiberium ed. Pusey c. 6, 7, III., p. 587 sq. Cyril
devoted a special work to this subject entitled κατὰ συνουσιαστῶν which I regard as
one of his last). Nevertheless he defended the word κρᾶσις as against Nestorius
(adv. Nestor. I., 1 c. 3) as an expression used by the fathers to bring out the
closeness of the union of the two natures, and unhesitatingly employs certain forms
of speech compounded of it or its synonyms. (Ehrhard op. cit., p. 44.) Further,
both of these, the amplifications of Tertullian and those of the anti-Apollinarian
Greek fathers, refer back to philosophical usage, but this usage explains at the
same time why Cyril and others could indeed adopt the expression κρᾶσις but
not σύγχυσις. The Stoics (see Zeller. Philos. d. Griechen III. 3, p. 127) drew a
distinction between παράθεσις, μῖξις, κρᾶσις and σύγχυσις. "The παράθεσις is
the σωμάτων συναφὴ κατὰ τὰς ἐπιφανείας, as in the case of the mixing of
different kinds of grain"—they have the Nestorians in view—: μῖξις on the
contrary is δύο ἢ καί πλειόνων σωμάτων ἀντιπαρέκτασις δι᾽ ὅλων, ὑπομενουσῶν τῶν
συμφυῶν περὶ αὐτὰ ποιοτήτων, as in the case of the union of fire with iron and
of the soul with the body; but speaking more accurately a mingling of this sort
of dry bodies should be called μῖξις, and of fluid bodies κρᾶσις (the κρᾶσις δι᾽
ὅλων of the Stoics presupposes the permeability of the bodies and assumes that
the smaller body when mingled with a larger body spreads itself over the entire
extent of the latter and is thus to be found in every particle of it [ὡς μηδὲν
μόριον ἐν αὐτοῖς εἶναι μὴ μετέχον πάντων τῶν ἐν τῷ μίγματι], but that both preserve their own peculiarities in the mingling; thus the "mixtio" does not exclude,
but on the contrary includes the salva proprietas utriusque substantiæ). The
σύγχυσις finally is δύο ἢ καί πλειόνων ποιοτήτων περὶ τὰ σώματα μεταβολὴ εἰς
ἑτέρας διαφερούσης τούτων ποιότητος γένεσιν, i.e., the old substances and their
qualities cease to exist (φθείρεσθαι) and a third body comes into existence." Tertullian, the Stoic, rested his ideas apparently on these philosophical theorems and
first of all applied this materialistic view to the relation of the two substances in

thing like an express repudiation of Nestorius, not to speak of the Antiochian Christology. [1]

The Council was opened at Ephesus in August 449. Dioscurus presided and assigned the second place to the represen-

Christ (he and Novatian, who was also a Stoic, accept the μῖξις and reject the σύγχυσις; but along with this Tertullian has further a juristic set of conceptions (una persona, duæ substantiæ). In his treatise "Ammonius Sakkas und Plotinus" (Archiv. f. Gesch. d. Philos. VII. Vol. H. 3) Zeller, however, has called attention to the fact that Ammonius Sakkas (Plotinus) described the relation of body and soul in man in the sense of the Stoic κρᾶσις (μῖξις) (the soul entirely permeates the body and unites itself with it so as to form one substance, but nevertheless remains unchanged and retains its proprietas salva) and that Nemesius expressly says that this view of the matter, in support of which he appeals to Porphyry, is to be applied to the relation of the two natures in Christ. Now, however, not only the Eastern bishops but also Leo I. expressly appeal in support of their Christology to the relation between body and soul. There can therefore be no doubt but that this is to be traced back to the Neo-Platonic school which had adopted a Stoic terminology. Plotinus calls the soul not only ἀπαθής but also ἄτρεπτος (because in the union it undergoes no change); but, as Zeller observes, he never speaks of ἀσύγχυτος. This word, however, once more occurs in Porphyry and is used to designate the union. Consequently so far as the Easterns are concerned the ἀτρέπτως is to be referred to Plotinus and the ἀσυγχύτως to Porphyry (Zeller), while the West through Tertullian took the "non confusus" direct from the Stoa.

[1] It may also be said that the speculations of Cyril and the Alexandrian theologians begin where Leo leaves off, and for this reason it is altogether astonishing to read in Thomasius (Dogmengesch., Vol. I., p. 365) that Leo in his epistle seeks to gather up both negatively and positively the results of the Christological movement so far as it had gone. Leo did not think of this. He contents himself with making the thought definite and confessing with full assurance that Christ was perfect God and perfect man, and points out that redemption demands the divinity and the humanity. But the question as to the relation into which the divinity and the humanity have come to each other, was one which really never gave him any concern when he thought of redemption. This, however, was the main question with Cyril, Eutyches and Dioscurus. It cannot accordingly be said that Leo and they are in direct contradiction. On the contrary, Cyril and his followers further developed the problem in concrete fashion in the name of the Faith, ex necessitate fidei so to speak, while with Leo it was in true Western fashion left in the indefinite form of conceptions. This is how the matter stands on a favourable view of Leo's position; for as soon as we take his development of the doctrine in a concrete sense and transfer it into the region of the Eastern controversy it can be understood only as Nestorian. With Leo it is not at all a question of a union of the two natures. It may, however, help towards forming a fair and correct estimate of Leo's position to note that he (mistakenly) saw in Eutychianism the recurrence of a danger which he had so energetically warded off in his struggle with Manichæism (see his sermon). He in fact opposes "Eutychianism" as if it were Manichæism.

tative of the Roman bishop.   There were one hundred and
thirty-five members present.   The bishops who had sat in judgment on Eutyches were not allowed to vote, since the Synod
meant to proceed with a revision of that process.   Dioscurus
put the Pope's letter to the Council amongst the Acts, but did
not have it read out, and in fact treated Rome as non-existent.
Not Rome but Alexandria was to speak.   It was a bold stroke,
but Dioscurus had got authority from the Emperor.   As regards
its proceedings the Council does not compare unfavourably with
other Councils.   What gave it its peculiar character was the
fact that it was guided by a powerful and determined will, that
of Dioscurus.   The latter got the Council simply to resolve not
to go beyond the conclusions come to at Nicæa and Ephesus.
The affair of Eutyches was next taken up; he declared that
he took his stand on the teaching of these Councils and repudiated Manes, Valentin, Apollinaris, and Nestorius.   In the course
of the debate it became evident that those present regarded
the formula "after the Incarnation one nature", as alone ortho-
dox—with the addition: "made flesh and made man" ($\sigma\epsilon\sigma\alpha\rho$-
$\varkappa\omega\mu\acute{\epsilon}\nu\eta\nu$ $\varkappa\alpha\grave{\iota}$ $\grave{\epsilon}\nu\alpha\nu\theta\rho\omega\pi\acute{\eta}\sigma\alpha\sigma\alpha\nu$), and that they condemned the doctrine of two natures after the Incarnation.   In this sense Euty-
ches was declared by all to be orthodox.   Rome's legates refrained
from voting.   Domnus of Antioch and Juvenal of Jerusalem
also concurred, and even three of the bishops who had condemned Eutyches at Constantinople did the same.   Dioscurus
now proceeded to take aggressive steps.   Each bishop was
required to state in writing whether he considered that those
should be punished who in the course of their theological
investigations had gone beyond the Nicene Creed.   Dioscurus
got the answer he wished, and even the Roman legate did not
oppose the question when put in this form.   On the basis of
this resolution the Council pronounced sentence of deposition
on Flavian and Eusebius of Doryläum, Domnus and Juvenal
concurring.   Both of the deposed bishops were present and
soon after appealed to the Pope, whose legates, moreover, had
at least shewn some hesitation at the Council, though after the
first session they took no further share in the proceedings.   In
the second and third sessions Dioscurus got the detested Ibas

deposed (to whom the saying was currently attributed "I do not envy Christ because He became God; for I too can become God if I wish"), the Sabinian bishop of Perrha and several others;[1] also Theodoret,[2] the pillar of the East, and finally even Domnus of Antioch.[3] The fact that he had for so long sided with Dioscurus availed him nothing. He had latterly drawn back, was unwilling to take part in the ecclesiastico-political revision of the Canons of Nicæa and Constantinople which Dioscurus was contemplating, and was generally in his road.

Never before at any Council had a Patriarch scored such a victory. The atmosphere was cleared; the triumph of the old Confession of Nicæa and Ephesus (431) which alone was recognised by the pious Greeks as embodying their faith, had been secured; the Christology of Cyril, the one incarnate nature of the God-Logos, had been acknowledged as the true one; those who opposed it had partly been deposed and partly had submitted; arrangements had already been made for securing suitable successors to those who had been deposed, and an Alexandrian priest, Anatolius, was appointed to Constantinople. The Church of the East lay at the feet of the Alexandrian Patriarch and he had attained everything with the concurrence of the Emperor.[4] He had doubtless made use of force; but it was the State in fact which stood behind him; the police and the monks of Barsumas had, to be sure, over-awed the Fathers; but far worse than the terrors of this Council were the calum-

---

[1] This has reference to the proceedings of the year 448 (Irenæus of Tyre) into which I cannot enter. The Syrian Acts first threw light on them as well as on the Councils of Tyre and Berytus.

[2] See Martin, op. cit. p. 186 sq.

[3] See Martin, p. 196 sq.

[4] The charges brought against him by Egyptians at the third sitting of the Council of Chalcedon (Mansi VI. p. 1006—1035) even after making all due allowance for the calumnies in them, afford interesting proofs of how he disregarded the imperial authority in Egypt and how he weakened the authority of the State there and also of the extent to which he was master of Egypt and now threatened to become master of the State. Tillemont XV. p. 589, very justly says: "Dioscore règne partout." See, above all, p. 1032: Διόσκορος πάντα ἀκαθοσιώτως πράττων, νομίζων τε ἀνωτέρω πάντων εἶναι, οὔτε τοὺς θείους τύπους οὔτε τὰς μεγίστας ἀποφάσεις συνεχώρησεν ἐκβιβασθῆναι, ἑαυτοῦ τὴν χώραν μᾶλλον ἢ τῶν κρατούντων εἶναι λέγων.

nies spread regarding it on the part of those who two years
later had to extenuate their dastardly treachery. If we consider
who were present at the Council we must conclude that Dioscurus, to whom even Theodoret on one occasion (ep. 60) bore
favourable testimony, cannot have found it necessary to employ
any very great amount of actual force. That Flavian was
trampled on and left half dead is anything but certain, and a
Council which more than any other gave expression to the
tradition of the religious feeling of the time and to what it
considered of vital importance, does not deserve the name
"Robber-Council" (Leo, ep. 95). Regarded from the standpoint
of the Church of the East something of importance had actually
been attained, and what had been thus attained had the guarantee of permanence so long as foreign elements did not come
in to disturb it.

But Dioscurus had not reckoned on the death of the Emperor
which was near at hand, nor with the Roman bishop, nor
finally on the widespread aversion felt towards the right wing
of his army which was Apollinarian in disguise. He had rehabilitated Eutyches without, however, getting the questionable
statements to which the latter had formerly given utterance,
proscribed, though the allegation that he endorsed them is a
falsehood asserted by his embittered opponents at Chalcedon.
This was a blunder in policy which was calculated to bring on
a reaction introduced from the outside, and the reaction taking
its start from this, might in the state in which matters then
were, overthrow the great work which had been accomplished
without in appearance abandoning the position gained in the
year 431. At first Dioscurus was still master of the situation.
While all those who felt themselves injured by him betook
themselves to Leo as the only refuge,[1] and while the latter
hastened to reject the resolutions of the Council, Dioscurus
pronounced sentence of excommunication upon Leo,[2] prepared

---

[1] See Theodoret's letters 113 and ff. Theodoret speaks in terms of high praise
of Leo's ep. dogmatica, and as a matter of fact he had no reason for suspecting
it in any way. In letter 121 he expressly says that Leo's letter agrees with τοῖς
παρ᾽ ἡμῶν καὶ συγγραφεῖσι καὶ ἐπ᾽ ἐκκλησίας κηρυχθεῖσιν ἀεί.

[2] See the Acts of the Council of Chalcedon in Mansi VI., p. 1009; the matter

now to measure his strength with the last remaining opponent too, whom he had treated at Ephesus as a nonentity. Leo was in an extremely difficult position, as letters 43—72 prove. If the decree of Ephesus were to become permanent it was all over with his orthodoxy as well as with the primacy of his chair. He assembled a Council and at the same time got all the members of the imperial family of the Western Empire, when they came to Rome, to write letters to Theodosius against the "episcopus Alexandrinus sibi omnia vindicans" (45, 2), against the Council in support of his just claim to be considered supreme judge in matters of faith,[1] and in favour of calling a new Council to meet in Italy. He saw himself under the necessity of repeatedly assuring the Emperor of the East that he also held firmly to the Nicene Faith; he took care not to mention what it was exactly that he found fault with in the dogmatic decrees of Ephesus; he simply insisted on the condemnation of Eutyches as a Manichean and a Doketist, and was slow about recognising the new bishop of Constantinople, the creature of Dioscurus. He yielded nothing as the successor of Peter, but neither did he gain anything. Theodosius stood firm, maintained that the Council had merely defended antiquity against the innovations of Flavian, and coldly replied to the letters of his imperial relations in the West, declining to take any action. A less politic Pope than he was, would have brought on a breach backed up as he would have been by the whole West and by the Emperor of the West, but Leo waited and did not wait in vain.

is, however, not quite certain. It is even probable that Dioscurus did not excommunicate Leo till shortly before the Council of Chalcedon.

    [1] Valentinian III. writes to Theod. II. (ep. Leon. 55): "The Faith must get into confusion, ἣν ἡμεῖς ἀπὸ τῶν προγόνων παραδοθεῖσαν ὀφείλομεν μετὰ τῆς προσηκούσης καθοσιώσεως ἐκδικεῖν καὶ τῆς ἰδίας εὐλαβείας τὴν ἀξίαν τῷ μακαρίῳ ἀποστόλῳ Πέτρῳ ἄτρωτον καὶ ἐν τοῖς ἡμετέροις χρόνοις διαφυλάττειν, ἵνα ὁ μακαριώτατος ἐπίσκοπος τῆς Ῥωμαίων πόλεως, ᾧ τὴν ἱερωσύνην κατὰ πάντων ἡ ἀρχαιότης παρέσχε, χώραν καὶ εὐπορίαν ἔχειν περί τε πίστεως καὶ ἱερέων κρίνειν. Flavian was right in appealing to him. It is a curious spectacle! Both Emperors are entirely in the hands of their Patriarchs, the one in the hands of Dioscurus, and the other as here in the hands of Leo. Never yet had the State been so much under priestly authority. The Emperors who were powerless to do anything themselves played the one primate against the other.

Theodosius II.[1] died on the 28th of July, 450, and the situation was at once altered. Pulcheria who mounted the throne and offered her hand to Marcian, had always deplored her brother's miserable misrule, and his protégés were her enemies. She specially guided the ecclesiastical policy of the Government, while Marcian fought its enemies outside. The Court resolved to free itself and the State from the Alexandrian despot. This could not be done without the help of Rome, for— and this is a fact of the highest importance—the Council of 449 had really pacified the Church of the East. Of course there were some who were discontented, but they were in the minority. The Court could not in carrying out its new policy reckon on the support of any united and reliable party. It was only in Constantinople that it was able to make way quickly, for there Flavian was not yet forgotten. The Church of the East had enjoyed peace since August. In order that the State might get back its independence, this Church which had been pacified, had to be disturbed anew and reduced to the most lamentable condition.

Marcian, whose recognition as Emperor Dioscurus had sought to prevent in Egypt, at once addressed a letter to Leo. He formally handed over to the latter the primacy with which his predecessor had actually invested Dioscurus, and announced besides his readiness to summon the Council desired by Leo.[2] Soon after an epistle reached Leo from Pulcheria which announced the change of view on the part of the bishop of Constantinople. He had subscribed Leo's dogmatic letter, that sent to Flavian, and had condemned the erroneous doctrine of Eutyches; the Emperor had also ordered the recall of the bishops who had been deposed by the Council, and their reinstatement

---

[1] He had, however, begun to shew a certain amount of hesitation during the last months, as is evident from the recall of Pulcheria and the banishment of his minister Chrysaphius. See Krüger, op. cit. p. 56.

[2] Marcian ep. in Leon. epp. 73: "Pro reverenda et catholica religione fidei Christianorum tuam sanctitatem principatum in episcopatu divinæ fidei possidentem sacris litteris in principio justum credimus alloquendam ... omni impio errore sublato per celebrandam synodum te auctore maxime pax circa omnes episcopos fidei catholicæ fiat!" It was in these terms that Marcian wrote to Leo! But he had in view merely an Eastern Council; see the second letter (ep. 76).

in office was reserved for the Council over which, if possible, Leo was to preside in person and which was to be held in the East. As a matter of fact in the capital itself, after a local Synod had been called, everything was already going as the Emperor, or rather, as the Empress, desired. The wretched toady, the patriarch, the creature and the betrayer of Dioscurus, was prepared to do everything the Court wished. In view of the completely changed circumstances Leo had no longer any wish for a Council, because a Council might always mean action which was dangerous for the Pope. He now took up the position that his letter was sufficient, that the bishops were individually to bind themselves to accept the doctrine set forth in it, and that by their return to orthodoxy and the erasure of the names of Dioscurus, Juvenal, etc., from the Diptychs, the Robber-Council would be rendered powerless for harm. He wished on his own initiative and apart from any Council, but with the assistance of his legates, to act the part of judge and to receive to favour or punish as impenitent each individual bishop; the bishop of Constantinople was to act with him in the matter as his mandatory. He therewith made an actual beginning with the business and it was now fairly on its way. And as a matter of fact Leo may have been naive enough to imagine that the solution of the dogmatic difficulty of the East was contained in his sorry letter, for it seems never to have occurred to the Pope that there could be any other Christ-ologies besides the "correct" one, Doketism, and the doctrine of Paul of Samosata. He had no appreciation of the subtle, though no doubt partly incorrect formulæ of the Greek theo-logians; but he was sure of his ground, and it was with this feeling that the letters 82—86 were composed, in which the Pope sought at all costs to prevent the calling of a Council as being unnecessary and inopportune. [1] But Marcian required the Council for himself and for the Eastern Church, in which, since the change of rulers, no one knew what he should believe, and in which, for the time, many bishoprics were held by two bishops or had no bishop at all. The Emperor had no desire

---

[1] The Westerns could not come, he writes, because of the distress occasioned by the Huns.

to surrender to the Pope while claiming his help. He issued
an edict ordaining the Council to meet at Nicæa in September
451, and Leo had to acquiesce, though with a very bad grace
(ep. 89). He arranged to send four legates and deputed to one
of them, Bishop Paschasinus, the duty of presiding in his stead;
for Marcian had designated Leo himself as leader of the future
Council, and so what Dioscurus had got for himself in 449
after a struggle, the Pope now secured without taking any
trouble. [1] Still Leo was extremely uneasy. His numerous letters
(89—95) prove that he was afraid of "innovations contrary to
the Nicene Creed", i.e., divergences from his doctrinal letter.
He accordingly kept constantly counselling mildness and forgiveness; whoever would only condemn Eutyches and recognise
the Nicene Creed was to be regarded as orthodox. The controversy regarding the Faith was in no case to be renewed,
everything was clear and finally decided. In his letter to the
Council (93) he expressly guarded his position by hinting that
besides the condemnation of Eutyches, that of Nestorius also in
the year 431, must remain in force. This request was rather
an act of self-justification than a demand; for there were very
few in the East who were disposed to rehabilitate Nestorius,
but then there was no actual repudiation of the "heretic" in
the *epistola dogmatica*. But all this did not in fine constitute
the Pope's greatest anxiety. What he dreaded above all was
the restoration of the power of the bishop whom his predecessors in alliance with the Alexandrians had humbled, the bishop
of Constantinople, behind whom was Constantius' idea of the
State. Now, however, he was at enmity with the old ally and
had in fact humiliated him to the dust, [2] but with the downfall
of the enemy the support he had given disappeared too. The
Pope's anxiety comes out in the precise instructions given to
the legates: [3] "You may not permit the constitution set up by

---

[1] Still the presidency was only an honorary presidency; even Hefele admits that "the
official conducting of the business" was looked after by the Imperial Commissioners.
As a matter of fact the Romish Legates were merely the first to record their vote.

[2] One of the instructions given by Leo to his legates is to the effect that Dioscurus ought not to have a seat in the Council, but should only be heard as a
defendant; Mansi VI, p. 580 sq.

[3] Mansi VII., p. 443.

the holy Fathers (the sixth Canon of Nicæa according to the
Roman forgery) to be violated or diminished by any rash
action .... and if perchance some trusting to the dignity of
their cities shall have attempted to appropriate anything for
themselves, this you may check with befitting firmness." ("Sanctorum patrum constitutionem prolatam nulla patiamini temeritate
violari vel imminui ... ac si qui forte civitatum suarum splendore
confisi aliquid sibi tentaverint usurpare, hoc qua dignum est constantia retundatis"). In order to ensure the Emperor's personal
presence which the Roman legates insisted upon, the Council was
at the last moment transferred to Chalcedon in the neighbour-
hood of the capital, and was opened on the eighth of October, 451.

As regards the number of those who took part in it—between
500 and 600 and perhaps over 600—no earlier Council can
compare with this one, which was "politically and ecclesiastically
one of the most important of all",[1] a memorial of the restoration of the authority of the State accomplished by Pulcheria
and Marcian, but for this very reason a memorial of the
enslavement of the spirit of the Eastern Church which here, in
connection with the most important doctrinal question, surrendered to the Western supreme bishop allied with the Emperor.
We have no right at all to say that possibly the "authorised
moment of truth" of the Antiochian Christology triumphed at
Chalcedon over the dogmatic ideas of the Alexandrians and
the monks, for the representatives of this Christology had long
ere this succumbed to the power of the Alexandrian Confession.
The unspeakably pitiful behaviour too of the Patriarchs of
Antioch and of the largest section of the bishops who were
theologians in sympathy with them,—the Antiochian middle-
party which dates from 433—proves that the members of this
school conscious of their miserable powerlessness, had of their
own free will long ere this renounced all attempts to influence
the Church. The disgrace attaching to this Council consists in

---

[1] Ranke, Weltgesch. IV. 1, p. 324.

[2] Luther, who is, speaking generally, not favourably disposed towards the Chalcedonian Council, says of it (von Conciliis und Kirchen, Erl. Ed., Vol., 25, p. 351):
"The Fourth Council of Chalcedon had 630 members, almost as many as all the
others, and yet they were quite unequal to the Fathers at Nicæa and Constantinople."

the fact that the great majority of the bishops who held the
same views as Cyril and Dioscurus finally allowed a formula to
be forced upon them which was that of strangers, of the Emperor and the Pope, and which did not correspond to their
belief. Judging by the Acts of the Council we can be in no
doubt as regards the following points:[1] (1) that the views of the
great majority of the Fathers assembled at Chalcedon agreed
neither with those of Leo nor with those of Flavian who
represented the Antiochian middle-party, that on the contrary
they, and above all the Illyrian, Palestinian, and Egyptian bishops, wished for nothing else beyond the ratification of the
Creeds of Nicæa and Ephesus as understood by Cyril ;[2] (2) that
for this reason the formula, "out of two natures Christ is," with
the addition either expressed or understood, that after the Incarnation the God-Logos had only one nature which had become
flesh, alone answered to the faith of the Constantinopolitan
Patriarch Anatolius and of the majority of the bishops; (3) that
far from Theodoret and his friends possessing the sympathy of
the majority of the members of the Council, they had to endure
the worst forms of abuse, being called "Jews", while Theodoret
succeeded in saving his orthodoxy only by allowing his opponents to extort from him the condemnation of Nestorius;[3] (4)

---

[1] From the Récits de Dioscore (Krüger op. cit. 12 ff. 61—68) we gather—what
was hitherto not known—that Dioscurus was to be won over in a friendly way
by the Court after he had arrived at Constantinople from Alexandria, accompanied by fewer bishops than he had intended to have with him, in consequence
of an intrigue. We now know that he was conducted to a meeting of ecclesiastical
notables and that there he also met the Emperor and Pulcheria. Every effort was
made to get him to agree to the ep. Leonis; but he remained firm and it is said
that by his glowing words against the two natures he for the time being again
won over the bishops (Anatolius, Juvenal, Maximus of Antioch and others) as well
as the Senate to his doctrine. This is very probable. The story given in Krüger,
p. 62, shews by what a spirit of rebellion against the State and Emperor he and
his followers were animated. It follows from the Acts that during the first session
of the Council of Chalcedon he was still a power.

[2] Those too who held Antiochian views were undoubtedly no small number,
namely, bishops from Syria, Asia, Pontus, and Thrace; they could accept Leo's
letter: but (1) they were in the minority. (2) Partly by their repudiation of
Nestorius and partly by what they did at Ephesus in 449 they had made the
sacrificium intellectus fidei and were thus spiritually demoralised. Others might
without trouble have gained all they wanted so far as they were concerned.

[3] The threatening and abusive language ("Whoever divides Christ ought to be

that the Imperial Commissioners directed all the proceedings
and were resolved from the first to get the deposition of Dioscurus carried through at the Council, although they gave the
Council the show of freedom; (5) that the Imperial Commissioners had been at the same time instructed to press for the
establishment of a new doctrinal formula on the basis of Leo's
letter in order to bring to an end the intolerable state of things
which had prevailed in the Church of the East owing to the
annulling of the resolution of 449; (6) that the Roman legates
were at one with the Commissioners in their determination to
get the Council to decree the deposition of Dioscurus and the
setting up of a dogmatic confession, but that they differed from
them so far in that they wished Dioscurus to be described as
a heretic, in other words, as a rebel against the Pope, and
at the same time exerted themselves simply towards getting
Leo's ep. dogmatica accepted in the Church; (7) that Dioscurus
had to submit to a judicial process of an extremely disgraceful
and unjust kind, that he acquitted himself worthily, and firmly
maintained his position as the successor of Athanasius, and that
in the end he was in no sense deposed on the ground of heresy,
nor on account of murder, but on the ground of certain
irregularities, including contempt for the divine canon, and dis-
obedience to the Council,[1] while his deceased opponent Flavian

---

divided himself; dismember them, cast them out, etc.") used at Chalcedon was not
any milder than that used at Ephesus in 449. Theodoret condemned Nestorius at
the eighth sitting, Mansi VII., p. 185 sq. From the time of Leo I., moreover, the
orthodox and those whose views were more of the type of the school of Antioch,
applied the worst term of abuse, "Jew", to the Eutychians (Monophysites) because
they ostensibly denied the Incarnation.

[1] Dioscurus protested that he did not assume that there was any mixing of the
natures; and nobody was able to prove the opposite against him; see Mansi VI.,
p. 676: Διόσκορος εἶπεν· οὔτε σύγχυσιν λέγομεν οὔτε τομὴν οὔτε τροπήν. ἀνάθεμα τῷ
λέγοντι σύγχυσιν ἢ τροπὴν ἢ ἀνάκρασιν. On the other hand he was not refuted
when he (p. 683) asserted: "Flavian was justly condemned because he still maintained two natures after the union. I can prove from Athanasius, Gregory, and
Cyril that after the union we ought rather to speak only of one incarnate nature
of the Logos. I will be rejected together with the Fathers, but I am defending
the doctrine of the Fathers, and yield on no point." He approved of the expression "out of two natures"; one can readily understand how as early as the second
session he no longer wished to appear at the Council.

was on the other hand rehabilitated;[1] (8) that the bishops who
had met together with him at Ephesus at first attempted to
make out that the vote they gave there had been extorted by
force, but that afterwards when they found they could not prove
this they described themselves in the most dishonourable way
as erring men who had gone wrong and begged forgiveness,
although as a matter of fact they did not deny their faith at
Ephesus in the year 449, but now at Chalcedon;[2] (9) that,
considering the views of the faith prevailing at the time, the
great majority of the bishops were able to comply with a new
rule of faith even though it might be expressed in the usual
terms, only by doing violence to their consciences, and that
they finally deceived themselves by drawing the delusive distinction that it was not a question of an exposition (ἔκθεσις)
but of an interpretation (ἑρμηνεία); (10) that spite of all the
pressure put on them by the Roman legates and the commissioners, the majority under the guidance of Anatolius while expressly emphasing the fact that Dioscurus was not deposed on
account of heresy—Anatolius had always in his heart agreed
with the views of Dioscurus—further attempted to set up a
doctrinal formula in which the distinction between the two
natures was made one *in thought* only, and which made it possible to speak of one nature after the Incarnation,[3] and that
three statements particularly, in the third and fourth chapters
of Leo's letter to Flavian, (see above) appeared to the bishops

---

[1] In connection with this affair Juvenal and the Palestinian bishops changed
their opinion in the most disgraceful fashion

[2] Some of them had agreed with Flavian in 448, with Dioscurus in 449, and
now they agreed with the Council! Even the Imperial Commissioners blamed the
bishops for the contradiction in which they entangled themselves when they gave
out that their vote of the year 449 had been purely extorted from them; see
Mansi VI., p. 637 fin. It has to be noted, moreover, that throughout the proceedings
it was much more—in fact it was almost exclusively—a question of persons, of
their standing, or of the right or wrong of their condemnation, and therefore as to
Nestorius, Cyril, Flavian, Eutyches, Theodoret, Dioscurus, Leo, than a question of
the actual matter in hand. In the first place everyone took care not to touch the
real point or to have anything to do with constructing formulæ, and in the second
place the personal question was with most of them the main thing.

[3] See the proceedings in Mansi VII., p. 97 sq.

to be intolerably Nestorian;[1] (11) that the bishops abandoned their proposed formula only after the most violent threats on the part of the Emperor, among which too was a threat to transfer the Council to Italy, and that they outwardly reconciled themselves to the statements of Leo with which they had found fault by deluding themselves with the false idea that Cyril said very much what Leo said and that both were in agreement; (12) that the new doctrinal formula[2] would nevertheless not have been carried through if it had not finally been established under severe pressure at a secret commission, and that this formula is so far lacking in veracity in that it is intended to contain the genuine doctrine of Cyril and recognises the resolution of the Cyrillian Council of 431, while it gives it the go-bye in so far as it sets aside the unity and union of the *natures*.

The imperial-papal formula was proclaimed and adopted at the fifth sitting.[3] It first of all confirms the decision of Nicæa, Constantinople, and Ephesus, it then explains that the Creed which had been handed down is sufficient in itself, but that on account of the teachers of false doctrine who on the one hand reject the designation $\theta\epsilon o\tau \acute{o}\kappa o\varsigma$ and on the other wish to introduce the idea of a confusion ($\sigma \acute{v}\gamma\chi v\sigma\iota\varsigma$) and mixing ($\kappa\rho\tilde{a}\sigma\iota\varsigma$) of the natures, "and absurdly fabricate only *one* nature for the flesh and the Godhead,"[4] and consider the divine nature of the only-begotten to be capable of suffering, the Council has adopted both the letters of Cyril to Nestorius[5] and the Easterns, as

---

[1] The expression so frequently used by the Westerns, God has assumed "a man", was also found fault with, but not officially.

[2] The formula was probably already drawn up when the Chalcedonian Council began; that commission cannot have got it ready in the short time it had; it even appears to follow from what is said in the Récits de Dioscore that it had already been laid before the Court previous to the meeting of the Council.

[3] See Mansi VII., p. 107 sq.

[4] Rarely had any one to my knowledge expressed himself in this way after Apollinaris ($\mu \acute{i}\alpha\nu$ $\epsilon \tilde{i}\nu\alpha\iota$ $\tau\tilde{\eta}\varsigma$ $\sigma\alpha\rho\kappa\grave{o}\varsigma$ $\kappa\alpha\grave{\iota}$ $\tau\tilde{\eta}\varsigma$ $\theta\epsilon \acute{o}\tau\eta\tau o\varsigma$ $\phi \acute{v}\sigma\iota\nu$), but the Bishops had first to distort the faith which they themselves had avowed and which they now nevertheless rejected, in order to turn it into a heresy. The "Eranistes" of Theodoret, however, attacks those who "make the divinity and humanity into one nature."

[5] The Anathemas of Cyril are also implicitly to be understood as included in these; see Loofs, op. cit. p. 50 f

well as the letter of Leo. It is therefore directed both against those who break up the mystery of the Incarnation into two sons, and also against those who consider the Godhead of the only-begotten to be capable of suffering, who imagine a mingling and a fusion and declare the human substance of Christ to be a heavenly substance: "those who on the one hand assert two natures in the Lord before the union and those on the other hand who imagine one after the union, be anathema." (καὶ τοὺς δύο μὲν πρὸ τῆς ἑνώσεως φύσεις τοῦ κυρίου μυθεύοντας, μίαν δὲ μετὰ τὴν ἕνωσιν ἀναπλάττοντας, ἀναθεματίζει). (This was the sacrifice of the thought of Faith.) "Following therefore the holy Fathers, we all agree in teaching plainly that it is necessary to confess one and the same Son our Lord Jesus Christ, perfect alike in His divinity and perfect in his humanity, alike truly God and truly man," ('Επόμενοι τοίνον τοῖς ἁγίοις πατράσιν ἕνα καὶ τὸν αὐτὸν ὁμολογεῖν υἱὸν τὸν κύριον ἡμῶν Ἰ. Χρ. συμφώνως ἅπαντες ἐκδιδάσκομεν, τέλειον τὸν αὐτὸν ἐν θεότητι καὶ τέλειον τὸν αὐτὸν ἐν ἀνθρωπότητι, Θεὸν ἀληθῶς καὶ ἄνθρωπον ἀληθῶς τὸν αὐτόν). This is further developed in detail, then we have: "We acknowledge one and the same Christ in two natures unconfusedly, unchangeably, indivisibly, inseparably; nowhere is the difference of the natures annulled because of the union, but on the contrary the property of each of the two natures is preserved; each nature coming together into one person and one hypostasis, not divided or separated into two persons, but one and the same Son and only-begotten, God-Logos." (ἕνα καὶ τὸν αὐτὸν Χριστὸν... ἐν δύο φύσεσιν [1] ἀσυγχύτως, ἀτρέπτως, ἀδιαιρέτως, ἀχωρίστως γνωρίζομεν· οὐδαμοῦ τῆς τῶν φύσεων διαφορᾶς ἀνῃρημένης διὰ τὴν ἕνωσιν, σωζομένης δὲ μᾶλλον τῆς ἰδιότητος ἑκατέρας φύσεως. καὶ εἰς ἓν πρόσωπον καὶ μίαν ὑπόστασιν συντρεχούσης, οὐκ εἰς δύο πρόσωπα μεριζόμενον ἢ διαιρούμενον, ἀλλὰ ἕνα

---

[1] It is here that the difficulty occurs which has been so much discussed, namely, that the Greek text gives ἐκ δύο φύσεων and the Latin "in duabus naturis". Judging from all that preceded this, one cannot but hold that Tillemont, Walch, Gieseler, Neander, Hefele and others are right (as against Baur and Dörner) and look for the original reading in the latter phrase. The form in which we have the Greek text is of course not a mere error, but is an ancient falsification. In the period from the fifth to the seventh century the falsification of acts was an important weapon for the defence of what was sacred.

καὶ τὸν αὐτὸν υἱὸν καὶ μονογενῆ, Θεὸν λόγον.). The decree appeals
in support of these statements to the Old Testament, to Jesus
Christ Himself, and—to the Nicene Creed; at the close it is
said that no one is to accept or teach any other creed, that
on the contrary only this form of belief is to be handed
down in connection with the instruction of Jews, heathen, and
heretics.

The Emperor had now got what he wished. He had shewn
that he ruled the Church, and he had got a formula according
to which he was able henceforth to decide what was orthodox
and what was heretical.[1] An end was put to the uncertain
state of things which permitted everyone to appeal to the 318
bishops and in doing this to think whatever he liked. In the
full consciousness of his triumph Marcian appeared in person
along with Pulcheria at the sitting immediately following (6),
and addressed the Council, making express reference to Constantine. He was greeted with acclamations from the whole
Council: "We all so believe; we are all orthodox; this Faith
has saved the world; hail to Marcian, the new Constantine, the
new Paul, the new David! You are the peace of the world;
Pulcheria is the new Helena!" But the Pope too had got
what he wanted, if not everything. His letter had not been

[1] This prospect was indeed a delusive one; for since the Council had expressly
appealed both to Cyril and to Leo, its decree could be interpreted according to
the views either of the one or of the other, and consequently the old trouble was
really there again. The three decrees of February 7th, March 13th, and July 28th,
452, (Mansi VII., pp. 476, 477, 501) are a proof of the energy and vigour with
which the Emperor purposed to enforce the Chalcedonian Creed. According to
the first of these all controversy was to cease, nobody was to dispute publicly
regarding the faith. Whoever does this is looking in broad daylight for a false
light, commits an act of sacrilege, insults the holy Council and betrays the secret
to the Jews and the heathen. He must accordingly expect severe punishment,
which has been already fixed and which will be of different degrees for the separate classes of the community. According to the third edict Eutychians and Apollinarians are forbidden to have pastors; those who contravene this order are to be
punished with confiscation of their goods and exile. The right of assemblage,
the right of building churches, and of being together in monasteries, is withdrawn
from them. Their property is to go to the Exchequer. So too they are deprived
of the power of inheriting anything and of bequeathing anything. Eutychian
monks are to be treated as Manicheans, are to be driven from their "stalls" and
removed from the soil of the Empire. Eutychian writings are to be burned, etc.
Eutyches and Dioscurus themselves must go into exile.

given straight off the place of a doctrinal ordinance, but the Conciliar-decree had proceeded from this letter; his dogmatic teaching was acknowledged, and in his address to the Council Marcian had given expression to this fact. The truth is that without the help of the Papal legates Marcian could not have effected anything. But the Church of the East had been deprived of its faith. [1] The ἕνωσις φυσική, the natural union, was not mentioned; no one could any longer unhesitatingly teach that the God-Logos had taken up the human nature into the unity of his unique substance and made it the perfect organ of His deity. The construction of a Christology based on the God-Logos was severely shaken; the "two hypostases (δύο ὑποστάσεις) were not expressly condemned. In the "coming together" (συντρέχειν) each nature continues to exist in its own mode of being; the divinity has not absorbed the humanity nor has the humanity been exalted to the height of the divinity, but the human and divine natures are simply united in the *person* of the Redeemer, and therefore only mediately and in an individual (individuum). No pious Greek who had had Athanasius and Cyril for his teachers could acknowledge that to be "the right mean"; it was not even a formula of compromise like that of the year 433; it was the abandonment of the work of developing the Christological formula strictly in accordance with soteriology. The latter itself now became uncertain. If humanity was not deified in Christ, but if in His case His humanity was merely united with the divinity by the *prosopon* or person, then what effect can a union such as that have for us? That formula can only be of advantage either to the detested "moralism" of the Antiochians, or to mysticism, which bases its hope of redemption on the idea that the God-Logos continually unites Himself anew with each individual soul so as to form a union. The four bald negative terms (ἀσυγχύτως etc.,) which are supposed to express the whole truth, are in the view of the classical theologians amongst the Greeks, profoundly

[1] In respect of its relation to the orthodox faith and of the fact that it owed its origin to the Emperor, the Chalcedonian Creed may be compared with the decrees of the last Councils of Constantius. It is true that orthodoxy afterwards found it easier to reconcile itself to the two natures than to the "likeness". Still perhaps it might have come to terms with the latter also.

irreligious. They are wanting in warm, concrete substance; of the bridge which his faith is to the believer, the bridge from earth to heaven, they make a line which is finer than the hair upon which the adherents of Islam one day hope to enter Paradise. One may indeed say that the Chalcedonian Creed preserved for the East the minimum of historical conception which the Church still possessed regarding the person of Christ, by cutting short the logical results of the doctrine of redemption, which threatened completely to destroy the Christ of the Gospels. But the Fathers who accepted the Creed did not think of that. They in fact accepted it under compulsion, and if they had thought of this, the price which they paid would have been too dear; for a theology which, in what is for it the most important of all questions, has recourse to mere negatives, is self-condemned. Nor is it of any use to point to the fact that the Council merely gave the mystery a definite standing and thereby furthered the interests of the Greek Church and the Greek theology. *The true mystery on the contrary was contained in the substantial union of the two natures themselves.* It was seriously damaged by being banished from its place here, and when in place of it the *conception* of the union, a conception which was supposed at the same time to involve a state of separation, was raised to the position of the secret of faith. The real mystery was thus shoved aside by a pseudo-mystery which in truth no longer permitted theology to advance to the thought of the actual and perfect union. Monophysitism which holds to the statement that, without prejudice to the homo-ousia of the body of Christ with our body, the God-Logos made this body His own body and for this reason took it up into the unity of His substance, is without doubt the legitimate heir of the theology of Athanasius and the fitting expression of Greek Christianity. [1] The proposition, however, which was

---

[1] We can only adduce one consideration here, namely, that it was essential to this Christianity which had the New Testament beside it, that it should never, just because of this, develop in a logical way as a mystical doctrine of redemption. Understood in this sense no objection can be taken to the statement that the logical development of the monophysite faith even in its least extravagant form, was bound to come into conflict with certain elements of the ecclesiastical tradition, or with certain New Testament passages which could not be given up.

now to pass for orthodox, "each nature in communion with the
other does what is proper to it," (agit utraque forma cum alterius communione, quod proprium est) actually makes two subjects out of one and betokens a lapse from the ancient faith.
That the view we have here expressed is correct is attested by
the previous history of the formula of the two natures and the
one person. Up to this time scarcely anything had been known
in the East of a "nature without hypostasis" (φύσις ἀνυπόστατος),
although the Antiochians had distinguished between φύσις and
πρόσωπον. It is attested further by the melancholy proceedings
at the Council itself, and, as will be shewn, it is attested above
all by the history which follows. A formula was now introduced
which could ultimately be traced to a legal source and which
for that reason could be transformed into a philosophical-theological formula only by a scholastic.

At Chalcedon only a part of the deputation of monks who
had approached the Council with the prayer that the ancient
faith might not suffer harm, and also the majority of the Egyptian monks, remained firm. [1] We cannot say, however, whether
the action of the latter was an instance of the courage of faith.
Their request that the Council should not compel them to
accept the formula since in this case they would be killed after
their return to Egypt, their despairing cry, "We shall be killed,
if we subscribe Leo's epistle; we would rather be put to death
here by you than there; have pity on us: we would rather die
at the hands of the Emperor and at your hands than at home,"
proves that they were still more afraid of Coptic fanaticism
than of the Emperor's police. They were allowed to postpone
their subscription till a new bishop should be appointed to
Alexandria, since they had explained that without a new bishop
they could do nothing. They were not, however, to stir from
Constantinople till then.

The Council was to be a Council of peace after the downfall
of Dioscurus. All were pardoned, even Ibas himself, and on
the other hand, the traitorous associates of Dioscurus at whose
head stood Juvenal of Jerusalem. All were restored to their
bishoprics so far as that was at all feasible. A series of Canons

[1] See the proceedings of the fourth sitting.

was then issued dealing with the regulation of ecclesiastical matters. The seventeenth Canon asserted in a blunt fashion what was a fundamental Byzantine principle: "let the arrangement also of the ecclesiastical districts follow that of the civil and state places." (τοῖς πολιτικοῖς καὶ δημοσίοις τόποις καὶ τῶν ἐκκλησιαστικῶν παροικιῶν ἡ τάξις ἀκολουθείτω). The twenty-eighth, under cover of an appeal to the third Canon [1] of 381, struck a blow at Rome by ordaining that the patriarch of Constantinople was to enjoy similar privileges to those possessed by the bishop of Rome, was to be second to him in rank, and was to get an enormous extension of his diocese—namely, over Pontus, Asia, and Thrace. The proceedings in connection with this matter do not belong to the history of dogma, although Leo combated the resolution with dogmatic arguments drawn from tradition. The Roman legates, we may note, entered their protest. The Emperor once more created for himself a patriarch *primi ordinis*, after that the patriarch of Alexandria had had to be overthrown, and it was the bishop of his own capital whom he put alongside of the Roman bishop. The Council had to ask the Pope to confirm the twenty-eighth Canon by way of return, as it was openly put, for the acknowledgment of his dogmatic letter in the East. [2] But the Pope remained firm; his letters 104—107 prove that he had no intention of surrendering the grand success he had secured just in the East. A primacy of the East in Constantinople was the greatest possible danger, and for this reason Leo at once again took up the cause of the chairs of Alexandria and Antioch. In fact he now even shewed some hesitation in giving his approval of the resolutions of the great Councils generally, so that the Monophysites came to be

---

[1] The Romans before this had no official knowledge whatever of this Canon, and *in praxi* it had not been entirely enforced, even in the East itself, as the Robber-Synod shews.

[2] Leo, ep. 98. The letter is full of flattery of the Pope; see c. I. It follows too from the formally very submissive epistle of Anatolius to Leo (ep. 101) that an attempt had been made to induce Leo by flattery to acknowledge the 28th Canon. We gather from Marcian's epistle to Leo (ep. 100) that the Emperor considered that Canon as the most important ordinance of the Council together with the doctrinal decision. For details see Kattenbusch, op. cit. I., p. 87 ff., where the Canons 9 and 17 are discussed.

under the pleasing delusion that he was inclined to side with them. (!) [1] He soon entirely broke with Anatolius and entered into negotiations with the new bishop of Alexandria (ep. 129) and with the bishop of Antioch (ep. 119) whose position in their patriarchates he sought to strengthen, and whom he begged to send him more frequently information regarding their affairs that he might be able to render them assistance. Soon, however, the Constantinopolitan bishop Anatolius found himself in such a difficult position owing to the new dogmatic controversies, that he preferred to shelve the Canon complained of and once more to seek the friendship of Leo which he did indeed secure.

§ 3. *The Monophysite Controversies and the Fifth Council.* [2]

1. The severest condemnation of the Chalcedonian Creed as decree wrung from the Eastern Churches, is to be found in the history of the next 68 years. These years are not only marked by the most frightful revolts on the part of the populace and the monks, particularly in Egypt, Palestine, and a part of Syria, but also by the attempts of the Emperors to get rid of the decree which had been issued with a definite end in view, and which was a source of difficulty and threatened the security

---

[1] See ep. 110; the approval followed in ep. 114, with certain reservations because of Canon 28; see ep. 115—117.

[2] The enormous and varied documentary material is given only in part in Mansi VII—IX. The Pope's letters are in Thiel, 1867. Much new in Mai's Script. Vet. Nova Coll.; Joh. of Ephesus (Monophysite) hist. eccl., German translation by Schönfelder, 1862, something different in Land, Anecd. Syr. Information regarding further sources in Möller, Monophysiten (R.-Encykl. X.) and Loofs, Leontius, 1887, (Texte u. Unters. III. 1, 2). Accounts by Tillemont, Gibbon, Walch, Schröckh, Hefele, Dorner, Baur, cf. the articles on the subject by Möller, Gass, and Hauck in the R.-Encykl.: in the same place the special literature in connection with the Theopaschitian, Tritheistic, and Origenist controversies and that of the Three Chapters. The special investigations, however, which had been carried on up till the beginning of the 18th century have rarely been resumed in recent times, but see Gieseler, Comment., qua Monophys. opin. illustr., 2 parts, 1835, 1838; Krüger, Monophys. Streitigkeiten, 1884 and Loofs, op. cit.; Kleyn, Bijdrage tot de Kerkgeschiedenis van het Oosten gedurende de zesde Eeuw, 1891 (from the chronicle of Dionysius of Tellmahre, who made extracts from the Church History of John of Ephesus. Kleyn gives the portions referring to the 6th century; they are identical with the

of the Empire.[1] They were all the more under the necessity
of making these attempts, that in the East energetic theologians
who could defend the Chalcedonian Creed were entirely lacking.
At this period it maintained its position only by means of the
great importance given to it by the imposing Council, by the
majority of the clergy in the capital, and by the Roman bishop.
These were strong forces; but the strength of the opposition
to it, which was supported by the increasing aversion to the
Byzantine Emperor and his Patriarch, by national aspirations
and personal antipathies,[2] was also great. In addition to this
the pious-minded felt as much aggrieved by the fact that a new
formula had been introduced at all as by what was in the
formula itself.[3] The Encyclical letter (ἐγκύκλιον) of the usurper

second and third parts of John's Church History. Kleyn has published for the
first time the sections for the years 481—561 [in Dutch]; they are of great importance for the history of Monophysitism, its spread, and the persecution it underwent).

[1] Leo I., Marcian's successor, had already made a beginning with this, though
he proceeded cautiously; see Leon. papæ ep. 145—158, 160—165, 169—173. One
can see here what trouble it cost the Pope to maintain the Chalcedonian Creed.
The opposition parties made the strongest efforts to prove that the Chalcedonian
Creed was Nestorian. Of the memorial of Timotheus Aelurus (Heruler? hardly)
the Monophysite Patriarch of Alexandria, Gennadius says (de vir. inl. 73): "librum
valde suasorium, quem pravo sensu patrum testimoniis in tantum roborare conatus
est, ut ad decipiendum imperatorem et suam hæresim constituendam pæne Leonem,
urbis Romæ pontificem, et Chalcedonensem synodum ac totos occidentales episcopos
illorum adminiculo Nestorianos ostenderet." The fact that the Emperor Leo called
for an expression of opinion regarding the Chalcedonian Creed, was a step towards
getting rid of it.

[2] Monasticism which was hostile to the State, the aspirations after independence on the part of the Egyptians, and jealousy of the influence of the Byzantine
Patriarch, all played a part behind Monophysitism. This feeling of jealousy was
shared by the Roman bishop who, however, felt himself under the necessity
primarily of guarding the dogmatic formula.

[3] See the opinion of a Pamphylian Council supplied to the Emperor, printed
in Mansi VII. p. 573—576. We can see from this that not only was the new
definition which went beyond the Nicene Creed felt to be objectionable by the
bishops, but that they disapprove too of the distinction of nature and person,
prefer to speak with Cyril of one nature and wish to make the Chalcedonian
Creed authoritative only in connection with controversies as being a formula which
originated in and was rendered necessary by controversy, but not for the instruction of ordinary Christians. The Armenian Church has kept to this position; it
is not Monophysite, but Cyrillian; see Arsak Ter Mikelian, Die Armenische Kirche
in ihren Beziehungen zur Byzantischen vom. 4—13 Jahrh., Leipzig 1892, cf.
Karapet, Die Paulikianer, (Leipzig 1893) p. 54 ff.

Basilikus (476) which abrogated the Chalcedonian Creed and decided in favour of Monophysitism, had certainly only a passing importance. [1] But state-policy was successful in uniting a section of the Chalcedonians and Monophysites by means of a Henoticon (482), which, when issued as an imperial edict by Zeno, virtually annulled the decree of 451. [2] The result was that soon instead of two parties there were three; for not only did the strict Monophysites renounce their allegiance to the Alexandrian patriarch Peter Mongus who had concluded a union with his Constantinopolitan colleague Acacius, but the Roman bishop too, Felix II., (see the epp.) rejected the Henoticon and pronounced sentence of excommunication on Acacius. Old and New Rome, which were already separated by political circumstances, now came to be divided ecclesiastically, and this schism lasted from 484 to 519. Since the Henoticon soon shewed itself to be ineffective, it would have been brought to an end sooner if Rome had not insisted on the condemnation of Acacius by his successors. The Monophysites soon came forward again openly rejecting the Chalcedonian Creed, and those in the Eastern Empire who adhered to it, and also the Henotics, had at first difficulty in preventing the new Emperor Anastasius from formally doing

[1] Basilikus had the ep. Leon. ad Flav. and the Chalcedonian Creed condemned. About 500 bishops of the South and West actually subscribed it, but not Acacius; see Euagr. h. e. III. 4. The decree takes its stand upon the Nicene Creed and the two following Councils, but orders the Chalcedonian canons to be burned. Basilikus afterwards withdrew it (Euagr. III. 7), see also the epp. Simplicii papæ.

[2] The Henotikon (Euagr. III. 14) declares in the first part that the sole authoritative creed is the Nicene-Constantinopolitan, and excludes all the other σύμβολα or μαθήματα; it then expressly condemns Nestorius and Eutyches while accepting the anathemas of Cyril. Then, however, there further follows a full Christological Confession in which the following statements are specially worthy of note: ὁμολογοῦμεν τὸν μονογενῆ τοῦ Θεοῦ υἱὸν ... ἕνα τυγχάνειν καὶ οὐ δύο· ἑνὸς γὰρ εἶναι φαμὲν τὰ τε θαύματα καὶ τὰ πάθη ἅπερ ἑκουσίως ὑπέμεινε σαρκί ... ἡ σάρκωσις ἐκ τῆς θεοτόκου προσθήκην υἱοῦ οὐ πεποίηκε. μεμένηκε γὰρ τριὰς ἡ τριὰς καὶ σαρκωθέντος τοῦ ἑνὸς τῆς τριάδος Θεοῦ λόγου ... πάντα δὲ τὸν ἕτερόν τι φρονήσαντα ἢ φρονοῦντα, ἢ νῦν ἢ πώποτε ἢ ἐν Καλχηδόνι ἢ οἵᾳ δήποτε συνόδῳ ἀναθεματίζομεν. An appeal on behalf of union is then made to the Egyptians to whom the epistle is addressed. Its dogmatic substance is not orthodox; the insincere way, however, in which the Council of Chalcedon is not condemned, but ignored, shews that there was a desire to tolerate Monophysitism. The Emperor indeed cannot be blamed for issuing the edict; in doing this he simply did his duty. But Petrus Mongus played a double game, and so too did Acacius.

away with the unfortunate decree. [1] The confusion was now
greater than it had ever been. People who used one and the
same Christological formula were often further apart and more
bitter against one another than were those who were separated by
the wording of the formulæ. If the Emperor had not been a capable ruler, things in the Empire would have got out of joint. He
was meanwhile always approaching nearer to Monophysitism with
which he was personally in sympathy, and on the side of which
stood not only the more fanatical, but also the more capable
theologians, such as Philoxenus of Mabug, and Severus. In Syria
and Palestine the Monophysite cause already triumphed amid
terrors of all sorts; but the capital, Constantinople, and Thrace,
with the true instinct of self-preservation held to the Chalcedonian Creed against the Emperor, the patron of heretics, and
Vitalian, [2] a fierce general, a semi-barbarian, and rebel who was
yet the forerunner of Justinian who taught him politics, made
common cause with the Chalcedonians against his monarch.
The Emperor had to submit to the powerful general; but it
was not possible, even by making all sorts of concessions in
regard to the dogmatic question, to get Rome, which put forward exorbitant claims, to agree to a policy of oblivion in
reference to Acacius. Anastasius did not come to any agreement with the Pope Hormisdas. But what he did not succeed
in doing was successfully accomplished by his successor Justin,
or rather by the nephew and director of the new Emperor
Justin, Justinian, in conjunction with Vitalian. They saw that
for the re-establishment of the authority of the Emperor and
the state in the Empire, the re-establishment of the Chalcedonian
Creed and of the league with Rome, was indispensable. After
that the authority of the four Councils had been once more
solemnly recognised in Constantinople, everywhere throughout
the Empire the orthodox raised their heads. Hormisdas did
not himself appear in the capital; but his legates succeeded in
getting almost everything he had asked. Again did the Roman
bishop, like Leo before him, help the Byzantine State to gain

---

[1] See Rose, Kaiser Anastasius I., Halle, 1882.
[2] On the importance of the part played by Vitalian, see Loofs, p. 243 ff.,
and in addition Joh. Antioch. in Müller, Fragm. hist. gr. V., p. 32 sq.

the victory over the ecclesiastical movements. Orthodoxy was again restored and the names of the authors and defenders of the Henotikon, from Acacius and Zeno downwards were erased from the sacred books (519). The purification of Syria and its chair from the monophysite heresy meanwhile created some difficulty. The attempt to get the more determined Monophysites out of the way was, it is true, successful, but as soon it became a question as to who were to be their successors, it at once became evident again that the Chalcedonian Creed was understood in a different way in Rome and in the East respectively, and that the East had not got rid of the suspicion of Nestorianism so far as Rome was concerned.

This difference emerged in a very characteristic form in the so-called Theopaschitian controversy.[1] The formulæ, "God has suffered", "God was crucified", were time-honoured forms[2] of speech in the Church and had never been quite forgotten. But after there had been so much speculation regarding the Trinity and the Incarnation, these formulæ came to be discussed too. Still, even after the formation of the Chalcedonian Creed, it seemed to be impossible to disapprove of them; for if Mary was to be called θεοτόκος this meant that they were approved of. Nevertheless opposition soon shewed itself when the Monophysite patriarch of Antioch, Petrus Fullo, with the approval of his co-religionists, formulated the Trishagion as follows: Holy God, Holy the mighty one, Holy the immortal one who was crucified for us: ἅγιος ὁ Θεός, ἅγιος ἰσχυρός, ἅγιος ἀθάνατος, ὁ σταυρωθεὶς δι' ἡμᾶς. The Emperor approved of this innovation which, however, at once met with opposition in Antioch itself, and which cost one of those who had to do with it his life. In the capital a controversy broke out when some Scythian monks, whose soundness in the faith was unimpeachable, defended the orthodoxy of the formula, "one of the Trinity was crucified —suffered in the flesh" ("unum de trinitate, esse crucifixum— passum carne"), about the year 518. The legates of Pope Hormisdas, bearing in mind Leo's doctrinal letter, opposed it as being incompatible with the Catholic Faith! The Pope him-

---

[1] See Hauck in the Realencyklop. Vol. XV. p. 534 ff.

[2] See Vol. I., p. 187.

self was now concerned in the matter. A decision was necessarily urgently desired—on the part of the Emperor too; for the
relations had become so strained that any sudden movement
might throw the whole Church into confusion. Hormisdas
hesitated about giving an answer; he neither wished to disavow
his legates nor too openly to reject the formulæ. The decision
which he finally gave in a letter to the Emperor Justin (521),
was to the effect that everything was already decided, without,
however, saying what was to be regarded as authoritative. This
declaration which shewed his perplexity roused just indignation
not only in Constantinople but also in North Africa. Justinian,
who at first did not approve of the formula,—so long, that is,
as he still followed in the wake of Vitalian,— afterwards held
to it all the more strongly, the more he urged the strictly
Cyrillian interpretation of the Chalcedonian Creed. When he
had the power he got the Popes too to acknowledge it, had the
faithful but impolitic partisans of Rome, the Akoimetan monks
in Constantinople, excommunicated, and finally got the formula
sanctioned at the Fifth Ecumenical Council, that our Lord who
was crucified in the flesh, Jesus Christ, was one of the Trinity. [1]

It is apparently necessary to make a sharp distinction between the attempt of the Monophysites to give an extension to
the Trishagion in a Theopaschitian sense, and the assertion of
the Scythian monks that the doctrinal formula: "One of the
Trinity suffered in the flesh", was orthodox. That attempt was
rejected because it involved an innovation in worship and
because it could be interpreted in a Sabellian sense. Orthodoxy
putting this meaning on it, gave the name "Theopaschitian"
a permanent place in its collection as a heretical name. On
the other hand it was, to begin with, purely owing to Roman
obstinacy that the formula proposed by the Scythians, and
which, moreover, rather justifies than adopts the monophysite
formula, was objected to. But it has been recently very justly
remarked [2] that the cause of the offence which the formula gave,

---

[1] See on the controversy Marcellinus, Euagr. Theophanes, Victor Tun., The
Letters of Hormisdas, Mansi VIII. c. IX. Noris, Hist. Pelag. Disser. I. 1702.
On the Scythian Monks, see Loofs, pp. 229—261.

[2] See Loofs, op. cit., pp. 53, 231 f., 248 ff., whose splendid investigations have
been made use of in what follows.

even to some of the Chalcedonians, is not to be looked for
within the Christological, but on the contrary within the Trinitarian, domain. This brings us to a complete change which
took place in the theology of that period and which claims the
most serious attention.

Attention has been already drawn to the fact, (Vol. III., p. 154
and above p. 126) that in the course of the transition from the fifth
to the sixth century Aristotelianism once more became the fashion
in science. This revolution helped to bring about the naturalisa-
tion of the Chalcedonian Creed in the Church, or what amounts
to the same thing, contributed towards reconciling Greek religious feeling to it. While up to the beginning of the sixth century orthodoxy was without any theologians, we come across
a man in the first half of the century who both as theologian
and student of dogma was as able as he was prolific, and in
the case of whom one feels that while he believes and thinks
as Cyril believed and thought, his determined defence of the
Chalcedonian Creed was nevertheless not in any way forced
out of him—Leontius of Byzantium (c. 485—543). [1] When, however, we try to find out by what means he, as a theologian of
the school of Cyril, succeeded in accommodating himself to the
Chalcedonian Creed, it becomes clear that he was helped to
this by the Aristotelian conceptual distinctions, and therefore
by scholasticism. Leontius was the first scholastic. [2] While,
owing to his faith, he stood in an intimate relation to Greek
religious feeling, the Chalcedonian formula presented itself to
him as an inviolable doctrine promulgated by the Church. But

---

[1] Loofs was the first to throw light on his works, his personality, and his
history.

[2] This description is to be taken with the qualification that in his theological
thinking he still shewed a certain freedom. While the proofs alleged by Loofs
in favour of the view that the "Origenist" Leontius is identical with the Byzantine (pp. 274—297) are indeed not absolutely decisive, though to my mind they are
convincing, one can see that Leontius held the great master in veneration without
following him in his doubtful statements. But nothing is more characteristic of
the period upon which the Church had now entered than the fact that even this
academic veneration for Origen was no longer tolerated. Leontius was described
as "Origenist" and Loofs' conjecture is quite correct (p. 296) that Joh. Damascenus, that in a certain sense the Eastern Church itself, consigned this theologian
of theirs to oblivion because he was still too liberal.

while he unweariedly defended it against Nestorians, Apollinarians, and Severians, dogmatic and religious considerations were put entirely into the background; their place was taken by an exposition of doctrine based on philosophical conceptions.[1] He treated of substance, genus, species, individual being, of the attributes which constitute the substance, of inseparable accidents and of separable accidents. It was on the result of these discussions that the conceptions of the natures and the hypostasis in Christ were based; the Aristotelian δευτέρα οὐσία, or second substance, was given a place of prominence, and thus the Chalcedonian Creed was justified. All the Aristotelian splitting of conceptions did not, it is true, cover the most crucial point of all—namely, the exposition of the unity. Here, however, Leontius had recourse to the idea of the Enhypostasis of the human nature; thus proving in the clearest way that he wished to keep the Chalcedonian definition on the lines laid down by Apollinaris and Cyril and not on those laid down in Leo's doctrinal letter.[3]   In the whole way in which Leontius

---

[1] See Loofs, p. 60: "It is neither exegetical, nor religious arguments which are given a foremost place, but philosophical, and the philosophical theory upon which the arguments of our author rest, has a decidedly Aristotelian and not a Platonic origin.   Our author is a forerunner of John of Damascus."

[2] See the explanations given by Loofs of the apparatus of conceptions used by Leontius, p. 60—74. The entire distinction between the Western conception and that which combines the views of Cyril and Leontius is to be found in scientific form in the statement of Leontius: οὐκ ἔστι φύσις ἀνυπόστατος ... ἀνυπόστατος μὲν οὖν φύσις, τουτέστιν οὐσία, οὐκ ἂν εἴη ποτέ. The Western legal fiction of a distinction between person and nature is here pitched aside. I do not enter into further detail regarding the theology of Leontius because in an outline of the History of Dogma it must suffice to ascertain its tendency and methods. Anything further belongs to the history of theology.

[3] The expedient of the enhypostasis was adopted in order to meet the objection urged by the Monophysite Severus against the Chalcedonian Creed and Leo's doctrine, that two energies necessarily lead to two hypostases. Leontius, following up a hint of Cyril herewith shews that if the relative standards of criticism are once abandoned, all Greeks who start from the doctrine of redemption, must be Apollinarians in disguise. Leontius was the first who definitely maintained that the human nature of Christ is not ἀνυπόστατις nor on the other hand an independent ὑπόστασις, but that it has its ὑποστῆναι ἐν τῷ λόγῳ. Leontius refers to the mode of the existence of the ποιότητες οὐσιώδεις in the ousia. The comparison is naturally defective since these ποιότητες do not in themselves constitute a φύσις. In fact all comparisons are defective. Neither Plato nor Aristotle is responsible for this philosophy. A pious Apollinarian monk would probably have been able

transferred the Nestorian-Monophysite controversy into the region
of Philosophy, we may accordingly see a momentous revolution.
This much, however, is certain, that his violent μετάβασις εἰς
ἄλλο γένος was the condition of the gradual reconciliation of the
East with the Chalcedonian Creed [1] and that in intrinsic importance it may be classed along with the method of counting
up authorities. Only in this way was it possible for Leontius to
accept the formula as authoritative, and, spite of the dry form
in which it was put, to regard it with respect from the religious
point of view and at the same time to see in it an inexhaustible subject for the display of dialectical skill. It is undeniable that Chalcedonian orthodoxy was first firmly established in
the East in the age of Justinian, that is to say, inner agreement with the Chalcedonian Creed was then first secured to
any large extent, and this without abandoning Cyril's religious
theology, but on the contrary while emphasising it and giving
it the preference. [2] If this is so then the only possible explanation of these facts is that supplied by the entrance of Aristotelian scholasticism into the Church. *The Chalcedonian dogma
is lost in philosophical theology.* The Faith and the Church
were to a certain extent relieved, feeling reassured by the
knowledge that the dogma was in safe keeping and in good
hands, as it were. One can forget the scruples to which it
gives rise, when one is confident that there are scholars who are
able by the aid of a definite set of technical terms to make everything right. Here, too, for this reason, the work of the historian
of dogma ceases; his place is taken by the historian of theology.

to say with regard to the ὑποστῆναι ἐν τῷ λόγῳ: " Apollinaris says pretty much
the same thing only in somewhat more intelligible words."

[1] Loofs, p. 72 ff. shews that the Chalcedonian element is strongly represented
in the doctrine of Leontius and that in the efforts he made to do it justice we see the
presence of the modern element of personality as distinguished from *physis*, though
indeed only as a kind of shadow of it.

[2] The energetic opposition to the Antiochian theology is specially worthy of
note in this connection. Up to the beginning of the Sixth Century the Chalcedonians were in such a state of alarm owing to the decree, that they could find no
fixed point from which to carry on the old and to them supremely important
struggle against the "dismemberment". Leontius was the first to resume Cyril's
attack on it and to carry on the interrupted work of repelling the most dangerous
of all enemies.

Leontius was himself one of the Scythian monks.[1] The fact that this great opponent of the Monophysites championed the Theopaschitian formula and his criticism of the Antiochian theology, prove how far removed he was from Nestorianism. But the formula by its characteristic difference from the older conception, that of Petrus Fullo, further proves that the introduction of the Aristotelian philosophy into theology called for a restatement of the doctrine of the Trinity. The "unus ex trinitate" is opposed to the "thrice holy" who was crucified for us. Tritheistic tendencies were not wanting at that period, and this is true of both sides in so far as attention was given to the Aristotelian philosophy. That Petrus Fullo, who as a Monophysite so energetically made the Trinity into a unity, was, it is true, no Aristotelian, but neither is his formula in any way typical of Monophysitism as a whole.

The latter on the contrary for the two or three generations after the Chalcedonian Creed, shews that it had in it sufficient life and vigour to be accessible to the influence of the most varied movements and thoughts. It shews during this period that it was the expression of spiritual and theological life in the East generally. The state of petrifaction, barrenness, and barbarism into which it afterwards got, did not yet actually exist, although signs of its approach were evident amongst the fanatical masses and the ignorant monks. It is significant, to begin with, that Monophysitism did not allow itself to be carried to extremes by the blow dealt it by the Chalcedonian Creed. That is a proof of the goodness of its cause and of its power. The Monophysites were strongly bent on keeping clear of "Eutychianism". Anything like mingling or transformation was out of the question, in fact Eutyches himself was abandoned to his fate.[2] Then the readiness shewn by a large section of the Monophysites to come to terms with orthodoxy if only the Chalcedonian Creed and the objectionable dogmatic development in Leo's doctrinal letter were got out of the way, is a proof that they really strictly maintained the position of Cyril. This is true very specially of the most important champion of

---

[1] See Loofs, p. 228 ff.
[2] See Martin, Pseudo-Synode, p. 53.

Monophysitism—Severus. The attempt has indeed been to draw a distinction, as regards doctrine, between Cyril and Severus, but the attempt does not seem to me to have been successful. [1] Cyril, equally with Severus, would have objected to Leo's assertion that each nature in Christ effects what is peculiar to it, though in conjunction with the other. The emphasis laid by Severus on the one energy is genuinely Cyrillian, and the expression borrowed from the Areopagite, ἐνέργεια θεανδρική, "theandric energy", by no means approaches so near the limits of the permissible as the expression θεοτόκος. But neither is there any difference in the formulæ, μία φύσις τοῦ λόγου σεσαρκωμένη, "one incarnate nature of the Logos" and μία φύσις τοῦ λογοῦ σεσαρκωμένου, "one nature of the incarnate Logos"; for Cyril too, logically attributed one nature not only to the God-Logos but also to the Christ. The communication of properties according to him, involves in every respect the natures. But there is not even any trace of a theological difference between Severus and Leontius. [2] The difference consists purely in the extent to which each was desirous of accommodating his views to the Chalcedonian Creed and interpreting Leo's doctrinal letter *in bonam partem*, and also in the philosophico-theological termi-

---

[1] See Loofs, p. 53 ff. The sources of information regarding the Christology of Severus are given there, p. 54. I refrain from giving any account of it (see Gieseler, op. cit. I., Dorner II., p. 166 ff.), since its identity with Cyril's doctrine seems to me to follow from the evidence brought forward by Loofs. It is interesting to note that Severus deduces from the Chalcedonian Creed the hypothesis of two natural energies and two wills, and further employs this deduction against his opponents as an *argumentatio ad absurdum*. No one in the East knew just at that time what was still to come in the succeeding century. The statement of Severus: οὐκ ἐνεργεῖ ποτὲ φύσις οὐχ ὑφεστῶσα, from which he concludes that in Leo's view there are two hypostases, is highly noteworthy and is quite in accordance with Cyril's ideas. Gieseler, op. cit. I., p. 9.

[2] See the 30 κεφάλαια of Leontius κατὰ Σευήρου (Migne 86, 2, p. 1901 sq.). See the notice in Loofs, p. 77 ff. It is highly amusing to notice how two authors whose ideas are exactly the same *appear* to have absolutely distinct views owing to the different terminology, "one nature", "two natures". In Thesis XI. where the Trinity and Christology are treated together in a scientific way, Leontius says: "If, according to Gregory, we have in the case of the Holy Trinity the reverse of what we have in the οἰκονομία κατὰ τὸν σωτῆρα, then in the case of the latter we must have two natures and one hypostasis, just as in that of the former we have three hypostases and one nature."

nology employed. The statements of Severus regarding the one composite nature, the μεταστοιχείωσις [1] or transformation etc., express absolutely nothing else than what is found in the formulæ of Leontius which are in part expressed in an entirely different and in fact in an opposite way. Leontius accepts the enhypostasis of the human nature in Christ, and Severus strictly defends himself against the supposition that he teaches that the human nature in any way loses its natural peculiarity in the union. It is simply that unfortunate Chalcedonian Creed which stands between the opponents, and what separates them therefore is the question as to whether the Western terminology is to be followed or not. That this is the case is proved by the attitude taken up by Severus to the Extreme Right of his party. The Henoticon had already split up the Egyptian Monophysites. One section of them had renounced connection with Petrus Mongus (ἀκέφαλοι). But in Syria, too, at the beginning of the Fifth Century we find several tendencies amongst them. The blow dealt them after the restoration of orthodoxy in 519 drove them to Egypt, and there actual splits took place. Even the strictest party amongst them did not put forth the catchword "transformation"; but in seriously reflecting on the problem as to how a human nature must be constituted after a God had made it His own, they arrived at propositions which were perfectly logical and which for this very reason referred back to Irenæus, Clemens Alex., Origen, Gregory Nyss., Hilary, Apollinaris, and to some utterances of Dioscurus and Eutyches. Their leader, Julian of Halicarnassus who was opposed by the Severians, developed the doctrine of the one nature into the doctrine of the identity of the substance and properties of the divinity and the humanity in Christ. The hypothesis of the indestructibleness of the body of Christ from the moment of the *assumptio*, became the shibloleth of the "Julianists" or Gaians, who, now nicknamed Aphthartodoketæ and Phantasiasts by the Severians, retorted with the word "Phthartolatry". The Julianists, whose point of view was determined solely by the thought of redemption, did not shrink from maintaining the perfect glorification of the body of Christ from the very first, and in accordance with this saw

---

[1] See Gieseler, op. cit. II. p. 3.

in the emotions and sufferings of Christ not the natural—though in reference to the Godhead the voluntary—states consequent on the human nature, but the acceptance of states κατὰ χάριν, which were regarded as having no inner connection with the nature of the Redeemer as that of the God-man. This nature being entirely free from all sin was also supposed to have nothing in common with suffering and death. [1] In opposition to this view the Severians laid so much stress on the relation of the sufferings of Christ to the human side of Christ's nature

[1] The extremely instructive second treatise of Gieseler supplies us with abundant material. Gieseler has brought out two things at the same time (1) that these Julianists (see the sixth anathema of Julius, p. 6) started from the idea of redemption, according to which the Logos assumed our flesh (ὁμοούσιος), but that as it (second Adam) was not subject to sin so neither was it subject to corruptio, and that in the moment of the assumptio He raised it to the state of the Divine. A homousia of the body of Christ with our body after the Incarnation would do away with all the comfort and the certainty of redemption. For the Logos assumed our nature just in order that He might free it from φθορά; if therefore the human nature of Christ had been still subject to φθορά then redemption would be rendered uncertain. Gieseler has shewn (2) that this idea is identical with the idea of the classic fathers of the Church, that while they undoubtedly shewed some hesitation as regards the conclusions to be drawn from it, still all the conclusions drawn by the Julianists, or by Philoxenus, are represented in one or other of the classical witnesses. Above all the Julianist and Philoxenian statement that in the case of Christ all passiones were not assumed naturally, but in the strictest sense voluntarily, κατ' οἰκονομίαν or κατὰ χάριν, (Gieseler, p. 7) is merely the vigorous echo of the oldest religious conviction. It was the sharper distinction between the divinity and the humanity in the incarnate one, worked out in the Arian controversy, that first endangered this conviction. Apollinaris sought to give some help here, but it was no longer of any avail. Gieseler very rightly calls attention to the fact that in the Apollinarian school the dispute between the Polemians and Valentinians corresponds exactly to the dispute between the Julianists and Severians, i.e., in the case of the former the same conclusions had been already drawn and had in turn been denied, which the Monophysites afterwards drew. Of these some went the length of assuming the divinity of Christ's blood and spittle (see besides, Athanasius, ad Serap. IV. 14; "Christ spat as a man, and His spittle was filled with the Godhead"), and, strictly speaking, the Church itself never could nor would dispense with this ancient idea spite of its doctrine of the two natures. The very same people who got excited about Aphthartodoketism had never any scruples in speaking about the blood of God, and in thinking of that blood as actually divine. We cannot therefore avoid seeing in Aphthartodoketism the logical development of the Greek doctrine of salvation, and we are all the more forced so to regard it that Julian expressly and ex necessitate fidei acknowledged the homousia of the body of Christ with our body at the moment when the Logos assumed it, and rejected everything of the nature of a heavenly body so far as its origin was concerned.

in order to rid them of anything doketic, that no Western could
have more effectively attacked doketism than they did.[1] We
find in general amongst the Severians such a determined rejection of all doctrinal extravagances—though these are not to be
regarded as absurdities, but as signs of the settled nature of
the belief in redemption—that we are glad to be able clearly
to see how unnecessary it was in the East to adopt the Chalcedonian Creed, and to replace the μία φύσις of Cyril by the
doubtful doctrine of the two natures. One section of the Monophysites nevertheless went the length of asserting that the
human soul of Christ was not omniscient ("Agnoetæ"), so that
as regards the one energy of the God-Man, a distinction is to
be drawn even in the sphere of knowledge between what it
did as possessed of divine knowledge and what it did as
humanly ignorant. This idea yields to none of the Monophysite eccentricities in absurdity,[2] and indeed it differs from them
for the worse by the fact of its having no religious thought as
its basis. While one section of the Monophysites thus did the
work of criticising their own party better than any Chalcedonian
could have done without incurring the reproach of Nestorianism, a philosophy of identity made its appearance amongst
certain individuals in the party itself, which might have raised
the fear that it would turn into Pantheism, if there had been
any danger of its doing this at the time. On the mystical side,
this had indeed been accomplished long ago, but this was very
far from involving an intellectual mode of conceiving of things.
Still it is of importance to note that an approach was made in
this direction from two sides. First there were Monophysites
who took up with the thought that the body of Christ from

[1] The passages are in Gieseler I. p. 20. The distinctions which were made are highly
significant in view of the period of scholasticism which was approaching. There
are two sorts of φθορά; Christ was subject to the natural πάθη of the body, but not
to the φθορά as ἡ εἰς τὰ ἐξ ὧν συνετέθη τὸ σῶμα στοιχεῖα διάλυσις. (Gieseler, p. 4).

[2] Thomasius indeed finds it "remarkable" (p. 375) that the majority of the
orthodox teachers of the Church, Jerome, Ambrose, the Patriarch Eulogius, the
Roman Gregory, rejected the doctrine of the Agnoetæ and attributed to Christ an
absolute knowledge which he concealed temporarily only κατ᾽ οἰκονομίαν. These
Fathers had not yet succeeded in doing what the Agnoetæ and the modern theologians
can manage and do—namely, to imagine a Christ who at the one and the same time
knew as God what he did not know as man and was yet all the while *one* person.

the moment of the *assumptio* was to be considered as uncreated, the view of the Aktistetæ. If the Father can communicate to the Son the attribute of unbegottenness, and at that time no one any longer doubted that he could, why should the Logos not also be able to give His body the attributes of the un-created; and in fact if it is His body, could He help doing this? Here already we meet with the thought that something created can nevertheless be something eternal. We hear no more of a flesh which was brought hither from heaven, but a kindred idea takes the place of this heretical thought. In the second place there were people, the Adiaphorites, [1] who refused to make any distinction between the divinity and the humanity in Christ, and this denial of all distinction further led some Syrian and Egyptian monks to the speculative idea, or to put it other-wise, gave increased strength to the speculative idea, that Nature in general is of one substance with God (see Vol. III., p. 302), a thought which had points of contact with mystical religious practices. [2] If all these movements illustrate the inner life of Monophysitism which within itself once more passed through old forms of development, the attention it gave to the Aristo-telian philosophy and such excellent works as those published by Joh. Philoponus, finally proves too that it did not in any way shrink from contact with the great spiritual forces of the time. The tritheistic controversy was in all essential respects fought out on its own ground, and the boldness and freedom shewn by the scholarly Monophysites, in the face too of tradition, [3] bears witness to the fact that in the Chalcedonian Creed a foreign power had imposed itself on the Church of the East. [4]

---

[1] See Möller, R.-Encykl. X., p. 248. Stephanus Niobes is mentioned as the originator of this line of thought.

[2] Frothingham in his Stephen bar Sudaili (1886) has now given us information regarding the Syrian Pantheistic thinkers amongst the Monophysites about the year 500 and further down. All Scotus Erigena is in Barsudaili. The Pantheistic mysticism of this Syrian and his friends merits the serious attention not of the historian of dogma, but of the historian of philosophy and culture. Scotus and the Pantheistic Mystics of the Middle Ages stand in closer connection with these Syrians than with the Areopagite. 1 Cor. XV. 28 supplies the central doctrine here.

[3] See Stephanus Gobarus in Photius, Cod. 232. He is also Aristotelian and Tritheist; noteworthy also for his bold criticism of tradition.

[4] On the Tritheists, see Schönfelder, Die Kirchengesch. des Johann v. Ephesus,

2. The restitution of orthodoxy in the year 519 coincides with the successful efforts of the theologians who were skilled in the Aristotelian philosophy, to furnish the Church which clung to the Chalcedonian Creed with a good conscience. *It is possible to accept the Chalcedonian Creed as authoritative and at the same time to think exactly as Cyril thought:* this was the result arrived at by the "new Cappadocians", the "new Conservatives", as Leontius and his friends came to be called, who made terms with the two natures in the same way as the oriental scholars in the Fourth Century did with the ὁμοούσιος; *and it is this conviction which lies at the basis of Justinian's policy in reference both to the Church and the State.* If the efforts of former emperors in so far as they favoured Monophysitism were directed towards getting rid of the Chalcedonian Creed or consigning it to oblivion, the policy of the Emperor, which had the support of the new conservative theology, was to make use of the power which every *fait accompli*, and therefore too a Council, supplies, and at the same time to do justice to the old tendencies of Greek piety. It was the Roman bishop who was hardest hit by such a policy. For the second time he had contributed towards giving the Emperor of the East a firmer position in the country, this time by doing away with the schism. But the friend had not become any more harmless than he was in the year 451. As at that time he was, after having done what was required of him, quietly pushed back within his own boundaries by the 28th Canon of the Council, so on this occasion too he was to get a poor reward for his services. It was not intended that Rome should triumph in the East, but that the Emperor of the East should once more become the Lord of Rome. The dogmatic union with the West represented the terms on which it was to be made ecclesiastically and politically subject to the Emperor.

Justinian's policy has in it an element of greatness. He once more set up the world-empire and pacified the Church, and yet his civil and ecclesiastical policy of conquest was unsound and

p. 267 ff. The works of Philoxenus, Bishop of Hierapolis, who has lately been termed the best Syrian stylist, have been hitherto wholly neglected and still await an editor.

its results lacked permanence. He did not know how to win over the Monophysites, and by his Western policy he did harm to the much more important Eastern policy. Some years after his accession Justinian arranged a grand religious discussion in Constantinople between the Severians and the Theopaschitian Orthodox (531). It is of some importance because it shews the extent of the advances made by the Orthodox towards the Monophysites under the guidance of Hypatius of Ephesus in conformity with the wish of the Emperor.[1] The orthodox held firmly to the Chalcedonian Creed, but allowed that the Council had also approved of the phrase, one incarnate nature (!);[2] on the other hand they rejected as Apollinarian forgeries the testimonies of their opponents in reference to the condemnation of the words "in duabis naturis" on the part of the ancient fathers.[3] About the same time the Emperor issued several edicts regarding the true Faith (533), which *in thesi* were based on the Chalcedonian Creed, but did not reproduce its formulæ; on the contrary they evaded the use of them and contained besides, the addition that it is necessary to believe that the Lord who suffered was one of the Holy Trinity.[4] The Emperor, who had himself an interest in dogma, already here shewed what his policy was, namely, to take back the Church in all that was essential entirely to Cyril, but to allow the Chalcedonian Creed to remain authoritative. Thus as matters stood, the formula: ἕνα τῆς ἁγίας τριάδος πεπονθέναι σαρκί, "one of the Holy Trinity suffered in the flesh", was a henotikon. But the Empress went still further. She had always favoured the Monophysites, one cannot even say secretly; the various threads of the undertaking the object of which was to assist "the pious doctrine" to triumph,

---

[1] See the Acts in Mansi VIII., p. 817 sq., Loofs, p. 263 f. Leontius took part in the discussion and it was dominated by his theology.

[2] See 823: "Sancta synodus utrosque sermones (two and one natures) *pari honore* suscepit et pertractat."

[3] It was here that the Areopagite was first cited as an authority—by the Severians, p. 820; his writings were, however, described by the orthodox as doubtful.

[4] Cod. Justinian (ed. Krüger), de summa trinit. 6—8. The words: ἑνὸς καὶ τοῦ αὐτοῦ τὰ τε θαύματα καὶ τὰ πάθη, ἅπερ ἑκουσίως ὑπέμεινεν σαρκί ... οὔτε τετάρτου προσώπου προσθήκην ἐπιδέχεται ἡ ἁγία τρίας, are worthy of note. Pope John II., 534, had to approve of the Theopaschitian addition.

all met in her cabinet, and it appeared not impossible that the
Emperor might in the end be got also to agree to the formal
abandonment of the Chalcedonian Creed and consequently to a
new actual henotikon. [1] The appointment of Anthimus, a Monophysite in disguise, as patriarch of the Capital, and the admission of Severus to the Court, prepared the way for the final
blow which was to be struck at the Chalcedonian Creed. But
once more did the Roman bishop, who was informed of what
was going on by Ephraem of Antioch, save orthodoxy. In the
year 536 Agapetus appeared at the Court of the Emperor and
succeeded in getting Anthimus removed from his post and excommunicated. A Council which was held under the presidency
of the new patriarch Mennas at Constantinople in the year 536,
after the death of Agapetus who died in the capital, and which
has left behind an extensive collection of Acts, [2] put an end
to the Monophysitism which was making overtures in an under-
hand way, acknowledged anew the expression: "ἐν δύο φύσεσι",
"in two natures", and deposed and anathematised Anthimus.
It is important that the Council which followed in the track of
the theology of Leontius and upon which Leontius himself had
some influence, roundly declared through its leader that nothing
whatever ought to be done in the Church contrary to the will
and command of the Emperor, but at the same time also added
the following: "We both follow and obey the apostolic throne
(Rome) and we regard those in communion with it as in communion, and those condemned by it we also condemn": ἡμεῖς τῷ
ἀποστολικῷ θρόνῳ ἐξακολουθοῦμέν τε καὶ πειθόμεθα καὶ τοὺς κοινωνικοὺς αὐτοῦ κοινωνικοὺς ἔχομεν, καὶ τοὺς ὑπ' αὐτοῦ κατακριθέντας
καὶ ἡμεῖς κατακρίνομεν. [3] The days when the names of Marcian
and Leo were mentioned together, seemed to have returned.
But the Pope at this time was no Leo, and Justinian was more
than Marcian. Besides Anthimus, Severus, about whom the
very worst calumnies were spread—that he was a heathen in
disguise—and the heads of the Monophysite party of conciliation,

---

[1] Loofs, p. 304 f., has shewn, however, that at this time Justinian was following
the lead of Leontius.

[2] Mansi VIII., pp. 877—1162.

[3] P. 970.

were condemned. Justinian confirmed this sentence [1] by a decree
(Aug. 536), while he threatened all adherents of the accused
with exile and ordered the books of Severus as also those of
Porphyry, [2] to be burned. At the first glance it seems paradoxical that the Emperor, who was himself not without Monophysite
leanings, was now so genuinely furious at Severus and accused
him at once of Nestorianism [3] and Eutychianism. But after
what has been remarked above, (p. 241) the charge of Nestorianism is quite intelligible, and we can understand too the aversion felt by the Emperor who had himself an interest in dogma.
A Monophysitism, such as that of Severus, which *merely* rejected
the Chalcedonian Creed, but which, moreover, in combating
Aphthartodoketism got the length of teaching in the most definite
way the "division" of Christ, when once it was thoroughly
understood, could be regarded only with antipathy by the
Imperial theologian who had on the contrary always wished to
have the Chalcedonian Creed *and* Aphthartodoketism. A Jerusalem Council repeated the decrees of the Council of Constantinople; [4] but it was impossible to restore tranquillity in Egypt.
The Severian Theodosius had to make way for the Julianist
Gajanus as Patriarch, and the Patriarch sent by the Emperor
so seriously compromised his patron that he had to be excommunicated. [5]

In the measures he took the Emperor, however, never lost
sight of his design which was to win over the Monophysites,
and it is at this point that the humiliation of the Roman bishop
begins, though he was himself undoubtedly mainly to blame.
The theology of Antioch was still something highly objectionable in the eyes of all pious-minded persons. It seemed to be
favoured by Leo's doctrinal letter and in fact to be put in
a place of honour, and yet a large section of the Eastern
Orthodox were at one with all Monophysites in holding
that the great Antiochians "would have betrayed the secret".
People hated it for the same reason that they hate the Li-

[1] P. 1150 sq.
[2] P. 1154.
[3] P. 1151.
[4] Mansi VIII., p. 1164 sq.
[5] Liberat. Brev. 23.

berals in the Church at the present day, and the Emperor certainly did not hate it least, not to speak of the Empress, the patroness of all pious monks. The Antiochians got the blame of "denying the divinity of Christ" and of dividing the one Christ into two. The influential bishop, Theodorus Askidas of Cæsarea in Cappadocia, is said to have advised the Emperor to make use of this widespread hatred in the interest of his ecclesiastical policy. This man, an enthusiastic pupil of Origen, had suffered seriously from the condemnation of the latter [1] to which he had assented against his will, and in order to divert attention from Origen (Euagr. E. H. IV. 38) he got the Emperor persuaded to believe that a great many Monophysites could be won over if a blow was struck at the Antiochians. [2] As a matter of fact what had given most serious offence to the Monophysites in connection with the Council of Chalcedon, was that it pronounced Ibas and Theodoret orthodox and was silent about Theodore. [3] The Emperor, supported by Theodora, who

[1] On this (in the year 544) see the concluding chapter. Since in the conflict with Origenism Christology did not constitute the main cause of offence, we can leave it out of account here. Still it must be admitted that certain features of the Christology of Origen were acceptable to the Monophysites and to the monks with Monophysite tendencies, and the discussions about Origen in the sixth century took their start from here.

[2] Regarding the Three Chapters' dispute and the Fifth Council, there has been a great controversy in the Catholic Church, which dates very far back and which is still continued. We owe this controversy to the writings of the Jesuit Halloix (for Origen; and unfavourable to the Fifth Council); the Augustinian Noris (Diss. historica de synodo V., in favour of the Council) the Jesuit Garnier, in the 17th century, and later, to those of the Ballerini. In more recent times Vincenzi has sought in a big work which falsifies history (In S. Gregorii Nyss. et Origenis scripta et doctrinam nova defensio, 5 Vols. 1864 sq.) to justify the theses of Halloix, to rehabilitate Origen and Vigilius, and on the other hand partly to "remodel" the Council and partly to bring it into contempt. The Romish Church is not yet quite clear as to the position it should take up in reference to the older Antiochians and Theodoret, and further, to Origen and Vigilius. I am not acquainted with the work of Punkes, P. Vigilius und der Dreicapitelstreit, München 1865. The fullest Protestant account is still that of Walch, Vol. VIII. The most thorough study of the chief opponent of the imperial policy, Facundus of Hermiane in North Africa, has been published by a Russian, Dobroklonskij (1880); see on his work Theol. Lit. Ztg. 1880, n. 26.

[3] Theodore had still in the East and even in the monasteries some secret adherents, apart from the Nestorians; see Loofs, pp. 274—297, 304.

had long ago established a Monophysite branch-regime which made its influence felt as far as Rome, issued, apparently in 543, an edict,[1] in which the person and writings of Theodore, the Anti-Cyrillian writings of Theodoret, and the letter of Ibas to the Persian Maris,[2] were condemned. This was the edict of the τρία κεφάλαια, the three points or chapters. The orthodox found themselves placed by it in a most painful position. It was a political move on the part of the Emperor forced on him by the circumstances in which he was placed, and a better one could not have been contrived.[3] The faithful adherents of the Fourth Council had to face the alternative either of actually departing from orthodoxy by the rejection of heterodox doctrines—for it was evident that a revision of the Chalcedonian Creed was intended, which limited freedom in the interpretation of it—or of having to defend what was questionable by way of protecting doctrinal unity; for nobody could deny but that Theodore in particular had actually taught heterodox doctrine. At the same time a sort of question *du fait* was to be decided in addition. The question as to the views held by the Council regarding things which it had not discussed, was to be settled. The Emperor dictated what these views were. Distinctions were to be made between what the whole Council had approved of and what had been approved of merely by individual members; for example, in reference to the letter of Ibas. It was plain that all this was bound only to be to the advantage of the Mono-physites. It might be easy to point out to the Western oppo-

---

[1] No longer preserved.

[2] Mansi VIII., p. 242 sq.

[3] Loofs, op. cit. has shewn that Justinian's policy, which struck at once at Origen and at Theodore, was occasioned by the disturbances in the monasteries of Palestine where both had their sympathisers who had already come into sharp conflict with each other. "The explanation of the fact that Justinian pretty much about the same time struck at Origen with the one hand and at the Three Chapters with the other, is to be found not in the ill-humour of Theodorus Askidas, but in the state of things in Palestine." The energetic attack already made by Leontius on Theodore in the years 531—538 had prepared the way for a decree which enjoined that the Chalcedonian Creed must positively not be interpreted in the sense in which it was understood by Theodore; see Loofs, p. 307. The resolution to add the writings of Ibas and Theodoret, seems only to have been come to at the last moment.

nents of the imperial decree that they had been too sharp-
sighted in hunting for traces of Monophysite leaven, but as
regards the main point they were entirely in the right. The
condemnation of the three chapters, so far as its tendency was
concerned, involved a revision of the Chalcedonian Creed. But
the Emperor was in the right too; for he corrected the conciliar-
decree in accordance with the spirit of the Eastern Church,
which had been repressed at Chalcedon itself. He destroyed
the Western influence; he carried the Chalcedonian Creed back
to Cyril; *he restored the dogmatic thought of the two Councils
of Ephesus, without meddling with the Creed of Chalcedon.*
All four patriarchs of the East took offence at the condemnation of the Three Chapters and all four signed it after a brief
hesitation. Thus powerfully did the Emperor make his rule
felt in the Church; there had been no such monarch since
Constantius and Theodosius I. The patriarchs worked their
bishops and they too all submitted, although they felt it difficult
to consent to the condemnation of a bishop who a hundred
years before this had died at peace with the Church. What,
however, they did not feel, was the desolation created by this
imperial measure. Origen was already condemned; the condemnation of the Antiochene theology now followed on his. It was
now that the Church first fully provided itself with a falsified
tradition, by shutting out its true Fathers as heretics under the
patronage of Justinian. It is pretended that its theology had
always been the same, and any one who at an earlier period
had taught otherwise, was no Father and Shepherd, but an
innovator, a robber and murderer. This Church tolerated no
recollection of the fact that it had once allowed room within it
for a greater variety of opinion. Justinian who closed the School
of Athens, also closed the schools of Alexandria and Antioch!
He is the Diocletian of theological science and the Constantine
of scholasticism! In doing this he did not, however, impose
anything on the Church; on the contrary he ascertained what were
the true feelings of the majority, probably realised them himself, and by satisfying them made the Church obedient to the
State; for the World-Church is to be feared only when provoked;
when satisfied it will allow any kind of yoke to be imposed upon it.

The outbreak of the controversy of the Three Chapters which followed on this and its history, have an interest for the history of dogma merely owing to the fact that the North African bishops and, speaking generally, most of the Western bishops made such an energetic resistance to the condemnation of the Three Chapters. The conduct of the Africans and especially the work of Facundus "pro tribus capitulis", are honourable pages in the history of the Punic Churches. On the other hand in the conduct of the Roman Bishop we have a tragedy, the hero of which was no hero, but on the contrary a rogue. Vigilius, the creature of Theodora, the intellectual murderer of his predecessor, the man who was Monophysite or Chalcedonian in accordance with orders, constantly changed his opinion in the course of the controversy, according as he considered compliance with feeling in the West or compliance with the commands of the Emperor, the more necessary. Twice over he was forced by the Emperor to appear before the tribunal of the Church as a liar when Justinian produced secret explanations of his which contradicted his public utterances. His conduct both before the great Council and after it was equally lamentable. The poorest of all the Popes was confronted with the most powerful of the Byzantine Emperors. [1]

Justinian considered a great Council to be necessary although he himself, about the year 551, issued a second edict dealing with the affair of the Three Chapters. This edict [2] which was framed by the Emperor himself who was always theologically inclined, contains in the most verbose form the strictly Cyrillian interpretation of the Chalcedonian decree. The Cyrillian formula of the "one nature" is approved of, attention being, however, directed to the fact that Cyril made no distinction between nature and hypostasis. Christ is one "composite hypostasis"— ὑπόστασις σύνθετος. The Antiochian theology is rejected in strong terms, the three chapters are condemned in this connection; but it is asserted that we must abide by the Chalce-

---

[1] Duchesne, Vigile et Pélage, 1884.

[2] Mansi IX., p. 537 sq. Loofs has briefly indicated the nature of the Emperor's theological writing (p. 310 f.) and has shewn how closely it is related to that of Leontius.

donian Creed. In order to sanction this edict, the Fifth Ecumenical Council was opened at Constantinople in May 553, Vigilius protesting. The patriarch of the capital presided. The Acts have not come down to us in their original form; we have only part of them in a Latin translation. But we know from the proceedings of the Sixth Council that interpolations were put into the Acts in the 7th century (on the part of the Monothelites?) and that these interpolations were traced at the time by means of palæographic investigations, though the documents which had been foisted in were in no sense forgeries. The proceedings of the Council which consisted of about 150 members amongst whom there were very few Westerns, were unimportant; all it had to do was to throw the halo of the Church round the imperial edicts. It condemned Origen, as Justinian desired;[1] it condemned the Three Chapters and consequently the Antiochian theology as Justinian desired; it sanctioned the theopaschitian formula as Justinian desired, and in its 14 long-winded anathemas it adopted the imperial edict of 551 as its own. But amongst those who thus said yes to everything, there were few who spoke contrary to their convictions. The Emperor was really the best dogmatist of his time and of his country—if it is the duty of the dogmatist to ascertain the opinions of the majority. While giving a position of exclusive authority to the interpretation of the Chalcedonian Creed on the lines of the theology of Cyril, he hit upon the sense in which it was understood by the Church of the East, i.e., by the majority in it.[2] The importance of the dogmatic

[1] So with reason Noris, the Ballerini, Möller (R. Encykl. XI., p. 113) and Loofs (pp. 287, 291) as against Hefele and Vincenzi.

[2] The anathemas so far as their positive form is concerned come very near Monophysitism without actually falling into it—the most distinct divergence is in No. 8. No. 7 goes furthest in the direction of meeting Monophysitism: εἴ τις ἐν δύο φύσεσι λέγων, μὴ ὡς ἐν θεότητι καὶ ἀνθρωπότητι τὸν ἕνα κύριον ἡμῶν Ἰησοῦν Χριστὸν γνωρίζεσθαι ὁμολογεῖ, ἵνα διὰ τούτου σημάνῃ τὴν διαφορὰν τῶν φύσεων, ἐξ ὧν ἀσυγχύτως ἡ ἄφραστος ἕνωσις γέγονεν, οὔτε τοῦ λόγου εἰς τὴν τῆς σαρκὸς μεταποιηθέντος φύσιν, οὔτε τῆς σαρκὸς πρὸς τοῦ λόγου φύσιν μεταχωρησάσης—μένει γὰρ ἑκάτερον ὅπερ ἐστὶ τῇ φύσει, καὶ γενομένης τῆς ἑνώσεως καθ᾽ ὑπόστασιν—, ἀλλ᾽ ἐπὶ διαιρέσει τῇ ἀνὰ μέρος τὴν τοιαύτην λαμβάνει φωνὴν ἐπὶ τοῦ κατὰ Χριστὸν μυστηρίου, ἢ τὸν ἀριθμὸν τῶν φύσεων ὁμολογῶν ἐπὶ τοῦ αὐτοῦ ἑνὸς κυρίου ἡμῶν Ἰησοῦ τοῦ Θεοῦ λόγου σαρκωθέντος, μὴ τῇ θεωρίᾳ μόνῃ τὴν διαφορὰν τούτων λαμβάνει, ἐξ ὧν

finding of 553 ought not to be underrated. In a certain sense the blow which the 'West gave to the East at the Fourth Council was parried by the Fifth Council—in the fashion in which this is done in general in matters of dogma. Rome had given the formula of the two natures to the East, but a hundred years later the East dictated to the West how this formula was to be understood, an interpretation of it which in no way corresponded to the actual wording of the formula. At first undoubtedly the decree of the Fifth Council called forth serious opposition in the West.[1] But first Vigilius submitted,[2] then five years later the African Church followed his example.[3] Still the position of the successor of Vigilius, Pelagius I., was very seriously endangered in the West. The Churches of Upper Italy under the guidance of Milan and Aquileia renounced their allegiance to Rome. Never in antiquity was the apostolic chair in such a critical condition as at that time. Its occupant appeared to many in the West in the light of a State bishop at the beck of Constantinople and deprived of ecclesiastical freedom. The Lombard conquests set him free and rescued him from his position of dependence on Byzantium. Gregory I. having once more regained strength politically and his help being regarded as indispensable by those in Upper Italy who were threatened by the Arians and the pagans, again gained over the larger part of Upper Italy together with the Archbishop of Milan, though indeed it was at the price of a temporary disavowal of the Fifth Council.[4] Another part stood

καὶ συνετέθη, οὐκ ἀναιρουμένην διὰ τὴν ἔνωσιν—εἷς γὰρ ἐξ ἀμφοῖν, καὶ δἰ ἑνὸς ἀμφότερα—ἀλλ᾽ ἐπὶ τούτῳ κέχρηται τῷ ἀριθμῷ, ὡς κεχωρισμένας καὶ ἰδιοϋποστάτους ἔχει τὰς φύσεις· ὁ τοιοῦτος ἀνάθεμα ἔστω. Observe how the conception of number too gets a new meaning in Dogmatics and how in the dogmatic sense the conception of number is to be taken in one way in connection with the dogma of the Trinity and again in a different way in connection with the Christological dogma. There we have already the whole of scholasticism! In the same way "θεωρία" is now a conception which has first to get a new form for Dogmatics. All throughout in these conceptions things which are irreconcileable must be shewn to be reconciled.

[1]   The opposition in the East was wholly unimportant; see Hefele, p. 903 f.
[2]   Two statements of Dec. 553 and Feb. 554. Hefele, 905 ff.
[3]   Hefele, p. 913 f.
[4]   Gregor I., epp. l. IV., 2—4, 38, 39. Gregory had to make his orthodoxy certain by acknowledging the four Councils. He was silent about the Fifth.

aloof from Rome for a whole century. But in the West too at the same period there was a decay of all independent interest in theological questions; when it once more revived, the Church had the Fifth Council and the Cyrillian Dogmatics. The East had revenged itself.

And yet one may doubt if Justinian's policy was the right one which *in dogmaticis* aimed at a mean between the Western and the Egypto-Syrian dogmatic. It stopped half-way. For the sake of the West and of the basis supplied by the Council of 451, the Emperor had adhered to the Chalcedonian Creed; for the sake of the Monophysites and of his own inclinations he decreed the Theopaschitian formula and the rejection of the Three Chapters. But in doing this he roused the West against the spirit of Constantinople and against the Byzantine State, at the very moment when he was making friendly overtures to it, and yet he did not gain over the Monophysites. [1] He could not find the right dogmatic formula for the World-Empire which he created; what he did settle was the specific formula for the patriarchate of Constantinople and its immediate belongings. He, however, saw that himself; he wished to sanction Aphthartodoketism (564) [2] which was in harmony with his own dogmatic views and which might perhaps win over the Monophysites. His policy was a logical one, and the Emperor set about carrying it out with his wonted energy, beginning as usual by deposing the patriarch of the capital. We cannot now say what would have happened; the opposition of the Bishops, led this time by the Patriarch of Antioch, Anastasius Sinaita, would perhaps have been overcome; but the Emperor died in November, 565, and his successor Justin II. did not continue this policy. Still, under Justin II. the attempts to gain over the Monophysites, by dragonnades and by friendly methods, did not cease. [3] Even at that time the Imperial bishops were throughout kept from acceding to the

---

[1] It was only temporally that the Melchites, led by some distinguished patriarchs, once more got the mastery in Egypt; see Gelzer, Leontios von Neapolis, Leben des h. Johannes des Barmherzigen, Erzbischofs v. Alexandrien 1893.

[2] Euagr. H. E. IV. 39, 40.

[3] A sort of henoticon of Justin's in Euagr. V. 4; cf. the Church History of John of Ephesus.

extreme demands of the Monophysites by their desire to preserve communion with the West. The vacillation in the imperial policy, its partial success and partial failure, and the divisions among the Monophysites themselves, etc., belong to Church-History. The way was being prepared for renouncing entirely the authority of Byzantium—and here the political-national movement everywhere preceded the other,—and for the organisation in each case of a separate ecclesiastical constitution. These aims were not definitely accomplished till the seventh century, under entirely altered political conditions. [1]

4. *The Monergist and Monothelite Controversies. The Sixth Council and Johannes Damascenus.* [2]

Paul of Samosata equally [3] with the old Antiochians [4] had affirmed the doctrine of the one will (μία θέλησις) in reference to Jesus Christ. The statement of the former, "the different natures and the different persons have one single mode of union,—agreement in will, from which it plainly appears that there is a unity as to energy in the things thus joined together," (αἱ διάφοροι φύσεις καὶ τὰ διάφορα πρόσωπα ἕνα καὶ μόνον ἑνώσεως ἔχουσι τρόπον τὴν κατὰ θέλησιν σύμβασιν, ἐξ ἧς ἡ κατὰ ἐνέργειαν ἐπὶ τῶν οὕτως συμβιβασθέντων ἀλλήλοις ἀναφαίνεται μονάς), lies at the basis of the Antiochene Dogmatic even after it had taken definite shape as a doctrine of two natures. They were thus Monothelites. On the other hand, Gregory of Nyssa, Cyril, and the Areopagite had taught the doctrine of one energy in Christ,

---

[1] On the Syro-Jacobite-Monophysite, the Coptic-Monophysite, the Abyssinian Church, as well as on the Armenian Church which continued to be Cyrillian, not Monophysite in the strict sense of word—see the article in Herzog's R. Encykl., and better in the Dict. of Christ. Biog. and in Kattenbusch, op. cit. I., p. 205 ff.; cf. also Sibernagl op. cit.

[2] See the material in Mansi X., XI.; in addition the works of Maximus Confessor, of Anastasius Biblioth., of Anastasius Abbas, and the Chronographs; see also the Lib. pontif. and the works of Joh. Damascenus. Accounts by Combefis (1648), Tamagnini (1678), Assemani (1764), Gibbon, Walch (Vol. 9), Schröckh, Hefele, Baur, and Dorner. Further, Möller in Herzog's R. Encykl. (Art. "Monothel."), Wagenmann, there also, Art. "Maximus Confessor".

[3] See Vol. III., p. 41.

[4] In the "Ekthesis" it is expressly admitted that Nestorius did not teach the doctrine of two wills.

the latter with the definite addition "θεανδρική". ¹ The Antiochians and those last mentioned meant, however, something different by their respective statements. The view of the Antiochians was that the human nature by placing itself at the service of the divine was wholly filled with the divine will—their μία θέλησις was not the product of a physico-psychological, but of an ethical, mode of regarding Christ. The Alexandrians regarded the God-Logos as the subject of the God-Man who had made the human nature His own and used it as his organ; they thus thought of a unity of energy having its roots in the unity of the mysterious constitution of the God-Man. In Leo's doctrinal letter there was what was for the East a new conception of it—"Agit utraque forma quod proprium est", "each nature does what is peculiar to it", though undoubtedly "cum alterius communione"—"in union with the other". This way of conceiving of it was indirectly sanctioned by the Chalcedonian decree. In the century following it gave great offence; it besides rendered it necessary to consider the nature of the energy, the willing and the acting of Christ, and as a matter of fact it was the most serious stumbling-block for the Severians whose thesis "one composite nature" (μία φύσις σύνθετος) naturally demanded the "one energy" (μία ἐνέργεια). But still owing to the Chalcedonian Creed a theory gradually got a footing in the Church according to which each nature was considered by itself while the unity was consequently conceived of as a product, and the doctrine of the Agnoetæ (see p. 239) which made its appearance amongst the Severians proves that even this party could not avoid what was a sort of splitting up of the one Christ. The neo-orthodox theology of a Leontius and Justinian spite of its Cyrillian character required that Christ should be conceived of as having two energies, although it is going too far to maintain

---

¹ Dionys. Areop. (Opp. ed. Corderius, edit. Veneta 1755, T. I., p. 593), ep. 4, (ad Caium): ἡμεῖς δὲ τὸν Ἰησοῦν οὐκ ἀνθρωπικῶς ἀφορίζομεν· οὐδὲ γὰρ ἄνθρωπος μόνον (οὐδὲ ὑπερούσιος ἢ ἄνθρωπος μόνον) ἀλλ᾽ ἄνθρωπος ἀληθῶς, ὁ διαφερόντως φιλάνθρωπος ὑπὲρ ἀνθρώπους καὶ κατὰ ἀνθρώπους ἐκ τῆς τῶν ἀνθρώπων οὐσίας ὁ ὑπερούσιος οὐσιωμένος... καὶ γὰρ ἵνα συνελόντες εἴπωμεν οὐδὲ ἄνθρωπος ἦν, οὐχ ὡς μὴ ἄνθρωπος, ἀλλ᾽ ὡς ἐξ ἀνθρώπων, ἀνθρώπων ἐπέκεινα, καὶ ὑπὲρ ἄνθρωπον ἀληθῶς ἄνθρωπος γεγονώς. Καὶ τὸ λοιπὸν οὐ κατὰ Θεὸν τὰ θεῖα δράσας, οὐ τὰ ἀνθρώπεια κατὰ ἄνθρωπον, ἀλλ᾽ ἀνδρωθέντος Θεοῦ καινήν τινα τὴν θεανδρικὴν ἐνέργειαν ἡμῖν πεπολιτευμένος.

that already in the time of Justinian the question had been decided[1] in accordance with the later orthodox view. [2]

One might try to explain the fact that the question was raised in the seventh century at all, from the "inner logic" of the matter; but the dogma in the form in which it was settled under Justinian, still left room for the raising of countless other questions which were not less important. As a matter of fact it was a purely political consideration, the desire, namely, to win back the Monophysite provinces, which conjured up the controversy. The latter accordingly essentially belongs to political history and it will be sufficient here to fix the most important points, since the doctrine of one will equally with that of two wills would have been in harmony with the decisions of the Fourth and Fifth Councils.

The patriarch of the capital, Sergius, advised his emperor, the powerful and victorious Heraclius, (610—641) to secure the conquests he had once more made in the South and East by meeting the Monophysites half way with the formula that the God-Man consisting of two natures effected everything by means of *one* divine-human energy. In support of this doctrine Sergius collected together passages from the Fathers, large numbers of which belonging both to ancient and recent times, lay to hand, won over influential clergy in Armenia, Syria, and Egypt, and succeeded in conjunction with the Emperor in filling the eastern Patriarchates with men whose views were similar to his own and actually laid the foundation of a union with the Monophysites (633). But a Palestinian monk named Sophronius, who was afterwards bishop of Jerusalem, came to Egypt, declared the μία ἐνέργεια to be "Apollinarianism", seriously embarrassed the imperial Patriarch, Cyrus, in Alexandria, and impressed even Sergius to whom he had recourse. As on the one hand, how-

---

[1] Loofs, p. 316.

[2] According to anathema No. 3 of the Fifth Council the active principle in the Redeemer is the undivided person who as such performs miracles and suffers. No. 8 is undoubtedly opposed to this: μενούσης ἑκατέρας φύσεως, ὅπερ ἐστίν, ἡνῶσθαι σαρκὶ νοοῦμεν τὸν λόγον. The dispute as to whether there was one will or two, dates at least as far back as the beginning of the 6th century; but the assertion of two wills is as a rule charged against the orthodox by their *opponents* as the logical result of their views.

ever, there was a desire not to abandon again the position gained in reference to the Monophysites, and as on the other it was necessary to avoid the appearance of endangering ortho-doxy, Sergius now declared that all discussion of the question of energies was to cease, and signified his wish in this matter to his colleagues in Alexandria and to the Emperor himself. He wrote at the same time to Bishop Honorius of Rome. [1] The latter at that time published the celebrated letter which played such an important part in 1870 and the treatment of which in the second edition of Hefele's History of the Councils has justly occasioned so much surprise. [2] Honorius in this letter describes Sophronius as a man who is stirring up new controversies, praises Sergius for his great prudence in discarding the new expression (μία ἐνέργεια) which might be a stumbling-block to the simple, declares that Holy Scripture makes no mention either of one energy or of two energies, that the latter ex-pression is suggestive of Nestorianism and the former of Euty-chianism, and incidentally states as something self-evident that "we confess one will of the Lord Jesus Christ" (ἓν θέλημα ὁμολογοῦμεν τοῦ κυρίου Ἰησοῦ Χριστοῦ), that is, the one will of the Godhead. This was not yet in any sense a controversial question; but Sergius in his letter to Alexandria had regarded it as like-wise self-evident that in putting the question of the energies into the background he could not in any case agree to the doctrine of two wills. [3] Meanwhile Sophronius in his character as the new bishop of Jerusalem had issued a work definitely based on the Chalcedonian Creed as interpreted by Leo's doctrinal letter. Two energies are to be recognised in the one Christ who is in both the same. One and the same Christ followed the energy both of his divine and also of his human nature. Still Sophronius does not say anything of two wills.

---

[1] Shortly before this the controversy between Rome and Byzantium regarding the title "Ecumenical Patriarch" had been going on; see Gelzer in the Jahrbb. f. Protest. Theol. 1887, p. 549 ff., and Kattenbusch, op. cit. I., p. 111 f.

[2] See S. Theol. Lit. Ztg., 1878, No. XI. The letter is in Mansi, XI., p. 538 sq.

[3] The heterodoxy of Honorius does not certainly amount to much, since he adheres to Leo's doctrinal letter and since nothing was yet decided regarding the energies and the will.

He likewise had recourse to Rome, and Honorius, like Sergius, made an effort to bring about union between the contending parties in the Eastern Church by dissuading them from employing the formulæ. Heraclius gave his support to these efforts and published an edict drawn up by Sergius (638), the Ecthesis, which forbade the use both of μία ἐνέργεια and of "two energies" as equally dangerous expressions. The latter expression, it was maintained, leads to the assumption of two conflicting wills in Christ, while Christ has only one will since the human nature acts only in accordance with the God-Logos who has assumed it. [1] The personality of the Redeemer thus appears, in strict accordance with the theology of Cyril, as built up on the basis of the God-Logos.

But already Rome and the West once more bethought themselves of their dogmatics. Every attempt to meet the views of the Monophysites always brought the Byzantine Emperor into conflict with Rome. Pope John IV. as early as the year 641 condemned Monothelitism at a Roman Council. Immediately thereafter Heraclius died, putting the responsibility of the Ecthesis on to Sergius. The latter had died previously to this; Pyrrhus, who held similar views, took his place. After severe struggles in the palace, which Pyrrhus had to pay for by his deposition, Constans II., a grandson of Heraclius, became emperor. Those at the Court were resolved to maintain the Ecthesis and not to submit to the Roman bishop, Theodore. [2] Meanwhile North Africa had become the second headquarters of the Dyothelites. The Byzantine governor there, Gregory, the patron of the monks, who was on bad terms with the Court, made use of the African dislike of Byzantium and its dogmatics in order, if possible, to detach the Province from Constantinople, and with him sided the most learned Chalcedonian of the East,

---

[1] Mansi, X., p. 931 sq.: "We must confess one will in our Lord Jesus Christ, the true God, implying that at no time did his flesh animated by a reasonable soul accomplish what was natural for it to do, separately, and by its own impulse, in opposition to the suggestion of the God-Logos who was hypostatically united with it, but that on the contrary it acted only when and how and in the way the Logos wished."

[2] John IV. had already, moreover, attempted to hush up the conduct of Honorius, to excuse it, that is.

Maximus (Confessor) and many other Easterns, monks especially, who had fallen out with the Emperor.[1] Pyrrhus too took up his quarters in North Africa and was easily converted to dyotheletism. In Rome he completed his change of opinion and was recognised by Theodore as the legitimate bishop of Constantinople. The Emperor was flooded with addresses from North Africa the aim of which was to induce him to enter the lists on behalf of orthodoxy. But the defeat of Gregory by the Saracens weakened the courage and interfered with the plans of the Anti-Byzantine coalition. Pyrrhus with all possible speed once more made his peace with the Emperor and with the Imperial dogmatics; but the Roman bishop stood firm, condemned Pyrrhus, and pronounced sentence of deposition on Paul who was at the time occupying the Byzantine chair. The Emperor, on the advice of Paul and in order to pacify the Empire, issued in the year 648 the Typus, which bears the same relation to the doctrine of the wills as the Ecthesis does to the doctrine of the energies. It simply prohibits under severe penalties all controversy regarding the question as to whether it is necessary to believe in one will and one energy or in two wills and two energies, and forbids the prosecution of any one because of his position on this question. For the sake of the Westerns the Ecthesis was removed from the principal church of the capital.[2]

But Rome was far from accepting this part-payment as a full discharge. It had wholly different plans. The situation seemed a favourable one for estranging from the Emperor the entire orthodoxy of the East and binding it to the successor of Peter,

---

[1] Battifol, L'abbaye de Rossano, Paris, 1891, has given us information of first-rate quality regarding the exodus of the Greek monks and priests to (North Africa) Sicily and Calabria. Lower Italy underwent at that time a new Hellenisation.

[2] Mansi X., p. 1019 sq. The form of the Typus as distinguished from the Ecthesis is worthy of note. It no longer speaks the theological language which Justinian above all had naturalised. Constans in fact more and more gave evidence of possessing qualities which make him appear akin in spirit to the iconoclastic Emperors of a later time. Conversely, amongst the most outstanding monks and priests of the seventh century we already meet with that enmity to the State, in other words, that desire to see the Church independent of the State, which occasioned the frightful struggle in the eighth and ninth centuries. In this respect the position taken up by Maximus Confessor who contested the right of the Emperor to interfere in dogmatic questions and disputed his sacerdotal dignity, is specially characteristic.

in order to shew the Byzantine ruler the power of the Apostolic chair. What Justinian had done to the latter was to be re-quited, although Constans was the Sovereign of Rome. The new Pope, Martin I., who, like many of his predecessors, had formerly been the Papal Apokrisiar in Constantinople, got together a large Council in the Lateran in October 649. Over a hundred Western bishops attended; they were surrounded by numerous Greek priests and monks who had fled from Constans, first to North Africa, and then after the catastrophe there, to Sicily, Calabria, and Rome. The Council was a con-spiracy against Constantinople, and he who was at the head of it was raised to the throne without the imperial sanction. We have here a continuation of the policy of Gregory I., but in a more energetic and menacing form. The dyothelite doc-trine after a discussion lasting over several sittings, was made a fixed dogma by the help of the huge patristic apparatus contributed by the Greeks, [1] and finally a symbol was adopted which added on to the Chalcedonian Creed the words, "two natural wills" ("duas naturales voluntates") "two natural opera-tions" (duas naturales operationes), without detriment to the unity of the person ("one and the same Jesus Christ our Lord and God as willing and effecting divinely and humanly our salvation"—"eundem atque unum dominum nostrum et deum I. Chr. utpote volentem et operantem divine et humane nostram salutem"), and allowing in fact the validity of the proposition when correctly understood; "one incarnate nature of the divine Logos"—μία φύσις τοῦ Θεοῦ λόγου σεσαρκωμένη. The twenty canons attached to the Creed define the doctrine more precisely and cover the whole of Christology. In the eighteenth canon Origen and Didymus are reckoned amongst the other "nefandissimi hæretici". In addition, the fathers of Monothe-litism, of the Ecthesis and the Typus, Theodore of Pharan, Cyrus of Alexandria, and also the three Constantinopolitan patriarchs, Sergius, Pyrrhus, and Paul were condemned. Mono-thelitism was designated as Monophysitism, while the Typus again was described as the godless decree which robbed Jesus

---

[1] "We have a library, but no manuscripts," wrote the Pope in that same year to Bishop Amandus.

Christ of His will, His action, and consequently of His natures generally. Maximus Confessor too stated this brilliant thought with many variations.[1] When we read the resolutions of this Council the impression produced is that of a polemic encounter arranged with some secret end in view.

Martin now made the most strenuous endeavours to get authority over the Churches of the East by the help of the decision of the Council. Like a second Dioscurus he interfered with Eastern affairs, made use of the desperate state of the Churches in the East which were in part in the possession of the Saracens and consequently were no longer in connection with Constantinople, in order to play the roll of supreme bishop, and accordingly worked in direct opposition to the imperial interests and perhaps even conspired with the Saracens. The Emperor now proceeded to take energetic measures. The first attempt to seize the Pope miscarried, it is true, owing to the faithlessness of the Exarch who was sent to Italy. But the new Exarch succeeded in getting Martin into his power (653). As a traitor who had secretly made common cause with the Saracens and as a bishop who had been illegally appointed, he was brought to Constantinople. Dishonoured and disgraced he was then banished to the Chersonesus where he died in the year 655. At the same time proceedings were taken against the dogmatic theologian of Dyothelitism, the monk Maximus, the mystic and scholastic, who for the sake of scholasticism was unwilling to do without the complicated formulæ of the two natures, two wills, two operations in the one person, and who had actually made a profound study of them. In Rome Eugenius was now chosen as Pope and he was disposed to come to some arrangement. At the same time the most reasonable proposal was made which could possibly have been made in the circumstances: It was allowable to speak of *two* natural wills which, however, in accordance with the hypostatic union, become one hypostatic will. Maximus probably endeavoured to prevent the West from falling into this "heresy", but the successor of Eugenius (+657) Vitalian, gave in without any

---

[1] The Acts of the Council, which even yet enjoys a special authority in the Romish Church, are in Mansi XI., the Creed, p. 1150; see also Hahn 2, § 110.

explanations and once more restored the communion with Constantinople which had for so long been interrupted. Constans himself visited Rome in the year 663; the peace lasted till the violent death of the Emperor (668) when he was staying at Syracuse. Rome's lofty plans seemed to be destroyed.

The revolution in policy which now followed in Constantinople is not perfectly comprehensible spite of the obvious explanation that the Monophysite provinces were lost and that consequently there was no longer any reason for shewing any enthusiasm on behalf of Monothelitism or for opposing the establishment of Dyothelitism. Then we may reflect further that, as a matter of fact, the Chalcedonian Creed the more it was regarded from the outside demanded the doctrine of two wills, and that this doctrine alone possessed in Maximus a theologian of weight. But these considerations do not entirely clear up the facts of the case. Constantine Pogonatus seems really to have held the memory of Pope Vitalian in honour because the latter had supported him in putting down the usurpers. For this very reason he hesitated to comply with the wish of the Eastern Patriarchs that Vitalian's name should be erased from the diptychs—the bishop of Constantinople could never desire to enter into alliance with Rome. [1] It was perhaps a real love of peace or still more a perception of the fact that Italy must not be lost to the Empire, and that Italy, moreover, could be retained only by an alliance with the Roman see, which induced the Emperor to arrange a meeting and a conference of the opposing parties. In the year 678, taking up an entirely impartial attitude, he requested the Roman bishop to send representatives to the capital to attend a gathering of this kind. Rome, i.e., the new bishop Agatho, said nothing at first; why is not quite clear. At any rate he once more set afloat in the West certain declarations in favour of the doctrine of two wills. Meanwhile the Patriarch Theodore of Constantinople and Macarius of Antioch who, however, resided in the Capital, succeeded in getting the Emperor's sanction for erasing Vitalian's name from the diptychs. Finally, Agatho sent the desired deputies,

---

[1] There was once more friction between Rome and the patriarch of Constantinople, and this threatened to make the old controversy a pretext for quarrelling.

together with a very comprehensive letter which was modelled in imitation of Leo's doctrinal letter, and in which at the same time the infallibility of the Roman see in matters of faith was expressed in a supremely self-conscious fashion. [1] From this time onwards the Emperor was resolved to yield to the Pope in everything (why?). By means of an edict addressed to George, the new patriarch of the Capital, who had shewn himself pliable, he now summoned a Council to meet, which though it was not originally intended by the Emperor himself to be ecumenical, did nevertheless come to be this. It lasted from November 680 to September 681, had 18 sittings and was attended by about 170 bishops. (The Byzantine East was already very seriously curtailed owing to the Mohammedan conquests.) It was presided over by the Emperor, or, what is the same thing, by the imperial representatives, while the Roman Legates voted first. It may be called the Council of antiquaries and palæographists; for really dogmatic considerations were hardly adduced. On the contrary, operations were conducted on both sides by the help of the voluminous collections of the Acts of earlier Councils and whole volumes of citations from the Fathers, which, however,—and this is in the highest degree characteristic—were after delivery *sealed* until the exact time when they were to be read out, so that they might not be secretly falsified at the very last moment. Moreover, palæographic investigations were conducted which were not without result. [2] Monothelitism had not a few supporters; the most energetic of these was the Patriarch of Antioch, Macarius, who amongst other things appealed to Vigilius, but was forbidden to do so; the letters, it was alleged, were tampered with, which was not the case. Other fathers expressed a desire that it should not be permissible to go beyond the conclusions of the Five Councils in any direction. A proposal was also made at the sixteenth sitting to grant two wills for the period of Christ's earthly life, but to allow of only one after the Resurrection. [3] But the new "Manichean" and "Apollinarian" was promptly expelled from

---

[1] Mansi XI., pp. 234—286.

[2] The Acts of the Council in Mansi, XI.

[3] Mansi XI., p. 611 sq.

the place of meeting. The experiment made by another Monothelite and which he carried on for two hours, of laying his
creed on the body of a dead person in order to restore him
to life and thus to prove the truth of the doctrine of one will,
miscarried. [1] The Council knew what the will of the Emperor
was, and following the lead of the Patriarch of the Capital,
placed itself at the disposal of "the new David" who "has
thoroughly grasped the completeness of the two natures of
Christ our God"! Vitalian's name was restored; in accordance
with the wish of Agatho a long series of Constantinopolitan
patriarchs from Sergius downward together with Macarius and
other Monothelites were condemned, *amongst whom Pope
Honorius too was put.* [2] Finally a creed full of coarse flattery
of the Emperor was adopted, [3] and this completed the triumph
of the Pope over Byzantium. Two natural θελήσεις ἢ θελήματα
were acknowledged and two natural energies existing indivisibly
(ἀδιαιρέτως), unchangeably (ἀτρέπτως), undividedly (ἀμερίστως), unconfusedly (ἀσυγχύτως) in the one Christ. They are not to be
thought of as mutually opposed, on the contrary, the human
will follows the divine and almighty will and far from resisting
or opposing it, is in subjection to it. The human will is thus
not done away with; but there is on the other hand a certain
interchange; it is the will of the divine Logos, just as the
human nature without being done away with has nevertheless
become the nature of the divine Logos. The Conciliar epistle
to Agatho extols the latter as an imitator of the prince of the
Apostles and as the teacher of the mystery of theology. [4] The
Monothelites who had been condemned by the Council were handed over to him to be further dealt with—an unheard of act
hitherto. In the West the decrees were universally accepted—in
Spain too, where, soon after, the Augustinian interpretation of the
Chalcedonian Creed was advanced yet a stage further (as we see

---

[1] Fifteenth Session, Mansi XI., p. 602 sq.

[2] For the mode in which this "problem" is treated by Roman theologians, see
Hefele III., pp. 290—313.

[3] Mansi XI., p. 631 sq.

[4] Mansi XI., p. 658 sq.

in Adoptianism). In the East again the adoption of Dyothelitism which, backed up by the authority of Rome had gained the victory, did not by any means proceed smoothly. Not only did a Monothelite reaction ensue, which was, however, definitely disposed of [1] in the year 713, but there was, above all, a reaction against the penetration of the Roman spirit into the East. This which began with the second Trullan Council in 692 was continued in the age of the iconoclastic Emperors and of Photius. Apart, however, from the controversy about the "filioque" which was dragged in and which has already been treated of above p. 126, it belongs entirely to political history, or to that of worship and discipline.

It is incontrovertible that Rome at the Fourth and Sixth Councils permanently gave *her* formula to the East and that this formula admits of a Græco-Cyrillian interpretation only by the use of theological artifice. But this interpretation had been given to it already at the Fifth Council and had an effect on Rome herself, who from this time onward had to tolerate *also* the μία φύσις τοῦ Θεοῦ λόγου σεσαρκωμένη—the one incarnate nature of the divine Logos. [2] This circumstance explains on the one hand the strange lack of vigour shewn by the Easterns in combating Dyothelitism, and on the other hand the paradoxical fact that the ablest of the Eastern theologians, even the Mystics, supported the doctrine of the two wills. But in order to explain the action of the Mystics it is necessary further to point to the fact that it was no longer possible to do without the scholastic theology of the neo-orthodox, Leontius and Justinian, which had the "duality" as its presupposition, and in conjunction with Mysticism presented a subject for endless speculations. To this was added the fact that the Eucharist and the whole system of worship, already satisfied in a much more certain and more living way than did the system of dogma which had become purely "sacred antiquity", the feeling of the Church as to what was of direct concern and of supreme

---

[1] On the Maronites, see Kessler in Herzog's R.-Encykl. IX., p. 346 ff.

[2] Why in accordance with this the use of the formula ἓν θέλημα θεανδρικόν was not allowed together with the doctrine of the two wills, is a point that is not easily understood. It was owing to Romish obstinacy.

importance in the past—namely, the thought of deification. This
is shewn by the nature of the discussions in the Sixth Council.
The impression we get that at that time believing thought, in the
sense of a direct and living interest in the spiritual and religious
substance of the Faith, had been entirely blighted, very strongly
induces us to look for the life of this Church in some other
sphere. And if we ask where we are to look for it, the image-
controversies on the one hand, and the scholastic investigations
of Johannes Damascenus on the other, supply the answer. The
dogma which had been already settled at the Fifth Council and
which at the Sixth Council had been once more revived and—
not without danger—meddled with, embodied itself in cultus
and science.

The Christological propositions which are worked out in the
Dogmatics of Johannes Damascenus, especially in the third
book, are—even according to Thomasius—stated in "what is
pretty much a scholastic form". It is the idea of distinction
which dominates the method of treatment. Christ did not assume
human nature in its generic form—for John as an Aristotelian is aware that the genus embraces all individuals—but
neither did he unite himself with a particular man; on the contrary he assumed the human nature in such a way that he
individualised what he assumed and what is not a part but the
whole. This is the kind of cross which had already been
recognised by Leontius, which has no hypostasis of its own
and yet is not without it, but which possessing its independent
existence in the hypostasis of the Logos is enhypostatic. Thus
Christ is the composite hypostasis. The "centaur" and "satyr"
against which Apollinaris had warned the Church, have thus
not been avoided The hypostasis belongs to both natures and
yet belongs wholly to each of them. But the divine nature
preponderates very considerably (cf. the old deceptive analogy
of the relation between soul and body in man, III., 7) and it
has been correctly remarked that with Johannes Damascenus
the Logos is at one time the hypostasis and then again
the composite being of Christ as something between. In any
case the humanity is in no way considered as formally entirely
homogeneous with the divinity. This is shewn too in the

doctrine of the interchange (μετάδοσις), appropriation, exchange, (οἰκείωσις, ἀντίδοσις) of the peculiarities of the two natures, which John conceives of as so complete that he speaks of a "coinherence or circumincession of the parts with one another"— εἰς ἄλληλα τῶν μέρων περιχώρησις. The flesh has *actually* become God, and the divinity has become flesh and entered into a state of humiliation. This exchange is to be conceived of as implying that the flesh also is permitted to permeate the divinity, but this is allowed only to the flesh which has itself first been deified; *i.e.*, it is not the actual humanity which permeates the divinity; hence the Logos too remains entirely untouched by the sufferings. Everything is accordingly in this way assigned to the two wills and the two operations. The religious point of view of the whole system is that of Cyril, but this point of view cannot be perfectly realised by means of the "duality" already laid down in the dogma. Just for this reason a certain amount of room is left for the human nature of Christ and for the work of the philosophers. That is why the Christology of Johannes Damascenus has become classical. [1]

---

[1] It is characteristic of the way in which John works out the doctrine, that his arguments throughout are based on passages quoted verbally from the Fathers, though the names of the authors are frequently not given. A mosaic of citations lies at the basis of the scholastic distinctions ; Leontius is most frequently drawn upon, but he is never mentioned by name. John is also dependent to a very great extent on Maximus. How scholasticism has stifled theology is most strikingly shewn in proposition III. 3 (ed. Lequien 1712, I., p. 207) : ἀλλὰ τοῦτό ἐστι τὸ ποιοῦν τοῖς αἱρετικοῖς τὴν πλάνην, τὸ ταὐτὸ λέγειν τὴν φύσιν καὶ τὴν ὑπόστασιν. I imagine that as late as the fifth century any theologian who would have drawn the inference of heresy in this fashion, would have made himself ridiculous. That was the achievement of the neo-orthodox, the Aristotelians from Leontius onwards. A detailed description of the Christology of the Damascene belongs to the history of theology. But it may not be without use to mention the topics which he dealt with here: III. 2: How the Word was conceived and concerning his divine incarnation. 3: Of the two natures in opposition to the Monophysites. 4: On the nature and mode of the antidosis. 5: On the number of the natures (ὁ ἀριθμὸς οὐ διαιρέσεως αἴτιος πέφυκεν. p. 211). 6: That the whole divine nature in one of its hypostases united itself with the whole human nature and not a part with a part. 7: On the one composite hypostasis of the divine Logos. 8: Against those who say that the natures of the Lord must be brought under the category either of continuous or discrete quantity. 9: An answer to the question whether there is an enhypostatic nature (here, p. 218, the enhypostasis). 10: On the Trishagion. 11: περὶ τῆς ἐν εἴδει καὶ ἐν ἀτόμῳ θεωρουμένης φύσεως καὶ διαφορᾶς, ἑνώσεώς τε καὶ

σαρκώσεως καὶ πῶς ἐκκληπτέον, τὴν μίαν φύσιν τοῦ Θεοῦ λόγου σεσαρκωμένην (one of the main chapters from the scholastic point of view). 12: On θεοτόκος as against the Nestorians. 13: On the properties of the two natures. 14: On the wills and the αὐτεξούσια of Christ (the fullest chapter together with 15: On the energies which are in Christ). 16: Against those who say: as man has two natures and two energies, so we must attribute to Christ three natures and the same number of energies—a very ticklish problem. 17: On the deification of the nature of the flesh of the Lord and of His will. (As is the case throughout the discussion here starts from the *contradictio in adjecto* and conceals it under distinctions: the flesh has become divine, but in the process has undergone neither a μεταβολή, nor τροπή nor ἀλλοίωσις nor σύγχυσις; it has been deified κατὰ τὴν καθ᾽ ὑπόστασιν οἰκονομικὴν ἕνωσιν or κατὰ τὴν ἐν ἀλλήλαις τῶν φύσεων περιχώρησιν. The old image of the glowing iron). 18: Once more regarding the wills, the αὐτεξούσια, the double-understanding, the double-gnosis, the double-wisdom of Christ. 19: On the ἐνέργεια θεανδρική. 20: Of the natural and blameless feelings (Christ possessed them, but the number of them given is very limited). 21: Of the ignorance and servitude of Christ (because of the hypostatic union neither ignorance nor servitude can be attributed to Christ relatively to God). 22: On the προκοπή in Christ (as a matter of fact the idea of προκοπή is plainly rejected: the "increase in wisdom" is explained: διὰ τῆς αὐξήσεως τῆς ἡλικίας τὴν ἐνυπάρχουσαν αὐτῷ σοφίαν εἰς φανέρωσιν ἄγων. This is genuine docetic Monophysitism; to this it is added that "he makes man's advance in wisdom and grace his own advance." John is here in the most patent perplexity). 23: Of fear (the fear which Christ had and which he did not have. He had natural fear "voluntarily"). 24: Of the Lord's praying (He prayed, not because there was any need for Him to do it, but because He occupied our place, represented what was ours in Himself, and was a pattern. Thus the prayer in Matt. XXVI. 39 was meant merely to convey a lesson; Christ wished at the same time to shew by it that He had two natures and two natural but not mutually opposed wills—this is just the explanation formerly given by Clemens Alex. when he stated that Christ, whom he himself conceived of in a docetic fashion, voluntarily did what was human, in order to refute the Docetae. Christ spoke the words in Matt. XXVII. 46 purely as our representative). 25: On the οἰκείωσις (this chapter too begins, like most of them, with the distinction, that there are two forms of assumption, the φυσική and προσωπική or σχετική. Christ assumed our nature φυσικῶς, but also σχετικῶς, *i.e.*, took our place by way of sympathy or compassion, took part in our forlorn condition and our curse and "in our place uttered words which do not suit His own case"). 26: Of the sufferings of the body of the Lord and of the absence of feeling in His godhead. 27: That the divinity of the Word was not separated from the soul and the body even in death, and continued to be an hypostasis. 28: Of the corruption and decay (as against Julian and Gajan; but here again a distinction is drawn between two kinds of φθορά). 29: Of the descent into Hades. The contents even of the Fourth Book are still Christological, but this may be due to an oversight. One may admire the energy and formal dexterity of Johannes, but still what we have is merely one and the same method of distinction, which, once discovered, can be easily and mechanically employed, as the application of a new chemical method to an indefinite number of substances. Even this brief synopsis will, however, have brought out one thing, if it was still necessary that this should be done—namely, that in Greek Dogmatics in their *religious* aspect *Apollinaris* had triumphed. The moderate docetism which the latter expressed in a plain, bold and frank way forms the basis of the orthodox idea of Christ, though it is indeed concealed under all sorts of formulæ. As regards these, orthodoxy approaches much nearer to the Antiochians than to Apollinaris; but as regards the matter of the doctrine, all that was preserved of the Antiochian doctrine was the statement that Christ had a real and perfect human nature. This statement came to have a great importance for the future, not of the East, but of the West; but, if I am not mistaken, it helped to preserve the Byzantine Church too from getting into that condition of desolation into which the Monophysite Churches got, though it is true that in the case of the latter other causes were at work.

C. *THE ENJOYMENT OF REDEMPTION IN THE PRESENT.*

CHAPTER IV.

THE MYSTERIES AND KINDRED SUBJECTS.

THERE is an old story of a man who was in a condition of ignorance, dirt, and wretchedness and who was one day told by God that he might wish for anything he liked and that his wish would be granted. And he began to wish for more and more and to get higher and higher, and he got all he wanted. At last he got presumptuous and wished he might become like God Himself, when at once he was back again in his dirt and wretchedness. The history of religion is such a story; but it is in the history of the religion of the Greeks and the Easterns that it came true in the strictest sense. They first wished to have material goods by means of religion, then political, æsthetic, moral, and intellectual goods, and they got everything. They became Christians and desired perfect knowledge and a supra-moral life. Finally they wished even in this world to be as God in knowledge, bliss, and life, and then they fell down, not all at once, but with a fall that could not be stopped, to the lowest stage in ignorance, dirt, and barbarity. Any one who at the present day studies the condition of Greek religion amongst the orthodox and the Monophysites, and not merely the religion of the untrained masses, but also the ritual of worship and the magical ceremonies practised by the ordinary priests and monks and their ideas of things, will with regard to many points get the impression that religion could hardly fall lower. [1]

---

[1] That an honest and genuine faith can live and does live within these husks is not to be denied.

It has really become "superstitio", a chaos of mixed and entirely diverse but at the same time rigidly fixed maxims and formulæ, an unintelligible and long-winded ritual of a patchwork kind, which is held in high esteem, because it binds the nation or the tribe together or unites it to the past, but which is still a really living ritual only in its most inferior parts.[1] If we were to imagine that we knew nothing, absolutely nothing, of Christianity in its original form and of its history in the first six centuries, and had to determine the genesis, the earlier stages, and the value of the original religion from a consideration of the present condition, say, of the Jacobite or of the Ethiopian Church, how utterly impossible this would be.[2] What we have here is a forbidding and well-nigh dead figure of which only some members and these not the principal members are still living, whose nobler parts are so crusted over that so far as their essence is concerned they defy any historical explanation.[3] Islam which swept violently over Christianity in this form was a real deliverer; for spite of its defects and barrenness it was a more spiritual power than the Christian religion which in the East had well-nigh become a religion of the amulet, the fetish, and conjurers, above which floats the dogmatic spectre, Jesus Christ.[4]

[1] Even in these, as experience teaches us, religion may still continue to live for some. Thus the symbol and cult of the Cross in the Greek Church keeps alive a feeling of the holiness of the suffering of the righteous one and a reverence for greatness in humility.

[2] This impossibility may serve as a warning to us in regard to the interpretation of other religions, of their mythologies and ritual formularies. We know most religions only in the form of "superstitio", *i.e.*, in the form in which they have come down to us they are for the most part already in an entirely degenerate state, or have become petrified. Who therefore would make bold to set about explaining these forms in the absence of all knowledge of the previous stages? It is an audacious undertaking.

[3] This judgment must stand although much that is ancient, genuine, and edifying is contained in the prayers and hymns of the liturgies of all the peoples belonging to the Greek Church. But it has become a formula and as a rule is not understood by the people. In this respect the orthodox churches are in a more favourable position, and much is now being done in order to make the liturgy more intelligible.

[4] See Fallmerayer, Fragmente aus dem Orient, 1877, further the descriptions of the Easter festivals kept by the different ecclesiastical parties in Jerusalem and

Many factors contributed to this final result, and above all, the stern march of political history and the economic distress. Closely connected with this was the abolition of the old distinctions between aristocrats, freemen, and slaves, and following upon this the penetration into the higher ranks of the religious and intellectual barbarism which had never been overcome in the lower ranks. Christianity itself contributed in the most effective fashion towards the decomposition of society; but having done this, it was not able to elevate the masses and to build up a Christian Society in the most moderate sense of the word, on the contrary it made one concession after another to the requirements and wishes of the masses. The fact, however, that it thus soon became weak and allowed the "Christian religion of the second order" which originally had been merely tolerated, to exercise an ever increasing influence on the official religion, is to be explained from the attitude which the latter itself had more and more come to take up.

The general idea of redemption which prevailed in the Greek Church had an eschatological character; redemption is deliverance from perishableness and death. But in Vol. III., pp. 163—190, attention was drawn to the fact that at all periods of its history the Greek Church was aware of possessing a means of salvation which already exists in the present and had its origin in the same source from which future redemption flows—namely, the incarnate person of Jesus Christ. The conception of this present means of salvation was originally of a spiritual kind; the knowledge of God and of the world, the perfect knowledge of the conditions attached to the future enjoyment of salvation, and the power of doing good works, in short "teaching of dogmas and good works" (μάθημα τῶν δογμάτων καὶ πράξεις ἀγαθαί) (Cyril of Jerus.), and in addition power over the demons (Athanasius). True, however, to the general mode of conceiving things and also to the heathen philosophies of religion of that period, this knowledge in reference to divine things soon came

---

their image worship. By the Mohammedans too the Christian priest is frequently regarded as a conjurer and when they happen to be living in the same place with Christians, and are in dire distress, they visit the holy places and have recourse to the miracle-working reliques and images.

to be regarded not as in its nature a clear knowledge, or as having an historical origin, or as in its working something to be spiritually apprehended, but on the contrary as a sophia or wisdom, which being only half comprehensible and mysterious, originates directly with God and is communicated by sacred initiation. [1] The uncertainty which in consequence seemed to attach to the content of this knowledge was more than counterbalanced by the consciousness that the knowledge so acquired and communicated, establishes a fellowship amongst those possessed of it and leads to real union with God and is thus not merely individual reflection.

This magical-mystical element which attaches to knowledge as the present possession of salvation, is certainly also to be considered as a clumsy expression of the view that the *summum bonum* is higher than all reason. [2] But the truth which the Eastern Christians wished to grasp and to retain, was not securely established by mystical rationalism. The combination, however, of the natural theology which had never been given up with mysticism, [3] with the magical and sacramental, entailed above all this serious loss that less and less attention was given to the positive moral element, while the downfall of pure science made it possible for the theologians to take up with all sorts of superstition. It was not that the *superstitio* of the masses was simply forced upon them; in their own theology they endeavoured in ever increasing measure to reach a transcendental knowledge which could be enjoyed, as it were, in a sensuous way. Like their blood-relations the Neo-Platonists, they were originally over-excited, and their minds became dulled, and thus they required a stronger and stronger stimulant. The most refined longing for the enjoyment of faith and knowledge was finally changed into barbarity. They wished to fill themselves with the holy and the divine as one fills oneself with

---

[1] The beginnings of this transformation are, it is true, to be found far back in the past. We can already trace them in Justin, and perhaps in fact even in the Apostolic Age missionaries like Apollos regarded religion in this way.

[2] See Vol. I., p. 111, Vol. II., p. 349, n. 2.

[3] See Vol. III., p. 253, and p. 272 f. Mysticism as a rule is rationalism worked out in a fantastic way, and rationalism is a faded mysticism.

some particular kind of food. In accordance with this the
dogma, the μάθησις, was embodied in material forms and
changed into a means of enjoyment—the end of this was the
magic of mysteries, which swallows up everything, the sacred
images, the sacred ritual. Christianity is no longer μάθησις and
πράξεις ἀγαθαί, it is μάθησις and μυσταγωγία, or rather for the
great majority it was to be only μυσταγωγία. The image-controversy shews us where the supreme interests of the Church
are to be looked for.

The development of what belongs to the sphere of mysteries
and of cultus from the time of Origen to the ninth century
does not form part of the History of Dogma. Together with
the conceptions of baptism, the Lord's Supper, sacraments, and
images it constitutes a history by itself, a history which has
never yet been written,[1] and which runs parallel with the
History of Dogma. In the Greek Church there was no "dogma"
of the Lord's Supper any more than there was a "dogma" of
grace. And quite as little was there up to the time of the
image-controversy a "dogma" of the saints, angels, and images; it was the θεοτόκος only that was found in the Catechism.
But ritual was practised here with all the more certainty. There
was a holy ritual; it was already firmly established in the days
of Athanasius when the State united with the Church, and it
was closely followed by a mystagogic theology. This mystagogic theology starting from a fixed point moved with the
greatest freedom in the direction of a definitely recognised goal.

The fixed starting-point it had in common with dogma. It
was the idea that Christianity is the religion which has made
the Divine comprehensible and offers it to us to be possessed
and enjoyed. The definitely recognised goal was the establishment of a system of divine economy of a strictly complete kind
as regards time and place, the factors of which it was composed and the means it employed, and which, while existing in
the midst of what is earthly, allows the initiated by the help

---

[1] The best treatment of the subject is in von Zezschwitz, System der Kirchl.
Katechetik, Vol. I.; see also his article "Liturgie" in Herzog's R.-Encyckl., 2nd
ed., and cf. the investigations of the *disciplina arcana* by Rothe, Th. Harnack
and Bonwetsch.

of sensuous media to enjoy the divine life. Those who above all developed this system did so with a certain reservation—it was not absolutely necessary. He who has speculation and ascetic discipline has in these as a personal possession, means which render it unnecessary for him to go in quest of sensuous signs and initiation in common. This was the view of Clemens and Origen, and after them the same opinion was expressed by the most important mystagogues of the earlier period, that is, by all those who created mystagogy; for no one creates anything without having the consciousness of being above his creation. But the Epigoni receive everything which has come to be what it is under the form of authority, and accordingly it becomes more and more impossible for them to distinguish between end and means, actual things and their substitutes, between what occupies a ruling place and what is subordinate. The spiritualism which, partly in self-protection and partly following its craving for fantastic creations and sensuous pictures, creates for itself in the earthly sphere a new world which it fills with its own ideas, is at the last menaced and crushed by its own creations. But then the spirit which has been artificially enclosed in it vanishes too, and there is nothing but a dead, inert remainder. On it accordingly that veneration is ever more and more bestowed which formerly was supposed to belong to the spirit which had been confined within the matter. Herewith polytheism in the full sense of the word is once more established, it matters not what form dogmatics may take. Religion has lost touch with spiritual truth. When for it a definite *space* is sacred—in the strictest sense of the word,—and in the same way a definite *place*, definite *vehicles*, bread, wine, images, crosses, amulets, clothes, when it connects the presence of the Holy with definite persons, vessels, ceremonies, in short with the exact carrying out of a carefully prescribed ritual, then though this ritual may have the form it always had and may even include in it the most sublime and exalted thoughts, it is played out as spiritual religion and has fallen back to a low level. But this was the final fate of the religion of the Greeks, which adorns itself with the name "Christian". The private religion of thousands of its adherents, measured by the Gospel or the Christianity of Justin may be genuinely Christian,—the *religio publica* has only the incontestable right to the Christian *name*,—and in possessing the Holy Scriptures it has what cannot be lost, the capability of reforming itself. Its fundamental dogma, which in the end determined its entire practice, namely, that the God-man Jesus Christ deified the human substance and in accordance with this attached a system of divine forces to earthly media, did not enable it to overcome the old polytheism of the Greeks and barbarians, but on the contrary rendered it incapable of resisting this.

This is not the place to discuss the question as to the extent to which religion succumbed to it and the consequences of this, nor as to the influence exercised by the Neo-Platonic ecclesiastical science and by the ancient religions and mysteries respectively. All we can aim at doing is to establish the fact that the μυσταγωγία which the μάθησις had in view, gradually brought about the decay of the latter. It is only now that we are able perfectly to understand why such a determined resistance was made in the Greek Church to all fresh attempts to give dogma a fixed form, a resistance which could be overcome only by the most strenuous efforts. It was not only the traditionalism native to all religions which thus offered resistance, but the interests bound up with the ritualistic treatment of dogma and to which serious injury was done by the construction of new formulæ. If the practical significance of dogma lay not only in the fact that salvation was attained hereafter on the basis of this Faith, but also in the fact that on the basis of this Faith Christians were already initiated in this world,—in worship,—into fellowship with the Godhead and were able to enjoy the divine, it was necessary that the expression of this truth should be raised above all possibility of change. The liturgical formula which is constantly repeated, is what can least of all stand being altered. Accordingly it is only when we consider how dogmatic controversies have necessarily always been controversies about words which demanded admission into the liturgy, as was the case with the foreign Nicene catchwords, the θεοτόκος, the theopaschitian formula etc., and finally the "filioque", that we can understand the suspicion which they necessarily roused. We can still see in fact from the state of things in our own churches at the present time how such a liturgy or such a book of praise which in no way corresponds to the creed, causes no difficulty, while even the best innovation has a most disturbing effect. The value of the ritual of worship lies always in its antiquity, not in its dogmatic correctness. Thus the μυσταγωγία which rested on the fundamental thoughts of the μάθησις, and which in fact issued from it, was the stoutest opponent of a *doctrina publica* which was advancing to greater precision of statement. In the end it actually reduced it to silence. In the controversy of Photius with Rome in reference to the Holy Spirit the charge brought against the West of having altered the *wording* of the Creed was urged quite as strongly as the charge of having tampered with the doctrine. One may in fact say that the Greeks regarded the former as worse than the latter. This is the most telling proof of the fact that the daughter became more powerful than the mother, that the μυσταγωγία had come to occupy a place of central importance. This, however, took place long before the days of Photius. The dogmatic controversies of the seventh century are in truth only a kind of echo of no importance, which merely gave dogma the illusory appearance of an independent life. The nature of the controversy makes it evident to any one who looks at the matter more closely, that the dogma had already become a petrifaction and that the kindred ideas of antiquity and of the stability of worship already dominated everything. It is the age of Justinian which brings the independent dogmatic development to an end. At that time the liturgy too received what was practically its final revision. The final completion of dogma ensued under the guidance of scholasticism which now established itself in the Church. Mystagogic theology, which now first began to spread widely, followed the completed liturgy. In this connection we may mention Leontius on the one side and Maximus Confessor who belonged to the seventh century on the other. Dogma as treated in the scholastic and ritualistic fashion is no longer μάθησις at all, in the strict sense of the word. It is, like the Eucharist or the "authentic" image, a divine marvel, a paradoxical, sacred datum, [1] which scholasticism labours to elevate to being μάθησις, and which mysteriosophy exhibits in worship as something to be enjoyed.

We might content ourselves with these hints regarding the fate of dogma. It will, however, be proper to select two subjects from the rich and complicated material of the history of worship and the mysteries and by means of them to give a somewhat more precise outline of the course of development. These are the ideas of the Lord's Supper in connection with which we have to pay attention to the mysteries in general, and the worship of angels, saints, the Virgin Mary, martyrs, relics, and images. As regards the latter, *the* action ensued in the eighth and ninth centuries which brings to an end the history of dogma or the history of religion in the Eastern Church generally. From this date onwards it has had merely an outward history, a history of theology, of mysticism, and ritualism.

§ I.

At the beginning of the Fourth Century the Church already possessed a large series of "mysteries" whose number and limits were, however, not in any way certainly defined. [2] They are τελεταί, mystic rites, which are based on λόγια τοῦ Θεοῦ, words of God; amongst these Baptism, together with the practice of anointing which was closely connected with it, and the Lord's Supper, [3] were the most highly esteemed; while

---

[1] The description of the doctrine, *i.e.*, the *fides quæ creditur*, as μυστήριον (sacrament), dated back to ancient times, hence too the practice of keeping the Creed secret.

[2] See Kattenbusch, op. cit. I., p. 393 ff. "The mysteries represent by their form the dogma"... "It is in this connection too that the comparison of the details in the Liturgy with the life of Jesus as known to us from the Gospel and for which Sophronius of Jerusalem had already prepared the way, first appears in the true light. The arrangement of the Liturgy represents the history of the Incarnation. In this way the whole form of the Liturgy came to share in the value attached to the dogma. Only he who acknowledges the orthodox Liturgy is a Chalcedonian."

[3] There are many passages which prove how closely Baptism and the Lord's Supper were linked together, and regarded as the chief mysteries. What Augustine de pecc. mer. et remiss. remarks (24, 34) can hardly be held to apply only to the

from them a part of the other mysteries had also been developed. Symbolic acts, originally intended to accompany these mysteries, got detached and became independent. It was in this way that Confirmation originated[1] which is already reckoned by Cyprian as a special "Sacramentum", which Augustine designates[2] a "Sacramentum Chrismatis", and which is called by the Areopagite a "mystery of the mystic oil" (μυστήριον τελετῆς μύρου). Augustine too knows of a "Sacramentum Salis" as well as many others,[3] and the Areopagite makes special mention of six mysteries: of enlightenment (φωτίσματος), of coming together or communion (συνάξεως εἴτ᾽ οὖν κοινωνίας), of the mystic oil (τελετῆς μύρου), of priestly consecrations (ἱερατικῶν τελειώσεων), of monastic consecration (μοναχικῆς τελειώσεως), and the mysteries in reference to the holy dead (μυστήρια ἐπὶ τῶν ἱερῶς κεκοιμημένων).[4] This enumeration is not, however, in any way typical, and its author can hardly have intended it to be taken as absolutely complete. "Mysterium" is every symbol, any material thing, in connection with which anything sacred is to be thought of, every action done in the Church, every priestly performance.[5] These mysteries correspond to the heavenly mysteries which have their source in the

Punic Christians. "Optime Punici Christiani baptismum ipsum nihil aliud quam 'salutem' et sacramentum corporis Christi nihil aliud quam 'vitam' vocant, unde nisi ex antiqua, ut existimo, et apostolica traditione" etc. It was chiefly through the Lord's Supper that the element of mysteries found an entrance into the religion of spirit and truth. This way of treating the elements used in it, which are nevertheless expressly described as symbols, supplied the point of departure for the development of the greatest importance.

[1] Cypr. ep. 72. 1. We find it first amongst the Gnostics alongside of Baptism and the Lord's Supper; see Excerpta ex Theodoto, the Coptic-gnostic writings and the ritual of the Marcianites. Cf. on this sacrament Schwane, Dogmengesch. II., p. 968 ff.

[2] C. litt. Petiliani II., c. 104, 239.

[3] De pecc. merit. II., 42.

[4] See de eccles. hierarch. 2—7. To the author the most of these mysteries are not separate mysteries, but represent a whole series of different mysteries. The last mentioned has nothing to do with extreme unction, but designates certain practices in connection with the treatment of the corpse.

[5] The "aliud videtur, aliud intellegitur" (Augustine) is the best definition of the sacrament or mystery.

Trinity and in the Incarnation. [1] As every fact of revelation is a *mysterium* in so far as the divine has through it entered into the sphere of the material, so conversely every material medium, and thus too the word or the action, is a *mysterium* as soon as the material is a symbol or vehicle of the divine. But even in the earliest times no strict distinction was made between symbol and vehicle. The development consists in this that the symbol more and more retreated behind the vehicle, that new heathen symbols and ritual actions were adopted in increasing numbers and that finally the vehicle was no longer conceived of as a covering for or outward embodiment of a truth, but as a deified element, as something essentially divine. [2]

It is obvious that this way of regarding the "mysteries", amongst which the sign of the cross, relics, exorcism, marriage, etc., were reckoned, made it impossible to think of them as having a marked and lofty *dogmatic* efficacy. The rigid dogmatic even forbade such an assumption. As Greek theology regards the Church as an institute for salvation only when it is thinking of heathen and lapsed members or members who are minors, because the doctrine of freedom and redemption does not allow of the thought of a saving institute or of a community of believers chosen by God, in the same way and for the same reasons it knows nothing of a means of grace for those who are already believers, so far as by this is meant the sin-destroying, reconciliatory activity of God attached to a material sign and always strictly limited in its range, and which has for its object the re-establishment of justice and charity or of the filial relation. The ancient Church knew nothing of such means of grace. Accordingly since it desired to have mysteries, believed it possessed them in actions which had been handed down, and was strongly influenced by the dying heathen cultus, it had

---

[1] The orthodox Greek Church came to reckon the sacraments as seven owing to the influence of the West, *i.e.*, gradually from the year 1274 onwards. Still the number seven never came to have the importance attached to it in the West.

[2] In Athanasius we already meet with both modes of expression: (1) "The Logos became flesh, in order that he might offer his body for all, and we by participating in his spirit may be made divine" (de decret. synod. Nic. 14); (2) "We are made divine inasmuch as we do not participate in the body of a man, but receive the body of the Logos Himself" (ad. Maxim. phil. 2).

to content itself with the *inexpressibleness* of the effect of the
mysteries. This conception forms the basis even where, following the directions of the New Testament, [1] regeneration, the
forgiveness of sins, the bestowal of the spirit, etc., are deduced
in rhetorical language from separate sacraments. The assumption that the sacramental actions had certain inexpressible
effects—the doctrine of freedom prevented the magical-mystical
effects which were specially included under this head from
being embodied in a dogmatic theory—logically led, however,
to these being performed in such a way that the imagination
was excited and the heavenly was seen heard, smelt, and felt,
as for example in incense and the relics and bones of martyrs.
The enjoyment of salvation on the part of him who participated
in these rites, was supposed to consist in the elevating impression made on the imagination and the sensuous feelings.
He was supposed to feel himself lifted up by means of it into
the higher world, and in this feeling to taste the glory of the
super-sensuous, and for this reason to carry away the conviction
that in a mysterious fashion soul and body had been prepared
for the future reception of the immortal life. Such being the
theory it was an easy step from this to combine all the mysteries into one great mystery in worship, and this was what
actually took place. With this as the starting-point the "Church"
too accordingly became a holy reality, the institution for worship, the holy mechanism, which supplies the believer with
heavenly impressions and raises him to heaven. The idea of
the Church which had the most vitality in the East was that
of something which, regarded as active, was "the lawful steward
of the mysteries (" ὁ γνήσιος τῶν μυστηρίων οἰκονόμος") and conceived of as passive, was the image of the "heavenly hierarchy."

In strict logical fashion it developed from beginnings which
already foreshadow the end. Although the beginnings are
characteristically different, we find them in Antioch as well as
in Alexandria and thus in both the centres of the East. In
the case of the former of these cities the beginnings are to be

---

[1] Here already at this early stage the difficult question emerges which even at
the present day troubles many amongst ourselves, as to whether the ceremonies of
the Old Testament, circumcision for instance, were sacraments.

looked for in Ignatius, the author of the Six Books of the
Apostolic Constitutions, the editor of the Eight Books, and in
Chrysostom, and together with them in Methodius. In the case
of the latter the starting-point was supplied by Clemens, Origen,
(Gregory of Nyssa) and Macarius. In the former everything
from the first was intimately associated with the bishop and
with worship, in the latter with the true Gnostic originally,
then next with the monk. In the former the bishop is the
hierurge and the representative of God, the presbyters represent
the apostles, and the deacons Jesus Christ. This is the earthly
hierarchy, the copy of the heavenly. Already with Ignatius
the cultus dominates the entire Christian life; the holy meal is
the heavenly meal, the Supper is the "medicine of immortality"—Φάρμακον ἀθανασίας. By means of the *one* Church-
worship we mount up to God; woe to him who takes no part
in it. All this is put in a stronger form in the Apostolical
Constitutions, and is developed in a worthy and sensible fashion
in the work of Chrysostom περὶ ἱερωσύνης. But in all this the
attitude of the laity is a passive one; they make no effort,
they allow themselves to be filled.[1] The influential Methodius
viewed the matter from a different standpoint. Although he is
the opponent of the Alexandrians, he does not deny the influence which he had received from them. His realism and traditionalism are, however, of a speculative kind. They constitute
the substructure of the subjectivity of the monkish mysticism.
Christ must be born "rationally" (νοητῶς) in the believer; every
Christian must by participating in Christ become a Christ.
Methodius knew how to unite the ideas of a powerful religious
individualism with the Mysticism which attaches itself to objective traditions. While protecting these latter against the in-
roads of a heterodox idealism, he nevertheless intended that

---

[1] I here leave out of account the Syrian mysticism of the fifth and sixth centuries
of which we first really got some idea from the admirable work of Frothingham,
Stephen bar Sudaili, 1886. The philosophico-logical element is not entirely absent
from the views of these Syro-Monophysite mystics who had relations with Egypt
too, but still it always was kept in the background. We have in their case
Pantheism of a strongly marked character represented by the consubstantiality of
God and the universe, and in accordance with this they had a fondness for the
"Origenistic" ideas of the history of the universe and of the restoration of all things.

they should merely constitute the premises of an individual religious life which goes on between the soul and the Logos alone.

This was the fundamental thought of the great theologians of Alexandria. But they rarely connected the substructure of their theosophy with earthly worship, and still more rarely with earthly priests. Nevertheless their substructure was of a much richer kind than that of the Antiochians. There is probably no single idea connected with religion or worship, no religious form, which they did not turn to account. Sacrifice, blood, reconciliation, expiation, purification, perfection, the means of salvation, the mediators of salvation,—all these, which were connected with some symbol or other, played a *rôle* in their system. It was the hierarchical element alone which was kept very much in the background, nor was much prominence indeed given to the idea of the ritual unity of the Church which was a leading one with the Antiochians. Everything is directed towards the perfection of the individual, the Christian Gnostic, and everything is arranged in stages, a feature which is wanting in the system of the Antiochians. The Christian does not merely allow himself to be filled with the Holy; on the contrary he is himself here always engaged in independent effort inasmuch as he advances from secret to secret. At every stage some remain behind; each stage down to the last presents a real thing and the covering of a thing. Blessed is he who knows the thing or actual fact, still more blessed he who presses on to the next stage, but he too is saved who grasps the thing in its covering only. But with the stages of the mysteries the stages of the knowledge of the world further correspond. He who makes the mysteries his own, *thinks* at the same time on the progressively ordered world. He advances from the external world upwards to himself, to his soul, his spirit, to the laws of the world and the world-spirits, to the one undivided Logos who rules the universe, to the incarnate Logos, to the highest Reason, which lies behind the Logos, to what is above all reason—to God. The Cosmos, the history of redemption, the Bible are the great graduated, ordered mysteries which have to be traversed: all divine things and all human things—πάντα θεῖα καὶ πάντα ἀνθρώπινα. When we have once reached the end aimed at, all helps may be dispensed with. There is a standpoint viewed from which every symbol, every sacrament, every thing that is holy, which appears in a material covering, becomes profane, for the soul lives in the Holiest of all. "Images and symbols which set forth other things were of value so long as the truth was not present, but when the truth is present, it is necessary to do the things of the truth and not of the image or representation of it," (αἱ εἰκόνες καὶ τὰ σύμβολα παραστατικὰ ὄντα ἑτέρων πραγμάτων καλῶς ἐγίνοντο, μέχρι μὴ παρῆν ἡ ἀλήθεια· παρούσης δὲ τῆς ἀληθείας τὰ τῆς ἀληθείας δεῖ ποιεῖν, οὐ τὰ εἰκόνος). This holds good of the aspiring theologian; it holds good also in the main of the humblest, barbarous monk. But Christianity would not be the universal religion if it did not present salvation in the symbolic form at all stages. This thought separates the ecclesiastical theosophs of Alexandria from their Neo-Platonic and Gnostic brethren. In it the universalism of Christianity finds expression, but the concession is too great. It sanctions a Christianity which is bound up with signs and formulæ, the Christianity of the "εἰκόνες". The most sublime spiritualism, as happened in expiring antiquity, made terms with the grossest forms of the religion of the masses,—or rather, here is expiring antiquity. That it could do this is a proof that a naturalistic or polytheistic element was inherent in itself. Because it did it, it was itself stifled by the power which it tolerated. The issue reveals the initial capital blunder.

The mystical cultus of Antioch which culminates in the priest and divine service, and the philosophical mysticism of Alexandria which has ultimately in view the individual, the gnostic and the monk, already converge in Methodius and the Cappadocians ;[1] they next converge in the works of the pseudo-Dionysius the Areopagite.[2] It was owing to Maximus Confessor

---

[1] Gregory of Nazianzus (in laud. Heron. c. 2) thus speaks from the altar to Hero "Approach hither, near to the Holy places, the mystic table and me, τῷ διὰ τούτων μυσταγωγοῦντι τὴν θέωσιν, οἷς σε προσάγει λόγος καὶ βίος καὶ ἡ διὰ τοῦ παθεῖν κάθαρσις."

[2] The article by Möller in Herzog's R.-Encyklop. III., p. 616 ff. enables us to understand how the Dionysius question stood in the year 1878 (the best analysis is by Steitz, in the Jahrbb. für deutsche Theol., 1866, p. 197 ff.; there are valuable if not quite convincing discussions by Hipler, 1861 and in the Kirchenlex. 2 III.,

that in this combination they became the power which dominates the Church.

Everything was grouped round the Lord's Supper, [1] and as
p. 1789 ff., cf. the work of Engelhardt, Die angebl. Schriften des A. Dionysius,
Sulzbach, 1823). Within recent years, however, several new publications based on
the sources, and discussions, have appeared, which shew that nothing has really
yet been certainly established; see Pitra, Analecta Sacra III., on this Loofs in the
ThLZ., 1884, Col. 554 f.; Frothingham, Stephen bar Sudaili, the Syrian Mystic
and the Book of Hierotheos, 1886; in addition Baethgen in the ThLZ, 1887,
No. 10; Skworzow, Patrologische Untersuchungen, 1875; Kanakis, Dion. d. Areopagite, 1881; Dräseke (Ges. Patrist. Abhandl., 1889, p. 25 ff.; Dionysios v. Rhino-
kolura, in addition Gelzer in the Wochenschrift f. Klass. Philol., 1892, separate
impression); Jahn, Dionysiaca, 1889; Foss, Ueber den Abt Hilduin von St. Denis
und Dionysius Areop. in the Jahresbericht des Luisenstädt. R.-Gymnasiums z. Berlin,
1886. The most ancient testimony to the existence of these works is to be found
in the Church History attributed to Zacharias of Mitylene (Land, Anecd. Syr. III.,
p. 228). Severus quoted them at a Council at Tyre which cannot have been held
later than the year 513. Still older would be Cyril's testimony in the work against
Diodorus and Theodore, which even if it ought not to be attributed to Cyril, belongs to the fifth century. "Although the manuscript reading in Liberatus Brev. 10
is corrupt still it ought probably to be emended thus : Dionysii Areopagitæ, (Dionysii) Corinthiorum episcopi" (Gelzer). Hipler, Pitra, Dräseke, Möller, Kanakis
(who wishes to fix the date of the writings definitely for about 120) have pronounced
against the old assumption of a (pious) fraud, and have referred the writings to
the second half of the fourth century. They have besides sought to shew that we
ought probably to make a distinction between the several works which now bear
the name of Dionysius, and that the oldest of the writings bearing this name are
in all probability not forgeries, though forgers and interpolators did seize upon
them in the fifth or sixth century, and that therefore, as is so frequently the case, it
was not the author, but tradition which first committed the forgery. But if Frothingham is right, the writings ought to be put later, and Gelzer as against Dräseke
has advanced some very strong arguments in favour of the idea of an original
pia fraus—after the analogy of the Neo-Platonic interpolations—that is in support
of the hypothesis "that the author of these writings purposely intended from the
first to secure a loftier authority from them than they would otherwise have had
by means of the prestige attaching to works contemporary with the Apostles." "The
author of the Dionysian writings was merely following the usages of the schools, in
transferring his works to the apostolic age." The question of date is consequently
not yet settled, (second half of the fourth and fifth century). The period previous
to 400 seems to me the more probable, but there are so many points connected
with these writings which are still obscure that one must refrain from pronouncing
an opinion until a new, thorough, and comprehensive investigation has been made.

[1] Baptism may be left out of account; for the views held regarding it did not
undergo any actual development within the period we treat of (see Vol. II., 140.)
Naturally the general and changing ideas of the mysteries exercised an influence
upon baptism, but it was rarely studied *ex professo*. It besides occupied an isolated
position since it could never be brought into intimate connection with worship.

was the case in an earlier period, it still continued to be regarded from a twofold point of view, the sacrificial and the

What was certain was that baptism actually purifies from sins committed previous
to it, *i.e.*, destroys them, and consequently constitutes the beginning of the process
which makes the mortal man imperishable. It is thus the source and beginning
of all gifts of grace. But as was the case in regard to the other mysteries, so
here too there were theologians who, in imitation of Origen, held the view that
there was a mysterious purification of the soul, and regarded the water as a symbol,
but all the same as the absolutely necessary symbol, which just for this very reason
is not simply a "symbol" in the modern sense of the word (see the Cappadocians).
The intellectualism of these theologians and their inability to believe in an actual
forgiveness of sins, led them in the case of baptism to prefer the idea of a
φωτισμός—the primitive designation of the sacrament—and thus of a physical
purification (κάθαρσις) or else to think of the proof it gave of such a purification.
Other theologians, however, from the days of Cyril of Alexandria downwards, in
accordance with their ideas of the Lord's Supper with which, following John XIX.
34, baptism was always ranged (Johannes Damascenus still gives prominence to
these two sacraments only), assumed that there was an actual μεταστοιχείωσις of the
water into a divine material, which took place by means of the descent of the
spirit which followed the invocation of God. Tertullian (de bapt.) and Cyprian had
already taught similar doctrine in the West. Cyril of Jerusalem too (cat. III. 3, 4)
held the view that there was a dynamic change in the water. But it is Cyril of
Alexandria (Opp. IV., p. 147) who first says: Διὰ τῆς τοῦ πνεύματος ἐνεργείας τὸ
αἰσθητὸν ὕδωρ πρὸς θείαν τινὰ καὶ ἀπόρρητον μεταστοιχειοῦται δύναμιν, ἁγιάζει δὲ
λοιπὸν τοὺς ἐν οἷς ἂν γένοιτο. Still the Church did not get the length of having
distinct and definite formulæ for the sacramental unity of water and spirit, for the
moment, and for the means whereby this unity was produced. Although the
statement held good that baptism was absolutely necessary to salvation, still people
shrank more from the unworthy reception of it than from the danger of definitely
dispensing with it. In the fourth century people kept postponing it repeatedly—
so as not to use this general means till the hour of death. Baptism was accordingly
regarded by many *in praxi* not as initiation into the Christian state, but as the
completion of it. Some very characteristic passages in Augustine's Confessions, *e.g.*,
show this (*e.g.*, Confess. VI. 4): it was possible in the fourth century to rank as
a Christian, though one was not yet baptised. But the great Church-Fathers of the
fourth century defended the practice of infant-baptism which had been already
handed down, and this was established in the fifth century as the general usage.
Its complete adoption runs parallel with the death of heathenism. As regards baptism by heretics, the view held in the Eastern Church at the beginning of the
fourth century was that it was not valid. But it gradually, though hesitatingly,
receded somewhat from this position (see the decisions of 325 and 381). A distinction was made between those sects whose baptism was to be recognised, or was to
be supplemented by the laying on of hands, and those whose baptism had to be
repeated (this is still what we have in the ninty-fifth canon of the Trullan Synod
692). The Church did not, however, arrive at any more fixed view on the matter,
since just those fathers of the fourth century who where held in the highest esteem
generally demanded re-baptism. Whether one ought to re-baptise the heretic or to

sacramental.[1] The mystery with which it came to be increasingly surrounded and the commemorations which took place at its celebration, preserved to the Lord's Supper in wholly altered conditions within the world-Church which embraced the Empire, its lofty and at the same time familiar, congregational character.[2] No rigidly doctrinal development of the Lord's Supper followed on this. But probably the presence of changes in the conceptions formed of the Lord's Supper both in its sacrificial and in its sacramental aspect, might be proved. These changes, however, take place throughout within the limits which were already fixed in the third century. The blend of a sublime spiritualism and a sensuous realism was already in existence in the third century. Any progress which took place could consist only in this, that religious materialism advanced further and further and forced spiritualism to retire. Its advance was, however, furthered above all by the fact that the dogma of the Incarnation was brought into connection with the Lord's Supper. This is the most important fact connected with this development, for now the Lord's Supper became, as it were, the intelligible exponent of the entire dogmatic system, and at the same time the hitherto vague ideas regarding the kind and nature of the body of Christ in the Lord's Supper, came to have a firmly fixed form. If previous to this Christians had never of set purpose thought of the body of the historical Christ when speaking of the body of Christ in the Lord's Supper, but of His spirit, His word, or the remembrance of His body offered up, or of something inexpressible, something glorified which

---

anoint him or merely to lay the hand upon him, is a point that is not certainly decided up to the present time. The Greek Church very frequently still repeats baptism at the present day; see Höfling, Sacr. der Taufe, 1848; Steitz, Art. "Ketzertaufe" in Herzog's R.-Encykl. 2nd ed.; Kattenbusch, op. cit. I., p. 403 ff.

[1] See Vol. II., p. 136, and p. 146.

[2] It is very worthy of note that already in the fourth century the Lord's Supper was regarded as the expression of a particular form of Confession. Philostorgius (H. E. III. 14) tells us that up to the time of Aëtius the Arians in the East had joined with the orthodox in prayers, hymns, etc., in short in almost all ecclesiastical acts, but not in the "mystic sacrifice." In the commemorations from that time onwards connection with the Church found public expression. Cancelling of Church membership was regularly expressed by erasure of the name in the commemoration from the diptychs.

passed for being His body, now the idea emerged that the
material element which is potentially already the body of Christ
according to Gregory of Nyssa, is by priestly consecration or
more correctly, by the Holy Spirit who also overshadowed
Mary, changed with the real body of Christ or else taken up
into it. The Incarnation is not repeated in the Lord's Supper,
but it is continued in it in a mysterious fashion, and the dogma
is practically attested in the most living and marvellous way
through this mystery. The priest is here, it is true, the minister
only, not the author; but in connection with such a transaction
to be the servant who carries out what is done, means to be
engaged in an inexpressibly lofty service which raises one even
above the angels. The whole transaction, which is based on
the Incarnation, is thus beyond a doubt itself the mystery of
the deification (θέωσις). The connection is exceptionally close;
for if the act gets its essence and its substance from the Incarnation, while the latter again has in view the deification, it is
itself the real means of the deification. It is the same thought
as that which had already been indicated by Ignatius when he
described the holy food as the "medicine of immortality"
(φάρμακον ἀθανασίας); but it is only now that this thought is
taken out of the region of uncertain authority and has fixity
given to it by getting a thoroughly firm foundation. But perhaps the point that is most worthy of note is, that in reference
to the elements phrases were used by the Greek Fathers of a
later period, which, as applied to the dogma of the Incarnation,
had to be discarded as Gnostic, doketic, Apollinarian, or Eutychian and Apthartodok_etic! People speak naïvely—up to the
time of Johannes Damascenus, at least—of the changing, transformation, transubstantiation of the elements into the Divine.
No attempt is made to form definite ideas regarding the where-
abouts of their material qualities; they are wholly and entirely
deified. In a word, the views held regarding the Lord's Supper
were for a long time Apollinarian-monophysite, and not dyophy-
site. But this makes it once more perfectly plain that what
was regarded by the Greek Church as of real importance from
the religious point of view, was adequately represented only by
the teaching of Apollinaris and Monophysitism, and that the

reasons which finally led to the adoption of Dyophysitism had
no strict connection with the dogmatic system.

As regards the sacrificial aspect of the holy action, the most
important development consists in the advance made in the
transformation of the idea of sacrifice, for which the way had
been already prepared in the third century. The offering of
the elements, the memorial celebration of the sacrifice of Christ
in the sacrifice of the Supper, the offering of the gifts (προσφέρειν τὰ δῶρα) and the offering of the memorial of the body
(προσφέρειν τὴν μνήμην τοῦ σώματος) was changed into an offering of the body, (τὸ σῶμα προσφέρειν) a propitiatory memorial
sacrifice. "The sacrifice of His Son on the Cross was, as it
were, put before God's eyes and recalled to memory in order
that its effects might be communicated to the Church." Thus,
owing to the influence of the heathen mysteries and in consequence of the development of the priestly notion, the idea
crept in that the body and blood of Christ were constantly
offered to God afresh in order to propitiate Him. And the
more uncertain men became as to God's feelings, and the more
worldly and estranged from God they felt themselves to be,
the more readily they conceived of the Supper as a real renewal
of the Sacrifice of Christ and of His saving death. Christians
had formerly made it their boast that the death of Christ had
put an end to every sort of outward sacrifice; they had spoken
of the "bloodless and rational and gentle sacrifice" (ἄναιμος
καὶ λογικὴ καὶ προσηνὴς θυσία) or of the "immaterial and mental
sacrifice" (θυσία ἀσώματος καὶ νοερά). These modes of expression
continued to be used in the third and fourth centuries, but the
desire for a sensuous expiatory sacrifice, which had been present,
though in a hidden form, at an early date, became stronger
and stronger, and thus "flesh and blood"—namely, the flesh
and blood of Christ—were described as sacrificial offerings.
Thus men had once more a bloody sacrifice, though indeed
without visible blood, and what it seemed not to have certainly
accomplished when offered once, was to be accomplished by a
repetition of it. And thus, as the act regarded as a sacrament
was connected in the closest way with the Incarnation, and
appeared as a mysterious, real representation of it, as something

to be enjoyed by the believer, so, regarded as a sacrifice, it was
now finally brought into the most intimate connection with the
death of Christ, but in such a way that in it the saving sacrificial death likewise appeared to be continued, *i.e.*, repeated.
Is it possible to give the sacramental act a loftier position than
this? Assuredly not! And yet it was nothing but pure Paganism
which had brought .this about. Since these developments took
place most of the Churches of Christendom in the East and
West have been fettered and enslaved by a "doctrine of the
Supper" and a "ritual of the Supper", which must be reckoned
amongst the most serious hindrances which the Gospel has experienced in the course of its history. Neither the calling out of
elevated feelings, nor the superabundance of intellectual force, of
acuteness and "philosophy" which has been expended in connection with this, can undo the mischief which has been incalculable and which is still going on. And as in the fifth and sixth
centuries the Supper was conceived of as the resultant of the
system of dogma as a whole (the Trinity and the Incarnation),
and was supposed to be equivalent to it, and to give a lively
representation of it, so the same is still the case at the present
day. The "doctrine" of the Supper has been treated in such
a way as in the first place to sanction the dogma of the Incarnation, and in the second place to gather up to a point the entire
confessional system of doctrine and the conception of the Church.
In the whole history of religions there is probably no second
example of such a transformation, extension, demoralisation and
narrowing of a simple and sacred institution!

Sure and logical as was the course of the development of
the ritual and doctrine of the Supper in the Greek Church, no
dogma in the strict sense of the word was set up, because
there was no controversy unless about points of no importance.
But just for this very reason the doctrinal pronouncements
scarcely ever get beyond the stage of unfathomable contradictions and insoluble oracles. Christians felt so comfortable in
the darkness of the mystery; they laid hold of this or the other
extravagant form of expression without being afraid of being
corrected or being forced to pay respect to a fixed form of
words sanctioned by ecclesiastical usage. Anything that sounded

pious and edifying, profound and mysterious, could be freely used in connection with the mystery. And since the words which were used in this connection, such as spirit (πνεῦμα), spiritually (πνευματικῶς), flesh (σάρξ), body (σῶμα) had a threefold and a manifold meaning [1] in ecclesiastical usage, since Scripture itself supplied various allegories in connection with this matter, using flesh of Christ as equal to the Church, flesh of Christ as equal to His words, etc., since John VI. as compared with the words of institution supplied endless scope for speculation and rhetoric, since the consequences and the terminology of the dogma of the Incarnation were on the same lines,—and in addition, the doctrine of the Holy Spirit and certain ideas of the Church,—since finally the sacramental and sacrificial elements were at one time kept strictly separate and at another ran into one another, the utterances of the Greek Fathers in reference to the Supper constitute as a rule the most forbidding portions of their works. But to give a logical solution and orderly reproduction of their thoughts is not at all the historian's business, for in attempting such a task he would constantly be in danger of missing the meaning of the Fathers. For this reason we here renounce any such attempt. It will be sufficient to note the tendency and progress of the development in the Fathers who are to be referred to in what follows. [2]   That the increasingly complex

---

[1] Let any one take a proposition such as this from Athanasius: πνεῦμα ζωοποιοῦν ἡ σάρξ ἐστι τοῦ κυρίου, διότι ἐκ πνεύματος ζωοποιοῦ συνελήμφθη, in order to form an idea of how one may twist and turn the words.

[2] In the essays by Steitz on the doctrine of the Supper in the Greek Church (Jahrbb. f. deutsche Theol. IX., pp. 409—481; X., pp. 64—152, 399—463; XI., pp. 193—253: XII., pp. 211—286; XIII., pp. 3—66) we possess an investigation of the subject which is as comprehensive as it is thorough. The author, however, does not seem to me always to have hit the mark in the judgments he passes. He makes too many distinctions, and in particular his view as to the existence of a strictly distinct symbolic doctrine of the Supper is hardly tenable in the form in which he seeks to develop it. A purely symbolic conception of the Supper never existed, for it was always harmoniously united with a ritual which was based on a very realistic way of conceiving of it. What we now call "symbol" is something wholly different from what was so-called by the ancient Church. On the other hand, after the sacramental magic in its coarsest form had found its way into the Church, "symbolic" statements were always tolerated because the symbol was really never a mere type or sign, but always embodied a mystery; see Vol. II., p. 143. On the doctrine of the Supper cf. further the monographs by Rückert, Kahnis, Ebrard.

form taken by doctrine was of no advantage to real religion
may be inferred from the one fact that the effects of the
Supper were always described in an absolutely vague fashion.
Nor did the θεώσις, that process to which was attached this
high-sounding name, really mean anything, for it was impossible
to understand it in any serious sense. The idea that freedom was the basis of all that was good, was in the way of
this. This θεώσις, which is experienced in imagination, threatened, in the case of the Greeks themselves, to change into a
mere play of fancy; for as soon as they realised that they
were moral beings, they thought of nothing else save of the
exalted God, of His demand that they should renounce the
world and do good, and of the duty which lay upon man of
living a holy life in order to die a blessed death. For this
very reason they were also unable to reach any complete
confidence in the promise of the forgiveness of sins given in the
Supper. In place of this, however, religious materialism went to
absurd lengths, while at the same time the ascetic theosoph
was always free respectfully to ignore the whole transaction.

Only a few hints regarding the course taken by the development of the doctrine can fitly be given here : Origen supplies
the starting-point. "In his view the eucharistic body was only
the Word of God or of the Logos as being a substitute for
his appearance in the flesh; the shew-bread was for him the type
of the Word in the old Covenant; for as this was placed, as
it were, before the eyes of God as a propitiatory memorial
object, so the Church also puts a bread before God which has
a great propitiatory power—namely, the commemoration, the
word regarding His passion and death with which Christ
introduced and founded the Supper. But the bread of blessing was in his view the symbol only of this word, only of
His eucharistic body, but not of His body offered up on the
Cross, and if he does once call the latter "the typical and
symbolic body", he did this only in the sense referred to. This
is just what is peculiar and characteristic in his standpoint, that
whenever he speaks of the Supper or indeed in a more general

sense of the eating of the flesh or of the drinking of the blood
of Christ, he does this without any reference to the body
which He had as man or to the blood which flowed in the
veins of this body." [1] The body and blood of Christ are knowledge, life, and immortality, not, however, as a mere thought
or as a symbol, but in inexpressible reality. In Eusebius we
already note an advance, and in fact in the "Demonstratio" and
in the work "de eccles. theologia" he has several new categories. In his case already the offering of the memorial of the
body (μνήμην τοῦ σώματος προσφέρειν) passes over into the offering of the body (τὸ σῶμα προσφέρειν). He has the propitiatory
memorial sacrifice. But from the sacramental point of view
the consecrated elements are still for him symbols of the *mystical*
body of Christ, *i.e.*, of His word : only from the sacrificial point
of view do they already possess the value of mysterious symbols
of the actual body, the body which was once offered up. [2] It
is impossible to extract a doctrine from the confused statements
of Athanasius, nor will it do to make him a "symbolist". [3]
Probably, however, Athanasius comes nearer to Origen in his
conception of the Supper than in any other part of his doctrine. [4]
The statement of Basil (ep. 8, c. 4) is genuinely Origenist :
"We eat the flesh of Christ and drink His blood in that by
His Incarnation and His life which was manifest to the senses,
we become partakers of the Logos and of wisdom. For he
described His whole mystical appearance as flesh and blood
and thereby indicated the doctrine which is based on practical,
physical, and theological science, and by which the soul is
nourished and is meanwhile prepared for the vision of the truly
existent." But the Cappadocians likewise had already advocated
a theurgy of the most palpable kind — in all the Fathers the
spiritualistic amplifications of the doctrine occur, always with
reference to John VI. As regards the doctrine of the Supper,
"Realism" and Real Presence of the true body of Christ (or
transubstantiation) are for us at the present day equivalent. In

---

[1]   Steitz X., p. 99.
[2]   Demonstr. ev. I. 10 ; de eccles. theol. III. 12 ; Steitz X., p. 97 ff.
[3]   So rightly Thomasius I., p. 431 ff. as against Steitz X., p. 109 ff.
[4]   See ad Serap. IV., espec. c. 19 and the Festival-letters.

ancient times, however, there was a "realism" which had no
reference whatever to that real presence, but which on the contrary regarded a spiritual mystical something as really present.
Hence the controversy on the part of historians of dogma and of
ecclesiastical parties regarding the doctrine of the Supper held
by the Fathers. They are "Symbolists" in respect of the real
presence of the true body; indeed as regards this they are
in a way not even symbolists, since they had not that body in
their minds at all. But they know of a mystical body of Christ
which is for them absolutely real—it is spirit, life, immortality,
and they transferred this as real to the celebration of the Supper.[1]
According to Macarius too, Christ gives Himself and the soul
to be eaten spiritually (hom. 27, 17), but this spiritual eating
is the enjoyment of something actual. Macarius, however, while
he had the individual soul in view always thought of the Church;
for to this noteworthy Greek mystic who, moreover, knew something of sin and grace, as to Methodius, the soul is the micro-
cosm of the Church and the Church is the macrocosm of the
soul. But the statements made by him and Methodius in respect
to this point, were not further followed out.[2] The influence
of the sacrificial conception of the consecrated elements, as being
the antitypes of the broken body of Christ, on the sacramental
conception, can be traced already in Eustathius and in the
Apostolical Constitutions;[3] its presence is perfectly apparent
in the mystagogic catechetics of Cyril of Jerusalem. But I
suspect that in their catechetical instruction Basil and Gregory
did not express themselves differently from him. Besides the
many other passages having reference to the subject, Catech.

---

[1] On Basil Steitz X., p. 127 ff., on Gregor Naz. the same, p. 133 ff. From
Basil's ninety-third letter in particular we see that for him spiritualism was in
no sense opposed to the most superstitious treatment of the Supper. Quite correctly
Ullmann, Gregor, p. 487: "It is difficult to determine what Gregory understood by
eating and drinking the blood of Christ, and in any case no dogma which may
be regarded as peculiarly belonging to Gregory can be deduced from it." In him
we find the expression for the consecrated elements "ἀντίτυπα τοῦ τιμίου σώματος
καὶ αἵματος", an expression which Eusebius in his day might have used and which
Eustathius did use (Steitz X., p. 402).

[2] On Macarius, see Steitz X., p. 142 ff.

[3] Steitz X., pp. 402—410.

V., 7 is specially important. "And next after we have sanctified ourselves (through prayer), we pray the gracious God that He will send down His Holy Spirit on the elements presented, in order that He may make the bread into the body of Christ and the wine into the blood of Christ; for 'what the Holy Spirit touches is wholly sanctified and transformed (μετα-βέβληται)." Here therefore we have a plain assertion of the μεταβολή which is effected by the Holy Spirit in the Supper, and Cyril in fact appeals to the miracle of Cana. At the same time "Cyril is the first church-teacher who treats of baptism, the oil, and the Eucharist, in their logical sequence, and in accordance with general principles." The element which may be termed the symbolic, or better, the spiritual element, is nowhere wanting in his theology, and in fact it still quite clearly constitutes its basis; but we see it supplemented by that "realism" which already regards the details of the act of ritual as the special subject of instruction. The epiklesis or invocation, brings with it a dynamic change in the elements in the Supper as in all mysteries. By partaking of the holy food one becomes "a bearer of Christ"; the flesh and blood of Christ is distributed amongst the members of the body. In Cyril's view the elements in their original form have after consecration wholly disappeared. "Since now thou art taught and convinced that the visible bread is not bread, although to the taste it appears to be such, but the body of Christ; and that the visible wine is not wine, although to taste it seems to be such, but the blood of Christ, comfort thine heart," (Catech. V., 9). But still we might make a mistake if we were to attribute to the theologian what is said by the catechist. Extravagances of this sort still belonged at that time to the liturgical and catechetical element, but were not a part of theology.[1] But the miracle of Cana and the multiplication of the bread now became important events for teachers, as indeed is evident from the sculpture of the Fourth Century, and even such a pronounced Origenist as Gregory of Nyssa for whom indeed σύμβολον was equivalent to ἀπόδειξις (a setting forth) and γνώρισμα (mark or token) and who laid down the principle "Christianity has its

[1] On Cyril, see Steitz X., pp. 412—428.

strength in the mystic symbols" (ἐν τοῖς μυστικοῖς συμβόλοις ὁ χριστιανισμὸς τὴν ἰσχον ἔχει), [1] as catechist propounded a *physiological* philosophically constructed theory regarding the spiritual nourishing power of the elements which were changed into the body of the Lord, which in religious barbarity far outstrips anything put forward by the Neo-Platonic Mysteriosophs. It makes it plain to us that in the fourth century Christianity was sought after not because it supplied a worship of God in spirit and in truth, but because it offered to men a spiritual sense-enjoyment with which neither Mithras nor any other god could successfully compete. Gregory wished for a spiritual and corporal "communion and mixing" (μετουσία καὶ ἀνάκρασις) with the Redeemer. The only help against the poison which has crept into our body is the antidote of the body of Him who was stronger than death. This antidote must be introduced into the body. It accordingly transforms and alters our body (μεταποιεῖν καὶ μετατιθέναι; μετάστασις, μεταστοιχείωσις, ἀλλοίωσις). The actual body of Christ as immortal is thus the remedy against death; it must therefore, like other sorts of good, be partaken of *bodily*. This partaking takes place in the Supper; for through the act of consecration the bread and wine are changed into the flesh and blood of the Lord (μεταποίησις) in order that through partaking of them our body may be transformed into the body of Christ (μεταστοιχείωσις; see Justin). These transubstantiations are proved by a philosophical exposition of matter and form, potentiality and actuality; at this point Aristotle had already to be brought forward to furnish the necessary proof. The paradox was held to be not really so paradoxical. The body of the Logos, it was affirmed, itself consisted of bread; the bread was virtually (δυνάμει) the body etc. But more important than these dreadful expositions of a pharmaceutical philosophy was the close connection which Gregory formed by means of them between the Eucharist and the Incarnation. He was the first, so far as I know, to do this. The older Fathers also, indeed, while by the eucharistic body they understood the word and the life, always regarded the Incarnation as the fundamental condition, which alone made that

[1] C. Eunomium XI., T. II., p. 704.

use of it possible. But since they did not entertain the idea of the real body of Christ, the Incarnation and Eucharist—apart from some attempts by Athanasius—still remained unconnected.

It was otherwise with Gregory. *For him the transformation of the consecrated bread into the body of Christ was the continuation of the process of the Incarnation.* "If the existence of the whole body depends on nourishment while this consists of food and drink; if, further, bread serves for food, and water mixed with wine for drink, and if the Logos of God, as has been already proved, is united (συνανεκράθη) in his character as God and Logos with human nature, and, having entered our body, produced no different or new constitution for human nature, but rather sustained his body by the usual and fitting means and supported life by food and drink, the food being bread; then, just as in our case, he who sees the bread to some extent perceives the human body therein, because when the bread enters the latter it becomes part of it, so in that case the body which conceals God within it, and which received the bread is to a certain extent identical with the bread... for what is characteristic of all was also admitted regarding the flesh of Christ, namely, that it was also supported by bread, *but the body was by the residence in it of the Divine Logos transformed* (μετεποιήθη) *to a divine sublimity and dignity.* We accordingly are now also justified in believing that the bread consecrated by the word of God is transformed into the body of the God-Logos. For that body was also virtually bread, but was consecrated by the residence in it of the Logos, who dwelt in the flesh. Accordingly as the bread transformed in that body was invested with divine energy we have the same thing happening here. For in the former case the grace of the Word sanctified the body which owed its existence to, and to a certain extent was, bread, and similarly, in the present instance, the bread, as the apostle says, is made holy by God's Word (Logos) and command; not that it is first changed into the body of the Logos by being eaten, but that it is at once transformed into his body by the Logos (by its consecration) in accordance with the saying of the Logos, 'This is my body'." Gregory argues similarly as regards the wine and blood, and

then continues: "Since then that flesh which received God also
received this portion (wine, blood) into its substance, and God
made manifest by that means interfused himself in the perishable nature of men, in order that by communion with deity
the human might be deified; therefore he implants himself in
all who have believed in the dispensation of grace, by means
of the flesh whose substance consists of both wine and bread,
condemning himself to the bodies of believers, so that by union
with that which is immortal man also might become a partici-
pator in immortality. And these things he grants to the power
of the blessing, having therefore transformed the nature of the
phenomena (Ἐπεὶ οὖν καὶ τοῦτο τὸ μέρος [wine, blood] ἡ θεοδόχος
ἐκείνη σὰρξ πρὸς τὴν σύστασιν ἑαυτῆς παρεδέξατο, ὁ δε Φανερωθεὶς
Θεὸς διὰ τοῦτο κατέμιξεν ἑαυτὸν τῇ ἐπικήρῳ τῶν ἀνθρώπων φύσει,
ἵνα τῇ τῆς θεότητος κοινωνίᾳ συναποθεωθῇ τὸ ἀνθρώπινον, τούτου χάριν
πᾶσι τοῖς πεπιστευκόσι τῇ οἰκονομίᾳ τῆς χάριτος ἑαυτὸν ἐνσπείρει
διὰ τῆς σαρκός ἧς ἡ σύστασις ἐξ οἴνου τε καὶ ἄρτου ἐστὶ, τοῖς σώμασι
τῶν πεπιστευκότων κατακρινάμενος, ὡς ἂν τῇ πρὸς τὸ ἀθάνατον
ἑνώσει καὶ ὁ ἄνθρωπος τῆς ἀθανασίας μέτοχος γένοιτο. Ταῦτα δὲ
δίδωσι τῇ τῆς εὐλογίας δυνάμει πρὸς ἐκεῖνο μεταστοιχειώσας τῶν
Φαινομένων τὴν Φύσιν). It was henceforth impossible for any
other theory to outbid this one, which followed the practice.
It is the foundation for all farther developments, especially the
liturgical, and is responsible for nominally Christian heathenism.
*It sprang from Gregory the "spiritualist", the disciple of Ori-
gen!* It explains why all purer science necessarily ceased. No
independent theology could long hold its ground side by side
with such an intoxicating speculation.[1] For the rest, Gregory
did not teach transubstantiation in the later Western sense.
According to him only the form (εἶδος) of the elements, not the
substance, was changed. His theory is therefore rightly described
as one of transformation. Nor was he quite clear about the
relation of the eucharistic to the real—transfigured—body. He
did not entertain the idea of a complete identity, but only of
a qualitative unity. The consecrated elements were qualitatively
identical with the body, which the Logos had employed as his
organ.

---

[1] Catech. magna 37, Steitz X., pp. 435—446.

Chrysostom, on the contrary, spoke of a complete identity, and did not shrink from the boldest and most repugnant expressions. "In proof of his love he has given us the body pierced with nails, that we might hold it in our hands and eat it; *for we often bite those whom we love much.*"[1] "Christ permits us to glut ourselves on his flesh." Chrysostom won't remove our horror of cannibalism by spiritualising the rite. "In order then that the disciples might not be afraid, he drank first, and thus introduced them undismayed into the Communion of his mysteries; therefore he drank his own blood." "Reflect, that the tongue is the member with which we receive the awful sacrifice." "Our tongue is reddened by the most awful blood." "He has permitted us who desire it not merely to see, but to touch and eat and bury our teeth in his flesh, and to intermingle it with our own being." The fact that at the same time the benefit contained in the Lord's Supper is described as being perceived by the mind, a νοητόν, hardly affects the result, for of course the body, however real, of a God is a νοητόν. Like Gregory, Chrysostom speaks of a refashioning and transforming (μεταρρυθμίζειν and μετασκευάζειν) of the elements, which Christ, the Holy Ghost, effects through the priest by means of the invocation—not of the words of institution which do not constitute the medium among the Greeks. Very instructive, moreover, is the reference to the Incarnation. "The Church sees the Lord lying in the crib wrapped in swaddling-clothes— an awful and wonderful spectacle; for the Lord's table takes the place of the crib, and here also lies the body of the Lord, not wrapped in swaddling-clothes, but surrounded on all sides by the Holy Ghost." Chrysostom, accordingly, went decidedly farther in this point also than Gregory, with whom he agreed in the assumption of an essentially corporeal effect of the participation.[3]

---

[1] Hom. 24 in 1 ep. ad. Cor. c. 4.

[2] Hom. de beato Philogono 3; see Steitz X., pp. 446—462, from whom also the above quoted passages are taken.

[3] Compare also the offensive expressions of Theodoret (Interpret. in cant. cantic. c. 3, Opp. II., p. 89 Schulze): οἱ τοίνυν ἐσθίοντες τοῦ νυμφίου τὰ μέλη καὶ πίνοντες αὐτοῦ τὸ αἷμα τῆς γαμικῆς αὐτοῦ τυγχάνουσι κοινωνίας. But the same author

To Dionysius, who was thoroughly Neoplatonic, the ethical central notion consists in mystical union [= θέωσις (deification) = ἀφομοίωσις (likeness) + ἕνωσις (union)]. The complicated "hierarchies" in heaven and in the Church—"purifying, illuminating, perfecting" = deacons, priests, and bishops—act as intermediaries. This they accomplish by the mysteries which likewise are graded; to the bishops is reserved the consecration of the priests, the consecration of the anointing oil and of the altar. So the Lord's Supper, as in the case of Cyril of Jerusalem, is no longer treated apart; it has its place along with five other mysteries. Dionysius was enabled to evolve a mystical doctrine dealing with each mystery by a close examination of its ritual performance. A deeper sense is given to each little detail; it has a symbolical significance; "symbolical" is indeed not a strong enough term. There is really a mystery present; but this conception does not prevent the expert in mysteries from after all regarding everything as the covering of a single inner process: the return of the soul from multiplicity to unity, from finitude and disunion to the ocean of the divine being. The Eucharist which accompanies and completes the process contributes to that which was begun in baptism. The liturgical performance is rendered symbolical in every part. Moreover, the consecrated elements are themselves treated as symbols. The realistic view of Chrysostom is not found in Dionysius. *The realism consists, so to speak, in the fixity and integrity of the liturgical performance.* Otherwise it is true of the Lord's Supper, what Dionysius says generally of all mysteries: "The majority of us do not believe in what is said regarding the divine mysteries; for we only see them through the sensible symbols attached to them. We ought to strip the symbols off and behold them by themselves when they have become naked and pure; for thus seeing them we should revere the spring of life pouring into itself, both beholding it existing by itself and being a kind of single force, simple, self-moved, self-acting, not abandoning itself, but furnishing the science of all sciences, and

---

writes (Dial. Inconfus.): οὐδὲ γὰρ μετὰ τὸν ἁγιασμὸν τὰ μυστικὰ σύμβολα τῆς οἰκείας ἐξίσταται φύσεως. μένει γὰρ ἐπὶ τῆς προτέρας οὐσίας καὶ τοῦ σχήματος καὶ τοῦ εἴδους καὶ ὁρατά ἐστι καὶ ἁπτά, οἷα καὶ πρότερον ἦν.

ever itself seen by itself." [1] And it is characteristic that it was precisely the consecration of the monk which constituted the highest mystery. Nothing but the tradition of the Church prevented Dionysius ranking it actually above the Eucharist. Dionysius does not discuss the Eucharistic sacrifice at all. [2] The following period was set the task of combining the crass realism of Gregory of Nyssa and Chrysostom with the ritualism of Dionysius, without at the same time wholly destroying the hidden spiritual element which depreciated all rites in comparison with the inner feeling and exaltation. But from the beginning of the fifth century conceptions of the Eucharist were very decidedly influenced by the Christological differences. If the conception of the Eucharist was connected with that of the Incarnation, then it could not be a matter of indifference to the former, whether in the latter the two natures were held to be fused in one or to remain separate. *Monophysites and Orthodox, however, had always been and remained of one mind regarding the Lord's Supper.* Cyril argued over and over again from the Lord's Supper in support of the Incarnation and *vice versâ*, and it was strictly due to him that the Church learned the connection between the two and never lost it. Even Leo I. can discuss it. [3] Nay, the incorruptibility of the Eucharistic body was now accepted without question, while this view, when applied to the Incarnation, was called, at least in later times, Aphthartodoketism. Cyril had no fixed doctrinal formula for the Lord's Supper; he did not go so far as Chrysostom. [4] But since the body was to him, because of the one

---

[1] Dionys. ep. 9, 1 ed. Corder (1755) I., p. 612: "'Απιστοῦμεν οἱ πολλοὶ τοῖς περὶ τῶν θείων μοστηρίων λόγοις· θεώμεθα γὰρ μόνον αὐτὰ διὰ τῶν προσπεφυκότων αὐτοῖς αἰσθητῶν συμβόλων. Δεῖ δὲ καὶ ἀποδύντας αὐτὰ ἐφ' ἑαυτῶν γυμνὰ καὶ καθαρὰ γενόμενα ἰδεῖν· οὕτω γὰρ ἂν θεώμενοι σεφθείημεν πηγὴν ζωῆς εἰς ἑαυτὴν χεομένην καὶ ἐφ' ἑαυτῆς ἑστῶσαν ὁρῶντες καὶ μίαν τινὰ δύναμιν, ἁπλῆν, αὐτοκίνητον αὐτοενέργητον, ἑαυτὴν οὐκ ἀπολείπουσαν, ἀλλὰ γνῶσιν πασῶν γνώσεως ὑπάρχουσαν, καὶ ἀεὶ δι' ἑαυτῆς ἑαυτὴν θεωμένην.

[2] Mönchsweihe de eccles. hierarch. I. 6, Abendmahl l. c. I. 3, pp. 187—198; on Dionysius' whole teaching on the Sacraments, see Steitz XI., pp. 216—229.

[3] Ep. 59.

[4] On the doctrine of the Lord's Supper as held by Theodore, Theodoret, Nestorius, and Pseudo-Chrysostom, see Steitz XII, pp. 217—435. Theodoret can be described with most reason as a believer in the symbolical character of the rite.

nature made flesh (μία φύσις σεσαρκωμένη), God's body, it was
in the full sense of the term "life-giving" (ζωοποιός). Accordingly
he also maintained that it was not, as Nestorius taught, the
body of a man that lay on the altar, but the body of God.[1]
When we partake of the flesh of Christ, he implants it in us;
he does not thereby become man in us—this mystical inference
is rejected,—but our body is transformed and becomes immortal. We do not yet find in Cyril, however, the contention
that the real body of Christ is present in the eucharistic body;
it is rather only an operative presence that is meant; the eucharistic body is identical in its effects with the real.[2] It was the strict
Monophysites who could bring the eucharistic and the earthly
body quite closely together, because they also held the earthly
body to be imperishable;[3] while the Severians still kept the
two apart. But even the strict Monophysites did not, so far as
is known, advance beyond identity in operative power.[4] The
decisive step was taken in the age of the orthodox renaissance
under the shield of Aristotle, accordingly by the scholastics of
the sixth century. Here we have above all and first to name
Eutychius, Patriarch of Constantinople in the time of Justinian.
He based his view "on the conception derived from the system
of Dionysius, that the cause exists by itself apart from its effects,
but multiplies itself potentially in them and enters wholly into
each, and proved that the ascended body abides complete [in
substance] and undivided in itself [in heaven], and yet is received completely by each communicant in the portion of
bread dispensed to him." Eutychius teaches a real *multiplication of one and the same body of Christ* in its antitypes—for
as such he still describes the consecrated elements; but this

---

Yet on the other hand it was maintained in the school of Theodore, in order to
separate deity and humanity in Christ, that in the Lord's Supper the humanity of
the Redeemer is received. This was very stoutly and acutely opposed by Leontius (in Mai, Vet. Script. nova coll. VI., p. 312) and that as a deification of man.

[1] Ep. 12 ad Cœlest.

[2] On Cyril, see Steitz XII., pp. 235—245. Nilus held the same view, l. c., pp.
245—248.

[3] Anastasius Sinaita made experiments to refute them, demonstrating that the
consecrated host actually did decay; Steitz XII., pp. 215, 271 f.

[4] Steitz XII., pp. 248—256.

multiplication is not one of substance, but of power. At any rate the separate existence of the eucharistic body side by side with the real is here for the first time given up. [1] Even before this, Isidore of Pelusium had demonstrated that the eucharistic body passed through the same stages of deification (θέωσις) as the real. "It is partaken as capable of suffering and mortal; for it is broken and is bruised by our teeth; yet it is not destroyed, but is transformed in the communicant into the immortal body." [2]

John of Damascus settled this question also. [3] In the 13th chapter of Book IV. of his system of doctrine he gave a theory of the mysteries—Baptism and the Lord's Supper—based on that of Gregory of Nyssa, but at the same time he was the first to perfect the conception of the identity of the eucharistic and the real body of Christ. John begins with the corruption of humanity and the Incarnation. From the latter we obtain the new birth and the twofold food, that we may become sons and heirs of God. The birth and food required to be spiritual as well as corporeal, for we are both. As regards the food, he himself in the last night ate the ancient passover, and then gave the New Testament. God is all powerful and creates by word and spirit. As he sent forth the light, as his spirit formed a body from the flesh of the virgin and without seed, so the same spirit, falling like rain on the field, changes bread and wine into the flesh and blood of Christ; an analogy drawn from the process of nourishment as in Gregory of Nyssa. We may ask here as Mary did: How can that be? And we must once more answer: The Holy Spirit comes upon it. And in fact God has taken for his purpose the commonest things that we through the common and natural may be transplanted into the supernatural. But he now writes: "The body is truly made one with the deity, *the body which came from the holy virgin,*

---

[1]   Steitz XII., pp. 214, 256—262.

[2]   Steitz XII., pp. 215, 262 ff.

[3]   On the mystics before him and after Dionysius, and their in part significant modification of the ideas of Dionysius under the influence of Aristotle, see Steitz. XI., pp. 229—253. How closely the Trinity, Incarnation, and Eucharist were conceived to be connected, in the 7th century, may be seen from the Confession of Macarius of Antioch at the sixth Council, Mansi XI., p. 350 sq.

not that the body which was assumed comes down from heaven, but the very bread and wine are transformed into the body and blood of God. And if you ask how this happens, it is enough for you to hear that it is by the Holy Spirit, just as the Lord also by the Holy Spirit assumed flesh for himself and in himself." [1] In what follows the view is expressly rejected that it is a different body of Christ that is in question: there are not two bodies, but one. Further: "The bread and wine are not types of the body and blood of Christ; not so, but the very body of the Lord deified." [2] The bread of the communion is not simple bread, but is united with the deity; it has accordingly two natures. The body united with the deity is, however, not one nature, but the one is that of the body, the other that of the deity combined with it, so that the two together constitute not one nature but two. Only the not yet consecrated elements, moreover, are to be called "antitypes"; in this way Basil also used the word (!). The mystery, however, is called "participation" because through it we possess a share in the deity of Jesus, but "communion" first, because we have communion with Christ, and secondly, because by the holy food we are united with one another, one body of Christ, members in his body, and therefore of one another. Therefore we have anxiously to watch lest we "participate" with heretics, or allow them to "participate" with us. Finally, it is still to be noticed that, according to John, the sacred food was not subject to the natural processes in the body.

This is the classical doctrine of the Lord's Supper in the Greek Church up to the present day. By the Holy Ghost bread and wine are received into the body of Christ. The eucharistic body is that which was born the virgin, not, however, by a transubstantiation, as if the body of Christ descended suddenly from heaven and took the place of the elements, but by trans-

---

[1] Σῶμά ἐστιν ἀληθῶς ἡνωμένον θεότητι, τὸ ἐκ τῆς ἁγίας παρθένου σῶμα, οὐχ ὅτι τὸ ἀναληφθὲν σῶμα ἐξ οὐρανοῦ κατέρχεται, ἀλλ' ὅτι αὐτὸς ὁ ἄρτος καὶ οἶνος μεταποιοῦνται εἰς σῶμα καὶ αἶμα Θεοῦ. εἰ δὲ τὸν τρόπον ἐπιζητεῖς, πῶς γίνεται, ἀρκεῖ σοι ἀκοῦσαι, ὅτι διὰ πνεύματος ἁγίου, ὥσπερ καὶ ἐξ τῆς ἁγίας θεοτόκου διὰ πνεύματος ἁγίου ἑαυτῷ καὶ ἐν ἑαυτῷ ὁ κύριος σάρκα ὑπεστήσατο.

[2] Οὐκ ἔστι τύπος ὁ ἄρτος καὶ ὁ οἶνος τοῦ σώματος καὶ αἵματος Χριστοῦ· μὴ γένοιτο, ἀλλ' αὐτὸ τὸ σῶμα τοῦ κυρίου τεθεωμένον.

formation and assumption, just as in the Incarnation. The bread-body is received into the real body and is thus identical with it. [1] That is the last word of the Greek Church—only now was the mystery perfect. Only now was the real presence of the true body originated, the doctrine which the Churches of to-day, except the Reformed, wrongly assign to antiquity, nay, to the Apostolic age itself. It is true that Scholastics and Mystics have taught much that was original on the Lord's Supper in the Greek Churches since John ; spiritualism also was not abolished ; but the history of dogma can give no place to these individual pronouncements. [2] The sacrificial character and the reference to the crucifixion, which are so strikingly neglected by John, were again made prominent in after times. [3] The physical and liturgical miracle was never, however, so logically analysed or reduced to the categories of being and phenomenon, substance and accident, in the Greek Church as in the West. Attempts at this were made ; but they never obtained any far-reaching importance in the official doctrine. The second Nicene Council of A.D. 787 took its stand on the conception of John. The last exclamations of the assembled Fathers were : " Whoever docs not confess that Christ, on the side of his humanity, has an unlimited form, let him be anathema. May the memory of Germanus (of Constantinople) and of John (of Damascus) endure for ever." [4]

---

[1] Steitz XII., pp. 216 f., 275—286.

[2] See Steitz XIII., pp. 3—66. The two controversies about the Lord's Supper of 1155 and 1199 are relatively the most important.

[3] The magical view of the Lord's Supper is also seen in the practice of children's communion, which first attested by Cyprian (by Leucius ?), became the rule in the East, after infant Baptism had been established. Participation in the Lord's Supper was even held to be absolutely necessary ; so already Cyprian, Testim. III. 25. See the Art. "Communion of Children" by v. Zezschwitz in Herzog's R.-Encykl., 2nd ed.

[4] See Mansi XIII., p. 398 sq. and Hefele III., p. 473. On the present doctrine and practice of the Greek Churches as regards the Eucharist, see Gass, Symbolik, pp. 252—277.; Kattenbusch l. c. I., p. 410 ff. There as also in the Index of Hefele's Conciliengesch. (esp. Vol III. under " Abendmahl", " Messe ") we obtain information also as to the numerous detailed decisions bearing on the rite (leavened bread, etc.); compare Heineccius, Abbildung der alten und neuen griechischen Kirche, 1711.

§ 2. *Christianity of the Second Rank.*

There existed in Christendom, ever since there was a *doctrina publica*, *i.e.*, from the end of the second century, a kind of subsidiary religion, one of the second rank, as it were subterranean, different among different peoples, but everywhere alike in its crass superstition, naïve doketism, dualism, and polytheism. "When religions change, it is as if the mountains open. Among the great magic snakes, golden dragons and crystal spirits of the human soul, which ascend to the light, there come forth all sorts of hideous reptiles and a host of rats and mice." Every new religion invigorates the products of the ancient one which it supersedes. In one aspect of it we know very little of the "Christianity" of the second rank, for it had no literary existence;[1] in another we are thoroughly familiar with it; for we only need to set before us, and to provide with a few Christian reminiscences, the popular conditions and rites with which Christianity came in contact in different provinces,[2] as also the tendencies, everywhere the same, of the superstitious mob, tendencies inert in the moral sphere, exuberant in the realm of fancy. Then we have this second-class Christianity. It consisted in worship of angels—demigods and demons, reverence for pictures, relics, and amulets, a more or less impotent enthusiasm for the sternest asceticism—therefore not infrequently strictly dualistic conceptions—and a scrupulous observance of certain things held to be sacred, words, signs, rites, ceremonies, places, and times. There probably never was an age in which Christendom was free from this "Christianity", just as there never will be one in which it shall have been overcome. But in the fully formed Catholic Church as it passes over into the Middle Ages, this Christianity was not only dragged along with it as a tolerated, because irremovable, burden, but it was to a very large extent legitimised, though under safeguards, and fused with the *doctrina publica*. Catholicism as it meets us in Gregory the Great and in the final decisions of the seventh

---

[1] Yet some of the apocryphal Gospels, Acts of the Apostles, Apocalypses, etc., come under this head.

[2] The works of Usener and Dieterich (Νεκυια, Leipzig, 1893) are valuable.

Council, presents itself as the most intimate union of Christianity
of the first order with that subterranean, thoroughly superstitious,
and polytheistic "Christianity"; and the centuries from the third
to the eighth mark the stages in the process of fusion, which
seems to have reached an advanced point even in the third
and was yet reinforced from century to century to a most extraordinary extent.

It is the business of the historian of the Church and of
civilisation to describe these developments in detail, and to
show how in separate provinces the ancient gods were transformed into Christian saints, angels, and heroes, and the ancient
mythology and cultus into Christian mythology and local worship.
This task is as æsthetically attractive as that other which is
closely allied to it, the indication of the remains of heathen
temples in Christian Churches. The temple of Mithras which
became St. George's Church, proves that St. George was
Mithras; in St. Michael the ancient Wotan had been brought
to life again, just as Poseidon in St. Nicholas; the different
"mothers of God", who were honoured with all sorts of sacred
offerings—one preferred fruits, another animals—only show that
Demeter, Venus, Juno, and countless other great mothers and
holy or unholy virgins, had merged in the one mother.—The
provincial calendars and various "Church Years" conceal significant reminiscences from the old heathen times.   Here, however, we are only interested in the questions of principle, how
far all this had forced its way into the *doctrina publica*, and
how it was possible for that religion, whose strong point had
once been a horror of idols, to admit this stuff as something
sacred.

As regards the second question, the points of contact existed
in the *doctrina publica* itself. The following may have been
the most important.   In the first place, the *doctrina* had been
constructed by the aid of Greek and Roman intellectual culture
and philosophy. These, however, were connected by a thousand
ties with mythology and superstition, which were not got rid
of by assigning a "noumenon" to everything. We need only
recall the single instance of Origen to see that the father of
free and spiritual theology was at the same time the patron of

every superstition that would admit of receiving the least grain of spiritual contents. Secondly, the *doctrina publica* sanctioned the Old Testament. Before this, indeed, and even to some extent in the time of the conflict with Gnosticism great pains had been taken to prove that the Old Testament was a Christian book, and to allegorise all its ceremonial features. But the power of interpretation had weakened more and more in comparison with the strength of the letter. What a wealth was embraced in the book of material drawn from the most varied stages of religious history! This material was sacred. No one indeed now got circumcised, or offered bloody sacrifices, or refrained from eating pork, but what did that signify if everything else gradually came somehow or other to be accepted? From the third century the Church needed infinitely more than a *doctrina publica*; it needed a sacred constitution, holy priests and a holy ritual. The Old Testament from which pretty nearly anything can be legitimised also legitimised this. Thus, side by side with revelation in the form of sacred doctrine, there arose an indefinitely increasing mass of sacred things which could be justified from the Old Testament alone. For its sake the old strict exclusion of the literal meaning of the book and of its ceremonies was abandoned, slowly indeed, but surely. At first the attempt was made to proceed circuitously, and to attribute the ceremonial decrees to the Apostles, because men were still unwilling to appeal directly to the Old Testament commands; but they then became bolder, and finally felt no scruple about using the Old Testament down to matters of detail, the special points of the Temple ritual—the cherubim being cited, for example, in support of the right to worship pictures.

Thirdly, the sacred rites of Baptism, and especially of the Eucharist, offered points of contact for the intrusion of Christianity of the second rank into official Christianity. The public doctrine had already, at a very early date, treated and regarded these rites as mysteries in the ancient sense. Thus the door was thrown wide open to the inrush of everything of the character of a mystery, magic, liturgical miracles, and fetishes. Fourthly, devils and angels had played a great part even in primitive Christianity. The official doctrine, however, at first paid comparatively little heed to them; yet they had always employed the imagination even of the most enlightened. Round these traditions the popular conceptions now gathered, and the *doctrina publica* was almost defenceless against them. When in the fourth and fifth centuries the masses streamed into the Church, it was not in a position, in spite of catechetical instruction, to exercise any control over them, or to examine the (mental) luggage of those desiring admission. Nay, more, the monks, who in the same period had with such extraordinary rapidity obtained full charge of piety, moved in this world of demons and angels, and cherished the ancient mythology under a Christian name. To live in the sphere of pure and impure spirits, to be visited, refreshed, strengthened by the former, and to be tempted and assailed by the latter, soon was held to be a sign of a heroic Christianity; and to this the official doctrine had to accommodate itself. Besides the cultus, men obtained their edification from a pious light literature whose dualism and exotic character might lead the critic to assign it wrongly to the Gnosticism of the second century. [1]   But the Church was perhaps even more strongly influenced by the Neoplatonic doctrine of spirits. In devoting itself to a lofty intuition, and, like the Gnostics of old, seeing between God and the world hosts of graded æons (angels) who as the " heavenly hierarchy "—in reality as cosmical powers —reduced the many to the one, this doctrine legitimised the superstitious and barbarous conceptions of demigods and genii. The one God, whom the people had never understood, threatened to disappear, even in the views of refined theologians, behind the whole complicated intermediaries who appeared more tangible and therefore more trustworthy. Who can wonder that now the cultured Christian, if a mystic, also preferred in his religious difficulties to resort to these courts rather than to turn directly to God? If the supreme God had appointed and set these courts between himself and his world, then it would

---

[1]   To the monks there fell as a rule in the East the role of mediators between Christianity of the first and second rank. They perhaps contributed most strongly to the transference of catchwords of the former into the latter, and of the spirit of the latter into the former.

be presumption and aimless effort to ignore them. Only the
strict ascetic might venture that. But he also would rather
dwell in fancy in the magnificent, beautifully ordered world
of spirits, where the golden buckets ascend;[1] he would rather
picture the fulness and variety of the immortal life than dwell
for ever on the desolate and terrifying thought of the One,
who was so incomprehensible, that not even his Being could
be conceived.

Fifthly, as a residuum of the idea that all Christians were
"saints", and that the Church possessed apostles, prophets, and
spiritual teachers, the conviction had remained that there had
been a Heroic Age, and that those who had then won a name
for themselves were "saints". They were added to the Patriarchs and Old Testament Prophets, and they continued to
receive successors in the martyrs and great ascetics. The most
cultured theologians had already set up theories of the power
of these heroes to intercede with God, and of their special
relation to Christ. The anniversaries of the birth or death of
the saints were celebrated, and thus they offered themselves in
the most natural way to take the place of the dethroned gods
and their festivals. They fell into line with the angelic powers,
and were held to be more trustworthy than the latter. Among
them Mary came to the front, and the course of the development of dogma specially favoured her, and her alone. A woman,
a mother, made her appearance in proximity to the deity; and
thus at last it became possible to include in Christianity the
recognition of that which had been most foreign to primitive
Christianity—homage paid to sex, the sacred, the divine, in a
female form. The Gospel to the Hebrews had already, indeed,
made the Lord say, "My mother the Holy Ghost"; but this
thought was yet sexless, so to speak, and was besides never
made use of in the great Church. Mary now became the
mother, the bearer, of God.

Sixthly, from the earliest times the Christians had looked on
death as holy; it was the birth-hour of the true life; for in
this world life meant for the Christians to practise dying, and
to have died was to live in immortality. Accordingly, every-

---

1 The Manichæans held a similar doctrine.

thing connected with blessed death, had already been touched by the breath of immortality. The martyrs exhaled this breath; therefore their very bones were more precious than gold or jewels. The worship of the dead began early, and only a few opposed it. The heathen use of fetishes and amulets revived in the cultus of the dead and of relics; in this form it was destitute of the æsthetic charm which antiquity knew how to give to its amulets and little sanctuaries, and for this reason the refined taste of enthusiastic Epigoni rose in disgust against the veneration of bones and corpses (see Julian's attacks). But the Christians satisfied themselves from the contrast between the sensuous appearance and its religious value that their faith was unique and elevated, since it found the divine in the very dust and fragments of death. Therefore they were certain of not being heathen in revering those amulets and relics; for heathenism sought and found its sacred things in the bloom of life, but Christianity in death. With the service of the relics was most intimately connected the veneration of the saints, and the two led to the veneration of pictures and idols.

For, seventhly, the *doctrina publica*, as has been shown in our whole account, contained to an increasing extent the impulse to transform the μάθησις (doctrine) into mysteries; this impulse it followed continually in the treatment of the Eucharist. But in doing so, it opened up the way to the boundless desire to enjoy the holy everywhere and with the whole five senses, and it then obeyed this desire itself. The Lord's Supper became the centre of an ever extending circle of material sacred things which could be seen, heard, tasted, smelt, and touched. The religious was much more closely connected with the material than with the moral. That, however, meant the relapse to religious barbarism and the worship of images. This might be transfigured in poetry—everything now showed a trace of God; it could even be spiritualised pantheistically—God is the world, and the world is the deity revealed; but within Christianity it was nothing but apostasy. But further, the senses which seek to perceive and therefore do perceive that which is holy, become dull and blind in presence of that which is actually perceptible, and dazzle the reason. The reason became

accustomed to a fabulous world of wonders, and more and
more lost all rational standards. Even the most cultured Fathers
from the fifth century ceased to be capable of distinguishing
between the real and unreal; they were defenceless against the
most absurd tales of the miraculous, and lived in a world of
magic and enchantment. Then there once more emerged
practices which date from the earliest age of civilisation. Sooth-
saying, auguries, examination of sacrifices, inquiries at oracles
of every sort:— they had lost their name and their ritual, but
they were now revived in all that was essential as Christian,
though in new forms. Bibliomancy, questioning the Bible like
a book of oracles, arose. Synods at first denounced it, but
even great doctors of the Church favoured the evil habit.
Ordeals, which were by no means originated by the Germans,
came into vogue. Two clerics of North Africa were suspected
of a scandalous act; both denied the charge; one must have
been guilty; Augustine sent them over sea to the grave of
S. Felix of Nola. There they were to repeat their assertions;
Augustine expected that the saint would at once punish the
liar. At the sixth Council a Monothelite offered to prove the
truth of his confession by writing it and placing it on the
breast of a dead man, when the dead would rise up. *The
Fathers of the Council accepted the test.* In cases of sickness
questions were addressed to this or that saint; the patient slept
in his chapel; on certain days lodging in the chapel was more
effective than on others, etc., etc. The sources of the fifth to
the eighth century contain hundreds of such cases; not only did
the foolish multitude take part in them, but, as the above
passages have shown, the spiritual leaders themselves. The
impulse to mystagogy, and the misguided craving to feel the
proximity of the deity, without being or becoming a new man,
were to blame for this decline and fall. Only two points can
be cited. First, the better Christians still continued to seek
and find an object of thought (νοητόν) in the thousand liturgical
sacred things, the thought and its envelopment interchanged
with each other in an attractive play. Thus these men defended
themselves against the charge of worshipping idols. Secondly,
the honour to be assigned to idols was and continued to be

uncertain; it was not equal to that of God or of Jesus Christ or to the authority of Holy Scripture, and one might even finally disown them; any one might confine himself to the *doctrina publica*, and privately interpret in his own way its sensuous and magical portions, if only he did not attack them. But the poor common people knew nothing of this secret privilege of the learned, nor might they share in it. And even scholars were themselves burdened with an immense amount of stuff to which they had to dedicate their piety. It is the same to-day. The pious regard which is required by the whole complex of ecclesiasticism, intimately interwoven as it is with nationality, restricts the capacity to win independent power in religion, and to take earnestly and devoutly what is really earnest and holy. No religion gains anything through time; it only loses. If a hurricane does not pass over it and purify it again and again, it gets stifled in its own withered foliage. No hurricane has yet swept over the Churches of the East. And yet they possess in the Gospel, which they too read, an element of movement which perhaps in some future time will bring life to the dry bones.

On the worship of angels, see Vol. III., Chap. IV. and Schwane, Dogmengeschichte II., pp. 299—328. The seventh general Synod decided that angels must also be portrayed because they were finite in form, and had appeared to many in a human shape. The theologoumenon of Dionysius, who was not the first to teach it, concerning the nine choirs of angels, obtained general acceptance. The conception of the manifold guardian ministry of the angels became more and more important. Even Schwane confesses here: "the doctrine that every man possessed such a guardian spirit appears to have been allied to the old heathen idea of genii, but was also founded on Holy Scripture" (p. 315). The worship and invocation of angels became established; but the Church held in principle to the position that the angelic cultus was not identified with the worship of God. [1]

---

[1] On the extension of angel-worship we have an interesting bit of evidence as early as the fourth century in Didymus, De trinit. II. 7, p. 250 (ed. Mingarelli): Διὸ μετὰ τὰς ἐκκλησίας καὶ οἶκοι εὐκτήριοι τῷ Θεῷ τῆς προηγορίας ὑμῶν (scil. of

In reference to the Saints, Cyril says in his fifth mystagogic catechism (c. 9); "Then we also remember those who have already fallen asleep, first the Patriarchs, Prophets, Apostles, and martyrs, that God through their prayers and intercession may accept our supplication." So also Augustine. This circle was extended after the fifth century by the addition of holy bishops, monks, and nuns. The power of the Saints to intercede was always the reason why honour and invocation (τιμὴ καὶ ἐπίκλησις) were due to them. The ancient little martyr-chapels of the saints now became great Churches. The complete apotheosis of the saints was denied in principle. The offerings brought on the anniversaries of Saints and Martyrs were always meant for God. But the connecting of the service of the Saints with the eucharistic sacrifice gave the former an extraordinary value. Banquets were regularly held on their anniversaries— a genuinely heathen custom, and in vain did men like Ambrose, Augustine, and Gregory of Nazianzus inveigh against them. The ideas of the communion of the Saints, and its typical import—every class gradually obtained its Saint—were certainly very valuable, and in this sense the worship of the Saints was not entirely unjustifiable; but the harm was greater than the benefit. The worship of God suffered, and crass superstition was introduced, especially in connection with the relics. This was first perceived by the Gallican priest Vigilantius who had witnessed the gross disorder prevalent at the sacred sites of Palestine.[1] Vigilantius (end of the fourth century) went to the roots of the worship of the Saints with his criticism, not only disputing the power of their intercession, but denying its existence, since the Saints were not yet in heaven with Christ. Against him Jerome maintained (c. Vigil. 6) a "ubique esse" of the saints, Apostles, and Martyrs, since they were wherever

the angels) ἐπώνυμοι, ᾧ εὐάρεστος ξυνωρὶς ἀρχαγγέλων, οὐκ ἐν μόναις ταῖς πόλεσιν, ἀλλὰ καὶ στενωποῖς ἰδίᾳ καὶ οἰκίαις καὶ ἀγροῖς ἱδρύθησαν, χρυσῷ καὶ ἀργύρῳ ἢ καὶ ἐλέφαντι κοσμηθέντες· ἴασίν τε οἱ ἄνθρωποι καὶ εἰς τὰ ἀπωτέρω τῆς ἐνεγκαμένης αὐτοὺς χωρία τὰ ἔχοντα οἷον ὡς πρυτάνια ἐπιτευγμάτων τὰ εὐκτήρια προβεβλημένα, οὐκ ὀκνοῦντες καὶ πέλαγος διαλαβεῖν ἣν δέοι μακρόν... ὡς πειραθησόμενοι πλείονος εὐνοίας μὲν τῆς περὶ τὴν πρεσβείαν ἀπὸ ὑμῶν, μετουσίας δὲ τῆς τῶν φιλοτιμουμένων ὑπὲρ τοῦ εὖ ἀγαθῶν παρὰ τοῦ Θεοῦ.

[1] Jerome c. Vigilant. and ep. ad Riparium.

Christ was. Augustine also, who refers to similar contentions, showed that the Saints continued to have the power and the will to participate in earthly things. Vigilantius had rightly perceived the danger of an actual fusion of the service of God and of the Saints, and his attack resulted, at least, in a sharper distinction being drawn in theory. This was also, however, done by the Greeks; they reserved worship (λατρεία) to God, and described the veneration of the Saints, in language already used by Cyril of Alexandria, as a becoming honour (τιμὴ σχετική).[1]

Most offensive was the worship of relics.[2] It flourished to its greatest extent as early as the fourth century, and no Church doctor of repute restricted it. All of them rather, even the Cappadocians, countenanced it. The numerous miracles which were continually wrought by bones and relics seemed to confirm their worship. The Church therefore would not give up the practice, although a violent attack was made upon it by a few cultured heathens, and besides by Manichæans. Moreover, in the Church itself a scanty opposition arose here and there. The strict Arians (Eunomians) appear to have been more backward about this worship (c. Vigil, 8), and Vigilantius assailed the worshippers of relics, with Julian-like acuteness, though he was moved by the thought of the divine worship in spirit and truth. He called the adorers of relics "suppliants to refuse and servants of idols." He would have nothing to do with the lights kindled before relics, the praying and kissing, or the pomp with which they

---

[1] Worship was more and more paid to the saints as ascetics and workers of miracles. Men wished to receive from the miracle-workers what they praised in the ascetics; for the worship was not platonic, but was always covetous. The great patterns for biographies of ascetics were the Life of Anthony by Athanasius, and the Lives of the Egyptian monks by Jerome. These were followed in the West by the saintly novels on Martin of Tours by Sulpicius Severus, and the Egyptian Tales of Johannes Cassianus. Comprehensive works soon appeared in the East, of which the φιλόθεος ἱστορία of Theodoret, the Historia Lausiaca of Palladius, and the corresponding sections of Sozomen's Church History, deserve special mention. The ἀποφθέγματα of Macarius are uniqne. The biographies of saints and martyrs of the Jacobites, Copts and Abyssinians are, thanks to a gloomy and desolate fancy, particularly repulsive. We need only here mention the collection (Simeon Metaphrastes) and the ritual use of the biographies (Menaen, Synaxarien, etc.).

[2] On the differences between East and West in the cultus of the relics, see Sdralek, Art. Reliquien in Kraus, Realencyklop. der Christl. Alterthümer.

were surrounded (c. 4). But that did as little good as his unsuccessful attacks on pilgrimage to the holy sites of Palestine.
Men continued to seek the living among the dead, and soon it
was enjoined as an universal command — and first in the West —
that every altar must have its relics; see Canon 17 of the 6th
Synod of Carthage, and Canon 2 of a Parisian Council in Hefele
III., p. 70. The altar was no longer merely the table of the
Lord, but at the same time the memorial of some Saint or
other. Yet in France it was still necessary for a long time to
defend the practice against Vigilantius who had obtained no
ally in Augustine, although that great theologian well knew
that God required a spiritual service.[1] In the East, after Constantine Copronymus had attacked the relics along with the
images, their worship was expressly enjoined by the seventh
Synod; see the transactions at the fourth and seventh sittings
(Hefele III., pp. 466, 472) as also the seventh Canon of the
Council: "As every sin is followed by others in its train, the
heresy of the iconoclasts dragged other impieties after it. They
have not only taken away the sacred pictures, but they have
abandoned other usages of the Church, which must now be renewed. We order therefore that relics be deposited with the
usual prayers in all temples which have been consecrated without
possessing any. But if in future a bishop consecrates a Church
not having relics he shall be deposed." On the worship of
saints and relics in the modern Greek Church, see Gass, Symbolik, p. 310 ff., Kattenbusch l. c. I., p. 465 f. Along with
relics and pictures the sign of the cross—this from an early
date: see even Justin—the volume of the Gospels, the eucharistic
vessels and many other things were held to be especially holy.
On the cross and the form in which it was to be made, on
which great stress is placed, see Gass, p. 184 f.

Mary takes the first place among the saints. She came into

---

[1] On the continued influence of Vigilantius in France, see the tractate of Faustus
of Reji de symbolo (Caspari, Quellen IV., p. 273); "Ut transeamus ad sanctorum
communionem. Illos hic sententia ista confundit, qui sanctorum et amicorum dei
cineres non in honore debere esse blasphemant, qui beatorum martyrum gloriosam
memoriam sacrorum reverentia monumentorum colendam esse non credunt. In
symbolum prævaricati sunt, et Christo in fonte mentiti sunt, et per hanc infidelitatem
in medio sinu vitæ locum morti aperuerunt."

notice even in the first three centuries.[1] So early began the
legends and aprocryphal narratives that dealt with her; her
place in the Symbol next the Holy Spirit insured a lofty position
to her for all time. Pierius, Alexander of Alexandria, and
Athanasius, already called her mother of God, and her virginity
was maintained before, during and after the birth, the birth
itself being embellished with miracle, as in the case of the
Gnostics. But Mary obtained her chief, her positively dogmatic significance from the fact that the dogma of the Incarnation became the central dogma of the Church. Even the
arguments of Irenæus are in this respect very significant (Mary
and Eve); but it was only from the fourth century that the
consequences were drawn. It would lead us too far to give
here a history of mariolatry even in outline.[2] The orthodox
Fathers of the Greek Church in the fourth century were still
comparatively reserved. Ambrose and Jerome, above all, in
their controversy with Jovinian, initiated the Church in the
worship of Mary.[3] Ambrose who exerted so strong an influence
upon Augustine is especially to be mentioned as patron of this
worship. He taught that Mary took an *active* share in the
work of redemption, and already applied Gen. III., 3 to the
holy virgin. In his time, again, the fables about Mary, which
had long been in existence, began to be recognised as authoritative in the Church. All that had been sung in her praise
by extravagant Latin, Greek, and Syrian poets and novelists,
was consolidated into a kind of doctrine. It was believed as
early as the end of the fourth century that Mary had not died,

---

[1] See Vol. I., p. 258; II., p. 277.

[2] A good review is given by Benrath, "Zur Gesch. der Marienverehrung", re-
printed from the Theol. Studien und Kritik., 1886. A list is given in it of Catholic
literature, in which the works of Marraci, Passaglia, Kurz (1881), Scheeben (1882),
and von Lehner (1881, also a 2nd ed.) are especially noteworthy. Art. "Maria"
by Steitz in the R.-Encykl., Rösch, Astarte Maria (Stud. u. Krit., 1888, pp. 265—
299). Kattenbusch, l. c. I., p. 464 f.

[3] Jovinian, so passionately handled by Jerome, had, in keeping with his depre-
ciatory view of virginity in general, denied among other things the perpetua virginitas of Mary. But other Western writers, like Bonosus and Helvidius, held the
same view, and found supporters in their own time in Illyria. Bonosus held
heterodox views, besides, of the person of Christ (compare the Art. on him in
Herzog's R.-Encykl.).

but had been removed from the earth by a miracle. Yet the
Arabian Collyridians, who presented her with offerings of bread-
cakes, as if she had been a goddess, were anathematised
(Epiph. H. 78). The Nestorian controversy brought Mary into
the centre next Christ. She was the rock from which was hewn
the deified body of the God-Logos. Nestorius cried in vain to
Cyril, and with him to the whole Church, "Don't make the
virgin into a goddess"; at Ephesus Cyril exalted her for ever
in the Catholic Church above all creatures, above Cherubim and
Seraphim, and set her at the right hand of the Son. He started
the *permutatio nominum* by which everything held true of the
Son might be said to a great extent of the mother, because
without her there would have been no God-man. She now
really became a factor in dogma, which cannot be said of any
saint or angel; for the name "she who bore God" (bride of the
Holy Spirit) was thoroughly meant. It may be said in many
respects that the orthodox now taught regarding Mary what
the Arians had taught regarding Christ; she was a demi-god
mediating between God and men. John of Damascus summarised the Greek theory in De fide orth. III., 12 and in the
three homilies devoted to Mary. "The name 'Bearer of God'
represents the whole mystery of the Incarnation. The Holy
Spirit purified Mary with a view to the conception." John adopted
the whole mass of legend up to the Ascension. Her share in
the work of redemption is strongly emphasised; her body remained uncorrupted. Yet it is noteworthy that John was much
more cautious in his dogmatic work than in his homilies.

The Synod of A.D. 754, hostile as it was to saints and
pictures, did not venture to interfere with mariolatry; indeed
it expressly avowed its orthodoxy on this point; but that was
not enough for the opposition. Theodorus Studita described
the iconoclasts as opponents of the worship of Mary—see his
ἐγκώμιον εἰς τὴν κοίμησιν of Mary; and it was only by the Synod
of 787 that feeling in the East was satisfied. But in spite of
all the extravagances with which she was honoured—the successive rise of numerous festivals, the annunciation, birth, death,
reception, introduction into the temple—she is only recognised
after all in Greek dogmatics as the great patroness and inter-

cessor for men. There is not a word of her having been free
from the stain of original sin. It has been rightly said that
she soon took a much more independent position in Western
piety. "The prayers to Mary in the Greek Euchologion have
a very uniform tone, because they dwell persistently on the
desire for support and help." (Gass, l. c. p. 183). In a word,
although she is also called "Lady" by the Greeks, she is not
the "Queen" who rules Christendom and the world, and commands in heaven. She is not the "Mother of sorrows"; that
itself gives a different meaning to the feeling in the two Churches.
But the superstition which is practised among the masses in
connection with her pictures is perhaps worse in the East than
in the West.

The distinctive character of the Greek Church was most
clearly expressed in the worship of pictures, in the form in
which it was dogmatically settled after the controversy on the
subject. [1] There had been pictures from early times, originally
for decorative purposes, and afterwards for instruction, in the
grave-yards, churches, memorial chapels, and houses, and fixed
to all sorts of furniture. Opposition had existed, but it came
to an end in the Constantinian age. The people were to learn
from the pictures the histories they depicted; they were looked
on as the books of the unlearned. [2] At the same time the

---

[1] On the controversy about images, see Mansi XII.—XIV., and the works of John of
Damascus, Theodore Studita, Theophanes, Gregory Hamartolus, Cedrenus, Zonaras,
Constantine Manasses, Michael Glycas, Anastasius and others. Works by Goldast
(1608), Dallaeus (1642), Maimbourg (1683), Spanheim (1686), Walch (Vol. X. of the
Ketzergesch.), Schlosser (1812), Marx (1839), Hefele (Concil. Gesch. III. 2, p. 366 ff.;
IV. 2, p. 1 ff.), Schenk, Kaiser Leo III. (Halle, 1880). On the relation of Armenia
to the image-controversy, see Karapet Ter Mkrttschian, Die Paulikianer (Leipzig,
1893), p. 52 ff., and there also the part on the controversies and the history of the
sects, p. 112 ff., etc.; see especially the K.-Gesch. of Hergenröther. Gass, Symbolik, p. 315 ff. Kattenbusch l. c. I., p. 467 ff., and the monograph by Schwarzlose,
Der Bilderstreit, ein Kampf der griechischen Kirche um ihre Eigenart und ihre
Freiheit, 1890.

[2] But at the same time, some ranked the pictures much higher than exegesis,
as is shown by the interesting letter of Bishop David of Mez-Kolmank on images
and drawings to John Mairogomier (translated by Karapet, l. c., p. 52): ... "This
sect arose after the time of the Apostles, and first appeared among the Romans,
wherefore a great Synod was held at Cæsarea, and the command was given to

picture was to adorn holy places. But still another interest gradually made itself felt, one that had formerly been most strenuously resisted by early Christianity. It is natural for men to desire relics and images of venerated beings, to withdraw them from profane use, and to treat them with deep devotion. Christianity had originally resisted this impulse, so far as anything connected with the deity was concerned, in order not to fall into idolatry. There was less repugnance, however, to it, when it dealt with Christ, and almost none from the first in the case of martyrs and heroic characters. From this point the veneration of relics and pictures slowly crept in again. But from the fifth century it was greatly strengthened, and received a support unheard of in antiquity, through the dogma of the incarnation and the corresponding treatment of the Eucharist. Christ was the image (εἰκών) of God, and yet a living being, nay, a life-giving spirit (πνεῦμα ζωοποιόν); Christ had by the incarnation made it possible to apprehend the divine in a material form, and had raised sensuous human nature to the divine: the consecrated elements were εἰκόνες of Christ and yet were his very body. These ideas introduced thought to a new world. It was not only the Areopagite and the mystics who saw in all consecrated finite things the active symbol of an eternal power, or perceived the superiority of the Christian religion to all others in the very fact that it brought the divine everywhere into contact with the senses. They merely raised to the level of a philosophic view what the common man and the monk had long perceived, namely, that everything secular which has been adopted by the Church became, not only a symbol, but also a vehicle of the sacred. But amid secular things the image, which bore as it were its consecration in itself, appeared to be least secular. Pictures of Christ, Mary, and the saints, had been already worshipped from the fifth

paint pictures in the House of God. These painters became arrogant, and sought to have their art placed above all other ecclesiastical arts. They said: "Our art is light, for, while few read the Holy Scriptures, it enlightens equally old and young." This and other passages by Armenius show, besides, that there were "iconoclastic heretics" long before the Emperor Leo. The Marcionites (Paulicians) also rejected pictures and crosses.

(fourth) century with greetings, kisses, prostration, a renewal of ancient pagan practices. In the naive and confident conviction that Christians no longer ran any risk of idolatry, the Church not only tolerated, but promoted, the entrance of paganism. It was certainly the intention to worship the divine in the material; for the incarnation of deity had deified nature ($\phi\acute{\upsilon}\sigma\iota\varsigma$). A brisk trade was carried on in the seventh and beginning of the eighth century in images, especially by monks; churches, and chapels were crowded with pictures and relics; the practice of heathen times was revived, only the sense of beauty was inverted. It was not fresh life that seemed fair, but, though a trace of the majestic might not be lacking, it was the life consecrated to asceticism and death. We do not know how far artistic incapacity, how far the dogmatic intention, contributed to the Byzantine ideal of the saints. "Authentic" pictures were in existence, and numberless copies were made from them. By their means, monkish piety, engaged in a stupid staring at sacred things, ruled the people, and dragged Christianity down to deeper and deeper depths.

But this monkish piety, which prevailed from the Bishops down, had become more and more independent in relation to the State. None of his successors had mastered the Church, like Justinian; and it was the aim of the iconoclastic emperors to reduce it to complete subjection to the State, to make it a department of the State. They sought at the same time to have a State Church into which they could force the sects, Jews and Mohammedans, without imposing what was most obnoxious to them, that which made official Christianity into heathenism —the worship of images. They meant therefore to decide what was Christian, and how the cultus ought to be framed, and in doing so they were aided by the fact that it could be shown without any difficulty that the worship of images was something relatively novel and alien. We cannot say more; for they themselves were violent and rude barbarians, military upstarts, who depended on the sword. They had abandoned the idea of the Church as the chief support of the empire; it was to be the chief servant. Instead of priests they had soldiers. They merely wished that the Church should not give trouble, and that it

should be possible in any given case to make whatever use of
it the State might require. Image-worship may look like religious barbarism; but it was associated with all the spiritual
forces still possessed at that time in Christendom. The iconoclastic imperial power was much more barbarous, though we
have to admit that Constantine Copronymus possessed brilliant
gifts as a ruler. However, the emperors found bishops who made
common cause with them, and it cannot be denied that some
of these had religious motives for attacking the images. Here
and there the hostility of the Jews and of Islam may have set
them thinking about the matter; others sought for means of
winning or conciliating the Mohammedans. Their opponents
described the Arabians as the teachers of the iconoclastic
emperors.

In A.D. 726 Leo the Isaurian took the matter in hand.[1] A
general opposition at once arose. "The king must not decide
concerning faith" (μὴ δεῖν βασιλέα περὶ πίστεως λόγον ποιεῖσθαι).
This general idea accompanied the whole dispute. From the
days of Maximus Confessor, the leaders of the Greek Church
insisted on the independence of the Church in relation to the
State, and the Roman Bishops supported them in their efforts.
They were for that very reason on the side of image-worship,
just as, conversely, Charlemagne and his Franks were averse

---

[1] Schwarzlose (l. c., p. 36 ff.) has anew examined the origin of the controversy, in order to determine the external causes. But the matter has not yet
been made clear. The following points fall to be considered. (1) Lesser reac-
tions against the worship of images, which proceeded from the bosom of the
Church even before the outbreak of the controversy, but which were only locally
important. (2) Accusations by the Jews that the Christians ran counter to the
prohibition of images in the Old Testament; the intervention of an Arabian Khalif,
A.D. 723 (Jezid II.), against the Christian worship of images and of Mary (influenced
by Judaism?); influence of the Jews on Leo the Isaurian (?). (3) A theological
iconoclastic party in Phrygia, gathered round the Bishop of Nacolia [on this Schwarzlose, as it seems to me rightly, lays particular stress]; this party perhaps took its
stand on ancient Montanistic and Novatian reminiscences—the Paulicians are also
said to have been inconoclasts; Leo's contact with the above party in his time of
military service. (4) The resolve of the Emperors no longer to depend for support
on the spiritual power of the Church, but on the army, yet on the other hand to
perfect the imperial papacy—after the pattern of the Khalif: βασιλεὺς καὶ ἱερεύς
εἰμι. Karapet, l. c., lays stress on the part played by Islam, but will have nothing to
do with Jewish influences. The Emperor wished to play the same part as the Khalif.

from it. At the same time the influence of other motives than those of ecclesiastical politics should not be denied. [1] It was perhaps the greatest and the least expected crisis ever experienced by the Byzantine Church. [2] The issue deprived it of any further independent history, of middle ages, or of a modern era. The image-worshippers, with the Pope at their head, replied to the imperial edict by referring to express divine statutes, to the Labarum of Constantine, and to the great Fathers of the fourth century, who had taught that the worship passed from the image to its prototype. [3] They appealed to a picture at Paneas of which Eusebius had spoken, but above all to the incarnation of the Logos. "Had God not become man, we would not portray him in a human form." The prohibitions of the Old Testament signified nothing to the contrary; for idols are only pictures of things which do not exist. We do not worship idols like the golden calf. He who makes use of the Old Testament in the Jewish fashion and charges the Church with idolatry is a reprobate Jew. Besides, Israel had possessed divine images of its own; it only refused to value them—Moses' rod, the golden pitcher, the cover of the ark etc.; had it worshipped these, it would not have fallen down before idols. All sculpture made in the name of God was venerable and holy. [4] These were the most important arguments.

But the Emperor appointed a Patriarch favourable to him in Constantinople, and sought to get the Pope of Rome into his power. The latter, in his letters to him [5] defending the images, emphasized the points, first, that there were χειροποίητα (images made with hands) which had been prompted by God, and were therefore sacred and, secondly, ἀχειροποίητα (not made with hands),

---

[1] Reuter, Gesch. der relig. Aufkläring in MA. I., p. 10 ff.

[2] On the external course of the controversy in detail, see Schwarzlose, l. c., p. 51 ff.

[3] A passage from the works of Basil was especially important (δι' εἰκόνος ἡ γνῶσις τοῦ ἀρχετύπου γίνεται); but Funk (Quartalschr., 1888) has shown that while Basil certainly uttered this saying, his meaning was different from that of the later image-worshippers; by εἰκών he meant Christ himself to whom the worship passed.

[4] Gregory II. Ep. ad German. in Mansi XIII., p. 91 sq.

[5] Mansi XII., pp. 959 sq., 975 sq.

as *e.g.*, the picture which Christ had sent to Abgar. The latter, the ἀχειροποίητα, played a great, indeed the decisive, role in the Church of the East. Moreover, we see from the Pope's letters that the imperial edict not only affected image worship as the veneration of idols, stones, walls, and boards, but also the veneration of martyrs as polytheism, and that the military Emperor plumed himself on his likeness to Josiah (Hezekiah). Thereupon the Pope wrote him that the dogmas of the Church were the affair of Bishops and not of the Emperor; as the former might not interfere in civil matters, so neither might the latter in ecclesiastical. The Emperor replied that he was at once Emperor and Priest. But Gregory was not to be dismayed; his second letter was even more forcible than his first. John of Damascus, securely protected by a Khalif, also raised his voice in three apologies on behalf of the images. [1] In these the adoration of images is made to form an integral part of the dogmatic theory of the Incarnation. We adore the Creator who became a creature; with him is inseparably connected the purple garment of the body. Therefore, while God himself cannot be portrayed, the incarnate God can. The Mosaic law only forbade the 'adoration of service' (προσκύνησις λατρείας), but not adoration (προσκύνησις) in general. Images are visible forms representative of the invisible; the Son alone indeed is a perfect (identical) copy; but other images are also connected with the subject they portray, and from eternity one of every creature has existed in the presence of God. Gregory and John have a very great deal in common in their arguments, so that we see clearly how dependent the former was on Greek writers, [2] but not only is the whole subject more thoroughly treated in John, but it is more strictly based on dogmatics. He even goes so

---

[1] Opp. ed. Lequien I., pp. 305—390; see Langen, Joh. von Damasc., p. 129 ff. Schwarzlose (l. c., pp. 202—223) has described very thoroughly the theology of the supporters of images. On the third of the Damascene's apologies, see l. c., p. 103 ff., on the spurious letter to the Emperor Theophilus, p. 109 ff.

[2] Apparently this opinion is not yet sufficient. Following doubts already expressed by Semler, Rössler, Malfatti, and Duchesner, Schwarzlose (l. c., p. 113 ff.) has brought forward reasons worth considering for holding that Gregory's two letters in their present form cannot have come from the hand of Gregory II. Interpolations have been inserted by a Greek.

far as to see in the rejection of images Manichæism, the contempt of matter which the God-Logos had hypostatically united
with himself.   We find a frightful confusion of ideas in an
apparently simple and solid argument.   All dogma, wherever
John lays his hands on it, culminates in the images. The doctrines of the Holy Ghost, of death, unction and the cross, all
require this worship.

But the freedom of the Church from the State was also
strongly emphasised by the subject of the Khalif, so that once
more the parallelism with Gregory's letters is striking, so much
so as almost to cast doubt on the genuineness of the latter or
of John's apologies.   It was the prerogative not of Emperors
but of Councils to control Church affairs.   The power of binding and loosing had been granted not to Emperors, but to
Apostles, Bishops, and Doctors.   In the second address John
assails the Emperor still more sharply.   At the same time, he
now maintains that the Church is governed by the written and
unwritten institutions of the Fathers; the worship of images
belongs to the latter.   It was difficult to produce proof from
tradition, and many patristic passages could be instanced against
it.   Hence "unwritten" tradition.   The adoration of the cross
and of relics was always embraced in the defence, and even
the Old Testament analogy was cited in its support.   In the
third address it is again declared that adoration is due only
to God and the body united with the Deity, and that the incarnate God is alone to be portrayed.   Then the abandonment
of Scriptural evidence for images is made up for by an indirect
proof.   Here it occurs to the apologist, that in fact all the
catchwords of orthodox dogma do not exist in the Bible.
Next, we have a detailed philosophy of images: the Son is the
perfect resemblance of God, and the Holy Ghost of the Son.
Images are the ideas of things; man is the likeness of God;
the word is the image of thought; recollection of the past and
representation of the future are images.   Everything is an image, and the image is everything.   The saints themselves are
worshipped in their pictures.   This is followed by the treatment of the Eucharist, next by a long section on the degrees
of worship; it is abasement in presence of the object revered.

To this is appended the mention of the curative shadow of the Apostles, the handkerchief, and the boys who ridiculed Elisha. Thus we are led up to relics, saints, and pictures, the crib, Golgotha, the cross, nails, sheets, swaddling-clothes, and vesture, and again to books of the Gospels, sacred vessels, candlesticks and crosses etc. in the Church. Even the adoration of princes is recalled. Numerous patristic passages, some of them forged, are quoted.

After the death of Leo, and the overthrow of an anti-emperor supported by those friendly to images, the son of the former, Constantine Copronymus, carried out his father's policy with an iron hand. He summoned the general Synod, already planned by his father, to Constantinople A.D. 754. Three hundred and thirty-eight bishops assembled, but the Patriarchs were absent. Archbishop Theodosius of Ephesus presided. [1] The proceedings are only in part known, through those of the seventh general Council. [2] In the decision (ὅρος) of the Synod Christianity is abruptly contrasted with idolatry, but the veneration of images is idolatry. There were hardly many Bishops who could or dared use such language honestly or from the heart. The majority played the hypocrite from dread of the emperor in declaring that the veneration of images was a work of Satan, introduced into the Church of the pure doctrine, in order to seduce men from the lofty adoration of God, or in describing painting as the sinful art by which the incarnation of Christ was blasphemed. But it sounds strangest of all to hear that these Bishops charged the image worshippers at once with Nestorianism and Eutychianism. They were Nestorians since it was of course only possible' to represent the humanity of Christ, and thus his divinity and humanity were sundered; and they were Eutychians in so far as they sought at the same time to represent his divinity and accordingly confounded it with his humanity. The only image allowed—and this is an

---

[1] Schwarzlose (l. c., pp. 76—101) has well described the iconoclastic party and its whole system. "The iconoclasts rejected the religious use and adoration of pictures, because not only according to their view were they contrary to Scripture, tradition, and dogma, but also seduced the Church into heresy and heathenism."

[2] Mansi XIII., p. 205 sq.

important declaration—were the bread and wine in the Lord's Supper. Starting from the prohibition of the portrayal of Christ, images in general were argued against. Further, Christianity rejected along with heathenism not only sacrificial, but pictorial, worship. The saints live with God; to recall them to earthly life by means of a dead art was blasphemy. Men ought to continue to worship and invoke them, but to condemn their pictures. No reference seems to have been made to relics. We have now a series of excellently chosen passages from the Bible and the Fathers. In conclusion, stringent penalties were attached to the worship of images, and a string of anathemas crowns the whole. "We also believe that we speak apostolic-ally and have the Holy Spirit." They had in fact uttered fine propositions, and used words which had ceased for centuries to be heard so distinctly in the Greek Church; but did they themselves believe in these words?

They were under the yoke of the Emperor. The clergy obeyed when the decrees were published; but resistance was offered in the ranks of the monks. Many took to flight, some became martyrs. The imperial police stormed the Churches, and destroyed those images and pictures that had not been secured. The iconoclastic zeal by no means sprang from enthusiasm for divine service in spirit and in truth. The Emperor now also directly attacked the monks; he meant to extirpate the hated order, and to overthrow the throne of Peter. We see how the idea of an absolute military state rose powerfully in Constantinople, how it strove to establish itself by brute force. The Emperor, according to trustworthy evidence, made the inhabitants of the city swear that they would henceforth wor-ship no image, and give up all intercourse with monks. Clois-ters were turned into arsenals and barracks, relics were hurled into the sea, and the monks, as far as possible, secularised. And the politically far-seeing Emperor at the same time entered into correspondence with France (Synod of Gentilly, A.D. 767) and sought to win Pepin, History seemed to have suffered a violent rupture, a new era was dawning which should supersede the history of the Church.

But the Church was too powerful, and the Emperor was not

even master of Oriental Christendom, but only of part of it. The orthodox Patriarchs of the East (under the rule of Islam) declared against the iconoclastic movement, and a Church without monks or pictures, in schism with the other orthodox Churches, was a nonentity. A spiritual reformer was wanting. Thus the great reaction set in, after the death of the Emperor (A.D. 775), the ablest ruler Constantinople had seen for a long time. This is not the place to describe how it was inaugurated and cautiously carried out by the skilful policy of the Empress Irene,[1] cautiously, for a generation had already grown up that was accustomed to the cultus without images. An important part was played by the miracles performed by the re-emerging relics and pictures. But the lower classes had always been really favourable to them; only the army and the not inconsiderable number of bishops who were of the school of Constantine had to be carefully handled. Tarasius,[2] the new Patriarch of Constantinople and a supporter of images, succeeded, after overcoming much difficulty, and especially distrust in Rome and the East, after also removing the excited army, in bringing together a general Council of about 350 bishops at Nicæa, A.D. 787, which annulled the decrees of A.D. 754.[3] The proceedings of the seven sittings[4] are of great value, because very important patristic passages have been preserved in them which otherwise would have perished; for at this Synod also the discussions turned chiefly on the Fathers. The decision (ὅρος) restored orthodoxy and finally settled it. The first six Synods with their anathemas and canons were first confirmed, and it went on: "We decide with all precision and fitness to set up, along with the form of the precious and life-giving cross, the august and holy images made with colours or of

---

[1] See Phoropulos, Εἰρηνη ἡ ᾿Αθηναια αὐτοκρατειρα ῾Ρωμαιων. Μερος ά ann 769—788. It is important that the iconoclastic emperors belonged to Asia Minor, while Irene was Athenian.

[2] Heikel (Helsingfors, 1889) has published in Greek for the first time the Vita Tarasii, written by Deacon Ignatius.

[3] A first attempt to hold a Synod failed A.D. 786, since the majority of the bishops were still adverse, and were supported by the army.

[4] See Mansi XIII., pp. 992—1052. The quotations in the Libri Carolini furnish many problems.

stone or other suitable material, in the holy churches of God, on sacred vessels and garments, on walls and tablets, in houses and on the streets: both the image of our Lord and God and Saviour Jesus Christ, and of our undefiled Lady, the holy mother of God, and of the august angels, and all saintly and pious men; for the prototypes being constantly seen represented in images, the spectators are excited to remember and long for them, and to bestow reverence and due veneration on the images, not indeed the true worship according to our faith which is due to God alone; but (as it becomes us) to make an offering of incense and lights in their honour to the form of the precious and life-giving cross, to the holy Gospels, and the other sacred erections, as was the pious custom of the ancients; for the honour paid to the image passes to the prototype; and he who adores the image adores in it the being or object portrayed." [1]

Just as at Trent, in addition to the restoration of mediæval doctrine, a series of reforming decrees was published, so this Synod promulgated twenty-two canons which can be similarly described. The attack on monachism and the constitution of the Church had been of some use. They are the best canons drawn up by an Œcumenical Synod. The bishops were enjoined to study, to live simply and be unselfish, and to attend to the care of souls; the monks to observe order, decorum, and also to be unselfish. With the State and the Emperor no compromise was made; on the contrary, the demands of Maximus

---

[1] Ὁρίζομεν σὺν ἀκριβείᾳ πάσῃ καὶ ἐμμελείᾳ παραπλησίως τῷ τύπῳ τοῦ τιμίου καὶ ζωοποιοῦ σταυροῦ ἀνατίθεσθαι τὰς σεπτὰς καὶ ἁγίας εἰκόνας, τὰς ἐκ χρωμάτων καὶ ψηφῖδος καὶ ἑτέρας ὕλης ἐπιτηδείως ἐχούσης ἐν ταῖς ἁγίαις τοῦ Θεοῦ ἐκκλησίαις, ἐν ἱεροῖς σκεύεσι, καὶ ἐσθῆσι, τοίχοις τε καὶ σανίσιν, οἴκοι τε καὶ ὁδοῖς· τῆς τε τοῦ κυρίου καὶ Θεοῦ καὶ σωτῆρος ἡμῶν Ἰησοῦ Χριστοῦ εἰκόνος, καὶ τῆς ἀχράντου δεσποίνης ἡμῶν τῆς ἁγίας θεοτόκου, τιμίων τε ἀγγέλων, καὶ πάντων ἁγίων καὶ ὁσίων ἀνδρῶν· ὅσῳ γὰρ συνεχῶς δι᾽ εἰκονικῆς ἀνατυπώσεως ὁρῶνται, τοσοῦτον καὶ οἱ ταύτας θεώμενοι διανίστανται πρὸς τὴν τῶν πρωτοτύπων μνήμην τε καὶ ἐπιπόθησιν, καὶ ταύταις ἀσπασμὸν καὶ τιμητικὴν προσκύνησιν ἀπονέμειν, οὐ μὴν τὴν κατὰ πίστιν ἡμῶν ἀληθινὴν λατρείαν, ἣ πρέπει μόνῃ τῇ θείᾳ φύσει· ἀλλ᾽ ὃν τρόπον τῷ τύπῳ τοῦ τιμίου καὶ ζωοποιοῦ σταυροῦ καὶ τοῖς ἁγίοις εὐαγγελίοις καὶ τοῖς λοιποῖς ἱεροῖς ἀναθήμασι, καὶ θυμιαμάτων καὶ φώτων προσαγωγὴν πρὸς τὴν τούτων τιμὴν ποιεῖσθαι, καθὼς καὶ τοῖς ἀρχαίοις εὐσεβῶς εἴθισται· ἡ γὰρ τῆς εἰκόνος τιμὴ ἐπὶ τὸ πρωτότυπον διαβαίνει· καὶ ὁ προσκυνῶν τὴν εἰκόνα, προσκυνεῖ ἐν αὐτῇ τοῦ ἐγγραφομένου τὴν ὑπόστασιν.

Confessor and John of Damascus are heard, though in muffled tones, from the canons.[1] Still, though the Byzantine Church possessed in the next period an abbot—Theodorus Studita[2]—who championed, as none but a Nicholas or Gregory could, the sovereignty over princes of God's law and the Church, it did not win freedom and independence. However, the repeated and for decades successful attempts made by military Emperors in the ninth century to get rid of the image-worship which had only brought defeat to the State, were finally frustrated.[3] The great Theodore maintained the orthodox cause unflinchingly against Leo the Armenian and Michael the Stammerer. Their successor Theophilus was a relentless foe to images and the monks. Then came an Empress, Theodora, who finally restored the worship. This took place at the Synod held at Constantinople A.D. 842. This Synod decreed that a Feast of Orthodoxy (ἡ κυριακὴ τῆς ὀρθοδοξίας) should be celebrated annually, at which the victory over the iconoclasts should be regularly remembered. Thus the whole of orthodoxy was united in image-worship.[4]

In this way the Eastern Church reached the position which suited its nature. We have here the conclusion of a development consistent in the main points. The divine and sacred, as that had descended into the sensuous world by the incarnation, had created for itself in the Church a system of material, supernatural things, which offered themselves for man's use. The theosophy of images corresponded to the Neo-platonic conception, connected with that of the Incarnation, of the one unfolding

---

[1] See the Canons 3, 6 and 12. Theodorus Studita a few years later triumphantly asserted the famous 3rd Canon: "Any choice of a bishop, priest or deacon emanating from a secular prince is invalid."

[2] See Thomas, Theodor von Studion, Leipzig 1892.

[3] The superstition indulged in by the image-worshippers is shown by the epistle of Michael the Stammerer to Ludwig the Pious (Mansi XIV., p. 399); see Hefele IV., p. 40.

[4] See also the decision of the 8th general Synod, sessio X. (Mansi XVI., p. 161). An Oriental Christian—an Armenian, but in this question all Orientals are agreed—writes at the present day : A Christianity which is stunted and disguised in pictorial forms, if it belongs to the Church, i.e., if it is determined by the history and the spiritual genius of a people, is much stronger and more justified than any conceptions coloured by sectarianism or rationalism, however much these may appeal to modern taste (Karapet l. c., p. 116).

itself in a plurality of graded ideas (original types) down to
the earthly. The theme had, as the image-worshippers said,
been already touched on by Basil ("the knowledge of the prototype comes through the image": δι᾽ εἰκόνος ἡ γνῶσις τοῦ ἀρχετύπου γίνεται); Gregory of Nazianzus ("it is the nature of the
image to be a copy of the prototype and of what is said":
αὕτη εἰκόνος φύσις μίμημα εἶναι τοῦ ἀρχετύπου καὶ οὗ λέγεται);
the Areopagite ("truly visible images are the seen [representa-
tives] of the unseen" ἀληθῶς ἐμφανεῖς εἰκόνες εἰσὶ τὰ ὁρατὰ τῶν
ἀοράτων); Theodoret ("sin alone has no copy") and others. [1] All
that had been wanting was a correct understanding and a bold
carrying out of the truth. And lastly, that nothing be left out,
Aristotelian scholasticism found its account here also. It had
been maintained long ago, and supported by reference to the
pictures "not made with hands" (ἀχειροποίητα), that not painting, but the tradition and law of the Church created the types—
see also the decision of the seventh Council. But Theodorus
Studita went still further. [2] To him the picture was almost
more important than the correct dogmatic formula; for in his
view the relation of the copy to the original was a necessary
one, and there was complete identity in so far as while the
material was different, the form (the hypostasis) was the same.
Theodore maintained that the material was indifferent, but that in
the form of the authentic pictures one possessed the real Christ,
the real Mary, and the real saints. They all bore their prototype in themselves, and this prototype was independent of the
personal impress; it went on imprinting itself from picture to
picture, at first spontaneously—for these men caught at the
absurdity of images not made with hands (εἰκόνες ἀχειροποίητοι),
then through the artist, if he reproduced the type faithfully. [3]

With this science of images composed of superstition, magic
and scholasticism we may fitly close the development. The

[1] See passages in Gass, p. 319 f.

[2] See Opp. Theodori ed. Sirmond T.V. Here we have collected the Antirrhetic.
(I.—III.) c. Iconomachos, Confutatio Poematum Iconomachorum, Quæstiones propo-
sitæ Iconomachis, the Capita VII. adv. Iconom., and the Ep. ad Platon. de cultu ss.
imag. The two books of epistles (l. c.) contain abundant material regarding the images.

[3] The chief passages are collected in great abundance and are well arranged
by Sirmond T.V. sub voce "Imagines" in the index.

Greek Church has almost entirely excluded plastic representations, and its practice of art has, in consequence of the ban
placed on it by the "authentic" picture, never been anything
but stunted. No one can deny that the image-worshippers had
some justification in their controversy with the iconoclasts; and
for Greek Christianity, as it was, image-worship was a vital
question. But in the great conflict waged for a century by the
Byzantine Church with the State, not only did its distinctive
character, but [its freedom, depend on the issue. Great monks
had tried to educate the Church up to the idea of freedom.
In the fight to retain its character it was victorious; but in
that for liberty it succumbed.

CHAPTER V.

APPENDIX.—SKETCH OF THE HISTORY OF THE GENESIS OF THE ORTHODOX SYSTEM.

ORIGEN had drawn up a system of Christian theology based on the four principles, God, the world, freedom, and Holy Scripture, and depending on the old Catholic Church doctrine. It is the only original scientific system ever produced by the Greek Church. The conception of a scientific system of truth is in itself philosophical; it has not come from religion which consists rather in faith in revelation. But the science of the time had conceded a lofty place within itself to this very belief in revelation, and, on the other hand, it was an innate instinct of the Christian faith to give an account of itself.

Origen's undertaking and the manner in which he carried it out contained as many repellent as attractive features for his Christian contemporaries and the future. As a whole it held its ground only in the narrow circle of friends and followers; [1] but its effects were nevertheless incalculable. If Origen had recast the whole faith (Pistis) into a science (Gnosis) the immediate consequence, by no means intended by him, was that some of his gnostic (theological) propositions were introduced into the faith, and that conversely others were amended in accordance with the language of the antignostic Catholic Kerygma. The system was thus dislocated, and with good reason ; for it was a system, simply because in spite of its scrupulous regard for the Bible, history, and freedom, it had transformed history into a natural process. In opposing the notoriously heterodox points of the system—the pre-existence of souls, pre-temporal

[1] Theognostus, Origen's disciple, made a new attempt at constructing a system, see Vol. III., p. 96.

fall of souls, eternal creation of the world, the doctrine of the
transfigured body, and Apokatastasis—an attack was made, if
not always consciously, on its principles which became conspicuous in these points.   For the above doctrines were not append-
ages which could be deleted; they rather expressed most clearly
the fundamental thought of the system, that God is all in all,
and that the doctrine of the Church was dealing with wholly
inadequate symbols in concerning itself with the conceptions of
the creation of the world in time, the historical fall and redemption, the judgment, and a twofold final destiny.   Men desired
science, and there was, as in all ages, only one science; then
it was simply that which Origen had represented.   But at the
same time none would abandon the traditional tenets as absolutely valid truths, partly in the interest of conservatism, partly
because it was vaguely felt that scientific theology did not do
justice to the distinctive character of Christian faith.   That was
the dilemma; but in one point all thinkers were agreed with
Origen, viz., that the final aim of faith and of the theology
accompanied by asceticism, was participation in the knowledge
and consequently the life of the Deity.   They were all intellect-
ualists, even, so far as we are acquainted with them, the earliest
opponents of Origen, including Methodius.[1]   And theology
brought about in the case of nearly all of them a loss to faith
incalculable in its consequences—the fading of moral responsibility and of the conception of the judgment.   No doubt the
"Judgment" was maintained as before, and that against Origen;
but the thought had lost and continued more and more to lose
its all-commanding position in doctrine.

At the beginning of the fourth century,[2] Christianity was,
again in consequence of the theology, on the point of disrup-
tion.   Eusebius has himself admitted the danger in the outward
organisation, and it was a result of the cleavage in thought.
Bishops spoke authoritatively in the East who had learned from
Origen all sorts of ideas that put the doctrine of the Church
in danger of running to seed.   A compact school was in the

---

[1] Besides him the earliest opponents—after Demetrius—were Peter of Alexandria
and Eustathius of Antioch.   Pamphilus and Eusebius wrote against Origen's enemies.

[2] See the details in Vol. III., pp. 121—162.

field that, while it considered itself very scientific and genuinely biblical, yet without knowing or intending it, secularised Christianity. Constantine on the one hand, and Athanasius on the other, saved Christendom. Athanasius was no follower of Origen; he was more akin to Irenæus. In giving the central place to the thought of Christ's essential unity with God, and in carrying it out, he also set the theology of the future, as it seems, on a new, or rather on the old Irenæan basis. But he was no theologian, or, better, he ceased to be one from the moment when he perceived the central significance of the above conception of faith. He hardly touched, let alone solved, the problem of correlating it with all the other results of contemporary knowledge, with the whole of natural theology. He had enough to do in showing that a conception still alien, at any rate to the majority, and clothed in an unfamiliar word, was scriptural, traditional, and fundamental, and in obviating objections. A kind of system was rather constructed by the strict Arians—Aëtius and Eunomius—by means of Aristotelian philosophy. Every professed system up till past the middle of the fourth century was heterodox, with the sole exception of that of Marcellus; but while he made a bold front against the whole doctrine of Origen, he seemed to fall into long refuted errors. His fate itself proves that one thing, in whose assertion orthodox and Arians were agreed, was already inseparably bound up with the Christianity of the cultured, viz., the Neo-platonic doctrine of God and his revelation. The one party—the Arians—might supplement it with Aristotelianism, the other might give the widest scope to the conception of salvation embodied in Jesus Christ, but in the above fundamental thought both were agreed, and the common veneration of Origen is proof of this.[1] Cyril's catechisms show the procedure followed in the catechetic instruction of the cultured. They are based on the Symbol, and its separate points are proved from Scripture. Agreement with Scripture is sufficient; it also guarantees, so to speak, the unity, or, better, it suppresses the craving for strict unity. Revelation, as contained in the oracles of Scripture, was to satisfy all wants. The catechist did not indeed renounce rational argument in

[1] On Arians and orthodox, see Chap. I.

support of separate points of doctrine, but he did not offer anything like a system. On the other hand, traditionalism and the mysticism of the cultus were already strongly marked. Nor was the latter unconnected with Origen; on the contrary, no theologian of early times did so much to further it as he.

The transference of Athanasius' thought into the scientific theology, *i.e.*, into Origenism, was the work of the Cappadocians. Among them Gregory of Nyssa was the most thorough adherent of Origen. Though not without some reservations, yet it can be said that he represented the fundamental conception of Origen.[1] His "Great Catechism" is the only writing of the fourth century which can be compared to the work "De principiis"; but it contains a much narrower range of ideas, and is by no means, even in Gregory's own view, a complete work on dogma.[2] Next to the Cappadocians, Didymus of Alexandria is to be named as a disciple of Origen. It was of immense importance that, just before complete traditionalism settled on the Church, these men took up the cause of theological science in Origen's sense, further, that at this very time men were found in the West to communicate the views of the Cappadocians

---

[1] The reservations are, certainly, not unimportant. If Gregory also shared Origen's starting-point, viz., the antithesis of the spiritually divine and the sensuous, yet he had a more distinct grasp of the notion of creation, and attempted to understand the sensuous as a necessary side of human nature. Finally, however, he also regards the whole development explored by Christian theology as a cosmical process; only the process does not appear so manifest as in Origen, who besides had also, judging from Clement of Alex., introduced ideas alien to it.

[2] Everything in the "Great Catechism" is rational. The author begins by expounding the doctrine of the Trinity as the just mean between Jewish monotheism and heathen polytheism. He also shows that it occurs in the Old Testament (c. 1—4). Then follows the account of the doctrine of the Incarnation (c. 5—32), which forms the subject proper of the Catechism. It is treated from the most varied sides; the reason, nature, and result of the incarnation are discussed. It is proved from the essential attributes of God as well as the state of men; and it is shown that on the one hand it corresponds to the goodness, justice, wisdom, and power of God, and on the other presupposes the condition of evil, death, and freedom in man. Christ became man for all, but he is the physician only for the virtuous. The old question why he appeared so late is also (c. 29) discussed. The conclusion is taken up with expositions of Baptism, the Last Supper, and faith, which constitute the new birth, *i.e.*, virtuous life (c. 33—40). Origen's conceptions, though grouped round a new centre in that of Athanasius, run through the whole; this is still more conspicuous in some of the other writings by the same author.

and Didymus to their native land, and, finally, that the Byzantine Church never ventured to condemn the works of the Cappadocians—of Gregory of Nyssa. The last is especially a fact which cannot fail to excite astonishment; but what would have been left to the Greek Church from the sixth century down, if to the condemned doctors of the Church and their writings we had further to add the main works of Gregory of Nyssa. Since, however, the Church has steadily acknowledged the orthodoxy of the Cappadocians,[1] Origen himself has after all been always looked at as only half a heretic. Up to the present day the members of the two Catholic Churches do not know exactly how they ought really to regard him. He has remained a thorn in the flesh of the Church.

At the close of the fourth century it was settled that the dogmas of the Trinity and the Incarnation constituted the faith; for they were most intimately connected, and the former was fixed in terms of the Incarnation. The great Apollinaris, a systematic theologian and besides an opponent of Origen's method, and the Cappadocians established this conviction. By this means an immense gain was made on the one hand, but on the other not much; for what good did it do to confess these doctrines, as long as it was possible by means of philosophy to furnish very different versions of them, or while the infinite number of other tenets, which fell within the range of theology and required absolutely to be discussed in terms of the Symbol or of Holy Scripture, were destitute of any fixed form? We must again, or, rather still conceive the state of matters during the whole of the fourth century on to its close as being *mutatis mutandis* the same as when Gnosticism flourished, though a consensus of opinion was not wanting in the Church.

[1] The Cappadocians were always held to be the foremost among theologians. Thus Theodore of Studion says (Antirrhet II. adv. Iconom., p. 123, edit. Sirmond.): καὶ δὴ ἀκουσόμεθα τῶν κορυφαιοτάτων πατέρων, Γρηγορίου μὲν τοῦ θεολόγου ... Βασιλείου δὲ τοῦ μεγάλου, and of the former (Iamb. 67, p. 766): Βροντῶν τὰ θεῖα τῇ βοῇ τῶν δογμάτων, Ἠχήσας ὄντως τὴν ὑπουράνιον, μάκαρ· Καὶ πάσας ἀπρὶξ μωράνας τὰς αἱρέσεις, Τον κόσμον ἐστήριξας ἐν τοῖς σοῖς λόγοῖς. From the sixth century Gregory of Nyssa put his admirers in a precarious position by his manifestly heterodox doctrines. They were hushed up; yet their author is not placed by the Greeks of to-day on quite the same high level as Basilius and Gregory of Nazianzus.

There was no recognised conception of the nature of the Incarnation, after the bold and sanguine attempt of Apollinaris
had been rejected as heretical, and the hundred and one
"doctrines" which floated round the Trinitarian and Christological dogma were as fickle and uncertain as the waves of the
sea.   It was not known what belonged to the "faith", whether
to include psychology, or natural science.   Everything offered
itself, and nothing could be declared indifferent without danger;
it was uncertain, too, in what form it did belong to faith.   No
one knew how the Bible was to be interpreted, whether lite-
rally, or typically, or spiritually; no form of interpretation could
be wholly accepted or wholly rejected.   It was not known what
was to be expected in a future state; and as much doubt prevailed about the beginning as about the end of things.   Conceptions still existed of God, the earth, heaven, Christ, the
glories of Paradise and the horrors of the judgment, like those
prevalent among the old "Saints" of the second century, and
they were firmly held with less sanctity, but the same fanaticism, by the new saints, the monks.

On the other hand, both among monks and others, conceptions
existed such as Origen cherished from which the many-coloured
pictures and dramatic scenes had disappeared: men believed in
eternal worlds, the original affinity of the human spirit with God,
in the one unfolding itself into the many, and the many necessarily
returning into the one.   And in the fourth century Christians, and
even clerics, went beyond Origen.   To them the coverings and
masks into which he had transformed the realistic doctrines of
the Church were still more transparent.   A man was now a
Christian because every one was or was becoming one; but he
would not cease being a philosopher.   It was hardly necessary
to come to terms with the doctrine of the Trinity, for, one or
two points being set aside, it was held to be correct, rational,
and Platonic.   The Incarnation caused greater difficulty, but
the Cappadocians themselves had shown how it could be understood rationally.   A still further step was taken; the humanity
assumed by God was dealt with in a free and easy manner.
Speculation found plenty of expedients by which to pare down
the paradox and to reduce it to the level of the intelligible.

But once one had formulated, somehow or other, his assent to the Trinity and Incarnation he was really free and could apply Greek learning (Ἑλληνικὴ παιδεία) as much as he pleased to Christian truth, interpreting its myths. [1] Moreover, there were Christianised philosophers who succeeded by an artifice in uniting the sublimest spiritualism with superstition; they inculcated a ritualistic immanence of the pneumatic in material, if consecrated, things, and transformed the whole world and history into a descending series of types and symbols, which appeared at the same time as effective vehicles of the divine. Creation was the evolution of the one into a world of ideas, symbols and types—every potency being the copy of a higher, and the pattern for a lower one; and redemption was completed in the mysteries of thought and the cultus, which led from type to type, from potency to potency, up to the all-embracing One. Thus Iamblichus had taught; Neoplatonic philosophers of the fourth and fifth centuries followed him, and as they were in a position to conserve heathen mythologies and cults by this view, Christians transferred the conception and method to Christianity. To them the Incarnation no longer appeared as an isolated paradox; it was a special instance, or the verification, or necessary result, of the cosmical process. The great Unknown, who probably belonged to Alexandria, and who is called Pseudo-Dionysius, "in an elaborate conception of the world, smuggled into the Greek Church and its theology the Neoplatonism into which the other doctors of the Church had only dipped timidly, (?) and on this foundation he constructed his theory of the heavenly hierarchy, and its copy, the hierarchy of the Church." [2] Diony-

[1] Nothing is more instructive here than the study of the noble Synesius. Thousands must have held the same views as he at the transition from the fourth to the fifth century; but few possessed the honesty of this Bishop or the clearness of his mind; see above all his letter to his brother Euoptius, when confronted by the question whether he should or should not accept the bishopric offered him. He was then still a Neoplatonist, and, though he afterwards modified his views to some extent, he never ceased to be one. But he openly declared that while he would not give up science, he would accept outwardly the mythical wrapping (τὰ δ᾽ ἔξω φιλομυθῶν), since the people did not endure the clear light.—Even at the end of the fourth century, Church Fathers found it necessary to oppose the idea first broached by Celsus, that Christ had borrowed from Plato.

[2] Steitz, Jahrbb. XI., p. 195.

sius seems to be a realist in the sense of the Church; he lets everything realistic stand; but it is all in fact simply a wrapping; nothing is and nothing happens which is not self-evolved in the process of the Cosmos. At the same time it is unmistakable that, though the form by which it is expressed is not satisfactory, the nature of the good is perceived—it consists in inner union with God.[1] It was of inexpressible importance that

[1] On the system of Dionysius, see Steitz l. c., pp. 197—229. The fundamental thought of Dionysius is the absolute transcendence of God; but God is to him, at the same time, absolute causality; as causality he still stands outside of the world (the many), but yet the forces emanating from him can on the other hand be regarded as a self-reduplication (πολλαπλασιάζεσθαι). Thus the attempt was made to combine the thought of the transcendence of the One with Pantheism. This One is force and movement in virtue of the ἔρως (ἀγάπη) dwelling in it, and thus it issues from itself in order to return to itself. This emanation, however, is identical with the fixing of προορισμοί and παραδείγματα; i.e., the finite conceived as pure forms exists from eternity in God himself, nay, treated and conceived as one, it is himself. In him and belonging to him the forces are always immaterial, undivided, identical. From the standpoint of God, accordingly, the whole process of the world is simply pure self-movement; but viewed from beneath it is one of unfolding, division, and descent, and again of ascent, unification, and return to the One. We must always maintain both, rest and movement, transcendence and immanence, unity and multiplicity. To this correspond the kataphatic and the apophatic theologies. The former descends from God to things in order from the effects to draw conclusions as to the absolute, inexhaustible, nature of the One. The latter rises from things to God, in order to deny regarding him all that may be conceived, and to find him exalted above the antithesis of error and truth, of not-being and being. The latter is to Dionysius the more appropriate, but the two methods ought not to contradict each other; for the Deity is placed even above the antithesis formed by the statements of the apophatic and kataphatic theology. In his fifth Epistle, Dionysius says (I., p. 594, ed. Corder): ὁ θεῖος γνόφος ἐστὶ τὸ ἀπρόσιτον φῶς—how often since that has been repeated by mystics!—ἐν ᾧ κατοικεῖν ὁ Θεὸς λέγεται· καὶ ἀοράτῳ γε ὄντι διὰ τὴν ὑπερέχουσαν φανότητα καὶ ἀπροσίτῳ τῷ αὐτῷ διὰ τὴν ὑπερβολὴν τῆς ὑπερουσίου φωτοχυσίας, ἐν τούτῳ γίγνεται πᾶς ὁ Θεὸν γνῶναι καὶ ἰδεῖν ἀξιούμενος αὐτῷ τῷ μὴ ὁρᾶν μηδὲ γινώσκειν, ἀληθῶς ἐν τῷ ὑπὲρ ὅρασιν κ:ὶ γνῶσιν γιγνόμενος. The thought of God's transcendence was the decisive point. To the unmoved mover every spirit, nay, everything in its own way strives to rise. "A nameless longing passes through all the veins of nature;" God himself comes not nearer; but men can force themselves up to him. Evil consists in being separated from him; it is a pure negation; it does not exist in relation to God; for it is a negative in the sphere of the many, which yet in view of God constitute a non-material unity: it is the unnatural, that which does not correspond to the nature of the various beings and things, each taken in its distinctive character. In so far as these *are*, they are good; but in so far as they are not what they ought to be, they contain evil in themselves. It remains obscure, however, how they cannot be what they ought. Is it due to the

from and after the sixth century the writings of the Unknown, which also betrayed the influence of Aristotle, were held to be the works of an Apostolic personage. Neoplatonism and the mysticism of the Cultus were thus declared to be part of classic Christianity. The representatives of the "common sense" of the Church at the end of the fourth century were quite aware of the multiplication in itself, or to an unknown hindrance ? In any case the good is union with God. At this point begins the most characteristic work of Dionysius, its mystical and scholastic feature. This union, like everything else, has its stages; it is consummated by purification, illumination, and perfecting. As the sun dispels darkness, then fills everything with light, and brings it to perfection, so also does the Deity. And everything in the Cosmos contributes to this process; it is the object and agent of redemption; it is a universe of symbols which lead to God, but which cannot be entirely transcended in this world; for we only see through a mirror in a dark saying. The process itself is no pure process of thought; thinking is only its accompaniment; it is a process of the action of being upon being; therefore the symbol and the rite which offer themselves to the feeling of the soul that is passive and yields itself up to them. Accordingly we have, at the close, the passive intuition, in which man no longer participates in anything external, is no longer conscious of anything positive, but negativing all things, loses himself in the inscrutable. Yet there is no negation from which it would not be necessary to separate the Deity by a ὑπέρ; the imagination must cast anchor before the portals of the inscrutable and incomprehensible. The purifying, illuminating, and perfecting rites are imparted to men by the heavenly and ecclesiastical hierarchies. But between these and the Deity Dionysius has placed the Church doctrines of the Trinity and the Incarnation. The former has been outwardly treated orthodoxly on the whole, yet in such a way that it after all merely assumes the form of a Trinity in revelation; *i.e.*, the persons are regarded as the first stages in the multiplication of the Deity which is continued in the heavenly hierarchy; however, this way of looking at the matter is disguised from view. As regards the Incarnation, the system has naturally no room for it; for regard for the transcendence of the Deity prevents it from recognising any incarnation, and in consequence of his immanence the whole process of the Cosmos itself is the materialising and manifestation of the Deity in the world. Yet the Incarnation is maintained; but, since this was impossible, it is not made the central point, but serves as the foundation of various speculations, and the illustration of valuable thoughts. The result of the Incarnation in Jesus is conceived as a raising of human nature to its highest power, and not properly as a fusion of two natures (yet we have the expression: καινὴ θεανδρικὴ ἐνέργεια); for even in the manifestation of Jesus the Deity remains concealed and incomprehensible. Like all symbols and phenomena the Incarnation is in a certain sense a disguising of the Deity. With Jesus Dionysius also connects a few realistic Church doctrines as to redemption, victory over the demons, and θεογενεσία; but the Incarnation really is the representation of God's unfolding of himself in general. As regards the actual redemption of individuals the main stress is placed in this system on the two hierarchies and the mysteries. These hierarchies are genuinely Neo-platonic. The heavenly was formed by the graded choirs of angels (Triads, see Vol. III., Chap. 4) which themselves consecrated severally by the higher, consecrate heterodoxies which existed in spite of, and side by side with, the confession of the Trinity and Incarnation; some of them indeed were themselves not content with the generally received doctrine. They desired a God with eyes, ears and limbs, a resurrection of the identical body, and a visible glorious kingdom of Christ at the end of the world. Even an exceedingly cultured exegete like Apollinaris made common cause with them in the last point. A founder was sought for heterodoxies; it was impossible to blame Manichæism for everything. Ἑλληνικὴ παιδεία was held to be the culprit, and therefore also Origen, the man who was said, not without reason, to have introduced it into Christian theology. A passionate opposition was raised in Egypt among the Scetian monks, and in Palestine where Origen had many admirers. It was, above all, the narrow but honest Epiphanius who saw in Origen the father of Arianism and many other heresies. The comprehensive chapter against him in the former's Panarion (H. 64) is the first polemical writing we possess of ecclesiastical traditionalism against Origen; it is by no means unskilful; it does not confine itself to details, but disputes *e fundamento* the title to a place in the Church of a theology such as Origen offered.[1] The "Expositio fidei catholicæ ecclesiæ" appended to the Panarion shows, indeed, the complete inability of Epiphanius to give an account of the faith; it loses itself as usual in irrelevant discussions, and the positive contents are extraordinarily scanty. But the attack on Origen (compare also the somewhat earlier "An-

severally the lower; the historical Christ even had his place among them. The ecclesiastical hierarchy consisted of the bishops, priests, and deacons; and the means which acted from beneath upwards were the six mysteries (see Chap. IV.). In the work on the ecclesiastical hierarchy these mysteries are minutely explained. Every openly heterodox opinion is, as generally, once more avoided. "The Areopagite has given the Church an exposition of all the mystic rites, such as it had not possessed till then, in which every act of the cultus has its peculiar, deeper reference and secret meaning. His exposition attaches itself in form to Christian dogma, and could therefore serve as a pattern to the Church theologians of the following centuries. As regards the matter, indeed, the case is different; for the Christian dogmas themselves merely appear as the dress of Neo-platonic ideas, to which the inflexible form offers a stubborn resistance."

[1] H. 64 c. 73; Σύ, Ὠριγένη, ἀπὸ τῆς Ἑλληνικῆς παιδείας τυφλωθεὶς τὸν νοῦν ἐξήμεσας τὸν ἰὸν τοῖς πειθεῖσί σοι, καὶ γέγονας αὐτοῖς εἰς βρῶμα δηλητηρίου, δι' ὧν αὐτὸς ἠδίκησαι ἀδικήσας τοὺς πλείους

coratus") opened the first great controversy over the question
whether scientific theology as understood by Origen was legitimate or not. Walch has described the history of this controversy
with his usual thoroughness. It is acknowledged how disagree-
ably the action of Epiphanius disturbed the circle of Origen's
monkish admirers, who were congregated in Palestine under
the protection of the like-minded John, Bishop of Jerusalem.
The dream that one might be both a pillar of the Church and
a theologian like Origen was dissipated. Jerome preferred to
remain a pillar and to abandon Origen. After his desertion
and his betrayal of his friend Rufinus, he became the father of
the "science of the Church." To some extent he is a type of
this "science" up to the present day. It lives on fragments
of the men whom it declares to be heretics. It accepts just as
much from them as circumstances permit, and retains of the
old what it can maintain with decency. It cultivates a little
literalness, a little allegory, and a little typology. It attacks
all questions with a parade of freedom from prejudice; but
anything inconvenient it surrounds with a thousand invented
difficulties. It is proud of its free-thought in matters of no
importance, and hides itself finally, when hot pressed, behind
a brazen stare. It characterises its friends as "well-disposed",
homines boni, and slanders its opponents. Where evasion is no
longer possible, it states the inexorable historical fact as a major
premise; to this it adds a minor taken from its prejudices, and
then it solves the syllogistic problem by the aid of piquant
conceits.[1] It can be incredibly frivolous and again pedantically
learned, just as it suits. Only one question does not occur in
its catechism, and it is always hard to drive it home, viz., what
is historical truth? That is the science of—Jerome.

---

[1] For a parallel to this characterisation compare Luther, Vom Papstthum zu Rom
wider den hochberühmten Romanisten zu Leipzig (Weimarer Ausgabe, Vol. VI. 304):
Lieber Romanist, wer hat daran gezweiffelt, dass das alt Gesetz und seine Figuren
mussen ym Neuen erfullet werden? man durfft deiner Meisterschaft hirynnen nichts
Aber hie soltestu dich lassen sehen und beweysen deine hohe Kunst, das die selb
Erfulling durch Petrum odder denn Bapst gescheh: Da schweygestu wie ein Stock,
da zu reden ist, und schwetzist da nit not zu redenn ist. Hastu dein logica nit
bass gelernet? Du probirst die maiores, die niemant anficht, und nympst fur gewiss
die minores, die ydermann anficht, und schleussist was Du wilt.

Epiphanius' breach with John led to the intervention of the
Alexandrian Bishop Theophilus, who, at the time, still refused
to yield to the "anthropomorphists", and adhered to Origen's
party. Rome also took part in the dispute which, settled as
between the bishops, broke out anew between the two scholars.
Rufinus was only able to defend Origen's orthodoxy by the
doubtful assumption that "heretics" had corrupted his works
But that helped neither him nor Origen. Origen was condemned and Rufinus censured in Rome in A.D. 399 by the
ignorant Anastasius. The errors charged against Origen (see
Hieron. ad Pammach.) were, a subordinationist doctrine of the
Trinity, the doctrine of the preëxistence of souls and their condemnation to enter into bodies, the view of the future conversion of the devil and the demons, the interpretation of the
skins in Gen. III. to mean the body, the spiritualising of the
doctrine of the resurrection of the body, the explanation of
Paradise as spiritual, and the too extensive use of the allegorical method, etc. Not only, however, did Rome renounce Origen, but Alexandria also. Theophilus saw that his power in
Egypt would be shaken if he did not rely upon the masses of
stupid and fanatical Coptic monks, the anthropomorphists, in
whose circles a material God was defended in doggerel rhymes,
and the ancient apocalyptic literature was greedily read. Theophilus wheeled round, abandoned, and that with strong personal
feeling, the admirers of Origen among the monks, and, with
the approval of Rome, hurled his anathemas against him.
Jerome, ever on the alert to blot out the stain that attached
to him from having once venerated the great theologian, translated into Latin Theophilus' slanderous Easter epistle against
Origenism, although he must have seen through its calumnies.
In Constantinople, however, the fight waged by Theophilus
against his former friends, the Nitrian monks, was followed by
that agitation of which Chrysostom was a victim. It was the
first violent attempt of the Alexandrian Patriarch, who by his
alliance with the masses had won a secure position in his own
diocese, to get possession of the Constantinopolitan patriarchate,
the capital, and whole Church of the East.

Meanwhile it was only in the West that the influence of

Origen was really deeply shaken by these endeavours. Jerome persuaded the Western Church that Origen was the father of Pelagianism; Vincentius of Lerinum held him up as an example along with Apollinaris and other heretics; Leo I. considered him a heretic, and Gelasius insisted that Jerome's criticism should be maintained in dealing with his works. [1] Orthodoxy held its ground unshaken as regards all the points of doctrine touching on the dogmas of the Trinity and Incarnation, which in the West were hardly ever subjects of controversy. Jerome now became the standard theologian and exegete. Everything ancient and distinctive, even where it did not lie in the direction of Origenism, disappeared more and more in the West. The Western Church became the Church of Jerome; but it became also—to its lasting benefit—the Church of Augustine (see Vol. V.).

It was different in the East. The transformation of the controversy about Origen into a conflict between two great Patriarchs, in which Origen was soon lost sight of, and the rehabilitation, belated indeed, of Chrysostom, favoured the impugned reputation of the great theologian. But even apart from this, his influence was too deeply rooted to be upset by a single bishop, no matter how powerful. His individuality represented the Ἑλληνική παιδεία, with which men would not dispense. They were willing to recognise the dogma of the Church, *i.e.*, the doctrines of the Trinity and Incarnation; but they sought besides freedom to interest themselves in (theological) science. The Church History of Socrates shows the undiminished influence of Origen—see above Vol. III., p. 146 and elsewhere; even before Socrates, the celebrated Evagrius of Pontus had sturdily defended him, and Sozomen himself, monkish and narrow as he was, was no opponent of Origen. The outbreak of the Nestorian and Monophysite controversies as to the nature of the Incarnation soon thrust everything else into the background, and procured for Origen's cause a temporary peace.

It is fitting that we should here take a glance at the Patri-

---

[1] The so-called decree of Gelasius, which obtained a far-reaching importance in the West is also otherwise important from the condemnation it passed on the whole of earlier Christian literature. The orthodox Church was determined to vilify and then to bury its own past in order to maintain undisputed the fiction that it had always remained the same.

archate of Antioch and its neighbouring territories. The circumstances there were wholly peculiar. The East swarmed with
old and new sects. All sorts betook themselves thither, and,
beside the official Christianity only to be met with in Greek
cities, there existed an assortment of the most varied Christian
communions. Even in the fifth century the Bishops had to face
conflicts there which had almost died out in Rome, Byzantium,
and Alexandria, as early as the third century. Therefore the
Bishops living in or sprung from that quarter still possessed
the lofty conviction that they were constantly fighting the
battles of the Lord, and hastening from victory to victory.
Nestorius, Theodoret, and others plume themselves in their
correspondence with their Western brethren on their merits as
antagonists of heretics;[1] even Chrysostom was their inexorable
enemy. As a matter of fact, the continuance of these conflicts
was of vast consequence to the whole Church. Gnosticism and
Manichæism dogged the steps of the Eastern Bishops, and compelled them to adhere strictly to the ancient *regula fidei* with
its antignostic impress. They could not, as in Alexandria and
Constantinople, confine their interest to the Incarnation. They
had to defend the doctrine, point by point, in its whole extent,
and were thus prevented from casting themselves into the arms
of one transcendent idea. They were pious after the monkish
fashion, like the Egyptians; nay, their Bishops outdid those of
Egypt in asceticism; they were not less realistic in what belonged to the Cultus than the rest; they were as much to the

---

[1] The later antignostic writings and compendiums, those of Ephraem, Epiphanius, Theodoret, Esnik, etc., are all, in so far as they are not mere extracts from
older works, from the East. Mohammedans, besides the later Nestorian and Jacobite
scholars, confessedly turned their attention to the Christian sects still existing in
the East, to one of which Islam owes the best of its teaching. Theodoret is full
of self-praise over his actions, and sports them over and over again to prop up
his imperilled orthodoxy. In Ep. 81 (IV., p. 1141, ed. Schulze) he writes: κώμας
ὄκτω τῆς Μαρκίωνος καὶ τὰς πέριξ κειμένας, ἀσμένας πρὸς τὴν ἀλήθειαν ἐφοδήγησα·
ἄλλην κώμην Εὐνομιανῶν—we see that the sects are tabulated according to their
origin—πεπληρωμένην καὶ ἄλλην Ἀρειανῶν τῷ φωτὶ τῆς θεογνωσίας προσήγαγον.
καὶ διὰ τὴν θείαν χάριν οὐδὲ ἓν παρ' ἡμῖν αἱρετικῶν ὑπελείφθη ζιζάνιον. Ep. 145.
(IV., p. 1246) he tells how he fought steadily against Greeks, Jews, Eunomians, Apollinarians, and Marcionites; ibid, p. 1252: πλείους ἢ μυρίους τῶν τοῦ
Μαρκίωνος πείσας προσήγαγον τῷ παναγίῳ βαπτίσματι. In Hæret. fab. I. 20 he
records that he had confiscated more than 200 copies of the Diatessaron.

front when it was necessary to defend an old doctrine. But their scientific theologians—Palestine stands by itself—were not followers of Origen, and in their fights with heretics they could not use his teaching. They used a more liberal and, again, a more rational, a less flighty, exegesis, and a sober philosophy. Both these were given them by Lucian, and it was, lastly, one and the same school which extended from Lucian to Theodoret, and stretched far beyond the latter into the Christian schools of the Persian kingdom.

The character and significance of this school have been discussed above in various chapters—see especially Vol. III., ch. 3. It sharply contested Origen's hermeneutics, but did not vilify the great man. Its own exegetical and biblical-theological method, with some admirable features, indeed, omitted, and a little of the literal and allegorical added, gradually became, in consequence of its appropriateness and thanks to the influence of Chrysostom, the ruling one. And the use of Aristotelian philosophy in the Antiochene school was an indication for the future. But the ablest of the Antiochenes finally came under censure on account of his Christology, and, over and above his Christology, he was charged with various heresies, especially Pelagianism. In fact, his whole system, and he possessed a system to a greater extent than any other after Origen, was a rational one; it was natural theology without any transcendentalism. He is therefore a source of great difficulty to the Church up to the present time; it declines to go further in condemning him than the fifth Council, indeed it only recognises conditionally the censure of the "chapters". Theodoret's work is without the boldness of Theodore, his anthropology and his doctrine of grace as well as his Christology approximating to the traditional teaching. Among other things, he appended to his compendium of heretical fables a fifth book, "θείων δογμάτων ἐπιτομή" (an epitome of divine dogmas), *which must be described as the first attempt at a system after Origen,* and which apparently exercised great influence on John of Damascus. This "epitome" has a lofty significance. It combines the Trinitarian and Christological dogma with the whole circle of the doctrines connected with the symbol. It reveals an attitude as markedly biblical as it is ecclesiastical and rational. It throughout observes the "just mean". It is almost complete, the Last Supper being omitted, and it especially takes realistic Eschatology once more into account.[1] It has adopted none of the obnoxious doctrines of Origen, and yet he himself is not treated as a heretic.[2] An actual system this epitome is not; but the consistent sobriety and lucidity in the discussion of details, and the careful biblical proof lend to the whole a stamp of unity. It could not yet indeed give satisfaction, firstly, because of the personality of its author, and, secondly, because there was an entire absence of mysticism and Neoplatonism from his doctrinal conception.

In the second half of the fifth century everyone was occupied with the decree of Chalcedon. Cyril of Alexandria, the Christo-logian whom bishops and monks had understood best, had to reconquer his whole influence side by side with the creed of Chalcedon. The only two great theologians whom the Eastern Church has possessed—Origen and Theodore, the former a follower of Plato, the latter of Aristotle, both biblicists though in very different ways,—were discredited, but not condemned. It was on the soil of Palestine, and among the monks there, that admiration for Origen came into collision with that for Theodore. We are well informed as to the living spiritual movements in the cloisters of Palestine at the beginning of the sixth century. Origenism experienced a regular renaissance, although it had never died out.[3] Its "peculiar doctrines", which had sprung from rational mysticism, were in particular taken up again, or at least declared to be arguable. The Cappadocians were

---

[1] Theodoret discusses (1) the First Principle and the Father, (2) the Son, (3) the Holy Spirit and the divine names, (4—9) creation, matter, æons, angels, demons, and man, (10) providence, (11—15) the Incarnation, and that in general as well as in reference to separate points of doctrine, *e.g.*, the assumption of a real body of a soul, and generally of the complete human nature, and the resuscitation of this nature, (16) the identity of the just and beneficent God, (17) God is the author of both Testaments, (18) Baptism, (19) the resurrection, (20) the judgment, (21) the promises, (22) the second advent of Christ, (23) Antichrist, (24) virginity, (25) marriage, (26) second marriage, (27—29) fornication, penitence and continence.

[2] Theodoret has not introduced him into his catalogue of heretics.

[3] Walch l. c., p. 618 ff.; Möller in the R.-Encykl. XI., p. 112 f.; Loofs, Leontius, p. 274 ff.; Bigg, l. c.

appealed to in support of their validity. Origenism was defended under very different shades. There was an extreme right, and even pillars of orthodoxy were found on this side,[1] and there was a left, which surpassed even Origen in daring. He led some of his admirers over to the Areopagite and the Neo-Platonists. The works of the Unknown were brought out, studied, and, as it appears, edited. Some went the length of undisguised Pantheism, like Stephen bar Sudaili, or the author of the book of Hierotheus, "On the hidden mysteries of the Deity."[2] No Gnostic of the second century had erected a nihilistic philosophy on the ground of Christianity so boldly as this writer.[3]

But the admirers of Origen met with opponents in Palestine, not only among the dull herd of monks and the traditionalists, but also among the adherents of the sober science and Christology of Theodore of Mopsuestia. And, in addition, there was rising up a new power, Aristotelian scholasticism, which took possession of the monophysite as well as the orthodox dogma, but only concluded a firm alliance with the latter, through Leontius, the great opponent of Nestorianism and of Theodore —see above, p. 232 f. The Antiochene school was smitten with its own weapons. The great dogmas of the Church, hallowed by age, seemed to receive their sanction from the re-invigo-

---

[1] Leontius, as Loofs has shown.

[2] See the analysis of this extraordinarily interesting work, not yet printed, in Frothingham's Stephen bar Sudaili, 1886, p. 92 f.; the writer ably calls attention also to the connection with the renaissance of Origenism.

[3] Frothingham rightly says, p. 49 f.: "His system was openly pantheistic, or, to speak more philosophically, Pan-nihilistic; for, according to him, all nature even to the lowest forms of animal creation, being simply an emanation from the Divinity-Chaos, finally returns to it; and, when the consummation has taken place, God himself passes away and everything is swallowed up in the indefinite chaos, which he conceives to be the first principle and the end of being and which admits of no distinction." The contents of the five books are according to Fr. as follows: I.—On God, the Universal Essence and distinct existences. II.—The various species of motion, the ascent of the mind towards God, during which it must endure the sufferings of Christ. III.—The resurrection of the mind, the vicissitudes of its conflict with the powers of evil, and its final identification with Christ. IV.—The mind becomes one, first with Christ, then with the Spirit and the Father, and finally becomes absorbed. V.—All nature becomes confounded with the Father; all distinct existence and God himself passes away; Essence alone remains.

rated Aristotelianism, because they were peculiarly adapted for dialectical treatment. Thus the age of Justinian shows the Church of the East in a state of the liveliest spiritual agitation. All the great powers of the past, Neoplatonism and Aristotelianism, Origen and Theodore, were again living forces; a new combination was drawing near, and all efforts to stifle by conciliar decrees the living spirit in the Church seemed to have been vain. But the movements were but limited in extent and energy; the "new combination" was in truth the death of real science—a thinking which started in the middle of its subject, and for which that which was alone worth reflection was held to be beyond the range of discussion. Trifling monks, who excommunicated and denounced each other, talked big; and there sat at Constantinople an emperor who, himself a theologian, thirsted for the fame of creating a uniform science as well as a uniform belief. The dispute of the Palestinian monks and the scholasticism of a theologian like Leontius gave him his chance. The Emperor did not need to publish an edict requiring the followers of Origen and Theodore to annihilate one another; they took care of that for themselves. The spectacle of the two "sciences", of Origen and the Antiochenes, tearing each other to pieces, in the age of Justinian, has something tragi-comical about it, recalling the tale of the two lions. The fifth Council confirmed this, after the Emperor had himself, in his epistle to Mennas, declared, and Vigilius—with other Patriarchs—had repeated, the condemnation of Origen. The fifteen anathemas against Origen, [1] on which his condemnation at the Council was based, contained the following points. (1) The preëxistence of souls and Apokatastasis; (2) the doctrine of the upper world of spirits, their original equality, and their fall; (3) the view that sun, moon, and stars belonged to this world of spirits, and had also fallen; (4) the doctrine that the differences in the bodies of the spirits was a consequence of this fall; (5) the opinion that the higher spirits become lower ones, or men, and *vice versâ*; (6) Origen's doctrine of creation, and that it was not accomplished by the Trinity; (7) the Christo-

---

[1] Compare with this the ten anathemas in the epistle to Mennas and the Vitæ Sabæ, Euthymii and Cyriaci, Loofs l. c, p. 290 f.

logy which taught that Christ became for all grades of spirits
—each in its own form—that which he had become for men
through the Incarnation, so that he assumed different bodies
and received different names; (8) the contention that the Logos
was only to be called Christ by a misuse of language (κατα-
χρηστικῶς), that accordingly a distinction was to be drawn between them; (9) the opinion that not the Logos, but a creaturely mind (νοῦς) which he had assumed became man; (10) the
assertion of the spherical and ethereal form of the resurrection-
body, and of the annihilation of the material body; (11) the
interpreting of the judgment to mean this annihilation, and the
view that at the end of the world there would only exist non-
material nature (spirit); (12) the view that the Logos united
with every man and spirit as he had done with the νοῦς he
had assumed: heresy of the Isochristians who appealed to
Origen, see, besides, Methodius; (13) the assertion of the similarity of the νοῦς, called Christ, to all other rational beings;
(14) the view of the ultimate cessation of all plurality of persons and of multiplicity of knowledge (gnosis), the doctrine of
reversion to unity and of apokatastasis; (15) the view of the
identity of the pretemporal with the final life of spirits.

Since the "Three Chapters" were condemned at the same
time, Origen and Theodore were both got rid of.[1] The latter
found more energetic defenders than the former; but the majority of his admirers held aloof. The fact that the Augustinian
West took up his cause best shows that we must not over-
value this championship. The condemnation of the "peculiar
doctrines" of Origenism meant much more. Henceforth buoys
were laid down, which marked off the Neo-platonic channel in
which men moved under the guidance of the "apostolic" Dionysius. Origen's doctrines of the consummation, and of spirits
and matter might no longer be maintained. The judgment was
restored to its place, and got back even its literal meaning.
The mysticism of the Cultus was carried continually further; it
received a new impetus; but it adhered much more closely to

---

[1] The religious policy of Justinian and the fifth Council had accordingly the
same significance for the (orthodox) East as the so-called Gelasian decree for the
West. In the former as in the latter history was extinguished and theology fettered.

tradition. The anti-gnostic *regula fidei* was finally restored, and the great cultus-mystic of the seventh century not only respected it, but worked within its lines. Maximus Confessor held the same relation to the Areopagite, as did the Cappadocians to Origen, and Theodoret to Theodore.[1] But he was not only a mystic; he was also a scholastic and dialectician. There were no longer any theologians who reflected independently " de principiis." God, the world, freedom, Christ, and Scripture were no longer the first principles, but, instead, the fixed doctrines regarding them drawn from tradition. Science took for granted the foundations guarded by the Church, and passing to the upper story went on building there. A latent free thought, indeed, still remained. If everything was symbolical and figurative, then, no matter how closely the spiritual might be combined with the material, the idea could not perish that the theologian who was in a position to grasp the subject matter did not require figures. While mysticism and scholasticism might not shrink from a figurative philosophy in the most daring sense of the term, they could not stifle the view that took every sort of figure and all history as a covering, nor could they blame the self-criticism of the Christian who was ashamed of being confined in this body.[2]

For learning (μάθησις) the Cappadocians (the two Gregorys, next to them Athanasius and Cyril) were regarded as the principal authorities; for mystagogy (μυσταγωγία), the Areopagite and Maximus; for philosophy, Aristotle; and for homiletics (ὁμιλία), Chrysostom. The man, however, who embraced all that, who had transferred the scholastic dialectic method, which had been brought by Leontius to bear on the dogma of the Incarnation, to the whole sphere of the " divine dogma " as that had been fixed by Theodoret, was John of Damascus. Through him the Greek Church gained the orthodox system, but not the Greek Church alone. John's work was no less

---

[1] See on him the Art. of Wagenmann in the R.-Encykl. and Steitz XI., p. 209; on the Cultus-mystics Sophronius of Jerusalem and Germanus of Constantinople, see Steitz XI., pp. 238 f. and 246 f.

[2] The saying is due to Porphyry who has used it of Plotinus (Vita I.): Πλω-τῖνος ὁ φιλόσοφος ἐῴκει μὲν αἰσχυνομένῳ ὅτι ἐν σώματι εἴη.

important to the West.[1] "He was the cope-stone of antiquity and the transition to a new age, because his writings, translated into Latin, became confessedly a foundation of the mediæval theology of the West." He was above all a scholastic. To him each difficulty was but an incitement to split up notions artificially, and to find a new one to which nothing in the world corresponds except that very difficulty which the new notion was meant to remove. John even put the fundamental question of mediæval science, that as to nominalism and realism; and he solved it by a modified Aristotelianism. All doctrines were in his view given already; he took them from findings of the Councils and the works of recognised Fathers. He held it to be the task of science to edit them. In this way the two chief dogmas were introduced into the circle of the doctrines of the old antignostically interpreted Symbol. A very modest use was made of the allegorical explanation of Holy Scripture. The letter ruled wholesale, at any rate much more thoroughly than in the case of the Cappadocians. In consequence of this, natural theology was shut out from sight; it was hedged round by extremely realistic Bible narratives confidingly accepted.[2] But the most serious fact was that the close connection which in Athanasius, Apollinaris, and Cyril of Alexandria had united the Trinity and Incarnation, or dogma in general, with the thought of salvation, was completely loosened. This process had begun with the Council of Chalcedon, and John had a mass of dogmas which it was necessary to believe; but they had ceased to be clearly subordinate to a uniform conception of their purpose. The object which dogma once served as the means remained; but the means had changed. Instead of dogma, we have the Cultus, the mysteries, into which Book IV. enters (IV. 17—25 are to be regarded as appendices). In consequence of this the system is destitute of inner vital unity.[3] It is really

---

[1] See Bach, Dogmengesch. des Mittelalters I., p. 49 ff. Bach begins with good reason, pp. 6—49, with Dionysius and Maximus.

[2] Yet the rational method was by no means given up; on the contrary, it was retained; see, *e.g.*, the rational arguments for the Trinity, I. 6, 7.

[3] The plan of the work is as follows : Book I. discusses the Deity, the Trinity and the attributes of God; Book II. the creation, angels, paradise, and man, giving an elaborate psychology ; Book III. the Incarnation, the two natures, and Christo-

not an account of faith, but of its presuppositions, and its unity depends on the form of treatment, the high antiquity of its doctrine, and Holy Scripture. The dogmas had become the sacred inheritance from the classic antiquity of the Church, but they had, as it were, fallen to the ground. The worship of images, mysticism, and scholasticism ruled the Church. The two latter bore much fair fruit in after times; for the spirit which strives towards God cannot be stifled by anything, and is capable even of constructing a restricted science. But the history of dogma came to an end in the Greek Church a thousand years ago, and its reanimation cannot easily be conceived. A reformation could only set in in the cultus. The adoption of a few Catholic or Protestant *theologumena* in later catechisms and books of doctrine has hitherto been without effect, and will in the future hardly obtain any.

Independent theology had been extinguished in the churches of the East; but alongside these churches there arose all the more energetically, from the seventh century, the sects, old enemies in new forms, Marcionites (as Paulicians) and Manichæans, and in addition many other curious bodies, the necessary products of religious movements among tribes falling into barbarism, and but little trained by the Church. On the shaping of the dogmas of the Church these sects exerted not the slightest influence; and for that very reason they do not belong to the history of dogma. [1]

logy—see above, Chap. 3, conclusion; Book IV. continues the Christology up to Chap. 8 and then discusses—very characteristically—baptism, including the μὖρον, faith, the sign of the cross and faith, adoration towards the East, the mysteries (the Eucharists), Mary the mother of God and the genealogy of Christ, the veneration of the saints and their relics, pictures and, only then, Scripture. To the chapter on Scripture a series of chapters are appended containing hermeneutical rules for the exposition of Scripture, dealing with the statements regarding Christ— where we have a precise distinction made between the τρόποι of the hypostatic union—those concerning God in his relation to evil, the apparent existence of two principles, the law of God, and the law of sin and the Sabbath. The conclusion consists of chapters on virginity, circumcision—the position of these headings is reversed—on Anti-Christ and the resurrection.

[1] Besides the old researches of Engelhardt (1827), Gieseler (1829, 1846, 1849), see now Döllinger, Beitr. z. Sectengesch. des Mittelalters (1890) and Karapet Ter Mkrttschian, Die Paulikianer (1893).

Again, this history has nothing to say about the scientific life of the Byzantine Church, or the many theories and disputes which arose out of it, and, on the other hand, from mystical speculations; for all that had little or no effect on dogma. No doubt an isolated theological question was decided at this or that Synod; or individual theologians elaborated in a praiseworthy fashion theological conceptions, as *e.g.*, in reference to the crucifixion of Christ, atonement, and substitution; no doubt another rather important dispute—the Hesychastic controversy— agitated the Church in the fourteenth century; but dogma, and to some extent the Church itself, remained ultimately unaffected. For centuries the intellectual work of the Church consisted in the development of Church legislation, and its theologians either wrote on exegesis, history, and biography, following traditional patterns, or composed ascetic books.

Finally, to the history of dogma belongs neither the development of the schism with the West, nor the silent process, in which the Eastern Church has taken over, since the thirteenth and fourteenth centuries, a great deal from the ecclesiastically more vigorous West. Apart from the "filioque" discussed above, the development of the schism was not determined by dogmatic factors, and the silent process [1] which lasted up to the end of the seventeenth century, and to which the Church owes, *e.g.*, the settling of its Canon of the Bible, the doctrine of the seven sacraments, a kind of doctrine of transubstantiation, a more certain doctrine of purgatory, development of the doctrines of sin and grace, a more sharply defined theory and practice of the sacrament of penance etc., has come to an end at a time when we have accurate knowledge, and will perhaps never be fully explained. The only definite dogmatic interests shown in it are anti-protestant.

---

[1] Compare as to this Kattenbusch, Vergleichende Confessionskunde I. passim. The general intellectual life in Eastern Rome is best discussed in the excellent work of Krumbacher, Gesch. d. Byzant. Litteratur, München, 1891.

HISTORY OF DOGMA

BY

Dr. ADOLPH HARNACK

Volume V

EDITORIAL NOTE.

THE present volume is the first of three, which will reproduce in English the contents of Vol. III. of Harnack's great work in the German original, third Edition. The author's prefaces to the first and second Editions and to the third Edition are here translated. This volume deals with the epoch-making service of Augustine as a reformer of Christian piety and as a theological teacher, and with the influence he exercised down to the period of the Carlovingian Renaissance. The following volume will complete the history of the Development of Dogma by telling the story of Mediæval Theology. The concluding volume will treat of the Issues of Dogma in the period since the Reformation, and will contain a General Index for the whole work.

A. B. BRUCE.

PREFACE TO FIRST AND SECOND EDITIONS.

THERE does not yet exist a recognised method for presenting the History of Dogma of the Mediæval and more modern period. There is no agreement either as to the extent or treatment of our material, and the greatest confusion prevails as to the goal to be aimed at. The end and aim, the method and course adopted in the present Text-Book, were clearly indicated in the introduction to the first volume. I have seen no reason to make any change in carrying out the work. But however definite may be our conception of the task involved in our branch of study, the immense theological material presented by the Middle Ages, and the uncertainty as to what was Dogma at that time, make selection in many places an experiment. I may not hope that the experiment has always been successful.

After a considerable pause, great activity has been shown in the study of our subject in the last two years. Benrath, Hauck, Bonwetsch, and Seeberg have published new editions of older Text-Books; Loofs has produced an excellent Guide to the History of Dogma; Kaftan has given a sketch of the study in his work on the Truth of the Christian Religion; Möller and Koffmane have devoted special attention to the sections dealing with it in their volumes on Ancient Church History. The study of these books, and many others which I have gratefully made use of, has shown me that my labours on this great subject have not remained isolated or been fruitless. The knowledge of this has outweighed many experiences which I pass over in silence.

This concluding volume counts, to a greater extent than its predecessors, on the indulgence of my learned colleagues; for its author is not a "specialist," either in the history of the Mediæval Church or in the period of the Reformation. But the advantage possessed by him who comes to the Middle Ages and the Reformation with a thorough knowledge of ecclesiastical antiquity perhaps outweighs the defects of an account which does not everywhere rest on a complete induction. One man can really review all the sources for the history of the Ancient Church ; but as regards the Middle Ages and the history of the Reformation, even one more familiar with them than the author of this Text-Book will prove his wisdom simply by the most judicious choice of the material which he studies independently. The exposition of Augustine, Anselm, Thomas, the Council of Trent, Socinianism, and Luther rests throughout on independent studies. This is also true of other parts ; but sections will be found in which the study is not advanced, but only its present position is reproduced.

I have spent a great deal of time on the preparation of a Table of Contents. I trust it will assist the use of the book. But for the book itself, I wish that it may contribute to break down the power that really dictates in the theological conflicts of the present, *viz.*, ignorance. We cannot, indeed, think too humbly of the importance of theological science for Christian piety ; but we cannot rate it too highly as regards the development of the Evangelical Church, our relation to the past, and the preparation of that better future in which, as once in the second century, the Christian faith will again be the comfort of the weak and the strength of the strong.

Berlin, 24th Dec., 1889.

PREFACE TO THIRD EDITION.

SINCE this volume first appeared, there may have been published about fifty monographs and more extensive treatises on the Western History of Dogma, most of which have referred to it. I have tried to make use of them for the new Edition, and I also proposed to make other additions and corrections on the

original form of the book, without finding myself compelled to
carry out changes in essential points. I have thankfully studied
the investigations, published by Dilthey in the Archiv f. Gesch.
d. Philosophie, Vols. V. to VII., on the reformed system of
doctrine in its relation to Humanism and the "natural system."
He has examined the reformed conceptions in connections in
which they have hitherto been seldom or only superficially considered, and he has, therefore, essentially advanced a knowledge
of them.

Among the many objections to the plan of this work, and the
critical standards observed in it, four are especially of importance.
It has been said that in this account the development of Dogma
is judged by the gospel, but that we do not learn clearly what
the gospel is. It has further been maintained that the History
of Dogma is depicted as a pathological process. Again, the
plan of Book III., headed "The threefold outcome of Dogma,"
has been attacked. And, lastly, it has been declared that,
although the account marks a scientific advance, it yet bears too
subjective or churchly a stamp, and does not correspond to the
strictest claims of historical objectivity.

As to the first objection, I believe that I have given a fuller
account of my conception of the gospel than has been yet done
in any text-book of the History of Dogma. But I gladly give
here a brief epitome of my view. The preaching of Jesus contains three great main sections. Firstly, the message of the
approaching Kingdom of God or of the future salvation; secondly,
the proclamation of the actual state of things and of thoughts,
such as are given in Matthew VI. 25-34; VII. 7-11; IX. 2; X.
28-33, etc. (see Vol. I., p. 74 f.); thirdly, the new righteousness
(the new law). The middle section connected with Matthew
XI. 25-30, and therefore also combined with the primitive
Christian testimony regarding Jesus as Lord and Saviour, I hold,
from strictly historical and objective grounds, to be the true
main section, the gospel in the gospel, and to it I subordinate
the other portions. That Christ himself expressed it under
cover of Eschatology I know as well (Vol. I., p. 58) as the anti-
quarians who have so keen an eye for the everlasting yesterday.

As to the second objection I am at a loss. After the new

religion had entered the Roman Empire, and had combined with
it in the form of the universal Catholic Church, the History of
Dogma shows an advance and a rise in all its main features
down to the Reformation. I have described it in this sense
from Origen to Athanasius, Augustine, Bernard, and Francis, to
mystic Scholasticism and to Luther. It is to me a mystery how
far the history should nevertheless have been depicted as a
"process of disease." Of course superstitions accumulated, as in
every history of religion, but within this incrustation the individual ever became stronger, the sense for the gospel more active,
and the feeling for what was holy and moral more refined and
pure. But as regards the development from the beginnings of
the evangelic message in the Empire down to the rise of the
Catholic Church, I have not permitted myself to speculate how
splendid it would have been if everything had happened differently from what it did. On the other hand, I grant that I have
not been able to join in praising the formation of that tradition
and theology which has lowered immediate religion to one that
is mediated, and has burdened faith with complicated theological
and philosophical formulas. Just as little could it occur to me
to extol the rise of that ecclesiastical rule that chiefly means
obedience, when it speaks of faith. But in this there is no
"pathology"; the formations that arose overcame Gnosticism.

My critics have not convinced me that the conception followed
by me in reference to the final offshoots of the History of Dogma
is unhistorical. But I readily admit that the History of Dogma
can also be treated as history of ecclesiastical theology, and that
in this way the account can bring it down to the present time.
Little is to be gained by disputing about such questions in an
either-or fashion. If we regard Protestantism as a new
principle which has superseded the *absolute* authority of Dogmas,
then, in dealing with the History of Dogma, we must disregard
Protestant forms of doctrine, however closely they may approximate to ancient Dogma. But if we look upon it as a particular
reform of Western Catholicism, we shall have to admit its
doctrinal formations into that history. Only, even in that case,
we must not forget that the Evangelical Churches, tried by the

notion of a church which prevailed for 1300 years, are no churches. From this the rest follows of itself.

Finally, as regards the last objection, I may apply chiefly to my account a verdict recently passed by a younger fellow-worker:—"The History of Dogma of to-day is, when regarded as science, a half thing." Certainly it is in its beginnings, and it falls far short of perfection. It must become still more circumspect and reserved ; but I should fear, lest it be so purified in the crucible of this youngest adept—who meantime, however, is still a member of the numerous company of those who only give advice—that nothing of consequence would remain, or only that hollow gospel, "religion is history," which he professes to have derived from the teaching of four great prophets, from whom he could have learnt better. We are all alike sensible of the labours and controversies which he would evade ; but it is one of the surprises that are rare even in theology, that one of our number should be trying in all seriousness to divide the child between the contending mothers, and that by a method which would necessarily once more perpetuate the dispute that preceded the division. The ecclesiastics among Protestants, although they arrogate to themselves the monopoly of "Christian" theology on the title-pages of their books, will never give up the claim to history and science; they will, therefore, always feel it their duty to come to terms with the "other" theology. Nor will scientific theology ever forget that it is the conscience of the Evangelical Church, and as such has to impose demands on the Church which it serves in freedom.

Berlin, 11th July, 1897.   ADOLF HARNACK.

CONTENTS.

PART II.

DEVELOPMENT OF ECCLESIASTICAL DOGMA.

BOOK II.

*Expansion and Remodelling of Dogma into a Doctrine of Sin,
Grace, and Means of Grace on the basis of the Church.*

Second Part.

DEVELOPMENT OF ECCLESIASTICAL DOGMA.

SECOND BOOK.

Expansion and Remodelling of Dogma into a Doctrine of Sin, Grace and means of Grace on the basis of the Church.

"Domini mors potentior erat quam vita . . .
Lex Christianorum crux est sancta Christi."
——*Pseudo-Cyprian.*

"Die Ehrfurcht vor dem, was unter uns ist, ist ein Letztes wozu die Menschheit gelangen konnte und musste. Aber was gehörte dazu, die Erde nicht allein unter sich liegen zu lassen und sich auf einen höheren Geburtsort zu berufen, sondern auch Niedrigkeit und Armuth, Spott und Verachtung, Schmach und Elend, Leiden und Tod als göttlich anzuerkennen, ja selbst Sünde und Verbrechen nicht als Hindernisse, sondern als Fördernisse des Heiligen zu verehren!"
——*Goethe.*

CHAPTER I.

HISTORICAL SITUATION.[1]

THE history of piety and of dogmas in the West was so thoroughly dominated by Augustine from the beginning of the fifth century to the era of the Reformation, that we must take this whole time as forming one period. It is indeed possible to doubt whether it is not correct to include also the succeeding period, since Augustinianism continued to exert its influence in the sixteenth century. But we are compelled to prefer the views that the Reformation had all the significance of a new movement, and that the revolt from Augustine was marked even in post-tridentine Catholicism, as well as, completely, in Socinianism.[2] In this second Book of the second Section, therefore, we regard the history of dogma of the West from Augustine to the Reformation as one complete development, and then, in accordance with our definition of dogma and its history,[3] we add the "final stages of dogma" in their triple form—Tridentine Catholicism, Socinianism, and Protestantism.

2. In order rightly to appreciate the part played by Augustine, it is necessary first (Chap. II.) to describe the distinctive character of Western Christianity and Western theologians

---

[1] Baur, Vorles. üb. die christl. D.-G., 2nd vol., 1866. Bach, Die Dogmengeschichte des Mittelalters, 2 vols., 1873, 1875. Seeberg, Die Dogmengesch. des Mittelalters (Thomasius, Die christl. Dogmengesch, 2 Ed., 2 vol., Division I.) 1888. All begin in the period after Augustine, as also Schwane, D.-G. der mittleren, Zeit 1882. Loofs, Leitfaden der D.-G., 3 Ed., 1893. Seeberg, Lehrbuch d. D.-G., Division I., 1895.

[2] The complete breach with Augustine is indeed marked neither by Luther nor Ignatius Loyola, but first by Leibnitz, Thomasius, and—the Probabilists of the seventeenth and eighteenth centuries.

[3] Vol. I., § 1.

anterior to his appearance. It will then appear that while the
West was prepared to favour Augustinianism, those very
elements that especially characterised Western Christianity—
the juristic and moralistic—resisted the Augustinian type of
thought in matters of faith. This fact at once foreshadows the
later history of Augustinianism in the Church.

3. Augustine comes before us, in the first place, as a reformer
of Christian piety, altering much that belonged to vulgar
Catholicism, and *carrying out monotheism strictly and thoroughly*.
He gave the central place to the living relation of the soul to
God ; he took religion out of the sphere of cosmology and the
cultus, and demonstrated and cherished it in the domain of the
deepest life of the soul. On the other hand, we will have to
show that while establishing the sovereignty of faith over all
that is natural, he did not surmount the old Catholic foundation
of the theological mode of thought ; further, that he was not
completely convinced of the supremacy of the religious over the
moral, of the personal state of faith over ecclesiasticism ; and
finally, that in his religious tendencies, as generally, he remained
burdened by the rubbish of ecclesiastical tradition. (Chap. III.)

4. Augustine falls next to be considered as a Church teacher.
The union of three great circles of thought, which he reconstructed and connected absolutely, assured him, along with the
incomparable impression made by his inexhaustible personality,
of a lasting influence. In the first place, he built up a complete
circle of conceptions, which is marked by the categories, " God,
the soul, alienation from God, irresistible grace, hunger for God,
unrest in the world and rest in God, and felicity," a circle in
which we can easily demonstrate the co-operation of Neoplatonic and monastic Christian elements, but which is really so
pure and simple that it can be taken as the fundamental form
of monotheistic piety in general. Secondly, he gave expression
to a group of ideas in which sin, grace through Christ, grace in
general, faith, love, and hope form the main points ; a Paulinism
modified by popular Catholic elements. Thirdly, he constructed
another group, in which the Catholic Church is regarded as
authority, dispenser of grace, and administrator of the sacraments, and, further, as the means and aim of all God's ordinances.

Here he always constructed, along with a wealth of ideas, a profusion of schemes—not formulas; he re-fashioned Dogmatics
proper, and, speaking generally, gave the first impulse to a study
which, as an introduction to Dogmatics, has obtained such an
immense importance for theology and science since the Scholastics.

5. On the other hand, Augustine always felt that he was, as regards *Dogma*, an *Epigone*, and he submitted himself absolutely to
the tradition of the Church. He was wanting in the vigorous energy
in Church work shown, *e.g.*, by Athanasius, and in the impulse
to force upon the Church in *fixed formulas* the truths that possessed his soul. Consequently the result of his life-work on
behalf of the Church can be described thus. (1) He established
more securely in the West the ancient ecclesiastical tradition as
authority and law. (2) He deepened and, comparatively speaking, Christianised the old religious *tendency*. (3) In the thought
and life of the Church he substituted a *plan of salvation*, along
with an appropriate doctrine of the sacraments, for the old
dogma[1] and the cultus, and instilled into heart and feeling the
fundamental conception of his Christianity ¡that divine grace
was the beginning, middle, and end ; but he himself sought to
harmonise the conception with popular Catholicism, and he expressed this in formulas which, because they were not fixed and
definite, admitted of still further concessions to traditional views.
In a word, he failed to establish without admixture the new and
higher religious style in which he constructed theology. Therefore the ancient Greek dogma which aimed at deification, as well
as the old Roman conception of religion as a legal relationship,
could maintain their ground side by side with it. *Precisely in
the best of his gifts to the Church, Augustine gave it impulses and
problems, but not a solid capital.* Along with this he transmitted
to posterity a profusion of ideas, conceptions, and views which,

---

[1] The ancient dogma has thus formed building material in the West since Augustine.
It has been deprived—at least in the most important respect—of its ancient purpose,
and serves new ones. The stones hewn for a temple, and once constructed into a
temple, now serve for the building of a cathedral. Or perhaps the figure is more
appropriate that the old temple expanded into a cathedral, and wonderfully transformed, is yet perceptible in the cathedral.

unsatisfactorily harmonised by himself, produced great friction, living movements, and, finally, violent controversies.

6. As at the beginning of the history of the Latin Church Cyprian followed Tertullian, and stamped the character of ancient Latin Christianity, so Gregory the Great succeeded Augustine, and gave expression to the mediæval character of Latin Christianity, a form which, under Augustinian formulas, often differs in whole and in details from Augustine. Dogma remains almost throughout, in the Middle Ages, the complex of Trinitarian and Christological doctrines which was handed down with the Symbol. But, besides this, an immense series of theological conceptions, of church regulations and statutes, already possessed a quasi-dogmatic authority. Yet, in acute cases, he could alone be expelled as a heretic who could be convicted of disbelieving one of the twelve articles of the Symbol, or of sharing in the doctrines of heretics already rejected, *i.e.*, of Pelagians, Donatists, etc. Thus it remained up to the time of the Reformation, although the doctrines of the Church—the Pope, and the sacraments, the ecclesiastical sacrament of penance, and the doctrine of transubstantiation—claimed almost dogmatic authority, though only by being artificially connected with the Symbol.

7. The consolidation of the ecclesiastical and dogmatic system into a legal order, in harmony with the genius of Western Christianity, was almost rendered perfect by the political history of the Church in the period of the tribal migrations. The Germans who entered the circle of the Church, and partly became fused with the Latins, partly, but under the leadership of Rome, remained independent, received Christianity in its ecclesiastical form, as something absolutely complete. Therefore, setting aside the Chauvinistic contention that the Germans were predisposed to Christianity,[1] no independent theological movement took place for centuries on purely German soil. No *German Christianity* existed in the Middle Ages in the sense that there was a Jewish, Greek, or Latin form.[2] Even if the

---

[1] Seeberg, (Dogmengesch. des Mittelalters, p. 3), has repeated it.

[2] Even the influence, which some have very recently sought to demonstrate, of German character on the formation of a few mediæval theologumena is at least doubt-

Germans may have attempted to make themselves more thoroughly familiar with Latin Christianity, as *e.g.*, the Slavs did with the Greek—we may recall the old Saxon harmony of the Gospels, etc.—[1] yet there was a complete absence of any independence in consciously appropriating it, up to the settlement of the Begging orders in Germany, properly speaking, indeed, up to the Reformation. Complaints of Papal oppressions, or of external ceremonies, cannot be introduced into this question. The complainers were themselves Roman Christians, and the never-failing sectaries paid homage, not to a "German" Christianity, but to a form of Church which was also imported. If up to the thirteenth century there existed in Germany no independent theology or science, still less was there any movement in the history of dogma.[2] But as soon as Germans, in Germany and England, took up an independent part in the inner movement of the Church, they prepared the way, supported indeed by Augustine, for the Reformation. The case was different on Roman territory. We need not, of course, look at Italy, for the land of the Popes steadily maintained its characteristic indifference to all theology as theology. Apocalyptic, socialistic, and revolutionary movements were not wanting ; Hippocrates and Justinian were studied ; but the ideals of thinkers seldom interested Italians, and they hardly ever troubled themselves about a dogma, if it was nothing more. Spain, also, very soon passed out of the intellectual movement, into which, besides, it had never thrown any energy. For eight centuries it was set the immense practical task of protecting Christendom from Islam : in this war it transformed the law of the Catholic religion into a military discipline. The Spanish history of dogma has been a blank since the days of Bishop Elipandus.

ful (against Cremer). Die Wurzeln des Anselm'schen Satisfactions-begriffs in the Theol. Stud. u. Kritik., 1880, p. 7 ff., 1893, p. 316 ff., and Seeberg, l.c. p. 123. Fuller details in I., ch. 7, Sect. 4.

[1] It was to the advantage, here and there, of simple piety that it had not co-operated in the construction of the Church.

[2] Nitzsch, Deutsche Gesch., II., p. 15 : "(Up to the middle of the eleventh century) the task of administering property was more important to the German Church than the political and dogmatic debates of the neighbouring French hierarchy." See also Döllinger Akad. Vorträge, vol. II., Lecture 1, at beginning.

Thus France alone remains. *In so far as the Middle Ages,
down to the thirteenth century, possessed any dogmatic history, it
was to a very large extent Frankish or French.*[1]   Gaul had been
the land of culture among Latin countries as early as the fourth
and fifth centuries.   'Mid the storms of the tribal migrations,
culture maintained its ground longest in Southern Gaul, and
after a short epoch of barbarism, during which civilisation
seemed to have died out everywhere on the Continent, and
England appeared to have obtained the leadership, France
under the Carlovingians—of course, France allied with Rome
through Boniface—came again to the front.   There it remained,
but with its centre of gravity in the North, between the Seine
and the Rhine.   Paris was for centuries only second to Rome,
as formerly Alexandria and Carthage had been.[2]   The imperial
crown passed to the Germans ; the real ruler of the world sat at
Rome ; but the "studium"—in every sense of the term—
belonged to the French.   Strictly speaking, even in France,
there was no history of dogma in the Middle Ages.   If the
Reformation had not taken place, we would have been as little
aware of any mediæval history of dogma in the West as in the
East ; *for the theological and ecclesiastical movements of the
Middle Ages, which by no means professed to be new dogmatic
efforts, only claim to be received into the history of dogma because
they ended in the dogmas of Trent on the one hand, and in the
symbols of the Reformed Churches and Socinian Rationalism on
the other.*   The whole of the Middle Ages presents itself in the
sphere of dogmatic history as a transition period, the period
when the Church was fixing its relationship to Augustine, and
the numerous impulses originated by him.   This period lasted
so long, (1) because centuries had to elapse before Augustine
found disciples worthy of him, and men were in a position *even
to understand* the chain of ecclesiastical and theological edicts

1 See the correct opinion of Jordanus of Osnabrück (about 1285) that the
Romans had received the *sacerdotium*, the Germans the *imperium*, the French the
studium (Lorenz, Geschichtsquellen, 2 ed., vol. II., p. 296).

2 See on the importance of North-Eastern France, Sohm in the Ztschr. d.
Savigny-Stiftung.   German Division I., p 3 ff., and Schrörs, Hinkmar, p. 3 f.   On
Rome and Paris see Reuter, Gesch. d. Aufkl. I., p. 181.

handed down from antiquity ; (2) because the Roman genius of
the Western Church and the Augustinian spirit were in part ill-
assorted, and it was therefore a huge task to harmonise them ;
and (3) because at the time when complete power had been
gained for the inaependent study of Church doctrine and
Augustine, a new authority, in many respects more congenial to
the spirit of the Church, appeared on the scene, *viz.*, Augustine's
powerful rival,[1] Aristotle. The Roman genius, the superstition
which, descending from the closing period of antiquity, was
strengthened in barbarous times, Augustine, and Aristotle—
these are the four powers which contended for their interpretation of the gospel in the history of dogma in the Middle
Ages.

8. The Middle Ages experienced no dogmatic decisions like
those of Nicæa or Chalcedon.   After the condemnation of
Pelagians and Semipelagians, Monothelites, and Adoptians, the
dogmatic circle was closed.   The actions in the Carlovingian
age against images, and against Ratramnus and Gottschalk
were really of slight importance, and in the fights with later
heretics, so many of whom disturbed the mediæval Church,
old weapons were used, new ones being in fact unnecessary.
The task of the historian of dogma is here, therefore, very
difficult.   In order to know what he ought to describe, to be as
just to ancient dogma in its continued influence as to the new
quasi-dogmatic Christianity in whose midst men lived, he must
fix his eyes on the beginning, Augustine, and the close, the
sixteenth century.   Nothing belongs to the history of dogma
which does not serve to explain this final stage, and even then
only on its dogmatic side, and this again may be portrayed only
in so far as it prepared the way for the framing of new doctrines,
or the official revision of the ancient dogmas.

If my view is right, there are three lines to which we have to
turn our attention.   In the first place we must examine the
history of *piety*, in so far as new tendencies were formed in it,
based on, or existing side by side with Augustinianism ; for the
piety which was determined by other influences led also to the

---

[1] The derisive title of Augustine—" Aristoteles Pœnorum "—was prophetic.   He
got this name from Julian of Eclanum, Aug. Op. imperf., III., 199.

construction of other dogmatic formulas. But the history of piety in the Middle Ages is the history of monachism.[1] We may therefore conjecture that if monachism really passed through a history in the Middle Ages, and not merely endless repetitions, it cannot be indifferent for the history of dogma. As a matter of fact, it will be shown that Bernard and Francis were also doctrinal Fathers. We may here point at once to the fact that Augustine, at least apparently, reveals a hiatus in his theology as dominated by piety; he was able to say little concerning the *work* of Christ in connection with his system of doctrine, and his impassioned love of God was not clearly connected in theory with the impression made by Christ's death, or with Christ's "work." What a transformation, what an access of fervour, Augustinianism had to experience, when impassioned love to the Eternal and Holy One found its object in the Crucified, when it invested with heavenly glory, and referred to the sinful soul, all traits of the beaten, wounded, and dying One, when it began to reflect on the infinite "merits" of its Saviour, because the most profound of thoughts had dawned upon it, that the suffering of the innocent was salvation in history! Dogma could not remain unaffected by what it now found to contemplate and experience in the "crucified" Saviour of Bernard, the "poor" Saviour of Francis.[2] We may say briefly that, by the agency of the mediæval religious virtuosi and theologians, the close connection between God, the "work" of Christ, and salvation was ultimately restored in the Tridentine and ancient Lutheran dogma. The Greek Church had maintained and still maintains it; but Augustine had loosened it, because his great task was to show what God is, and what salvation the soul requires.

In the second place, we have to take the doctrine of the Sacraments into consideration; for great as were the impulses

---

[1] See Ritschl, Gesch. des Pietismus, vol. I., p. 7 ff., and my Vortrag über das Monchthum, 3 ed.

[2] Bernard prepared the way for transforming the Neoplatonic exercitium of the contemplation of the All and the Deity into methodical reflection on the sufferings of Christ. Gilbert says: "Dilectus meus, inquit sponsa, candidus et rubicundus. In hoc nobis et candet veritas et rubet caritas."

given here also by Augustine, yet everything was incomplete
which he transmitted to the Church. But the Church as an
institution and training-school required the sacraments above
all, and in its adherence to Augustine it was precisely his
sacramental doctrine, and the conception connected therewith
of gradual justification, of which it laid hold. We shall have to
show how the Church developed this down to the sixteenth
century, how it idealised itself in the sacraments, and fashioned
them into being its peculiar agencies. In the third place, we
have to pursue a line which is marked for us by the names of
Augustine and Aristotle—fides and ratio, auctoritas and ratio
intelligentia and ratio. To investigate this thoroughly would
be to write the history of mediæval science in general. Here,
therefore, we have only to examine it, in so far as there were
developed in it the same manifold fashioning of theological
thought, and those fundamental views which passed into the
formulas, and at the same time into the contents of the doctrinal
creations, of the sixteenth century, and which ultimately almost
put an end to dogma in the original sense of the term. But we
have also to include under the heading "Augustine and Aristotle"
the opposition between the doctrine of the enslaved will and
free grace and that of free will and merit. The latter shattered
Augustinianism within Catholicism.

We cannot trace any dogma regarding the Church in the
Middle Ages until the end of the thirteenth century, but this
is only because the Church was the foundation and the latent
co-efficient of all spiritual and theological movement.[1] Our
account has to make this significance of the Church explicit,
and in doing so to examine the growth of papal power ; for in
the sixteenth century the claim of the Pope was in dispute. On
this point the Western Church was split up. But further,
Augustine had given a central place to the question of the
personal position of the Christian, confusing it, however, by uncertain references to the Church and to the medicinal effect of

---

[1] The opposition to a sacerdotal Church which existed at all times, and was
already strong in the thirteenth century, left no lasting traces down to the fourteenth.
In this century movements began on the soil of Catholicism which led to new forms
of the conception of the Church and compelled it to fix definitively its own.

the means of grace. And the mediæval movement, in proportion as the Church and the sacraments came to the front without any diminution of the longing for an independent faith,[1] was led to the question of *personal assurance.* On this point also— justification—the Western Church was rent asunder.[2] Thus an account of the history of dogma in the Middle Ages will only be complete if it can show how the questions as to the power of the Church (of the Pope, the importance of the Mass and sacraments) and justification came to the front, and how in these questions the old dogma, not indeed outwardly, but really, perished. In Tridentine Catholicism it now became completely, along with its new portions, a body of law; in Protestantism it was still retained only in as far as it showed itself, when compared with the Divine Word, to express the Gospel, to form a bond with the historical past, or to serve as the basis of personal assurance of salvation.

There can be no doubt about the division into periods. After an introduction on Western Christianity and Theology before Augustine, Augustinianism falls to be described. Then we have to discuss the epochs of (1) the Semipelagian controversies and Gregory I.; (2) the Carlovingian Renaissance; (3) the period of Clugny and Bernard (the eleventh and twelfth centuries); and (4) the period of the mendicant orders, as also of the so-called Reformers before the Reformation, *i.e.*, of revived Augustinianism (thirteenth and fifteenth centuries). The Middle Ages only reached their climax after the beginning of the thirteenth century and, having grown spiritually equal to the material received from the ancient Church, then developed all individual energies and conceptions. But then at once began the crises which led to the

---

[1] In the Middle Ages every advance in the development of the authority and power of the Church was accompanied by the growing impression that the Church was corrupt. This impression led to the suspicion that it had become Babylon, and to despair of its improvement.

[2] On this most important point the schism went beyond Augustine; for in the Middle Ages, as regards the ground and assurance of faith, Augustine of the Confessions and doctrine of predestination was played off against Augustine the apologist of the Catholic Church. Luther, however, abandoned both alike, and followed a view which can be shown to exist in Augustine and in the Middle Ages at most in a hidden undercurrent.

Renaissance and Humanism, to the Reformation, Socinianism and Tridentine Catholicism. It is, therefore, impossible to delimit two periods within the thirteenth to the fifteenth century; for Scholasticism and Mysticism, the development of the authoritative, Nominalist, dogmatics, and the attempts to form new doctrines, are all interwoven. *Reformation and Counter-reformation have a common root.*

CHAPTER II.

WESTERN CHRISTIANITY AND WESTERN THEOLOGIANS BEFORE AUGUSTINE.

THE distinctive character of Western Christianity has been frequently referred to in our earlier volumes. We may now, before taking up Augustine and the Church influenced by him, appropriately review and describe the Christianity into which he entered, and on which he conferred an extraordinarily prolonged existence and new vital energies by the peculiar form and training to which he subjected it. It was the Roman Church that transmitted Christianity to the Middle Ages. But it might almost be named the Augustinian-Gregorian[1] with as much justice as that of the Augsburg Confession is called the Lutheran.

If, however, we ascend the history of the Latin Church to as near its origin as we can, we find ourselves confronted by a man in whom the character and the future of this Church were already announced, *viz.*, Tertullian. Tertullian and Augustine are the Fathers of the Latin Church in so eminent a sense that, measured by them, the East possessed no Church Fathers at all.[2] The only one to rival them, Origen, exerted his influence in a more limited sphere. Eminently ecclesiastical as his activity was, his Christianity was not really ecclesiastical, but esoteric. His development and the import of his personal life were almost without significance for the mass; he continued to live in his books and among theologians. But with Tertullian and Augus-

---

[1] After Gregory I.

[2] Möhler says very justly, from the Catholic standpoint (Patrologie, p. 737) : " We are often surprised for a moment, and forget that in Tertullian we have before us a writer of the beginning of the third century, we feel so much at home in reading the language, often very familiar to us, in which he discusses difficult questions concerning dogmatics, morals, or even the ritual of the Church."

tine it was different. It is true that only a fraction of Tertullian's teaching was retained, that he was tolerated by posterity only in Cyprian's reduced version, and that Augustine became more and more a source of uneasiness to, and was secretly opposed by, his Church. Yet both passed into the history of the Western Catholic Church with their personality, with the characteristics of their Christian thought and feeling. The frictions and unresolved dissonances, in which they wore themselves out, were transmitted to the future as well as the concords they sounded, and the problems, which they could not master in their own inner experience, became the themes of world-historical spiritual conflicts.[1] We can exhibit the superiority of Western to Eastern Christianity at many points ; we can even state a whole series of causes for this superiority ; but one of the most outstanding is the fact that while the East was influenced by a commonplace succession of theologians and monks, the West was moulded by Tertullian and Augustine.

Roman Christianity, still (c. 180) essentially Greek in form, but already with important features of its own,[2] had won the Great African to its service.[3] It had already transmitted to him Latin translations of Biblical books ; but on this foundation Tertullian laboured, creating both thought and language, because he was able thoroughly to assimilate the new faith, and to express his whole individuality in it.[4]

In doing so he adopted all the elements which tradition offered him. First, as a Christian Churchman, he took up the old enthusiastic and rigorous, as well as the new anti-heretical, faith. He sought to represent both, and in his sovereign law to verify the strict *lex* of the ancient *disciplina*, founded on eschato-

---

[1] Ultimately men were content, indeed, with preserving the inconsistencies, treating them as problems of the schools, and ceasing to attempt to solve them ; for time makes even self-contradictions tolerable, and indeed to some extent hallows them.

[2] See the 1 Ep. of Clement, also the tractate on The Players, and the testimonies of Ignatius, Dionysius of Corinth and others as to the old Roman Church.

[3] De praescr. 36 : " Si Italiæ adjaces habes Romam, unde nobis auctoritas quoque praesto est."

[4] On Church Latin, see Koffmane's work, which contains much that is valuable, Gesch. des Kirchenlateins, 1879-1881.

logical hopes, and allied with unrestrained pneumatic dogmatics, and also the strict *lex* of the new rule of faith, which seemed ancient, because the heretics were undoubtedly innovators. He sought to be a disciple of the prophets and an obedient son of his Episcopal teachers. While he spent his strength in the fruitless attempt to unite them,[1] he left both forces as an inheritance to the Church of the West. If the history of that Church down to the sixteenth century exhibits a conflict between orthodox clerical and enthusiastic, between biblical and pneumatic elements, if monachism here was constantly in danger of running into apocalyptics and enthusiasm, and of forming an opposition to the Episcopal and world-Church, all that is foreshadowed in Tertullian.

A further element, which here comes before us, is the juristic. We know that jurisprudence and legal thought held the chief place in mediæval philosophy, theology, and ethics.[2] Post-apostolic Greek Christians had, indeed, already put Christianity forward as the "law," and the Roman community may have cultivated this view with peculiar energy;[3] but in and by itself this term is capable of so many meanings as to be almost neutral. Yet through the agency of Tertullian, by his earlier profession a lawyer, all Christian forms received a legal impress. He not only transferred the technical terms of the jurists into the ecclesiastical language of the West, but he also contemplated, from a legal standpoint, all relations of the individual and the Church to the Deity, and *vice versâ*, all duties and rights, the

---

[1] See our expositions of this in Vol. II., p. 67 ff., 108 ff., 128 f., 311 f.

[2] See v. Schulte, Gesch. der Quellen und Lit. d. kanonischen Rechts, Vol. I., pp. 92-103, Vol. II., p. 512 f. Also his Gedanken über Aufgabe und Reform d. jurist. Studiums, 1881 : " The science of law was in practice the leading factor in Church and State from the twelfth century." That it is so still may, to save many words, be confirmed by a testimony of Döllinger's. In a memorable speech on Phillips he says, (Akad. Vorträge, Vol. II., p. 185 f.) : " Frequent intercourse with the two closely-allied converts, Iarcke and Phillips, showed me how an ultramontane and papistical conception of the Christian religion was especially suggested and favoured by legal culture and mode of thought, which was dominated, even in the case of German specialists like Phillips, not by ancient German, but Roman legal ideas."

[3] On the designation of Holy Scripture as "lex" in the West, see Zahn, Gesch. d. neutestamentlichen Kanous, I. 1, p. 95 f.

moral imperative as well as the actions of God and Christ, nay, their mutual relationship. He who was so passionate and fanciful seemed never to be thoroughly satisfied until he had found the scheme of a legal relationship which he could proclaim as an inviolable authority; he never felt secure until he had demonstrated inner compulsions to be external demands, exuberant promises to be stipulated rewards. But with this the scheme of personal rights was applied almost universally. God appears as the mighty partner who watches jealously over his rights. Through Tertullian this tendency passed into the Western Church, which, being Roman, was disposed to favour it; there it operated in the most prejudicial way. If we grant that by it much that was valuable was preserved, and juristic thought did contribute to the understanding of some, not indeed the most precious, Pauline conceptions, yet, on the whole, religious reflection was led into a false channel, the ideas of satisfaction and merit becoming of the highest importance, and the separation of Western from primitive and Eastern Christianity was promoted.[1]

Another element is closely connected with the legal, *viz.*, the syllogistic and dialetical. Tertullian has been extolled as a speculative theologian; but this is wrong. Speculation was not his forte; we perceive this very plainly when we look at his relation to Irenaeus. Notice how much he has borrowed from this predecessor of his, and how carefully he has avoided, in doing so, his most profound speculations! Tertullian was a Sophist in the good and bad sense of the term. He was in his element in Aristotelian and Stoic dialectics; in his syllogisms he is a philosophising advocate. But in this also he was the pioneer of his Church, whose theologians have always reasoned more than they have philosophised. The manner in which he rings the changes on *auctoritas* and *ratio*, or combines them, and spins lines of thought out of them; the formal treatment of problems, meant to supply the place of one dealing with the matter, until it ultimately loses sight of aim and object, and falls a prey to the delusion that the certainty of the conclusion

[1] Consider, *e.g.*, a sentence like this of Cyprian De unit. 15: "Justitia opus est, ut promereri quis possit deum judicem."

guarantees the certainty of the premises—this whole method only too well known from mediæval Scholasticism, had its originator in Tertullian.[1]   In the classical period of eastern

---

[1] A series of legal schemes framed by Tertullian for his dogmatics and ethics have been given in Vol. II., 279 f., 294 f., Vol. IV. pp. 110, 121. In addition to his speculation on *substantia, persona,* and *status,* the categories *offendere, satisfacere, promereri, acceptare,* and *rependere,* etc., play the chief part in his system.   Most closely connected with the legal contemplation of problems is the abstract reference to authority ; for one does not obey a law because he finds it to be good and just, but because it is law. (Tertullian, indeed, knows very well, when defending himself against heathen insinuations, that the above dictum is not sufficient in the sphere of religion and morals, see *e.g.,* Apolog. 4.)   This attitude of Tertullian, led up to by his dialectical procedure and his alternations between *auctoritas* and *ratio,* produces in many passages the impression that we are listening to a mediæval Catholic.   In regard to the alternation above described, the work De corona is especially characteristic ; but so is Adv. Marc. I., 23 f.   He writes, De pænit. 4 : " Nos pro nostris angustiis unum inculcamus, bonum atque optimum esse quod deus præcipit.   Audaciam existimo de bono divini præcepti disputare.   Neque enim quia bonum est, idcirco auscultare debemus, sed quia deus præcepit.   Ad exhibitionem obsequii prior est majestas divinæ potestatis, prior est auctoritas imperantis quam utilitas servientis."   (Compare Scorp. 2, 3 ; De fuga, 4; De cor. 2.)   But the same theologian writes, De pæn. 1 : "Res dei ratio, quia deus nihil non ratione providit, nihil non ratione tractari intellegique voluit."   The work De pænit. is in general peculiarly fitted to initiate us into Tertullian's style of thought.   I shall in the sequel pick out the most important points, and furnish parallels from his other writings.   Be it noticed first that the work emphasises the three parts, *vera poenitentia* (deflere, metus dei), *confessio* and *satisfactio,* and then adds the *venia* on the part of the *offensus deus.*
    In chap. II. we already meet with the expression "merita pænitentiæ."   There we read : "ratio salutis *certam formam* tenet, ne bonis umquam factis cogitatisve quasi violenta aliqua manus injiciatur.   Deus enim *reprobationem* bonorum ratam non habens, utpote suorum, quorum cum auctor et defensor sit necesse est, proinde et *acceptator,* si acceptator etiam *remunerator* . . . bonum factum deum habet *debitorem,* sicuti et malum, *quia judex omnis remunerator est causæ."*   (De orat. 7 : "pænitentia demonstratur *acceptabilis deo ;"* we have also "commendatior ").   Chap. III. ; " Admissus ad dominica præcepta ex ipsis statim eruditur, id peccato deputandum, a quo deus arceat."   (The distinction between præcepta and consilia dominica is familiar in Tertullian ; see Ad. uxor. II. 1 ; De coron. 4 ; Adv. Marc. II. 17.   In Adv. Marc. I. 29, he says that we may not reject marriage altogether, because if we did there would be no meritorious sanctity.   In Adv. Marc. I. 23, the distinction is drawn between "debita" and "indebita bonitas ").   Chap. III. : "Voluntas facti origo est ;" a disquisition follows on *velle, concupiscere, perficere.*   Chap. V. : "Ita qui per delictorum pænitentiam instituerat dominus *satisfacere,* diabolo per aliæ pænitentiæ pænitentiam *satisfaciet,* eritque tanto magis *perosus* deo, quanto æmulo ejus *acceptus."*   (See De orat. 11 ; "fratri satisfacere," 18 ; "disciplinæ satisfacere," 23 ; satisfacimus deo domino nostro " ; De jejun. 3 ; De pud. 9, 13 ; De pat. 10, 13, etc., etc. : "peccator patri satisfacit," namely, through his penances ; see De pud. 13 : "hic jam carnis interitum in officium pænitentiæ interpretantur, quod videatur

theology men did not stop at *auctoritas* and *ratio ;* they sought to reach the inner convincing phases of authority, and understood by *ratio* the reason determined by the conception of the matter jejuniis et sordibus et incuria omni et dedita opera malæ tractationis carnem exterminando satis deo facere "). In ch. V. it is explained quite in the Catholic manner that *timor* is the fundamental form of the religious relation. Here, as in countless other passages, the "deus offensus" moves Tertullian's soul (see De pat. 5 : "hinc deus irasci exorsus, unde offendere homo inductus.") Fear dominates the whole of penitence. (De pænit. 6 : "metus est instrumentum pænitentiæ." In general "offendere deum" and "satisfacere deo" are the proper technical terms ; see De pæn. 7 : "offendisti, sed reconciliari adhuc potes ; habes cui satisfacias et quidem volentem." Ch. X. : "intolerandum scilicet pudori, domino offenso satisfacere." Ch. XI. : "castigationem victus atque cultus offenso domino præstare." Along with satisfacere we have "deum iratum, indignatum mitigare, placare, reconciliare." Ch. VI : "omnes salutis *in promerendo deo* petitores sumus." Compare with this "promereri deum" Scorp. 6 : "quomodo multæ mansíones apud patrem, si non pro varietate meritorum . . . porro et si fidei propterea congruebat sublimitati et claritatis aliqua prolatio, tale quid esse opportuerat illud *emolumenti*, quod magno constaret labore, cruciatu, tormento, morte . . . *eadem pretia quæ et merces.*" De orat. 2 : "meritum fidei." 3 : "nos angelorum, si meruimus, candidati" ; 4 : "merita cujusque." De pænit. 6 : "catechumenus mereri cupit baptismum, timet adhuc delinquere, ne non mereretur accipere." De pat. 4 : "artificium promerendi obsequium est, obsequii vero disciplina morigera subjectio est." De virg. vel., 13 : "deus justus est ad *remuneranda* quæ soli sibi fiunt." De exhort. 1 : "nemo indulgentia dei utendo promeretur, sed voluntati obsequendo ;" 2 : "deus quæ vult præcipit et *accepto* facit et æternitatis mercede dispungit." De pud. 10 : "pænitentiam deo immolare . . . magis merebitur fructum pænitentiæ qui nondum ea usus est quam qui jam et abusus est." De jejun. 3 : "ratio promerendi deum" [jejunium iratum deum homini reconciliat, ch. VII.]; 13 : "ultro officium facere deo." How familiar and important in general is to Tertullian the thought of performing a service, a favour to God, or of furnishing him with a spectacle ! He indeed describes as a heathen idea (Apolog. 11) the sentence : "conlatio divinitatis meritorum remunerandorum fuit ratio" ; but he himself comes very near it ; thus he says (De exhortat. 10) : "per continentiam *negotiaberis magnam substantiam sanctitatis*, parsimonia carnis spiritum acquires." He sternly reproves, Scorp. 15, the saying of the "Lax" : Christus non vicem passionis sitit ; he himself says (De pat. 16) : "*rependamus* Christi patientiam, quam pro nobis ipse dependit." De pænit. 6 : "Quam porro ineptum, quam pænitentiam non adimplere, ei veniam delictorum sustinere ? *Hoc est pretium non exhibere, ad mercem manum emittere.* Hoc enim pretio dominus veniam addicere instituit ; hac pænitentiæ *compensatione redimendam* proponit impunitatem," (see Scorp. 6 : "nulli *compensatio* invidiosa est, in qua aut gratiæ aut injuriæ communis est ratio"). In Ch. VI. Tertullian uses "imputare," and this word is not rarely found along with "reputare" ; in Ch. VII. we have "indulgentia" (indulgere), and these terms are met somewhat frequently ; so also "restituere" (ch. VII. 12 : "restitutio peccatoris"). De pat. 8 : "tantum relevat *confessio* delictorum, quantum dissimulatio exaggerat ; *confessio omni satisfactionis consilium est.*" Further, ch. IX.: "Hujus igitur pænitentiæ secundæ et unius quanto in arte negotium est, *tanto operosior probatio*

in question.   In the West, *auctoritas* and *ratio* stood for a very
long time side by side without their relations being fixed—see
the mediæval theologians from Cassian—and the speculation
introduced by Augustine was ultimately once more eliminated,
(that sounds quite mediæval), ut non sola conscientia præferatur, sed aliquo etiam actu
administretur.   Is actus, qui magis Græco vocabulo exprimitur et frequentatur, ex-
omologesis est, qua delictum domino nostro confitemur, non quidem ut ignaro, *sed
quatenus satisfactio confessione disponitur*, confessione pænitentia nascitur, *pænitentia
deus mitigatur*.   Concerning this exhomologesis, this tearful confession, he goes on :
"commendat pænitentiam deo *et temporali afflictatione æterna supplicia non dicam
frustratur sed expungit.*"   ("Commendare" as used above is common, see *e.g.*, De
virg. vel. 14, and De pat. 13 : "patientia corporis [penances] precationes commendat,
deprecationes affirmat ; hæc aures Christi aperit, clementiam elicit.").   The conception
is also distinctly expressed by Tertullian that in the ceremony of penance the Church
completely represents Christ himself, see ch. X. : "in uno et altero ecclesia est,
ecclesia vero Christus.   Ergo cum te ad fratrum genua protendis, *Christum contrectas,
Christum exoras.*"   De pudic. 10, shows how he really bases pardon solely on the
"cessatio delicti" ; "etsi venia est pænitentiæ fructus, hanc quoque consistere non
licet sine cessatione delicti.   *Ita cessatio delicti radix est veniæ ut venia sit pænitentiæ
fructus.*"   Further ch. 11. : "omne delictum aut venia dispungit aut poena, venia ex
castigatione, poena ex damnatione"; but "satisfactio" is implied in the "castigatio."
In De pudic. 1 the notorious lax edict of Calixtus is called "liberalitas" (venia) *i.e.*,
"indulgence."   Let us further recall some formulas which are pertinent here.   Thus
we have the often-used figure of the "militia Christi," and the regimental oath—
sacramentum.   So also the extremely characteristic alternation between "gratia" and
"voluntas humana," most clearly given in De exhort. 2 : "non est bonæ et solidæ
fidei sic omnia ad voluntatem dei referre et ita adulari unum quemque dicendo nihil
fieri sine nutu ejus, ut non intelligamus, *esse aliquid in nobis ipsis.* . . . Non debemus
quod nostro expositum est arbitrio in domini referre voluntatem"; Ad uxor. 1, 8 :
"quædam enim sunt divinæ liberalitatis, quædam nostræ operationis."   Then we
have the remarkable attempt to distinguish two wills in God, one manifest and one
hidden, and to identify these with præcepta and consilia, in order ultimately to
establish the "hidden" or "higher" alone.   De exhort. 2 f. : "cum solum sit in
nobis velle, et in hoc probatur nostra erga deum mens, an ea velimus quæ cum voluntate ipsius faciunt, alte et impresse recogitandum esse dico dei voluntatem, quid etiam
in occulto velit.   Quæ enim in manifesto scimus omnes."   Now follows an exposition on the two wills in God, the higher, hidden, and proper one, and the lower :
"Deus ostendens quid magis velit, minorem voluntatem majore delevit.   Quantoque
notitiæ tuæ utrumque proposuit, tanto definiit, id te sectari debere quod declaravit se
magis velle.   Ergo si ideo declaravit, ut id secteris quod magis vult, sine dubio, nisi
ita facis, contra voluntatem ejus sapis, sapiendo contra potiorem ejus voluntatem,
magisque offendis quam promereris, quod vult quidem faciendo et quod mavult re-
spuendo.   Ex parte delinquis ; ex parte, si non delinquis, non tamen promereris.
Non porro et promereri nolle delinquere est ?   Secundum igitur matrimonium, *si est
ex illa dei voluntate quæ indulgentia vocatur,* etc., etc."   On the other hand, see the
sharp distinction between sins of ignorance ("natural sins") and sins of "conscientia
et voluntas, ubi et culpa sapit et gratia," De pud. 10.

as is proved by the triumph of Nominalism.   Stoic, or "Aristotelian" rationalism, united with the recognition of empirical
authority under cover of Augustinian religious formulas, remained the characteristic of Roman Catholic dogmatics and
morality.[1]

But the Western type of thought possessed, besides this, an
element in which it was considerably superior to the Eastern,
the psychological view.   The importance due to Augustine in
this respect has been better perceived in recent years, and we
may look for better results as regards the share of Scholasticism
in the development of modern psychology.[2]   In Augustine himself Stoic rationalism was thrust strongly into the background by
his supreme effort to establish the psychology of the moral and
immoral, the pious and impious on the basis of actual observation.   His greatness as a *scientific* theologian is found essentially
in the psychological element.   But that also is first indicated in
Tertullian.   As a moralist he indeed follows, so far as he is a
philosopher, the dogmatism of the Stoa ; but Stoic physics
could lead into an empirical psychology.   In this respect Tertullian's great writing, "De anima," is an extremely important
achievement.   It contains germs of insight and aspirations
which developed afterwards; and another Western before Augustine, Arnobius, also did better work in grasping problems
psychologically than the great theologians of the East.[3]   This

---

[1] Augustine has also employed both notions in countless places since the writings
De Ordine (see II. 26 : ad discendum necessarie dupliciter ducimur, auctoritate
atque ratione) and De vera religione (45 : animae medicina distribuitur in auctoritatem
atque rationem).

[2] See Kahl, Die Lehre vom Primat des Willens bei Augustin, Duns Scotus und
Descartes 1886, as also the works of Siebeck ; cf. his treatise " Die Anfänge der
neueren Psychologie in der Scholastik " in the Ztschr. f. Philos. u. philosoph.
Kritik.   New series.   93 Vol., p. 161 ff., and Dilthey's Einl. in d. Geisteswiss.
Vol. I.

[3] See Franke, Die Psychologie und Erkenntnisslehre des Arnobius, 1878, in which
the empiricism and criticism of this eclectic theologian are rightly emphasised.   The
perception that Arnobius was not original, but had taken his refutation of Platonism
from Lucretius, and also that he remained, after becoming a Christian, the rhetorician
that he had been before (see Röhricht Seelenlehre des Arnobius, Hamburg, 1893),
cannot shake the fact that his psychology is influenced by the consciousness of
redemption.

side of Western theology undoubtedly continued weak before
Augustine, because the eclecticism and moralism to which Cicero
had especially given currency held the upper hand through the
reading of his works.[1]

Finally, still another element falls to be mentioned which
distinguishes the features of Western Christianity from the Eastern, but which it is hard to summarise in one word. Many have
spoken of its more practical attitude. But in the East, Christianity received as practical a form as people there required.
What is meant is connected with the absence of the speculative
tendency in the West. To this is to be attributed the fact that
the West did not fix its attention above all on deification, nor, in
consequence, on asceticism, but kept real life more distinctly in
view ; it therefore obtained to a greater extent from the gospel
what could rule and correct that life. Thus Western Christianity appears to us from the first more popular and biblical, as
well as more ecclesiastical. It may be that this impression is
chiefly due to our descent from the Christianity in question, and
that we can never therefore convey it to a Greek[2]; but it is undeniable that as the Latin idiom of the Church was from its
origin more popular than the Greek, which always retained
something hieratic about it, so the West succeeded to a greater
extent in giving effect to the words of the gospel. For both of
these facts we have to refer again to Tertullian. He had the
gift, granted to few Christian writers, of writing attractively, both
for theologians and laymen. His style, popular and fresh,
must have been extremely effective. On the other hand,
he was able, in writings like De patientia, De oratione, De
pænitentia, or De idololatria, to express the gospel in a concrete
and homely form ; and even in many of his learned and polemical works, which are full of paradoxes, antitheses, rhetorical

---

[1] Compare especially Minucius Felix and Lactantius.

[2] Conversely it is quite intelligible that he who has started with the ideals of classic
antiquity, and has assimilated them, should derive more pleasure from men like
Clemens Alex. Origen and Gregory of Nazianzus than from Tertullian and
Augustine. But this sympathy is less due to the Christianity of the former scholars.
We are no longer directly moved by the religious emotions of the older Greeks, while
expressions of Tertullian and Augustine reach our heart.

figures, frigid sentences, and wild exaggerations, we do not fail
to find the clear and pertinent application of evangelical sayings,
astonishing only by its simplicity, and reminding us, where the
thought takes a higher flight, not infrequently of Augustine.[1]

The Christianity and theology of Tertullian, whose elements
we have here endeavoured to characterise, were above all
headed by the primitive Christian hope and morality. In these
was comprehended what he felt to be his inmost thought. Both
phases recur in a large section of Latin literature of the third

---

[1] Not only is the distinction between "natura" and "gratia" (*e.g.*, De anima 21),
or between "gratia" and "virtus" common in Tertullian, not only has he—in his
later writings—laid great stress on the continued effect of Adam's sin and the transmission of death, but there also occur many detached thoughts and propositions which
recall Augustine. (For the transmission of sin and death see De exhort. 2; Adv.
Marc. I., 22; De pud. 6, 9; De jejun. 3, 4: "mors cum ipso genere traducto,"
"primordiale delictum expiare," cf. the expression "vitium originis"; further, also,
the writing De pascha comput. 12, 21.)—De orat. 4: "summa est voluntatis dei salus
eorum, quos adoptavit." De pat. 1: "Bonorum quorundam intolerabilis magnitudo
est, ut ad capienda et præstanda ea sola gratia divinæ inspirationis operetur. Nam
quod maxime bonum, id maxime penes deum, nec alius id, quam qui possidet, dispen-
sat, ut cuique dignatur." De pænit. 2: "Bonorum unus est titulus salus hominis
criminum pristinorum abolitione præmissa." De pat. 12: "Dilectio summum fidei
sacramentum, Christiani nominis thesaurus." De orat. 4: In order to fulfil the will
of God "opus est dei voluntate . . . Christus erat voluntas et potestas patris." 5:
"quidquid nobis optamus, in illum auguramur, et illi deputamus, quod ab illo exspec-
tamus." 9: "Deus solus docere potuit, quomodo se vellet orari." De pænit. 2:
"Quod homini proficit, deo servit." 4: "Rape occasionem inopinatæ felicitatis, ut
ille tu, nihil quondam penes deum nisi stilla situlæ et areæ pulvus et vasculum figuli,
arbor exinde fias illa quæ penes aquas seritur, etc." 4: "Obsequii ratio in similitudine animorum constituta est." De orat. 7: "debitum in scripturis delicti figura est.'
De bapt. 5: exempto *reatu* eximitur et *poena*. De pud. 22: "Quis alienam mortem
sua solvit nisi solus dei filius." Tertullian imputed the proposition "peccando pro-
meremur" (De pud. 10) to his ecclesiastical opponents. The religious elements in his
mode of thought seem to have been decided—apart from the New Testament books—
by the reading of Seneca's writings. In these Stoic morality seems to have been
deepened, and in part transcended, by a really religious feeling and reflection, so that
it was possible to pass from them to Pauline Christianity. Seneca, however, influenced Western thinkers generally : see Minucius Felix, Novatian, and Jerome De inl.
vir. 12. Even in Cyprian there occur traits that might be termed Augustinian :
notice how he emphasises the immanence of Christ in believers, *e.g.*, Ep. 10, 3, and
cf. the remarkable statement Ep. 10, 4: "Christus in certamine agonis nostri et coronat pariter et coronatur." Add Ep. 58, 5: "Spiritus dei, qui cum a confitentibus
non discedit neque dividitur, ipse in nobis loquitur et coronatur." See also the
Roman epistle Ep. 8, 3.

and of the first half of the fourth century.¹ There it is hardly possible to find any traces of Antignostic dogmatics; on the contrary, Apocalyptics were developed with extreme vividness, and morality, often Stoic in colouring, received a stringent form.² The whole of the abundant literary labours and dogmatic efforts of Hippolytus seem to have been lost on the West from the first and completely.

But Tertullian also was deprived by his Montanism of the full influence which he might have exerted on the Church.³ The results of his work passed to Cyprian, and, though much abbreviated and modified, were circulated by him. *For the period from* A.D. 260 *down to Ambrose—indeed, properly speaking, to Augustine and Jerome—Cyprian became the Latin Church author par excellence.* All known and unknown Latin writers of his time, and after him, had but a limited influence : he, as an edifying and standard author, dictated like a sovereign to the Western Church for the next 120 years. His authority ranked close after that of the Holy Scriptures, and it lasted up to the time of Augustine.⁴

---

¹ Compare especially also the writings which are falsely headed with the name of Cyprian, and have begun to be examined in very recent years.

² Compare the characteristics of the Christianity taught by Commodian, Arnobius, and Lactantius, vol. III. p. 77 ff. Novatian was accused of Stoicism by his opponents. Several of the writings headed by the name of Cyprian are very old and important for our knowledge of ancient Latin Christianity. I have verified that in the tractates De aleatoribus (Victor), Ad Novatianum (Sixtus), and De laude mart. (Novatian) (Texte und Unters, VI., 1 ; XIII., 1 and 4 ; see also the writings, to be attributed to Novatian, De spectac, and De bono pudic.) ; but let anyone read also "De duobus montibus" in order to gain an idea of the theological simplicity and archaic quality of these Latins. And yet the author of the above treatise succeeded in formulating the phrase (c. 9) : "Lex Christianorum crux est sancta Christi filii dei vivi." Most instructive are the Instructiones of Commodian. The great influence of Hermas' Pastor, and the interest directed accordingly to the Church, are character-istic of this whole literature. Even unlearned authors continued to occupy themselves with the Church, see the Symbol of Carthage : "credo remissionem peccatorum per sanctam ecclesiam."

³ See my treatise on "Tertullian in der Litteratur der alten Kirche" in the Sitzungsber, d. K. Preuss. Akad. d. Wissensch, 1895, p. 545 ff.

⁴ See a short demonstration of this in my Texten und Unters, V 1, p. 2, and elaborated in my Altchristl. Litt.-Gesch., Part I., p. 688 ff. Pitra has furnished new material for the acquaintance also of the East with Cyprian in the Analecta

Cyprian had hardly one original theological thought; for even the work "De unitate ecclesiæ" rests on points of view which are partly derived from the earlier Catholic Fathers, and partly borrowed from the Roman Church, to which they were indigenous. In the extremely authoritative work, "De opere et eleemosynis" the Tertullian conceptions of merit and satisfaction are strictly developed, and are made to serve as the basis of penance, almost without reference to the grace of God in Christ. Cyprian's chief importance is perhaps due to the fact that, influenced by the consequences of the Decian storm he founded, in union with the Roman bishop Cornelius, what was afterwards called the sacrament of penance; in this, indeed, he was the slave rather than the master of circumstances; and in addition, he was yielding to Roman influences which had been working in this direction since Calixtus. He established the rule of the hierarchy in the Church in the spheres of the sacrament, sacrifice, and discipline; he set his seal on Episcopalianism; he planted firmly the conceptions of a legal relation between man and God, of works of penance as means of grace, and of the "satisfactory" expiations of Christ. He also created clerical language with its solemn dignity, cold-blooded anger, and misuse of Biblical words to interpret and criticise contemporary affairs—a metamorphosis of the Tertullian genius for language. Cyprian by no means inherited the interest taken by Tertullian in Antignostic theology. Like all great princes of the Church, he was a theologian only in so far as he was a catechist. He held all the more firmly by the symbol, and knew how to state in few words its undoubted meaning, and to turn it skilfully even against allied movements like that of Novatian.

This had been learnt from Rome, where, since as early as the end of the second century, the "Apostles'" creed had been used with skill and tact against the motley opinions held about doctrine by Eastern immigrants. The Roman Bishops of the

Sacra. Cyprian's unparalleled authority in the West is attested especially by Lucifer, Prudentius, Optatus, Pacian, Jerome, Augustine, and Mommsen's catalogue of the Holy Scriptures. The see of Carthage was called in after times " Cathedra Cypriani," as that of Rome "Cathedra Petri." Optat. I., 10.

third century did not meddle with dogmatic disputes ; the only
two who tried it, and undoubtedly rendered great services to the
Church, Hippolytus and Novatian, could not keep the sympathies of the clergy or the majority.　In the West men did not
live as Christians upon dogma, but they were obedient to the
short law (lex) presented in the Symbol;[1] they impressed the
East by the confidence with which, when necessary, they adopted
a position in dogmatic questions, following in the doctrine of
the Trinity and in Christology an original scheme formed by
Tertullian and developed by Novatian;[2] while at the same time
they worked at the consolidation of the constitution of the
Church, the construction of a practical ecclesiastical moral
code, as also the disciplining and training of the community through Divine Service and the rules of penance.[3]
The canons of Elvira, which, for the rest, are not lax, but are
even distinguished by their stringency, show how strictness and
clemency were united, Christendom being marked off from the
world, while at the same time a life in the world was rendered
possible, and even the grossest sins were still indulged in.　The
result was a complete ecclesiastical constitution, with an almost
military organisation.　At its head stood the Roman Bishop,
who, in spite of the abstract equality of all Bishops, occupied a
unique position, not only as representative, but also as actual
defender of the unity of the Church, which, nevertheless, was

---

[1] The perversions adopted in order to represent the Christians as being bound to
the "lex" are shown, *e.g.*, by the argument in the, we admit, late and spurious
writing attributed to Cyprian De XII., abusivis sæculi, chap. 12: "Dum Christus
finis est legis, qui sine lege sunt sine Christo sunt ; igitur populus sine lege populus
sine Christo est."　As against this, verdicts such as that cursorily given by Tertullian
(De spect. 2), that the natural man "deum non novit nisi naturali jure, non etiam
familiari," remained without effect.

[2] See on this Vol. II., p. 279 f. 312 f., and Vol. III. and IV. in various places ;
cf. Reuter, Augustin. Studien, pp. 153-230.　Since the West never perceived clearly
the close connection between the result of salvation (ἀφθαρσία) and the Incarnation,
there always existed there a rationalistic element as regards the person of Christ,
which afterwards disclosed itself completely in Pelagianism.　The West only completed its own theory as to Christ after it had transferred to His work conceptions
obtained in the discipline of penance.　But that took place very gradually.

[3] Here again the Instructiones of Commodian are very instructive.

severely shaken, first by Novatianism, and afterwards by Donatism.

When Constantine granted toleration and privileges to the Church, and enabled the provincial Churches to communicate with all freedom, Rome had already become a Latin city, and the Roman community was thoroughly Latinised ; elsewhere also in the West the Greek element, once so powerful, had receded. Undoubtedly, Western Christians had no other idea than that they formed a single Church with the East ; they were actually at one with the Eastern tendency represented by Athanasius in the fundamental conceptions of the doctrines of God, Christ, and eternal salvation. But their interests were often divided, and, in fact, there was little mutual understanding, particularly after Cappadocian orthodoxy triumphed in the East. From the middle of the third century the weakening of the central power had once more restored their independence to all the provinces, and had thus set free the principle of nationality ; and this would have led to a complete reaction and wholesale particularism had not some energetic rulers, the migrations of the tribes, and the Church set up a barrier, which, indeed, ultimately proved too weak in the East.

It was the great dogmatic controversies which compelled the provincial Churches to look beyond their own borders. But the sympathy of the West for the East—there never developed any vital interest in the opposite direction[1]—was no longer general or natural. It sprang, as a rule, from temporary necessities or ambitious purposes. Yet it became of incalculable importance for Western theology ; for their relations with the East, into which the Western Church was brought by the Arian conflict, led Western Christians to observe more closely two great phenomena of the Eastern Church, the *scientific theology (of Origen) and monachism.*

It may here be at once said that the contact and influence which thus arose did not in the end change the genius and

---

[1] An exception of short duration is formed by the interest taken by the Antiochenes in the Western scheme of Christology during the Eutychian controversy : see the epistolary collection of Theodoret and his Eranistes, as also the works of Theodore of Mopsuestia.

tendency of the Western Church to its depths. In so far as a
lasting change was introduced in the fifth century, it is not to be
derived from this quarter. But for their suggestiveness, the
capital and impulse which were received from the East cannot
be highly enough appreciated. We need only compare the
writings of the Latin theologians who were not influenced by
the Greeks, [1] with Hilary, Victorinus Rhetor, Ambrose, Jerome,
Rufinus, and the others dependent on them, in order to perceive
the enormous difference. *The exegetical and speculative science*
of the Greeks was imported into the West, and, besides monachism and the ideal of a virginity devoted to God, as the practical application of that science.

The West was not disposed to favour either of these, and
since it is always hardest to carry through changes in the rules
of practical life, the implanting of monachism cost embittered
conflicts.[2] But the ideal of virginity, as denoting the love-bond
with Christ, very soon established itself among the spiritual
leaders of the West. (Even before this, Cyprian says, De hab.
virg. 22 : and you virgins have no husband, your lord and head
is Christ in the similitude and place of a man.) [3] It then won
through Ambrose the same significance for the West as it had
obtained through Origen's expositions of the Song of Songs
and Methodius in the East. Nay, it was in the West that the
ideal was first, so to speak, individualised, and that it created a
profusion of forms in which it was allied with or excited the
impassioned love of Christ.[4] The theological science of the

---

[1] E.g. Lucifer, so far as he does not simply imitate the Greeks. See on his
"theology" Krüger's Monograph, 1886.

[2] See Jovinian and Vigilantius, as also the conflicts of monachism in Spain and
Gaul (cf. the works of Sulpicius Severus).

[3] "Virginibus nec maritus dominus, dominus vester ac caput Christus est ad instar
et vicem masculi." Before this he says of the Church (Cypr., de unit. 6) : "sponsa
Christi, unius cubiculi sanctitatem casto pudore custodit." Afterwards this far from
beautiful thought was transferred to the individual soul, and thus erotic spiritualism
was produced.

[4] See details in Vol. III., p. 129 f. The conception of Methodius was quite current
in Latin writers at the end of the fourth century, *viz.*, that Christ must be born in
every Christian, and that only so could redemption be appropriated. Thus Prudentius
sings, "Virginitas et prompta fides Christum bibit alvo cordis et intactis condit
paritura latebris." Ambrose, Expos. in ev. sec. Luc. l. II., c. 26 : "Vides non

Greeks could not have domesticated itself, even if the time had
been less unfavourable; just then its authority was tottering even
in the East, after the Cappadocians seemed to have reconciled
faith and knowledge for a brief period. Where one has once
been accustomed to regard a complex of thoughts as an inviolable law, a legal order, it is no longer possible to awaken for it
for a length of time the inner sympathy which clings to spheres
in which the spiritual life finds a home; and if it does succeed
in obtaining an assured position, its treatment assumes a different
character; there is no freedom in dealing with it. As a matter
of fact, the West was always less free in relation to dogma
proper than the East in the classic period of Church theology.
In the West men reflected *about*, and now and again *against*,
dogma; but they really thought little *in* it.

But how great, nevertheless, were the stores rescued to the
West from the East[1] by Greek scholars, especially Hilary,
Ambrose, and Jerome, at a time when the Greek sun had
already ceased to warm the West! In the philosophical,
historical, and theological elements transplanted by them, we
have also one of Augustine's roots. He learned the science of
exegetical speculation from Ambrose, the disciple of the Cappadocians, and it was only by its help that he was delivered from
Manichæism. He made himself familiar with Neoplatonic
philosophy, and in this sphere he was apparently assisted by
the works of another Greek scholar, Victorinus Rhetor. He
acquired an astonishing amount of knowledge of the Egyptian
monks, and the impression thus received became of decisive
importance for him. These influences must be weighed if we
are to understand thoroughly the conditions under which such a

---

dubitasse Mariam, sed credidisse et ideo fructum fidei consecutam. . . . Sed et vos
beati, qui audistis et credidistis; quæcunque enim crediderit anima et concipit et
generat dei verbum et opera ejus agnoscit. Sit in singulis Mariæ anima, ut magnificet
dominum; sit in singulis spiritus Mariæ, ut exultet in deo. Si secundum carnem
una mater est Christi, *secundum fidem tamen omnium fructus est Christus.* Omnis
enim anima accipit dei verbum, si tamen immaculata et immunis a vitiis intemerato
castimoniam pudore custodiat."

[1] We must pass by the older importer of Greek exegesis, Victorinus of Pettau, since,
in spite of all his dependence on Origen, the Latin spirit held the upper hand, and
his activity seems to have been limited.

phenomenon as that which Augustine offers us was possible.[1]
But, on the other hand, Augustine continues the Western line
represented by Tertullian, Cyprian, Ambrosiaster, Optatus,
Pacian, Prudentius, and also by Ambrose. Extremely characteristic is his relation to the Stoic Christian popular philosophy of Western teachers. We shall see that he retained a
remnant of it. But his importance in the history of the Church,
and of dogma, consisted essentially in the fact *that he gave to
the West, in place of Stoic Christian popular morality as that was
comprised in Pelagianism, a religious and specifically Christian
ethic, and that he impressed this so strongly on the Church that its
formulas at least maintain their supremacy up to the present day
in the whole of Western Christendom.* In getting rid, however,
of Stoic morals, he also thrust aside its curious complement, the
realistic eschatology in which the ancient Latin Christians had
given specific expression to their Christian faith.

Ambrose was sovereign among Western Bishops, and at the
same time the Greek trained exegete and theologian. In both
qualities he acted on Augustine, who looked up to him as
Luther did to Staupitz.[2] He comes first to be considered here

---

[1] We may disregard Jerome ; he had no importance for Augustine, or if he had
any, it was only in confirming the latter in his conservative attitude. This, indeed,
does not refer to Jerome's learning, which to Augustine was always something
uncanny and even suspicious. Jerome's erudition, acquired from the Greeks, and
increased with some genius for learned investigations, became a great storehouse of
the mediæval Church; yet Jerome did not mould the popular dogmatics of the Church,
but confirmed them, and as a rhetorician made them eloquent, while his ascetic
writings implanted monachism, and held out to it ideals which were in part extremely
questionable. At the first glance it is a paradoxical fact that Jerome is rightly regarded as the *doctor ecclesiæ Romanæ* κατεξοχήν, and that we can yet pass him over
in a history of dogma. The explanation of the paradox is that after he threw off the
influence of Origen, he was exclusively the speaker and advocate of vulgar Catholicism, and that he possessed a just instinct for the "ecclesiastical mean" in controversies which were only to reveal their whole significance after his time (see the
Semipelagian question and his relation to Augustinianism.) If that is a compliment
to him, it is none to his Church. After Augustine's time influences from the East
were very scanty ; yet we have to recall Junilius and Cassiodorus.

[2] See Augustine's testimony as to Ambrose in the Ballerinis' ed. of the latter's works.
Contra Jul. I. 4, 10: "Audi excellentem dei dispensatorem, quem veneror ut patrem ; in Christo Jesu enim per evangelium me genuit et eo Christi ministro lavacrum
regenerationis accepi. Beatum loquor Ambrosium cujus pro Catholica fide gratiam,

in the latter respect. His education, his Episcopal chair in
Milan, the Arian and Apollinarian conflict into which he had to
enter, directed him to Greek theological literature. Philo, Hippolytus, Origen, and Basil were industriously read by him ; he
made extracts from them, and edited them in Latin.[1] He was
united with Basil, not only by similiarity of situation, but above
all by agreement in character and attitude. Basil was his real
teacher in doctrine, and while the former was met with distrust
in Alexandria and Rome, Ambrose highly honoured him, and
fully recognised his orthodoxy. The importance of this attitude
of the Milanese Bishop for the closing of the Arian controversy,
and for the reconciliation of Roman and Alexandrian orthodoxy
with that of the Cappadocians, has been described in an earlier
volume.[2] It has indeed been recently shown, beyond dispute,
that, in spite of his dependence on the Greeks, Ambrose preserved and further developed the Western system in his
Christology.[3] Tertullian, Novatian—directly or indirectly—and
Hilary influenced him. But on the other hand there is no
mistake that he emphasised more strongly than Augustine the
fundamental position of the Nicene decision,[4] and that he was
confirmed in his doctrine of the Two Substances by the Cappadocians, who had been involuntarily led to something approaching it in their fight against Apollinaris. Further, he treats the
Logos in Jesus Christ so much as the subject, the human
substance so much as form and matter, that here again Greek

constantiam, labores, pericula sive operibus sive sermonibus et ipse sum expertus et
mecum non dubitat orbis prædicare Romanus." Op. imperf. c. Julian. I., 2: "Quem
vero judicem poteris Ambrosio reperire meliorem? De quo magister tuus Pelagins
ait, quod ejus fidem et purissimum in scripturis sensum ne inimicus quidem ausus est
reprehendere." Pelagius' own words in De gratia Christi et lib. arb. 43 (47):
"Beatus Ambrosius episcopus, in cujus præcipue libris *Romana* elucet fides, qui
scriptorum inter Latinos flos quidam speciosus enituit, cujus fidem et purissimum in
scripturis sensum ne inimicus quidem ausus est reprehendere" (see c. Jul. I., 30). The
fame of Ambrose is also proclaimed by Rufinus, who defends him against Jerome,
"who, as an envious Augur, censured Ambrose's plagiarisms from the Greeks, while
he himself was much more culpable since he always posed as original."

[1] See detailed references in Förster, Ambrosius, p. 99 ff.
[2] See Vol. IV., p. 93.
[3] See Reuter, August. Studien, pp. 207-227.
[4] See Ambrose de fid. I. prol et al. loc. in Reuter, l.c. p. 185; on Augustine's
neutral position, id. p. 185 f.

influence—as in Hilary, who was similarly dependent on the
Greeks—cannot be overlooked ; for his own conception of the
work of Christ conflicts with this stunted view of his human
nature. But the most important influence of the East upon
Ambrose does not lie in the special domain of dogmatics. It
consists in the reception of the allegorical method of exegesis,
and of many separate schemes and doctrines. It is true
Ambrose had his own reservations in dealing with Plato and
Origen ; he did not adopt the consequences of Origen's
theology ; [1] he was much too hasty and superficial in the sphere
of speculative reflection to appropriate from the Greeks more than
fragments. But he, as well as the heavier but more thorough
Hilary, raised the West above the "meagreness" of a pedantically literal, and, in its practical application, wholly planless
exegesis; and they transmitted to their countrymen a profusion
of ideas attached to the text of Holy Scripture. Rufinus and,
in his first period, Jerome also completed the work. Manichæism would hardly have been overcome in the West unless it had
been confronted by the theosophic exegesis, the "Biblical
alchemy" of the Greeks, and the great theme of virginity was
praised with new tongues after Western Christians heard of the
union of the soul with its bridegroom, Christ, as taught by Origen
in his commentary on the Song of Songs.[2] The unity, so far as
at all attainable, of ecclesiastical feeling in East and West, was
restored in the loftiest regions of theology about A.D. 390. But
the fight against Origen, which soon broke out with embittered
hatred, had, among other sad consequences, the immediate
result that the West refused to learn anything further from the

---

[1] Not a few passages might here be quoted from Ambrose's works. He rejects
questionable principles held by Origen with tact and without judging him a heretic,
always himself holding to the common Christian element. In a few important
questions, the influence of Origen—Plato—is unmistakable ; as in the doctrine of
souls and the conception of hell. Greek influence appears to me to be strongest in
the doctrine of the relative necessity and expediency of evil ("amplius nobis profuit
culpa quam nocuit"). Therefore, I cannot see in this doctrine a bold theory of evil
peculiar to Ambrose, like Deutsch (Des Ambrosius Lehre von der Sünde, etc., 1867,
p. 8) and Förster (l.c. pp. 136, 142, 300). The teleological view from the standpoint
of the fuller restoration is alone new perhaps.

[2] Ambrose, De Isaac et anima.

great theologian. The West never attained a strict system in the science of allegorical exegesis.

The sacred histories of the Old Testament were also transformed into spiritual narratives for the West by Hilary,[1] Ambrose, Jerome, and Rufinus.[2] In this transformation Western Christians obtained a multitude of separate mystical Neoplatonic conceptions, though they failed to obtain any insight into the system as a whole. Another Western, the rhetorician Victorinus, that "aged man, most learned and skilled in the liberal sciences, who had read and weighed so many works of the philosophers ; the instructor of so many noble Senators, who also, as a monument of his excellent discharge of his office, had deserved and obtained a statue in the Roman Forum," had initiated his fellow-countrymen into Neoplatonism by translations and original works.[3] That happened before he became a Christian. Having gone over to Christianity at an advanced age, and become a prolific ecclesiastical writer, he by no means abandoned Neoplatonism. If I am not mistaken, Augustine made him his model in the crucial period of his life, and although he understood enough Greek to read Neoplatonic writings, yet it was substantially by Victorinus that he was initiated into them. Above all, he here learned how to unite Neoplatonic speculation with the Christianity of the Church, and to oppose Manichæism from this as his starting-point. We do not require to describe in detail what the above combination and polemic meant to him. When Neoplatonism became a decisive element in Augustine's religious and philosophical mode of thought, it did so also for the whole of the West. The religious philosophy of the Greeks was incorporated in the spiritual assets of the West, along with

---

[1] On Hilary's exile in the East, epoch-making as it was for the history of theology, and his relation to Origen, see Reinken's Hilarius, p. 128, 270, 281 ff. Augustine held him in high honour.

[2] In the interpretation of the New Testament, Ambrose kept more faithfully to the letter, following the Western tradition, and declining the gifts of the Greeks. He describes Origen (Ep. 75) as "Longe minor in novo quam in veteri testamento." But Western Christians were first made familiar with the Old Testament by the Greeks.

[3] Aug. Confess. VIII., 2. See there also the story of his conversion.

its ascetic and monachist impulses.[1] But, unless all signs
deceive, Augustine received from Victorinus the impulse which
led him to assimilate Paul's type of religious thought ; for it
appears from the works of the aged rhetorician that he had
appropriated Paul's characteristic ideas, and Augustine demon-
strably devoted a patient study to the Pauline epistles from the
moment when he became more thoroughly acquainted with
Neoplatonism. Victorinus wrote very obscurely, and his works
found but a slender circulation. But this is not the only case in
history where the whole importance of an able writer was merged
in the service he rendered to a greater successor. A great,
epoch-making man is like a stream : the smaller brooks, which
have had their origin perhaps further off in the country, lose
themselves in it, having fed it, but without changing the course

---

[1] If we disregard the fragments which reached the West through translations of
Origen's works, and plagiarisms from the Cappadocians, Neoplatonism, and with it
Greek speculation in general, were imparted to it in three successive forms :—(1) By
Victorinus and Augustine, and by Marius Mercator in the fourth and fifth centuries ;
(2) by Boethius in the sixth ; (3) by the importation of the works of the Pseudo-
Areopagite in the ninth century. Cassiodorus praises Boethius (Var. epp. 1, 45) for
having given the Latins by translations the works of Pythagoras, Ptolemy, Nico-
machus, Euclid, Plato the theologian, Aristotle the logician, Archimedes, and other
Greeks. It seems now to me proven (Usener, Anecdoton Holderi, 1877) that
Boethius was a Christian, and that he also wrote the frequently-suspected writings De
sancta trimitate, Utrum pater et filius et spiritus s. de divinitate substantialiter præ-
dicentur, Quomodo substantiæ in eo quod sint bonæ sint, cum non sint substantialia
bona, De fide Catholica and Contra Eutychen et Nestorium. But he has influenced
posterity, not by his Christian writings, but by his treatise, wholly dependent on
Aristotle, " De consolatione philosophiæ," which for that very reason could have been
written by a heathen, and by his commentaries on Aristotle. He was really, along
with Aristotle, the knowledge of whom was imperfect enough, the philosopher of the
early Middle Ages. On the system of Boethius, see Nitzsch's monograph, 1860.
Many of his ideas recall Seneca and Proclus ; an examination of his relation to Victorinus would be desirable. " In his system the foundation is formed by Platonism,
modified by certain Aristotelian thoughts ; besides this we have unmistakably a Stoic
trait, due to the Roman and personal character of the philosopher and the reading of
Roman thinkers. In this eclecticism Christianity occupies as good as no position.
For that reason we must renounce the attempt to give a place to the system of
Boethius among those which represent or aim at a harmonising or fusion of Christianity with Platonism (e.g., Synesius, Pseudo-Dionysius) " ; compare Nitzsch, l.c.p.
84 f. The fact that this man, who, in view of death, consoled himself with the ideas
of heathen philosophers, wrote treatises on the central dogma of the Church, affords
us the best means of observing that the dogma of Christ presented a side on which it
led to the forgetting of Christ himself.

of its current.   Not only Victorinus,[1] but ultimately also Ambrose himself, Optatus, Cyprian, and Tertullian were lost to view in Augustine ; but they made him the proud stream in

---

[1] It is to the credit of Ch. Gore that he has described, in his article "Victorinus" (Dict. of Christ. Biog. IV., pp. 1129-1138), the distinctive character of the theology of Victorinus and its importance for Augustine. He says rightly : " His theology is Neoplatonist in tone . . . he applied many principles of the Plotinian philosophy to the elucidation of the Christian mysteries. His importance in this respect has been entirely overlooked in the history of theology. He preceded the Pseudo-Dionysius. He anticipated a great deal that appears in Scotus Erigena." In fact, when we study the works of Victorinus (Migne T. VIII., pp. 999-1310), we are astonished to find in him a perfect Christian Neoplatonist, and an Augustine before Augustine. The writings "Ad Justinum Manichæum," and " De generatione verbi divini, and the great work against the Arians, read like compositions by Augustine, only the Neoplatonic element makes a much more natural appearance in him than in Augustine, who had to make an effort to grasp it. If we substitute the word " natura " for " deus " in the speculation of Victorinus, we have the complete system of Scotus Erigena. But even this exchange is unnecessary ; for in Victorinus the terminology of the Church only rests like a thin covering on the Neoplatonic doctrine of identity. God in himself is " motus "—not mutatio : " moveri ipsum quo est esse " ; but without the Son he is conceived as ὁ μὴ ὤν (speculation on the four-fold sense of the μὴ εἶναι as in the later mystics). The Son is ὁ ὤν. It appears clearly in the speculation on the relation of Father and Son, that consequent—pantheistic—Neoplatonism is favourable to the doctrine of the Homoousia. Because the Deity is movere, the Father finds himself in a " semper generans generatio." So the Son proceeds from him, " re non tempore posterior." The Son is the " potentia actuosa " ; while the Father begets him, " ipse se ipsum conterminavit." The Son is accordingly the eternal object of the divine will and the divine self-knowledge ; he is the form and limitation of God, very essence of the Father ; the Father in perceiving the Son perceives himself ("alteritas nata "). "In isto sine intellectu temporis, tempore . . . est alteritas nata, cito in identitatem revenit ; " therefore the most perfect unity and absolute consubstantiality, although the Son is subordinate. Victorinus first designated the Spirit as the copula of the Deity (see Augustine) ; it is he who completes the perfect circle of the Deity ; "omnes in alternis exsistentes et semper simul ὁμοούσιοι divina affectione, secundum actionem (tantummodo) subsistentiam propriam habentes." This is elaborated in speculations which form the themes of Augustine's great work " De trinitate." The number three is in the end only apparent ; "ante unum quod est in numero, plane simplex." "Ipse quod est esse, subsistit tripliciter." While anyone who is at all sharp-sighted sees clearly from this that the "Son " as " potentia actuosa " is the world-idea, that is perfectly evident in what follows. All things are potentially in God, actually in the Son ; for " filius festinat in actionem." The world is distinguished from God, as the many from the one, *i.e.*, the world is God unfolding himself and returning to unity *sub specie æternitatis*. That which is alien and God-resisting in the world is simply not-being, matter. This is all as given by Proclus, and therefore, while the word " creare " is indeed retained, is transformed, in fact, into an emanation. The distinction between *deus ipse* and *quæ*

whose waters the banks are mirrored, on whose bosom the ships
sail, and which fertilises and passes through a whole region of
the world.

a deo is preserved ; but, in reality, the world is looked at under the point of view of
the Deity developing himself.   Ad Justinum 4 : " Aliter quidem quod ipse est, aliter
quæ ab ipso.   Quod ipse est unum est totumque est quidquid ipse est ; quod vero ab
ipso est, innumerum est.   Et hæc sunt quibus refletur omne quod uno toto clauditur
et ambitur.   Verum quod varia sunt quæ ab ipso sunt, qui a se est et unum est, variis
cum convenit dominare.   Et ut omnipotens apparet, contrariorum etiam origo ipse
debuit inveniri."   But it is said of these "varia," that "insubstantiata sunt omnia
ὄντα in Jesu, hoc est, ἐν τῷ λόγῳ.   He is the unity of nature, accordingly elementum,
receptaculum, habitaculum, habitator, locus naturæ.   He is the "unum totum" in
which the universum presents itself as a unity.   And now follows the process of
emanation designated as " creation," in whose description are employed the Christian
and Neoplatonic stages : deus, Jesus, spiritus, νοῦς, anima (as world-soul) angeli et
deinde corporalia omnia subministrata."   Redemption through Christ, and the return
ad deum of all essences, in so far as they are *a deo*, is Neoplatonically conceived, as
also we have then the doctrine of the pre-existence of souls and their pre-temporal
fall.   The Incarnation is admitted, but spiritualised, inasmuch as side by side with
the conception of the assumption of a human form, which occurs once, the other
prevails that Christ appears as burdened with humanity in its totality ; "universalis
caro, universalis anima ; in isto omnia universalia erant" (Adv. Arian. III., 3).
" Quia corpus ille catholicum ad omnem hominem habuit, omne quod passus est
catholicum fecit ; id est ut omnis caro in ipso crucifixa sit" (Ad Philipp, pp. 1196-
1221 ; Adv. Arian. III., 3).   But the most interesting features, because the most
important for Augustine are (1), that Victorinus gives strong expression to the
doctrine of Predestination—only he feels compelled in opposition to Manichæism to
maintain the freedom of the will ; and (2), that, especially in his commentaries, he
places the highest value on *Justification by faith alone* in opposition to all moralism.
Neoplatonism had won his assent, or had prepared him in some measure to assent, to
both these doctrines ; we know, indeed, from other sources, that heathen Neoplatonists felt attracted to John and Paul, but not to the Synoptics or James.   Thus
Victorinus writes : " non omnia restaurantur sed quæ in Christo sunt " (p. 1245),
" quæ salvari possent " (p. 1274), "universos sed qui sequerentur" (p. 1221).   In a
mystical way Christ is believing humanity (the Church), and believing humanity is
humanity in general.   Everything undergoes a strictly necessary development ; therefore Victorinus was a predestinationist.   The passages in which Victorinus expresses
himself in a strictly Pauline, and, so to speak, Antipelagian sense, are collected by
Gore, p. 1137 ; see Ad Gal. 3, 22 ; Ad Philipp, 3, 9 ; " 'non meam justitiam '
tunc enim mea est vel nostra, cum moribus nostris justitiam dei mereri nos putamus
perfectam per mores.   At non, inquit, hanc habens justitiam, sed quam ?   Illam ex
fide.   Non illam quæ ex lege ; væ in operibus est et carnali disciplina, sed hanc quæ
ex deo procedit ' justitia ex fide ; ' " Ad Phil. 4, 9 ; Ad Ephes. 2, 5 : "non nostri
laboris est, quod sæpe moneo, ut nos salvemus ; sed sola fides in Christum nobis
salus est . . . nostrum pene jam nihil est nisi solum credere qui superavit omnia.
Hoc est enim plena salvatio, Christum hæc vicisse.   Fidem in Christo habere,

For not only the work of those Greek Latins, but also the
line of representatives of genuine Western theology and ecclesiasticism ended in Augustine.[1]

plenam fidem, nullus labor est, nulla difficultas, animi tantum voluntas est . . .
justitia non tantum valet quantum fides " ; Ad Ephes. i, 14 ; 3, 7 ; Ad Phil. 2, 13 :
" quia ipsum velle a deo nobis operatur, fit ut ex deo et operationem et voluntatem
habeamus." Victorinus has been discussed most recently by Geiger (Programme von
Metten, 1888, 1889), and Reinhold Schmid (Marius Victorinus Rhetor u. s. Bez. z.
Augustin. Kiel, 1895)—compare also the dissertation by Koffmane, De Mario Victor-
ino, philosopho Christiano, Breslau, 1880.   Geiger has thoroughly expounded
the complete Neoplatonic system of Victorinus ; Schmid seeks, after an excellent
statement of his theological views, to show (p. 68 ff.), that he exerted no, or, at least,
no decisive influence on Augustine.   I cannot see that this proof has really been
successful ; yet I admit that Schmid has brought forward weighty arguments in
support of his proposition.   The name of Victorinus is not the important point for the
history of dogma, but the indisputable fact that the combination of Neoplatonism
and highly orthodox Christianity existed in the West, in Rome, before Augustine,
under the badge of Paulinism.   Since this combination was hardly of frequent
occurrence in the fourth century, and since Augustine gives a prominent place to
Victorinus in his Confessions, it will remain probable that he was influenced by him.
The facts that he was less Neoplatonic than Victorine, and afterwards even opposed
him, do not weigh against the above contention.   But it is positively misleading to
argue like Schmid (p. 68) against Augustine's Neoplatonism by appealing to the fact
that from the moment of his rejection of Manichæism and semi-scepticism, he was a
" decided Christian."

   [1] Little is yet known regarding the history of ecclesiastical penance in the East ;
but I believe I can maintain that in the West the shock was less violent in its effect,
which all official Church discipline received through the rapid extension of Christianity
after Constantine.   Here confidence in the Church was greater, the union of "sancta
ecclesia " and " remissio peccatorum " closer ("credo remissionem peccatorum per
sanctam ecclesiam " : Symbol. Carthag.), and the sense of sin as guilt, which was to
be atoned for by public confession and satisfactio, more acute.   Whence this came,
it is hard to say.   In the East it would appear that greater stress was laid on the
operations of the cultus as a collective institution, and on the other hand on private
self-education through prayer and asceticism ; while in the West the feeling was
stronger that men occupied religious legal relationships, in which they were responsible
to the Church, being able, however, to expect from the Church sacramental and inter-
cessory aid in *each individual case.*   The individual and the Church thus stood nearer
each other in the West than in the East.   Therefore, ecclesiastical penance asserted
a much greater importance in the former than in the latter.   We can study this
significance in the works of the Africans on the one hand, and of Ambrose on the
other.   They have little else in common, but they agree in their view of penance
(Ambrose, De pænitentia).   The practice of penance now acquired an increasing
influence in the West on all conditions of the ecclesiastical constitution and of
theology, so that we can ultimately construct from this starting-point the whole of
Western Catholicism in the Middle Ages and modern times, and can trace the subtle

Augustine studied, above all, very thoroughly, and made himself familiar with Cyprian's work.   Cyprian was to him the
"saintly," the Church Father, κατ᾽ ἐξοχήν, and his view of
heresy and the unity of the Church was dependent on Cyprian.
But standing as a Bishop, unassailed, on the foundation which
Cyprian had created, Augustine did not find it necessary to
state Episcopalianism so uncompromisingly as the former,
and being occupied with putting an end to a schism which was
different from the Novatian, he learned to take a different view
of the nature of schisms from the Bishop whom he venerated as
a hero.[1] Cursory remarks show, besides, that Augustine had
made himself familiar with the literature of the Novatian controversy, and had learned from it for his notion of the Church.
Some works quoted by him we no longer possess—e.g., that of
Reticius against the Novatians.[2] What has been preserved to
us of this literature,[3] proves that the Western Church was continually impelled, by its opposition to the Novatians in the
course of the fourth century, to reflect on the nature of the
Church.[4]

But even when he entered into the Donatist controversy,
Augustine did so as a man of the second or indeed of the third
generation, and he therefore enjoyed the great advantage of

workings of the theory of penance to the most remote dogmas.   But Augustine once
more marks the decisive impetus in this development.   With him began the process
by which what had long existed in the Church was elevated into theory.   He indeed
created few formulas, and has not even once spoken of a sacrament of penance ; but,
on the one hand, he has clearly enough expressed the thing itself, and, on the other,
where he has not yet drawn the theoretical consequences of the practice of penance,
he has left such *striking gaps* (see his Christology) that they were filled up by unosten-
tatious efforts, as if inevitably, in after times.

[1] See Reuter, August. Studien, pp. 232 ff., 355.

[2] Lib I. c. Julian. 3 Op. imperf. c. Jul I., 55 ; Jerome de vir. inl., 82.

[3] Pseudo-Cyprian = Sixtus II. ad Novatianum, Ambrosiaster in the Quæst. ex Vet.
et Novo Testam. [the inserted tractate against Novatian] Pacianus c. Novat.

[4] From Pacian's Ep. I. ad Sempron. comes the famous sentence : "Christianus
mihi nomen est, catholicus cognomen."   In the tractate of Ambrosiaster against
Novatian, the objectivity of the Divine Word and of baptism, and their independence
in their operation of the moral character of the priest, are consistently argued.   In
some of the sentences we imagine that we are listening to Augustine.   On the whole,
there is not a little in Ambrosiaster's commentary and questions which must be
described as leading up to Augustine, and is therewith genuinely Western.

having at his disposal a fund of conceptions and ideas already collected. In this sphere Optatus had especially wrought before him.[1] This is not the place to describe the rise of Donatism ; for the dispute did not originate in a dogmatic controversy.[2] It arose in the first place out of Cæcilian's action against the exaggerated veneration of martyrs, which disturbed the order and endangered the existence of the Church. Some of the clergy who did not desire a strong episcopal power seem to have made common cause with the discontented and refractory enthusiasts, to whom Cæcilian had been obnoxious even when Deacon. In any case, a point of principle did not immediately emerge in the controversy. But it was soon introduced, and indeed there is no doubt that Cyprian was played off against himself.[3] The Donatist party, which was at the same time, it appears, the African national party, found support both in Cyprian's conception that the Bishop was only a Bishop if he possessed a certain Christian and moral quality, and in his defence of heretical baptism. The opposition, also carrying out ideas taught by Cyprian, gave such prominence to the official character of the episcopate, and the objective efficacy of the sacrament, that the personal quality of the official or dispenser became indifferent.[4] It may be that those martyrs and relic-

---

[1] Aug adv. Parmen. 1, 3 : "Venerabilis memoriæ Milevitanus episcopus catholicæ communionis Optatus." Fulgentius ranks Optatus along with Ambrose and Augustine.

[2] See Deutsch, Drei Actenstücke z. Gesch. des Donatismus, 1875, p. 40 f. Völter, Der Ursprung des Donatismus, 1882 ; Harnack, Theol. Lit-Zeit., 1884, No. 4 ; on the other side, Reuter l.c. 234 ff. whose contradiction, however, partly rests on a misunderstanding of my view. Seeck. Zitschr. für K.-Gesch. X. 4. Duschesne gives the best account, Le doissier du Donatisme, 1890.

[3] See Vol. II., p. 114 ff.

[4] Here these Africans abandoned the position, in the question of heretical baptisms, taken up by Cyprian ; see the 8th Canon of Arles (A.D. 316) : "De Afris quod propria lege sua utuntur, ut rebaptizent, placuit, ut si ad ecclesiam aliquis de hæresi venerit, interrogent eum symbolum ; et si perviderint eum in patre et filio et spiritu sancto esse baptizatum, manus ei tantum imponatur ut accipiat spiritum sanctum. Quod si interrogatus non responderit hanc trinitatem, baptizetur." Can. 13 : "De his, qui scripturas s. tradidisse dicuntur vel vasa dominica vel nomina patrum suorum, placuit nobis, ut quicumque eorum ex actis publicis fuerit detectus, non verbis nudis, ab ordine cleri amoveatur. Nam si iidem aliquos ordinasse fuerint deprehensi et

worshipping enthusiasts in Carthage were inclined from the first
to the conception once held by Cyprian against Calixtus and
his successors, and that they thus required a standard of active,
personal holiness for bishops, which could no longer be sustained in the great Church and during the devastating storms
of the last persecution. But this cannot be proved. On the
other hand, it is indisputable that, after the Synod of Arles,
the controversy had reached a point where it must be regarded
as the last link in the chain of the great phenomena (Encratites
Montanists, adherents of Hippolytus and Novatians) in which
Christendom strove against the secularisation that was imposed
upon it by the removal of the attribute of holiness, and with it
of the truth of the Church, from *persons* to *institutions*—the
office and mysteries;[1] this change being due to the fact that

hi quos ordinaverunt rationales (able? capable?) subsistunt, *non illis obsit ordinatio*"
(that is the decisive principle ; even ordination by a traditor was to be valid).

[1] Crises, similar to that of the Donatists, also arose elsewhere--as in Rome and
Alexandria—at the beginning of the fourth century ; but our information regarding
them is wholly unsatisfactory ; see Lipsius, Chronologie der römischen Bischöfe, p.
250 ff., where the epitaphs by Damasus on Marcellus and Eusebius are copied, and
rightly compared with the passage in the Liber prædest., c. 16 on Heracleon (who is
really Heraclius). Heraclius appears already (A.D. 307-309) to have exaggerated
the view of the "objectivity" and power of the sacraments to such an extent as o
declare all sins by baptised persons to be "venial," and to hold a severe public penance to be unnecessary. Therefore it was said of him, "Christus in pace negavit"
and "vetuit lapsos peccata dolere" ; more precisely in Lib. prædest. : "Baptizatum
hominem sive justum sive peccatorem *loco sancti* computari docebat nihilque obesse
baptizatis peccata memorabat, dicens, sicut non in se recipit natura ignis gelu *ita
baptizatus non in se recipit peccatum*. Sicut enim ignis resolvit aspectu suo nives
quantæcunque juxta sint, sic semel baptizatus non recipit *peccatorum reatum*, etiam
quantavis fuerint operibus ejus peccata permixta." In this we can truly study the
continuity of Western Christianity ! How often this thought has cropped up on into
the nineteenth century, and that precisely among evangelicals ! It marks positively
the "concealed poison," which it is hard to distinguish from the wholesome medicine
of evangelic comfort. But it is very noteworthy that this phase in the conception of
the favoured position of the baptised can be first proved as existing in Rome. Developments always went furthest there, as the measures taken by Calixtus also show.
Yet this one was rejected, after a schism had broken out in the community, and that
is perfectly intelligible ; for apart from the ruinous frivolity which had come in with
the above view, what importance could the priestly class retain if every baptised
person might, without further ceremony, and if he only willed it, feel and assert himself to be a member of the congregation even after the gravest sin ? It is not very
probable that Heraclius developed his ecclesiastical attitude on the basis of the

otherwise men would have had to despair of the Christian character of the Church as Catholic. The Donatists denied the validity of any ordination conferred by a traditor, and therefore also of sacraments administered by a bishop who had been consecrated by a traditor. *As a last remnant of a much more earnest conception, a minimum of personal worthiness was required of the clergy alone, and received into the notion of the Church itself:* it was no longer Christian if this minimum was wanting, if the clergy—nothing being now said of the laity—were not free from every idolatrous stain. Compared with the measure of agreement which prevailed between Catholics and Donatists, the separate thesis of the latter looks like a caprice, and certainly much obstinacy, personal discontent, and insubordination lurked behind it. But we may not overlook the question of principle any more here than in the case of Novatianism. The legend of the Sybilline Books is constantly repeating itself in the history of spiritual conflicts. The remnant saved from the flames stands at as high a price as the whole collection. And what a price the Church has paid in order to escape the exhortations of separatists ! The Novatian crisis—after the Decian persecution —drew from it the sacrament of penance, and thereby gave the impulse in general to substitute a system of sacraments for the sacrament that blotted out sin. (The formal establishment of the new sacrament had, indeed, still to be waited for for a long time.) The Donatist crisis—after the Diocletian persecution— taught the Church to value ordination as imparting an inalienable title (character indelebilis) and to form a stringent view of the " objectivity " of the sacraments ; or, to use a plainer expression, to regard the Church primarily as an *institution* whose

Pauline theory of baptism and of the faith that lays hold of Christ. If we were to understand the matter so, he would have been a Luther before Luther. We have probably to suppose that he saw in baptism the magical bestowal of a stamp, as in the conception taken of certain heathen mysteries. In the Meletian schism in Egypt, the difference in principles as to the renewed reception of the lapsed, co-operated with opposition to the monarchial position of the Alexandrian Bishop. The dispute, which thus recalls the Donatist controversy, soon became one of Church politics, and personal. (Compare Meletius and the *later* Donatists ; the limitation of the whole question to the Bishops is, however, peculiar to the Donatists.) See Walch, Ketzerhistorie, Vol. IV., and Möller in Herzog's R.-E. IX., p. 534 ff.

holiness and truth were inalienable, however melancholy the
state of its members.

In this thought Catholicism was first complete. By it is explained its later history down to the present day, in so far as it
is not a history of piety, but of the Church, the Hierarchy,
sacramental magic, and implicit faith (fides implicita). But
only in the West did the thought come to be deliberately and
definitely expressed. It also made its way in the East, because it was inevitable; but it did so, as it were, unconsciously.
This was no advantage; for the very fact that this conception
of the Church was definitely thought out in the West, led over
and over again to the quest for safeguards, or a form which
could be reconciled with living faith, and the requirements of a
holy life. Even Augustine, who stated it definitely and fully,
aimed at reconciling the Christian conscience with it. But he
was not the first to declare it ; he rather received it from
tradition. The first representative of the new conception known
to us, and Augustine also knew him, was Optatus.

The work of Optatus, " De schismate Donatistarum," was
written in the interests of peace, and therefore in as friendly and
conciliatory a tone as possible. This did not, indeed, prevent
violent attacks in detail, and especially extremely insulting
allegorical interpretations of texts from Scripture. But the
author every now and then recalls the fact that his opponents
are after all Christian brethren (IV., 1., 2), who have disdainfully
seceded from the Church, and only decline to recognise what is
gladly offered them, Church fellowship. At the very beginning
of his book, which, for the rest, is badly arranged, because it is
a reply point by point to a writing by the Donatist, Parmenian,
Optatus (I., 10 sq.)—differing from Cyprian—indicates the
distinction in principle between heretics and schismatics, and he
adheres firmly to the distinction—already drawn by Irenæus—
to the end of his statement.[1] Heretics are " deserters from or
falsifiers of the Symbol " (I., 10, 12 ; II., 8), and accordingly are
not Christians ; the Donatists are seditious Christians. Since
the definition holds (I., 11) that " a simple and true understand-

---

[1] Parmenian denied this distinction.

ing in the law (*scil.* the two testaments), the unique and most true sacrament, and unity of minds constitute the Catholic (*scil.* Church),"[1] the Donatists only want the last point to be genuinely Catholic Christians.   The heretics have " various and false baptisms," no legitimate office of the keys, no true divine service ; " but these things cannot be denied to you schismatics,[2] although you be not in the Catholic Church, because you have received along with us true and common sacraments " (I., 12). He says afterwards (III., 9) : " You and we have a common ground in the Church (ecclesiastica una conversatio), and if the minds of men contend, the sacraments do not."   Finally, we also can say : " We equally believe, and have been stamped with one seal, nor did we receive a different baptism from you ; nor a different ordination.   We read equally the Divine Testament ; we pray to one God.   Among you and us the prayer of our Lord is the same, but a rent having been made, with the parts hanging on this side and on that, it was necessary that it should be joined."   And (III., 10) he remarks very spiritually, founding on a passage in Ezechiel : " You build not a protecting house, like the Catholic Church, but only a wall ; the partition supports no corner-stone ; it has a needless door, nor does it guard what is enclosed ; it is swept by the rain, destroyed by tempests, and is unable to keep out the robber.   It is a house wall, but not a home.   *And your part is a quasi ecclesia, but not Catholic.*"   V., 1 : " That is for both which is common to you and us : *therefore it belongs also to you, because you proceed from us ;* " that is the famous principle which is still valid in the present day in the Catholic Church.   " Finally, both you and we have one ecclesiastical language, common lessons, the same faith, the very sacraments of the faith, the same

---

[1] " Catholicam (scil. ecclesiam) facit simplex et verus intellectus in lege (scil. duobus testamentis) singulare ac verissimum sacramentum et unitas animorum."

[2] Cyprian would never have admitted that.   He accused the Novatians (Ep. 68) of infringing the Symbol like other heretics, by depriving the " remissio peccatorum " of its full authority ; and he commanded all who had not been baptised in the Catholic Church to be re-baptised.   Cyprian had on his side the logical consequence of the Catholic dogma of the Church ; but since this consequence was hurtful to the expansion of the Church, and the development of its power, it was rejected with a correct instinct in Rome (see Ambrosiaster), and afterwards in Africa.

mysteries." Undoubtedly Optatus also held ultimately that those things possessed by the schismatics were in the end fruit-less, because their offence was especially aggravated. They merely constituted a "quasi ecclesia." For the first mark of the one, true, and holy Church was not the holiness of the persons composing it; but exclusively the possession of the sacraments. II., 1 : "*It is the one Church whose sanctity is de-rived from the sacraments, and not estimated from the pride of persons.* This cannot apply to all heretics and schismatics; it remains that it is (found) in one place." The second mark con-sists in territorial Catholicity according to the promise : "I will give the heathen for an inheritance, and the ends of the world for a possession." II., 1 : "To whom, then, does the name of Catholic belong, since it is called Catholic because it is reason-able and diffused everywhere?"[1]

Optatus did not succeed in clearly describing the first mark in its negative and exclusive meaning; we could indeed easily charge him with contradicting himself on this point. The second was all the more important in his eyes,[2] since the Dona-tists had only taken hold in Africa and, by means of a few emigrants, in Rome. In both signs he prepared the way for Augustine's doctrine of the Church and the sacraments, in which Optatus' thought was, of course, spiritualised. Optatus has himself shown, in the case of Baptism (V., 1-8), what he meant by the "sanctity of the sacraments." In Baptism there were

---

[1] Compare l.c. : " Ecclesiam tu, frater Parmeniane, apud vos solos esse dixisti ; nisi forte quia vobis *specialem sanctitatem* de superbia vindicare contenditis, ut, ubi vultis, ibi sit ecclesia, et non sit, ubi non vultis. Ergo ut in particula Africæ, in an-gulo parvæ regionis, apud vos esse possit, apud nos in alia parte Africæ non erit?"

[2] In connection with the territorial *catholicity* of the Church, Optatus always treats the assertion of its *unity*. Here he is dependent on Cyprian ; see besides the details in Book 2 those in Book 7 : " Ex persona beatissimi Petri forma unitatis retinendæ vel faciendæ descripta recitatur;" ch. 3 : " Malum est contra interdictum aliquid facere ; sed pejus est, unita'em non habere, cum possis . . . " " Bono *unitatis* sepelienda esse peccata hinc intellegi datur, quod b. Paulus apostolus dicat, *caritatem* posse obstruere multitudinem peccatorum" (here, accordingly, is the identification of unitas and caritas). . . . " Hæc omnia Paulus viderat in apostolis ceteris, qui bono unitas per caritatem noluerunt a communione Petri recedere, ejus scil. qui negaverat Christum. Quod si major esset amor innocentiæ quam utilitas pacis unitatis, dicerent se non debere communicare Petro, qui negaverat magistrum." That is still a dangerous fundamental thought of Catholicism at the present day.

three essentials : the acting Holy Trinity ("confertur a trinitate"), the believer ("fides credentis"), and the administrator. These three were not, however, equally important ; the two first rather belonged alone to the dogmatic notion of Baptism ("for I see that two are necessary, and one as if necessary [quasi necessariam]¹"), for the baptisers are not "lords" (domini), but "agents or ministers of baptism" (operarii vel ministri baptismi). (Ambrosiaster calls them advocates who plead, but have nothing to say at the end when sentence is passed.) They are only ministering and changing organs, and therefore contribute nothing to the notion and effect of Baptism ; for "it is the part of God to cleanse by the sacrament." But if the sacrament is independent of him who, by chance, dispenses it, because the rite presupposes only the ever the same Trinity and the ever the same faith,² then it cannot be altered in its nature by the dispenser (V. 4 : "the sacraments are holy in themselves, not through men : sacramenta per se esse sancta, non per homines"). That is the famous principle of the objectivity of the sacraments which became so fundamental for the development of the dogmatics of the Western Church, although it never could be carried out in all its purity in the Roman Church, because in that case it would have destroyed the prerogatives of the Clergy. It is to be noticed, however, that Optatus made the holiness of the sacraments to be effective only for the faith of the believer (fides credentis), and he is perfectly consistent in this respect, holding faith to be all important, to the complete exclusion of virtues. Here again he prepared the way for the future theology of the West by emphasising the sovereignty of faith.³ It is all

---

¹ Notice that there already occur in Optatus terms compounded with "quasi" which were so significant in the later dogmatics of Catholicism.

² Here stands the following sentence (V., 7) : "Ne quis putaret, in solis apostolis aut episcopis spem suam esse ponendam, sic Paulus ait : 'Quid est enim Paulus vel quid Apollo? Utique ministri ejus, in quem credidistis. Est ergo in universis servientibus non dominium sed ministerium."

³ At this point there occur especially in V., 7, 8, very important expositions anticipating Augustine. "Ad gratiam dei pertinet qui credit, non ille, pro cujus voluntate, ut dicitis, sanctitas vestra succedit."—"Nomen trinitatis est, quod sanctificat, non opus (operantis)."—"Restat jam de credentis merito aliquid dicere, cujus est fides, quam filius dei et sanctitati suae anteposuit et majestati ; non enim potestis sanctiores esse, quam Christus est." Here follows the story of the Canaanitish woman, with

the more shocking to find that even Optatus uses the whole reflection to enable him to depreciate claims on the life of the
members of the Church.   We see clearly that the Catholic
doctrine of the sacraments grew out of the desire to show that
the Church was holy and therefore true, in spite of the irreligion
of the Christians belonging to it.   *But in aiming at this, men lit,
curiously, upon a trace of evangelical religion.*   Since it was impossible to point to active holiness, faith and its importance
were called to mind.   A great crisis, a *perplexity*, in which, seeing the actual condition of matters, the Catholic Church found
itself involved with its doctrine of Baptism, virtue, and salvation,
turned its attention to the promise of God and faith.   *Thus the
most beneficent and momentous transformation experienced by
Western Christianity before Luther was forced upon it by circumstances.*   But it would never have made its way if it had not
been changed by the spiritual experiences of a Catholic Christian,
Augustine, from an extorted theory[1] into a joyful and confident
confession.

Parmenian gave Optatus occasion to enumerate certain " endowments " (dotes) of the Church, *i.e.*, the essential parts of its
possession.   Parmenian had numbered six, Optatus gives five :
(1) cathedra (the [Episcopal] chair); (2) angelus; (3) spiritus; (4)
fons ; (5) sigillum (the symbol).   The enumeration is so awkward that one can only regret that it is adapted to the formula
of an opponent.   But we learn, at least, in this way that
Cyprian's ideal of the unity of the Episcopate, as represented in
Peter's chair, had been received and fostered unsuspiciously in
Africa.   "Peter alone received the keys" (I., 10, 12).   "You
cannot deny your knowledge that on Peter, in the city of Rome,
was first conferred the Episcopal chair, in which he sat, the
head of all the Apostles, whence he was also called Cephas, in
which one chair unity might be observed by all, lest the rest of

the remarkable application : "Et ut ostenderet filius dei, *se vacasse, fidem tantummodo operatam esse* : vade, inquit, mulier in pace, *fides tua te salvavit."*   So also faith
is extolled as having been the sole agent in the stories of the Centurion of Capernaum
and the Issue of Blood.   "Nec mulier petiit, nec Christus promisit, sed fides tantum
quantum praesumpsit, exegit."   The same thoughts occur in Optatus' contemporary,
Ambrosiaster.

[1] This it was in the case of Ambrosiaster as well as in that of Optatus.

the Apostles should severally defend one, each for himself, in order that he might now be a schismatic and sinner, who should appoint a second as against the one unique chair " (II., 2). The connection with Peter's chair was of decisive importance, not only for Optatus, but also for his opponent (II., 4), who had appealed to the fact that Donatists had also possessed a Bishop in Rome. Optatus, besides, discusses the second point, the angelus, who is the legitimate Bishop of the local community, the chair (cathedra) guaranteeing the œcumenical unity, and he emphasises the connection of the African Catholic Churches with the Oriental, and especially the seven-fold *ecclesia* of Asia (Rev. II., 3), almost as strongly as that with the Roman Church (II., 6 ; VI., 3). His disquisitions on spiritus,[1] fons, and sigillum, are devoid of any special interest (II., 7-9). On the other hand, it is important to notice that he expressly subordinates the consideration of the endowments (dotes) of the Church, to the verification of "its sacred members and internal organs" (sancta membra ac viscera ecclesiæ), about which Parmenian had said nothing. These consisted in the sacraments and the names of the Trinity " in which meet the faith and profession of believers " (cui concurrit fides credentium et professio). Thus he returns to his natural and significant line of thought.[2]

---

[1] The Donatist had said (II., 7) : " Nam in illa (catholica) ecclesia quis spiritus esse potest, nisi qui pariat filios gehennæ ? " That is the genuine confession of separatists.

[2] We may here select a few details from the work of Optatus as characteristic of Western Christianity before Augustine. He regularly gives the name of " lex " to both the Testaments ; he judges all dogmatic statements by the *symbolum apostolicum*, in which he finds the doctrine of the Trinity, to him the chief confession, without therefore mentioning the Nicene Creed ; he confesses " per *carnem* Christi deo reconciliatus est mundus " (I., 10) ; he declares (VI., 1) : " quid est altare, nisi sedes et corporis et sanguinis Christi, cujus illic *per certa momenta* corpus et sanguis habitabat ? " He speaks of the *reatus peccati* and *meritum fidei ;* he has definitely stated the distinction between *præcepta* and *consilia* (VI., 4) in his explanation of the parable of the Good Samaritan. The innkeeper is Paul, the two pence are the two Testaments, the additional sum still perhaps necessary are the consilia. He describes the position of the soteriological dogma in his time by the following exposition (II., 20) :—" Est Christiani hominis, quod bonum est velle et in eo quod bene voluerit, currere ; sed homini non est datum perficere, ut post spatia, quæ debet homo implere, restet aliquid deo, ubi deficienti succurrat, quia ipse solus est perfectio et perfectus solus dei filius Christus, cæteri *omnes semi-perfecti* sumus." Here we perceive the great task that awaited Augustine. But even as regards Church politics Optatus betrays himself as

If Ambrosiaster and Optatus prepared the way for Augustine's doctrines of the sacraments, faith, and the Church,[1] Ambrose did so for those of sin, grace, and faith. We have endeavoured above to estimate his importance to Augustine as a disciple of the Greeks ; we have now to regard him as a Western.[2] But we have first of all to consider not the theologian, but the Bishop. It was the royal priest who first opened Augustine's eyes to the authority and majesty of the Church. Only a Roman Bishop—even if he did not sit in the Roman chair—could teach him this, and perhaps the great work, De civitate Dei, would never have been written had it not been for the way in which this majesty had been impressed on Augustine by Ambrose ; for great historical conceptions arise either from the fascinating impression made by great personalities or from political energy ; and Augustine never possessed the latter. It was, on the contrary, in Ambrose, the priestly Chancellor of the State, that the imperial power (imperium) of the Catholic Church dawned upon him,[3] and his experiences of the confusion and weakness of the civil power at the beginning of the fifth century completed the impression. Along with this Ambrose's sermons fall to be considered.[4] If, on one side, they were wholly dependent on Greek models, yet they show, on the other hand, in their practical tone, the spirit of the West. Augustine's demand that the preacher should " teach, sway, and move ' (docere, flectere, movere) is as if drawn from those sermons. In spite of the asceticism and virginity which he also mainly preached, he constantly discussed all the concrete affairs of the time and the

---

an Epigone of the Constantinian era, and as a precursor of the Augustinian. See his thesis on the disloyalty of the Donatists to the State (III., 3) : "Non respublica est in ecclesia, sed ecclesia in republica est, id est in imperio Romano."

[1] In the West, before Augustine, the conception of *gratia* exhausted itself in that of the *remissio peccatorum*. We can see this in propositions like the following from Pacian, sermo de bapt. 3 :—"Quid est gratia ? peccati remissio, *i.e.*, donum ; gratia enim donum est."

[2] In this respect Ambrose takes an isolated position ; thus it is, *e.g.*, characteristic that he does not seem to have read Cyprian's works.

[3] I express myself thus intentionally ; for Ambrose never, in words, thrust the actual, hierarchical Church into the foreground.

[4] See proofs by Förster, l.c., p. 218 ff.

moral wants of the community.[1]   Thus Ambrose represents the intimate union of the ascetic ideal with energetic insistence on positive morality, a union which the Western mediæval Church never lost, however much practical life was subordinated to the contemplative.

Three different types of thought are interwoven in Ambrose's doctrine of sin and grace.   First, he was dependent on the Greek conception that regarded evil as not-being, but at the same time as necessary.[2]   Secondly, he shows that he was strongly influenced by the popular morality of Ciceronian Stoicism,[3] which was widespread among cultured Western Christians, and which had, by its combination with monastic morality, brought about, in Pelagianism, the crisis so decisive for the dogmatics of the West.   Thirdly and finally, he carried very much further that view taken by Tertullian of the *radical* nature of evil and the *guiltiness* of sin which was made his fundamental principle by Augustine.   *Evil was radical, and yet its root was not found in the sensuous, but in "pride of mind" (superbia animi); it sprang from freedom, and was yet a power propagating itself in mankind.*   The Greeks had looked on the universal state of sinfulness as a more or less accidental product of circumstances ; Ambrose regarded it as the decisive fact, made it the starting-point of his thought, and referred it more definitely than any previous teacher—Ambrosiaster excepted—to Adam's Fall.[4]   Passages occur in his works which in this respect do not fall a whit behind the famous statements of Augustine.[5]

---

[1] See at an earlier date the Instructiones of Commodian.   Ambrose was not such an advocate of Monachism as Jerome.

[2] See above, p. 31.

[3] See Ewald, Der Einfluss der stoisch-ciceronianischen Moral auf die Darstellung der Ethik bei Ambrosius, 1881.   " De officiis," with all its apparent consistency, shows merely a considerable vacillation between virtue as the supreme good (in the Stoic sense) and eternal life—which latter term, for the rest, is not understood in its Christian meaning.   The moralism of antiquity, as well as the eudaimonist trait of ancient moral philosophy dominate the book, in which ultimately the "true wise man " appears most clearly.   In such circumstances the distinction drawn between *præcepta* and *consilia*, in itself so dangerous to evangelical morality, constitutes an advantage ; for specifically Christian virtues appear in the form of the *consilia.*

[4] Hilary also speaks of the *vitium originis.*

[5] See Deutsch, Des Ambrosius Lehre von der Sünde und Sündentilgung, 1867.

But important as this phase was, in which thought was no longer directed primarily to sin's results, or to the single sinful act, but to the sinful *state* which no virtue could remove, yet it is just in this alone that we can perceive the advance made by Ambrose. As regards religion, none is to be found in his works ; for his doctrine of the traducian character and tenacity of sin was in no way connected with the heightened consciousness of God and salvation. *Ambrose did not submit evil to be decided upon in the light of religion.* Therefore he merely groped his way round the guilty character of sin, without hitting upon it ; he could once more emphasise the weakness of the flesh as an essential factor ; and he could maintain the proposition that man was of himself capable of willing the good. For this reason, finally, his doctrine of sin is to us an irreconcilable mass of contradictions. But we must, nevertheless, estimate very highly the advance made by Ambrose in contemplating the radical sinful *condition*. It was undoubtedly important for Augustine. And to this is to be added that he was able to speak in a very vivid way of faith, conceiving it to be a living communion with God or Christ. The religious individualism which shines clearly in Augustine already does so faintly in Ambrose : " Let Christ enter thy soul, let Jesus dwell in your minds. . . . What advantage is it to me, conscious of such great sins, if the Lord do come, unless He comes into my soul, returns into my mind, unless Christ lives in me ? "[1]　And while

---

Förster, l. c., p. 146 ff. All human beings are sinners, even Mary. The "hæreditarium vinculum" of sin embraces all. " Fuit Adam, et in illo fuimus omnes ; periit Adam, et in illo omnes perierunt." It is not only an inherited infirmity that is meant, but a guilt that continues active. " Quicunque natus est sub peccato, quem ipsa nosciæ conditionis hæreditas adstrinxit ad culpam." No doctrine of imputation, indeed, yet occurs in Ambrose ; for as he conceived it, mankind in Adam was a unity, in which took place a *peccatrix successio*, a continuous evolution of Adam's sin. Accordingly no imputation was necessary. Ambrosiaster (on Rom. V., 12) has also expressed Ambrose's thought : " Manifestum itaque est, in Adam omnes peccasse quasi in massa ; ipse enim per peccatum corruptus, quos genuit, omnes, nati sunt sub peccato. Ex eo igitur cuncti peccatores, quia ex eo ipso sumus omnes." In the West this thought was traditional after Tertullian. See Cyprian, Ep. 64, 5 ; De opere 1, and Commodian, Instruct. I., 35.

[1] "Intret in animam tuam Christus, inhabitet in mentibus tuis Jesus. . . . Quid mihi prodest tantorum conscio peccatorum, si dominus veniat, nisi veniat in meam animam, redeat in meam mentem, nisi vivat in me Christus." In Ps. CXIX., exp.

in many passages he distinctly describes the merit gained by works, and love as means of redemption, yet in some of his reflections, on the other hand, he rises as strongly to the lofty thought that God alone rouses in us the disposition for what is good, and that we can only depend on the grace of God in Christ.[1]   St. Paul's Epistles occupied the foreground in Ambrose's thought,[2] and from them he learned that faith as confidence in God is a power by itself, and does not simply fall into the realm of pious belief.   However much he adds that is alien, however often he conceives faith to be an act of obedience to an external authority, he can speak of it in different terms from his predecessors.   Faith is to him the fundamental fact of the Christian life, not merely as belief in authority (" faith goes before reason," fides prævenit rationem),[3] but as faith *which lays hold of redemption through Christ*, and justifies because it is the foundation of perfect works, and because grace and faith are alone valid before God.   " And that benefits me because we are not justified from the works of the law.   I have no reason, therefore, to glory in my works, I have nothing to boast of ; and therefore I will glory in Christ.   I will not boast because I am just, but because I am redeemed.   I will glory, not because I am without sins, but because my sins have been remitted.   I will not glory because I have done good service, or because anyone has benefited me, but because the blood of Christ was

---

IV., 26 : in Luc. enarr., X., 7 ; in Ps. XXXVI., exp. 63.   The passages are collected by Förster (see esp. De poenit., II., 8).   See also Vol. III., p. 130.   For the rest, the author of the Quæstiones ex Vet. et. Nov. Testam. (Ambrosiaster) could also speak in tones whose pathetic individualism recalls Augustine ; cf. *e.g.*, the conclusion of the inserted tractate c. Novat. : "ego . . . te (scil. deum) quæsivi, te desideravi, tibi credidi ; de homine nihil speravi . . . ego verbis antistitis fidem dedi, quæ a te data dicuntur, quæque te inspirant, te loquuntur, de te promittunt ; huic de se nihil credidi nec gestis ejus, sed fidei quæ ex te est, me copulavi."

[1] On Ps. CXIX., exp. XX., 14 : " Nemo sibi arroget, nemo de meritis, nemo de potestate se jactet, sed omnes speremus per dominum Jesum misericordiam invenire— quæ enim spes alia peccatoribus ? "

The interrogation mark in Reuter, August. Studien, p. 493, is due to exaggerated caution.   The antithesis of nature and grace, which, wherever it occurs, has one of its roots in Paulinism, and was already familiar to Tertullian, is anew proclaimed in Ambrose ; see De off. I., 7, 24 ; see also the address on the death of his brother.   Ambrosiaster, too, makes use of the natura-gratia antithesis.

[3] De Abrah., I., 3, 21.

shed for me."[1]   That is Augustinianism before Augustine, nay, it is more than Augustinianism.[2]

In the dogmatic work of Western theologians of the fourth century, the genius of Western Christianity, which found its most vigorous expression in Cyprian's De opere et eleemosynis, fell away to some extent. But it only receded, remaining still the prevailing spirit. *The more vital notion of God, the strong feeling of responsibility to God as judge, the consciousness of God as moral power, neither restricted nor dissolved by any speculation on nature*—all that constituted the superiority of Western to Eastern Christianity is seen in its worst form under the deteriorating influence of the legal doctrine of *retribution*, and the pseudo-moral one of *merit*.[3]   In view of this, the inrush of Neoplatonic mysticism was highly important; for it created a counterpoise to a conception which threatened to dissolve religion into a series of legal transactions. But the weightiest counterpoise consisted in the doctrine of faith and grace as proclaimed by Augustine. However, it will be shown that Augustine taught his new conception in such a form that it did not shatter the prevailing system, but could rather be admitted into it ; perhaps the greatest triumph ever achieved in the history of religion by a morality of calculations over religion.

The conception of religion as a legal relationship, which was concerned with the categories lex (law) delictum (fault) satisfactio, pœna (punishment) meritum, præmium, etc., was not destroyed by Augustine. Grace was rather inserted in a legal and objective form into the relationship, yet in such a way that it remained possible for the individual to construe the whole relationship from the point of view of grace.

---

[1] De Jacob et vita beata I., 6, 21 ; other passages in Förster, pp. 160 ff, 303 ff.

[2] A detailed account would here require to discuss many other Western writers, *e.g.*, Prudentius (see monographs by Brockhaus, 1872, and Rösler, 1886), Pacian, Zeno, Paulinus of Nola, etc. ; but what we have given may serve to define the directions in which Western Christianity moved. As regards Hilary, Förster has shown very recently (Stud. u. Krit., 1888, p. 645 ff.) that even he, in spite of his dependence on the Greeks, did not belie the practical ethical interest of the Westerns.

[3] The East knew nothing of this excessive analysis ; it took a man more as a whole, and judged him by the regular course taken by his will.

We have attempted, in the above discussion, to exhibit the
different lines existing in the West which meet in Augustine.
Let us, in conclusion, emphasise further the following points.

1. Along with Holy Scripture, the Symbol, the Apostolic
"law" (lex), was placed in the West on an unapproachable
height. This law was framed in opposition to Marcionitism,
Sabellianism, Arianism, and Apollinarianism, without essential
variations, and without any process of reasoning, as a confession
of faith in the *unity of God* in three persons, as also in the *unity
of Christ* in two substances. The Western Church, therefore,
apparently possessed a lofty certitude in dealing with Trinitarian
and Christological problems. But with this certitude was contrasted the fact, of which we have many instances, that under
cover of the official confession many more Christological heresies
circulated, and were maintained in the West than in the
Churches of the East, and that in particular the Christological
formula, where it was not wholly unknown, was, for the laity
and for many of the clergy, simply a noumenon.[1] This fact is
further confirmed when we observe that Western theologians, as
long as they were not directly involved in Eastern controversies,
*did not turn their attention to the principles contained in the above
"law," but to quite different questions.* Augustine was not the
first to write " expositions of the Symbol," in which questions,
wholly different from what his text would lead us to expect,

---

[1] I have already discussed this briefly in Vol. III., p. 33 ff. Augustine (Confess.
VII., 19) believed, up to the time of his conversion, that the doctrine of Christ held
by the Catholic Church was almost identical with that of Photinus ; his friend Alypius
thought, on the contrary, that the Church denied Christ a human soul. We see
from Hilary's work, De trinitate, how many Christological conceptions circulated in
the Western communities, among them even " quod in eo ex virgine creando efficax
Dei sapientia et virtus exstiterit, et in nativitate ejus divinæ prudentiæ et potestatis
opus intellegatur, sitque in eo efficientia potius quam natura sapientiæ." Optatus (I.,
8) had to blame Parmenian for calling the body of Christ *sinful*, and maintaining
that it was purified by his baptism. Further, in spite of the doctrine of " two
natures," and the acceptance of Greek speculations, the thought of Hippolytus
(Philos. X., 33) : εἰ γὰρ ὁ θεὸς θεόν σε ἠθέλησε ποιῆσαι, ἐδύνατο· ἔχεις τοῦ λόγου τὸ
παράδειγμα, runs like a concealed thread through the Christological utterances of the
West. We shall see that even in Ambrose and Augustine there is to be found a
hidden, but intentionally retained, remnant of the old Adoptian conception. (How
this is to be regarded, see above under 2). We may here pass over the influence of
Manichæan Christology on many secondary minds in the Western Churches.

were discussed. On the contrary, Western theologians from Cyprian show that they lived in a complex of ideas and questions which had little to do with the problems treated by Antignostics and Alexandrians, or with dogma.

2. In connection with the development of penance on the basis of works and merits (in the sense of satisfactions), and in harmony with the legal spirit characteristic of Western theological speculation, Christ's expiatory work came now to the front. It was not so much the Incarnation — that was the antecedent condition—as the death of Christ, which was regarded as the salient point (punctum saliens);[1] and it was already treated from all conceivable points of view as a sacrificial death, atonement, ransom, and vicarious consummation of the crucifixion. At the same time, Ambrose discussed its relationship (reconciliatio, redemptio, satisfactio, immolatio, meritum) to sin as guilt (reatus). In such circumstances the accent fell on the human nature of Christ; the offerer and offering was the mediator as man, who received his value through the divine nature, though quite as much so by his acceptance on the part of the Deity. Thus the West had a Christological system of its own, which, while the formula of the two natures formed its starting-point, was pursued in a new direction : *the mediator was looked on as the man whose voluntary achievement possessed an infinite value in virtue of the special dispensation of God.*[2] (Optat I., 10 : " the world [was] reconciled to God by means of the flesh of Christ " : *mundus reconciliatus deo per carnem Christi.*) From this we can understand how Augustine, in not a few of his arguments, opposed, if in a veiled fashion, the doctrine of the divine nature of Christ, discussing the merits of the historical Christ as if that nature did not exist, but everything was given to Christ of *grace.*[3] The same reason

---

[1] Pseudo-Cyprian, De duplici martyrio, 16 : " Domini mors potentior erat quam vita."

[2] For fuller details, see Vol. III., p. 310 ff. Ritschl, Lehre v.d., Rechtfertigung u. Versöhnung, 2nd. ed., I., p, 38, III., p. 362. Gesch. des Pietism. III., p. 426 ff.

[3] See *e.g.*, the remarkable expositions ad Laurentium, c. 36 sq. The divine nature is indeed regarded as resting in the background ; but in Jesus Christ there comes to the front the " individual " man, who, without previous merit, was of grace received into the Deity.

further explains why afterwards modified Adoptianism was constantly re-emerging in the West,[1] it being from the standpoint of the consistent Greek Christology the worst of heresies because it dislocated the whole structure of the latter, and threw its purpose into confusion. Finally, the same fact also explains why, in later times, Western Christians, particularly such as had acquired the mystical monachist observance of intercourse with Christ, the chaste bridegroom, substantially reduced the Christological conception to " Ecce homo." The vividness and thrilling power which this figure possessed for them, raising them above sorrow and suffering, cannot deceive us as to the fact that the Church Christology was no longer anything to them but a formula. But while the ancient Western form had become the basis of a view which left fancy and disposition to fix the significance of Christ's Person, that must not be described as a necessary deduction from it. That form—in which Christ was the object of the Father's grace, carried out what the Father entrusted him with, and by Him was exalted—rather corresponded to the clearest passages of the New Testament, and was the only protection against the superstitious conceptions of the Greeks which emptied the Gospel of all meaning. Of decisive value, however, are not the various mediæval attempts to appraise Christ's *work*, but rather the whole tendency to understand Christianity as the religion of *atonement ;* for in this tendency is expressed characteristically the *fear of God as judge*, which, in the East, disappeared behind mystic speculations.[2]

3. An acute observer perceives that the soteriological question —How does man get rid, and remain rid, of his sins and attain eternal life ?—had already, in the fourth century, actively engaged the earnest attention of thinkers in the Western Church, and, indeed, in such a way that, as distinguished from the East, *the religious and moral sides of the problem are no longer found separate.* But the question was not clearly put before the Pelagian conflict, since the controversies with Heraclius and Jovinian were not followed by a lasting movement. Opinions were still jumbled together in a motley fashion, sometimes in

[1] See the evidence in Bach's Dogmengesch. des Mittelalters, Vol. II.
[2] See Vol. III., p. 189.

one and the same writer. If I see aright, five different conceptions can be distinguished for the period about 400 A.D.
First we have the *Manichæan* which insinuated its way in the
darkness, but was widely extended, even among the clergy;
according to it evil was a real physical power, and was overcome in the individual by goodness, equally a physical force
which was attached to natural potencies and Christ.[1] Secondly,
we have the *Neoplatonic and Alexandrian* view which taught
that evil was not-being, that which had not yet become, the
necessary foil of the good, the shadow of the light, the transitoriness cleaving to the " many " in opposition to the " one." It
held that redemption was the return to the one, the existent, to
God; that it was identification with God in love; Christ was
the strength and crutches for such a return; for "energies and
crutches come from one hand." [2]　Thirdly, there was the *rationalistic Stoic* conception; this held that virtue was the supreme
good; sin was the separate evil act springing from free will;
redemption was the concentration of the will and its energetic
direction to the good. Here again the historical and Christological were really nothing but crutches.[3] All these three
conceptions lay the greatest stress on asceticism. Fourthly,
there was the *sacramental* view, which may be characterised
partly as morally lax, partly as "evangelical"; we find it, *e.g.*,
in Heraclius [4] on the one hand, and in Jovinian [5] on the other.
According to it he who was baptised possessing genuine faith
obtained the guarantee of felicity; sin could not harm him; no
impeachment of sin (reatus peccati) could touch him. It is
proved that really lax and "evangelical" views met: a man
could always rely as a Christian on the grace of God; sin did
not separate him from God, if he stood firm in the faith. Nay,
from the second century, really from Paul, there existed in the

---

[1] See on the extension of Manichæism in the West, Vol. III., p. 334 ff. It was
always more Christian and therefore more dangerous there. On its importance to
Augustine, see under.

[2] See the conceptions of Ambrose, Victorinus, and Augustine.

[3] See the Western popular philosophies in the style of Cicero, but also Ambrose'
De officiis.

[4] See above, p. 40 f.

[5] Ambrose, Jerome, Augustine and Siricius give us information regarding him.

Gentile Church movements which deliberately defended reliance
on faith alone (the " sola fide ") and " the most assured salvation through grace granted in baptism " (salus per gratiam in
baptismo donatam certissima.) [1]   A fifth conception was closely
related to, yet different from, the last.   We can call it briefly
the *doctrine of grace and merit.*   We have pointed out strong
traces of it in Victorinus, Optatus, and Ambrose.   According
to it, evil as the inherent sin of Adam was only to be eradicated
by divine grace in Christ ; this grace produced faith to which,
however, redemption was only granted when it had advanced
and become the habitual love from which those good works
spring that establish merit in the sight of God.   Evil is
godlessness and the vice that springs from it ; goodness is the

---

[1] I have demonstrated this in the Ztschr. f. Theol. u. Kirche I. (1891), pp. 82-178,
and cannot repeat the proof here.   From the I. Ep. of John onwards undercurrents
can be traced in the Gentile Church which required to have the saying addressed to
them : " Be not deceived, he who *does* righteousness is righteous."   My main references are to the erroneous views opposed in the Catholic Epistles ; the lax Christians
mentioned by Tertullian ; the edict on penance of Calixtus, with its noteworthy
evangelical basis (see also Rolffs in the Texten u. Unters, Vol. XI., part 3) ; Heraclius
in Rome ; the counter-efforts of the lax against the monachism which was establishing
itself in the West ; Jovinian ; and to the opponents assailed by Augustine in his
very important writing, " De fide et operibus."   This writing is, along with Jovinian's
discussions, the most important source.   There can be no doubt that in the majority
of cases an unbridled and accommodating trust in the sacrament—accordingly a
strained form of the popular Catholic feeling—was the leading idea, and that the
reference to Gospel texts, which bore witness to the unlimited mercy of God, was
only a drapery ; that accordingly the " sola fide "—the catchword occurs—was not
conceived evangelically, but really meant " solo sacramento "—*i e.*, even if the life
did not correspond to the Christian demand for holiness.   But there were Christian
teachers who had really grasped the evangelical thesis, and Jovinian is to be counted
one of them, even if his opponents be right (and I am doubtful of this) in taking
offence at his conduct ; and even if it be certain that his doctrine, in the circumstances
of the time, could and did promote laxity.   His main positions were as follows :—
1. The natural man is in the state of sin.   Even the slightest sin separates from God
and exposes to damnation.   2. The state of the Christian rests on baptism and faith ;
these produce regeneration.   3. Regeneration is the state in which Christ is in us,
and we are in Christ ; there are no degrees in it, for this personal relationship either
does or does not exist.   Where it does, there is righteousness.   4. It is a relation
formed by love that is in question : Father and Son dwell in believers ; *but where
there is such an indweller, the possessor can want for nothing.*   5. Accordingly all
blessings are bestowed with and in this relationship ; nothing can be thought of as
capable of being added.   6. Since all blessings issue from this relationship, there
can be no special meritorious works ; for at bottom there is only one good, and that

energy of grace and the good works that flow from it. Here,
accordingly, nature and grace, unbelief and faith, selfishness and
love of God are the antitheses, and the work of the historical
Christ stands in the centre. Nevertheless, this view did not
exclude asceticism, but required it, since only that faith was
genuine and justified men which evinced itself in sanctification,
i.e., in world-renouncing love. Thus a middle path was here
sought between Jovinian on the one side and Manichæan and
Priscillian asceticism on the other.[1]

These different conceptions met and were inextricably
mingled. The future of Christianity was necessarily to be
decided by the victory of one or other of them.

we possess as the best beloved children of God, who now participate in the divine
nature, and that good will be fully revealed in Heaven. 7. In him who occupies
this relationship of faith and love there is nothing to be condemned ; he can commit no sin which would separate him from God ; the devil cannot make him fall,
for he ever recovers himself as a child of God by faith and penitence. The relationship fixed in baptism through faith is something lasting and indissoluble. 8. But
such an one must not only be baptised ; he must have received baptism with perfect
faith, and by faith evince baptismal grace. He must labour and wrestle earnestly
—though not in monkish efforts, for they are valueless—not in order to deserve
something further, but that he may not lose what he has received. To him, too, the
truth applies that there are no small and great sins, but that the heart is either with
God or the devil. 9. Those who are baptised in Christ, and cling to Him with confident faith, form the one, true Church. To her belong all the glorious promises :
she is bride, sister, mother, and is never without her bridegroom. She lives in one
faith, and is never violated or divided, but is a pure virgin. We may call Jovinian
actually a "witness of antiquity to the truth," and a "Protestant of his time,"
though we must not mistake a point of difference : the indwelling of God and Christ
in the baptised is more strongly emphasised than the power of faith.

The Spaniard, Vigilantius, even surpassed Jovinian, both in range and intensity,
in the energy with which he attacked the excrescences of monkery, relic-worship,
virginity, etc.; but he does not belong to this section, for he was moved by the
impression made upon him by the superstition and idolatry which he saw rising to
supremacy in the Church. Jerome's writing against him is miserable, but is surpassed
in meanness by the same author's books against Jovinian.

[1] The puzzling phenomenon of Priscillianism has not been made much clearer by
the discovery of Priscillian's homilies. I believe we may pass them over, since, important as were the points touched on in the Priscillian controversy (even the question
as to the claims of the "Apocrypha" compared with the Bible), they neither evoked
a dogmatic controversy, nor obtained a more general significance. The meritorious
work by Paret, Priscillianus, ein Reformator des 4 Jahrh. (Würzburg, 1891) is not
convincing in its leading thoughts (see on the other side Hilgenfeld in his Zeitschr.
Vol. 35, 1892, pp. 1-85).

4. In the West, interest in the question of the relation of grace and means of grace to the Church was awakened by the Novatian, heretical baptism, and Donatist controversy. This interest was, however, still further strengthened by the fact that the Church detached itself more forcibly from the State than in the East. The fall of the West Roman Empire, opposition to the remains of a still powerful heathen party in Rome, and finally dislike to the new Arian German forms of government all contributed to this.

One perhaps expects to find here by way of conclusion a characterisation of the different national Churches of the West; but little can be said from the standpoint of the history of dogma. The distinctive character of the North African Church was strongly marked. A darkness broods over the Churches of Spain, Gaul, and Britain, in which the only clear spot is the conflict of the priests with the monachism that was establishing itself. The conflict with Priscillianism in Spain, the attacks on Martin of Tours in Gaul, and, on the other hand, Vigilantius, come in here. It is not unimportant to notice that Southern Gaul was distinguished by its culture and taste for æsthetics and rhetoric about A.D. 360 (see Julian's testimony) and A.D. 400 (see Sulp. Severus, Chron. init.). Rome only became a Christian city in the fifth century, but even in the time of Liberius and Damasus the Roman Bishop was the foremost Roman. What was wrested by Damasus, that unsaintly but sagacious man, from the State and the East, was never again abandoned by his energetic successors ; they also tried vigorous intervention in the affairs of the provincial Churches. Holding faithfully to its confession, the Roman Church was, not only from its position, but also by its nature, the connecting link between East and West, between the monachist leanings of the former, and the tendency to ecclesiastical politics and sacramentarianism of the latter. It also united South and North in the West. Rome, again, from the time of Liberius pursued and explained that religious policy towards paganism, "by which the Catholic Church gained the means not only of winning but of satisfying the masses of the people who were, and, in spite of the confession, remained heathen " (Usener, Relig. Unters., I., p. 293): "it rendered heathenism harmless by giving its blessing to it, *i.e.*, to all that belonged to the pagan cultus." But that magnanimous way of opposing paganism, which has been rightly adduced, and which Usener (op. cit.) has begun to exhibit to us so learnedly and instructively, concealed within it the greatest dangers. In such circumstances it was of supreme value both for the contemporary and future fortunes of the Church that, just when the process of ethnicising was in full swing, Augustine, equally at home in North Africa, Rome, and Milan, appeared and reminded the Church what Christian faith was.

CHAPTER III.

THE HISTORICAL POSITION OF AUGUSTINE AS REFORMER OF CHRISTIAN PIETY.[1]

"VIRTUES will so increase and be perfected as to conduct thee without any hesitation to the truly blessed life which only is eternal : where evils, which will not exist, are not discriminated from blessings by *prudence*, nor adversity is borne *bravely*, because there we shall find only what we love, not also what we tolerate, nor lust is bridled by temperance, where we shall not feel its

[1] Of the immense literature about Augustine, the following works may be mentioned (with special regard to the Pelagian controversy) : The critical investigations of the Benedictines in their editions of Aug.'s Opp., and the controversies over his doctrine of grace in the 16th to the 18th century; the works of Petavius, Noris (Hist. Pelag.), Tillemont, Garnier, Mansi, Hefele ; Bindemaun, Der hl. Aug. 3 vols., 1844-69 ; Böhringer, Aur. Aug., 2 ed., 1877-78 ; Reuter, August. Studien, 1887 (the best of later works) ; A. Dorner, Aug., sein theol. System und seine relig.-philos. Anschauung, 1873 ; Loofs, "Augustinus in the 3 Ed. of the R.-Encykl. v. Hauck, Vol. II., pp. 257-285 (an excellent study, with an especially good discussion of the period to 395). Comprehensive expositions in Ritter, Baur, Nitzsch, Thomasius, Schwane, Huber (Philos. der KVV.), Jul. Müller (L. v. d. Sünde), Dorner (Entwicklgesch. d. L. v. d. Person Christi), Prantl (Gesch. d. Logik), Siebeck (Gesch. d. Psychologie), Zeller ; see esp. Eucken, Die Lebenanschauungen der grossen Denker (1890) p. 258 ff.—Naville, S' Aug., Etude sur le devéloppement de sa pensée jusqu à l'époque de son ordination (Geneva 1872). Bornemann, Aug.'s Bekenntnisse, 1888; Harnack, Aug.'s Confessionen, 1888; Boissier, La conversion de S. Aug. in the Rev. de deux mondes, 1888 Jan. ; Wörter, Die Geistesentw. d. h. Aug. bis zu seiner Taufe, 1892 ; Overbeck, Aug. u. Hieronymus in the Histor. Ztschr. N. F., Vol. VI. ; Feuerlein, Ueb. d. Stellung Aug.'s in the Kirchenund Culturgesch. Histor. Ztschr., XXII., p. 270 ff. (see Reuter, l.c. p. 479 ff.) ; Ritschl, Ueber die Methode der ältesten D.-G. in the Jahrbb. f. deutsche Theol., 1871 (idem, Rechtfert. und Versöhn. Vol. I., Gesch. d. Pietismus Vol. I.) ; Kattenbusch, Studien z. Symbolik in the Stud. u. Krit. 1878 ; Reinkens, Geschichtsphilos. d. hl. Aug., 1866 ; Seyrich, Geschichts philosophie Aug.'s, 1891 ; Gangauf, Metaphys. Psychologie d. hl. Aug., 1852 ; Bestmann, Qua ratione Aug. notiones philosophiæ græcæ, etc., 1877 ; Lœsche, De Aug. Platonizante 1880 ; Ferraz, Psychologie de S. Aug., 1862 ; Nourissou, La philosophie de S. Aug., 2 Ed., 1866 ; Storz, Die Philosophie des hl. Aug., 1882 ; Scipio, Des Aurel. Aug. Metaphysik, etc., 1886 ; Melzer, Die augus . Lehre vom Causalitätsverhältniss Gottes zur Welt, 1892; Melzer, Augustini et Cartesii

incitements, nor the needy are aided *justly,* where we will have no need and nothing unworthy. *There virtue will be one, and virtue and the reward of virtue will be* that spoken of in sacred phrase by the man who loves it : " *But to me to cling to God is a good thing.*" This virtue will be there the full and eternal wisdom, and it will also truly be the life that is blessed. *Surely this is*

placita de mentis humanæ sui cognitione, 1860 ; Siebeck, Die Anfänge der neueren Psychologie in the Ztschr. f. Philos., 1888, p. 161 ff. ; Kahl, Der Primat des Willens bei Aug., 1886 ; Schütz, August. non esse ontologum, 1867 ; Heinzelmann, Aug.'s Ansichten vom Wesen der menschlichen Seele, 1894 ; van Endert, Gottesbeweis in d. patrist. Zeit, 1869 ; Clauren, Aug. s. script. interpret., 1822 ; Gangauf, Des hl. Aug. Lehre von Gott dem Dreieinigen, 1865 ; Nitzsch, Aug.'s Lehre v. Wunder, 1865. Walch, De pelagianismo ante Pelagium, 1783 ; idem. hist. doctrinæ de peccato orig., 1783 ; Horn, Comm. de sentent. patrum . . . de pecc. originali, 180: ; Dunker, Pecc. orig. et act., 1836; Krabinger, Der angebliche Pelagianismus d. voraugust. VV. Tüb Quartalschr., 1853 ; Kuhn, Der vorgebl. Pelagianismus d. voraugust. VV., in same journal ; Walch, Ketzerhistorie, Vols. IV. and V. ; Wiggers, Pragmat. Darstell. des Augustinismus u. Pelagianismus, 2 Vols., 1831-33 (the continuation on Semipela- gianism in the Zeitschr. f. d. histor. Theol., 1854 ff.) ; Rottmanner, Der Augustinis- mus, 1892 ; Jacobi, Die Lehre des Pelagius, 1842 ; Leutzen, de Pelagianorum doctrinæ principiis, 1833 ; Jul. Muller, Der Pelagianismus in the deutsche Zeitschr f. christl. Wissensch., 1854, Nr. 40 f. ; Wörter, Der Pelagianismus, 1866; Klasen, Die innere Entw. des Pelagianism., 1882; Geffcken, Histor. semipelag., 1826 ; Wiggers, de Joanne Cass., 1824-25 ; Wörter, Prosper v. Aquitanien über Gnade und Freiheit, 1867 ; Landerer, Das Verhältniss v. Gnade u. Freiheit in the Jahrbb. f. deutsche Theol., Vol. II., 1857; Luthardt, Die L. v. freien Willen u. s. Verh. z. Gnade, 1863 ; Kihn, Theodor. v. Mopsueste, 1880 ; Ritschl, Expos. doctr. S. Aug. de creat., peccato, gratia, 1843 ; Zeller, Die Lehre des Paulus u. Augustinus v. d. Sünde u. Gnade in ihrem Verhältniss z. protest. Kirchenlehre (Theol. Jahrbb., 1854, p. 295 ff.) ; Ehlers, Aug. de origine mali doctrina, 1857 ; Nirschl, Ursp. u. Wesen des Bösen nach Aug., 1854 ; Hamma, Die L. des hl. Aug. uber die Concupiscenz in the Tüb. Quartalschr., 1873 ; Voigt, Comment. de theoria August., Pelag., Semi- pelag. et Synergist., 1829 ; Kühner, Aug.'s Anschauung v. d. Erlösungsbedeutung Christi, 1890 ; Dieckhoff, Aug.'s L. v. d. Gnade in the Mecklenb. Theol. Ztschr. I., 1860 ; Weber, Aug. de justificatione doctr. ; Ernst, Die Werke der Ungläubigen nach Aug., 1871 ; Beck, Prädest.—Lehre in the Stud. u. Krit., 1847, II. ; Koch, Autori- tät Aug.'s in der Lehre v. der Gnade u. Prädest., in the Tüb. Quartalschr., 1891, p. 95 ff. ; H. Schmidt, Origenes u. Aug. als Apologeten, in the Jahrbb. f. deutsche Theologie, Vol. VIII. ; Bigg, The Christian Platonists of Alexandria, 1886.—On Aug.'s doctrine of Baptism see Reuter, Kliefoth (Liturg. Abhandl.), and Höfling. Wilden, Die L. d. hl. Aug. v. Opfer d. Eucharistie, 1864 ; Ginzel L. d. hl. Aug. v. d. Kirche, in the Tüb. Theol. Quartalschr., 1849 ; Köstlin, Die kathol Auffass. v. d. Kirche, etc., in the deutschen Zeitschrift f. christl. Wissensch., 1856, Nr. 14 ; H. Schmidt, Aug.'s L. v. d. Kirche, in the Jahrbb. f. deutsche Theol., 1861 (id. Die Kirche, 1884) ; Seeberg, Begriff d. christl. Kirche, Pt. I., 1885 ; Roux, Diss. de. Aug. adversario Donatistarum, 1838 ; Ribbeck, Donatus und Augustinus, 1858.

to attain to the eternal and supreme blessing, to which to cling for ever is the end of our goodness. Let this (virtue) be called *prudence*, because it will cling to the good too eagerly for it to be lost, and *fortitude*, because it will cling to the good too firmly for it to be torn away, and *temperance*, because it will cling to the good too chastely to be corrupted, and *justice*, because it will cling to the good too justly to be inferior in any merit. *Although even in this life the only virtue is to love what ought to be loved.* But what should we choose chiefly to love except that than which we find nothing better? This is God, and if we prefer anything or esteem anything equal to love to him we fail to love ourselves. For it is the better for us, *the more we enter into him,* than whom there is nothing better. But we move not by walking, but by loving. We may not go (to him) afoot, but with our character. But our character is wont to be judged, not from what anyone knows, but from what he loves. *Nothing makes character good or bad but good or bad affections.* Therefore, by our corruption, we have been far from the righteousness of God. Whence we are corrected by loving the right, that being just we may be able to cling to the right."[1]

[1] August. Ep. 155 c. 12. 13. "Virtutes ita crescent et perficientur, ut te ad vitam vere beatam, quæ nonnisi æterna est, sine ulla dubitatione perducant : ubi jam nec *prudenter* discernantur a bonis mala, quæ non erunt, nec *fortiter* tolerentur adversa, quia non ibi erit nisi quod amemus, non etiam quod toleremus, nec *temperanter* libido frenetur, ubi nulla ejus incitamenta sentiemus, nec *juste* subveniatur ope indigentibus, ubi inopem atque indignum non habebimus. *Una ibi virtus erit, et idipsum erit virtus præmiumque virtutis,* quod dicit in sanctis eloquiis homo qui hoc amat : *Mihi autem adhærere deo bonum est.* Hæc ibi erit plena et sempiterna *sapientia* eademque veraciter *vita* jam beata. *Perventio quippe est ad æternum ac summum bonum, cui adhærere est finis nostri boni.* Dicatur hæc et *prudentia* quia prospectissime adhærebit bono quod non amittatur, et fortitudo, quia fermissime adhærebit bono unde non avellatur, et temperantia, quia castissime adhærebit bono, ubi non corrumpatur, et *justitia,* quia rectissime adhærebit bono, cui merito subjiciatur. *Quamquam et in hac vita virtus non est nisi diligere quod diligendum est.* Quid autem eligamus quod præcipue diligamus, nisi quo nihil melius invenimus? Hoc deus est, cui si diligendo aliquid vel præponimus vel aequamus, nos ipsos diligere nescimus. Tanto enim nobis melius est, *quanto magis in illum imus,* quo nihil melius est. Imus autem non ambulando, sed amando. Ad eum non pedibus ire licet, sed moribus. Mores autem nostri, non ex eo quod quisque novit, sed ex eo quod diligit, dijudicari solent. *Nec faciunt bonos vel malos mores, nisi boni vel mali amores.* Pravitate ergo nostra a rectitudine dei longe fuimus. Unde rectum amando corrigimur, ut recto recti adhærere possimus."

Augustine reveals his soul in these words ; they therefore also mark his importance in the history of dogma. If, as we have attempted in the preceding chapter, we pursue and let converge the different lines along which Western Christianity developed in the fourth and fifth centuries, we can construct a system which approximates to " Augustinianism "; indeed we can even deduce the latter, as a necessary product, from the internal and external conditions in which the Church and theology then found themselves. But we cannot, for all that, match the man who was behind the system and lent it vigour and life. Similarly we can attempt—and it is a remunerative task—to make Augustine's Christian conception of the world intelligible from the course of his education, and to show how no stage in his career failed to influence him. His pagan father, and pious, Christian mother, Cicero's Hortensius, Manichæism, Aristotelianism, Neoplatonism, with its mysticism and scepticism, the impression produced by Ambrose and monachism—all contributed their share.[1] But even from this standpoint we cannot finally do complete justice to the distinctive character of this man. That is his secret and his greatness, and perhaps all or any analysis itself is an injury : *he knew his heart to be his worst possession, and the living God to be his highest good ; he lived in the love of God, and he possessed a fascinating power of expressing his observations on the inner life.* In doing this, he taught the world that the highest and sweetest enjoyment was to be sought in the feeling that springs from a soul that has triumphed over its pain, from the love of God as the fountain of good, and therefore from the certainty of grace. Theologians before him had taught that man must be *changed* in order to be blessed ; he taught that man could be *a new being* if he let God find him, and if he found himself and God, from the midst of his distraction and dissipation.

He destroyed the delusion of ancient popular psychology and morality; he gave the final blow to the intellectualism of antiquity ; but he resuscitated it in the pious thought of the man who found true being and the supreme good in the living

---

[1] Compare my lecture " Augustin's Confessionen," 1888. See also Essay by G. Boissier in the Rev. de deux mond., 1 Jan., 1888.

God. He was the first to separate *nature* and *grace*, two spheres
which men had long attempted unsuccessfully to divide ; but by
this means he connected religion and morality, and gave a new
meaning to the idea of the good. He was the first to mark off
the scope and force of the heart and will, and to deduce from
this what moralists and religious philosophers imagined they
had understood, but never had understood ; he set up
a fixed goal for the aimless striving of asceticism :
perfection in the love of God, suppression of selfish
ambition, *humility*. He taught men to realise the horror
of the depth of sin and guilt which he disclosed, at the same
time with the blessed feeling of an ever-comforted misery, and a
perennial grace. He first perfected Christian pessimism, whose
upholders till then had really reserved for themselves an
extremely optimistic view of human nature. But while showing
that radical evil was the mainspring of all human action, he
preached also the regeneration of the will, by which man
adapted himself to the blessed life. He did not bridge for
feeling and thought the gulf which Christian tradition disclosed
between this world and the next ; but he testified so thrillingly
to the blessedness of the man who had found rest in God, that
nothing was reserved for the future life but an indescribable
"vision." But above all and in all, he exhibited to every soul
its glory and its responsibility : God and the soul, the soul and
its God. He took religion—a transfigured and moulded
monachism, dominated by positive conceptions and trust in
Christ—out of its congregational and ritualistic form, and set it
in the hearts of individuals as a gift and a task. He preached
the sincere humility which blossoms only on ruins—the ruins
of self-righteousness ; but he recognised in this very humility
the charter of the soul, and even where he assigned an imperious
power to the authority of the Church, he only did so in the end
in order to give the individual soul an assurance which it could
not attain by any exertion, or any individual act of pardon.
Therefore, he became not only a pedagogue and teacher, but a
Father of the Church. He was a tree, planted by the waters,
whose leaves do not fade, and on whose branches the birds of
the air dwell. His voice has pealed forth to the Church through

the centuries, and he preached to Christendom the words
" Blessed is the man whose strength Thou art ; in whose heart
are Thy ways."

We do not require to prove that, for a man with such a personality, all that tradition offered him could only serve as
material and *means*, that he only accepted it in order to work it
into the shape that suited him.   In this respect Augustine was
akin to the great Alexandrians, and plenty of evidence can be
adduced in support of this affinity, which was conditioned on
both sides by the same loftiness of soul, as well as by dependence
on Neoplatonic philosophy.   But in spite of all they possessed
in common, the distinction between them was extremely significant.   It did not consist merely in the fact that while the former
lived about A.D. 200, Augustine was a member of the Theodosian
imperial Church, nor that he had passed through Manichæism,
but it was due in a much greater degree to his having, in spite
of his Neoplatonism, a different conception of the nature of the
Christian religion, and also other ideas about the nature and
authority of the Church.

I. He thought of *sin*, when he reflected on God and Christ,
and he thought of the *living God*, who has created and redeemed
us, when he reflected on evil : the steadfastness with which he
referred these factors to each other was the novel feature which
distinguished him above all his predecessors.   But not less novel
was the energy with which he combined the categories God,
Christ, the word of God, the sacraments, and the Catholic Church
for practical piety, compressing what was fullest of life and
freest, the possession of God, into, as it were, an objective property, which was transferred to an institution, the Church.   As
he accordingly begot the feeling that Christian piety was *grief
of soul comforted,* so, on the other hand, *he created that interweaving,* characteristic of Western Catholicism, of the freest,
most personal surrender to the divine, with constant submission
to the Church as an institution in possession of the means of
grace.

According to this he is, in the first place, to be estimated, even for the history of dogma, not as a theologian, but as a reformer of Christian piety. The characteristic feature of the old Christian piety was its vacillation between hope and fear (Tertull., De uxor. II., 2 : " Fear is the foundation of salvation, confidence is the barrier against fear " : *timor fundamentum salutis est, præsumptio impedimentum timoris*).[1] It was known that Jesus accepted sinners ; but in that case men were accepted through baptism. The action of God was, as it were, exhausted.[2] The whole Dogmatic (Trinity, Christology, etc.) had its practical culmination, and therewith its end, in the merely retrospective blessing received in baptism. What next ? Men feared the judge, and hoped in an uncertain fashion for a still existent grace. The fear of the judge led to fasting, almsgiving, and prayer, and the uncertain hope groped after new means of grace. Men wavered between reliance on their own powers and hope in the inexhaustibility of Christ's grace. But did they not possess faith ? They did, and prized it as a lofty possession ; but they valued it as a condition, as an indispensable card of admission. In order actually to enter, there were other and wholly different conditions to be fulfilled. *Piety, when it concerned itself with the task of the present, did not live in faith.* The psychological form of piety was *unrest, i.e.*, fear and hope.[3] Reliance was placed on free-will ; but what was to be done if it led to one defeat after another ? Repentance and amendment were required. No doubt was felt that repentance was sufficient wherever sins " against our neighbour " were in question, and where the injury could be made good. Repentance and compensation had the widest possible scope in relation to sin. Sin consisted in evil action ; the good action united with repentance balanced it. One's neighbour could forgive the offence committed against

---

[1] In what follows the fundamental tendency is alone characterised. It is not to be denied that in some cases evangelical features were more marked.

[2] After the exposition given in Vols. I.-IV., and the indications in Chap. II. of this vol., I need not adduce further evidence that for the ancient Church the grace of God in Christ was exhausted in the gifts received in baptism. All other grace, which was hoped for, was beset with uncertainty.

[3] Read the striking avowals of II. Clement, the Shepherd of Hermas, Tertullian, the confessions of monks, and of the great theologians of the fourth century who were prevented by circumstances from becoming monks.

him, and the sin no longer existed ; the Church could forgive what affected its constitution, and guilt was effaced.

But he who was baptised sinned also "against God." However widely the Church might extend the circle of sins in which she was the injured party, the judge, and the possessor of the right to pardon, there were sins against God, and there were transgressions which could not be made good. Who could cancel murder and adultery, or a misspent life on the part of the baptised ? *Perhaps* even these sins were not in such evil case ; *perhaps* God did not impute them to the baptised at all—though that would be an Epicurean error ; *perhaps* the power of the Church did not break on the rock of accomplished facts ; *perhaps* there were other means of grace besides baptism. *But who could know this?* The Church created a kind of sacrament of penance in the third and fourth centuries ; but it did not say clearly what was to be expected of this sacrament. Did it reconcile with the Church or with God ; did it do away with sin, guilt, or punishment ; was it effective through the penances of the penitent, or through the power of grace ?[1] Was it necessary ? Was there in that case a sinful state, one that lasted, when the disposition had changed, when the will strove with all its powers after the good ? Was there such a thing as *guilt ?* Was not everything which man could do in accordance with his nature involved in the eternal alternation marked by good and evil actions, by knowledge, repentance, and striving? *Knowledge* and *action* decide. The man of to-day, who does the good, has no longer anything in common with the man of yesterday who did evil. But sins against God persisted in troubling them. Whence came fear, lasting fear? The Church threw its doors wider and wider ; it forgave sin, all sin ; but the earnest fled into the desert. There they tried to succeed by precisely the same means they had used in the world, and their mood remained the same—one of hope and fear. There was no consolation which was not confronted by a three-fold horror.

---

[1] Rothe says very truly, Kirchengesch., II., p. 33 : "Men secretly distrusted inevitably the presupposed purely supernatural and accordingly magical operation of God's grace, and they therefore arranged their plans on the eventuality that in the end everything might still require to be done by man alone."

That was the temper of the ancient Christians from the day when we can first observe them in the wide framework of the Roman Empire until the epoch with whose dawn we are here concerned. The "evangelical" ideas which are sometimes formed of the nature of their piety are not at all appropriate. The two most restless elements which can agitate a human breast, hope and fear, ruled over those Christians. These elements shattered the world and built the Church. Men, indeed, had a faith, and created a dogmatic for themselves ; but these were insufficient to satisfy them regarding their daily life, or any life. They gave wings to hope, but they did not eradicate fear. They did not tell what the sins were with which the Christian daily fights, and what Christ had done for *these* sins. They left those questions to the individual conscience, and the answers given in ecclesiastical practice were not answers to soothe the heart. The only sure issue of the whole system of dogmatics was in the benefits of baptism. He who rose from the font had henceforth to go his way alone. If he reflected earnestly he could not doubt that all the Church could afterwards give him was a set of crutches.

"Against Thee only have I sinned." "Thou, Lord, hast made us for Thyself, and our heart is restless, until it finds rest in Thee." "Grant what Thou dost command, and command what Thou dost desire" (da quod jubes, et jube quod vis).[1] "The just by *faith* will live." "No one enjoys what he knows, unless he also loves it, nor does anyone abide in that which he perceives unless by love" (eo quod quisque novit, non fruitur, nisi et id diligit, neque quisquam in eo quod percipit permanet nisi dilectione).[2] These are the new tones sounded by Augustine, that is the mighty chord which he produced from Holy Scripture, from the most profound observations of human nature, and speculations concerning the first and last things. Everything in the mind that was without God was absolutely sinful ; the only good thing left to it was that it existed. Sin

---

[1] De pecc. mer. et remiss., II., 5; De spiritu et lit., 22; see Confessions, X, 40, and De dono persever., 53. The substance is given already in Soliloq., I., 5 : "Jube quæso atque impera quidquid vis, sed sana et aperi aures meas." Enchir., 117, " Fides impetrat quod lex imperat."

[2] De fide et symb., 19,

was the sphere and form of the inner life of every natural man. It had been maintained in all theological systems from Paul to Origen, and later, that a great revolt lay at the root of the present state of the human race. But Augustine was the first to base all religious feeling and all theological thought on this revolt as still existent and damning in every natural man. The Apologists regarded the revolt as an uncertain datum; Origen looked upon it as a premundane fatality. To Augustine it was the most vital fact of the present, one which, at work from the beginning, determined the life of the individual and of the whole race. Further, *all sin was sin against God;* for the created spirit had only one lasting relationship, that to God. Sin was self-will, the proud striving of the heart (superbia); therefore it took the form of *desire* and *unrest.* In this unrest, *lust,* never quieted, and fear revealed themselves. Fear was evil; but in this unrest there was also revealed the inalienable goodness of the spirit that has come from the hand of God : "We wish to be happy, and wish not to be unhappy, but neither can we will."[1] We cannot but strive after blessings, after happiness. But there is only one good, one happiness, and one rest. "It is a good thing that I should cling to God." All is included in that. Only in God as its element does the soul live. "Oh! who will give me to repose in Thee? Oh! that Thou wouldest enter into my heart, and inebriate it, that I may forget my ills, and embrace Thee, my only good! What art Thou to me? Of Thy mercy teach me to declare it. What am I to Thee that Thou demandest my love, and if I give it not, art angry with me, and threatenest me with grievous miseries? . . . For Thy mercies' sake tell me, O Lord my God, what Thou art to me. Say unto my soul : '*I am thy salvation.*' Say it so, that I may hear. Behold, Lord, the ears of my heart are before Thee; open Thou them, and say to my soul : *I am thy salvation.* I will run after this voice, and take hold on Thee. Hide not Thy face from me; let me die seeing it—

---

[1] De Trinit., XIII., 4 : " Felices esse volumus et infelices esse nolumus, sed nec velle possumus." De civit. dei, XI., 26 : "Tam porro nemo est qui esse se nolit, quam nemo est qui non esse beatus velit   Quo modo enim potest beatus esse, si nihil sit ?"

only let me see it. Narrow is the tenement of my soul ; en-
large Thou it, that it may be able to receive Thee. It is ruinous ; repair Thou it. Within, it has these things that must
offend Thine eyes ; I confess and know ; but who will cleanse
it ? or to whom shall I cry save Thee ? "[1]

The same God who created us has redeemed us through Jesus
Christ. That simply means that he has restored us to communion with himself. This takes place through grace and love,
and in turn through faith and love. Through grace which lays
hold of us and makes the unwilling willing (ex nolentibus
volentes), which gives us an incomprehensibly new nature by
imparting a new birth ; and through love, which strengthens the
weak spirit, and inspires it with powers of goodness. Through
faith which holds to the saying, " He who is just by faith will
live," "which was written and confirmed by the all-powerful
authority of apostolic teaching " (quod scriptum est et apostolicæ
disciplinæ robustissima auctoritate firmatum) ; and through love,
which *humbly* renounces all that is its own and longs for God
and his law. Faith and love spring from God ; for they are
the means by which the living God enables us to appropriate
him. The soul regards those possessions, in which it has
obtained all that God requires of us, as an everlasting gift and a
sacred mystery ; for a heart equipped with faith and love fulfils
the righteousness that is accepted by God. The peace of God
is shed upon the soul which has the living God for its friend ;
it has risen from unrest to rest, from seeking to finding, from
the false freedom to the free necessity, from fear to love ; for
perfect love casts out fear. It cannot for a moment forget that
it is entangled in worldliness and sin, as long as it lives in this

---

[1] Confess., I., 5 : Quis mihi dabit acquiescere in te?   Quis mihi dabit ut venias in
cor meum et inebries illud, ut obliviscar mala mea et unum bonum amplectar te ?
Quid mihi es ?   Miserere, ut loquar.   Quid tibi sum ipse, ut amari a me jubeas a me,
et nisi faciam irascaris mihi et mineris ingentes miserias ? . . . Dic mihi per misera-
tiones tuas, domine deus meus, quid sis mihi.   Dic animæ meæ : *Salus tua ego sum.*
Sic dic, ut audiam.   Ecce aures cordis mei ante te, domine ; aperi eas, et dic animæ
meæ : *Salus tua ego sum.*   Curram post vocem hanc et apprehendam te.   Noli
abscondere a me faciem tuam ; moriar ne moriar, ut eam videam.   Angusta est
domus animæ meæ quo venias ad eam ; dilatetur abs te.   Ruinosa est ; refice eam.
Habet quæ offendant oculos tuos ; fateor et scio ; sed quis mundabit eam ? aut cui
alteri præter te clamabo ?

world ; but it does not let its thoughts rest for a moment on sin, without remembering the living God who is its strength. The misery of sin overcome by *faith, humility* and *love*—that is Christian piety. In this temper the Christian was to live. He was constantly to feel the pain caused by sin, separation from God ; but he was at the same time to console himself with the conviction that the grace of God had taken possession of him, that the Lord of heaven and earth had instilled His love into his heart, and that this love worked as mightily after as in baptism.[1] Thus Augustine dethroned the traditional feelings of the baptised, fear and hope, the elements of unrest, and substituted the elements of rest, faith, and love. For an uncertain and vacillating notion of sin he substituted the perception of its power and horror, for a still uncertain notion of grace he substituted the perception of its omnipotence. He did not abolish hope, he rather confirmed with all his power the old feeling that this life is not worthy to be compared with the glory that is to be revealed. But in realising and preaching the *rest* bestowed by faith and love, he transformed the stormy and fanatical power of hope into a gentle and sure conviction.[2]

I have here reproduced Augustine's teaching, as we find it chiefly in his Confessions. This book has the advantage of giving us an account which is not influenced by any particular aims. Our exposition is by no means complete ; we should require to add more than one caution, in order to be perfectly just.[3] Further, the description has intentionally only considered the fundamental lines, and given expression to but one direction in which the epoch-making importance of Augustine comes to the front. But there can be no doubt that it is the *most decisive*. If we Western Christians are shut up to the conviction that religion moves between the poles of sin and grace—nature and grace ; if we subordinate morality to faith, in so far as we reject

---

[1] Enchir., 64 : "Excepto baptismatis munere ipsa etiam vita cetera, quantalibet præpolleat fœcunditate justitiæ, sine peccatorum remissione non agitur."

[2] We will afterwards discuss how far Augustine failed to surmount this uncertainty and unrest, owing to the reception of popular Catholic elements into his piety.

[3] The most important caution—that Augustine fitted his new form of feeling and reflection into the old—will be discussed later on ; it has been only mildly suggested in the above exposition.

the thought of an independent morality, one indifferent to religion ; if we believe that it is necessary to pay much greater heed to the essence of sin than to the forms in which it is manifested—fixing our attention on its roots, not on its degrees, or on sinful actions ; if we are convinced that universal sinfulness is the presupposition of religion; if we expect nothing from our own powers; if we comprise all means of salvation in the thought of God's grace and of faith ; if the preaching of faith and the love of God is substituted for that of fear, repentance, and hope ;[1] if, finally, we distinguish between law and gospel, gifts and tasks appointed by God—then we feel with the emotions, think in the thoughts, and speak with the words of Augustine.[2]

Who can deny that in this way religion disclosed deeper truths to feeling and thought, that the disease was recognised more surely, and the means of healing were demonstrated more reliably ?   Who can mistake the gain in laying bare the living heart, the need of the soul, the living God, the peace that exists in the disposition to trust and love ?   Even if he merely seeks to study these phenomena as a disinterested " historian of culture," who can escape the impression that we have here an advance, at least in psychological knowledge, that can never

---

[1] I need hardly guard against the misapprehension that I represent faith as not having been of fundamental importance to the Pre-Augustinian and Greek Church. The question here is as to the feeling and disposition of the Christian. The Pre-Augustinian Christian regarded faith as the self-evident presupposition of the righteousness which he had to gain by his own efforts.

[2] It need not be objected that this is the doctrine of Scripture. In the first place, Scripture has no homogeneous doctrine ; secondly, even Paul's range of thought, to which Augustine's here most closely approximates, does not perfectly coincide with it. But we must undoubtedly recognise that the Augustinian reformation was quite essentially a *Pauline reaction* against the prevailing piety. Augustine, to some extent, appears as a second Marcion, see Vol. I., p. 136, Reuter, August. Studien, p. 492 : " We can perhaps say that Paulinism, which the growing Catholic Church only half-learned to understand, which Marcion attempted to open up in an eccentric one-sidedness that the Church, in its opposition to him, had all but rejected, was exploited by our Church Father for the second time, in such a way, that much hitherto belonging to popular Catholicism was remodelled." This is followed by a parallel between Augustine and Marcion. The triad " Faith, Love, and Hope," is Pauline, and occurs in almost all Church Fathers ; but Augustine first made it fruitful again (perhaps he learned here from Jovinian).

again be lost? In fact, history seems to teach that the gain can
never perish within the Christian Church; nay, it attests more,
it would appear, than this: it tells us that a limit has been
reached, beyond which the pious mood cannot receive a further
development. If we review all the men and women of the
West since Augustine's time, whom, for the disposition that
possessed them, history has designated as prominent Christians,
we have always the same type; we find marked conviction of
sin, complete renunciation of their own strength, and trust in
grace, in the personal God who is apprehended as the Merciful
One in the humility of Christ. The variations of this frame of
mind are indeed numerous—we will speak of these later on;
but the fundamental type is the same. And this frame of mind
is taught in sermons and in instruction by truly pious Catholics
and Evangelicals; to it youthful Christians are trained, and
dogmatics are framed in harmony with it. It always produces
so powerful an effect, even where it is only preached as the experience of others, that he who has once come in contact with
it can never forget it; it accompanies him as a shadow by day
and as a light in the dark; he who imagines that he has long
shaken it off sees it rising up suddenly before him again.
Since the days of Leibnitz, indeed, and the "Illumination," a
powerful opponent has grown up, an enemy that seemed to
have mastered it during a whole century, that reduced the
Christian religion, when it gave any countenance to it at all,
once more to energetic action, and furnished it with the foil
of a cheerful optimism, a mode of thought which removed the
living God afar off, and subordinated the religious to the moral.
But this opponent succumbed in our century, at least, within
the Churches, before the power of the old frame of mind.
Whether this triumph of Augustine is guaranteed to last, none
but a prophet could tell. It is only certain that the constella-
tion of circumstances in the fray has been favourable to the
victor.

On the part of the Church no doubt prevails that the
Augustinian feeling and type of thought are alone legitimate in
Christianity, that they are alone Christian; for the conception
of redemption (by God himself), in the sense of regeneration,

dominates everything. But we cannot fail to be puzzled when
we consider that it cannot by any means be directly deduced
from the surest words of Jesus, and that the ancient and Greek
Church was ignorant of it. Further, we cannot but be doubtful
when we weigh its consequences ; for their testimony is not all
favourable. A *quietistic*, I might almost say a *narcotic*, element
is contained in it, or is, at least, imperceptibly associated with
it.   There is something latent in it which seems to enervate the
vital energies, to hinder the exertion of the will, and to substitute *feelings* for *action*. Is there no danger in substituting a
general consciousness of sin for evident evil tendencies, heartless
words and shameful deeds ? [1] Is it safe to rely on the uniform
operation of Grace, when we are called to be perfect and holy
like God ? Are all the energies of the Will actually set free,
where the soul lives constantly in the mood shown in the
" Confessions " ? Are fear and hope really phases, necessarily
to be superseded by faith and love ? Perhaps it is correct to
answer all these questions in accordance with the type of
thought here considered ; but even then a doubt remains.
Is it advisable—apart from the variety in men's temperaments
—to present this ideal as the aim at all stages of spiritual
development ? Here, at least, the answer cannot be doubtful.
That which is the last stage reached by the advanced Christian
who has passed through a rich experience is a *refinement* to him
who is in process of development. But a refined piety or
morality is always pernicious ; for it no longer starts at the
point of duty and conscience. It *deceives* regarding our need
and its satisfaction. And since it is strong enough to fascinate,
and can also be comprehended as a doctrine by an intelligence
that is far from advanced, in order, once comprehended, never
to pass away again, so it can become dangerous to morality, and
therefore also to piety. For, after all, in both these spheres,

---

[1] I say nothing of the arrogant habit of those who, because they agree with the
Augustinian doctrine, not only openly credit themselves with possessing " positive "
Christianity, but also denounce their opponents as " half-believers." For this nonsense Augustine is not responsible, and it only made its appearance in the nineteenth
century. It is only in our days that evangelical Christendom has permitted itself to
be terrorised by people who bear the deeper " knowledge of sin " as a motto, and
with this shield guard themselves against the counsel to be just and modest.

that only has any value which heightens the power to be and
do good ; everything else is a poisonous fog. Perhaps, if we
consider the matter fairly, no feeling or mood, and no theory of
the factors in the religious process, are alone legitimate. As
man requires sleep and wakefulness, so also he must, if he is to
preserve his moral and religious life in health, alternate between
the sense of his freedom and power and that of his bondage and
helplessness, between the sense of full moral responsibility and
the conviction that he is a favoured child of God. Or is there a
way of so grasping Augustine's type of feeling and thought,
that it may fashion faith into the strongest lever of *moral
energy and action ? Are not the difficulties that rise against his
type of piety due perhaps just to his not having developed it forcibly
and absolutely enough ?*

This question will obtain its answer later on. Here we have
to point out that the dissemination of the religious views,
peculiar to Augustine, was not in every respect beneficial.
They constituted his greatness ; they conducted him to the
wonderful path he trod ; they led him to conceive redemption
no longer as a solitary intervention, by means of baptism, in
the course of human life, but as the element in which the soul
lived—baptismal grace being therefore a continuously operative
force. "Personal characteristics" lie beyond the sphere of
errors and truths ; they may be erroneous, looked at from without, true from within. They may for that very reason be even
hurtful as *influences*, for "when they introduce disproportion-
ately what is foreign, the question arises, how these adventitious
peculiarities harmonise with those that are native to the soul,
and whether by the very act of mingling they do not produce a
sickly condition."[1] Nevertheless, there can be no doubt that
Augustine submitted the traditional religious feeling to as
thorough-going a revision as is conceivable, and even he who is
not in a position to praise it unreservedly will not seek to
minimise its benefits.[2]

[1] Compare Goethe in his wonderful reflections on Sterne, Werke (Hempel's Ed.),
Vol. XXIX., p. 749 f.

[2] Augustine's Exposition of the Church I neither count one of his greater achievements, nor can I hold it to be the central idea which determines what is essential to him.

II. No one was further than Augustine from intending to correct the tradition of the Church. If he has done this so emphatically, he was himself merely actuated by the feeling that he was thus assimilating more and more thoroughly the faith of the Church. Having forced his way through scepticism to the truth of the Catholic Church, he regarded the latter as the rock on which his faith was founded. We should misunderstand him were we to blink this fact. He rather sets us reflecting how it was possible for the most vital piety to have a double ground of conviction, inner experience, and external, nay, extremely external, attestation. We can make a still stronger assertion. *Augustine first transformed the authority of the Church into a factor in religion;* he first expressed pious contemplation, the view of God and self, in such a way that the religious man always found the authority of the Church side by side with sin and grace.[1] Paul and post-apostolic teachers, especially Tertullian, had, indeed, already introduced the Church into the religious relationship itself;[2] but they were not thinking of its authority.

When we fix our attention on Augustine's distinctive type of Christian piety as the foundation of his significance for Church and dogmatic history, we must not only consider the decisive tendency of his doctrine of sin and grace, but we must also review his reception and characteristic revision of traditional elements. For from these his piety, *i.e.*, his sense of God, and sin and grace, obtained the form which is familiar to us as specifically Catholic. In addition to (1) the above-mentioned element of the authority of the Church, there are, if my view is

---

[1] Reuter says excellently (l.c., p. 494) : " Many phases of the hitherto traditional and authoritative doctrine were transformed by him into really religious factors ; he effected a revolution in the religious consciousness in those circles in and upon which he worked, yet without seeking to endanger its Catholicity." Cf., also p. 102 (71-98) : " Much, but very far from all, that belonged to popular Catholicism was revised by Augustine."

[2] See De bapt., 6 : " Cum antem sub tribus et testatio fidei et sponsio salutis pignerentur, necessario adicitur ecclesiæ mentio, quoniam ubi tres, id est pater et filius et spiritus sanctus, ibi ecclesia, quæ trium corpus est." De orat., 2 : " Pater . . . filius . . . ne mater quidam ecclesia præteritur. Si quidem in filio et patre mater recognoscitur, de qua constat et patris et filii nomen." De monog., 7 : " Vivit enim unicus pater noster et mater ecclesia." All this is based on the Symbol.

correct, other three ; (2) *the confusion of personal relationship to God with a sacramental communication of grace ;* (3) *uncertainty as to the nature of faith and the forgiveness of sins ;* (4) *uncertainty as to the significance of the present life.* Even in the way he felt and wrote about these things he created new states of feeling; but they appear merely to be modifications of the old ; or, rather, he first enabled the old moods fully to understand themselves, in other words, enriched them from the dead material which they brought with them. This exerted in turn a very strong influence on the fundamental feeling—the sense of sin and grace, and first gave it the form which enabled it to take possession of souls, without creating a revolution, or producing a violent breach with tradition.

In the sequel we only discuss the fundamental features of these four elements. [1]

1. Augustine introduced the authority of the Church as a religious factor for two reasons. Like the thought of redemption, the significance of the Church seems, on a superficial examination, to have received so sovereign and fixed an impress in the conception formed by the ancient Catholic and Greek Fathers, that any further accentuation of it is impossible. But, if we look more closely, redemption was presented as a solitary

---

[1] We don't need now to say for the first time that Augustine was as closely as possible united to the past of the Church in all else (Scripture, doctrinal confession, etc.). Besides this, he shared with his contemporaries in the conception of the Church's science in its relation to faith, and had on many points as naïve ideas as they of the limits and scope of knowledge. If he possessed the faculty of psychological observation in a much higher degree than his predecessors, he retained the absolute type of thought, and, with all the sceptical reserve which he practised in single questions, he further developed that conglomerate of cosmology, ethics, mythology, and rationalism, which was then called science. So also he was implicated in all the prejudices of contemporary exegesis. It is to be added, finally, that, although less credulous than his contemporaries, he was, like Origen, involved in the prejudices, the mania for miracles, and the superstition of the age. His works, sober in comparison with many other elaborations of the epoch, are yet full of miracles. A slave learns to read in answer to prayer, in three days, and without human help ; and we have divine judgments, miracle-working relics, etc. He certainly made the absurd indispensable to the Church. Since Augustine's time there are wholly absurd Church doctrines, whose abandonment would not be without danger, because they have excited, or at least have supported, like the vine-pole, the virtues of conscientiousness, strictness in self-examination, and tenderness of soul (see, *e.g.*, his doctrine of original sin). But like all absurdities, they have also excited blind fanaticism and fearful despair.

intervention, and the significance of the Church was exhausted in the fact that, while it was the presupposition of Christian life and the guarantee of Christian truth, it did not enter into the separate acts in which the religious and moral life ran its spiritual course.   Here also Rothe's saying is true that Christians tacitly " laid their plans to meet the chance that in the end everything might require to be done by men alone." These " plans " were based since the days of the Apologists on the *optimistic* conception of the inalienable goodness of human nature, and the demonstrability (clearness and intelligibility) of the Christian religion.   The course of a spontaneously moral life was ultimately modified, neither by the doctrine of redemption nor by that of the Church.

In both these respects Augustine's experience had led to wholly different conclusions.   His conflict with himself had convinced him of the badness of human nature, *and Manichæism had left him in complete doubt as to the foundations and truth of the Christian faith.* [1]   His confidence in the rationality of Christian truth had been shaken to the very depths, *and it was never restored.*   In other words, as an individual *thinker* he never gained the subjective certitude that Christian truth and as such everything contained in the two Testaments had to be regarded, was clear, consistent, and demonstrable. [2]   When he threw himself into the arms of the Catholic Church, he was perfectly conscious that he needed its

---

1 See Reuter, l.c. p. 490 f.

2 The few tendencies to this conception, which are also found in his works, are always combined with that neutralising of the historical displayed by the Apologists. We cannot here discuss more fully this undercurrent in his writings.   But it is important to show clearly the main current, namely, that scholars were by no means confident of the rationality of the Catholic faith.   The attacks made by heathens and Manichæans had shaken them.   Some speak, partly with self-satisfaction, partly with pain, of " modern " doubts of the faith of the Church.   But these doubts are so far from modern that the creation of the Augustinian and mediæval authority of the Church is their work.   That ecclesiasticism is so powerful, nay, has become a dogmatic quantity, is due to the defective morality of Christians in the second and third centuries, and to their defective faith in the fourth and fifth.   The distinction between Justin and Augustine is in this respect much greater than that between Augustine and a Christian of the sixteenth or nineteenth centuries.

authority, not to sink in scepticism or nihilism.[1] For example, nothing but the authority of the Church could remove the stumbling-blocks in the Old Testament. The thousand doubts excited by theology, and especially Christology, could only be allayed by the Church. As regards the former case, allegorical interpretation, of course, helped to get one over the difficulties ; but it (as contrasted with the literal which solves everything) did not justify itself; the Church alone gave the right to apply it. *The Church guaranteed the truth of the faith, where the individual could not perceive it ;* that is the new thought whose open declaration proves the thinker's scepticism, as well as the man's love of truth. He would not impose upon himself; he would not become the sophist of his faith. Openly he proclaimed it : I believe in many articles only on the Church's authority ; nay, I believe in the Gospel itself merely on the same ground.[2] Thereby the Church had gained an enormous importance, an importance which it was henceforth to retain in Western Catholicism ; upon it, an entity above all incomprehensible— for what and where is the Church?—a great part of the responsibility was rolled, which had hitherto to be borne by the individual. Thus henceforth the Church had its part in every act of faith. By this, however, a vast revolution was brought about in the relation to the "faith which is believed" (fides quæ creditur). *Acts of faith were, at the same time, acts of obedience.* The difficulties were recognised which the Alexandrians overcame by distinguishing between exoteric and

---

[1] See the middle Books of the Confessions, *e.g.*, VI., 11 : "Scripturæ sanctæ, quas ecclesiæ catholicæ commendat auctoritas." VI., 7 : "Libris tuis, quos tanta in omnibus fere gentibus auctoritate fundasti. . . . Non audiendos esse, si qui forte mihi dicerent ; unde scis illos libros unius veri et veracissimi dei spiritu esse humano generi ministratos ? *idipsum enim maxime credendum erat.*" VI., 8 : "Ideoque cum essemus infirmi ad inveniendam liquida ratione veritatem, et ob hoc nobis opus esset auctoritate sanctarum litterarum, jam credere cœperam nullo modo te fuisse tributurum tam excellentem illi scripturæ per omnes jam terras auctoritatem, nisi et per ipsam tibi credi et per ipsam te quæri voluisses. Jam enim absurditatem quæ me in illis litteris solebat offendere, cum multa ex eis probabiliter exposita audissem, ad sacramentorum altitudinem referebam." See also the treatise De utilit. credendi, and, in general, the writings against Manichæism.

[2] Contra Ep. Manichæi, 5 : "Ego vero evangelio non crederem, nisi me catholicæ (ecclesiæ) commoveret auctoritas." Innumerable parallels exist, especially in the writings against Manichæism, but also elsewhere.

esoteric religion, but this distinction was itself rejected. In its place was now openly proclaimed what had long—especially in the West (see ch. I., Scripture and Dogma as Law)—been secretly the expedient of thousands : partial renunciation of independent faith, and the substitution for it of obedience. It is obvious that thus a great body of dogmas, or of the contents of Scripture, was placed beyond the reach of the believing subject, that a wholly different relation to them was introduced, that, in a word, the doctrines of Scripture and the Church obtained a new meaning. Augustine was the father of the conception of implicit faith (fides implicita), by associating with the individual believer the Church, with which he believes and which believes for him, in as far as it takes the place for him in many points of a psychological element of faith, namely, inner conviction. In openly proclaiming this conception, which, as has been said, already lurked in darkness, Augustine, on the one hand, disburdened individual faith, and directed it more energetically to those spheres in which it could rest without difficulties, but, on the other hand, introduced all the evil consequences which spring from faith in authority.[1]

However, this championship of faith in authority had an additional root, in the case of Augustine, besides scepticism. Tradition and grace are connected by secret ties. A genius, who was never a sceptic, and who was therefore never possessed by a mania for authority, has confessed : " The dew in which I bathe and find health is tradition, is grace." Augustine was also led, both as a psychologist and a Christian of living faith, to tradition and therewith to the Church. In breaking with moralism, he broke too with the individualism and atomism of the ancient school. The "mass of perdition" (massa perditionis) was always confronted for him by grace (gratia) as a force *working in history*. I will not here yet go into his notion of the Church ; it is certain that he possessed a lively sense that all great bene-

---

[1] Reuter, who by no means over-values the importance of the idea of the Church in Augustine, declares (p. 499) : " By Augustine the idea of the Church was rendered the central power in the religious state of mind and ecclesiastical activity of the West in a fashion unknown to the East." "Central power " is almost saying too much (see Theol. Lit.—Zeit., 1887, No. 15).

fits, even communion with God himself, were attached to
historical tradition, and it is manifest that religious individualism,
as developed by him, was paralleled by and compatible with a
conception, according to which the individual was supported by
other persons, and by forces in the direction of goodness which
he received through a visible medium.   Augustine concentrated
this correct historical conception in the idea of the Church.   It
was to him the organism and—for the individual—the womb of
grace ; it was further the communion of righteousness and love ;
and he felt this significance of the Church in his most personal
piety much more acutely than any one before him.

But the sceptic who needs the authority of the Church, and
the Christian of quick feeling and sure observation, who
perceives and prizes the value of Church communion, do not part
company.   There has never yet existed in the world a strong
religious faith, which has not appealed, at some *decisive* point or
other, to an *external authority*.   It is only in the colourless expositions of religious philosophers, or the polemical systems of
Protestant theologians, that a faith is constructed which derives
its certitude exclusively from its own inner impulses.   These
undoubtedly constitute the *force* by which it exists and is preserved.   But are not *conditions* necessary, under which this force
becomes operative ?   Jesus Christ appealed to the authority of
the Old Testament, ancient Christians to the evidence of prophecy, Augustine to the Church, and Luther himself to the
written Word of God.   Only academic speculation thinks that
it can eliminate external authority ; life and history show that
no faith is capable of convincing men or propagating itself,
which does not include obedience to an external authority, or
fails to be convinced of its absolute power.   The only point is
to determine the rightful authority, and to discover the just
relationship between external and internal authority.   Were it
otherwise, we should not be weak, helpless beings.   We cannot
think too highly of the nobility of human talents; but they are not
lofty enough to enable men so to appropriate the sum of all the
ideal elements which compose the inner life, that these simply
grow with the growth of the soul, or become its product.
Above all, the thought of God, the thought of the love of God,

can never receive an irrefragable certainty, without being supported by an external authority.   It is not a false view of religion that the restless quest of the soul only ceases when there has dawned upon it an authority whose validity is independent of the degree of strength with which its justification is felt *within the breast*.[1]

All this Augustine perceived and expressed.   Therefore "the traditional, exclusively authoritative doctrine" of the Church was transformed by him into a conception, according to which the Church is a *religious* factor.   By this, however, the distinctive character of piety itself received a new definition.[2]

2.   The perception that *religion is the possession of the living God*, a personal relationship between the soul and God, is conspicuous in Augustine's Confessions, but also in other writings by him.   That nothing but God himself could give the soul rest and peace is the fundamental note of the Confessions: "Say unto my soul: I am thy salvation."   His great place in

---

[1] This argument has been very badly received by some critics, but I find nothing to change in it.   Perhaps it will help to its being understood if I add that the spiritual man is directly conscious of the Divine Spirit as his Lord—who constrains him to obedience, even where he himself does not perceive the inner authority—but the non-spiritual require some sort of intervening authority, whether consisting in persons, or a book, or Church.   But in both cases we are dealing with a controlling power, whose authority rises above one's own individuality and knowledge.   I hope that in disclosing this state of the case I am safe from being (wrongly) understood to draw a fixed line between the spiritual and non-spiritual.   Throughout it is only a question of the proportion in which the apocalyptic and mediated elements appear and are connected in personal religion.   Even the spiritual man who holds direct communion with God has, as history shows, extremely seldom, perhaps never entirely, freed himself from all intermediate authority ; on the contrary, he has clung to it firmly, in spite of his intercourse with the Deity.   This is not the place to explain this phenomenon ; but personal religion is not shown to be valueless by its being proved that its authorities are not sound (against Baumann, Die Grundfrage der Religion, 1895, p. 21 f.).   The important point is what the pious man has derived from his authorities.

[2] It is only to a superficial observer that Eastern Christians seem to cling more strongly to the Church than Western.   In the East the historical course of events welded ecclesiasticism and nationality into one, and the internal development made the cultus of the Church the chief matter.   But what other rôle does the Church play in personal piety than being the scene of Christian life, the teacher of doctrine, and the administrator of the mysteries ?   All these are, in fact, *presupposed conditions ;* in the West, on the contrary, the Church has thrust itself into all relations and points of contact of the pious soul to God and Christ, as far as the Augustinian tradition is accepted.

the history of piety is bound up with this perception, as we find
it attached to Rom. VIII., 31-39. He is to be compared, in
this also, to the great Alexandrians, especially Clement. But
as Augustine did not merely reach this conclusion by means of
a laborious speculation, so it assumed a much more forcible and
purer form in his life and works than in theirs.[1]

But the sure application of what is simplest in dogma is ever
the hardest thing. Augustine found himself confronted by a
tradition which taught that men enjoyed intercourse with God
through *laws* and *communications of grace ;* nay, the prevailing
tradition was constantly in danger of reducing the latter to the
former. In opposition to this, a great advance was at once
made by insisting on the distinction between law and gospel,
commands and grace. We now perceive that Augustine substantially limited himself to this in his polemical dogmatic writings. That is, he was not in a position to translate into his
dogmatic theory the vital perception that God himself, as he
appeared in Christ, was the possession of the soul. *He substantially left standing the old scheme that God came to man's assistance, like a benevolent judge with acts of pardon, or like a
physician with medicines.* In other words, he gave the force of
absolute conviction to what had been uncertain, *viz.,* that God
operates continuously by a mysterious and omnipotent imparta-
tion of grace, *i.e.,* by powers of grace.[2] Thus grace (gratia per
Christum) preserved even with him an objective character, and

[1] Let anyone read attentively the Confessions B. VII. and VIII., as also the writings and epistles composed immediately after his conversion, and he will find that
Augustine's Neoplatonism had undoubtedly a share in giving him this perception.
But he was brought to it in a much higher degree by his inner experience, and the
reading of Paul and the Psalms. The Psalmists' piety was revived in him (see esp.
Confess., IX., 8-12). His style even was modelled on theirs. In Clement of Alex.
and Origen, Neoplatonic speculation, on the contrary, prevailed. Even in the
most glorious of their expositions, in which the power of feeling is clearly conspicuous, we cannot forget the speculative path by which they *thought* they had attained
to the possession of God.

The final ground of this view with Augustine consists naturally in the fact that he
never wholly got rid of the old Catholic scheme that the ultimate concern of Christianity was to transform human nature physically and morally for eternal life. He
took a great step forward ; but he was not able to give clear expression to the
Pauline thought that the whole question turned on forgiveness of sins and sonship to
God, or to frame all dogmatics in harmony with it.

in his controversy with Donatists and Pelagians he completely
developed this view of grace in connection with his doctrines of
the Church and sacraments.   He understood how to harmonise
this, in his own feeling and self-criticism, with the conviction
that the question involved was the possession of the living God.
But as teacher of piety he did not succeed in doing so ; indeed,
we can say that, just because he laid all emphasis on grace
through Christ, while conceiving it to consist in portions or in-
stalments of grace, he was the means of establishing, along with
the perception of its importance as beginning, middle, and end,
the delusion that grace had an objective character.   His age
could understand, though with a great effort, his exposition of
grace, as something imparted by the sacraments or the Church.
It could bring that down to its own level.   The magical element
which adhered to this conception, the external solidity which
the notion of grace received in the sacrament, the apparent
clearness of the view, the possibility of instituting theological
computations with sin and grace—all these phases in the
Augustinian doctrine of grace were greedily seized.   Thus, in
making grace the foundation and centre of all Christian theological reflection, it was due to his way of thinking that the
living God and the *personality* of Christ lost ground in the consciousness of the Church he influenced.   The believer had to do
with the inheritance left by Christ, with what he had gained,
with his merit, but not with Christ himself.   The love of God
was instilled into the soul in portions ; but Augustine did not
perceive that dogmatic was imperfect, nay, formed a hindrance
to religion, as long as the supreme place was withheld from
the principle : " Our heart is restless, *until it rests in Thee.*"
The violent agitation which he had himself experienced, the
crisis in which the sole question was whether he should or
should not find God to be *his* God, he has extremely imper-
fectly expressed in the dogmatic theory of his later period.   He
poured the new wine into old bottles, and was thus partly to
blame for the rise of that Catholic doctrine of grace, which is
perhaps the most dreadful part of Catholic dogmatics ; for " the
corruption of the best is the worst " (corruptio optimi pessima).
When a Roman Catholic dogmatist very recently called the

doctrine of grace " thorny ground," this description alone must
have sufficed to show every common-sense Christian that the
whole treatment of this main article had stumbled on a false
path since the days of Augustine. Could there be a sadder admission than this, that reflection on what God grants the soul
in Christ leads us among nothing but thorns ? And could we
conceive a greater contrast than that which exists between the
sayings of Jesus and the Catholic doctrine of grace ? But Protestantism, in its actual form, need not boast of having surmounted this pernicious Catholic doctrine. As it rests on the
Augustinian doctrine of grace in the good sense of the term,
and is distinguished thereby as Western Christianity from
Eastern, it also bears the greatest part of the burden of this
doctrine, and is therefore subject to the same dangers as
Catholicism. It runs the risk of concealing the personal Christ
by grace and the sacraments, of hedging in the living God
through grace itself, and of setting up calculations about grace
which make an account out of what is freest and holiest, and
either dull the soul or leave it in unrest.

But as Augustine knew, for his part, by what his soul lived,
and was able to testify to it in words that lived, and, indeed, in
some of his discussions also doctrinally, he exerted a powerful
influence in this respect, too, on posterity. He became the
father not only of the Catholic doctrine of grace, but also of
that mysticism which was naturalised in the Catholic Church,
down to the Council of Trent, indeed, till the Jansenist controversy. In more than a hundred passages of his works, above
all by his Christian personality, he incited men to gain a life
with God, within which they apprehended the personal God in
grace. We may here also recall his doctrine of predestination.
One of its roots indisputably grew out of the thought of the
supremacy of personal relationship to God. It was understood,
too in this way, wherever it was the means in after-times of
obviating the pernicious consequences of the Church doctrine of
grace and sacraments. But there can undoubtedly be no mistake,
that wherever Augustine threw into the background his questionable doctrine of grace, he at once also incurred the danger of neutralising Christ's general significance. According to him, Christ's

work referred to, and exhausted itself in the forgiveness of sins. But, as we shall see in what immediately follows, forgiveness did not bestow all that the Christian requires for salvation. Therefore the doctrine of grace was relatively independent of the historical Christ. This danger of conceiving positive grace without reference to Christ, or of connecting it with him only in the form of æsthetic observations, continued to exert an influence. Luther, who started from Augustinianism, first overcame it, in as far as, in his relation to God, he only thought of God at all as he knew him in Christ. Augustine was prevented from doing so by his religious philosophy, and also his Biblicism, both of which had established independent claims upon him. Thus it happened that he influenced the piety of Western Christians by a doctrine of grace which met their lower inclinations, as well as by a promulgation of the immediateness of the religious relationship which failed to do justice to Christ's significance as mirror of God's fatherly heart and as the eternal mediator. In the latter as the former case, he set his seal on and gave vitality to elements which existed in the traditional doctrine only as dead material or stunted germs.

3. Augustine shared with the whole of contemporary Christendom the thought, held to be all-important, that a time would come when at the judgment-seat of Christ "every one would receive in accordance with his actions"; and none will impugn the Christian character of this thought. But he went a step further, and also accepted the conception of merits current in the Church from the days of Tertullian and Cyprian. He did not get beyond the idea that in the final decision merits could alone be considered. He reconciled this principle, however, with his doctrine of grace, by teaching that God crowned his gifts (munera) in crowning our merits (merita).[1] This seemed to correspond to both considerations, and the certainty with which this conception established itself in the Church appeared

---

[1] See e.g., Confess. IX. 34 : "Quisquis tibi enumerat vera merita sua, quid tibi enumerat nisi munera tua." Ep. 194, n. 19 : "cum deus coronat merita nostra, nihil aliud coronat quam munera sua." De gratia et lib. arb., 15 : "Dona sua coronat deus non merita tua . . . si ergo dei dona sunt bona merita tua, non deus coronat merita tua tamquam merita tua sed tamquam dona sua." De gestis Pelag., 35 :

to guarantee that the correct view had now been reached. But, first, the question arises whether the ambiguity of the reconciliation did not contribute to its being received ; secondly, it cannot fail to surprise us that there is not a word about faith in the principle. We are once more at a point where Augustine, in reforming the prevailing piety, paid it a very considerable tribute. He certainly expressed the importance and power of faith in a striking and novel fashion. He who disregards the formulas, but looks to the spirit, will everywhere find in Augustine's works a stream of Pauline faith. None before him but his teachers Victorinus and Ambrose, in some of their expositions, had used similar language. Numerous passages can be cited in which Augustine extolled faith as the element in which the soul lives, as beginning, middle, and end of piety. But in the sphere of dogmatic reflection Augustine spoke of faith with extreme uncertainty, and, indeed, as a rule, not differently from his predecessors.

Different points meet here. Firstly, it was simply the power of tradition which prevented him from perceiving more in faith than the act of initiation. Secondly, Scriptural 'texts led him to the assumption that something else than faith, namely, *habitual goodness* (righteousness), must finally fall to be considered at the divine tribunal. Thirdly and lastly, he limited the significance of the forgiveness of sins. The last point is in his case the most paradoxical, but here the most important. He for whom the supreme thing was the certainty of possessing a God, and who called to his whole period : " You have not yet considered of how great weight sin is " (nondum considerasti, quanti ponderis sit peccatum), never realised the strict relation that exists between faith and forgiveness, nor could explain clearly that the assurance of forgiveness is life and salvation. At this point the moral element suddenly entered with sovereign power into religious reflection. It is as if Augustine had here sought to escape

" Redditur quidem meritis tuis corona sua, sed dei dona sunt merita tua." De trinit., XIII., 14 : " Et ea quæ dicuntur merita nostra, dona sunt eius," etc. XV. 21 : " Quid animam faciet beatam, nisi meritum suum et præmium domini sui ? Sed et meritum ejus gratia est illius, cujus, præmium erit beatitudo ejus." De prædest. sanct., 10. For this very reason the fundamental principle holds good, that grace is not granted *secundum merita nostra.*

the quietistic consequences of his doctrine (see above), and, in his inability to deduce positive virtue from faith in forgiveness of sin, turned from faith to works.   Or was he prevented by the remnants of religious philosophy and cosmology that still clung to his theory of religion from perceiving absolutely that religion is bound up in faith in forgiveness of sins ? [1]   Or, again, is this perception itself erroneous and untenable, one that paralyses the power of moral exertion?   We do not intend to examine these questions here.   The fact is that Augustine conceived faith to be a preliminary stage, because he regarded forgiveness of sins as preliminary.   If we look closely, we find that in his dogmatic theory sin was not *guilt*, but loss and infirmity.   The very man who strove for, and found, a lasting relationship with God, was not capable of reproducing and stating his experience correctly in the shape of doctrine.   He came back to the customary moralistic view, in so far as in his doctrine of grace he thought not of enmity to God, but the disease of sin, not of divine sonship, but of the restoration of a state in which man was rendered capable of becoming good, *i.e.*, sinless.   Therefore faith was merely something preliminary, and it is this that makes it so difficult to define Augustine's conception of the forgiveness of sins.   It appears to have been really identical with the external and magical idea of his predecessors, with the exception that he had a firmer grasp of the forgiveness being an act of God, on which the baptised might constantly rely.   But his reflection rarely took the form of regarding assurance of forgiveness as something whereby the soul receives energy and wings.   He substantially never got beyond the impression that something was *actually* swept away by it, though that was indeed the gravest of facts, sin.

The impossibility of carrying out this conception will always, however, leave a latent doubt.   In spite of his new feeling, Augustine, for this reason, moved entirely in the lines of the old scheme when he sought to supplement and to build upon forgiveness of sin, and looked about him for a positive force which was required to take its place alongside of the negative effect.

[1] In his 177th letter, *e.g.* (Ad Innocent., c. 4), he expressly declares that it is an error to say that *gratia* is *liberum arbitrium* or *remissio peccatorum*.

This he found in love. It was not in faith, but only in love, that
he could recognise the force that really changed a man's nature,
that set him in a new relationship. But then, in spite of the empirical objections that confronted him, he did not doubt that love
could be infused like a medicine. Certain that God alone effects
everything, he transferred to love the conception applicable to
faith (trust)—that it ceases to be itself where it is felt to be other
than an assimilative organ (ὄργανον ληπτικόν)—as if love could
also be as simply regarded as a gift of God through Christ
(munus dei per Christum). The result of these reflections is that
Augustine held that the relation of the pious soul to God was
most appropriately described as a *gradually advancing process of
sanctification.* To this he believed he could reduce all legitimate
considerations, the fundamental importance of faith, the conception of (sacramental) grace as beginning, middle, and end, the
need of positive forces capable of changing man's state, the view
that only the just could be saved, and that no one was righteous
whose works were not perfect, *i.e.,* the necessity of merits, etc.
He believed that he had found a means of adjusting the claims
of religion and morality, of grace and merits, of the doctrine of
faith and eschatology. Omnipotent love became for him the
principle that connected and supported everything. Faith, love,
and merit were successive steps in the way to final salvation, and
he has impressed this view on the Catholic Church of after times,
and on its piety up to the present day. It is the ancient scheme
of the process of sanctification leading to final salvation, but so
transformed that grace acts upon all its stages. Excellent and
—for many stages of development—appropriate as this conception appears, yet it cannot be mistaken that in it Augustine
lagged behind his own experience, and that against his will he
subordinated the religious sphere to moral goodness ; for this
subordination was by no means precluded by the equation "our
merits, God's gifts " (nostra merita, dei munera). Where merits
play a part there is a failure to understand that there is a
relationship to God which is maintained mid weakness and sin,
as well as in misery and death. [1]

---

[1] But, besides, the final and supreme question as to assurance of salvation is not less
misunderstood.

Of this even Augustine had a presentiment, and he therefore also imparted to the Church, to which he transmitted his doctrine of faith, love, and merit, germs of a conception which could not but be fatal to that doctrine. They are not only included in his doctrine of predestination, but at least as much so in every passage of his writings, where he gives voice to the confession, "To me to cling to God is a good thing." In this avowal the religious possession and moral goodness coincide, and are referred to God, their source. But even apart from this, his idea of love : "in this life also virtue is nothing but loving what ought to be loved ; good affections make a good character,"[1] was so excellent and forcible that all criticism looks like impudent coxcombry. Nevertheless, we must criticise it from the standpoint of the gospel. We have already remarked above that Augustine's doctrine of infused love is indifferent to the work of the historical Christ. Therefore he had a two-fold Christology : on the one hand, Christ is God, a member of the Trinity (unus ex trinitate) ; on the other hand, the chosen man, who *was as much under grace as we are*. All that leads us back ultimately to the fact that he under-estimated the significance of the forgiveness of sins and of the publican's faith : that his piety was not yet *simple* enough.[2]

4. Finally, it is to be pointed out that Augustine in his reformation of Christian piety did not disturb its character as a preparation for the next world. He could have changed nothing here without wounding the Christian religion itself; for the view of some Protestants, that Christianity can be transformed into a religion of this world, is an illusion. Augustine lived as much in the future world as Justin and Irenæus. His eschato-

---

[1] Et in hac vita virtus non est nisi diligere quod diligendum est ; faciunt boni amores bonos mores.

[2] It has seemed necessary to concede to Augustine's conception of sanctification that it had the merit of correcting the quietistic phase that clung dangerously to his doctrine of grace. But, on a closer inspection, we find that love did not certainly mean to him the exemplification of morality in serving our neighbour, but sentiments, or such works of love, as owed their value to reflex action at least as strongly as to philanthropy. Here again, in very many expositions, he did not advance beyond the old Catholic Christians, or Cyprian and Ambrose ; man attends best to his own interests by means of *caritas*, and pleases God in divesting himself of what is worldly.

logical reflections are inexhaustible, and if, as will be shown afterwards, he set aside a few of the older ideas, yet that affords no standard of the whole trend of his piety. He only intensified the pessimistic view of *this* life, this mortal life and living death (vita mortalis, mors vitalis), by his doctrine of sin. "What flood of eloquence would ever suffice to portray the tribulations of this life, to describe this wretchedness, which is, as it were, a kind of hell in our present existence? Verily, the new-born infant comes to our mortal light, not laughing but weeping, and by its tears prophesies in some fashion, even without knowing it, to what great evils it has come forth. . . . A heavy yoke burdens all the children of Adam from the day of birth to that of burial, when they return to the common mother of all. . . . And the sorest thing of all is that we cannot but know how, just by the grievous sin committed in Paradise, this life has become a punishment to us."[1] Just as he has retained the pessimistic view of our present life, he has also described blessedness as the state of the perfect knowledge of God. He has done so in one of his earliest writings, De vita beata, and he substantially adhered to it.

But the very perception, that misery was not a mere fatality, but was incurred by guilt, and the confidence that grace could make man free and happy even upon this earth, exerted a certain counterpoise. He undoubtedly does not call the present life of the Christian "joy of felicity," "but comfort of misery," and declares that to be an extremely false felicity which is devised by men who seek here another happiness than that entertained by hope.[2] But in not a few passages he yet speaks of the joy in God which creates blessedness even here. He seldom obeyed this feeling. For that very reason he found this

[1] See also the thrilling description, De civitat, XIX., 4.

[2] In his Soliloquies, one of his earliest writings, he awards felicity to the soul that perceives God here below. But in his Retractations, I., 4, he says expressly, "Nec illud mihi placet, quod in ista vita deo intellecto jam beatam esse animam (in Soliloquiis) dixi, *nisi forte spe.*" In general, Augustine at a later date disavowed many arguments in his works written immediately after his conversion; nay, even in his Confessions, in which he is disposed to describe his conversion as instantaneous, he has admitted in one important sentence how imperfect his Christian thought was at that time: IX. 7, "Ibi (in Cassiciacum) quid egerim in litteris, jam quidem servientibus

life in itself objectless, and there are only a few indications, especially in the work, De civitate dei, in which he tried to show that a kingdom of Christ may be built up even in this world, and that the just, who live by faith, constitute it, and have a present task to perform (see also De trinit. I., 16 and 21). Speaking generally, he propagated the feeling shown in ancient Christian eschatology in every respect, and prepared the ground for monachism. If he seems to have instigated the development of the Catholic Church in its tendency to masterful rule over this world, yet external circumstances, and the interpretation they produced of his work " De civitate dei," contributed much more to the result than any intentional impulses given by him.[1] Where, however, there has developed in Catholicism in after times a strong sense of the blessedness which the Christian can receive even in this state, it has always assumed a mystical and ecstatic character. This is a clear proof that in any case this life was disregarded ; for the mystical feeling of blessedness, even as Augustine knew it, really exists, by means of an *excess*, already in the future state.

In the preceding pages the attempt has been made to show how the piety was constituted in which Augustine lived, and which he transmitted to posterity. It is extraordinary difficult to understand it aright ; for experience and tradition are interwoven in it in the most wonderful way. Yet we cannot understand

---

tibi, sed *adhue superbiæ scholam tanquam in pausatione anhelantibus*, testantur libri disputati cum præsentibus (libr. c. Academ.—de beata vita—de ordine) et cum ipso me solo (Soliloquia) coram te ; quæ autem cum absente Nebridio, testantur epistolæ "). But our judgment must here be divided. What was written earlier was undoubtedly in many respects less complete, less churchly, more Neoplatonic ; but on the other hand it was more direct, more personal and determined to a smaller degree by regard for the Catholicism of the Church. Yet he was already determined to have nothing to do with a felicity of inquiry and seeking ; but only saw it in its *possession* (Adv. Acad. lib., I.).

[1] On Augustine's pessimistic and eschatological tendency, his view of the secular and clerical life, as also the efforts to surmount the popular Catholic conception, see Reuter, l.c., Studie VI. We return briefly to these subjects further on.

him as teacher of the Church, until we have formed our estimate of him as reformer of piety ; for, besides Scripture and tradition, his theories have their strongest roots in the piety that animated him. They are in part nothing but states of feeling interpreted theoretically. But in these states of feeling there gathered round the grand experience of conversion from bondage to freedom in God all the manifold religious experiences and moral reflections of the ancient world. The Psalms and Paul, Plato and the Neoplatonists, the Moralists, Tertullian and Ambrose, we find all again in Augustine, and, side by side with the new psychological view constructed by him as disciple of the Neoplatonists, we come once more upon all the childish reflections and absolute theories which these men had pursued.

CHAPTER IV.

THE HISTORICAL POSITION OF AUGUSTINE AS TEACHER OF THE CHURCH.

THE ancient Church before Augustine only possessed a single great dogmatic scheme, the *Christological.* Augustine also knew it and made use of it ; but in inserting it into a greater and more living group, he deprived it of its original meaning and object. It has been said of Socrates that he brought philosophy down from heaven ; we may maintain of Augustine that he did the same for dogmatics, by separating it from speculations about the finite and infinite, God the Logos and the creature, mortal and immortal, and connecting it with questions as to moral good, freedom, sin, and blessedness. *Goodness became for him the point on which turned the consideration of blessings ;* moral goodness (virtue) and the possession of salvation were not merely to occupy corresponding positions, but to coincide (ipsa virtus et præmium virtutis). If we may use a figure, we can say that Augustine formed into one the two centres of popular Catholic theology, the renewing power of redemption and the free effort to attain virtue ; of the ellipse he made a circle—God, whose grace delivers the will and endows it with power to do what is good. In this is comprehended his significance in the history of the Christian religion. He did not, however, vindicate the new portion consistently, but built the old into it. Indeed, in the new cathedral erected by him, the old building formed, as it were, the holy of holies, which is seldom entered.

When we seek to determine what has been accomplished by an ancient Church theologian as teacher of the Church, we must examine his expositions of the Symbol. We possess several by Augustine. It is extremely instructive to compare the earliest (De fide et symbolo, A.D. 393) with one of the latest (De fide,

95

spe et caritate, A.D. 421, or later). In the former Augustine is still substantially a theologian of the ancient Church. The questions discussed by him are the same as were then dealt with, in both halves of the Church, in the Symbol, and are suggested by its language. Even the manner in which he discusses them is but slightly distinguished from the customary one. Finally,the polemic is the one that was usual: Arians, Manichæans, Apollinarians, Pneumatomachoi occupy the foreground ; the last named especially are very thoroughly refuted. On the other hand, Augustine's characteristics declare themselves even in this early exposition.[1] Thus we have, above all, his love of truth and frankness in the sections on the Holy Spirit, and his sceptical reserve and obedient submission to Church tradition. Further, in the Christology we find his characteristic scheme " Christ invested in man " (Christus indutus in homine), as well as the strong emphasis laid on the humility of Christ contrasted with pride (superbia). Compare, besides, sentences like the following. Chapter VI.—" Since he is only-begotten he has no brothers ; but since he is first-begotten, he has deigned to name all those his brothers who after and through his headship are born again into the grace of God through the adoption of sons." Or (Chapter XI.) : " Our Lord's humility was lowly in his being born for us ; to this it was added that he deigned to die for

---

[1] The foundation of Augustine's religious characteristics can be best studied in the writings that are read least, namely in the tractates and letters written immediately after his conversion, and forming an extremely necessary supplement to his Confessions (see above, p. 92, note 2). In these writings he is not yet at all interested in Church dogmatics, but is wholly absorbed in the task of making clear to himself, while settling with Neoplatonism, the new stage of religious philosophical reflection and inner experience, in which he finally found rest (see De vita beata, Adv. Academ., Soliloquia, De ordine, and the Epistles to Nebridius). The state of feeling expressed by him in these works never left him ; but it was only in a later period that he gave it its dogmatic sub-structure. In consequence of this, as is proved even by the Confessions and also the Retractations, he himself lost the power of rightly estimating those writings and the inner state in which he had found himself in the first years after his conversion. But he never lost the underlying tone of those first fruits of his authorship : " Rest in the possession of God," as distinguished from the unrest and unhappiness of a seeking and inquiry that never reach their aim, or the essentially Neoplatonic version of the loftiest problems (see e.g., De ordine II., 11 ff., " mala in ordinem redacta faciunt decorem universi " ; the same view of evil is still given in De civit., XI., 18). Those writings cannot be more fully discussed in a history of dogma.

mortals." Or (Chapter XIX.): "The writers of the Divine Scriptures declare that the Holy Spirit is God's gift *in order that we may believe that God does not bestow a gift inferior to himself.*" Or (ibid.): "No one enjoys that which he knows, unless he also loves it . . . nor does anyone abide in that which he apprehends unless by love."[1] But if Augustine had died before the Donatist and Pelagian controversies, he would not have been the dogmatist who changed the whole scheme of doctrine; for it was these controversies that first compelled him to reflect on and review what he had long held, to vindicate it with all his power, and to introduce it also into the instruction of the Church. But since it had never entered his mind that the ancient doctrinal tradition, as attached to the Symbol, could be insufficient,[2] since it had still less occurred to him to declare the Symbol itself to be inadequate, it was a matter of course to him that he should

---

[1] Secundum id, quod unigenitus est, non habet fratres ; secundum id autem quod primogenitûs est, fratres vocare dignatus est omnes qui post ejus et per ejus primatum in dei gratiam renascuntur per adoptionem filiorum." "Parva erat pro nobis domini nostri humilitas in nascendo ; accessit etiam ut mori pro mortalibus dignaretur." "Divinarum scripturarum tractatores spiritum sanctum donum dei esse prædicant, *ut deum credamus non se ipso inferius donum dare.*" "Eo quod quisque novit non fruitur, nisi et id diligat . . . neque quisquam in eo quod percipit permanet nisi dilectione."

[2] He undoubtedly noticed, and with his love of truth frankly said, that the Church writers gave throughout an insufficient statement of the grace of God ; but he contented himself with the plea that the Church had always duly emphasised grace in its prayers and institutions. See prædest. sanct., 27 : "Quid opus est, ut eorum scrutemur opuscula, qui prius quam ista hæresis (Pelagianorum) oriretur, non habuerunt necessitatem in hac difficili ad solvendum quæstione versari ? quod procul dubio facerent, si respondere talibus cogerentur. Unde factum est, ut de gratia dei quid sentirent, breviter quibusdam scriptorum suorum locis et transeunter adtingerent, immorarentur vero in eis, quæ adversus inimicos ecclesiæ disputabant, et in exhortationibus ad quasque virtutes, quibus deo vivo et vero pro adipiscenda vita æterna et vera felicitate servitur. Frequentationibus autem orationum simpliciter apparebat dei gratia quid valeret ; non enim poscerentur de deo quæ præcipit fieri, nisi ab illo donaretur ut fierent." He himself had indeed learned from experience in his struggle with the Manichæans, that the defence of truth has to be regulated by the nature of the attack. When he was twitted by his opponents with what he had formerly written about freewill against the Manichæans, he appealed to the claims of advancing knowledge, as well as to the duty of offering resistance both to right and left. He thus saw in the earlier Church teachers the defenders of the truth of the Church against fatalism, Gnosticisim, and Manichæism, and from this standpoint explained their attitude.

make everything which he had to present as religious doctrine
hinge on that Confession. In this way arose the characteristic
scheme of doctrine, which continued to influence the West in
the Middle Ages ; nay, on which the Reformed version is based
—a combination of ancient Catholic theology and system with
the new fundamental thought of the doctrine of grace, forced
into the framework of the Symbol. It is evident that by this
means a mixture of styles arose which was not conducive to the
transparency and intelligibility of doctrine. But we have not
only to complain of want of clearness, but also of a complexity
of material which, in a still higher degree than was the case in the
ancient Catholic Church, necessarily frustrated the demand for
a closely reasoned and homogeneous version of religious doctrine. We are perhaps justified in maintaining that the Church
never possessed in ancient times another teacher so anxious as
Augustine to think out theological problems, and to secure unity
for the system of doctrine. But the circumstances in which he
was placed led to him above all others necessarily confusing that
system of doctrine, and involving it in new inconsistencies.[1]
The following points fall to be considered.

1. As a Western theologian, he felt that he was bound by the
Symbol ; but no Western theologian before him had lived so
much in Scripture, or taken so much from it as he. The old vari-
ance between Symbol and Scripture,[2] which at that time indeed
was not yet consciously felt, was accordingly intensified by him.
The uncertainty as to the relation of Scripture and Symbol was
increased by him in spite of the extraordinary services he had
rendered in making the Church familiar with the former.[3] The
Biblicism of later times, which afterwards took up an aggressive
attitude to the Church in the West, is to be traced back to
Augustine ; and the resolute deletion of Scriptural thoughts by

---

[1] It is self-evident that for this reason dogma, *i.e.*, the old Catholic doctrine of the
Trinity and Christology, necessarily became less impressive. Reuter's objection (l.c.
p. 495) rests on an incomprehensible misunderstanding.

[2] See on this and on what follows, Vol. III., pp. 203 ff., 207 ff.

[3] The attempts to define their relationship, *e.g.*, in Book I. of the treatise De
doctrina Christiana, are wholly vague, and indeed scarcely comprehensible. The
" substance " of Scripture is to form the propositions of the Rule of Faith ; but yet
every sentence of Scripture is an article of faith.

an appeal to the authority of the Church's doctrine may equally
refer to him.[1] If we are asked for the historical justification
of pre-reformers and reformers in the West, in taking their
stand exclusively on Scripture, we must name Augustine ; if we
are asked by what right such theologians have been silenced, we
may refer similarly to Augustine ; but we can in this case undoubtedly go back to the authority of Tertullian (De præscr.
hær.).

2. On the one hand, Augustine was convinced that everything
in Scripture was valuable for faith, and that any thought was at
once justified, ecclesiastically and theologically, by being proved
to be Biblical—see his doctrine of predestination and other
tenets, of which he was certain simply because they were found
in the Bible. By this principle any unity of doctrine was nullified. [2] But, on the other hand, Augustine knew very well that
religion was a practical matter, that in it faith, hope, and love, or
love alone, were all-important, and that only what promoted the
latter had any value. Indeed he advanced a considerable step
further, and approximated to the Alexandrian theologians : he
ultimately regarded Scripture merely as a *means*, which was dispensed with when love had reached its highest point, and he
even approached the conception that the very facts of Christ's
earthly revelation were stages beyond which the believer passed,
whose heart was possessed wholly by love. [3] This latter point—
which is connected with his individualistic theology, but slightly

---

[1] After his conversion Augustine was firmly of opinion that nothing stood in Scripture that contradicted the doctrine of the Church ; he was not so certain that the interpretation of Scripture must follow the authority of tradition. Yet what a profusion of
"dangerous" ideas would have been evolved from the Bible by his rich and acute
genius if once he had freed his intellect from the fetters of obedience ! The perception
that no less than everything would have been doubtful, that a thousand contradictions
would have taken the place of a unanimous doctrine, certainly helped in determining
him not to shake the bars of his prison. He felt he would never be able to escape,
but would be buried by the ruins of the collapsing edifice. Hence the principle
declared in De nat. et grat. 22, that we must first submit to what stands in Scripture,
and only then ask "quomodo id fieri potuerit." What a difference from Origen !

[2] See Vol. II., 331, n. 3.

[3] De doctr. Christ. I., 34 : an extremely noteworthy exposition, which, so far as I
know, has very few clear parallels in Augustine's works, but forms the background of
his development.

influenced by the historical Christ—will be discussed below. It is enough here to formulate sharply the inconsistency of making Scripture, on the one hand, a *source*, and, on the other, a *means*.[1] —a means indeed which is finally dispensed with like a crutch.[2] The mystics and fanatics of the West have given their adhesion to the last principle, advancing the inner light and inner revelation against the written. Now Augustine, in his excellent preface to his work "De doctrina Christiana," has undoubtedly, as with a flash of prophetic illumination, rejected all fanatical inspiration, which either fancied it had no need at all of Scripture, or, appealing to the Spirit, declared philological and historical interpretation to be useless. But yet he opened the door to fanaticism with his statement that there was a stage at which men had got beyond Scripture. Above all, however, he created the fatal situation, in which the system of doctrine and theology of the Western Church are still found at the present day, by the vagueness which he failed to dispel as to the importance of the letter of Scripture. The Church knows, on the one hand, that in the Bible, so far as meant for faith, the "matter" is alone of importance. But, on the other hand, it cannot rid itself of the prejudice that every single text contains a Divine and absolute direction, a "revelation." Protestant Churches have in this respect not gone one step beyond Augustine ; Luther himself, if we compare his "prefaces" to the New Testament, *e.g.*, with his position in the controversy about the Lord's Supper, was involved in the same inconsistency as burdened Augustine's doctrinal structure.

3. Augustine brought the practical element to the front more than any previous Church Father. Religion was only given to produce faith, love, and hope, and blessedness itself was bound up in these virtues bestowed by God, or in love. But the act of reform, which found expression in the subordination of all materials to the above intention, was not carried out by him

---

[1] See the details in "De doctr. Christiana" copied in Vol. III., p. 203, n. 2, of this work.

[2] De doctr. Christ., 35-40, especially c. 39, "Therefore a man who depends on faith, hope, and love, and holds by them invincibly, only needs Scripture to instruct others." Scripture even only offers patchwork ; but a man may rise to such perfection even in this life as no longer to require the patchwork.

unalloyed. In retaining the old Catholic scheme, knowledge and eternal life (ἀφθαρσία) remained the supreme thoughts; in pursuing Neoplatonic mysticism, he did not cast off the acosmic view that regarded all phenomena as transient, and all that was transient as figurative, retaining finally only the majesty of the concealed Deity; in despising the present life, he necessarily also depreciated faith and all that belonged to the present. Thus, his theology was not decided, even in its final aims, by one thought, and he was therefore unable really to carry out his doctrine of grace and sin in a pure form. As the intellectualism of antiquity, of course in a sublimated form, was not wholly superseded by him, his profoundest religious utterances were accompanied by, or entwined with, philosophical considerations. Often one and the same principle has a double root, a Neo-platonic and a Christian (Pauline), and accordingly a double meaning, a cosmological and a religious. Philosophy, saving faith, and Church tradition, disputed the leading place in his system of faith, and since Biblicism was added to these three elements, the unity of his type of thought was everywhere disturbed.

4. But apart from the intention, the execution contains not only inconsistencies in detail, but opposite views. In his con-flict with Manichæism and Donatism, Augustine sketched a doctrine of freedom, the Church, and the means of grace, which has little in common with his experience of sin and grace, and simply conflicts with the theological development of that ex-perience—the doctrine of predestinating grace. We can positively sketch two Augustinian theologies, one ecclesiastical, the other a doctrine of grace, and state the whole system in either.

5. But even in his ecclesiastical system and his doctrine of grace, conflicting lines of thought meet; for in the former a hierarchical and sacramental fundamental element conflicts with a liberal, universalist view inherited from the Apologists; and in the doctrine of grace two different conceptions are manifestly combined, namely, the thought of grace through (per, propter) Christ, and that of grace emanating, independently of Christ, from the essential nature of God as the supreme good

and supreme being (summum bonum, summum esse). The
latter inconsistency was of greatest importance for Augustine's
own theology, and for the attitude of Western theology after
him. The West, confessedly, never thoroughly appropriated the
uncompromising Eastern scheme of Christology as a statement
of saving faith. But by Augustine the relation of the doctrine
of the two natures (or the Incarnation) to that of salvation was
still further loosened. It will be shown that he really prepared
the way much more strongly for the Franciscan feeling towards
Christ than for Anselm's satisfaction theory, and that, in general,
as a Christologian—in the strict sense of the term—he be-
queathed more gaps than positive material to posterity. But in
addition to this antithesis of a grace through Christ and without Christ, we have, finally, in Augustine's doctrine of sin a
strong Manichæan and Gnostic element; for Augustine never
wholly surmounted Manichæism.

From our exposition up to this point—and only the most
important facts have been mentioned—it follows that we cannot
speak of Augustine having a system, nor did he compose any
work which can be compared to Origen's περὶ ἀρχῶν. Since he
did not, like the latter, boldly proclaim the right of an esoteric
Christianity, but rather as Christian and churchman constantly
delayed taking this liberating step,[1] everything with him stands
on one level, and therefore is involved in conflict.[2] But it is
"not what one knows and says that decides, but what one
loves"; he loved God, and his Church, and he was true. This
attitude is conspicuous in all his writings, whether it is the Neoplatonist, the earlier Manichæan, the Pauline Christian, the
Catholic Bishop, or the Biblicist, that speaks, and it lends to all
his expositions a unity, which, though it cannnot be demonstrated in the doctrines, can be plainly felt. Therefore, also, the
different movements that started or learned from him, were
always conscious of the complete man, and drew strength from

---

[1] Tendencies in this direction are found everywhere; but they were never more
than tendencies.

[2] It is one of Reuter's chief merits that he has proved the impossibility of constructing a system from Augustine's thought, and of removing the inconsistencies that
occur in it.

him. He would not have been the teacher of the future if he had not stood before it as a Christian personality who lent force and weight to every word, no matter in what direction it led. As preacher of faith, love, and the dispensation of grace, he has dominated Catholic piety up to the present day. By his fundamental sentiment: "Mihi adhærere deo bonum est," as also by his distinction between law and gospel, letter and spirit, and his preaching that God creates faith and a good will in us, he called forth the evangelical Reformation.[1] By his doctrine of the authority and means of grace of the Church, he carried forward the construction of Roman Catholicism; nay, he first created the hierarchical and sacramental institution. By his Biblicism he prepared the way for the so-called pre-reformation movements, and the criticism of all extra-Biblical ecclesiastical traditions. By the force of his speculation, the acuteness of his intellect, the subtlety of his observation and experience, he incited, nay, partly created, scholasticism in all its branches, including the Nominalistic, and therefore also the modern theory of knowledge and psychology. By his Neoplatonism and enthusiasm for predestination he evoked the mysticism as well as the anti-clerical opposition of the Middle Ages.[2] By the form of his ideal of the Church and of felicity, he strengthened the popular Catholic, the monachist, state of feeling, domesticating it, moreover, in the Church, and thereby rousing and capacitating it to *overcome* and *dominate* the world as contrasted with the Church. Finally, by his unique power of portraying himself, of expressing the wealth of his genius, and giving every word an individual impress, by his gift of individualising and self-observation, he contributed to the rise of the Renaissance and the modern spirit.

These are not capricious combinations, but historical facts :[3] the connecting lines that lead back to him, can everywhere be

---

[1] See the testimonies to Augustine of the Reformers and their confessional writings ; yet the difference that still existed was not unknown to them.

[2] Even the Anti-Gregorian party in the Middle Ages frequently appealed to Augustine. It was possible to find in him welcome statements as to the meaning of the Empire, the possibility of correcting Councils, and, generally, anti-hierarchical passages.

[3] Compare Reuter, Studie VII.

clearly demonstrated. But where, then, in the history of the West is there a man to be compared to him? Without taking much to do with affairs—Augustine was Bishop of a second-rate city, and possessed neither liking nor talent for the *rôle* of an ecclesiastical leader or practical reformer—by the force of his ideas he influenced men, and made his life permeate the centuries that followed.

It has been attempted to depict Augustine's significance as Church teacher, by dividing absolutely the various directions in which his thought moved, and by giving separate accounts of the Neoplatonist, the Paulinist, the earlier Manichæan, and the Catholic Bishop.[1] But it is to be feared that violence is done him by such an analysis. It is safer and more appropriate, within the limits of a history of dogma, to keep to the external unity which he has himself given to his conceptions. In that case his *Enchiridion ad Laurentium,* his matured exposition of the Symbol, presents itself as our best guide. This writing we mean to bring forward at the close of the present chapter, after preliminary questions have been discussed which were of supreme importance to Augustine, and the controversies have been reviewed in which his genius was matured. We shall, in this way, obtain the clearest view of what Augustine achieved for the Church *of his time,* and of the revolution he evoked. It is a very attractive task to centralise Augustinian theology, but it is safer to rest content with the modest result of becoming acquainted with it, in so far as it exerted its influence on the Church. One difficulty meets us at the very outset which can *not* be removed, and went on increasing in after times. *What portion of Augustine's countless expositions constituted dogma in his own eyes, or became dogma at a later period?* While he extended dogma to an extraordinary extent, he at the same time

---

[1] It is unmistakable that there are three planes in Augustine's theological thoughts, Neoplatonic mysticism (without means of grace, without the Church, nay, in a sense, even without Christ), Christological soteriology, and the plane of the authority and sacraments of the Church. Besides these, rationalistic and Manichæan elements have to be taken into account.

sometimes relaxed, sometimes—as regards ancient tradition— specifically stiffened, the notion to be held of it. The question as to the extent of dogmas was neither answered, nor ever put precisely, in the West, after the Donatist and Pelagian contro- versies. In other words, no necessity was felt for setting up similarly express positive statements in addition to the express refutations of Pelagians, Donatists, etc. But the necessity was not felt, because Churchmen possessed neither self-confidence nor courage to take ecclesiastical action on a grand scale. They always felt they were Epigones of a past time which had created the professedly adequate tradition. This feeling, which was still further accentuated in the Middle Ages, was gradually overcome by the Popes, though solely by them. Apart from a few exceptions, it was not till the Council of Trent that dogmas were again formed. Till then the only dogmas were the doctrines contained in the Symbols. Next these stood the catalogues of heretics, from which dogmas could be indirectly deduced. This state of matters induces us to present the doctrine of Augustine as fully as possible, consistently with the design of a text-book. Many things must here be brought forward from his works which bore no fruit in his own time, but had a powerful influence on the course of doctrinal develop- ment in the following centuries, and came to light in the dogmas of Trent.[1]

In what follows we shall proceed (1) to describe Augustine's fundamental view, his doctrines of the first and last things;[2]

---

[1] Reuter also recognises (p. 495 f., note) that Augustine held the contents of the Symbol alone to be dogma. But we have here to remember that the most elaborate doctrine of the Trinity and Christology were evolved from the Symbol, and that its words "sancta ecclesia" and "remissio peccatorum" contained theories from which equally far-reaching dogmas could be formed, or heretics be convicted. Even Cyprian refuted the Novatians from the Symbol, and Augustine used it against the Pelagians. A peculiar difficulty in the way of discussing Augustine in the history of dogma consists further in the fact that he created countless theological *schemes*, but no dogmatic *formulas*. He was too copious, too earnest, and too sincere to publish catch-words.

[2] Augustine was the first dogmatist to feel the need of considering for himself the questions, which we are now accustomed to treat in the "prolegomena to dogmatics." The Alexandrians undoubtedly attempted this also; but in their case formal and material, original and derived, were too much intertwined. Nor did they advance to

for they were fixed when he became a Catholic Christian; (2)
and (3) we then describe his controversies with Donatists and
Pelagians, in which his conception of faith was deepened and
unfolded ; and (4) we expound his system of doctrine by the
help of the *Enchiridion ad Laurentium.*

1. *Augustine's Doctrines of the First and Last Things.*[1]

It has been said of Fiesole that he prayed his pictures on to
the walls.   It can be maintained of Augustine that his most
profound thoughts regarding the first and the last things arose
out of prayers; for all these matters were contained for him in
God.   If the same can be said of innumerable mystics down to
the private communities of Madame de Guyon and Tersteegen,
it is true of them because they were Augustine's disciples.   But
more than anyone else he possessed the faculty of combining
speculation about God with a contemplation of mind and soul
which was not content with a few traditional categories, but
analysed the states of feeling and the contents of consciousness.
Every advance in this analysis became for him at the same time
an advance in the knowledge of God, and *vice versâ*; concentration of his whole being in prayer led him to the most abstract
observation, and this, in turn, changed to prayer.   No philosopher before or after him has verified in so conspicuous a
fashion the profound saying that " the fear of the Lord is the
beginning of wisdom."   *Godliness* was the very atmosphere of
his thought and life.   " Piety is the wisdom of man " (Hominis
sapientia pietas est, Enchir., 2; De civ. dei XIV., 28).   Thus
Augustine was the *psychological,* because he was the *theological,*
genius of the Patristic period.[2]   Not unversed in the domains
of objective secular knowledge, he yet discarded them more

---

the last problems of psychology and the theory of perception.   Enchir., 4 : " Quid
primum, quid ultimum, teneatur, quæ totius definitionis summa sit, quod certum
propriumque fidei catholicæ fundamentum."   (Questions by Laurentius.)

[1] Augustine taught that it was only possible to obtain a firm grasp of the highest
questions by earnest and unwearied independent labour.   Herein above all did his
greatness consist.

[2] Compare with what follows, Siebeck, in the Ztschr. f. Philos. und philos. Kritik,
1888, p. 170 ff.

resolutely than his Neoplatonic teachers, to whom he owed much, but whom he far surpassed. " The contents of the inner life lay clearly before Augustine's eyes as a realm of distinctive objects of perception, outside and independent of sense experience, and he was convinced by his own rich insight that in this sphere quite as genuine knowledge and information, based on inner experience, were to be gained, as by external observation in surrounding nature." Augustine brought to an end the development of ancient philosophy by completing the process which led from the naïve objective to the subjective objective.[1] He found what had been long sought for : the making of the inner life the starting-point of reflection on the world.[2] And he did not give himself up to empty dreams, but investigated with a truly " physiological psychology " all conditions of the inner life, from its elementary processes up to the most sublime moods ; he became, because he was the counterpart of Aristotle, the true Aristotle of a new science,[3] which seems indeed to

[1] See the Appendix on Neoplatonism, Vol. I., p. 336 ff.

[2] The method of the Neoplatonists was still very uncertain, and this is connected, among other things, with their polytheism. It is easy to show that Augustine went so much further in psychology because he was a monotheist. So far as I know we are still, unfortunately, without any investigation of the importance of monotheism for psychology.

[3] See the excellent parallel between them in Siebeck, l.c. p. 188 f. : " Among the important personalities of Antiquity two could hardly be found with characters so different as Aristotle and Augustine. In the former we have the Greek, restful and clear, and yet moved by energetic warmth of thought, who gives its purest scientific expression to the Hellenic ideal of the life of the cultured, contentment with the even and constant advance of the life of the thinker, examining the depths and wants of the soul, only in so far as they appear on the surface, in the external nature and garb of the affections, and discussing this whole domain, not properly in order to know the heart, but only for rhetorical purposes. The internal world of the soul is here described and criticised only in so far as it evinces itself in reciprocal action with the external, and in the form it assumes as determined by the co-operation of the latter. For the comprehensive and final problem with Aristotle is the scientific construction and form of the external world in nature and social life. Augustine's tendency and frame of mind are quite the opposite. The external owes all its importance and value in his eyes to the form it assumes as reflected in the internal. Everything is dominated not by problems of nature and the State and secular ethics, but by those of the deepest wants of mind and heart, of love and faith, hope and conscience. The proper objects and the moving forces of his speculation are not found in the relation of inward to outward, but of inner to innermost, to the sense and vision of God in the heart. Even the powers of the intellect are looked at from a

have forgotten that as a theory of perception, and as inner observation, it originated in the monotheistic faith and life of prayer. He disposed of all that we call the ancient classical temper, the classical conception of life and the world. With the last remains of its cheerfulness and naïve objectivity, he buried for a long time the old truth itself, and showed the way to a new truth of things. But this was born in him amid pains, and it has kept its feature of painfulness. Mohammed, the barbarian, smote into ruins, in the name of Allah, who had mastered him, the Hellenistic world which he did not know. Augustine, the disciple of the Hellenes, completed in the West the long prepared dissolution of this world, in the name of God, whom he had

new point of view, owing to the influence exerted on them by the heart and will, and they lose, in consequence, their claim to sole supremacy in scientific thought. The cool analysis made by Aristotle of the external world, which also dissected and discriminated between the states of the soul, as if they were objects that existed externally, disappears in Augustine before the immediate experience and feeling of states and processes of the emotional life ; but the fact that he presents them to us with the warmest personal interest in them, entirely prevents us from feeling the absence of the Aristotelian talent of acuteness in analytical dissection. While Aristotle avoids all personal and individual colouring in his views, and labours everywhere to let the matter in hand speak for itself, Augustine, even when bringing forward investigations of the most general purport, always speaks as if only of himself, the individual, to whom his personal feelings and sensations are the main thing. He is *a priori* certain that they must have a farther reaching meaning, since feeling and wishing are found to be similar potencies in every human heart. Questions of ethics, which Aristotle handles from the standpoint of the relation of man to man, appear in Augustine in the light of the relations between his own heart and that of this known and felt God. With the former the supreme decision is given by clear perception of the external by reason ; with the latter, by the irresistible force of the internal, the conviction of feeling, which in his case—as is given in such perfection to few—is fused with the penetrating light of the intellect. . . . Aristotle knows the wants of the inner life only so far as they are capable of developing the life, supported by energetic effort and philosophic equanimity, in and with society. He seems to hold that clear thinking and restfully energetic activity prevent all suffering and misfortune to society or the individual. The deeper sources of dispeace, of pain of soul, of unfulfilled wants of the heart, remain dark in his investigation. Augustine's significance begins just where the problem is to trace the unrest of the believing or seeking soul to its roots, and to make sure of the inner facts in which the heart can reach its rest. Even the old problems which he reviews and examines in their whole extent and meaning from the standpoint of his rich scientific culture, now appear in a new light. Therefore he can grasp, and, at the same time, deepen everything which has come to him from Hellenism. For Aristotle, everything that the intellect can see and analyse in the

perceived to be the only reality;[1] but he built up a new world in his own heart and mind.[2] However, nothing really perished entirely, because everything was accomplished by a protracted transformation, and, besides, the old Hellenistic world continued in part to exist on the North-East coast of the Mediterranean. It was possible to travel back along the line which had been traced by a millennium down to Augustine, and the positive

inner and outer world constitutes a problem ; for Augustine, that holds the chief place which the life of feeling and desire forces on him as a new fact added to his previous knowledge. In the one case it is the calm, theoretical mind ; in the other, the conscience excited by the unrest caused by love of God and consciousness of sin, from which the questions spring. But along with this, scientific interest also turned to a wholly novel side of actual life. No wonder that the all-sufficiency of the dissecting and abstracting intellect had its despotism limited. The intellect was now no longer to create problems, but to receive them from the depths of the world of feeling, in order then to see what could be made of them. Nor was it to continue to feel supremacy over the will, but rather the influence to which it was subject from it. The main subject of its reflections was to consist, henceforth, not in the external world, nor in the internal discussed by means of analogy with, and the method of, the external, but in the kernel of personality, conscience in connection with emotion and will. Only from this point might it return, in order to learn to understand them anew, to previous views of the inner and outer life. Aristotle, the Greek, was only interested in the life of the soul, in so far as it turned outward and helped to fathom the world theoretically and practically ; Augustine, *the first modern man* (the expression occurs also in Sell, Aus der Gesch. des Christenthums, 1888, p. 43 ; I had already used it years ago), only took it into consideration, in so far as reflection upon it enabled him to conceive the inner character of personal life as something really independent of the outer world." Aristotle and Augustine are the two rivals who contended in the science and tendency of the following centuries. Both, as a rule, were indeed degraded, Aristotle to empty distinctions and categories, and a hide-bound dogmatism, Augustine to a mysticism floating in all conceivable media, having lost the guidance of a sure observation of the inner nature. Even in the Pelagians Augustine energetically opposed Aristotelian rationalism, and his controversy with them was repeated over and over again in after ages. In the history of religion it was a fight between a really irreligious, theologically, labelled morality and religion ; for even in its classical form, Aristotelianism is a morality without religion.

[1] All Christian Hellenistic thinkers before Augustine were still refined polytheists, or, more correctly, the polytheistic element was not wholly eradicated in their case, seeing that they preserved a part of nature-religion. This is most evident among Origen's successors.

[2] Weh ! Weh !   Wir tragen
Du hast sie zerstört,   Die Trümmer ins Nichts hinüber
Die schöne Welt,   Und klagen
Mit mächtiger Faust ;   Ueber die verlorene Schöne.
Sie stürzt, sie zerfällt !   Prächtiger baue sie wieder,
Ein Halbgott hat sie zerschlagen !   In deinem Busen baue sie auf !

capital, which Neoplatonism and Augustine had received from
the past and had changed into negative values, could also be
re-established with a positive force. But something had undoubtedly been lost; we find it surviving in almost none but
those who were ignorant of theology and philosophy; we do
not find it among thinkers; and that is frank joy in the phenomenal world, in its obvious meaning, and in calm and energetic
work.[1] If it were possible to unite in science and in the disposition, the piety, spirituality, and introspection of Augustine,
with the openness to the world, the restful and energetic activity,
and unclouded cheerfulness of antiquity, we should have reached
the highest level! We are told that such a combination is a
phantom, that it is an absurd idea. But do we not honour the
great minds, who have been granted us since Luther, simply
because they have endeavoured to realise the " fancy picture "?
Did not Goethe declare this to be his ideal, and endeavour to
present it in his own life, in his closing epoch? Is it not in the
same ideal that the meaning of evangelical and reforming Christianity is contained, if it is really different from Catholicism ?

" I desire to know God and the soul. Nothing more? Nothing at all." [2] In these words Augustine has briefly formulated
the aim of his spiritual life. That was the *truth* [3] for which
"the marrow of his soul sighed." All truth was contained for
him in the perception of God. After a brief period of sore
doubting, he was firm as a rock in the conviction that there was
a God, and that he was the supreme good (summum bonum); [4] [5]
but who he was, and how he was to be found, were to him the
great questions. He was first snatched from the night of uncertainty by Neoplatonism: the Manichæan notion of God had

[1] Compare even the state of feeling of Petrarch and the other Humanists.

[2] Soliloq., I. 7.   Deum et animam scire cupio.   Nihilne plus? Nihil omnino. In
the knowledge of God was also included that of the Cosmus, see Scipio, Metaphysik,
p. 14 ff.

[3] Playing with husks and shells disgusted Augustine; he longed for facts, for the
knowledge of actual forces.

[4] Augustine became a Manichæan because he did not get past the idea that the
Catholic doctrine held God to be the originator of sin.

[5] Confess., VII. 16: " Audivi (verba Ego sum qui sum) sicut auditur in corde, et
non erat prorsus unde dubitarem ; faciliusque dubitarem vivere me, quam non esse
veritatem (VI., 5).

proved itself to be false, since its God was not absolute and omnipotent. Neoplatonism had shown him a way by which to escape the flux of phenomena, and the mysterious and harassing play of the transient, to reach the fixed resting-point he sought, and to discover this in the absolute and *spiritual* God (Confess. VII., 26: "incorporea veritas"). Augustine traversed this ascending path from the corporeal world through ever higher and more permanent spheres, and he also experienced the ecstatic mood in the "excess" of feeling.[1] But at the same time he turned more energetically to those observations for which the Neoplatonists had only been able to give him hints—to his spiritual experience, and psychological analysis. He was saved from scepticism by perceiving that even if the whole of external experience was subject to doubt, the facts of the inner life remained and demanded an explanation leading to certainty. There is no evil, but we are afraid, and this fear is certainly an evil.[2] There is no visible object of faith, but we see faith in us.[3] Thus—*in his theory of perception*—God and the soul entered into the closest union, and this union confirmed him in

---

[1] Suggestions in Confess., VII. 13-16, 23. Here is described the intellectual "exercise" of the observation of the mutabilia leading to the incommutabile. "Et pervenit cogitatio ad id quod est, *in ictu trepidantis aspectus*. Tunc vero invisibilia tua, per ea quæ facta sunt, intellecta conspexi (this now becomes his dominant saying); *sed aciem figere non valui*: et repercussa infirmitate redditus solitis, non mecum ferebam nisi amantem memoriam et quasi olfacta desiderantem (quite as in Plotinus) quæ comedere nondum possem," VIII. 1. But again in his famous dialogue (IX. 23-25), with his mother in Ostia, a regular Neoplatonic "exercise" is really described which ends with ecstasy (attigimus veritatem modice toto ictu cordis"). We afterwards meet extremely seldom with anything of the same kind in Augustine; on the other hand, the anti-Manichæan writings still show many echoes ("se rapere in deum," "rapi in deum," "volitare," "amplexus dei"). Reuter says rightly (p. 472) that these are unusual expressions, only occurring exceptionally. But he must have forgotten the passages in the Confessions when he adds that no instructions are given as to the method to be followed.

[2] Confess., VII. 7 : "Ubi ergo malum et unde et qua huc irrepsit? Quæ radix ejus et quo semen ejus? An omnino non est? Cur ergo timemus et cavemus quod non est? Aut si inaniter timemus, certe vel timor ipse malum est . . . et tanto gravius malum, quanto non est quod timeamus. *Idcirco aut est malum quod timemus, aut hoc malum est quia timemus.*"

[3] De trinit., XIII. 3: "Cum propterea credere jubeamur, quia id quod credere jubemur, videre non possumus, ipsam tamen fidem, quando inest in nobis, videmus in nobis."

his belief in their *metaphysical* connection. Henceforth the investigation of the life of the soul was to him a *theological* necessity. No examination seemed to him to be indifferent; he sought to obtain *divine knowledge* from every quarter. The command to "know thyself" (Γνῶθι σεαυτόν) became for him the way to God. We cannot here discuss the wealth of psychological discoveries made by him.[1] But he only entered his proper element when he was inquiring into the practical side of spiritual life. The popular conception, beyond which even philosophers had not advanced far, was that man was a rational being who was hampered by sensuousness, but possessed a free will capable at every moment of choosing the good—a very external, dualistic view. Augustine observed the actual man. He found that the typical characteristic of the life of the soul consisted *in the effort to obtain pleasure*[2] (cupido, amor); from this type no one could depart. It was identical with the striving to get possessions, enjoyment. As the attempt to attain the pleasant it was desire (libido), cupiditas, and was perfected in joy; as resistance to the unpleasant, it was anger (ira), fear (timor), and was completed in sadness (tristitia). All impulses were only evolutions of this typical characteristic; sometimes they partook more of the form of passive impression, sometimes they were more of an active nature, *and they were quite as true of the spiritual as of the sensuous life.*[3]

According to Augustine, the will is most closely connected with this life of impulse, so that impulses can indeed be conceived as contents of the will, yet it is to be distinguished from them. For the will is not bound to the nexus of nature; it is a force existing above sensuous nature.[4] It is free, in so far as it

---

[1] As regards memory, association of ideas, synthetic activity of spontaneous thought, ideality of the categories, *a priori* functions, "determinant" numbers, synthesis of reproduction in the imagination, etc. Of course all this is only touched on by him; we have, as it were, merely flashes of it in his works; see Siebeck, l.c. p. 179. He has applied his observations on self-consciousness in his speculation on the Trinity.

[2] He meant by this the legitimate striving after self-assertion, after *Being*, which he attributed to all organic, nay, even to inorganic, things; see De civ. dei, XI., 28.

[3] This is the most important advance in perception.

[4] See Siebeck l.c. p. 181 f.; Hamma in the Tüb. Theol. Quartalschr., vol. 55, pp. 427 ff. 458; Kahl, Primat des Willens, p. 1 f. Augustine's psychology of the

possesses formally the capacity of following or resisting the various inclinations; but concretely it is never free; that is, never free choice (liberum arbitrium), but is always conditioned by the chain of existing inclinations, which form its motives and determine it. The theoretical freedom of choice therefore only becomes actual freedom when desire (cupiditas, amor) of good has become the ruling motive of the will; in other words, *it is only true of a good will that it is free*: freedom of will and moral goodness coincide. But it follows just from this that the will truly free possesses its liberty not in caprice, but in *being bound* to the motive which impels to goodness ("beata necessitas boni"). This bondage is freedom, because it delivers the will from the rule of the impulses (to lower forms of good), and realises *the destiny and design of man to possess himself of true being and life.* In bondage to goodness the higher appetite (appetitus), the genuine impulse of self-preservation, realises itself, while by satisfaction "in dissipation" it brings man "bit by bit to ruin." It does not follow, however, from Augustine's assertion of the incapacity for good of the individual spontaneous will, that the evil will, because it is not free, is also irresponsible; for since the will is credited with the power of yielding to the love of good (amor boni), it is guilty of the neglect (the defect).

From this point Augustine, combining the results of Neoplatonic cosmological speculation with the above analysis, now built up his metaphysic, or more correctly, his *theology.* But since in the epoch in which he pursued these observations, he turned to the asceticism of Catholic monachism, and also studied profoundly the Psalms (and the Pauline epistles), the simple grandeur of his living notion of God exerted a tremendous influence on his speculations, and condensed the different, and in part artificially obtained, elements of his doctrine of God,[1] again and again into the supremely simple confession: "The

---

will is undoubtedly rooted in indeterminism; but in his concrete observations he becomes a determinist.

[1] They have all besides a practical object, *i.e.*, they correspond to a definite form of the *pious* contemplation of the divine, and a definite relation to it (a definite self-criticism). For details of the theology, see Dorner, Augustin, pp. 5-112.

Lord of heaven and earth is love; He is my salvation; of whom
should I be afraid?"

By the Neoplatonic speculation of the ascent [of the soul]
Augustine reached the supreme unchangeable, permanent Being,[1]
the incorporeal truth, spiritual substance, incommutable and
true eternity of truth, the light incommutable[2] (incorporea
veritas, spiritalis substantia, incommutabilis et vera veritatis
æternitas, the lux incommutabilis). Starting with this, everything which was not God, including his own soul, was examined
by Augustine from two points of view. On the one hand, it
appeared as the absolutely transient, therefore as non-existent;
for no true being exists, where there is also not-being; *therefore
God exists alone (God the only substance)*. On the other hand,
as far as it possessed a relative existence, it seemed good, very
good, as an evolution of the divine being (the many as the embodiment, emanating, and ever-returning, of the one). Augustine
never tires of realising the beauty (pulchrum) and fitness (aptum)
of creation, of regarding the universe as an ordered work of art,
in which the gradations are as admirable as the contrasts. The
individual and evil are lost to view in the notion of beauty; nay,
God himself is the eternal, the old and new, the only, beauty.
Even hell, the damnation of sinners, is, as an act in the ordination of evils (ordinatio malorum), an indispensable part of the
work of art.[3] But, indeed, the whole work of art is after

---

[1] In Confess. VII. 16, he could now put the triumphant question : " Numquid nihil
est veritas, quoniam neque per finita, neque per infinita locorum spatia diffusa est."

[2] Not common light ; "non hoc illa erat ; sed aliud, aliud valde ab istis omnibus.
Nec ita erat supra mentem meam sicut oleum super aquam, nec sicut coelum super
terram, sed superior, quia ipsa fecit me, et ego inferior, quia factus sum ab ea. Qui
novit veritatem novit eam, et qui novit eam, novit æternitatem. Caritas novit eam. O
æterna veritas, et vera caritas, et cara æternitas ! tu es deus meus ; tibi suspiro die
ac nocte." (Confess. VII. 16.)   Further the magnificently reproduced reflection,
I X. 23-25, De Trin. IV. 1.   By being, Augustine did not understand a vacuous existence, but being full of life, and he never doubted that being was better than not-
being.   De civit. dei, XI. 26: "Et sumus et nos esse novimus et id esse ac nosse
diligimus."   The triad, "esse, scire, amare" was to him the supreme thing; he
never thought of the possibility of glorifying not-being after the fashion of Buddhism
or Schopenhauer.

[3] We cannot here discuss Augustine's cosmology more fully (see the works by
Gangauf and Scipio).   His reflections on life and the gradation of organic and inorganic ("ordo, species, modus") were highly important to later philosophy and

all—nothing; a likeness, but ah! only a likeness of the infinite fulness of the one which alone *exists*. How deeply in earnest Augustine was with this acosmic Pantheism, which threatened to degenerate into cosmic Monism, how he never wholly abandoned it, is shown even by the expression " pulchri-tudo " (beauty) for God,[1] by his doctrine of predestination, which has one of its roots here, and, finally, by the æsthetic optimism of his view of the world which comes out here and there even in his latest writings,[2] and by his uncertainty as to the notion of creation.[3] But the very fact that, as a rule, Augustine was governed by a wholly different temper is a guar-antee that the element here obtained was only a grounding to which he applied new colours. He would not have been the reformer of Christian piety if he had only celebrated, albeit in the most seductive tones,[4] that Neoplatonic notion of God, which, indeed, ultimately rested on a pious *natural sentiment*.

The new elements resulted first from the psychological analysis briefly indicated above. He found in man, as the fundamental form of existence, the desire to reach happiness,

theology, and especially continued to exert an influence in mediæval mysticism. So also the view that evil and good are necessary elements in the artistic composition of the world continued to make its presence actively felt in the same quarter. Yet—as in Augustine—the idea of the privative significance of evil always preponderated.

[1] This expression is frequent in all his writings. Even utterances like " vita vitæ meæ," etc., have at first an acosmic meaning, but, of course, were given a deeper sense by Augustine.

[2] Augustine never lost his optimistic joy in life in the sense of the true life, as is proved in his work, De civit. dei ; but in contrasting the moods caused by contem-plation of the world—æsthetic joy in the Cosmus, and sorrow over the world per-verted by sin—the latter prevailed. Existence never became to Augustine a torment in itself, but that existence did which condemned itself to not-being, bringing about its own ruin.

[3] Where Augustine put the question of creation in the form, " How is the unity of being related to plurality of manifestation ? " the notion of creation is really always eliminated. But he never entirely gave up this way of putting the question ; for, at bottom, things possess their independence only in their manifestation, while, in so far as they *exist*, they form the ground of knowledge for the existence of God. But besides this, Augustine still asserted vigorously the *creatio ex nihilo* (" omnes naturæ ex deo, non de deo," De nat. bon. c. Manich., I.). See note 4, p. 120.

[4] He discovered these, and inspired hundreds of mystics after him. We have no right to deny that this contemplative view of being, not-being, and the harmony of being evolving itself in the phenomenal, is also a sphere of piety.

goods, *being*, and he could harmonise this desire excellently
with his Neoplatonic doctrine. He farther found the desire to
obtain an ever higher happiness, and ever loftier forms of good,
an inexhaustible and noble longing, and this discovery also
agreed with the doctrine. Unrest, hunger and thirst for God,
horror and disgust at the enjoyment of lower kinds of good,
were not to be stifled ; for the soul, *so far as it exists*, comes
certainly from God, and belongs to Him (ex deo and ad deum).
But now he discovered a dreadful fact : *the will, as a matter of
fact, would not what it would, or at least seemed to will.* No, it
was no seeming ; it was the most dreadful of paradoxes ; we
will to come to God, and we cannot, *i.e.*, we will not.[1] Augustine
felt this state along with the whole weight of responsibility; that
responsibility was never lessened for him by the view that the
will in not seeking God was seeking nothing, that it therefore by
self-will was properly "annulling itself until it no longer existed."
Nor was it mitigated for him by the correlative consideration, that
the individual will, ruled by its desire, was not free. Rather,
from the dread sense of responsibility, God appeared as *the good*,

1 We have the most profound description of this state in Confess. VIII. 17-26 ;
Augustine calls it a "monstrum" (monstrous phenomenon). He solves the problem
disclosed, in so far as it is capable of solution, not by an appeal to the enslaved will,
accordingly not by the "non possumus," but as an indeterminist by the reflection,
"non ex toto volumus, non ergo ex toto [nobis] imperamus." (21), "I was
afraid that Thou mightest soon hear me, and heal me of the sickness of lust, whose
satisfaction I wished more than its eradication. . . . And I was deluded, therefore I
put off following Thee alone from day to day, because I had not yet seen any certain
aim for my striving. And now the day was at hand, and the voice of my conscience
exhorted me : 'Didst thou not say thou wouldst not cast the vain burden from
thee, only because the truth was still uncertain ? *Behold now thou art certain of the
truth*, but (thou wilt not).' . . . The way to union with God, and the attainment of
the goal, *coincide with the will to reach this goal*, though, indeed, only with the
determined and pure will. . . . And thus during this inner fever and irresoluteness I
was wont to make many movements with my body, which can only be performed
when the will makes definite resolves, and become impossible if the corresponding
limbs are wanting, or are fettered, worn out, asleep, or hindered in any way. If,
e.g., I tore a hair out, beat my brow, or embraced my knee with folded hands, I did
it because I willed it. But I might have willed and not done it, if the power of
motion in my limbs had forsaken me. So many things, then, I did in a sphere,
where to will was not the same as to be able. And yet I did not that which both I
longed incomparably more to do, and which I could do whenever I really earnestly
willed it ; *because, as soon as I had willed it, I had really already made it mine in
willing. For in these things the ability was one with the will, and really to resolve*

and the self-seeking life of impulse, which determined the will and gave its motive, constituted *evil*. The "summum bonum" now first obtained its deeper meaning—it was no longer merely the permanent resting point for disturbed thinkers, or the exhilarating enjoyment of life for jaded mortals : it now meant *that which ought to be*,[1] that which should be the fundamental motive ruling the will, should give the will its liberty, and therewith for the first time its power over the sphere of the natural, freeing the inexhaustible longing of man for the good from the dire necessity of sinning (misera necessitas peccandi), and accordingly first making that innate longing effectual. In a word, it now meant *the good*. And thus the notion of the good itself was divested of all accretions from the intellect, and all eudaimonist husks and wrappings. In this contemplation that overpowered him, the sole object was *the good will*, the moral imperative vitalised, to renounce selfish pleasure. But at the same time he acquired the experience which he himself could not analyse, which no thinker will undertake to analyse, that this good laid hold of him as love, and snatched him from

---

was to do. And yet, in my case, it was not done ; and more readily did my body obey the weakest willing of my soul, in moving its limbs at its nod, *than the soul obeyed itself where it was called upon to realise its great desire by a simple effort of the will.* How is such a prodigy possible, and what is its reason ? The soul commands the body, and it obeys instantly ; the soul commands itself, and is resisted. The soul commands the hand to be moved, and it is done so promptly that command and performance can scarcely be distinguished ; and yet the soul is spirit, but the hand is a member of the body. The soul commands the soul itself to an act of will ; it is its own command, yet it does not carry it out. How is such a prodigy possible, and what is its reason ? The soul commands an act of will, I say ; *its command consists simply in willing;* and yet that command is not carried out. *Sed non ex toto vult ; non ergo ex toto imperat.* Nam in tantum imperat, in quantum vult, et in tantum non fit quod imperat, in quantum non vult. Quoniam voluntas imperat ut sit voluntas, nec alia sed ipsa. *Non itaque plena imperat ideo non est quod imperat. Nam si plena esset, nec imperaret ut esset, quia jam esset.* Non igitur monstrum partim velle, partim nolle, sed ægritudo animi est, quia non totus assurgit, veritate sublevatus, consuetudine prægravatus. Et ideo sunt duæ voluntates, quia una earum tota non est, et hoc adest alteri quod deest alteri."

1 "What ought to be ? How cannot the inner nature exhibit itself by reflection, but can by action?" (Scipio, Metaphysik des Aug., p. 7.) Augustine was the first to put this question clearly. "Antiquity conceived the whole of life, we might say, in a naive fashion from the standpoint of *science :* the spiritual appeared as natural, and virtue as a natural force.

the misery of the monstrous inconsistency of existence.[1]
Thereby the notion of God received a wholly new content:
the good which could do that was omnipotent. In the *one act* of
liberation was given the identity of omnipotent being and the
good, *the summum ὄν (supreme being) was holiness working on the
will in the form of omnipotent love.* This was what Augustine
felt and described. A stream of divine conceptions was now
set loose, partly given in the old language, but with a meaning
felt for the first time, wonderfully combined with the statement
of the philosophical knowledge of God, but regulating and
transforming it. The Supreme Being (summum esse) is the
Supreme Good ; He is a *person ;* the ontological defect of
creaturely being becomes the moral defect of godlessness of
will ; evil is here as there negative ;[2] but in the former case it
is the negation of substance (privatio substantiæ), in the
latter that of good (privatio boni), meaning the defect
arising from freedom. The good indeed still remains

---

[1] Augustine indeed could further explain why the form, in which the good takes
possession of and delivers the soul, must consist in the infusion of love. So long as
the soul along with its will is confronted by duty (an ought), and commands itself to
obey, it has not completely appropriated the good ; "nam si plena esset, nec
imperaret ut esset, quia jam esset" (Confess. VIII. 21). Accordingly, the fact that
it admits the duty, does not yet create an effective will *ex toto.* It must accordingly
so love what it ought, that it no longer needs command itself ; nay, duty (the
ought) must be its only love ; only then is it *plena in voluntate bona.* The "abyssus
corruptionis nostræ" is only exhausted when by love we "totum illud, quod vole-
bamus nolumus et totum illud, quod deus vult, volumus (Confess. IX. 1).

[2] Confess. VII. 18 : "Malum si substantia esset, bonum esset. Aut enim esset
incorruptibilis substantia, magnum utique bonum ; aut substantia corruptibilis esset,
quæ nisi bona esset, corrumpi non posset." But since evil thus always exists in a
good substance (more accurately : springs from the bad will of the good substance),
it is absolutely inexplicable ; see *e.g.,* De civitat. dei, XII. 7 : "Nemo igitur quærat
efficientem causam malæ voluntatis ; non enim est efficiens sed deficiens (that is, the
aspiration after nothing, after the annulling of life, constitutes the content of the bad
will), quia nec illa effectio sed defectio. Deficere namque ab eo, quod summe est, ad
id, quod minus est, hoc est incipere habere voluntatem malam. Causas porro
defectionum istarum, cum efficientes non sint, ut dixi, sed deficientes, velle invenire
tale est, ac si quisquam velit videre tenebras vel audire silentium, quod tamen utrumque nobis notum est, neque illud nisi per oculos, neque hoc nisi per aures, non sane
in specie, sed in speciei privatione. Nemo ergo ex me scire quærat, quod me nescire
scio, nisi forte, ut nescire discat, quod scire non posse sciendum est. Ea quippe
quæ non in specie, sed in ejus privatione sciuntur, si dici aut intelligi potest
quodammodo nesciendo sciuntur, ut sciendo nesciantur."

the divine being as fulness of life; but for man it is summed up in the "common morality" which issues from the divine being and divine love. That is, he cannot appropriate it save in the will, which gladly forsakes its old nature, and loves that which dwells above all that is sensuous and selfish. *Nothing is good except a good will:* this principle was most closely combined by Augustine with the other: *nothing is good but God;* and love became for him the middle term. For the last and highest point reached in his knowledge was his combination of the thought that "all substance was from God" (omnis substantia a deo) with the other that "all good was" from God (omne bonum a deo). The conception of God as universal and sole worker, shaded into the other that God, just because he is God and source of all being, is also the only author and source of good in the form of self-imparting love.[1] *It belongs just as essentially to God to be grace (gratia) imparting itself in love, as to be the uncaused cause of causes* (causa causatrix non causata). If we express this anthropologically: goodness does not make man independent of God— that was the old conception—but in goodness the constant natural dependence of all his creatures on God finds expression as a *willed* dependence securing the existence of the creaturely spirit. The latter only exists in yielding himself, only lives in dying, is only free when he suffers himself to be entirely ruled by God, is only good if his will is God's will. These are the grand paradoxes with which he contrasted the "monstrous" paradoxes discussed above. But meanwhile there is no mistake that the metaphysical background everywhere shows in the ethical view; it is seen, first, in the ascetic trait which clings to

---

[1] Augustine says of love (De civ. XI. 28), that we not only love its objects, but itself. "Amor amatur, et hinc probamus, quod in hominibus, qui rectius amantur, ipse magis amatur." This observation led him to see God everywhere in love. As God is in all being, so is he also in love; nay, his existence in being is ultimately identical with his existence in love. Therefore love is beginning, middle, and end. It is the final object of theological thought, and the fundamental form of true spiritual life. "Caritas inchoata inchoata justitia est; caritas provecta provecta justitia est; caritas magna magna justitia est; caritas perfecta perfecta justitia est" (De nat. et grat. 84). But since in life in general voluntas = caritas (De trin. XV. 38): "quid est aliud caritas quam voluntas?", we here find once more the profound connection between ethics and psychology.

the notion of the good in spite of its simple form (joy in God);
secondly, in uncertainty as to the notion of love, into which an
intellectual element still enters ; thirdly, in the conception of
grace (gratia), which appears not infrequently as the almost
natural mode of the divine existence.

The instruction how to hold communion with God displays
still more clearly the interweaving of metaphysical and ethical
views, that wonderful oscillation, hesitancy, and wavering between the intellectual and that which lives and is experienced
in the depths of the soul.[1] On the one hand, it is required to
enjoy God ; nay, he is the only " thing " (res) which may be
enjoyed, all else may only be used. But to enjoy means " to
cling to anything by love for its own sake " (alicui rei amore
inhærere propter se ipsam ").[2] God is *steadfastly* to be enjoyed
—the Neoplatonists are reproached with not reaching this.[3]
This enjoying is inseparably connected with the thought of
God's " beauty," and in turn with the sense that he is all in all
and indescribable.[4] But, on the other hand, Augustine thrust

---

[1] Augustine's ability to unite the Neoplatonic ontological speculation with the
results of his examination of the practical spiritual life was due *inter alia* especially
to his complete abstinence, in the former case, from accepting ritualistic elements, or
from introducing into his speculation matter taken from the Cultus and the religion
of the second order. If at first the stage of spiritual development which he occupied
(when outside the Church), of itself protected him from admitting these deleterious
elements, yet it was a conspicuous and hitherto unappreciated side of his greatness
that he always kept clear of ritualistic mysticism. Thereby he rendered an invaluable
service not only to his disciples in mysticism, but to the whole Western Church.

[2] De doctr. christ., I., 3 sq.

[3] See Confess., VII. 24 : " et qæerebam viam comparandi roboris quod esset
idoneum ad fruendum te, etc.," 26 : " certus quidem in istis eram, nimis tamen in-
firmus ad fruendum te."

[4] Augustine has often repeated the old Platonic assertion of the impossibility of de-
fining the nature of God, and that not always with a feeling of dissatisfaction, but as
an expression of romantic satisfaction (" ineffabilis simplex natura " ; "facilius dicimus
quid non sit, quam quod sit "). He contributed much, besides, to the relative elucidation of negative definitions and of properties and accidents, and created scholastic
terminology ; see especially De trinit., XV. He is the father of Western theological
dialectic ; but also the inventor of the dialectic of the pious consciousness. From the
anti-Manichæan controversy sprang the desire to conceive all God's separate attributes
as identical, *i.e.*, the interest in the indivisibility of God—God is essence, not substance ; for the latter cannot be thought of without accidents ; see De trinit., VII.,
10 ; and this interest went so far as to hold that even *habere* and *esse* coincided in
God (De civ., XI. 10 : " ideo simplex dicitur quoniam quod habet hoc est "). In

aside the thought that God was a substance (res) in the interest
of a living communion with him.   God was a person, and in
the phrase " to cleave by love " ("amore inhærere ") the emphasis falls in that case on the love (amor) which rests on faith

order to guard God from *corruptibilitas*, compositeness of any sort was denied.   But,
at this point, Augustine had, nevertheless, to make a distinction in God, in order to
discriminate the divine world-plan from him, and not to fall completely into Pantheism.   (The latter is stamped on many passages in the work De trinit., see *e.g.*,
IV., 3, " Quia unum verbum dei est, per quod facta sunt omnia, quod est incommutabilis veritas, ibi principaliter atque incommutabiliter sunt omnia simul, et omnia
vita sunt et omnia unum sunt.")   But since he always harked to the conviction that
being, and wisdom, and goodness, are identical in God, he did not reach what he
aimed at.   This difficulty increased still further for him, where he combined speculation as to the nature of God with that regarding the Trinity.   (Dorner, p. 22 ff.)
It is seen most clearly in the doctrine of the divine world-plan.   It always threatens
to submerge the world in the Son as a unity, and to take away its difference (it is
wrong, however—at least for the period after c., A.D. 400—to say conversely that
the intelligible world is for Augustine identical with the Son, or is the Son).   The
vacillation is continued in the doctrine of creation.   But Dorner (p. 40 f.) is wrong
when he says : " Augustine had no conception as yet that the notion of causality,
clearly conceived, is sufficient to establish the distinction between God and the world."
Augustine had undoubtedly no such conception, but this time it is not he, but Dorner,
who shows his simplicity.   The notion of causality, " clearly conceived," can never
establish a distinction, but only a transformation.   If he had meant to give expression
to the former, he required to introduce more into the cause than the effect ; that is,
it was necessary to furnish the cause with properties and powers which did not pass
into the *causatum* (effect).   But this already means that the scheme of cause and
effect is inadequate to establish the difference.   Augustine, certainly, had no clear
conception of such a thing ; but he felt that mere causality was useless.   He adopted
the expedient of calling in "nihil " (nothing) to his aid, the negation : *God works in
nothing*.   This "nothing" was the cause of the world not being a transformation
or evolution of God, but of its appearing as an inferior or irridescent product, which,
because it is a *divina operatio*, exists (yet not independently of God), and which, so
far as independent, does not exist, since its independence resides in the *nihil*.   The
sentence " mundus de nihilo a deo factus "—the root principle of Augustinian cosmology—is ultimately to be taken dualistically ; but the dualism is concealed by the
second element consisting in negation, and therefore only revealing itself in the
privative form (of mutability, transitoriness).   But in the end the purely negative
character of the second element cannot be absolutely retained (Augustine never, certainly, identified it with matter); it purported to be absolute impotence, but combined with the divine activity it became the resisting factor, and we know how it does
resist in sin.   Accordingly, the question most fatal to Augustine would have been :
Who created this nothing ?   As a matter of fact this question breaks down the whole
construction.   Absurd as it sounds, it is justified.   Augustine cannot explain negation
with its determinative power existing side by side with the *divina operatio;* for it is
no explanation to say that it did not exist at all, since it merely had negative effects.

(fides), and includes hope (spes). "God to be worshipped with faith, hope, and love ("Fide, spe, caritate colendum deum").[1] Augustine was so strongly possessed by the feeling, never, indeed, clearly formulated, that *God is a person* whom we must trust and love, that this conviction was even a latent standard in his Trinitarian speculations.[2] Faith, hope, and love had, in that case, however, nothing further to do with "freedom" in the proper sense of the word. They were God's *gifts*, and constituted a spiritual relation to Him, from which sprang good resolves (bonum velle) and righteousness (justitia). But, indeed, whenever Augustine looked from this life to eternal life, the possession of faith, love, and hope assumed a temporary aspect. "But when the mind has been imbued with the commencement of faith which works by love, it aspires by a good life to reach the manifestation in which holy and perfect hearts perceive *the ineffable beauty whose complete vision is the highest felicity.* This is surely what thou requirest, 'what is to be esteemed the first and the last thing,' *to begin with faith, to be perfected in sight*" (Enchir. 5 ; see De doctr., II. 34 sq.).[3] Certain as it is that the Neoplatonic tendency comes out in this, it is as certain that we have more than a mere "remnant of mystical natural religion"; for the feeling that "presses upward and forward" from the faith in what is not seen, to the

---

Yet theory, sometimes acosmic, sometimes dualistic, in form, is everywhere corrected in Augustine, whether by the expression of a wise nescience, or by faith in God as Father. The criticism here used has been attacked by Loofs (R.-Encypl. 3, Vol. II., p. 271). We have to admit that it goes more deeply into the reason of his views than Augustine's words require. But I do not believe that the statement given by Loofs is adequate : "God so created his creatures from nothing that some are less fair, less good than others, and, therefore, have less being (esse)." Could Augustine have actually contented himself with these facts without asking whence this "less"?

[1] Enchirid. 3.

[2] See Vol. IV., p. 129 ff. I do not enter further into the doctrine of the Trinity, but remark that the term "tres personæ" was very fatal to Augustine, and that all his original efforts in dealing with the Trinity lead away from cosmical and hypercosmical plurality to conceptions that make it express inner, spiritual self-movement in the *one* God.

[3] Cum autem initio fidei quæ per dilectionem operatur imbuta mens fuerit, tendit bene vivendo etiam ad *speciem* pervenire, ubi est sanctis et perfectis cordibus nota *ineffabilis pulchritudo, cujus plena visio est summa felicitas.* Hoc est nimirum quod requiris, "quid primum, quid ultimum teneatur," *inchoari fide, perfici specie.*

seeing of what is believed, is not only the innate germ of religion, but its enduring stimulus.[1] The idea of the world sketched from contemplation of the inner life and the sense of responsibility, which was combined with that of metaphysical cosmological speculation, led finally to a wholly different state of feeling from the latter. The optimism founded on æsthetics vanished before the " monstrum " of humanity which, infirm of will,[2] willed not and did not what at bottom it desired, and fell into the abyss of perdition. They are only a few who suffer themselves to be saved by grace. The mass is a *massa perditionis*, which death allures. "Woe is thee, thou torrent of human custom! Who shall stop thy course? How long will it be before thou art dried up? and whom wilt thou, O offspring of Eve, roll into the huge and hideous ocean, which even they

---

[1] We may here touch briefly on the question several times recently discussed, as to the supremacy of the will in Augustine. Kahl has maintained it. But Siebeck (l.c. 183 f.) has with reason rejected it ; (see also my notice of Kahl's book in the ThLZ., 1886, No. 25) ; and Kahl has himself to admit " that at the last stage of knowledge Neoplatonic intellectualism, which explains volition away in view of thought, has frequently traversed the logical consequences of Augustine's standpoint." But it is just the last stage that decides. On the other hand, Kahl is quite right in appreciating so highly the importance of the will in Augustine. The kernel of our nature exists indisputably according to Augustine in our will ; therefore, in order that the *veritas*, the *scire deum et animam* may be able to obtain supremacy, and become, as it were, the unique function of man, the will must be won on its behalf. This takes place through God's grace, which leads the soul to will and love spiritual truth, *i.e.*, God. Only now is it rendered possible for the intellect to assume supremacy. *Accordingly the freeing of the will is ultimately the substitution of the supremacy of the intellect for that of the will.* (Compare, *e.g.*, the passage Confess. IX. 24 : " regio ubertatis indeficientis, ubi pascis Israel in æternum veritatis pabulo, *et ubi vita sapientia est* "; but for this life it holds true that " sapientia hominis pietas.") Yet in so far as the supremacy of the intellect could not maintain itself without the *amor essendi et sciendi*, the will remains the co-efficient of the intellect even in the highest sphere. That is, briefly, Augustine's view of the relation of the will and intellect. It explains why the return to Augustine in the Middle Ages brought about the complete subordination of the intellect to the will ; for Augustine himself so presented the case that no inner state and no activity of thought existed apart from the will. But if that were so, Augustine's opinion, that the vision (visio) of God was the supreme goal, could not but in the end pass away. It was necessary to demonstrate a goal which corresponded to the assured fact that man was will (see Duns Scotus).

[2] See De civit. dei, XIV. 3 sq. ; it is not the body (sensuousness) that is the ultimate cause of sin.

scarcely overpass who have climbed the tree [the Church]?"[1]
The misery of the earth is unspeakable ; whatever moves and
cherishes an independent life upon it is its own punishment;
for he who decreed sins (the ordinator peccatorum) has
ordained that every sin judges itself, that every unregulated
spirit is its own punishment. [2]

But from the beginning the historical Christian tradition
penetrated with its influence the sequence of thoughts (on
nature and grace), which the pious thinker had derived from his
speculations on nature and his spiritual experience. Brought
up from boyhood as a Catholic Christian, he has himself confessed that nothing ever satisfied him which did not bear the
name of Christ.[3] The description of the years when he
wandered in doubt is traversed as with a scarlet cord by the
bond that united him with Christ. Without many words,
indeed with a modest reserve, he recalls in the Confessions the
relation to Christ that had never died out in him, until in VII.
24 f., he can emphasise it strongly. We cannot doubt that even
those expositions of his which are apparently indifferent to the
Church traditions of Christianity—on the living personal God,
the distinction between God and the world, on God as Creator,
on grace as the omnipotent principle—were already influenced
by that tradition. And we must remember that his intense
study of Paul and the Psalms began whenever, having broken

---

[1] Confess. I. 25 : Væ tibi flumen moris humani ? quis resistet tibi ? quamdiu non
siccaberis ? quosque volves Evæ filius in mare magnum et formidolosum, quod vix
transeunt qui lignum [ecclesiam] conscenderint ?

[2] There is a wonderful contrast in Augustine between the profound pessimistic view
of the world, and the conception, strictly held in theory, that everything takes place
under the uniform and unchangeable activity of God. What a difference between
the statement of the problem and the result ! And in order to remove this difference
the metaphysician refers us to the—nothing. The course of the world is so confidently regarded as caused in whole and in detail by God, nay, is, as it were, taken
up into the unchangeableness of God himself, that even miracles are only conceived
to be events contrary to nature as known to us (Genes. ad lit. VI. 13 ; cf. De civ.
X. 12 ; XXI. 1-8 ; nothing happens against nature ; the world is itself the greatest,
nay, the sole miracle ; see Nitzsch, Aug's Lehre v. Wunder, 1865 ; Dorner, p. 71 f.),
and yet everything shapes itself into a vast tragedy. In this nothing there still indeed
lurks in Augustine a part of Manichæism ; but in his vital view of the world it is not
the " nothing " which plays a part, but the sin of wicked pleasure—self-will.

[3] Confess. III. 8 ; V. 25 ; etc.

with Manichæism, he had been convinced by Neoplatonism that God was a spiritual substance (spiritalis substantia). Even the expositions in the earliest writings which are apparently purely philosophical, were already dominated by the Christian conviction that God, the world, and the Ego were to be distinguished, and that room was to be made for the distinction in mystical speculation. Further, all attempts to break through the iron scheme of God's unchangeableness (in his active presence in the world) are to be explained from the impression made by Christian history upon Augustine.

However, we cannot here take in hand to show how Christ and the Church gradually obtained a fixed fundamental position in his mode of thought. His reply to Laurentius in the Enchiridion, that " Christ is the sure and peculiar foundation of the Catholic faith," (certum propriumque fidei catholicæ fundamentum Christus est), would have been made in the same terms many years before, and, indeed, though his conceptions of Christ were then still uncertain, as early as about A.D. 387.[1] *Christ, the way, strength, and authority,* explained for him the significance of Christ. It is very noteworthy that in the Confessions VII., 24 sq., and other passages where he brings the Christian religion into the question as to the first and last things, he does not produce general theories about revelation, but at once gives the central place to Christ and the Church.[2] The

---

[1] See the avowals in Confess. VII. 25.

[2] Naturally, general investigations are not wanting of the nature of revelation as a whole, its relation to *ratio*, its stages (punishment of sin, law, prophecy), etc., but they have no secure connection with his dogmatics ; they are dependant on the occasions that called them forth, and they are not clearly thought out. In any case, however, so many elements are found in them which connect them with Greek speculations, and in turn others which exerted a powerful influence at a later date (see Abelard), that one or two references are necessary (cf. Schmidt, Origenes and Aug. als Apologeten in the Jahrbb. f. deutsche Theol. VIII.; Böhringer, p. 204 ff.; Reuter, p. 90 f., 350 ff., 400). Augustine occupies himself here, as always, with a problem whose factors ultimately do not admit of being reconciled. On the one hand, he never gave up the lofty appreciation of reason (ratio), of independent knowledge, in which being and life are embraced. Originally (in his first period, after A.D. 386), although he had already seen the importance of *auctoritas*, he set up as the goal of the *ratio* the overcoming of *auctoritas*, which required to precede it only *for a time* (De ord. II., 26, 27). " Ratio was to him the organ in which God reveals himself to man, and in which man perceives God." *In after times this thought was*

two decisive principles on which he laid stress were that the
Catholic Church alone introduces us into communion with
Christ, and that it is only through communion with Christ
that we participate in God's grace. That is, *he is only*

never given up ; but it was limited by the distinction between subjective and objective
reason, by the increasing perception of the extent of the influence exerted on human
reason by the will, by the assumption that one consequence of original sin was ignorance, and, finally, by the view that while knowledge, due to faith, would always be
uncertain here below, the soul longed after the real, *i.e.*, the absolute and absolutely
sure, knowledge. The latter alone superseded *ratio* as the organ by which God is
known, as guide to the *vita beata ;* the other limitations were limitations pure and
simple. And the constancy with which, in spite of these, Augustine *at all times*
valued *ratio* is proved by those striking expositions, which occur in his earliest and
latest writings, *of Christianity as the disclosure of the one* true religion which had
always existed. The whole work De civitate dei is, indeed, built upon this thought
—the *civitas dei* not being first created by the appearance of Christ—which, indeed,
has two other roots besides Rationalism, namely, the conception of the absolute
immutability of God, and the intention to defend Christianity and its God against
Neoplatonic and pagan attacks. (The first two roots, as can be easily shown, are
reducible ultimately to one single conception. The apologetic idea is of quite a
different kind. Christianity is held to be as old as the world, in order that the reproach of its late arrival may fall to the ground. Here the wholly incongruous idea
is introduced that Christians before Christ had believed on his future appearance.
Reuter has shown excellently (p. 90 ff.) how even the particularist doctrine of predestination has its share in the universalist and humanist conception ; he also deserves
the greatest gratitude for collecting the numerous passages in which that conception
is elaborated.) Even before the appearance of Christ the *civitas dei* existed ; to it belonged pagans and Jews. Christianity is as old as the world. It is the natural religion
which has existed from the beginning under various forms and names. Through Christ
it received the *name* of the Christian religion ; " res ipsa quæ nunc Christiana religio
nuncupatur, erat apud antiquos, nec defuit ab initio generis humani, quousque ipse Christus venit in carne, unde vera religio, quæ jam erat, cœpit appellari Christiana " (Retract.
I., 12, 3) ; see especially Ep. 102 and De civit. XVIII., 47, where the incongruous
thought is inserted that the *unus mediator* was revealed to the heathens who belonged to
the heavenly Jerusalem in the earliest time. The latter idea is by no means inserted
everywhere ; there was rather up to the end of his life, in spite and because of his
doctrine of particular predestinating grace, an undercurrent in Augustine's thought :
co-ordinating God and free knowledge, he recognised behind the system of the
Church a free science, and in accordance therewith conceived also God and the
world to be the abiding objects of knowledge. With this idea, however, as in
the case of Origen, Christ at once disappears. The ultimate reason of this consists
in the fact that Augustine, with all his progress in knowledge, *never advanced to
history*. The great psychologist was still blind to the nature of historical development, to what personality achieved in history, and what history had accomplished
for mankind. He had only two methods of observation at his disposal—either the
mythological contemplation of history, or a rationalistic neutralising. The man who
felt so clearly and testified so convincingly that freedom lay in the change of will

*certain of the speculative conception of the idea of the good, and its
real activity as love when it is proclaimed authoritatively by the
Church and supported by the conception of Christ.*
By the *conception formed of Christ.* Here a new element

when it received a strength binding us to the good, was yet incapable as a thinker of
drawing clearly the consequences of this experience.   But those should not blame
him who cannot free themselves from the illusion that an absolute knowledge of
some sort must be possible to man ; for the effort to obtain such a knowledge
is the ultimate cause of the inability to understand history as history. He
who is only happy with absolute knowledge is either blind to history, or it
becomes a Medusa's head to him.   Yet rationalism is only the undercurrent, though
here and there it does force its way to the surface.   More surely and more constantly
Augustine appeased with revelation his hunger for the absolute, which he was unable
to distinguish from aiming at force and strength (God and goodness).   His feelings
were the same as Faust's : "We long for revelation."   Now, it is very characteristic
that in dealing with the notion of revelation, Augustine has expounded nothing more
clearly than the thought that revelation is *absolutely authoritative.*   We can leave out
of account his other views on its necessity, nature, etc.   The decisive fact for him is
that revelation does not merely recommend itself by its intrinsic worth.   Accordingly,
the *external attestation* is the main point.   Augustine discussed this (especially in his
work De civit.) much more carefully and comprehensively than earlier Apologists,
in order to establish the right to demand *simple submission to the contents of revelation.*
Auctoritas and *fides* were inseparably connected ; indeed, they occupied an almost
exclusive relation to each other (see De util. cred., 25 sq.).   We indeed find him
explaining in his writings of all periods that authority is milk-food, and that, on the
other hand, the demand in matters of religion for faith resting on authority is not
exceptional, but that all the affairs of life of a deeper nature rest on such a faith.   But
these are simply sops to Cerberus.   *Man needs authority to discipline his mind, and to
support a certainty not to be obtained elsewhere.*   Augustine was especially convinced
of this as against heretics (Manichæans).   Heathens he could refute to a certain
extent from reason, heretics he could not.   But even apart from this, since the
power which binds the will to God presented itself to him as the rock-fast conviction
of the unseen, even the "strong" could not dispense with faith in authority.   The
gradual progress from faith to knowledge, which was well-known to him ("Every
one who knows also believes, although not every one who believes knows,") was still
a progress constantly accompanied by faith.   The saying, "fides præcedit rationem,"
of which he has given so many variations (see *e.g.*, Ep. 120, 2 sq.: "fides præcedit
rationem," or paradoxically : "rationabiliter visum est, ut fides præcedat rationem,")
did not signify a suspension of faith at the higher stages.   Or, rather, and here the *Sic
et Non* holds good, Augustine was never clear about the relation of faith and
knowledge ; he handed over this problem to the future.   On the one hand he trusted
ratio ; but, on the other hand, he did not, relying only on God, and his Genius ruling
in experience.   Faith's authority was given for him in Scripture and the Church.
But here, again, he only maintained and transmitted the disposition to obey, while
his theoretical expositions are beset by sheer contradictions and ambiguities ; for he
has neither worked out the sufficiency, infallibility, and independence of Scripture,
nor demonstrated the infallibility of the Church, nor defined the relation of Scripture

entered. Augustine supported, times without number, the old
Western scheme of the twofold nature (utraque natura), the
word and man one person (verbum et homo una persona)—
(we may leave unnoticed the rare, inaccurate expressions
"permixtio," "mixtura," *e.g.* Ep. 137, 11, 12), the form of
God and form of a slave, and he contributed much to fortify
this scheme in the West with its sharply defined division
between what was done by the human, and what by the
divine. But the unusual energy with which he rejected
Apollinarianism—from his earliest to his latest writings—is
enough to show *that his deepest interest centred in the human
soul of Jesus.* The passages are extremely rare in which he
adopts the same interpretation as Cyril of the confession : "the
Word became flesh," and the doctrine of the deification of all
human nature by the Incarnation is not represented, or, at any
rate, only extremely doubtfully represented, by him. (Passages
referring to it are not wholly awanting, but they are extremely
rare.) He rather explains the incarnation of the Word from
another point of view, and accordingly, though he has points of
contact with Origen, he describes it quite differently from the
Greeks. Starting from the speculative consideration, to him a
certainty, that it is always the whole Trinity that acts, and that
its operation is absolutely invariable, the Incarnation was also a
work of the whole Trinity. The Trinity produced the manifestation held to signify the Son (De trin. in many places). The
Word (verbum) was not really more closely related than the

and the Church. Sometimes Scripture is a court of appeal which owes its authority
to the Church, sometimes the Church doctrine and all *consuetudo* are to be measured
by Scripture (Scripture is the only source of *doctrina Christiana*), sometimes Church
and Scripture are held to constitute one whole ; in one place the Church seems to
find in the Council its infallible mouthpiece, in the other, the perfectibility of Councils
themselves is maintained. "The idea of the Church's infallibility belongs to
Augustine's popular Catholic presuppositions which grew out of his Catholic faith.
It was never directly or expressly expounded by him, or dogmatically discussed.
Therefore he cannot have felt the necessity of adjusting an exhaustive or precise
doctrine regarding the legitimate form of the supreme representation of the Church
by supposition infallible. This uncertainty and vagueness perhaps " (rather, indisputably) "spring from the vacillations of his thought regarding authority and reason,
faith and knowledge " (see Reuter, pp. 345-358 ; Böhringer, pp. 217-256 ; Dorner, pp.
233-244 ; further, above pp. 77-83, and Vol. III., p. 203 ff.).

whole Trinity to the Son.   But since the Trinity could not act upon Jesus except as it always did, *the uniqueness and power of the Person of Jesus Christ were to be derived from the receptiveness with which the man Jesus met the operatio divina;* in other words, Augustine started from the human nature (soul) in his construction of the God-man.   The human nature received the Word into its spirit ; the human soul, because it acted as intermediary (medians), was also the centre of the God-man. Accordingly, the Word did not *become* flesh, if that be taken to mean that a transformation of any sort took place, but the *divina operatio trinitatis* could so work upon the human spirit of Jesus, that the Word was permanently attached to him, and was united with him to form one person.[1]   This receptiveness of Jesus was, as in all other cases, caused by the election of grace ; it was a gift of God (munus dei), an incomprehensible act of divine grace ; nay, it was the same divine grace that forgives us our sins which led the man Jesus to form one person with the Word and made him sinless.   The Incarnation thus appeared simply to be parallel to the grace which makes us willing who were unwilling, and is independent of every historical fact.[2]

---

[1] The figure often used by Augustine that the Word was united with the man Jesus as our souls are with our bodies is absolutely unsuitable.   Augustine borrowed it from antiquity without realising that it really conflicted with his own conception.

[2] Enchir., 36 : "Hic omnino granditer et evidenter dei gratia commendatur. Quid enim natura humana in homine Christi meruit ut in unitatem personæ unici filii dei singulariter esset assumpta!   Quæ bona voluntas, cujus boni propositi studium, quæ bona opera præcesserunt, quibus mereretur iste homo una fieri persona cum deo? Numquid antea fuit homo, et hoc ei singulare beneficium præstitum est, cum singulariter promereretur deum?   Nempe ex quo homo esse cœpit. non aliud cœpit esse homo quam dei filius : et hoc unicus, et propter deum verbum, quod illo suscepto caro factum est, utique deus. . . .   Unde naturæ humanæ tanta gloria, nullis præcedentibus meritis sine dubitatione gratuita, nisi quia magna hic et sola dei gratia fideliter et sobrie considerantibus evidenter ostenditur, *ut intellegant homines per eandem gratiam se justificari a peccatis, per quam factum est ut homo Christus nullum habere posset peccatum.*"   40 : "Natus Christus insinuat nobis gratiam dei, qua homo nullis præcedentibus meritis in ipso exordio naturæ suæ quo esse cœpit, verbo deo copularetur in tantam personæ unitatem, ut idem ipse esset filius dei qui filius hominis, etc." De dono persev., 67.   Op. imperf., I., 138 : "Qua gratia homo Jesus ab initio factus est bonus, eadem gratia homines qui sunt membra ejus ex malis fiunt boni." De prædest. 30 : "Est etiam præclarissimum lumen prædestinationis et gratiæ ipse salvator, ipse mediator dei et hominum homo Christus Jesus, qui ut hoc esset, quibus

But it was not so meant. While, indeed, it is here again
evident, that the conception of the divine grace in Christ
was, at bottom, subordinate to predestinating grace, and
that the latter was independent of the former,[1] yet Augustine
by no means confined himself to dealing with the ultimate
grounds of his conceptions. Rather the Incarnation benefited
us; the salvation bestowed was dependent on it for us "who
are his members" (qui sumus membra ejus).[2] But how far?
Where Augustine speaks as a Churchman, he thinks of the
sacraments, the powers of faith, forgiveness and love, which
were the inheritance left the Church by the God-man (see
under). But where he expresses the living Christian piety
which actuated him, he had three wholly distinct conceptions by which he realised that Christ, the God-man,
was the rock of his faith.[3] The Incarnation was the great

tandem suis vel operum vel fidei præcedentibus meritis natura humana quæ in illo est
comparavit? . . . Singulariter nostra natura in Jesu nullis suis præcedentibus meritis accepit admiranda (*scil.* the union with deity). Respondeat hic homo deo, si
audet, et dicat : Cur non et ego? Et si audierit : O homo, tu quis es qui respondeas
deo, etc." De corrept. et grat. 30 : "Deus naturam nostram id est animam rationalem carnemque hominis Christi suscepit, susceptione singulariter mirabili vel mirabiliter singulari, ut nullis justitiæ suæ præcedentibus meritis filius dei sic esset ab initio
quo esse homo cœpisset, ut ipse et verbum, quod sine initio est, una persona esset."
De pecc. mer. II. 27. Augustine says in Confess. VII. 25 : "Ego autem aliquanto posterius didicisse me fateor. in eo quod verbum caro factum est, quomodo
catholica veritas a Photini falsitate dirimatur." Our account given above will have
shown, however, that he never entirely learnt this. His Christology, at all times,
retained a strong trace of affinity with that of Paul of Samosata and Photinus (only all
merit was excluded on the part of the man Jesus), because he knew that his faith
could not dispense with the man Jesus, and he supplanted the pseudo-theological
speculation as to the Word by the evangelical one that the Word had become the
content of Christ's soul.

  [1] Therefore, also, the uncertainty which we find already in Augustine as to whether
the Incarnation was necessary. In De Trinit. XIII. 13, he answers the momentous
question whether God might not have chosen another way, by leaving the possibility
open, but describing the way selected as *bonus, divinæ dignitati congruus* and *con-
venientior.* By this he opened up a perilous perspective to the Middle Ages.

  [2] Op. imperf. l.c.

  [3] He definitely rejects the idea held by him before his conversion that Christ was
only a teacher ; see, *e.g.*, Confess. VII. 25 : "Tantum sentiebam de domino
Christo meo, quantum de excellentis sapientiæ viro, cui nullus posset æquari ; præsertim quia mirabiliter natus ex virgine ad exemplum contemnendorum temporalium
pro adipiscenda immortalitate divina pro nobis cura tantam auctoritatem magisterii
meruisse videbatur."

proof of God's love towards us ;[1] the humility of God and Christ attested in it breaks down our pride and teaches us that "all goodness is made perfect in humility" (omne bonum in humilitate perficitur) ; the truth which was eternal is made comprehensible to us in Christ : lying in the dust we can apprehend God who redeems us by revealing himself in our lowliness. Throughout all this we are met by the living impression of Christ's person,[2] and it is humility, which Paul also regarded as so important, that stands out as its clearest and most weighty attributes.[3] *The type of humility exhibited in majesty*—this it was that overpowered Augustine : *pride was sin, and humility was the sphere and force of goodness.* From this he learned and implanted in the Church the new disposition of *reverence* for

---

[1] De trin. XIII. 13 : "Quid tam necessarium fuit ad erigendam spem nostram, quam ut demonstraretur nobis, *quanti nos penderet deus quantumque diligeret?*" That takes place through the Incarnation.

[2] The "work" of Christ falls to be discussed afterwards ; for we cannot include Augustine's views concerning it among his fundamental conceptions. In part they alternate (between redemption from the devil, sacrifice, and removal of original sin by death), and in part they are dependant on his specific view of original sin. Where he indulges in expositions of practical piety, he has no theory at all regarding Christ's work.

[3] The clearest, and on account of the historical connection the most decisive, testimony is given in Confess. VII. 24-27, where, in telling what Christ had become to him, he at the same time explains why Neoplatonism was insufficient. He knew what the Neoplatonists perceived, but "quærebam *viam* comparandi *roboris* quod esset idoneum ad fruendum te, nec inveniebam donec amplecterer mediatorem dei et hominum, hominem Christum Jesum vocantem et dicentem : Ego sum via et veritas et vita, et cibum, cui capiendo invalidus eram, miscentem carni ; quoniam verbum caro factum est, *ut infantiæ nostræ lactesceret sapientia tua* per quam creasti omnia. Non enim tenebam dominum meum Jesum, *humilis humilem, nec cujus rei magistra esset ejus infirmitas noveram.* Verbum enim tuum æterna veritas . . . subditos erigit ad se ipsam : in inferioribus autem ædificavit sibi *humilem* domum de limo nostro, *per quam subdendos deprimeret a seipsis et ad se trajiceret, sanans tumorem* et nutriens amorem, *ne fiducia sui progrederentur longius, sed potius infirmarentur videntes ante pedes suos infirmam divinitatem ex participatione tunicæ pelliceæ nostræ, et lassi prosternerentur in eam, illa autem surgens lavaret eos.*" He then explains in the sequel that the Neoplatonic writings led him to thoroughly understand the nature of God, but : "garriebam plane *quasi peritus,* et nisi in Christo salvatore nostro *viam* tuam quærerem, non peritus, sed periturus essem." I sought to be wise, puffed up by knowledge. "Ubi enim erat illa *ædificans caritas a fundamento humilitatis, quod est Christus Jesus?*" This love rooted in humility those writings could not teach me. It was from the Bible I first learned : "quid interesset inter *præsumptionem et confessionem, inter videntes quo eundum sit nec videntes qua, et viam*

humility. The new bias which he thus gave to Christology
continued to exert its influence in the Middle Ages, and displayed itself in rays of varying brilliancy and strength; although,
as a consequence of the Adoptian controversy, Greek Christology once more entered in force, from the ninth century, and
hindered piety from expressing its knowledge clearly in dogma.
We now understand also why Augustine attached such value
to the human element (homo) in Christ. This was not merely
due to a consequence of his theology (see above), but it was in
a much higher degree the pious view of Christ that demanded
this conception. He could not realise Christ's humility with
certainty in the Incarnation; for the latter sprang from the
universal working of God, predestinating grace, and Jesus' receptiveness; but humility was the constant "habit" of the
divino-human personality. Thus the true nature of Jesus Christ
was really known: "strength is made perfect in weakness"
(robur in infirmitate perficitur). That lowliness, suffering, shame,
misery, and death are means of sanctification; nay, that self-
less and therefore ever suffering love is the only means of sanctification ("I sanctify myself for them"); that what is great and

---

ducentem ad beatificam patriam, non tantum cernendam, sed et habitandam." Now
I read Paul. "Et apparuit mihi una facies eloquiorum castorum. Et cœpi et inveni
quidquid illac verum legeram, *hac cum commendatione gratiæ tuæ dici*, ut qui videt
non sic glorietur quasi non acceperit, non solum id quod videt, sed etiam ut videat,
et ut te non solum admoneatur ut videat, *sed etiam* sanetur ut teneat, et qui de
longinquo videre non potest, viam tamen ambulet, qua veniat et videat et teneat."
For if a man delights in the law of God after the inner man, what does he do with
the other law in his members? . . . What shall wretched man do? Who shall
deliver him from the body of this death? Who but thy grace through our Lord
Jesus Christ by whom the handwriting which was against us was abolished. "Hoc
illæ litteræ non habent. Non habent illæ paginæ vultum pietatis hujus, lacrimas
confessionis, sacrificium tuum, spiritum contribulatum. . . . Nemo ibi cantat:
Nonne deo subdita erit anima mea. Ab ipso enim salutare meum. Nemo ibi audit
vocantem: *Venite ad me, omnes qui laboratis. Dedignantur ab eo discere quoniam
mitis est et humilis corde.* Abscondisti enim hæc a sapientibus et prudentibus, et
revelasti ea parvulis." "For it is one thing from the mountain's wooded top to see
the land of peace and yet to find no way to it, and another to keep steadfastly on
the way thither." Compare with this the elaborate criticism of Platonism in De
civit. dei, X., esp. ch. 24 and 32, where Christ is presented as "universalis animæ
liberandæ via," while his significance is for the rest explained much more in the
popular Catholic fashion than in the Confessions. In ch. 1 ff. there is even an
attempt to conceive the angels and saints as a heavenly hierarchy as the Greeks do.

good always appears in a lowly state, and by the power of the contrast triumphs over pride ; that humility alone has an eye wherewith to see the divine ; that every feeling in the good is accompanied by the sense of being pardoned—that was the very core of Augustine's Christology. He, for his part, did not drag it into the region of æsthetics, or direct the imagination to busy itself with separate visions of lowliness. No, with him it still existed wholly on the clear height of ethical thought, of modest reverence for the purport of Christ's whole life, whose splendour had been realised in humility. " Reverence for that which is beneath us is a final stage which mankind could and had to reach. But what was involved not only in despising the earth and claiming a higher birthplace, but in recognising low-liness and poverty, ridicule and contempt, shame and misery, suffering and death as divine, nay, in revering sin and trans-gression not as hindrances, but as furtherances of sanctification." Augustine could have written these words ; for no idea was more strongly marked in his view of Christ than that he had ennobled what we shrank from—shame, pain, sorrow, death— and had stripped of value what we desired—success, honour, enjoyment. " By abstinence he rendered contemptible all that we aimed at, and because of which we lived badly. By his suffering he disarmed what we fled from. No single sin can be committed if we do not desire what he despised, or shirk what he endured."

But Augustine did not succeed in reducing this conception of the person of Christ to dogmatic formulas. Can we confine the sun's ray in a bucket ? He held by the old formulas as forming an element of tradition and as expressing the uniqueness of Christ ; but to him the true foundation of the Church was Christ, because he knew that the impression made by his character had broken down his own pride, and had given him the power to find God in lowliness and to apprehend him in humility. Thus the living Christ had become to him the truth [1] and the way to

---

[1] Augustine accordingly testifies that in order that the truth which is perceived should also be loved and extolled, a person is necessary who should conduct us and that on the path of humility. This is the burden of his Confessions. The truth itself had been shown clearly to him by the Neoplatonists ; but it had not become his

blessedness, and he who was preached by the Church his authority.[1]

But what is the beatific fatherland, the blessed life, to which Christ is the way and the strength? We have already discussed it (p. 91 f.), and we need only here mention a few additional points.

The blessed life is eternal peace, the constant *contemplation* of God in the other world.[2] Knowledge remains man's goal; even the notion of the enjoyment of God (fruitio dei), or that other of heavenly peace, does not certainly divert us from it.[3] Knowledge, is, however, contrasted with action, and the future state is wholly different from the present. From this it follows that Augustine retained the popular Catholic feeling that directed men in this life wholly to hope, asceticism, and the contemplation [of God] in worship, for though that can never be attained in this world which the future will bring, yet life here must be regulated by the state which will be enjoyed afterwards. Hence Augustine championed monachism and opposed Jovinian so decidedly; hence he regarded the world in the same light as the ancient Catholic Fathers; hence he valued as highly as they did the distinction between precepts and counsels; hence he never looked even on the highest blessings (munera dei) which we can here enjoy as containing the reality, but only a

spiritual possession. Augustine knew only one person capable of so impressing the truth as to make it loved and extolled, and he alone could do this, because he was the revelation of the *verbum dei in humilitate*. When Christendom has attained securely and clearly to this "Christology," it will no longer demand to be freed from the yoke of Christology.

1 This is linked together by Augustine in a wonderful fashion. The scepticism of the thinker *in genere* and the doubts, never overcome in his own mind as to the Catholic doctrine *in specie*, demanded that Christ should be the indisputable authority of the Church. To this is added, in connection with *gratia infusa*, the Christ of the sacraments. I do not discuss this authoritative Christ more fully, because he coincides with the authority of the Church itself, and we have already dealt with the latter.

2 De civ. dei XIX. 13 : "Pax cælestis civitatis ordinatissima et concordissima societas fruendi deo et invicem in deo." Enchir. 29 : "Contemplatio ejus artificis, qui vocat ea quæ non sunt tamquam ea quæ sunt, atque in mensura et numero et pondere cuncta disponit," see 63.

3 Yet the conception of blessedness as peace undoubtedly involves a tendency to think primarily of the will.

pledge and similitude ; for set in the sphere of the transitory they were themselves transitory ; hence, finally, he did not think of the earthly Church when seeking to realise the first and last things, for God alone, constantly seen and enjoyed, was the supreme blessing; and even the divine kingdom, so far as it was earthly, was transitory.

But even here much that was new emerged in the form of undercurrents, and the old was modified in many respects, a few details being almost set aside. It is therefore easy to point to numerous dissonances in Augustine's idea of the goal ; but he who does not criticise like an irresponsible critic or impartial logician will admit that he knows no more than Augustine, and that he also cannot do better than alternate between different points of view. Let us pick out the following points in detail.

1. Augustine put an end to the doubt whether virtue was not perhaps the supreme good ; he reduced virtues to dependance on God—to grace ; see Ep. 155, 12 sq.[1] He, indeed, re-admitted the thought at a new and higher stage—merits called forth by grace, righteousness made perfect by love. But the mood at any rate is changed.

2. Augustine did not follow the lead of the Greek Church : he did not cultivate systematic mysticism with a view to the future state, or regard and treat the cultus as a means by which to anticipate deification. He set aside the elements of physical magic in religious doctrine, and by this means spiritualised the ideas of the other world. The ascetic life of the churchman was to be *spiritual* and *moral.* Statements, indeed, are not wholly wanting in his works to the effect that eternal life can be experienced in ecstatic visions in this world ; but he is thinking then especially of Biblical characters (Paul), and in the course of his Christian development he thrust the whole conception more and more into the background.

3. Augustine's profound knowledge of the *will,* and his perception of the extent to which the latter swayed even know-ledge, led to his discovery of the principle, that goodness and

---

[1] The whole of Book XIX. of De civit. dei—it is perhaps on the whole the most important—comes to be considered here. In Ch. IV., it is expressly denied that virtue is the supreme good.

blessing, accordingly also final salvation, coincided in the
dependance of the will on God. By this means he broke
through intellectualism, and a superlative blessing was shown
to exist even in this world. " It is a good thing for me to
cleave to God." This "cleaving" is produced by the Holy
Spirit, and he thereby imparts love and blessedness to the
heart.[1] In presence of the realisation of this blessedness, the
antithesis of time and eternity, life and death, disappears.[2]

4. Starting from this, he arrived at a series of views which
necessarily exerted a powerful influence on the popular frame
of mind.

(a) Of the three virtues, graces, by which man clings to God
—faith, love, and hope—love continues to exist in eternity.
Accordingly, love, unchanging and grateful, connects this world
with the next.

(b) Thereby, however, the quietism of knowledge is also
modified. Seeing is to be nothing but loving ; an element of
adjustment of all discords in feeling and will is introduced into
the notion of blessedness, and although "rational contempla-

---

[1] See De spiritu et lit. 5 (the passage follows afterwards).

[2] That Augustine was able from this point of view to make the conscious feeling of
blessedness a force entering into the affairs of this world, is shown by the passage De
civit. dei XIX. 14, which, indeed, so far as I know, is almost unique. " Et
quoniam (Christianus) quamdin est in isto mortali corpore, peregrinatur a domino,
ambulat per fidem non per speciem ; ac per hoc omnem pacem vel corporis vel
animæ vel simul corporis et animæ refert ad illam pacem, quæ homini mortali est
cum immortali deo, ut ei sit ordinata in fide sub æterna lege obœdientia. Jam vero
quia duo præcipua præcepta, hoc est dilectionem dei et dilectionem proximi, docet
magister deus . . . consequens est, ut etiam proximo ad diligendum deum consulat,
quem jubetur sicut se ipsum diligere (sic uxori, sic filiis, sic domesticis, sic ceteris quibus
potuerit hominibus), et ad hoc sibi a proximo, si forte indiget, consuli velit ; ac per
hoc erit pacatus, quantum in ipso est, omni homini pace hominum, id est ordinata
concordia cujus hic ordo est, primum ut nulli noceat, deinde ut etiam prosit cui
potuerit. Primitus ergo inest ei suorum cura ; ad eos quippe habet opportuniorem
facilioremque aditum consulendi, vel naturæ ordine vel ipsius societatis humanæ.
Unde apostolus dicit : ' Quisquis autem suis et maxime domesticis non providet,
fidem denegat et est infideli deterior.' Hinc itaque etiam pax domestica oritur, id
est ordinati imperandi obœdiendique concordia cohabitantium. Imperaut enim, qui
consulunt : sicut vir uxori, parentes filiis, domini servis. . . . Sed in domo justi
viventes ex fide et adhuc ab illa cælesti civitate peregrinantis etiam qui imperant
serviunt eis, quibus videntur imperare. Neque enim dominandi cupiditate imperant,
sed officio consulendi, nec principandi superbia, sed providendi misericordia."

tion" (contemplatio rationalis) is always ranked above "rational action" (actio rationalis), a high value is always attached to practical and active love.[1]

(c) A higher meaning was now given, not indeed to the earthly world, but to the earthly Church and its peculiar privileges (within it) in this world. The idea of the city of God on earth, formulated long before by others, was yet, as we shall see in the next section, first raised by Augustine into the sphere of religious thought. In front of the Holy of Holies, the first and last things, he beheld, as it were, a sanctuary, the Church on earth, with the blessings granted it by God. He saw that it was a self-rewarding task, nay, a sacred duty, to cherish this sanctuary, to establish it in the world, to rank it higher than worldly ties, and to devote to it all earthly goods, in order again to receive them from it as legitimate possessions. He thus, following, indeed, the impulses given by the Western tradition, also created, if we may use so bold a phrase, a religion of the second order. But this second-order religion, was not, as in the case of the Greeks, the formless creation of a superstitious cultus. It was on the contrary a doctrine which dealt with the Church in its relation to the world as an active and moral power transforming and governing society, as an organism, in which Christ was actively present, of the sacraments, of goodness and righteousness. Ecclesiasticism and theology were meant to be thoroughly united, the former serving the latter, the one like Martha, the other like Mary.[2] They ministered to

---

[1] The element of " pax " obtains a value higher than and independent of knowledge (see above). That is shown also in the fact that the definitive state of the unsaved (De civit. dei, XIX., 28) is not described as ignorance, but as *constant war :* " Quod bellum gravius et amarius cogitari potest, quam ubi voluntas sic adversa est passioni et passio voluntati, ut nullius earum victoria tales inimicitiæ finiantur. et ubi sic confligit cum ipsa natura corporis vis doloris, ut neutrum alteri cedat ? Hic [in terra] enim quando contingit iste conflictus, aut dolor vincit et sensum mors adimit, aut natura vincit et dolorem sanitas tollit. Ibi autem et dolor permanet ut affligat, et natura perdurat ut sentiat ; quia utrumque ideo non deficit, ne pœna deficiat." Undoubtedly, as regards the sainted (see Book, XXII.), the conception comes again and again to the front that their felicity will consist in seeing God.

[2] Augustine has (De trin. I. 20) applied this comparison to the Churches of the future and present world ; we may also adopt it to the relations of his doctrines of the Church and of God.

the same object, and righteousness made perfect by love was
the element in which both lived.[1]

(*d*) While the ascetic life remained the ideal for the individual, Augustine modified the popular tendency also in
monachism by never forgetting, with all his appreciation of
external works (poverty, virginity, etc.), that faith, hope, and
charity were alone of decisive importance, and that therefore
the worth of the man who possessed these virtues might no
longer be determined by his outward performances.   He knew,
besides, better than anyone else, that external works might be
accomplished with a godless heart—not only by heretical
monks, where this was self-evident, but also by Catholics, Ep.,
78, 79, and, uniting ascetics as closely as possible to the Church,
he urged them to engage in active work.   Here, again, we see
that he broke through the barren system which made blessedness consist in *contemplatio rationalis* and that alone.

This is, in brief, Augustine's doctrine of the first and last
things, together with indications that point to that sphere which
belongs though not directly yet indirectly to those things, *viz.*,
the equipment and tasks of the Church in our present state.
" Doctrine " of the first and last things is really an incorrect expression ; for, and this is the supreme thing to be said in closing the subject, it was not to him a matter of " doctrine," but of
the faithful reproduction of his *experiences*.   The most thorough-
going modification by Augustine of traditional dogmatic
Christianity consisted in his perception " that Christianity is

---

[1] Ritschl published in his Treatise on the method of the earliest history of dogma
(Jahrb. f. deutsche Theol., 1871) the grand conception that the Areopagite in the
East, and Augustine in the West, were parallels ; that the former founded a ritualistic ecclesiasticism, the latter an ecclesiasticism of moral tasks, in the service of a
world-wide Christianity ; that both thus modified in the same direction, but with entirely different means, the old state of feeling (the bare hope of the future life).   This
conception is substantially correct if we keep firm hold of the fact that the traditional
popular Catholic system was not modified by either to its utmost limit, and that both
followed impulses *which had been at work in their Churches even before their time.*
The doctrine regarding the Church was not Augustine's " central idea," but he took
what every Catholic was certain of, and made it a matter of clearer, in part for the
first time of any clear, conviction ; and moved by very varied causes, he finally produced an ecclesiasticism whose independent value he himself never thoroughly perceived.

ultimately different from everything called ' doctrine '" (Reuter, p. 494). The law is doctrine ; the gospel is power. The law produces enlightenment; the gospel peace. This Augustine clearly perceived, and thereby set religion in the sphere of a vital, spiritual experience, while he disassociated it from knowledge and inference. He once more, indeed, placed his newly-discovered truth on the plane of the old ; for he was a Catholic Christian ; but the connection with the past which belongs to every effective reformer need not prevent us from exhibiting his originality. Anyone who seeks to give effect to the "whole " Augustine and the "whole " Luther is suspected of seeking to evade the "true " Augustine and the "true " Luther ; for what man's peculiarity and strength are fully expressed in the breadth of all he has said and done ? One or two glorious passages from Augustine should show, in conclusion, that he divested the Christian religion of what is called "doctrine " or "dogma." " I possess nothing but will ; I know nothing but that what is fleeting and transitory ought to be despised, and what is certain and eternal ought to be sought for. . . . If those who flee to thee find thee by faith, grant faith ; if by virtue, grant virtue ; if by knowledge, grant knowledge. Increase in me faith, hope, love." " But we say that man's will is divinely aided to do what is righteous, so that, besides his creation with free-will, and besides the doctrine by which he is taught how he should live, *man receives the Holy Spirit in order that there may be created in his mind, even now when he still walks by faith, and not by appearance, the delight in and love of that supreme and unchangeable good which is God ;* in order that this pledge, as it were, having been given him of the free gift, a man may fervently long to cling to his Creator, and be inflamed with desire to enter into the participation of that true light, that he may receive good from him from whom he has his being. For if the way of truth be hidden, free-will is of no use except for sinning, and when that which ought to be done, or striven for, begins to reveal itself, nothing is done, or undertaken, and the good life is not lived, unless it delights and is loved. But that it may be loved, the love of God is diffused in our hearts, not by free choice emanating from ourselves, but by the Holy

Spirit given unto us." "What the law of works commands by threatening, the law of faith effects by believing. *This is the wisdom which is called piety*, by which the father of lights is worshipped, by whom every excellence is given, and every gift made perfect. . . . By the law of works God says: Do what I command; by the law of faith we say to God: Grant what thou commandest. . . . We have not received the spirit of this world, says the most constant preacher of grace, but the spirit which is from God, that we may know what things have been granted us by God. But what is the spirit of this world but the spirit of pride? . . . Nor are they deceived by any other spirit, who, being ignorant of God's righteousness, and seeking to establish their own, are not subject to God's righteousness. *Whence it seems to me that he is a son of faith who knows from whom he hopes to receive what he does not yet possess, rather than he who attributes to himself what he has.* We conclude that a man is not justified by the letter, but by the spirit, not by the merits of his deeds, but by free grace."[1]

2. *The Donatist Controversy. The Work: De civitate Dei. Doctrine of the Church, and Means of Grace.*

Augustine was still occupied with the controversy with the Manichæans, in which he so sharply emphasised the authority

---

[1] Solil. I. 5: "Nihil aliud habeo quam voluntatem; nihil aliud scio nisi fluxa et caduca spernenda esse, certa et æterna requirenda . . . si fide te inveniunt, qui ad te refugiunt, fidem da, si virtute, virtutem, si scientia, scientiam. Auge in me fidem, auge spem, auge caritatem." De spiritu et lit., 5: "Nos autem dicimus humanam voluntatem sic divinitus adjuvari ad faciendam justitiam, ut præter quod creatus est homo cum libero arbitrio voluntatis, præterque doctrinam qua ei præcipitur quemadmodum vivere debeat, accipiat spiritum sanctum, quo fiat in animo ejus delectatio dilectioque summi illius atque incommutabilis boni quod deus est, etiam nunc cum adhuc per fidem ambulatur, nondum per speciem: ut hac sibi velut arra data gratuiti muneris inardescat inhærere creatori atque inflammetur accedere ad participationem illius veri luminis, ut ex illo ei bene sit, a quo habet ut sit. Nam neque liberum arbitrium quidquam nisi ad peccandum valet, si lateat veritatis via, et cum id quod agendum et quo nitendum est cœperit non latere, nisi etiam delectet et ametur, non agitur, non suscipitur, non bene vivitur. Ut autem diligatur, caritas dei diffunditur in cordibus nostris, non per arbitrium liberum quod surgit ex nobis, sed per spiritum sanctum qui datus est nobis." L.c., 22: "Quod operum lex minando imperat, hoc fidei lex credendo impetrat. Ipsa est illa sapientia quæ pietas vocatur, qua colitur

of the Catholic Church,[1] when his ecclesiastical position—Presbyter, A.D. 392, Bishop, A.D. 396, in Hippo—compelled him to take up the fight with the Donatists. In Hippo these formed the majority of the inhabitants, and so violent was their hatred that they even refused to make bread for the Catholics. Augustine fought with them from 393 to 411, and wrote against them a succession of works, some of these being very comprehensive.[2] We must here take for granted a knowledge of the course of the controversy at Synods, and as influenced by the intrusion of the Civil power.[3] It was carried on upon the ground prepared by Cyprian. His authority was accepted by the opponents. Accordingly, internal antitheses developed in the dispute which had remained latent in Cyprian's theory. The new-fashioned Catholic theory had been already stated impressively by Optatus (see above, p. 42 ff.). It was reserved to Augustine to extend and complete it. But, as it usually happens in such questions, every newly-acquired position opened up new questions, and for one solution created any number of

pater luminum, a quo est omne datum optimum et omne donum perfectum. . . . Lege operum dicit deus : Fac quod jubeo ; lege fidei dicitur deo : Da quod jubes. . . . Non spiritum hujus mundi accepimus, ait constantissimus gratiæ prædicator, sed spiritum qui ex deo est, ut sciamus quæ a deo donata sunt nobis. Quis est autem spiritus mundi hujus, nisi superbiæ spiritus ? . . . Nec alio spiritu decipiuntur etiam illi qui ignorantes dei justitiam et suam justitiam volentes constituere, justitiæ dei non sunt subjecti. Unde mihi videtur magis esse fidei filius, qui novit a quo speret quod nondum habet, quam qui sibi tribuit id quod habet. Colligimus non justificari hominem littera, sed spiritu, non factorum meritis, sed gratuita gratia."

[1] The Manichæans professed, in the controversy of the day, to be the men of "free inquiry " ("docendi fontem aperire gloriantur " De utilit. 21). We cannot here discuss how far they were ; Augustine did not conscientiously feel that his breach with them was a breach with free inquiry. Therefore the efforts from the outset to define the relations of *ratio* and *auctoritas*, and to save what was still possible of the former.

[2] Psalmus c. partem Donati—C. Parmeniani epist. ad Tichonium b. III.—De bapt. c. Donatistas, b. VII.—C. litteras Petiliani, b. III.—Ep. ad Catholicos c. Donatistas —C. Cresconium, b. IV.—De unico bapt. c. Petilianum—Breviculus Collationis c. Donatistis—Post collationem ad Donatistas. Further, at a later date : Sermo ad Cæsareensis ecclesiæ plebem—De gestis cum Emerito—C. Gaudentium Donatistam episcopum, b. II. The Sermo de Rusticiano is a forgery by the notorious Hieronymus Viguerius.

[3] Augustine supported, at least from A.D. 407, the suppression by force of the Donatists by the Christian state in the interest of " loving discipline." The discussion of A.D. 411 was a tragi-comedy. Last traces of the Donatists are still found in the time of Gregory I., who anew invoked the aid of the Civil power against them.

problems. And thus Augustine left more problems than he had solved.

The controversy did not now deal directly with the hierarchical constitution of the Church. Episcopacy was an accepted fact. The competency of the Church was questioned, and therewith its nature, significance, and extent. That ultimately the constitution of the Church should be dragged into the same peril was inevitable; for the hierarchy is, of course, the tenderest part in a constitution based upon it.

The schism was in itself the greatest evil. But in order to get over it, it was necessary to go to its roots and show *that it was utterly impossible to sever oneself from the Catholic Church, that the unity, as well as truth of the Church, was indestructible.* The main thesis of the Donatists was to the effect that the empirical is only the true Church when those who propagate it, the priests, are " pure "; for no one can propagate what he does not himself possess.[1] The true Church thus needs pure priests; it must therefore declare consecration by *traditores* to be invalid; and it cannot admit the efficacy of baptism administered by the impure—heretics, or those guilty of mortal sins; finally, it must exclude all that is manifestly stained and unworthy. This was followed by the breach with such Christian communions as did not strictly observe these rules, and by the practice of re-baptism.[2] Separation was imperative, no matter how great or small the extent of the Church. This thesis was supplemented, during the period of the State persecutions, by a second, that the persecuted Church was the true one, and that the State had nothing to do with the Church.

Augustine's counter-argument, based on Cyprian, Ambrosiaster, and Optatus, but partly disavowing, though with due respect, the first-named, went far beyond a bare refutation of

---

[1] C. litt. Petil I. 3 : " Qui fidem a perfido sumpserit non fidem percipit, sed reatum." I. 2 : " Conscientia dantis adtenditur, qui abluat accipientis." Other Donatistic theses ran (l.c.) " Omnes res origine et radice consistit, et si caput non habet aliquid, nihil est." " Nec quidquam bene regenerat, nisi bono semine (boni sacerdotis) regeneretur." " Quæ potest esse perversitas ut qui suis criminibus reus est, alium faciat innocentem ? "

[2] The Donatists, of course, did not regard it as re-baptism, l.c. " non repetimus quod jam erat, sed damus quod non erat."

the separatists. He created the beginnings of a doctrine of the Church, and means of grace, of the Church as institute of salvation, the organism of the good, *i.e.*, of divine powers in the world. Nor did the Donatist controversy furnish him with his only motive for developing this doctrine. The dispute with the Manichæans had already roused his interest in the authority of the Church, and led him to look more closely into it than his predecessors (see above, p. 79 ff.), who, indeed, were quite at one with him in their *practical* attitude to the Church. The Pelagian controversy, the state of the world, and the defence of Christianity against heathen attacks, had an extremely important influence on conceptions of the Church. Thus Augustine created the Catholic doctrine of the Catholic Church on earth, and we attempt in what follows to give, as far as possible, a complete and connected account of it. Finally, the earthly Church was and remained absolutely nothing but a means for the eternal salvation of the individual, and therefore the doctrine[1] of the Church was also meant to be nothing but a subsidiary doctrine. But if all dogmatic ran the risk, with its means and subsidiary conceptions, of obscuring the important point, the danger was imminent here. Does not the doctrine of salvation appear in Catholicism to be almost nullified by the "subsidiary doctrine," the doctrine of the Church?

Grace and Authority—these two powers had, according to Augustine's self-criticism, effected his conversion. The authority was the Church. Every one knew what the Church was : the empirical, visible Church, which had triumphed ever since the days of Constantine. A "logical definition" of the Church was therefore unnecessary. The important point was to show that men needed an authority, and why it was the authority. The weak intellect needed revelation, which brings truth to the individual, before he himself is capable of finding it ; this revelation is bound up in the Church. The fact that the

---

[1] Doctrine is, strictly speaking, inaccurate ; for Catholicism does not know of any "doctrines" here, but describes an actual state of matters brought about by God.

Church was the authority for doctrine constituted for long Augustine's only interest in it. He produced in support of this principle proofs of subjective necessity and of an objective nature ; yet he never reached in his exposition the stringency and certainty which as a Catholic he simply felt ; for who can demonstrate that an *external* authority *must* be authoritative ? The most important point was that the Church proclaimed itself to be the authority in doctrine. One was certainly a member of the Church only in so far as he submitted to its authority. There was no other way of belonging to it. Conversely, its significance seemed, on superficial reflection, to be entirely limited to doctrinal authority. We occupy our true relation to God and Christ, we possess and expect heavenly blessings only when we follow the doctrinal instructions given by the Church.

Augustine embraced this "superficial reflection" until his ecclesiastical office and the Donatist controversy led him to more comprehensive considerations. He had arrived at his doctrine of predestinating grace without any external instigation by independent meditation on the nature of conversion and piety. The development of his doctrine regarding the Church, so far as it carried out popular Catholic ideas, was entirely dependent on the external circumstances in which he found himself placed. But he did not himself feel that he was stating a doctrine ; he was only describing an actual position accepted all along by every Catholic, one which each had to interpret to himself, but without subtraction or addition. In addition to the importance of the Church as a doctrinal authority, he also felt its significance as a sacred institution which imparted grace. On its latter feature he especially reflected ; but the Church appeared to him much more vividly after he had gained his doctrine of grace : it was the one communion of saints, the dwelling-place of the Spirit who created faith, love, and hope. We condense his most important statements.

1. The Catholic Church, held together by the Holy Spirit, who is also the bond of union in the Trinity, possesses its most important mark in its unity, and that a unity in faith, love, and hope, as well as in Catholicity.

2. This unity in the midst of the divisions existing among men is the greatest of miracles, the proof that the Church is not the work of men, but of the Holy Spirit.

3. This follows still more clearly when we consider that unity presupposes love. Love is, however, the proper sphere of the Spirit's activity; or more correctly, all love finds its source in the Holy Spirit;[1] for faith and hope can be acquired to a certain extent independently—therefore also outside of the Church—but love issues only from the Holy Spirit. The Church, accordingly, because it is a unity, is the alliance of love, in which alone sinners can be purified; for the Spirit only works in " love the bond of unity " (in unitatis vinculo caritate). If then the unity of the Church rests primarily on faith, yet it rests *essentially* on the sway of the spirit of love alone, which presupposes faith.[2]

4. The unity of the Church, represented in Holy Scripture by many symbols and figures, obtains its strongest guarantee from the fact that Christ has made the Church his bride and his body. This relationship is so close that we can absolutely call the Church " Christ ";[3] for it constitutes a *real* unity with Christ. Those who are in the Church are thus "among the members of Christ " (in membris Christi); the means and bond of this union are in turn nothing but love, more precisely the love that resides in unity (caritas unitatis).

---

[1] Grace is love and love is grace : " caritas est gratia testamenti novi."

[2] C. Crescon. I. 34 : " Non autem existimo quemquam ita desipere, ut credat ad ecclesiæ pertinere unitatem eum qui non habet caritatem. Sicut ergo deus unus colitur ignoranter etiam extra ecclesiam nec ideo non est ipse, et fides una habetur sine caritate etiam extra ecclesiam, nec ideo non est ipse, ita et unus baptismus, etc." God and faith also exist *extra ecclesiam* but not "*pie.*" The relevant passages are so numerous that it would give a false idea to quote singly. The conception given here constitutes the core of Augustine's doctrine of the Church : The Holy Ghost, love, unity, and Church occupy an exclusive connection : " caritas christiana nisi in unitate ecclesiæ non potest custodiri, etsi baptismum et fidem teneatis " (c. Pet. litt. II. 172).

[3] De unit eccl. 7 : " totus Christus caput et corpus est." De civit. XXI. 25. De pecc. mer. I. 59 : " Homines sancti et fideles fiunt cum homine Christo unus Christus, ut omnibus per ejus hanc gratiam societatemque adscendentibus ipse unus Christus adscendat in cælum, qui de cælo descendit." Sermo 354, 1 : " Praedicat Christus Christum."

5. Heretics, *i.e.*, those who follow a faith chosen by themselves, cannot be in the Church, because they would at once destroy its presupposition, the unity of faith ; the Church, however, is not a society like the State, which tolerates all sorts of philosophers in its midst. Expelled heretics serve the good of the Church, just as everything must benefit those who love God, for they exercise them in *patience* (by means of persecutions), in *wisdom* (by false contentions), and in *love to their enemies*, which has to be evinced on the one hand in saving beneficence, and on the other in the terrors of discipline.[1]

6. But neither do the Schismatics, *i.e.*, those who possessed the true faith, belong to the Church ; for in abandoning its unity—being urged thereto by pride like the heretics—they show that they do not possess love, and accordingly are beyond the pale of the operations of the Holy Spirit. Accordingly the Catholic Church is the only Church.

7. From this it follows that salvation (salus) is not to be found outside the Church, for since love is confined to the visible Church, even heroic acts of faith, and faith itself, are destitute of the saving stamp, which exists through love alone.[2] Means of sanctification, a sort of faith, and miraculous powers may accordingly exist outside of the Church (see afterwards), but they cannot produce the effect and afford the benefit they are meant to have.

8. The second mark of the Church is holiness. This consists in the fact that it is holy through its union with Christ and the activity of the Spirit, possesses the means—in the Word and sacraments—of sanctifying its individual members, *i.e.*, of perfecting them in love, and has also actually attained this end. That it does not succeed in doing so in the case of all who are in its midst[3]—for it will only be without spot or wrinkle in the world beyond—nay, that it cannot entirely destroy sin except

---

[1] De civit. dei, XVIII. 51, 1.

[2] Ep. 173, 6 : Foris ab ecclesia constitutus et separatus a compagine unitatis et vinculo caritatis æterno supplicio puniveris, etiam si pro Christi nomine vivus incenderis."

[3] The Biblical texts are here used that had been already quoted against Calixtus and the Anti-Novatians (Noah's Ark, The Wheat and Tares, etc.).

in a very few, detracts nothing from its holiness. Even a pre-ponderance of the wicked and hypocritical over the good and spiritual[1] does not lessen it, for there would be no Church at all if the Donatist thesis were correct, that unholy members put an end to the Church's existence. The Donatists required to limit their own contention in a quite capricious fashion, in order to avoid destroying the Church.[2]

9. Although the tares are not to be rooted out, since men are not omniscient, and this world is not the scene of the consumma-tion, yet the Church exercises its discipline, and in certain circumstances even excommunicates; but it does not do so properly in order to preserve its holiness, but to educate its members or guard them against infection. But the Church can also tolerate. "They do not know the wicked in the Catholic unity, or they tolerate those they know for the sake of unity."[3] It can even suffer manifest and gross sinners, if in a particular case the infliction of punishment might result in greater harm.[4] It is itself secured from contamination by the profane by never approving evil, and always retaining its control over the means of sanctification.[5]

10. But it is indeed an attribute of its holiness also to beget actually holy members. It can furnish evidence of this, since a few have attained perfection in it, since miracles and signs have constantly been wrought, and a general elevation and sanctifica-tion of morals been achieved by it, and since, finally, its whole membership will in the end be holy.

11. Its holiness is, however, shown more clearly in the fact

---

[1] Augustine seems to have thought that the bad were in the majority even in the Church. He at anyrate held that the majority of men would be lost (Enchir. 97).

[2] De bapt. II. 8 : If the Donatists were right, there would have been no Church even in Cyprian's time ; their own origin would therefore have been unholy. Augustine often reproaches them with the number of gross sinners in their midst. Their grossest sin, it is true, was—schism (c. litt. Pet. II. 221).

[3] C. Petil. I. 25 : "Malos in unitate catholica vel non noverunt, vel pro unitate tolerant quos noverunt."

[4] Here and there in Augustine the thought occurs that the new covenant was throughout milder than the old.

[5] C. litt. Pet. III. 4 : "Licet a malis interim vita, moribus, corde ac voluntate separari atque discedere, quæ separatio semper oportet custodiatur. Corporalis autem separatio ad sæculi finem fidenter, patienter, fortiter exspectatur."

that it is *only within the Church* that personal holiness can be attained (see above sub. 7).[1]

12. The unholy in the Church unquestionably belong to it; for being in its unity they are subject to the operation of the means of sanctification, and can still become good and spiritual. Yet they do not belong to the inner court of the Church, but form a wider circle in it. [They are "vessels to dishonour in the house of God" (vasa in contumeliam in domo dei); they are not themselves, like the "vessels to honour" (vasa in honorem), the house of God, but are "in it"; they are "in the communion of the sacraments," not in the proper society of the house, but "adjoined to the communion of the saints" (congregationi sanctorum admixti); they are in a sense *not* in the Church, because they are not the Church self; therefore the Church can also be described as a "mixed body" (corpus permixtum).][2]   Nay, even the heretics and schismatics, in so far as they have appropriated the Church's means of sanctification (see under), belong to the Catholic Church, since the latter makes them sons without requiring to impart a second baptism.[3]   The character of the Church's holiness is not modified by these wider circles in the sphere to which it extends; for, as regards its foundation, means, and aim, it always remains the same, and a time will come when the holiness of all its members—for Augustine does not neglect this mark—will be an actual fact.

---

[1] Sermo 4, 11 : " Omnes quotquot fuerunt sancti, ad ipsam ecclesiam pertinent."

[2] " Corpus permixtum " against the second rule of Tichonius, who had spoken of a bipartite body of the Lord, a term rejected by Augustine.   Not a few of Augustine's arguments here suggest the idea that an invisible Church present " in occulto " in the visible was the true Church (De bapt. V. 38).

[3] De bapt. I. 13 : The question of the Donatists was whether in the view of Catholics baptism begot "sons" in the Donatist Church.   If the Catholics said it did, then it should follow that the Donatists had a Church, and since there was only one, the Church ; but if the question was answered in the negative, then they drew the inference : " Cur ergo apud vos non renascuntur per baptismum, qui transeunt a nobis ad vos, cum apud nos fuerint baptizati, si nondum nati sunt ? "   To this Augustine replies : " Quasi vero ex hoc generet unde separata est, et non ex hoc unde conjuncta est.   Separata est enim a vinculo caritatis et pacio, sed juncta est in uno baptismate.   *Itaque est una ecclesia, quæ sola Catholica nominatur ;* et quidquid suum habet in communionibus diversorum a sua unitate separatis, *per hoc quod suum in eis habet, ipsa utique generat, non illæ.*"

13. The third mark of the Church is *Catholicity*. It is that which, combined with unity, furnishes the most impressive external proof, and the surest criterion of its truth. That is, Catholicity—extension over the globe—was prophesied, and had been realised, although it must be described as a miracle, that an association which required such faith and obedience, and handed down such mysteries, should have obtained this extension. The obvious miracle is precisely the evidence of the truth. Donatists cannot be the Church, because they are virtually confined to Africa. The Church can only exist where it proves its Catholicity by union with Rome and the ancient Oriental Churches, with the communities of the whole globe. The objection that men's sin hinders the extension is without weight; for that would have had to be prophesied. But it is the opposite that was prophesied and fulfilled.[1] The reminder, also, that many heresies were extended over the world is of no consequence; for, firstly, almost all heresies are *national*, secondly, even the most wide-spread heresy finds another existing at its side, and thereby reveals its falsehood. [This is the old sophism : on the one hand, disintegration is regarded as the essential characteristic of heresies ; on the other, they are represented as forming a unity in order that the existence of others side by side with it may be urged against each in turn.]

14. The fourth mark of the Church is its *apostolicity*. It was displayed in the Catholic Church, (1) in the possession of apostolic writings,[2] and doctrine, (2) in its ability to trace its existence up to the Apostolic communities and the Apostles, and to point to its unity (communicatio) with the churches founded by the latter.[3] This proof was especially to be adduced in the

---

[1] A Donatist, "historicus doctus," indeed urged the telling objection (Ep. 93, 23) : " Quantum ad totius mundi pertinet partes, modica pars est in compensatione totius mundi, in qua fides Christiana nominatur." Augustine, naturally, was unable really to weaken the force of this objection.

[2] We have already remarked that Augustine held these to have—at least in many respects—an independent authority ; see Doctrina Christ. and Ep 54, 55. In not a few expositions it seems as if the appeal to the Church was solely to the Church that possessed Scripture.

[3] Besides the whole of the anti-Donatist writings, see, *e.g.*, Ep. 43, 21 ; 44, 3 ; 49, 2, 3 ; 51, 5 ; 53, 3.

succession of the Bishops, though their importance is for the rest not so strongly emphasised by Augustine as by Cyprian ; indeed passages occur in his works in which the universal priesthood, as maintained by Tertullian, is proclaimed.[1]

15. While among the apostolic communities those of the East are also very important, yet that of Rome, and in consequence its Bishop, hold the first place.   Peter is the representative of the Apostles, of Christians in general (Ep. 53, 2 : "totius ecclesiæ figuram gerens "), of weak Christians, and of Bishops, or the Episcopal ministry.   Augustine maintained the theory of Cyprian and Optatus regarding Peter's chair : it was occupied by the Roman Bishop and it was necessary to be in accord with it, because it was the apostolic seat *par excellence*, *i.e.*, the bearer of the doctrinal authority and unity of the Church.   His statements as to the infallibility of the Roman chair are as uncertain and contradictory as those dealing with the Councils and Episcopate.   He had no doubt that a Council ranked above the Roman Bishop (Ep. 43, 19).[2]

16. Augustine was convinced of the *infallibility* of the Catholic Church ; for it is a necessary consequence of its *authority* as based on Apostolicity.   But he never had any occasion to think out this predicate, and to establish it in the representation and decisions of the Church.   Therefore he made many admissions, partly without thought, partly when hard pressed, which, logically understood, destroyed the Church's infallibility.

17. So also he holds the *indispensableness* of the Church, for it follows from the exclusive relation to Christ and the Holy Spirit revealed in its unity and holiness.   This indispensableness is expressed in the term " Mother Church "[3] (ecclesia mater or corpus Christi); on modifications, see later.

18. Finally, he was also convinced of the *permanence* of the

---

[1] De civit. dei, XX. 10 : Distinction between *sacerdotes* and *proprie sacerdotes.*

[2] Augustine's attitude to the Roman Bishop, *i.e.* to the infallible Roman tradition, is shown clearly in his criticism of Zosimus (Reuter p. 312 ff., 325 ff.) and in the extremely valuable 36 Epistle, which discusses the work of an anonymous Roman writer, who had glorified the Roman Church along with Peter (c. 21 " Petrus, apostolorum caput, cœli janitor, ecclesiæ fundamentum "), and had declared statutory institutions of the Roman Church to be universally binding.

[3] C. litt Pet. III. 10 : "deum patrem et ejus ecclesiam matrem habere."

Church, and therewith also of its *primeval* character ; for this follows from the exclusive relation to God ; yet ideas entered into the conception of permanence and primevalness, which did not flow from any consideration of the empirical Church (" the heavenly Church " on the one hand, the " city of God " on the other ; on this see under).

19. The empirical Catholic Church is also the " Kingdom of God " (regnum dei, civitas dei). As a matter of fact these terms are primarily employed in a view which is indifferent to the empirical Church (see under) ; but since to Augustine there was ultimately only one Church, everything that was true of it was also applicable to the empirical Church. At all times he referred to the Catholic Church the old term which had long been applied to the Church, " the kingdom (city) of God," of course having in mind not that the Church was the mixed, but the true body (corpus permixtum, verum).[1]

20. But Augustine gave a much stronger hold than his predecessors to the conception that the Church is the kingdom of God, and by the manner in which in his " Divine Comedy," the " De civitate dei," he contrasted the Church with the State, far more than his own expressed view, he roused the conviction that the empirical Catholic Church *sans phrase* was the kingdom of God, and the independent State that of the devil. That is, although primarily the earthly State (civitas terrena) consisted for Augustine in the society of the profane and reprobate, inclusive of demons, while the city of God (civitas dei) was the

---

[1] Perhaps the most cogent evidence of this is Ep. 36, 17. The anonymous Roman Christian had appealed to the verse " Non est regnum dei esca et potus," *and simply identified "regnum dei" with "ecclesia,"* to prove that the Roman command to fast on the Sabbath was apostolic. Augustine does not reject this identification, but only the inference drawn from it by the anonymous writer. Here, however, ecclesia is manifestly the Catholic Church. In De trinit. I. 16, 20, 21, Augustine has no doubt that the *regnum,* which Christ will hand over to the Father, " omnes justi sunt, in quibus nunc regnat mediator," or the " credentes et viventes ex fide ; fideles quippe ejus quos redemit sanguine suo dicti sunt regnum ejus." That is the Church ; but at the same time it is self-evident that its " wrinkles " are ignored, yet not so its organisation ; see on Ps. CXXVI. 3 : " Quæ autem domus dei et ipsa civitas ? Domus enim dei populus dei, quia domus dei templum dei . . . omnes fideles, quæ est domus dei, cum angelis faciunt unam civitatem. *Habet custodes. Christus custodiebat, custos erat. Et episcopi hoc faciunt.* Nam ideo altior locus positus est episcopis, ut ipsi superintendant et tamquam custodiant populum."

heavenly communion of all saints of all times, comprising the
angels, yet he held that the former found their earthly historical
form of expression and manifestation in the secular State, the
latter in the empirical Church ; for there were by no means
two cities, kingdoms, temples, or houses of God.   Accordingly
the kingdom of God is the Church.   And, carried away by the
Church's authority and triumph in the world, as also profoundly
moved by the fall of the Roman world-empire, whose internal
and external power manifestly no longer existed save in the
Church, Augustine saw in the present epoch, *i.e.*, in the Church's
History, the millennial kingdom that had been announced by
John (De civit. XX.).   By this means he revised, without completely abolishing, the ancient Chiliasm of the Latin Church.[1]
*But if it were once determined that the millennial kingdom was
now, since Christ's appearance, in existence, the Church was elevated to the throne of supremacy over the world;* for while this
kingdom consists in Christ's reign, he only reigns in the present
through the Church.   Augustine neither followed out nor
clearly perceived the hierarchical tendency of his position ; yet
he reasoned out the present reign of Christ which he had to
demonstrate (XX. 9-13) by reflecting that only the "saints"
(sancti) reign with Christ, and not, say, the "tares"; that thus
only those reign in the kingdom who themselves constitute the
kingdom ; and that they reign because they aim at what is
above, fight the fight of sanctification, and practise patience in
suffering, etc.   But he himself prepared the way directly for
the sacerdotal interpretation of his thought, or positively expressed it, in two of his arguments.   The one was drawn from
him by exegesis,[2] the other is a result of a manifest view of his
own.   In the first place, *viz.*, he had to show that Rev. XX. 4

---

[1] How far he went in this is shown by observing that in B. XX. he has connected
with the present, as already fulfilled, not a few passages which plainly refer to Christ's
Second Advent ; see c. 5 : "Multa praeterea quae de ultimo judicio ita dici videntur,
ut diligenter considerata reperiantur ambigua vel magis ad aliud pertinentia, *sive
scilicet ad eum salva oris adventum, quo per totum hoc tempus in ecclesia sua venit,
hoc est in membris suis, particulatim atque paulatim, quoniam tota corpus est ejus*, sive ad
excidium terrenae Hierusalem, quia et de illo cum loquitur, plerumque sic loquitur
tamquam de fine saeculi atque illo die judicii novissimo et magno loquatur." Yet he
has left standing much of the dramatic eschatology.

[2] See Reuter, Studie III.

("those sitting on thrones judge") was even now being fulfilled. *He found this fulfilment in the heads of the Church, who controlled the keys of binding and loosing, accordingly in the clergy* (XX. 9). Secondly, he prepared the way for the supremacy of the Church over the State [1] in his explicit arguments both against and in favour of the latter (XIX., and even before this in V.). The earthly State (civitas terrena) and accordingly secular kingdoms are sprung from sin, the virtue of the ambitious, and simply because they strive for earthly possessions—summed up in the *pax terrena*, carried out in all earthly affairs—they are sinful, and must finally perish, even if they be legitimate and salutary on earth. The secular kingdom is finally, indeed, a vast robbery (IV. 4): "righteousness being abolished, what are kingdoms but great robberies?") [2] which ends in hell in everlasting war; the Roman Republic never possessed peace (XIX. 21). From this point of view the Divine State is the only legitimate association.

But Augustine had yet another version to give of the matter. The establishment of earthly peace (pax terrena)—see its manifold forms in XIX. 13—is necessary upon earth. Even those who treasure heavenly peace as the highest good are bound to care on earth by love for earthly peace. (Already the Jewish State was legitimate in this sense; see the description IV. 34, and the general principle XV. 2: "We therefore find two forms in the earthly State, one demonstrating its present existence, the other serving to signify the heavenly State by its presence"; [3] here the Divine State is also to be understood by the earthly, in so far as the former is copied on earth.) The Roman kingdom has become Christian, and Augustine rejoices in the fact. [4] But it is only by the help of *justitia* that rests on love that the State can secure earthly peace, and lose the

---

[1] Augustine had already written in Ep. 35 (A.D. 396, c. 3) : " Dominus jugo suo in gremio ecclesiæ toto orbe diffuso omnia terrena regna subjecit."

[2] " Remota justitia quid sunt regna nisi magna latrocinia " ?

[3] " Invenimus ergo in terrena civitate duas formas, unam suam præsentiam demonstrantem, alteram cælesti civitati significandæ sua præsentia servientem."

[4] It is not, accordingly, involved under all circumstances in the notion of the earthly State that it is the organism of sin. Passages on the Christian State, Christian ages, and Catholic emperors, are given in Reuter, p. 141.

character of being a robbery (latrocinium). But righteousness
and love only exist where the worship of the true God is found,
in the Church, God's State.[1] Accordingly the State must be
dependent on the kingdom of God ; in other words, those who,
as rulers, administer the earthly peace of society, are legitimate
and "blessed" (felices), when they make "their power sub-
servient to the divine majesty for the extension as widely as
possible of the worship of God, *if they love that kingdom more,
where they do not fear having colleagues.*"[2] Rulers, therefore,
must not only be Christians, but must serve the Church in order
to attain their own object (pax terrena) ; for outside the Divine
State—of love and righteousness—there are no virtues, but only
the semblance of virtues, *i.e.*, splendid vices (XIX. 25). However much Augustine may have recognised, here and elsewhere,
the relative independence and title of the State,[3] the proposition
stands, that since the Church is the kingdom of God it is the
duty of the State to serve it, because the State becomes more
legitimate by being, as it were, embodied in it.[4] It is especially
the duty of the State, however, to aid the Church by forcible
measures against idolatry, heretics, and schismatics ; for compulsion is suitable in such cases to prevent the good from being
seduced, to instruct the wavering and ignorant, and to punish
the wicked. But it by no means follows from this that in
Augustine's view the State was to pursue anything that might
be called an *independent* ecclesiastical or religious policy. It
rather in matters of religion constantly supports the cause of
the Church, and this at once implies that it is to receive its

---

[1] Augustine, indeed, also holds that there is an earthly justitia, which is a
great good contrasted with flagitia and facinora ; he can even appreciate the value of
relative blessings (Reuter, p. 135 ff.), but this righteousness finally is dissipated,
because, not having itself issued from "the Good," it cannot permanently institute
anything good.

[2] V. 24 : If they "suam potestatem ad dei cultum maxime dilatandum majestati
ejus famulam faciunt, si plus amant illud regnum, ubi non timent habere consortes."

[3] What holds true of the State applies equally, of course, to all particular blessings
marriage, family, property, etc.

[4] Augustine, therefore, holds a different view from Optatus (see above, p. 48) ; at
least, a second consideration is frequent, in which the Church does not exist in the
Roman empire, but that empire is attached to the Church. In matters of *terrena
felicitas* the Church, according to Augustine, was bound to obey the State.

instructions from the Church. And this was actually Augustine's procedure. His conception of the "Christian State" did not include any imperial papistical title on the part of the civil power; such a title was rather absolutely precluded. Even if the Church begged for clemency to heretics, against whom it had itself invoked the arm of the State, this did not establish the independent right of the latter to inflict punishment: it served the Church in punishing, and it gratified it in practising clemency.[1]

II. 21. Augustine was compelled by the Donatist practice of re-baptism and re-ordination to examine more closely, following Optatus, the significance and efficacy of the functions of the Church. It was inevitable that in doing so he should give a more prominent place to the notion of the Church as the communion of the Sacraments, and at the same time have instituted extremely sophistical discussions on the Sacraments—which, however, he did not yet carry out to their conclusion—in order to prove their objectivity, and make them independent of men, yet without completely externalising them, while vindicating them as the Church's exclusive property.

22. To begin with, it was an immense advance, only possible to so spiritual a man as Augustine, to rank the Word along with the Sacraments. It is to him we owe the phrase "the Word and Sacraments." If he did not duly appreciate and carry out the import of the "Word," yet he perceived that as gospel it lay at the root of every saving rite of the Church.[2]

---

[1] On the relation of Church and State, see Dorner, pp. 295-312, and the modifications considered necessary by Reuter in Studien, 3 and 6. Augustine did not at first approve the theory of inquisition and compulsion (c. Ep. Man. c. 1-3), but he was convinced of its necessity in the Donatist controversy ("coge intrare"). He now held all means of compulsion legitimate except the death penalty ; Optatus approved of the latter also. If it is not difficult to demonstrate that Augustine always recognised an independent right of the State to be obeyed, yet that proves little. It may, indeed, be the case that Augustine valued the State relatively more highly than the ancient Christians, who were still more strongly influenced by eschatological views. But we may not forget that he advanced not only the *cælestis societas*, but the *catholica*, in opposition to the State.

[2] Ep. 21, 3 : "sacramentum et verbum dei populo ministrare." Very frequently *verbum* = *evangelium* = Christ and the first cause of regeneration. C. litt. Pet. I. 8 : "Semen quo regeneror verbum dei est." The objective efficacy of the Word is

23. Exhaustively as he dealt with the Sacraments, he was far from outlining a doctrine regarding them ; he contented himself rather with empirical reflections on ecclesiastical procedure and its defence. He did not evolve a harmonious theory either of the number or notion of the Sacraments.[1] Every material sign with which a salvation-conferring word was connected was to him a Sacrament. " The word is added to the element, and a Sacrament is constituted, itself being, as it were, a visible word."[2] The emphasis rests so strongly on the Word and faith (on John XXV. 12 : " believe and thou hast eaten ") that the sign is simply described in many places, and indeed, as a rule, as a figure. But this view is modified by the fact that in almost as many passages the Word, with its saving power, is also conceived as a sign of an accompanying invisible entity,[3] and all are admonished to take whatever is here presented to the senses as a guarantee of the reality. But everything beyond this is involved in obscurity, since we do not know to what signs Augustine would have us apply his ideas about the Sacrament ;

---

sharply emphasised, but—outside of the Church it does not succeed in infusing love. C. Pet. III. 67 : " minister verbi et sacramenti evangelici, si bonus est, consocius fit evangelii, si autem malus est, non ideo dispensator non est evangelii." II. 11 : " Nascitur credens non ex ministri sterilitate, sed ex veritatis fœcunditate." Still, Luther was right when he included even Augustine among the new-fashioned theologians who talk much about the Sacraments and little about the Word.

[1] "Aliud videtur aliud intelligitur" (Sermo 272) is Augustine's main thought, which Ratramnus afterwards enforced so energetically. Hahn (L. v. d. Sacram., p. 11 ff.) has detailed Augustine's various statements on the notion of the Sacrament. We learn, e.g., from Ep. 36 and 54, the strange point of view from which at times he regarded the conception of the Sacrament : see 54, 1 : " Dominus noster, sicut ipse in evangelio loquitur, leni jugo suo nos subdidit et sarcinæ levi ; unde sacramentis numero paucissimis, observatione facillimis, significatione præstantissimis societatem novi populi colligavit." Baptism and the Lord's Supper follow "et si quid aliud in scripturis canonicis commendatur. . . . Illa autem quæ non scripta, sed tradita custodimus, quæ quidem toto terrarum orbe servantur, datur intelligi vel ab ipsis apostolis, vel plenariis conciliis, quorum est in ecclesia saluberrima auctoritas, commendata atque statuta retineri, sicut quod domini passio et resurrectio et ascensio in cælum et adventus de cælo spiritus sancti anniversaria sollemnitate celebrantur, et si quid aliud tale occurrit quod servatur ab universa, quacumque se diffundit, ecclesia."

[2] On John T. 80, 3 : " Accedit verbum ad elementum et fit sacramentum, etiam ipsum tamquam visibile verbum.

[3] De catech. rud. 50 : " Signacula quidem rerum divinarum esse visibilia, sed res ipsas invisibiles in eis honorari."

in De doctr. Christ. he speaks as if Baptism and the Lord's
Supper were almost alone in question, but in other passages his
language is different.[1]

24. He himself had no occasion to pursue his reflections
further in this direction. On the other hand, the Donatist
thesis that the efficacy of the Sacrament depended on the cele-
brant, and the Donatist practice of re-baptism, forced him to
set up two self-contradictory positions. First, the Sacraments
are *only* efficacious in the Church, but they are also efficacious
in circles outside the Church. If he abandoned the former principle, he denied the indispensableness of the Church ; if he
sacrificed the second, he would have required to approve of re-
baptism. Secondly, the Sacraments are independent of any
human disposition, and they are inseparably attached to the
Catholic Church and faith. To give up the one thesis meant
that the Donatist was right ; to doubt the other was to make the
Sacrament a magical performance indifferent to Christianity and
faith. In order to remove these contradictions, it was necessary
to look for *distinctions.* These he found, not, say, by discriminating between the offer and bestowal of grace, but by assuming a twofold efficacy of the Sacraments. These were (1) an
indelible *marking* of every recipient, which took place wherever
the Sacrament was administered, no matter by whom,[2] and (2)
an administration of grace, in which the believer participated
only in the union of the Catholic Church. According to this he
could teach that : the Sacraments belong exclusively to the
Catholic Church, and only in it bestow grace on faith ; but they
can be purloined from that Church, since, " being holy in them·
selves," they primarily produce an effect which depends solely
on the Word and sign (the impression of an indelible " stamp "),

---

[1] Hahn (p. 12) gives the following definition as Augustinian : " The Sacrament is
a corporeal sign, instituted by God, of a holy object, which, from its nature, it is
adapted by a certain resemblance to represent, and by means of it God, under certain conditions, imparts his grace to those who make use of it."

[2] Ep. 173, 3 : " Vos oves Christi estis, characterem dominicum portatis in sacramento." De bapt. c. Donat. IV. 16 : " Manifestum est, fieri posse, ut in eis qui
sunt ex parte diaboli sanctum sit sacramentum Christi, non ad salutem, sed ad judicium eorum . . . signa nostri imperatoris in eis cognoscimus . . . desertores sunt."
VI. 1 : " Oves dominicum characterem a fallacibus deprædatoribus foris adeptæ."

and not on a human factor.[1]   Heretics have stolen it, and
administer it validly in their associations.   Therefore the
Church does not again baptise repentant heretics (schismatics),
being certain that at the moment of faithful submission to the
Catholic communion of love, the Sacrament is "efficacious for
salvation" (ad salutem valet) to him who had been baptised
outside its pale.[2]

25. This theory could not but leave the nature of the
"stamp" impressed and its relation to the communication of
grace obscure.[3]   The legal claim of schismatics and heretics to
belong to the Catholic Church appears to be the most important,
and, indeed, the sole effect of the "objectivity" of the Sacraments outside the Church.[4]   But the theory was only worked
out by Augustine in baptism and ordination, though even here
he did not succeed in settling all the problems that arose, or in
actually demonstrating the "objectivity."   But in his treatment
of the Lord's Supper, e.g., it cannot be demonstrated at all.   For

---

[1] De bapt. IV. 16 : " Per se ipsum considerandus est baptismus verbis evangelicis,
non adjuncta neque permixta ulla perversitate atque malitia sive accipientium sive
tradentium . . . non cogitandum, quis det sed quid det." C. litt. Pet. I. 8 :
"(Against various Donatist theses, e.g., ' conscientia dantis adtenditur, qui abluat accipientis') Sæpe mihi ignota est humana conscientia, sed certus sum de Christi
misericordia . . . non est perfidus Christus, a quo fidem percipio, non reatum . . .
origo mea Christus est, radix mea Christus est . . . semen quo regeneror, verbum
dei est . . . etiam si ille, per quem audio, quæ mihi dicit ipse non facit . . . me
innocentem non facit nisi qui mortuus est propter delicta nostra et resurrexit propter
justificationem nostram. Non enim in ministrum, per quem baptizor, credo, sed in
eum, qui justificat impium."

[2] We have to emphasise the distinction between " habere " and "utiliter habere "
often drawn in the writings against the Donatists ; c. Cresc. I. 34 : " Vobis
(Donatistis) pacem nos annuntiamus, non ut, cum ad nos veneritis, alterum baptismum
accipiatis, sed ut eum qui jam apud vos erat *utiliter habeatis*," or " una catholica
ecclesia non in qua sola unus baptismus habetur, sed in qua sola unus baptismus
salubriter *habetur*." De bapt. c. Donat. IV. 24 : " Qui in invidia intus et malevo-
lentia sine caritate vivunt, verum baptisma possunt et accipere et tradere. (Sed)
salus, inquit Cyprianus, extra ecclesiam non est. Quis negat ? Et ideo quæcumque
ipsius ecclesiæ habentur, extra ecclesiam non valent ad salutem. *Sed aliud est non
habere, aliud non utiliter habere.*"

[3] In the Catholic Church the seal and salvation coincide where faith is present.
Augustine's primary concern was that the believer should receive in the Sacrament a
firm conviction of the mercy of Christ.

[4] Augustine did not really lay any stress on legal relation ; but he did, as a matter
of fact, a great deal to set matters in this light.

since, according to him, the reality of the Sacrament (res sacramenti) was invisible incorporation in the body of Christ (Augustine deals with the elements symbolically), and the eucharistic sacrifice was the sacrifice of love or peace, *the co-operation of the Catholic Church is always taken to be essential to the Lord's Supper.* Accordingly there is here no "stamp" independent of the Church.[1] But in the case of Baptism, he could assume that

---

[1] Sermo 57, 7 : "Eucharistia panis noster quotidianus est ; sed sic accipiamus illum, ut non solum ventre sed et mente reficiamur. Virtus enim ipsa, quæ ibi intelligitur, unitas est, ut redacti in corpus ejus, effecti membra ejus, simus quod accipimus." 272 : "panis est corpus Christi . . . corpus Christi si vis intelligere, apostolum audi : vos estis corpus Christi." Augustine maintains the traditional conception that, in speaking of the "body of Christ," we may think of all the ideas connected with the word (the body is πνευματικόν, is itself spirit, is the Church), but he prefers the latter, and, like the ancient Church, suffers the reference to forgiveness of sins to fall into the background. *Unitas* and *vita* (De pecc. mer. I. 34) occupy the foreground. Therefore in this case also, nay, more than in that of any other *signum*, the sign is wholly irrelevant. This "sacramentum unitatis" assures believers and *gives them what they are*, on condition of their po-sessing faith. (On John XXVI. 1 : "credere in eum, hoc est manducare panem vivum "; De civit. XXI. 25.) No one has more strongly resisted the realistic interpretation of the Lord's Supper, and pointed out that what "visibiliter celebratur, oportet invisibiliter intelligi " (On Ps. XCVIII. 9 fin.). "The flesh profits nothing," and Christ is not on earth "secundum corporis præsentiam." Now it is possible that, like the Greeks, Augustine might here or there have entertained the thought that the sacramental body of the Lord must also be identified with the real. But I have found no passage which clearly supports this (see also Dorner, p. 267 ff.). All we can say is that not a few passages at a first glance can be, and soon were, understood in this way. Augustine, the spiritual thinker, has in general greatly weakened the *dogmatic* significance of the Sacrament. He indeed describes it, like Baptism, as necessary to salvation ; but since he hardly ever cites the argument that it is connected with the resurrection and eternal life, the necessity is reduced to the unity and love which find one expression along with others in the Lord's Supper. The holy food is rather, in general, a declaration and assurance, or the avowal of an existing state, than a gift. In this Augustine agrees undoubtedly with the so-called pre-Reformers and Zwingli. This leads us to the import of the rite as a sacrifice ("sacrificium corporis Christi "). Here there are four possible views. The Church presents itself as a sacrifice in Christ's body ; Christ's sacrificial death is symbolically repeated by the priest in memory of him ; Christ's body is really offered anew by the priest ; and Christ, as priest, continually and everywhere presents himself as a sacrifice to the Father. Of these views, 1, 2, and 4 can certainly be instanced in Augustine, but not the third. He strictly maintains the prerogative of the priest ; but there is as little mention of a "conficere corpus Christi " as of Transubstantiation ; for the passage (Sermo 234, 2) to which Catholics delight to appeal : "non omnis panis sed accipiens benedictionem fit corpus Christi," only means that, as in all Sacraments, the *res* is now added to the *panis*, and makes it the *signum rei invisibilis ;* by consecration the bread becomes something

it could establish, even outside of the Church, an *inalienable* relation to the triune God, *whose place could not be supplied by anything else,* which in certain circumstances created a kind of faith, but which only bestowed salvation within the pale of the Church.[1]

different from what it was before. The *res invisibilis* is not, however, the real body, but incorporation into Christ's body, which is the Church. According to Augustine, the unworthy also obtain the valid Sacrament, but what they do receive is indeed wholly obscure. I could not say with Dorner (p. 274) : " Augustine does not know of any participation in the real (?) body and blood on the part of unbelievers."

[1] It is now the proper administration of baptism (rite) that is emphasised. The Sacrament belongs to God ; therefore it cannot be rendered invalid by sin or heresy. The indispensableness of baptism rests of sheer necessity on the " stamp," and that is the most fatal turn it could take, because in that case faith is by no means certainly implied. The " Punici " are praised in De pecc. mer. I. 34, because they simply call baptism " salus " ; but yet the indispensableness of the rite is not held to consist in its power of conferring salvation, but in the stamp. This indispensableness is only infringed by the baptism of blood, or by the wish to receive baptism where circumstances render that impossible. In the corresponding line of thought baptism rightly administered among heretics appears, because possessed unlawfully, to be actually inefficacious, nay, it brings a judgment. The Euphrates, which flows in Paradise and in profane countries, only brings forth fruit in the former. Therefore the controversy between Dorner and Schmidt, whether Augustine did or did not hold the Sacrament to be dependent on the Catholic Church, is idle. It is independent of it, in so far as it is necessary ; dependent, if it is to bestow salvation. Yet Dorner (l.c. p. 252 f., and elsewhere) seems to me to be advancing not an Augustinian conception, but at most a deduction from one, when he maintains that Augustine does not contradict the idea that the Church is rendered holy by its membership, by emphasising the Sacraments, but by laying stress on the sanctity of the *whole*, namely the Church. He repeatedly makes the suggestion, however, in order to remove the difficulties in Augustine's notion of the Sacraments, that he must have distinguished between the offer and bestowal of grace ; even the former securing their objective validity. But this is extremely questionable, and would fall short of Augustine ; for his correct religious view is that grace operates and does not merely make an offer. Augustine, besides, has wavered to such an extent in marking off the place of the stamp, and of saving efficacy in baptism, that he has even supposed a momentary forgiveness of sin in the case of heretics (De bapt. I. 19 ; III. 18 : "rursus debita redeunt per hæresis aut schismatis obstinationem et ideo necessarium habent hujusmodi homines venire ad Catholicam pacem ; " for, on John XXVII. 6 : " pax ecclesiæ dimittit peccata et ab ecclesiæ pace alienatio tenet peccata ; petra tenet, petra dimittit ; columba tenet, columba dimittit ; unitas tenet, unitas dimittit "). The most questionable feature of Augustine's doctrine of baptism (within the Church) is that he not only did not get rid of the magical idea, but strengthened it by his interest in infant baptism. While he intended that baptism and faith should be connected, infant baptism made a cleavage between them. He deduced the indispensableness of infant baptism from original sin, but by no means also from the tendency to make the salvation of all men dependent on the Church (see Dorner, p. 257). In order to conserve faith in baptism, Augustine assumed a kind

And in the case of Ordination he could teach that, properly bestowed, it conveyed the inalienable power to administer the Sacraments, although the recipient, if he stood outside the Church, only officiated to his own perdition.[1] In both cases his

---

of vicarious faith on the part of god-parents, but, as it would appear, he laid no stress on it, since his true opinion was that baptism took the place of faith for children. However, the whole doctrine of baptism is ultimately for Augustine merely preliminary. Baptism is indispensable, but it is, after all, nothing more. The main thing is the active presence of the Holy Spirit in the soul ; so that, from this point of view, baptism is of no real importance for salvation. But Augustine was far from drawing this inference.

[1] Little reflection had hitherto been given in the Church to ordination. The Donatists furnished a motive for thinking about it, and it was once more Augustine who bestowed on the Church a series of sacerdotal ideas, without himself being interested in their sacerdotal tendency. The practice had indeed for long been sacerdotal ; but it was only by its fateful combination with baptism, and the principle that ordination did not require (as against Cyprian) a moral disposition to render it valid, that the new sacrament became perfect. It now conferred an inalienable stamp, and was, therefore, if it had been properly administered, even though outside the Church, not repeated, and as it communicated an objective holiness, it gave the power also to propagate holiness. From Book I. c. 1 of De bapt. c. Donat. onwards, the *sacramentum baptismi* and the *sacramentum baptismi dandi* are treated in common (§ 2 : " sicut baptizatus, si ab unitate recesserit, sacramentum baptismi non amittit, sic etiam ordinatus, si ab unitate recesserit, sacramentum dandi baptismi non amittit." C. ep. Parm. II. 28 : " utrumque in Catholica non licet iterari." The clearest passage is De bono conjug. 32 : " Quemadmodum si fiat ordinatio cleri ad plebem congregandam, etiamsi plebis congregatio non subsequatur, manet tamen in illis ordinatis sacramentum ordinationis, et si aliqua culpa quisquam ab officio removeatur, sacramento domini semel imposito non carebit, quamvis ad judicium permanente "). The priests are alone appointed to administer the sacraments (in c. ep. Parm. II. 29 we have the remarkably tortuous explanation of lay-baptism ; Augustine holds that it is a *veniale delictum*, even when the necessity is urgent ; he, at least, believes it possible that it is so. But baptism, even when unnecessarily usurped by laymen, is valid, although *illicite datum ;* for the " stamp " is there. Yet Augustine warns urgently against encroaching on the office of the priest.) None but the priest can celebrate the Lord's Supper. That was ancient tradition. The judicial functions of priests fall into the background in Augustine (as compared with Cyprian). We do not find in him, in a technical form, a sacrament of penance. Yet it actually existed, and he was the first to give it a substructure by his conception that the *gratia Christi* was not exhausted in the retrospective effect of baptismal grace. In that period, baptism and penance were named together as if they were the two chief Sacraments, without the latter being expressly called a Sacrament ; see Pelagius' confession of faith (Hahn, § 133) : " Hominem, si post baptismum lapsus fuerit, per pænitentiam credimus posse salvari ; " which is almost identical with that of Julian of Eclanum (l. c. § 155) : " Eum, qui post baptismum peccaverit, per pænitentiam credimus posse salvari ; " and Augustine's (Enchir. 46) : " Peccata, quæ male agendo postea

view was determined by the following considerations. First, he sought to defend the Church, and to put the Donatists in the wrong. Secondly, he desired to indicate the mark of the Church's holiness, which could not, with certainty, be established in any other way, in the objective holiness of the Sacraments. And, thirdly, he wished to give expression to the thought that there must exist somewhere, in the action of the Church, an element to which faith can cling, which is not supported by men, but which sustains faith itself, and corresponds to the assurance which the believer rests on grace. Augustine's doctrine of grace has a very great share in his doctrine of the sacraments, or, more accurately, of the sacrament of baptism. On the other hand, he had by no means any sacerdotal interest in this conception. *But it could not fail afterwards to develop in an essentially sacerdotal sense.* But, at the same time, men were impelled in quite a different direction by the distinction between the outward rite and accompanying effect, by the value given to the " Word " and the desire to maintain the objectivity of the Sacrament. The above distinction could not but lead in later times to a spiritualising which refined away the Sacraments, or, on the other hand, centred them in the " Word," where stress was laid on a given and certain authority, and therewith on the supremacy of the Word. Both these cases occurred. Not only does the Mediæval Catholic doctrine of the Sacraments go back to Augustine, but so do the spiritualists of the Middle Ages, and, in turn, Luther and Calvin are indebted to him for suggestions.[1]

---

committuntur, possunt et pœnitendo sanari, sicut etiam post baptismum fieri videmus ;" (c. 65) : " Neque de ipsis criminibus quamlibet magnis remittendis in sancta ecclesia dei misericordia desperanda est agentibus pœnitentiam secundum modum sui cujusque peccati." He is not speaking of baptism, but of the Church's treatment of its members after baptism, when he says (l.c. c. 83) : " Qui vero in ecclesia remitti peccata non credens contemnit tantam divini muneris largitatem et in hac obstinatione mentis diem claudit extremum, reus est illo irremissibili peccato in spiritum sanctum."

[1] A passage in Augustine's letter to Januarius (Ep. 55, c. 2) on the nature of the sacrament became very important for after ages : " Primum oportet noveris diem natalem domini non in sacramento celebrari, sed tantum in memoriam revocari quod natus sit, ac per hoc nihil opus erat, nisi revolutum anni diem, quo ipsa res acta est,

Augustine's conception, above described, of the visible Church and means of grace is full of self-contradictions. His identification of the Church with the visible Catholic Church was not a success. He meant that there should be only one Church, and that none but believers should belong to it ; but the wicked and hypocrites were also in it, without being it ; nay, even heretics were in a sense in it, since they participated in the Sacraments. But in that case is the Church still visible ? It is—in the Sacraments. But the Church which is visible in the Sacraments is certainly not the bride and body of Christ, the indispensable institution of salvation ; that is alone the Church which is possessed by the spirit of love ; and yet it is masked by the presence of the wicked and hypocritical. And the Sacrament cannot be relied upon ; for while it is certainly not efficacious for salvation outside the Catholic Church, it is by no means certainly efficacious within it. The one Church is the true body of Christ, a mixed body, and the outward society of the Sacraments ; in each instance we have a different circle ; but it is as essential and important that it should be the one as the other. What is the meaning, then, " of being in the Church " (in ecclesia esse) ? Every speculation on the notions of things is fated to stumble on contradictions ; everything can be something else, anything is everything, and everything is nothing. The speculation surprises us with a hundred points of view—that is its strength—to end in none of them being really authoritative.

But all Augustine's deliverances on this subject are seen to be merely conditional in their value, not only from their self-contradictions, *but from the fact that the theologian is not, or is only to a very limited extent, expressing his religious conviction.* He felt and wrote as he did because he was the defender of the practice of the Church, whose authority he needed for his faith. But this faith took quite other directions. Even those incon-

festa devotione signari. *Sacramentum est autem in aliqua celebratione, cum rei gestæ commemoratio ita fit, ut aliquid etiam significari intelligatur, quod sancte accipiendum est.* Eo itaque modo egimus pascha ut non solum in memoriam quod gestum est, re-vocemus, id est, quod mortuus est Christus et resurrexit, sed etiam cetera, quæ circa ea adtestantur ad sacramenti significationem non omittamus."

sistencies, which indeed were partly traditional, show that his
conception of the Church was penetrated by an element which
resisted the idea that it was visible. This element, however,
was itself by no means congruous throughout, but again comprehended various though intertwined features.

1. The Church is *heavenly ;* as bride and body of Christ it is
quite essentially a heavenly society (cælestis societas). This
ancient traditional idea stood in the foreground of Augustine's
practical faith. *What the Church is, it cannot at all be on earth ;*
it possesses its truth, its seat, in heaven. There alone is to be
found the true sphere of its members ; a small fragment wander
as pilgrims here upon earth for a time. It may indeed be said
that upon earth we have only the *copy* of the heavenly Church
for in so far as the earthly fragment is a " civitas terrena " (an
earthly state) it is not yet what it will be. It is united with
the heavenly Church by hope. It is folly to regard the present
Church as the Kingdom of Heaven. " What is left them but
to assert that the kingdom of heaven itself belongs to the
temporal life in which we now exist ? For why should not
blind presumption advance to such a pitch of madness ? And
what is wilder than that assertion ? For although the Church
even as it now exists is sometimes called the kingdom of
heaven, it is surely so named because of its future and eternal
existence ? " [1]

2. The Church is *primeval,* and its members are therefore not
all included in the visible institution of the Catholic Church.
We now meet with the conception expounded by Augustine in
his great work " De civitate dei," at which he wrought for
almost fifteen years. The *civitas dei, i.e.,* the society in which
there rules " the love of God to the contempt of self " (amor dei
usque ad contemptum sui, XIV. 28), and which therefore aspires
to " heavenly peace " (pax cælestis), began in the angelic world.
With this the above conception (see sub. 1) is combined : the

[1] De virgin. 24 : " Quid aliud istis restat nisi ut ipsum regnum cælorum ad hanc
temporalem vitam, in qua nunc sumus, asserant pertinere ? Cur enim non et in hanc
insaniam progrediatur cæca præsumptio ? Et quid hac assertione furiosius ? Nam
etsi regnum cælorum aliquando ecclesia etiam quæ hoc tempore est appellatur ad
hoc utique sic appellatur, quia futuræ vitæ sempiternæque colligitur." It is needless
to quote more passages, they are so numerous.

city of God is the heavenly Jerusalem. But it embraces all
believers of the past, present, and future ; it mingled with the
earthly State (civitas terrena) before the Deluge,[1] ran through a
history on earth in six periods (the Deluge, Abraham, David,
the Exile, Christ, and Christ's second Advent), and continues
intermingled with the secular State to the end. With the transcendental conception of the City of God is thus combined,
here and elsewhere,[2] the universalist belief applied to the
present world : [3] Christianity, old as the world, has everywhere
and in all ages had its confessors who " without doubt" have
received salvation ; for the " Word " was ever the same, and
has always been at work under the most varied forms (" prius
occultius, postea manifestius ")[4] down to the Incarnation. He
who believed on this Word, that is Christ, received eternal
salvation.[5]

3. The Church is the communion of those who believe in the
crucified Christ, and are subject to the influences of his death,
and who are therefore *holy and spiritual* (sancti et spiritales).
To this view we are conducted by the conclusion from the
previous one, the humanist and universalist element being
stript away. If we ask : Where is the Church ? Augustine
answers in innumerable passages, wherever the communion of
these holy and spiritual persons is found. They are Christ's
body, the house, temple, or city of God. Grace on the one
hand, faith, love, and hope on the other, constitute accordingly
the notion of the Church. Or briefly : " the Church which is
on earth exists by the remission of sins," or still more certainly
" the Church exists in love." [6] In any number of expositions
Augustine ignores every idea of the Church except this, which
leads him to think of a *spiritual* communion alone, and he is as

---

[1] See on this above, p. 151.

[2] *E.g.*, Ep. 102, quæst 2, esp. § 12.

[3] See above, p. 152, n. 2.

[4] Formerly more hiddenly, afterwards more manifestly.

[5] In this line of thought the historical Christ takes a very secondary place ; but it
is quite different in others ; see Sermo 116, 6 : " Per Christum factus est alter
mundus."

[6] " Per remissionem peccatorum stat ecclesia quæ est in terris." " In caritate stat
ecclesia."

indifferent to the conception of the Church being an outward
communion of the Sacraments as to the last one now to be
mentioned.[1]

4. The Church is the *number of the elect.* The final consequence of Augustine's doctrine of grace (see next section)
teaches that salvation depends on God's inscrutable predestination (election of grace) and on that alone. Therefore the
Church cannot be anything but the number of the elect. This
is not, however, absolutely comprehended in the external communion of the Catholic Church—for some have been elect, who
were never Catholics, and others are elect who are not yet
Catholics. Nor is it simply identical with the communion of
the saints (that is of those who submit themselves in faith to
the operation of the means of grace); for these may include
for the time such as will yet relapse, and may not include others
who will ultimately be saved. *Thus the thought of predestination
shatters every notion of the Church*—that mentioned under 2 can
alone to some extent hold its ground—and renders valueless all
divine ordinances, the institution and means of salvation. The
number of the elect is no Church. The elect of God are to be
found inside and outside the Church, under the operation and
remote from the operation of sacramental grace; God has his
subjects among the enemy, and his enemies among those who
for the time being are "good."[2] Augustine, the Catholic, did
not, however, venture to draw the inexorable consequences of
this conception; if he was ever led to see them he contented himself with bringing more closely together the notions of the external communion, communion of saints, Christ's body, city of God,
kingdom of heaven, and number of elect, and with thus making

---

1 We see here that the assumption that the Church was a *corpus permixtum* or an
externa communio sacramentorum was only a make-shift conception; see the splendid
exposition De baptis. V. 38, which, however, passes into the doctrine of predestination.

2 De bapt. V. 38: "Numerus ille justorum, qui secundum propositum vocati
sunt, ipse est (ecclesia). . . . Sunt etiam quidam ex eo numero qui adhuc nequiter
vivant aut etiam in hæresibus vel in gentilium superstitionibus jaceant, et tamen
etiam illic novit dominus qui sunt ejus. Namque in illa ineffabili præscientia dei
multi qui foris videntur, intus sunt, et multi, qui intus videntur, foris sunt." We
return to this in dealing with Augustine's doctrine of predestination.

it appear as if they were identified. He stated his conviction that the number of the elect was substantially confined to the empirical Catholic Church, and that we must therefore use diligently all its benefits. But on the other hand, the faith that actuated his own life was too personal to let him bind grace, the source of faith, love, and hope, indissolubly to mechanical means and external institutions, and he was too strongly dominated by the thought of God's majesty and self-sufficiency to bring himself to examine God narrowly as to the why and how of his actions. He never did maintain that predestination was realised by means of the Church and its communication of grace.[1]

Augustine's different conceptions of the Church are only united in the person of their originator, whose rich inner life was ruled by varied tendencies. The attempts to harmonise them which occur in his writings are, besides being few in number, quite worthless. But the scholastic endeavour to combine or pack together the different notions by new and flimsy distinctions leads to theological chatter. Even Augustine's opponents apparently felt only a small part of the inconsistencies. Men at that time were far from seeking in religious conceptions that kind of consistency which is even at the present day felt as a want by only a small minority, and in any case is no necessary condition of a sincere piety. Perhaps the most important consequence of Augustine's doctrine of the Church and Sacraments consists in the fact that a complex of magical ceremonies and ideas, which was originally designed to counter-balance a *moralistic* mode of thought based on the doctrine of free-will, now held its ground alongside of a religious frame of mind. The Sacrament had a deteriorating effect on the latter; but, on the other hand, it was only by this combination that it was itself rendered capable of being reformed. It is impossible to mistake, even in the case of Augustine himself, that the notion of the Church in which his own life centred was swayed by the thought of the certainty of grace and earnestness of faith and love, and that, similarly, his supreme intention, in his doctrine of the means of grace, was to establish the comfort derived from the sure grace of God in Christ, which was

---

[1] Here Reuter is entirely right as against Dorner.

independent of human agency. Augustine subordinated the notions of the Church and Sacraments to the spiritual doctrine of God, Christ, the gospel, faith and love, as far as that was at all possible about A.D. 400.

3. *The Pelagian Controversy. The Doctrine of Grace and Sin.*

Augustine's doctrine of grace and sin was constructed independently of the Pelagian controversy. It was substantially complete when he entered the conflict ; but he was by no means clear as to its application in separate questions in the year of his conversion. At the time of his fight with Manichæism (see the Tres libri de libero arbitrio) he had rather emphasised, following the tradition of the Church teachers, the independence of human freedom, and had spoken of original sin merely as inherited evil. It was his clerical office, a renewed study of Romans, and the criticism of his spiritual development, as instituted in the Confessions, that first led him to the Neoplatonic Christian conviction that all good, and therefore faith, came from God, and that man was only good and free in dependence on God. Thus he gained a point of view which he confessed at the close of his life he had not always possessed, and which he opposed to the earlier, erroneous conceptions [1] that friends and enemies frequently reminded him of. It can be said that his doctrine of grace, in so far as it was a doctrine of God, was complete as early as A.D. 387 ; but it was not, in its application to Bible history, or to the problem of conversion and sanctification (in the Church), before the beginning of the fifth century. It can also be shown that he was at all times slightly influenced by the popular Catholic view, and this all the more as he was not capable of drawing the whole consequences of his system, which, if he had done so, would have led to determinism.

This system did *not* evoke Pelagianism. Pelagius had taken offence, indeed, before the outbreak of the controversy, at Augustine's famous sentence : " Grant what thou commandest,

---

[1] De praed. 7 ; De dono persev. 55 ; c. Jul. VI. 39 ; also the Retract.

and command what thou dost desire," and he had opposed it at Rome;[1] but by that date his doctrine was substantially settled. *The two great types of thought,* involving the question whether virtue or grace, morality or religion, the original and inalienable constitution of man, or the power of Jesus Christ was supreme, *did not evolve themselves in the controversy.* They gained in clearness and precision during its course,[2] but both arose, independently of each other, from the internal conditions of the Church. We can observe here, if anywhere, the " logic " of history. There has never, perhaps, been another crisis of equal importance in Church history in which the opponents have expressed the principles at issue so clearly and abstractly. The Arian dispute before the Nicene Council can alone be compared with it ; but in this case the controversy moved in a narrow sphere of formulas already marked off by tradition. On the other hand, in spite of the exegetical and pseudo-historical materials that encumbered the problems in this instance also, there is a freshness about the Pelagian controversy and dis-putants that is wanting in the Greek contentions.[3] The essentially literary character of the dispute, the absence of great central incidents, did not prejudice it any way ; the main issue was all the freer of irrelevant matter. But it is its most

---

[1] De dono persev. 53 : " Cum libros Confessionum ediderim ante quam Pelagiana hæresis exstitisset, in eis certe dixi deo nostro et sæpe dixi : Da quod jubes et jube quod vis. Quæ mea verba Pelagius Romæ, cum a quodam fratre et episcopo meo fuissent eo præsente commemorata, ferre non potuit et contradicens aliquanto commotius pæne cum eo qui illa commemoraverat litigavit.

[2] De doctr. Christ. III. 46 : " Hæresis Pelagiana multum nos, ut gratiam dei quæ per dominum nostrum Jesum Christum est, adversus eam defenderemus, exercuit."

[3] Pelagius and his friends were always convinced that the disputed questions, while extremely important, were not dogmatic. We can once more, therefore, study very clearly what at that time was held to be dogma ; (see De gestis Pelag. 16 : Pelagius denied at the Synod at Diospolis that statements of high dogmatic import were his ; when it was proposed that he should anathematise those who taught them, he replied : " Anathematizo quasi stultos, non quasi hæreticos, *si quidem non est dogma.*" Cælestius says of Original sin (De pecc. orig. 3) : " licet quæstionis res sit ista, non hæresis." He also declared in the Libellus fidei (26) submitted at Rome : " si quæ vero præter fidem quæstiones natæ sunt . . . non ego quasi auctor alicujus dogmatis definita hæc auctoritate statui." Hahn, § 134. This was also the view at first of Pope Zosimus (Ep. 3, 7). Julian (Op. imp. III. 106) saw dogmas in the doctrine of the Trinity and Resurrection, " multisque aliis similibus."

memorable feature that the Western Church so speedily and definitely rejected Pelagianism, while the latter, in its formulas, still seemed to maintain that Church's ancient teaching. In the crucial question, whether grace is to be reduced to nature, or the new life to grace, in the difficulty *how* the polar antitheses of " creaturely freedom and grace " are to be united,[1] the Church placed itself resolutely on the side of religion. In doing so it was as far from seeking to recognise all the consequences that followed from this position as it had been a hundred years earlier at Nicæa ; indeed it did not even examine them. But it never recalled—perhaps it was no longer possible to recall— the step taken as soon as rationalistic moralism clearly revealed its character.

Not only is the inner logic of events proved by the simultaneous and independent emergence of Augustinianism and Pelagianism, but the *how* strikes us by its consistency. On the one side we have a hot-blooded man who had wrestled, while striving for truth, to attain *strength* and *salvation*, to whom the sublimest thoughts of the Neoplatonists, the Psalms, and Paul had solved the problems of his inner life, and who had been over-powered by his experience of the living God. On the other, we have a monk and a eunuch,[2] both without traces of any inner struggles, both enthusiasts for virtue, and possessed by the idea of summoning a morally listless Christendom to exert its will, and of leading it to monachist perfection ; equally familiar with the Fathers, desirous of establishing relations with the East, and well versed in Antiochene exegesis ;[3] but, above all, following that

---

[1] Augustinianism and Pelagianism were akin in form, and opposed to the previous mode of thought, in that both conceptions were based on the desire for unity. They sought to get at the root of religion and morality, and had ceased to be satisfied with recognising freedom and grace as independent and equivalent original data, as if religion with its blessings were at the same time superior and subordinate to moral goodness. The " either—or " asserted itself strongly.

[2] Pelagius, a monk leading a free life—Cælestius, "naturæ vitio eunuchus matris utero editus," both laymen, Cælestius *auditorialis scholasticus.* Pelagius was a Briton (an Irishman ? called Morgan ?), but in view of the intercourse between different countries at the time, the birthplace is somewhat indifferent. Cælestius was won over by Pelagius in Rome, and then gave up his worldly career.

[3] It is uncertain whether Pelagius had been in the East before he appeared in Rome. Cælestius had heard Rufinus in Rome, and stated that the latter would have

Stoic and Aristotelian popular philosophy—theory of knowledge, psychology, ethics and dialectics—which numbered so many adherents among cultured Christians of the West. The third member of the league, Julian of Eclanum, the early widowed Bishop, was more active and aggressive than the reserved and prudent Pelagius,[1] more circumspect than Cælestius, the agitator, and more cultured than either. Overbearing in manner, he had a talent for dialectics, and, more stubborn than earnest, was endowed with an insatiable delight in disputing, and a boyish eagerness to define conceptions and construct syllogisms. He was no monk, but a child of the world, and jovial by nature. He was, indeed, the first, and up to the sixteenth century, the unsurpassed, unabashed representative of a self-satisfied Christianity. Pelagius and Cælestius required the aid of Julian, if the moralistic mode of thought was not to be represented from one side alone—the religious view needed only one representative. Certainly no dramatist could have better invented types of these two contrasted conceptions of life than those furnished by Augustine on the one hand, and the two earnest monks,

---

nothing to do with the "tradux peccati" (De pecc. orig. 3). Marius Mercator has even sought to deduce Pelagianism from Theodore of Mopsuestia's teaching, and supposed that Rufinus "the Syrian" (identical (?) with Rufinus of Aquileia) brought it to Rome. Others have repeated this. While the direct points of contact at the beginning are problematical, it is certain (1) that Pelagianism and Theodore's teaching approximate very closely (see Gurjew, Theodor v. Mopsu. 1890 [in Russian] p. 44 ff.) ; (2) that Theodore took up sides in the controversy against the teaching of Augustine and Jerome : he wrote a work "against those who maintain that men sin by nature, and not at their own discretion ;" (see Photius cod. 177) ; (3) that the Pelagians looked to him as a protector and Julian of Eclanum fled to him ; (4) that the Pelagians and Semi-Pelagians were convinced that they could count on the East (and even on the Church of Constantinople) for support, and that some of them studied in Constantinople. Theodore's distinctive doctrine of Grace is not found in Pelagian writings ; for this reason he could not ally himself thoroughly with Julian (see Kihn, Theodor v. Mopsu. p. 42 ff.). But their affinity was unquestionable. It is therefore no mere inference that leads Cassian (c. Nestor. I. 3 sq.) to combine the Nestorians with the Pelagians ("cognata hæresis"). The interests and methods of both were the same. The comparison with Eunomius and Aëtius is also pertinent.

[1] De pecc. orig. 13 : " Quid inter Pelagium et Cælestium in hac quæstione distabit, nisi quod ille apertior, iste occultior fuit ; ille pertinacior, iste mendacior, vel certe ille liberior, hic astutior." "Cælestius incredibili loquacitate." Many adherents of the new teaching preferred to be called "Cælestiani."

Pelagius and Cælestius, and the daring, worldly bishop Julian on the other.[1]

We have thus already indicated the origin of Pelagianism. *It is the consistent outcome of the Christian rationalism* that had long been wide spread in the West, especially among the more cultured, that had been nourished by the popular philosophy influenced by Stoicism and Aristotelianism,[2] and had by means of Julian received a bias to (Stoic) naturalism.[3] (We may not

---

[1] The earnestness and "holiness" of Pelagius are often attested, especially by Augustine himself and Paulinus of Nola. His untruthfulness, indeed, throws a dark shadow on his character ; but we have not the material to enable us to decide confidently how far he was entrapped into it, or how far he reserved his opinion in the legitimate endeavour to prevent a good cause being stifled by theology. Augustine, the truthful, is here also disposed to treat charitably the falsehoods of his opponent. But we must, above all, reflect that at that time priests and theologians lied shamelessly in self-defence, in speeches, protocols, and writings. Public opinion was much less sensitive, especially when accused theologians were exculpating themselves, as can be seen from Jerome's writings, though not from them alone. The people who got so angry over Pelagius' lies were no small hypocrites. Augustine was entitled to be wroth ; but his work De gestis Pelagii shows how considerate and tolerant he remained in spite of everything. Pelagius and Cælestius must have belonged to those lucky people who, cold by nature and temperate by training, never notice any appreciable difference between what they ought to do and what they actually do. Julian was an emotional character, a young man full of self-confidence (c. Julian II. 30 : "itane tandem, juvenis confidentissime, consolari te debes, quia talibus displices, an lugere?"), who, in his youth, had had dealings with the Roman Bishop Innocent (c. Julian I. 13) and Augustine, "vir acer ingenio, in divinis scripturis doctus, Græca et Latina lingua scholasticus ; prius quam impietatem Pelagii in se aperiret, clarus in doctoribus ecclesiæ fuit" (Gennad. script. eccl. 46). In particular, he was unusually learned in the history of philosophy. Early author and bishop, he seems, like so many precocious geniuses, never to have got beyond the stage reached by the clever youth. Fancy and passionate energy checked his growth, and made him the fanatical exponent of the moralistic theory. In any case he is not to be taken lightly. The ancient Church produced few geniuses so bold and heedless. His criticism is often excellent, and always acute. But even if we admitted that his whole criticism was correct, we would find ourselves in the end in possession of nothing but chaff. We also miss in his case that earnest sense of duty which we do not look for in vain in Pelagius. For this very reason, the delightful impression produced by a serene spirit, who appeared to avenge despised reason and authoritative morality, is always spoiled by the disagreeable effect caused by the creaking sound of a critical chopping-machine. An excellent monograph on Julian by Bruckner will appear immediately in the "Texten und Unters."

[2] Cicero's words : "virtutem nemo unquam acceptam deo retulit," could be inscribed as a motto over Pelagianism.

[3] Pelagianism and Augustinianism are also akin in form, in that in both the old dramatic eschatological element, which had hitherto played so great a *rôle* in the

overlook the fact that it originally fell back upon monachism, still in its early stages in the West, and that the two phenomena at first sought a mutual support in each other.)[1] Nature, free-will, virtue and law, these—strictly defined and made independent of the notion of God—were the catch-words of Pelagianism : self-acquired virtue is the supreme good which is followed by reward. Religion and morality lie in the sphere of the free spirit ; [2] they are won at any moment by man's own effort. The extent to which this mode of thought was diffused is revealed, not only by the uncertain utterances of theologians, who in many of their expositions show that they know better,[3] but above all by the Institutes of Lactantius.[4] In what follows we have first to describe briefly the external course of the controversy, then to state the Pelagian line of thought, and finally to expound Augustine's doctrine.[5]

I. We first meet with Pelagius in Rome. In every century there have appeared preachers in Italy who have had the power of thrilling for the moment the vivacious and emotional Italians. Pelagius was one of the first (De pecc. orig. 24 : " He lived for

West, and had balanced moralism, wholly disappears.   But Julian was the first to secularise the type of thought.

[1] The Antiochene theologians also were notoriously zealous defenders of monachism.

[2] Here we have a third point (see p. 170, n. 1) in which Pelagianism and Augustinianism are akin in form.   Neither is interested in the mysticism of the cultus ; their authors rather strive to direct spiritual things in spiritual channels, though Augustine, indeed, did not entirely succeed in doing so.

[3] See the remarks on Ambrose, p. 50.   Perhaps the three rules of Tichonius best show the confusion that prevailed (Aug. de doctr. christ. III. 46 : " opera a deo dari merito fidei, ipsam vero fidem sic esse a nobis ut nobis non sit a deo."   Yet Augustine sought (c. Julian. L. I.) to give traditional evidence for his doctrine.

[4] One passage (IV. 24 sq.) became famous in the controversy : " oportet magistrum doctoremque virtutis homini simillimum fieri, ut vincendo peccatum doceat hominem vincere posse peccatum . . . ut desideriis carnis edomitis doceret, non necessitatis esse peccare, sed propositi ac voluntatis."

[5] Our sources are the writings of Pelagius, Cælestius, and Julian (chiefly in Jerome and Augustine) Augustine's works (T. X. and c. 20, letters among which Epp. 186, 194 are the most important), Jerome, Orosius, Marius Mercator, and the relevant Papal letters. Mansi T. IV., Hefele, Vol. II.   For other literature see above, p. 61.   Marius was the most active opponent of the Pelagians towards the close of the controversy, and obtained their condemnation in the East (see Migne, T. 48, and the Art. in the Dict. of Chr. Biog).

a very long time in Rome "). Roused to anger by an inert
Christendom, that excused itself by pleading the frailty of the
flesh and the impossibility of fulfilling the grievous commandments of God, he preached that God commanded nothing impossible, that man possessed the power of doing the good if
only he willed, and that the weakness of the flesh was merely a
pretext. " In dealing with ethics and the principles of a holy
life, I first demonstrate the power to decide and act inherent
in human nature, and show what it can achieve, lest the mind
be careless and sluggish in pursuit of virtue in proportion to its
want of belief in its power, and in its ignorance of its attributes
think that it does not possess them." [1]   In opposition to Jovinian,
whose teaching can only have encouraged laxity, he proclaimed
and urged on Christians the demands of monachism ; for with
nothing less was this preacher concerned.[2] Of unquestioned
orthodoxy,[3] prominent also as exegete and theologian in the
capital of Christendom,[4] so barren in literary work, he was so
energetic in his labour that news of his success penetrated to
North Africa.[5] He took to do with the practical alone. Apparently he avoided theological polemics ; but when Augustine's
Confessions began to produce their narcotic effects, he opposed

---

[1] Pelag. Ep. ad Demetr. : " ne tanto remissior sit ad virtutem animus ac tardior,
quanto minus se posse credat et dum quod inesse sibi ignorat id se existimet non
habere."

[2] He was, perhaps, not the first ; we do not know whom Augustine meant in De
pecc. orig. 25 (" Pelagius et Cælestius hujus perversitatis auctores vel perhibentur
vel etiam probantur, vel certe si auctores non sunt, sed hoc ab aliis didicerunt,
assertores tamen atque doctores "), and De gest Pelag. 61 (" post veteres
hæreses inventa etiam modo hæresis est non ab episcopis seu presbyteris vel
quibuscumque clericis, sed a quibusdam veluti monachis "). Pelagius and Cælestius
may themselves be understood in the second passage.

[3] The Confession of Faith, afterwards tendered (Hahn, § 133), is clear and confident
in its dogmatic parts.   The unity of the Godhead is not so strongly pronounced in
the doctrine of the Trinity as with Augustine ; Pelagius resembled the Greeks more
strongly in this respect also.

[4] At Rome Pelagius wrote the Ep. to Paulinus of Nola, the three books De fide
trinitatis, his Eulogia and Commentaries on Paul's Epistles, to which Augustine
afterwards referred.   The latter have been preserved for us among Jerome's works ;
but their genuineness is suspected.   Augustine mentions, besides, an Ep. ad Constantium episc. (De grat. 39) ; it is not known when it was written.

[5] De gestis Pelag. 46 : " Pelagii nomen cum magna ejus laude cognovi."

them. Yet positive teaching, the emphasising of the freedom of the will, always remained to him the chief thing. On the other hand, his disciple and friend Cælestius [1] seems to have attacked original sin (tradux peccati) from the first. His converts proclaimed as their watchword that the forgiveness of sin was not the object of infant baptism.[2] When Alaric stormed Rome, the two preachers retreated by Sicily to North Africa. They intended to visit Augustine ; but Pelagius and he did not meet either in Hippo or Carthage.[3] Probably the former left suddenly when he saw that he would not attain his ends in Africa, but would only cause theological strife. On the other hand, Cælestius remained, and became candidate for the post of Presbyter in Carthage. But as early as A.D. 412 (411) he was accused by Paulinus, Deacon in Milan (afterwards Ambrose's biographer), at a Synod held in Carthage before Bishop Aurelius.[4] The points of the complaint, reduced to writing, were as follows :—He taught "that Adam was made mortal and would have died whether he had or had not sinned—that Adam's sin injured himself alone, and not the human race— infants at birth are in that state in which Adam was before his falsehood—that the whole human race neither dies on account of Adam's death or falsehood, nor will rise again in virtue of Christ's resurrection—the law admits men to the kingdom of heaven as well as the gospel—even before the advent of our Lord there were impeccable men, i.e., men without sin—that man can be without sin and can keep the divine commands easily if he will."[5] Cælestius declared at the conference that

---

[1] By him are three works de monasterio. "Cælesti opuscula," De gratia, 32.

[2] So Augustine heard when in Carthage ; see De pecc. mer. III. 12.

[3] De gestis Pelag. 46.

[4] Marius Merc. Common. and Aug., De pecc. orig., 2 sq. It is worthy of note that the complaint came from a disciple of Ambrose. This establishes the continuity of the Antipelagian teaching.

[5] "Adam mortalem factum, qui sive peccaret sive non peccaret moriturus fuisset— peccatum Adæ ipsum solum læsit, non genus humanum—parvuli qui nascuntur in eo statu sunt, in quo fuit Adam ante prævaricationem—neque per mortem vel prævari- cationem Adæ omne genus hominum moritur, nec per resurrectionem Christi omne genus hominum resurget—lex sic mittit ad regnum cœlorum quomodo et evangelium —et ante adventum domini fuerunt homines impeccabiles, i.e., sine peccato—hominem

infants needed baptism and had to be baptised; that since he
maintained this his orthodoxy was proved; that original sin
(tradux peccati) was at any rate an open question, "because I
have heard many members of the Catholic Church deny it,
and also others assent to it."[1] He was, nevertheless, excommunicated. In the *Libellus Brevissimus*, which he wrote in his
own defence, he admitted the necessity of baptism if children
were to be saved; but he held that there was a kingdom of
heaven distinct from eternal life. He would not hear of forgiveness of sin in connection with infant baptism.[2] He was
indisputably condemned because he undid the fixed connection
between baptism and forgiveness, thus, as it were, setting up
two baptisms, and offending against the Symbol. He now
went to Ephesus,[3] there became Presbyter, and afterwards
betook himself to Constantinople.

posse esse sine peccato et mandata dei facile custodire, si velit." On the transmission of these propositions, see Klasen, Pelagianismus, p. 48 f.

[1] "Quia intra Catholicam constitutos plures audivi destruere nec non et alios
adstruere."

[2] De pecc. mer. I. 58, 62.

[3] He is said to have stayed before this in Sicily, but that is merely a guess on
Augustine's part, an inference from the spread of Cælestian heresies there. See
Augustine's interesting letters, Epp. 156, 157, 22, 23 sq. From these we learn that
Cælestius actually taught : "divitem manentem in divitiis suis regnum dei non posse
ingredi, nisi omnia sua vendiderit ; nec prodesse eidem posse, si forte ex ipsis divitiis
mandata fecerit." In the "definitiones Cælestii" a document which came to Augustine from Sicily, and whose origin is indeed uncertain, the Stoic method of forming
definitions is noteworthy. In it there also occurs the famous definition of sin—"that
which can be let alone"—(Gœthe gives the converse description : "What, then, do
you call sin ? With everyone I call it what can *not* be let alone.") The whole argument serves to prove that since *peccatum vitari potest*, man can be sinless (De perfect.
just. 1 sq.). In the passage just cited, and again at Diospolis (De gestis Pelag. 29—
63) a work by Cælestius is mentioned, whose title is unknown. Not a few sentences
have been preserved (l.c.) : "Plus facimus quam in lege et evangelis jussum est—
gratiam dei et adjutorium non ad singulos actus dari, sed in libero arbitrio esse, vel in
lege ac doctrina—dei gratiam secundum merita nostra dari, quia si peccatoribus illam
dat, videtur esse iniquus—si gratia dei est, quando vincimus peccata, ergo ipse est in
culpa, quando a peccato vincimur, quia omnino custodire nos aut non potuit aut no-
luit—unumquemque hominem omnes virtutes posse habere et gratias—filios dei non
posse vocari nisi omni modo absque peccato fuerint effecti—oblivionem et ignorantiam
non subjacere peccato, quoniam non secundum voluntatem eveniunt, sed secundum
necessitatem—non esse liberum arbitrium, si dei indigeat auxilio, quoniam in propria
voluntate habet unusquisque aut facere aliquid aut non facere—victoriam nostram non

Pelagius had gone to Palestine. He followed different tactics from his friend, who hoped to serve the cause by his maxim of " shocking deeply " (fortiter scandalizare). Pelagius desired peace ; he wrote a flattering letter to Augustine, who sent him a friendly but reserved answer.[1] He sought to attach himself to Jerome, and to give no public offence. He plainly felt hampered by Cælestius with his agitation for the sinlessness of children, and against original sin. He wished to work for something positive. How could anyone thrust a negative point to the front, and check the movement for reform by precipitancy and theological bitterness ? He actually found good friends.[2] But his friendly relations with John, Bishop of Jerusalem, could not please Jerome. Besides, reports of Pelagius' questionable doctrines came from the East, where, in Palestine, there always were numerous natives of the West. Jerome, who at the time was on good terms with Augustine, broke with Pelagius,[3] and wrote against him the Ep. ad Ctesi-

---

ex dei esse adjutorio, sed ex libero arbitrio—si anima non potest esse sine peccato, ergo et deus subjacet peccato, *cujus pars, hoc est anima,* peccato obnoxia est—pænitentibus venia non datur secundum gratiam et misericordiam dei, *sed secundum merita et laborem eorum, qui per pœnitentiam digni fuerint misericordia.*" We readily see, what indeed has not hitherto been clearly perceived, *that this writing of Cœlestius must have been the real cause of offence.* It could not but open the eyes even of the waverers. We return to it in the text.

[1] De gestis Pelag. 51, 52. The interpretation added by Augustine to a few conventional phrases used in the letter seems to us superfluous and laboured. He, besides, spared Pelagius in Carthage itself ; for in his first great work against Pelagianism, De pecc. mer. et remiss. et de bapt. parvulorum ad Marcellinum (412), the name of Pelagius is not yet mentioned. Before this, Augustine had sought to influence the Church only by sermons and discourses. Even the Tractate De spiritu et litera, which followed immediately, is not directed against Pelagius.

[2] I am disposed to regard as a forgery the letter of condolence to the widow Livania (Fragments in Aug. De gestis Pel. 16, 19, Hieron. and Marius ; partly reported in the indictment at Diospolis). Yet we cannot decide with certainty. We must allow the possibility of Pelagius having so expressed himself in a flattering letter, not meant to be published, to a sanctimonious widow. Indeed, words like the following sound like mockery : " Ille ad deum digne elevat manus, ille orationem bona conscientia effundit qui potest dicere, tu nosti, domine, quam sanctæ et innocentes et mundæ sunt ab omni molestia et iniquitate et rapina quas ad te extendo manus, quemadmodum justa et munda labia et ab omni mendacio libera, quibus offero tibi deprecationem, ut mihi misereris."   Pharisee and Publican in one !

[3] The latter afterwards complained (c. Jul. II. 36), " quod Hieronymus ei tamquam æmulo inviderit."   That is very credible.

phontem (Ep. 133), and the Dialogi c. Pelag., writings which
constitute a model of irrational polemics. He put in the foreground the question, " whether man can be without sin," and
at the same time did all he could to connect Pelagius with the
" heretic " Origen and other false teachers. But still greater
harm was done to Pelagius [1] by the appearance, at this precise
moment, of the work already known to us, in which Cælestius
played so regardlessly the rôle of the *enfant terrible* of the
party (see above). [2]

Augustine's disciple, the Spanish priest Orosius, who had
come to Jerome in order to call his attention to the dangers of
Pelagianism, ultimately succeeded in getting John of Jerusalem
to cite Pelagius, and to receive a formal report on his case in
presence of his presbyters (A.D. 415). But the inquiry ended
with the triumph of the accused. Orosius referred to the
authority of his celebrated teacher, and to that of Jerome and
the Synod of Carthage, but without success, and when Pelagius
was charged with teaching that man could be sinless and needed
no divine help, the latter declared that he taught that it was not
possible for man to become sinless without divine grace. With
this John entirely agreed. Now since Orosius for his part
would not maintain that man's nature was created evil by God,
the Orientals did not see what the dispute was all about. The
conference, irregular and hampered by Orosius' inability to
speak Greek, was broken off : it was said that the quarrel might
be decided in the West, or more precisely in Rome. [3] Pelagius
had repelled the first attack. But his opponents did not rest.

---

[1] From motives of prudence he did not answer Jerome publicly ; for he wished to
avoid all controversy. Jerome was, for the rest, much more akin to him really than
Augustine. The former maintained, *e.g.*, in a later controversial work, that it was
orthodox to teach that the beginning of good resolves and faith is due to ourselves.

[2] Pelagius himself wrote to the nun Demetrias (A.D. 413 or 414) a letter still preserved, and forming the clearest memorial of his doctrine, and shortly before the
Synod of Diospolis he composed his book De natura, in which there is much that he
abjured at the Synod. It is extremely probable that this book also was not meant
for the public, but only for his friends (against the charges of Jerome). Augustine,
as soon as he got it, refuted it in his tractate De natura et gratia (415). Pelagius had
essayed to give a dialectical proof of his anthropology in the book. Augustine's
work, De perfectione justitiæ, composed also in A.D. 415, was aimed at Cælestius.

[3] See Orosii Apolog.

They succeeded, in December, 415, in getting him brought before a Palestinian Synod, presided over by Eulogius of Cæsarea, at Diospolis, where, however, he was not confronted by his accusers.[1] He was at once able to appeal to the favourable testimonies of many Bishops, who had warmly recognised his efforts to promote morality. He did not disown the propositions ascribed to him regarding nature and grace, but he succeeded in explaining them so satisfactorily, that his judges found him to be of blameless orthodoxy. The extravagant sentences taken from the letter to Livania he in part set right, and in part disowned, and when the Synod required him expressly to condemn them, he declared: " I anathematise them as foolish, not as heretical, seeing it is no case of dogma "[2] Hereupon the Synod decided : " Now since with his own voice Pelagius has anathematised the groundless nonsense, answering rightly that a man can be without sin with the divine help and grace, let him also reply to the other counts."[3]   There were now laid before him the statements of Cælestius as to Adam, Adam's sin, death, new-born children, the perdition of the rich, sinlessness of God's children, the unessential character of divine assistance—in short, all those propositions which had either been already condemned at Carthage, or were afterwards advanced by Cælestius in a much worse form.   Pelagius was in an awkward position.   He hated all theological strife ; he knew that Christian morality could only lose by it ; he wished to leave the region of dogma alone.[4]   Cælestius had only said,

---

[1] The indictment was composed by two Gallic Bishops, Heros and Lazarus, who had been forced to fly from their own country. It was very comprehensive ; but no strict line was drawn between what Pelagius had himself said, and what belonged to Cælestius.   The two Bishops were, for the rest, afterwards treated as under suspicion at the conferences in Rome.

[2] " Anathematizo quasi stultos, non quasi hæreticos, si quidem non est dogma."

[3] " Nunc quoniam propria voce anathematizavit Pelagius incertum stultiloquium, recte respondens, hominem cum adjutorio dei et gratia posse esse sine peccato, respondeat et ad alia capitula."

[4] The above quoted phrase, " non est dogma," is extremely characteristic. It shows how painfully anxious Pelagius was not to extend the sphere of dogma. In this he quite shared the feeling always entertained even to the present day by the Greeks.   A Greek priest once said to the author that the great freedom of the Greek Church, compared with the Western, consisted in the possibility of holding very dif-

indeed, what he himself had described as correct when among his intimate friends; but the former had spoken publicly and regardlessly, and—"the tone makes the music." Thus Pelagius considered himself justified in disowning almost all those statements : " but the rest even according to their own testimony was not said by me, and for it I am not called upon to give satisfaction." But he added: "I anathematise those who hold or have held these views." With these words he pronounced judgment on himself; they were false. The Synod rehabilitated him completely: " Now since we have been satisfied by our examination in our presence of Pelagius the monk, and he assents to godly doctrines, while condemning those things contrary to the faith of the Church, we acknowledge him to belong to our ecclesiastical and Catholic Communion."[1]

No one can blame the Synod :[2] Pelagius had, in fact, given expression to its own ideas; Augustinianism was neither known nor understood; and the "heresy of Cælestius"[3] was condemned.[4]

But Pelagius now found it necessary to defend himself to his

ferent views of sin, grace, justification, etc., if only the dogmas were adhered to. Pelagius accordingly opposed the introduction of a great new tract being included in the dogmatic sphere. He saw merely the inevitable evils of such an advance. We must judge his whole attitude up to his death from this point of view. Seeberg (Dogmengesch. I., p. 282 f,) holds that the phrase, "non est dogma," was merely meant to provide a means of defence ; but if we consider Pelagius' whole attitude, we have no ground for taking any such view.

[1] De gestis Pelag. 44 : " Reliqua vero et secundum ipsorum testimonium a me dicta non sunt, pro quibus ego satisfacere non debeo." " Anathematizo illos qui sic tenent aut aliquando tenuerunt." " Nunc quoniam satisfactum est nobis prosecutionibus præsentis Pelagii monachi, qui quidem piis doctrinis consentit, contraria vero ecclesiæ fidei anathematizat, communionis ecclesiasticæ eum esse et catholicæ confitemur."

[2] " Synodus miserabilis," Jerome, Ep. 143, 2.

[3] Jerome, Ep. 143, 1.

[4] In his work, De gestis Pelagii, Augustine, following a written account, criticises the proceedings of the Synod, and shows that Pelagius uttered the falsehood. The latter, always anxious to keep peace, addressed a report of his own after the Synod to Augustine (l.c. 57 sq.), in order to influence him in his favour. But Augustine rightly gave the preference to the other account, since Pelagius had omitted from his the " anathematizo." Again in the work De pecc. orig., Augustine shows, from the writings of Pelagius with which he was acquainted, that the latter had got off by evasions at Diospolis, and that he really held the same opinions as Cælestius.—We can only excuse the man by repeating that he wished to do practical work, and felt himself put out by dogmatic questions as to original sin, etc.

own adherents.   While on the one hand he was zealous in pro-
moting in the West the effect of the impression produced by
the decision in his favour, he wrote to a friendly priest,[1] that his
statement, " that a man can be without sin and keep the commands of God easily [2] if he will," had been recognised as orthodox.   His work, De natura, made its appearance at the same
time, and he further published four books, De libero arbitrio,[3]
which, while written with all caution, disclosed his standpoint
more clearly than his earlier ones.[4]

But North Africa [5] did not acquiesce in what had taken place.
The prestige of the West and orthodoxy were endangered.
Synods were held in A.D. 416 at Carthage and Mileve, Augustine
being also present at the latter.   Both turned to Innocent of
Rome, to whom Cælestius had appealed long before.   Soon
after the epistles of the two Synods (Aug. epp. 175, 176,) the
Pope received a third from five African Bishops, of whom
Augustine was one (Ep. 177).[6]   It was evidently feared that
Pelagius might have influential friends in Rome.[7]   The letters
referred to the condemnation, five years before, of Cælestius;
they pointed out that the Biblical doctrine of grace and the
doctrine of baptism were in danger, and demanded that, no

---

[1] De gestis, 54 sq.

[2] There was no word of " easily " at Diospolis.

[3] Augustine's tractates, De gratia Christi et De peccato originali, are directed against
this book.

[4] De pecc. orig. 20 : " Denique quomodo respondeat advertite et videte latebras
ambiguitatis falsitati præparare refugia, offundendo caliginem veritati, ita ut etiam nos
cum primum ea legimus, recta vel correcta propemodum gauderemus.   Sed latiores
disputationes ejus in libris, ubi se quantumlibet operiat, plerumque aperire compel-
litur, fecerunt nobis et ipsa suspecta, ut adtentius intuentes inveniremus ambigua."

[5] Orosius had carried there information of the events.

[6] The letter was accompanied by Pelagius' work De natura and Augustine's reply.

[7] Ep. 177, 2.—To about this date belong, according to Caspari's investigations, the
Pelagian letters and tractates published by him A.D. 1890 (Briefe, Abhandlungen und
Predigten, etc. pp. 3-167, 223-389, Christiania), and ascribed on good grounds to Agricola, of Britain.   The fragments were written, however, in Italy.   They add nothing
new to our knowledge of Pelagianism.   But they confirm the fact that the earliest
Pelagianism—before Julian—was associated with the most stringent monastic demands, and was extremely rigorous.   In particular, Agricola flatly forbids the possession of wealth.   He also regards ignorance of the divine will as no excuse for the
sinner, but as an aggravation.

matter how Pelagius might express himself, those should be excommunicated who taught that man could overcome sin and keep God's commands by virtue of his own nature, or that baptism did not deliver children from a state of sin. It was necessary to defeat the enemies of God's grace. It was not a question of expelling Pelagius and Cælestius, but of opposing a dangerous heresy.[1]

The Pope had, perhaps, never yet received petitions from North African Synods which laid such stress on the importance of the Roman Chair. Innocent sought to forge the iron while it was hot. In his four replies (Aug. Epp. 181-184 = Innoc. Epp. 30-33) he first congratulated the Africans on having acted on the ancient rule, " that no matter might be finally decided, even in the most remote provinces, until the Roman Chair had been informed of it, in order that every just decision might be confirmed by its authority ; " for truth issued from Rome, and thence was communicated in tiny streams to the other Churches. The Pope then praised their zeal against heretics, declared it impious to deny the necessity of divine grace, or to promise eternal life to children without baptism ; he who thought otherwise was to be expelled from the Church, unless he performed due penance. " Therefore (Ep. 31, 6) we declare in virtue of our Apostolic authority that Pelagius and Cælestius are excluded from the communion of the Church until they deliver themselves from the snares of the devil ; " if they did so, they were not to be refused readmission. Any adherents of Pelagius who might be in Rome would not venture to take his part after this condemnation ; besides, the acquittal of the man in the East was not certain ; nothing indubitably authentic had been laid before him, the Pope, and it appeared even from the proceedings, if they were genuine, that Pelagius had got off by evasions ; if he felt himself to be innocent, he would have

---

[1] Epp. 177, 3 : " Non agitur de uno Pelagio, qui jam forte correctus est." The consideration for him is very remarkable ; it is explained by his prestige and his justification at Diospolis. The letter of the five Bishops composed by Augustine and sent afterwards was obviously meant thoroughly to instruct the Pope, who was held to be insufficiently informed as to the importance of the question. Yet we have at the close, (c. 19) : " Non rivulum nostrum tuo largo fonti augendo refundimus."

hastened to Rome that he might be acquitted by us; he would not summon him, however; those among whom he resided might try him once more ; if he recanted, they could not condemn him ; there lurked much that was blasphemous, but still more that was superfluous, in the book, De Natura; "what orthodox believer might not argue most copiously about the potentiality of nature, free-will, the whole grace of God and daily grace ? "[1] He who can read between the lines will readily observe that the Pope left more than one back-door open, and had no real interest in the controversy.[2]

Pelagius now sent his remarkably well-composed confession of faith [3] to Rome, along with an elaborate vindication of himself.[4] The accusation that he refused baptism to children, or promised them admission to heaven without it, and that he taught that men could easily fulfil the divine commands, he declared to be a calumny invented by his enemies. As already at Diospolis, so now he guarded himself against the worst charges, though they were not indeed unwarranted, partly by mental reservations, and partly by modifications; but we cannot say that he was unfaithful to his main conception. He declared that all men had received the power to will aright from God, but that the divine aid (adjutorium) only operated in the case of Christians. It was blasphemous to maintain that God had given impossible commands to men. He took his stand between Augustine and Jovinian. This letter did not reach Innocent, he having died. It was thus received by his successor Zosimus. Cælestius, who had come to Rome and submitted a *Libellus fidei* that left nothing to be desired in

---

1 Ep. 183, 2-5 : "Nam de naturæ possibilitate, de libero arbitrio, et de omni dei gratia et quotidiana gratia cui non sit recte sentienti uberrimum disputare?"

2 This is not the view that has hitherto been taken of the letters; Zosimus has rather been simply contrasted with Innocent. Seeberg (p. 283) sees in the letter a monument of the Pope's helplessness in dogma : he was so ignorant as to admit that the Africans were right, and yet to make them talk like Pelagians. That seems to me an exaggeration.

3 Hahn. 133. In it we have the words "liberum sic confitemur arbitrium, ut dicamus nos indigere dei semper auxilio" (but in what does the auxilium consist?), and "baptismum unum tenemus quod iisdem sacramenti verbis in infantibus, quibus etiam in majoribus, asserimus esse celebrandum."

4 Fragments in Aug., De Gratia Christi et de pecc. orig.

point of submission to the Pope, vindicated himself to the
latter. Cælestius, on the whole, seems now, when matters had
become critical, to have sounded the retreat;[1] he at least modified his statements, and took care not to come into conflict with
the theory, deducible from the Church's practice, that infant
baptism did away with sin.[2] After these similar declarations of
the two friends, Zosimus did not see that the dogma or Church
practice of baptism was endangered in any respect. At a
Roman Synod (417), Cælestius, who was ready to condemn
everything banned by the Pope, was rehabilitated;[3] and
Pelagius, for whom Orientals interceded, was likewise declared
to have cleared himself. The complainants were described as
worthless beings, and the Africans were blamed for deciding too
hastily; they were called upon to prove their charges within
two months. This result was communicated in two letters[4] to
the African Bishops.[5] They were told that Pelagius had never
been separated from the Church, and that if there had been
great joy over the return of the lost son, how much greater
should be the joy of believing that those about whom false
reports had been circulated were neither dead nor lost (Ep.
4, 8)!

The Carthaginians were indignant, but not discouraged. A

---

[1] Fragments of the Libellus in Aug., De pecc. orig. 5 sq.

[2] L.c.: "Infantes debere baptizari in remissionem peccatorum secundum regulam
universalis ecclesiæ et secundum evangelii sententiam confitemur, quia dominus
statuit, regnum cœlorum non nisi baptizatis posse conferri ; quod, *quia vires naturæ
non habent*, conferri necesse est per gratiæ libertatem. In remissionem peccatorum
baptizandos infantes non idcirco diximus, ut peccatum *ex traduce* firmaie videamur
(he thus clung to this point), quod longe a catholico sensu alienum est, quia peccatum
non cum homine nascitur, quod postmodum exercetur ab homine, quia non naturæ
delictum, sed voluntatis esse demonstratur. Et illud ergo confiteri congruum, ne
diversa baptismatis genera facere videamur, et hoc præmunire necessarium est, ne per
mysterii occasionem ad creatoris injuriam malum, antequam fiat ab homine, tradi
dicatur homini per naturam."

[3] He wisely refused to discuss the separate points of complaint.

[4] Zosim., Epp. 3, 4.

[5] The Bishops are arrogantly rebuked. For the rest, the whole question in
dispute is regarded as due to an epidemic of curiosity, as superfluous and pernicious :
one ought to abide by Scripture. No wonder that Rome hesitated to declare a question
important in which the disputants were agreed as regards Holy Scripture, dogma, and
Church practice. The Church only took hesitatingly the momentous step involved in
acknowledging anything outside of these to be of equal importance to "dogmas."

Synod (417) determined to adhere to the condemnation until it was ascertained that both heretics saw in grace not merely an enlightenment of the intellect, but the only power for good (righteousness), without which we can have absolutely no true religion in thought, speech, and action.[1] This resolution was conveyed to Zosimus. Paulinus of Milan declared at the same time in a letter to the Pope that he would not come to Rome to prosecute Cælestius, for the case had been already decided.[2] This energetic opposition made the Pope cautious. In his reply,[3] he glorified Peter and his office in eloquent language, but changed his whole procedure, declaring now that the Africans were under a mistake if they believed that he had trusted Cælestius[4] in everything, and had already come to a decision. The case had not yet been prejudiced, and was in the same position as before (March, 418). Immediately after the arrival of this letter in Africa, a great Council was held there—more than 200 Bishops being present—and Pelagianism was condemned, without consulting the Pope, in 8 (9) unequivocal Canons;[5] indeed, such was the indignation felt against Zosimus—and on different grounds—that the Council, in its 17 Canon, threatened with excommunication any appeal to Rome.[6] But it had first assured itself of the Emperor's support, who had published on the 30th April, 418, an edict to the Prefect of the Prætorium, banishing the new heretics with their followers from Rome, permitting their prosecution, and threatening the guilty with stringent penalties.[7]

---

[1] Prosper, c. collat. 5.

[2] Zosim., Ep. 10.

[3] Zosim., Ep. 15.

[4] It was with Cælestius that he was chiefly concerned.

[5] Let him be condemned : who derives death from natural necessity ; who denies the presence of original sin in children and rebels against Paul (Rom. V. 12) ; who assigns any form of salvation to unbaptised children ; who refers God's justifying grace in Christ merely to past sins ; who applies grace to knowledge alone, while not perceiving in it the power necessary to us ; who sees in grace merely a means of rendering the good easier, but not its indispensable condition ; or who derives the confessions of sin by the pious from humility alone, and interprets their prayer for pardon of guilt as applying solely to the guilt of others.

[6] The proceedings in Mansi III., p. 810 sq.

[7] The edict in Aug. Opp. X. app., p. 105. It is certainly doubtful whether the

Zosimus, whose action had been hitherto influenced by the
strength of Pelagius' party in Rome, now laid down his arms.
In his *Ep. tractatoria* to all the Churches,[1] he informed them of
the excommunication of Cælestius and Pelagius, was now
convinced *that the doctrines of the absolute importance of justifying grace, and of original sin, belonged to the faith* (*de fide*),
and required all Bishops to signify their assent by their signa-
tures. But eighteen Bishops refused;[2] *they appealed to a
General Council,* and recalled with reason the fact that the Pope
had himself formerly considered a thorough conference to be
necessary. In their name Julian of Eclanum wrote two bold
letters to the Pope,[3] while also rejecting the propositions once
set up by Cælestius.[4] From now onwards the stage was occupied by this "most confident young man," for whom Augustine,
a friend of his family, possessed so much natural sympathy, and
whom, in spite of his rudeness, he always treated, as long as the
case lasted, affectionately and gently.[5] At the instigation of
the new Pope, Boniface, Augustine refuted one of the letters
sent to Rome and circulated in Italy, as well as another by
Julian (addressed to Rufus of Thessalonica) in his work *c. duas
epp. Pelagianorum* (420). Julian, who had resigned or been
deposed from his bishopric, now took up his sharp and

Africans effected this; perhaps it was instigated from Milan or by Italian Anti-
Pelagians. The attempt has been made to prove that Zosimus' change of front was
independent of the edict.

[1] Aug. Opp. X. app., p. 108.

[2] C. duas epp. Pel. I. 3.

[3] See Op. imperf. I. 18.　Fragments in Marius.

[4] The confession of faith contained in one of the letters (Hahn, § 135) shows also
that Julian wished to stand by Pelagius.

[5] We must remember in excuse of Julian's violent and unmeasured polemics that
he was defending an already hopeless case. He himself knew this—Op. imp. I. 1, 2 :
"magnis impedimentis angoribus, quos intuenti mihi hac tempestate ecclesiarum
statum partim indignatio ingerit partim miseratio"—"labentis mundi odia promere-
mur" —"rebus in pejorem partem properantibus, quod mundi fini suo incumbentis
indicium est" (l.c. I. 12). His violence is in any case not explained from secret
uncertainty, for there certainly have been few theologians so thoroughly convinced as
he of being on the right path. Religious pioneers, besides, have as a rule surpassed
their opponents in strength of conviction. They also possess it more readily ; for the
certainty of religion and morality, as they understand it, is involved for them in
personal assurance.

restless pen.   No one else pressed Augustine so hard as he ; he compelled him to work out the consequences of his line of thought; he displayed inexorably the contradictions in his works, and showed how untenable was the great man's doctrine when it was fully developed; he pointed out the traces of a Manichæan type of thinking in Augustine, traces of which the latter tried in vain to get rid.   He could indeed explain that he did not mean them, but could not show that they were not there.   Julian's charge that Augustine's teaching desecrated marriage had made an impression on the powerful Comes Valerius in Rome.   Augustine sought to weaken the force of the charge in his writing, De nuptiis et concupiscentia, Lib. I. ; but Julian now wrote a work in four volumes against the treatise.   Augustine based a reply on extracts from the latter (De nupt. et concup., l. II.), and when he received the work itself, he substituted, for this preliminary answer, a new work : Libri sex c. Julianum hæresis Pelagianæ defensorem.   Julian replied to the " Preliminary pamphlet " with a work in eight volumes (written already in Cilicia).   Augustine was engaged with the answer to this work, *Opus imperf. c. Julianum* (l. sex), up to his death. Since he follows Julian almost sentence by sentence, we possess the most accurate information as to the latter's positions.[1]   In his latest years, Augustine composed other four writings which are not aimed directly at the Pelagians, but discuss objections raised against his own doctrine by Catholics or Semi-Pelagians [2] (De gratia et libero arbitrio ; De correptione et gratia : to the monks of Hadrumetum ; De prædestinatione sanctorum and De dono perseverantiæ : to Prosper and Hilary as against the Gallic monks).   In these works the doctrine of predestinating grace is worked out in its strictest form.

The Pelagians nowhere came to form a sect or schismatical party.[3]   They were suppressed in the years after A.D. 418, without it being necessary to apply any special force.   The Emperor

---

[1] When we realise the exceptional qualities of two such outstanding opponents, we wish that nature had rolled them into one.   What a man that would have been !

[2] This name appears first in the Middle Ages.   In ancient times men spoke of the " reliquiæ Pelagianorum."

[3] They still hoped for their rehabilitation up to A.D. 430, and urged it in Rome on every new Pope.

once more published a sharp edict. Cælestius, who had hitherto escaped punishment, was still chiefly dealt with. He was forbidden to reside in Italy, and sentence of exile was pronounced on anyone who should harbour him. Pelagius is said to have been condemned by a Synod in Antioch. But this information, given by Marius, is uncertain. He disappears from history.[1] Julian and other Pelagians took refuge with Theodore in Cilicia. There they were at first left in peace ; for either the controversy was not understood, or the attitude to Augustinianism was hostile. The indefatigable Cælestius was able in A.D. 424 to demand once more an inquiry in Rome from Bishop Cælestine, but then betook himself, without having obtained his object, to Constantinople, where, since Julian and other friends were also assembled, the party now pitched their headquarters.[2] The Patriarch Nestorius joined hands with them, a proceeding fatal to both sides ; for Nestorius thereby incurred the displeasure of the Pope, and the Pelagians fell into the ranks of the enemies of the dominant party in the East (Cyril's). Marius Mercator agitated successfully against them at the Court, and in the comedy at Ephesus Cyril obliged the Roman legates by getting the Council to condemn the doctrine of Cælestius, Rome having concurred in his condemnation of Nestorius.[3] Thus Pelagianism had brought upon itself a kind of universal anathema, while in the East there were perhaps not even a dozen Christians who really disapproved of it,[4] and the West, in turn, was by no means clear as to the consequences to which it would necessarily be led by the condemnation of the Pelagians.

II. As regards the history of dogma, the "system" of Pelagianism, *i.e.* of Julian of Eclanum, is tolerably indifferent ;

---

[1] It is noteworthy that Julian speaks in his works as if he now alone represented the *destituta veritas*, a claim that Augustine tells him shows extreme arrogance (see c. Jul. II. 36).

[2] I do not here discuss more minutely the history of Julian, who once more paid a passing visit to Rome ; see art. in the Encycl. of Christ. Biogr.

[3] Julian's name was expressly mentioned ; perhaps he was in Ephesus with Nestorius. It is maintained by Marius that he had been already condemned in his absence (with Theodore's concurrence) at a Cilician Synod.

[4] Bishop Atticus of Constantinople was undoubtedly a decided enemy of the Pelagians ; but we do not know his motives.

for it was only produced after the whole question was already decided, and its author was a theologian, who, by renouncing his ecclesiastical office, had himself thrown away much of his claim to be considered. From the standpoint of the history of dogma, the controversy closed simply with rejection of the doctrines, (1) that God's grace (in Christ) was not absolutely necessary—before and after baptism—for the salvation of every man, and (2) that the baptism of infants was not in the fullest sense a baptism for remission of sins (in remissionem peccatorum). *The contrary doctrines were the new "dogmas."* But, since those two doctrines and the main theses of Pelagianism involved a multitude of consequences, and since some of these consequences were even then apparent, while others afterwards occupied the Church up till and beyond the Reformation, it is advisable to point out the fundamental features of the Pelagian system, and the contrary teaching of Augustinianism.[1] In doing so we have to remember that Pelagius would have nothing to do with a system. To him "De fide" (of the faith) meant simply the orthodox dogma and the ability of man to do the good. All else were open questions which might be answered in the affirmative or negative, among the rest original sin, which he denied. He laid sole stress on preaching practical Christianity, *i.e.*, the monastic life, to a corrupt and worldly Christendom, and on depriving it of the pretext that it was impossible to fulfil the divine commands. Cælestius, at one with his teacher in this respect, attacked original sin more energetically, and fought by the aid of definitions and syllogisms theological doctrines which he held to be pernicious. But Julian was the first to develop their mode of thought systematically, and to elevate it into a Stoic Christian system.[2] Yet he really added nothing essential to what occurs scattered through the writings of Pelagius and Cælestius. He only gave it all a naturalistic tendency, *i.e.*, he did away with the monastic intention of the type of thought. But even in Pelagius, arguments occur which completely contra-

---

[1] This is also necessary because the mode of thought at the root of Pelagianism never reappeared—up to the time of Socinianism—in so pure a form as in Julian.

[2] Augustine says very gracefully (c. Jul. VI. 36): "Quæ tu si non didicisses, Pelagiani dogmatis machina sine architecto necessario remansisset."

dict the ascetic monastic conception. In his letter to Demetrius he shows that fasting, abstinence and prayer are not of
such great importance ; they should not be carried to excess, as
is often done by beginners ; moderation should be observed in
all things, therefore even in good works. The main thing
is to change one's morals and to practise every kind of virtue.
And thus no one is to think that the vow of chastity can let
him dispense with the practice of spiritual virtues and the fight
with anger, vanity, and pride, etc. *It was the actual development
of the character in goodness on which he laid stress.* The monastic idea appears subordinate to this thought, which in some
passages is expressed eloquently. The ancient call to wise
moderation has not a naturalistic impress in Pelagius. In
treating the thought of these three men as a whole we have to
remember this distinction, as also the fact that Pelagius and
Cælestius for the most part paid due heed to Church practice,
and besides avoided almost entirely any appeal to the ancient
philosophers.[1] They were all actuated by a courageous confi-

---

[1] As regards form (Klasen, pp. 81-116), *i.e.* in their teaching as to Scripture, tradition, and authority, no innovations occur in Pelagius and Cælestius. Pelagianism,
indeed, implicitly involves the rejection of every doctrine, *quæ ratione defendi non
potest*, and he interpreted Scripture accordingly (see examples of exegesis in Klasen
l.c.). In his treatise, De natura, he quotes the Fathers in support of his form of doctrine, as Augustine did for his (Chrysostom was especially often quoted, but so also
were Jerome, Ambrose, and Lactantius). Julian, on the contrary, expressly gave the
first place to *ratio :* "Quod ratio arguit, non potest auctoritas vindicare" (Op. imp.
II. 16). With Origen—in sharp contrast to Augustine—he observes the rule not
that a thing is good, because God wills it and it stands in Scripture, but that reason
establishes what is good: "Hæreat hoc maxime prudentis animo lectoris, omnibus scripturis sacris solum illud, quod in honorem dei catholici sapiunt, contineri, sicut frequen-
tium sententiarum luce illustratur, et sicubi durior elocutio moverit quæstionem, certum
quidem esse, non ibi id quod injustum est loci illius auctorum sapuisse ; secundum id autem
debere intelligi, quod et *ratio perspicua* et aliorum locorum, in quibus non est ambigu-
itas, splendor apparuerit" (l.c. II. 22 ; cf. I. 4). "Sanctas quidem apostoli esse
paginas confitemur, non ob aliud, nisi quia *rationi*, pietati, fidei congruentes erudiunt
nos" (II. 144). Julian declares time and again that "wrong" and right must be the
standard to be applied to all traditions regarding God. Now if the interpretations of
Scripture given by Pelagius and Cælestius are "shallow," Julian's are sometimes
quite profane. Our first parents clothed themselves after the Fall, because they were
cold, and had learned for the first time the art of making clothes (c. Jul. IV. 79 sq.).
But the rationalist standpoint of historical criticism appears most clearly in Julian's
attitude to tradition. He is the author of the famous saying that we ought to weigh
and not count opinions (c. Julian, II. 35 : "non numerandas, sed ponderandas esse

dence in man's capacity for goodness, along with the need for clearness of thought on religious and moral questions.

1. God's highest attributes are his goodness and justice, and, in fact, righteousness is the quality without which God cannot

sententias; ad aliquid inveniendum multitudinem nihil prodesse cæcorum"). He says boldly that in dogmatic questions we must set aside the *strepitus turbarum de omni ordine conversationis hominum*, all *de plebeia fæce sellularii, milites, scholastici auditoriales, tabernarii, cetarii, coqui, lanii, adolescentes ex monachis dissoluti*, and further the *turba qualiumcumque clericorum;* " *honorandam esse paucitatem*, quam ratio, eruditio, libertasque sublimat." Compare Op. imperf. I. 41, where Julian says "et si philosophorum ego senatum advocavero, tu continuo sellularios, opifices omneque in nos vulgus accendas," and II. 14 : "Traduciani pro se sursum deorsum plebecularum aut ruralium aut theatralium scita commendant." He justifies the setting aside of laymen and the uneducated clergy; he says: "*quia non possunt secundum categorias Aristotelis de dogmatibus judicare.*" Here (c. Julian. II. 36, 37) Julian's chief interest becomes clearly evident. *Without Aristotle, no theology;* everything else is clod-hoppers' theology ; *but we have the cultured on our side* (l.c. V. 1., Augustine suggests that is a contention of all heretics, already soiled and worn by frequent use). Julian adhered to Aristotle and Zeno ; he knew their ethics thoroughly and reflected on their differences (c. Jul. II. 34 ; VI. 36 ; VI. 64 : " de scholis Peripateticorum sive Stoicorum ;" Op. impf. I, 35, 36). In contents and method his teaching was closely related to that of these philosophers—Augustine alludes very often to this. Besides, he quotes (c. Jul. IV .75) Thales, Anaximander, Anaximenes, Anaxagoras, Xenophanes, Parmenides, Leucippus, Democritus, Empedocles, Heraclitus, Melissus, Plato, and Pythagoras ("quis non ipso nominum sectarumque conglobatarum strepitu terretur?" remarks Augustine). Of these philosophers—along with whom Sallust and Cicero are quoted—Julian says (l.c.), while granting they were idolaters ("licet in scholis aliud disserentes"), that they had enjoyed, in the midst of many errors, "de naturalibus aliquas veritatis partes," and that these were rightly to be preferred to the dogma of original sin. Augustine justly speaks of "nebulæ de Aristotelicis categoriis ;" but the Stoic element prevails in Julian. The whole conception of *ratio* and Nominalism is Stoic. The mania for definitions is also Stoic and Ciceronian. Without definition no knowledge (Op. imp. II. 30, said against Augustine : "Ad quid ergo persuadendum aut scripturas releges aut conscios nominabis, *qui adhuc quod sentis non potes definire*"). But these definitions never rise out of the actual and thoroughly observed case—and that was indeed also usual in the Stoa—but glide over it. Julian by no means despised altogether the appeal to the Fathers. Here also he proved himself reasonable. It was only their formal authority that he would have nothing to do with. His standpoint is most clearly expressed in c. Jul. I. 29 : "Cum igitur liquido clareat hanc sanam et veram esse sententiam, quam primo loco *ratio*, deinde *scripturarum* munivit auctoritas et quam *sanctorum virorum* semper celebravit *eruditio, qui tamen veritati auctoritatem non suo tribuere consensu*, sed testimonium et gloriam de ejus suscepere consortio, nullum prudentem conturbet conspiratio perditorum." Here we perceive the descending series of authorities, which is yet only authoritative, in so far as the witnesses are rational. The " Fathers " he really regarded as nothing, and well he knew how to

be thought of at all ; indeed, it can even be said that there is a God, because there is righteousness.[1] "Justice, as it is wont to be defined by the learned (s. Aristotle) and as we can understand, is (if the Stoics will allow us to prefer one to the other) the greatest of all virtues, discharging diligently the duty of restoring his own to each, without fraud, without favour."[2] Its genus, is God ; its species are the promulgation and administration of the laws; its difference consists in its being regulated by circumstances; its modus in its not requiring from anyone more than his powers permit, and in not excluding mercy; its quality in sweetness to pious souls. This notion of righteousness is so sure that it appears also to be ideally superior to Holy Scripture (see Op. imperf. II. 17): "Nothing can be proved by the sacred writings which righteousness cannot support."[3]

2. It follows, from the goodness and righteousness of God, that everything created by him is good—and that not only at the beginning—but what he now creates is likewise good.[4] Ac-

---

make use of the admissions wrung from Augustine regarding their authority (Op. imp. IV. 112): "Sed bene quod nos onere talium personarum prior levasti. Nam in libro ad Timasium cum s. Pelagius venerabilium virorum tam Ambrosii quam Cypriani recordatus fuisset, qui liberum arbitrium in libris suis commendaverant, respondisti nulla te gravari auctoritate talium, ita ut diceres eos processu vitæ melioris, si quid male senserant, expiasse." "Numquid"—exclaims Julian (l.c. IV. 110)— "legi dei aut operi dei scripta disputatorum præjudicant !" Julian felt most acutely his having to call to its senses the West, in bondage to "stupid and godless" dogma ; in the East alone did he now see salvation. The rock on which he stood was *reason ;* his winged organ was the *word*. He knew that God would honour him for having *alone* to lead the cause of righteousness. He confronted, as the most resolute "Aufklärer" of the ancient Church, its greatest religious personality.

[1] Cælestius in Aug., De perf. just. 15 ; Julian in the Op. imp. I. 27-38 and often. The thought of goodness—characteristically enough—is dropped, or accompanies it, as it were, incidentally. The idea of righteousness as legislative, distributive, and social, governs the whole system. "Lex dei fons ac magistra justitiæ," Op. imp. I. 4.

[2] Op. imp. I. 35 : "Justitia est, ut ab eruditis definiri solet (s. Aristoteles), et ut nos intelligere possumus, virtus (si per Stoicos liceat alteri alteram præferre), virtutum omnium maxima fungens diligenter officio ad restituendum sua unicuique, sine fraude, sine gratia." By this is gained for religion and morality the supreme principle by which man confronts God as judge in complete independence.

[3] "Nihil potest per sanctas scripturas probari, quod justitia non possit tueri."

[4] Op. imp. VI. 16.

cordingly, the creature is good, and so also are marriage, the law, free will, and the saints. [1]

3. Nature, which was created good, is not convertible, "because the things of nature persist from the beginning of existence (substance) to ˙ᵗᶜ end." [2] " Natural properties are not converted by accident.'   .. ˙ ʋrdingly, there can be no "natural sins" (peccata naturalia); for they could only have arisen if nature had become evil.

4. Human nature is thus indestructibly good, and can only be modified accidentally. To its constitution belongs—and that was very good—the will as free choice ; for "willing is nothing but a movement of the mind without any compulsion." [4] This free choice, with which reason is implied,[5] is the highest good in man's constitution, " he who upholds grace praises human nature." [6] We know that Pelagius always began in his sermons by praising man's glorious constitution, his nature which shows itself in free will [7] and reason, and he never wearied of extolling our "condition of willing" (conditio

[1] Aug. c. duas epp. Pelag. III. 24 : " Hae sunt nebulæ Pelagianorum de laude creaturæ, laude nuptiarum, laude legis, laude liberi arbitrii, laude sanctorum, IV. 1, 2.

[2] " Quia naturalia ab initio substantiæ usque ad terminum illius perseverant." (Op. imp. II. 76).

[3] Naturalia per accidens non convertuntur." " Quod innascitur usque ad finem ejus, cui adhæserit, perseverat." L.c. I. 61.

[4] " Voluntas est nihil aliud quam motus animi cogente nullo" (Op. imp. l. V.). More precisely (I. 78-82) : " Libertas arbritii, *qua a deo emancipatus homo est*, in admittendi peccati et abstinendi a peccato possibilitate consistit. . . Posse bonum facere aula virtutis est, posse malum facere testimonium libertatis est. Per hoc igitur suppetit homini habere proprium bonum, per quod ei subest posse facere malum. *Tota ergo divini plenitudo judicii tam junctum habet negotium cum hac libertate hominum, ut harum qui unam agnoverit ambas noverit*. . . . Sic igitur et libertas humani custodiatur arbitrii, quemadmodum divina æquitas custoditur . . . Libertas igitur arbitrii possibilitas est vel admittendi vel vitandi peccati, expers cogentis necessitatis, quæ in suo utpote jure habet, utrum surgentium partem sequatur, *i.e.*, vel ardua asperaque virtutum vel demersa etpa lustria voluptatum."

[5] The Pelagians were very silent as to the relation of *ratio* and *liberum arbitrium*. They did not even notice that it involved a main difficulty. All that they found it necessary to say consisted in quite childish arguments. Even the above definition of the will is absolutely untenable. After all, reason impels to what is bad as well as good ; the wicked man does not act, at least, without reason. But what does *justitia* mean, if the separate acts of will always pass into vacancy ? The original equilibrium, forsooth, remains fixed

[6] Op. imp. III. 188 : " Qui gratiam confirmat, hominum laudat naturam."

[7] " Libertas utriusque partis."

voluntatis), as contrasted with the "condition of necessity" (conditio necessitatis) of irrational creatures. "Nature was created so good that it needs no help."[1] With reason as guide (duce ratione) man can and should do the good, *i.e.*, righteousness (jus humanæ societatis).[2] God desires a voluntary performer of righteousness (voluntarius executor justitiæ); it is his will that we be capable of both, and that we do one. *According to Pelagius freedom of will is freedom to choose the good; according to Julian it is simply freedom of choice.* The possibility of good as a *natural faculty* is from God,[3] willing and action are our business;[4] the possibility of both (possibilitas utriusque) is as a psychological faculty inevitable (a necessario); for this very reason a continual change is possible in it.[5]

5. Evil, sin, is willing to do that which righteousness forbids, and from which we are free to abstain,[6] accordingly what we can avoid.[7] It is no element or body, no nature—in that case God would be its author; nor is it a perverted nature (natura conversa), but it is always a momentary self-determination of the will, *which can never pass into nature so as to give rise to an evil nature.*[8] But if this cannot happen, so much the less can evil be inherited; for that would do away with the goodness

---

[1] Ep. ad Demetr.

[2] Op. imp. I. 79. Here the humanist notion of the good is clear. To this Julian adhered, in so far as he followed out the thought at all.

[3] De grat. Christi 5; de nat. et gratia, passim. (Expositions by Pelagius).

[4] The notion of freedom taught by the Pelagians lies in the *possibilitas*, and that according to Julian, the *possibilitas utriusque*, not merely *boni*. In Pelagius the *possibilitas boni*, and therewith responsibility, are more prominent. He does not merely say that man has freedom of choice, but also (ep. ad Demetr.) that "in animi nostris naturalis quædam sanctitas est."

[5] Klasen (pp. 229-237) distinguishes a threefold *possibilitas* in the Pelagians' teaching, *i.e.*, so many distinctions are, in fact, required, if we would escape the contradictions covered by the notion.

[6] Op. imp. I. 44; V. 28, 43; VI, 17 and often.

[7] Cælest. in Aug. de perfect. 1.

[8] Besides the indefiniteness of the relation of reason to freedom, the wrong definition of the will, the obscurity as to the notion of *ratio*, and the contradictions in the notion of *possibilitas*, especially characteristic are the inability to give a concrete definition of evil, and the mythological fashion in which nature and will are distinguished. Why should will and nature be so completely divided, if the *possibilitas* belongs to nature? What is nature in general over and above will, since it is by no means held to be merely the flesh?

and righteousness of God, the notion of sin (as that which can
be avoided), and the notion of redemption ; a " natural " guilt
could never be got rid of.[1]

6. Pelagius deduced the actual existence of sin from the
snares of the devil and *sensuous* lusts (gula and libido), and condemned concupiscence accordingly. It was necessary to overcome it by virginity and continence. It sprang not from the
substance of the flesh (de substantia carnis), but from its works
(ex operibus carnis), otherwise God would be its author.
Pelagius took a serious view of this whole matter ; but he was
certain, on the other hand, that the body was subject to the
soul, and that thus the relationship willed by God could be
restored.[2] But Julian felt that this was a vexed point. Whence
came the evil desires of the flesh (desideria carnis mala) if the
substance was good, and if it was yet manifest that they frequently did not spring from the will ? The case of marriage,
which is unthinkable without sexual desire, showed Julian that
libido was permitted by God, and he attacked inexorably the
artificial distinctions which Augustine sought and was compelled to make between *nuptiæ* and *concupiscentia*.[3] Julian
taught that *concupiscence was in itself indifferent and innocent;*
for the actual creation was of all conceivable kinds the best ;
but this creation embraced sexual and all other desires.[4] *Libido*
was guilty *non in genere suo, non in specie, non in modo*, but *only
in excessu;* genus and species were from God, the modus depended on an honest decision (arbitrium honestatis), excess

---

[1] To this point the Pelagians applied their greatest acuteness, and made just objections, see under. Pelag. in Aug. de pecc. orig. 14 : " Omne bonum ac malum, quo
vel laudabiles vel vituperabiles sumus, non nobiscum oritur, sed agitur a nobis :
capaces enim utriusque rei, *non pleni* nascimur, et ut sine virtute ita et sine vitio
procreamur atque ante actionem propriæ voluntatis id solum in homine est, quod
deus condidit."

[2] See the Ep. ad Demetr. ; De nat. et grat. 60-71. A grave experience is revealed in the confession (Ep. ad Demetr. 26) that the devil may often fill even those
who are separated from the world with such foul and impious thoughts, that they
imagine they are as wicked as when they loved the *res sæculi*.

With his distinction of marriage as good and bad, Augustine resembles the charla-
tan who would exhibit a beast that devours itself ; Jul. III. 47.

[4] See especially Op. imp. Book V., and c. Julian, Book V. Augustine calls him
" laudator concupiscentia ; " c. Jul. III. 44.

followed from a fault of will (vitium voluntatis).[1] If it were otherwise, then baptism would necessarily eradicate, and not merely regulate, concupiscence.[2]   Accordingly the latter, within limits (intra modum), was good ;[3] he who used it moderately, used a blessing rightly ; he who indulged in it immoderately, used a blessing badly ; but he who from love to virginity despised even moderate indulgence, *did not thereby use a good thing better.*[4] The shame alluded to by Augustine, which is felt even at the lawful enjoyment of desire, was explained by Julian, following the Cynics, as mere convention and custom.[5] Christ himself possessed concupiscence.[6]

7. It follows from this teaching that there can always have been sinless men :[7] Pelagius, indeed, argued further that since every man could resist sin (easily), he who sinned passed into hell at the Judgment;[8] for every sin was really mortal, the sinner having acted against his ability to do better.   Julian, moreover, taught that every excess was a mortal sin, since it was done absolutely without compulsion.[9] In the end, it is said, God punishes the wicked and rewards the virtuous.   But it remains wholly obscure how there can exist virtue (righteousness) and sin at all if, in practising them, a character can never be gained, if we are only concerned with fragmentary actions from which no deposit is left or sum-total formed.

In the foregoing the fundamental conceptions of the Pelagians are described.   But they were also, of course, Catholic Christians;

[1] C. Jul. IV. 7 ; III. 27.

[2] L.c. IV. 8.

[3] L.c. IV. 52.

[4] Asceticism is thus declared to be superfluous, l.c. III. 42.

[5] Op. imp. IV. 37-43. There undoubtedly occur other passages in Julian in which the " blessing " of libido appears small, and virginity is admired.

[6] L.c. IV. 45-64, and elsewhere.

[7] We must here, indeed, remember the twofold meaning of *posse.*

[8] De gest. Pelag. 11.

[9] On this Pelagius laid great stress (see Op. imp. V.), expressly denying (against Augustine) that man sins because he was created *ex nihilo.* By referring evil to the will, every possibility of explaining its origin comes to an end ; for any such explanation means proving its necessity. V. 41 : " Quæritis necessitatem rei quæ esse non potest si patitur necessitatem.   Huic motui animi libero, sine coactu originis inquieto, si causa ipso motu detur antiquior, non gignitur omnino sed tollitur." V. 57-60 : " ideo habuit voluntatem malam, quia voluit."

they were accordingly compelled to harmonise these doctrines of theirs with Holy Scripture and its historical contents, with Christ and the teaching of the Church. How they did so we have still briefly to discuss in what follows. It is apparent that the difficulties in showing this agreement were extraordinarily great, and, indeed, not only for them, but for everyone who would harmonise a coherent rational doctrine with Gen. I.-III., and with hundreds of passages in Scripture.

8. Adam was created with free will—according to Pelagius— also with "what is called natural holiness " (naturalis quæ dicitur sanctitas), which consisted just in free will and reason. Julian considered this state to be morally very high and intellectually low.[1] All are, however, agreed that Adam's endowments were the peculiar and inalienable gift of divine grace (gratia).

9. Adam sinned through free will (Julian esteemed this sin of slight account);[2] but by this sin his nature was not corrupted. Nor was natural death a consequence of it, for it is natural ; but spiritual death, the condemnation of the soul on account of sin, was the result of sin.[3]

10. Natural death was accordingly not inherited from Adam ; moreover, spiritual death was only in so far as his descendants likewise sinned. If all men died through Adam's death, then all would necessarily rise again through the resurrection of Christ.[4]

11. Still much less was Adam's sin or guilt transmitted. The doctrine of transmitted and original sin (tradux peccati and peccatum originis) is Manichæan and blasphemous; it is equally absurd whether viewed in relation to God, or man, or the notion of sin, or

---

[1] Op. imp. VI. 14-23.

[2] Op. Imp. VI. 23 ; VI. 14, he lets it appear plainly enough that the Fall was an advantage for Adam : " porro ignorantia quam profunda quamque patiendi ejus dura conditio, ut liberari ab ea nisi prævaricatione non posset, scientiam quippe boni malique absque ansa condemnabili nequaquam capessiturus."

[3] Thus first Cælestius (Karthago, s. Diospolis ; de pecc. mer. 2). So also Julian, op. imp. II. 66. Common death is natural. Yet here Julian has tried to compromise. He will not deny that natural death has a connection with sin ; i.e., it had really to be annulled by merits ; but his explanations in Book II. are very tortuous. Without sin death would have been " levissima " ; but God cannot do away with it entirely even for saints, for (VI. 30) : " non est tanti unius meritum, ut universa quæ naturaliter sunt instituta perturbet."

[4] Thus already Cælestius.

Christ, or Holy Scripture. In relation to God, for his righteousness is annulled by imputing the sins of others, and regarding as sinful a nature that has not yet sinned, just as much as it would be by ushering into the world, laden with sin, human beings born after Adam's fall. In relation to man, for a vitiated nature is then equivalent to a bad nature ; if a nature possesses evil, it is bad ; but in that case the guilt falls upon God, for he is responsible for our nature ; further, sin could only propagate itself, if we assumed a procreation of souls ; but this assumption is absurd ; finally, if sin is propagated through marriage, so that desire in marriage is and transmits sin, marriage is thereby condemned. In relation to the notion of sin, for sin is absolutely embraced by the will, so that it does not exist at all, where there is no free-will ; further, even if it could propagate itself, it could not be transmitted by baptised parents ; lastly, Augustine's contention that sin is itself used by God as a punishment of sin, that there is a divine law of sin, etc., is absurd and immoral. In relation to Christ, for were nature bad, it could not be redeemed, or, were there an inherited sin which became natural to man, Christ also must have possessed it. In relation to Holy Scripture, as countless passages show that sin is a matter of the will, and that God punishes each for his own sins alone. Rom. V. 12, merely asserts that all die because they themselves sin like Adam, or something similar ; in any case it contains nothing to support inherited sin.[1]

12. Thus all men created by God are in the position in which Adam was before the fall.[2] An unessential difference exists only in so far as Adam possessed at once the use of reason, while children do not ; that Adam was still untaught, while children are born into a society *in which the custom of evil prevails.* Pelagius at least teaches this.[3] The mere capa

---

[1] It is superfluous to quote passages ; see the detailed account in Klasen, pp. 116-182. Julian's explanation of Rom. V. 12 occurs in c. Jul. VI. 75-81. Besides charging him with Manichæism, Julian also accused Augustine of Traducianism, though he was no Traducian. The heretical name of "Traduciani" was originated by Julian (Op. imp. I. 6).

[2] De pecc. orig. 14.

[3] Ep. ad Demetr. The reign of sin in the world is also elsewhere strongly emphasised by Pelagius.

city of either (mera capacitas utriusque) is the original innocence.[1]

13. The habit of sinning, working by example, according to Pelagius, weakens the will (?). Yet nothing can be said as to how it really works; for otherwise the indifference of the will[2] is destroyed. Probably the meaning was that the possibility of good remained wholly intact, but the habit of sinning darkened reason.[3]

14. It is when we come to discuss grace that it is hardest to reproduce the view of the Pelagians; for it was here that they found it most necessary to accommodate their opinions. Very strong assertions occur in Pelagius and Julian—Cælestius was more reserved[4]—as to the necessity of divine grace (adjutorium) for every good work.[5] We also find statements to the effect

---

[1] This talk of primitive innocence is already in Julian a case of accommodation; for innocence of course always remains really the same. C. Jul. III. 36: "homo igitur innocentia quidem plenus, sed virtutis capax nascitur, aut laudem aut reprehensionem ex proposito accedente meriturus . . . nec justos nasci parvulos nec injustos, quod futuri sunt actibus suis, sed tantummodo infantiam innocentiæ dote locupletem." But the same chapter shows what is after all meant by this "innocence": Perfecta ignorantia (in scripturis justitia nominatur).

[2] Op. imp. I. 91: "liberum arbitrium et post peccata tam plenum est quam fuit ante peccata."

[3] Here, as in Stoicism, there is a gap in the system. Why is rational man irrational and bad? How can he possess *ratio* and an evil will at the same time? And how is the sinful habit explained?—Julian also says, besides (Op. imp. I. 16) "consuetudo peccati amorem delicti facit et exstinguit pudorem;" but he means in the teaching of Augustine.

[4] "The will is not free, if it needs God's help" (De gestis 42). "Si per gratiam (De gestis 30) omnia facimus, quando vincimur a peccato, non nos vincimur, sed dei gratia, quæ voluit nos adjuvare omni modo et non potuit."

[5] We can, indeed, exemplify almost all the principles of Augustinianism from the utterances of Pelagius and Julian. The number of passages in their works which sound like good Church doctrine is very great. We should require to quote these also in order to give an idea of the figure presented by the two men to the world; but this would carry us beyond our present limits. We do not, however, do injustice to their thought by omitting them; for they are only characteristic of their mode of expression. Pelagius never denied publicly that man always needed the divine grace, that he could only *adjuvante gratia esse* sine peccato (see De gestis 16, 22, 31; De gratia 2: "anathemo qui vel sentit vel dicit, gratiam dei, qua Christus venit in hunc mundum peccatores salvos facere, non solum per singulas horas aut per singula momenta, sed etiam per singulos actus nostros non esse necessariam, et qui hanc conantur auferre, pœnas sortiantur æternas"; see also his Confession to the Pope). Julian used, if possible, still stronger expressions; but both very often said exactly

that grace *facilitated* goodness.[1] Finally, others occur which teach that grace is superfluous, nay, strictly speaking, in itself impossible.[2] It is no injustice to the Pelagians to take the two latter positions, which, to a certain extent can be combined, as giving their true opinion ; for it was assuredly the chief intention of Pelagius to deprive Christians of their indolent reliance on grace, and Julian's main object was to show that the human constitution bore merit and salvation in its own lap. The proposition "homo libero arbitrio emancipatus a deo" really contains the protest against any grace.[3]

15. By grace we have throughout to understand in the first place the grace of creation ;[4] it is so glorious that

the opposite of what is here given. But they never did say that the grace of God through Christ established freedom from sin and salvation.

[1] These are the usual ones : free will exists in all men, but it is only supported by grace in the case of Christians (De gratia, 34) ; the rest only possess the "nudum et inerme conditionis bonum." Similarly Julian, but still more strongly (Op. imp. I. 40) : "quos fecit quia voluit nec condemnat nisi spretus ; si cum non spernitur, faciat consecratione meliores, nec detrimentum justitiæ patitur et munificentia miseiationis ornatur." I. 111 : "malæ voluntati veniam pro inæstimabili liberalitate largitur et innocentiam, quam creat bonam, facit innovando adoptandoque meliorem" (but can anything be better than good?). III. 106 : "Quod ais, ad colendum recte deum sine ipsius adjutorio dici a nobis sufficere unicuique libertatem arbitrii, omnino mentiris. Cum igitur cultus dei multis intelligatur modis, et in custodia mandatorum et in execratione vitiorum et in simplicitate conversationis et in ordine mysteriorum et in profunditate dogmatum . . . qui fieri potest, ut nos in confuso dicamus, sine adjutorio dei liberum arbitrium sufficiens ad ejus esse culturam . . . cum utique ista omnia, tam quæ dogmatibus quam quæ mysteriis continentur, libertas arbitrii per se non potuerit *invenire*, etc." There we see clearly how we are to understand the "adjutorium" ; it consists solely in the law of dogmas and mysteries given by God and not discovered by man, but not in a power. Therefore, because God had invented so many institutions, Julian can proceed : "hominem innumeris divinæ gratiæ speciebus juvari . . . præcipiendo, benedicendo, sanctificando, coercendo, provocando, illuminando."

[2] Impossible as a power, since the will cannot actually be determined. On this point Cælestius has alone expressed himself clearly, but Julian holds the same view, as he is never tired saying : "cunctarum origo virtutum in rationabili animo sita est."

[3] This proposition of Julian's is properly the key to the whole mode of thought : man created free is with his whole sphere independent of God. He has no longer to do with God, but with himself alone. God only re-enters at the end (at the judgment).

[4] The statements of the Pelagians as to grace are very often rendered intentionally (*e.g.*, De gestis Pel. 22) ambiguous, by their understanding it to mean the grace of

there have been perfect men even among heathens and
Jews.[1]

16. In the seeond place, it denotes the law (lex) of God ;
indeed, all grace, in so far as it is not nature, can at bottom
have no other character than that of illumination and instruction (doctrina). This facilitates the doing of the good.[2]

17. Thirdly, grace means the grace of God through Christ.
This also is at bottom *illuminatio et doctrina ;*[3] Christ works
by his example.[4] Pelagius and Julian admit that the habit of
sinning was so great that Christ's appearance was necessary.[5]
Julian's conception of this appearance was that Christ owed
what he became to his free will.[6] But it was necessary, over
and above instruction (doctrina), to assume, in conformity with
Church teaching and practice, an effective action through Christ

creation, and accordingly nature. Yet this is not the rule. Pelagius and Julian
distinguish three states : ex natura, sub lege, sub gratia (Chiisti) ; see C. duas epp, 1.
39.

[1] " Perfecta justitia " also in the old covenant (l.c.) and among "antiqui homines."
Julian often cites the perfect heathens, and sneers at Augustine's "splendida vitia.'
If the virtues of the heathens are not virtues, their eyes are not eyes (c. Jul. IV. 26-
30). Pelagius has made wholly contradictory statements on this point ; Julian
afterwards became more prudent ; but, finally, he always held the opinion that there
was no difference between a good Christian and a good heathen.

[2] The law was the first *augmentum beneficiorum dei ;* but it was at the same time
the fundamental form of all that God could further do after creation. Pelagius has
expressed himself very plainly (De gestis 30) : "giatiam dei et adjutorium non ad
singulos actus dari (in other places he says the opposite) sed in libero arbitrio esse *vel
in lege ac doctrina.*" That accordingly is all. Augustine therefore says very rightly
that Pelagius only admitted the grace "qua demonstrat et revelat deus quid agere
debeamus, non qua donat atque adjuvat ut agamus."

[3] See preceding note and Cælestius' statement : "lex sic mittit ad regnum
coelorum quomodo et evangelium."

[4] Example and imitation, see Op. imp. II. 146 sq.   C. Jul. V. 58 : "tolle
exempli causam, tolle et pretii, quod pro nobis factus est." Julian also ultimately
reduced the death of Christ to a type, Op. imp. II. 223.

[5] Op. imp. II. 217-222.

[6] It is very instructive that to Julian (as to Augustine) it is the man that forms the
peisonality in Jesus. He is distinguished from Augustine by saying that the man
Jesus was chosen by God and united with Christ *secundum merita.* The *profectus* is
also more plainly marked : Jesus was gradually adopted by the Word of God ; the
filius hominis gradually became the *filius dei* through the achievement of his will.
Accordingly, unless Augustine has greatly exaggerated, this still might be taught with
impunity at that time in the West (see Op. imp. IV. 84).

on the part of God. The Pelagians did not deny that this was
represented in baptism and the remissions granted by God;
they taught the forgiveness of sins through baptism. But they
could not show wherein this forgiveness consisted without
coming into conflict with freedom. As regards infant baptism,
they dared no longer dispute its necessity; indeed, they dared
no longer flatly declare that it was not given for the remission
of sins. They derived a certain consecration and sanctification
from it, but they disputed the doctrine that children dying
unbaptised were lost; these would only fail to enter the kingdom of heaven, the highest grade of felicity.[1]

18. Finally, the Pelagians taught that this grace through
Christ was compatible with the righteousness (justitia) of God,
because the latter did not preclude an increase of benefits,[2] but
that grace was given *secundum merita* (according to the merits
of the rational spirit) because in any other case God would have
been unjust.[3] The contention, however, that it was absolutely
necessary was never seriously advocated by them, and was frequently denied, and in the thesis that the operation of the
gospel is not different from that of the law, the former is in
point of fact completely reduced to the level of the latter. But
the law is itself nothing but a crutch not necessary to everyone.
Man is to be sinless: this state we can attain by our will; but
sinlessness (impeccantia) is rendered easy to the Christian; for
by looking to Christ he can easily turn, and in baptism, the

---

[1] The evasions in the case of baptism are so numerous that it is not worth while
mentioning separate instances. The notion of forgiveness was in itself very irksome
to the Pelagians; it could be at most a kind of indulgence, with difficulty compatible
with justice. They also touched on the question whether baptism extirpates sin or
removes guilt; but for them the question was senseless. As regards infant baptism,
all their statements are to be derived from the fact that they would neither abolish it,
nor admit baptisms of different value. The distinction between *regnum cœlorum* and
vita æterna was an eschatological *rudiment*, in this case welcome.

[2] Op. imp. I. 72, III. 163 : " augmenta beneficiorum divinorum utilia esse et neces-
saria omnibus in commune ætatibus dicimus, ita tamen ut nec virtus nec peccatum
sine propria cuiquam voluntate tribuatur."

[3] De gestis 30 : " De gratiam secundum merita nostra dari, quia si peccatoribus
illam det, videtur esse iniquus." This destroys the notion of grace; for it is only as
gratuitous that it is grace. Here it takes the form of a means of rewarding the good.
But if grace is neither *gratis* nor a power, it is nothing but an empty word.

mysteries, dogmas, and the commandments, he from the first
possesses nothing but means to promote virtue. All that Christ
did and the Church does is considered not as action but as
teaching.

The Pelagians deserve respect for their purity of motive, their
horror of the Manichæan leaven and the *opus operatum*, their
insistence on clearness, and their intention to defend the Deity.[1]
But we cannot but decide that their doctrine fails to recognise
the misery of sin and evil, that in its deepest roots it is godless,
that it knows, and seeks to know, nothing of redemption, and
that it is dominated by an empty formalism (a notional mythology) which does justice at no single point to actual quantities,
and on a closer examination consists of sheer contradictions.
In the *form* in which this doctrine was *expressed* by Pelagius—
and in part also by Julian—*i.e.*, with all the accommodations to
which he condescended, it was not a novelty.[2] But in its fundamental thought it was ; or, rather, *it was an innovation because
it abandoned, in spite of all accommodations in expression, the pole of
the mystical doctrine of redemption, which the Church had steadfastly maintained side by side with the doctrine of freedom.*[3]

III. The fundamental notion of Pelagianism is nature em-
bracing free will (liberum arbitrium); the fundamental notion
of Augustinianism is grace, and in the Pelagian controversy the
grace of God through Christ.[4] In Pelagianism the doctrine of
grace amounts to an " appendix " badly connected with the
main subject ; in Augustinianism the doctrine of nature is beset

---

[1] That Augustinianism is identical with Manichæism runs through Julian's polemic
like a red line. " Sub laude baptismatis eructat Augustinus Manichæorum sordes ac
naturale peccatum, ut ecclesiæ catholicæ pura hactenus sacramenta contaminet " (Op.
imp. I. 9).

[2] His condemnation was, therefore—from a legal standpoint—not above question ;
the rejection of his energetic appeal to freedom in Church instruction not in every
respect salutary.

[3] But from this point of view it could not be thoroughly opposed. Augustinianism
could alone overcome it. Augustine's criticism of this system will be best given
through an exposition of his own.

[4] Therefore the Pelagians attacked Augustine's doctrine of nature, and he their
doctrine of grace. Everything that Augustine has to say to the Pelagians springs
properly from the proof that they were ignorant of the nature of grace, and therefore
also of that of sin.

with contradictions, because *it is impossible to give a rational account of nature and history from the standpoint of the grace of experience.* For it is absolutely impossible to develop as a rational doctrine the conviction of the *transforming* grace of God who is also the *creator;* it must begin and end with the confession : " How incomprehensible are God's judgments and how inscrutable his ways!" Augustine, sneered at as "Aristoteles Pœnorum" as "philosophaster Pœnorum" (Op. imperf. III. 198, V. 11), knew this also. But living in an age when it was held to be culpable ignorance and unbelief not to answer all possible questions, and penetrated by the vulgar conviction that Holy Scripture solved all problems, he, too, made the highest facts and the feelings of the inner life which he had gained in the gospel the starting-point of a description of "primitive history" and the history of mankind that could not but end in contradictions. At the same time, the pathological experiences of the course of his life are mirrored in this description. The stream of living water still bears in its depths traces of the gloomy banks past which it once had flowed, and into which it had almost sunk.[1]

1. Mankind is, as experience shows, a "mass of sin" [massa peccati (perditionis)], waited on by death, and incapable of raising itself to the good ; for having revolted from God, it could no more return to him than an empty vessel could refill itself. But in Christ the Redeemer—and in him alone—the grace of God manifested itself and entered on the work of man's deliverance. Christ by his death removed the gulf between God and mankind—breaking the rule of the devil—so that the grace of God, which for that reason is *gratia per (propter) Christum,* could pursue its work.[2] This free grace (*gratia gratis*

---

[1] Since Augustine's fundamental theological conceptions have been already discussed above (see p. 94 ff.), we have here only to examine the doctrine of grace, and that of sin and the primitive state. This order is self-evident, while Pelagianism started at the doctrine of an indestructible nature.

[2] Expositions of the death of Christ as the ground of salvation are frequent in Augustine. But they refer mostly to the reign of the devil, which was *legally* abrogated by Christ's death ; on the other hand, they are much rarer when Augustine speaks of *positive* redemption. This deliverance from the devil's power was the common conception of Christ's death ; it was the *pretium* paid for us to the devil,

data)[1] working in the Church, is beginning, middle, and end.   Its aim is the rescue from the *massa perditionis*, that as guilty falls justly a prey to eternal death, of a fixed number of elect (certus numerus electorum), who enter eternal life.   They are saved because God, in virtue of his eternal decree of salvation, has pre-destinated, chosen, called, justified, sanctified, and preserved them.[2]   This is done through grace, which thus is (1) *pre-*

which he could not, however, retain.   But it plays a subordinate part in Augustine's whole system ; even the thought that God must be propitiated, of which we have echoes in Augustine, is not strictly carried out.   The grace of God to him means, as a rule, the annulling of the *state of sin*.   It is involved, however, in the nature of the case, that the reference is uncertain ; for it is hard to demonstrate how a "state" is changed *effectively* by the death of Christ.   But the looseness of connection was also a result of Augustine's conception of God ; for grace, at bottom, emanated from the inscrutable decree of God, or the *bonum esse*.   Augustine rarely connects *gratia infusa* in his thought with Christ, but with *caritas*, which is the essence of the Good.   Heie we have once more to remember that Christ himself, as a historical manifestation, was an instance in Augustine's view of predestinating grace (see above, p. 129).   "Therefore the activity of Christ, who, as living eternally, works directly in us, is loosely connected with the historical process of propitiation" (Dorner, p. 182).   That is, this "ever living Christ" is himself nothing but grace.   In Enchir. 108, Augustine has summed up all he had to say on the import of Christ's work ; but it will be found that, although the *reconciliatio cum deo*—only, indeed, as restoration to God—is not wanting, what is called "objective redemption" is left pretty much in the background.   Augustine accordingly conceived the import of Christ *spiritually* : "Neque per ipsum liberaremur unum mediatorem dei et hominum hominem Jesum Christum, nisi esset et deus.   Sed cum factus est Adam homo, scil. rectus, mediatore non opus erat.   Cum vero genus humanum peccata *longe separaverunt a deo*, per mediatorem, qui solus sine peccato natus est, vixit, occisus est, reconciliaii nos oporte-bat deo usque ad carnis resurrectionem in vitam æternam, *ut humana superbia per humilitatem dei argueretur* (that is the main thought, see above, p. 131 f.) *ac sanaretur et demonstraretur homini quam longe a deo recesserat* (to-day this conception of Christ's work would be called rationalistic), *cum per incarnatum deum revocaretur et exemplum obedientiæ per hominem-deum* (this expression, "homo-deus" was not used, so far as I know, before Augustine) *contumaci homini præberetur*, et unigenito suscipiente formam servi, quæ nihil ante meruerat, fons gratiæ panderetur *et carnis etiam resurrectio redemptis promissa in ipso redemptore præmonstraretur*, et per eandem naturam quam se decepisse lætabatur, diabolus vinceretur, nec tamen homo gloriaretur, *ne iterum superbia nasceretur*, etc."

  [1] Enchir. 107 : "Gratia vero nisi gratis est, gratia non est."
  [2] See the writings De corrept. et gratia, De dono perseverantiæ, De prædest. sanctorum, as well as expositions in all the works of Augustine's last years ; for they never fail to prove that he more and more recognised the doctrine of predestinating grace to be the main one.   Predestination does not rest on the foreknowledge that those particular men would follow grace, but it effects this result.   The scriptural proof is Rom. IX. (see De prædest. 34).

venient;[1] for it must first create the good will (faith).[2] (This prevenient grace can be combined with "the call" (vocatio);[3] but we must even here remember that the call comes to some who are not "called according to the purpose."[4] In the strict sense the whole transactions of grace apply only to those who are predestinated;[5] in the wider sense, grace operates as far as sanctification in a much greater circle, who, however, finally perish, because they have not received its last work.)[6] Augustine has inserted his whole religious experience in the confession of free and prevenient grace. He nowhere speaks with greater conviction, more simply and grandly, than where he praises the grace that snatches man from his sinful condition. But grace (2) works *co-operatively.*[7] This work evolves itself in a series of stages, since naturally it is only possible slowly and gradually to reach the goal whose attainment is desired, *viz.*, the perseverance and complete and actual regeneration of man [8]—re-creation

---

[1] Enchir. 32 : "Nolentem prævenit ut velit, volentem subsequitur, ne frustra velit." De gratia et lib. arb. 33 : " præparat voluntatem et cooperando perficit, quod operando inficit. Quoniam ipse ut velimus operatur incipiens." There are countless other passages.

[2] De spir et litt. 34 : "Non credere potest quodlibet libero arbitrio, si nulla sit suasio vel vocatio cui credat ; profecto et ipsum velle credere deus operatur in homine et in omnibus miseiicoidia ejus prævenit nos : consentire autem vocationi dei vel ab ea dissentire propriæ voluntatis est." Augustine's favourite text was, " Quid habes, quod non accepisti."

[3] See preceding note.

[4] See Augustine's last writings, *e.g.,*, De corr. 39 ; De præd. 32. The means of grace are uncertain ; the universal vocatio should be successful, but it is not.

[5] Here it is true that "deus ita suadet ut persuadeat." De prædest, 34 : " Electi sunt ante mundi constitutionem ea prædestinatione, in qua deus sua futura facta præscivit ; electi sunt autem de mundo ea vocatione, qua deus id, quod prædestinavit, implevit. Quos enim prædestinavit, ipsos et vocavit, illa scilicet vocatione secundum propositum, *non ergo alios sed quos prædestinavit ipsos et vocavit,* nec alios, sed quos prædestinavit, vocavit justificavit, ipsos et glorificavit, illo utique fine, qui non habet finem."

[6] Therefore it was possible for Augustine to conceive the means of grace as acting in the case of heietics, because he felt their efficacy in general to be in the end uncertain.

[7] See above, note 1. The commonest term is "adjutorium," which the Pelagians also used, but with a quite different meaning. They thought of a crutch, Augustine of a necessary power.

[8] That is, this regeneration, surpassing forgiveness of sin and faith, is always considered the goal. That is the moral phase of the religious movement. Renovatio=

into good men—accordingly his being rendered capable of doing
good works of piety and possessing merit.   The calling (vocatio)
first results in *faith* as God's gift.   This faith is itself subject to
growth, *i.e.*, it begins as unquestioning acceptance based on the
authority of the Church and Scripture ; it presents itself further
as obedience, then trust (fiducia) believing God, belief about
God, belief on God (credere deum, credere de deo, credere in
deum) and as such passes into love.[1] Parallel with this goes
the effective (visible) action of grace in the Church,[2] which
begins with the remission of sins.[3]   This is administered in baptism, and since the latter removes the guilt of original sin,[4] and
blots out sins previously committed, it is the "bath of regeneration."   But it is so only as an initiatory act ; for the actual
justification, which corresponds to co-operating grace, is not yet
gained, where sin is no longer imputed, but only where the irreligious man has *become* just, where accordingly an actual renovation has taken place.   This is effected through the infusion of
love into the heart by the Holy Spirit, and this love substitutes

---

justificatio = sanctificatio = sanctitas.   Thus even regeneration is only perfect at the
close.   Enchir. 31 : "We become free when God fashions us into good men."

[1] On faith as an advancing process of faith see Dorner, pp. 183-195.   Originally,
faith is contrasted with knowledge ; it is the acceptance on authority of things we
cannot know, nay, of what is contrary to reason ; but it grows into *assensus, fiducia*,
and spiritual perception, and thus passes into love, or, according to Paul and James,
into the faith that works in love.

[2] Yet, as follows from the above exposition, the whole process of grace is completely subjective, although the parallel of the rites of the Church is maintained.

[3] Augustine was the first to make baptism a real act of initiation (Ench. 64 : "a
baptismate incipit renovatio ").   The forgiveness of sins has an independent value
only for the baptised child if it dies ; otherwise it is an initiation.   Here, and for this
reason, we have Luther's divergence in the notion of faith.   De grat. et lib. arb. 27 :
"neque scientia divinæ legis, neque natura *neque sola remissio peccatorum* est illa
gratia per Christum, sed ipsa facit, ut lex impleatur."

[4] For Augustine's system it is a grave defect, sufficiently animadverted on also by
the Pelagians, that baptism only removes the guilt of inherited sin ; for with him
removal of guilt is really a slight matter, in any case not the chief concern.   But in
the formulas the "non imputare," as well as *fides*, undoubtedly appears as the chief
thing.   In reality, while the removal of guilt is the object of *fides historica*, sin is
blotted out by *gratia infusa*.   Where Augustine seeks to retain guilt as the supreme
conception, he always turns to its punishment.   Man is emptied by sin.   Thus sin
bears its punishment in itself.   Man despoiled, however, is much too dependent, too
much of a cipher, to be able to possess guilt.

good for evil desire (concupiscence). That is, the man now not
only makes the joyful confession : " To me to cleave to God is
a good thing," and delights in God as the *summum bonum*,
instead of in perishable possessions (the humility of faith, love
and hope in place of pride of heart), but gains also the power to
do good works. This new frame of mind and capacity, which
grace begets through the gift of the Holy Spirit, is the experience of justification by faith (justificatio ex fide).[1]

Justification is an act that takes place once for all, and is
completed *sub specie æternitatis,* and with reference to the fact
that everything can be comprised in faith. As an empirical
experience, however, it is a *process* never completed in this
world, because the being replenished with faith, which through
love labours to effect the *complete* transformation of man, is
itself subject to limitation in our present life.[2] This operation

---

[1] The formula *justificatio ex fide* is very frequent in Augustine. De spiritu et litt.
45 : " cum dicat gratis justificari hominem per fidem sine operibus legis, nihil aliud
volens intelligi in eo, quod dicit *gratis,* nisi quia justificationem opera non præce-
dunt. . . Quid est aliud justificati quam justi facti ab illo scilicet qui justificat impium
ut ex impio fiat justus." 15 : " non quod sine voluntate nostra justificatio fiat, sed
voluntas nostra ostenditur infirma per legem, ut *sanet* gratia voluntatem et sanata
voluntas impleat legem." C. Jul. II. 23 : " justificatio in hac vita nobis secundum tria
ista confertur : prius lavacro regenerationis, quo remittuntur cuncta peccata, deinde
congressione cum vitiis, a quorum reatu absoluti sumus, tertio dum nostra exaudiatur
oratio, qua dicimus, Dimitte nobis debita nostra." The whole process up to the
meritis and *vita æterna* in De gratia et lib. arb. 20. Love alone decides salvation,
because it alone replenishes the man despoiled by sin. Man receives his final salvation by being restored through the spirit of love to goodness, being, and God, and by
being united with him mystically yet really. The depreciation of faith follows necessarily from the notions of God, the creature and sin, all three of which have the mark
of the acosmic. Since there is no independence beside God, the act of faith on the
part of a subject in the presence of God only obtains any value when it is transformed
into union with God—the " being filled " by God. This union, however, is a product of the freed will and *gratia (cooperans).*

[2] This is argued very often by Augustine. The *boni concupiscentia* can, as experience shows, never wholly supplant on earth the *mala.* (De spiritu 6 : " adjuvat
spiritus sanctus inspirans pro concupiscentia mala concupiscentiam bonam, hoc est
caritatem diffundens in cordibus nostris.") For this very reason *diffusio caritatis*
(gratia infusa, inspiratio dilectio—Augustine has many synonyms for this power of
justification) is never perfected. Thus justification, which is identical with sanctification, is never completed because " opera " also are essential to it. Augustine appealed
expressly to James. *Gratia,* however, is never imparted *secundum merita bonæ
voluntatis,* let alone *bonorum operum* ; it first calls them forth.

of the spirit of love has its parallel in the effective (visible) dealings of grace in the Church, and that in the Lord's Supper (the incorporation into the love and unity of Christ's body) as well as in the Eucharistic sacrifice, penance, and Church works, so far as these are capable of blotting out sin.[1] These works, however, possess still another value. Renunciation of worldly pleasure is only completed in asceticism, and since at the Judgment God will deal with us in accordance with our works, the completion of justification can only consist in the sanctification, in virtue of which particular possessions—marriage, property, etc.—are wholly abandoned. It is not, indeed, absolutely necessary for everyone to fulfil the counsels of the gospel (consilia evangelica); we can live in faith, hope, and love without them. God's grace does not make everyone a saint,[2] to be worshipped, and to be implored to intercede for us. But everybody who is to be crowned must ultimately possess merits in some degree; for, at the Judgment, merits will alone be crowned, these ever being, indeed, like all good, God's gifts.[3] But the perseverance of the elect in love through the whole course of their life until the Judgment is (3) the highest and last gift of grace, which now appears as irresistible. Perseverance to the end is the good, without which all that went before is nothing. Therefore, in a sense, it alone is grace; for only those are finally saved who have obtained this irresistible grace. The called who do not possess it are lost. But why only a few

---

[1] See above, p. 155. We have to notice here also the juxtaposition of the two processes, the outer and inner. For the rest, the whole account of the process of salvation is not yet reduced to a strict plan. Augustine still confuses the stages, and, fortunately, has no fixed terminology. Scholasticism first changed all this.

[2] No one can wholly avoid sin ; but the saints can refrain from crimes (Enchir. 64).

[3] The work " De fide et operibus " is especially important at this point. Augustine expressly denies, c. 40, that faith and knowledge of God suffice for final blessedness. He holds by the saying : " Hereby we know him, if we keep his commandments." Against reformers like Jovinian, and not only against them, he defended the *consilia*, monachism, the higher morality, and the saints. De gratia et lib. arb. 1 : " per gratiam dei bona merita comparamus quibus ad vitam perveniamus æternam." By these *merita*, works thoroughly ascetic are to be understood ; see also the writings, De sancta virgin., and De bono viduit., in which, for the rest, Augustine is still more favourable to marriage than at a later date. His writings are at all times marked by a lofty appreciation of almsgiving.

obtain this gift, though it is bestowed *secundum merita*, is God's secret.[1] Eternal life and eternal damnation are decreed by one and the same justice.[2]

2. The doctrine of sin, the Fall, and the primitive state is sketched from the standpoint of free and prevenient grace. It follows from the doctrine of grace that sin characterises mankind as they now exist. Sin presents itself essentially as being without God (carentia dei), the voluntary diminution of strength of being.[3] The failure to possess God (privatio boni), the *non inhærere deo*, constitutes sin, and, indeed, the two thoughts—the one metaphysical, that sin is defect of being, the other ethical, that it is defect of goodness—coincide as we reflect on them,[4] just as in the examination of grace the metaphysical (the finding of being from not-being) and the ethico-religious elements always accord. This sin is a *state*: the wretched necessity of being unable to refrain from sinning (misera necessitas non posse non peccandi). Freedom in the sense of free choice is *not* destroyed;[5] but the freedom still existing always leads to sin; and this state is all the more dreadful, as there exists a certain knowledge of the good, nay, even a powerless desire for it, which invariably succumbs.[6] Positively, however, the sinful state presents itself as the *rule of the devil* over men,

---

[1] That grace is *gratis data* only appears certain to Augustine from the contention that it is irresistibilis, and embraces the *donum perseverantiæ*. The doctrine that the election of grace is unconditioned thus appears most plainly at the close of the whole line of thought ; see De corrept et grat. 34, and the writings De dono persev. and De prædest. sanct. But, according to Augustine, no one can be certain that he possesses this grace. Therefore with all his horror of sin, Augustine had not experienced the horror of uncertainty of salvation. For this reason Christ can take so secondary a place in the working out of the process of grace. Christ is for him the Redeemer, and is actively present in the Sacraments ; but he is not the pledge of the inner assurance of salvation.

[2] But Augustine assumes different degrees also in definitive salvation and perdition. That is characteristic for his moral theory.

[3] Dorner, p. 124 ff.

[4] See above, p. 114 f.

[5] This was constantly admitted by Augustine.

[6] We find in Augustine the two positions, that sinful man does not will goodness, and that he yet, under a blind impulse, pursues blessings, nay, even the good, but without ever attaining them.

as *pride*[1] and *concupiscence*.[2]   From that rule it follows that man must be redeemed *from without* before he can be helped.[3] Pride in relation to God and concupiscence show that man is sinful in soul and body.   Yet the emphasis falls on concupiscence ;[4] it is the lower desire, sensuous lust, which shows itself above all in the lust of the flesh.   The *motus genitalium, independent even of the will,* teaches us *that nature is corrupt ;* it has not become vice (vitium), but it is vitiated (natura vitiata).[5]   *It*

---

[1] The inclination to nothing (not-being) is always at the same time a striving for independence, which is false, and ends in being resultless.

[2] Pride is the sin of the soul, concupiscence *essentially* that of the body which masters the soul.   The inner evolution of sin from *privatio (defectus) boni* to *ignorantia, concupiscentia, error, dolor, metus, delectatio morbida,* see Enchir. 23.   What Augustine always regarded most in sin was the infirmity, the wound.

[3] The work of the *historical* Christ is *essentially* redemption from the power of the devil.

[4] Here enters the popular Catholic element, still further accentuated, however, by Augustine.   Enchir. 117 : " Regnat carnalis cupiditas, ubi non est dei caritas."

[5] The extremely disgusting disquisitions on marriage and lust in the polemical writings against Julian (also De civ. dei XIV.) are, as the latter rightly perceived, hardly independent of Augustine's Manichæism : (Julian, indeed, traces Traducianism to Manichæism ; see Op. imperf. III. 172).   (Manichæism, besides, already appears, in the treatment of the " ex nihilo," as if it were an evil substance ; Neoplatonism alone does not, in my opinion, explain this conception ; yet the above dependence cannot be strictly proved—see Loofs, D.-Gesch., 3 Ed., p. 215.)   And the disquisitions are by no means a mere outwork in Augustine's system ; they belong to its very centre.   The most remarkable feature in the sexual sphere was, in his view, the involuntariness of the impulse.   But instead of inferring that it could not therefore be sinful—and this should have been the inference in keeping with the principle " omne peccatum ex voluntate "—he rather concludes that there is a sin which belongs to nature, namely, to *natura vitiata,* and not to the sphere of the will.   He accordingly perceives a sin rooted in *natura,* of course in the form which it has assumed, a sin that propagates itself with our nature.   It would be easy now to prove that in thinking of inherited sin, he always has chiefly in view this very sin, the lust of procreation; but it is impracticable to quote his material here.   *It is clear that inherited sin is the basis of all wickedness, and that it is in quite a different position from actual sins, because in it nature, having become evil, infects the whole being.*   But it is obvious that this was an unheard of novelty in the Church, and must be explained by reference to Manichæism.   Of course Augustine did not intend to be a Manichæan.   He distinguishes sharply between *vitium* and *natura vitiata* (De nupt. 36 ; Op. imp. III. 188, etc., etc.,) ; he strives to introduce the " voluntarium " even into inherited sin (Retract. I. 13, 5) ; but dualism is not surmounted simply by supposing nature to have *become* " mala," and yet to propagate itself as evil, and the *voluntarium* is a mere assertion.   The dualism lies in the proposition that children possess original sin, because their parents have procreated them in lust—and by this proposition stands

therefore propagates sin. That it does so is attested by the evidence of the senses, the sensuous, and therefore sinful pleasure in the act of procreation, and by Holy Scripture (Rom. V. 12 f.). Thus mankind is a *massa perditionis* also in the sense that it procreates sin in itself from a corrupt nature. But since the soul in all probability is not procreated at the same time, it is in each case created by God,[1] so the body, begotten in the lust of the flesh, is quite essentially the bearer of sin.[2] That the latter thus descends is decreed by God; for sin is not always merely sin, but also, or often only, the punishment of sin (*peccatum* and *malum* combine in the sense of evil).[3] The sin which descends in the *massa perditionis* (peccatum originis, tradux peccati) is at once sin and sin's punishment. This has been ordained by him who decreed sins (the "ordinator peccatorum)." Every desire involves infatuation. It is the penalty of sin that we do the evil we would not. Every sin carries with it dissolution, the death of the sinner. It rends and

or falls the doctrine of original sin (De nupt. II. 15). So also Christ has sinlessness attributed to him, because he was not born of marriage (Ench. 41, 34), and Augustine imagined paradisaical marriages in which children were begotten without lust, or, as Julian says jestingly, were to be shaken from trees. All that he here maintains had been long ago held by Marcion and the Gnostics. One would have, in fact, to be a very rough being not to be able, and that without Manichæism, to sympathise with his feeling. But to yield to it so far as Augustine did, without rejecting marriage in consequence, could only happen at a time when doctrines were as confused as in the fifth century. Those, indeed, have increased the confusion still further, who have believed that they could retain Augustine's doctrine of inherited sin while rejecting his teaching as to concupiscence. But the history of dogma is the history of ever increasing confusions, and of a growing indifference not only to the absurd, but also to contradictions, because the Church was only with difficulty capable of giving up anything found in tradition. It cannot also be said that Augustine by his theory simply gave expression to the monastic tendency (Jerome, indeed, has gone just as far in his rejection of marriage—see lib. adv. Jovin.) ; for this was a tendency and not a theory. The legitimate point in Augustine's doctrine lies in the judgment passed by the child of God on himself, *viz.*, that without God he is wretched, and that this wretchedness is *guilt*. But this paradox of the verdict of faith is no key to the understanding of history.

1 See the correspondence with Jerome on this point which was never settled by Augustine.

2 This destroys the beautiful proposition (pride and humility) out of which, of course, no historical theories could be constructed.

3 On sin and sin's punishment (inherited sin is both), see Op. imp. I. 41-47, but even in the Confessions often, and De pecc. mer. II. 36.

dismembers him, it empties him and exhausts him, until he no longer exists. Thus death reigns in its various forms, till it reaches eternal death, in the *massa perditionis*. This humanity which is subject to the dreary necessity of not being able to refrain from sin (non posse non peccare) is therefore also and at the same time subject to the dreadful necessity of not being able to escape death (non posse non mori).[1] No power of its own can rescue it. Its best deeds are all stained from the roots; therefore they are nothing but splendid vices. Its youngest offspring, even if they have done nothing sinful, must necessarily be lost ; for since they possess original sin, *i.e.*, are destitute of God, and are burdened with concupiscence, they pass justly into damnation.[2] This is attested also by the Church when it baptises newly-born children.[3]

How did this state arise—a state which could not have been due to God the creator? Scripture and the Church answer : through Adam's Fall. The magnitude of this Fall had already been depicted in the Church; but from his standpoint Augustine had rightly to say that Adam's sin, and therewith sin in general, had not yet been duly perceived—yet the Church, as its institutions prove, had, it was alleged, appreciated it truly ; writers, however, had fallen short of this estimate. Adam's Fall was

---

[1] Even inherited sin is quite enough for damnation, as Augustine has very often maintained—and rightly, if there is such a thing.

[2] " Mitissima pœna " (Enchir. 103)—thus the man permits himself to soften the inscrutable righteousness of God which he teaches elsewhere. He answered the question why then should God continue to create men if they must almost all be lost, by referring to baptism, and the peculiar power of Divine Omnipotence to make good out of evil. Had God not been omnipotent, then he could not have permitted evil (Enchir. 11) ; " melius judicavit, de malis bene facere, quam mala nulla esse permittere " (c. 27, 100). But he himself was shaken by the problem presented by the death, unbaptised, of Christian children (De corr. et gr. 18). All who are lost are juste prædestinati ad pœnam (mortem)—see Enchir. 100 ; De civ. XXII. 24. Whether God damns all, or pardons some—nulla est iniquitas ; for all have deserved death (Enchir. 27). " Tenebatur justa damnatione genus humanum et omnes erant iræ filii (c. 33). Here in the later writings arises the doctrine of God's twofold will (judicium), the secret and the manifest. God does not will that all be blessed (Enchir. 103).

[3] It was very incorrect to derive Augustine's whole conception of original sin from the practice of infant baptism. It was, of course, very important to him as a means of proof.

inconceivably great.[1] When, in the hope of becoming like God, he transgressed God's command not to eat the apple, all conceivable sins were compressed into his sin: the revolt to the devil, pride of heart, envy, sensuous lust—all in all : self-love in place of love of God.[2] And it was all the more dreadful, as it was easy for Adam to refrain from sin.[3] Therefore also came the unspeakable misery, *viz.*, the punishment of sin, with and in sin, working itself out in death. Adam lost the possession of God.[4] This was followed by complete deprivation (defectio boni), which is represented as the death of the soul ; for the latter without God is dead (spiritual death).[5] The dead soul is now drawn downwards; it seeks its blessings in the mutable and perishable, and is no longer capable of commanding the body. The latter then asserted itself with all its wanton impulses, and *thus corrupted the whole human nature.*[6]

The corruption is manifest in sexual lust, whose sinfulness is evidenced by compulsion and shame, and it must be inherited since the central seat of nature is disordered.[7] It indeed still

[1] The description of the magnitude of Adam's Fall is in most of the anti-Pelagian writings, but also elsewhere.

[2] In the case of Adam's Fall Augustine gives the greatest prominence to the sin of the soul : "in paradiso ab animo cœpit elatio" (c. Jul. V. 17). We have "amor sui" as chief and radical sin in the Confessions ; Enchir. 45 gives a precise enumeration of all the sins committed in one act by Adam.

[3] That is, he was not only created good, but grace stood by him also as *adjutorium :* see under.

[4] The grace supporting him (adjutorium).

[5] Augustine always thinks first of this death. That the Pelagians accepted for their own purposes, since they held natural death to be natural. Augustine never maintained that formal freedom had been lost by Adam's sin, nay, in C. duas epp. Pelag. I. 5 he distinctly disputed this : "libertas periit, sed illa, quæ in paradiso fuit, non liberum arbitrium." But Augustine has represented the latter to be hopelessly hampered. See also the writing De gratia et lib. arb. In it he says (c. 45) : "deus induravit per justum judicium, et ipse Pharao per liberum arbitrium. But (Enchir. 105) : "Multo liberius erit arbitrium, quod omnino non poterit servire peccato."

[6] Thus sensuousness appears as the main detriment.

[7] Enchir. 26 : "Hinc post peccatum exul effectus stirpem quoque suam, quam peccando in se tamquam in radice vitiaverat, pœna mortis et damnationis obstrinxit, ut quidquid prolis ex illo et simul damnata per quam peccaverat conjuge per carnalem concupiscentiam, in qua inobedientiæ pœna similis [so far as the flesh here is not obedient to the will, but acts of itself] retributa est, nasceretur, traheret originale peccatum, quo traheretur per errores doloresque diversos ad illud extremum supplicium."

continues to be capable of redemption—it does not become an evil substance—but it is so corrupt that even grace can only blot out the guilt (reatus) of original sin ; it cannot completely extirpate concupiscence itself in the elect, as is proved by the survival of the evil sexual lust.　This inheriting of sin and of Adam's death is, however, not merely a fact, but it is just, because Scripture says that we have all sinned in Adam,[1] because all owe their life to sinful lust,[2] and because—God is just.

Adam's Fall presupposes that his previous constitution had been good.　This is taught, too, by Scripture, and it follows likewise from the assurance that God is the creator, and the good creator, of all things.[3]　If Adam was created good, then he possessed not only everything that a rational creature needs (body and soul and their due relationship as servant and master, reason and *free will*), but, above all, grace ever supporting and preserving him, the *adjutorium*, that is the bond of union with the living God ; for the virtuous man is not independent of God ; he is only independent when completely dependent on God.　Adam, accordingly, not only had a free will, *but this will was influenced in the direction of God*.[4]　For this very reason he was free (in God) ; but he was also free (able) to will evil ; *for evil springs from freedom*.　If Adam had not possessed a free will, he would have been unable to sin ; but in that case he would not have been a rational creature.　So he possessed the

---

[1] Augustine's exposition of the ἐφ᾿ ᾧ in De pecc. mer. I. 11 ; c. Jul. VI. 75 sq. ; Op. imp. II. 48-55 (against mere imitation).　The translation "in quo" was received by Augustine from tradition, and in general his doctrine of original sin is at this point closest to tradition.　If he had contented himself with the mystical, *i.e.*, the postulated, conception that all are sinners, because they somehow were all in Adam, his theory would have been no novelty.　But this "in quo" does not include, but excludes, original sin in the strict sense ; all are sinners personally, because they were all in Adam, or were Adam.　The conception that Adam's sin passed to all as actual sin, and affected them through contagion (by means of the parents who infect their children, Enchir. 46 ; doubts as to the extent of descent by inheritance, 47), is the complete antithesis of that mystical conception.

[2] See above, p. 210 f.

[3] On the doctrine of the primitive state, see Dorner, p. 114 ff.

[4] Both formal freedom and the true freedom which established Adam's obedience as the *mater omnium virtutum* are very strongly emphasised by Augustine as belonging to the primitive state ; De civ. XIV. 12 ; De bono conjug. 32.　On the primitive state, l.c. XI.-XIV. ; De corrept. 28-33.

power not to sin, or die, or forsake the good (posse non peccare,
—mori,—deserere bonum), but this through the *adjutorium*
(auxiliary grace) went so far in the direction of inability to sin
(non posse peccare) that it would have been easy for Adam to
attain it.[1] Had he attained it by means of free will (liberum
arbitrium), he would have received perfect blessedness in return
for the merit involved in his perseverance, he would have remained, and escaped death, in Paradise, and would have begotten children without sinful lust.   We see that the primitive state
was meant to be portrayed in accordance with the state of grace
of the present ; but an important difference prevailed, since in
the former case, the *adjutorium* was only the condition, under
which Adam could use his free will lastingly in being and doing

---

[1] This "ease" is strongly emphasised in De civ. XIV. 12-15. The whole
doctrine of the primitive state, like all teaching on this subject, is full of contradictions ; for we have here a grace that is meant to be *actual*, and is yet merely a condition, *i.e.*, it by no means *makes* a man good, but only leaves scope to the will.
Thereby the whole doctrine of grace is upset ; for if there is a grace at all which only
produces the *posse non peccare*, is not this the sole significance of all grace ? and if
that is correct, were not the Pelagians right ?   They, of course, maintained that
grace was only a condition.   *Augustine's doctrine of grace in the primitive state (the
adjutorium) is Pelagian*, and contradicts his doctrine of grace elsewhere.   We have
here the clearest proof that it is impossible to construct a history from the standpoint
of predestinating grace.   Augustine falls back on the assumption that God wished to
bestow on man a higher good than that he had received at first.   Enchir. 25, 105 :
" Sic enim oportebat prius hominem fieri, ut et bene velle posset et male, nec gratis
si bene, nec impune, si male ; postea vero sic erit, ut male velle non possit, nec ideo
libero carebit arbitrio . . . ordo prætermittendus non fuit, in quo deus ostendere
voluit, quam bonum sit animal rationale quod etiam non peccare possit, quamvis sit
melius quod peccare non possit."   But how does that accord with irresistible grace ?
Therefore the question rightly arises (De corrept. et gratia) : " Quomodo Adam non
perseverando peccavit, qui perseverantiam non accepit ?"   Is not the whole doctrine
of grace upset if we have to read (Enchir. 106) : "Minorem immortalitatem (*i.e.*,
posse non mori) natura humana perdidit per liberum arbitrium, majorem (*i.e.*, non
posse mori) est acceptura per gratiam, quam fuerat, si non peccasset, acceptura per
meritum, quamvis sine gratia nec tunc ullum meritum esse potuisset?"   Accordingly,
at the beginning and end (the primitive state and the Judgment) the moral view is set
above the religious.   The whole doctrine of predestinating irresistible grace is set in
a frame incompatible with it.   Thus Augustine is himself responsible if his Church in
after times, arguing from the primitive state and the Judgment (secundum merita),
has eliminated practically his doctrine of *gratia gratis data*.   He, indeed, said himself
(107) : " ipsa vita æterna merces est operum bonorum."   That would have been the
case with Adam, and it is also ours.   The *infralapsarian* doctrine of predestination,
as understood by Augustine, is very different from Calvin's.

good, while in the latter, it is the power, that, being irresistible, brings fallen man to perfection.

Contemporary criticism on this system may here be briefly summed up. Augustine contradicted himself in maintaining that all ability to attain goodness had been lost, and in yet admitting that freedom of choice—the decisive thing—remained. His notion of freedom was self-destructive, since he defined freedom as lasting dependence on God. His conception of original sin was self-contradictory, because he himself admitted that sin always springs from the will. He was compelled to teach Traducianism, which, however, is a heresy. And his Scriptural exegesis was arbitrary. In particular, God provokes sins, if he punishes sin with sin, and decrees the reign of sin ; he is unjust if he imputes to men the sins of others, while forgiving them their own, and, further, if he accepts some, and not others, just as he pleases. This contention leads to despair. Above all, however, the doctrine of original sin leads to Manichæan dualism, which Augustine never surmounted, and is accordingly an impious and foolish dogma. For, turn as he will, Augustine affirms an *evil nature*, and therewith a *diabolic creator of the world*. His doctrine of concupiscence conduces to the same view. Besides, he depreciates the glorious gift of human freedom, nay, even divine grace in Christ, since he holds that original sin is never entirely removed. Finally, his doctrines of the exclusive efficacy of grace and predestination put an end not only to asceticism and the meritoriousness of good works, but also to all human doings. It is useless to exhort, intercede for, or blame sinners, etc. In the end, even the connection with the Church, which Augustine insisted on so energetically in the Donatist controversy, seemed to be superseded.

Truth and error exist side by side in these observations. Perhaps the following considerations will be more pertinent. (1) The impossibility of determining the fate of the whole body of mankind and of every separate individual from the standpoint of *gratia gratis data*, is shown in the thesis of the damna-

tion of children who die unbaptised.   Here Augustine impugns
the thought of God's righteousness.   But this thought must
become worthless altogether if everything is overruled by predestinating and irresistible grace.   Thereby a grave injury is
inflicted on piety.   (2) The carrying out of the conception of
predestinating grace, which should be no more than a sentiment, *confined to himself*, of the redeemed, leads to a *determinism*
that conflicts with the gospel and imperils the vigour of our
sense of freedom.   Besides, the assumption of irresistible grace
rests above all experience, even above that of the believer, and
the doctrine of God's twofold will (see de grat. et lib. arb. 45)
makes everything affecting faith uncertain.   (3) Augustine did
not by any means hold so certainly that grace was grace through
Christ, as that it proceeded from the secret operation of God.
The acosmic Neoplatonic element in the doctrine of predestination imperilled not only the efficacy of the Word and Sacrament
(vocatio and justificatio), but also redemption through Christ in
general.   (4) The religious tendency in the system, the belief
that the decisive point was cleaving or not cleaving to God, received in the sequel a new version, and the moral attitude
became rather the crucial question—the will, of course when
freed, was an efficient cause of righteousness.   For this reason
the meaning of forgiveness, of the new fundamental relation to
God, and of the assurance of faith, was misunderstood.   The
former became an act of·initiation, the relation became temporary, and the assurance of faith, which even according to the
doctrine of predestination need not arise, was lost in the conception of a process of sanctification never or almost never
completed in this world, a process to which various grades of
salvation, just as there were various degrees of damnation, corresponded in the world beyond.   What a proof of moralism![1]
Between the thesis of the ancient (Greek) Church : " Where the
knowledge of God is, come also life and salvation," and Luther's
principle : " Where we have forgiveness of sins, we have also
life and salvation," we find Augustine's : " Where love is there
also follows a salvation corresponding to the measure of love."

[1] Enchir. 93 : "Tanto quisque *tolerabiliorem* ibi habebit damnationem, quanto hic
minorem habuit iniquitatem !"   Also 111.

Augustine examined the equation remission of sins=grace
through Christ, and expressly rejected it. This turn he gave
his doctrine also explains the contention that God, in the end,
crowns our merits, a view that conflicts with predestinating
grace, and opens the door to a refined form of righteousness by
works.[1] (5) The Neoplatonic notion of God and the monastic
tendency demand that all love should at the same time present itself in the form of asceticism. Thereby love drifts still further
apart from faith (as fiducia), threatens the sovereignty of the
latter, and gives free scope for all sorts of popular Catholic conceptions. (6) The conception—necessary in the system—of Adam's
Fall and original sin contains—apart from the mythology which
here takes the place of history—a bundle of inconsistencies and
extremely questionable ideas. The latter Augustine also perceived, and he tried, but without success, to guard against them.
Absolutely Manichæan is the view that man sins because he
was created from nothing, " nothing " being here treated as an
evil principle. (The Neoplatonic doctrine also sees in this
" nothing " the ground of sin ; but to it sin is merely finitude.
Augustine took a more profound view of sin, but he had also to
conceive the *nihil* as " more evil " in proportion, *i.e.*, to convert it
into the evil substance of Manichism.) Manichæan also is the
opinion that sexual desire is sinful, and that inherited sin is
explained simply from procreation as the propagation of a
vitiated nature (natura vitiata).[2] Absolutely contradictory are

---

[1] Augustine attempted, in opposition to Pelagianism, to exhibit the difference
between the law and faith : " fides impetrat quod lex imperat." He also succeeded
as far as the difference can be evolved from the notion of grace as the exclusive operation of God. But since he had not obtained an insight into the strict and exclusive
cohesion of grace and faith, he did not succeed in thinking out and holding fast the
distinction between law and faith to the end. He had no assured experience that the
law prepared the way for wrath and despair. At this point Luther intervened.

It is perhaps the worst, it is at any rate the most odious, consequence of Augustinianism, that the Christian religion in Catholicism is brought into particularly close
relations to the sphere of sex. The combination of grace and sin (in which the latter
takes above all the form of original sin identified with the sexual impulse and its
excesses) became the justification of that gruesome and disgusting raking up of
human filth, which, as is proved by the moral books of Catholicism, is a chief business
of the priest, the *celibate* priest and monk, in the confessional. The dogmatic
treatises of mediæval and modern times give, under the heading " sin," a wholly
colourless idea of what is really considered " sin," of that which incessantly occupies

the positions that all sin springs from freedom (the will), and that children just born are in a state of sin. It is extremely suspicious to find that, when sin is more minutely dealt with, concupiscence is practically ranked above alienation from God (deo non adhærere), this *also*, indeed, resulting from uncertainty as to Traducianism. It again raises our doubts when we see original sin treated as if it were more serious than actual sin; for while the former can only be washed out by baptism, the latter can be atoned for by penance. The whole doctrinal conception at this point shows that the conviction of the redeemed, that without God he is lost and unfit to do any good work, is a verdict of the believer on himself, a verdict that marks a *limit*, but can never become a principle by which to consider the history of mankind. *At this point, just because the contradictions were so enormous, the development of dogmatic with Augustine was on the verge of casting off the immense material in which it had been entangled, and of withdrawing from the interpretation of the world and history; but as Augustine would not abandon that material, so men will not, even at the present day, let it go,* because they suppose that the Bible protects it, and because they will not learn the humility of faith, that shows itself in renunciation of the attempt to decide on God's government of the world in history.[1]

the imagination of common Christians, priests, and, unfortunately, also many "saints." We have to study the mirrors of the confessional, the moral books and legends of the saints, and to surprise the secret life, to perceive to what point in Catholicism religious consolation is especially applied. Truly, the renowned educational wisdom of this Church makes a sad shipwreck on this rock! It seeks here also to oppose sin; but instead of quieting the imagination, which is especially interested in it, it goes on exciting it to its depths, drags the most secret things shamelessly to the light in its dogmas of the virgin, etc., and permits itself to speak openly of matters of which no one else ventures to talk. Ancient naturalism is less dangerous, at any rate for thousands less infectious, than this seraphic contemplation of virginity, and this continual attention to the sphere of sex. Here Augustine transmitted the theory, and Jerome the music. But how far the beginnings reach back! Tertullian had already written the momentous words (De pudic. 17): "Quid intelligimus carnis sensum et carnis vitam nisi quodcunque pudet pronunciare?" Later writers were nevertheless not ashamed to utter broadly what the far from prudish African only suggested.

[1] We have at the same time to notice that no Church Father was so keenly conscious as he of the limitations of knowledge. In almost all his writings—a bequest

(7) But apart from original sin, Augustine's notion of sin raises doubts, because it is constructed at least as much on the thought of God as the supreme and true being (summum and verum esse) as on that of his goodness (bonum esse). Although the stamp of guilt is not wholly misunderstood, yet it is the thought of the misery produced by sin with its destructiveness and hideousness that comes to the front. Hence we understand why Augustine, passing over justifying faith, perceived the highest good in " infused love " (caritas infusa). (8) Finally the doctrine of the primitive state is beset by inconsistency, because Augustine could not avoid giving grace another meaning in that state from that it possessed in the process by which the redeemed is justified. With him grace is ultimately identical with irresistible grace—anything else is a semblance of it ; but though Adam possessed grace, it was not irresistible.

But all these grave objections cannot obscure the greatness of the perception that God works in us " to will and to accomplish," that we have nothing that we have not received, and that dependence on God is good, and is our possession. It is easy to show that in every single objectionable theory formulated by Augustine, there lurks a true phase of Christian self-criticism, which is only defective because it projects into history, or is made the foundation on which to construct a " history." Is not the doctrine of predestination an expression of the confession : " He who would boast, let him boast in the Lord " ? Is not the doctrine of original sin based on the thought that behind all separate sins there resides sin as want of love, joy, and divine peace? Does it not express the just view that we feel ourselves guilty of all evil, even where we are shown that we have no guilt?

of the Academy and a result of his thought being directed to the main matter—he exhorts his hearers to refrain from over-curiousness, a pretence of knowledge that runs to seed.   He set aside as insoluble very many problems that had been and were afterwards often discussed, and he prepared the way for the concentration of the doctrinal system on its own material.

4. *Augustine's Interpretation of the Symbol (Enchiridion ad Laurentium). The New System of Religion.*

After the exposition given above p. 106 f., we shall best conclude our account of Augustine's *rôle* in the history of dogma,
by reviewing the expositions given in the Enchiridion of the
contents of the Catholic religion. Everything is combined in
this book to instruct us as to the nature of the revision (and on
the other hand of the confirmation) by Augustine of the popular
Catholic dogmatic doctrine that gave a new impress to the
Western Church. We shall proceed first to give a minute
analysis of the book, and then to set down systematically what
was new and at the same time lasting.

Augustine begins by saying that the wisdom of man is piety
("hominis sapientia pietas est" or more accurately " θεοσέβεια ")
(2). The answer to the question how God is to be worshipped,
is—by faith, hope, and love. We have accordingly to determine
what is meant by each of these three virtues (3). In them is
comprised the whole doctrine of religion. They cannot, however, be established by reason or perception, but must be
derived from Holy Scripture, and be implicitly *believed in* on
the testimony of the sacred writers (4). When the soul has
attained this faith, it will, if faith works in love, strive to reach
that *vision* by which holy and perfected souls perceive the
ineffable beauty, the complete contemplation of which is
supreme blessedness. "The beginning in faith, the completion
in sight, the foundation Christ." But Christ is the foundation
only of the Catholic faith, although heretics also call themselves
by his name. The evidence for this exclusive relationship
between Christ and the Catholic Church would carry us too far
here (5). We do not intend to enter into controversy, but to
expound (6). The *Symbol* and the *Lord's Prayer* constitute the
contents of faith (symbol), and of hope and love (prayer); but
faith also prays (7). Faith applies also to things which we do
not hope for, but fear ; and further to our own affairs and those
of others. So far as it—like hope—refers to invisible, future
blessings, it is itself hope. But without love it profits nothing,

because the devils also believe. Thus everything is comprehended in *faith, which works by love and possesses hope* (8)

Augustine now passes to the Symbol (the ancient Apostolic
creed), in order to state the contents of faith. In §§ 9-32, he
deals with the first article. The knowledge of nature and
physics does *not* belong to faith—besides, scholars conjecture
rather than know in this matter (opinantes quam scientes).
It is enough for the Christian to believe that the goodness
of the creator is simply the first cause of all things, so that
there is no nature unless either it is he himself, or is of him.
Further, that this creator is the " Trinity, supremely and equally,
and unchangeably good " (trinitas summe et æquabiliter et
immutabiliter bona), and that while created things do not
possess this quality, they are good ; nay, everything collectively
is very good, and produces a wonderful beauty, in which evil,
set in its right place, only throws the good into relief (9, 10).
Augustine at once passes to the doctrine of evil. God permits
it only because he is so powerful that he can make good out of
evil, *i.e.*, he can restore the defect of the good (privatio boni),
evil being represented as such defect (morbus [disease] vulnus
[wound]). In the notion of that which is not supremely good
(non summum bonum esse) we have the capacity for deteriora-
tion ; but the good, which is involved in the existence of any
substance, cannot be annihilated, unless the substance itself be
destroyed. But in that case corruption itself also ceases, since
it can never exist save in what is good : evil can only exist in
what is good (in a *bonum*). This is expounded at length (11-15).
The causes of good and evil must be known, in order to escape
the errors and infirmities (ærumnæ) of this life. On the other
hand, the causes of great movements in nature—Augustine
returns to § 9—need not be known ; we do not even know the
conditions of our health, which yet lie nearest us (16)!

But is not every error an evil, and what are we to think of
deception, lying? These questions are minutely discussed in
§§ 17-22. Every case of ignorance is not an error, but only
supposed knowledge is, and every error is not hurtful ; there is
even a good error, one that is of use. But since it is unseemly
(deforme atque indecens) for the mind to hold the truth to be

false, and the uncertain certain, our life is for that very reason wretched, because at times we need error that we may not lose our life. Such will not be that existence, "where truth itself will be the life of our soul" (ubi ipsa veritas vita animæ nostræ erit). But the lie is worst, so bad that even liars themselves hate being lied to. But yet falsehood offers a difficult problem. (The question of lying in an emergency, whether it can become a duty for a righteous man, is elaborately discussed.) Here again the most important point is to determine wherein one errs : "*it is far more tolerable to lie in those things that are unconnected with religion than to be deceived in those without belief in, or knowledge of, which God cannot be worshipped*" (18).[1] Looked at accurately, every error is an evil, though often, certainly, a small one. It is possible to doubt whether every error is also sinful—*e.g.*, a confusion about twins, or holding sweet to be bitter, etc.; at all events, in such cases the sin is exceedingly small and trivial (minimum et levissimum peccatum), since it has nothing to do with the way that leads to God, *i.e.* with the faith that works in love. Error is, indeed, rather an evil than a sin, a sign of the misery of this life. In any case, however, we may not, in order to avoid all error, seek to hold nothing to be true—like the Academicians ; for it is our duty to *believe*. Besides the standpoint of absolute nescience is impracticable ; for even he who knows not must deduce his existence from this consciousness of nescience (20). We must, on the contrary, avoid the lie ; for even when we err in our thought, we must always say what we think.[2] Even the lie which benefits another is sinful, although men who have lied for the general advantage have contributed a great deal to prosperity (22). Augustine returns to § 16 : we must know the causes of good and evil. The sole first cause of the good is the goodness of God; the cause of evil is the revolt of the will from the unchangeable God

---

[1] " Longe tolerabilius est in his quæ a religione sunt sejuncta mentiri, quam in iis, sine quorum fide vel notitia deus coli non potest, falli." *E.g.*, to tell anyone falsely that a dead man is still alive is a much less evil than to believe erroneously that Christ will die once more.

[2] C. 22. "Et utique verba propterea sunt instituta, non per quæ se homines invicem fallunt, sed per quæ in alterius quisque notitiam cogitationes suas perferat." (Compare Talleyrand).

on the part of a being, good but changeable, first, an angel, then man (23). From this revolt follow all the other infirmities of the soul [ignorance, concupiscence, etc.] (24). But the craving for blessedness (appetitus beatitudinis) was not lost

We now have an exposition of Adam's endowment, the Fall, *original sin*, the sen ence of death, the *massa damnata*, which suffers along with the doomed angels, etc. God's goodness is shown, however, in his grant of continued existence to the wicked angels, for whom there is no conversion besides, and in his preservation of men. Although it would have been only justice to give them also over to eternal punishment, he resolved to bring good out of evil (25-27). It was his merciful intention, *i.e.*, to supplement from mankind the number of the angels who persevered in goodness, rendered incomplete by the fall of some, in order that the heavenly Jerusalem might retain its full complement, nay, should be increased by the "sons of our Holy Mother" [filii sanctæ matris] (28-29). But the men chosen owe this not to the merits of their own works (to free will); for in themselves they are dead like the rest (suicides), and are only free to commit sin. Before they are made free, accordingly, they are slaves ; they can only be redeemed by grace and faith. Even faith is God's gift, and works will not fail to follow it. Thus they only become free, when God fashions them anew (into the *nova creatura*), producing the act of will as well as its accomplishment ("quamvis non possit credere, sperare, diligere homo rationalis, nisi velit"—although rational man cannot believe, hope, or love, unless he will).[1] That is, God makes the will itself good (misericordia præveniens) and constantly assists it [miseric. subsequens] (30-32).

The exposition of the second article follows in §§ 33-55. Since all men are by nature children of wrath, and are burdened by original sin and their own sins, a mediator (reconciliator) was necessary, who should appease this wrath (justa vindicta) by presenting a unique sacrifice. That this was done, and we from being enemies became children, constitutes the grace of God through Jesus Christ (33). We know that this mediator is the "Word" that became flesh. The Word was not transformed,

---

[1] C. 32 : " Ex utroque fit, id est, ex voluntate hominis et misericordia dei."

but assumed our complete human nature from the virgin, being conceived not by the *libido matris*, but by faith—and therefore sinlessly.[1] The mother remained a virgin in giving birth (in partu) (34). We have now a short discussion on Christ as "God and man in unity of person, equal to God, and as man less than God" (35). Christ, the man who was deemed worthy to be assumed by God to form one person with him, is the most splendid example of grace given *gratis*, and not according to merits. The same grace that fell to the man Christ and made him sinless falls to us in justification from sins. It also revealed itself in Christ's miraculous birth, in connection with which, besides, the Holy Ghost did not act like a natural father. It was rather the whole Trinity that created the offspring of the virgin : the man Jesus, like the world, is the creation of the Trinity. But why precisely the Holy Ghost is named, it is hard to say. In any case, the man Jesus was not the son of the Spirit, but the latter is probably named in order to point to the grace that, existing without any preceding merits, had become in the man Jesus an attribute which in some way was natural (quodammodo naturalis); for the Holy Spirit is "so far God that he may be called the gift of God" [sic deus, ut dicatur etiam dei donum] (36-40). This is followed again by a long section (41 to 52) on sin and the relation of Christ to it. Christ

---

[1] Augustine's whole conception of the sinfulness mingled with all procreation, and his view that sexual desire is due not to nature as originally created, but to sin, have admittedly their roots in the earliest period. But they were expressed with Augustine's thoroughness only by the Gnostics, Marcion and—the author of the fragment *De resurrectione* ascribed to Justin. The parallel offered by the latter (c. 3) is extremely striking. There is not yet, naturally, any question of sin being propagated through sexual union ; that union is held simply to be sinful ; μήτρας ἐστὶν ἐνέργεια τὸ κυΐσκειν καὶ μορίου ἀνδρικοῦ τὸ σπερμαίνειν· ὥσπερ δέ, εἰ ταῦτα μέλλει ἐνεργεῖν ταύτας τὰς ἐνεργείας, οὕτως οὐκ ἀναγκαῖον αὐτοῖς ἐστιν τὸ τὴν ἀρχὴν ἐνεργεῖν (ὁρῶμεν γοῦν πολλὰς γυναῖκας μὴ κυΐσκούσας, ὡς τὰς στείρας, καὶ μήτρας ἐχούσας), οὕτως οὐκ εὐθέως καὶ τὸ μήτραν ἔχειν καὶ κυΐσκειν ἀναγκάζει· ἀλλὰ καὶ μὴ στεῖραι μὲν ἐξ ἀρχῆς, παρθενεύουσαι δέ, κατήργησαν καὶ τὴν συνουσίαν, ἕτεραι δὲ καὶ ἀπὸ χρόνου· καὶ τοὺς ἄρσενας δὲ τοὺς μὲν ἀπ' ἀρχῆς παρθενεύοντας ὁρῶμεν, τοὺς δὲ ἀπὸ χρόνου, ὥστε δι' αὐτῶν καταλύεσθαι τὸν δι' ἐπιθυμίας ἄνομον γάμον· There are also beasts that refrain from having connection, ὥστε καὶ δι ἀνθρώπων καὶ δι ἀλόγων καταργουμένην συνουσίαν πρὶν τοῦ μέλλοντος αἰῶνος ὁρᾶσθαι· καὶ ὁ κύριος δὲ ἡμῶν Ἰησοῦς ὁ Χριστὸς οὐ δι' ἄλλο τι ἐκ παρθένου ἐγεννήθη, ἀλλ' ἵνα καταργήσῃ γέννησιν ἐπιθυμίας ἀνόμου καὶ δείξῃ τῷ ἄρχοντι καὶ δίχα συνουσίας ἀνθρωπίνης δυνατὴν εἶναι τῷ θεῷ τὴν ἀνθρώπου πλάσιν·

was free from original and actual sin, but was himself—on account of similarity to sinful flesh—absolutely called sin. That is, he became a sacrifice for sin, representing our sin in the flesh in which he was crucified, " that in some way he might die to sin, in dying to the flesh,"[1] and from the Resurrection might seal our new life (41). That is bestowed on us in baptism. *Everyone* dies to sin in baptism—even the children, who die to original sin—and in this respect sin is to be understood collectively; for even in Adam's sin many forms of sin were contained. But children are obviously infected not only by Adam's sin, but also by those of their parents. For their birth is corrupt, because by Adam's sin *nature was perverted*; moreover the actual sins of parents "although they cannot thus change nature, impose guilt on the children" (etsi non ita possunt mutare naturam, rcatu tamen obligant filios). But Augustine refrains from deciding how far the sins of ancestors project their influence in the chain of descent. It is all expiated by the mediator, the man Jesus Christ, who was alone equipped with such grace as not to need regeneration ; for he only accepted baptism by John in order to give a grand example of humility, just as he also submitted to death, not from compulsion, but in order to let the devil receive his rights (42-49). Christ is thus Adam's anti-type ; but the latter only introduced one sin into the world, while Christ took away all that had since been committed. All were condemned in Adam; none escapes the condemnation without Christ. Baptism is to be solemnised as " the grand mystery in the cross of Christ" (mysterium grande in cruce Christi); for according to Paul baptism is " nothing but the similitude of Christ's death ; but the death of Christ crucified is nothing but the similitude of the remission of sin, that as in him a true death took place, so in us a true remission of sins."[2] This is elaborated in accordance with Rom. VI ; we are dead to sin through baptism (50-52). The clauses of the Symbol are now enumerated down to the "sitting at the right hand"

---

[1] " Ut quodammodo peccato moreretur, dum moritur carni."

[2] " Nihil aliud nisi similitudo mortis Christi ; nihil autem aliud mortem Christi crucifixi nisi remissionis peccati similitudinem, ut quemadmodum in illo vera mors facta est, sic in nobis vera remissio peccatorum."

with the observation: "*It was so carried out that in these matters the Christian life which is borne here should be typified not only mystically by words but also by deeds*."[1] That is established in connection with each separate article. Thus the "sitting at the right hand" means: "set your affections on those things that are above" (quæ sursum sunt sapite). On the other hand, the Return of Christ has no reference to *our* earthly life. It belongs entirely to the future. The judgment of the living and dead may also suggest to us the just and unjust (53-55).

To the third article §§ 56-113 are devoted; it is accordingly most elaborately elucidated. §§ 56-63 treat of the Holy Ghost, who completes the Trinity, and so is no part of creation, and also of the Holy Church. This is the temple and city of the Trinity. But it is here regarded as a whole. That is, it includes the section which exists in heaven and has never experienced a fall—the angels who aid the pilgrim part (pars peregrinans) being already united with it by love (56). The Church in heaven is void of evil and unchangeable. Augustine admits that he does not know whether there are degrees of rank among the angels, whether the stars belong to them, or what the truth is as to their bodily form (57-59). It is more important to determine when Satan invests himself in the form of an angel of light (60). We shall only know the state of the heavenly Church when we belong to it ourselves. The Church of this world, for which Christ died, we do know; for the angels he did not die; yet the result of his work also extends to them, in so far as enmity to them is at an end, and their number is once more complete. Thus by the one sacrifice the earthly host is again united with the heavenly, and the peace is restored that transcends all thought—not that of angels, but of men; but even angels, and men who have entered the state of felicity, will never comprehend the peace of God as God himself does (61-63).

Augustine now passes to the "remission of sins" (64-83): "by this stands the Church on earth" (per hanc stat ecclesia quæ in terris est). So far as our sins are forgiven, "the angels

---

[1] "Ita gestum est, ut his rebus non mystice tantum dictis sed etiam gestis configuraretur vita Christiana quæ hic geritur."

are even now in harmony with us" (concordant nobiscum angeli etiam nunc). In addition to the "great indulgence," there is a continuous remission of sins, which even the most advanced of the righteous need, for they often descend to their own level and sin. Certainly the life of the saints may be free from transgressions, but not from sin (64). But even for grave offences there is forgiveness in the Church after due penance; and the important point is not the time of penance, but the anguish of the penitent. But since this emotion is concealed from our fellow-men, and cannot be inspected, the bishops have rightly instituted penitential seasons "that the Church may also be satisfied," the Church beyond whose pale there is no forgiveness; for it alone has received the pledge of the Holy Ghost (65). Evils remain in this world in spite of the *salutaria sacramenta*, that we may see that the future state is their goal. There are punitive evils; for sins last on, and are punished in this life or the next (66). We must certainly not fancy that faith by itself protects from future judgment ($\dot{\omega}\varsigma$ $\delta\iota\dot{\alpha}$ $\pi\upsilon\rho\dot{o}\varsigma$), it is rather only the faith that works in love (faith and works). By "wood and stubble" we are not to understand sins, but desires after earthly things lawful in themselves (67, 68). It is credible that a purifying fire exists for *believers* even after death (69)—sinners can only be saved by a corresponding penance combined with almsgiving. Almsgiving is now discussed in detail (69-77). At the Last Judgment the decision turns on it (Mat. XXV. 34 ff.). Of course we are at the same time to amend our lives; "God is to be propitiated for past sins by alms, not by any means to be bribed that we may always be allowed to commit sins with impunity."[1] God blots out sins "if due satisfaction is not neglected" (si satisfactio congrua non negligatur), without giving permission to sin (70). Daily prayer furnishes satisfaction for small and light daily sins (71).[2] The forgiveness, also, that we bestow on others is a kind of alms. Speaking generally, everything good we give to others,

---

[1] " Per eleemosynas de peccatis præteritis est propitiandus deus, non ad hoc emendus quodam modo, ut peccata semper liceat impune committere." Accordingly some Catholics must even then have looked on alms as conferring a license.

[2] " Delet omnino hæc oratio minima et quotidiana peccata."

advice, comfort, discipline, etc., is alms. By this we besides
help to gain forgiveness of our own sins (72). But the highest
stages of almsgiving are forgiveness of sins and love of our
enemies (73).[1] Those virtues everyone must practise, that he
himself may be forgiven (74). But all these alms fail to benefit
us unless we amend ourselves; that is, the alms we give to ourselves are the most important. Of him alone who has mercy
on himself is the saying true : " Give alms and all is right (pure)
with you." We must love ourselves with the love that God has
bestowed on us ; this the Pharisees, who only gave outward
alms, did not do, for they were the enemies of their own souls
(75-77). The divine judgment, however, can alone determine what sins are light or grave. Many things permitted by
the apostles—*e.g.*, matrimonial intercourse prompted by desire
—are yet sinful ; many sins which we consider wholly trifling
(*e.g.*, reviling), are grave ; and many—*e.g.*, unchastity—which
custom has brought us to look on lightly, are dreadful, even
though Church discipline itself has become lax in dealing with
them (78-80). All sin springs either from ignorance or weakness. The latter is the more serious ; but divine grace alone
aids us to overcome either (81). Unfortunately, from false
weakness and shame, public penance is frequently withheld.
Therefore God's mercy is not only necessary in the case of
penitence, but also that men may resolve to show penitence.
But he who disbelieves in and despises the forgiveness of
sin in the Church commits the sin against the Holy Ghost
(82, 83).

The resurrection of the body is dealt with in §§ 84-113.
First, the resurrection of abortions and monstrosities is discussed (85-87); then the relation of the new body to its old
material—every particle of which need not pass into the former ;
and further, the corporeal difference, the stainlessness and
spirituality of bodies in the future state (88-91). We must not
concern ourselves with the constitution of the bodies of the lost
who also rise again, although we are here confronted by the

---

[1] Augustine here says with great truth that love of our enemies is possible only to a
small minority (the perfect). But even those who do not attain it are heard if they
utter the fifth petition in faith.

great paradox that a corruptible body does not die nor an incorruptible feel pain.[1] (92). Those will have the mildest punishment who have only original, but not actual, sin. Damnation in general will be marked by degrees, depending in each case on the measure of sin (93). Augustine now comes to speak of predestination in detail (94-108): "no one is saved except by undeserved mercy, and no one is condemned except by a deserved judgment."[2] That is the theme. It will become manifest in eternal life *why* of two children the one is accepted out of mercy, and the other rejected in accordance with justice. God's refusal of salvation is not unjust, though all might have been saved if he had willed; for nothing happens without his will or permission (95). Even in permitting evil his action is good, or the first article of the Symbol would no longer hold true (96). But if God's will cannot be frustrated by any choice of his creatures, how does the fact that all are not saved agree with the assurance that "he wills that all should be saved" (1 Tim. II. 4)? The usual answer, that men will not, is obviously false; for they cannot hinder God's will, as he can certainly turn even the bad into a good will. Accordingly, God does not will that all be saved, but he justly sentences sinners to death (Rom. IX.), that he who receives salvation may boast in the Lord. God is free in his election to grace; he would not have been to be blamed if he had redeemed no one after Adam's Fall; so neither is he to be blamed if in his mercy he redeems only a few, that none may boast of his own merits, but in the Lord. God's will is expressed in the case of the lost as much as in that of the saved ("in the very deed by which they opposed his will, his will regarding them was done").[3] So great are the works of the Lord that nothing that takes place against his will happens outside (præter) of it. A good son wishes his father to live, but God, whose will is good, decides that he should die. Again, a bad son wishes his father to die, and God

---

[1] In hell "mors ipsa non moritur."

[2] "Nisi per indebitam misericordiam nemo liberatur et nisi per debitum judicium nemo damnatur."

[3] "Hoc ipso quod contra voluntatem fecerunt ejus, de ipsis facta est voluntas ejus."

also wills this. The former wills what God does not ; the latter
what he does. Yet the former stands nearer God ; for in the
case of men it is the final intention that counts, while God
accomplishes his good will even through the bad will of men.
He is always just and always omnipotent (97-102). Therefore
1 Tim. II. 4 can only mean that God wills all *classes* of men to
be saved, or that all those whom he resolves to save will be
saved. In any case it is not to be imagined that he desires to
save all, but is prevented (103).

Had God foreknown that Adam, in keeping with his constitution, would have retained forever the will to avoid sin, he
would have preserved him in his original state of salvation.
But he knew the opposite, and therefore shaped his own will to
effect good through him who did evil. For man must have
been so created originally as to be able to do good and evil.
Afterwards he will be changed, and will no longer be able to
will evil ; " nor will he therefore be without free choice " (nec
ideo libero carebit arbitrio) ; for free will still exists, even if a
time comes when we cannot will evil, just as it even now exists,
although we can never will our own damnation. Only the
order of things had to be observed, first the " posse non," then
the " non posse." But grace is always necessary, and would
have been even if man had not sinned ; for he could only have
attained the " non posse " by the co-operation of grace. (Men
can indeed starve voluntarily, but mere appetite will not keep
them alive ; they require food.) But since sin entered, grace is
much greater, because the will had itself to be freed in order
that it might co-operate with grace (104-106.) Eternal life,
though a reward of good works, is also a gift of grace, because our
merits are God's gifts. God has made one vessel to honour and
another to dishonour, that none should boast. The mediator
who redeemed us required also to be God, " that the pride of
man might be censured by the humility of God " (ut superbia
humana per humilitatem dei argueretur), and that man might
be shown how far he had departed from God, etc. (107, 108).
After this long excursus, Augustine returns to § 93, and deals
(109) with the intermediate state (in abditis receptaculis), and
the mitigation obtained by departed souls through the Mass,

and the alms of survivors in the Church ; for there are many
souls not good enough to be able to dispense with this provi-
sion, and not bad enough not to be benefited by it. " Wherefore here (on the earth) all merit is acquired by which anyone
can be relieved or burdened after this life."[1] What the Church
does for the dead (pro defunctis commendandis) is not inconsistent with Rom. XIV. 10 ; II. Cor. V. 10. For those who are
wholly good it is a thanksgiving, for those not altogether bad
an atonement, for those entirely wicked it is resultless, but
gives comfort to the survivors ; nay, while it makes remission
complete (plena), it renders damnation more tolerable (110).
After the Judgment there are only two states, though there are
different grades in them. We must believe in the eternal
duration of the pains of hell, although we may perhaps suppose
that from time to time God lightens the punishment of the lost,
or permits some sort of mitigation. " Death will continue
without end, just as the collective eternal life of all saints will
continue " (111-113).[2]

Following his programme, Augustine ought now to have
discussed in detail hope and love (prayer) ; but he omits doing
so, because he has really touched on everything already. He
therefore confines himself to affirming that hope applies solely
to what we pray for in the Lord's Prayer, that three petitions
refer to eternal, four to temporal, benefits, and that Matthew
and Luke do not really differ in their versions of the Prayer
(114-116). As regards love, he points out that it is the greatest
of all. It, and not faith and hope, decides the measure of goodness possessed by a man. Faith and hope can exist without
love, but they are useless. The faith that works in love, i.e., the
Holy Spirit by whom love is infused into our hearts, is all-
important ; for where love is wanting, fleshly lust reigns (117).
There are four human conditions : life among the deepest
shades of ignorance (altissimis ignorantiæ tenebris), under the
law (which produces knowledge and conscious sin), under grace
or good hope, and under peace (in the world beyond). Such

---

[1] Quocirca hic (in terra) omne meritum comparatur, quo possit post hanc vitam
relevari quispiam vel gravari.

[2] Manebit sine fine mors, sicut manebit communiter omnium vita æterna sanctorum.

has also been the history of God's people ; but God has shown
his grace even at the first and second stages (118), and thus
even now man is laid hold of sometimes at the first, sometimes
at the second, stage, all his sins being forgiven in his regeneration (119), so that death itself no longer harms him (120). All
divine commands aim at love, and no good, if done from fear of
punishment or any other motive than love, is done as it ought.
All precepts (mandata) and counsels (consilia) given by God
are comprised in the command to love God and our neighbour,
and they are only rightly performed when they spring, at
present in faith, in the future in immediate knowledge, from
love.   In the world of sight each will know what he should love
in the other.   Even now desire abates as love increases, until it
reaches the love that leads a man to give his life for another.
But how great will love be in the future state, when there no
longer exists any desire to be overcome !

No one can mistake the popular Catholic features of this
system of religion.   It is based on the ancient Symbol.   The
doctrines of the Trinity and the Two Natures are faithfully
avowed.   The importance of the Catholic Church is strictly
guarded, and its relation to the heavenly Church, which is the
proper object of faith, is left as indefinite as the current view
required.   Baptism is set in the foreground as the " grand
mystery of renovation," and is derived from Christ's death, in
which the devil has obtained his due.   Faith is only regarded
as a preliminary condition ; eternal life is only imparted to
merits which are products of grace and freedom.   They consist
of works of love, which are summed up in almsgiving.   Almsgiving is freely treated ; it constitutes penance.   Within the
Church forgiveness is to be had for all sins after baptism, if only
a fitting satisfaction is furnished (satisfacere ecclesiæ ; satisfactio
congrua).   There is a scale of sins, from crimes to quite trivial
daily offences.   For this reason, wicked and good men are
graded ; but even the best (sancti, perfecti) can only be sinless
in the sense that they commit none but the lightest sins.   The

saints are the perfect ascetics ; asceticism is the culmination of
love ; but all do not need to practise it ; we must distinguish
between commands and counsels. In the future state both
felicity and perdition will also be graded. Departed souls, if at
death they have only left trivial sins unatoned for by penance,
will be benefited by the masses, alms, and prayers of survivors.
They are placed in a purgatory that cleanses them in the form
of a decreed punishment.[1] If here popular Catholic elements
are already strengthened, and the way prepared for their future
elaboration, that is equally true of the doctrines of the intermediate state, the temporary mitigation of the punishment of
the lost, the help afforded by holy angels to the Church of the
present world, the completion—by means of redeemed mortals
—of the heavenly Church reduced in number through the Fall
of the wicked angels, the virginity of Mary even *in partu*,[2] and
the grace of Christ as being greater than Adam's sin. This
also applies to the opinion that the ignorant adherence to a
false religion is worse than the knowing utterance of a lie, and
to many other doctrines developed by Augustine in other
writings. Finally, the conception of salvation that holds it to

---

[1] The Enchiridion is not the only work in which Augustine has spoken of this *ignis
purgatorius.*

[2] The growing Marian dogma (see Vol. IV., p. 314) was thus strengthened rather
than weakened by Augustine. He agreed entirely with Ambrose and Jerome
(against Jovinian). By a woman came death, by a woman came life ; Mary's faith
conceived the Saviour. Julian's remarkable objection to the doctrine of original sin,
that it made Mary to be subject to the devil (nascendi conditione), Augustine met by
saying (Op. imp. IV. 122) : "ipsa conditio nascendi solvitur gratia renascendi."
We may not maintain it to be certain (see Schwane II., p. 691 f.) that Augustine thus
implicitly taught Mary's immaculate conception. On the other hand, he undoubtedly held her to be without active sin ; see De nat. et gr. 36 : " Excepta itaque s.
virgine Maria, de qua propter honorem domini nullam prorsus, cum de peccatis
agitur, haberi volo quæstionem ; unde enim scimus, quid ei plus gratiæ collatum
fuerit ad vincendum omni ex parte peccatum, quæ concipere et parere meruit, quem
constat nullum habuisse peccatum ? hac ergo virgine excepta si omnes illos sanctos
et sanctas, cum hic viverent, congregare possimus et interrogare, utrum essent sine
peccato, quid fuisse responsuros putamus, utrum hoc quod ista dicit an quod Johannes
apostolus ? " Gen. ad litt. X. 18-21. Augustine helped to give Mary a special position between Christ and Christians, simply because he first emphasised strongly the
sinfulness of all men, even the saints, and then *excepted Mary.* Mary's passive
receptivity in relation to grace is emphasised with the same words as that of the man
Jesus.

consist in "vision" and "fruition" is at the root of and runs
through everything.   Yet the most spiritual fact, the process of
sanctification, is attached to mysteriously operating forces.

But on the other hand, this system of religion is new.   The
old Symbol—the Apostles interpreted by the Nicene—was
supplemented by new material which could only be very loosely
combined with it, and which at the same time modified the
original elements.   *In all three articles the treatment of sin, forgiveness, and perfecting in love is the main matter* (10-15 ; 25-33 ;
41-52 ; 64-83).   Everything is presented as a spiritual process,
to which the briefly discussed old dogmatic material appears
subordinated.   Therefore, also, the third article comes into the
foreground ; a half of the whole book is devoted to the few
words contained in it.   Even in the outline, novelty is shown :
religion is so much a matter of the inner life that faith, hope,
and love are all-important (3-8).   *No cosmology is given in the
first article ;* indeed, physical teaching is expressly denied to
form part of dogmatics (9, 16 f.).   *Therefore any Logos doctrine
is also wanting.*   The Trinity, taught by tradition as dogma, is
apprehended in the strictest unity ; *it is the creator.*   It is
really one person ; the "persons," as Augustine teaches us
in other writings, are *inner* phases (moments) in the *one God ;*
they have no cosmological import.   Thus the whole Trinity
also created the man Christ in Mary's womb ; the Holy Ghost
is only named because "spiritus" is also a term for "God's
gift" (donum dei).   Everything in religion relates to God as
only source of all *good*, and to *sin ;* the latter is distinguished
from *error*.   Hereby a breach is made with ancient intellectualism, though a trace of it remains in the contention that errors
are very small sins.   Wherever sin is thought of, so is free,
predestinating grace (gratia gratis data).   The latter is contrasted with the sin inherited from Adam ; it first gives freedom
to the enslaved will.   The exposition of the first article closes
with the reference to prevenient and subsequent mercy.   How
different would have been the wording of this article if Augustine had been able to give an independent version !

The case is not different with the second article.   The actual
contents of the Symbol are only briefly touched on—the

Second Advent is merely mentioned without a single Chiliastic observation. On the other hand, the following points of view come to the front. On the one side we have the *unity* of Christ's personality as the man (homo) with whose soul the Word united itself, *the predestinating grace*, that introduced this man into personal unity with the Deity, although he possessed no merits (hence the parallel with our regeneration); the close connection of Christ's death with redemption from the devil, atonement, and baptism (forgiveness of sins). But on the other side we find *the view of Christ's appearance and history as loftiness in humility, and as the pattern of the Christian life.* Christ's significance as redeemer [1] is quite as strongly expressed for Augustine in this humility in splendour, and in his example of a Christian life (see S. Bernard and S. Francis), as in his death. He fluctuates between these two points of view. The Incarnation wholly recedes, or is set in a light entirely unfamiliar to the Greeks. Thus the second article has been completely changed.

The chief and novel point in the third article consists in the freedom and assurance with which Augustine teaches that the forgiveness of sins in the Church is inexhaustible. When we consider the attitude of the ancient Church, Augustine, and Luther, to the sins of baptised Christians, an external criticism might lead us to say that men grow more and more lax, and that the increasing prominence given to grace (the religious factor) was merely a means of evading the strict demands made by the gospel on morality—the Christian life. And this view is also correct, if we look at the great mass of those who followed those guides. But in their own case their new ideas were produced by a profounder consciousness of sin, and an absorption in the magnitude of divine grace as taught by Paul. Augustine stands midway between the ancient Church and Luther. The question of personal assurance of salvation had not yet come home to him; but the question: " How shall I get rid of my sins, and be filled with divine energy?" took the

---

[1] Sin and original sin are again discussed in §§ 41-52, but they are now looked at from the standpoint of their removal through the baptism that emanates from Christ's death.

first place with him. Following the popular Catholic view, he
looked to good works (alms, prayer, asceticism); but he conceived them to be the product of grace and the will subject to
grace; further, he warned Christians against all external doing.
As he set aside all ritualistic mysticism, so he was thoroughly
aware that nothing was to be purchased by almsgiving pure
and simple, but that the issue depended on an inner transformation, a pure heart, and a new spirit. At the same time he was
sure that even after baptism the way of forgiveness was ever open
to the penitent, and *that he committed the sin against the Holy
Ghost who did not believe in this remission of sins in the Church.*
That is an entirely new interpretation of the Gospel saying.
The concluding section of the Symbol (resurrectio carnis) is
explained even more thoroughly than the forgiveness of sins in
its third treatment in the third article. But after a short discussion of the subject proper—the *doctrine of predestination* [1]
and a view which as doctrine is likewise virtually new, and
takes the place of Origen's theory of Apokatastasis—the main
theme is the supposition of an intermediate state, and of a
cleansing of souls in it, to which the offerings and prayers of
survivors can contribute.

Piety: *faith* and *love* instead of fear and hope. Theory of

---

[1] The doctrine of predestination—before Augustine almost unheard of in the
Catholic Church—constituted the power of his religious life, as Chiliasm did that of
the post-apostolic, and mysticism that of the Greek Church. In Augustine,
in addition to its Biblical and Neoplatonic supports, the doctrine had indeed
a strong religious root—free grace (gratia gratis data). But the latter by
itself does not explain the importance which the doctrine had gained in his
case. As everything that lives and works in nature is attached to something else,
and is never found in an *independent* state, so, too, there is no distilled piety.
On the contrary, so long as we men are men, precisely the most vital piety
will be least isolated and free. None but the dogmatist can construct such a religion.
But history teaches that all great religious personalities have connected their saving
faith inextricably with convictions which to the reflecting mind appear to be irrelevant
additions. In the history of Christianity there are the three named—Chiliasm,
mysticism, and the doctrine of predestination. It is in the bark formed by these
that faith has grown, just as it is not in the middle of the stem, but at its circum-
ference, where stem and bark meet, that the sap of the plant flows. Strip the tree,
and it will wither ! Therefore it is well-meant, but foolish, to suppose that Augustine would have done better to have given forth his teaching without the doctrine of
predestination.

religion : something higher than aught we call doctrine, a new *life* in the power of love. The doctrine of Scripture : the substance—the gospel, faith, love and hope—God. The Trinity : the one living God. Christology : the one mediator, the man Jesus into union with whose soul the Deity entered, without that soul having deserved it. Redemption : death for the benefit of enemies and humility in greatness. The Sacraments : the Word side by side with the Symbols. Salvation (felicity): the *beata necessitas* of the *good*. *The good :* blessedness in *dependence on God.* History : *God works everything in accordance with His good pleasure.* With that compare the dogmatics of the Greeks ! [1]

The extent and position of dogma were also modified by this revolution. The old dogmas of the undivided Church, simply because they passed into the background, and were no longer expressive of piety itself, became more rigid ; they more and more received the character of a legal system. The new dogmas, on the contrary, the doctrines of sin and grace in which piety lived, did *not yet* receive in their positive form the position and value of the old, nor were they definitely stated in rounded formulas.[2] Thus, through the instrumentality of Augustine, the extent and importance, in the history of dogma, of the doctrine of the Church became more uncertain. On the one hand, that doctrine was referred back to the gospel itself; on the other, it was much less sharply marked off than before from theology, since the new thoughts were not enclosed in fixed formulas. There was formed round the old dogma, which held its ground as an inflexible authority, a vast indefinite circle of doctrines, in

---

[1] An excellent comparison between Origen and Augustine occurs in Bigg, The Christian Platonists, pp. 284-290. He has sharply emphasised the inconsistencies in Augustine's doctrine of the primitive state, original sin, and grace, but he has not overlooked the advance made by Augustine on Origen. If we evolve Augustine's doctrine from predestination, then Bigg is right when he says : "Augustine's system is in truth that of the Gnostics, the ancestors of the Manichees. For it makes no real difference whether our doom is stamped upon the nature given to us by our Creator, or fixed by an arbitrary decree."

[2] The resistance of the Pelagians and their associates was also a *resistance to the formation of new dogmas in general.* Exactly like the Eusebians in the Arian conflict, they also fought against the new construction of dogmas by the North African Church on formal grounds.

which the *most important* religious conceptions lived, and which yet no one was capable of examining and weaving into a fixed connection. That is the state of dogma in the Middle Ages. *Side by side with the growing inflexibility, the process of internal dissolution had already begun.*

During the storms of the tribal migrations, just before the power of barbarianism broke in, God bestowed on the Church a man who judged spiritual things spiritually, and taught Christendom what constituted Christian piety. So far as we can judge, the young Germano-Roman peoples, like the Slavs, would have remained wholly incapable of ever appropriating independently and thoroughly the contemporary Christian religion, the Church system transmitted to them as law and cultus in fixed formulas, they would never have pierced through the husk to the kernel, if along with that system they had not also received Augustine. It was from him, or rather from the Gospel and Paulinism under his guidance, that they derived the courage to reform the Church and the strength to reform themselves.

CHAPTER V.

HISTORY OF DOGMA IN THE WEST DOWN TO THE BEGINNING OF THE MIDDLE AGES (A.D. 430-604).

WE have already described in Vol. III. of our present work, as far as it bore on the history of dogma, the part taken by the West during this period in the Christological controversies of the East, the great impetus given to the papacy by the successors of Damasus, and further by Leo I. and his successors. We have shown how the papal power was in the sixth century embroiled, and (under Justinian) almost perished, in the East Gothic and Byzantine turmoils; how the fifth Council produced a schism in the West, and shook the position of the papacy, and how on the other hand the latter regained and strengthened its importance through the instrumentality of Gregory I.[1][2] We also

---

[1] Gregory, certainly, had almost to abandon the fifth Council.

[2] The papal power received its greatest accession of authority from the days of Damasus to the end of the fifth century: it was then settled that the primacy was to be a permanent institution of the Catholic Church. This accession of strength was partly due to the fact that in that century the Chair of St. Peter was occupied by a number of peculiarly capable, clever, and energetic Bishops. But the advance was caused to a still greater extent by external conditions. The most important may be mentioned here. (1) The dogmatic complications in the East gave the Popes an opportunity of acting as umpires, or of exhibiting in full light the doctrinal correctness "characteristic of the Chair of St. Peter." (2) The Western Roman Empire leant ultimately for support, in its decline, on the Roman Bishop (see the Ep. Valent. III. to Leo. I.); when it perished the latter was its natural heir, since the central political power in the West was gone, and the Byzantine Emperor had not the power, the leader of the German hosts not the prestige, necessary to restore it. (3) The storms of the tribal migration drove the Catholics of Western countries, which were seized by Arians, into the arms of Rome; even where this did not happen at once, the opposition ceased which had been previously offered to the claims of the Roman Bishop by the provinces, especially North Africa. (4) The patriarchal constitution never got established in the West, and the Metropolitan only succeeded in part; thus the development into the papal constitution was ensured for the future. (5) The transactions with the political power of Eastern Rome and the Imperial Bishop there now

reviewed the important work, in which Vincentius of Lerinum
standing on Augustine's shoulders, described the *antiquitas
catholicæ fidei, i.e.,* the Catholic conception of tradition.[1] The
whole West was agitated in our period by the storms of the
tribal migrations. The ancient world received its final blow,
and the Church itself, so far as it was composed of Romans,
seemed to run wild under the horror and pressure of the times.[2]
The young peoples which streamed in were Christian, but Arian.
In the kingdom of the Franks alone there arose a Catholic,
German nation, which began slowly to be fused with the ancient
Roman population ; but the Church, with its cultus, law, and
language, remained Latin : *victus victori legem dat.* The Franks
were at the outset in the Latin Church, as at the present day
the Mongolian tribes of Finland are in the Greek Church of
Russia. This Latin Church, which, however, had parted in
Franconia with the Roman Bishop, or was only connected with
him by respect for him, preserved its old interests in Gaul and
Spain, and continued its former life until the end of the sixth
century.[3] Even up till that time the old civilisation had not
wholly perished in it, but it was almost stifled by the barbarian-

---

compelled the Roman Bishops, that they might not be at a disadvantage in dealing
with Constantinople, to deduce their peculiar position, which they owed to the capital
of the world, entirely from their spiritual (their apostolic or Petrine) dignity. But
this *exclusive* basing of the Roman Chair on Peter afforded the firmest foundation
at a time when all political force tottered or collapsed, but the religious was respected.
Even the thought of political sovereignty, so far as such a thought could arise in the
Roman Empire at all, seems to have dawned on Leo's successors. In any case, the
position of the papacy was so secure at the close of the fifth century, that even the
frightful storms of the sixth century were unable to uproot it. That in the West—
outside of Rome—the *theory* of the Roman Bishop (following Matt. XVI.) came but
slowly to be recognised, and that the attempt was made to retain independence as far
as the exigencies of the case permitted, ought to be expressly noticed. Theologians
only admitted that the Roman Bishop represented ecclesiastical unity, and did not
assent to the papistical inference that it was the prerogative of Rome to govern the
Churches.

Vol. III., p. 230 ff.

Salvian. de gubern. III. 44 : "Ipsa ecclesia, quæ in omnibus esse debet placatrix
dei, quid est aliud quam exacerbatrix dei ? aut præter paucissimos quosdam, qui
mala fugiunt, quid est aliud pæne omnis cœtus Christianorum quam sentina vitiorum ?"

[3] See Hatch, "The Organisation of the Early Christian Churches," Lecture viii.,
and "The Growth of Church Institutions," p. 1 f.

ism, which resulted from fusion with the invading populace.   In North Africa, in spite of dreadful sufferings, Catholic Latin ecclesiasticism held its ground till on into the seventh century. But the Church, once so independent in its relations with Rome, found itself compelled more than once in this period to turn for succour to Rome for its self-preservation.   The position of Italy, *i.e.*, of the Roman Bishop, was wholly peculiar, for the *Church* of Middle and Lower Italy never played any part in Church history.   So far as a Catholic Church still existed in the West in the German Empire, it represented the remnant of the shattered Western Roman Empire, and therefore lay in the sphere of power of the Roman Bishop, even if this relationship might not take any definite shape for the moment.   But this Roman Bishop was himself fettered to the East, and political and ecclesiastical ties compelled him to look more to the East than the West.   The fact that he nevertheless did not lose his connection with the latter, he, in the sixth century, owed more to his past, and his impregnable position in Rome, than to a deliberate policy.[1]

Under the Catholic Bishops who had survived in Gaul and North Africa as representatives of the Roman Empire, a not altogether unimportant part of the history of dogma was enacted in our period, *viz.*, the fight for and against complete Augustinianism.   The Roman Bishop, though much more concerned with the Christological and political questions of the East, intervened also in this matter.   At the close of our period, when absolute darkness had settled on the West, the great monachist Pope and "father of superstitions" introduced the ecclesiastical world to the Middle Ages in the form required by uncivilised peoples.   In doing so, he had not to do violence to his own convictions ; for the civilisation that was passing away inclined to barbarism.[2]

---

[1] The recognition in Rome of the fifth Council had almost alienated Italy and North Africa from the Pope.

[2] Yet classical culture was never quite extinct in Italy (Rome).   Its representatives in the sixth century were Cassiodorus, the pious churchman, on the one hand, and Boethius, the latitudinarian, on the other.   The former laboured earnestly on behalf of the Church and monachism of his time (compare also the exertions of Junilius) ; the latter was the instructor of a later age (see above, p. 34).

We have only therefore to consider, in what follows, the conflict waged round Augustinianism, and the position of Gregory
the Great in the history of dogma.[1]

[1] On the history of the Apostolic Symbol in our period see my article in Herzog's
R. E. 3 Ed. ; Caspari, Quellen I.-IV. Vols. ; v. Zezschwitz, System der Katechetik
II. 1.   Of the additions made to the ancient Roman Symbol, and afterwards universally accepted, the only one important dogmatically is the phrase " communio sanctorum." It can be proved from the second homily of Faustus of Rhegium (Caspari,
Kirchenhist. Anekdota, p. 338), and his Tractat de symbolo, which he certainly did
not edit himself (Caspari, Quellen IV., p. 250 ff.), that South Gallican Churches had
the words " communio sanctorum " in the Apostolicum in the second half of the fifth
century.   It is debatable whether they already stood in the Symbol of Nicetas, whom
I identify with Nicetas of Romatiana—the friend of Paulinus of Nola ; they may also
have merely belonged to the exposition, which was strongly influenced by Cyril's
Catechisms (see Kattenbusch, Apost. Symbolum, 1894, Vol. I).   If it were certain
that they were merely meant in the Gallican Symbol to stand in exegetical apposition
to " sancta ecclesia," then we would have to suppose that that Symbol had been
influenced by the countless passages in which Augustine describes the Church as
communio sanctorum, i.e., of the angels and all the elect, inclusive of the simple
justi (or with synonymous terms).   But, firstly, one does not conceive how a mere
exegetical apposition should have got into the Symbol, and why that should have
happened particularly in Gaul ; secondly, the explanation of the words by Faustus
points in another direction.   We read in his second homily : " Credamus et sanctorum communionem, sed sanctos non tam pro dei parte, quam pro dei honore
veneremur.   Non sunt sancti pars illius, sed ipse probatur pars esse sanctorum.
Quare ? quia, quod sunt, de illuminatione et de similitudine ejus accipiunt ; in sanctis
autem non res dei, sed pars dei est.   Quicquid enim de deo participant. divinæ est
gratiæ, non naturæ.   Colamus in sanctis timorem et amorem dei, non divinitatem dei,
colamus merita, non quæ de proprio habent, sed quæ accipere pro devotione
meruerunt.   Digne itaque venerandi sunt, dum nobis dei cultum et futuræ vitæ
desiderium contemptu mortis insinuant."   And still more clearly in the Tractate (p.
273 f.) : ". . . transeamus ad sanctorum communionem.   Illos hic sententia ista
confundit, qui sanctorum et amicorum dei cineres non in honore debere esse blasphemant, qui beatorum martyrum gloriosam memoriam sacrorum reverentia monumentorum colendam esse non credunt.   In symbolum prævaricati sunt, et Christo in
fonte mentiti sunt."   Faustus accordingly understands by the " sancti " not all the
justi, but—as Augustine not infrequently does—the specifically " holy," and he con-
tends that the words aimed at the followers of Vigilantius who rejected the worship
of the saints.   In that case " communio sanctorum " means communion of or with
the specifically " holy."   It is still matter of dispute whether this is really the idea to
which the Apostolicum owes its questionable acquisition, or whether the latter is
only a very early artificial explanation.   On the " filioque " in the Constantinopolitan
Creed, see Vol. IV., p. 126 f.

1. *The Conflict between Semi-Pelagianism and Augustinianism.*

Augustine and the North-African Church had succeeded in getting Pelagianism condemned ; but this did not by any means involve the acceptance of Augustinianism in the Church. Augustine's authority, indeed, was very great everywhere, and in many circles he was enthusiastically venerated ;[1] but his doctrine of *gratia irresistibilis* (absolute predestination) met with opposition, both because it was new and unheard of,[2] and because it ran counter, not only to prevalent conceptions, but also to clear passages of Holy Scripture. The fight against it was not only a fight waged by the old conception of the Church against a new one—*for Semi-Pelagianism was the ancient doctrine of Tertullian, Ambrose, and Jerome*—but the old *gospel* was also defended against novel teaching ; *for Semi-Pelagianism was also an evangelical protest, which grew up on Augustinian piety, against a conception of the same Augustine that was intolerable as doctrine.*[3]   Accordingly, it is not strange that " Semi-Pelagianism " raised its head in spite of the overthrow of Pelagianism ; rather it is strange that it was ultimately compelled to submit to Augustinianism.   This submission was never indeed perfectly honest.   On the other hand, there lurked an element of " Semi-Pelagianism " in Augustinianism itself, *viz.*, in the doctrines of the primitive state, of righteousness—as the product of grace

---

[1] See the Ep. Prosperi ad Aug. [225].   Here Augustine is called " ineffabiliter mirabilis, incomparabiliter honorandus, præstantissimus patronus, columna veritatis ubique gentium conspicua, specialis fidei patronus."

[2] See Vincentius' Commonitorium.

[3] Semi-Pelagianism also rests undoubtedly on Augustinian conceptions. Loof's designation of it as " popular Anti-Pelagian Catholicism " is perfectly just (see Theol. Lit. Ztg. 1895, Col. 568, against Krüger, l.c. Col. 368).   " Semi-Pelagianism " is a malicious heretical term.   The literary leaders of this doctrine were in no respect influenced, so far as I see, by Pelagius, nor did they learn anything from him ; on the contrary, they take their stand—the later the more plainly (but not more Augustinian)—on doctrines of Augustine, and it is impossible to understand them apart from his teaching.   " Semi-Pelagianism " is popular Catholicism made more definite and profound by Augustine's doctrines.   The Semi-Pelagians are accordingly the Eusebians of the doctrine of grace.   See also Sublet, Le Semi-Pélagianisme des Origines. Namur, 1897.

and the will—and of merits.   When Augustinianism triumphed, these points necessarily came to the front.   But a situation was thus created that was wholly insecure, capable of various interpretations, and untrue in itself.

Augustine himself found by experience that his doctrine of grace produced internal disturbances among the monks at Hadrumetum.   Free-will was done with ; men could fold their hands ; good works were superfluous ; even at the Last Judgment they were not taken into account.   Augustine sought to appease them by his treatise, De gratia et lib. arbitrio, and he followed this with his work, De correptione et gratia, when he heard that doubts had risen whether the erring and sinful should still be reprimanded, or if their case was sufficiently met by intercession.   Augustine strove in these writings to remove the misunderstandings of the monks, but he formulated his doctrine of grace more sharply than ever, trying, however, to retain free choice and the popular Catholic view.   A year or two afterwards (428-9) he was informed by his devoted friends, Prosper, Tyro,[1] and Hilary[2] (Epp. 225, 226,), that at Marseilles and other places in France there was an unwillingness to admit the strict doctrine of predestination, and the view that the will was *completely* impotent,[3] because they paralysed Christian preaching.   Augustine replied, confirming his friends, but giving new offence to his opponents by his two writings, De præ-destinatione sanctorum and De dono perseverantiæ.   He died soon afterwards, bequeathing his mantle to disciples whose fidelity and steadfastness had to atone for their want of independence.   The Gallican monks (" servi dei ") now advanced to open opposition.[4]   It is quite intelligible that monks, and Greek-trained monks, should have first entered the lists. Among them the most prominent were Johannes Cassianus,

---

[1] On him see Wörter's Progr., Freiburg, 1867, and Hauck in the R. E.

[2] Not to be confounded with Hilary of Arles, the Semi-Pelagian.

[3] The opposition was at first cautious.

[4] An accurate description of the controversy has been given by Wiggers in the 2nd vol. of his "Pragmatische Darstellung des Augustinismus und Pelagianismus (1833) ; see also Luthardt, Die L. v. fr. Willen (1863).   The later development from Gregory I. to Gottschalk is described by Wiggers in the Ztsch. f. d. hist. Theol, 1854-55-57-59.

father of South Gallican monachism[1] and disciple of Chrysostom and Vincentius of Lerinum.[2] The former has especially formulated his standpoint in the 13th Conference of his " collationes patrum," which bears the title " De protectione dei."[3] He takes objection above all to *absolute* predestination, the *particularism* of grace, and the *complete* bondage of the will. His teaching as to grace and liberty is as follows.

God's grace is the foundation of our salvation ; every beginning is to be traced to it, in so far as it brings the chance of salvation and the possibility of being saved. But that is external grace ; inner grace is that which lays hold of a man, enlightens, chastens, and sanctifies him, and penetrates his will as well as his intelligence. Human virtue can neither grow nor be perfected without this grace—therefore the virtues of the heathens are very small.[4] But the *beginnings* of the good resolve, good thoughts, and faith—understood as the preparation for grace— can be due to ourselves. Hence grace is absolutely necessary in order to reach final salvation (perfection), but not so much so in order to make a start. It accompanies us at all stages of our inner growth, and our exertions are of no avail without it (libero arbitrio semper co-operatur) ; but it only supports and accompanies him who really strives, "who reaches forward to the mark." Yet *at times* God anticipates the decision of men, and first renders them willing—*e.g.*, at the call of Matthew and Paul ; but even this—rare—action of grace is not irresistible. Free-will is never destroyed by God—that we must hold, even if we admit the incomprehensibleness of divine grace. Similarly, we must hold firmly to the conviction that God wills earnestly the salvation of all, and that therefore Christ's redemption applies not only to the small number of elect, but to all men.

---

[1] See De cœnobiorum institutis l. XII. Cf. Hoch, L.d. Johannes Cass. v. Natur u. Gnade, 1895 (besides Krüger, Theol. Lit.-Ztg. 1895, Col. 368 ff).

[2] The Commonitorium is directed exclusively against Augustine. The fact that it has reached us only in a mutilated form is explained, indeed, by its opposition to him. Apart from it, Prosper has preserved for us Vincentius' objections to Augustine.

[3] He speaks still more frankly and therefore " more like a Pelagian " in the Institutions.

[4] Here Cassian has learned thoroughly Augustine's teaching, and we see that he not only accommodated himself to it, but had been convinced by it.

The contrary doctrine involved "a huge blasphemy" (ingens sacrilegium). Predestination can therefore be only grounded on prescience—and the proposition that it was foreknown what anything would have been, if it had been at all, had at that time arisen in connection with the question of those dying in infancy.[1] But Cassian has hardly given an opinion on the relation of prescience and predestination. Regarding the primitive state, he taught that it was one of immortality, wisdom, and perfect freedom. Adam and Eve's Fall had entailed corruption and inevitable sinfulness on the whole race. But with a free, though a weakened, will, there also remained a certain ability to turn to the good.[2]

---

[1] Some maintained, namely, that the fate of these children was decided by how they would have acted if they had lived ; for that was known to God.

[2] Statements by Cassian. (Coll. XIII. 3): " non solum actuum, verum etiam cogi_ tationum bonarum ex deo esse principium, qui nobis et initia sanctæ voluntatis inspirat et virtutem atque opportunitatem eorum quæ recte cupimus tribuit peragendi . . . deus incipit quæ bona sunt et exsequitur et consummat in nobis, nostrum vero est, ut cotidie adtrahentem nos gratiam dei humiliter subsequamur." 5 : " gentiles veræ castitatis (and that is the virtue κατ' ἐξοχήν) virtutem non agnoverunt." 6 : "semper auxilio dei homines indigere nec aliquid humanam fragilitatem quod ad salutem pertinet per se solam i.e., sine adiutorio dei posse perficere." 7 : "propositum dei, quo non ob hoc hominem fecerat, ut periret, sed ut in perpetuum viveret, manet immobile, cuius benignitas cum bonæ voluntatis in nobis quantulamcunque scintillam emicuisse perspexerit vel quam ipse tamquam de dura silice nostri cordis excuderit, confovet eam et exsuscitat et confortat . . . qui enim ut pereat unus ex pusillis non habet voluntatem, quomodo sine ingenti sacrilegio putandus est non universaliter omnes, sed quosdam salvos fieri velle pro omnibus? ergo quicumque pereunt, contra illius pereunt voluntatem . . . deus mortem non fecit." 8 : " tanta est erga creaturam suam pietas creatoris, ut non solum comitetur eam, sed etiam præcedit iugiter providentia, qui cum in nobis ortum quendam bonæ voluntatis inspexerit, inluminat eam confestim atque confortat et incitat ad salutem, incrementum tribuens ei quam vel ipse plantavit vel nostro conatu viderit emersisse." 9 : "non facile humana ratione discernitur quemadmodum dominus petentibus tribuat, a quærentibus inveniatur et rursus inveniatur a non quærentibus se et palam adpareat inter illos, qui eum non interrogabant." 10 ; " libertatem scriptura divina nostri confirmat arbitrii sed et infirmitatem." 11 : "ita sunt hæc quodammodo indiscrete permixta atque confusa, ut quid ex quo pendeat inter multos magna quæstione volvatur, i.e., utrum quia initium bonæ voluntatis præbuerimus misereatur nostri deus, an quia deus misereatur consequamur bonæ voluntatis initium (in the former case Zacchæus, in the latter Paul and Matthew are named as examples)." 12 : " non enim talum deus hominem fecisse credendus est qui nec velit umquam nec possit bonum . . . cavendum nobis est, ne ita ad dominium omnia sanctorum merita referamus, ut nihil nisi id quod malum atque perversum est humanæ adscribamus naturæ . . . dubitari non potest, inesse quidem omni animæ

It is usual to condemn "Semi-Pelagianism." But absolute condemnation is unjust. *If a universal theory is to be set up, in the form of a doctrine, of the relation of God to mankind (as object of his will to save), then it can only be stated in terms of " Semi-Pelagianism " or Cassianism.* Cassian did not pledge himself to explain everything ; he knew very well that " God's judgments are incomprehensible and his ways inscrutable." Therefore he rightly declined to enter into the question of predestination. In refusing, however, to probe the mystery to the bottom, he demanded that so far as we affirmed anything on the subject, we should not prejudice the universality of grace and the accountability of man, *i.e.*, his free-will. That was an evangelical and correct conception. *But as Augustine erred in elevating the necessary self-criticism of the advanced Christian into a doctrine, which should form the sole standard by which to judge the whole sphere of God's dealings with men, so Cassian erred in not separating his legitimate theory from the rule by which the individual Christian ought to regard his own religious state.* He thus opened the door to self-righteousness, because from fear of fatalism he would not bluntly say to himself and those whose spiritual guide he was, that the faith which does not know that it is produced by God is still entangled in the life of self.[1]

Prosper, himself an ascetic and a frequenter of the famous cloisters of Provence, had already attacked his friends as Troubadour of Augustinianism during the lifetime of Augustine (Carmen de ingratis, see also the Ep. ad Rufinum). Now, after 430, he wrote several works in which he defended Augustine, and also himself, against charges that had been brought against Augustinianism.[2] He did not succeed in convincing the monks ;

---

naturaliter virtutum semina beneficio creatoris inseita, sed nisi hæc opitulatione dei fuerint excitata, ad incrementum perfectionis non potuerunt pervenire."

[1] Semi-Pelagianism is no " half truth." It is *wholly* correct as a theory, if any theory is to be set up, but it is *wholly* false if taken to express our self-judgment in the presence of God.

[2] Pro Augustino responsiones ad capitula objectionum Gallorum calumniantium (against the Gallican monks) ; Responsiones pro Augustino ad excerpta quæ de Genuensi civitate sunt missa (against Semi-Pelagian priests who desired *aufklärung*) ; Responsiones pro Augustino ad capitula objectionum Vincentiarium (here we have the most acute attacks by opponents). The " Galli " adhered to Cassian, though he

for his admission that Augustine spoke too harshly ("durius") when he said that God did not will that all men should be saved,[1] did not satisfy, and their scruples were not even removed by his contention that there was only one predestination (to salvation), that we must distinguish between this and prescience (as regards the *reprobati*), and in doing so be certain that God's action was not determined by caprice, but by justice and holiness.[2] He did, however, succeed in getting Pope Celestine to send a letter to the Gallican monks, supporting Augustine and blaming the opposition for presumption. The Pope was, however, very reserved in dealing with the matter in question, although he stated strongly the activity of grace as prevenient.[3] Prosper now wrote (432) his chief work against the 13th Collatio of Cassian, in which he showed more controversial skill, convicted his opponent of inconsistencies, and stated his own standpoint in a more cautious form, but without any concession in substance. He left Gaul, and took no further part in the dispute, but showed in his "Sentences" and "Epigrams" that as a theologian he continued to depend on Augustine alone.[4]

Another Augustinian, unknown to us, author of the work, De vocatione omnium gentium,[5] sought to do justice to the

---

hardly mentions original sin, while they taught it, and he does not speak so definitely as they about predestination.

[1] Sentent. sup. VIII. on the respons. ad capp. Gallorum.

[2] Even Augustine, in addition to expressing himself in a way that suggests the two-fold doctrine of predestination, said (De dono persev. 14) : " Hæc est prædestinatio sanctorum nihil aliud : præscientia scil. præparatio beneficiorum dei quibus certissime liberantur, quicunque liberantur." Prosper takes his stand on this language (see resp. ad excerpt. Genuens. VIII.) : " We confess with pious faith that God has fore-known absolutely to whom he should grant faith, or what men he should give to his Son, that he might lose none of them ; we confess that, foreknowing this, he also foresaw the favours by which he vouchsafes to free us, and that predestination consists in the foreknowledge and preparation of the ;divine grace by which men are most certainly redeemed." The reprobate accordingly are not embraced by predestination, but they are damned, because God has *foreseen* their sins. In this, accordingly, pre-science is alone at work, as also in the case of the regenerate, who fall away again. But prescience compels no one to sin.

[3] Cælest. ep. 21. The appendix was added later, but it perhaps was by Prosper.

[4] Gennadius relates (De script. eccl. 85) that Prosper dictated the famous letters of Leo I. against Eutyches. But he gives this as a mere rumour.

[5] Included among the works of Prosper and Leo I.

opposition by undertaking to combine the doctrine of the exclusive efficacy of divine grace with the other that God willed that all men should be saved. His intention proves that even among Augustine's admirers offence was taken at his principle of the particularism of God's purpose to save. But the laudable endeavour to combine the truth of Augustinianism with a universalist doctrine could not but fail. For all the author's distinctions between universal grace (creation and history) and special (Christ), and between the sensual, animal, and spiritual will (voluntas sensualis, animalis, spiritalis), as well as his assertions that grace, while preparing the will, does not supersede it, and that God desires the salvation of all, could not remove the real causes of offence (the damnation of children who died unbaptised, and reprobation in general) since Augustinianism was to be strictly upheld.[1] The work was at all events written with the honourable intention of removing doubts and establishing peace. On the other hand, attempts had been made on the Semi-Pelagian side from the first to make Augustinianism impossible, by an unsparing exposure of its real and supposed consequences, and these efforts culminated (about 450?) in the notorious " Prædestinatus" first discovered in A.D. 1643. The mystery that overhangs this work has not yet been fully solved; but it is probable that the writing of a predestinationist, introduced into Book II., and refuted, from the standpoint of Semi-Pelagianism, in Book III., is a forgery. For Augustine's teaching is unfolded in it entirely in paradoxical, pernicious, and almost blasphemous propositions, such as no Augustinian ever produced.[2] (We have both kinds of predestination strictly carried out : "those whom God has once predestined will, even if they neglect, sin, or refuse, be brought unwillingly to life, while those whom he has predestined to death labour in

---

[1] A minute analysis of the work is given by Wiggers, II. p. 218 ff. and Thomasius, I. pp. 563-570. It is to be admitted that the work marks an advance by its desire to admit the universality of God's purpose of salvation. But the doctrine of the *universitas specialis* is only a play on words, if *universitas* does not here mean more than with Augustine and Prosper, namely, that men of all nations and periods will be saved.

[2] See Wiggers, II., pp. 329-350.

vain, even if they run or hasten)."[1] And the contention that
the "sect of the predestinationists"[2] covers itself with Augustine's name, like the wolf in sheep's clothing, is a bold, controversial trick of fence.

Of the effects produced by this venomous writing nothing is
known ; on the other hand, we do know that Semi-Pelagianism
continued to exist undisturbed in Southern Gaul,[3] and, indeed,
found its most distinguished defender in Faustus of Rhegium
(died shortly before 500), formerly Abbot at Lerinum.[4] This
amiable and charitable Bishop, highly respected in spite of
many peculiar theories, took an active part in all the controversies and literary labours of his time. He was the forerunner
of Gregory I. in establishing, from the Episcopal Chair, monastic Christianity in the Gallican communities. He had entered
the lists against Pelagius (" pestifer "), and he now fought as
decidedly against the tenet of the extinction of free-will and
the doctrine of predestination, which he declared to be erroneous, blasphemous, heathen, fatalistic, and conducive to immo-
rality. The occasion was furnished by Lucidus, a Presbyter of
Augustinian views, who made an uncompromising statement of
the doctrine of predestination. He recanted formally after the
" error prædestinationis " had been condemned at a Synod at
Arles (475), with the assistance, if not on the instigation, of
Faustus.[5] After this Synod, and a second at Lyons, Faustus

---

[1] " Quos deus semel prædestinavit ad vitam, etiamsi negligant, etiamsi peccent,
etiamsi nolint, ad vitam perducentur inviti, quos autem prædestinavit ad mortem,
etiamsi currant, etiamsi festinent, sine causa laborant."

[2] Of any such sect absolutely nothing is known. There is no original authority to
show that there actually existed " libertines of grace," i.e., Augustinians who, under
cover of the doctrine of predestination, gave themselves up to unbridled sin. The
Semi-Pelagians would not have suffered such " Augustinians " to escape them in their
polemics. There may have arisen isolated ultra-Augustinians like Lucidus, but they
were not libertines.

[3] North Africa was removed from theological disputes by the dreadful invasion of
the Vandals. The majority there were certainly Augustinians, yet doubts and opposition were not wanting ; see Aug. Ep. 217 ad Vitalem.

[4] See Tillemont, Vol. XVI., and Wiggers, II. 224-329 ; Koch, Der h. Faustus von
Riez, 1895 (further, Loofs, Theol. Lit.-Ztg. 1895, Col. 567 ff.).

[5] See Mansi VII., where we have also (p. 1010) Lucidus' recantation in a Libellus
ad episcopos. Even before the Synod Faustus had an interview with his friend, and

composed his work, De gratia dei et humanæ mentis libero arbitrio, lib. II., meant to explain the dogmatic attitude of the Synods—against Pelagius and predestination.[1] Grace and freedom are parallel ; it is certain that man, since Adam's Fall, is externally and internally corrupt, that original sin and death as the result of sin reign over him, and that he is thus incapable of attaining salvation by his own strength ; but it is as certain that man can still obey or resist grace. God wills the salvation of all ; all need grace ; but grace reckons on the will which remains, though weakened ; *it always co-operates with the latter ;* otherwise the effort of human obedience (labor humanæ obedientiæ)[2] would be in vain. Original sin and free-will, in its infirm, weakened state (infirmatum, attenuatum), are not mutually exclusive. But those who ascribe everything to grace fall into heathen and blasphemous follies.[3] Our being saved is God's gift ; it does not rest, however, on an absolute predestination, but God's predetermination depends on the use man makes of the liberty still left him, and in virtue of which he can amend himself (prescience). Faustus no longer shows himself to be so strongly influenced by Augustine's thoughts as Cassian,[4] although, as a theologian, he owes more to him than the latter does. He is " more of a monk." Faith also is a work and a

---

he wrote a doctrinal letter to him (VII. 1007 sq.) which, however, was equally unsuccessful.

[1] Further, the Professio fidei (to Leontius) contra eos, qui dum per solam dei voluntatem alios dicunt ad vitam attrahi, alios in mortem deprimi, hinc fatum cum gentilibus asserunt, inde liberum arbitrium cum Manichæis negant.

[2] " Obedientia " plays the chief part with Faustus next to castitas. In this the mediæval monk announces himself.

[3] Faustus took good care not to contend against Augustine ; he only opposed Augustinianism. This is true of the Catholic Church at the present day.

[4] Yet he expressed himself very strongly as to original sin, and even taught Traducianism. As with Augustine, pro-creation is the means of transmitting original sin, which rises " per incentivum maledictæ generationis ardorem et per inlecebro-um utriusque parentis amplexum." Since Christ was alone free from this heritable infection, because he was not born of sexual intercourse, we must acknowledge the pleasure of intercourse and vice of sensuality to be the origin of the *malum originale.* We readily see that everything in Augustinianism met with applause that depreciated marriage. And these monks crossed themselves at the thought of Manichæism !

human achievement;[1] ascetic performances are in general
brought still more to the front by him, and the possibility of
grace preceding the movement of the will towards good is
understood to mean that salvation is first offered to a man
from without by means of preaching, law, and reproof. (In this
sense Faustus is even of opinion that the beginning is always
the work of grace.) The most questionable (Pelagian) feature,
however, consists in Faustus giving a very subordinate place to
internal grace—the *adjutorium* essentially means for him external aid in the form of law and doctrine—and that he clearly
returns to the Pelagian conception of nature as the original
(universal) grace [gratia prima (universalis)]. It is manifest, on
the other hand, that he sought to lead precisely ascetics to
humility; even where they increase their own merits they are
to remember that "whatever we are is of God," (dei est omne
quod sumus), *i.e.*, that perfect virtue is impossible without grace.[2]
We see when we look closely that Faustus already distinctly
preached implicitly the later doctrine of *meritum de congruo et
de condigno*.[3] In faith as knowledge, and in the exertions of the
will to amend ourselves, we have a merit supported by the first
grace (gratia prima); to it is imparted redeeming grace, and
the latter now co-operates with the will in producing perfect
merits.

In his own time Faustus hardly met with an opponent, not to
speak of one his equal.[4] But in Rome Augustine was held in

---

[1] Faustus even supposes that *fides* remained as the knowledge of God after the
Fall.
  See lib. II. 4. On the other hand, Abel, Enoch, etc., were saved by the first
grace, the law of nature, II. 6, 7. Since Enoch preceded the rest, in that so early
age, by the merit of faith (fidei merito), he showed that faith had been transmitted to
him with the law of nature; see also II. 8 ("et ex gentibus fuisse salvatos," 7).

[3] Wiggers calls attention (p. 328) to Faustus' principle, important for the sake of
later considerations in the Church : "Christus plus dedit quam totus mundus vale-
bat" (De grat. et lib. arb. 16).

[4] The most distinguished writers of the age held similar views, *e.g.*, Arnobius the
younger, Gennadius of Marseilles, Ennodius of Ticinum. Augustine's own authority
was already wavering; for Gennadius permitted himself to write of him (De script.
eccl. 39) : "unde ex multa eloquentia accidit, quod dixit per Salomonem spiritus
sanctus : ex multiloquio non effugies peccatum" and "error tamen illius sermone
multo, ut dixi, contractus, lucta hostium exaggeratus necdum hæresis quæstionem

high honour, without anyone, certainly, saying how far he was prepared to go with him, and doctrines which directly contradicted him were not tolerated.   If we may ascribe the decree, De libris recipiendis et non recipiendis, to Gelasius, then that Pope, who is also proved by other facts to have been a strong opponent of Pelagianism, declared Augustine and Prosper's writings to be in harmony with the Church, but those of Cassian and Faustus "apocryphal."   But the course of affairs in Rome at the beginning of the sixth century makes the ascription of this decree to Gelasius—in its present form—improbable.   That is, as Pelagianism had formerly amalgamated with Nestorianism, to which it gravitated, and had thus sealed its doom, so Semi-Pelagianism did not escape the fate of being dragged into the Christological controversy, and of being assailed by the dislike which orthodoxy influenced by Monophysitism cherished against all "that was human."   Those Scythian monks in Constantinople, who wished to force Theopaschitism on the Church,[1] handed to the Legate of Pope Hormisdas a Confession of faith, in which they opposed the remains of Nestorianism as well as the doctrine that grace did not effect the act of will and its accomplishment (519).[2]   Dismissed by the Legate, they brought their view in person before the Pope, and sent a report to the banished North African Bishops, who were residing in Sardinia, and among whom the most important was Fulgentius of Ruspe, a practised disputant against Arianism, and a faithful adherent of Augustine.   The report of the Scythians, which discussed Christology as well as the doctrine of grace, and quoted in support of the latter—in its Augustinian form—Eastern and Western authorities, closes with the words: " We hold it necessary

absolvit."   Many MSS. have suppressed these passages !   We find it said of Prosper (c. 85) that in his work against Cassian he " quæ ecclesia dei salutaria probat, infamat nociva."   Cassian and Faustus are highly praised.—As sources for Semi-Pelagianism there fall further to be considered the homilies, only in part by Faustus, which are printed in the Max. Bibl. Lugd. T. VI., pp. 619-686 ; see on them Caspari, Briefe, Abhandlungen u. Predigten (1890) p. 418 ff.

[1] See Vol. IV., p. 231.

[2] These " Scythians " were well versed in Western thought, their leader, Maxentius, who wrote in Latin, belonged himself to the West.   In the Confession of faith they treat of grace, " non qua creamur, sed qua recreamur et renovamur."   Pelagius, Cælestius, and Theodore of Mopsuestia are grouped together.

to add this; not as if you did not know it, but we have considered it useful to insert it in our short paper, in order to refute
the folly of those who reject it as containing tenets novel and
entirely unheard of in the churches. Instructed in the teaching
of all these holy Fathers, we condemn Pelagius, Cælestius,
Julian, and those of a similar type of thought, *especially the
books of Faustus of the cloister of Lerinum*, which there is no
doubt were written against the doctrine of predestination. In
these he attacks the tradition not only of these holy Fathers, but
also of the Apostle himself, annexing the support of grace to
human effort, and, while doing away with the whole grace of
Christ, avowing impiously that the ancient saints were not
saved, as the most holy Apostle Peter teaches, by the same
grace as we are, but by natural capacity."

The North Africans assented to this, and Fulgentius in reply
wrote his work, De incarnatione et gratia, in which, as in earlier
writings, he defended the Augustinian standpoint, and especially
derived original sin from the lust of sexual intercourse. Free-
will in the state of sin was wickedly free (male liberum), and
Christ's grace was to be sharply distinguished from grace in
creation (gratia creans) [c. 12]; the act of willing is not ours,
and assistance God's, business, but "it is the part of God's grace
to aid, that it may be mine to will, believe" (c. 16: gratiæ dei
est adjuvare, ut sit meum velle credere). Rom. II. 14, is to be
applied to the Gentiles justified by faith (c. 25); and the particularism of grace is also maintained.' The Scythians left
Rome, leaving behind them an anathema on Nestorians, Pelagians, and all akin to them. The celebrated name of Faustus
appeared in a bad light, and Possessor, an exiled African
Bishop who lived in Constantinople, hastened to recommend
himself to the Pope by the submissive query, What view was
now to be taken of Faustus? assuring him at the same time that
distinguished State officials equally desired enlightenment.[2]
Hormisdas gave a reserved answer (Aug. 520). The Scythian
monks were branded as vile disturbers of orthodoxy; Faustus

---

[1] See Wiggers II., pp. 369-4 9. According to Fulgentius, even Mary's conception
was stained, and therefore not free from original sin, see c. 6.

[2] All these transactions in Mansi VIII.

was described as a man whose private views need disquiet nobody, as the Church had not raised him to the post of a teacher ; *the doctrine of the Roman Church as regards sin and grace could be seen from Augustine's writings, especially those to Prosper and Hilary.* The Scythians sent a vigorous reply, sparing the Pope in so far as they questioned the authenticity of his letter. If Augustine's teaching was that of the Catholic Church, then Faustus was a heretic ; that is what the Pope would have necessarily said. The heresy was perfectly clear ; for Faustus only understood by prevenient grace, *external* grace —the preaching of the gospel. At the same time, the monks instigated Fulgentius now to write directly against Faustus, which he did in the Seven Books c. Faustum (lost) and—on his return to Africa A.D. 523—in his work, De veritate prædestinationis et gratiæ dei (l. III.) In this work Fulgentius expounds out and out Augustinianism (particularism of the will to save), but rejects the idea of a predestination to sin (nevertheless to punishment).[1] The Bishops remaining in Sardinia concurred fully with their colleague in the Ep. Synodica addressed to the Scythian monks : grace is the light, the will the eye ; the eye needs light in order to be able to see the light. Faustus' theses are "inventions, contrary to the truth, entirely hostile to the Catholic faith" (commenta, veritati contraria, catholicæ fidei penitus inimica).

These conflicts could not be without consequence for Southern Gaul. Still greater effect was produced by the reading of Augustine's writings, especially his sermons. In an age that thought solely in contrasts, the dilemma whether Augustine was a holy doctor or a heretic could only be decided ultimately in favour of the incomparable teacher. Cæsarius of Arles, the most meritorious and famous Bishop at the beginning of the sixth century, had, though trained in Lerinum and never wholly belying his training, so steeped himself in Augustine's works, that he would not abandon him, and his theology and sermons became a mirror of the master's important thoughts and forms of expression (though not of all or the most characteristic of

---

[1] On the derivation of original sin, see I. 4 : "proinde de immunditia nuptiarum mundus homo non nascitur, quia interveniente libidine seminatur."

them).[1]   He fought against (+542) the writings and authority
of Faustus.[2]   In Southern Gaul he at first met with much opposition, but still more indifference—for how many Bishops were
there at the beginning of the sixth century capable of understanding Augustinianism? In Rome, on the contrary, he found
approval.[3]   This approval was not without effect in Gaul.[4]   A
mixed Synod at Orange[5] in A.D. 529 under the presidency of
Cæsarius approved of twenty-five Canons, i. e., headings extracted
by Pope Felix IV. from Augustine and Prosper's writings, and
sent by him to the South Gallicans as the doctrine of the
"ancient Fathers," in order to support Cæsarius in his fight
against Semi-Pelagianism.[6]

These Canons[7] are strongly anti-Semi-Pelagian :—3 : " The
grace of God is not granted in response to prayer, but itself
causes the prayer to be offered for it." 4 : "That we may be

---

[1] See Arnold's interesting monograph, Cäsarius von Arelate und die gallische Kirche
s. Zeit, 1894. An edition of the Opp. Cæsarii is forthcoming.

[2] Avitus of Vienne is usually named along with him ; but after Arnold's authoritative account of the former (p. 202 ff.), he must be disregarded. On the other hand,
Mamertus Claudianus is to be named as an opponent of Faustus (Arnold, p. 325) ;
he is an Augustinian and Neoplatonist, and thus an enemy of Semi-Pelagianism as a
metaphysician.

[3] Cæsarius' work, however, De gratia et libero arbitrio, and its approval by Felix
IV. belong to the realm of fiction (Arnold, p. 499). On the other hand, we have to
notice some indirect manifestations on the part of Rome about A.D. 500 in favour of
Augustinianism and against Faustus. Yet Rome never took the trouble really to
comprehend Augustinianism.

[4] We only know of the Synod of Valencia, at which Cæsarius was not present,
owing to illness, but where he was represented by a friendly Bishop, from the Vita
Cæsarii by his disciple Cyprian (Mansi VIII., p. 723). Hefele has shown (Conciliengesch., II.[2] p. 738 ff.), that it is to be dated before the Synod of Orange. It seems
necessary to infer from the short account that the Bishops met to oppose Cæsarius,
and published a decree condemning, or at least disapproving his teaching (see also
Arnold, p. 346 ff.). At Orange Cæsarius justified himself, or triumphantly defended
his doctrine from "Apostolic tradition," and Pope Boniface agreed with him, and
not with his Valencian opponents.

[5] See Arnold p. 350 ff.

[6] We cannot now decide whether the 25 Canons are absolutely identical with
those transmitted heads, or whether the Synod (perhaps even the Pope?) proposed
trifling modifications ; see Chap. XIX. of the Treves Codex in Mansi VIII., p. 722.
However, it is very improbable that the Bishops made important changes in these
heads (yet see Arnold, p. 352) since according to them they expounded their own
view in the Epilogue.

[7] See Hahn, § 103 ; Hefele, p. 726 f.

cleansed from sin, God does not wait upon, but prepares, our will." 5: "The beginning of faith is not due to us, but to the grace of God—that state of believing by which we believe in him who justifies the impious, and attain the regeneration of holy Baptism, is brought about through the gift of grace, *i.e.*, the inspiration of the Holy Spirit correcting our will from unbelief to faith, and is not ours naturally." 6: "It is the work of grace that we believe, will, desire, attempt, knock, etc., and not *vice-versâ.*" 7: "We cannot without grace think or choose, by our natural powers, anything good that pertains to salvation." 8 : "It is untrue that some attain baptismal faith by mercy, others by free-will." 9: "As often as we do good, God works in and with us, that we may work." 10: "Even the regenerate and holy always need the divine aid." 11 : "We can only vow to God what we ourselves have received from him." 12 : "God loves us as we shall be by his gift, not as we are by our merit." 13: "Choice of will, weakened in the first man, cannot be repaired except by the grace of Baptism." 16: "Let no one boast of what he seems to have as if he did not receive it, or think that he has received, because the letter appeared or was sounded outwardly that it might be read or heard." 17: "On the love of God diffused in hearts by the Holy Spirit." 18: "Undeserved grace precedes meritorious works." 19 : "Even if it had remained in the sound state in which it was created, human nature would by no means preserve itself without the aid of its creator." 21 : "The law does not justify, and grace is not nature ; therefore Christ died not gratuitously, but that the law might be fulfilled, and that nature, ruined by Adam, might be repaired by him." 22 : "No one has anything of his own but falsehood and sin," and "The virtue of heathens is produced only by worldly desire, that of Christians springs not from free will, but from the gift of the Holy Ghost."[1] 23: "In (doing) evil men carry out their own will, but when they do what they resolve in order to serve the divine will, although their actions are willed by them, yet it is his will by which their act of will is both prepared and commanded." 24: "The twig

---

[1] This Canon caused the greatest distress to the Catholic Church in the sixteenth, seventeenth, eighteenth, and nineteenth centuries (see Hefele, p. 733 f.).

does not benefit the stem, but the stem the twig; so also those who have Christ in them and abide in him do not benefit Christ, but themselves." 25 : " To love God is the gift of God."

The definition given by the Bishops, after drawing up these heads, is likewise strongly anti-Semi-Pelagian.[1] *But no mention is made of predestination,*[2] *nor is the inner process of grace, on which Augustine laid the chief stress, properly appreciated.* The former fact would have been no blemish in itself; but at that time, when the question was whether the *whole* Augustine was authoritative or not, silence was dangerous. Those who were disposed to Semi-Pelagianism could appeal to the fact that Augustine's doctrine of predestination was not approved, and might then introduce into this unsanctioned tenet a great deal that belonged to the doctrine of grace. This actually took place. *Accordingly the controversy only came apparently to an end here.* But the continued vitality of Semi-Pelagian ideas, under cover of Augustinian formulas, was further promoted by that external conception of grace as the sacrament of Baptism, which lay at the root of the decree. " Love," it is true, was also discussed ; but we see easily that the idea of the sacrament was all-predominant. " Even Augustine's adherents," it has been truly remarked, " lost sight of the distinction between Augustinianism and Semi-Pelagianism in relation to all who were baptised." It was Augustine himself, who, because he had not comprehended the notion of *faith*, was to blame for the fact that, at the close of the dispute, a conception was evolved as his doctrine which, while explaining grace to be beginning and end, really held to the magical miracle of Baptism, and to "faithful working with the aid of Christ" (fideliter laborare auxiliante Christo).

---

[1] Yet Augustine would not have written the sentence : " hoc etiam credimus, quod accepta per baptismum gratia *omnes baptizati* Christo auxiliante et co-operante, quæ ad salutem animæ pertinent, possint et debeant, *si fideliter laborare voluerint*, adimplere." Besides, the words "quæ ad salutem pertinent adimplere" and "fideliter laborare" are ambiguous.

[2] The word only occurs in the epilogue, and there merely to reject *prædestinatio ad malum :* "aliquos vero ad malum divina potestate prædestinatos esse non solum non credimus, sed etiam, si sunt qui tantum malum credere velint, cum omni detestatione illis anathema dicimus." The decree is also silent as to *gratia irresistibilis*, and the particularism of God's will to bestow grace.

The new Pope, Boniface II., approved of these decrees in a letter to Cæsarius ;¹ they have retained a great esteem in the Catholic Church, and were very thoroughly considered by the Council of Trent.² Henceforth, the doctrine of prevenient grace, on which the Pope also laid particular stress, is to be regarded as Western dogma ; the Semi-Pelagians have to be acknowledged heretics. But the controversy could begin anew at any moment, as soon, namely, as any one appeared, who, for the sake of prevenient grace, also required the recognition of particular election to grace. If we consider which of Augustine's doctrines met with acceptance, and which were passed over, if further we recollect why the former were approved, we are compelled to say that, next to anxiety to secure to the Sacrament of Baptism its irreplaceable importance, *it was the monastic view of the impurity of marriage that especially operated here.* All are sinful, and grace must come before our own efforts, because all are born from the sinful lust of sexual intercourse. The Catholic system of doctrine has risen from a compromise between two equally monastic conceptions : the meritoriousness of works and the impurity of marriage. Both thoughts were Augustinian in themselves and in their working out ; but the moving soul of Augustinianism was starved. It is a fact that has not yet been sufficiently appreciated *that Catholic doctrine did not adhere to Semi-Pelagianism*, because the former declared sexual desire to be sinful.³

¹ Mansi VIII., p. 735 sq. The resolutions were also subscribed by laymen, a thing almost unheard of in the dogmatic history of the ancient Church, but not so in Gaul in the sixth century ; see Hatch, " The Growth of Church Institutions " chap. VIII.

² The Roman Bishops evidently felt their attitude in the Semi-Pelagian controversy prejudiced by the decisions of their predecessors against Pelagius. We look in vain for an independent word coming from internal conviction (Gelasius is perhaps an exception), and yet it is quite essentially " thanks " to them that the Semi-Pelagian dispute ended with the recognition of the Augustinian doctrine of prevenient grace and with silence as to predestination.

³ Seeberg (Dogmengesch. I., p. 326), has disputed this, because the representatives of Semi-Pelagianism made the strongest assertions on this point (see especially Faustus), and because the opposition between them and the Augustinians actually depended on quite different issues. Both objections are quite correct, but they do not meet the above statement ; the Semi-Pelagian doctrine of grace could not but react upon and modify Augustine's doctrine of original sin, and therefore also the view of the evil of sin as necessarily propagated by sexual intercourse, involving damnation, and de-

2. *Gregory the Great.*

The doctrine of grace taught by Pope Gregory the Great (590 to 604) shows how little Augustinianism was understood in Rome, and how confused theological thought had become in the course of the sixth century. A more motley farrago of Augustinian formulas and crude work-religion (ergismus) could hardly be conceived. Gregory has nowhere uttered an original thought; he has rather at all points preserved, while emasculating, the traditional system of doctrine, reduced the spiritual to the level of a coarsely material intelligence, changed dogmatic, so far as it suited, into technical directions for the clergy, and associated it with popular religion of the second rank. All his institutions were wise and well considered, and yet they sprang from an almost naïf monastic soul, which laboured with faithful anxiety at the education of uncivilised peoples, and the training of his clergy, ever adopting what was calculated by turns to disquiet and soothe, and thus to rule the lay world with the mechanism of religion.[1] Because Gregory, living in an age when the old was passing away and the new presented itself in a form still rude and disjointed, looked only to what was necessary and attainable, he sanctioned as religion an external legality, as suited to train young nations, as it was adapted to the Epigones of ancient civilisation, who had lost fineness of feeling and thought, were sunk in superstition and magic, and did homage to the stupid ideals of asceticism.[2] It is the accent that changes the melody, and the tone makes the music. Gregory created the vulgar type of mediæval Catholicism by the way he accented the various traditional doctrines and Church usages,[3] and the tone to which he tuned Christian

---

structive of all goodness. As regards this it is quite indifferent how individual Semi-Pelagian monks looked at sexual desire and marriage, as also whether this point came at once to light in the controversy.

[1] After reading Gregory's abundant correspondence, we gain a high respect for the wisdom, charity, tolerance, and energy of the Pope.

[2] Yet side by side with this external legality there are not wanting traits of Gospel liberty ; see the letters to Augustine.

[3] So Lau. Gregor d. Grosse, p. 326 : " Without perceiving, perhaps, the signific-

souls is the key we hear echoed by Catholicism down to the present day.[1] The voice is the voice of Gregory, and also of Jerome, but the hands are Augustine's. Only in one respect he was not Augustine's disciple. Akin to Cyprian and Leo I. and well versed in jurisprudence, he laid stress on the *legal* element in addition to the ritual and sacramental. *Through him the amalgamation of doctrine and Church government made a further advance in the West.*[2]

A few lines are sufficient to depict the emasculated Augustinianism represented by Gregory. Reason, science, and philosophy, are more strongly depreciated by him than by Augustine (Evang. II. hom. 26);[3] miracle is the distinguishing mark of the religious. Reason can, indeed, establish the existence of God, but it is only "by faith that the way is opened to the vision of God" (per aditum fidei aperitur aditus visionis dei; Ezech. II. hom. 5, following Augustine). The doctrine of angels and the devil comes to the front, because it suited popular and monastic piety. We can call Gregory the "Doctor angelorum et diaboli." As regards the angels, he took particular delight (see Evang. II. hom. 34) in working out their ranks (under the influence of Greek mysticism), in glorifying Michael, Gabriel, and Raphael—the hero of miracle, the great messenger and warrior against the spirits of the air, and the medicine-man—in the exact division of angelic tasks and the idea of guardian spirits; he held that angels watched over men, as the latter did over cattle. He who thought so little of Græco-Roman culture sanctioned its most inferior parts in his

---

ance of what he did, he prepared the way for the development of later Catholicism by imperceptibly altering the conception of the tradition received from a preceding age."

[1] Gregory was most read of the Western Church Fathers, as the literature of the Middle Ages and our libraries show. Even in the seventh century he was extolled by tasteless and uncritical writers as wiser than Augustine, more eloquent than Cyprian, more pious than Anthony ("nihil illi simile demonstrat antiquitas" Ildefond. de script. 1).

[2] Lau gives a detailed account of Gregory's teaching; l.c. pp. 329-556. We see here the extent of Gregory's dependence on Augustine. He especially lays as great stress on Holy Scripture being the rule of life and doctrine. The most profound of Augustine's thoughts are touched on, but they are all rendered superficial.

[3] "Fides non habet meritum, cui humana ratio præbet experimentum" (§ 1). Tertullian, certainly, had already said that (Apolog. 21) once.

doctrine of the angels.   His monkish fancy dealt still more
actively in conceptions about the devil and demons, and he
gave new life to ideas about Antichrist, who stood already at
the door, because the world was near its end.   As the Logos
had assumed human nature, so the devil would be incarnate
at the end of the world (Moral. 31, 24 ; 13, 10).   Before Christ
appeared, the devil possessed all men of right, and he still
possesses unbelievers.   He raged through the latter ; but as
regarded believers he was a powerless and cheated devil.   The
doctrines of redemption, justification, grace, and sin show an
Augustinianism modified in the interests of miracle, sacred
rites and monachism.   The God-man—whose mother remained
a virgin at and after the birth—was sinless, because he did not
come into the world through fleshly lust.   He is our redeemer
(redemptor) and mediator—these titles being preferred—and he
especially propitiated the devil by purchasing men from him
with his death,[1] and he abolished the disunion between angels
and men.   It is also remarked incidentally that Christ bore
our punishments and propitiated God's wrath.   But, besides
redemption from the devil, the chief thing is deliverance from
sin itself.   It was effected by Christ putting an end to the
punishment of original sin, and also destroying sin itself,
by giving us an example.[2]   This amounts to saying that
Christ's work was incomplete, *i.e.*, that it must be supplemented by our penances, for it transformed the eternal punishment of original sin into temporary penalties, which must be
atoned for, and it acts mainly by way of example.[3]   In fact, in

---

[1] The deception theory is thus given by Gregory in its most revolting form.   The
devil is the fish snapping at Christ's flesh, and swallowing the hidden hook, his
divinity ; see Moral. 33, 7, 9.

[2] Moral. I. 13 : "Incarnatus dominus in semetipso omne quod nobis inspiravit
ostendit, ut quod præcepto diceret, exemplo suaderet." II. 24 : "Venit inter homines
mediator dei et hominum, homo Christus Jesus, ad præbendum exemplum vitæ
hominibus simplex, ad non parcendum malignis spiritibus rectus ad debellandum
superbiam timens deum, ad detergendam vero in electis suis immunditiam recedens
a malo."

[3] Lau. p. 434 : "The chief stress is placed on instruction and example ; reconciliation with God, certainty of which is absolutely necessary to man's peace of mind, is
almost entirely passed over ; and deliverance from punishment is inadequately conceived, as referring merely to original sin, or is regarded purely externally. . . . All

Gregory's teaching, Christ's death and penance appear side by side, as two factors of equal value.[1]

We must remember this, or we may assign too high a value to another line of thought. Gregory regards Christ's death as an offering (oblatio) for our purification : Christ presents it constantly for us, ever showing God his (crucified) body.[2] But this apparently high pitched view after all means very little. It has risen from the observance of the Lord's Supper. What was constantly done by the priest has been transferred to Christ himself. But both oblations, related as they are to our "puri-fication," possess their sole value in the mitigation of sin's *penalties*. Still another consideration was at work in this case, one that, though relying on Biblical statements, sprang in reality from wholly different sources. It is the conception of Christ's continual intercession. But this intercession must be combined with the whole apparatus of intercessions (of angels, saints, alms and masses for the dead, which were conceived as personi-fied forces), to see that we are here dealing with a *heathen* conception, which, though it had indeed long been established in the practice of the Church, was only now elevated into a theory—that of "aids in need." Gregory's candid avowal that

that Gregory can do to give man peace is to direct him to penance and his good works." He speaks of even the holiest remaining in constant uncertainty as to their reconciliation. He can make nothing of the thesis that our sins are forgiven for Christ's sake. God rather punishes every sin not atoned for by penance, even if he pardons it ; see Moral. IX. 34 : "Bene dicit Hiob (IX. 28) : Sciens quod non parceris delinquenti, *quia delicta nostra sive per nos sive per semetipsum resecat, etiam cum relaxat.* Ab electis enim suis iniquitatum maculas studet temporali afflictione tergere, quas in eis in perpetuum non vult videre." In his commentary on 1 Kings (l. IV. 4, 57), which was hardly transcribed indeed in its present form by Gregory himself, we even read : "Non omnia nostra Christus explevit, per crucem quidem suam omnes redemit, sed remansit, ut qui redimi et regnare cum eo nititur, crucifigatur. Hoc profecto residuum viderat, qui dicebat : si compatimur et conregnabimus. Quasi dicat : *Quod explevit Christus, non valet nisi ei, qui id quod remansit adimplet.*"

[1] Therefore we find over and over in the Moral. in reference to the expiation of sins : "sive per nos, sive per deum."

[2] Moral. i. 24 : "Sine intermissione pro nobis holocaustum redemptor immolat, qui sine cessatione patri suam pro nobis incarnationem demonstrat ; ipsa quippe ejus incarnatio nostræ emundationis oblatio est ; cumque se hominem ostendit, delicta hominis interveniens diluit. Et humanitatis suæ mysterio perenne sacrificium immolat, quia et hæc sunt æterna, quæ mundat."

the death of Christ was not absolutely necessary, showed how
indefinite was his view of the part it played in this mediation.
As God created us from nothing, he could also have delivered
us from misery without Christ's death. But he willed to show
us the greatness of his compassion by taking upon himself that
from which he desired to deliver us; he willed to give us an
example, that we should not dread the misfortune and miseries
of the world, but should avoid its happiness; and he sought
to teach us to remember death.[1] Nor has Gregory yet sketched
a theory of Christ's merit—after the analogy of the merits
which we can gain. That was reserved for the Middle Ages;
but he has examined Christ's work from the point of view of
masses for the dead and the intercession of saints.

In the doctrines of the primitive state, original sin, sin, faith and
grace, the Augustinian formulas are repeated—after the Canons
of Orange, without irresistible grace and particular election.[2]
But a very real significance was attributed to free-will, which
Augustine had abstractly admitted. Here we have the fully
developed doctrines of free and prevenient grace, of the primitive state and original sin; (the carnal lust of parents is the
cause of our life, therefore the latter is sinful; the "disobedi-
ence" or "disorderliness" of the genital organs is the proof of
original sin; intercourse in marriage is never innocent). And
side by side with all this, we have a calm statement of the
doctrine of the will, which is merely weakened, and of free
choice (liberum arbitrium) which must follow grace, if the latter
is to become operative,[3]—and yet grace is first to determine the
will to will. From the first two powers co-operate in all good,
since free-will must accept what grace offers. It can therefore
be said "that we redeem ourselves because we assent to the
Lord redeeming us."[4] Predestination is simply reduced in the

[1] Moral. 20, 36; 2, 37.   Ezek. l. II. hom. 1, 2.   Here occur fine ideas: "Nos
minus amasset, nisi et vulnera nostra susciperet" (M. 20, 36).

[2] See the proof of positive points of agreement between Gregory and the Canons of
Oranges in Arnold, Cæsarius, p. 369 f.   Yet Gregory never himself appealed to those
resolutions.

[3] How could a bishop, who felt himself to be the pastor of all Christendom, have
then made pure Augustinianism the standard of all his counsels?

[4] Moral. 24, 10; see also 33, 21; "Bonum quod agimus et dei est et nostrum,

case of sinners and elect to prescience, while at the same time
it is maintained in other passages that it rests on God's free
power and grace.   The latter assumption was necessary, because
Gregory also adhered to "a fixed and definite number of the
elect"—to supply the place of angels ; but ultimately all belong
to that number whose perseverance in faith and good works
God knew beforehand.

After all, everything spiritual is reduced to the rites of the
Church.   As in the East, these come to the front ; but they are
regarded in a different way.   In the East more scope is given
to religious sentiment, which exalts itself and luxuriates in the
whole of the Cultus as a divino-human drama ; in the West, as
befitted the Roman character, everything is more prosaic and
calculating.   Man accomplishes and receives ; submissive obedience is the chief virtue ; merits are rewarded, but on the
humble a merit not his own is also bestowed : that is grace.
Baptism, the Lord's Supper, and penance are the central points
in the legal process of grace.   We are baptised : thereby inherited guilt is expiated, and all sins committed before baptism
are blotted out ; but original sin is not obliterated, and the
guilt of later sins remains.[1]   It must be cancelled or atoned for.
For this there are numerous means, which are as necessary as
they are uncertain.   A man must make himself righteous ; for
righteousness is the supreme virtue (radix virtutum).   He is
instructed to pray, give alms, and mourn over life.   But he
is further told : "Those who trust in no work of their own run
to the protection of the holy martyrs, and throng to their sacred

dei per prævenientem gratiam, nostrum per obsequentem liberam voluntatem. . . .
Si nostrum non est, unde nobis retribui præmia speramus ?   Quia ergo non immerito
gratias agimus, scimus, quod ejus munere prævenimur ; *et rursum quia non immerito
retributionem quærimus, scimus, quod obsequente libero arbitrio bona eligimus, quæ
ageremus.*"   See Ep. III. 29 : Christ will comfort us richly at the Judgment, when
he observes that we have punished our faults by ourselves.

[1] Moral. IX. 34 : "Salutis unda a culpa primi parentis absolvimur, sed tamen
reatum ejusdem culpæ diluentes absoluti quoque adhuc carnaliter obimus."   The
casuistical treatment of sins is by no means puritanical in Gregory.   He displays in
this matter a lofty wisdom united with charity, and gives directions which were
certainly the best for the circumstances of the time.   He says once (Ep. XI. 64) :
"It is characteristic of pious souls to imagine that they are guilty of faults when
there is absolutely none."

bodies with tears, entreat that they may merit pardon at the intercession of the saints."[1] This practice of resorting to saints and relics had existed for a long time, but Gregory has the merit of systematising it, at the same time providing it with abundant material by means of his "Dialogues," as well as his other writings.[2] A cloud of "mediators" came between God and the soul: angels, saints, and Christ; and men began already to compute cunningly what each could do for them, what each was good for. Uncertainty about God, perverse, monkish humility, and the dread entertained by the poor unreconciled heart of sin's penalties, threw Christians into the arms of pagan superstition, and introduced the "mediators" into dogmatics. But in terrifying with its principle: "sin is in no case absolved without punishment" (nullatenus peccatum sine vindicta laxatur),[3] the Church not only referred men to intercessors, alms, and the other forms of satisfaction, to "masses for the dead," which obtained an ever-increasing importance, but it even modified hell, placing purgatory in front of heaven; it thereby confused conscience and lessened the gravity of sin, turning men's interest to sin's punishment. Gregory sanctioned and developed broadly the doctrine of purgatory,[4] already suggested by Augustine.[5] The power of the *Church*, of prayers,

---

[1] Moral. XVI. 51 : " Hi qui de nullo suo opere confidunt, ad sanctorum martyrum protectionem currunt atque ad sacra eorum corpora fletibus insistunt, promereri se veniam iis intercedentibus deprecantur."

[2] Similar things to those recorded by Gregory were often narrated at an earlier date ; but no Western writer before him had developed these superstitions to such an extent—and he was the most influential bishop. Miracles wrought by relics were to him every-day events ; the miraculous power of some was so great that everyone who touched them died. Everything that came in contact with them was magnetised. What powerful intercessors and advocates must then the saints be, when even their bodies did such deeds ! Gregory therefore sought to preserve the attachment of influential people by sending relics and—slaves. On pictures, see Ep. IX. 52 ; IX. 105 ; XI. 13.

[3] Moral. IX. 34, or : " delinquenti dominus nequaquam parcit, quia delictum sine ultione non deserit. Aut enim ipse homo in se pænitens punit, aut hoc deus cum homine vindicans percutit."

[4] See Dial. IV. (25) and 39. After God has changed eternal punishments into temporary, the *justified* must expiate these temporary penalties for sin in purgatory. This is inferred indirectly from Matth. XII. 31, directly from 1 Cor. III. 12 f. There are perfect men, however, who do not need purgatory.

[5] See above, p. 232.

and intercessors extended, however, to this purgatory of his.[1] The whole life even of the baptised being still stained at least by small sins, their constant attitude must be one of penitence, *i.e.*, they must practise penance, which culminates in satisfactions and invocations to " Aids in need." Gregory systematised the doctrine of penance in the exact form in which it passed over into the Middle Ages.[2] Penance included four points, perception of sin and dread of God's judgments, regret (contritio), confession of sin, and satisfaction (satisfactio). The two first could also be conceived as one (conversio mentis).[3] The chief emphasis was still held to fall on "conversion," even penance was not yet attached to the institution of the Church and the priest; but "satisfaction" was necessarily felt to be the main thing. The last word was not indeed yet said; but already the order of penance was taking the place due to faith; nay, it was called the "baptism of tears."[4] And the Lord's Supper was also ultimately drawn into the mechanism of penance. In this case, again, Gregory had only to accentuate what had long been in use. The main point in the Lord's Supper was that it was a sacrifice, which benefited living and dead as a means of mitigation (laxatio). As a sacrifice it was a repetition of Christ's—hence Gregory's development of the

---

[1] Dial. IV. 57 : " Credo, quia hoc tam aperte cum viventibus ac nescientibus agitur, ut cunctis hæc agentibus ac nescientibus ostendatur, quia si insolubiles culpæ non fuerint, ad absolutionem prodesse etiam mortuis victima sacræ oblationis possit. Sed sciendum est, quia illis sacræ victimæ mortuis prosint, qui hic vivendo obtinuerunt, ut eos etiam post mortem bona adjuvent, quæ hic pro ipsis ab aliis fiunt."

[2] On the older Western order of penance, see Preuschen, Tertullian's Schriften de pænit. and de pudicit. 1890; Rolff's Das Indulgenzedict des röm. Bischofs Kallist 1893 (Texte und Unters. Vol. 11, Part 3) ; Götz, Die Busslehre Cyprian's 1895 ; Karl Muller, Die Bussinstitution in Karthago unter Cyprian (Zeitschr. f. K.-Gesch., Vol. 16 [1895-96] p. 1 ff., p. 187 ff.).

[3] 1 Reg. l. VI. 2, 33 : " tria in unoquoque consideranda sunt veraciter pænitente, videlicet conversio mentis, confessio oris et vindicta peccati." Moral 13, 39 : " convertuntur fide, veniunt opere, convertuntur deserendo mala, veniunt bona faciendo." Voluntarily assumed pains constitute *satisfactio*.

[4] Evang. l. I. hom. 10 : " Peccata nostra præterita in baptismatis perceptione laxata sunt, et tamen post baptisma multa commisimus, sed laxari iterum baptismatis aqua non possumus. Quia ergo et post baptisma inquinavimus vitam, baptizemus lacrimis conscientiam."

ceremonial ritual—and it is self-evident that this was conceived altogether realistically. In this rite (eucharistia, missa, sacrificium, oblatio, hostia, sacramentum passionis, communio), the passion of Christ;[1] who "is entire in the single portions" (in singulis portionibus totus est), was repeated for our atonement. Yet even here the last word was not yet uttered, transubstantiation was not yet evolved. Indeed, we find, accompanying the above, a view of the Lord's Supper, which lays stress on *our* presenting ourselves to God as the victim (the host), in yielding ourselves to him, practising love, rendering daily the sacrifice of tears, despising the world, and—daily offering the *host* of the body and blood of Christ.[2]

What has been left here of Augustinianism? All the popular Catholic elements which Augustine thrust aside and in part remodelled have returned with doubled strength! The moral and legal view has triumphed over the religious. What we see aimed at in Cyprian's work, De opere et eleemosynis, now dominates the whole religious conception, and the uncertainty left by Augustine as to the notion of God, *because his ideas regarding God in Christ were only vague*, has here become a source of injury traversing the whole system of religion. For what does Gregory know of God? *That, being omnipotent, he has an inscrutable will;[3] being the requiter, he leaves no sin unpunished; and that because he is beneficent, he has created an immense multitude of institutions for conveying grace, whose use enables the free will to escape sin's penalties, and to exhibit merits to God the rewarder.* That is Gregory's notion of God, and it is

---

[1] Evang. l. II. hom. 37, 7 : "Singulariter ad absolutionem nostram oblata cum lacrimis et benignitate mentis sacri altaris hostia suffragatur, quia is, qui in se resurgens a mortuis jam non moritur, adhuc per hanc in suo mysterio pro nobis iterum patitur. Nam quoties ei hostiam suæ passionis offerimus, toties nobis ad absolutionem nostram passionem illius reparamus."

[2] See Dial. IV. 58, 59. Gregory already laid great stress on the frequency of masses. He also approved of their use to avert temporal sufferings. He tells with approval of a woman having delivered her husband from prison by their means, and he sees in them generally the remedy against all torments in this world and in purgatory. Only to eternal blessedness the mass does not apply.

[3] That is the impression that was preserved of Augustine's doctrine of predestination.

the specific conception held by the Roman Catholic Church:
Christ as a person is forgotten. He is a great name in dogmatics, *i.e.*, at the relative place; but the fundamental questions
of salvation are not answered by reference to him, and in life
the baptised has to depend on "means" which exist partly
alongside, partly independently of him, or merely bear his
badge. From this standpoint is explained the whole structure
of Gregory's theory of religion, which once more sets up *fear* [1]
and *hope* instead of *faith* and *love*, and for the grace of God in
Christ substitutes not an improved, but merely a more complicated doctrine of merit. And yet Augustine could not have
complained of this displacement of his ideas; for he had left
standing, nay, had himself admitted into his system, all the
main lines of this theory of religion. Even the manifest and
grave externalisation of sin, the direction that we must be ever
bathed in tears, while at the same time zealous and watchful to
escape the penalties of sin, the perversion of the notion of God
and sin, as if God's sole concern was to be *satisfied*, since he
was the requiter—all these thoughts have their points of contact
in the range of Augustine's conceptions.[2] The darkest spot in
mediæval piety, the fact that it commanded constant contrition,
while at the same time it incited the penitent to make *calcula-*
tions which deadened the moral nerve and changed regret for
sin into dread of punishment—this source of evil, which makes
religious morality worse than non-religious, was from this time
perpetuated in the Catholic Church of the West.[3]

---

[1] "Deus terrores incutit"--often.

[2] The term "tutius," and the *via tutior* already play a great part in Gregory's
writings; see *e.g.*, Dial. IV. 58: "Pensandum est, quod *tutior* sit via, ut bonum
quod quisque post mortem suam sperat agi per alios, agit ipse dum vivit per se."
Accordingly that is only *tutius*, and not a self-evident duty.

[3] Gregory also expressly forbids anyone to be certain of his salvation; for this he
could, indeed, appeal to Augustine. His letter to the Empress Gregoria's lady of
the bed-chamber is most instructive (V. 25). This poor woman wished to have
assurance of her salvation, and had written the Pope that she would ply him with
letters until he should write that *he knew by a special revelation that her sins were*
forgiven. What an evangelical impulse in A.D. 596! The Pope replied, first, that
he was unworthy of a special revelation; secondly, that she should not be certain of
forgiveness until, the last day of her life having come, she should no longer be in a
position to deplore her sins. Till then she must continue to fear; for certainty is the
parent of indolence; she must not strive to obtain it lest she go to sleep. "Let thy

But in the case of Gregory himself, this system of religion is traversed by many other ideas gained from the Gospel and Augustine. He could speak eloquently of the impression made by the person of Christ, and describe the inner change produced by the Divine Word [1] in such a way as to make us feel that he is not reproducing a lesson he has learnt from others, but is speaking from his own experience. "Through the sacred oracles we are quickened by the gift of the Spirit, that we may reject works that bring death; the Spirit enters, when God touches the mind of the reader in different ways and orders." The Spirit of God works on the inner nature through the Word. Thus, many of Augustine's best thoughts are reproduced in Gregory's writings.[3] Again, in his Dogmatics he was not a sacerdotalist. If, as is undeniable, he gave an impetus to the further identification of the empirical Church with *the* Church, if all his teaching as to the imputed merit of saints, oblations, masses, penance, purgatory, etc., could not but benefit the sacerdotal Church, and favour the complete subjection of poor souls to its power, if, finally, his ecclesiastical policy was adapted to raise the Church, with the Pope at its head, to a supremacy that limited and gave its blessing and sanction to every other power, yet his dogmatic was by no means mere ecclesiasticism. We wonder, rather, that he has nowhere drawn the last, and apparently so obvious consequences,[4] in other

soul tremble for a little while just now, that it may afterwards enjoy unending delight."

[1] Divinus sermo. The phrase " verbum fidei " is also very common.

[2] Ezech. I., h. 7. " Per sacra eloquia dono spiritus vivificamur, ut mortifera a nobis opera repellamus ; spiritus vadit, cum legentis animum diversis modis et ordinibus tangit deus."

[3] Gregory's veracity, indeed, is not altogether above suspicion. His miraculous tales are often not ingenuous, but calculated ; read *e.g.*, Ep. IV. 30. His propaganda for the Church did not shrink from doubtful means. The Jews on papal properties were to be influenced to accept Christianity by the remission of taxes. Even if their own conversion was not sincere, their children would be good Catholics (Ep. V. 8). Yet Gregory has expressed himself very distinctly against forcible conversions (Ep. I. 47).

[4] Besides, he by no means sought to introduce the usages of the Roman Church by tyrannical force, but rather directed Augustine, the missionary, to adopt what good he found in other national Churches ; see Ep. XI. 64. On the other hand, the bewildering identification of Peter and the Pope made a further advance in the

words, that he did not rigidly concentrate the whole immense apparatus in the hand of the priest, and give the latter the *guidance* of every single soul.   Already this had been frequently done in practice ; but the thought still predominated that every baptised person was alone responsible for himself, and had to go *his own way* in the sight of God and within the Church, by aid of penance and forgiveness.   It was reserved for the mediæval development first to set up *dogmatically* the demand that the penitent, *i.e.*, every Christian from baptism to death, should depend wholly on the guidance of the priest.[1]

hands of Gregory.   He means the Pope when he says : " s. ecclesia in apostolorum principis soliditate firmata est." And he declares (Ep. IX. 12) : " de Constantino-politana ecclesia quod dicunt, quis eam dubitet sedi apostolicæ esse subjectam ; " see also the fine passage Ep. IX. 59 : " si qua culpa in episcopis invenitur, nescic quis Petri successori subjectus non sit ; cum vero culpa non exigit, omnes secundum rationem humilitatis æquales sunt."

[1] Gregory's extensive correspondence shows how far even at this time strictly theological questions had come to be eclipsed by practical ones as to pastoral super-vision and education by means of the cultus and church order.   On Gregory's importance in connection with the cultus, see Duchesne's excellent work, Orig. du culte chrétien (1888), esp. p. 153 sq.

CHAPTER VI.

HISTORY OF DOGMA IN THE PERIOD OF THE CRALOVINGIAN RENAISSANCE.

AMONG the young uncivilised peoples, all ecclesiastical institutions occupied a still more prominent place than had been given them even by the development of the Church in the Roman Empire. The philosophical and theological capital of antiquity, already handed down in part in compendia, was propagated in new abridgements (Isidore of Seville, Bede, Rabanus, etc.). John Scotus the unique excepted,[1] no one was now able to probe that intellectual world to its ultimate ideas and perceptions,

---

[1] Johannes Scotus Erigena's system (chief work : De divisione naturæ, see Migne CXXII. ; Christlieb 1860, Huber 1861, see Ritter and Baur), does not belong to the history of dogma in the West, for it is an entirely free, independent reproduction of the Neoplatonic (pantheistic) type of thouoht, as represented by the Areopagite and especially "the divine philosopher Maximus Confessor," whom Scotus had read. Augustine also undoubtedly influenced him ; but he has not brought his speculation any nearer Christianity. The most learned and perhaps also the wisest man of his age, he maintained the complete identity of *religio vera* and *philosophia vera*, and thus restored to its central place the fundamental thought of ancient philosophy. But to him, only nominally conceding a place to authority beside reason, the *philosophia vera* was that monism of view in which the knowledge of nature and that of God coincide, thought and bëing in that case also coinciding. (Everything is nature, and finally indeed, "nature which does not create and is not created," and the notion of being existing in the human mind is the substance of being itself: "intellectus rerum veraciter ipsæ res sunt.") Acosmic idealism is carried by Scotus (as by Stephan bar Sudaili) to the point at which even deity disappears in the intellect of man. All agreements with Church doctrines rest with Scotus on accommodation ; they do not spring, however, from perplexity, but from the clear insight that wrappings must exist. In reality, even the living movement of nature itself is only an appearance. Without influence, indeed regarded with suspicion in his own time, he did not afterwards become the instructor of the West, though Western mystics have learnt much from him. He was too much of a Greek. In love and power of systematic construction he was phenomenal, and speculative philosophers rightly revere him as a master.

and make it part of their own spiritual experience.[1] To the historian of *civilisation* everything in the epoch is interesting; in the Carlovingian age, the foundations were laid for the developments of the Middle Ages; but to the historian of *dogma*, if we are to consider not the appropriation of familiar material, but the *advance* of evolution, that period does not offer much.

The Carlovingian epoch was a great, and in many respects an unsuccessful, essay at a renaissance of antiquity. It was not the product of the slow natural evolution of the Germano-Roman peoples, but Charlemagne and his circle sought to gain by storm a higher culture for the Frankish Empire, by a frequently forced return to antiquity, or by the establishment in their midst of Byzantine culture. Antiquity was still a living thing in Constantinople. Springer has shown, in dealing with the history of art, that the Carlovingian school is to be regarded as the after-bloom of ancient, and not as the beginning of mediæval, art; and this applies also to theological and philosophical efforts. *The Carlovingian period marks the epoch-making beginnings in the history of institutions ;* [2] *in the history of spiritual life it is an appendix to that of the ancient world.* Therefore the history of dogma in the Middle Ages begins, strictly speaking, with the age of Clugny.[3] It is also useless to discuss, in connection with this branch of study, the so-called popular forms of German Christianity found in poetical and prose fragments. For, firstly, their popular character is very limited; secondly, popular Christianity has hardly exercised any influ-

---

[1] It is, on the other hand, wonderful with what strength of memory and intellect men like Alcuin and Paulinus of Aquileia familiarised themselves with the *separate* lines of Augustine's thought. Alcuin also lived a life of Augustinian piety.

[2] See Hatch : An introductory lecture on the study of ecclesiastical history, 1885.

[3] On the history of dogma in the Carlovingian age, see Schwane, Dogmengesch. der mittleren Zeit. 1882 ; Bach, Dogmengesch. des Mittelalters I. Th. 1873, Thomasius-Seeberg, Dogmengesch. II. 1, 1888 : Reuter, Gesch. der relig. Aufklärung im Mittelalter, 1875, I. pp. 1-64. The last book discusses the efforts to promote culture. Cf. also Göbl, Gesch. der Katechese im Abendland 1880, and Spiess, Gesch. des Unterrichtswesens in Deutschland von den ältesten Zeiten bis zur Mitte des 13 Jahrhunderts, 1885. Further the histories of the German Church by Rettberg and Hauck. On "popular theology" among Anglo-Saxons, Saxons, and Franks, see Bach, l.c. I., p. 81 ff.

ence at all on institutions, not to speak of dogma. He who
wished to reach a higher theological culture, read Augustine
and Gregory, Gregory and Augustine, and he felt himself to be
merely a disciple in relation to these and the other Latin
Fathers, having still to learn the lessons delivered to him.[1]

At that time many of the clergy were undoubtedly keenly
desirous of culture; to see this we have only to look at the
manuscripts preserved from the eighth and ninth centuries.[2]
Nor must we overlook the fact that a small number of scholars
went further than those belonging to the period A.D. 450-650,
that they advanced beyond Isidore and Gregory to Augustine
himself, saw through the emasculation of religion and its
perversion into a ceremonial service and belief in miracle, and
returned to the spiritual teaching of Augustine.[3] But the lofty
figure of the African Bishop set bounds to any further advance.
The best looked up to him, but none saw past him, not even
Alcuin and Agobard, though the latter has also studied Tertullian.[4] It is very attractive to study, in connection with
Church history, the energetic efforts of the Carlovingian Augus-

---

[1] John Scotus forms an exception, and so also does, in some sense, Fredegis of
Tours, so far as the latter took an independent view of the ominous "nihil" presented by Augustinian metaphysics. Ahner has, however, shown in his Dissertation
on Fredegis and his letter "De nihilo et tenebris" (1878) that this work has been
over-estimated by earlier scholars.

[2] Our gratitude is due to Schrörs for having given in his monograph on Hinkmar
(1884), pp. 166-174, an account of the ancient works read or quoted by the great
Bishop. What an amount of learning and reading is evident from this comparison,
and yet Hinkmar was by no means the greatest scholar. It is also interesting to
notice that Hinkmar held strictly to the edict of Gelasius.

[3] A greater interest in Dialectics was also shown by many teachers of the Carlovingian period than by earlier theologians. Compare Alcuin's work, De fide
trinitatis, which also displays a valiant effort to reach systematic unity in theological
thought. Fredegis, Alcuin's *discipulus dulcissimus*, was also reproved by Agobard
as a "philosopher" for his preference for dialectics, the syllogism, and vexed questions. ("Invenietis nobilitatem divini eloquii non secundum vestram assertionem
more. philosophorum in tumore et pompa esse verborum" Agobardi lib. c. object.
Fredegisi abb.) Yet his teaching as to *auctoritas* and *ratio* was not different from
Augustine's; but distrust was caused by the earnest attempt, on the basis of authority,
to use reason in dealing with dogma. In the dispute between Agobard and Fredegis
many controversial questions emerged which would have become important if the
opponents had really developed them.

[4] On Alcuin, see Werner's monograph (1881). Radbert had also read Tertullian.

tinians, to observe their attempts, following but surpassing the great Emperor, to purify the traditional form of religion, and to narrow the range of a stupid awe of the mysteries and of a half-heathen superstition. But it would merely lead to confusion in the history of dogma if we were to try to examine these attempts.[1]

The transactions and determining events important to the history of dogma in our epoch divide into the following groups. 1. Controversies as to Byzantine and Roman Christology contrasted with that of Augustine and the West, and between the Gregorian system of doctrine and Augustine's theory of predestination.[2] 2. Disputes shared in by Rome against the East regarding the *filioque*, and against Rome and the East about

---

[1] The conditions which heralded the Carlovingian Renaissance consisted in the political position of the Frankish Empire, the flourishing of theological studies among the Anglo-Saxons (Bede), the ecclesiastical activity of Boniface on the Continent, and the partly new, partly revived, relations of the Empire to Rome and Constantinople. The fact that elements of culture from England, Rome, Lombardy, and finally also the East converged at Charlemagne's Court, and found so energetic a Mæcenas in the king, made possible the renaissance, which then continued to exist under Louis the Pious, and at the Court of Charles the Bald. We cannot over-estimate the contribution made by Constantinople. We need only recall the works of the Pseudo-Dionysius, Maximus, and John of Damascus, which at that time had reached the Frankish Kingdom. Not only John Scotus, but *e.g.*, Hinkmar, read or quoted the Pseudo-Dionysius. Some knowledge of Greek was possessed by a few Anglo-Saxons from the days of Archbishop Theodore of Tarsus in Canterbury ; but they were to a much greater extent teachers of Augustinianism ; yet not in the Christological question (see under). It was in Augustine along with the Areopagite that the mediæval mysticism of the West—and also Scotus—found its source ; for it is very one-sided to make the latter alone responsible for mysticism. The Franks' love of culture received its greatest strength from the acquisition of the Crown of Imperial Rome, A.D. 800. What had formerly been a voluntary aspiration now assumed the appearance of a duty and obligation ; for the king-emperor of the Franks and Romans was the successor of Augustine and Constantine. But how rapidly all this blossom withered ! Walafrid writes truly in the prologue to Einhard's Life of Kaiser Karl : "When King Karl assembled wise men, he filled with light, kindled by God, the mist-shrouded, and so to speak almost entirely dark, expanse of the kingdom entrusted to him by God, by the new radiance of all science such as till then had been in part wholly unknown to these barbarians. But now, since these studies once more relapse into their opposite, the light of wisdom, which finds few who love it, becomes ever rarer."

[2] In these conflicts the controversy as to Augustine is represented. See also the dispute as to the Lord's Supper.

images.[1] 3. The development of the practice and theory of the
Mass and of penance.[2]

§ I. (a.) The Adoptian Controversy.[3]

After the Western Christological formula of the two natures
had been forced on the East at the fourth Council, the latter
had at the fifth Council given the formula a Cyrillian interpretation, which it confirmed by condemning the Three
Chapters. Since the Roman Bishop had to accede to the new
definition, which was regarded in the West as a revolt from that
of Chalcedon, a schism took place in Upper Italy, which was
only got over with difficulty, extending into the seventh century,
and damaging the Pope's prestige in the West. The Monothelite controversies brought the schism to an end,[4] and the sixth
Council restored the formula of Chalcedon in the new version
of the problem—the question as to the will in Christ. But men
were far from drawing the consequences of the formula in the
East, or in Rome itself. Mysticism, which taught the complete
and inseparable union of the divine and human, and celebrated
its triumph in all the ritual institutions of the Church, had long
overgrown the intractable dogmatic formula and stifled its
influence. But the case was different with many Western
Bishops, so long as they had not yet been reached by Greek
mysticism, and still were under the influence of the ancient
Western tradition, especially Augustine. They held the Christological theory that the Holy Trinity had effected the Incarnation by the second Person of the Godhead, the Son, selecting a
man (homo) in virtue of eternal election—without antecedent

---

[1] These controversies are of universal interest in Church history.

[2] In this development the dogmatic interest of the Carlovingians was alone really
acute, leading to new definitions, if not at once expressed in strictly dogmatic forms.
To this subject also belongs the doctrine of the saints (Mary), relics, and indulgences.

[3] See Bach, l.c. Walch, Ketzerhistorie, Vol. IX. ; Hefele, Concil. Gesch. III.,[2] p.
642 ff. (628 ff.) ; Helfferrich, D. westgothische Arianismus u. die spanische Ketzer-
geschichte 1860 ; Gams, Kirchengesch. Spaniens, Vol. II. ; Dorner, Entwickel.
Gesch. Vol. II. ; Hauck, K.-Gesch. Deutschlands, Vol. II., p. 256 ; Opp. Alcuini
ed. Froben ; Mansi, T. XII., XIII. ; Migne, T. XCVI.—CI.

[4] Yet not yet everywhere.

merits on the part of the man—by uniting with him to form a personal unity, and by thus adopting him to perfect sonship.[1] This scheme is distinguished *toto coelo* from the Greek one (received in Rome) of the fifth Council, even if—as happened— the whole of human nature was also understood by the *homo*. For, according to the prevailing Greek conception, the God-Logos, in the moment of the Incarnation, so *assumed* human nature and received it into the unity of his being ($\mathit{\iota\delta\iota\sigma\pi\sigma\iota\epsilon\hat{\iota}\nu}$), that it participated completely in the dignity, and accordingly in the *sonship*, of the Son, the incarnate Logos thus being in every respect as much the *one real* Son of God as the pre-existent. To hold Jesus Christ as Son of Man to be merely the *adopted* Son of God destroyed, according to Greek ideas, the whole mystery of the Incarnation, and took the Church back to the abyss of Nestorianism. Conversely, it was possible for one who took his stand on Augustinian Christology to feel that the contention that the Son of Man was as essentially Son of God as the Logos, was a relapse into *Docetism* or even *Pantheism*— the fusion of divine and human. The great claim of Cyril's conception consisted in its maintenance of the perfect *unity* of the Redeemer's personality,[2] the justification of the other in its adherence to Christ's real humanity. This humanity was to the opposite party in truth only a *theorem*, whose avowal permitted them to deify *in concreto* everything human in Christ,[3] while the Adoptians were only able to postulate the unity of the Son of God and Son of Man.[4]

---

[1] See Augustine's Christology above, p. 127 ff. The idea of the *adoptio* of the man Jesus, or human nature, also occurs in Tertullian, Novatian, Marius Victorinus, and Hilary.

[2] So far as the retention of this is the condition of understanding Jesus Christ, the Greek conception is superior to the Adoptian.

[3] The defenders of the anti-Adoptian Christology (Alcuin's) have not latered their tactics at the present day. Thus Bach says (l.c. I., p. 109 ff.) : " The Adoptians had no presentiment of that which the (Greek) Fathers call the *pneumatic* quality of Christ's flesh. Christ's body is to them that of common human nature in *every respect*. In this kenotic (!!) we have the basis of Adoptian dualism. . . . Felix, like Elipandus, does not understand the *pneumatic* human nature in Christ." If these words suggest any meaning at all, they show that the modern historian of dogma is as honest a Docetic as the orthodox after Justinian's heart.

[4] The case is precisely the same as in Christological conflicts generally from the

It is the old antagonism of Monophysitism and Nestorianism,
toned down, indeed, in phraseology, but not lessened in substance—how could it be lessened ?   It is not wonderful that it
broke out once more after the sixth Council, and that in
connection with the term "adoptio." It is only surprising
that it arose at the outskirts of Christendom ; and that the
controversy occasioned by it in the Church was so rapidly
and thoroughly quieted.   If we reflect that Augustine had
unhesitatingly taught that Christ, on his human side, was
the adopted Son of God and the supreme example of
prevenient free grace (gratia gratis data præveniens), that he
was read everywhere, that many passages in the Western
Fathers gave evidence of Adoptianism,[1] and that even Isidore
of Seville had written without being questioned : " he is called
sole-begotten from the excellence of his divinity, because he is
without brothers, first-begotten *on account of the assumption of a
man, in which act he has deigned to have brothers by the adoption
of grace*, with regard to whom he should be the first-begotten," [2]
we are seized with astonishment at the secret, energetic counter-
action of the Christological mysticism of Cyril and the
Areopagite.   It captivated thoughtful and superstitious
Christians in Rome, and thence in England, Upper Italy, and
France.   It succeeded in doing so, because it was allied both
with the philosophical speculation of the time and the superstitious craving for mysteries.   Plato and Aristotle, as they
were understood, were its evangelists, and, again, every celebration of the Lord's Supper, yea, every relic, was a silent missionary
for it.   In this men experienced the identity of the heavenly and
earthly ; accordingly, that identity had to be recognised above all
in Christ himself.   Thus the Western and Augustinian Christ-

---

days of Apollinaris.   There is right and wrong on both sides, but after all on neither,
because the conception of a divine nature in Christ leads either to Docetism or the
double personality.   All speculations that seek to escape these consequences can
display at most their good intentions.

[1] This was bluntly asserted by Marius Victorinus (adv. Arium I.) to whom is entirely
due the Augustinian view of Christology *sub specie prædestinationis*.

[2] Migne, CI., p. 1322 sq. : " Unigenitus vocatur secundum divinitatis excellentiam,
quia sine fratribus, primogenitus secundum susceptionem hominis, in qua per adoptionem gratiæ fratres habere dignatus est, de quibus esset primogenitus."

ology, with its last, and yet so significant, remnant of a historical view of Christ—*his subjection to divine grace*—was effaced, not by a conflict, but much more certainly by a silent revolution.[1] But Augustinian Christology was advocated in Arabian Spain about A.D. 780 by Elipandus, Metropolitan of Toledo, and soon afterwards in Frankish Spain by Felix, Bishop of Urgel; it being also supported by the Mozarabian liturgy.[2] They strongly emphasised the view that Christ was adopted as man, and the redeemed were accordingly, in the fullest sense, brothers of the man Jesus. There has been a good deal of argument as to how the two bishops, who, for the rest, had the approval of the majority of their colleagues in Spain, were influenced thus to emphasise the *adoptio*. After what we have observed above we ought rather to ask why the other Western Bishops did not do the same. In any case, the hypothesis that this Adoptianism is to be explained from Ancient West Gothic Arianism [3] is still less tenable than its derivation from Arab influences.[4] Nor do we obtain much enlightenment from the reference to the controversy which Elipandus had previously waged with a heretic named Migetius,[5] since the doctrines ascribed to him do not seem to have been the reverse of Adoptianism, while the whole figure is obscure.[6] All that is clear is that at that date the

---

[1] Western Augustinian Christology, like Nestorianism, deserved its fall ; for since it taught that the God-Logos existed behind the man Jesus who was supported by divine grace, the relation of the work of redemption to that *homo* was extremely uncertain. The result was a duplicity of view which could only produce confusion, and which had to come to an end, until the conception of faith should be thoroughly accepted, unhampered by pernicious speculations as to the two natures, that God himself was in the man Jesus.

[2] See the seven, though not equally valuable passages in Hefele, l.c., p. 650 f. : "adoptivi hominis passio"—"adoptivi hominis non horruisti vestimentum"— "salvator per adoptionem carnis sedem repetiit deitatis," etc.

[3] So Helfferich, l.c. ; also Hauck, R.-Encyklop I[3]., p. 185, leaves it open.

[4] Gfrörer, K.-Gesch. III., p. 644 ff. Graf. Baudissin, Eulogius und Alvar 1872, p. 61 f. The traces cited of a connection between Elipandus and Felix with the Saracens are very slight ; besides, the objections felt by the latter to the doctrine of the Trinity are not lessened by Adoptianism. Elipandus defended the doctrine with peculiar emphasis.

[5] Hefele, Op. cit., p. 628 ff.

[6] Besides his enthusiasm for Rome, Migetius' main heresy seems to have been that he conceived God strictly as a single person, and maintained that he had revealed

Spanish Church possessed no connection with Rome, that it
rejected the alliance sought by Hadrian I., and, while relatively
uninfluenced by the Roman and Byzantine Church tradition,[1]
was in a state of great confusion internally.[2] It is further
evident that Elipandus gladly seized the opportunity to extend
the sphere of his metropolitan power to Asturia under the sure
protection of the unbelievers.   A dogmatic *Spanish* formula was

himself in three persons, namely, David (Father ?), Jesus, and Paul (the Holy Ghost ?).
Besides this "Sabellianism," one might be tempted to discover "Priscillian"
errors in him.   But the slight information we possess (see Hadrian and Elipandus'
letters) do not warrant a confident decision.

[1] This explains the uninterrupted prestige of Augustinian theology.   Isidore of
Seville, *e.g.*, felt it so strongly, that he even taught twofold predestination (Sentent.
II. 6): "gemina predestinatio . . . sive reproborum ad mortem."

[2] The comparatively slight influence exerted by the great main current of Church
development is also shown by the fact that the opposition of the Spaniard Vigilantius to
saints and relics continued to influence Spain, as is evidenced, *e.g.*, by the attack made
upon him by Faustus of Rhegium (see above, p. 244, note 1).   Paradoxical as it sounds,
the veneration of these objects lay in the *van* of Church evolution, in so far as it was
most closely connected with the development of Christology.   Those who resisted
this worship soon ceased to do so on evangelical grounds, but because ecclesiastically
they were "laggards."   The dislike to relics and pictures, however, is as closely connected with the Adoptian theory, as their worship and the materialistic dogma of the
Lord's Supper are with the Christology of Cyril, Justinian, and Alcuin (see under).
But even after Reccared passed over to Catholicism, the Spanish Church showed its
disorderly state, not only in the persistent mingling of Pagan and Christian morals,
and (in some circles) the continuance of certain Arian leanings, but still more in
numerous heretical intrigues.   To this class belong Priscillianism, degenerated into
dualism, Migetius, that Marcus who rejuvenated Basilidianism, and above all the sect
of Bonosians that held its ground in Spain—phenomena that were profoundly opposed
to Catholicism, and prove how hard it was for the rising Roman Catholic Church in
Spain to adopt the sentiments of Roman Catholicism.   No other Western Church
had at this date still to strive so keenly with powerful heresies as the Spanish.   Hence
is explained the growth in this Church, especially after contact with Islam, of the
cold, determined fanaticism of its orthodoxy and persecution of heretics.   Wherever
it arises, this is a sign that men have forced themselves after severe sacrifices to submit to the sacred cause, and that they now seek to compensate themselves by making
others do the same.   As regards the sect of Bonosians in particular, their founder,
Bonosus, Bishop of Sardica, advanced from a denial of Mary's perpetual virginity to
the doctrine of Photinus (see the Synod of Capua, A.D. 391; Ambrose's letters,
Siricius, and Innocent I., and Marius Mercator).   Strange to say, he found adherents
in South Gaul, and especially in Spain, up till into the eighth century; in Spain, as it
appears, they were numerous; see the 2 Synod of Arles (443?) c. 17, Synod of Clichy
(626) c. 5, Synod of Orleans (538) c. 31, Gennad. de vir. inl. 14, Avitus Vienn.,
Isidore de script. eccl. 20, de hær. 53.   In the sixth century Justinian of Valentia
opposed them in Spain, and in the seventh the Synod of Toledo (675), referred in

welcome to him as a means of doing this.   It is probable, finally,
that Latin translations of Nestorian writings (*i.e.*, of Theodore
of Mopsuestia) were read in Spain.   This cannot, indeed, be
proved ; but there can be no doubt that *Felix of Urgel gave a
Nestorian (Theodorian) development to Augustine's Christology,
and thus went beyond Augustine,* and it is on the other hand
certain that from the sixth century *Latin* translations of works
by Nestorian (and Syrian) writers were current in the West.[1]

Elipandus was a loyal adherent to the Augustinian and
Chalcedonian Christology ; this is attested by his epistles ; see
also the two books written against him by Beatus and Eterius of
Asturia, as well as Alcuin's writings.   He meant to maintain
the unity of person throughout ; but this unity did not, in his
view, do away with the strict distinction of natures.   The human
nature remained human, being thence raised to the dignity of
divinity, and for this reason he held the term "adoptio" to be
peculiarly fitting : "the son adoptive in his humanity but not in

the Symbol to the doctrine of the Bonosians that Christ had only existed after Mary
bore him, and was merely a *filius adoptivus,* by confessing : " hic etiam filius dei
natura est filius, non adoptione." Naturally Elipandus and Felix were conjoined by
their opponents with the Bonosians, but with the greatest injustice ; they were rather
their most implacable enemies, since they never denied that Christ as Son of God was
filius dei naturalis. They even tried to hurl back the charge of Bonosianism at their
enemies (Beatus and Eterius), an attempt, indeed, that could not succeed. It was at
any rate prejudicial, seeing that men cling to catchwords, to place in the Toledan
Symbol of 675 the words "non filius adoptione," although by them the Photinian
error, which Elipandus himself "condemned to hell," was exclusively meant. We
may, indeed, say of Bonosianism, but not of Elipandus' teaching, that its circulation
in Spain s explained by the Arian leanings of the Western Goths ; for not only in
the Arianism of scholarly theologians, but still more in its popular form, there lurked
an element of the doctrine of Paul of Samosata and Photinus.

1 Since the Three Chapter controversy. We have to remember, further, that Theodore's commentary on Paul's Epistles still exists in a Latin translation, and that the work
of Junilius comes from a Syrian copy ; see Neander's Dogmengesch. II., p. 25 f., and
Jacobi's note there, p. 26 f.   Möller (Art. Adoptianism in Herzog's R.-E., 2nd Ed.) has
stated, on the basis of Gam's discoveries, a conjecture that is worth noting : " Perhaps
we ought to regard the orthodox brethren in Cordova extolled by Elipandus (Ep. ad
Felic. in Alcuin's letters, ep. 123), who provided him with scholarly material, and to
whom Alcuin (ep. ad Leidrad. 141) supposes the evil originally to have been due,
as Eastern Christians of Nestorian culture who had come in the train of the Arabs,
and who, if they did not produce, supported the Adoptian tendency." It is further
important that Elipandus has not mentioned Nestorianism among the ancient heresies
rejected by him.

his divinity " (filius adoptivus humanitate nequaquam divinitate). Everyone in the West (even Alcuin) still spoke at that time of the *assumtio hominis,* and not merely of the *assumtio humanæ naturæ* (assumption of a man not of human nature). It was a correct inference that *assumtio hominis = adoptio hominis.* If the word "adoptio" was not exactly common in the more ancient literature,[1] the matter designated by it was correctly expressed in Augustine's sense.[2] The sonship of Christ was therefore twofold ; as God he was son by race and nature (genere et natura), as man by adoption and grace. Elipandus quoted texts in support of this, and inferred quite correctly that he who disputed the Redeemer's *adoptio* had to deny the reality of his human nature, and consequently to suppose that Christ derived his humanity, which would be unlike ours, from the substance of the Father. Elipandus therefore designates his opponents Docetics or Eutychians.

If we find that even he was interested really in Christ's complete humanity *for his work's sake,* the same fact shows much more clearly in the important case of Felix (see the writings directed against him by Paulinus and Alcuin). He has also left the God-Logos resting in the background ; but his theory of religion deals with the second Adam in a way that had not been heard of in the Church since the days of Theodore. Since the Son of Man was actually a man, the whole stages of his humiliation were not voluntarily undertaken, but were necessary. It was only the resolve of the Son of God to adopt a man that was freely made. After this resolve was realised the Son of Man *had* to be a *servant, had* to be subject to the Father in everything, *had* to fulfil his will and not his own. Like all men he was only good so far as, and because, he was subject to the Father's grace ; he was not omniscient and omnipotent, but his wisdom and power were bounded by the limits imposed on humanity. He derived his life from the Father, and to him he also prayed for

---

[1] Alcuin says too much when he exclaims (adv. Elip. IV. 2) : "Ubi latuit, ubi dormivit hoc nomen adoptionis vel nuncupationis de Christo ?" or Ep. 110 : "Novitas vocum in adoptione, nuncupatione, omnino fidelibus omnibus detestanda est."

[2] Compare how also Facundus of Hermiane (pro defens. trium capp. p. 708, ed. Paris, 1616, II.) acknowledges that Christ accepted the "Sacrament of Adoption."

himself.[1] Felix's final interest consisted in the fact *that only
thus can we be certain of our adoption*. He insisted very strongly
on raising to the central place in the conception of redemption
the thought that the adoption of believers is only certain if
Christ adopted a man like other men, or *humanity :* we are only
redeemed if Christ is our *oldest brother*. The assurance of the
redemption of humanity rests, as with Augustine, on the sole-
begotten (in the divine sphere) having united with himself the
first-begotten (in the human) ["adoptivi cum adoptivo, servi cum
servo, Christi cum Christo, deus inter deos"]. Christ, who as
man was sacrificed for sakes, was the head of humanity, not by
his divinity, but by his humanity. For this very reason the
members are only certain of their adoption if the head is
adopted.[2] If we are not dealing in Christ's case with an
adoption as in our own, the then Incarnation was enacted
outside of our sphere, and is of no benefit to us. But Felix
went a step farther. He did not, like Augustine, satisfy himself
with stopping at the simple contention that the man (homo)
Christ was adopted in virtue of the prevenient grace of predestination, and with combining, by a mere assertion, this contention with the thesis of personal unity. On the contrary he
rigidly separated the natures, and sought to form a clear idea of
the way *in which the adoption was accomplished* (see the
Antiochenes.)

As regards the first point, he applied the phrase "true and
peculiar son" (verus et proprius filius) to the God-Logos alone,
and did not shrink from the proposition "the son is believed one
in two forms" (duobus modis unus creditur filius); he distinguished between "the one" and "the other" (*alter* and *alter*),
"this one" and "that" (*ille* and *ille*), nay, he called the Son of
Man "God by adoption" (*nuncupativus deus :* meaning that he
became God). He speaks, like the Antiochenes, of a "dwelling"
of God in man, of the man who is united (conjunctus ; appli-
catus) with deity, or bears deity. He has, indeed, compared the
union of the two natures in Christ with the relation of soul and
body ; but the figure is still more inapt from his standpoint than

---

[1] See passages cited by Bach, Opp. cit., p. 110 ff.
[2] The clearest passages—Felix's own words—occur in Agobard, lib. adv. Fel. 27-37.

from Augustine's; for the community of attributes is to him not real, but nominal, and "we must by no means believe that the omnipotent divine Father, who is a spirit, begets the body from himself" (nullo modo credendum est, ut omnipotens deus pater, qui spiritus est, de semetipso carnem generet). The man Christ has *two* fathers, one natural (David), and the other by his adoption.

With reference to the second point, Felix taught that the Son of Man underwent two births: he was born of the virgin— that was his natural birth, and of grace or *adoption in baptism*— his spiritual birth. Christ, accordingly, like all Christians, experienced a twofold birth. His spiritual birth, as indispensable for him as for the rest, was accomplished, as in every other case, in baptism; but in this instance also baptism was only the beginning. It was not completed till the Resurrection.[1] As the Son of Man, therefore, was subject to the different stages of divine grace arising from his election, he was also originally, though sinless,[2] the "old man" (vetus homo), and passed through the process of regeneration until he reached complete adoption—undergoing everything that and as we do. But we follow the Head, and it is only because he experienced this that he can be our redeemer and intercessor. For the rest, it is besides to be held that the *Son of God* also accepted human birth for himself, as in that case he is further to be conceived as sharing in all the acts of the Son of Man.[3]

Elipandus had given currency to his teaching in letters. His

---

[1] Alcuin adv. Felic. II. 16 (Felix says): "Christus qui est secundus Adam, accepit has geminas generationes, primam vid. quæ secundum carnem est, secundam vero spiritualem, quæ per adoptionem fit, idem redemptor noster secundum hominem complexus in semetipso continet: primam vid. quam suscepit ex virgine nascendo, secundam vero quam *initiavit* in lavacro a mortuis resurgendo."

[2] Alcuin indeed does not believe that Felix was sincere in professing to hold the sinlessness of Christ, for, if he had been, he would not have spoken of a regeneration of Christ (l.c., c. 18).

[3] Felix's words in Agobard 33: "Propter singularitatem personæ, in qua divinitas filii dei cum humanitate sua communes habeat actiones, qua ex causa aliquando ea quæ divina sunt referuntur ad humana, et ea quæ humana fiunt interdum adscribuntur ad divina, et hoc ordine aliquando dei filius in hominis filio filius hominis appellari dignatur et hominis filius in dei filio filius dei *nuncupatur*." The Nestorians, too, maintained such a double personality.

first opponents were the Abbot Beatus and the youthful Bishop
Eterius. Their opposition inflamed the anger of the ageing
Metropolitan, jealous of his orthodoxy. All who refused to see
in the two natures more than one *filius proprius* he called
" servants of Antichrist " (A.D. 785). Those he attacked, however, did not keep silent, but exposed the heretical character of
Adoptianism in an elaborate document ; they also noted the
fact that the controversy had already excited the Bishops of all
Spain, and had extended into France.[1] Hadrian I. entered into
the dispute at this time. He could not but welcome the chance
of proving to the Spanish Metropolitan, whose independence
rendered him obnoxious, that he had fallen into the heresy of
Nestorius, and that the Spanish Bishops were therefore bound
to adhere to the teaching of Rome and the Fathers.[2]

Soon afterwards Felix of Urgel energetically championed the
thesis laid down by Elipandus. Thereby the question at issue
became important for the kingdom of the Franks. The Synod
of Regensburg (792), whose transactions are unfortunately lost,
was convened to deal with Adoptianism. Felix himself required
to appear. He defended himself before Charlemagne,[3] but is

---

[1] See the analysis of this writing in Bach, p. 116 ff. It follows Cyril. The old
charge formerly made against the Nestorians is also urged against the Adoptians, that
by making the Son of Man independent they expanded the Trinity into a Quaternity.
A few Western reminiscences are, however, not wanting, although the human nature is
substantially conceived to be the impersonal *caro ;* see *e.g.*, II. 68, where the *filius secundum carnem* is named as mediator (" reconciliati sumus per solum filium secundum
carnem, sed non soli filio secundum divinitatem ") ; also II. 40 : " dominus ac
redemptor noster cum sancta ecclesia, quam redemit secundum carnem, una substantia
est."

[2] Ep. 97 in the Cod. Carol. in Migne, T. CII., see analysis in Hefele III., p. 661
ff., which is also to be compared with what follows.

[3] In the controversy the King proved that he felt fully his responsibility as a
Christian ruler, and was at the same time thoroughly anxious to be just. He was
really convinced by the propositions of his theologians. They extolled him highly as
protector of the faith, as a David and a Solomon. Alcuin says of the King (adv.
Elipand. I. 16) : " Catholicus in fide, rex in potestate, pontifex in prædicatione, judex
in æquitate, philosophus in liberalibus studiis, inclytus in moribus (?) et omni honestate
præcipuus." Ep. 100 ad dominum regem : " hoc mirabile et speciale in te pietatis
dei donum prædicamus, quod tanta devotione ecclesias Christi a perfidorum doctrinis
intrinsecus purgare tuerique niteris, quanta forinsecus a vastatione paganorum defen-
dere vel propagare conaris. *His duobus gladiis* vestram venerandam excellentiam
dextra lævaque divina armavit potestas."

said to have ultimately recanted, since all the Bishops declared his teaching to be erroneous. The recantation is, indeed, supported by several witnesses, but is not placed beyond doubt, for we hear that Felix was sent to Rome, and was kept in prison by the Pope until he yielded to swear to an orthodox confession. He now returned to Spain (to his bishopric ?) but soon renounced his forced recantation, and withdrew to Toledo in Saracen territory, in order to escape the censorship of the Franks. Alcuin's attempt to recover for the Church its highly prized bishop by means of a very friendly letter that breathed Augustine's spirit (A.D. 793) perhaps crossed the effort made by the heads of the Adoptianists to maintain their teaching in the Church by an encyclical to the Bishops of the Frankish kingdom, and a letter to Charlemagne, which took the form of a remonstrance, and contained a petition for a new investigation. Elipandus always regarded the "sleek" Beatus as the chief enemy, who had instilled his poison into the Church and seduced the Bishops. He adjures the King to judge justly ; to reinstate Felix, and be warned by Constantine's revolt to Arianism. The heresy that through Beatus now threatened the whole Church was nothing less than the denial that Christ received his body from the Virgin. At the brilliant Synod of Frankfurt, Charlemagne, after reporting to the Pope, set on foot a new investigation (794). Learned bishops and theologians were summoned from all quarters. The assembly rejected Adoptianism in two Synodal deeds—the Italian Bishops under Paulinus of Aquileia voted separately. The same course was followed by a Synod assembled contemporaneously at Rome. All these resolutions were transmitted, along with a letter of his own, by Charlemagne to Elipandus.

We are not interested in following the controversy further, for new phases did not appear. But we have the impression that Adoptianism made advances in Saracen Spain and the neighbouring province until about A.D. 799. Even the personal influence of famous doctors (Benedict of Aniane, Leidrad of Lyons) met at first with little success. But Frankish Spain could not resist the influence of the whole empire, and Felix himself was ultimately induced once more to recant at the

Synod of Aachen (799).   At this date, besides Paulinus,[1] Alcuin was indefatigable in producing works, some of them extensive, against the heresy (Libell. adv. Felic. hær., IV. lib. adv. Elipandum, VII. lib. adv. Felic.).   It is interesting to notice how this Anglo-Saxon, the disciple of Bede, was entirely dependent in his Christology on the Greeks, and had abandoned the Augustinian tradition.   Augustine as well as Græco-Roman speculative theology had become domesticated in England through the Romanising of that country.   But in those questions on which the Greeks had pronounced their views, they were ever regarded as the more honourable, reliable, and learned.   They were the representatives of the sublime theology of the mystery of the Incarnation.[2]   The Latins were only after all to be considered in so far as they agreed with the Greeks.   How great is the imposing prestige and power of an ancient culture, and how cogent is every " advance " that it experiences, even if that advance passes imperceptibly into a refinement which produces a new barbarianism !   Alcuin's arguments might have occurred just as well in the works of Cyril, Leontius, or John of Damascus, and they are sometimes actually to be found there word for word :—Christ is the personal God-Logos who assumed impersonal human nature, and fused it into the complete unity of his being.   Accordingly, even apart from sin, Christ's humanity was by no means like ours in all points, but was very different.   Since it acquired all the attributes of deity, all human limitations shown in the life of Jesus were voluntarily accepted, in other words were due to accommodation, were pedagogic or illusory.   Alcuin dissipates the records of the gospels as thoroughly as the Monophysite and Crypto-Monophysite Greeks.   This form of piety had ceased to regard Christ in any sense as a human person ; nay, it felt itself gravely hurt if it was told that it ought to suppose a really human consciousness in Christ.   Not only was the dismemberment of the one Christ disowned as blasphemous, but still more the application to him of categories that were held to describe believers.[3]   In

---

[1] See on his polemics, Bach, p. 121 ff.

[2] This is true above all of Cyril.

[3] See the analysis of Alcuin's Christology in Bach, p. 128 ff.   Alcuin seeks to show

fact, we are correct in saying that faith in Christ as Redeemer
had no interest in expounding broadly wherein Christ is like us.[1]
But the Adoptians had, consistently with this likeness, which
they asserted, characterised him as *head* of the community,
and demonstrated a way in which the man Christ could be
apprehended as redeemer and intercessor.[2] But then, as now,

(1) that all the statements of Scripture and the Fathers regarding Christ have for their
subject the concrete person in two natures ; (2) that the notion of adoption occurs
neither in Scripture nor the Fathers, and is thus novel and false ; and (3) that the
Adoptianist theory is inconsistent, and upsets the basis of faith. He tries to show that
adoptio, if taken to mean anything different from *assumptio*, leads to heresy. Assumption is held to express the *natural relation* in which humanity is connected with
deity by the Incarnation, and which is annulled by the *adoptio* that designates a
relation due to grace. Alcuin indeed also speaks (following Augustine) of grace
having been in Christ, for it does not, like *adoptio*, exclude the natural relation of
sonship. But his strongest argument consists in his explanation that passive adoption
was impossible, because the Son of Man *did not exist at all* before he was actual Son
of God. Neither he nor Paulinus supposes that the man Christ was a person before
the God-man. He certainly possessed his personality from the first in the Son of
God. Accordingly, if we think abstractly, we may not conceive of a man (homo)
Christ who existed before the Incarnation, but of human nature, which only became
personal by its assumption, and was at once made an essential constituent of the
person of the God-man. Therefore this nature, even apart from sin, was infinitely
superior to and unlike ours. Therefore the doctrine of the Agnoetes, who had besides been already strongly assailed by Gregory I. in his letters, was to be condemned;
and the servile form of the Son of God was in every respect worthy of adoration,
because it was not necessary to his nature, but was at every point freely undertaken.
Accordingly Christ required neither baptism nor adoption, and even as man was no
ordinary creature, but always the God-man. " In spite of the assumption of human
nature, the God-man retained sole property in the person of the Son." Humanity
was merely added like something impersonal to this unity of person of the Son of
God, "and there remained the same property in two natures in the name of the Son
that formerly existed in one substance." But Alcuin adds very inaptly (c. Felic. II.
12) : "in adsumtione carnis a deo persona perit hominis, non natura ;" for he
certainly did not assume that a " persona hominis " had existed previously. We can
only explain this lapse by supposing that Alcuin had not yet let Cyril's Christology
expunge from his mind every reminiscence of Augustine's. Bach rightly remarks
(p. 136 f. : against Dorner) " that no opponent of the Adoptians imagined that personality was essential to the completeness of the human nature ; (like Bach himself)
they taught exactly the opposite." Bach's own explanation of the above passage,
which is only intelligible as a lapse, is, for the rest, wholly incorrect. By *persona* he
would understand "the person of man as such, of *humanitas*, and not of the man
Christ."

　　1 Epist. ad Carol. M. : " Quid enim prodest ecclesiæ dei Christum appellare
adoptivum filium vel deum nuncupativum ? "
　　2 The explanations given by Felix as to the man Christ as *sacerdos, sacrificium,*

no one who had once been initiated into the mysteries was influenced by this.   He who has once but sipped the intoxicating cup of that mysticism, which promises to transform every worthless stone into gold, sees everywhere the mystery of deification, and then it is not easy for the watchman to recall the dreamer to life.[1]   For this is the last motive of this speculation : *from the transformation of the impersonal human substance into the divine (in the case of Christ) to derive the divino-human means of enjoyment in this world.*   Even in the instance of Beatus, the realistic conception of the Lord's Supper turns out to be a decisive motive against Adoptianism,[2] and this motive can also be demonstrated in Alcuin's works.[3]   Thus the Christological controversy is closely connected with the magical conceptions of the Lord's Supper as the centre of Church doctrine and practice.   It is all the more instructive that, as we shall see, *images* were not yet thought of, while the East had long had them in view, as well as the Lord's Supper, in connection with its Crypto-Monophysite Christology.   In this matter the Anglo-Saxon and Frankish Church still " lagged " behind its guide.

caput ecclesiæ are Augustinian, and in part more precise than they occur in Augustine. The part played in the controversy by the thought of Christ as head of the Church is worthy of note.   We are not prepared for it, if we start from the more ancient tradition.   The greater emphasis laid on Christ as priest and sacrifice was already determined by the all-prevailing reference to the Mass.

[1] Adoptianism, like Nestorianism, necessarily remained a half thing, because it did not correct this pseudo-Christian motive.   This is the ultimate cause of its speedy death.   Adoptianism and the Eucharistic Christ do not suit each other.

[2] See Bach, p. 119 f.   Beatus has pointed out, like Cyril, that the concrete unity of Christ's person is shown most clearly in the fact that in the Lord's Supper the whole Christ is adored, and that his flesh is the principle of eternal life.   Bach (p. 120) has eloquently evolved as his own view the cause for which the opponents of the Adoptians ultimately contended.   " Beatus and Eterius, in opposition to the externality of Elipandus, pointed with a profoundly realistic glance to the central significance of Christ in the collective ethical and sacramental constitution of Christianity, and the morally free life of humanity.   The organic and *physical* relation of Christ to humanity, and the *physiology* of grace in its inner relation to human freedom, which has its living roots in the concrete God-man, are hereby indicated.   A divided Christ cannot be a new *physical* ethical *ferment* of life to mankind."   This materialistic ghost unfortunately also announces its presence in Protestant Christianity.

[3] With him and Paulinus, only indeed in unimportant hints, wherefore Bach calls Paulinus " less profound and thorough " than Beatus.   How the speculation reached the latter is not known.

Felix secluded himself with Leidrad in Lyons. The re-conversion of the Frankish Adoptians now made great strides, and Felix himself had to exhort his congregation to abandon the error which he had formerly taught them. But he was by no means thoroughly convinced at heart, as is shown by papers found, after the death of the unfortunate Bishop, by Leidrad's successor, Agobard. Agobard held it necessary to refute the dead Felix. If aggressive Adoptianism soon expired in the Frankish kingdom, it was revived by the daring dialectic of the eleventh and twelfth centuries as a doctrine of the schools,[1] and it afterwards continued during all centuries of the Middle Ages, though without rousing more than a theological dispute. Little is known of how the "heresy" gradually died out in Saracen Spain. Even in the time of Elipandus it did not escape censure. It still had power to attract about A.D. 850;[2] but then there came times when it was necessarily worth more to Christian Spaniards to feel that they were in agreement with the whole Church than to defend the legitimacy of a distinctive position.

The decisive result of the whole controversy was that the West set aside its own earlier Christological system, and—for the sake of the Lord's Supper and the imposing tradition of the Greeks—thought like the latter *within the sphere of dogma*. Christ's *unity* was maintained; but this unity absorbed his humanity, and removed far off the dread incarnate Son of God (dei filius incarnatus tremendus). Strict dogmatic only permitted him to be approached in the Lord's Supper. But that did not prevent the vision of the lowly Man of Sorrows continuing, still secretly at first, to make its way side by side with dogmatic theory, that vision that had dawned upon Augustine, and was in ever-increasing vividness to form the strength of piety in the future.

§ I. (*b*). *The Controversy as to Predestination.*[3]

The revival of theological science in the ninth century led

---

[1] See Bach, II., p. 390 ff.
[2] See the letters of Alvar, Bandissin, l.c. Bach I., p. 146 ff.
[3] Sources, collected by the Jansenist Maugin, Veterum auct. qui IX. sæc. de

to a thorough study of Augustine. But the theology of Gregory I. had already accustomed men to combine the formulas of Augustinianism with the Pelagianism required by the system of the cultus. Hence a renewal of the controversy would hardly have taken place had not the monk Gottschalk of Orbais asserted the doctrine of predestination with as much energy as Augustine had done in his latest writings, and had he not been opposed by Hinkmar, whom his jealous colleagues would gladly have charged with heresy. It was not his use of Augustinian formulas that lifted Gottschalk out of the mass of theologians, and gave a startling effect to his confession. It was the fact that the doctrine of predestination had become the strength and support of his being after a misspent life. Here again it is palpable that words are not everything, that they remain a tinkling cymbal as long as they are not the expression of experience. Many joined and followed Gottschalk in speaking as he did at the time; but he alone was persecuted as a heretical teacher, because the opposition felt that he alone was dangerous to their Church system.

Gottschalk's teaching regarding predestination was not different, either in matter or form, from that of Augustine, Fulgentius, and Isidore ;[1] but it must also be said that he taught nothing but predestination. With the devotion, at first of resignation, and afterwards of fanaticism, he committed himself to the hands of God who does all things according to his good pleasure, and does nothing without having determined it irrevocably from the beginning. Predestination is the content of

præedest. et gratia scripserunt, Paris 1650 ; see the works of Carlovingian theologians in the time of Charles the Bald, Mansi, T. XIV. and XV.; Gfrörer, Gesch. der Karol. Vol. I., and K.-Gesch., Vol. III. 2 ; Dümmler, Gesch. des ostfränk. Reichs, Vol. I. ; Hauck, K.-Gesch. Deutschlands, Vol. II. : Wiggers in the Ztschr. f. d. hist. Theol. 1859 ; Weizsäcker in the Jahrbb. f. deutsche Theol. 1859 ; Hefele, Concil.-Gesch. IV²., p. 130 ff. ; Bach, Op. cit. I., p. 219 ff ; Reuter l.c. I., p. 43 ff ; Borrasch, Der Mönch Gottschalk, 1868 ; Monographs on Hinkmar by v. Noorden and Schrörs ; Freystedt, Der wissensch. Kampf im Prädest.-Streit des 9 Jahrh. ; also, Der synodale Kampf im Prädest.-Streit des 9 Jahrh. (Ztschr. f. wissensch. Theol. Vol. 36, pp. 315-368 ; New Series, Vol. I., pp. 447-478), and Studien zu Gottschalk (Ztschr. f. K. Gesch., Vol XVIII., p. 1 ff.).

[1] Gottschalk is especially dependent on Fulgentius. On Isidore's doctrine of predestination, see Wiggers, Ztschr. f. d. hist. Theol. 1855 ; on Bede's, l.c. 1857.

the Gospel, is the object of faith. It is the truth—that twofold predestination to life and death, according to which eternal life is decreed for the good, and death for the sinner, in which, therefore, some are appointed to life, and the rest to death. Nothing is to be set aside that the Church elsewhere teaches, or that it does; but it is a revolt from the Gospel to obscure in the hearts of men the certainty of this eternal unchangeable dispensation of divine grace—for justice and punishment are also good. Until his death Gottschalk defended inflexibly this faith of his, in the living and original language of the convinced advocate.[1]

But what did the historical Christ, or the Christ of the sacramentally ordered Church, mean here? If the hidden God with his hidden will was a comfort to Gottschalk, then that comfort consisted in the assurance that this God had *also* predestinated some to life, and the assurance flowed from the economy which culminated in Christ. For from what other source was it known that eternal predestination also embraced the *pardon* of a section of mankind? The assurance of the individual gained nothing by this; but among the opposition also no one would have anything to do with certainty of salvation; the individual did not count for much to himself or others. Individualism was not yet developed. Christ accordingly was not in question. Even the resolute defender of predestination looked to him when he thought of election to life. But the system of the Sacraments, legal demands and works, which constituted the Church itself, tottered, as it must always totter, wherever religion is recalled from externality to the *inner life*. This recall was accomplished in a much more abstract way in the present instance than by Augustine. The most profound of the African's expositions on liberating grace and the blessed necessity of goodness (beata necessitas boni), which form the

---

[1] On Gottschalk's life till the outbreak of the dispute, see Hefele, l.c. The Augustinian spirit, and Augustine's language in the Confessio prolixior (Migne, CXXI., p. 349): "Tui profecto sic semper indigent omnes electi tui, quo videlicet tibi de te solo semper valeant placere. Quemadmodum palmites indigent vite, quo fructum queant ferre, vel aër aut oculi luce, quo vel ille lucidus esse vel illi possint videre. . . . te igitur supplex invoco . . . ut largiaris indigentissimo mihi *per gratuitæ gratiæ tuæ invictissimam virtutem, etc.*"

background of the doctrine of predestination, do not tell strongly upon Gottschalk. Nor had the Frankish monk been able to appropriate the Neoplatonic speculation, that had been toned down or transferred to a wholly different sphere of ideas by Augustine's teaching. And, again, he did not know the dialectic of the notion of time, which is inseparable from Augustine's conception. Yet he was not unfamiliar with dialectics; indeed, if we may trust the accounts given us, he at first took pleasure in the problem on dialectical grounds; but the fire he played with afterwards mastered him. The subject matter itself became precious to him. It corresponded to his own mood, ever growing gloomier, and he championed it with the zeal of the missionary. It was not original sin, or sin that he regarded as the chief subject, but the unchangeableness and wisdom of God. He was a theologian in the narrowest sense of the term.

Gottschalk was first opposed by Rabanus in his letters to Noting and Eberard—shortly before A.D. 848.[1] He was accused of teaching that right faith and good works were of no avail to him who was not appointed to salvation, and that God forced men to sin and perdition (invitum hominem facit peccare).[2] Other opponents soon arose, and it was declared that he taught a predestination to sin. At the Council of Mainz (848) Rabanus got him condemned,[3] and handed over, by command of King Lewis, to Hinkmar to whose province as monk he belonged.[4] In his letter to Hinkmar, Rabanus declares a predestination as regards wickedness to be simply erroneous, and he is able to tell already of people, who, seduced by Gottschalk, gave up pious practices

---

[1] See Opp. Raban. in Migne, CXII., p. 1530 sq., Kunstmann, Rabanus Magnentius Maurus 1841.

[2] The view of Rabanus himself, that great, pure, truly pious and unpolitical prince of the Church, was Semi-Pelagian.

[3] Fragment of a confession of Gottschalk laid before the Synod in Hinkmar, De prædest. 5, Migne, CXXV., p. 89 sq. (Hefele, p. 138) : " gemina prædestinatio . . . similiter omnino omnes reprobos, qui damnabuntur propter ipsorum mala merita, incommutabilis deus per justum judicium suum incommutabiliter prædestinavit ad mortem merito sempiternam."

[4] Migne, CXII., p. 1574.

because, forsooth, they were wholly useless.[1] Hinkmar got the
judgment against the "miserable monk" repeated at an imperial
synodal diet at Chiersey (849). He was deposed from his office,
scourged, and rendered harmless in prison.[2] Neither Rabanus
nor Hinkmar seems at first to have formed as yet any idea of
the difficulty of the whole question—caused by the authority of
Augustine and other Fathers. Hinkmar contented himself with
referring God's prescience to good or evil, but predestination to
goodness alone.[3] But the position of the case soon changed.
Gottschalk composed two confessions, in which he stated his
teaching, supporting it from Scripture and the Fathers,[4] and he
also wrote essays in which he emphasised the particularism of
Christ's saving work,[5] subordinating the latter strictly to the
premundane decree of God. He also, in a letter to Amolo, gave

[1] Op. cit.

[2] Hincm. De prædest. 2; Migne, CXXV., p. 85; cf. Migne, CXXI, p. 1027.

[3] Hinkmar's large works on the question in dispute were not written till several years
later; (yet see the writing Ad reclusos et simplices, A.D. 849-50; Gundlach in the
Ztschr. für K.-Gesch., Vol. X., p. 258 ff.; Freystedt, l.c. p. 320 ff., 358 ff.). The first
in three books (856 and 857) was so extensive, that it was not transcribed, and so has
perished (see Schrörs, p. 136 f.). The second, De prædestinatione dei et libero arbitrio,
was also prolix enough and very meaningless (written 859 to 860, Schrörs, p. 141 ff.).
In the introduction to this work, the history of the sect of predestinationists, which is
said to have risen even in St. Augustine's lifetime, is described in a very unhistorical
fashion. The sect has now revived, and its newer members adhere to Fulgentius, who
never enjoyed a lofty prestige in the Church (c. 3, 8, 13). Hinkmar's main proposition
is that predestination to punishment embraces compulsion to commit sin. " Præscivit
deus hominem ad pœnam." Accordingly there is only a predestination *of*, not *to*,
punishment.

[4] Migne, CXXI., pp. 347-349: "Confiteor, deum omnipotentem et incommutabilem
præscisse et prædestinasse angelos sanctos et homines electos ad vitam gratis æternam,
et ipsum diabolum . . . cum ipsis quoque hominibus reprobis . . . propter præscita
certissime ipsorum propria futura mala merita prædestinasse *pariter* per justissimum
judicium suum in mortem merito sempiternam." " Credo siquidem atque confiteor
præscisse teante sæcula quæcunque erant futura, sive bona sive mala, prædestinasse vero
tantummodo bona. Bona autem a te prædestinata bifariam sunt tuis a fidelibus in-
dagata . . . *i.e.* in gratiæ beneficia et justitiæ simul judicia . . . Frustra electis
prædestinasses vitam, nisi et illos prædestinasses ad ipsam. Sic etiam . . . omnibus
quoque reprobis hominibus perennem merito prædestinasti pœnam, et eosdem similiter
prædestinasti ad eam, quia nimirum sine causa et ipsis prædestinasses mortis perpetuæ
pœnam, nisi et ipsos prædestinasses ad eam : non enim irent, nisi destinati, neque
profecto destinarentur, nisi essent prædestinati." From Gottschalk's standpoint both
confessions are conciliatory.

[5] Gottschalk frequently maintained that Christ did not die for the *reprobi*, though

expression to the particularly objectionable principle "that baptism and the other sacraments were given in vain to those who perished after receiving them ; " for "those of the number of the faithful who perish were never incorporated in Christ and the Church." [1] But it was perceived in the more cultured South, apart from Mainz and Rheims, that it was not Gottschalk but his opponents who diverged from Augustine's teaching. The best theologians ranged themselves on the side of the Confessor *e.g.*, Prudentius of Troyes, Ratramnus of Corbie, then also the learned and acute Lupus of Ferrières,[2] the priest Servatus Lupus and Remigius of Lyons, for the most part disciples of Alcuin.[3]

There now began a lively theological controversy (849-50), which was not, however, violent enough to involve the rest of the Church and the Pope, and which was unspeakably unsatisfactory, because staunch Augustinians neither could nor would abandon the ruling ecclesiastical system, and had therefore to seek for compromises where Gottschalk's results endangered it, and because the Frankish Semi-Pelagians soon saw that they would have to approximate their *phraseology* to Augustinianism. Among the writings in defence of Gottschalk there were accordingly many shades of opinion, but so were there also on the other side.[4] Florus Magister, *e.g.*, advocated the twofold (gemina) predestination, but yet opposed Gottschalk, since he rejected the thought of the irresistibleness of grace.[5] Amolo of Lyons treated him in a friendly spirit ; but no one else showed so emphatically that Gottschalk's teaching did away with the historical redemption, the fruits of Christ's death, and *sacra-*

he taught a certain general redemption of all the baptised ; see Hincm. De præd. 29, 34, 35 ; Migne, CXXV., p. 289 sq., 349 sq., 369 sq.

[1] Hefele, p. 169 : " baptistum et alia sacramenta frustatorie eis dari, qui post eorum perceptionem pereunt ; " for " qui ex numero fidelium pereunt, Christo et ecclesiæ nunquam fuerunt incorporati."

[2] See Freystedt, l.c., p. 329 ff.

[3] Bach (I., p. 232 ff.) has analysed and discussed the various writings of these men.

[4] Men at that time disputed about predestination, just as " positive " theologians to-day quarrel among themselves about the right of historical criticism. Some defend this right, others would restrict or abolish it ; but even the former don't really believe in it, since they take care not to carry out its conclusions.

[5] Bach, I., p. 240.

mental grace.[1] The only one who took up a consistent stand-point, and from it opposed the monk, was John Scotus. His teaching did not rest on Augustine's doctrine of predestination but on the Neoplatonic and Augustinian ontology, which he developed boldly. According to this, evil and death were nothing. Unchangeable being had only one unchangeable will, namely itself, and it evolved itself alone. Everything else consisted in negation, was nothing actual, and bore this very not-being in itself as a punishment. Applying this to the question of predestination, it followed that those were right who would only admit one predestination.[2] But friend and foe felt, without seeing through the pantheism of Scotus, that this was a case of casting out the devil by the aid of Beelzebub (" commentum diaboli "). There was only one way out of the difficulty besides that given by Scotus. This was to give up altogether putting the question in the form of the predestination problem, to hold to the historical Christ, and to do justice to Augustine's doctrine of grace by reducing the Church system to the experience of the new birth and faith. But no one discovered this expedient,[3] and so the whole controversy necessarily became a maze of insincerity, partly objective, partly conscious. Augustine's authority, however, was so powerful that the result, if we may speak of such a thing, came nearer Gottschalk's teaching in *words* than to the original utterances of Rabanus and his comrades (of whom Pardulus also was one). The latter sought to carry their distinction between prescience and predestination (as regards evil and punishment), and would therefore have nothing said of *persons* being predestined to punishment. When God foresaw evil, he predestined punishment for those who should not deserve to be redeemed by grace ; room, accordingly, is left indirectly to free-will, although, so far as words go, the saved are saved solely in virtue of election. The artificial distinction here made (predestination

---

[1] Bach, I., p. 241 ff.

[2] De divina prædest. Migne, CXXII., p. 355 sq. The Synods at Valencia and Langres (859) condemned the work, after Prudentius and Florus Magister had written against it.

[3] Amolo came nearest it.

of life and of the good, prescience of the wicked, predestination
of punishment) is apparently defensible, even on an Augustinian
basis, since Hinkmar now spoke of a complete loss of freedom
through Adam's Fall. But the distinction was in truth meant
to open a door for the entrance of Semi-Pelagianism. This
doctrine was adopted at a new Synod of Chiersey (853) under
Hinkmar's leadership.[1]

But what took place here was not authoritative in the Arch-
bishopric of Sens[2] and the Empire of Lothar. Remigius of
Lyons sharply attacked the four chapters of Chiersey as running
counter to Scripture and the Fathers.[3] At the great Synod
held at Valencia of the provinces of Lyons, Vienne and Arles
(855), canons were adopted which adhered much more closely
to Augustine, and contained the teaching of Remigius. Dislike
to the powerful Hinkmar also played a part in their composition. The Synod rejected the four chapters : they had been

---

[1] The four chapters of Chiersey yielded more to Augustinianism than was consistent
with truthfulness : I. "Deus hominem sine peccato rectum cum libero arbitrio condidit et in paradiso posuit, quem in sanctitate justitiæ permanere voluit. Homo
libero arbitrio male utens peccavit et cecidit, et factus est massa perditionis totius
humani generis. Deus autem bonus et justus elegit ex eadem massa perditionis
secundum præscientiam suam, quos per gratiam prædestinavit ad vitam, et vitam illis
prædestinavit æternam. Ceteros autem, quos justitiæ judicio in massa perditionis
reliquit, perituros præscivit, sed non ut perirent prædestinavit, pœnam autem illis,
quia justus est, prædestinavit æternam. Ac per hoc *unam* dei prædestinationem
tantummodo dicimus, quæ aut ad donum pertinet gratiæ, aut ad retributionem
justitiæ." II. "Libertatem arbitrii in primo homine *perdidimus*, quam per Christum
dominum nostrum recepimus. Et habemus liberum arbitrium ad bonum, præventum
et adjutum gratia. Et habemus liberum arbitrium ad malum, desertum gratia.
Liberum autem habemus arbitrium quia gratia liberatum et gratia, de corrupto
sanatum." III. "Deus omnes homines sine exceptione vult salvos fieri, licet non
omnes salventur. Quod autem quidem salvantur, salvantis est donum ; quod autem
quidem pereunt, pereuntium est meritum." The fourth chapter says that Christ
adopted the nature of each man, and accordingly died for each, though all are not redeemed. The cause of this fact is that those not redeemed are *infideles* or are defi-
cient in the faith that works by love; "poculum humanæ salutis, quod confectum
est infirmitate nostra et virtute divina, habet quidem in se, ut omnibus prosit, sed si
non bibitur non medetur." Mansi, XIV., p. 919.

[2] See on Prudentius and the Synod of Sens, Hefele, p. 188 f. The four chapters
of this Synod, which teach the *gemina prædestinatio*, are by Prudentius ; see Migne,
CXXV., p. 64.

[3] Migne, CXXI., p. 1083 : "Libellus de tenenda immobiliter scripturæ veritate"
as an official paper of the Church of Lyons.

entered on with too little prudence ("minus prospecte suscepta.") It taught the double predestination, applied the latter
to persons also, and maintained that Christ shed his blood for
believers. The question whether God willed to save all men
was carefully evaded. If the Synod disowned a predestination
to sin, it did not thereby abandon strictly Augustinian ground.
On the contrary, the contention that condemnation was based
on prescience, and that in the Church's Sacraments "nothing
was futile or delusive" (nihil sit cassum, nihil ludificatorium)
shows the anxiety felt not to give up what was held valid by
the Church.[1] If we compare the resolutions of the two Synods
word for word, the differences are extremely subtle, and yet the
little addition (plus) of the alien co-efficient attached to Augustinianism in the Chiersey decrees is highly significant.
Rabanus, Hinkmar, and Charles's Synod take their stand on
ecclesiastical empiricism, and try, because they must, to come
to terms with Augustinianism, therein yielding more than can
have been agreeable to them. Remigius, Prudentius, and
Lothar's Synod take their stand on Augustinianism, and yet
would not give up this ecclesiastical empiricism. But in neither
case did anyone permit the suggestion of a doubt as to whether
this empiricism and Augustinianism were compatible.

Political affairs prevented the threatened breach from being
consummated. The matter was taken up again in the reign of
King Charles, Lothar's son. A few slight modifications of the
chapters of Valencia were decided on at Langres (859) in order
to enable Charles the Bald, who had subscribed those of
Chiersey, to approve of them.[2] The great Synod of Savonières
(859), at which there were present bishops from three kingdoms,
as well as the sovereigns themselves, Charles the Bald, Charles
of Provence, and Lothar of Lothringen, adopted the modified
chapters of Valencia, and also, as it appears, those passed at
Chiersey; the members did not condemn one another on
account of disbelief or belief in twofold predestination (gemina
predestinatio), and this meant the greatest advance towards

---

[1] It is superfluous to give the canons here—they are very prolix ; see Mansi, XV.,
p. 3 ; Hefele, IV., p. 193 ff. ; Schröis, p. 133 ff.

[2] Mansi, XV., p. 537 ; Hefele, p. 205.

peace.[1] Hinkmar, indeed, did not doubt that there had been and was a predestinationist heresy, which it was necessary to oppose, and whose adherents appealed unjustifiably to Augustine. He composed at the time his prolix work, De prædestinatione (against Remigius and others), under the auspices of his theological king. But the kings' need of peace was stronger than the zeal of bishops fighting in the dark. At the great Synod of the three realms at Toucy (860), the case postponed at Savonières was brought to an end in a comprehensive synodal edict, which dealt indefinitely with the real kernel of the question, and was destitute of meaning and badly arranged. Controversial points were left alone, and those were confessed on which all were agreed. Hinkmar composed this document. Besides predestination to life, which was set forth in good Augustinian language, it was declared that God willed to save *all*, that Christ died for *all*, and that while free-will required to be redeemed and healed after the Fall, it had never been wholly lost. [2] If the worth of a confession depends on its really expressing the existing belief, then the triumph of Hinkmar's formula was really more valuable than would have been that of the contrary doctrine. The avowal of twofold predestination, in itself even more the expression of a theological speculation than of Christian faith in God the Father, would have meant less than nothing coupled with the retention of ecclesiastical empiricism. Of course the formula of Hinkmar, which no artifice could reconcile with that of Orange, did not mean much either; for, in spite of words, Augustine remained deposed. Gregory I.'s system of doctrine held the field. Men thought of the sacramental Christ, as they rejected, along with Adoptianism, the Augustinian Christology, and it was still this Christ and the good works of believers to which they looked, when, along with twofold predestination, they in fact set aside Augustine's doctrine of grace.

Gottschalk died in prison, irreconcilable and unreconciled (869), clinging to the *predestinatio ad mortem*, which he understood in

---

[1] Mansi, XV., p. 529; Hefele, p. 206.

[2] The prolix Ep. synodalis in Mansi, XV., p. 563; Hefele, p. 217 ff. *Prædestinatio ad mortem* is not mentioned.

so " erroneous a sense " that he did not abandon it as Remigius
seems to have done. He had prophesied in vain the unmasking
and fall of his mortal enemy Hinkmar as Antichrist, that great
exemplar of predestination to death.[1]

§ 2. *The Controversy regarding the Filioque and Pictures.*

By the position it had taken up in the Adoptianist as well as
in the predestination controversy, the Church of the Frankish
kingdom identified itself, abandoning tendencies to higher
characteristics of its own,[2] with the popular Church ideas as
represented by Constantinople and Rome. The theology it had
inherited from Augustine was transformed into an ecclesiastical
system such as had long prevailed in those chief Churches.
But the West at that time still held tenaciously to its own
characteristic position as compared with the East in two
doctrines ; it supported the *filioque* and rejected images. Both
these subjects have been already discussed in Vol. IV., pp. 133,
317, therefore only a little falls to be added.

Even if we had not known it already, we see very clearly in
the controversy regarding the *filioque* clause that the doctrine
of the Trinity and Christology constituted dogma and the legal
basis of the Church κατ᾽ ἐξοχήν even for the West—see the

---

[1] The ill-usage he had suffered seems to have rendered Gottschalk at times irresponsible for his actions in the last years of his life. His dispute with Hinkmar about
the phrase "trina deitas" is noteworthy. The latter would not permit it on the ground
that it was Arian ; Gottschalk and Ratramnus defended it by accusing Hinkmar of
Sabellianism. Both phrases "una deitas" and "trina deitas" can be defended from the
Augustinian standpoint ; see Hinkmar's writing, De una et non trina deitate (Migne,
CXXV., p. 473 ; Schrörs, Hinkmar, p. 150 ff.), in which Boethius' notion of personality ("rationabilis naturæ individua subsistentia") plays a part. The number of
theological problems discussed at the date of this renaissance of theology was very
great ; see Schrörs, Hinkmar, p. 88 ff. But the questions were almost all exceedingly
minute and subtle, like those suggested by clever children. Nor was the culture of
the period possessed of the scholastic technique required for their treatment.

[2] Of course only tendencies—the confusion that still prevailed at the close of the
eighth century as regards Augustinianism is best shown by the fact that the Symbol
admitted into the Libri Carolini (symbolum Hieronymi, sermo Augustini) was Pelagius'
Confession of Faith *ad Innocentium.* But it was also, as late as A.D. 1521, produced
by the Sorbonne against Luther as Augustine's confession.

Athanasian Creed.[1]   The *filioque*, which originated in Augustinian theology, came to the Frankish kingdom from Spain, but
we know nothing more precisely as to how it did.   It was held
to be certain that it belonged to the Symbol, and this conviction

---

[1] I have dealt with the origin and authority of the Athanasian Symbol in Vol. IV.,
p. 134.   Since then Loofs (R. Encykl., Vol. II.[3], pp. 177-194) has published an investigation regarding it, distinguished by a comprehensive knowledge of sources and
literature.   We are agreed as to the following points.   (1) The Symbol, whether we
may think it to have risen out of two originally independent documents or not, belongs
to Roman Southern Gaul.   (2) Its first, longer, Trinitarian half, as well as the second,
shorter, Christological portion belongs to the period c. 450—(at latest) 600.   In the
pre-Carlovingian age the Symbol had only a partial authority—the Canon of Autun
proves that it was accepted there c. 670.   Not till the Carlovingian period was the
way prepared for its universal acceptance.   Thus only two important points are in
dispute.   (1) Did the Symbol originate in a sermo de symbolo, or was it directly
conceived as a formulary of the faith ?   (2) Does it consist of two portions originally
independent, or was it framed from the first in its present extent ?   I may here leave
the first question alone.   As regards the second, I had supported the original independence of the Trinitarian first half, and supposed that the Christological section
was only added a considerable time later, *perhaps* not till the Carlovingian epoch.
Loofs (p. 185 ff.) has convinced me, by his evidence as to the Cod. Paris, 3836, that
this date has been put too late.   But I never *based* my opinion of an original independence of the two parts on this external testimony invalidated by Loofs, but on the
internal matter of the Symbol.   The latter Loofs has practically left alone.   The
following facts fall to be considered.   (1) In the opening of the Symbol, §§ 1-3, the
doctrine of the Trinity is alone announced as " catholica fides " (compare the edict
of Theodosius I. of A.D. 380) ; there is nothing to suggest that the author means also
to deal with Christology.   (2) In § 26 we find, consistently with this, the solemn conclusion reverting to the beginning ; " Qui vult ergo salvus esse, ita de trinitate
sentiat." This whole first half is accordingly a rule of faith complete in itself and
entire, elaborated by the aid of Augustine and Vincentius, and anti-Arian.   Nothing
essential is to be found in it which could not have been written by Augustine, if of
course the sentences may have been only gradually polished afterwards.   (3) The
following section, not hitherto introduced, is, indeed, bracketed with the preceding
one by §§ 27 and 48 ; but these brackets testify plainly enough that an original organic
unity is not to be supposed.   For (a) § 40 is a replica of § 26, yet (b) the language is
somewhat different (in the second section we have " fideliter credere," " fides recta,
ut credamus et confiteamur," " fideliter et firmiterque credere " ; in the first section :
" catholicam fidem tenere," or " integram inviolatamque fidem servare ").   (4) Looking to the contents, the Christological section, §§ 28-39, shows, first, the Antinestorian
(32) and Antimonophysite attitude (34, 35) completely balanced ; secondly, the
Gallican rescension of the Apostle's Creed (" passus," " descendit ad inferos," " sedet
ad dexteram *dei patris omnipotentis*—these could only be attributed to Spain) ;
thirdly, the influence of the Nicene Constantinopolitan Creed (" passus est *pro nostra
salute*"), so that we can hardly ascend beyond the beginning of the sixth century for
this part.   (5) Weight is to be given to the fact that the author, who has adhered
strictly in §§ 36, 37 to the curt form of the Symbol, has considered it necessary in

was already expressed at the Synod of Gentilly (767) [1] Charles's
learned theologians confirmed it, as is proved by Alcuin's work
De processione spiritus sancti, and the Libri Carolini. [2] Official
action was provoked by Western monks having had to submit
to grave injustice in Jerusalem, because in the Liturgy they
added, " sicut erat in principio " to the " Gloria patri," and " tu
solus altissimus " to the " Gloria in excelsis," and in the Symbol
" filioque " to " a patre." They complained to the Pope, who
turned to the Emperor. The latter commissioned Theodulf of
Orleans to compose a work, " De spiritu sancto," and got it
decreed at the Synod of Aachen (809) that the *filioque* belonged to the Symbol. [3] The Pope, however, who had to
approve of this decision, still took the East into consideration,
and did not permit the admission of the word, though he
assented to the doctrine. Even the remonstrance of the Franks
that the *filioque* was necessary to salvation did not move him.[4]
The matter continued thus till the great controversy under
Photius, until the *filioque* became the Symbolic watchword in
the whole of the West. [5] The most worthless formula of

§§ 38, 39 to make a wordy addition, that at Christ's coming all men " reddituri sunt de
factis *propriis* rationem, et qui bona egerunt ibunt in vitam æternam, qui vero mala in
ignem æternum." Is this addition not to be understood as in the interests of Semi-
Pelagianism ? The two portions may have been combined as early as the sixth century.
If we could date the Sermo Trevir. we would know more accurately about this.

[1] See Hefele, III., p. 432.

[2] Hefele, III., p. 704 ; see Libr. Carol. III. 3 (Migne, Vol. 98), where Tarasius is
blamed for teaching that the Holy Spirit proceeds *ex patre per filium* instead of *ex
filio*.

[3] Hefele, III., 750-755.

[4] See Mansi, XIV., p. 18 sq. It is very important that the Pope objected to the
last-mentioned argument of the Franks, saying that other things were also necessary
for salvation, and were yet not received into the Symbol, since it could admit of no
change at all. *This meant* (as opposed to the Eastern view) *that the Symbol did not
embrace everything that belonged to salvation.* The Pope says (p. 20) : " Verumtamen,
quæso, responde mihi : num universa hujusmodi fidei mystica sacramenta, quæ symbolo
non continentur, sine quibus quisque, qui ad hoc pertingere potest, catholicus esse
non potest, symbolis inserenda et propter compendium minus intellegentium, ut
cuique libuerit, addenda sunt ? " The Pope, besides, asserted, in a very remarkable
way, in the interview with the Frankish *missi,* he thought that all stages of culture
could not take up the same attitude to dogma, hat accordingly what was important
to some was not to others.

[5] The papal legates in Constantinople (A.D. 880) still subscribed the Symbol without

Augustinianism, once recommended by its opposition to Arianism, was thus preserved in the West.

If in this controversy between the West and East the former at first received only a lukewarm support from Rome, which was still half Byzantine, the Pope ranged himself entirely on the side of the pious Eastern theologians in the Oriental controversy about images, and therewith his relations became strained with Frankish theology or the efforts made by Charles I. to promote civilisation. The attitude of that theology in the great conflict is extremely characteristic of the transition time in which it found itself. The spiritual (*inner*) element introduced into it by Augustine no longer reacted in Christology, and in the conception of the Mass, against mystical superstition and magic sacramentalism. It had been swallowed up by the more powerful Byzantine Roman current. But the Franks could not yet force themselves to adopt the Oriental *worship of images*. [1] A halt was made at the Host. A spiritual, Augustinian element reacted against image-worship, but, paradoxical as it sounds, the lower state of dogmatic culture had also its effect here. It would indeed seem, on a superficial view, that he who rejects the veneration of images is always the more cultured. But that only holds in circumstances that did not then exist. Where men had once entered, as was the case in the Frankish kingdom, the magic circle of the Byzantine mysticism that enveloped Christ and the cultus, it was simply the sign of a religious faith not yet fully developed on this basis to halt at the Host, and to disdain the riches offered by images to theological thought and pious fancy. The East and Rome made their Christology living for themselves in pictures, and so saw the past mystery in the abiding present. How could a faith dispense with them that already aimed at the sensuous enjoyment of heavenly things and revelled in the worship of relics? But dogmatic culture was still backward in the West, the theosophy of images had not yet

filioque. On John VIII., see Hefele IV., p. 482. The Frankish kingdom took the liveliest interest in the controversy in that period; but the grounds on which it rested its own view were always the same. It is not known how and when the "filioque" was admitted in Rome into *the Symbol;* and we know just as little about how and when Rome accepted the Gallican Apostles' Creed and the Athanasian.

[1] This is true of the cultured, and at that time governing, portion of the clergy.

been learnt, and—what was most important—but few pictures were possessed.

It has been maintained,[1] but it is not absolutely certain, that the Synod of Gentilly (767) emitted a declaration as to image-worship satisfactory to the Pope. The Synod of Frankfort (794) unanimously condemned the decision of the seventh Œcumenical Council, which required "service and adoration" (servitium, adoratio) to be rendered to images. The decisions of the Council were undoubtedly extant only in a very bad translation.[2] "Certain chapters" had been previously sent to Rome against the worship of images, these being an extract (85 ch.) from the Libri Carolini, which Alcuin had composed shortly before, at the Emperor's command, in conjunction with other theological Court officials; they were written against the Oriental Councils of 754 and 787.[3] In these iconoclasm, but still more strongly image-worship, are forbidden as foolish and mischievous. It was right to have pictures for decoration and recollection, but not to adore them (Gregory I., Ep. VII. 111: "therefore the picture is used in Churches that those who are ignorant of letters may at least read by seeing upon the walls what they cannot read in books," and, further, Libri Carol. præf.: "having images in the ornaments of our churches and in memory of past events, and worshipping God alone, and exhibiting fit veneration to his saints, we are neither iconoclasts with the one party nor worshippers with the other"). Image-worship is then refuted at greater length, and the addition of the seventh to the six Œcumenical Councils is condemned; the two Synods (of 754 and 787) are "infamous" and "most foolish" (infames, ineptissimæ). Some would see in these books a proof of the Carlovingian "illumination";[4] but the enlightenment, which is unmistakable in other respects, only went the length of ignorance of the theosophy of images, failure to understand the subtle distinctions between λατρεία (worship) and προσκύνησις (venera-tion), and the king's effort to advance civilisation. What the books really show is the self-reliance and sense of power of the

---

[1] Hefele, III., p. 433; Hauck, K.-Gesch. II., p. 278 f.

[2] Mansi, XIII., p. 909.

[3] Migne, CII., p. 999 sq.

[4] Reuter, l.c. I., p. 10 f.

Frankish Church, which break out with youthful audacity, con-
victing with mischievous glee the older and wiser sister of error,
and actually summoning, and requiring the Pope formally
to prosecute, the Byzantine Emperor and the Empress-Regent.

These books already show that the Roman West and the East
could no longer go together, because the former sought to take
command. They also reveal a trace of Augustinian spiritual
teaching, but knowing what we do of the sort of thing held
sacred at that time in the Frankish kingdom, they cannot be
taken as proving that men were more enlightened in the
Western than in the Eastern Church.[1] Pope Hadrian refuted
the chapters,[2] but took care not to exaggerate the difference.
Under Louis the Pious, a Synod convoked at Paris on account
of an embassy from Michael the Stammerer (825) pronounced
itself decidedly against the image-worshipping Pope, and held
strictly to the line laid down in the Libri Carolini: pictures
might be set up " in memory of pious love " (pro amoris pii
memoria), as ornaments, and, above all, for the sake of the uneducated; but they were not to be adored, and their erection
might therefore be dispensed with.[3] Louis adopted more
stringent measures against image-worship than Charles.[4] Pope
Eugene II. wrapped himself in silence; nay, even in A.D. 863 a
Lateran Synod, while it recognised image-worship in guarded
language, said nothing about the seventh Œcumenical Council.[5]
Image-worship and the seventh Synod of 787 were gradually
accepted only after the time of the eighth general Synod (869).[6]

[1] The most vigorous defenders of Augustinian spiritual teaching were Claudius of
Turin and Agobard; see Reuter, I., p. 16 ff. We are reasonably astonished that
Claudius did not fare worse than he did. The study of Augustine had opened his as
well as Agobard's eyes to the contrast between the external, superstitious Christianity
of their time and the ideal type of Catholicism that had taken shape to itself in the
work of the great African.

[2] Mansi, XIII., p. 759.

[3] Mansi, XIV., p. 415 sq.   Hefele, IV., 38 ff.

[4] See Claudius' mission in Upper Italy, where iconoclasm broke out, and the worship
was described as idolatry.

[5] Mansi, XV., p. 178, 244; XIV., p. 106.   Hefele, IV., p. 272.

[6] But the dispute between Rome and Byzantium had already become acute, the
gap impassable, so that the West was unable to take part in the great renaissance of
the sciences experienced by Byzantium from the time of Photius until the beginning
of the tenth century.

Yet the Carlovingian theologians were still hostile to image-worship at the close of the period. Hinkmar, who wrote a work, no longer preserved, "on the worship of pictures of the Redeemer and the Saints,"[1] would only admit them as means of instruction (or for ornament) ; and Agobard,[2] Jonas of Orleans,[3] Walafrid Strabo,[4] and Æneas of Paris[5] held the same view. Hinkmar also calls the Council of 787 a Pseudo-Synod, and all Frankish authorities known to us, of the ninth century, reckon only six Councils. Even the (eighth) Council of 869 was at first not recognised by Hinkmar. It was only when the Frankish German Church again came to the light after the dark ages that it also saw the seventh and eighth Councils. Yet the difference with the Pope regarding the pictures hardly did any harm to his prestige in the ninth century. His authority, that is, had not been carried so high or become so sensitive that such shocks could bring about its fall.[6] Image-worship was never able to domesticate itself thoroughly where antiquity was not the ruling spirit. Even at the present day Italy is still the classic land of image-worship in the West. While, however, in the East that worship expresses the religious faith and the philosophy of religion themselves, because it is evolved from the Christology, in the West pictures form part of the system of *intercessors and helpers in need*. In practice, indeed, the difference is pretty well obliterated.

§ 3. *The Development of the Practice and Theory of the Mass (the Dogma of the Lord's Supper) and of Penance.*

Three factors co-operated to promote a development of the theory of the Lord's Supper in the West in the Carlovingian

---

[1] See Schrörs, l.c., p. 163.

[2] Contra eorum superstitionem, qui picturis et imaginibus sanctorum adorationis obsequium deferendum putant. Migne, CIV., p. 199.

[3] De cultu imaginum, l. III. Migne, CVI., p. 305.

[4] De eccles. rerum exordiis. Migne, CXIV., p. 927.

[5] Lib. adv. Græc. Migne, CXXI., p. 685 sq.

[6] On the authority of Peter's Chair itself in Hinkmar's view, see Schrörs, l.c., p. 165 f. But when men spoke of the Pope, they did not always think of the primacy (which, besides, included no administrative power in other dioceses), but also of the Roman Church. She is the "nurse and teacher" of all churches (Hinkmar).

age. Firstly, the influence of Byzantium, where the controversy about images had led their worshippers to disconnect the symbolical conception from the consecrated elements, in order to avoid the necessity of identifying the Sacrament with the images, and of thus robbing the great mystery of its unique character.[1] Secondly, the practice of the Western Church. The divine service of the Mass was the central point of all Christianity, to which everything referred, and from which every saving influence flowed for the baptized Christian. But if the ordinary life of the Christian was connected with miraculous powers and mysteries, if miracles were in the present, and still more in the accounts of the past, every-day events,[2] then the sacred act effected in the Lord's Supper had to be developed into the wonder of wonders, lest its significance should be impaired by comparison with hundreds of miracles of a common stamp.[3] Thirdly, theology and Christology come before us in this connection. The greater the prominence given in the notion of God to the idea that God, because omnipotent, was a mysterious arbitrary power, and the more vague became the perception of God in Christ and the knowledge measured by moral holiness, the more firmly did men cling to the *institutions* of the Church as the alone manifest, and seek in them, *i.e.*, in mystery and miracle, to apprehend the hidden God. Further,

---

[1] On the development of the mysteries and Lord's Supper in the Greek Church, see Vol. IV. p. 268. John of Damascus (De fide orth. IV. 13), declared expressly : οὔκ ἐστι τύπος ὁ ἄρτος τοῦ σώματος ἀλλ' αὐτὸ τὸ σῶμα τοῦ κυρίου τεθεωμένον. After the Synod of 754 (Mansi, XIII., p. 261 sq.), had called the consecrated elements types and images, the second Nicene Synod of 787 (l.c. p. 265) expressly declared that they were not that, since neither the Apostles nor Fathers had so named them ; by consecration they rather became αὐτὸ σῶμα καὶ αὐτὸ αἷμα. Yet Transubstantiation, taken strictly in the Western sense, was admittedly never taught by the Greeks.

[2] See Reuter, I., pp. 24 ff. 41 ff.

[3] In order to perceive that the Lord's Supper needed a special prominence to be given to it, notice the view taken by Hinkmar of ordeals, on which Augustine, indeed, had already laid great stress (Schrörs, p. 190 ff.) ; he regarded them, namely, as sacraments instituted in Scripture, and placed them on a level with the baptismal ceremonies. Hinkmar was not alone in the value he attached to the oath of purgation and divine judgments (see Rozière, Recueil général des formules, Paris, 1859, n. DLXXXI.-DCXXV. ; on p. 70, the ceremony is described as *christianæ religionis officium*), but Agobard, who opposed them, stood almost alone ; see Reuter, I., p. 32 ff.

the more the historical Christ was lost in light which no man
can approach, and the more resolutely religious speculation, in
order to be truly pious, only saw in him the God, who had
added human nature to his fulness (see the Adoptian controversy), the more clearly did men feel themselves constrained to
seek Christ not in the historical picture or the Word, but where the
mystery of his Incarnation and death was present and palpable.[1]

[1] The controversies *de partu virginis* (Bach, I., p. 152 ff. ; see Ratramnus, Liber
de eo, quod Christus ex virgine natus est ; Radbertus, Opusculum de partu virginis,
d'Achery, Spicil. I. p. 52, 44), show still better than the Adoptian controversy, the
kind of Christology that was honoured by the religion of the community and monks.
Ratramnus described as the poison of the old serpent the fact that some Germans
denied that Christ had issued from Mary's womb in the natural way, for thus the
reality of Christ's birth was destroyed, *although he also acknowledged Mary's perpetual
virginity and taught the partus clauso utero:* "clausa patuit dominanti." Radbert
on the other hand, without answering Ratramnus, consoled some nuns, who had
been unsettled by the alleged denial of Mary's virginity, by saying that the Church
held firmly to the "clauso utero"; for if Christ had come to the light in the natural
way, he would have been like an ordinary man ; everything connected with the
incarnation, however, was miraculous. He who did not admit Christ to have
been born *clauso utero*, set him under the common law of nature, *i.e.* sinful nature,
and in that case Christ was not free of sin. The difference between the two scholars
thus consisted solely in the fact that while Ratramnus maintained the natural process
of birth to have taken place miraculously *clauso utero*, Radbert taught that the birth
was a supernatural process, and that Christ had left his mother in a different way from
other children. Radbert here also is the more consistent ; Ratramnus seeks to unite
natural and supernatural. Radbert, at least, in imparting his curious instruction to
the virgins of the cloister, does not display the pruriency of Jerome, who is the father
of these gynæcological fancies, and the nuns may have taken this question very
seriously, as seriously as Marcion and Augustine, because they recognised all that
was sexual to be the hearth of sin. To later scholasticism is due the credit of having
explained the *partus clauso utero* scientifically from the ubiquity of Christ's body.
Such miraculous conceptions having been diffused as to the body of the *historical*
Christ, it being held, in a word, to be already *pneumatic* in itself, it was by that very
reason *sacramental* (mysterious). But, in that case, it was impossible not to take
the next step, and finally and completely identify the real with that sacramental
(mysterious) body that was offered in the Lord's Supper. The lines drawn from the
incarnation dogma and the Lord's Supper necessarily converged in the end. That
this did not happen earlier was due, apart from the material hindrance presented by
Augustine with his sober conceptions of the historical Christ as a real *homo*, to formal
difficulties caused by the traditional idiom (the sacramental body is figura corporis
Christi). These had to be removed. Bach remarks very justly (I. p. 156): "The
cause of present day misunderstandings of the ancient controversies regarding the
Lord's Supper, consists in mistaking the law that governs the formation of language,
and that also applies to theological idiom. We refer here to *the gradual change of
meaning of theological words, even when they have become, as regards their outward*

The active influence of these combined factors undoubtedly
received an extremely significant check in the case of Bede,
and in the first decades of the Carlovingian age, from the rise
of the study of Augustine, whose teaching on the Lord's Supper
had been predominantly spiritual. Charles's theologians, or
Charles himself, frequently used quite Augustinian language,
in speaking of the Lord's Supper. But even in their case
variations occur,[1] and towards the end of the period of Louis
the Pious, Paschasius Radbertus was able to assert as *doctrine*,
what had long been felt by the majority, that the real (historical)
body of Christ was sacrificed in the Mass, and partaken of in
the Lord's Supper.[2]

verbal form, fixed categories, i.e. termini technici." The admission here frankly made
by the Catholic historian of dogma is, we know, not always granted by Lutheran
theologians. We have indeed had to listen, in the controversy of our own days, to
the wonderful cry that we ought to restore to words their *original* meaning. As if
any one still possessed the old die!

[1] Bede's teaching was thoroughly Augustinian. (" In redemptionis memoriam,"
"corporis sanguinisque sacramentum," "ad corpus Christi mystice refertur,"
"spiritualiter intellegite," "non hoc corpus, quod videtis—Christus inquit—mandu-
caturi estis, sacramentum aliquod vobis commendavi, spiritualiter intellectum vivifica-
bit vos," "lavat nos a peccatis nostris quotidie in sanguine suo, cum beatæ passionis
ad altare memoria replicatur, cum panis et vini creatura in sacramentum carnis et
sanguinis ejus ineffabili spiritus sanctificatione transfertur"); passages in Münter
(D.-Gesch. II., 1 [1834] p. 223 f.). But we then see how the conception changed
step by step until the middle of the ninth century. Alcuin repeats his teacher's
principles; but both his opposition to the Council of A.D. 754 (De impio imag. cultu
IV. 14: "non sanguinis et corporis dominici mysterium *imago* jam nunc dicendum
est, sed *veritas*, non umbra, sed corpus "), and in part his study of Greek Christology
and adoption of sentiments expressed in the Church practice led him to make statements like the following (Ep. 36): "profer nomen amici tui eo tempore opportuno,
quo panem et vinum in substantiam corporis et sanguinis Christi consecraveris."
Münter justly remarks (l.c.) that this is not yet synonymous with "in substantiam
corporis convertere;" but it approaches it. The *general* notion of the Sacrament is
completely identical in the cases of Isidore, Rabanus Maurus, Ratramnus, and
Paschasius Radbertus, and so entirely follows Augustine in its construction that we
are not prepared by it for the strictly realistic version in the doctrine of the Lord's
Supper.

[2] See Radberti Lib. de corp. et sang. domini (831), new edition, with an Ep. ad
Carolum, thirteen years later (Migne, CXX., p. 1267). Steitz in the R.-Encykl. XII.,
p. 474. Rückert in Hilgenfeld's Ztschr. 1858. Bach. I., p. 156 ff. Reuter, I., p.
41 ff. Choisy, Paschase Radbert, Genève, 1888. Hausher, Der hl. Paschasius, 1862.
Ernst, Die Lehre d. h. P. Radbert v. d. Eucharistie, 1896. Geschichte der Abend-
mahlsfeier by Dieckhoff, p. 13 ff., Ebrard, Kahnis, etc. Ebert, Gesch. d. Lit. des

Paschasius Radbertus was perhaps the most learned and able theologian, after Alcuin, as well versed in Greek theology as he was familiar with Augustinianism, a comprehensive genius, who felt the liveliest desire to harmonise theory and practice, and at the same time to give due weight to everything that had been taught till then by Church tradition regarding the Lord's Supper.[1] *His great work on the Lord's Supper was the first Church monograph on the subject.*[2]   It is a one-sided description of its contents to sum them up in the phrase : " Paschasius taught transubstantiation." [3]   The importance of the book lies rather in the fact that the Lord's Supper is exhaustively discussed from all possible points of view, and that a certain unity is nevertheless attained. Paschasius did for this dogma what Origen did for the whole of dogmatics; he is the Origen of the Catholic doctrine of the Lord's Supper, which was placed by him as a theory in the central position that it had long held in practice.   We can only appreciate Paschasius' teaching if we keep it in mind that Greek Christological mysticism, Augustinian spiritualism, and— unconsciously to the author himself—the practice of the Frankish Church, had an equal share in it.   But we must also remember that the notion of God as inscrutable omnipotence, *i.e.*, arbitrary power, was dominant.   Without this conception of deity the doctrine of transubstantiation would never have been reached.[4]

Mittelalters, II.   Mabillon, in the second and third parts of the Benedictine Annals. Ratramnus' work (De corpore et sanguine domini ad Carolum) in Migne CXXI., p. 125.   Köhler, Rabanus' Streit mit Paschasius, in Hilgenfeld's Zeitschr. 1879, p. 116 ff.   A detailed account of the doctrine of the Lord's Supper from Paschasius to Berengar is given by Schnitzer, Berengar von Tours (1890), pp. 127-245.

[1] Radbert's work, De fide, spe et caritate is also important, because it shows greater power to grasp religious doctrine as a whole than we expect at this date.

[2] So far as I know, no inquiry has yet been undertaken as to the homily, De corpore et sanguine Christi, which is found in Jerome's works (Migne, T. XXX., Col. 271 ff.), being ascribed by tradition to Eusebius of Emesa, and of which a copy is also given among the works of Faustus of Riez.   In it occurs the sentence : " Visibilis sacerdos visibiles creaturas in substantiam corporis et sanguinis sui verbo suo secreta potestate convertit."   The homily belongs to a whole group, on which consult Caspari, Briefe, Abhandlungen und Predigten (1890), p. 418 ff. (see above, p. 254).

[3] Choisy seeks to show that Paschasius was the father of the Catholic dogma even to the *manducatio infidelium*, and that the spiritual form of the dogma of the Lord's Supper is in his case only apparent, since ultimately everything is dominated by crass realism.

[4] Compare Radbert's extremely characteristic introduction to his treatise : he

To begin with, Paschasius has given most vigorous expression to Augustinian doctrine not as something foreign to him, but as if he had thoroughly assimilated it.[1] The sacrament is a spiritual food for faith; to eat Christ's flesh means to be and remain in Christ. The rite is given to faith, and faith is to be roused by it. Faith, however, is always related to the invisible; and thus the sacrament in its deepest sense can only be received by the faith that has withdrawn into the invisible world. Christ, the soul, faith, heaven, and the sacrament are most intimately connected—the bodily eye must always look beyond the sensuous to the heavenly behind it. Therefore the meal is a meal for the holy, the elect. Only he who belongs to Christ and is a member in his body enjoys the food worthily, nay, he alone enjoys the food of faith actually. Unbelievers receive the sacrament, but not its virtue (virtus sacramenti). But even Augustine had so distinguished between these two notions that *virtus sacramenti* sometimes describes its saving efficacy alone, sometimes the miraculous nature of the holy food itself, so that in the former case the sacrament itself signifies the totality of the rite without its corresponding effect, and in the latter merely something objective incapable of further definition. Radbert, like Augustine, prefers the latter version. The believer alone receives the *virtus sacramenti* as food of faith and incorporation into Christ's body—there was no eating on the part of unbelievers (manducatio infidelium); Christ's flesh as contained in the sacrament did not exist apart from faith. The unbeliever, indeed, receives the sacrament—what that is is indefinable—but he does

---

discusses the almighty will of God as ground of all natural events. God's arbitrary power is the ultimate cause; therefore his actions can be described as contrary to nature as well as natural (the latter, because even the regular course of things is subject to divine absolutism). The new dogma is explicitly based on this conception of God. Notoriously everything can be deduced from it, predestination, accommodation, transubstantiation, etc. Radbert holds the Lord's Supper to be the miracle of miracles, towards which all others point; see 1, 5.

[1] Radbert expressly attacks the Capernaite coarse conception of participation in the Lord's Supper; he declines to adopt the crudely sensuous ideas diffused in the widest circles (Bach, I. 167 ff.); see De corp. et sang. 8, 2. Expos. in Mat. l. XII., 26. Reality in its common sense is "natura" in Radbert's view; but he never says that the elements are *naturaliter* transformed. Therefore also Christ's body is not digested.

so to his condemnation ; for without the *virtus sacramenti* the sacrament exists *ad judicium damnationis*.[1]

In addition to this Augustinianism, a Greek element is very strongly marked in the description of the effects of the holy food ; for besides incorporation in Christ and forgiveness of venial sins, the chief emphasis is laid on our soul *and body* being nourished by this food *for immortality*. The combination contained in the statement that this is effected *by baptism, the Lord's Supper, and Holy Scripture* (c. 1, 4), is Western ; but the intention to which prominence is given in connection with the Lord's Supper alone, *viz.* "that even our flesh may be renewed by it to immortality and incorruption,"[2] is Greek. Indeed Radbert even says conversely : "the flesh of Christ spiritually digested is transformed into our flesh."[3] But he now went still further with the Greeks—Cyril and John of Damascus. He had learned from them that although the rite existed for faith only, yet the *reality* of Christ's body was present.[4] This assumption was rendered easy, nay imperative, to the Greeks by their view that Christ's historical body was itself pneumatic from the moment of the Incarnation. Although they then (John of Damascus) completed the identification, and assumed a real presence of Christ's body in the Sacrament, they still hesitated secretly, because they did not get over the difficulty caused by the fact that the body once received into heaven did not return.

---

[1] See esp. ch. VIII., but also 5-7, 14, 21. This spiritual conception, on which Steitz (l.c.) has rightly laid great stress, runs through the whole book. But when Radbert positively calls the body present in the Lord's Supper a *corpus spiritale*, he does not mean this in contrast with the natural, but the lower bodily nature (caro humana) confined to space. C. 21, 5 : "Non nisi electorum cibus est." 6, 2 : "Quid est, quod manducant homines ? Ecce omnes indifferenter quam sæpe sacramenta altaris percipiunt. Percipiunt plane, sed alius carnem Christi spiritaliter manducat et sanguinem bibit, alius vero non, quamvis buccellam de manu sacerdotis videatur percipere. Et quid accipit, *cum una sit consecratio*, si corpus et sang. Chr. non accipit ? Vere, quia reus indigne accipit, judicium sibi manducat."

[2] "Ut etiam caro nostra per hoc ad immortalitatem et incorruptionem reparetur."

[3] "Carni nostræ caro Christi spiritaliter conviscerata transformatur." See c. 11 and 19, 1 : "Non sicut quidam volunt anima sola hoc mysterio pascitur, quia non sola redimitur morte Christi et salvatur, verum etiam et caro nostra, etc. etc. ; "nos per hoc in incorruptionem transformamur" (therefore as in Justin) ; the same thought already in I. 4, 6.

[4] "Spiritale" and "verum" are thus not mutually exclusive.

Therefore they assigned the form of the miracle (sacramental transformation and assumption) to the "mystery." Radbert took up the matter here, at the same time influenced by the popular conception and his certainty that the practice of the Church was justified. *For the first time in the Church he declares without hesitancy that the sacramental body is that which had been born of Mary, and that this is due to a transformation which only leaves the sensuous appearance unchanged.* This is a miracle against nature (or *quasi contra naturam :* for nature always depends on the will of God); but it is to be believed for that very reason, for we only think worthily of God, who can do anything, when we acknowledge him to be the power that works miracles. What he does here is a miraculous creative act, effected, as always, through the word, in this case the word of institution, and this is spoken not by the priest, but on each occasion by God through the eternal Word (Christ), so that the priest only issues the appeal to God. This constantly repeated creation by God is exactly parallel to the Incarnation—Christ's word corresponds to the Holy Spirit, the elements to the virgin's womb ; the effect is the same. The sacramental is the historical body, of course also historically transfigured ; for from Cyril's standpoint the trans-figuration of the body in the Resurrection is only the *manifestation* of the properties which it always possessed.[1] In order to

---

[1] C. 1, 2 : "Nullus moveatur de hoc corpore Christi et sanguine, quod *in mysterio vera sit caro et verus* sit sanguis, *dum sic voluit ille qui creavit :* omnia enim quæcumque voluit fecit in cælo et in terra, et quia voluit, licet in figura panis et vini, hæc sic esse, omnino nihil aliud quam caro Christi et sanguis post consecrationem credenda sunt. Unde ipsa veritas ad discipulos : Hæc, inquit, caro mea est pro mundi vita, et *ut mirabilius loquar,* non alia plane quam quæ nata est de Maria et passa in cruce et resurrexit de sepulcro." Further 7, 2 : "corpus quod natum est de Maria virgine . . . resurrexit a mortuis, penetravit cœlos *et nunc pontifex factus in æternum quotidie interpellat pro nobis.*" 12, 1 : "ubi catholica fide hoc mysterium celebratur, nihil a bono majus nihilque a malo minus percipi sacerdote, nihilque aliud quam caro Christi et sanguis dum catholice consecratur, *quia non in merito con-secrantis sed in verbo efficitur creatoris et virtute spiritus s.,* ut caro Chr. et sanguis, non alia quam quæ de spiritu s. *creata* est, vera fide credatur et spiritali intellegentia degustetur . . . *Christi* est qui per s. s. hanc suam *efficit* carnem." Cf. 15, 1 : "non æstimandum est, quod alterius verbis, quod ullius alterius meritis, quod potestate alicujus ista fiunt, sed verbo *creatoris,* quo cuncta creata sunt." 8, 2 : "substantia panis et vini in Christi carnem et sanguinem *efficaciter interius commutatur.*" 2, 2 : "sensibilis res intelligibiliter virtute dei per verbum Christi in carnem ipsius divinitus transfertur."

explain the startling fact that the results of the transformation
were not capable of being perceived by the senses, Radbert had
a number of reasons ready : it was unnecessary and repulsive,[1]
and besides it would happen often.[2] The most important of
these was that—it was necessary the rite should remain a mystery given to faith alone. We are as far as possible from
being prepared for this idea, and yet it was very important to
Radbert. The Lord's Supper always presupposes faith and is
meant to rouse faith, where it exists, to advance to the undisguised
Christ who is not daily sacrificed. Hence the sacrament cannot
be a manifest, but is always a disguised, miracle. Hence, moreover, the elements, in so far as they are *not perceptibly* transformed (colour, taste, and smell remaining), must be regarded as
symbols of Christ's body, from which faith penetrates to the
mysterious but really created source of salvation. *The sensuous
appearance of the consecrated elements is the symbol of Christ's
body, their essence is the true historical body itself.*[3]

We readily perceive that in this phase the bridge to the
Augustinian conception has been recovered. Paschasius intended to unite and did unite two positions in his doctrine of

---

[1] See c. 10 and 13, and esp. 4, 1 : "quia Christum vorari fas dentibus non est,
voluit in mysterio hunc panem et vinum vere carnem suam et sanguinem consecratione
spiritus s. potentialiter (*i.e.* efficaciter) creari, creando vero quotidie pro mundi vita
mystice immolari."

[2] See c. 14 ; besides Bach I., p. 168 ff. A lamb, or real blood, or the Christ-child
appeared.

[3] On this point Radbert speaks like Ratramnus ; see 1, 5 : "visu corporeo et gustu
propterea non demutantur, quatenus fides exerceatur ad justitiam." 13, 1, 2, "quod
colorem aut saporem carnis minime præbet, virtus tamen fidei et intellegentiæ, quæ
nihil de Christo dubitat, totum illud spiritaliter sapit et degustat . . . Sic debuit hoc
mysterium temperari, ut et arcana secretorum celarentur infidis et *meritum* cresceret
de virtute fidei et nihil deesset interius vere credentibus promis-æ veritatis." Nay the
disguise incites to loftier aspiration (as with the Greeks) : "insuper et quod majus est
per hæc secretius præstita ad illam tenderent speciem *satietatis ubi jam non pro peccatis
nostris quotidie Christus immolabitur,* sed satietate manifestationis ejus sine ulla
corruptione omnes sine fine fruemur." (One imagines that he is listening to Origen
or Gregory of Nyssa.) On figura and veritas, see 4, 1 : ". . . ut sicut de virgine
per spiritum vera caro sine coitu creatur, *ita per eundem ex substantia panis ac vini
mystice idem Christi corpus et sanguis consecretur . . . figura* videtur esse cum
frangitur, dum in *specie visibili* aliud intelligitur quam quod visu carnis et gustu sentitur.
Veritas appellatur, dum corpus Christi et sanguis virtute spiritus in verbo ipsius ex
panis vinique substantia efficitur."

the Lord's Supper: the Augustinian, that the sacraments are given to faith and everything in them is spiritually handled, and the Greek, which also seemed to him commended by the letter of Scripture, the Fathers, and a few miracles, that we are confronted by a *reality* existent prior to all faith, since only the true body and the blood actually shed can redeem us, and since we need the corporeal indwelling of Christ.   Both considerations seemed to be served by the view, *that in the elements we are dealing with a miraculous creation of Christ's body, which is, however, effected in such a way that faith alone can rise from the still existent semblance of the mere bodily figure (figura corporis) to the apprehension of the heavenly reality.*

The voluminous books, afterwards written by Catholics and Lutherans on the Lord's Supper, prove that Radbert's theory opened up a perspective to hundreds of questions, which he did not solve, and, indeed, did not even put.   His treatment of the part played by the priest at the sacrament seemed unsatisfactory. His brief expositions as to the creation of the body failed to make certain the identity of the heavenly and the sacramental Christ.   There was still no definition of the relation of the unconverted to the converted object of sense-perception.   When men began to attempt this definition, nothing short of the whole of philosophy necessarily passed before the mind of the cultured theologian.   The claim of the symbolical view had to be determined, and thereby the sacrament, symbol, virtue, reality (res) and, again, the graded and yet identical bodies of Christ (the historical on earth, the transfigured in heaven, the sacramental on earth, the body as Church in heaven and on earth) had to be defined, as it were geologically, as intersecting boulders.   " One deep called to the others " ; and the fact that in after times the most intelligent men leant an ear to this clamour, and yet remained sane in other respects, proved that the most absurd speculations in the sphere of religion do not necessarily make the whole reason sick.[1]

---

[1] The doctrine of the real conversion of the elements in the West is to be regarded as an importation from the East, and is closely connected with the anti-Adoptian version of Christology.   But it was first in the West that the legal mind and dialectics cast themselves on this subject, and produced a complicated and never to be completed doctrine of endless extent.

But the most remarkable feature in Radbert's fundamental theory is that he did not refer primarily to the Mass, or indeed to Christ's death on the Cross ; in other words, he did not draw all the consequences which resulted from it.   Radbert is not the theologian of the Catholic Mass.   The *Incarnation* and Lord's Supper were for him more intimately connected, as it seems, than Christ's *sacrificial death* and the dogma of the Lord's Supper.   From this we see that Radbert was a disciple of the Greeks, that he was really a *theologian,* and his interest did not centre *primarily* on the Church institution of penance, and the divine service of the Mass connected with it.[1]

Rabanus [2] and Ratramnus alone opposed him.   The opposition is as obscure, logically, as in the controversy about the virgin birth.   As Ratramnus had then taught that the natural had come to pass by a miracle, while Radbert held that the event was contrary to nature ; so here again Rabanus and, above all, Ratramnus taught that, while the external miracle (contra naturam)—the communication in the Lord's Supper of the body that was born, that died and rose again—did not take place, the true body was *potentialiter* (effectively) created, yet *in mysterio,* by the consecration of the Holy Spirit.[3]   Ratramnus examines elaborately the problem that the king had set him, whether that which is received into his mouth by the believer, is in mystery or reality Christ's body.   From the king's question he himself formulates other two : whether participation, in the cultus, in the body of Christ was an act *in mysterio* or *in veritate,* and whether the sacramental body was identical with the historical which now sits at the right hand of the Father.[4]   To the second question he replies that that which lies *consecrated*

---

[1] Not *primarily ;* for undoubtedly he more than once in his work thinks of the Mass, and draws the inference of the daily sacrifice of Christ's body *pro peccatis ;* see 13, 2 ; 4, 1, etc.

[2] Ep. ad Eigil. Migne, CXII., p. 1510.

[3] Ratramnus and Rabanus are nearer each other than is currently supposed ; but Bach (I. p. 191 ff.) is wrong, when, after the precedent of other Catholics, he tries by an interpretation of Ratramnus' use of language to make him a genuine Catholic. Ratramnus also holds that a miracle takes place, but not the miracle that magically produces the body worn by Christ as a person.

[4] See the opening of the work.

on the altar is by no means the historical body, but only the *mystery* of the body, as also the mystery of the Church. As regards the historical body the consecrated elements are thus only a figure (figura), means of reminiscence for our present earthly life, since we cannot yet see what we believe.[1] But nevertheless *believers* receive Christ's body and blood in this rite ; for faith does not receive what it sees, but what it believes, *Accordingly in the Lord's Supper Christ's body exists in an in-*

---

[1] Following on a reference to Ambrose, he writes (c. 75 sq.) : "De carne Christi quæ crucifixa et sepulta est, ait, ' Vera utique caro Christi est.' At de illo quod sumitur in sacramento dicit, ' Veræ carnis illius sacramentum est,' distinguens sacramentum carnis a veritate carnis.   Veritas carnis quam sumpsit de virgine ; quod vero nunc agitur in ecclesia mysterium, veræ illius carnis . . . sacramentum . . . non est specie caro, sed sacramentum, siquidem in specie panis est, in sacramento vero verum Christi corpus . . . (elementa) secundum quod spiritualiter vitæ substantiam subministrant corpus et sanguis Christi sunt.   Illud vero corpus, *in quo semel passus est Christus*, non aliam speciem præferebat quam in qua consistebat ; hoc enim erat vere quod esse videbatur ; . . . at nunc sanguis Christi quem credentes ebibunt et corpus quod comedunt, *aliud sunt in specie et aliud in significatione*, aliud quod pascunt corpus esca corporea et aliud quod saginant mentes æternæ vitæ substantia . . . aliud igitur est, quod exterius geritur, aliud item quod per fidem capitur ; ad sensum corporis quod pertinet, corruptibile (Radbert also said this) est, quod fides vero capit incorruptible.   Exterius igitur quod apparet non est res sed imago rei, mente vero quod sentitur et intelligitur, veritas rei." Even to the last sentence a Radbertian meaning can be given ; but this ceases to be possible where Ratramnus—as often happens—designates the whole *rite* (and it is the *rite* with which he is generally concerned) as "figura," in "figuram sive memoriam dominicæ mortis," "repræsentatio memoriæ dominicæ passionis," and, further, as "pignus" (see c. 10, 11, 16 : "figurate facta" ; c. 88 : "corpus et sanguis quod in ecclesia geritur, differt ab illo corpore et sanguine quod in Christi corpore jam glorificatum cognoscitur ; et hoc corpus pignus est et species, illud vero ipsa veritas.   Hoc enim geretur, donec ad illud perveniatur ; ubi vero ad illud perventum fuerit hoc removebitur." Reconciliation with Radbert is absolutely impossible where Ratramnus strictly disowns the "permutatio corporalis," and reduces everything to a memorial meal ; c. 12 : "et quomodo jam Christi corpus dicitur, in quo nulla permutatio facta cognoscitur ?" c. 15 : "dicant, secundum quod permutata sunt ; corporaliter namque nihil in eis cernitur esse permutatum." Catholics excuse him here by saying that he meant to deny "conversion" into a crassly realistic body. "Fatebuntur igitur necesse est aut mutata esse secundum aliud quam secundum corpus, ac per hoc non esse hoc quod in veritate videntur, sed aliud quod non esse secundum propriam essentiam cernuntur.   Aut si hoc profiteri noluerint, negare corpus esse sanguinem Christi, quod nefas est non solum dicere verum etiam cogitare." c. 100 : "iste panis et sanguis qui super altare ponuntur, in figuram sive memoriam dominicæ mortis ponuntur, et quod gestum est in præterito, præsenti revocet (dominus) memoriæ, ut illius passionis memores effecti, per eam efficiamur divini muneris consortes."

visible reality for faith as real food of the soul.[1] The extremely
obscure and at least seemingly contradictory statements of
Ratramnus make it hard to hit on his meaning correctly. In
any case he taught no mere figurative conception. We shall
perhaps be most certain to do him justice if we observe what
above all he did, and what he did not, intend. He meant above
all to emphasise and verify the absolute necessity of faith
throughout the rite ; the sacrament belonged to faith, existed
for it alone, etc.[2] In this he coincides entirely with Radbert,
who shared the same interest equally strongly. But in what he
would not allow he is distinguished to his advantage from
Radbert ; *since everything is given to faith he would not recognise
the common reality,* because in view of the latter faith and
disbelief are indifferent. To Ratramnus reality (veritas) is
concrete being as it presents itself to the senses ; for this very
reason " sub figura " and " in veritate " he looks on as mutually
exclusive opposites. Faith has its own realities, which are real,
but only disclose themselves to faith ; Ratramnus designates
them—mistakenly—as " sub figura," because they are copied by
sensuous realities, or, better, rest behind the latter. Radbert, on the
other hand, believed himself compelled, precisely as an Augustinian, to conceive *veritas* as reality in general ; hence to him " sub
figura " and *in veritate* are not opposites, since heavenly realities
when they appeared as earthly had in his view to manifest themselves *sub figura. But Ratramnus was superior to Radbert as a
Christian, in that he did not conceive the presence of the heavenly
in the earthly to be a miracle against nature, i.e.,* he followed a
different notion of God from the latter.[3] The mysteries of
faith are not brought to pass by a continual interruption of the

---

[1] C. 101 : " Fides non quod oculus videt sed quod credit accipit, quoniam spiritualis
est esca et spiritualis potus, spiritualiter animam pascens et æternæ satietatis vitam
tribuens, sicut ipse salvator mysterium hoc commendans loquitur : spiritus est qui vivi-
ficat." C. 49 : " Christ's true body is distributed in the Lord's Supper according to
its *invisibilis substantia,* and that because the *invisibilis substantia* is like the *potentia
divini verbi.* Many similar passages elsewhere."

[2] C. 11 : " Nam si secundum quosdam figurate hic nihil accipitur, sed totum in
veritate conspicitur, *nihil hic fides operatur, quoniam nihil spiritale geritur . . . nec
jam mysterium erit, in quo nihil secreti, nihil abditi continebitur.*"

[3] Ratramnus always thinks of the God who excites and nourishes faith.

natural order, but they rest as a world administered by the
Holy Spirit behind the phenomenal world, and what takes place
in the Lord's Supper is not a departure, by means of a special
miracle, from operations such as are carried out, *e.g.*, in Baptism
(c. 17, 25, 26.) In a word, Ratramnus would have the mystery
of the Lord's Supper recognised as in harmony with the method
by which God bestows salvation through Baptism and the Word,
because as an Augustinian and Christian he shrank from the
brutal miracle (the idea of God is here involved), and because
he was afraid that otherwise nothing would be left to faith.

It is in this that the importance of Ratramnus consists. But
it is questionable whether the learned king for whom he wrote
was any the wiser for his book ; for not only is Ratramnus confused in his terminology, but also in his matter,[1] *because he would
not give up the idea that the efficacy of the sacrament was objective*,
whence it always follows that the miraculous efficacy depends
not on the recipients, but on the means. Hence we find numerous expositions in which he talks like Radbert : by the ministry
of the priest the bread becomes Christ's body, nay, it is transformed.[2] He does not venture to pursue consistently the
parallel he seeks to establish with baptismal water ; for the
words " body and blood of Christ " are too strong for him. It
is sinful to deny that the consecrated elements are Christ's
body.[3] Thus the difference between Radbert and Ratramnus
can be reduced to the following formula. The former openly
and deliberately transferred the spiritual teaching of Augustinianism into the realistic conception, and gave clear expression to
the belief of the Church. The latter *attempted* to maintain
complete spiritualism in the interests of a loftier notion of God
and of faith, but he was not in a position to carry this out
absolutely, because he himself was far too much under the
influence of the *formula*. Therefore he only speaks clearly

---

[1] The difference between Paschasius and Ratramnus is really very subtle if we confine our attention to the question of the reality of Christ's body (and the transformation) ; but it is not quite so subtle as is represented by Schnitzer (l.c., 167-174). It
was, besides, long before Ratramnus' work was held to be heretical.

[2] C. 16, a *commutatio* is taught, " sed non corporaliter sed spiritualiter facta est . . .
spiritualiter sub velamento corporei panis . . . corpus et sanguis Christi existunt."

[3] See C. 15.

where he is disowning the miracle.[1] The future belonged to
Radbert ;[2] nay, Ratramnus' book, it would seem, did not even
excite attention, but afterwards met with the most curious
history down to the present day.[3]

The doctrine expressed by Radbert, a Pandora's casket of
problems to future scholars, was extremely intelligible to the
simple. Nothing can guarantee the success of a dogma more
fully than the possession of these two qualities. It received its
application, above all, in the Mass. The thought of the repeated
sacrificial death of Christ, long since conceived, was now as
firmly established as that of the repeated assumption of the
flesh. What could now approach the Mass? There was no
need to alter the ancient wording of missal prayers, which still,
when they dealt with the sacrifice, emphasised the sacrifice of
praise ; for who attended to words? The Mass as a sacrificial
rite, in which the holiest thing conceivable was presented to
God, had, however, ceased long ago to end in participation, but
found its climax in the act that expiated sin and removed evil.
It was received into the great institution that conferred atonement. On this a few further remarks are necessary, although
no dogmatic conflicts arose.

The frequent repetition of the Mass (in one and the same
Church), and its simple celebration (without communion), show
that this rite was not intended so much for the congregation as for
God: *God was to be appeased.* The ancient element of commemoration on the part of the celebrants had, especially since the days
of Gregory I., been made an independent service, and the communion had been, as it were, changed into a *second* celebration.[4]
The practice, according to which the laity looked on while the
priests partook, the laity taking merely a passive part—the rite
being consummated on their behalf—while the priests performed

---

[1] Ratramnus has the elements of Zwingli and Calvin's doctrines. Besides, in relation to the invisible substance, he assumes the identity of the eucharistic and historical
body, or, at any rate, will not give it up.

[2] In connection with Matt. XXVI. 26, he defended himself skilfully against Ratramnus, whom, for the rest, he does not name.

[3] Bach, I., p. 191 ff.

[4] Walafried Strabo was the first to justify expressly the celebration of the Lord's
Supper without communicants, and therefore Masses (Migne, T. 114, col. 943 ff).

the ceremony, corresponded to the prevailing view, especially among German peoples, that laymen were second-class Christians, and that partaking in the Lord's Supper was for them associated with grave dangers. *The holy rite belonged to the laity, so far as it represented a form of the Church's intercession peculiarly effective for the mitigation of sin's penalties.*

The Mass was thereby included in the Church's atoning institute ; but for laymen the Church had long been essentially a baptismal institution, and an establishment for the reconciliation necessary after baptism.   In order to understand this, and the immense extent and value acquired by the practice of Confession in the West, we have to observe the following points.

1. The prevailing notion of God was that of *omnipotent absolutism, requital and remission.*   It was in these conceptions that God was a present and really living God, and they directed the thought and practice of trained theologians and laymen.   The hidden God was manifest in the fact that he suffered no sin to be unatoned ; but he was merciful because he granted remissions (through the mediation of heavenly persons and the Church) a fact which, indeed, did not contravene the general rule that everything must be expiated or punished.   *This notion of God was already complete when the Church entered into the national life of Germany.*   It is accordingly not to be regarded as a German modification, but as a conception in harmony with and rising from the unrefined religious consciousness, and especially the Latin spirit.   Cyprian and Gregory I. attest this.   But as this conception of God could easily combine with German ideas of justice, it was also well adapted to train uncivilised peoples. It had long been settled on purely Latin soil that no sin committed after Baptism could be simply forgiven, but that due penitence (pænitentia legitima), or fitting satisfaction (satisfactio congrua) formed the necessary condition of remission.   In keeping with the strict regard for law and sense of duty, which distinguished the Latin Church more than the Greek, ecclesiastical methods paid more heed to the sins of Church members in general.   And in accordance with the conviction that sins represented breaches of contract or outrages, of greater or less gravity, the Church had been working at the codification

of *pœnitentia legitima*, or the definition of the measure of satisfaction, since the second half of the third century. All this took
place without German influence.

2. This system had originally been elaborated with a view
to public penance, in presence of the congregation, for the sake
of reconciliation, and thus referred to open and gross sins, for
which as a rule only a single act of penance was possible. It
therefore suffered a severe blow when all society became
Christian, and magistrates, being themselves Christians, punished these gross offences of different kinds, even such as the
State had not formerly dealt with. The whole ancient institution of penance collapsed in the East. It came almost entirely
to an end in the West also in its old form, in so far as the list
of public sins, punished by the Church alone, was always
growing smaller.[1] But in the German kingdoms, where the
Church had not sunk to the level of an institution for worship in
the State, and had not entirely abandoned higher religion to the
monks, where, on the contrary, it long went hand in hand with
the State as a Latin institution with its old Roman law, and
trained the nations as a *universal* power, it did not renounce
its penance regulations, which besides suited the German spirit.
But a change was necessary in this case also, a change in which
German dislike to public humiliations had perhaps as great a
share as fear of purgatory and the tendency of the Church to
establish throughout the regulations of its *monkish castes*, in
other words, to monachise the secular clergy, and finally also
the laity. From this there sprang a deepening of the notion of
sin, since new sins, namely, the "roots of sin" themselves were
put in the place of the old mortal sins,[2] but there also resulted
an externalising of the notion, as "satisfactions," which are
more tolerable in the case of great overt offences, were now
also applied to these "roots" (intemperance, fornication, greed,
anger, ill-temper, secret fear and dislike, presumption and
pride).

But, above all, this was followed by the intrusion of the

---

[1] When the State punished, *e.g.*, in cases of murder and theft, the ecclesiastical
consequences followed without further trial.

[2] This was also effected in the Greek Church through the action of the monks.

Church into all affairs of private life. What had been the rule in primitive times, namely, the subjection of the private life of the individual to the control of the Church, returned in an entirely new form. But then it was a congregation of brethren which lived together like a family, and in which each was the conscience of the other ; now one *institution* and one *class* ruled the irresponsible community ; and while the latter was restrained, indeed, from extremes, yet, since no one was really capable of properly controlling the life of the individual, consciences were sophisticated by incentives and sedatives, by a frequently over-refined morality (legislation as to fasting and marriage), and by extremely external directions as to satisfaction. The transition to the new practice resulted in the laity themselves demanding the intercession of the Church, the reading of the Mass, invocations of the saints, etc., to an increasing extent, since preachers had always been telling them that they were a sinful people, incapable of coming near God,[1] that the priests held the keys, and that the Church's intercession was the most effective. But the gradual settlement of *monachist practice* in the world-Church alone explains the facts that actual confession of all sins to the priest, and the imposition of all sorts of satisfactions,[2] for the hundred and one offences in life and conduct, in a word, that *private penance in the presence of the priest*, became the rule. This state of matters began in the Iro-Scottish Church, which was in an eminent degree monachist. There penitential regulations—meaning private penance—were, so far as we know, first drawn up for the laity, who were directed to confess their sins to the priest, as the monks had long been enjoined to do in their cloisters. From Ireland, books dealing with penance came to the Anglo-Saxons (Theodore of Canterbury), to the Franks and Rome ; they did not establish this footing without opposition, and after they had become a settled institution, they very soon gave offence again, since their directions became more and more

---

[1] See the view taken of the laity in the forged fragments of the pseudo-Isidorian decretals.

[2] Among these, pilgrimages of a year's duration played a great part, a fact that shows the monks' contempt of family life and civic occupations ; for these were severely affected by pilgrimages.

external and questionable. To the practice of private penance
which thus arose is to be ascribed the new conception of *sin*,
and the new attitude to it, which now became the ruling one
in the West, namely, the facile and deadening readiness with
which every one confessed himself to be a mortal sinner. What
was more tolerable in the ranks of the monks, nay, was in many
cases the expression of a really sensitive conscience—I mean
the readiness at once to confess oneself a sinner, and to make
a less and less distinction between sins and sins—threatened
when transferred to the masses to become a worthless practice,
because one that blunted the moral sense. Men sinned, and
coolly confessed wholesale to a host of sins, lest they might
miss the miraculous help of the Church, for some one or other
actually committed. If the men of those days had not been so
simple, this system would even then have made them thorough
hypocrites. But as it was, it worked more like an external
system of law—a police institution, which punished wantonness
and barbarianism, outbreaks of wild energy and passion. This
was not the intention, but it was its *actual* import, so far as a
certain salutary effect cannot be denied it.

3. The institution was already certain in its operations, and
made great strides especially in the later Carlovingian period,
since the complete separation of the clergy and laity, which
had been obliterated in the Merovingian age, was only then
made once more complete, and measures began at the same
time to be taken to make monks of the former. Nevertheless
the dogmatic theory was still entirely awanting. It was not
settled that the priest alone could forgive sins—it was still
conceded that trifling sins could be expiated without the priest,
by means of prayer and alms. Nor were the value and result
of priestly forgiveness fixed : was it declaratory or deprecatory ?
Nor had it been stated to be absolutely necessary to confess
all sins to the priest.[1] And finally no fixed definitions had

---

1 I adhere to these statements, in spite of Karl Müller's arguments in his treatise
" Der Umschwung in der Lehre von der Busse während des 12 Jahrh." (Abhandl.
für Weizsäcker, 1892, p. 287 ff.) If I am not mistaken, Müller has been misled by
Morinus, and has looked at the state of penance and confession, at the close of ancient
and the beginning of mediæval Church history, too much from the standpoint of the

been deduced from the matter itself of mortal and venial sins, or of the treatment of public and private offences. It was only long afterwards that all these points were decided. We see clearly here that ecclesiastical practice does not wait for dogmatic, indeed, that it does not really need it, as long as it goes with the great stream. The Church possessed a sacrament of penance with all its subtleties for many centuries, during which dogmatic knew of no such thing, but span a finer thread.

4. This is not the place to give the interesting history of the growth of satisfactions. Let us, however, notice four points. (1) The old, more or less arbitrary, definitions dealing with the selection (prayers, alms, lamentations, temporary exclusion), and duration of compensatory punishments were supplemented to an increasing extent by new ones (pilgrimages), as well as by *definitions taken from the Old Testament law and German legal ordinances.* Charlemagne took a great stride in advance with reference to dependence on the Old Testament. *But this led to the computation of compensatory penalties being itself looked at in the light of a divine dispensation,* and definitions not taken from the Old Testament were also regarded from the same stand-point. (2) The performance of penance was a means of compensation, so far as—if no sin had preceded it—it would have established *merit* in the sight of God, or would have bestowed something upon him. (It was accordingly not *merely* a substitution for punishment, but also a positive property in the sight of God, and therefore a compensation for injury.) Accordingly the whole institution was included under the conception of *merit*, from of old connected with works and alms (operibus et eleemosynis). But if the performance of penance was after all the presentation of something valuable (sacrifice) to God, something which gave him pleasure, and that *for its own sake*, it became more effective if as *many* and as *good*

modern Roman conception; he has at least pre-supposed too great a uniformity of theoretical ideas—if one may speak of such. I cannot accept the blunt assertion on p. 292, that down to the twelfth century the priest's absolution was always regarded as simply identical with divine forgiveness, and therefore as indispensable. There was no doctrine proper on this question for centuries, but almost only a practice. As soon as the doctrine is again introduced, doubts also arise, to be once more gradually allayed.

persons as possible took part in it. If a saint helped by his intercession, then God could not really resist; for there was nothing to be made good by the saint, and therefore his offering was a pure present to God. This dreadful idea that the mighty Judge in Heaven could demand nothing more of the saints, while they were able to bestow much upon him, makes it evident that the system of *intercessions* necessarily played the most important rôle in the system of penance. The conception of Christ taken by faith, that he represents men in the Father's presence, was perverted in the saddest way, and he was dragged into this system; and since nothing was too lofty or precious to be included as investments in this petty calculation, the repeated *sacrificial death* of Christ was itself the most important instalment. Masses were the surest protection against sins' penalties in purgatory, because in them Christ himself was presented to the Father, and the infinite value [1] of his Passion was anew brought before him, in other words, the merit of that Passion was multiplied. Hence the accumulation of a treasury of masses was the best "palliative" against the fire, or the most reliable means of abridging it.

(3) Since performances of penance [2]—the penitent disposition was always presupposed in theory—had an *objective* value to God, and were at the same time in part equivalents, they could be *bartered*. Not only, however, could like be bartered for like, but a less valuable act could be taken as full payment, if circumstances rendered a complete discharge difficult, or if it was supplemented by the intercession of others, or if the slighter performance sufficiently displayed the penitent mood. It had been the custom in earlier times to shorten the duration and diminish the number of penances imposed by the *Church* after the penitent had proved his sincerity. This was appropriate enough, for the purpose was to effect reconciliation with the community; but it was now applied to the penitent's relation to

---

[1] In the fourth ch. of the Synod of Chiersey, 853, it is called " pretii copiositas mysterii passionis ; " that is also an anticipation of Anselm's theory of satisfaction.

[2] The *peregrinationes* also belong to them. That indulgences rest quite essentially on the custom of pilgrimages and their commutation is shown by Götz, Ztschr. f. K.-Gesch., vol. XV., p. 329 ff.

God. It was at the same time remembered that the strict Judge was also merciful, *i.e.*, indulgent. Thus arose the system of *remissions, i.e.*, of *commutations* and *redemptions*, or of *substitutions*. The latter originated in German conceptions, but they had a latent root even in ancient times. Commutations and redemptions are first met with in any number in the eighth and ninth centuries. "Weregeld" or blood-money is found sanctioned then; but they already follow from the ancient system, and had certainly been practised in the cloisters long before the Carlovingian age. Therewith, however, indulgences were created, as soon, namely, as the possibility of commutation was admitted and legally fixed, independently of the special circumstances of the individual case. These commutations, which were only established against opposition, completely externalised the whole system. Above all, they interested the Church financially, and made it, already the great landed proprietor, into a banking establishment. How poor was the Greek Church, with its scanty trade in relics, pictures, and lights, compared with her rich sister, who drew bills on every soul!

(4) The whole system of merits and satisfactions had really no reference to sins, but only to their punishment. But since everything ultimately served this system, men were trained to evade sins' penalties as well, securely, and cheaply as possible. The element which seemingly mitigated the dangers of this whole view—namely, that sin itself was left out of sight, since it must be forgiven by God who ʼexcites penitence and faith— necessarily resulted in the case of the multitude in their paying little or no attention to sin, and in their thinking only of punishment. Even if they finally entered the cloister, or gave their goods to the poor, they did so, not because they loved God, but because they wished to escape his punishments. Punishment ruled the world and the consciences for whose possession good and evil angels contend.

It would not have been necessary to discuss this practice within the limits of the history of dogma if it had not had a very active influence on dogma in the succeeding period. It had wound itself round Augustinianism from the beginning, and had prevented it from obtaining complete sway in the Church; it influenced Christology even in the time of Gregory I., and then in the classic period of the Middle Ages it acted decisively upon and remodelled all the dogmas that had come down from antiquity.[1]

[1] On the history of penance, see Steitz, Das römische Busssacrament, 1854 ; Wasserschleben, Bussordnungen d. Abendl. Kirche, 1851 ; v. Zezschwitz Beichte, in Herzog's R.-E. II., p. 220 ff., System der Katechetik I., p. 483 ff., II. 1, p. 208. ff. ; Göbl,. Gesch. der Katachese in Abendland, 1880. Further, on the history of the ordinances of penance, Wasserschleben, Die irische Kanonensammlung, 2 ed., 1855 ; and Schmitz, Die Bussbücher und die Bussdisciplin der Kirche, 1883. On the latter's attempt to refer the regulations of penance to Rome, see Theol. Lit.-Ztg., 1883, col. 614 ff. On the development of the separation of clergy and laity in the 9th century, and the beginning of the monachising of the clergy, see Hatch, " Growth of Christian Institutions," Chap. IX.

On divine service and discipline in the Carlovingian age, see Gieseler II., 1 (1846) pp. 152-170 ; on the constitution of German law-courts, feuds, and penance, outlawry and death of the victim, see Brunner, Deutsche Rechtsgesch. I., pp. 143 ff., 156 ff., 166 ff.; on the principle of personality and the amount of blood-money and penances, l.c., p. 261 ff.; on the personal rights of the clergy, p. 269 f.; and on the rise of written law, p. 282 ff. If we review the state of the development of German law in the age of the Merovingians, and compare it with the ecclesiastical discipline of penance, as it was independently evolved on Latin ground until Gregory I., we are astonished at the ease with which these systems could be and actually were dovetailed into each other. The Roman law received by the Church underwent great modifications within its pale caused by the conceptions of the *Communio* of the Church militant with the saints, of satisfactions, merits, and the claim of the Church to remit sins. Above all, the Church's right to punish, which had originally accepted the Roman thought of the *public character* of crimes, and had treated them accordingly, became more and more a private right. That is, transgressions against God were regarded as *injuries* done to God—not the violation of public order and the holy, inviolable divine law ; and accordingly the idea arose, and got more and more scope, that they were to be treated, as it were, like private complaints. In such cases the alternative, *either punishment or satisfaction* (compensation), was appropriate. But as regards satisfactions, all the liberties were necessarily introduced that are inherent in that conception, namely, that the injured party himself, or the Church as his representative, could indulgently lessen their amount, or could commute or transfer them, etc. It is obvious how easily this view could fuse with the German one. One or two examples are sufficient. German law held the principle : either outlawry or penance. This corresponds to the Church principle : either excommunication or the performance of satisfactory acts of penance. According to German law, vengeance did not require to be executed on the evil-doer himself, but might be on a member of his clan ; nay, it was held in Norway to be a more severe vengeance to strike the best man of the clan instead of the murderer. The Church looked on Christians as forming a " clan " with the saints in heaven, and the performance of penance could to a certain extent, or entirely, be passed on to the latter ; Christ had, above all, borne beforehand by his death God's vengeance on the ill-doing race of his brethren. German law held, similarly, that the compensation, the payment of the fine, could be divided. According to the practice of the Church, the saints interceded if prayed to, and presented their merits to God, taking from the sinner a part of the penance imposed upon him. Afterwards the Church positively adopted the German institution, and let earthly friends, comrades, members of the family, and bondmen share in the performance of penance in order to lighten the task.   In one respect, however, the action of the Church had a softening and beneficial effect.   It restricted to an extraordinary extent the capital punishments closely connected with outlawry.   They were objectionable in themselves, and doubly so where they were regarded, on the ground of a primitive priestly law of punishment, as a human sacrifice offered to the gods (Brunner, pp. 173-177).   Even in the Roman period the Church in Gaul exerted itself to soften the Roman administration of justice where the latter admitted capital punishment.   It continued its efforts with success in the Merovingian age, so that arrangements were more and more frequently made in substitution for the death penalty.   The chief argument urged by the Church was doubtless that God did not will the death of the sinner, and that Christ died an atoning and sacrificial death for all.   Thus Christ's death obtained an extraordinary importance.   It became the grand achievement, whose value even softened the earthly right of punishment.

CATALOGUE OF DOVER BOOKS

The more difficult books are indicated by an asterisk (*)

Books Explaining Science and Mathematics

WHAT IS SCIENCE?, N. Campbell. The role of experiment and measurement, the function of mathematics, the nature of scientific laws, the difference between laws and theories, the limitations of science, and many similarly provocative topics are treated clearly and without technicalities by an eminent scientist. "Still an excellent introduction to scientific philosophy," H. Margenau in PHYSICS TODAY. "A first-rate primer . . . deserves a wide audience," SCIENTIFIC AMERICAN. 192pp. 5⅜ x 8.   S43 Paperbound **$1.25**

THE NATURE OF PHYSICAL THEORY, P. W. Bridgman. A Nobel Laureate's clear, non-technical lectures on difficulties and paradoxes connected with frontier research on the physical sciences. Concerned with such central concepts as thought, logic, mathematics, relativity, probability, wave mechanics, etc. he analyzes the contributions of such men as Newton, Einstein, Bohr, Heisenberg, and many others. "Lucid and entertaining . . . recommended to anyone who wants to get some insight into current philosophies of science," THE NEW PHILOSOPHY. Index. xi + 138pp. 5⅜ x 8.   S33 Paperbound **$1.25**

EXPERIMENT AND THEORY IN PHYSICS, Max Born. A Nobel Laureate examines the nature of experiment and theory in theoretical physics and analyzes the advances made by the great physicists of our day: Heisenberg, Einstein, Bohr, Planck, Dirac, and others. The actual process of creation is detailed step-by-step by one who participated. A fine examination of the scientific method at work. 44pp. 5⅜ x 8.   S308 Paperbound **75¢**

THE PSYCHOLOGY OF INVENTION IN THE MATHEMATICAL FIELD, J. Hadamard. The reports of such men as Descartes, Pascal, Einstein, Poincaré, and others are considered in this investigation of the method of idea-creation in mathematics and other sciences and the thinking process in general. How do ideas originate? What is the role of the unconscious? What is Poincaré's forgetting hypothesis? are some of the fascinating questions treated. A penetrating analysis of Einstein's thought processes concludes the book. xiii + 145pp. 5⅜ x 8.   T107 Paperbound **$1.25**

THE NATURE OF LIGHT AND COLOUR IN THE OPEN AIR, M. Minnaert. Why are shadows sometimes blue, sometimes green, or other colors depending on the light and surroundings? What causes mirages? Why do multiple suns and moons appear in the sky? Professor Minnaert explains these unusual phenomena and hundreds of others in simple, easy-to-understand terms based on optical laws and the properties of light and color. No mathematics is required but artists, scientists, students, and everyone fascinated by these "tricks" of nature will find thousands of useful and amazing pieces of information. Hundreds of observational experiments are suggested which require no special equipment. 200 illustrations; 42 photos. xvi + 362pp. 5⅜ x 8.   T196 Paperbound **$1.95**

THE UNIVERSE OF LIGHT, W. Bragg. Sir William Bragg, Nobel Laureate and great modern physicist, is also well known for his powers of clear exposition. Here he analyzes all aspects of light for the layman: lenses, reflection, refraction, the optics of vision, x-rays, the photoelectric effect, etc. He tells you what causes the color of spectra, rainbows, and soap bubbles, how magic mirrors work, and much more. Dozens of simple experiments are described. Preface. Index. 199 line drawings and photographs, including 2 full-page color plates. x + 283pp. 5⅜ x 8.   T538 Paperbound **$1.85**

SOAP-BUBBLES: THEIR COLOURS AND THE FORCES THAT MOULD THEM, C. V. Boys. For continuing popularity and validity as scientific primer, few books can match this volume of easily-followed experiments, explanations. Lucid exposition of complexities of liquid films, surface tension and related phenomena, bubbles' reaction to heat, motion, music, magnetic fields. Experiments with capillary attraction, soap bubbles on frames, composite bubbles, liquid cylinders and jets, bubbles other than soap, etc. Wonderful introduction to scientific method, natural laws that have many ramifications in areas of modern physics. Only complete edition in print. New Introduction by S. Z. Lewin, New York University. 83 illustrations; 1 full-page color plate. xii + 190pp. 5⅜ x 8½.   T542 Paperbound **95¢**

CATALOGUE OF DOVER BOOKS

THE STORY OF X-RAYS FROM RONTGEN TO ISOTOPES, A. R. Bleich, M.D. This book, by a member of the American College of Radiology, gives the scientific explanation of x-rays, their applications in medicine, industry and art, and their danger (and that of atmospheric radiation) to the individual and the species. You learn how radiation therapy is applied against cancer, how x-rays diagnose heart disease and other ailments, how they are used to examine mummies for information on diseases of early societies, and industrial materials for hidden weaknesses. 54 illustrations show x-rays of flowers, bones, stomach, gears with flaws, etc. 1st publication. Index. xix + 186pp. 5⅜ x 8.   T622 Paperbound **$1.35**

SPINNING TOPS AND GYROSCOPIC MOTION, John Perry. A classic elementary text of the dynamics of rotation — the behavior and use of rotating bodies such as gyroscopes and tops. In simple, everyday English you are shown how quasi-rigidity is induced in discs of paper, smoke rings, chains, etc., by rapid motions; why a gyrostat falls and why a top rises; precession; how the earth's motion affects climate; and many other phenomena. Appendix on practical use of gyroscopes. 62 figures. 128pp. 5⅜ x 8.   T416 Paperbound **$1.00**

SNOW CRYSTALS, W. A. Bentley, M. J. Humphreys. For almost 50 years W. A. Bentley photographed snow flakes in his laboratory in Jericho, Vermont; in 1931 the American Meteorological Society gathered together the best of his work, some 2400 photographs of snow flakes, plus a few ice flowers, windowpane frosts, dew, frozen rain, and other ice formations. Pictures were selected for beauty and scientific value. A very valuable work to anyone in meteorology, cryology; most interesting to layman; extremely useful for artist who wants beautiful, crystalline designs. All copyright free. Unabridged reprint of 1931 edition. 2453 illustrations. 227pp. 8 x 10½.   T287 Paperbound **$3.00**

A DOVER SCIENCE SAMPLER, edited by George Barkin. A collection of brief, non-technical passages from 44 Dover Books Explaining Science for the enjoyment of the science-minded browser. Includes work of Bertrand Russell, Poincaré, Laplace, Max Born, Galileo, Newton; material on physics, mathematics, metallurgy, anatomy, astronomy, chemistry, etc. You will be fascinated by Martin Gardner's analysis of the sincere pseudo-scientist, Moritz's account of Newton's absentmindedness, Bernard's examples of human vivisection, etc. Illustrations from the Diderot Pictorial Encyclopedia and De Re Metallica. 64 pages.   **FREE**

THE STORY OF ATOMIC THEORY AND ATOMIC ENERGY, J. G. Feinberg. A broader approach to subject of nuclear energy and its cultural implications than any other similar source. Very readable, informal, completely non-technical text. Begins with first atomic theory, 600 B.C. and carries you through the work of Mendelejeff, Röntgen, Madame Curie, to Einstein's equation and the A-bomb. New chapter goes through thermonuclear fission, binding energy, other events up to 1959. Radioactive decay and radiation hazards, future benefits, work of Bohr, moderns, hundreds more topics. "Deserves special mention . . . not only authoritative but thoroughly popular in the best sense of the word," Saturday Review. Formerly, "The Atom Story." Expanded with new chapter. Three appendixes. Index. 34 illustrations. vii + 243pp. 5⅜ x 8.   T625 Paperbound **$1.45**

THE STRANGE STORY OF THE QUANTUM, AN ACCOUNT FOR THE GENERAL READER OF THE GROWTH OF IDEAS UNDERLYING OUR PRESENT ATOMIC KNOWLEDGE, B. Hoffmann. Presents lucidly and expertly, with barest amount of mathematics, the problems and theories which led to modern quantum physics. Dr. Hoffmann begins with the closing years of the 19th century, when certain trifling discrepancies were noticed, and with illuminating analogies and examples takes you through the brilliant concepts of Planck, Einstein, Pauli, Broglie, Bohr, Schroedinger, Heisenberg, Dirac, Sommerfeld, Feynman, etc. This edition includes a new, long postscript carrying the story through 1958. "Of the books attempting an account of the history and contents of our modern atomic physics which have come to my attention, this is the best," H. Margenau, Yale University, in "American Journal of Physics." 32 tables and line illustrations. Index. 275pp. 5⅜ x 8.   T518 Paperbound **$1.50**

SPACE AND TIME, E. Borel. Written by a versatile mathematician of world renown with his customary lucidity and precision, this introduction to relativity for the layman presents scores of examples, analogies, and illustrations that open up new ways of thinking about space and time. It covers abstract geometry and geographical maps, continuity and topology, the propagation of light, the special theory of relativity, the general theory of relativity, theoretical researches, and much more. Mathematical notes. 2 Indexes. 4 Appendices. 15 figures. xvi + 243pp. 5⅜ x 8.   T592 Paperbound **$1.45**

FROM EUCLID TO EDDINGTON: A STUDY OF THE CONCEPTIONS OF THE EXTERNAL WORLD, Sir Edmund Whittaker. A foremost British scientist traces the development of theories of natural philosophy from the western rediscovery of Euclid to Eddington, Einstein, Dirac, etc. The inadequacy of classical physics is contrasted with present day attempts to understand the physical world through relativity, non-Euclidean geometry, space curvature, wave mechanics, etc. 5 major divisions of examination: Space; Time and Movement; the Concepts of Classical Physics; the Concepts of Quantum Mechanics; the Eddington Universe. 212pp. 5⅜ x 8. T491 Paperbound **$1.35**

CATALOGUE OF DOVER BOOKS

*THE EVOLUTION OF SCIENTIFIC THOUGHT FROM NEWTON TO EINSTEIN, A. d'Abro. A detailed account of the evolution of classical physics into modern relativistic theory and the concomitant changes in scientific methodology. The breakdown of classical physics in the face of non-Euclidean geometry and the electromagnetic equations is carefully discussed and then an exhaustive analysis of Einstein's special and general theories of relativity and their implications is given. Newton, Riemann, Weyl, Lorentz, Planck, Maxwell, and many others are considered. A non-technical explanation of space, time, electromagnetic waves, etc. as understood today. "Model of semi-popular exposition," NEW REPUBLIC. 21 diagrams. 482pp. 5⅜ x 8.
T2 Paperbound **$2.00**

EINSTEIN'S THEORY OF RELATIVITY, Max Born. Nobel Laureate explains Einstein's special and general theories of relativity, beginning with a thorough review of classical physics in simple, non-technical language. Exposition of Einstein's work discusses concept of simultaneity, kinematics, relativity of arbitrary motions, the space-time continuum, geometry of curved surfaces, etc., steering middle course between vague popularizations and complex scientific presentations. 1962 edition revised by author takes into account latest findings, predictions of theory and implications for cosmology, indicates what is being sought in unified field theory. Mathematics very elementary, illustrative diagrams and experiments informative but simple. Revised 1962 edition. Revised by Max Born, assisted by Gunther Leibfried and Walter Biem. Index. 143 illustrations. vii + 376pp. 5⅜ x 8.
S769 Paperbound **$2.00**

PHILOSOPHY AND THE PHYSICISTS, L. Susan Stebbing. A philosopher examines the philosophical aspects of modern science, in terms of a lively critical attack on the ideas of Jeans and Eddington. Such basic questions are treated as the task of science, causality, determinism, probability, consciousness, the relation of the world of physics to the world of everyday experience. The author probes the concepts of man's smallness before an inscrutable universe, the tendency to idealize mathematical construction, unpredictability theorems and human freedom, the supposed opposition between 19th century determinism and modern science, and many others. Introduces many thought-stimulating ideas about the implications of modern physical concepts. xvi + 295pp. 5⅜ x 8. T480 Paperbound **$1.65**

THE RESTLESS UNIVERSE, Max Born. A remarkably lucid account by a Nobel Laureate of recent theories of wave mechanics, behavior of gases, electrons and ions, waves and particles, electronic structure of the atom, nuclear physics, and similar topics. "Much more thorough and deeper than most attempts . . . easy and delightful," CHEMICAL AND ENGINEERING NEWS. Special feature: 7 animated sequences of 60 figures each showing such phenomena as gas molecules in motion, the scattering of alpha particles, etc. 11 full-page plates of photographs. Total of nearly 600 illustrations. 351pp. 6⅛ x 9¼. T412 Paperbound **$2.00**

THE COMMON SENSE OF THE EXACT SCIENCES, W. K. Clifford. For 70 years a guide to the basic concepts of scientific and mathematical thought. Acclaimed by scientists and laymen alike, it offers a wonderful insight into concepts such as the extension of meaning of symbols, characteristics of surface boundaries, properties of plane figures, measurement of quantities, vectors, the nature of position, bending of space, motion, mass and force, and many others. Prefaces by Bertrand Russell and Karl Pearson. Critical introduction by James Newman. 130 figures. 249pp. 5⅜ x 8. T61 Paperbound **$1.60**

MATTER AND LIGHT, THE NEW PHYSICS, Louis de Broglie. Non-technical explanations by a Nobel Laureate of electro-magnetic theory, relativity, matter, light and radiation, wave mechanics, quantum physics, philosophy of science, and similar topics. This is one of the simplest yet most accurate introductions to the work of men like Planck, Einstein, Bohr, and others. Only 2 of the 21 chapters require a knowledge of mathematics. 300pp. 5⅜ x 8.
T35 Paperbound **$1.75**

SCIENCE, THEORY AND MAN, Erwin Schrödinger. This is a complete and unabridged reissue of SCIENCE AND THE HUMAN TEMPERAMENT plus an additional essay: "What Is an Elementary Particle?" Nobel Laureate Schrödinger discusses such topics as nature of scientific method, tne nature of science, chance and determinism, science and society, conceptual models for physical entities, elementary particles and wave mechanics. Presentation is popular and may be followed by most people with little or no scientific training. "Fine practical preparation for a time when laws of nature, human institutions . . . are undergoing a critical examination without parallel," Waldemar Kaempffert, N. Y. TIMES. 192pp. 5⅜ x 8.
T428 Paperbound **$1.35**

CONCERNING THE NATURE OF THINGS, Sir William Bragg. The Nobel Laureate physicist in his Royal Institute Christmas Lectures explains such diverse phenomena as the formation of crystals, how uranium is transmuted to lead, the way X-rays work, why a spinning ball travels in a curved path, the reason why bubbles bounce from each other, and many other scientific topics that are seldom explained in simple terms. No scientific background needed—book is easy enough that any intelligent adult or youngster can understand it. Unabridged. 32pp. of photos; 57 figures. xii + 232pp. 5⅜ x 8. T31 Paperbound **$1.35**

*THE RISE OF THE NEW PHYSICS (formerly THE DECLINE OF MECHANISM), A. d'Abro. This authoritative and comprehensive 2 volume exposition is unique in scientific publishing. Written for intelligent readers not familiar with higher mathematics, it is the only thorough explanation in non-technical language of modern mathematical-physical theory. Combining both history and exposition, it ranges from classical Newtonian concepts up through the electronic theories of Dirac and Heisenberg, the statistical mechanics of Fermi, and Einstein's relativity theories. "A must for anyone doing serious study in the physical sciences," J. OF FRANKLIN INST. 97 illustrations. 991pp. 2 volumes. T3 Vol. 1, Paperbound **$2.00**
T4 Vol. 2, Paperbound **$2.00**

SCIENCE AND HYPOTHESIS, Henri Poincaré. Creative psychology in science. How such concepts as number, magnitude, space, force, classical mechanics were developed and how the modern scientist uses them in his thought. Hypothesis in physics, theories of modern physics. Introduction by Sir James Larmor. "Few mathematicians have had the breadth of vision of Poincaré, and none is his superior in the gift of clear exposition," E. T. Bell. Index. 272pp. 5⅜ x 8.
S221 Paperbound **$1.35**

THE VALUE OF SCIENCE, Henri Poincaré. Many of the most mature ideas of the "last scientific universalist" conveyed with charm and vigor for both the beginning student and the advanced worker. Discusses the nature of scientific truth, whether order is innate in the universe or imposed upon it by man, logical thought versus intuition (relating to mathematics through the works of Weierstrass, Lie, Klein, Riemann), time and space (relativity, psychological time, simultaneity), Hertz's concept of force, interrelationship of mathematical physics to pure math, values within disciplines of Maxwell, Carnot, Mayer, Newton, Lorentz, etc. Index. iii + 147pp. 5⅜ x 8.
S469 Paperbound **$1.35**

THE SKY AND ITS MYSTERIES, E. A. Beet. One of the most lucid books on the mysteries of the universe; covers history of astronomy from earliest observations to modern theories of expanding universe, source of stellar energy, birth of planets, origin of moon craters, possibilities of life on other planets. Discusses effects of sunspots on weather; distance, age of stars; methods and tools of astronomers; much more. Expert and fascinating. "Eminently readable book," London Times. Bibliography. Over 50 diagrams, 12 full-page plates. Fold-out star map. Introduction. Index. 238pp. 5¼ x 7½.
T627 Clothbound **$3.50**

OUT OF THE SKY: AN INTRODUCTION TO METEORITICS, H. H. Nininger. A non-technical yet comprehensive introduction to the young science of meteoritics: all aspects of the arrival of cosmic matter on our planet from outer space and the reaction and alteration of this matter in the terrestrial environment. Essential facts and major theories presented by one of the world's leading experts. Covers ancient reports of meteors; modern systematic investigations; fireball clusters; meteorite showers; tektites; planetoidal encounters; etc. 52 full-page plates with over 175 photographs. 22 figures. Bibliography and references. Index. viii + 336pp. 5⅜ x 8.
T519 Paperbound **$1.85**

THE REALM OF THE NEBULAE, E. Hubble. One of great astronomers of our day records his formulation of concept of "island universes." Covers velocity-distance relationship; classification, nature, distances, general types of nebulae; cosmological theories. A fine introduction to modern theories for layman. No math needed. New introduction by A. Sandage. 55 illustrations, photos. Index. iv + 201pp. 5⅜ x 8.
S455 Paperbound **$1.50**

AN ELEMENTARY SURVEY OF CELESTIAL MECHANICS, Y. Ryabov. Elementary exposition of gravitational theory and celestial mechanics. Historical introduction and coverage of basic principles, including: the ecliptic, the orbital plane, the 2- and 3-body problems, the discovery of Neptune, planetary rotation, the length of the day, the shapes of galaxies, satellites (detailed treatment of Sputnik I), etc. First American reprinting of successful Russian popular exposition. Follow actual methods of astrophysicists with only high school math! Appendix. 58 figures. 165pp. 5⅜ x 8.
T756 Paperbound **$1.25**

GREAT IDEAS AND THEORIES OF MODERN COSMOLOGY, Jagjit Singh. Companion volume to author's popular "Great Ideas of Modern Mathematics" (Dover, $1.55). The best non-technical survey of post-Einstein attempts to answer perhaps unanswerable questions of origin, age of Universe, possibility of life on other worlds, etc. Fundamental theories of cosmology and cosmogony recounted, explained, evaluated in light of most recent data: Einstein's concepts of relativity, space-time; Milne's a priori world-system; astrophysical theories of Jeans, Eddington; Hoyle's "continuous creation;" contributions of dozens more scientists. A faithful, comprehensive critical summary of complex material presented in an extremely well-written text intended for laymen. Original publication. Index. xii + 276pp. 5⅜ x 8½.
T925 Paperbound **$1.85**

BASIC ELECTRICITY, Bureau of Naval Personnel. Very thorough, easily followed course in basic electricity for beginner, layman, or intermediate student. Begins with simplest definitions, presents coordinated, systematic coverage of basic theory and application: conductors, insulators, static electricity, magnetism, production of voltage, Ohm's law, direct current series and parallel circuits, wiring techniques, electromagnetism, alternating current, capacitance and inductance, measuring instruments, etc.; application to electrical machines such as alternating and direct current generators, motors, transformers, magnetic magnifiers, etc. Each chapter contains problems to test progress; answers at rear. No math needed beyond algebra. Appendices on signs, formulas, etc. 345 illustrations. 448pp. 7½ x 10.
S973 Paperbound **$2.95**

ELEMENTARY METALLURGY AND METALLOGRAPHY, A. M. Shrager. An introduction to common metals and alloys; stress is upon steel and iron, but other metals and alloys also covered. All aspects of production, processing, working of metals. Designed for student who wishes to enter metallurgy, for bright high school or college beginner, layman who wants background on extremely important industry. Questions, at ends of chapters, many microphotographs, glossary. Greatly revised 1961 edition. 195 illustrations, tables. ix + 389pp. 5⅜ x 8.
S138 Paperbound **$2.25**

CATALOGUE OF DOVER BOOKS

BRIDGES AND THEIR BUILDERS, D. B. Steinman & S. R. Watson. Engineers, historians, and every person who has ever been fascinated by great spans will find this book an endless source of information and interest. Greek and Roman structures, Medieval bridges, modern classics such as the Brooklyn Bridge, and the latest developments in the science are retold by one of the world's leading authorities on bridge design and construction. BRIDGES AND THEIR BUILDERS is the only comprehensive and accurate semi-popular history of these important measures of progress in print. New, greatly revised, enlarged edition. 23 photos; 26 line-drawings. Index. xvii + 401pp. 5⅜ x 8. **T431 Paperbound $2.00**

FAMOUS BRIDGES OF THE WORLD, D. B. Steinman. An up-to-the-minute new edition of a book that explains the fascinating drama of how the world's great bridges came to be built. The author, designer of the famed Mackinac bridge, discusses bridges from all periods and all parts of the world, explaining their various types of construction, and describing the problems their builders faced. Although primarily for youngsters, this cannot fail to interest readers of all ages. 48 illustrations in the text. 23 photographs. 99pp. 6⅛ x 9¼. **T161 Paperbound $1.00**

HOW DO YOU USE A SLIDE RULE? by A. A. Merrill. A step-by-step explanation of the slide rule that presents the fundamental rules clearly enough for the non-mathematician to understand. Unlike most instruction manuals, this work concentrates on the two most important operations: multiplication and division. 10 easy lessons, each with a clear drawing, for the reader who has difficulty following other expositions. 1st publication. Index. 2 Appendices. 10 illustrations. 78 problems, all with answers. vi + 36 pp. 6⅛ x 9¼. **T62 Paperbound 60¢**

HOW TO CALCULATE QUICKLY, H. Sticker. A tried and true method for increasing your "number sense" — the ability to see relationships between numbers and groups of numbers. Addition, subtraction, multiplication, division, fractions, and other topics are treated through techniques not generally taught in schools: left to right multiplication, division by inspection, etc. This is not a collection of tricks which work only on special numbers, but a detailed well-planned course, consisting of over 9,000 problems that you can work in spare moments. It is excellent for anyone who is inconvenienced by slow computational skills. 5 or 10 minutes of this book daily will double or triple your calculation speed. 9,000 problems, answers. 256pp. 5⅜ x 8. **T295 Paperbound $1.00**

MATHEMATICAL FUN, GAMES AND PUZZLES, Jack Frohlichstein. A valuable service for parents of children who have trouble with math, for teachers in need of a supplement to regular upper elementary and junior high math texts (each section is graded—easy, average, difficult —for ready adaptation to different levels of ability), and for just anyone who would like to develop basic skills in an informal and entertaining manner. The author combines ten years of experience as a junior high school math teacher with a method that uses puzzles and games to introduce the basic ideas and operations of arithmetic. Stress on everyday uses of math: banking, stock market, personal budgets, insurance, taxes. Intellectually stimulating and practical, too. 418 problems and diversions with answers. Bibliography. 120 illustrations. xix + 306pp. 5⅝ x 8½. **T789 Paperbound $1.75**

GREAT IDEAS OF MODERN MATHEMATICS: THEIR NATURE AND USE, Jagjit Singh. Reader with only high school math will understand main mathematical ideas of modern physics, astronomy, genetics, psychology, evolution, etc. better than many who use them as tools, but comprehend little of their basic structure. Author uses his wide knowledge of non-mathematical fields in brilliant exposition of differential equations, matrices, group theory, logic, statistics, problems of mathematical foundations, imaginary numbers, vectors, etc. Original publication. 2 appendixes. 2 indexes. 65 illustr. 322pp. 5⅜ x 8. **S587 Paperbound $1.75**

*MATHEMATICS IN ACTION, O. G. Sutton. Everyone with a command of high school algebra will find this book one of the finest possible introductions to the application of mathematics to physical theory. Ballistics, numerical analysis, waves and wavelike phenomena, Fourier series, group concepts, fluid flow and aerodynamics, statistical measures, and meteorology are discussed with unusual clarity. Some calculus and differential equations theory is developed by the author for the reader's help in the more difficult sections. 88 figures. Index. viii + 236pp. 5⅜ x 8. **T440 Clothbound $3.50**

*INTRODUCTION TO SYMBOLIC LOGIC AND ITS APPLICATIONS, Rudolph Carnap. One of the clearest, most comprehensive, and rigorous introductions to modern symbolic logic, by perhaps its greatest living master. Not merely elementary theory, but demonstrated applications in mathematics, physics, and biology. Symbolic languages of various degrees of complexity are analyzed, and one constructed. "A creation of the rank of a masterpiece," Zentralblatt für Mathematik und Ihre Grenzgebiete. Over 300 exercises. 5 figures. Bibliography. Index. xvi + 241pp. 5⅜ x 8. **S453 Paperbound $1.85**

*HIGHER MATHEMATICS FOR STUDENTS OF CHEMISTRY AND PHYSICS, J. W. Mellor. Not abstract, but practical, drawing its problems from familiar laboratory material, this book covers theory and application of differential calculus, analytic geometry, functions with singularities, integral calculus, infinite series, solution of numerical equations, differential equations, Fourier's theorem and extensions, probability and the theory of errors, calculus of variations, determinants, etc. "If the reader is not familiar with this book, it will repay him to examine it," CHEM. & ENGINEERING NEWS. 800 problems. 189 figures. 2 appendices; 30 tables of integrals, probability functions, etc. Bibliography. xxi + 641pp. 5⅜ x 8. **S193 Paperbound $2.25**

THE FOURTH DIMENSION SIMPLY EXPLAINED, edited by Henry P. Manning. Originally written as entries in contest sponsored by "Scientific American," then published in book form, these 22 essays present easily understood explanations of how the fourth dimension may be studied, the relationship of non-Euclidean geometry to the fourth dimension, analogies to three-dimensional space, some fourth-dimensional absurdities and curiosities, possible measurements and forms in the fourth dimension. In general, a thorough coverage of many of the simpler properties of fourth-dimensional space. Multi-points of view on many of the most important aspects are valuable aid to comprehension. Introduction by Dr. Henry P. Manning gives proper emphasis to points in essays, more advanced account of fourth-dimensional geometry. 82 figures. 251pp. 5⅜ x 8.   T711 Paperbound **$1.35**

TRIGONOMETRY REFRESHER FOR TECHNICAL MEN, A. A. Klaf. A modern question and answer text on plane and spherical trigonometry. Part I covers plane trigonometry: angles, quadrants, trigonometrical functions, graphical representation, interpolation, equations, logarithms, solution of triangles, slide rules, etc. Part II discusses applications to navigation, surveying, elasticity, architecture, and engineering. Small angles, periodic functions, vectors, polar coordinates, De Moivre's theorem, fully covered. Part III is devoted to spherical trigonometry and the solution of spherical triangles, with applications to terrestrial and astronomical problems. Special time-savers for numerical calculation. 913 questions answered for you! 1738 problems; answers to odd numbers. 494 figures. 14 pages of functions, formulae. Index. x + 629pp. 5⅜ x 8.   T371 Paperbound **$2.00**

CALCULUS REFRESHER FOR TECHNICAL MEN. A. A. Klaf. Not an ordinary textbook but a unique refresher for engineers, technicians, and students. An examination of the most important aspects of differential and integral calculus by means of 756 key questions. Part I covers simple differential calculus: constants, variables, functions, increments, derivatives, logarithms, curvature, etc. Part II treats fundamental concepts of integration: inspection, substitution, transformation, reduction, areas and volumes, mean value, successive and partial integration, double and triple integration. Stresses practical aspects! A 50 page section gives applications to civil and nautical engineering, electricity, stress and strain, elasticity, industrial engineering, and similar fields. 756 questions answered. 556 problems; solutions to odd numbers. 36 pages of constants, formulae. Index. v + 431pp. 5⅜ x 8.
T370 Paperbound **$2.00**

PROBABILITIES AND LIFE, Emile Borel. One of the leading French mathematicians of the last 100 years makes use of certain results of mathematics of probabilities and explains a number of problems that for the most part, are related to everyday living or to illness and death: computation of life expectancy tables, chances of recovery from various diseases, probabilities of job accidents, weather predictions, games of chance, and so on. Emphasis on results not processes, though some indication is made of mathematical proofs. Simple in style, free of technical terminology, limited in scope to everyday situations, it is comprehensible to laymen, fine reading for beginning students of probability. New English translation. Index. Appendix. vi + 87pp. 5⅜ x 8½.   T121 Paperbound **$1.00**

POPULAR SCIENTIFIC LECTURES, Hermann von Helmholtz. 7 lucid expositions by a pre-eminent scientific mind: "The Physiological Causes of Harmony in Music," "On the Relation of Optics to Painting," "On the Conservation of Force," "On the Interaction of Natural Forces," "On Goethe's Scientific Researches" into theory of color, "On the Origin and Significance of Geometric Axioms," "On Recent Progress in the Theory of Vision." Written with simplicity of expression, stripped of technicalities, these are easy to understand and delightful reading for anyone interested in science or looking for an introduction to serious study of acoustics or optics. Introduction by Professor Morris Kline, Director, Division of Electromagnetic Research, New York University, contains astute, impartial evaluations. Selected from "Popular Lectures on Scientific Subjects," 1st and 2nd series. xii + 286pp. 5⅜ x 8½.   T799 Paperbound **$1.45**

SCIENCE AND METHOD, Henri Poincaré. Procedure of scientific discovery, methodology, experiment, idea-germination—the intellectual processes by which discoveries come into being. Most significant and most interesting aspects of development, application of ideas. Chapters cover selection of facts, chance, mathematical reasoning, mathematics, and logic; Whitehead, Russell, Cantor; the new mechanics, etc. 288pp. 5⅜ x 8.   S222 Paperbound **$1.35**

HEAT AND ITS WORKINGS, Morton Mott-Smith, Ph.D. An unusual book; to our knowledge the only middle-level survey of this important area of science. Explains clearly such important concepts as physiological sensation of heat and Weber's law, measurement of heat, evolution of thermometer, nature of heat, expansion and contraction of solids, Boyle's law, specific heat. BTU's and calories, evaporation, Andrews's isothermals, radiation, the relation of heat to light, many more topics inseparable from other aspects of physics. A wide, non-mathematical yet thorough explanation of basic ideas, theories, phenomena for laymen and beginning scientists illustrated by experiences of daily life. Bibliography. 50 illustrations. x + 165pp. 5⅜ x 8½.   T978 Paperbound **$1.00**

History of Science and Mathematics

THE STUDY OF THE HISTORY OF MATHEMATICS, THE STUDY OF THE HISTORY OF SCIENCE, G. Sarton. Two books bound as one. Each volume contains a long introduction to the methods and philosophy of each of these historical fields, covering the skills and sympathies of the historian, concepts of history of science, psychology of idea-creation, and the purpose of history of science. Prof. Sarton also provides more than 80 pages of classified bibliography. Complete and unabridged. Indexed. 10 illustrations. 188pp. 5⅜ x 8.   T240 Paperbound **$1.25**

A HISTORY OF PHYSICS, Florian Cajori, Ph.D. First written in 1899, thoroughly revised in 1929, this is still best entry into antecedents of modern theories. Precise non-mathematical discussion of ideas, theories, techniques, apparatus of each period from Greeks to 1920's, analyzing within each period basic topics of matter, mechanics, light, electricity and magnetism, sound, atomic theory, etc. Stress on modern developments, from early 19th century to present. Written with critical eye on historical development, significance. Provides most of needed historical background for student of physics. Reprint of second (1929) edition. Index. Bibliography in footnotes. 16 figures. xv + 424pp. 5⅜ x 8.   T970 Paperbound **$2.00**

A HISTORY OF ASTRONOMY FROM THALES TO KEPLER, J. L. E. Dreyer. Formerly titled A HISTORY OF PLANETARY SYSTEMS FROM THALES TO KEPLER. This is the only work in English which provides a detailed history of man's cosmological views from prehistoric times up through the Renaissance. It covers Egypt, Babylonia, early Greece, Alexandria, the Middle Ages, Copernicus, Tycho Brahe, Kepler, and many others. Epicycles and other complex theories of positional astronomy are explained in terms nearly everyone will find clear and easy to understand. "Standard reference on Greek astronomy and the Copernican revolution," SKY AND TELESCOPE. Bibliography. 21 diagrams. Index. xvii + 430pp. 5⅜ x 8.   S79 Paperbound **$1.98**

A SHORT HISTORY OF ASTRONOMY, A. Berry. A popular standard work for over 50 years, this thorough and accurate volume covers the science from primitive times to the end of the 19th century. After the Greeks and Middle Ages, individual chapters analyze Copernicus, Brahe, Galileo, Kepler, and Newton, and the mixed reception of their startling discoveries. Post-Newtonian achievements are then discussed in unusual detail: Halley, Bradley, Lagrange, Laplace, Herschel, Bessel, etc. 2 indexes. 104 illustrations, 9 portraits. xxxi + 440pp. 5⅜ x 8.   T210 Paperbound **$2.00**

PIONEERS OF SCIENCE, Sir Oliver Lodge. An authoritative, yet elementary history of science by a leading scientist and expositor. Concentrating on individuals—Copernicus, Brahe, Kepler, Galileo, Descartes, Newton, Laplace, Herschel, Lord Kelvin, and other scientists—the author presents their discoveries in historical order, adding biographical material on each man and full, specific explanations of their achievements. The full, clear discussions of the accomplishments of post-Newtonian astronomers are features seldom found in other books on the subject. Index. 120 illustrations. xv + 404pp. 5⅜ x 8.   T716 Paperbound **$1.65**

THE BIRTH AND DEVELOPMENT OF THE GEOLOGICAL SCIENCES, F. D. Adams. The most complete and thorough history of the earth sciences in print. Geological thought from earliest recorded times to the end of the 19th century—covers over 300 early thinkers and systems: fossils and hypothetical explanations of them, vulcanists vs. neptunists, figured stones and paleontology, generation of stones, and similar topics. 91 illustrations, including medieval, renaissance woodcuts, etc. 632 footnotes and bibliographic notes. Index. 511pp. 5⅜ x 8.
T5 Paperbound **$2.25**

THE STORY OF ALCHEMY AND EARLY CHEMISTRY, J. M. Stillman. "Add the blood of a red-haired man"—a recipe typical of the many quoted in this authoritative and readable history of the strange beliefs and practices of the alchemists. Concise studies of every leading figure in alchemy and early chemistry through Lavoisier, in this curious epic of superstition and true science, constructed from scores of rare and difficult Greek, Latin, German, and French texts. Foreword by S. W. Young. 246-item bibliography. Index. xiii + 566pp. 5⅜ x 8.
S628 Paperbound **$2.45**

HISTORY OF MATHEMATICS, D. E. Smith. Most comprehensive non-technical history of math in English. Discusses the lives and works of over a thousand major and minor figures, from Euclid to Descartes, Gauss, and Riemann. Vol. I: A chronological examination, from primitive concepts through Egypt, Babylonia, Greece, the Orient, Rome, the Middle Ages, the Renaissance, and up to 1900. Vol. 2: The development of ideas in specific fields and problems, up through elementary calculus. Two volumes, total of 510 illustrations, 1355pp. 5⅜ x 8. Set boxed in attractive container.   T429,430 Paperbound the set **$5.00**

CATALOGUE OF DOVER BOOKS

Classics of Science

THE DIDEROT PICTORIAL ENCYCLOPEDIA OF TRADES AND INDUSTRY, MANUFACTURING AND THE TECHNICAL ARTS IN PLATES SELECTED FROM "L'ENCYCLOPEDIE OU DICTIONNAIRE RAISONNE DES SCIENCES, DES ARTS, ET DES METIERS" OF DENIS DIDEROT, edited with text by C. Gillispie. The first modern selection of plates from the high point of 18th century French engraving, Diderot's famous Encyclopedia. Over 2000 illustrations on 485 full page plates, most of them original size, illustrating the trades and industries of one of the most fascinating periods of modern history, 18th century France. These magnificent engravings provide an invaluable glimpse into the past for the student of early technology, a lively and accurate social document to students of cultures, an outstanding find to the lover of fine engravings. The plates teem with life, with men, women, and children performing all of the thousands of operations necessary to the trades before and during the early stages of the industrial revolution. Plates are in sequence, and show general operations, closeups of difficult operations, and details of complex machinery. Such important and interesting trades and industries are illustrated as sowing, harvesting, beekeeping, cheesemaking, operating windmills, milling flour, charcoal burning, tobacco processing, indigo, fishing, arts of war, salt extraction, mining, smelting iron, casting iron, steel, extracting mercury, zinc, sulphur, copper, etc., slating, tinning, silverplating, gilding, making gunpowder, cannons, bells, shoeing horses, tanning, papermaking, printing, dying, and more than 40 other categories. 920pp. 9 x 12. Heavy library cloth.   T421 Two volume set **$18.50**

THE PRINCIPLES OF SCIENCE, A TREATISE ON LOGIC AND THE SCIENTIFIC METHOD, W. Stanley Jevons. Treating such topics as Inductive and Deductive Logic, the Theory of Number, Probability, and the Limits of Scientific Method, this milestone in the development of symbolic logic remains a stimulating contribution to the investigation of inferential validity in the natural and social sciences. It significantly advances Boole's logic, and describes a machine which is a foundation of modern electronic calculators. In his introduction, Ernest Nagel of Columbia University says, "(Jevons) . . . continues to be of interest as an attempt to articulate the logic of scientific inquiry." Index. liii + 786pp. 5⅜ x 8.
S446 Paperbound **$2.98**

*DIALOGUES CONCERNING TWO NEW SCIENCES, Galileo Galilei. A classic of experimental science which has had a profound and enduring influence on the entire history of mechanics and engineering. Galileo based this, his finest work, on 30 years of experimentation. It offers a fascinating and vivid exposition of dynamics, elasticity, sound, ballistics, strength of materials, and the scientific method. Translated by H. Crew and A. de Salvio. 126 diagrams. Index. xxi + 288pp. 5⅜ x 8.   S99 Paperbound **$1.75**

DE MAGNETE, William Gilbert. This classic work on magnetism founded a new science. Gilbert was the first to use the word "electricity," to recognize mass as distinct from weight, to discover the effect of heat on magnetic bodies; invented an electroscope, differentiated between static electricity and magnetism, conceived of the earth as a magnet. Written by the first great experimental scientist, this lively work is valuable not only as an historical landmark, but as the delightfully easy-to-follow record of a perpetually searching, ingenious mind. Translated by P. F. Mottelay. 25 page biographical memoir. 90 fix. lix + 368pp. 5⅜ x 8.   S470 Paperbound **$2.00**

*OPTICKS, Sir Isaac Newton. An enormous storehouse of insights and discoveries on light, reflection, color, refraction, theories of wave and corpuscular propagation of light, optical apparatus, and mathematical devices which have recently been reevaluated in terms of modern physics and placed in the top-most ranks of Newton's work! Foreword by Albert Einstein. Preface by I. B. Cohen of Harvard U. 7 pages of portraits, facsimile pages, letters, etc. cxvi + 412pp. 5⅜ x 8.   S205 Paperbound **$2.25**

A SURVEY OF PHYSICAL THEORY, M. Planck. Lucid essays on modern physics for the general reader by the Nobel Laureate and creator of the quantum revolution. Planck explains how the new concepts came into being; explores the clash between theories of mechanics, electrodynamics, and thermodynamics; and traces the evolution of the concept of light through Newton, Huygens, Maxwell, and his own quantum theory, providing unparalleled insights into his development of this momentous modern concept. Bibliography. Index. vii + 121pp. 5⅜ x 8.
S650 Paperbound **$1.15**

A SOURCE BOOK IN MATHEMATICS, D. E. Smith. English translations of the original papers that announced the great discoveries in mathematics from the Renaissance to the end of the 19th century: succinct selections from 125 different treatises and articles, most of them unavailable elsewhere in English—Newton, Leibniz, Pascal, Riemann, Bernoulli, etc. 24 articles trace developments in the field of number, 18 cover algebra, 36 are on geometry, and 13 on calculus. Biographical-historical introductions to each article. Two volume set. Index in each. Total of 115 illustrations. Total of xxviii + 742pp. 5⅜ x 8.   S552 Vol I Paperbound **$1.85**
S553 Vol II Paperbound **$1.85**
The set, boxed **$3.50**

CATALOGUE OF DOVER BOOKS

*THE THIRTEEN BOOKS OF EUCLID'S ELEMENTS, edited by T. L. Heath. This is the complete EUCLID — the definitive edition of one of the greatest classics of the western world. Complete English translation of the Heiberg text with spurious Book XIV. Detailed 150-page introduction discusses aspects of Greek and medieval mathematics: Euclid, texts, commentators, etc. Paralleling the text is an elaborate critical exposition analyzing each definition, proposition, postulate, etc., and covering textual matters, mathematical analyses, refutations, extensions, etc. Unabridged reproduction of the Cambridge 2nd edition. 3 volumes. Total of 995 figures, 1426pp. 5⅜ x 8.   S88, 89, 90 — 3 vol. set, Paperbound **$6.75**

*THE GEOMETRY OF RENE DESCARTES. The great work which founded analytic geometry. The renowned Smith-Latham translation faced with the original French text containing all of Descartes' own diagrams! Contains: Problems the Construction of Which Requires Only Straight Lines and Circles; On the Nature of Curved Lines; On the Construction of Solid or Supersolid Problems. Notes. Diagrams. 258pp.   S68 Paperbound **$1.60**

*A PHILOSOPHICAL ESSAY ON PROBABILITIES, P. Laplace. Without recourse to any mathematics above grammar school, Laplace develops a philosophically, mathematically and historically classical exposition of the nature of probability: its functions and limitations, operations in practical affairs, calculations in games of chance, insurance, government, astronomy, and countless other fields. New introduction by E. T. Bell. viii + 196pp.   S166 Paperbound **$1.35**

DE RE METALLICA, Georgius Agricola. Written over 400 years ago, for 200 years the most authoritative first-hand account of the production of metals, translated in 1912 by former President Herbert Hoover and his wife, and today still one of the most beautiful and fascinating volumes ever produced in the history of science! 12 books, exhaustively annotated, give a wonderfully lucid and vivid picture of the history of mining, selection of sites, types of deposits, excavating pits, sinking shafts, ventilating, pumps, crushing machinery, assaying, smelting, refining metals, making salt, alum, nitre, glass, and many other topics. This definitive edition contains all 289 of the 16th century woodcuts which made the original an artistic masterpiece. It makes a superb gift for geologists, engineers, libraries, artists, historians, and everyone interested in science and early illustrative art. Biographical, historical introductions. Bibliography, survey of ancient authors. Indices. 289 illustrations. 672pp. 6¾ x 10¾. Deluxe library edition.   S6 Clothbound **$10.00**

GEOGRAPHICAL ESSAYS, W. M. Davis. Modern geography and geomorphology rest on the fundamental work of this scientist. His new concepts of earth-processes revolutionized science and his broad interpretation of the scope of geography created a deeper understanding of the interrelation of the landscape and the forces that mold it. This first inexpensive unabridged edition covers theory of geography, methods of advanced geographic teaching, descriptions of geographic areas, analyses of land-shaping processes, and much besides. Not only a factual and historical classic, it is still widely read for its reflections of modern scientific thought. Introduction. 130 figures. Index. vi + 777pp. 5⅜ x 8.
                                                                 S383 Paperbound **$2.95**

CHARLES BABBAGE AND HIS CALCULATING ENGINES, edited by P. Morrison and E. Morrison. Friend of Darwin, Humboldt, and Laplace, Babbage was a leading pioneer in large-scale mathematical machines and a prophetic herald of modern operational research—true father of Harvard's relay computer Mark I. His Difference Engine and Analytical Engine were the first successful machines in the field. This volume contains a valuable introduction on his life and work; major excerpts from his fascinating autobiography, revealing his eccentric and unusual personality; and extensive selections from "Babbage's Calculating Engines," a compilation of hard-to-find journal articles, both by Babbage and by such eminent contributors as the Countess of Lovelace, L. F. Menabrea, and Dionysius Lardner. 11 illustrations. Appendix of miscellaneous papers. Index. Bibliography. xxxviii + 400pp. 5⅜ x 8.   T12 Paperbound **$2.00**

*THE WORKS OF ARCHIMEDES WITH THE METHOD OF ARCHIMEDES, edited by T. L. Heath. All the known works of the greatest mathematician of antiquity including the recently discovered METHOD OF ARCHIMEDES. This last is the only work we have which shows exactly how early mathematicians discovered their proofs before setting them down in their final perfection. A 186 page study by the eminent scholar Heath discusses Archimedes and the history of Greek mathematics. Bibliography. 563pp. 5⅜ x 8.   S9 Paperbound **$2.25**

Psychology

YOGA: A SCIENTIFIC EVALUATION, Kovoor T. Behanan. A complete reprinting of the book that for the first time gave Western readers a sane, scientific explanation and analysis of yoga. The author draws on controlled laboratory experiments and personal records of a year as a disciple of a yoga, to investigate yoga psychology, concepts of knowledge, physiology, "supernatural" phenomena, and the ability to tap the deepest human powers. In this study under the auspices of Yale University Institute of Human Relations, the strictest principles of physiological and psychological inquiry are followed throughout. Foreword by W. A. Miles, Yale University. 17 photographs. Glossary. Index. xx + 270pp. 5⅜ x 8. T505 Paperbound $1.75

CONDITIONED REFLEXES: AN INVESTIGATION OF THE PHYSIOLOGICAL ACTIVITIES OF THE CEREBRAL CORTEX, I. P. Pavlov. Full, authorized translation of Pavlov's own survey of his work in experimental psychology reviews entire course of experiments, summarizes conclusions, outlines psychological system based on famous "conditioned reflex" concept. Details of technical means used in experiments, observations on formation of conditioned reflexes, function of cerebral hemispheres, results of damage, nature of sleep, typology of nervous system, significance of experiments for human psychology. Trans. by Dr. G. V. Anrep, Cambridge Univ. 235-item bibliography. 18 figures. 445pp. 5⅜ x 8. S614 Paperbound $2.25

EXPLANATION OF HUMAN BEHAVIOUR, F. V. Smith. A major intermediate-level introduction to and criticism of 8 complete systems of the psychology of human behavior, with unusual emphasis on theory of investigation and methodology. Part I is an illuminating analysis of the problems involved in the explanation of observed phenomena, and the differing viewpoints on the nature of causality. Parts II and III are a closely detailed survey of the systems of McDougall, Gordon Allport, Lewin, the Gestalt group, Freud, Watson, Hull, and Tolman. Biographical notes. Bibliography of over 800 items. 2 Indexes. 38 figures. xii + 460pp. 5½ x 8¾. T253 Clothbound $6.00

SEX IN PSYCHO-ANALYSIS (formerly CONTRIBUTIONS TO PSYCHO-ANALYSIS), S. Ferenczi. Written by an associate of Freud, this volume presents countless insights on such topics as impotence, transference, analysis and children, dreams, symbols, obscene words, masturbation and male homosexuality, paranoia and psycho-analysis, the sense of reality, hypnotism and therapy, and many others. Also includes full text of THE DEVELOPMENT OF PSYCHO-ANALYSIS by Ferenczi and Otto Rank. Two books bound as one. Total of 406pp. 5⅜ x 8. T324 Paperbound $1.85

BEYOND PSYCHOLOGY, Otto Rank. One of Rank's most mature contributions, focussing on the irrational basis of human behavior as a basic fact of our lives. The psychoanalytic techniques of myth analysis trace to their source the ultimates of human existence: fear of death, personality, the social organization, the need for love and creativity, etc. Dr. Rank finds them stemming from a common irrational source, man's fear of final destruction. A seminal work in modern psychology, this work sheds light on areas ranging from the concept of immortal soul to the sources of state power. 291pp. 5⅜ x 8. T485 Paperbound $2.00

ILLUSIONS AND DELUSIONS OF THE SUPERNATURAL AND THE OCCULT, D. H. Rawcliffe. Holds up to rational examination hundreds of persistent delusions including crystal gazing, automatic writing, table turning, mediumistic trances, mental healing, stigmata, lycanthropy, live burial, the Indian Rope Trick, spiritualism, dowsing, telepathy, clairvoyance, ghosts, ESP, etc. The author explains and exposes the mental and physical deceptions involved, making this not only an exposé of supernatural phenomena, but a valuable exposition of characteristic types of abnormal psychology. Originally titled "The Psychology of the Occult." 14 illustrations. Index. 551pp. 5⅜ x 8. T503 Paperbound $2.00

THE PRINCIPLES OF PSYCHOLOGY, William James. The full long-course, unabridged, of one of the great classics of Western literature and science. Wonderfully lucid descriptions of human mental activity, the stream of thought, consciousness, time perception, memory, imagination, emotions, reason, abnormal phenomena, and similar topics. Original contributions are integrated with the work of such men as Berkeley, Binet, Mills, Darwin, Hume, Kant, Royce, Schopenhauer, Spinoza, Locke, Descartes, Galton, Wundt, Lotze, Herbart, Fechner, and scores of others. All contrasting interpretations of mental phenomena are examined in detail — introspective analysis, philosophical interpretation, and experimental research. "A classic," JOURNAL OF CONSULTING PSYCHOLOGY. "The main lines are as valid as ever," PSYCHO-ANALYTICAL QUARTERLY. "Standard reading . . . a classic of interpretation," PSYCHIATRIC QUARTERLY. 94 illustrations. 1408pp. 2 volumes. 5⅜ x 8. Vol. 1, T381 Paperbound $2.50 Vol. 2, T382 Paperbound $2.50

THE DYNAMICS OF THERAPY IN A CONTROLLED RELATIONSHIP, Jessie Taft. One of the most important works in literature of child psychology, out of print for 25 years. Outstanding disciple of Rank describes all aspects of relationship or Rankian therapy through concise, simple elucidation of theory underlying her actual contacts with two seven-year olds. Therapists, social caseworkers, psychologists, counselors, and laymen who work with children will all find this important work an invaluable summation of method, theory of child psychology. xix + 296pp. 5⅜ x 8. T325 Paperbound $1.75

Music

A GENERAL HISTORY OF MUSIC, Charles Burney. A detailed coverage of music from the Greeks up to 1789, with full information on all types of music: sacred and secular, vocal and instrumental, operatic and symphonic. Theory, notation, forms, instruments, innovators, composers, performers, typical and important works, and much more in an easy, entertaining style. Burney covered much of Europe and spoke with hundreds of authorities and composers so that this work is more than a compilation of records . . . it is a living work of careful and first-hand scholarship. Its account of thoroughbass (18th century) Italian music is probably still the best introduction on the subject. A recent NEW YORK TIMES review said, "Surprisingly few of Burney's statements have been invalidated by modern research . . . still of great value." Edited and corrected by Frank Mercer. 35 figures. Indices. 1915pp. 5⅜ x 8. 2 volumes. **T36 The Set, Clothbound $12.50**

A DICTIONARY OF HYMNOLOGY, John Julian. This exhaustive and scholarly work has become known as an invaluable source of hundreds of thousands of important and often difficult to obtain facts on the history and use of hymns in the western world. Everyone interested in hymns will be fascinated by the accounts of famous hymns and hymn writers and amazed by the amount of practical information he will find. More than 30,000 entries on individual hymns, giving authorship, date and circumstances of composition, publication, textual variations, translations, denominational and ritual usage, etc. Biographies of more than 9,000 hymn writers, and essays on important topics such as Christmas carols and children's hymns, and much other unusual and valuable information. A 200 page double-columned index of first lines — the largest in print. Total of 1786 pages in two reinforced clothbound volumes. 6¼ x 9¼. **The set, T333 Clothbound $17.50**

MUSIC IN MEDIEVAL BRITAIN, F. Ll. Harrison. The most thorough, up-to-date, and accurate treatment of the subject ever published, beautifully illustrated. Complete account of institutions and choirs; carols, masses, and motets; liturgy and plainsong; and polyphonic music from the Norman Conquest to the Reformation. Discusses the various schools of music and their reciprocal influences; the origin and development of new ritual forms; development and use of instruments; and new evidence on many problems of the period. Reproductions of scores, over 200 excerpts from medieval melodies. Rules of harmony and dissonance; influence of Continental styles; great composers (Dunstable, Cornysh, Fairfax, etc.); and much more. Register and index of more than 400 musicians. Index of titles. General Index. 225-item bibliography. 6 Appendices. xix + 491pp. 5⅝ x 8¾. **T705 Clothbound $10.00**

THE MUSIC OF SPAIN, Gilbert Chase. Only book in English to give concise, comprehensive account of Iberian music; new Chapter covers music since 1941. Victoria, Albéniz, Cabezón, Pedrell, Turina, hundreds of other composers; popular and folk music; the Gypsies; the guitar; dance, theatre, opera, with only extensive discussion in English of the Zarzuela; virtuosi such as Casals; much more. "Distinguished . . . readable," Saturday Review. 400-item bibliography. Index. 27 photos. 383pp. 5⅝ x 8. **T549 Paperbound $2.00**

ON STUDYING SINGING, Sergius Kagen. An intelligent method of voice-training, which leads you around pitfalls that waste your time, money, and effort. Exposes rigid, mechanical systems, baseless theories, deleterious exercises. "Logical, clear, convincing . . . dead right," Virgil Thomson, N.Y. Herald Tribune. "I recommend this volume highly," Maggie Teyte, Saturday Review. 119pp. 5⅜ x 8. **T622 Paperbound $1.25**

WILLIAM LAWES, M. Lefkowitz. This is the definitive work on Lawes, the versatile, prolific, and highly original "King's musician" of 17th century England. His life is reconstructed from original documents, and nearly every piece he ever wrote is examined and evaluated: his fantasias, pavans, violin "sonatas," lyra viol and bass viol suites, and music for harp and theorbo; and his songs, masques, and theater music to words by Herrick ("Gather Ye Rosebuds"), Jonson, Suckling, Shirley, and others. The author shows the innovations of dissonance, augmented triad, and other Italian influences Lawes helped introduce to England. List of Lawes' complete works and several complete scores by this major precursor of Purcell and the 18th century developments. Index. 5 Appendices. 52 musical excerpts, many never before in print. Bibliography. x + 320pp. 5⅜ x 8. **T706 Clothbound $10.00**

THE FUGUE IN BEETHOVEN'S PIANO MUSIC, J. V. Cockshoot. The first study of a neglected aspect of Beethoven's genius: his ability as a writer of fugues. Analyses of early studies and published works demonstrate his original and powerful contributions to composition. 34 works are examined, with 143 musical excerpts. For all pianists, teachers, students, and music-minded readers with a serious interest in Beethoven. Index. 93-item bibliography. Illustration of original score for "Fugue in C." xv + 212pp. 5⅝ x 8⅜. **T704 Clothbound $6.00**

Dover Classical Records

Now available directly to the public exclusively from Dover: top-quality recordings of fine classical music for only $2 per record! Almost all were released by major record companies to sell for $5 and $6. These recordings were issued under our imprint only after they had passed a severe critical test. We insisted upon:

First-rate music that is enjoyable, musically important and culturally significant.

First-rate performances, where the artists have carried out the composer's intentions, in which the music is alive, vigorous, played with understanding and sensitivity.

First-rate sound—clear, sonorous, fully balanced, crackle-free, whir-free.

Have in your home music by major composers, performed by such gifted musicians as Elsner, Gitlis, Wührer, Beveridge Webster, the Barchet Quartet, Gimpel, etc. Enthusiastically received when first released, many of these performances are definitive. The records are not seconds or remainders, but brand new pressings made on pure vinyl from carefully chosen master tapes. "All purpose" 12" monaural 33⅓ rpm records, they play equally well on hi-fi and stereo equipment. Fine music for discriminating music lovers, superlatively played, flawlessly recorded: there is no better way to build your library of recorded classical music at remarkable savings. There are no strings; this is not a come-on, not a club, forcing you to buy records you may not want in order to get a few at a lower price. Buy whatever records you want in any quantity, and never pay more than $2 each. Your obligation ends with your first purchase. And that's when ours begins. Dover's money-back guarantee allows you to return any record for any reason, even if you don't like the music, for a full, immediate refund—no questions asked.

MOZART: STRING QUARTETS: IN A (K. 464) AND C ("DISSONANT") (K. 465), Barchet Quartet. The final two of the famous Haydn Quartets, high-points in the history of music. The A Major was accepted with delight by Mozart's contemporaries, but the C Major, with its dissonant opening, aroused strong protest. Today, of course, the remarkable resolutions of the dissonances are recognized as major musical achievements. "Beautiful warm playing," MUSICAL AMERICA. "Two of Mozart's loveliest quartets in a distinguished performance," REV. OF RECORDED MUSIC. (Playing time 58 mins.) HCR 5200 **$2.00**

MOZART: STRING QUARTETS: IN G (K. 80), D (K. 156), and C (K. 157), Barchet Quartet. The early chamber music of Mozart receives unfortunately little attention. First-rate music of the Italian school, it contains all the lightness and charm that belongs only to the youthful Mozart. This is currently the only separate source for the composer's work of this period. "Excellent," HIGH FIDELITY. "Filled with sunshine and youthful joy; played with verve, recorded sound live and brilliant," CHRISTIAN SCI. MONITOR. (playing time 51 mins.) HCR 5201 **$2.00**

MOZART: SERENADES: #9 IN D ("POSTHORN") (K. 320), #6 IN D ("SERENATA NOTTURNA") (K. 239), Pro Musica Orch. of Stuttgart, under Edouard van Remoortel. For Mozart, the serenade was a highly effective form, since he could bring to it the immediacy and intimacy of chamber music as well as the free fantasy of larger group music. Both these serenades are distinguished by a playful, mischievous quality, a spirit perfectly captured in this fine performance. "A triumph, polished playing from the orchestra," HI FI MUSIC AT HOME. "Sound is rich and resonant, fidelity is wonderful," REV. OF RECORDED MUSIC. (Playing time 51 mins.) HCR 5202 **$2.00**

MOZART: DIVERTIMENTO FOR VIOLIN, VIOLA AND CELLO IN E FLAT (K. 563); ADAGIO AND FUGUE IN F MINOR (K. 404a), Kehr Trio. The divertimento is one of Mozart's most beloved pieces, called by Einstein "the finest and most perfect trio ever heard." It is difficult to imagine a music lover who will not be delighted by it. This is the only recording of the lesser known Adagio and Fugue, written in 1782 and influenced by Bach's Well-Tempered Clavichord. "Extremely beautiful recording, strongly recommended," THE OBSERVER. "Superior to rival editions," HIGH FIDELITY. (Playing time 51 mins.) HCR 5203 **$2.00**

SCHUMANN: KREISLERIANA (OPUS 16) AND FANTASIA IN C (OPUS 17), Vlado Perlemuter, Piano. The vigorous Romantic imagination and the remarkable emotional qualities of Schumann's piano music raise it to a special eminence in 19th-century creativity. Both these pieces are rooted to the composer's tortuous romance with his future wife, Clara, and both receive brilliant treatment at the hands of Vlado Perlemuter, Paris Conservatory, proclaimed by Alfred Cortot "not only a great virtuoso but also a great musician." "The best Kreisleriana to date," BILLBOARD. (Playing time 55 mins.) HCR 5204 **$2.00**

CATALOGUE OF DOVER BOOKS

SCHUMANN: TRIOS #1 IN D MINOR (OPUS 63) AND #3 IN G MINOR (OPUS 110), Trio di Bolzano. The fiery, romantic, melodic Trio #1 and the dramatic, seldom heard Trio #3 are both movingly played by a fine chamber ensemble. No one personified Romanticism to the general public of the 1840's more than did Robert Schumann, and among his most romantic works are these trios for cello, violin and piano. "Ensemble and overall interpretation leave little to be desired," HIGH FIDELITY. "An especially understanding performance," REV. OF RECORDED MUSIC. (Playing time 54 mins.) HCR 5205 **$2.00**

SCHUBERT: QUINTET IN A ("TROUT") (OPUS 114), AND NOCTURNE IN E FLAT (OPUS 148), Friedrich Wührer, Piano and Barchet Quartet. If there is a single piece of chamber music that is a universal favorite, it is probably Schubert's "Trout" Quintet. Delightful melody, harmonic resources, musical exuberance are its characteristics. The Nocturne (played by Wührer, Barchet, and Reimann) is an exquisite piece with a deceptively simple theme and harmony. "The best Trout on the market—Wührer is a fine Viennese-style Schubertian, and his spirit infects the Barchets," ATLANTIC MONTHLY. "Exquisitely recorded," ETUDE. (Playing time 44 mins.) HCR 5206 **$2.00**

SCHUBERT: PIANO SONATAS IN C MINOR AND B (OPUS 147), Friedrich Wührer. Schubert's sonatas retain the structure of the classical form, but delight listeners with romantic freedom and a special melodic richness. The C Minor, one of the Three Grand Sonatas, is a product of the composer's maturity. The B Major was not published until 15 years after his death. "Remarkable interpretation, reproduction of the first rank," DISQUES. "A superb pianist for music like this, musicianship, sweep, power, and an ability to integrate Schubert's measures such as few pianists have had since Schnabel," Harold Schonberg. (Playing time 49 mins.) HCR 5207 **$2.00**

STRAVINSKY: VIOLIN CONCERTO IN D, Ivry Gitlis, Cologne Orchestra; DUO CONCERTANTE, Ivry Gitlis, Violin, Charlotte Zelka, Piano, Cologne Orchestra; JEU DE CARTES, Bamberg Symphony, under Hollreiser. Igor Stravinsky is probably the most important composer of this century, and these three works are among the most significant of his neoclassical period of the 30's. The Violin Concerto is one of the few modern classics. Jeu de Cartes, a ballet score, bubbles with gaiety, color and melodiousness. "Imaginatively played and beautifully recorded," E. T. Canby, HARPERS MAGAZINE. "Gitlis is excellent, Hollreiser beautifully worked out," HIGH FIDELITY. (Playing time 55 mins.) HCR 5208 **$2.00**

GEMINIANI: SIX CONCERTI GROSSI, OPUS 3, Helma Elsner, Harpsichord, Barchet Quartet, Pro Musica Orch. of Stuttgart, under Reinhardt. Francesco Geminiani (1687-1762) has been rediscovered in the same musical exploration that revealed Scarlatti, Vivaldi, and Corelli. In form he is more sophisticated than the earlier Italians, but his music delights modern listeners with its combination of contrapuntal techniques and the full harmonies and rich melodies charcteristic of Italian music. This is the only recording of the six 1733 concerti: D Major, B Flat Minor, E Minor, G Minor, E Minor (bis), and D Minor. "I warmly recommend it, spacious, magnificent, I enjoyed every bar," C. Cudworth, RECORD NEWS. "Works of real charm, recorded with understanding and style," ETUDE. (Playing time 52 mins.) HCR 5209 **$2.00**

MODERN PIANO SONATAS: BARTOK: SONATA FOR PIANO; BLOCH: SONATA FOR PIANO (1935); PROKOFIEV, PIANO SONATA #7 IN B FLAT ("STALINGRAD"); STRAVINSKY: PIANO SONATA (1924), István Nádas, Piano. Shows some of the major forces and directions in modern piano music: Stravinsky's crisp austerity; Bartok's fusion of Hungarian folk motives; incisive diverse rhythms, and driving power; Bloch's distinctive emotional vigor; Prokofiev's brilliance and melodic beauty couched in pre-Romantic forms. "A most interesting documentation of the contemporary piano sonata. Nadas is a very good pianist." HIGH FIDELITY. (Playing time 59 mins.) HCR 5215 **$2.00**

VIVALDI: CONCERTI FOR FLUTE, VIOLIN, BASSOON, AND HARPSICHORD: #8 IN G MINOR, #21 IN F, #27 IN D, #7 IN D; SONATA #1 IN A MINOR, Gastone Tassinari, Renato Giangrandi, Giorgio Semprini, Arlette Eggmann. More than any other Baroque composer, Vivaldi moved the concerto grosso closer to the solo concert we deem standard today. In these concerti he wrote virtuosi music for the solo instruments, allowing each to introduce new material or expand on musical ideas, creating tone colors unusual even for Vivaldi. As a result, this record displays a new area of his genius, offering some of his most brilliant music. Performed by a top-rank European group. (Playing time 45 mins.) HCR 5216 **$2.00**

LÜBECK: CANTATAS: HILF DEINEM VOLK; GOTT, WIE DEIN NAME, Stuttgart Choral Society, Swabian Symphony Orch.; PRELUDES AND FUGUES IN C MINOR AND IN E, Eva Hölderlin, Organ. Vincent Lübeck (1654-1740), contemporary of Bach and Buxtehude, was one of the great figures of the 18th-century North German school. These examples of Lübeck's few surviving works indicate his power and brilliance. Voice and instrument lines in the cantatas are strongly reminiscent of the organ: the preludes and fugues show the influence of Bach and Buxtehude. This is the only recording of the superb cantatas. Text and translation included. "Outstanding record," E. T. Canby, SAT. REVIEW. "Hölderlin's playing is exceptional," AM. RECORD REVIEW. "Will make [Lübeck] many new friends," Philip Miller. (Playing time 37 mins.) HCR 5217 **$2.00**

CATALOGUE OF DOVER BOOKS

J. S. BACH: PARTITAS FOR UNACCOMPANIED VIOLIN: #2 in D Minor and #3 in E, Bronislav Gimpel. Bach's works for unaccompanied violin fall within the same area that produced the Brandenburg Concerti, the Orchestral Suites, and the first part of the Well-Tempered Clavichord. The D Minor is considered one of Bach's masterpieces; the E Major is a buoyant work with exceptionally interesting bariolage effects. This is the first release of a truly memorable recording by Bronislav Gimpel, "as a violinist, the equal of the greatest" (P. Leron, in OPERA, Paris). (Playing time 53 mins.) HCR 5212 **$2.00**

ROSSINI: QUARTETS FOR WOODWINDS: #1 IN F, #4 IN B FLAT, #5 IN D, AND #6 IN F, N. Y. Woodwind Quartet Members: S. Baron, Flute, J. Barrows, French Horn; B. Garfield, Bassoon; D. Glazer, Clarinet. Rossini's great genius was centered in the opera, but he also wrote a small amount of first-rate non-vocal music. Among these instrumental works, first place is usually given to the very interesting quartets. Of the three different surviving arrangements, this wind group version is the original, and this is the first recording of these works. "Each member of the group displays wonderful virtuosity when the music calls for it, at other times blending sensitively into the ensemble," HIGH FIDELITY. "Sheer delight," Philip Miller. (Playing time 45 mins.) HCR 5214 **$2.00**

TELEMANN: THE GERMAN FANTASIAS FOR HARPSICHORD (#1-12), Helma Elsner. Until recently, Georg Philip Telemann (1681-1767) was one of the mysteriously neglected great men of music. Recently he has received the attention he deserved. He created music that delights modern listeners with its freshness and originality. These fantasias are free in form and reveal the intricacy of thorough bass music, the harmonic wealth of the "new music," and a distinctive melodic beauty. "This is another blessing of the contemporary LP output. Miss Elsner plays with considerable sensitivity and a great deal of understanding," REV. OF RECORDED MUSIC. "Fine recorded sound," Harold Schonberg. "Recommended warmly, very high quality," DISQUES. (Playing time 50 mins.) HCR 5210 **$2.00**

Nova Recordings

In addition to our reprints of outstanding out-of-print records and American releases of first-rate foreign recordings, we have established our own new records. In order to keep every phase of their production under our own control, we have engaged musicians of world renown to play important music (for the most part unavailable elsewhere), have made use of the finest recording studios in New York, and have produced tapes equal to anything on the market, we believe. The first of these entirely new records are now available.

RAVEL: GASPARD DE LA NUIT, LE TOMBEAU DE COUPERIN, JEUX D'EAU, Beveridge Webster, Piano. Webster studied under Ravel and played his works in European recitals, often with Ravel's personal participation in the program. This record offers examples of the three major periods of Ravel's pianistic work, and is a must for any serious collector or music lover. (Playing time about 50 minutes). Monaural HCR 5213 **$2.00** / Stereo HCR ST 7000 **$2.00**

EIGHTEENTH CENTURY FRENCH FLUTE MUSIC, Jean-Pierre Rampal, Flute, and Robert Veyron-Lacroix, Harpsichord. Contains Concerts Royaux #7 for Flute and Harpsichord in G Minor, Francois Couperin; Sonata dite l'Inconnue in G for Flute and Harpsichord, Michel de la Barre; Sonata #6 in A Minor, Michel Blavet; and Sonata in D Minor, Anne Danican-Philidor. In the opinion of many Rampal is the world's premier flutist. (Playing time about 45 minutes) Monaural HCR 5238 **$2.00** / Stereo HCR ST 7001 **$2.00**

SCHUMANN: NOVELLETTEN (Opus 21), Beveridge Webster, Piano. Brilliantly played in this original recording by one of America's foremost keyboard performers. Connected Romantic pieces. Long a piano favorite. (Playing time about 45 minutes) Monaural HCR 5239 **$2.00** / Stereo HCR ST 7002 **$2.00**

Language Books and Records

GERMAN: HOW TO SPEAK AND WRITE IT. AN INFORMAL CONVERSATIONAL METHOD FOR SELF STUDY, Joseph Rosenberg. Eminently useful for self study because of concentration on elementary stages of learning. Also provides teachers with remarkable variety of aids: 28 full- and double-page sketches with pertinent items numbered and identified in German and English; German proverbs, jokes; grammar, idiom studies; extensive practice exercises. The most interesting introduction to German available, full of amusing illustrations, photographs of cities and landmarks in German-speaking cities, cultural information subtly woven into conversational material. Includes summary of grammar, guide to letter writing, study guide to German literature by Dr. Richard Friedenthal. Index. 400 illustrations. 384pp. 5⅜ x 8½.
T271 Paperbound **$2.00**

FRENCH: HOW TO SPEAK AND WRITE IT. AN INFORMAL CONVERSATIONAL METHOD FOR SELF STUDY, Joseph Lemaitre. Even the absolute beginner can acquire a solid foundation for further study from this delightful elementary course. Photographs, sketches and drawings, sparkling colloquial conversations on a wide variety of topics (including French culture and custom), French sayings and quips, are some of aids used to demonstrate rather than merely describe the language. Thorough yet surprisingly entertaining approach, excellent for teaching and for self study. Comprehensive analysis of pronunciation, practice exercises and appendices of verb tables, additional vocabulary, other useful material. Index. Appendix. 400 illustrations. 416pp. 5⅜ x 8½.
T268 Paperbound **$2.00**

DICTIONARY OF SPOKEN SPANISH, Spanish-English, English-Spanish. Compiled from spoken Spanish, emphasizing idiom and colloquial usage in both Castilian and Latin-American. More than 16,000 entries containing over 25,000 idioms—the largest list of idiomatic constructions ever published. Complete sentences given, indexed under single words—language in immediately useable form, for travellers, businessmen, students, etc. 25 page introduction provides rapid survey of sounds, grammar, syntax, with full consideration of irregular verbs. Especially apt in modern treatment of phrases and structure. 17 page glossary gives translations of geographical names, money values, numbers, national holidays, important street signs, useful expressions of high frequency, plus unique 7 page glossary of Spanish and Spanish-American foods and dishes. Originally published as War Department Technical Manual TM 30-900. iv + 513pp. 5⅜ x 8.
T495 Paperbound **$1.75**

SPEAK MY LANGUAGE: SPANISH FOR YOUNG BEGINNERS, M. Ahlman, Z. Gilbert. Records provide one of the best, and most entertaining, methods of introducing a foreign language to children. Within the framework of a train trip from Portugal to Spain, an English-speaking child is introduced to Spanish by a native companion. (Adapted from a successful radio program of the N. Y. State Educational Department.) Though a continuous story, there are a dozen specific categories of expressions, including greetings, numbers, time, weather, food, clothes, family members, etc. Drill is combined with poetry and contextual use. Authentic background music is heard. An accompanying book enables a reader to follow the records, and includes a vocabulary of over 350 recorded expressions. Two 10″ 33⅓ records, total of 40 minutes. Book. 40 illustrations. 69pp. 5¼ x 10½.
T890 The set **$4.95**

AN ENGLISH-FRENCH-GERMAN-SPANISH WORD FREQUENCY DICTIONARY, H. S. Eaton. An indispensable language study aid, this is a semantic frequency list of the 6000 most frequently used words in 4 languages—24,000 words in all. The lists, based on concepts rather than words alone, and containing all modern, exact, and idiomatic vocabulary, are arranged side by side to form a unique 4-language dictionary. A simple key indicates the importance of the individual words within each language. Over 200 pages of separate indexes for each language enable you to locate individual words at a glance. Will help language teachers and students, authors of textbooks, grammars, and language tests to compare concepts in the various languages and to concentrate on basic vocabulary, avoiding uncommon and obsolete words. 2 Appendixes. xxi + 441pp. 6½ x 9¼.
T738 Paperbound **$2.45**

NEW RUSSIAN-ENGLISH AND ENGLISH-RUSSIAN DICTIONARY, M. A. O'Brien. Over 70,000 entries in the new orthography! Many idiomatic uses and colloquialisms which form the basis of actual speech. Irregular verbs, perfective and imperfective aspects, regular and irregular sound changes, and other features. One of the few dictionaries where accent changes within the conjugation of verbs and the declension of nouns are fully indicated. "One of the best," Prof. E. J. Simmons, Cornell. First names, geographical terms, bibliography, etc. 738pp. 4½ x 6¼.
T208 Paperbound **$2.00**

96 MOST USEFUL PHRASES FOR TOURISTS AND STUDENTS in English, French, Spanish, German, Italian. A handy folder you'll want to carry with you. How to say "Excuse me," "How much is it?", "Write it down, please," etc., in four foreign languages. Copies limited, no more than 1 to a customer.
FREE

CATALOGUE OF DOVER BOOKS

Say It language phrase books

These handy phrase books (128 to 196 pages each) make grammatical drills unnecessary for an elementary knowledge of a spoken foreign language. Covering most matters of travel and everyday life each volume contains:

Over 1000 phrases and sentences in immediately useful forms — foreign language plus English.

Modern usage designed for Americans. Specific phrases like, "Give me small change," and "Please call a taxi."

Simplified phonetic transcription you will be able to read at sight.

The only completely indexed phrase books on the market.

Covers scores of important situations: — Greetings, restaurants, sightseeing, useful expressions, etc.

These books are prepared by native linguists who are professors at Columbia, N.Y.U., Fordham and other great universities. Use them independently or with any other book or record course. They provide a supplementary living element that most other courses lack. Individual volumes in:

Russian 75¢	Italian 75¢	Spanish 75¢	German 75¢
Hebrew 75¢	Danish 75¢	Japanese 75¢	Swedish 75¢
Dutch 75¢	Esperanto 75¢	Modern Greek 75¢	Portuguese 75¢
Norwegian 75¢	Polish 75¢	French 75¢	Yiddish 75¢
Turkish 75¢		English for German-speaking people 75¢	
English for Italian-speaking people 75¢		English for Spanish-speaking people 75¢	

Large clear type. 128-196 pages each. 3½ x 5¼. Sturdy paper binding.

Listen and Learn language records

LISTEN & LEARN is the only language record course designed especially to meet your travel and everyday needs. It is available in separate sets for FRENCH, SPANISH, GERMAN, JAPANESE, RUSSIAN, MODERN GREEK, PORTUGUESE, ITALIAN and HEBREW, and each set contains three 33⅓ rpm long-playing records—1½ hours of recorded speech by eminent native speakers who are professors at Columbia, New York University, Queens College.

Check the following special features found only in LISTEN & LEARN:

● **Dual-language recording.** 812 selected phrases and sentences, over 3200 words, spoken first in English, then in their foreign language equivalents. A suitable pause follows each foreign phrase, allowing you time to repeat the expression. You learn by unconscious assimilation.

● **128 to 206-page manual** contains everything on the records, plus a simple phonetic pronunciation guide.

● **Indexed for convenience. The only set on the market** that is completely indexed. No more puzzling over where to find the phrase you need. Just look in the rear of the manual.

● **Practical.** No time wasted on material you can find in any grammar. LISTEN & LEARN covers central core material with phrase approach. Ideal for the person with limited learning time.

● **Living, modern expressions,** not found in other courses. Hygienic products, modern equipment, shopping—expressions used every day, like "nylon" and "air-conditioned."

● **Limited objective.** Everything you learn, no matter where you stop, is immediately useful. You have to finish other courses, wade through grammar and vocabulary drill, before they help you.

● **High-fidelity recording.** LISTEN & LEARN records equal in clarity and surface-silence any record on the market costing up to $6.

"Excellent . . . the spoken records . . . impress me as being among the very best on the market," **Prof. Mario Pei,** Dept. of Romance Languages, Columbia University. "Inexpensive and well-done . . . it would make an ideal present," CHICAGO SUNDAY TRIBUNE. "More genuinely helpful than anything of its kind which I have previously encountered," **Sidney Clark,** well-known author of "ALL THE BEST" travel books.

UNCONDITIONAL GUARANTEE. Try LISTEN & LEARN, then return it within 10 days for full refund if you are not satisfied.

Each set contains three twelve-inch 33⅓ records, manual, and album.

SPANISH	the set $5.95	GERMAN	the set $5.95
FRENCH	the set $5.95	ITALIAN	the set $5.95
RUSSIAN	the set $5.95	JAPANESE	the set $5.95
PORTUGUESE	the set $5.95	MODERN GREEK	the set $5.95
MODERN HEBREW	the set $5.95		

Trubner Colloquial Manuals

These unusual books are members of the famous Trubner series of colloquial manuals. They have been written to provide adults with a sound colloquial knowledge of a foreign language, and are suited for either class use or self-study. Each book is a complete course in itself, with progressive, easy to follow lessons. Phonetics, grammar, and syntax are covered, while hundreds of phrases and idioms, reading texts, exercises, and vocabulary are included. These books are unusual in being neither skimpy nor overdetailed in grammatical matters, and in presenting up-to-date, colloquial, and practical phrase material. Bilingual presentation is stressed, to make thorough self-study easier for the reader.

COLLOQUIAL HINDUSTANI, A. H. Harley, formerly Nizam's Reader in Urdu, U. of London. 30 pages on phonetics and scripts (devanagari & Arabic-Persian) are followed by 29 lessons, including material on English and Arabic-Persian influences. Key to all exercises. Vocabulary. 5 x 7½. 147pp.   Clothbound **$1.75**

COLLOQUIAL PERSIAN, L. P. Elwell-Sutton. Best introduction to modern Persian, with 90 page grammatical section followed by conversations, 35-page vocabulary. 139pp.
Clothbound **$1.75**

COLLOQUIAL ARABIC, DeLacy O'Leary. Foremost Islamic scholar covers language of Egypt, Syria, Palestine, & Northern Arabia. Extremely clear coverage of complex Arabic verbs & noun plurals; also cultural aspects of language. Vocabulary. xviii + 192pp. 5 x 7½.
Clothbound **$2.50**

COLLOQUIAL GERMAN, P. F. Doring. Intensive thorough coverage of grammar in easily-followed form. Excellent for brush-up, with hundreds of colloquial phrases. 34 pages of bilingual texts. 224pp. 5 x 7½.   Clothbound **$1.75**

COLLOQUIAL SPANISH, W. R. Patterson. Castilan grammar and colloquial language, loaded with bilingual phrases and colloquialisms. Excellent for review or self-study. 164pp. 5 x 7½.
Clothbound **$1.75**

COLLOQUIAL FRENCH, W. R. Patterson. 16th revision of this extremely popular manual. Grammar explained with model clarity, and hundreds of useful expressions and phrases; exercises, reading texts, etc. Appendixes of new and useful words and phrases. 223pp. 5 x 7½.
Clothbound **$1.75**

COLLOQUIAL CZECH, J. Schwarz, former headmaster of Lingua Institute, Prague. Full easily followed coverage of grammar, hundreds of immediately useable phrases, texts. Perhaps the best Czech grammar in print. "An absolutely successful textbook," JOURNAL OF CZECHO-SLOVAK FORCES IN GREAT BRITAIN. 252pp. 5 x 7½.   Clothbound **$3.00**

COLLOQUIAL RUMANIAN, G. Nandris, Professor of University of London. Extremely thorough coverage of phonetics, grammar, syntax; also included 70-page reader, and 70-page vocabulary. Probably the best grammar for this increasingly important language. 340pp. 5 x 7½.
Clothbound **$2.50**

COLLOQUIAL ITALIAN, A. L. Hayward. Excellent self-study course in grammar, vocabulary, idioms, and reading. Easy progressive lessons will give a good working knowledge of Italian in the shortest possible time. 5 x 7½.   Clothbound **$1.75**

COLLOQUIAL TURKISH, Yusuf Mardin. Very clear, thorough introduction to leading cultural and economic language of Near East. Begins with pronunciation and statement of vowel harmony, then 36 lessons present grammar, graded vocabulary, useful phrases, dialogues, reading, exercises. Key to exercises at rear. Turkish-English vocabulary. All in Roman alphabet. x + 288pp. 4¾ x 7¼.   Clothbound **$4.00**

DUTCH-ENGLISH AND ENGLISH-DUTCH DICTIONARY, F. G. Renier. For travel, literary, scientific or business Dutch, you will find this the most convenient, practical and comprehensive dictionary on the market. More than 60,000 entries, shades of meaning, colloquialisms, idioms, compounds and technical terms. Dutch and English strong and irregular verbs. This is the only dictionary in its size and price range that indicates the gender of nouns. New orthography. xvii + 571pp. 5½ x 6¼.   T224 Clothbound **$2.75**

LEARN DUTCH, F. G. Renier. This book is the most satisfactory and most easily used grammar of modern Dutch. The student is gradually led from simple lessons in pronunciation, through translation from and into Dutch, and finally to a mastery of spoken and written Dutch. Grammatical principles are clearly explained while a useful, practical vocabulary is introduced in easy exercises and readings. It is used and recommended by the Fulbright Committee in the Netherlands. Phonetic appendices. Over 1200 exercises; Dutch-English, English-Dutch vocabularies. 181pp. 4¼ x 7¼.   T441 Clothbound **$2.25**

CATALOGUE OF DOVER BOOKS

INVITATION TO GERMAN POETRY record. Spoken by Lotte Lenya. Edited by Gustave Mathieu, Guy Stern. 42 poems of Walther von der Vogelweide, Goethe, Hölderlin, Heine, Hofmannsthal, George, Werfel, Brecht, other great poets from 13th to middle of 20th century, spoken with superb artistry. Use this set to improve your diction, build vocabulary, improve aural comprehension, learn German literary history, as well as for sheer delight in listening. 165-page book contains full German text of each poem; English translations; biographical, critical information on each poet; textual information; portraits of each poet, many never before available in this country. 1 12" 33⅓ record; 165-page book; album. The set **$4.95**

ESSENTIALS OF RUSSIAN record, A von Gronicka, H. Bates-Yakobson. 50 minutes of spoken Russian based on leading grammar will improve comprehension, pronunciation, increase vocabulary painlessly. Complete aural review of phonetics, phonemics—words contrasted to highlight sound differences. Wide range of material: talk between family members, friends; sightseeing; adaptation of Tolstoy's "The Shark;" history of Academy of Sciences; proverbs, epigrams; Pushkin, Lermontov, Fet, Blok, Maikov poems. Conversation passages spoken twice, fast and slow, let you anticipate answers, hear all sounds but understand normal speed. 12" 33⅓ record, album sleeve. 44-page manual with entire record text. Translation on facing pages, phonetic instructions. The set **$4.95**

Note: For students wishing to use a grammar as well, set is available with grammar-text on which record is based, Gronicka and Bates-Yakobson's "Essentials of Russian" (400pp., 6 x 9, clothbound; Prentice Hall), an excellent, standard text used in scores of colleges, institutions. Augmented set: book, record, manual, sleeve **$10.70**

DICTIONARY OF SPOKEN RUSSIAN, English-Russian, Russian-English. Based on phrases and complete sentences, rather than isolated words; recognized as one of the best methods of learning the idiomatic speech of a country. Over 11,500 entries, indexed by single words, with more than 32,000 English and Russian sentences and phrases, in immediately useable form. Probably the largest list ever published. Shows accent changes in conjugation and declension; irregular forms listed in both alphabetical place and under main form of word. 15,000 word introduction covering Russian sounds, writing, grammar, syntax. 15-page appendix of geographical names, money, important signs, given names, foods, special Soviet terms, etc. Travellers, businessmen, students, government employees have found this their best source for Russian expressions. Originally published as War Department Technical Manual TM 30-944. iv + 573pp. 5⅚ x 8⅜. T496 Paperbound **$2.75**

THE GIFT OF LANGUAGE, M. Schlauch. Formerly titled THE GIFT OF TONGUES, this is a middle-level survey that avoids both superficiality and pedantry. It covers such topics as linguistic families, word histories, grammatical processes in such foreign languages as Aztec, Ewe, and Bantu, semantics, language taboos, and dozens of other fascinating and important topics. Especially interesting is an analysis of the word-coinings of Joyce, Cummings, Stein and others in terms of linguistics. 232 bibliographic notes. Index. viii + 342pp. 5⅜ x 8. T243 Paperbound **$1.85**